THE KAUṬILĪYA ARTHAŚĀSTRA

PART II

THE KAUṬILĪYA ARTHAŚĀSTRA

PART II

AN ENGLISH TRANSLATION
WITH CRITICAL AND EXPLANATORY NOTES

R. P. KANGLE

MOTILAL BANARSIDASS
Delhi Varanasi Patna
Bangalore Madras

Second Edition: Bombay University, 1972
Reprint: Delhi, 1986, 1988

MOTILAL BANARSIDASS
Bungalow Road, Jawahar Nagar, Delhi 110 007

Branches
Chowk, Varanasi 221 001
Ashok Rajpath, Patna 800 004
24 Race Course Road, Bangalore 560 001
120 Royapettah High Road, Mylapore, Madras 600 004

Reprint from a copy procured by courtesy of Shri Radheshyam Shastri of Bhiwani

ISBN: 81–208–0040–0 (Part II)
ISBN: 81–208–0042–7 (Set)

PRINTED IN INDIA
BY JAINENDRA PRAKASH JAIN AT SHRI JAINENDRA PRESS, A-45 NARAINA INDUSTRIAL AREA, PHASE I, NEW DELHI 110 028 AND PUBLISHED BY NARENDRA PRAKASH JAIN FOR MOTILAL BANARSIDASS, DELHI 110 007.

PREFACE TO THE SECOND EDITION

SOME slight modifications and a few corrections have been necessitated in the Notes. In particular, references to explanations found in the commentaries Cj and Cp have been further checked. This opportunity has also been availed of to incorporate in the appropriate places the Notes based on the Russian translation, which had been added in an Appendix in the First Edition.

Further studies of the *Arthaśāstra* have appeared since the publication of the First Edition. I regret that it has not been possible for me to take full note of all this work, owing mainly to the rather long time that has elapsed since the submission of the Press copy.

I am thankful for the welcome generally accorded to this work by the world of scholars.

September, 1972. R. P. KANGLE

PREFACE TO THE FIRST EDITION

Dr. Shamasastry's translation of the *Kauṭilīya Arthaśāstra* was first published nearly five decades ago. In subsequent editions he, no doubt, added notes derived from Bhaṭṭasvāmin's Commentary as well as the Malayalam Commentary. However, in view of the discovery of fragments of other Commentaries, and particularly in view of the many important contributions made to the study of this text by a large number of scholars since then, it has long been felt that a new English translation of the text is a necessity. The present is an attempt to supply this need.

This translation is prepared after consulting the available ancient Commentaries—unfortunately none of them complete—as well as the works of many modern scholars. Among the latter I must make special mention of R. Shamasastry himself, the pioneer of studies in this field, T. Ganapati Sastri, editor of the text and author of a complete Sanskrit Commentary on it, J. J. Meyer, author of the German translation with voluminous notes, and B. Breloer, the author of three volumes of penetrating studies of this text. My debt to these and numerous other scholars is incalculable. The Russian translation of this work which was published a few years ago, came to my hands only after most of the present translation was already printed; it was, therefore, not possible to make use of it in the body of the notes. Some of the noteworthy renderings found in that translation are added at the end.

This translation aims at providing as accurate a rendering of the text as is possible. The *Arthaśāstra* is admittedly a difficult work, and very often it is not possible to be quite sure of the exact meaning of the author. Hence, in the notes a reference is made to the different interpretations found in the ancient commentaries as well as to those offered by modern scholars. In most important cases, the source of the interpretation adopted in the translation is mentioned, while brief comments are made on interpretations not found acceptable. An endeavour is also made in the notes to bring out the meaning of passages where the literal translation does not seem to make it quite clear. All important variant readings are, of course, referred to and discussed in the notes, though the discussion could not be very detailed in every case for obvious reasons.

During the course of the printing of the translation it was found that the text as printed in Part I needs revision in a few places. In about a dozen cases the translation presupposes readings different from those adopted in the text. These are listed separately at the end of this volume, along with misprints in the text that had escaped notice.

A few points referred to in the Introduction to Part I require further elaboration :—

(1) In connection with the transcript in the Government Library at Munich, viz., G_2, it was suggested there that the transcript was made from the Malayalam ms. M_1 rather than from any Grantha ms., as stated in the Punjab Edition. Subsequently I had occasion to visit the Staatsbibliothek in Munich and to go through the transcript myself. That left no room for any doubt that the ultimate source of that transcript is M_1. It seems that the transcript was made in 1907 by one Venkayya in Madras. And it is not unlikely that use was made by him of M_2, an earlier transcript of M_1, that was in Madras at that time. G_2 thus loses much of its independent value. Of Grantha mss. of the *Arthaśāstra*, therefore, we have only one, viz., G_1.

(2) Before this translation could go through the Press, the rest of Cb, the Malayalam Commentary, became available in print : *Bhāṣākauṭalīyam*, 4-7, edited by K. N. Ezhuthachan (University of Madras, 1960). Fortunately, it was posssible for me to make use of this Commentary in the notes on Books 4 to 7 as well. In a learned Introduction, Ezhuthachan has analysed in detail the structure of the language of this Commentary and has argued that though it shows some Tamil forms and words, the language is different from Tamil. It represents, according to him, the earliest form of Malayalam, as it evolved from West Coast Tamil about the 12th Century A.D. It is, therefore, not correct to say that the language of the Commentary is Tamil or that it is a hotch-potch of Tamil and Malayalam.

(3) As regards the Commentary referred to as Cj, it transpires that it really contains fragments of two different Commentaries. The Commentary on Book 1 alone is a fragment of the *Jayamaṅgalā*, the rest being a fragment of another Commentary called *Cāṇakyaṭīkā*. It is only the latter which is the work of Bhikṣu Prabhamati. The author of the *Jayamaṅgalō* fragment is probably the same as the author of the Commentaries on Vātsyāyana's *Kāmasūtra*, Kāmandaka's *Nītisāra* and other works, which also bear the name *Jayamaṅgalā*. This is shown by G. Harihara Sastri in the Introduction to his edition of the *Jayamaṅgalā* on Book 1 (published by the Kuppuswami Sastri Research Institute, Madras, 1958). The fragment of the *Cāṇakyaṭīkā* by Bhikṣu Prabhamati is also being edited by G. Harihara Sastri and published in the pages of the *Journal of Oriental Research*, Madras. I regret that when I went through the transcript in the Government Oriental Manuscripts Library in Madras, I failed to realise that it really contained fragments of two separate Commentaries.

(4) The fragment of the Devanagari ms. from Patan, D, is now published along with the fragment of Yogghama's Commentary, Cnn, by the Bharatiya Vidya Bhavan, Bombay : *A Fragment of the Kouṭalya's Arthaśāstra alias Rājasiddhānta*, edited by Muni Jina Vijay (Bombay, 1959).

In an article in the Schubring Commemoration Volume, Prof. L. Alsdorf refers to the existence of Folios 12-88 of a Commentary on the *Arthaśāstra* found in the Baḍā Bhaṇḍāra at Jaisalmer. My attention to this reference was kindly drawn by Sir Harold Bailey at Cambridge. I made inquiries about this fragment, especially of Muni Punya Vijayaji of Ahmedabad and Muni Jina Vijayaji now in Jaipur. Neither of them is aware of the existence of any such Commentary on the *Arthaśāstra* from the Jaisalmer Bhandar. Muni Jina Vijayaji tells me that he has ransacked all Jain Bhandars for anything that may concern the *Arthaśāstra*, and that if there really had been in existence such a fragment in the Jaisalmer Bhandar, he would have certainly obtained it and published it along with the other fragments from Patan. In any case, I have not succeeded in getting any fresh help as a result of the reference by L. Alsdorf.

This new translation of the *Arthaśāstra* is offered not without diffidence. I am keenly aware of the possibility that I may have very often misunderstood the text, and that such a misunderstanding may sometimes well be due to my own shortcomings rather than to the difficult nature of the text. Nevertheless, I am hopeful that scholars will find the translation generally acceptable. They will, no doubt, set me right where I may have gone astray.

I must repeat my feelings of gratefulness to the authorities of the University of Bombay for making the publication of this entire work possible.

Finally, I must record my sincere thanks to Shri B. A. Olkar, Superintendent of the Publications Section of the Bombay University, whose unstinted help in seeing this work through the Press has been of inestimable value to me. And to Shri V. G. Moghe, Superintendent of the Bombay University Press and his staff my best thanks are due for the great patience and diligence with which they carried out this rather exacting job.

The Errata at the end will, it is hoped, not be found inordinately long in a work of this nature.

October, 1963. R. P. KANGLE

TABLE OF CONTENTS

Book 1 Concerning the Topic of Training 1-54

Chapter 1			Enumeration of Sections and Books	1
2	Sec.	1	Enumeration of the Sciences	5
3	Sec.	1	(Continued)	7
4	Sec.	1	(Continued)	9
5	Sec.	2	Association with Elders	10
6	Sec.	3	Control over the Senses	12
7	Sec.	3	(Continued)	13
8	Sec.	4	Appointment of Ministers	15
9	Sec.	5	Appointment of Councillors and Chaplain	17
10	Sec.	6	Ascertainment of the Integrity of Ministers by Means of Secret Tests	18
11	Sec.	7	Appointment of Persons in Secret Service	21
12	Sec.	7	(Continued)	
	Sec.	8	Rules for Secret Servants	23
13	Sec.	9	Keeping a Watch over One's Seducible and Non-seducible Parties	28
14	Sec.	10	Winning over the Enemy's Seducible and Non-seducible Parties	30
15	Sec.	11	The Topic of Counsel	32
16	Sec.	12	Rules for the Envoy	36
17	Sec.	13	Guarding against Princes	39
18	Sec.	14	Conduct of the Prince in Disfavour	
	Sec.	15	Behaviour towards a Prince in Disfavour	43
19	Sec.	16	Rules for the King	45
20	Sec.	17	Regulations for the Royal Residence	48
21	Sec.	18	Protection of the King's Person	51

Book 2 The Activity of the Heads of Departments 55-189

Chapter 1	Sec.	19	Settlement of the Countryside	55
2	Sec.	20	Disposal of Non-agricultural Land	59

3	Sec.	21	Construction of Forts	61
4	Sec.	22	Lay-out of the Fortified City	67
5	Sec.	23	Duties of the Director of Stores	72
6	Sec.	24	The Setting up of Revenue by the Administrator	75
7	Sec.	25	Records and Accounts and Audit Office	80
8	Sec.	26	Misappropriation of Revenue by Officers and Its Recovery	85
9	Sec.	27	Inspection of Officers' Work	89
10	Sec.	28	The Topic of Edicts	92
11	Sec.	29	Examination of Precious Articles Received in the Treasury	97
12	Sec.	30	Starting of Mines and Factories	105
13	Sec.	31	The Superintendent of Gold in the Workshop	110
14	Sec.	32	The Royal Goldsmith in the Market Highway	116
15	Sec.	33	The Superintendent of the Magazine	122
16	Sec.	34	The Director of Trade	127
17	Sec.	35	The Director of Forests	129
18	Sec.	36	The Superintendent of the Armoury	131
19	Sec.	37	Standardisation of Weights and Measures	134
20	Sec.	38	Measures of Space and Time	138
21	Sec.	39	The Collector of Customs	141
22	Sec.	39	(Continued)	144
23	Sec.	40	The Superintendent of Yarns	146
24	Sec.	41	The Director of Agriculture	148
25	Sec.	42	The Controller of Spirituous Liquors	153
26	Sec.	43	The Supervisor of Animal Slaughter	157
27	Sec.	44	The Superintendent of Courtesans	158
28	Sec.	45	The Controller of Shipping	162
29	Sec.	46	The Superintendent of Cattle	165
30	Sec.	47	The Superintendent of Horses	170
31	Sec.	48	The Superintendent of Elephants	174
32	Sec.	48	(Continued)	177

33	Sec. 49	The Superintendent of Chariots	
	Sec. 50	The Superintendent of Foot Soldiers	
	Sec. 51	The Commandant of the Army	179
34	Sec. 52	The Superintendent of Passports	
	Sec. 53	The Superintendent of Pastures	181
35	Sec. 54	The Administrator's Activity	
	Sec. 55	Activity of Secret Agents	182
36	Sec. 56	The City Superintendent	185

Book 3 Concerning Judges 190-253

Chapter 1	Sec. 57	Valid and Invalid Transactions	
	Sec. 58	Filing of Law-suits	190
2	Sec. 59	Concerning Marriage	196
3	Sec. 59	(Continued)	201
4	Sec. 59	(Continued)	205
5	Sec. 60	Partition of Inheritance	208
6	Sec. 60	(Continued)	211
7	Sec. 60	(Continued)	213
8	Sec. 61	Concerning Immovable Property	216
9	Sec. 61	(Continued)	219
10	Sec. 61	(Continued)	
	Sec. 62	Non-observance of Conventions	222
11	Sec. 63	Non-payment of Debts	226
12	Sec. 64	Concerning Deposits	230
13	Sec. 65	Law Concerning Slaves and Labourers	235
14	Sec. 65	(Continued)	
	Sec. 66	Undertakings in Partnership	239
15	Sec. 67	Rescission of Sale and Purchase	242
16	Sec. 68	Non-conveyance of Gifts	
	Sec. 69	Sale without Ownership	
	Sec. 70	The Relation of Ownership	243
17	Sec. 71	Forcible Seizure	245
18	Sec. 72	Verbal Injury	246
19	Sec. 73	Physical Injury	247
20	Sec. 74	Gambling and Betting	
	Sec. 75	Miscellaneous Offences	250

Book 4			**The Suppression of Criminals**	**254-291**
Chapter 1	Sec.	76	Keeping a Watch over Artisans	254
2	Sec.	77	Keeping a Watch over Traders	259
3	Sec.	78	Remedies during Calamities	262
4	Sec.	79	Guarding against Persons with Secret Income	265
5	Sec.	80	Detection of Criminals through Secret Agents	267
6	Sec.	81	Arrest on Suspicion, with the Article and by the Act	268
7	Sec.	82	Inquest on Sudden Deaths	272
8	Sec.	83	Investigation through Interrogation and through Torture	274
9	Sec.	84	Keeping a Watch over Departments	277
10	Sec.	85	Redemption from Corporal Punishment	281
11	Sec.	86	Capital Punishment	283
12	Sec.	87	Violation of Maidens	285
13	Sec.	88	Punishment for Transgressions	288
Book 5			**Secret Conduct**	**292-313**
Chapter 1	Sec.	89	Infliction of Secret Punishment	292
2	Sec.	90	Replenishment of the Treasury	296
3	Sec.	91	The Salaries of State Servants	302
4	Sec.	92	Conduct Proper for a Dependent	305
5	Sec.	93	Proper Behaviour of a Courtier	307
6	Sec.	94	Continuance of the Kingdom	
	Sec.	95	Continuous Sovereignty	309
Book 6			**The Circle of Kings as the Basis**	**314-320**
Chapter 1	Sec.	96	Excellences of Constituents	314
2	Sec.	97	Concerning Peace and Activity	317
Book 7			**The Six Measures of Foreign Policy**	**321-384**
Chapter 1	Sec.	98	Enumeration of the Six Measures	
	Sec.	99	Use of Measures in Decline, Stable Condition and Advancement	321

2	Sec. 100	Conduct when Seeking Shelter	325
3	Sec. 101	Policies for the Equal, the Weaker and the Stronger Kings.	
	Sec. 102	Peace-Treaties by the Weaker King	327
4	Sec. 103	Staying Quiet after Making War	
	Sec. 104	Staying Quiet after Making Peace	
	Sec. 105	Marching after Making War	
	Sec. 106	Marching after Making Peace.	
	Sec. 107	Marching with Other Kings	331
5	Sec. 108	Considerations about Attack on a Vulnerable King and the Enemy	
	Sec. 109	Causes Leading to Decline, Greed and Disaffection among Subjects	
	Sec. 110	Confederated Allies	334
6	Sec. 111	March of two Allied Kings	
	Sec. 112	Treaties with Stipulations, without Stipulations and with Deserters	338
7	Sec. 113	Peace and War Connected with Dual Policy	342
8	Sec. 114	Conduct of the King about to be Attacked	
	Sec. 115	Allies Fit to be Helped	346
9	Sec. 116	Pacts for Securing an Ally, Money, Land and an Undertaking	349
10	Sec. 116	(Continued)	353
11	Sec. 116	(Continued)	355
12	Sec. 116	(Continued)	359
13	Sec. 117	Considerations about the King Attacking in the Rear	361
14	Sec. 118	Recoupment of Powers Become Weak	366
15	Sec. 119	Entrenching Oneself in a Fort in War with a Stronger King	
	Sec. 120	Conduct of the King Surrendering with Troops	369
16	Sec. 121	Conduct of the King Subjugating by Force	372
17	Sec. 122	The Making of Peace	
	Sec. 123	Liberation of the Hostage	375

18	Sec. 124	Conduct towards the Middle King	
	Sec. 125	Conduct towards the Neutral King	
	Sec. 126	Conduct towards the Circle of Kings	380

Book 8 Concerning the Topic of Calamities 385-405

Chapter 1	Sec. 127	Calamities of the Constituent Elements	385
2	Sec. 128	Calamities of the King and Kingship	390
3	Sec. 129	Vices of Man	393
4	Sec. 130	Afflictions	
	Sec. 131	Hindrances	
	Sec. 132	Stoppages of Payment to the Treasury	397
5	Sec. 133	Calamities of the Army	
	Sec. 134	Calamities of the Ally	401

Book 9 The Activity of the King About to March 406-432

Chapter 1	Sec. 135	Relative Strength of Powers, Place and Time	
	Sec. 136	Seasons for Marching on an Expedition	406
2	Sec. 137	Employment of Different Troops	
	Sec. 138	Enquipping Troops for war	
	Sec. 139	Employing Suitable Troops against Enemy Troops	409
3	Sec. 140	Revolts in the Rear	
	Sec. 141	Measures against Risings by Constituents	413
4	Sec. 142	Consideration of Losses, Expenses and Gains	417
5	Sec. 143	Dangers from Officers	420
6	Sec. 144	Dangers from Traitors and Enemies	422
7	Sec. 145	Dangers with Advantage, Disadvantage and Uncertainty	
	Sec. 146	Overcoming Dangers by Different Means	427

Book 10 Concerning War 433-453

Chapter 1	Sec. 147	Setting up of the Camp	433
2	Sec. 148	March from the Camp	
	Sec. 149	Guarding Troops during Calamities and at the Time of Attack	435

3	Sec. 150	Covert Fighting	
	Sec. 151	Encouraging the Troops	
	Sec. 152	Disposition of Troops	438
4	Sec. 153	Grounds Suitable for Fighting	
	Sec. 154	Functions of Infantry, Cavalry, Chariots and Elephants	442
5	Sec. 155	Arrangement of Battle-arrays	
	Sec. 156	Distribution of Strong and Weak Troops	
	Sec. 157	Modes of Fighting of Infantry, Cavalry, Chariots and Elephants	445
6	Sec. 158	Staff, Snake, Circle and Diffuse Arrays	
	Sec. 159	Counter-arrays against Them	450

Book 11 Policy towards Oligarchies **454-459**

Chapter 1	Sec. 160	The Policy of Sowing Dissensions	
	Sec. 161	Forms of Silent Punishment	454

Book 12 Concerning the Weaker King **460-473**

Chapter 1	Sec. 162	The Mission of the Envoy	460
2	Sec. 163	Fight with the Weapon of Diplomacy	
	Sec. 164	Assassination of Army Chiefs	462
3	Sec. 164	(Continued)	
	Sec. 165	Stirring up the Circle of Kings	465
4	Sec. 166	Secret Use of Weapons, Fire and Poison	
	Sec. 167	Destruction of Supplies, Reinforcements and Raids	467
5	Sec. 168	Overreaching the Enemy by Trickery	
	Sec. 169	Overreaching by Force	
	Sec. 170	Victory of the Single King	470

Book 13 Means of Taking a Fort **474-493**

Chapter 1	Sec. 171	Instigation to Sedition	474
2	Sec. 172	Drawing the Enemy out by Means of Stratagems	477

3	Sec. 173	Employment of Secret Agents	481
4	Sec. 174	Laying Siege to a Fort	
	Sec. 175	Storming a Fort	485
5	Sec. 176	Pacification of the Conquered Territory	491

Book 14 Concerning Secret Practices **494-511**

Chapter 1	Sec. 177	Secret Practices for the Destruction of Enemy Troops	494
2	Sec. 178	Deceiving through Occult Practices	499
3	Sec. 178	(Continued)	503
4	Sec. 179	Counter-measures against Injuries to One's Own Troops	510

Book 15 The Method of the Science **512-516**

Chapter 1	Sec. 180	Devices Used in the Science	512

INDEX OF PRINCIPAL TOPICS 517

Book One

CONCERNING THE TOPIC OF TRAINING

CHAPTER ONE

ENUMERATION OF SECTIONS AND BOOKS

Om. Salutation to Śukra and Bṛhaspati.

1 This single (treatise on the) Science of Politics has been prepared mostly by bringing together (the teaching of) as many treatises on the Science of Politics as have been composed by ancient teachers for the acquisition and protection of the earth.

2 Of that (treatise), this is an enumeration of Sections and Books :—

3 Enumeration of the Sciences, Association with Elders, Control over the Senses, Appointment of Ministers, Appointment of Councillors and Chaplain, Ascertainment of the Integrity or the Absence of Integrity of Ministers by means of Secret Tests, Appointment of Persons in Secret Service, Rules for Secret Servants, Keeping a Watch over the Seducible and Non-seducible Parties in One's Own Territory, Winning over the Seducible and Non-seducible Parties in the Enemy's Territory, The Topic of Counsel,

The first of the fifteen Books in this work deals mainly with the training of the prince for the arduous duties of rulership. It also discusses the question of the appointment of ministers and other officers necessary for the administration of a state. This prepares the ground for the establishment of a benevolent monarchy.

1.1

The First Chapter of this Book is called *prakaraṇādhikaraṇasamuddeśaḥ* in the colophon in D. The other mss. do not give this name. But that is the only appropriate name for this chapter which gives a table of contents of the work.

The work begins, as usual, with a *maṅgala*. The sacred syllable *om* is auspicious for purposes of all study. The homage to Śukra and Bṛhaspati, the preceptors of the demons and the gods respectively and the supposed promulgators of the science of politics, is quite appropriate in a work dealing with that science.

1 *Pṛthivyā lābhe pālane ca* : the aim of the *Arthaśāstra* is thus to teach the ruler how to acquire and protect a kingdom. 15.1.1-2 below state that *artha* refers to *pṛthivī* and that *Arthaśāstra* is the science dealing with its acquisition and protection. The plu. in *Arthaśāstrāṇi* refers to the numerous earlier works on the science. — *pūrvācāryaiḥ* : many of these earlier teachers and the schools founded by some of them are mentioned in the present work. — *prasthāpitāni* : 'established', i.e., composed. The reading *prastāvitāni* has the sense of 'set going, promulgated.' — *prāyaśas tāni saṁhṛtya* : this implies that the work is in the main based on earlier works, though in a few places the author expresses different views. The idea in *saṁhṛtya* is that of bringing together rather than that of abridgment.

2 *prakaraṇādhikaraṇasamuddeśaḥ* : A *prakaraṇa* is a 'section' dealing with a particular topic of the *śāstra*. An *adhikaraṇa* is a 'book' dealing with one of the fifteen principal topics into which the entire *śāstra* is divided. There is no reference here to the division of the work into chapters.

Rules for the Envoy, Guarding against Princes, The Conduct of a Prince in Disfavour, Behaviour towards a Prince in Disfavour, Rules for the King, Regulations for the Royal Residence, Concerning the Protection of the King's Own Person,—these constitute the First Book 'Concerning the Topic of Training'.

4 Settlement of the Countryside, Disposal of Non-agricultural Land, Construction of Forts, Lay-out of the Fortified City, The Work of Store-keeping by the Director of Stores, The Setting up of Revenue by the Administrator, The Topic of Accounts in the Records and Audit Office, Recovery of Revenue Misappropriated by State Employees, Inspection of (the work of) Officers, The Topic of Edicts, Examination of the Precious Articles to be Received into the Treasury, The Starting of Mines and Factories, The Superintendent of Gold in the Workshop, The Activity of the Goldsmith in the Market-highway, The Superintendent of the Magazine, The Director of Trade, The Director of Forest-produce, The Superintendent of the Armoury, Standardisation of Weights and Measures, Measures of Space and Time, The Collector of Customs and Tolls, The Superintendent of Yarns (and Textiles), The Director of Agriculture, The Controller of Spirituous Liquors, The Supervisor of (Animal-) Slaughter, The Superintendent of Courtesans, The Controller of Shipping, The Superintendent of Cattle, The Superintendent of Horses, The Superintendent of Elephants, The Superintendent of Chariots, The Superintendent of Foot-soldiers, The Activity of the Commandant of the Army, The Superintendent of Passports, The Superintendent of Pasture-lands, The Activity of the Administrator, Secret Agents in the Disguise of Householders, Traders and Ascetics, Rules for the City Superintendent,—these constitute the Second Book 'The Activity of the Heads of Departments'.

5 Determination of (Valid and Invalid) Transactions, Filing of Law-suits, Concerning Marriage, Partition of Inheritance, Concerning Immovable Property, Non-observance of Conventions, Non-payment of Debts, Concerning Deposits, Law concerning Slaves and Labourers, Undertakings in Partnership, Rescission of Sale and Purchase, Non-conveyance of Gifts, Sale without Ownership, The Relation of Ownership, Forcible Seizure, Verbal Injury, Physical Injury, Gambling and Betting, Miscellaneous—these constitute the Third Book 'Concerning Judges'.

4 *-cchidrāpidhānam* is from D as in 2.2 below. There is little doubt that this is the original reading. *-cchidrāvidhānam* of M is an obvious corruption, which G has tried to correct to *-cchidravidhānam*. *chidra* presupposes *apidhāna* 'covering'. — G2 M read *durgaviniveśaḥ* here but even they show *durganiveśaḥ* in the colophon of the actual chapter 2.4. — G1 reads *-ceyakarma* for *nicayakarma* : that is faulty. — Cb reads *kośaprāveśya-* both here and in 2.11. — D G read *gṛhapati-* here, but the form *gṛhapatika-* is found even in them in other places.

5 G M read *prakīrṇakāni* for *prakīrṇakam* of D. The actual passage, 3.20.14, supports the latter and there seems little doubt that the sing. is to be preferred as the name of a title of law.

6 Keeping a Watch over Artisans, Keeping a Watch over Traders, Remedial Measures during Calamities, Guarding against Persons with Secret (Means of) Income, Detection of Criminals through Secret Agents in the Disguise of Holy Men, Arrest on Suspicion, with the (Stolen) Article and by (Indications of) the Act, Inquest on Sudden Deaths, Investigation through Interrogation and through Torture, Keeping a Watch over (Officers of) All Departments, Redemption from the Cutting of Individual Limbs, The Law of (Capital) Punishment, Simple and with Torture, Violation of Maidens, Punishment for Transgression,—these constitute the Fourth Book 'The Suppression of Criminals'.

7 Concerning the Infliction of (secret) Punishment, Replenishment of the Treasury, Concerning the Salaries of (State) Servants, Conduct (proper) for a Dependent, Concerning Proper Behaviour (for a Courtier), Continuance of the Kingdom, Continuous Sovereignty,—these constitute the Fifth Book 'Secret Conduct'.

8 Excellences of the Constituent Elements, Concerning Peace and Activity,—these constitute the Sixth Book 'The Circle (of Kings) as the Basis'.

9 Enumeration of the Six Measures of Foreign Policy, Determination of (Measures in) Decline, Stable Condition and Advancement, Conduct when Seeking Shelter, Adherence to Policies by the Equal, the Weaker and the Stronger (King), Peace-treaties by the Weaker King, Staying Quiet after Making War, Staying Quiet after Making Peace, Marching after Making War, Marching after Making Peace, Marching together (with other Kings), Considerations regarding an Attack on a Vulnerable King and the (Natural) Enemy, Causes leading to Decline, Greed and Disaffection among the Subjects, Reflection on Confederated Allies, Concerning the March of Two (Kings) who have entered into a Treaty of Alliance, Treaties with Stipulations, without Stipulations and with Deserters, Peace and War connected with the Dual Policy, Conduct (proper) for the King about to be Attacked, The Different Kinds of Allies Fit to be Helped, Pacts for (securing) an Ally, Money, Land and an Undertaking, Considerations regarding the King Attacking in the Rear, Recoupment of Powers that have become Weak, Reasons for Entrenching Oneself (in a Fort) after Making War with a Powerful King, Conduct (proper) for the King Surrendering with his Troops, Conduct (proper) for the King Subjugating (other Kings) by Force, The Making of Peace, Liberation of the Hostage, Conduct towards the Middle King, Conduct towards the Neutral King, Conduct towards the Circle of Kings,—these constitute the Seventh Book 'The Six Measures of Foreign Policy'.

6 G M read *aticāradaṇḍaḥ* in the sing. The plu., however, though not quite necessary, seems more appropriate. The word *aticāra* is found with a short *ti* as in 3.3.32 or a long *tī* as in the colophon after 3.3.29. The reading adopted here as well as in 4.13 is supported by Cb.

9 *sāmavāyita-* in G1 is due to the usual confusion between *ka* and *ta* in Grantha mss. — G and Cb read *saṁdhimokṣaḥ*, but the actual passage at 7.17.32 supports *samādhimokṣaḥ* of the other mss.

10 The Group of Calamities of the Constituent Elements, Considerations regarding Calamities of the King and Kingship, The Group of the Vices of Man, The Group of Afflictions, The Group of Hindrances, The Group of Stoppages of Payment to the Treasury, The Group of Calamities of the Army, The Group of Calamities of the Ally,—these constitute the Eighth Book 'Concerning the Topic of Calamities'.

11 Ascertainment of the (relative) Strength or Weakness of Power, Place and Time, Seasons for Marching on an Expedition, Occasions for the Employment of (the different kinds of) Troops, Merits of Equipping (the different kinds of Troops) for War, The Work of (employing suitable) Troops against Enemy Troops, Consideration of Revolts in the Rear, Counter-measures against Risings of Constituents in the Outer Regions and in the Interior, Consideration of Losses, Expenses and Gains, Dangers from (Officers in) the Outer Regions and the Interior, (Dangers) Connected with Traitors and Enemies, (Dangers) Associated with Advantage, Disadvantage and Uncertainty (as to either), Overcoming These (Dangers) by the Use of the Different Means,—these constitute the Ninth Book 'The Activity of the King about to March'.

12 Setting up of the Camp, March from the Camp, Guarding (Troops) during the Calamities of the Army and at the Time of Attack, Various Types of Covert Fighting, Encouraging One's Own Troops, Disposition of One's Troops to Counter-act Enemy Troops, Ground Suitable for Fighting, Functions of the Infantry, the Cavalry, the Chariots and the Elephants, Arrangement of Battle-arrays in Wings, Flanks and Front in accordance with the Strength of Troops, Distribution of Strong and Weak Troops, Modes of Fighting of the Infantry, the Cavalry, the Chariots and the Elephants, Arrangement of the Staff, the Snake, the Circle and the Diffuse Arrays, Arranging Counter-arrays against Them,—these constitute the Tenth Book "Concerning War'.

13 (Ways of) Resorting to the Policy of (sowing) Dissensions, Forms of Secret Punishment, —these constitute the Eleventh Book 'Policy towards Oligarchies'.

14 The Mission of the Envoy, Fight with (the weapon of) Diplomacy, Assassination of (the enemy's) Army Chiefs, Stirring up the Circle of Kings, Secret Use of Weapons, Fire and Poison, Destruction of (the enemy's) Supplies, Reinforcements and Foraging Raids, Over-reaching (the enemy) by Trickery, Over-reaching (the enemy) by Force, Victory of the Single King, — these constitute the Twelfth Book 'Concerning the Weaker King'.

12 G1 has *-saṁhatavyūhanam,* which is clearly faulty for *-saṁhatavyūhavyūhanam*; cf. 10.6.

13 M1 has *prāṁśudaṇḍaḥ* which is an obvious corruption.

14 Cb reads *vivadha* for *vīvadha*; the latter form is, however, preferred in the text; cf. 7.6.8; 7.7.2; etc.

15 Instigation to Sedition, Drawing Out (the enemy) by means of Stratagems, Employment of Secret Agents, The Work of Laying Siege (to a Fort), Storming (a Fort), Pacification of the Conquered Territory, —these constitute the Thirteenth Book 'Means of Securing a Fort'.

16 Secret Practices for the Destruction of Enemy Troops, Deceiving (by means of Occult Practices), Counter-measures against Injuries to One's Own Troops, —these constitute the Fourteenth Book 'Concerning Secret Practices'.

17 Devices used in the (treatment of the) Science, —this constitutes the Fifteenth Book 'The Methods of the Science'.

18 The enumeration of the (contents of the) Science amounts to fifteen Books, one hundred and fifty Chapters, one hundred and eighty Sections and six thousand *ślokas.*

19 Easy to learn and understand, precise in doctrine, sense and word, free from prolixity of text, thus has this (work on the) Science been composed by Kauṭilya.

CHAPTER TWO

SECTION 1 ENUMERATION OF THE SCIENCES

(i) Establishing (the necessity of) Philosophy

1 Philosophy, the three Vedas, economics and the science of politics—these are the sciences.

18 *sapañcāśad adhyāyaśatam*: it is to be noted that the 150 chapters include this First Chapter, though it does not contain any *prakaraṇa*, but gives only a table of contents. The 180 *prakaraṇas* are distributed over the other 149 chapters. — *sāśītiḥ* of M1 is clearly faulty. — *ṣaṭ ślokasahasrāṇi*: it is a bit strange that a work which is mainly in prose but which has about 380 actual *ślokas* should be described as containing *ślokas* only. Moreover, on the usual basis of 32 prose syllables constituting a *śloka*, we get not 6,000, but less than 5,000 *ślokas* in the present text. It does not also appear very likely that 6,000 refers to the number of *sūtras*, of which there are about 5,370 in the present edition.

19 *sukhagrahaṇavijñeyam*: despite the rather unusual form of the compound, 'easy to learn and understand' seems better than 'easy to understand even for those with a weak, ease-loving intellect' (Cs). *grahaṇa* in the sense of *buddhi* would be unusual. *tattva* 'doctrine, teaching'. — *Kauṭilyena*: many mss. show Kauṭalya as the form of the name, though a few of them, e.g., D and M1 sometimes show the form with *ṭi*, with an attempt made to correct it to *ṭa*. The question is considered in a separate *Study*. — Cb does not read these two ss. which state the extent of the work and refer to its author. It is quite possible that they do not stem from the author himself, but are due to some later hand.

G reads *rājavṛttiḥ* 'the king's life' in the colophon, apparently as the title of this chapter. But the word is more appropriate as a description of the entire work than as the title of a chapter. D M and Cj include the word at the beginning of the next chapter. There it seems out of place. It can hardly be construed with the other words in sūtra 1.2.1. For the word, cf. 1.9.4.

1.2

The first *prakaraṇa* is spread over three chapters 1.2-4.

1 This is clearly the traditional enumeration of the *vidyās*, though some schools held different views.

2 'The three Vedas, economics and the science of politics (are the only sciences),' say the followers of Manu. 3 'For, philosophy is only a special branch of the Vedic lore.'

4 'Economics and the science of politics (are the only sciences),' say the followers of Bṛhaspati. 5 'For, the Vedic lore is only a cloak for one conversant with the ways of the world.'

6 'The science of politics is the only science,' say the followers of Uśanas. 7 'For, with it are bound up undertakings connected with all the sciences.'

8 'Four, indeed, is the number of the sciences,' says Kauṭilya.

9 Since with their help one can learn (what is) spiritual good and material well-being, therefore the sciences (*vidyās*) are so called.

10 Sāṁkhya, Yoga and Lokāyata—these constitute philosophy. 11 Investigating, by means of reasoning, (what is) spiritual good and evil in the Vedic lore, material gain and loss in economics, good policy and bad policy in the science of politics, as well as the relative strength and weakness of

2 *Mānavāḥ*: this refers to a school of Arthaśāstra and not to the *Manusmṛti*. The latter, in 7.43, recommends all the four *vidyās* and not three only. All other references to *Mānavāḥ* in this work are also unconnected with the *Manusmṛti*. 3 *Trayīviśeṣo hyānvīkṣikī*: *Ānvīkṣikī* as described below can hardly be regarded as a branch of the Vedic lore, though Sāṁkhya and Yoga claim to hold the Veda as authoritative.

4 *Bārhaspatyāh*: the *Bārhaspatya Arthaśāstra* published in the Punjab Sanskrit Series is a very late work and does not represent the views of this school as referred to in this work. 5 *saṁvaraṇa* 'a covering, a cloak.' As Cb says, it only serves the purpose of preventing people from calling him a *nāstika*.

6 *Auśanasāḥ*: the *Śukranītisāra* is an extremely late work and is not to be understood as representing the views of the school of Uśanas referred to here.

8 The four *vidyās*, on the study of all of which Kauṭilya himself insists, practically cover all branches of learning known at the time.

9 *tābhir* etc.: the etymology of *vidyā* is given in the manner of the Brāhmaṇa works. Only *dharma* and *artha* are mentioned, not *kāma* also, as objects of study; apparently a work on *kāma* would not constitute a *vidyā*, at any rate for a ruler, according to the author.

10 *Sāṁkhyaṁ Yogo Lokāyataṁ ca*: this enumeration of the philosophical systems is interesting. Sāṁkhya and Yoga, it is admitted, are the oldest among the philosophical systems of India. The Lokāyata, it appears from this passage, once held an equally honourable place. It is the system said to have been founded by Bṛhaspati and later associated with the name of Cārvāka. Cj says '*Lokāyataṁ Bārhaspatyam. lokāya buddhiṁ tanoti iti nairuktam*', i.e., it gives knowledge about worldly affairs. Similarly, Somadeva in the *Nītivākyāmṛta* (sec. 6) says '*aihikavyavahāra-prasādhana-paraṁ Lokāyatikam; Lokāyatato hi rājā rāṣṭra-kaṇṭakān ucchedayati*.' According to Cb, however, Lokāyata is the Nyāyaśāstra as taught by Brahman, Gārgya and others. But if by Nyāyaśāstra is meant the science of reasoning, this cannot be a correct explanation. — Ānvīkṣikī, as the present passage shows, is so called because of the use of reasoning for arriving at conclusions (*hetubhir anvīkṣamāṇā*). This led to its identification with Tarkavidyā (cf. *Mahābhārata*, 12.173.45 etc.) and the Nyāyaśāstra, even with the *Nyāyasūtras* of Gautama (cf. Vātsyāyana in his Bhāṣya on 1.1.1). But in this text Ānviksikī is not the science of reasoning or logic, but

these (three sciences), (philosophy) confers benefit on the people, keeps the mind steady in adversity and in prosperity and brings about proficiency in thought, speech and action.

12 Philosophy is ever thought of as the lamp of all sciences, as the means of all actions (and) as the support of all laws (and duties).

CHAPTER THREE

SECTION 1 (Continued)

(ii) Establishing (the necessity of) the Vedic Lore

1 The Sāmaveda, the Ṛgveda and the Yajurveda, — these three are the three Vedas. 2 (These three), the Atharvaveda and the Itihāsaveda are the Vedas.

3 Phonetics, Ritual, Grammar, Etymology, Prosody and Astronomy,— these are auxiliary sciences.

4 The law laid down in this Vedic lore is beneficial, as it prescribes the respective duties of the four *varṇas* and the four stages of life.

5 The special duties of the Brahmin are : studying, teaching, performing sacrifices for self, officiating at other people's sacrifices, making gifts and receiving gifts.

6 Those of the Kṣatriya are : studying, performing sacrifices for self, making gifts, living by (the profession of) arms and protecting beings.

7 Those of the Vaiśya are : studying, performing sacrifices for self, making gifts, agriculture, cattle-rearing and trade.

certain philosophical systems based on reasoning. 11 *nayāpanayau* : see 6.2.6-11 for these terms. — Cs (following in the main Cb) reads a stop after *Daṇḍanītyām* and supplies *prādhānyena pratipādyau* as the predicate for the clauses. It seems better, however, to construe *dharmādharmau* etc. also with *hetubhir anvīkṣamāṇā*. That is shown by the *ca* after *balābale* and supported by *pradīpaḥ sarvavidyānām* in s. 12 below.

12 Every chapter in this text closes with one or more stanzas. This stanza is found in Vātsyāyana's Bhāṣya on the *Nyāyasūtras* 1.1.1, where the last line appears as *vidyoddeśe prakīrtitā*. This clearly shows that Vātsyāyana had the present text before him; for, the present section does bear the name *vidyāsamuddeśa*.

1.3

1-2 Cs does not read the stop after *Trayī*, so that a single s. is understood to enumerate the five Vedas. An explanation of *Trayī* by itself would, however, seem to be necessary as in the other cases. It is not unlikely that the text originally read *Sāmargyajurvedās Trayī. Trayī Atharvavedetihāsavedau ca Vedāḥ.* — The *Chāndogya Upaniṣad* (7.1.2) refers to *Itihāsa-Purāṇa* as the fifth Veda.

4 *Trayīdharmaḥ* : actually it is only in the Dharmasūtras, a branch of the Vedāṅga Kalpa, that the duties of the *varṇas* and *āśramas* are laid down in detail.

8 Those of the Śūdra are : service of the twice-born, engaging in an economic calling (viz., agriculture, cattle-rearing and trade) and the profession of the artisan and the actor.

9 Those of the householder are : earning his living in accordance with his own special duty, marrying into families of the same caste but not of the some *gotra*, approaching the wife during the period, worship of the gods, manes and guests, making gifts to dependents and eating what is left over (after the others have eaten).

10 Those of the student of the Veda are : studying the Veda, tending the (sacred) fires and (ceremonial) bathing, keeping the vow of living on alms only, residing till the end of his life with the preceptor or, in his absence, with the preceptor's son or with a fellow-student.

11 Those of the forest-anchorite are : observing celibacy, sleeping on bare ground, wearing matted locks and an antelope-skin, worship of the (sacred) fires and (ceremonial) bathing, worshipping the gods, manes and guests and living on forest produce (only).

12 Those of the wandering ascetic are : having full control over the senses, refraining from all active life, being without any possessions, giving up all attachment to worldly ties, keeping the vow of begging alms, residing not in one place and in the forest, and observing external and internal cleanliness.

13 (Duties) common to all are : abstaining from injury (to living creatures), truthfulness, uprightness, freedom from malice, compassionateness and forbearance.

14 (The observance of) one's own special duty leads to heaven and to endless bliss. 15 In case of its transgression, people would be exterminated through (the) mixture (of duties and castes).

8 The Smṛtis generally allow to the Śūdra only service of the twice-born as his duty (cf. Manu, 9.334 ; *Gītā*, 18.44). Gautama (10.60) and Yājñavalkya (1.120) allow him trade or an artisan's profession only if service of the twice-born is not possible. The present text probably represents the actual state of things more accurately.

9 *svadharmājīvaḥ* from D seems preferable to *svakarmājīvaḥ*. — *tulyaiḥ*, i.e., those belonging to the same *varṇa*. — *asamānarṣibhiḥ*, i.e., not belonging to the same *gotra*, marriages between *sagotras* being prohibited. — D's *-tithipūjā bhṛtyeṣu tyāgaḥ* is distinctly better as shown by s. 11 below. — *śeṣa* ' remnants of the sacrifice ' (Russ.).

10 *bhaikṣavratitvam* from D seems better. Cb explains the other reading (with *-vratatvam*) ' begging alms and observing *vratas* ending with *godāna*.' Two ideas do not appear to be intended.

12 *bhaikṣavratam anekatra araṇye ca vāsaḥ* is again from D ; others read *bhaikṣam* and omit *ca*. In view of s. 10, *bhaikṣavratam* seems preferable and as *anekatra* is to be construed with *vāsaḥ*, *ca* seems better. — The stop after *ca śaucam* is necessary ; what follows forms a new sentence, laying down duties for all *varṇas* and *āśramas*, as in *Manusmṛti*, 6.91-93, *Āpastamba*, 1.8.23.6, *Mahābhārata*, 12.60.7-8, etc.

14 *ānantyāya* : this is mentioned over and above *svarga* ' heaven,' and hence obviously indicates the ' endless ' bliss of *mokṣa*. 15 *saṁkara* : this refers to *karmasaṁkara* doing the duties of a different *varṇa* ; it also refers to *varṇasaṁkara*, ' mixing ' of the *varṇas* through inter-marriages.

16 Therefore, the king should not allow the special duties of the (different) beings to be transgressed (by them); for, ensuring adherence to (each one's) special duty, he finds joy after death as well as in this life.

17 For, people, among whom the bounds of the Aryan rule of life are fixed, among whom the *varṇas* and the stages of life are securely established and who are guarded by the three Vedas, prosper, do not perish.

CHAPTER FOUR

SECTION 1 (Continued)

(iii) Establishing (the necessity of) Economics, and
(iv) the Science of Politics

1 Agriculture, cattle-rearing and trade,—these constitute economics, (which are) beneficial, as they yield grains, cattle, money, forest produce and labour. 2 Through them, the (king) brings under his sway his own party as well as the party of the enemies, by the (use of the) treasury and the army.

3 The means of ensuring the pursuit of philosophy, the three Vedas and econcmics is the Rod (wielded by the king); its administration constitutes the science of politics, having for its purpose the acquisition of (things) not possessed, the preservation of (things) possessed, the augmentation of (things) preserved and the bestowal of (things) augmented on a worthy recipient. 4 On it is dependent the orderly maintenance of worldly life.

5 'Therefore, the (king), seeking the orderly maintenance of worldly life, should ever hold the Rod lifted up (to strike). 6 For, there is no such means for the subjugation of beings as the Rod,' say the (ancient) teachers.

16 *na vyabhicārayet* is causal and hence 'should not allow the people to transgress.' — *saṁdadhānaḥ*: the substantive is clearly *rājā*, 'ensuring adherence to.'

17 *Trayyābhirakṣito* is from D; the *hi* in the other reading has little significance.

1.4

1 The word *vārttā* is clearly derived from *vṛtti* 'livelihood.' — *viṣṭi* 'labour,' i.e., labourers. The root in the word is *viṣ* 'to be active.'

3 *yogakṣema-*: *yoga* is the acquistion of things and *kṣema* is their secure possession; the two together convey the idea of security and well-being or prosperity. 4 *lokayātrā* 'the going of the world', i.e., worldly intercourse. — Meyer would include this s. in the opinion of the *ācāryāḥ*, stated in the following sutras; but it seems that Kauṭilya does not object to the statement in this s.; his objection is to *nityam udyatadaṇḍatva* only.

6 *vaśopanayanam* 'a means of bringing under subjugation.'

7 'No,' says Kauṭilya. 8 For, the (king), severe with the Rod, becomes a source of terror to beings. 9 The (king), mild with the Rod, is despised. 10 The (king), just with the Rod, is honoured.

11 For, the Rod, used after full consideration, endows the subjects with spiritual good, material well-being and pleasures of the senses. 12 Used unjustly, whether in passion or anger, or in contempt, it enrages even forest-anchorites and wandering ascetics, how much more then the householders? 13 If not used at all, it gives rise to the law of the fishes. 14 For, the stronger swallows the weak in the absence of the wielder of the Rod. 15 Protected by him, he prevails.

> 16 The people, of the four *varṇas* and in the four stages of life, protected by the king with the Rod, (and) deeply attached to occupations prescribed as their special duties, keep to their respective paths.

CHAPTER FIVE

SECTION 2 ASSOCIATION WITH ELDERS

1 Therefore, the three sciences have their root in the (just administration of) the Rod. 2 (Administration of) the Rod, (when) rooted in self-discipline, brings security and well-being to living beings.

3 Discipline is (twofold), acquired and inborn. 4 For, training disciplines suitable stuff, not one unsuited. 5 A science imparts discipline to one, whose intellect has (the qualities of) the desire to learn, listening (to the teacher), learning, retention, thorough understanding, reflection, rejection (of false views) and intentness on truth, (and) not to any other person.

8 *udvejanīyaḥ* ' one who is to be feared,' i.e., a source of terror or fright.

12 *avajñānād* is from D for *ajñānād*. The former is more likely to lead to rage than the latter. It is proposed to read a *vā* after *avajñānād*, as it is necessary. It seems to have dropped out because of the *vā-* with which the next word begins. 13 *mātsyanyāya* ' the law of the fishes,' according to which the bigger fish swallow the smaller ones. Cf. 1.13.5 below. 15 *sa tena guptaḥ prabhavati* : *tena* seems to refer to the *daṇḍadhara* rather than to *daṇḍa*. G M omit *sa*, but it seems necessary as referring to the *abala*. After *sa* D adds *ca*, which is not necessary. It is impossible to see in *guptaḥ* any reference to a patron of the author.

16 *vartmasu* : M reads *veśmasu* which yields a very colourless idea. Cb text shows *karmasu*, but the actual comment has *mārga*, which presupposes *vartmasu*. Moreover, *karmasu* is little likely, as the people are already *karmābhirata*.

1.5

1 *daṇḍamūlās tisro vidyāḥ* : this is so because unless there is a just administration, no pursuit of learning or avocations would be possible. 2 *vinayamūlo* etc: the idea is, administration by a disciplined ruler alone can lead to prosperity and security of the people.

4 *kriyā hi dravyam* etc. : cf. *Raghuvaṁśa*, 3.29, where Mallinātha quotes the present passage as from Kauṭilya. Cf. also *Mudrārākṣasa*, 7.14. 5 *śuśrūṣā-* etc.: these are called *prajñāguṇāḥ* 'qualities of the intellect' in 6.1.4 below. — *abhiniviṣṭa* may be understood in the sense of *abhiniveśa* or as standing for *abhiniveśayukta*.

6 But training and discipline in the sciences (are acquired) by (accepting) the authoritativeness of the teachers in the respective sciences.

7 When the ceremony of tonsure is performed, the (prince) should learn the use of the alphabet and arithmetic. 8 When the initiation with the preceptor is performed, he should learn the three Vedas and philosophy from the learned, economics from the heads of departments (and) the science of politics from theoretical and practical exponents.

9 And (he should observe) celibacy till the sixteenth year. 10 Thereafter (should follow) the cutting of the hair and marriage for him.

11 And (he should have) constant association with elders in learning for the sake of improving his training, since training has its root in that.

12 During the first part of the day, he should undergo training in the arts of (using) elephants, horses, chariots and weapons. 13 In the latter part, (he should engage) in listening to Itihāsa. 14 The Purāṇas, Itivṛtta, Ākhyāyikā, Udāharaṇa, Dharmaśāstra and Arthaśāstra, —these constitute Itihāsa. 15 During the remaining parts of the day and the night, he should learn new things and familiarise himself with those already learnt, and listen repeatedly to things not learnt. 16 For, from (continuous) study ensues a (trained) intellect, from intellect (comes) practical application, (and) from practical application (results) self-possession ; such is the efficacy of sciences.

17 For, the king, trained in the sciences, intent on the discipline of the subjects, enjoys the earth (alone) without sharing it with any other (ruler), being devoted to the welfare of all beings.

6 *vidyānām* is to be construed with *vinayo niyamaś ca*, though it has also to be understood with *yathāsvam*. Whereas *vinaya* refers to actual instruction, *niyama* seems to refer to the life of discipline that is to accompany the period of study.

7 *vṛttacaulakarmā* : the tonsure ceremony is to be performed in the first year or the third after birth. — *upayuñjīta*, i.e., should learn to make use of. 8 *śiṣṭebhyaḥ* 'those who are trained,' i.e., the learned teachers. — *vaktṛprayoktṛbhyaḥ* 'those who teach the theory and those actually engaged in practising it.'

9 *ā ṣodaśād varṣād* : as 3.3.1 shows, a man is supposed to have attained majority when he has completed his sixteenth year. 10 *godānam*, also known as *keśānta*, is the second tonsure, done at puberty. Cf. *Raghuvaṁśa* 3.28-33 which are clearly based on the present passage. For the *saṁskāras* mentioned here, see works on *Dharmaśāstra*. — G1 reads a stop after *ca* and includes *asya* in the next s. That makes an odd beginning for that s.

14 *Itivṛttam* 'such as the *Rāmāyaṇa*, *Bhārata* etc.' (Cj). — *ākhyāyikā* is '*divyamanuṣyādicaritam*' (Cb). — *udāharaṇam* 'e.g., *Tantrākhyāyikā*, etc.' (Cj). — G1 and M omit *Arthaśāstram*. — It is not unlikely that s. 14 is a marginal gloss (in explanation of Itihāsa occurring in s. 13) which later got into the text. 16 *prajñāyā*: G M and Cj read *prajñayā*; D has the original *jñā* changed to *jña*. A ms. collated in M2 shows the former reading, which is supported by Cb. The ablative would appear preferable as in the other clauses. — G2 reads *ātmavidyāsāmarthyam* and Jolly-Schmidt prefer it ; however, a reference to the science of the supreme spirit is out of place here. *ātmavattā* 'self-possession' is what is intended for the ruler.

CHAPTER SIX

SECTION 3 CONTROL OVER THE SENSES

(i) Casting out the Group of Six Enemies

1 Control over the senses, which is motivated by training in the sciences, should be secured by giving up lust, anger, greed, pride, arrogance and foolhardiness. 2 Absence of improper indulgence in (the pleasures of) sound, touch, colour, taste and smell by the senses of hearing, touch and sight, the tongue and the sense of smell, means control over the senses ; or, the practice of (this) science (gives such control). 3 For, the whole of this science means control over the senses.

4 A king, behaving in a manner contrary to that, (and hence) having no control over his senses, quickly perishes, though he be ruler right up to the four ends of the earth. 5 For example, the Bhoja king, Dāṇḍakya by name, entertaining a sinful desire for a Brahmin maiden, perished along with his kinsmen and kingdom; and (so did) Karāla, King of the Videhas. 6 Janamejaya, using violence against Brahmins, out of anger, (likewise perished); and (so did) Tālajaṅgha, (using violence) against the Bhṛgus. 7 Aila, extorting money from the four *varṇas* out of greed, (perished); and (so did) Ajabindu of the Sauvīras. 8 Rāvaṇa, not restoring the wife of another through pride, (perished); and (so did) Duryodhana (not returning) a portion of the kingdom. 9 Dambhodbhava, treating creatures with contempt out of arrogance, (perished) ; and (so did) Arjuna of the Haihayas.

1.6

The third *prakaraṇa* is spread over two chapters, 1.6-7.

1 *vidyāvinayahetuḥ* : this is a Bahuvrīhi compound (Cj Meyer) rather than a Tatpuruṣa (Cb Cs). — *māna* appears to be the feeling of great conceit owing to an exaggerated opinion about oneself; *mada* is arrogance resulting from the possession of great power; *harṣa* appears to be the feeling of great exhilaration resulting in playful pranks and fool hardy behaviour (*atikrīḍanonmatiḥ* or *krīḍāsukham* —Cj). 2 *avipratipattiḥ* : this is the absence of *vipratipatti* (*viruddhā pravṛtti* or improper behaviour, i.e., over-indulgence). 3 *kṛtsnaṁ hi śāstram* etc. : apparently a study of a work on the political science like the present text is expected to give the ruler control over the senses.

5 Dāṇḍakya Bhoja: the *Rāmāyaṇa*, 7.80-81, narrates how King Daṇḍa who had violated Arajā, the daughter of his chaplain Uśanas, was destroyed together with his whole kingdom by the latter's curse; thus was the Daṇḍakāraṇya made. Cnn in D gives Bṛhadaśva as the name of this king. — Karāla Vaideha: he seems to have been known also as Karāla Janaka, King of the Videhas. The *Buddhacarita* 11.31 refers to him as Maithila and mentions him along with Daṇḍaka. 6 Janamejaya : he is said to have whipped the Brahmin priests, whom he suspected of having violated his queen when it was really Indra, who had done that (Cj). — Tālajaṅgha was a descendant of Śaryāti, according to the *Mahābhārata*. The *Saundarananda* 7.39, 44 refers to these two kings in the same connection. Aśvaghoṣa had clearly the present passage before him. 7 Aila is Purūravas, the son of Ilā and Budha. He is said to have seized the golden vessels in the sacrifice he was called upon to protect. — *atyāhṛ* 'to extort money from.' — Sauvīra Ajabindu : little is known about him. 9 Dambhodbhava : the *Mahābhārata*, 5.94.5ff. narrates how Dambhodbhava wanted to fight with Nara and Nārāyana, but was rendered helpless by them with a handful of grass and was asked to give up his haughtiness. — Haihaya Arjuna is well-known; he is credited with the possession of a thousand arms. His over-bearing attitude towards Jamadagni cost him his life.

10 Vātāpi, trying to assail Agastya, out of foolhardiness, (perished); and (so did) the clan of the Vṛṣṇis (trying to assail) Dvaipāyana.

11 These and many other kings, giving themselsves up to the group of six enemies, perished with their kinsmen and kingdoms, being without control over their senses.

12 Casting out the group of six enemies, Jāmadagnya, who had full control over his senses, as well as Ambarīṣa, the son of Nabhāga, enjoyed the earth for a long time.

CHAPTER SEVEN

SECTION 3 (Continued)

(ii) The life of a Sage-like King

1 Therefore, by casting out the group of six enemies he should acquire control over the senses, cultivate his intellect by association with elders, keep a watchful eye by means of spies, bring about security and well-being by (energetic) activity, maintain the observance of their special duties (by the subjects) by carrying out (his own) duties, acquire discipline by (receiving) instruction in the sciences, attain popularity by association with what is of material advantage and maintain (proper) behaviour by (doing) what is beneficial.

10 Vātāpi: the *Mahābhārata* 3.94-97 and the *Rāmāyaṇa* 3.11.55-66 narrate the story of the demon Vātāpi and his brother Ilvala. The latter by his magic powers used to change his brother into a goat and offer him to Brahmins at a *śrāddha*. After they had taken their meals, Ilvala used to call his brother, who came out tearing open the bellies of those Brahmins and causing their death. Vātāpi met his doom when the same trick was tried on Agastya, who managed to digest Vātāpi. — *atyāsādayan*: 'encountering, going very near;' the idea of an actual assault is probably not intended. — Vṛṣṇisaṁgha: N. C. Banerjee states that the account of the downfall of the Vṛṣṇis by Dvaipāyana does not tally with the account in the *Mahābhārata*, but agrees with the tradition in the Ghaṭa Jātaka (IHQ, I, p. 97 and n.). According to the *Mahābhārata*, it was Nārada of whom the Vṛṣṇis made fun.

12 Jāmadagnya: this is clearly the celebrated Paraśurāma. But he is not elsewhere known to have 'enjoyed the earth for a long time,' though he had repeatedly cleared it of Ksatriyas. He is said to have made a gift of the earth to Brahmins, especially to Kaśyapa. Cf. *Rāmāyaṇa*, 1.75.25 etc. — For Ambarīṣa, see *Māhābhārata*, 12.29.

1.7

rājarṣivṛttam, i.e., the kind of life that would be appropriate to a sage-like king.

1 *kurvīta* is to be understood with all the following clauses as well. — *vinayaṁ vidyopadeśena*: this seems to refer to the ruler's own training rather than to that of the subjects. — Cj reads *lokapriyam*, explaining it by *lokasukham* 'happiness of the people.' — *arthasaṁyogena*: this seems to refer to doing beneficial things rather than only to acceptance and proper disposal of money (as in Cb Cs). — *hitena vṛttim*: this may refer to the ruler himself leading a life that is beneficial or to his securing for the subjects a livelihood by doing beneficial things. The former seems meant.

2 With his senses thus under control he should avoid another man's wife or property as well as doing injury to others, also (avoid) sleepiness, capriciousness, falsehood, wearing an extravagant dress, association with harmful persons and any transaction associated with unrighteousness or harm.

3 He should enjoy sensual pleasures without contravening his spiritual good and material well-being ; he should not deprive himself of pleasures. 4 Or, (he should devote himself) equally to the three goals of life which are bound up with one another. 5 For, any one of (the three, viz.,) spiritual good, material well-being and sensual pleasures, (if) excessively indulged in, does harm to itself as well as to the other two.

6 'Material well-being alone is supreme,' says Kauṭilya. 7 For, spiritual good and sensual pleasures depend on material well-being.

8 He should set the preceptors or ministers as the bounds of proper conduct (for himself), who should restrain him from occasions of harm, or, when he is erring in private, should prick him with the goad in the form of (the indication of time for the performance of his regular duties by means of) the shadow (of the gnomon) or the *nālikā* (water-clock).

9 Rulership can be successfully carried out (only) with the help of associates. One wheel alone does not turn. Therefore, he should appoint ministers and listen to their opinion.

2 *svapnalaulyam* of G1 is obviously faulty. — Cj seems to support D's *uddhataveṣam* for *-veṣatvam*. — *anarthya-* is a common word in the sense of 'a harmful person' such as a dancer, actor, singer, etc. (Cj). *anartha-* for it (as in G2) is unlikely, as *anarthasaṁyukta* is separately mentioned.

4 After *anyonyānubaddham*, D adds *parasparānupaghātakam*, which seems to be a marginal gloss on the former expression, which has got into the text. 5 The reading *kāmānātmānam* is due to the dropping of the letter *mā* between *nā* and *tmā* through a scribal error. The genitive is obviously necessary.

6-7 D omits s. 6 ; also, it seems, Cj. But s. 7 definitely presupposes it. The *hi* in it would otherwise have no significance. It appears that Kauṭilya was the first to assign a high place to *artha* as against *dharma* and *kāma*.

8 *maryādām*, i.e., the boundary beyond which he must not go ; in other words, he must not transgress their advice. — *chāyānālikāpratodena*: the *ācāryas* are to use the goad in the form of either *chāyā* or *nālikā*, which are the two ways of ascertaining time. For *nālikā* see 2.20.34-35 and for *chāyā* 2.20.39 below. The idea is that the teachers are to remind the prince of the time and the specific duties fixed for him at that time. This reminder serves like a goad to the erring prince. *pratoda* can hardly refer to the 'striking' of a drum or gong to indicate time, as F. E. Pargiter, JRAS, 1915, pp. 701-702, says. As *abhitudeyuḥ* shows, the idea of pricking an elephant with a goad, when he strays from the right path, is at the basis of the metaphor. As Cj has '*paśum iva; iyam anuṣṭhānāntaravelā vartate iti.*' *pratoda* has the same root *tud* and must mean a goad. — *rahasi* is to be construed with *pramādyantam* (Cb Cj) rather than with *abhitudeyuḥ* (Meyer).

9 *sacivān* is a general term for all who help in the work of administration, *mantrin*, *adhyakṣa*, *dūta* etc. — Cb includes ss. 8-9 in the next chapter at the beginning ; but though they appear more appropriate there, the *śloka* is s.9 indicates rather the end of a chapter.

CHAPTER EIGHT

SECTION 4 APPOINTMENT OF MINISTERS

1 'He should make his fellow-students his ministers, their integrity and capability being known (to him),' says Bhāradvāja. 2 'For, they enjoy his confidence.'

3 'No,' says Viśālākṣa. 4 'Having been his play-mates, they treat him with disrespect. 5 He should make those his ministers who are of a like nature to him in secret matters, since they have the same character and vices. 6 For, through fear that he is conversant with their secrets they do not offend him.'

7 'This defect is common (to both),' say the followers of Parāśara. 8 'For, through fear that they too are conversant with his secrets, he would acquiesce in what they do and what they omit to do.

> 9 'To as many persons the lord of men communicates a secret, to so many does he become subservient, being helpless by that act (of his).

10 'He should make those his ministers who may have helped him in calamities involving danger to life, since their loyalty is (thus) proved.'

11 'No,' says Piśuna. 12 'This is devotion, not a trait of intellect. 13 He should make those his ministers who, when appointed to tasks, the income from which is calculated (beforhand), would bring in the income as directed or more, since (thus) their qualities are proved.'

14 'No,' says Kauṇapadanta. 15 'For, these are not endowed with other qualities necessary in a minister. 16 He should make those his

1.8

1 *Bhāradvājaḥ* : he is generally identified with Droṇa, the celebrated teacher of the Kuru princes. But unlike Bhīṣma he is not known to have been a teacher of politics. Jolly-Schmidt identify him with Kaṇiṅka Bhāradvāja mentioned in 5.5.11 as a minister who ran away in time on noticing certain signs of his master's displeasure. The *Mahābhārata* 12.58.3 mentions Bhāradvāja as a teacher of *rājadharmas,* and contains a discourse on politics by Kaṇiṅka Bhāradvāja in 12.138.

3 *Viśālākṣaḥ* : this is the name of Śiva. In the *Mahābhārata* 12.59.80ff. he is said to have abridged the *Daṇḍanīti* composed by Svayaṁbhū, his work being known as the *Vaiśālākṣa Śāstra.* 5 *guhyasadharmāṇaḥ,* lit. 'those who possess the same characteristics in respect of secret affairs', i.e., his associates in secret affairs. 6 Here as well as in s. 8, *marmajña* seems to stand for *marmajñatva.* Cj shows *marmajñatva* in s. 8.

7 *Pārāśarāḥ* : G M read *Parāśaraḥ* here ; but in 1.15.23 and 1.17.9 even they show the former. Cj has *Pārāśarāḥ.* 9 The *śloka* makes it highly probable that we have here a regular quotation from a work of this school.

11 *Piśunaḥ* : he is usually identified with the sage Nārada. It is possible, however, that he is the same as the minister Piśuna mentioned in 5.5.11, who ran away on seeing signs of his master's displeasure. 13 *saṁkhyātārtheṣu* : in view of *saṁkhyāta* 'calculated,' *artha* should mean 'income, revenue,' accruing from the undertaking.

14 *Kauṇapadantaḥ* 'with goblin's teeth' is said to be a nickname of Bhīṣma ; *pūtidantasya Śaṁtanorayaṁ putra iti,* says Cj. Cnn remarks that Śaṁtanu had 'stinking teeth' because of a curse of Gaṅgā. 16 *dṛṣṭāvadānatvāt* : this is from D. We have to distinguish

ministers who have come (as hereditary servants) from his father and grandfather, since their pure conduct is known. 17 They do not desert him even when he misbehaves, being of the same kin. 18 This is observed even among animals. 19 For, cattle, passing by a herd of cattle not their kin, abide only with those that are their kin.'

20 'No,' says Vātavyādhi. 21 'For, bringing under their control everything belonging to him, they behave like masters (themselves). 22 Therefore, he should make new men well-versed in politics his ministers. 23 New men, indeed, looking upon the wielder of the Rod as occupying the position of Yama, do not give offence.'

24 'No,' says Bāhudantīputra. 25 'One, conversant with the science, (but) not experienced in practical affairs, would come to grief in (carrying out) undertakings. 26 He should appoint as ministers such (persons) as are endowed with nobility of birth, intellect, integrity, bravery and loyalty, because of the supreme importance of qualities (in this matter).'

27 'Everything (stated above) is justifiable,' says Kauṭilya. 28 For, from the capacity for doing work is the ability of a person judged. 29 And in accordance with their ability,

> by (suitably) distributing rank among ministers and assigning place, time and work (to them), he should appoint all these as ministers, not, however, as councillors.

avadāna 'good or pure conduct' from *apadāna* 'offence, crime.' For the latter, cf. 2.36.36; 3.12.35 etc. Cnn paraphrases *avadāna* by *upadhāśuddhi* integrity proved by a secret test. Cb renders it by *parākrama*, which unnecessarily restricts the sense. 17 *sagandha*: Cnn paraphrases *gandha* by '*paricayajanitasneha* affection produced by close acquaintance.' *sagandha*, however, seems rather to convey the idea of kinship. 19 *sagandheṣu* etc.: *Śākuntala* 5.21.27 seems influenced by the present passage.

20 *Vātavyādhiḥ*: this is said to be the name of Uddhava, a minister of Kṛṣṇa. Little is known about this teacher of politics. 21 *avagṛhya*: the root *ava-grah* is common in this text in the sense of 'to check, to bring under control.' —*iti* at the end of s. 21 found in some mss. is clearly out of place.

24 *Bāhundantīputraḥ* 'the son of one whose teeth are her arms' is said to be Indra. According to Cnn, Bāhudantī is the name of Indra's mother. The *Mahābhārata*, 12.59.82-83, refers to a further abridgment of Svayaṁbhū's work by Indra; it was called *Bāhudantaka*.

27 *sarvam upapannam*: this evidently means that all considerations for and against the various views can be justified according to circumstances. Meyer thinks that Kauṭilya agrees with Bāhudantīputra, though he does not discard altogether the opinions of others. Cj also seems to understand that a person endowed with *abhijana* etc. (mentioned by Bāhudantīputra) is able to accomplish anything. 28 Cb Cs read the stop not after *kalpyate* but after *sāmarthyataś ca* and explain 'the capability of a person (such as *viśvāsyatva* etc.) for different kinds of duties is established by the power (*sāmarthya*) of such actions as fellow-studentship, etc. (*kārya*), and by the possession in a greater or less degree of wisdom, study of science and other qualities (*sāmarthyataḥ*).' This appears hardly possible; *sāmarthyataś ca* quite obviously belongs to the stanza that follows. Russ. follows Cs.

29 *sāmarthyataḥ amātyavibhavaṁ vibhajya*, i.e., assigning the position or rank of *amātya* according to the capacity of the persons. —*sarva eva ete*, i.e., *sahādhyāyin* etc. mentioned above. Cnn remarks that each of the 18 principal officers in a state has three subordinates, so that 72 posts have to be filled in all. That allows room for choice from among *sahādhyāyins* and others.

CHAPTER NINE

SECTION 5 APPOINTMENT OF COUNCILLORS AND CHAPLAIN

1 A native of the country, of noble birth, easy to hold in check, trained in the arts, possessed of the eye (of science), intelligent, persevering, dexterous, eloquent, bold, possessed of a ready wit, endowed with energy and power, able to bear troubles, upright, friendly, firmly devoted, endowed with character, strength, health and spirit, devoid of stiffness and fickleness, amiable (and) not given to creating animosities,—these are the excellences of a minister.
2 One, lacking in a quarter and a half of these qualities is the middling and the lowest (type, respectively).

3 Of these (qualities), he should make inquiries about nationality, nobility of birth and tractability from (his) kinsmen, test his (training in) arts and possession of the eye of science through those learned in the same sciences, learn about his intelligence, perseverence and dexterity from his handling of undertakings, test his eloquence, boldness and presence of mind on occasions of conversation, his energy and power as well as ability to bear troubles during a calamity, his uprightness, friendliness and firmness of devotion from his dealings with others, learn about his character, strength, health and spirit as well as about freedom from stiffness and fickleness from those living with him, (and) about his amiability and absence of a disposition to animosity by personal observation.

4 For, the affairs of a king are (of three kinds, viz.,) directly perceived, unperceived and inferred. 5 What is seen by (the king) himself is directly perceived. 6 What is communicated by others is unperceived (by him).
7 Forming an idea of what has not been done from what is done in respect of undertakings is inferred. 8 But, because of the simultaneity of undertakings, their manifoldness and their having to be carried out in many different places, he should cause them to be carried out by ministers, unperceived (by him), so that there may be no loss of place and time.

1.9

1 *svavagrahaḥ* : Cb explains 'having good relations'; Cj has 'possessed of benevolent friends,' or 'who is able to restrain (the king) gently.' The word, however, rather means 'easy to control,' as contrasted with *anavagraha* 'unrestrained,' also used of a minister in 1.15.36 below; cf. also 6.1.6. — *dhārayiṣṇuḥ* 'with a good memory' (Cj Cs); but *prajñā* includes memory as its *guṇa*. — *stambha* 'rigidity' seems to refer to haughtiness. Cnn explans '*mithyābhimānād avinayaḥ*, insolence due to false pride.' — *-cāpalahīnaḥ* from D is supported by Cb.

3 *abhijanam* is missing in G M, evidently through a scribal error. — M Cj read *āpyataḥ* and the latter explains it by '*svajanataḥ*'; that is also Cb's explanation of *āptataḥ*. The word *āpta* may also mean 'a reliable person.' — *āpadyutsāhaprabhāvau kleśasahatvaṁ ca* is missing in D, clearly through a scribal error.

4 *rājavṛttiḥ* seems to refer to the carrying out of all kinds of state work. This is *pratyakṣa*, or *parokṣa* or *anumeya* from the king's point of view. The discussion brings out the necessity of appointing ministers. 8 *ayaugapadyāt* of G1 is clearly corrupt. The idea is, because a number of state works have to be carried out simultaneously, some works must be done when the king is not present and hence ministers become necessary.

So Far the Work of (Appointing) Ministers.

9 He should appoint a chaplain, who is very exalted in family and character, thoroughly trained in the Veda with its auxiliary sciences, in divine signs, in omens and in the science of politics and capable of counteracting divine and human calamities by means of Atharvan remedies. 10 And he should follow him as a pupil (does) his teacher, a son his father (or) a servant his master.

11 Kṣatriya power, made to prosper by the Brahmin (chaplain), sanctified by spells in the form of the counsel of ministers, (and) possessed of arms in the form of compliance with the science (of politics), triumphs, remaining ever unconquered.

CHAPTER TEN

SECTION 6 ASCERTAINMENT OF THE INTEGRITY OR THE ABSENCE OF INTEGRITY OF MINISTERS BY MEANS OF SECRET TESTS

1 After appointing ministers to ordinary offices in consultation with the councillors and the chaplain, he should test their integrity by means of secret tests.

2 The king should (seemingly) discard the chaplain on the ground that he showed resentment when appointed to officiate at the sacrifice of a person not entitled to the privilege of a sacrifice or to teach (such a person).

9 *uditoditakulaśīlam* : the repetition of *udita* seems only to emphasize the exalted character of the *kula* and *śīla*. Cb has ' when there is nothing blameworthy for four generations ' ; Cj ' when the ancestors and descendants upto four or seven generations are pure in birth and conduct.' Cs however has ' whose family and character are such as belong to those richly endowed (*udita*) with qualities prescribed (*udita*) in the *śāstra*.' This is too involved and seems due to the influence of the *Mitākṣarā* on *Yājñavalkya* 1.313, where, however, the word is only *uditoditam* (curtailed apparently for metrical reasons). — *sāṅge vede* of D is clearly a better expression than *ṣaḍaṅge vede* of the other mss. — Cb reads *sāmudre daivanimitte* for *daive nimitte* and explains ' signs connected with palmistry etc., and omens due to divine agencies such as earthquakes etc. ' *sāmudre* is not found in any ms. ; and Daiva and Nimitta would appear to be two distinct sciences, that of divine portents and that of omens such as the flight of birds etc., respectively.

11 *edhitam* and *mantrimantrābhimantritam* contain a punning reference to the kindling of fire and its sanctification by *mantras*. Cb renders *abhimantrita* by ' protected.' — *śāstrānugamaśastritam* ' possessed of weapons in the form of obedience to the *śāstra*,' or ' possessed of weapons on account of obedience to the *śāstra* ' (Cb). Cj however explains ' following the *śāstra* (*śāstrānugam*), though not making use of weapons (*aśastritam*).' Jolly-Schmidt refer to a pun, apparently in the word *śastrita* ' possessed of a weapon ' and ' accompanied by a hymn of praise or litany (*śastra*).' The reading *-nugama-* is obviously better than *-nugata-*.

1.10

upadhā ' a secret test ' is a term peculiar to this science.

1 *-sakhaḥ* 'in the company of ', i.e., in consultation with. — *sāmānyeṣu*: 'common', i.e., not carrying any responsiblity. — *śodhayet* from D Cj is preferable to *śaucayet* ; the latter is unusual and has to be understood in the sense of ' *śaucaṁ parīkṣayet*.'

2 Cb shows *ayājyayājane* for *ayājyayājanādhyāpane*. That would appear better, for *adhyāpana* can with difficulty be construed with *ayājya*. — *avakṣipet* : the root *ava-kṣip* ' to throw out, discard, dismiss ' is common in this text ; cf. 5.4.10 ; 11.1.20 ; 13.3.8.

3 He should (then) get each minister individually instigated, through secret agents, under oath, (in this manner) : ' This king is impious ; well, let us set up another pious (king), either a claimant from his own family or a prince in disfavour or a member of the (royal) family or a person who is the one support of the kingdom or a neighbouring prince or a forest chieftain or a person suddenly risen to power ; this is approved by all ; what about you ? ' 4 If he repulses (the suggestion), he is loyal.

This is the test of piety.

5 The commander of the army, (seemingly) dismissed by reason of support given to evil men, should get each minister individually instigated, through secret agents, to (bring about) the king's destruction, with (the offer of) a tempting material gain, (saying) : ' This is approved by all ; what about you ? ' 6 If he repulses (the suggestion), he is upright.

This is the test of material gain.

7 A wandering nun, who has won the confidence (of the different ministers) and is treated with honour in the palace, should secretly suggest to each minister individually : ' The chief queen is in love with you and has made arrangements for a meeting (with you) ; besides, you will obtain much wealth.' 8 If he repulses (the proposal), he is pure.

This is the test of lust.

9 On the occasion of a festive party, one minister should invite all the (other) ministers. 10 Through (seeming) fright at this (conspiracy), the

3 *śapathapūrvam*, i.e., the *amātyas* are first made to swear that they will not desclose what is being suggested to them. — *tatkulīna* : this word is used to refer to a claimant or pretender to the throne from the ruler's family. — *aparuddha* : See Chapter 1.18 below. — *kulya* is any other member of the royal family. — *ekapragraha* : in view of 5.6.28, this can only refer to the chief minister who is the ' one support ' of the dynasty. Cj Cnn explain 'honoured equally with the king (*rājñā sahaikapūjam* — Cj).' — *aupapādikam* : Cj, reading *upapādakam*, explains ' a person suddenly risen to power, i.e., not of royal descent ' and adds the illustration of Candragupta. Similarly Cnn. 'One belonging to a region at the foot of a mountain or one who is to be considered or determined by us' (Cs) appears little likely. Cf. 5.2.39. — *dharmopadhā* : this name is given to the test apparently because the *dhārmikatva* of the king is supposedly denied in it or because the officer's devotion to *dharma* (represented by the *purohita*) is put to test.

5 *asatpragraheṇa* : according to Cb Cs, the *senāpati* is ordered by the king to honour evil men, which he refuses to do ; that is then made the ground for his dismissal. This is hardly possible in view of the use of the expression elsewhere, specially in 7.5.19. It is the support given to worthless persons by the *senāpati* (may be at the king's secret instance as in Cj) that is made the ostensible ground for his seeming dismissal. 6 *arthopadhā* : the name is due to the offer of money involved in it.

7 *parivrājikā*, also called *bhikṣukī*, is a secret agent. See 1.12.4 below. — *te* after *ca* is from Cj and seems necessary ; cf. Śaṁkarārya on Kāmandaka, 4.26. — Cj offers an alternative explanation of *mahānarthaḥ* ' a great calamity will befall you etc. ' That is hardly likely.

9 *prahavaṇa* is from D G2 Cj ; *pravahaṇa* of the other mss. means practically the same thing. *prahavaṇa* is a festive party (*prahūyante'smin svajanamitrāṇīti prahavaṇam udvāhādir utsavaḥ*—Cj) or a picnic (*prītibhojana*—Cb). 10 *tena udvegena* : the fright is due to an

king should put them in prison. 11 A sharp pupil, imprisoned there earlier, should secretly suggest to each of those ministers individually, when they are deprived of property and honour, (in this manner): 'This king is behaving wickedly; well, let us kill him and install another; this is approved by all; what about you?' 12 If he repulses (the suggestion), he is loyal.

This is the test of fear.

13 From among them, he should appoint those proved loyal by the test of piety to posts in the judiciary and for suppression of criminals, those proved upright by the test of material gain to offices of the Administrator and in the stores of the Director of Stores, those proved pure by the test of lust to guardianship of (places of) recreation inside (the palace) as well as outside, those proved loyal by the test of fear to duties near the (person of the) king. 14 Those proved honest by all tests, he should make (his) councillors. 15 Those (found) dishonest by every test, he should employ in mines, in forests for material produce, in elephant-forests and in factories.

16 'He should appoint ministers, who have been cleared by the (tests of the) group of three (goals of life) and fear, to duties appropriate to them in accordance with their integrity;' thus have the (ancient) teachers laid down.

17 'However, under no circumstances must the king make himself or the queen the target for the sake of ascertaining the probity of ministers;' this is the opinion of Kauṭilya.

18 He should not effect the corruption of the uncorrupted as of water by poison; for, it may well happen that a cure may not be found for one corrupted.

19 And the mind, perverted by the fourfold secret tests, may not turn back without going to the end, remaining fixed in the will of spirited persons.

apparently suspected conspiracy of the ministers. 11 *kāpaṭikaś cātra* is from D. It is easy to see how the other readings *kāpaṭikaś chātraḥ* and *kāpaṭikacchātraḥ* arose successively out of this, under the influence of 1.11.2. Cj reads *kāpaṭikaś ca tatra*. — Jolly-Schmidt read *sahasainam* for *sādhu enam* on the authority of Śaṁkarārya on Kāmandaka, 4.26. But the reading of the mss. seems quite all right. Cj seems to have read *ata enam*. 12 *bhayopadhā*: the name has reference to the fear in which the arrested ministers live.

13 *dharmasthīya*: cf. Book 3. — *kaṇṭakaśodhana*: cf. Book 4. — *samāhartṛ*: cf. 2.6 below. — *saṁnidhātṛnicayakarma*: cf. 2.5 below. — *bābhyābhyantaravihārarakṣāsu*: Cnn rightly explains '*bāhyam udyānādi, ābhyantaram antaḥpurādi*' understanding *vihāra* in the sense of *vihārasthāna*. The explanation of Cb Cs '*vihāra*, objects of pleasure, i.e., women, and *bāhya*, i.e., mistresses (*bhoginī*) and *ābhyantara*, i.e., queens (*devī*)' is hardly acceptable. 15 *sarvatrāśucīn*: on the analogy of Manu 7.62, Meyer suggests that *sarvatra śucīn* should be read. That is hardly right, since it would place the councillor practically on the same footing as miners and factory workers. The *Manusmṛti* has evidently misunderstood the present passage.

16. From these stanzas it is clear that Kauṭilya does not agree with the traditional view regarding the tests in its entirety. 17 *Kauṭilyadarśanam*: *darśana* here is no philosophical or other 'system', only 'opinion, view.' 19 *nāgatvāntar* (m p) is clearly faulty.

20 Therefore, the king should make an outsider the object of reference in the fourfold work (of testing) and (thus) investigate through secret agents the integrity or otherwise of ministers.

CHAPTER ELEVEN

SECTION 7 APPOINTMENT OF PERSONS IN SECRET SERVICE

(i) Creation of Establishments of Spies

1 With the body of ministers proved upright by means of secret tests, the (king) should appoint persons in secret service, (viz.), the sharp pupil, the apostate monk, the seeming householder, the seeming trader and the seeming ascetic, as well as the secret agent, the bravo, the poison-giver and the begging nun.

2 A pupil, knowing the secrets of others, (and) bold, is the sharp pupil. 3 Encouraging him with money and honour, the minister should say, 'Regarding the king and me as your authority, report to us at once any evil of any person which you may notice.'

4 One, who has relinquished the life of a wandering monk, (and) is endowed with intelligence and honesty, is the apostate monk. 5 Equipped with plenty of money and assistants, he should get work done in a place assigned (to him), for the practice of some occupation. 6 And from the profits of (this) work, he should provide all wandering monks with food, clothing and residence. 7 And to those (among them), who seek a (per-

— *dhṛti* is 'firm will' rather than 'intellect.' 20 *adhiṣṭhānam* : Cnn suggests that a traitorous officer should be substituted for the king and the wife of such an officer in place of the queen for purposes of the tests. It is not easy to see how the tests can retain their efficacy in such a case. — *kārye* : M reads *cārye* and Cs explains 'for the employment of a test.' *kārye*, however, seems better.

1.11

1 *śuddhāmātyavargaḥ* : this is a Bahuvrīhi, describing the king, and not a Karmadhāraya, as Meyer thinks. A group of ministers could hardly be concerned with the appointment of spies.

2 *kāpaṭikaḥ* : derived from *kapaṭa* 'deceit,' (*kapaṭena carati iti*—Cj Cnn). — *chātraḥ* 'a pupil' or 'an apprentice.' Cb explains 'who has only his own person to care for (*śarīramātraparicchadaḥ*).' Cnn has '*kapālikāmātraparicchadaḥ*' implying the idea of a beggar. It is not unlikely that the word is derived from *chad* 'to conceal, to cover' and implies the idea of one concealing his movements, intentions etc. 3 *mantrī* : it is the *samāhartṛ*, who may have been meant. In the case of *gṛhapatikavyañjana* and others, the *samāhartṛ* is in charge, as is shown by 2.35.8-13. — *pratyādiśa* 'report, intimate,' a rather unusual sense.

4 *pravrajyāpratyavasitaḥ*, i.e., one who wants to give up the monk's life and return to the householder's life. 5 *vārttākarma-* : according to Meyer, *vārttā* is here the profession of spying, *karma* is the work of spying and *phala* the remuneration for this work. This is hardly likely. *vārttā* in the usual sense is quite all right.—*antevāsin* is used in the sense of an assistant in general, not merely an apprentice. 6 *karmaphalāt*, i.e., from the income derived from agriculture or trade or cattle-rearing. 7 *vṛttikāmān* : those who are anxious to find a secure livelihood and not depend on a life of mendicancy. — *etenaiva*

manent) livelihood, he should secretly propose, 'In this very garb, you should work in the interest of the king and present yourself here at the time of meals and payment.' 8 And all wandering monks should make similar secret proposals to (monks in) their respective orders.

9 A farmer, the means of whose livelihood are depleted, (and) who is endowed with intelligence and honesty, is the seeming householder. 10 In a place assigned (to him) for agricultural work, he should etc.— exactly as before.

11 A trader, the means of whose livelihood are depleted, (and) who is endowed with intelligence and honesty, is the seeming trader. 12 In a place assigned (to him) for his trade, he should etc.— exactly as before.

13 A hermit with shaven head or with matted hair, who seeks a (permanent) livelihood, is the seeming ascetic. 14 (Living) in the vicinity of a city with plenty of disciples with shaven heads or with matted hair, he should eat, openly, a vegetable or a handful of barley at intervals of a month or two, secretly, (however), meals as desired. 15 And assistants of traders (who are secret agents) should adore him with occult practices for becoming prosperous. 16 And his disciples should announce, 'That holy man is able to secure prosperity (for any one).' 17 And to those who have approached him with hopes of (securing) prosperity, he should specify events happening in their family, which are ascertained by means of the science of (interpreting the touch of) the body and with the help of signs made by his disciples, (events) such as a small gain, burning by fire, danger from thieves, the killing of a traitorous person, a gift of gratification, news about happenings in a foreign land, saying, 'this will happen today or tomorrow,' or 'the king will do this.'

veṣeṇa, i.e., the peculiar outward garb of the particular ascetic sect is not to be given up. 8 *svaṁ svaṁ vargam*: the different orders of wandering monks are to be under a member of the same order.

10 *samānaṁ pūrveṇa*, i.e., other indigent farmers are to accept secret service under him.

13 *muṇḍajaṭila-*: Cnn has '*muṇḍa* such as Śākya, Ājīvaka and others, *jaṭila* such as Pāśupata and others.' 14 *yavasamuṣṭim* of G M is obviously corrupt; 'grass' could not have been intended. 15 *vaidehakāntevāsinaḥ*: these are assistants of the trader-spy. — *samiddhayogair* 'practices which are intended to secure prosperity.' Cb paraphrases by '*pūrṇamanorathayoga*'. Meyer suggests that *samiddha* is a Prakritism for *samṛddha*; that seems likely in view of *samedhā* and *sāmedhika* presently used in the same sense, the root *edh* being synonymous with *ṛdh*, not with *idh*. 16 *asau siddhaḥ sāmedhikaḥ*: Cb Cs Meyer regard *siddhaḥ* also as predicate. It is better to understand *sāmedhikaḥ* alone as the predicate. *sāmedhika* is 'one who grants prosperity.' 17 *samedhāśāsti* 'hope or expectation of prosperity.' — *aṅgavidyā*: according to Cnn, it is the science by which one touches the body of the person putting the question and finds the answer to it in that touch (*yayā praṣṭuḥ praśnasamaye aṅgasparśaṁ dṛṣṭvā ādeśaḥ kriyate*). Cf. 1.12.1.— *abhijanepsitāni* of D is not likely, as *agnidāha*, *corabhaya* can hardly be regarded as *īpsita* 'desired.' *avasita* in the reading adopted means 'what has happened,' implying also the idea of 'what is going to happen'. — *ādiśet* with the implied sense of 'to foretell' is preferable to *pratyādiśet* of D. — *tuṣṭidānam* 'a gift in consequence of gratification' is preferable to *tuṣṭadānam*, though the latter can mean 'a gift to one who is contented (with the ruler).' — *idaṁ vā rājā* etc.: G2 M do not read *vā*; but it is necessary to show the option between the two kinds of prophecies. Cb seems to have read a single prophecy—*idaṁ adya śvo vā rājā kariṣyati*. For *alpalābha*,

18 Secret servants and agents should cause that (prophecy) of his to be fulfilled. 19 To those (among the visitors) who are richly endowed with spirit, intelligence and eloquence, he should predict good fortune at the hands of the king and speak of (their imminent) association with the minister. 20 And the minister should arrange for their livelihood and work.

21 And he should pacify with money and honour those who are resentful for good reason, those resentful without reason, by silent punishment, also those who do what is inimical to the king.

22. And favoured by the king with money and honour, they should ascertain the integrity of the king's servants. Thus these five establishments (of spies) have been described.

CHAPTER TWELVE

SECTION 7 (Continued)

(ii) Appointment of Roving Spies

SECTION 8 RULES FOR SECRET SERVANTS

1 And those who are without relations and have to be necessarily maintained, when they study the (science of the interpretation of) marks, the science of (the touch of) the body, the science of magic, that pertaining to (the creation

agnidāha and *corabhaya*, however, *idaṁ bhaviṣyati* seems necessary. 18 *gūḍhāḥ sattriṇaś ca* : *gūḍha* would refer to agents other than *sattrin*. D omits *ca*; in that case *gūḍha* merely emphasizes the secret character of the *sattrin*. 19 *vākyaśakti-* 'speech and power' (Cb); rather ' power of speech, i.e., eloquence '; cf. 1.14.9 below.— *rājabhāgyam* is from Cb Cj. D has *rājyabhāgyam*, the others *rājabhāvyam*. *bhāgya* is distinctly preferable to the colourless *bhāvya* 'what is going to happen, future.' What is meant is 'good fortune at the hands of the king (*asya rājñaḥ sakāśāt tava bhāgyaṁ lakṣmīr bhaviṣyati*—Cnn).' Cj seems to have some kind of honour in mind (*paṭṭasaṁbandhādi*). D's *rājya-* does not yield a very happy sense. —Meyer would interchange ss. 19 and 20, making *mantrī* the subject for *anuvyāharet*. There is no doubt, however, that *tāpasaḥ* is to be understood as the subject for this verb; with *mantrisaṁyogam* also as the object in the same s., *mantrī* cannot possibly be the subject. And *sattvaprajñā-* etc. describes visitors to the *tāpasa*, not the spies as Meyer thinks. *brūyāt* isn't quite necessary. G M do not show it. 20 *eṣām* refers to *sattvaprajñā-* etc.; they are to be given employment in state service, may be in secret service. — *viyateta* 'should arrange for'; cf. 1.17.25. Cj has '*viśeṣeṇa yateta*.'

21 *ye ca* etc.: this clearly refers to *kāpaṭika* and other agents described in this chapter. That is shown by the next s. — *rājñaḥ kāraṇakruddhāḥ* is found in D; *kāraṇakruddhāḥ* in it goes better with *akāraṇakruddhān* that follows. — *tūṣṇīṁdaṇḍena*, i.e., by assassination, poisoning etc.

22 *saṁsthāḥ* are so called because they are stationed in one place (*samyag ekasmin sthāne sthitāḥ*. — Cnn).

1.12

praṇidhi seems to mean 'what is laid down, what is prescribed, duties, rules for conduct, etc.' Cf. *rājapraṇidhiḥ* 1.19, *niśāntapraṇidhiḥ* 1.20. It can also mean in some cases 'employment, appointment.'

1 *ye cāpyasaṁbandhino'vaśyabhartavyāḥ* : we have to understand *ca api asaṁbandhinaḥ*, the last word meaning 'without relatives, orphans'; these are to be maintained by the state as we read in 2.1.26 (*anāthāṁś ca rājā bibhṛyāt*). Cb Cj read *ye cāsya* etc. and explain 'the relatives of the king who have necessarily to be maintained by him.' It is doubtful if spies were to be recruited only from the ranks of the king's relations. Cj mentions the former reading, but explains *āpya* by 'related'; that is little likely, when *saṁbandhinaḥ* is there. Cnn explains '*āpyānāṁ mantripurohitopādhyāyādīnāṁ saṁbandhinaḥ*, relations of ministers,

of) illusions, the duties of the *āśramas*, (the science of) omens, the 'wheel with the spaces' and so on, are the secret agents; or, (when they study) the art of association (with men).

2 Those in the land who are brave, have given up all (thought of) personal safety (and) would fight, for the sake of money, an elephant or a wild animal, are the bravoes.

3 Those who are without affection for their kinsmen and are cruel and indolent are the poison-givers.

4 A wandering nun, seeking a (secure) livelihood, poor, widowed, bold, Brahmin (by caste) and treated with honour in the palace, should (frequently) go to the houses of high officers. 5 By her (office) are explained (similar offices for) the shaven nuns of heretical sects.

These are the roving spies.

6 The king should employ these with a credible disguise as regards country, dress, profession, language and birth, to spy, in conformity with their loyalty and capability, on the councillor, the chaplain, the commander-in-chief, the crown-prince, the chief palace usher, the chief of the palace guards, the director, the administrator, the director of stores, the magistrate,

chaplain etc.' These could hardly be referred to as *avaśyabhartavyāḥ* for the king. — *lakṣaṇam*, i.e., the science of interpretation of the marks on the body. — *aṅgavidyā*: see 1.11.17 above. – *jambhakavidyā* is the 'magical lore by which one brings others under control, becomes invisible and so on' (Cb). — *antaracakram* is, according to Cb Cs, the science of the omens of birds, according to Cj, the cries of jackals and other animals. According to Meyer, it may indicate the magic circle of Tantric or other mystic sciences. In the *Bṛhatsaṁhitā*, Ch. 87, *antaracakra* refers to the interpretation of omens from the *dikcakra* which is divided into 32 parts in a building. — *sattrin* is apparently derived from *sattra* frequently used in the sense of 'an ambush' from *sad* 'to sit in ambush or to lie in wait unseen'; cf. 7.17.56; 10.2.15; 8.5.11 etc. The *sattrin*'s work is akin to an ambuscade without the element of an actual attack. Cnn explains '*(sat) vidyamānam api trāyati gopāyati iti sattraṁ chadma, tad vidyate yeṣāṁ te*'. — *saṁsargavidyā* 'the art of association,' i.e., the science of love and allied arts, such as singing, dancing etc. (Cb). So Cnn '*saṁsṛjyante janā yasyāṁ sā saṁsargavidyā gītanṛtyādikā*.'

2 D adds *puruṣam agnyādikaṁ vā* after *vyālaṁ vā*; the words do not appear to be original. — The point of *janapade*, according to Cb, is that people from the countryside tend to be so foolhardy.

4 *vidhavā* : Cj states that some read *avidhavā* and explain it by *puṁskāmā* 'longing for a man'. That is not at all likely. — *Brāhmaṇī*: apparently women of the Brāhmaṇa *varṇa* alone could become *parivrājikās*. — *abhigacchet* from D is necessary for sense. 5 *muṇḍā vṛṣalyaḥ* : Cb Cs explain 'Buddhist nuns and Śūdra females'; the 'and' seems hardly justified. Meyer too has 'shaven nuns and dissolute women' which accords with Cj as to the explanation of *vṛṣalī*, '*parityaktacāritradharmā*'. Cnn's explanation of *vṛṣalī*, '*veśyāmātaro devatāliṅgadhāriṇyaḥ*, old prostitutes showing themselves as devotees' is also doubtful. It seems that *vṛṣala* in this text refers to the follower of a heretical sect and *muṇḍā* describes the custom of shaving the head prevalent among nuns of such sects. — *saṁcārāḥ*: these are not settled in one place and do not belong to a *saṁsthā*. They also work individually. Cb adds that the *saṁsthāḥ* are appointed by the minister, the *saṁcārāḥ* by the king himself.

6 *mantripurohita*- etc. : we have here obviously a list of the 18 *tīrthas* referred to in s. 20 below. — *praśāstṛ* so high in the list can hardly be the same as the officer who looks after the camp and its supplies according to 10.1.17. Like the *dauvārika* and the *āntarvaṁśika* he seems to be a palace official in charge of its administration. — *pauravyāvahārika* : such an officer is not mentioned elsewhere in the text except in the salary lists in 5.3. Perhaps he is the same as the *nāgarika* of 2.36. Cj understands the *dharmastha* of Book 3. — *kārmāntika* 'the officer in charge of factories' is also mentioned again only in 5.3.7. — *mantripariṣad-adhyakṣa* : this is usually understood as 'the president of the council of ministers.' However,

the commandant, the city-judge, the director of factories, the council of ministers, the superintendents, the chief of the army staff, the commandant of the fort, the commandant of the frontier-fort and the forest chieftain, in his own territory.

7 Bravoes, (serving as) bearers of umbrella, water-vessel, fan, shoes, seat, carriage and riding animal, should (spy on and) ascertain the out-of-door activity of those (officers). 8 Secret agents should communicate that (information) to the (spy-) establishments.

9 Poison-givers, serving as cooks, waiters, bath-attendants, shampooers, bed-preparers, barbers, valets and water-servers, those appearing as hump-backs, dwarfs, Kirātas, dumb, deaf, idiotic or blind persons, (and) actors, dancers, singers, musicians, professional story-tellers and minstrels as well as women should (spy on and) ascertain the indoor activity (of those officers). 10 Nuns should communicate that (information) to the (spy-) establishments.

11 Assistants of the establishments should carry out the transmission of spied out news by means of sign-alphabets. 12 And neither the establishments nor these (assistants) should know one another.

13 In case of prohibition (of entry into the house) for nuns, (secret agents) appearing at the door one after another (or) appearing as the mother or father (of servants in the house), or posing as female artists, singers or female slaves, should get the secret information that is spied out conveyed outside by means of songs, recitations, writings concealed in musical instru-

such a president is unlikely, when the king is there to preside. Moreover, *adhyakṣa* in the sense of 'president' is doubtful for this text. Clearly, two categories, council of ministers (i.e., each of its members) and superintendents (i.e., heads of departments) are to be understood. Cf. 5.3 below, where we have *mantripariṣad* in s.7 and *adhyakṣa* separately in s.13. —*pāla* is to be construed with each of *daṇḍa-*, *durga-* and *anta-*. Of these *daṇḍapāla* seems to be a sort of chief of staff. — *āṭavika* 'the forest chieftain' is strictly not a *tīrtha* or high state officer. We get the number 18 by excluding him. — *bhaktitaḥ* : Cb Cs explain 'making him appear as the devotee of that god whose devotee the officer (spied on) happens to be.' The expression, however, seems to mean only 'in conformity with the devotion (of the spy) to the king.' — *sāmarthyayogāt* : Meyer understands *sāmarthya* and *yoga* as two ideas. A single idea, however, appears better.

7 *cāra* lit. 'movement, activity' which is spied upon, hence, also 'information spied out.'

9 *sūdārālika* : according to Cb, *sūda* is the cook, *ārālika* is one who serves food.— '*vāgjīvanāḥ kathakādayaḥ*' (Cj). — *kuśīlava*, though often used to include actors, dancers etc., seems here restricted to minstrels or rhapsodes.

11 *saṁjñālipibhiḥ* : 'a secret alphabet previously agreed upon' (Cb) is better than 'signals and writing' (Meyer).

13 *dvāḥsthaparaṁparā* : this refers to spies disguised as acrobats, beggars, jugglers etc. who appear at the door at intervals and beg or do their acts. Spies in the house take advantage of their appearance to communicate information to them. — *mātāpitṛvyañjanāḥ* : these claim to be the parent of some servant in the house, whom they wish to visit and from whom they get the secret information. — *gītapāṭhya-* etc.: it seems best to understand four items, viz., *gīta*, *pāṭhya*, *vādyabhāṇḍagūḍhalekhya* and *saṁjñā*. Apparently, the *vā* shows

ments or signs. 14 Or, a secret get-away (from the house should be made by the spies) by (taking advantage of a pretended) long illness or madness or by setting (something) on fire or administering poison (to someone).

15 When there is agreement in the reports of three (spies), credence (should be given). 16 In case of continuous mistakes on their part, 'silent' punishment is (the means of) their removal.

17 And spies mentioned in 'The Suppression of Criminals' should live with enemies receiving wages from them, in order to find out secret information, without associating with one another. 18 They are 'persons in the pay of both.'

19 And he should appoint 'persons in the pay of both,' after taking charge of their sons and wives. And he should know such agents when they are employed by the enemies. And (he should ascertain) their loyalty through (spies of) their type.

20 Thus he should sow spies among the enemy, the ally, the middle king, the neutral king, as well as among the eighteen high officers of (each of) those (kings).

21 Humpbacks, dwarfs, eunuchs, women skilled in arts, dumb persons and different types of Mleccha races (should be employed as spies) living inside their houses.

the option between these alternatives in the compound. 14 *agnirasavisargeṇa*, i.e., setting something on fire or poisoning someone and then escaping in the commotion that would follow. Meyer, however, has 'by pretending a fire (in his own house) or a case of poisoning (at his place) or for evacuation of the body (*visarga*, i.e., clearing of the bowels).' This is hardly possible.

15 *saṁpratyayaḥ* 'belief, credence.' 16 *vinipāta* 'falling away', i.e., bringing in false information. —*pratiṣedha* 'removal from office, dismissal from the job.' In the present case, it is brought about by death.

17 *kaṇṭakaśodhanoktāḥ* : spies mentioned in 4.4.3 are to be thought of. — D alternates between *avasarpa* and *apasarpa*, but has mostly the former. However, *apasarpa* is usual later. Cf. *Raghuvaṁśa*, 17.51 etc. — It is proposed to read *asaṁpātinaś cārārtham*, 'not associating together, for the sake of spying out information secretly.' The idea is, the *ubhayavetanas* are to operate independently in the enemy's territory, each being unaware of the other *ubhayavetanas* though from the same country. *saṁpāta*, in this text, has the sense of 'coming together, crowding etc.'; cf. 4.6.2; 9.2.2; 2.25.3 etc. For *asaṁpātin* cf. 2.36.21. Meyer proposes *saṁpātinaś cārārtham* 'going out there for the work of spying.' Most mss. read *saṁpātaniścārārtham*; it is possible that *niścāra* means 'sending out (spied out information from the enemy's territory)'; in that case, *saṁpāta* would have to mean 'information spied out,' which seems hardly possible. Cb renders *saṁpāta* by 'spy' and explains 'in order that his own spies may be able to work easily and the enemy spies may be unable to operate.' This is equally unsatisfactory.

19 *gṛhītaputradārāṁś ca* : i.e., the sons and wives of the *ubhayavetanas* are held as hostages. — *ariprahitān*, i.e., when *ubhayavetanas* are used by the enemies against him. — *tadvidhaiḥ* : if the *ubhayavetana* is disguised as a *kuśīlava*, the spy to watch over him should also appear as a *kuśīlava* and so on.

21 *-paṇḍakāḥ* of most mss. means the same as *-ṣaṇḍakāḥ* of Cb. — *citrāś ca mlecchajātayaḥ*, such as Kirāta, Śabara etc.

22 In fortified towns traders (should constitute) the spy establishments, on the outskirts of fortified towns ascetics, farmers and apostate monks in the countryside (and) herdsmen on the borders of the country.

23 In the forest should be placed forest-dwellers (such as) monks, foresters and others,—a series of spies, quick in their work,—in order to find out news of (the activity of) the enemy.

24 And such (spies) of the enemy should be found out, those of the different types by (his own spies) of the same types, (whether) roving spies or spy-establishments, secret servants not bearing the marks of a secret servant.

25 In order to discover espionage by enemies, he should station at frontiers principal officers, who are non-seducible, but are shown to be impelled by motives for action that are associated with seducible parties.

22 *rāṣṭra* is the same as *janapada*, distinguished from *durga* or *pura*.

23 It is to be noted that *Śramaṇas*, i.e., Buddhist or Jain monks (Cnn) are here included among *vanacaras*. — Cj shows *-jñānārtham* (for *-jñānārthāḥ*). That seems also Medhātithi's reading on Manu, 7.154. That would appear a more usual expression. D. Schlingloff ('Arthaśāstra-Studien, I. Kauṭilya und Medhātithi,' WZKSO, IX, 1965, 1-38) has made a critical comparison of Arthaśāstra quotations in Methātithi with passages in the present text. J. Duncan M. Derrett ('A Newly-discovered Contact between Arthaśāstra and Dharmasāstra,' ZDMG, 115, 1965, 134-152) has, in addition, also compared quotations in Bhāruci, an earlier commentator on the *Manusmṛti*.

24 *gūḍhāś cāgūḍhasaṁjñitāḥ* : in spite of the *ca* being placed after instead of before *gūḍhāḥ*, the latter does not form a third category as Meyer thinks. *agūḍhasaṁjñita* seems to mean 'who do not bear signs of being secret agents.' Cj reads *agūḍhasaṁjñitaiḥ*; that would describe his own spies. Medhātithi on Manu 7.154 reads *gūḍhasaṁjñitāḥ* 'who are equipped with, i.e., make use of secret signs.'

25 The translation follows in the main the explanation in Cnn '*krodhalobhabhayamānaiḥ kāraṇabhūtaiḥ pratirūpitān mantrisenāpatyādīn kṛtakakṛtyān kṛtvā mānādhikārabhraṣṭān rāṣṭrān nirvāsayet.*' The idea is, some important officers about whose loyalty there is no doubt are stationed at the frontier; it is made out (*darśita*) that they have a motive (*hetu*) such as *krodha*, *lobha* etc. for turning traitor (*kṛtyapakṣīya*). The enemy's spies feel tempted to try to seduce these officers; if they do so, the enemy's intentions become known to these officers and through them to the king. Cb seems to agree though it does not show a clear explanation of some expressions. Meyer has 'whose loyalty is unshakably demonstrated (*akṛtyān darśitān*) through men of the seceders' party (*kṛtyapakṣīyaiḥ*) who approach them for work of their own (*kāryahetubhiḥ*).' In the foot-note, he prefers *kṛtyapakṣīyaiḥ* as an adjective to *kāryahetubhiḥ* 'by those means of accomplishing an object which are useful in the case of *kṛtyas*, i.e., such means as test the likely seceders.' Cs explains 'such principal men as are difficult to win over (*akṛtyān*, i.e., *asādhyān*) and may even be hostile, should be first enlightened with reasons which are sufficient to win over a person, i.e., they should be won over with reasoning and then stationed etc.' This is hardly satisfactory. Russ. has 'should station his own chief spies (*mukhyān*), meriting trust (*akṛtyān*) revealed (*darsitān*) on the ground of their actions in the matter of traitors (*kṛtyapakṣīyaiḥ hetubhiḥ*).'

CHAPTER THIRTEEN

SECTION 9 KEEPING A WATCH OVER THE SEDUCIBLE AND NON-SEDUCIBLE PARTIES IN ONE'S OWN TERRITORY

1 When he has set spies on the high officials, he should set spies on the citizens and the country people.

2 Secret agents, opposing one another, should carry on a disputation at holy places, in assemblies, in communal gatherings and (other) congregations of people. 3 (One of them should say,) 'This king is said to be endowed with all virtues and yet no virtue is to be seen in him, as he oppresses citizens and country people with fines and taxes.' 4 The other should contradict him as well as those who may commend his views there. 5 (He should say,) 'People, overwhelmed by the law of the fishes, made Manu, the son of Vivasvat, their king. 6 And they assigned one-sixth of the grains, one-tenth of the commodities and money as his share. 7 Maintained by that, kings bring about the well-being and security of the subjects. 8 Those who do not pay fines and taxes take on themselves the sins of those (kings) and (kings) who do not bring about well-being and security (take on themselves the sins) of the subjects. 9 Therefore, even forest-dwellers offer a sixth part of their gleaned grains, saying "This is the share for him who protects us." 10 This is the office of Indra and Yama, viz., (that of) the kings, whose wrath

1.13

kṛtyas are defined in s. 22 below. — *rakṣaṇam* conveys the idea of being vigilant in the matter of these persons, protection of oneself from these persons, not protection of these persons.

2 *dvandvinaḥ* 'contending among themselves (*dvandvaṁ vairaṁ yeṣāṁ te*—Cj)' is more likely than 'moving in pairs' (Cb). — *tīrthasabhā-* etc.: *śālā-* added after *-sabhā-* in G M does not appear to be original. Four things seem meant, *tīrtha, sabhā, pūga* and *janasamavāya*, as in Cnn Cs. *pūga* is a sort of guild or communal group (*pūgāḥ śreṇīgaṇās tantuvāyādīnām*—Cnn). *janasamavāya* refers to congregations of people for dramatic shows, festivals etc. (*prekṣotsavādiṣu yatra janāḥ samavayanti*—Cnn). Meyer construes *samavāya* with *pūga* as well as *jana*. — It is not possible to agree with K. P. Jayaswal (*Hindu Polity*, II, p. 84) that *tīrthasabhāśālāsamavāya* refers to the sectional sub-assembly of the Paura Assembly in charge of sacred places and public buildings, that *pūgasamavāya* is the sub-assembly in charge of trade and manufactures and that *janasamavāya* is the Popular Assembly. 3 *ayaṁ rājā* etc.: according to Ghoshal (HPT, pp. 133-134 and n.) *ayaṁ rājā* means 'this class of kings,' *yaḥ* refers to *guṇaḥ* and *pīḍayati* is causal, 'which makes him harass the subjects.' This is very doubtful. *yaḥ* can easily refer to *asya*. 4 *ye'nupraśaṁseyuḥ* : these are possible *kṛtyas*. 5 *Manuṁ rājānam* etc.: the *Mahābhārata* 12.67.20-32 narrates how Manu was induced to undertake the task of rulership. 6 This theory of an original contract between the subjects and the ruler is merely a device used by agents for securing the allegiance of subjects. 8 *teṣāṁ kilbiṣam* etc. : the translation follows in the main Cnn which explains 'subjects not paying fines and taxes (*adaṇḍakarāḥ prajāḥ*) take on themselves the sins of the kings, and kings not securing the subjects' welfare take on themselves the sins of the subjects.' It would have been better if we had *prajāḥ* after *adaṇḍakarāḥ* and *rājānaḥ* after *-kṣemāvahāś ca*. Cj, reading *adaṇḍadharo harati*, seems to explain, ' a king who fails to wield the *daṇḍa* takes on himself the sins of those kings who do it, and kings failing to secure *yogakṣema* take on themselves the subjects' sins.' If the s. is looked upon as containing a single clause, we may understand 'kings who do not take fines and taxes take on themselves the sins of those other dutiful kings, and they also fail to secure the welfare of

and favour are visibly manifest. 11 Even divine punishment strikes those who slight them. 12 Therefore, kings must not be slighted.' 13 Thus he should restrain the common people. 14 And they should also find out rumours (spreading among the subjects).

15 And spies appearing as ascetics with shaven heads or with matted hair should ascertain the contentedness or discontentedness of those, who live on his grains, cattle or money, who help him with these in calamity or prosperity, who restrain a rebellious kinsman or region, (or) who repel an enemy or a forest chieftain. 16 He should favour those who are contented, with additional wealth and honour. 17 He should propitiate with gifts and conciliation those, who are discontented, in order to make them contented. 18 Or, he should divide them from each other as well as from neighbouring princes, forest-chieftains, pretenders from his family and princes in disfavour. 19 If they are even then discontented, he should make them incur the odium of the country by (appointing them to) the office of collecting fines and taxes. 20 When they have incurred the odium, he should bring about their end by 'silent' punishment or by an insurrection in the country. 21 Or, he should post them in mines or factories, after taking their sons and wives under his protection, for fear that they might be the object of designs by enemies.

22 Those, however, who are enraged or greedy or frightened or proud, are likely to be seduced by enemies. 23 Spies appearing as fortune-tellers, soothsayers and astrologers should ascertain their mutual relations as well as their contacts with enemies or forest chieftains. 24 He should favour those, who are contented, with wealth and honour. 25 He should manage those who are discontented by means of conciliation, gifts, dissension or force.

26 In this way, the wise (king) should guard from the secret instigations of enemies those likely to be seduced and those not likely to be seduced in his own territory, whether prominent persons or common people.

the subjects.' Meyer suggests *tāsām* for *teṣām* 'kings who do not receive fines or taxes and are therefore unable to secure welfare take on themselves the sins of those subjects.' Cs reads *daṇḍakarāh* and *yoga-* (for *ayoga-*) "punishments and taxes imposed by those kings (*teṣāṁ daṇḍakarāḥ*) remove distress (*kilbiṣa* evil) from the people and secure their welfare.' This seems very unlikely. Russ. follows Cs. 11 *daivo daṇḍaḥ*, i.e., some divine calamity. 13 *kṣudrakān* 'the common people, the masses' as distinguished from *pradhānāḥ* described in s. 15. — *pratiṣedhayet*, i.e., controvert their views and dissuade them from entertaining seditious thoughts.

15 *ājīvanti* 'live on,' i.e., receive as wages or salary. — *kupita* 'rebellious' from a root commonly used in this sense in this text. — *vyāvartayanti* 'turn back,' i.e., dissuade them from taking any rash steps. — *pratiṣedhayanti* 'repel,' may be, even by fighting. 17 *tyāga* is the same as *dāna*. 19 *daṇḍakarasādhana-* 'securing or recovering of fines and taxes.' *daṇḍasādhana* does not seem to mean 'raising an army.' The *vā* read in G M after *-dhikāreṇa* is not necessary and D omits it. We need not suppose, as Meyer does, that some word before *vā* has dropped out. *vā*, if read, can show the option between *daṇḍasādhana* and *karasādhana*. 20 *sādhayet* 'should manage, secure,' i.e., get rid of him.

22 According to Cb Cs the 9th *prakaraṇa* really begins only with this s., the earlier ss. forming part of the 8th. Even those ss., however, also refer to possible *kṛtyas* and *akṛtyas*. — *māninaḥ* from D is supported by 1.14.5 below.

CHAPTER FOURTEEN

SECTION 10 WINNING OVER THE SEDUCIBLE AND NON-SEDUCIBLE PARTIES IN THE ENEMY'S TERRITORY

1 The winning over of the seducible and non-seducible parties in one's own territory has been explained; that in the enemy's territory is to be described.

2 One who is cheated after being promised certain things, of two persons equally skilled in some art or useful service the one who is humiliated, one who is in disfavour because of a favourite (of the king), one who is defeated after being challenged (to a contest), one who is distressed by banishment, one who has not achieved his object after incurring expenditure, one who is hindered from doing his duty or receiving his inheritance, one deprived of honour or office, one held back by members of the family, one whose womenfolk are molested by force, one who is put in prison, one who is fined after losing his suit (in court), one prevented from indulging in wrong conduct, one whose entire property is confiscated, one tormented in confinement, one whose kinsmen are exiled (or, killed),—this is the group of the enraged.

3 One who has himself thwarted (someone), one who has committed a serious wrong, one who has become known for a sinful act, one frightened by punishment meted out to another with a like offence, one who has seized (some

1.14

upagraha is 'winning over to one's side, seducing.' '*upagrahaḥ anukūlanam*'—*Medinī*.

2 *tulyakāriṇoḥ* : 'of two persons who can do a thing equally efficiently.' Cj reads *tulyakāriṇaḥ* which may be understood as ablative, 'one humiliated as compared with his equal.' D reads *tattulyakāriṇaḥ* which may be similarly understood. —*vallabhāvaruddhaḥ* : following D, *-paruddhaḥ* should rather be read ; for, the idea is 'one in disfavour because of some favourite of the king,' hardly 'put in restraint by a favourite of the king.' —*pravāsa-* 'banishment,' rather than 'constant journeying on king's account.' —*kulyaiḥ* seems to refer to the king's kinsmen rather than to his own. —*kārābhinyastaḥ* 'put in prison' (Cb), though, as Meyer points out, *kārā* 'prison' is not found elsewhere in the text and *bandhanaparikliṣṭaḥ* appears to render this expression superfluous. Cj explains 'one who is urged to recover fines quickly (*kāro daṇḍaḥ, tatra abhiniveśena tvayedam āśūpaneyam iti niyuktaḥ*),' which is hardly convincing. Meyer would read *kārābhiyastaḥ* or *karābhiyastaḥ* 'over-oppressed by taxes' ; *karābhitrastaḥ* might be better in this sense. —*paroktadaṇḍitaḥ* : 3.1.19–20 show *parokta* in the sense of the person who has lost his suit and is fined in consequence. Therefore, 'who is fined without proper consideration on the testimony of another' (Cb Cj) does not seem to be right. —*mithyācāravāritaḥ* : Cb Cs explain 'who has been wrongly (*mithyā*) prevented from some practice such as the performance of the *Agniṣṭoma* sacrifice.' This case seems to be covered by *svadharmād uparuddhaḥ*. 'Prevented from indulging in some wrong conduct' is better. —*pravāsita-* may be 'exiled' or 'executed.' Cnn has '*yamapuraṁ preṣitabāndhavaḥ*.'

3 *svayam upahataḥ viprakṛtaḥ* : both participles appear used in the active sense 'who has hindered or thwarted (some highly placed individual), and who has committed some serious wrong (to such an individual).' If understood as 'who is thwarted' and 'who is wronged,' that would hardly suit. The consequence would be anger, rather than fear. Cnn explains *upahata* 'who has failed to carry out the task after spending a lot of money and troops (*kośaṁ daṇḍaṁ ca vināśya akṛtakāryo*), i.e. frustrated by his own actions' and *viprakṛta* 'who has done an act of treason like black magic etc. (*viruddhaṁ prakarṣeṇa kṛtaṁ rājadviṣṭam abhicārādi*).' Cj has 'who has been thwarted by his own evil deed

one's) land, one who is subdued by force, one in any (state) department who has suddenly amassed wealth, one hoping for a pretender from the (king's) family (coming to the throne), one disliked by the king, and one who entertains hostility towards the king,—this is the group of the frightened.

4 One who is impoverished, one whose property is taken by another, a miser, one in a calamity (or, indulging in a vice) and one indulging in rash transactions,—this is the group of the greedy.

5 One who is filled with self-conceit, one desirous of honour, one resentful of the honour done to his enemy, one placed in a low position, one fiery in temper, one given to violence, and one dissatisfied with his emoluments,—this is the group of the proud.

6 Among them, he should cause instigation through spies appearing as holy men with shaven heads or matted hair,—of each person of the seducible party by that (spy) to whom he may be devoted.

7. 'Just as an elephant, blinded by intoxication and mounted by an intoxicated driver, crushes whatever it finds (on the way), so this king, not possessed of the eye of science, and (hence) blind, has risen to destory the citizens and the country people; it is possible to do harm to him by inciting a rival elephant against him; show (your) resentment;'—in this way he should cause the group of the enraged to be instigated.

(*ātmaduścaritena upahataḥ rājakāryavināśād sa bibheti*)' and 'accused (*viprakṛto abhiśastaḥ*).' —*paryāttabhūmiḥ* 'whose lands are taken away from him' (Cb Meyer) is hardly likely to be afraid; 'who has seized the land of another (Cs) would appear better. Cj thinks of king's land being seized by him. —*daṇḍenopanataḥ*: usually this refers to a prince who has surrendered with his troops; cf. 7.15 below. As state officers are primarily thought of, 'subdued by force' is clearly meant. 'Impoverished by fines' (Cs) is hardly likely. —*tatkulīnopāśaṁsuḥ*: Cb explains 'who has sought shelter with or is dependent on a pretender to the throne.' Cj, reading *tatkulīno vāśaṁsuḥ*, explains 'a member of the king's family who is eagerly looking forward to becoming the king.' The reading with *vā* does not appear very likely.

4 *anyāttasvaḥ* from D appears preferable to *atyāttasvaḥ* 'whose property has been taken away by way of taxes or fines' (Cs) or 'who has taken to himself excessive property' (Meyer). —*atyāhitavyavahāraḥ*: the rashness of the undertaking apparently involves a financial loss or expectation of great gain.

5 *nīcair upahitaḥ* 'one who is placed in a low position (*nīcaiḥ* as adverbial)' appears better than 'placed along with low persons (either in rank or for some work)' (Cj Cs Meyer) or 'involved in the same matter along with low persons' (Cb). —*bhogena*, i.e., with what he receives in return for service rendered.

6 *yo yadbhaktis taṁ tena*: the idea is that the instigation is to be made by that spy (*tena*) disguised as a holy man, to whom the *kṛtya* may be devoted. Thus Cj. It is possible to refer *yad* and *tena* to *krodha*, *bhaya* etc. to which the *kṛtya* may be attached (*yadbhaktiḥ*); but this is less likely. Meyer proposes *yadabhaktiḥ tena* 'through that (*krodha* etc.) by which he has become disaffected (*abhaktiḥ*) towards his master.' This is hardly satisfactory. Cb has 'by the offer of whatever he may be desirous of.' What follows does not contain any reference to the desires of the *kṛtya*.

7 After *andho rājā*, Cb Cs add *andhena mantriṇā 'dhiṣṭhitaḥ*. Though it corresponds to *mattena adhiṣṭhitaḥ* in the upamāna, it isn't necessary. In fact, it may well have been a marginal gloss. Cf. Śaṁkarārya on Kāmandaka, 18.39. —*amarṣaḥ*: the resentment is apparently to be shown by going over to the enemy.

8 'Just as a serpent, lying in hiding, emits poison at the place from which it expects danger, so this king, having become apprehensive of harm (from you), will ere long emit the poison of anger at you; go elsewhere;'—in this way he should cause the group of the frightened to be instigated.

9 'Just as the cow of the hunters is milked for hounds, not for Brahmins, so this king is milked for those devoid of spirit, intelligence and eloquence, not for those endowed with qualities of the self; that (other) king knows (how to appreciate) persons of distinction; go to him;'—in this way he should cause the group of the greedy to be instigated.

10 'Just as the well of the Caṇḍālas is of use only to the Caṇḍālas, not to others, so this king, being low, is of benefit only to low persons, not to Āryas such as you; that (other) king knows (how to appreciate) persons of distinction; go to him;'—in this way he should cause the group of the proud to be instigated.

11 When they have agreed with the words 'So (we shall do)' and have become allied (to him) by the making of terms, he should employ them according to their capacity in his own works, with spies (to watch over them).

12 And he should win over the seducible in the enemy's territories by means of conciliation and gifts and those not seducible by means of dissension and force, pointing out (to them) the defects of the enemy.

CHAPTER FIFTEEN

SECTION 11 THE TOPIC OF COUNSEL

1 When he has secured the allegiance of his own party and the party of the enemy, he should think of the undertaking of works.

2 All undertakings should be preceded by consultation. 3 The place for that should be secluded, not allowing talks to be heard outside, incapable

8 *purā utsṛjati* : as usual the sense of the immediate future is to be understood. Meyer has 'before he emits, you should go.' Though possible, this doesn't appear intended.

9 *duhyate* is as in D Cj. *dugdhe* is equally good. — *-vākyaśakti-* cf. 1.11.19 above. — *asau rājā* is the king on whose behalf the secret agent is working. — In the reading *sevyatām* of G1 M (for *tatra gamyatām*), a *sa* would appear to be necessary before it; Cj seems to have read it here as well as in s.10.

10 This clearly implies the existence of separate arrangements for water for the untouchables.

11 *saṁhitān paṇakarmaṇā* : a treaty (*saṁdhi*) with terms (*paṇa*) laid down is meant.

1.15

3 *kathānām aniḥśrāvī* is from D, also implied in Cb. That is better than *anisrāvī* (*aniḥsrāvī* necessary as in Cs) 'not allowing (talk) to flow out.' Cj, with *anisrāvī*, has 'free

of being peeped in even by birds. 4 For, it is known that deliberations are divulged by parrots and starlings, even by dogs and other animals. 5 Therefore, an unauthorised person must not approach the place of counsel. 6 One who divulges secret counsel should be extirpated.

7 Secret counsel is indeed betrayed by the gestures and the expressions of the envoy, the minister and the monarch. 8 Gesture is behaviour other than normal. 9 The putting on of an expression (on the face) is expression. 10 Concealment of that (and) vigilance over officers appointed (should be maintained) till the time of (completion of) the undertaking. 11 For, their prattle through negligence or in intoxication or during sleep, their immoderation such as amorousness and the like, or, a person concealed or despised, betrays secret counsel. 12 Therefore, he should guard counsel.

13 'The divulgence of secret counsel is fatal to the security and well-being of the king and the officers appointed by him. 14 Therefore, he should deliberate alone over a confidential matter,' says Bhāradvāja. 15 'For, even councillors have (other) councillors, and these have others still. 16 Thus this series of councillors leads to the divulgence of secret counsel.

> 17 'Therefore, others should not know about any work sought to be done by him. Only those who undertake it should know (about it) when it is begun or even when it is actually completed.'

18 'There is no attainment of deliberation by a single person,' says Viśālākṣa. 19 'For, the affairs of a king are (threefold,) directly perceived, unperceived and inferred. 20 Coming to know what is not known, definite strengthening of what has become known, removal of doubt in case of two possible alternatives in a matter, finding out the rest in a matter that is partly known,—this can be achieved (only) with the help of ministers. 21 Therefore, he should sit in counsel with those who are mature in intellect.

from echoes.' 4 *śukasārikābhir* : Jolly-Schmidt refer to the *Harṣacarita* p. 268 (BSS edition) for illustrations. 5 Cj reads *ayukto* for *anāyukto*.

8 *iṅgita* derived from *iṅg* 'to move,' refers to movements or gestures indicative of the thoughts of a person. 9 *ākṛtigrahaṇam* 'putting on an expression other than natural, such as paleness of the face, etc.' (Cb). 10 A *ca* would seem necessary after *-rakṣaṇam*. — *iti* has no significance; a verb like *kuryāt* or *kārayet* would have been better. 11 *-pralāpāḥ* is from D. Since *kāma* etc. constitutes *utseka* as shown by 9.7.1 and *pramāda* etc. are unconnected with it, this reading is clearly necessary. Perhaps *pralāpaḥ* in the sing. which seems to be the reading of Cj, would be better, in view of the verb *bhinatti*. — *utsekaḥ* 'immoderation, excess' rather than 'haughtiness' (Cs) or 'self-forgetfulness' (Meyer).

13 D's *hyayoga-* is supported by Cb. — *ayogakṣemakaro rājñaḥ* : Cnn gives the illustration of Rāmagupta betrayed by Dhruvadevī (*yathā Dhruvadevyā kṛto Rāmaguptaśarīrasya*). 17 D has a slightly different form of the first line, which is found in s. 60. — An *iti* at the end of the stanza would be better to mark the end of the quotation from Bhāradvāja's work. That this is a quotation can hardly be doubted.

19 Cf. 1.9.4 above. It is possible that even there the s. is derived from Viśālākṣa's work. 20 *niścitabalādhānam* : Jolly-Schmidt have adopted *niścayo niścitasya balādhānam* from Somadeva's *Nītivākyāmṛta*, where the passage is quoted.

22 'He should despise none, (but) should listen to the opinion of every one. A wise man should make use of the sensible words of even a child.'

23 'This is ascertainment of counsel, not guarding of counsel,' say the followers of Parāśara. 24 'He should ask the councillors concerning a matter exactly similar to the undertaking he has in mind, "this work was like this, or, if it were to happen like this, how then should it be done ?" 25 As they might advise, so should he do that (work). 26 In this way is counsel ascertained and secrecy maintained at the same time.'

27 'No,' says Piśuna. 28 'For, councillors, questioned about a remote affair, whether it has taken place or not, give their opinion with indifference or disclose it. 29 That is a defect. 30 Therefore, he should deliberate with those who are approved for the particular undertakings. 31 Holding counsel with these (only), he achieves success in consultation as well as its secrecy.'

32 'No', says Kauṭilya, 33 For, this is a condition without fixity. 34 He should hold consultations with three or four councillors. 35 For, holding a consultation with one (only), he may not (be able to) reach a decision in difficult matters. 36 And a single councillor behaves as he pleases without restraint. 37 Holding consultations with two, he is controlled by the two if united and ruined by them if at war (with each other). 38 With three or four, that becomes possible (only) with difficulty. 39 However, if it does become possible, it involves great danger. 40 With more (councillors) than that, it is with difficulty that decisions on matters are reached or counsel

22 After this, too, an *iti* seems necessary.

23 *Pārāśarāḥ* : see 1.8.7. above. 24 *pratirūpakam* ' an exact counterpart.'

28 *vyavahitam* ' distant, ' i.e., not the matter which the king has in view at the time. 30 *abhipretāḥ* ' approved,' i.e., considered by the king as experts in the particular matter. 31 *mantrasiddhim* of D is distinctly better than *-buddhim* (in the sense of *upalabdhim*) or *-vṛddhim*. Cf. s. 18 above.

33 *anavasthā* : because every time the king would be consulting new men and there would be no stable group of councillors to advise the king. 38 *tat triṣu caturṣu vā* : this reading of D is found in Cj and supported by *tatriṣu* of M ; the omission of *naikāntam* (after *vā*) is supported by Cb. *tat* refers to the possibility of *avagraha* or *vināśa* which is there, when there are two ministers. Cnn includes the possibility of *mantraniścayānadhigama* and *yatheṣṭācaraṇa* also which are there when there is a single minister. 39 *mahādoṣam* etc. : the idea seems to be : if, however, the possibility of *avagraha* etc. does arise, it would spell disaster. It is not unlikely that this s. is a marginal gloss that has got into the text. Cj seems to explain 'that in which there is the great disadvantage (*doṣa*) of absence of security (*ayogakṣema*), is thus counteracted (*upapanna* i.e. *pratividhita*).' Without *tat* and with the addition of *naikāntam* in s. 38 Meyer explains the two ss. 'absence of conclusion or uncertainty (*naikāntam*) is reached (*upapadyate*) with difficulty. When it is reached, however, it becomes highly dangerous.' Cs includes *mahādoṣam* in s. 38 and explains 'a thing resulting in a great calamity (*mahādoṣam* as subject) such as *avagraha* etc. does not necessarily follow (*na ekāntam upapadyate*) ; if at all it follows, it does so with difficulty. (The matter under consideration *cintyamānaṁ kāryam*) becomes properly dealt with (*upapannaṁ bhavati*).' This explanation is very doubtful.

guarded. 41 However, in conformity with the place, time and work to be done, he should deliberate with one or two, or alone by himself, according to (their and his own) competence.

42 The means of starting undertakings, the excellence of men and materials, (suitable) apportionment of place and time, provision against failure (and) accomplishment of the work—this is deliberation in its five aspects.

43 He should ask them individually as well as jointly. 44 And he should ascertain their different opinions along with (their) reasons (for holding them). 45 Having found a matter (for deliberation) he should not allow time to pass. 46 He should not deliberate for a long time, nor with the partisans of those to whom he would (like to) do harm.

47 'He should appoint a council consisting of twelve ministers,' say the followers of Manu. 48 'Sixteen,' say the followers of Bṛhaspati. 49 'Twenty,' say the followers of Uśanas. 50 'According to capacity,' says Kauṭilya.

51 They should think over the (king's) own party and the enemy's party. 52 And (they) should bring about the commencement of what is not done, the carrying out of what is commenced, the improvement of what has been carried out and the excellence of (the execution of) orders, in the case of works.

53. He should look into the affairs with those who are present. 54 With those who are not present he should hold consultations by sending out letters.

41 *yathāsāmarthyam*, i.e., according to his own and the councillors' capability. Cnn remarks that capability implies proficiency in politics, brilliant intellect and skill in practical affairs '*mantre sāmarthyaṁ śāstracakṣuṣmattā niratiśayā prajñā lokavyavahāra-kauśalaṁ ca.*'

44 *matipravivekān*: distinctions of opinion, i.e., individual opinions. The reading of Jolly-Schmidt is derived from a commentary on Kāmandaka's *Nītisāra* and is in no way preferable. —*hetu* 'the motive' which apparently led the councillor to hold the opinion offered by him. Reading *matipravekān*, Cj paraphrases it by '*buddhiprakarṣānvitān* (possessed of outstanding intellect)', and supplies '*sahasaivānutiṣṭhet* (should carry out at once).' It is difficult to see how the former could be the object of this predicate. 45 *avāptārthaḥ*: this may mean 'when there is a matter on which the holding of a consultation is necessary' or 'when he has come to a decision after consultation.' The former is slightly better, since the next s. still refers to the consultation stage. 46 There can be no doubt that *na teṣāṁ pakṣīyair* of D is the original reading. *parakṣyer* in M1 is a scribal error for *pakṣyair* which means the same as *pakṣīyair*. The idea is, the king should not hold consultations with the relatives or partisans of those whom he wishes to harm. Cnn gives the illustration of Duryodhana consulting Vidura, a partisan of the Pāṇḍavas.

47 The opinion here attributed to the Mānavas is not found in the *Manusmṛti* (cf. 7.54). 49 Cb has *ekaviṁśatim* for *viṁśatim*. 50 *yathāsāmarthyam*: the *sāmarthya* may refer to the capacity of the ministers or the strength of the kingdom.

52 *akṛtārambham* etc.: these functions of the *mantripariṣad*, as distinguished from those of the *mantrins* in s. 42 above, suggest that the *pariṣad* is a body of executive officers, though

55 Indra indeed has a council of ministers consisting of a thousand sages. 56 He has that as his eye. 57 Therefore, they call him 'the thousand-eyed one,' though he is two-eyed.

58 In an urgent matter, he should call together the councillors as well as the council of ministers and ask them. 59 What the majority among them declare or what is conducive to the success of the work, that he should do.

60 And while he is doing that,

the enemies should not come to know of his secret; he should, however, find out the weaknesses of the enemy. He should conceal, as a tortoise does his limbs, any (limb) of his own that may have become exposed.

61 Just as a person not learned in the Veda does not deserve to eat the Śrāddha-meal of good persons, so a (king) who has not learnt the teaching of the science (of politics) is unfit to listen to counsel.

CHAPTER SIXTEEN

SECTION 12 RULES FOR THE ENVOY

1 When consultation has led to a choice of decision, the employment of the envoy (should follow).

2 One endowed with the excellences of a minister is the plenipotentiary. 3 One lacking in a quarter of the qualities is (the envoy) with a limited mission. 4 One lacking in half the qualities is the bearer of a message.

5 He should start after making proper arrangements for vehicles, draught-animals and retinue of servants. 6 'The message is thus to be delivered to the enemy; he will (probably) say this (in reply); for that this will be the suitable reply; thus is (the enemy) to be outwitted;'—reflecting

consultation with it is also recommended (ss. 54, 58–59). The *mantripariṣad* can hardly be regarded as a cabinet. — *niyogasaṁpadam* refers to the excellence of the way in which commands or instructions have been carried out.

59 *brūyuḥ* after *bhūyiṣṭhāḥ* as in D is better than after *vā* ; cf. 1.16.28 below. — This s. shows that the majority opinion is not intended to be followed as a rule. Cf. Kāmandaka, 12.40 : *dhṛte 'pi mantre mantrajñaiḥ svayaṁ bhūyo vicārayet.*

60 *yat* may refer to *chidra* or *aṅga* ; either yields a good sense, though the latter appears slightly better. — Cf. Manu, 7.105.

61 After this stanza D has two stanzas quoted as from Bṛhaspati. They are clearly not original and seem to be marginal notes that have got into the text.

1.16

For *praṇidhi* see 1.12 above.

1 *udvṛtamantraḥ* is from D for *uddhṛta-*. As an adjective to *dūtapraṇidhiḥ*, it means 'in which the counsel has been selected or accepted,' i.e., when a decision has been taken after deliberation.

2 *amātyasaṁpad* : cf. 1.9.1 above. — *nisṛṣṭārtha* lit. 'to whom the matter has been entrusted (with full powers of negotiation).'

in this manner, he should proceed. 7 And he should establish contacts with forest chieftains, frontier-chiefs and chief officials in the cities and the countryside (on the way). 8 He should observe terrains suitable for the stationing of an army, for fighting, for reserves and for retreat, for his own (state) and for the enemy. 9 And he should find out the size of the forts and the country as well as the strong points, sources of livelihood, defences and weak points (in the enemy's territory).

10 He should enter the enemy's residence with permission. 11 And he should deliver the message as given to him, even when danger to his life is seen (in so doing)).

12 He should notice graciousness in speech, expression and eyes of the enemy, esteem of the (envoy's) words, inquiries about (his) wishes, keen interest in talk about the qualities (of the envoy's master), offer of a seat close by, respectful welcome, remembering (the envoy) on pleasant occasions, and putting trust in him, as the signs of one pleased; the opposite of these as the signs of one displeased. 13 To such a one he should say, 'Kings indeed have envoys as their mouthpieces, you no less than others. 14 Therefore, envoys speak out as they are told even when weapons are raised (against them). 15 Of them even the lowest born are immune from killing; what to speak then of Brahmins ? 16 These are the words of another. 17 This is the duty of an envoy.'

18 If not permitted to depart, he should stay on, not feeling elated by honour (shown). 19 Among the enemies he should not think of (himself) being possessed of strength. 20 He should put up with disagreeable words. 21 He should avoid women and drink. 22 He should sleep alone. 23 For, it is (often) seen that the intentions of a person are revealed in sleep or intoxication.

5 *parivāpa*, when used by itself, refers to personal belongings as in 3.6.6, 8 ; when used with *puruṣa-* as here, it conveys the idea of a retinue or train of servants ; cf. 2.24.28 ; 3.3.3. 8 *pratigrahabhūmi* 'the place where reserves are held in readiness' ; cf. 10.5.58 ; 10.2.20 ; 10.6.1. *yuddhapratigraha* as a single idea 'acceptance of a fight' (Cs Meyer) seems little likely. — *apasāra* 'retreat ;' cf. 10.2.8 ; 7.13.25 etc. 9 *chidra* can be construed with the preceding *gupti*, hardly with *sāra* and *vṛtti* as well, as Meyer seems to do. It is best to understand it independently.

10 *adhiṣṭhāna* refers to the palace and the assembly-hall where the envoy would be received.

12 *guṇa-* seems to refer to the good points of the envoy's master, though the envoy's own merits may also be considered as possible. — *iṣṭeṣu smaraṇam* : cf. *bhakṣyeṣu smarati* 5.5.7 below. 13 *dūtamukhā hi* : Cb has *vai* for *hi* ; that is equally good. 15 Cj reads *antevāsinaḥ* 'attendants,' though it mentions the other reading.

18 In the reading *prapūjayā*, *pra* has little significance. 19 *pareṣu balitvaṁ na manyeta* : the idea seems to be, he should not commit any rash act at the enemy's court thinking that his own king is quite powerful. Cnn has 'he should not use harsh words (*vākpāruṣyaṁ na brūyāt*) because of his master's or his own strength (*svāmibalād ātmabalād vā*).' Meyer's 'he should consider for nought the strength of the enemies' is hardly likely in the context ; it contradicts the next clause. 'He should not disclose to the enemies that he is strong' (Cb Cs) seems also less likely.

24 He should find out (about) the instigation of seducible parties, the employment of secret agents against non-seducible parties, the loyalty or disaffection (of the enemy's subjects) towards their master and the weak points in the constituent elements (of the enemy's realm), through spies appearing as ascetics or traders, or through their disciples or assistants or through agents in the pay of both appearing as physicians or heretics. 25 In case conversation with them is not possible, he should find out secret information from the utterances of beggars, drunken persons, insane persons or persons in sleep, or, from pictures, writings or signs in holy places or temples of gods. 26 When (such information is) found out, he should make use of instigation.

27 And when asked by the enemy, he should not declare the size (and strength) of his own constituents. 28 He should say, 'Your Majesty knows every thing,' or (should say) what is conducive to the success of his mission.

29 When he is being detained although his mission has not succeeded, he should thus reflect—'Is he detaining me because he sees an imminent calamity befalling my master, or because he wants to take remedial steps against his own calamity, or because he wants to rouse (against my master) the enemy in the rear or his ally or (to stir up) an internal revolt or a forest chieftain, or because he wishes to obstruct my master's ally in front or ally in the rear, or because he wants to take remedial steps in a war of his own with another enemy or against an internal revolt or a forest chieftain (of his own), or because he wants to spoil the season for expedition for which my master has thoroughly prepared, or because he wants to collect stores of grains, commodities and forest produce or carry out fortifications or raise troops, or because he is awaiting time and place suitable for the operations of his own forces, or because of (a feeling of) contempt or through negligence, or because he seeks a continuation of (close) association (with my master)?' 30 Having found out (the enemy's motive), he should stay on or escape. 31 Or, he should take into consideration some purpose (regarded as) desirable.

24 *bhartari*, i.e., towards their own king, not towards the envoy's master. 25 *citralekhyasaṁjñā* : Cb has 'the drawing (*lekhya*) of pictures and signs,' Cs 'signs in the pictures and writings,' Meyer 'paintings, writings and signs.' The last seems best. 26 *upajāpam upeyāt*, i.e., resort to instigation of the party found amenable to it.

29 *paśyan* : D's *paśyati* is clearly not right. — *pārṣṇigrāham āsāram* of D is to be preferred, as each of these kings could be individually roused against his master. — *ākrandaṁ vā* from Cb Cj (for *ākrandābhyām*) is quite necessary. — *vyāghātayitukāmaḥ* : the idea is of hindering, foiling, and that is preferable to the idea of killing in the reading *vyāpādayitukāmaḥ*. — It is proposed to add *vā* after *saṁsiddham*, since it is quite necessary as in the other clauses. Perhaps Cj reads the *vā*. —The reading *yātrākāram*, though perhaps possible in the sense of 'the undertaking of a campaign,' seems hardly original. *yātrākāla* is definitely intended. — *pramādābhyām* : Cb Cs read *-pramadābhyām* 'out of affection;' that is unlikely. *pramāda* is commonly used along with *paribhava*. — *saṁsargānubandhārthī* : Meyer has 'wishing to have an association with or a following with.' But a single idea 'wishing to have a continuous association' seems better. Cnn has 'seeking relationship between the progeny of both through marriage (*saṁsargo yaunaḥ saṁbandhaḥ, tena anubandhaḥ ubhayasaṁbandhaḥ, tadarthī*).' *anubandha* is explained as *doṣotpāda* in Cs, which is little likely. 31 D's *upekṣeta* is unlikely, though its omission of *vā* may appear to be an improvement.

32 After delivering an unpleasant message, he should, for fear of imprisonment or death, go away even when not permitted; else he might be put under restraint.

33 Sending communications, guarding the terms of a treaty, (upholding his king's) majesty, acquisition of allies, instigation, dividing (the enemy's) friends, conveying secret agents and troops (into the enemy's territory),

34 kidnapping (the enemy's) kinsmen and treasures, ascertainment of secret information, showing valour, (helping in) the escape of hostages, and resort to secret practices,—these are the functions of an envoy.

35 He should cause all this to be carried out by his envoys, and should cause a watch to be kept over the envoys of the enemy by means of counter-envoys and spies as well as through open and secret guards.

CHAPTER SEVENTEEN

SECTION 13 GUARDING AGAINST PRINCES

1 A king protects the kingdom (only) when (he is himself) protected from persons near him and from enemies, first from his wives and sons. 2 Protection from wives we shall explain in 'Regulations for the Royal Residence.'

3 As to protection from sons, however :

4 'He should guard against princes right from their birth. 5 For, princes devour their begetters, being of the same nature as crabs. 6 Before love (for them) is produced in the father, silent punishment for them is best;' says Bhāradvāja.

33 *preṣaṇam* 'sending communications'; cf. 2.21.27. — *pratāpaḥ* : since *parākrama* is also used, 'valour' can hardly be understood by *pratāpa*. Meyer understands 'majesty, dignity,' i.e., the maintenance of his master's prestige at the foreign court. Cb refers to Hanūmat showing *pratāpa* in the Aśokavanikā, implying a pun 'causing trouble' and 'burning.' — *gūḍhadaṇḍātisāraṇam* : cf. 7.14.24.

34 Meyer thinks that *ratna*, like *ratnin* in the Brāhmaṇa texts, refers to big personalities in the state. That seems hardly possible in this text. — *samādhimokṣaḥ* : cf. 7.17.32ff. — *yogasya* : *yoga* refers to the secret methods used to do away with undesirables, particularly the use of weapons, poison etc. (*yogasya śastrāgnirasapraṇidhānasya*—Cj).

1.17

For *rakṣaṇa* in the sense of 'keeping a watch over, guarding oneself against,' see 1.13 above.

2 *niśāntapraṇidhau*, i.e., in Chapter 1.20 below.

4 *janmaprabhṛti* etc. : Cb Cs do not include ss. 4-5 in Bhāradvāja's opinion. It seems, however, that they contain the opinion of this cynical teacher alone and not the general view of the science. — Cj reads *rājā putrān*. 6 *ajātasnehe pitari* : this is a locative absolute 'before the father begins to feel affection.' *pitari ajātasnehe* (*putre*) *upāṁśudaṇḍaḥ* 'secretly doing away with a son who feels no affection for the father' is possible, but does not seem intended.

7 'This is cruel, (as it involves) the killing of innocent persons and the destruction of the Kṣatriya race,' says Viśālākṣa. 8 'Therefore, confinement in one place is best.'

9 'This is danger as from a snake,' say the followers of Parāśara. 10 'For, the prince, realising "through fear of my valour my father has confined me," might get the father himself in his power. 11 Therefore, making him stay in a frontier fortress is best.'

12 'This is danger as from a (fighting) ram,' says Piśuna. 13 'For, realising that alone to be the means of his return, he might become the ally of the frontier chief. 14 Therefore, making him stay in the fortress of a neighbouring (vassal) prince, far removed from his own territory, is best.'

15 'This is the position of a calf (for the prince),' says Kauṇapadanta. 16 'For, the neighbouring prince might milk his father as (one milks) a cow with the help of the calf. 17 Therefore, making him stay with the kinsmen of his mother is best.'

18 'This is the position of a flag (for the prince),' says Vātavyādhi. 19 'For, with him as the flag, his mother's kinsmen would be making demands

7 There can be no doubt that *adṛṣṭa-* of G M is faulty, being corrupted from *aduṣṭa-* (D). 8 *ekasthāna-* 'one place,' i.e., the place where the king himself is; '*yatra pitā tatraivāvarodhaḥ*' as in Cnn; similarly Cj.

9 *ahibhayam* : a simile is implied in this expression. 10 *tameva aṅke kuryāt* : D reads *tadeva*; the neuter *tad* cannot easily be made to refer to any preceding word. Cnn refers it to *ahibhayam* and explains 'he may bring about the same danger of a snake, as he is stationed near (*tadeva ahibhayaṁ vināśalakṣaṇam aṅke samīpe sthitaḥ kuryāt*).' This is far from convincing. Cj, with *tadeva*, refers *tad* to *vikramabhaya* or *avarodhana*, explaining *aṅke* by *samīpe vartamānaḥ*. *tam* in the other reading may refer to the father, 'might kill the father himself' as in Cb. In 7.19.40 *aṅkam upasthita* seems to mean 'who is in one's power,' so that here 'he may bring the father himself in his power' may be the sense intended. (Cf. *aṅkāgatasattvavṛtti*—*Raghuvaṁśa*, 2.38). *tam* may also refer to *vikramam* 'might resort to valour.' Cs refers *tam* to *vikramam*, but explains 'might show valour in a nearby place, i.e., in his own house.' This is less satisfactory.

12 *aurabhram* : the idea, as Cs explains, is, just as a ram taken to the ends of the fighting ring returns to the centre with greater vehemence to meet his rival, so the prince might return to attack the king with the help of the *antapāla*. Meyer's 'this is the fear of sheep' is hardly possible. 13 *pratyāpatteḥ kāraṇam* : Cb has 'reason for keeping him away', Cnn 'the cause of his going away from the father (*pituḥ sakāśād anyatra gamanam*)', Meyer 'the cause of the father holding aloof from the son,' Russ. 'the cause of the father's disgust with him.' It seems rather that *kāraṇam* is 'means,' not 'cause,' and that *tat* refers to *antapālasakhatva*, not *vikramabhaya* (as in Cnn), so that we have to understand 'the means of his return' to the capital. Cj has 'the means of ending his loss of liberty,' and refers *tad* to *vikrama* or to *antapālopagrahaṇa* 'winning the *antapāla* over.' The explanation of *pratyāpatteḥ* (understood as ablative) in Cs 'because his nature of being hostile to the king cannot be changed' is little likely.

19 *aditikauśikavad* : according to commentators 'mendicants earning their livelihood by showing images of gods (*aditi*) and snake-charmers (*kauśika*).' Cnn : '*aditivad devadhvajaṁ darśayitvā; aditigrahaṇam aditiputrāṇāṁ kālādidevānāṁ parigrahārtham. kauśikas tvāhituṇḍikaḥ kośena sarpagraheṇa caratīti*.' It may be that *aditikauśika* conveys a single idea, that of a sect of mendicants who make demands (which cannot be refused) in the name of some god whose flag, along with the image, they carry. Snake-charmers do not carry flags. Meyer suggests that as Kauśika is a name of Indra, we have to understand a mendicant woman in the garb of Aditi and a boy in the garb of Indra, the begging

like Aditikauśikas. 20 Therefore, he should let him free to indulge in vulgar pleasures. 21 For, sons kept engrossed in pleasures do not become hostile to the father.'

22 'This is living death,' says Kauṭilya. 23 For, like a piece of wood eaten by worms, the royal family, with its princes undisciplined, would break the moment it is attacked. 24 Therefore, when the chief queen is in her *ṛtu* (-period), priests should offer a *caru*-oblation to Indra and Bṛhaspati. 25 When she is pregnant, a childern's specialist should arrange for the nourishment of the foetus and for delivery. 26 When she has given birth, the chaplain should perform the sacraments for the son. 27 When he is ready for it, experts should train him.

28 'And one of the secret agents should tempt him with hunting, gambling, wine and women, (suggesting to him,) "Attack your father and seize the kingdom." 29 Another secret agent should dissuade him from that;' say the followers of Āmbhi.

30 'This awakening of one not awake is highly dangerous,' says Kauṭilya. 31 For, a fresh object absorbs whatever it is smeared with. 32 Similarly, this prince, immature in intellect, understands as the teaching of the science whatever he is told. 33 Therefore, he should instruct him in what conduces to spiritual and material good, not in what is spiritually and materially harmful.

34 On the contrary, secret agents, declaring 'We belong to you,' should guard him. 35 If in the exuberance of youth he were to entertain a longing for the wives of others, they should produce abhorrence in him through unclean women posing as noble ladies in lonely houses at night time. 36 If he were to long for wine, they should frighten him with drugged liquor. 37 If he were to long for gambling, they should create aversion in him through deceitful players. 38 If he were to long for hunting, they should frighten him through agents disguised as highway robbers. 39 If he were to entertain the idea

being done for the sake of the boy. A boy is unlikely, as there is the *dhvaja*, to which the prince corresponds.

25 *kaumārabhṛtyaḥ* : 'a physician who has specialised in bringing up children,' was also experienced in midwifery, as the present passage shows. Jolly-Schmidt point out that *kumārabhṛtya* 'treatment of infants' diseases' is the subject of a part of one of the ancient Buddhist medical treatises in the Bower Ms. and that Jīvaka, a famous contemporary of Buddha, was called *komārabhacca*.

28 This is a sort of *upadhā* or secret test. 29 *Āmbhīyāḥ* : the teacher's name appears to be Āmbhi. Pāṇini 4.1.96 (*bāhvādi gaṇa*) derives Āmbhi as a patronymic from Ambhas. Nothing is known about this teacher or his school. Ganapati Sastri understands Bhīṣma by Āmbhi (Intro. to Vol. III of the Trivandrum edition).

31 *upadihyate...ācūṣati* : the figure, as Cs says, is that of an earthen vessel or a mud wall.

35 *udvejayeyuḥ* : the root may mean 'create disgust or aversion' or 'frighten, inspire terror' according to context. 36 *yogapāna* is a drink to which some substance is added

of attacking his father, they should enter into his confidence (by pretending to agree) and then dissuade him (saying), 'The king should not be attacked; if the attack fails, (there will be) death; if it succeeds, (there will be) a fall in hell (for you), an uproar and (your) annihilation by the subjects as of a single clod of earth.'

40 They should inform (the king) if the prince is disaffected. 41 He should put an only, favourite son (if disaffected) in prison. 42 If he has many sons, he should send (the disaffected son) to the frontier or some other region where he may not become as a child in the womb (for the people there) or a commodity for sale (for those people) or a (source of) disturbance. 43 If he is possessed of the excellences of self, he should install him in the position of the commander-in-chief or the crown prince.

44 One possessed of sagacity, one with intellect requiring to be goaded and one of evil intellect—these are the different kinds of sons. 45 He who, when taught, understands spiritual and material good and practises the same is one possessed of sagacity. 46 He who understands but does not practise (them) is one with intellect requiring to be goaded. 47 He who is ever full of harm and hates spiritual and material good is one of evil intellect.

that creates a nausea for drink. 39 *anupraviśya* : this means 'entering into and winning the confidence of'; cf. 2.9.26 etc. — *aprārthanīyo* 'not fit to be attacked.' For *prārth* 'to attack,' cf. 3.10.34; 6.2.38. Cb's 'not to be killed' seems less likely. — *saṁkrośaḥ* 'an outcry, an uproar' rather than 'censure among the people' (Cs). — *ekaloṣṭavadhaḥ* 'destruction as of a single clod of earth' (Meyer) is to be preferred to 'death by people throwing one clod of earth each' (Cs). For the latter, *ekaika-* would seem necessary. 'Killing by a single throw with a stone' (Jolly) seems out of the question. — Meyer includes *virāgam* from the next s. at the end of s. 39 after *iti* and supplies *kuryuḥ* after it, 'with these words (*iti*) they should make him give up (*vi-*) his desire (*rāga*) (to attack his father).' This is very unlikely.

40 *virāgaṁ vedayeyuḥ* : i.e., they should inform the king about the prince who cannot be made to give up his disloyal intentions. With *vedayeyuḥ* (from D) continuity with the preceding is maintained. 42 *pratyantam* is a noun in the sense of 'the frontier' rather than an adjective to *viṣaya* in the next word. — *yatra garbhaḥ paṇyaṁ ḍimbo vā na bhavet* : Cj explains 'where the prince is not likely to be as a son or son-in-law to the people there (making them take his side against the father) or where he would not be treated as a commodity for disposal (the people there increasing their own power at his expense) or where no trouble would be caused by people there by finding support in him and trying to win over others on his behalf (*garbha iva garbhaḥ; yatrainaṁ putratayā jāmātṛtayā garbhīkṛtya snehāt...na vikurvate. paṇyavat paṇyam; yatrainaṁ pracārya bhikṣayā na śaktiṁ ātmanaḥ pūrayanti. ḍimbakāraṇatvāt ḍimbaḥ; yatra tadāśrayāt kṛtyān upagṛhya nopadravaṁ kuryuḥ*).' Cnn is more or less similar. Cb seems to have read *garvaḥ* and explains 'where there is no pride, where the prince is not treated as a commodity and where no injury may be done to him.' This is less satisfactory. Cs has 'where there is no food fit for the prince (*garbha*, i.e., food) or no commodity fit for him or no commotion among the people because of him.' This also is unsatisfactory. Meyer has made a number of suggestions, the final one being to read *garbhaḥ ṣaṇḍo ḍimbo vāno vā bhavet* 'where there is a foetus (in the queen's womb) or an impotent prince or a silly prince (*ḍimba*) or an exhausted prince (*vāna* from *vai*) as the only heir to the throne,' the idea being that the exiled prince would in such a case stand a chance of succeeding to the throne in that foreign land. This is very doubtful. *anyaviṣaya* hardly means 'foreign land'.

46 The definition shows that the *āhāryabuddhi* is unable or unwilling to put into practice what he knows to be right. Ministers and others are however able to induce him to do what is right, '*ācāryādibhiḥ pratikṣaṇam āhāryā buddhir yasya*' (Cnn). *āhārya* 'which can be brought near'; cf. *āhāryodaka setu* 2.1.20.

48 If such be the only son, he should endeavour to get a son born of him.
49 Or, he should get sons begotten on an appointed daughter.

50 An old or a diseased king, however, should get a child begotten on his wife by one of the following, (viz.), his mother's kinsman, a member of his own family, and a virtuous neighbouring prince. 51 But he should not install on the throne an only son, if undisciplined.

52 Of many (sons, who are undisciplined) confinement in one place (is best); (however), the father should be beneficently disposed towards the sons. Except in case of a calamity, sovereignty passing on to the eldest son is praised.

53 Or, the kingdom should belong to the (royal) family; for, a family oligarchy is difficult to conquer, and remains on the earth for ever without (having to face) the danger of a calamity befalling the king.

CHAPTER EIGHTEEN

SECTION 14 THE CONDUCT OF A PRINCE IN DISFAVOUR
SECTION 15 BEHAVIOUR TOWARDS A PRINCE IN DISFAVOUR

1 The disciplined prince, who finds living difficult, shou'd obey his father when appointed to an unworthy task, except when it is dangerous to life or rouses the subjects (against him) or involves a heinous sin.

2 If he is assigned some agreeable task, he should ask for an officer to supervise his work. 3 And under supervision of the officer, he should carry

48 *sa* refers to the *durbuddhi*; *ekaputraḥ* is a Karmadhāraya; Cj's *ekaḥ putraḥ* makes this clear. *asya* refers to this only son. The idea is, the king should try to secure a grandson. Hillebrandt's suggestion that we should read *yadyaputraḥ* (ZDMG, 70, p. 41 n. 1) makes no improvement. —*putrikā-*: cf. Manu, 9.127ff.

50 For *niyoga*, referred to here, the kinsmen on the mother's side are shown a preference, which is rather strange. Cf. also 3.6.24 below.

52 Cj has 'if there are many disaffected princes they should be confined in one place;' Cb 'of many sons each one should be put in confinement;' Cs 'from among many sons, he should confine one son, who may be *durbuddhi*, in *pratyanta* etc.' Meyer understands the first half as a single clause 'the father of many sons (*bahūnāṁ pitā*) who keeps out of succession one (*ekasaṁrodhaḥ* as adj. to *pitā*) cares only for the good of the sons'. Cj's explanation seems best. 53 *kulasya* : this is the group of all sons (Cb Cs). All male members of the royal family forming a sort of ruling council may appear better. Cj seems to understand a division of the kingdom forming a sort of confederation (*sarveṣāṁ vā vibhaktaṁ bhaved rājyam anyonyasaṁśrayam*). A council formed by a number of noble families is possible as the meaning of *kulasaṁgha*, but does not seem intended here. For *saṁgha* cf. 11.1 below. — *arājavyasanābādhaḥ*: this is an adj. to *kulasaṁghaḥ*. The idea is, even if one member is in *vyasana*, the others are there to carry on. For *rājavyasana* see 8.2 below.

1.18

D reads *aparuddha* throughout and that form is adopted in this edition. It is found in *Atharvaveda* 3.3.5 (*anyakṣetre aparuddhaṁ carantam*), *Taittirīya Saṁhitā* 2.2.8.4, *Kauśikasūtra* 16.30 and the Aihole Inscription, stanza 14.

1 G M omit *vinīto*; but it is better to read it, as the prince discussed here is assumed to be well-behaved and unjustly treated by his father. — *kṛcchravṛttiḥ* shows that he is made to work for his living and that he finds it difficult

out the task assigned with special zest. 4 And he should get despatched to his father the normal produce of the work as well as any (extra) gain received as a present.

5 If (the father is) even then not pleased and shows affection for another son or wife (other than his mother), he should ask for leave to repair to the forest. 6 Or, in case of fear of imprisonment or death, he should seek refuge with a neighbouring prince who is justly behaved, pious, truthful in speech, not given to breach of faith and welcomes and honours those who have approached him (for help). 7 Staying there and becoming enriched with treasure and troops, he should enter into marriage relations with heroic men, make contacts with forest chieftains and win over seducible parties (from his father's kingdom).

8 If he has to act alone, he should maintain himself by working mines and factories for gold-smelting, colouring gems and manufacturing gold and silver articles. 9 Or, he should secretly rob the wealth of heretical corporations or the wealth of temples except that to be used by Brahmins learned in the Vedas or the wealth of rich widows after entering into their confidence, and plunder caravans and sailing vessels after cheating (the men) by administering a stupefying drink. 10 Or, he should practise 'the stratagems for the conquest of an enemy town.' 11 Or, he should act after securring the support of persons from the side of his mother. 12 Or, with his appearance changed by disguising himself as an artisan, an artist, a minstrel, a physician, a professional story-teller or a heretical monk, (and) accompanied by associates in the same disguise, he should enter by taking advantage of some vulnerable point, and, striking the king with weapon or poison, announce, 'I am that prince; this kingdom is to be enjoyed jointly; a single person does not deserve to enjoy it; those who desire to serve me, them will I reward with double food and wages.'

Thus ends (the topic of) the conduct of a prince in disfavour.

4 *abhirūpam* 'appropriate', i.e., what would normally accrue from that work.

5 D adds *tadanurodhād vā dveṣeṇa*; the words do not appear to be original; at least *dviṣantam* would be necessary in place of *dveṣeṇa*. 7 *kṛtyapakṣa* are those in the father's kingdom who can be won over to his side.

8 *ekacaraḥ*, i.e., when he has not sought refuge with any neighbouring prince. Cb understands the idea of his being without *kośa* and *daṇḍa*. — *suvarṇapāka* seems to refer to the smelting of gold ore ; Cj says '*suvarṇasya varṇotkarṣārthaṁ pākaḥ*.' — *maṇirāga* 'colouring of crystals, in order to impart new qualities to them, *sphaṭikasya jātyantaraguṇādhānārthaṁ rañjanam*' (Cj). 9 *āḍhyavidhavādravyam* is from Cb and seems necessary to make it conform to the preceding expressions. — For *anupraviśya*, see 1.17.39 above. — It would have been better if we had *anupraviśya gūḍham apaharet* in this order before *sārthayāna-* etc. — *madanarasa* is a drink prepared from some narcotic drug that brings on stupefaction. 10 *pāragrāmikaṁ yogam*, i.e., tricks recommended for capturing an enemy's town in 13.1 below. 12 *kāruśilpi-* etc. : the compound should be understood as a Tatpuruṣa construed with *naṣṭarūpaḥ* and not as a Bahuvrīhi as in Cs, where *tadvyañjanasakhaḥ* is then rendered by 'appearing like the men dressed as craftsmen etc.' This latter is clearly unlikely. — *brūyāt* : the announcement is made in the presence of officers and other servants of the assassinated father. — *ye kāmayante* etc. : the reading adopted is with *mām* from D and *bhartum* from G

13 But sons of principal officers acting as secret agents should bring the prince in disfavour (to the king) after securing his consent; or, the mother, if she enjoys favour, (should bring him). 14 If he is given up (as incorrigible), secret agents should kill him with weapon or poison. 15 If not given up, they should make him addicted to women of the same character or to drinking or hunting, and seizing him at night, should bring him (to the king).

> 16 And when he has come, he should conciliate him by the (offer of the) kingdom, saying 'After me, (this is yours).' Then he should confine him in one place (if still recalcitrant); but if he has (other) sons, he should kill him.

CHAPTER NINETEEN

SECTION 16 RULES FOR THE KING

1 When the king is active, the servants become active following his example. 2 If he is remiss, they too become remiss along with him. 3 And they consume his works. 4 Moreover, he is over-reached by enemies. 5 Therefore, he should himself be (energetically) active.

M; the idea obviously is that the prince offers to share the kingdom with these officers, promising to double their salary so that they may have no qualms about serving the parricide. The reading proposed is *māṁ bhartuṁ tān aham*, with *bhṛ* understood in the sense of 'to support,' hence also 'to serve.' Cj reading *bhoktum* (for *bhartum*) explains 'who desire me (as their king) I shall give them double the salary for their maintenance (*bhoktum*, i.e., *poṣayitum*).' It is not certain that *bhoktum* could be so understood. We can get this sense with *māṁ tān bhartum aham*. D reads *bhartuḥ* which is not easy to construe; 'those who prefer me to the (late) master' seems hardly possible. If *bhartâram* were read, we could understand 'those who desire me as their master.' Meyer, rejecting *bhartum* and reading *martuṁ tān nāham*, translates 'such of you as desire to die (by refusing to accept me), them I shall not serve even for double food and wages.' This is highly problematical.

13 *mukhyaputrāpasarpāḥ*: the sons of principal officers are to serve as agents to fetch the prince. They are likely to succeed, as Cj says, because they had been his playmates. —*pratipādya*: Cb understands the idea of promising him *yauvarājya*. So Cnn has '*rājyaṁ pratipādya*.' That is possible, though 'making him agree, persuading him' would appear sufficient. —*pratigṛhītā*, i.e., enjoying the king's favour '*rājñā upacārair āvarjitā*' (Cnn). 'Acceptable' to the prince, i.e., enjoying his confidence is also not unlikely. 14 *tyaktam*, i.e., given up as incorrigible. 15 *tulyaśīlābhiḥ* of the same character as the prince and enjoying his confidence. —*prasañjayitvā* is presupposed in D. This is more in keeping with the usual causal form of this participle in this text. *prasajya* isn't a happy reading.

16 *ekastham*: Cb Cs Meyer understand this in the sense of 'the only son.' 'Stationed in one place' seems however all right.—*pravāsayet* 'should kill' rather than 'should exile.'— Cnn remarks that *sāntvayet* applies to the *buddhimān*, *saṁrundhyāt* to the *āhāryabuddhi* and *pravāsayet* to the *durbuddhi*.

1.19

For *praṇidhi* see 1.12 above.

1-5 *utthāna* 'being (energetically) active' is the opposite of *pramāda* 'being remiss in doing work.'

6 He should divide the day into eight parts as also the night by means of *nālikās*, or by the measure of the shadow (of the gnomon).

7 (A shadow) measuring three *pauruṣas*, one *pauruṣa*, (and) four *aṅgulas*, and the midday when the shadow disappears, these are the four earlier eighth parts of the day. 8 By them are explained the later (four). 9 Out of them, during the first eighth part of the day, he should listen to measures taken for defence and (accounts of) income and expenditure. 10 During the second, he should look into the affairs of the citizens and the country people. 11 During the third, he should take his bath and meals and devote himself to study. 12 During the fourth, he should receive revenue in cash and assign tasks to heads of departments. 13 During the fifth, he should consult the council of ministers by sending letters, and acquaint himself with secret information brought in by spies. 14 During the sixth, he should engage in recreation at his pleasure or hold consultations. 15 During the seventh, he should review elephants, horses, chariots and troops. 16 During the eighth, he should deliberate on military plans with the commander-in-chief. 17 When the day is ended, he should worship the evening twilight.

18 During the first (eighth) part of the night, he should interview secret agents. 19 During the second, he should take a bath and meals and engage in study. 20 During the third, he should go to bed to the strains of musical instruments and sleep during the fourth and the fifth (parts). 21 During the sixth, he should awaken to the sound of musical instruments and ponder over the teaching of the science (of politics) as well as over the work to be done. 22 During the seventh, he should sit in consultation (with councillors) and despatch secret agents. 23 During the eighth, he should receive blessings from priests, preceptors and chaplain, and see his physician, chief cook and astrologer. 24 And after going round a cow with her calf and a bull, he should proceed to the assembly hall.

6 *nālikābhir* : cf. 2.20.34-35. A *nālikā* measures 24 minutes. Because the eighth part of a day comes to 3¾ *nālikās*, Fleet (in a footnote to Shama Sastri's translation, p. 37) thinks that this *nālikā* is different from the *nālikā* of 2.20.35. How, he asks, are three-fourths of a *nālikā* to be marked by the water-bowl ? This *nālikā*, therefore, is one of 90 minutes according to him, its real name being *chāyānālikā* mentioned in 1.7.8 above. It is, however, very unlikely that two different kinds of *nālikās* would be referred to in the same work, particularly because a definition of *chāyānālikā* would also be then expected. It seems, moreover, that *chāyānālikā* in 1.7.8 refers to two separate methods of marking measures of time. Besides, it is not unlikely that the *nālikā* was graduated so that divisions of a *nālikā* could be easily read off it. — *chāyāpramāṇena vā*: this alternative is available only in day-time when it is clear.

7 *tripauruṣī* : *pauruṣa*, a measure used for measuring the length of the shadow of the gnomon on the sun-dial, is 12 *aṅgulas* (about 9 inches). See 2.20.10. — After s. 7 a long passage from a commentary has crept into the text in D. 9 *rakṣāvidhānam* : in view of 9.4.8 and 12.5.32 this refers to arrangements for defence, not to 'protection afforded (to citizens) during the night' (Cs). 12 *adhyakṣān kurvīta* refers to assigning tasks to these officers as well making new appointments when necessary. 13 *patrasaṁpreṣaṇena* : see 1.15.53-54 above. Letters become necessary only when some members are absent.

20 *saṁviṣṭaḥ* : '*śayyām ārūḍhaḥ. saṁviṣṭaśabdaprayogaḥ kāmaṁ sūcayati suratuprakārāṇāṁ saṁveśanābhidhānāt*' (Cnn). 23 *-purohitasvastyayanāni* is necessary as in D, because the blessings are to be received from the *purohita* and others, not from anyone else. It is

25 Or, he should divide the day and night into (different) parts in conformity with his capacity and carry out his tasks.

26 Arriving in the assembly hall, he should allow unrestricted entrance to those wishing to see him in connection with their affairs. 27 For, a king difficult of access is made to do the reverse of what ought to be done and what ought not to be done, by those near him. 28 In consequence of that, he may have to face an insurrection of the subjects or subjugation by the enemy. 29 Therefore, he should look into the affairs of temple deities, hermitages, heretics, Brahmins learned in the Vedas, cattle and holy places, of minors, the aged, the sick, the distressed and the helpless and of women, in (this) order, or, in accordance with the importance of the matter or its urgency.

30 He should hear (at once) every urgent matter, (and) not put it off. An (affair) postponed becomes difficult to settle or even impossible to settle.

31 He should look into the affairs of persons learned in the Vedas and of ascetics after going to the fire sanctuary (and) in the company of his chaplain and preceptor, after getting up from his seat and saluting (those suitors).

32 But he should decide the affairs of ascetics and of persons versed in the practice of magic, (in consultation) with persons learned in the three Vedas, not by himself (alone), for the reason that they might be roused to anger.

33 For the king, the (sacrificial) vow is activity, sacrifice the administration of affairs; the sacrificial fee, however, is impartiality of behaviour, (and) sacrificial initiation for him is the coronation.

34 In the happiness of the subjects lies the happiness of the king and in what is beneficial to the subjects his own benefit. What is dear to himself is not beneficial to the king, but what is dear to the subjects is beneficial (to him).

35 Therefore, being ever active, the king should carry out the management of material well-being. The root of material well-being is activity, of material disaster its reverse.

not likely that the king would be seeing other Brahmins just yet. Cj reads *-purohitebhyaḥ svastya-*, but mentions the reading of D.

26 *advārāsaṅgam* 'not being held up at the door,' i.e., free entry. Cj reads *dvāram asaṅgam* 'the door open."

29 *devatā*, i.e., temple affairs. *ātyayika-* : *ātyayikatva-* would seem to be necessary.

30 *atikrāntam* 'what has been passed over', i.e., postponed.

31 *agnyagāragataḥ* : cf. *Śākuntala*, Act 5, where this procedure is strictly followed by Duṣyanta when looking into the hermits' affair.

32 *māyāyoga* 'practice of magic' as a single idea seems intended.

33 There can be no doubt about *dīkṣā tasyābhiṣecanam* from D Cj being the original reading; it completes the elaborate metaphor in the stanza, the comparison of rulership

36 In the absence of activity, there is certain destruction of what is obtained and of what is not yet received. By activity reward is obtained, and one also secures abundance of riches.

CHAPTER TWENTY

SECTION 17 REGULATIONS FOR THE ROYAL RESIDENCE

1 On a site recommended by experts in building, he should cause the royal residence to be built, with a rampart, a moat and gates and provided with many halls.

2 He should cause to be constructed a living chamber in the centre in accordance with the procedure laid down for the treasury, or a maze-house with concealed passages in walls and in its centre a living chamber, or an underground room with its opening covered by the wooden image of a deity in a nearby sanctuary and having many subterranean passages (and) above it a palace with a stair-case concealed in a wall or having an entrance and an exit through a hollow pillar as a living chamber with the floor fixed to a mechanism (and thus) capable of sinking below, in order to counteract a calamity or when a calamity is apprehended. 3 Or he should vary the construction in ways other than these, because of the fear of fellow-students.

with a sacrifice. — After s. 33 D introduces another stanza with the words *tathā coktam.* It couldn't be original. That is not how quotations are introduced in this text. The stanza seems to be derived from some commentary.

1.20

niśānta from *ni-śam* is primarily a place of retirement, a residence. In particular it refers to the royal palace. For *praṇidhi*, see 1.12 above.

1 *vāstuka* ' an expert in the science of building ' (Cb Cj Cnn). — D has *kakṣā* for *kakṣyā* throughout ; both forms are possible. — *antaḥpuram* : this clearly is the same as *niśānta*, the royal residence ; as Cj has, ' *antaḥpuraṁ rājavāsakam.*' It is not merely the harem ; it includes the council hall and the assembly hall as well (s.12 below). The *Rāmāyaṇa* (2.14. 29-31 ; 2.16.1) shows the use of *antaḥpura* in this wider sense.

2 *kośagṛhavidhānena* : i.e., as laid down in 2.5.2-3 below. — *madhye*, i.e., in the centre of the area constituting the *antaḥpura* ; the word is not read in G M, but seems necessary. — *gūḍha-* etc. is an option to the method of the *kośagṛha* ; *mohanagṛha* is a maze or labyrinth where a stranger would get lost. It is to have ' passages concealed in walls ' ; the *vāsagṛha* is to be in its centre. *mohanagṛha* in the sense of ' a love-chamber ' (Meyer) is unlikely. — *bhūmigṛham* etc. states another alternative arrangement for the *vāsagṛha.* The idea is that an underground chamber is to be built with an emergency exit through a subterranean passage, leading to an opening covered by the wooden image of the deity in a nearby sanctuary. A person escaping from the *bhumigṛha* would arrive at the opening under the image, which, being made of wood, can be easily pushed aside ; thus he would make good his escape without being noticed by those besieging or searching the *vāsagṛha.* This is the explanation of Cj Cnn and the only right one. Cb reads *-caityāṣṭadevatā-* and explains ' covered by the abodes of *caityadevatās* and *aṣṭadevatās* nearby.' This isn't very happy. Cs, understanding *kāṣṭhā* ' direction ', explains ' with the door stamped with the image of a deity in a temple which is in a nearby quarter. ' What purpose the stamping of the door with the image of a deity is expected to serve it is difficult to see. — *tasyopari* from D is necessary, because the *bhūmigṛha* by itself could not constitute the *vāsagṛha* ; there is to be a *prāsāda* above it ; the *vā* after *prāsādam* needs also to be omitted as in D. *prāsāda* seems primarily to convey the idea of an elevated chamber to be reached (*pra-ā-sad*) by steps. — *gūḍhabhittisopānam*

4 When fire churned from human bones is taken round the royal residence three times (from right) towards the left, no other fire burns it nor does another fire blaze up there ; also when it is smeared with ashes caused by lightning and hailwater mixed with earth.

5 Serpents or poisons do not have (their) power in a (residence) protected by (a string of) shoots of the *Aśvattha* growing on wet land together with (shoots of) *Jīvantī*, *Śvetā*, *Muṣkaka* and *Puṣpavandākā* (plants).

6 Letting loose peacocks, ichneumons and spotted deer (on the premises) destroys serpents. 7 The parrot, the starling or the fork-tailed shrike shrieks when there is fear of serpents or poison. 8 The heron becomes frantic in the proximity of poison, the pheasant becomes faint, the intoxicated cuckoo dies, the eyes of the *Cakora*-partridge become discoloured.

9 Thus he should take precautions against fire, poison and serpents.

10 In a part of the apartments at the back (should be) ladies' rooms, establishments for maternity and sickness and places for trees and water.

'with stair-cases concealed in walls' is better than 'with concealed walls and stair-cases,' though *bhittigūḍha-* would have been better for the former ; cf. 2.3.22. — *suṣira-* etc. is an option to *gūḍhabhitti-* etc. — *yantrabaddha-* etc. also goes with *prāsādam*. The floor of the *prāsāda* is so constructed that with the release of a mechanism it can fall down into the cellar below. Its use is illustrated in 12.5.45. Meyer seems to understand *prāsādam...sopānam* as one alternative and *suṣira...-talāvapātam* as another. Cs has *prāsādam...-pasāram vā* and *vāsagṛham... -talāvapātam* as independent alternatives. — *āpatpratīkārārtham āpadi vā*: the former refers to the case where the clamaity is already there and steps have to be taken against it, while *āpadi* means when a calamity is feared (*āpadi vā bhaviṣyantyām* — Cnn). It doesn't seems necessary to read *kārayet* again after *āpadi vā* ; it is proposed to omit it. 3 *sahādhyāyi-* 'persons who have studied the same *śāstra* (of politics) and its rules, viz., the enemy kings' (Cb Cj). Meyer proposes *sahasādhyāyi-* or *sāhasādhyāyi-* 'who contemplate acts of daring against the king.' That is hardly plausible. 'Fellow-students' of the king who know him intimately and are likely to be conversant with the secrets of his chamber is, however, a possible idea.

4 *mānuṣeṇāgninā*, i.e., fire churned out of human bones ; see 14.2.38 below. — *apasavyam* is the opposite of *pradakṣiṇam* (Cb Cs), though Cj seems to understand it in the sense of '*prādakṣiṇyena*' and Cnn has '*pradakṣiṇena parigatam, nīrājitam.*' For the former meaning, cf. Caraka, 8.9 '*na pūjyamaṅgalāni apasavyaṁ gacchet,*' also Utpala on *Bṛhatsaṁhitā*, 33.13.

5 *Jīvantī-* etc. : cf. 14.4.12 below. Meyer understands the flowers (*puṣpa*) of the first three plants and the plant *Vandākā*, instead of understanding *Puṣpavandākā* as the name of a plant ; that appears also to be the explanation in Cj. — *akṣīve* : Cj has *akṣībe*, which appears to be explained by 'in a place that is not dry.' That seems to be the meaning intended. *akṣīva* can here hardly be understood as the name of a tree such as *Śigru* (Cs). — *pratānena*: 'a string of shoots' hung at the entrance, a *vandanamālā* as Cnn paraphrases it. The *vā* read after this word in G M is not original. A single string of *Aśvattha* shoots along with *Jīvantī* etc. is to be hung at the door-way and no option is intended, as is clear from 14.4.12. 6 The omission of *mārjāra-* as in D Cj seems necessary, as cats are not known to be snake-killers. 7 *Bhṛṅgarāja* 'the *Dhūmyāṭa* (fork-tailed shrike) or the *ali* (bee)' (Cs). The bee is clearly unlikely. 8 *Jīvaṁjīvaka* is a kind of pheasant usually identified with *Cakora*, but is here distinguished from it. — *virajyete*, i.e., their naturally red eyes become white (*svabhāvato rakte śuklatvaṁ pratipadyete*—Cj).

10 *garbhavyādhisaṁsthāḥ*, i.e., rooms for maternity and for sickness, the latter not necessarily restricted to women alone (as in Cj). G M add *-vaidyaprakhyāta-* after *-vyādhi* in the compound, Cb Cs *-vaidyapratyākhyāta-*. Cb Cs explain the latter 'rooms for queens

11 Outside (that) should be quarters for princesses and princes. 12 In front (should be) the dressing room, the council chamber, the assembly hall and a place for the ministers in charge of princes. 13 In the (open) spaces between the apartments, the palace guards should be stationed.

14 In the inner aprtments he should visit the queen after she is cleared (of suspicion) by old women. 15 For, concealing himself in the queen's chamber, his brother killed Bhadrasena, and lying (concealed) in his mother's bed his son killed Kārūṣa. 16 The queen killed the king of Kāśī by mixing fried grain with poison under the guise of honey; (the queen killed) Vairantya with an anklet smeared with poison, the king of the Sauvīras with a (poison-smeared) girdle-jewel, Jālūtha with a (poison-smeared) mirror; the queen killed Vidūratha by keeping a weapon concealed in the braid of her hair. 17 Therefore, he should avoid these occasions.

18 He should forbid (the queens') contact with ascetics with shaven heads or matted hair and with jugglers as well as with female slaves from outside. 19 Nor should members of their families visit these (queens) except in establishments for maternity and sickness. 20 Courtesans should see them after their bodies are cleansed by a bath and rubbing and after

given up as incurable by physicians.' This is extremely doubtful. The additions do not appear genuine, as shown by s. 19 below. 12 *alaṁkārabhūmiḥ* is the king's dressing room. — *kumārādhyakṣa* 'the minister in charge of princes' as a single idea is to be preferred; all *adhyakṣas* as such wouldn't have quarters in the palace grounds. Cf. O Stein, AOr, X, p. 164 and n. 5. 13 *antarvaṁśika* from *antarvaṁśa* (apparently the same as *antaḥpura*). Cf. 1.21.3.

14 *antargṛha* refers evidently to the sleeping chambers of the queens, obviously different from his own chamber. — *na kāṁcid abhigacchet* (found in G M) seems a marginal gloss which has got into the text. Cj, however, distinguishes between *paśyet* (see in his room) and *abhigacchet* (go to her room). 15 The addition of *śrūyate hi* at the beginning as in D might appear better. The *Harṣacarita* gives more details of these tales (pp. 199-200); the *Bṛhat-saṁhitā*, 78.1-2 refers to some of these and Śaṁkarārya on Kāmandaka, 7.51ff. mentions some details. — Bhadrasena was a King of the Kaliṅgas and his brother's name was Vīrasena. After *śayyāntargataś ca*, D adds details which are obviously derived from some commentary. According to this comment, the name of the King was Vajra; according to the *Harṣacarita* it was Dadhra, the reason for murder being the father's intention to crown another prince as *yuvarāja*. 16 The names of the King of Kāśī and his queen were Mahāsena and Suprabhā, according to the *Harṣacarita*, where the Vairantya king is named Rantideva. According to Cj Cnn the queen of Kāśī was unwilling (because her son was in disfavour — Cj) and the King approached her forcibly (*anicchantī balād abhigacchantam*). The *Bṛ. Saṁ.* makes Kāśirāja (and not Vairantya) the victim of a poisoned *nūpura*. — *Sauvīram* : Cj Cnn give Paraṁtapa as the name, but it was Vīrasena and his queen's name Haṁsavatī, according to the *Harṣacarita*. — *Jālūtham* : the *Harṣacarita* has Jārūtha, the king of Ayodhyā, also called Paraṁtapa, the queen's name being Ratnavatī. Cj Cnn also have Ayodhyā-pati and add that she was not approached even in *ṛtu*, or the king was attached to other queens, and hence the trouble. — Vidūratha was a Vṛṣṇi and his queen was Bindumatī (*Harṣacarita*). Cnn adds that she was enraged because her wealth was taken away by the king (*dravyāpahārād vidviṣṭā*); her wealth was spent on prostitutes (Cj). — Cf. S. K. Dikshit, Indian Culture, Vol. VI, p. 43.

18 *kuhaka* 'a magician, a juggler' (*māyāyogavid*—Cnn) is a puppet-player in the *Bhāgavata purāna*, 10.54.12 (*yathā dārumayī yoṣin nṛtyate kuhakecchayā*) 19 *-saṁsthābhyaḥ* : cf. s. 10 above. Neither 'at the time of following the husband in death' (Cs) nor 'medical treatment' (Meyer) seems possible for *saṁsthā*. 20 *rūpājīvāḥ* : this word is usually explained as 'who lives by her beauty,' hence a courtesan, a prostitute. A connection with *rūpa* (as *rūpaka*) 'a drama' is not unlikely, implying that the *rūpājīvā* was primarily an actress.

changing their garments and ornaments. 21 Men eighty years of age or women fifty years of age, appearing as a father or a mother, and aged and eunuch domestic servants should ascertain the purity or impurity of the inmates of the harem and should make them firmly devoted to what is beneficial to the master.

22 And every one (in the palace) should live in his own quarters and should not move to the quarters of another. And no one staying inside should establish contacts with an outsider.

23 And every object should go out of or come into (the palace) after it is examined and its arrival or departure recorded, its transport to its destination being under a seal.

CHAPTER TWENTY-ONE

SECTION 18 CONCERNING THE PROTECTION OF (THE KING'S) OWN PERSON

1 When risen from the bed, he should be surrounded by female guards bearing bows, in the second hall by eunuch servants wearing robes and turbans, in the third by humpbacks, dwarfs and Kirātas, in the fourth by ministers, kinsmen and door-keepers, lances in hand.

2 He should keep near him persons descended hereditarily from his father and grand-father, bound (to him) by some relationship, trained, loyal and of proved service, not anyone belonging to another country who has not been given money and honour nor even anyone belonging to his own country if taken in service after he had been harmed. 3 The palace guards should protect the king and the royal residence.

Here they are attendants of the harem. —*paśyeyuḥ* : the object is *enāḥ*, rather than *taṁ rājānam* (Cs). The king's own attendants are mentioned in 1.21.13 below. Cj reads *paśyet*, making *rājā* the subject and *rūpājīvāḥ* the object. 21 *mātāpitṛvyañjanāḥ*, i.e., posing as the parents of some harem attendants (*antaścarāṇām kṛtakamātāpitaraḥ rājapraṇihitāḥ*—Cnn). — *abhyāgārika* 'a servant of the inner apartments;' he could be a *sthavira* or a *varṣadhara* 'eunuch.'

22 *sarvaḥ*, i.e., all inmates of the palace.

23 *mudrāsaṁkrāntabhūmikam* : this seems to mean that it should proceed to its destination only after being sealed. *bhūmi* can hardly mean 'a container' as Cs seems to understand it. Russ. has 'provided with a seal with an indication of the place of destination.'

1.21

1 *strīgaṇair dhanvibhiḥ* : the female archers are attendants or guards in the bed-chamber. Cj reads *vandibhiḥ* 'bards.' — *varṣadharābhyāgārikaiḥ* : cf. 1.20.21 above.

2 *saṁbandhānubaddham* is from a reading in M2. The mss. read *mahāsaṁbandhā-*; the *mahā-* seems due to repetition from the last two syllables of the preceding word. For the expression cf. *saṁsargānubandhārthī* 1.16.29 above. With *mahā* Cb has 'descended from big families,' Cs 'connected with persons born in noble families (*saṁbandha*, i.e., *anvaya*),' Cj 'connected by close relationship,' Meyer 'with important relations and mighty connections.' — *kṛtakarmāṇam* suggests one who has proved his worth by accomplishing some work. — The s. is quoted in the *Nītivākyāmṛta* (sec. 24) with the remark, *ata evoktaṁ nayavidbhiḥ*.

4 The head cook should cause all cooking work to be done in a guarded place, by tasting it many times. 5 The king should partake of that in that same condition, after first making an offering to the (sacred) fire and to birds.

6 Blue colour of the flames and smoke, and a crackling sound of the fire (are signs of a thing) mixed with poison, also the death of birds (who eat it). 7 Of boiled rice, steam having the colour of the peacock's neck, coldness, sudden change of colour as when stale, being full of (unabsorbed) water, and not being moist; of broths, quick drying up as well, remaining in a state of boiling, having a soiled appearance, presence of foam, becoming curdled and the destruction of smell, touch and flavour; among liquids, the appearance of a shade (of colour) fainter or deeper (than usual) and the appearance of upward lines at the edges of the mass of foam,—in the case of juice a blue line in the middle, of milk a reddish (line), of wine and water black, of curds dark, of honey white; of wet substances, becoming quickly faded, becoming over-cooked and having a dark blue colour in boiling; of dry (substances), a quick falling to pieces and loss of colour; of hard substances softness and of soft substances hardness, and in their proximity the death of small creatures; of bed-sheets and covers, possession of dirty circles and the shedding of threads, wool or hair; of objects made of metals and gems, being smeared with mud-like dirt and the destruction of the smoothness, colour, weight, power, class and touch;—these are the indications of (these objects when) mixed with poison.

4 *āsvādabāhulyena*: this seems to mean 'by tasting it himself again and again to see that it is tasteful' (Cj), hardly 'by getting them tasted by servants, grinders, cooks etc. (*paricārakapeṣakapācakādibhiḥ krameṇa āsvāditaiḥ* — Cnn). It may also mean 'with plenty of taste (i.e., tasteful dishes).'

6 *viṣayuktasya* may be construed with *agneḥ* or we may supply *annasya prakṣepeṇa*; with *vayasām*, we may understand (*viṣayuktasya*) *annasya bhakṣaṇena*. 7 *annasya*: cooked rice is primarily thought of. — *kliṣṭasya*: *kliṣṭa* is *hastamṛdita* (soiled by hand), according to Cnn. — *aklinnatvam* 'not being moist,' i.e., with the rice-grains unsaturated. — *vyañjanānām*: these are broths prepared from pulses, vegetables, etc. — *ca* after *śuṣkatvam* shows that we have also to understand *śaityam* and *vaivarṇyam* from the preceding. — *kvāthadhyāma-* etc.: the translation follows Cnn 'remaining on the boil even when removed from fire (*kvāthabhāvo 'gnivyavadhāne 'pi*), appearing soiled even when not touched by any other object (*dhyāmabhāvo dravyāntarāsparśe 'pi*), having foam and appearing broken without cause (*phenabhāvo vicchinnabhāvaś ca taddhetvabhāve 'pi*).' In conformity with this *-paṭala-* may be dropped as in D. Cj (which reads *śyāma* for *dhyāma* and omits *paṭala*) seems to have a similar explanation. A single idea 'the state of breaking up of a mass of soiled (*dhyāma*) or dark (*śyāma*) foam on the surface while boiling,' may also appear possible. *phenapaṭala-* etc.: Cs has 'the appearance of scum, of its separation from the broth (*sīmanta*) and of lines above.' Meyer has 'bits of scum at the edges seem to move upwards in streaks.' We may understand 'upward lines rising from the edge of the mass of foam (on the surface)'; the upward lines may be those of steam or of some substance in the liquid or of the foam itself; Meyer has the last. — *madhye* seems to distinguish this from *sīmanta* of liquids in general, though it is possible that this is in addition to the preceding. — D has *śyāma* for *śyāva* in this and the following s. — *tantu-roma-pakṣman* refer to cotton, wool and fur respectively. *pakṣman* can harldy mean 'minute portions' (Cs). — *paṅkamala-* seems to mean 'mud-like dirt.' — *rāga* is 'colour' while *varṇa* conveys the idea of 'class' or quality. — *prabhāva* refers to the 'power' which certain gems are supposed to possess.

8 (The signs) of one who has administered poison, however, (are): having a dry, dark face, hesitation in speech, excessive perspiration and yawning, trembling, stumbling, looking about during speech, agitation in work and not remaining steady in his own place.

9 Therefore, experts in the science of poison-cure and physicians should be in attendance on him. 10 The physician, taking from the medicine-store a medicine proved pure by tasting, and making the cook, the pounder and himself taste it beforehand, should offer it to the king. 11 (Precautions for) drink and water are explained by (those for) medicine.

12 Barbers and valets, with their garments and hands clean after a bath, should wait (on the king) after receiving sealed implements from the hands of palace-attendants. 13 Female slaves of proved integrity should do the work of bath-attendants, shampooers, bed-preparers, laundresses and garland-makers, or artists supervised by them (should do it). 14 They should offer garments and flowers after (first) putting them to their eyes, and unguents to be used after bath, rubbing powder, perfumes and bath-cosmetics (after first putting them) on their own bosoms and arms. 15 By this is explained (the procedure for) what has come from another person.

16 Actors should entertain (the king) avoiding plays involving (the use of) weapons, fire or poison. 17 And their musical instruments should remain inside (the palace), as also the trappings of horses, chariots, and elephants.

8 *ca* shows that *atimātram* is to be construed with *svedaḥ* as well as *vijṛmbhaṇam*. —*vākyaviprekṣaṇam*: Cj has 'taking a long time to find a suitable reply (*kiṁ vakṣyāmīti viśeṣeṇa prekṣaṇam nibhālanam*),' Cnn 'listening to another's speech, being apprehensive that he may come to know about him and be talking about him (*paravākyākarṇanaṁ kim ahaṁ jñāto 'smi matkathām eva kurvantītyāśaṅkayā*).' Meyer has 'casting glances all round when speaking'; 'looking restlessly about when some one is speaking to him' is also possible. *karmaṇi* to be construed with *āvegaḥ*, hardly with *anavasthānam*.

9 *jāṅgulī* 'the science of poison-cure.' Cnn remarks 'it is well-known among the Buddhists (*Bauddhaprasiddhā vidyā*).'

10 *peṣaka*: pounding is essential in Indian medicine as is *pāka* or making a decoction.

13 *snāpaka* etc.: D shows *prasādhaka* along with *udakaparicāraka* in this compound though the preceding s. had already referred to the *prasādhaka*; that is probably due to 1.12.9. 14 *snānānulepana-* etc.: Cb Cs have 'fragrant myrobalans etc. (*snāna*), unguents like sandalwood (*anulepana*), the five astringents (*pragharṣa*), fragrant powder for garments (*cūrṇavāsa*) and powder used on the head during bath (*snānīya*).' Cj agrees except that *cūrṇa* and *vāsa* are understood separately as '*jambūkaṣāyādi*' and '*paṭavāsādi*' respectively. Cnn has 'fragrant substance used on the head (*snānaṁ sugandhadravyanirmitaṁ sārdraṁ yacchirasi prayujyate*), unguents like *kuṅkuma* etc. (*anulepanaṁ kuṅkumādi*), unguents (*udvartanam eva pragharṣaḥ*), dry fragrant powder used for the hair after bath (*cūrṇaḥ śuṣkaḥ snānottarakālaṁ keśavāsāya yaḥ prayujyate*), fragrant incense (*vāsaḥ sugandhakalpaḥ dhūpaḥ*)'; there is no explanation of *snānīya*. It might appear better to understand *snānānulepana*, *pragharṣacūrṇa*, *vāsa* and *snānīya* as the items intended.

16 *kuśīlavāḥ* appear here as actors and acrobats rather than as minstrels, as the latter would harldy have an occasion to use fire or weapon. Cf. 1.12.9.

18 He should ride a carriage or an animal when these are attended by trustworthy servants, and a boat when it is attended by a trustworthy boatman. 19 He should not go to a boat which is tied to another boat or is caught in a violent wind. 20 At the water's edge, troops should stand on guard.

21 He should plunge in water that has been cleared by fish-catchers. 22 He should go to a park after it is cleared by snake-catchers.

23 He should go to a forest containing game, for practising on moving targets, after the danger of harm from thieves, wild animals and enemies has been removed from it by fowlers and hunters.

24 He should grant an interview to a holy ascetic in the company of trusted armed guards, to an envoy of a neighbouring prince in the company of the council of ministers. 25 Being fully armoured and riding a horse, an elephant or a chariot, he should inspect fully equipped troops.

26 At the time of his departure from and entry into (the palace) he should go along the royal highway, with guards stationed on both sides and with persons carrying arms, ascetics and cripples removed from it by armed men and staff-bearers. 27 He should not plunge in a crowd of men. 28 He should go to fairs, gatherings, festivals and parties (only when these are) supervised by officers in command of ten soldiers each.

29 And just as the king keeps a watch over others through secret agents, so should he, being self-possessed, guard himself against danger from others.

Herewith ends the First Book of the Arthaśāstra of Kauṭilya
'CONCERNING THE TOPIC OF TRAINING'

21 *matsyagrāha* seems to mean 'a fish-catcher' (Cj), though 'fish and crocodiles' is also possible, as in Cnn. 22 *vyālagrāha* 'one who catches snakes' (Cj) is clearly intended, though Cnn has '*vyāla*, i.e., lions etc. and *grāha*, i.e., crocodile.' Lions can hardly be thought of as possible in an *udyāna*.

24 Cj seems to have read only *āptaśastragrāhādhiṣṭhitaḥ sāmantadūtaṁ paśyet*.

26 *śastribhir* from D is clearly better, since armed men are to be removed from the highways. — *pravrajita-vyaṅga*: these are likely to be enemy agents and hence they have to be removed. Perhaps we should read *nyaṅga* (for *vyaṅga*) as in 2.23.2 and other places. — *yātrā* is a festival or a fair in honour of some deity in a temple, while *utsava* is any other festival. — *prahavaṇa*: see 1.10.9. — *daśavargika* 'an officer in charge of ten soldiers or units.' He is probably the same as the *patika* described in 10.6.45; cf. also 10.3.46.

29 *adhitiṣṭhati* 'does harm' (Cs); however, 'supervises over,' i.e., 'keeps a strict watch over' seems a more likely idea. — *ābādha* from D Cj is the usual form of the word in the text, not *bādha*.

Book Two

THE ACTIVITY OF THE HEADS OF DEPARTMENTS

CHAPTER ONE

SECTION 19 SETTLEMENT OF THE COUNTRYSIDE

1 He should cause settlement of the country, which had been settled before or which had not been settled before, by bringing in people from foreign lands or by shifting the overflow (of population) from his own country.

2 He should cause villages to be settled consisting mostly of Śūdra agriculturists, with a minimum of one hundred families and a maximum of five hundred families, with boundaries extending over one *krośa* or two *krośas*, (and) affording mutual protection. 3 He should fix, at the boundary lines, a river, a mountain, a forest, a stretch of pebbles, sand etc., a cavern, an embankment, a *Śamī* tree, a *Śālmalī* tree or a milk-tree (like *Aśvattha*, *Nyagrodha* etc.).

In the Second Book, which deals with the activity of the various state departments we have a fairly full account of the internal administration of a state. Only the administration of justice and the maintenance of law and order are reserved for the Third and Fourth Books.

2.1

This chapter deals primarily with the settlement of new lands; a few rules, however, might appear to be applicable to old established settlements as well.

1 *bhūtapūrvam* 'which was settled before,' but was apparently abandoned by its inhabitants because of famine etc. *abhūtapūrva* 'not settled before' is virgin land. According to Cnn (which is available in full for the first three chapters of this Book), the former is easy to work (*sukhasādhya*), the latter difficult. — The expression *bhūtapūrva* is used in connection with a kingdom in 13.5.2, 22; there it means 'which had formerly belonged to him.' — *apavāhana* includes the idea of enticement as well as displacement by force. Mallinātha quotes this passage on *Raghuvaṁśa*, 15.29.

2 *Śūdrakarṣaka*- 'Śūdra agriculturists' (Cnn) rather than 'Śūdras and agriculturists' (Cb). Acutal workers on land could have been only Śūdras. — *kulaśatāvaram* etc.: according to Cnn, *kula* means land that can be ploughed by one, two or three ploughs (being respectively best, middling and worst); the smallest village area has 100 such fields with a boundary of one *krośa*, while the largest has 500 fields with a boundary of two *krośas*. It is not certain that all this is meant here. — *krośadvikrośasīmānam*: apparently the boundary of each village is to be at a distance of one or two *krośas* from the houses in it. Cj states that the village area should be four *krośas* on each side giving 16 square *krośas*; of these 10 are to be used for fields, 5 should be given over to houses and pasture and one reserved for *devasthāna* and common. According to Cs the distance between two villages is to be one *krośa* or two. *krośa* is the same as *goruta* of 2.20.25, though *krośa* itself is not mentioned in that chapter. Cnn explains '*niśāvasāne yāvantaṁ pradeśaṁ gavāṁ rutaṁ kṛṣṭaṁ vyāpnoti.*' — *anyonyārakṣam* 'giving protection to each other,' though, 'protected against each other's encroachments' is also possible. 3 *bhṛṣṭi* is from D, explained in Cnn as 'a stretch of pebbles, sand etc.', suggesting the dry bed of a rivulet. The *Medinī* gives *śūnyavāṭikā* 'a deserted garden' as the meaning. The word occurs in the *Ṛgveda* 1.56.3 (*girer bhṛṣṭiḥ*) in the sense of a ridge or edge. Meyer proposes *ghṛṣṭi* and explains *vanaghṛṣṭi* by 'the edge of a forest.' The reading *gṛṣṭi* is explained as 'a small hill' in Cb and 'a plant named *Badarā* or a kind of tree' in Cs. This latter is unlikely. As a tree it would have been put later in the compound with *Śālmalī*, etc, Russ. has 'prickly shrubbery'.

4 He should establish a *sthānīya* in the middle of eight hundred villages, a *droṇamukha* in the middle of four hundred villages, a *kārvaṭika* in the middle of two hundred villages. (and) a *saṁgrahaṇa* in a group of ten villages.

5 On the frontiers, he should erect the fortresses of frontier chiefs (as) the gates of the country, under the command of frontier chiefs. 6 Trappers, Śabaras, Pulindas, Caṇḍālas and forest-dwellers should guard the intervening regions between them.

7 He should grant (lands) to priests, preceptors, chaplains and Brahmins learned in the Vedas (as) gifts to Brahmins, exempt from fines and taxes, with inheritance passing on to corresponding heirs, (and) to heads of departments, accountants and others, and to *gopas*, *sthānikas*, elephant-trainers, physicians, horse-trainers and couriers, (lands) without the right of sale or mortgage.

8 He should allot to tax-payers arable fields for life. 9 Unarable fields should not be taken away from those who are making them arable.

10 He should take away (fields) from those who do not till them and give them to others. 11 Or, village servants and traders should till them. 12 Or, those who do not till should make good the loss (to the treasury).

13 And he should favour them with grains, cattle and money. 14 These they should pay back afterwards at their convenience. 15 And he should grant to them favours and exemptions which would cause an increase in the treasury, (but) avoid such as would cause loss to the treasury. 16 For, a king with a small treasury swallows up the citizens and the country people themselves. 17 He should grant exemptions at the time of settlement or as people come. 18 He should, like a father, show favours to those whose exemptions have ceased.

4 ***kārvaṭikam*** : the form ***khārvaṭikam*** is also possible. — These towns are established for purposes of revenue, being the headquarters of revenue officers like ***gopa***, ***sthānika***, etc. Cf. 2.35.1-6 below.

7 ***brahmadeyāni*** : the substantive may be ***grāmāṇi*** or ***kṣetrāṇi*** : perhaps the latter is to be understood. — ***abhirūpadāyādakāni***: Cnn explains ' with heirs of the same type as the person to whom the gift was originally made.' D's ***anirūpa-*** is obviously corrupt, but suggests that ***anurūpadāyādakāni*** may have been the original reading. Cj has ' of which sons, grandsons etc. endowed with learning and character are to be owners and which are not to revert to the king.' ***abhirūpadāyakāni*** of G M is possible in the sense of ' as worthy gifts ' or ' yielding suitable revenue, ' but does not seem original.

8 ***aikapuruṣikāṇi*** 'for one generation,' not to pass on to their heirs. Waste land being state property, it is to revert to the state on the death of the donee. 9 ***nādeyāni*** is from Cnn (supported by D's corruption ***nā. .ni***). ***nādeyāt*** is grammatically impossible.

10 ***ācchidya*** : confiscation is possible because the newly settled land was originally state property. 11 ***grāmabhṛtaka*** : these would appear to be state servants since they are included in the salary lists in 5.3.23. Their precise duties are not mentioned anywhere in the text. Cj understands ' barbers etc.' Cnn ' potters, smiths etc.' apparently corresponding to the modern ***balutedārs***, though these receive no salary. 12 ***vāvahīnam*** : ***vā*** found in D seems necessary. Meyer's explanation of ***apahīnam*** as 'a smaller rent or tax' is not very likely. Loss suffered by the state is to be understood ; ' ***vinaṣṭakṣetraphalam*** ' (Cnn).

14 ***anu*** as a conjunctive in the sense of ' afterwards ' is not very common. Cf., however, the ***Rāmāyaṇa***, 2.84.4 (***asmān vadhiṣyati anu Dāśarathiṁ Rāmam***). 17 ***yathāgatakam***, i.e., even if they come to settle there some time after the first settlement.

19 He should set going work in mines, factories, produce-forests, elephant-forests, cattle-herds and trade-routes and (establish) water-routes, land-routes and ports.

20 He should cause irrigation works to be built with natural water sources or with water to be brought in from elsewhere. 21 Or, to others who are building (these), he should render aid with land, road, trees and implements, and (also render aid) to (the building of) holy places and parks. 22 If one walks out of the joint building of an irrigation work, his labourers and bullocks should (be made to) do (his share of) the work. 23 And he should be a sharer in the expenses and yet should receive no portion (of the benefits derived). 24 The ownership of the fish, ducks, and green vegetables in the irrigation works should go to the king.

25 The king should enforce discipline on slaves, persons kept as pledges and kinsmen who do not obey (their masters etc.).

26 And the king should maintain children, aged persons and persons in distress when these are helpless, as also the woman who has borne no child and th sons of one who has (when these are helpless).

27 The elders of the village should augment the property of a minor till he comes of age, also the property of a temple.

28 If a person with means does not maintain his children and wife, his father and mother, his brothers who have not come of age, and his unmarried and widowed sisters, a fine of twelve *paṇas* (shall be imposed), except when these have become outcasts, with the exception of the mother.

19 *paṇyapattana* is ordinarily 'a market town'; but in the text, it refers principally to 'a port', not an inland town. Cf. 2.28.7,10,12; 7.12.21; etc. This may suggest that market towns were principally situated on river-banks or the sea-coast.

20 *setum*: this refers primarily to an embankment or dam built for storing water, also to the building of tanks. The *setu* is *sahodaka* when there are natural springs of water or a natural flow of water; it is *āhāryodaka* when it is a sort of a storage tank with water brought into it through channels. Cf. 7.12.4-5. 21 *mārga*: according to Cj this refers to the 'channel' for the *āhāryodaka setu*. 22 *saṁbhūyasetubandhāt*, i.e., when all settlers decide to pool their resources to build a tank for common use. 23 The punishment for a person backing out of a joint venture appears rather severe; hence Meyer proposes to include *puṇyasthānārāmāṇāṁ ca* in s. 22, to read *anapakrāmantaḥ* and to understand *rājā* as the subject in s.23, 'labourers and bullocks coming together shall do work for irrigation in connection with holy places and parks, without staying away. And the king shall share in the expenses and shall receive no benefit.' This is extremely unlikely. The harshness of the punishment may be justified on the ground that the person who agreed to join in the work of new settlement, is backing out of what is beneficial to the entire village. 24 *plava* 'a kind of duck' (Cs) or 'birds' (Cb Cj), rather than 'a boat'. — '*harita*, i.e., *nālikā* (reeds) and *paṇya*, i.e., *śṛṅgāṭaka*, *kaseruka*, etc.' (Cnn). — *rājā svāmyaṁ gacchet*: this is apparently because the land on which the tank is built is state property.

25 *-āhitaka-*: see 3.12.9 ff.

26 *-vyādhita-* (read after *-vṛddha-* in G M) does not appear to be original. — *anātha* is to be understood with each of *bāla* etc. '*bālādīnām antaḥpatito 'pyanāthaśabdo viśeṣaṇam, anyathā atiprasaṅgaḥ syāt*' (Cnn); and *anātha* is also to be understood with *striyam* and *putrān* as well. Cf. Breloer (KSt, III, 137 n. 4).

27 The reading *varjayeyuḥ* is quite unlikely. About elders being in charge of the property of minors see 3.5.20.

29 If one renounces home (to become an ascetic) without providing for his sons and wife, the lowest fine for violence (shall be imposed), also if one induces a woman to renounce home. 30 One who has lost his capacity for activity may renounce home after securing permission from the judges. 31 Otherwise, he shall be put under restraint.

32 An ascetic sect other than the (Brahmanical) forest hermit, a corporation other than that of those born in the same place or an association with agreements except one for a joint undertaking shall not settle in his countryside.

33 And there should be no parks there nor halls for recreation. 34 Actors, dancers, singers, musicians, professional story-tellers or minstrels shall not create obstruction in the work (of the people). 35 Because of villages being without shelter (for outsiders) and because of men being engrossed in (work on the) fields, an increase in the treasury, labourers, goods, grains and liquids follows.

36 The king should exempt from taxes a region laid waste by the army of an enemy or by foresters, or afflicted by disease or famine, and he should prohibit expensive sports.

37 He should protect agriculture that is oppressed by the troubles of fines, labourers and taxes, and herds of cattle (oppressed) by thieves, wild animals, poison and crocodiles as well as by diseases.

28 *kanyā vidhavāś ca* describe the two kinds of sisters who must be maintained. —*anyatra mātuḥ*, i.e., a mother, even if *patita*, must be maintained. Cf. *Baudhāyana Dharma Sūtra*, 2.2.48 : *patitām api tu mātaraṁ bibhṛyād anabhibhāṣamāṇaḥ*.

29 *striyaṁ ca pravrājayataḥ* : Cnn remarks that the woman meant is *anivṛttarajaskā* and still able to bear children. 30 *luptavyāyāmaḥ* is from D Cj. The latter explains 'devoid of internal and external powers (*bāhyābhyantaraśaktivikalaḥ*).' Cnn has '*prajananaśaktyabhāvād*.' The word *vyavāya* read in G1 means 'coitus' and does not appear to be original.

32 *vānaprasthād anyaḥ* etc. : this would exclude all heretical sects from the land. — *sajātād anyaḥ saṁghaḥ* : though *sajāta* means 'born together', it seems to refer to those who live at the same place, the idea being to prevent foreign tribal groups (*saṁghas*) from settling in the country. Only native or indigenous *saṁghas* are to be favoured. Cj explains 'which was formed at the time of settlement or which was there before in a *bhūtapūrva janapada*.' Cb explains *sajāta* by 'who are conversant with the four *vidyās*.' Cs, reading *sujātād* explains 'formed for the good of the king and the country.' Cnn thinks that this forbids the formation of *śreṇīs*. — *sāmutthāyikād anyaḥ samayānubandhaḥ* : *sāmutthāyika* refers to those who join together for some common undertaking; in the present case settlers on land joining together for some specific undertaking like the building of a tank are to be understood. That is how the commentators understand. — Cnn remarks that these restrictions apply only to the time of settlement; heretics and others may enter the villages with the king's permission (*ayaṁ niveśaviṣayo niyamaḥ; āgantavas tu pāṣaṇḍādayo rājñānujñātāḥ praviśanti*).

35 *nirāśrayatvāt* : *āśraya* 'shelter' for *naṭa*, *nartaka*, etc.

36 *pariharet* : in the context, 'should exempt from taxes' has to be understood; '*daṇḍakarādi na gṛhṇīyāt*' as Cnn has it, or *parihāreṇa pālayet* (Cj).

37 *viṣagrāha* seems to mean 'poison and crocodiles' in view of 2.29.13,24. The expression can hardly mean 'a poisonous creature.'

38 He should keep clear trade-routes that are harassed by (the king's) favourites, works-officers, robbers and frontier-chiefs or are reduced by herds of cattle.

39 Thus the king should protect produce-forests, elephant-forests, irrigation works and mines that were made in ancient times and should start new ones.

CHAPTER TWO

SECTION 20 DISPOSAL OF NON-AGRICULTURAL LAND

1 On land unsuitable for agriculture, he should allot pastures for cattle. 2 And he should grant to ascetics wildernesses for Veda-study and *soma*-sacrifices, with safety promised to (everything) immovable and movable in them, one *goruta* in extent at the most.

3 He should cause an animal park for the king's recreation to be laid out, with the same extent (i.e. one *goruta*), with a single entrance, protected by a moat, containing shrubs and bushes bearing sweet fruits, having trees without thorns, with shallow pools of water and stocked with tamed deer and (other) animals, containing wild animals with their claws and teeth removed (and) having male and female elephants and cubs useful for hunting. 4 And he should establish on its border or in conformity with the (suitability of the) land, another animal park where all animals are (welcomed) as guests (and given full protection).

5 And he should establish forests, one each for the products indicated as forest produce, as well as factories for goods made from forest produce, and (settle) foresters, attached to the produce-forests.

38 *kārmikaiḥ* ; these are the state officers in charge of state undertakings. See 2.7.22-23. — *śodhayet* 'should keep clear of noxious elements,' the noxious elements being the favourites, officers etc.

39 *dravyadvipavanam* : these are referred to in the next Chapter.

2.2

For the correct form of the name of this Section, *bhūmicchidrāpidhānam*, see 1.1.4 above. Cj too shows the correct form. *bhūmicchidra*, is *kṛṣyayogyā bhūḥ*—Yādava's *Vaijayantī*.

1 *vivītāni* : the root is *vī* 'to eat' according to Cnn (*vī khādane 'tra draṣṭavyaḥ*). 2 There is little doubt that *Brāhmaṇebhyo* and the consequential *tapovanāni ca* (in G M) are not original. Cb does not show the additional words. The regions are meant not for Brahmins as such, but for ascetics. As Cnn has it '*brahmāraṇyaṁ yatra Āraṇyakādivedopaniṣad adhīyate, somāraṇyaṁ yajñabhūmiḥ*.' — *goruta-parāṇi* : for *goruta*, see 2.20.25.

3 '*gulmāḥ karamardakādayaḥ gucchā badarāmalakādayaḥ*' (Cnn). — *mārgayuka* : Cj explains '*mṛgayāśīlā mṛgayavaḥ, teṣāṁ karma mārgayukam* ;' Cnn '*mṛgayur vyādhaḥ tasya karma*.' *mārgāyuka* is grammatically indefensible. 4 *sarvātithimṛgam* : this appears to be a sort of a zoological garden.

5 *kupyapradiṣṭānām*, i.e., those enumerated in 2.17 below. These are *dravyavanas*. D adds *tarūṇām* after *dravyāṇām* ; it seems to have been a marginal gloss on the latter word. — *aṭaviś ca* : as often in this text, *aṭavī* refers to forest-dwellers or foresters, not to forests ; cf. 1.18.7 ; 2.1.36 etc. '*aṭaviś ca āṭavikāṁś ca*' (Cnn).

6 On the border (of the kingdom), he should establish a forest for elephants guarded by foresters. 7 The superintendent of the elephant-forest should, with the help of guards of the elephant-forest, protect the elephant-forest (whether) on the mountain, along a river, along lakes or in marshy tracts, with its boundaries, entrances and exits (fully) known. 8 They should kill anyone slaying an elephant. 9 To a person bringing in the pair of tusks of an (elephant) dying naturally, a reward of four *paṇas* and a quarter (shall be given).

10 Guards of elephant-forests, aided by elephant keepers, foot-chainers, border guards, foresters and attendants, with their own odours suppressed by the urine and dung of elephants, with their bodies covered with branches of the *Bhallātakī*, (and) moving with five or seven female elephant decoys, should ascertain the size of the herds of elephants, by means of indications provided by sleeping places, foot-prints, dung and damage caused to river-banks. 11 They should maintain a record in writing of (every) elephant, (whether) moving in a herd, moving alone, lost from a herd or lord of a herd, (and whether) wild, intoxicated, cub or released from captivity.

12 They should catch elephants whose outward marks and behaviour are excellent in the judgment of elephant-trainers. 13 Victory (in battle) for a king depends principally on elephants. 14 For, elephants, being possessed of very big-sized bodies and being capable of life-destroying activities, pound the troops, battle-arrays, fortresses and camps of enemies.

> 15 Elephants from the Kaliṅgas and the Aṅgaras are best ; those from the east, those from Cedi and Karūṣa and those from the Daśārṇas and the Aparāntas are considered as of medium quality among the elephants.

6 *pratyante* ' on the border ' of the kingdom, hardly on the border of the *dravyavana*. Cj refers to the region between Lauhitya in the east, Prayāga in the west, Gaṅgā in the south and Himavat in the north, describing it as the *prācya vana* and implies that the *janapada* should not be inside this region. — *aṭavyārakṣam* ' of which the protection is secured by foresters.' 7 *nāgavanādhyakṣaḥ* : this officer is different from the *hastyadhyakṣa* of 2.31–32. Cnn quotes mnemonic verses giving descriptions of the *pārvata, nādeya, sārasa* and *ānūpa* regions.

10 Cj reads *sīmaka* for *saimika* and *padya* for *padyā*. — *leṇḍa-* : this form of the word is adopted throughout on the strength of D Cnn. Cf. also ' *padapracārair leṇḍaiś ca* ' in *Mānasollāsa*, 2.182. — *kūlaghāta-* is damage done to riverbanks when elephants but in sport. 11 *ekacaraṁ niryūtham* : according to Cnn the former has left the herd of his own accord, the latter is driven out of the herd (*ekacaraṁ svayam eva yūthān niḥsṛtam, niryūthaṁ yūthān nirdhāritam*).

14 *-anīkavyūha-* as two ideas ' troops and battle-arrays ' (Cnn) is preferable to ' arrays of an army. ' — *prāṇaharakarmāṇo* : Cnn quotes ' *spṛśannapi gajo hanti*.'

15 *kāliṅgāṅgarajāḥ* is from D ; M's *-rājāḥ* is corrupted from it, the editions making an attempt to correct it by reading *-gajāḥ*. Cnn, which has intruded into the text of D, gives a definition of *āṅgareyaka vana*, showing that the Aṅga region is not to be thought of here. Cb reads *kaliṅgavaṅgajāḥ*. According to mnemonic verses quoted in Cnn the *kāliṅga vana* lies between Utkala, the southern ocean, the Sahya Mountain and Kaliṅga ; the *āṅgareyaka vana* lies between Vidiśā, the Narmadā, Brahmavardhana and the Pāriyātra Mountain. According to Cnn, only these two types of elephants are best, those from *prācya* etc. being

16 Those from the Surāṣṭras and the Pañcanadas are declared to be of the lowest quality among them. Of all of these, valour, speed and spirit increase by training.

CHAPTER THREE

SECTION 21 CONSTRUCTION OF FORTS

1 In all four quarters, on the frontiers of the country, he should cause a nature-made fortress, equipped for fight, to be made: a water-fort (either) an island in the midst of water or high land shut in by water, (or) a mountain fort (either) consisting of rocks or a cave, (or) a desert fort (either) one without water and shrubs or a salty region, or a jungle fort (either) a marshy tract with water or a thicket of shrubs. 2 Among them a river fort and a mountain fort are places for the protectors of the country, a desert fort and a jungle fort are places for foresters or places of retreat in times of calamity.

3 In the centre of the country, he should lay out a *sthānīya*, the headquarters for revenue, on a site recommended by experts in the science of

madhyama. — *prācyāś cedikarūṣajāḥ*: the *prācya vana* lies between the Lauhitya, Prayāga, the Gaṅgā and Himavat; the *cedikarūṣaka vana* between Mekalā, Tripurī, Daśārṇa and the Unmattagaṅgā (Cnn). — *dāśārṇāḥ* is from Cb; a derivative as in the other cases is better. The *dāśārṇa vana* lies between Daśārṇa, Mahāgiri, Vindhya and the Vetravatī (Cnn). No description of the *āparānta vana* is found in these verses. 16 *saurāṣṭrakāḥ*: the *saurāṣṭraka vana* lies between Avantī, the Narmadā, Dvārakā and Arbuda (Cnn). — *pāñcanada vana* lies between Kurukṣetra, Kālikākānana, the Sindhu and Himavat (Cnn). — Very similar details are found in the *Mānasollāsa* of Someśvara (2.177 ff.).

2.3.

Many of the details concerning the building of a fort are far from clear. Meyer calls this 'the most frightful' among the chapters of this text.

In WZKSO, XI, 1967, 44-80, 'Arthaśāstra-studien II: Die Anlage einer Festung', D. Schlingloff has interpreted at great length the details of this chapter in the light of the excavations at the sites of ancient fortresses at Rājagṛha, Vaiśālī, Kauśāmbī etc.

1 *daivakṛtam* 'made by fate,' i.e., provided by nature; the reading *devakṛtam* 'made by the gods' conveys the same idea perhaps a little more clearly. There are two varieties of each of the four kinds of *durgas*. — *nimnāvaruddham* 'surrounded on all sides by water' (*nimnena jalena* —Cnn). Cb renders *nimna* by 'lakes.' — *prāstaram*: this seems to mean 'made of or consisting of rocks.' Cj understands 'a peak on top of a mountain with the sides chiselled off (*śikharam eva samantataḥ ṭaṅkacchinnapārśvatvād durgamam*).' — *nirudakastambam* 'without water and without shrubs,' rather than 'where shrubs grow on waterless ground' (Meyer). — *khañjanodakam*: *khañjana* is a marshy place, a bog; cf. 10.4.8; 12.4.25. That and water surround this kind of fort; '*sapaṅkajalam, khaji gativaikalye iti pāṭhāt*' —Cnn. Its mention as *vanadurga* seems due to the growth of weeds etc. in the morass. Cj, reading *khaṇḍanodakam*, explains '*vicchinnapravāhodakam, kvacit kvacid udakam iti yāvat*.' All these are 'nature-made' and hence no man-made fortification is necessary in their case. 2 *nadīdurga*: the same as *udakadurga*. — *janapadārakṣa-*: this expression is understood as in Cnn in the sense of *antapāla* frontier-chiefs. It corresponds to *aṭavī*, i.e., foresters in the next clause. The expression may also mean 'protection of the country.' — The *Devīpurāṇa*, 72.53-55, agrees with this text in the matter of these eight *durgas*.

3 *samudayasthānam*, i.e., the place where revenue is ultimately brought and kept. — *sthānīyam*: this is the headquarters for eight hundred villages (2.1.4. above). In most cases, it is the fortified capital of the state. — It seems that *hrada* is illustrated by *saras*,

building, at the confluence of rivers or on the bank of a lake that never dries up, either a (natural) lake or a (man-made) tank, round, rectangular or square or in accordance with the nature of the building site, with water flowing from left to right, a market town, served by a land-route and a water-route.

4 He should cause three moats to be dug round it, at a distance of one *daṇḍa* from each other, fourteen, twelve and ten *daṇḍas* broad, three-quarters or a half of the breadth deep, one-third (of the surface-breadth) at the bottom or square with the bottom, paved with stones or with the sides (only) built of stones or bricks, reaching down to (natural springs of) water or filled with water coming from elsewhere, with (arrangements for) draining excess water, and stocked with lotuses and crocodiles.

5 At a distance of four *daṇḍas* from the moat, he should cause a rampart to be made out of the earth dug out, six *daṇḍas* high, made compact, twice that in breadth, piled upwards with a platform-like (flat) surface (at the top) or with a jug-like side, pounded by elephants and bullocks (and) having (on the sides) clusters of thorny bushes and poisonous creepers. 6 With the remainder of the earth, he should cause the low places in the residential areas or palace grounds to be filled up.

a natural lake, and *taṭāka*, an artificial tank; *hrada* appears to be a common name for the two. — *pradakṣiṇodakam*, i.e., in effect on the right bank of the river. — *paṇyapuṭabhedanam* is evidently a market town, 'where packages coming from different places are opened for sale' (Cj Cs). According to Meyer *puṭabheda* is 'a bend in the river' (*nadīvakram*, says the *Medinīkośa*). According to Charpentier (ZDMG, 70, 237-242) it means a fork in the river where it breaks into two. — *aṁsapatha* is the same as *sthalapatha*.

4 *daṇḍāntarāḥ*: D adds *dvidaṇḍāntarāḥ vā* after this. Cnn, however, shows no explanation of it. A *daṇḍa* is about six feet. In 2.20.19 a *dhanus* of 108 *aṅgulas* (about 6′ 9″) is mentioned as a measure for *prākāra* and roads. In the present passage, however, *dhanus* is not used at all, only *daṇḍa*. — We may, with Cnn, understand the widest of the three moats as being nearest the rampart and the narrowest furthest away from it. — *tribhāgamūlāḥ*, i.e., the width at the bottom is to be one-third the width at the surface. Meyer understands *tribhāga* in the sense of three-fourths; that doesn't appear likely, though it would make the sides less sloping. — *mūle caturaśrapāṣāṇopahitāḥ* was an emendation suggested by Meyer, the meaning being that the bottom should be paved with square stones. But the emendation is unnecessary. We should read with D *mūlacaturaśrā vā* and regard it as an option to *tribhāgamūlāḥ* in the sense 'or, square with the bottom,' i.e., with straight instead of sloping sides. The translation is in conformity with this. With this reading, *pāṣāṇopahitāḥ* 'paved with stones (all through)' becomes an option to the following *pāṣāṇeṣṭakābaddhapārśvā vā* 'with sides (alone) paved with stones or bricks.' — *saparivāhāḥ* refers to arrangements for draining away excess water. — *padmagrāhavatīḥ* 'having lotuses and crocodiles,' the former for beauty, the latter as a danger to enemies. Cf. *Samarāṅgaṇasūtradhāra*, 10.17-22. Meyer thinks that *padmagrāha* may refer to some contrivance for letting water in or out by closing or opening it. That is possible though uncertain.

6 *avaruddham* 'enclosed firmly' seems to refer to firmness of foundation and the compactness of the structure. Cnn explains 'with both sides tiled with stones etc. (*pāṣāṇādibhir baddhobhayapārśvam*).' That seems hardly intended. — *ūrdhvacayam*: 'with a high pile'; Cj Cnn explain 'in the shape of an ant-hill (*valmīkanikarasaṁsthānam* —Cj).' — *mañcapṛṣṭham* 'with the top shaped like a platform, i.e., flat.' Cnn understands 'slightly depressed in the middle to make the parapet wall on it firm (*madhye kiṁcin nimnaṁ prākāradārḍhyārtham*).' This is not an option to *ūrdhvacayam* as Cs understands it. — *kumbhakukṣikaṁ vā*: 'with jar-like sides,' i.e., bulging in the middle to make climbing difficult. This is an option to *ūrdhvacayam*, *mañcapṛṣṭham* obviously being common to both. 6 *vāstucchidram* refers to areas in the city unsuitable for building purposes because they are not level. — *rājabhavanam* from D appears genuine in view of *vā*.

7 On top of the rampart, he should cause a parapet to be built, double the breadth in height, built of bricks, from twelve *hastas* upwards up to twenty-four *hastas*, either odd or even in number (of *hastas* in height), with a passage for the movement of chariots, shaped like a palm-stem and with the top decked with 'drums' and 'monkey-heads'. 8 Or, he should cause it to be made of stones, close-knit with big slabs, but under no circumstances (should he have it) made of wood. 9 For, fire remains lurking in it.

10 He should cause turrets to be made, square with the breadth, provided with steps for going down, (of the) same (length) as the height, and at a distance of thirty *daṇḍas* from each other. 11 Midway between (every) two turrets, he should cause a tower to be built, with two stories inclusive of a hall, (and) one and a half times in length. 12 Between each turret and

7 The height of the brick parapet is to be 12, 13, ... upto 24 *hastas* and the width to be half the height in each case. For *hasta* see 2.20.12. —*rathacaryāsaṁcāram* : evidently this passage for the movement of carts is to be on the top of the parapet, though in the case of smaller widths, it is not easy to suppose that *rathas* could move freely on top. Meyer makes *ratha-* etc. as the substantive and *tāla- . .ācitāgram* and *pṛthu . . . śailam* as adjectives to it. That seems hardly possible. All the expressions only describe the *vapra*. —*tālamūlam* as in D Cb is better. As an adjective to *vapram*, it is explained 'shaped like the root of a palm tree, i.e., broad at the base and narrow at the top' (Cb). —*murajakaiḥ kapiśīrṣakaiś ca* : the two expressions describe the shape of the coping stones on top. Cj thinks that these were covers for fighters, the former 'with even tops (*samaśirobhiḥ*),' the latter 'shaped like the *Aśvattha* leaf (*aśvatthapatrasaṁsthānaiḥ*).' Meyer's rendering '(a chariot passage) with a palm base and with figures of female breasts (*uraja*) and monkey-heads' is quite unlikely. 8 *pṛthuśilāsaṁhataṁ vā śailam* is an option to *aiṣṭakam* above. 9 *avahitaḥ* 'placed in,' i.e., lurking.

10 *viṣkambhacaturaśram* 'square with the width (of the parapet) ; ' the turret is thus a square structure, each side being as long as the parapet-width. — *utsedhasamāvakṣepasopānam* : Cnn explains 'with a flight of steps for descent (on the inside) in conformity with the height of the parapet together with the rampart (*savaprasya prākārasya ya utsedhas tasya samo yo 'vakṣepaḥ tatra sopānāni ārohaṇārthaṁ niśreṇīpadānīva yasya*)' and adds that soliders can then easily go to the top even when they carry weapons in both hands. This, however, can hardly be understood appropriately with the *aṭṭālaka* or turret. The steps may be only from the turret to the top of the parapet. And *avakṣepasopāna* as 'ladder for throwing down (and taking up) at will' is not unlikely. Cj remarks that there should be *murajakas* and *kapiśīrṣakas* in places on top where there are no *aṭṭālakas* (*aṭṭālakātiriktadeśe copariṣṭān murajāḥ kapiśīrṣakāś ca syuḥ*). 11 *saharmyadvitalām*, i.e., having two floors, one of them (the upper one) being a room or hall. It seems that the lower floor was without walls, there being only pillars to support the upper hall. — *adhyardhāyāmām* 'with a length one and a half times the width, ' the width apparently being co-extensive with the width of the parapet. The *pratolī* tower is thus bigger and loftier than the *aṭṭālaka*. With the reading *dvyardhā-* Meyer understands 'two and a half times.' 12 *sāpidhāna-* etc. : It seems that a board of planks is fixed at the outer edge of the parapet ; through holes, in it, archers could shoot at the enemy outside and the holes could be covered at will so that arrows from outside could not come in. Cnn which has this explanation (*sacchidraphalakatvaṁ śaranirgamārtham, sāpidhānatvaṁ paraśarapratiskhalanārtham*) adds that the name *indrakośa* is due to the many eye-like holes in it (*akṣisamānasahasracchidropetatvāt*). 13 *antareṣu*, i.e., in the spaces between the various structures, just described. —*pārśve* 'at the side ' means according to Cnn 'on the outer side of the parapet (*prākārabahiḥpārśve*) ' since the *devapatha* is intended for the protection of the base of the parapet on the outside. The *devapatha* is, according to it, made of strong wood fixed with copper-strips, with openings for shooting arrows but otherwise covered on all sides (*sāradārumayaṁ tāmrapatrikābaddham adhaḥkṛtaśaramārgaṁ sarvataś chāditam*). It is so called apparently because entry into it was difficult. That such a structure should be designated *-patha* is rather odd. — G M add *anuprākāram aṣṭahastāyatam* in the s., but the words seem to be merely a paraphrase of

tower, in the centre, he should cause to be erected a board, compact with planks having holes with coverings, as a place (from which to fight) for three archers. 13 In the intervening spaces, he should cause a 'gods' way' to be made, two *hastas* in breadth and four times that in length, at the side.

14 He should cause tracks to be made of a width of one *daṇḍa* or two *daṇḍas*, and in an unassailable place a run-way and an exit-door.

15 Outside (the fort), he should cause a covered road to be made that is strewn with knee-breakers, a mass of pikes, pits, concealed traps, barbed wires, 'serpent-backs', 'palm-leaves,' 'three peaks,' 'dog's jaws', bars, 'jumping sandals,' frying pans and ponds.

16 Having made on both sides of the parapet a 'ram's head' one *daṇḍa* and a half (in extent), he should cause the gate-way to be laid out, with

pārśve caturguṇāyāmaṁ and appear to have got into the text from a marginal gloss. — It should be remarked that in view of the structures on the parapet, *rathacaryā* (s. 7) would be difficult on it.

14 *daṇḍāntarāḥ* : *antara* is 'width' as in 2.4.3 below. — *caryāḥ* 'tracks, courses' seems to refer to steps for going up and down from the *devapatha* to the *pradhāvanikā*. The tracks would naturally be well protected as they are apparently on the outside of the wall. — *pradhāvanikām* : Cnn explains 'a run-way protected by a small zig-zag wall of the height of a man, extending from the *prākāra* to the big moat, intended as a cover for the fighters (*gomūtrikākārā puruṣapramāṇamuṇḍaprākāreṇa agrāhye pareṣāṁ niṣkiradvārair nirgatya parikhārakṣārthaṁ pradhāvanti yodhā asyām*).' Cj has a similar explanation. Cb understands *pradhāvitikā* merely as 'a screen for the protection of soldiers from the arrows of the enemy.' — *niṣkiradvāram* : Cnn has 'a small exit door made of iron at the end of a stair-case leading down from the *devapatha* in the outer wall of the rampart; through this door soldiers come out into the *pradhāvanikā* for the protection of the moat (*devapathasya adhastāt prākārakukṣipradeśeṣu niṣkiradvāram niṣkiryante bahiḥparikhārakṣārthaṁ yodhā yena tad ārohaṇāvataraṇārthaṁ kṛtaṁ tiryak prākārabāhyabhittiṣu svalpatarasopānaṁ kālāyasadṛḍhakapāṭam*).' Cj seems to have a similar explanation. For this door, cf. 13.4.12.

15 *ahipṛṣṭha*, *tālapatra*, *śṛṅgāṭaka* etc. have reference to the shape of the contraptions which may have been made of iron or strong wood. — *śvadaṁṣṭra* : in 10.4.9 it is obviously the name of a plant dangerous to elephants; here, however, a contraption shaped like a dog's jaws made of iron may be understood as in Cnn. — *upaskandanapādukā* 'sandals that make one jump' (Meyer). Cj has '*upaskanda*, i.e., much broken ground, and *pādukā*, i.e., a hole of the size of the foot, filled with thorns and covered with dust etc.'

16 *meṇḍhakam* : there is little doubt about this being the original reading. According to Cnn Cj, it refers to a structure on the rampart on both sides of the gate-way, resembling a ram's head with two horns. It seems that according to Cnn the two heads are above the level of the height of the *prākāra* and face each other in the opening made for the gate-way. Cj is not quite clear but seems to imply that the two ram's heads face inside the wall as well as outside, apparently above the gate extending over its entire width (*meṣaśṛṅgadvayasaṁsthānaṁ dvārasuṣirābhimukhāgrabāhuprākāram*—Cnn; *antar bahiś ca bāhū prasārya meṣaśṛṅgavat mārgābhimukhau*—Cj). — *adhyardhadaṇḍam* : this according to Cnn, refers to the extent of the projection of the ram's heads in the gate-way opening. As the gate-way area is 5-*daṇḍa* square, we get an opening of two *daṇḍas* (1½ into 2, i.e., 3, and 5 minus 3), i.e., 8 *hastas* for the gates between the two rams's heads. (*ubhayameṇḍhakaśṛṅgacatuṣṭayamadhye'ṣṭahastaṁ dvāramārgāvakāśaṁ muktvā* — Cnn). Apparently in Cj this referred to the extent of the projection on the inside and on the outside of the gate-way area. — *pratolīṣaṭtulāntaraṁ dvāram* : according to Cj *pratolī* is the name of the gate described here. That seems also to be Cnn's idea. Apparently the gate resembles the *pratolī* or tower of s. 11, as it has two floors, one of them a walled-in hall. The expression seems to mean 'a gate, having

space for six beams of the tower, from five *daṇḍas* (square) onwards increased by one *daṇḍa* upto eight *daṇḍas* square, or one-sixth part more than the length or one-eight part (more). 17 From fifteen *hastas* onwards increased by one *hasta* upto eighteen *hastas* (should be) the height of the floor. 18 The circumference of a pillar (should be) one-sixth of the length, double that the portion fixed in the ground ; the capital (should be) one-fourth (the length) in circumference).

19 Occupying one-fifth part of the ground floor (should be) a hall, a well and a border-room. 20 There should be two platforms facing each other, occupying one-tenth part (of the space) and in between two doors and a room. 21 And at half the height of the floor, there should be a structure with

space for six beams of the *pratolī*.' *tulā* is a beam and the six beams apparently are necessary for the ceiling of the ground floor ; in a gate-way 5 *daṇḍa* square in area, each *tulā* would be 5 *daṇḍa* long and there would be a space of a little less than one *daṇḍa* between every two *tulās*. Cb reads *talāntaram*, explaining *tala* as 'an archway pillar to support the gate-way.' Pillars, of course, would be necessary, but it is doubtful if *tala* could be understood in that sense ; *tulā*, however, might be so understood. — After *caturaśram*, Cb Cs add *dvidaṇḍaṁ vā*. The words, if genuine, are misplaced. They should come after *adhyardhadaṇḍaṁ kṛtvā* above. — *ṣaḍbhāgam āyāmād adhikam* is a modification of the idea in *caturaśram*. Apparently, if, e.g., the parapet ran north-south, the slightly longer side of the gate-way would be east-west. 17 *talotsedhaḥ* : the height referred to is apparently that of the ground floor. Cb Cs read *tulotsedhaḥ* 'the height of the pillars' which comes to the same thing. 18 *stambhasya* : as this word for pillar is used, *tulā* as pillar (Cb Cs in s. 17) appears less likely. — *ṣaḍāyāmaḥ* has to be understood as 'one-sixth of the length,' i.e., *āyāmaṣaḍbhāgaḥ*. Meyer thinks that *ṣaḍāyāmād* should be read for this sense. — *dviguṇaḥ* 'double' the one-sixth, i.e., one-third. — *cūlikāyāḥ* : we have to supply *parikṣepaḥ*. The capital of the pillar is thicker than the rest of it.

19 *āditalasya* : this refers to the ground floor area. — *pañcabhāgāḥ*, i.e., occupying one-fifth part of the area. Cb Cs read *pañca bhāgāḥ* as two words, understanding five divisions, a *vāpī*, two *śālās* and two *sīmāgṛhas*. This is extremely doubtful. As the two *pratimañcas* occupy one-tenth part each and the *kapāṭayogas* three-fifth part, one-fifth part would indeed be left over for *śālā*, *vāpī* and *sīmāgṛha* together. — *śālā vāpī sīmāgṛhaṁ ca* : according to Cnn the three are on the inner side. The *śālā* is innermost and serves as a sort of armoury (*praharaṇāvaraṇādisthānam*). The *vāpī* in front of the *śālā* is a hole six *aṅgulas* (about 4½″) in width, through which persons stationed above strike at advancing enemies (*śālāgrataḥ sthitaṁ ṣaḍaṅgulāntaraṁ suṣiraṁ vāpī yayā praviśataḥ śatrūn uparisthitāḥ praharanti*). In front of the *vāpī* and of the same size as the *śālā* is the *sīmāgṛha*, so called because it is on the border between the outside and the inside (*agrasthito śālāpramāṇo bhāgaḥ sīmāgṛhaṁ bāhyābhyantarabhāgayoḥ sīmni sthitatvāt, sīmāgṛhaṁ yuddhārtham*). 20 *pratimañcau* : these are two platforms opposite each other, evidently between the gate-leaves and the *sīmāgṛha*. They are intended for sentries (*dvārarakṣakāvasthānabhūtau* — Cnn). Cnn places the platforms on the two sides of the *vāpī* (*vāpībhāgasyobhayataḥ*). This would appear doubtful, as the *vāpī*, according to Cnn, is only a hole six *aṅgulas* in width.— After *pratimañcau*, D has a passage which is again derived from Cnn. — *antaram āṇī harmyaṁ ca* : Cnn on this is not quite clear. *antara* seems understood in the sense of the region enclosed by *śālā*, *vāpī*, *sīmāgṛha* and the *pratimañcas* ; in this region are to be two *āṇis*, i.e., doors opening to staircases ; in the rest of the region there is to be a *harmya*, a white-washed room for the sentries to sleep etc. (*śālāvāpīsīmāgṛhapratimañcāvaruddhapradeśe ... mantaram ityucyate, tatra āṇī ityāṇidvayaṁ sopānamārgadvāradvayam, śeṣapradeśadvaye harmyaṁ rakṣakaśayanāsanārthaṁ dhavalagṛham*). Cj also seems to understand *āṇi* in the sense of a door. It is not easy to see where exactly the doors and the room would be situated. 21 *samucchrayād ardhatale sthūṇābandhaś ca* : according to Cnn this describes the *dvitīyatala*, i.e., the first floor. Its height is to be half that of the ground floor, i.e., 7½ *hastas*, the floor area remaining the same. Apparently, rows of pillars, not regular walls, support the ceiling of this floor (*sārdhasaptahastaḥ samucchrayaḥ ucchrayāpekṣayā ardhatalam ucyate ; kṣetraṁ tu āditalasamānam ; atra sthūṇāḥ kṣudrastambhāḥ āditalasyopari sthūṇānyāsaṁ kṛtvā bandho dvitīyatalabandhaḥ*). It is

pillars. 22 There should be an upper chamber measuring half the built-in area or having a space one-third of it, with sides constructed with bricks, with a stair-case on the left running from left to right and on the other side a stair-case concealed in the wall. 23 The crest of the arch should be two *hastas* (in height). 24 The two door-leaves should occupy three-fifths (of the space). 25 There should be two bars (to the doors). 26 The stake (should be) one *aratni* (n height). 27 There should be a side-door five *hastas* in height. 28 There should be four elephant-bars. 29 The 'elephant-nail' (passage) should be half (the width of) the structure. 30 The bridge should be equal (in width) to the opening and capable of being withdrawn, or it should be made of earth where there is no water.

31 Having fixed an opening equal to (the width of) the parapet, he should cause the *gopura*-(gate) to be made, with one-third shaped like a lizard's mouth. 32 Having made a well in the middle of the parapet, he should erect the *puṣkariṇī*-gate ; with four halls at a distance of one (*daṇḍa*) and a half

also possible that the 7½ *hastas* of the first floor are taken out of the total height of 15 *hastas*, so that the *āditala* too would be 7½ *hastas* high. 22 *uttamāgāram* 'the upper chamber' is the second floor (*tṛtīyatala*) according to Cnn, which adds that it should be shaped like a bell or a jar (*ghaṇṭākalaśādiracanayā*). — *vāmataḥ* : apparently to the left of a person standing in the gate-way and facing outside. — *pradakṣinasopānam*, i.e., with stairs turning to the right at the landings, requiring a clockwise movement for going up. — *gūḍhabhittisopānam*, i.e., with stairs concealed in walls ; see 1.20.2 above. 23 *toraṇaśiraḥ* : this is the part above the frame of the gates. Cnn seems to understand an opening of two *hastas* for ventilation as well as for discharging arrows (*uttaradehalyāṁ suṣiraṁ...vātapraveśanārthaṁ śaramokṣārthaṁ ca*). 24 *kapāṭayogau* : *yoga* conveys the idea of fixing the leaves of the gate. For their movement when opening or closing, three-fifths of the area would seem to be quite necessary. 25 G M read *dvau dvau*, implying two bars for each gate-panel. That is how Cnn understands even with a single *dvau*. Two bars running the full width may however appear sufficient. 26 *indrakīlaḥ* 'an iron stake or bolt' to be fixed in the ground inside after the gate is closed. Cnn remarks that Indra was 'fixed' by Indrajit with such a stake, hence the name (*tasmin Indrajitā kila Indro baddhaḥ*). 27 *āṇidvāram* 'small door' in one of the panels of the gate. Five *hastas* is its height. 28 *hastiparighāḥ* : the purpose of these, as Cj says, is to prevent the gate being broken down by elephants. They seem to be iron stakes fixed in the gates on the outside (*bahiḥ hastipratighātakṣamā vāryām iva parighāḥ syuḥ dvārarakṣārtham*—Cj). So Cnn '*kapāṭarakṣārtham...hastināṁ asādhyāḥ*'. 29 *niveśārdham* 'half the structure,' i.e., half the width of the gate-way, e.g., 2½ *daṇḍas* for a five-*daṇḍa* gate. This is the passage for going down. Cj seems to read *niveśārtham* and include it in the preceding s. 'for the protection of the settlement, i.e., of the fort..' That is not happy. — — *hastinakha* is the name of the passage, so called perhaps because it resembled a nail of the *vapra* appearing like an elephant's foot. Cnn says it is paved with stones (*śilāmayam*) and, of course, sloping (*kramān nimnam*). 30 *saṁhāryo*, i.e., a drawbridge. G M read *asaṁhāryo vā*, where *vā* serves no purpose. Meyer proposes *saṁhāryo* '*saṁhāryo vā*, which is not very likely. Cb Cs render *asaṁhāryo* by 'firm, made of wood.' — *bhūmimayo vā nirudake*, i.e., ground of so much width should be left unexcavated, the moat being on either side (*tāvatīṁ bhūmim apahāya khātavyam ityarthaḥ*—Cnn).

31 According to the commentators we have in this and the next s. a description of different types of gates, *gopura* being the name of the gate described here. — *tribhāgagodhāmukham* 'with one-third shaped like a lizard's mouth'; apparently the top one-third would be so shaped and possibly it would be between the *two meṇḍhakas* on either side. The explanation in Cnn is far from clear owing to lacunae, but it seems that according to it, the gate-way opening (*mukha*) is to be of the same height as the *prākāra*, i.e., 12 *hastas*, and not 15 as in the *pratolī*. It adds that the gate is so called because cattle generally go out of this gate for the pastures (*prāyo vivītābhimukhaṁ gavāṁ etad dvāram iti gopuram*). 32 *puṣkariṇīdvāram* : this is the name of another type of gate ; in this there is to be only a *vāpī*, hence the name *puṣkariṇi* 'lotus-pond gate.' The *vāpī* would appear to be a sort of hollow into which the enemy soldiers would be trapped, should they happen to surge through the

(from each other) and with holes, the *kumārīpura*-(gate); a bare house with two stories, as the *muṇḍaka*-gate; or (he should erect gates) in accordance with the (availability of) land and materials.

33 He should cause channels to be made for storing goods, one third more in length (than the breadth).

34-35 In them should be stored stones, spades, axes, arrows and choppers, clubs and hammers, sticks, discuses, machines and 'hundred-killers,' pikes prepared by smiths and bamboos with piercing points, 'camel-necks,' incendiary objects as well as all the materials described in the section on forest produce.

CHAPTER FOUR

SECTION 22 LAY-OUT OF THE FORTIFIED CITY

1 Three royal highways running west to east and three running south to north, that should be the division of the residential area. 2 It should have

gate. Cnn seems to imply that the floor corresponding to the hole between the two *meṇḍhakas* is made of planks (*prākārayor meṇḍhakayor madhye yat suṣiraṁ tatsama...phalakāstāro bhūmikābandho...yuddhasaukaryārtham*). That the weapons are discharged from the ceiling above is clearly to be understood. — *catuḥśālam* etc.: this describes the gate called *kumārīpura* 'the princess gate' so called because it is enclosed by walls on all sides. Actually, it has rooms on the four sides. Apparently the rooms would contain soldiers ready to shoot at the enemy intruding in the inner quadrangle. — *adhyardhāntaram* 'with a space of 1½ *daṇḍas*;' this apparently describes the area of the quadrangle, one and a half *daṇḍas* on each side; in this area would the enemy be trapped. Cnn seems to understand 'one and a half times the *pratolī* gate,' understanding this of *vāpī* (i.e., the *vāpī* is to be a hole of nine *aṅgulas*?). — *sāṇikam* 'with holes' in the walls through which to shoot arrows (Cnn). — *muṇḍaharmyadvitalaṁ muṇḍakadvāram*: this is the 'bare' gate, without a roof on top or without the *uttamāgāra* (Cnn). Cb understands *muṇḍa* in the sence of 'round.' — *bhūmidravyavaśena vā*: this allows further variation in conformity with the land, materials etc. According to Cnn, this option has reference to the entire *durga*, not merely the gate.

33 *tribhāgādhikāyāmāḥ*, i.e., the length of the channels or pits is to be one-third more than the width, the actual length or width to vary according to need. Cnn's illustration '*yadi daśahasto viṣkambhas tadā pañcadaśahasta āyāma ityādi*' presupposes a different reading *ardhādhikā-*. — *bhāṇḍa* 'goods' here refers to weapons. — The pits are to be inside along the rampart (*anuprākāram antaḥ*—Cnn).

34 *kāṇḍakalpanāḥ* 'arrows of various kinds' (Meyer), 'instruments for repairing or sharpening arrows (*śarasaṁskāropakaraṇāni*)' (Cnn). *kalpana* or *kalpanā* may also mean 'a cutter, a chopper.' — *muṣuṇḍhī* is '*gadādi* mace and so on' (Cnn), 'a round piece of wood with many nails, *kīlabahulo vartulaḥ kāṣṭhaviśeṣaḥ*' (Cj). — *śataghnī* 'a huge bar with a thousand spikes (*kīlasahasrācitaḥ sthūlaparighaḥ*)' (Cj). 35 *uṣṭragrīvyaḥ*: according to Cj, this is the same as *kacagrahaṇī*, i.e., a long pole with a hook at one end. Cnn has a lacuna, but it seems to understand some long-necked vessel, for it has *tailādikāni yaiḥ kṣipyante*. That seems better. Hot oil would be poured from above over the enemies below from such vessels. Perhaps then *uṣṭragrīvī* is the same as the *uṣṭrikā* of 14.1.33; 14.2.44. — *kupyakalpe ca yo vidhiḥ*: a reference to 2.17; plants, poisons etc. seem to be meant.

2.4

1 *vāstuvibhāgaḥ*: with three east-west and three north-south roads, the town would be divided into 16 squares. Cnn seems to bring the highways into some sort of relation with the *paramaśāyika* plan of Indian architecture which has 81 squares. Referring to *navabhāge* in s.7 below, it remarks that without this plan that expression cannot be understood (*na hi ekāśītipadaṁ vihāya navabhāgasaṁbhavaḥ*). Its remarks concerning the situation of the roads are, however, far from clear. Unfortunately, the fragment containing this important commentary by Yogghama, comes to an end at this point. 2 *yuktodakabhramac-*

twelve gates (and be provided) with suitable (places for) water, drains and underground passages.

3 Roads should be of a width of four *daṇḍas*. 4 The royal highway and roads in a *droṇamukha*, a *sthānīya*, the countryside and pasture-lands as well as paths in a harbour town, a battle array, a cremation ground and a village (should be) eight *daṇḍas* (in width). 5 Paths on irrigation works and in forests four *daṇḍas*, paths for elephants and along fields two *daṇḍas*, five *aratnis* the chariot path, four the cattle-path (and) two the path for small animals and men.

6 On an excellent building site, fit for the four *varṇas* to live on, the royal residence (should be erected). 7 In the ninth part to the north of the heart of the residential area he should cause the royal palace to be built in accordance with the procedure laid down, facing the east or the north.

8 The residence of the preceptor and the chaplain, the places for sacrifices and for water as well as councillors should occupy its north-by-east part, the kitchen, the elephant stables and the magazine the south-by-east part. 9 Beyond that, dealers in perfumes, flowers and liquids, makers of articles of toilet and Kṣatriyas should live in the eastern quarter.

channapathaḥ : the position of *yukta* in the compound shows that it should be understood in the sense of 'suitable, proper.' *udaka* stands for *udakasthāna* 'places where (drinking) water is available, such as wells etc.' Cf. 2.36.43, also 1.20.10. *bhrama* is a water-course, particularly a drain for taking water out of the city. *channapatha* 'a covered road' seems to be underground. Cj understands *udakapatha* 'a channel for bringing water into the city,' *bhramapatha* 'a drain for taking water out of the city' and *channapatha* 'a sub-terranean passage'. It is doubtful if *patha* is to be construed in this way.

3 *caturdaṇḍāntarāḥ* : *antara* has clearly the sense of 'width.' Cj reads *caturdaṇḍottarāḥ* and seems to include *rathyā-* in the following compound. — *rathyāḥ* : these are roads in the city other than the six highways. 4 *rāṣṭravivītapathāḥ* i.e., roads passing through the countryside and pastures. That these are as broad as the royal highways is perhaps because they connect the towns and villages. — *saṁyānīya* : *saṁyāna* is a 'sea voyage' so called because a number of vessels sail together (*sam-yā*) like a *sārtha* on land. *saṁyānīya* is a harbour town. — *vyūhapatha* refers apparently to the open spaces between the different parts of a battle array. — *śmaśānapatha* : apparently a path leading to a cremation ground is meant. 5 *kṣetrapatha* would be along the fields rather than through them. — *rathapatha*, different from *rathyā*, seems to be a cart-road in the countryside.

6 *pravīre* : according to Cb, this means 'full of fertility.' 7 *vāstuhṛdayād uttare navabhāge* : it seems necessary to agree with the commentators and think of a *paramaśāyika* plan for the city area. This has 9 by 9, i.e., 81 squares. The central 1/81st square would be the *vāstuhṛdaya*. 1/9th part (consisting of 9 smaller squares) to the north of this central square is meant to be reserved for the *antaḥpura*, i.e., the royal palace and contingent buildings. In other words, the grounds for the palace etc. would occupy one-ninth of the city area a little to the north of the centre. Cf. 10.1.2 for the same idea. — *yathoktavidhānam antaḥpuram* : see 1.20.1-2.

8 *tasya*, i.e., *antaḥpurasya* — *pūrvottaram*, i.e.,the northern half of the area to the east (*pūrvasyāṁ diśi uttaraḥ*—Cj). — *āvaseyuḥ* shows that these places are within the huge area of the *antaḥpura*, while *adhivaseyuḥ* of the next s. has reference to residences of citizens unconnected with the *antaḥpura*. 9 All mss. add *-dhānya-* after *-mālya-* ; it is proposed to drop it in view of *dhānya* in s. 11 below. This is supported by the actual comment in Cb. — There can be no doubt about *prasādhanakāravaḥ* of D being the original reading. *pradhānakāravaḥ* is unlikely.

10 The store-house for goods, the records and audit office, and workmen's quarters (should occupy) the east-by-south part, the storehouse for forest produce and the armoury the west-by-south part. 11 Beyond that, grain-dealers of the city, factory officers and army officers, dealers in cooked food, wine and meat, courtesans, dancers and Vaiśyas should live in the southern quarter.

12 Stables for donkeys and camels and the workshop (should occupy) the south-by-west part, stables for carriages and chariots the north-by-west part. 13 Beyond that, workers in wool, yarn, bamboo, leather, armours, weapons and shields, and Śūdras should live in the western quarter.

14 The rooms for wares and medicines (should occupy) the west-by-north part, the treasury and cattle and horses the east-by-north part. 15 Beyond that, the tutelary deities of the city and the king, and workers in metals and jewels and Brahmins should live in the northern quarter.

16 In enclosures in the non-residential areas, quarters for guilds and foreign merchants should be situated.

10 *karmaniṣadyā* : this clearly refers to quarters for servants employed in the royal precincts. 11 *nagaradhānyavyāvahārika* 'those who deal in grains in the city, *nagarasthāne dhānyena ye krayavikrayādi kurvanti*' (Cj) . Cb seems to understand two things, possibly 'city-administrators and grain-dealers.'

12 *kharoṣṭra-* : donkeys (or mules) and camels could be used in war ; cf. 10.4.18. — *karmagṛha* 'a workshop' for work connected with the palace. Cj's paraphrase by *yātanāgṛham* presupposes *karman* in the sense of 'torture' as in Ch. 4.8 below.

15 *nagararāja-* etc. : we may understand 'city-deity, king's tutelary deity, and artisans in metals and jewels' or 'workers in metal and precious stones for the city, the king and deities (i.e., temples).' The former seems meant. — In the lay-out as described here, the area to the north where mostly Brahmins live would be smallest in extent, while that to the south where Vaiśyas live would be largest. That might appear to be in conformity with the likely ratio between the two *varṇas*. O. Stein has discussed the details of this chapter in AOr, vol. 8, pp. 72ff. and has arrived at rather different conclusions regarding the lay-out. He places the *antaḥpura* right on the border in the north, and his plan does not take into account the words *tataḥ param* used in all four directions. His kitchen thus becomes separated from the *antaḥpura* by a number of localities intervening, so that he himself is forced to ask what kitchen could be meant at this great distance from the *antaḥpura*. There is little doubt that the items mentioned in ss. 8, 10, 12 and 14 are proximate to the palace and are part of the *rājaniveśa*, and that items in ss. 9, 11, 13, and 15 refer to the extensive areas outside the palace grounds. — Stein also interprets *karmagṛha* in the sense of 'a prison-house' from *karman* in the sense of 'torture' as in 4.8 below. That is hardly right. For the prison-house the word is *bandhanāgāra*.

16 *vāstucchidrānuśāleṣu* : *anuśāla* seems to mean 'an enclosure or a hall' ; *anulāsa* of G M hardly conveys any sense. Cj with *-anusāleṣu* explains 'in unoccupied areas (*vāstucchidreṣu*, i.e., *avyāpteṣu*) and in regions near the city wall (*prākārasamīpeṣu ca deśeṣu*).' This is also the explanation of Cb, which however has *-anulāseṣu*. Perhaps the original reading was *vāstucchidre 'nusālam* 'in non-residential areas along the rampart (*sāla*).' — *śreṇī* 'washermen etc.' (Cj), 'i.e., weavers, washermen, tailors etc.' (Cb). — *prapaṇi-* is from D and seems to mean 'a foreign merchant.' The word is apparently derived from *prapaṇa* 'barter, exchange' which is Vedic. Cj reading *pravaṇi* has 'small merchants from Gandhāra etc.' ; Cb with *pravaṇika* has 'merchants from foreign lands.' — *nikāya* 'groups' (Cj). Perhaps 'residences, quarters' may appear better.

17 He should cause to be built in the centre of the city shrines for Aparājita, Apratihata, Jayanta and Vaijayanta as well as temples of Śiva, Vaiśravaṇa, Aśvins, Śrī and Madirā. 18 He should install the presiding deities of the dwelling places according to their respective regions. 19 The city gates (should be) presided over by Brahman, Indra, Yama and Senāpati. 20 Outside (the city), at a distance of one hundred *dhanuses* from the moat, should be made sanctuaries, holy places, groves and water-works, and the deities of the quarters in the respective quarters.

21 The northern or the eastern part of the cremation ground should be for the best among the *varṇas*, to the south the cremation ground for the lower *varṇas*. 22 For transgression of that, the lowest fine for violence (shall be imposed).

23 The quarters for heretics and Caṇḍālas (should be) on the outskirts of the cremation ground.

17 *Aparājita-* etc. : As all the four names signify invincibility in some form or the other, they appear to be spirits of victory. Meyer thinks that they are all forms of Kumāra or Skanda. Cj understands by these four, Viṣṇu, Indra, Indra's son and Skanda respectively, Cb Cs Durgā (Aparājitā), Viṣṇu, Subrahmaṇya and Indra respectively. The feminine form of the first name appears questionable. — *koṣṭha* 'a shrine' is a walled-in compound, with one or more structures inside. — Śiva and Vaiśravaṇa are mentioned in a Devatā-dvanda compound by Patañjali on Pāṇini 6.3.26 (Stein, AOr 8, 337 n.6). — Śrī is Lakṣmī, the Goddess of Wealth and Prosperity. — Madirā 'the Intoxicating One, the Fascinating One' is apparently some form of Durgā or Kālī. Meyer thinks that the association of drink in connection with the worship of this deity was responsible for this name. — *puramadhye* : this would be in front of the palace grounds, to its south, in the central 1/81st part. 18 *koṣṭhakālayeṣu* (found in G M) does not appear to be original. The *vāstudevatās* appear to be unconnected with Aparājita etc. and their *koṣṭhas*. They are the tutelary deities that are supposed to preside over the different parts of the *vāstupuruṣa*. — *yathoddeśam* can hardly mean 'according to the prescription (of the Śilpaśāstra)' (Stein AOr, 8, 338). 19 *brāhmaindra* etc. : this shows that Brahman presided over the north and Senāpati over the west, and not Kubera and Varuṇa respectively as later. Only the four principal gates are thought of here and hence there is no contradiction between the number four of the gates here and the number twelve in s. 2 above, as Stein (AOr, 8, 338) thinks. 20 *bahiḥ* might mean 'outside (the city)' or may be connected with *parikhāyāḥ* 'from the outermost moat.'

21 *varṇottamānām* etc. : the readings from D are preferred as being more likely. *varṇottamānām* seems to be understood by Cb as referring to Śūdras, which is unlikely. It may be, however, that Cb had before it *śmaśānabhāgo varṇāvarāṇāṁ dakṣiṇena varṇottamānām*. Cj has ' The cremation ground should be divided into four parts ; beginning with the part for Śūdras, those for Vaiśyas, Kṣatriyas and Brāhmaṇas should be successively to the north or to the east. The cremation ground should be to the south of the city. ' — The discrepancy that Stein finds between this passage and 2.36.31-33 (AOr, 8, 348) is due to the different character of the offences mentioned in the two places. The use of the wrong cremation ground is not a light offence as Stein thinks, and the lowest *sāhasa-daṇḍa* in this text is not 250 *paṇas*, but 48-96 *paṇas* (see 3.17.8 below).

23 *-ante*, i.e., *samīpe* (Cb). Stein points out that 2.36.14 shows *pāṣaṇḍāvāsa* to be inside (*abhyantare*). Perhaps the difference is due to difference in sources. It is more likely, however, that the present s. is not original, but a later addition. It seems to represent the Brahmanical ideal of an age characterised by bigotry.

24 He should fix boundaries for householders in accordance with areas (necessary) for their workshops. 25 In them they should make, with permission, flower-gardens and fruit-orchards, as well as stores of grains and commodities. 26 An enclosure for a group of ten families should be a place for a well (for them).

27 He should cause to be made stores, capable of being used over a number of years, of all kinds of fats, grains, sugar, salts, perfumes, medicines, dried vegetables, fodder, dried meat, hay, wood, metals, hides, charcoal, tendons, poisons, horns, bamboos, barks, strong timber, weapons, shields and stones. 28 He should cause the old to be constantly replaced by new.

29 He should station (a force consisting of) elephants, horses, chariots and infantry-men, under more than one chief. 30 For, a (force) under more than one chief does not fall a prey to enemy instigations, through mutual fear.

31 By this is explained the making of frontier forts.

32 And he should not allow in the city 'outsiders' who cause harm to the country. He should cast them out in the countryside or make them pay all the taxes.

24 *karmāntakṣetravaśena* : the *vā* after this in G M serves no purpose. According to Stein, this s. states an option to the entire plan of the town described so far. That is not likely. We have here a reference to the fixing of boundaries of the individual households. This is to depend on the nature of the work in which the household is engaged. 25 *-vāṭān dhānya-* is emended from D's reading *-vāṭadhānya-*. It is clear that *ṣaṇḍa* and *kedāra* are out of place in the city area. And we must have a separate expression from *dhānya-* onwards, for *nicayān* is not to be construed with *puṣpaphalavāṭa*. — *anujñātāḥ* : this implies that all private stores are known to the state, which can requisition them in times of emergency. 26 *daśakulīvāṭaṁ kūpasthānam* : Cb reads *-vāpam* and explains 'as much land as can be ploughed by ten bullocks or as much area as can be irrigated by one well.' This implies the presence of fields in the city area, which appears extremely doubtful. The idea intended seems to be that there should be one well for every ten families. *vāṭa* seems to convey the idea of a compact unit formed by the ten families.

27 *-gandha-* seems to have dropped out inadvertently in G M. — For *kṣāra* see 2.15.14 below.

31 *saṁskāra* means everything concerning the making of a fort, building, layout, making stores, etc. In 9.1.34-36 the idea of repairs also seems implied.

32 *bāhirikān* : Cb understands 'gamblers, beggars, dancers, actors etc.'. Stein suggests (AOr, 8, 356) that these are wandering tribes, something like the gypsies. That seems probable. — *pure rāṣṭropa-* is proposed for *purarāṣṭropa-* of the mss. That makes the idea of *kṣipet janapade* more clear. — Cb Cs read *janapadasyānte* and explain 'should settle them on the frontiers and (*vā* as *ca*) make them pay all taxes (or taxes like all other persons—Cs).' It seems, however, that *vā* shows an option, the idea being that if they stay in the city, they must be made to pay the usual taxes. Cj seems to have read *bāhirikām...-ghātikām* '(a part of a suburb) outside the city, (residents in) which might cause harm to the city and the country'.

CHAPTER FIVE

SECTION 23 THE WORK OF STORE-KEEPING BY THE DIRECTOR OF STORES

1 The Director of Stores should cause to be built a treasury, a ware-house, a magazine, a store for forest produce, an armoury and a prison-house.

2 Having caused to be dug a four-cornered well free from water and dampness, and having paved the walls on both sides and the bottom with big slabs of stone, he should cause an underground cellar to be made with a frame-work of strong timber, level with the ground, with three floors, with various arrangements, with ground and upper floors having well-made surfaces, with a single door, (and) with a stair-case provided with a mechanism. 3 On that he should cause a treasure-house to be made with a prohibition (to enter) on two sides, with an entrance-hall, built of bricks, and surrounded by (channels) storing goods ; or, (he should cause to be built only) an (above-the-ground) palace. 4 On the border of the country, he should cause a permanent treasure to be laid by persons condemned to death, as a provision against calamity.

5 He should cause to be made a ware-house and a magazine with pillars of baked bricks, with four halls (opening on to a quadrangle), with many,

2.5

1 The inclusion of the *bandhanāgāra* here seems to suggest that prisoners were, like the other objects, to be taken charge of and treated with care.

2 *ubhayataḥ* : Cj understands it in the sense of *ubhayam*, referring to *pārśva* and *mūla*. It mentions an alternative explanation 'along both (the length and breadth), *ubhayataḥ* . . . *āyāmaviṣkambhābhyām*.' In any case, it can hardly be understood with *pārśvam* alone. — *bhūmisamaṁ tritalam*: Cb, reading *-samatritalam*, explains 'with two floors under-ground and one above.' It seems rather that all three floors are underground. — *aneka-vidhānam*, i.e., with different arrangements for different types of goods. — *kuṭṭima-* etc. : Cb Cs explain 'of which the upper floor (*deśa*), the middle floor (*sthāna*) and the ground floor (*tala*) are firmly fixed (*kuṭṭima*).' This is doubtful. Cj has 'with paved sides (*deśa*) ground floor (*sthāna*) and upper floor (*tala*).' This is better. But *deśa* may be understood in the sense of 'surface', both of the walls and the floors. — *devatāpidhānam* : this expression, read in the text on the authority of Cb (supported by G M) is dropped in the translation. It does not seem original. In the absence of any reference to a secret passage here, the expres-sion has little significance, as it has in 1.20.2. A secret subterranean passage leading from the underground treasury to a nearby temple does not appear contemplated here. D Cj do not show the expression. 3 *ubhayatoniṣedham*: the idea seems to be that the two walls along the length are without doors, as Cj seems to imply (*ubhayapārśvāyatakuḍyam*). Cb has 'with a two-fold prohibition, to enter and to leave' ; that is not convincing. — *pragrīva* 'an entrance-hall' ; cf. 2.30.4 ; 2.31.2. — *bhāṇḍavāhinī-* : we have to understand *kulyā* as in 2.3.33 ; the channels may also serve as obstacles to people trying to get inside. — *prāsādaṁ vā* : this is an option to the *bhūmigṛha* (with *kośagṛha* above it). In this alternative there is no cellar, only an above-the-ground structure as a *kośagṛha*. 4 *dhruvanidhim* : as the word *nidhi* shows, the treasure is to be buried in the ground. — *abhityaktaiḥ* : these are to be executed after the work is over, so that the king alone would know where the treasure lies buried.

5 *anekasthānatalam* : here, too, *sthāna* may be understood as 'ground-floor', though it may also mean 'an apartment,' as in *vibhaktastrīpuruṣasthānam* that follows. — *vivṛta-* etc. : the idea seems to be that of escape (*apasāra*) through pillars that are open, i.e., hollow

ground and upper floors, (and) with a (secret) passage for escape through hollow pillars on two sides, in between, a store for forest produce with many long halls (and) with the walls surrounded by rooms, a similar (structure) with an under-ground cellar as an armoury, (and) separate prison-houses for those convicted by judges and for those punished by high officers, with separate apartments for women and men (and) with their rooms well-guarded against escape.

6 And in all (structures) he should cause the halls to be provided with a ditch, a well, a latrine and a bath-room, with precautions against fire and poison, with protection by means of cats and ichneumons and with (arrangements for) worship of their respective deities.

7 In the magazine, he should place a basin with a mouth one *aratni* (in width) as a rain-gauge.

8 Presiding over bureaus of experts for the different products, he should receive gems, articles of high value, articles of small value and forest produce,

(*vivṛta*). The purpose of such a passage in the stores, is, however, not quite clear ; perhaps it is meant as a precaution in case of fire. — *ubhayataḥ* : Meyer construes this with the preceding, i.e., 'with hollow pillars on both sides.' In view of *antaḥ* used with *kupyagṛham*, it seems that *ubhayataḥ* means rather 'on the two sides (of the *kupyagṛha*).' — *dīrghababulaśālam* : as timber is the principal commodity in the *kupyagṛha*, long and many halls are necessary. — *kakṣyāvṛtakuḍyam* : the walls of the halls are surrounded by rooms, in which apparently minor *kupya* products would be stored. The implication may be that the halls themselves are open to the sky. — *tadeva*, i.e., on the same plan as the *kupyagṛha*, big halls surrounded by rooms. — *dharmasthīyam*, i.e., for those convicted by the judges. In the 3rd Book, terms of imprisonment are not actually laid down as punishment, only fines. Those who cannot pay fines are apparently taken to prison. — *apasārataḥ* : D Cj read *aparādhataḥ* 'in accordance with the offence.' But this cannot be properly understood with either the preceding or the following expressions. Cj construes it with the preceding, 'separate rooms for men and women, for the reason that a crime may be committed if men and women are confined together.' In the alternative it construes it with the following, 'with rooms having greater or less protection according to offence (*yathāparādhaṁ sutamāṁ sutarāṁ ca guptā kakṣyā yasya*).' *apasārataḥ* however, seems definitely better, to be construed *suguptakakṣyam*.

6 This s. is missing in D. There is however no reason to doubt its genuineness. — *śālāḥ* is read as a separate word following Cj. The compound that follows is also read as in Cj. *khāta* is a ditch all round as a moat, *udapāna* is for drinking water. *varca* as 'latrine' is found in 3.8.28. — *svadaivata-* (*daivata* is from Cb) : these are the tutelary deities of the various structures, 'Vaiśravaṇa of the *kośagṛha*, Sītā of the *koṣṭhāgāra*, Śrī of the *paṇyagṛha*, Īśāna of the *kupyagṛha*, Skanda of the *āyudhāgāra*, Yama and Varuṇa of the *bandhanāgāras*' (Cj). Cb has Śrī in *paṇyakoṣṭhāgāra* and Viśvakarman in *kupyagṛha*. With the reading *-vacca*, Meyer includes *sarveṣām* . . . *vacca* in the preceding s. as a description of the *bandhanāgāra* (*sarveṣām*, i.e., for all prisoners). He also understands *agniviṣa-* etc. as applicable to prisons only, *svadaiva* being the deity of each individual prisoner. This is hardly satisfactory.

7 *aratnimukham* : according to Cb the gauge is square, each side being one cubit. The *Bṛhat Saṁhitā*, 23.2, also refers to a *hastaviśāla kuṇḍaka*, adding that it should measure one *āḍhaka* of rain. Perhaps the vessel was cubical in shape. Cj adds that the capacity of the vessel should be one *droṇa*, for rain is measured in *droṇas* (2.24.5).

8 *tajjāta* 'one born to it,' i.e., an expert (*tadabhijña ityarthaḥ* — Cj). — *adhiṣṭhitaḥ* is used in an active sense. In spite of 2.11.1, *kośādhyakṣaḥ* is not to be understood as the subject here (Stein, *Megasthenes und Kauṭilya*, p. 211) ; this officer has not been mentioned in this chapter. The *saṁnidhātṛ* as the officer in over-all charge has to be understood. —

whether old or new. 9 Among these (articles), in case of fraud concerning gems the highest fine for violence (shall be imposed) on the perpetrator and the instigator, in case of fraud concerning articles of high value the middle fine for violence, in case of fraud concerning articles of small value and forest produce (making good) the same and an equal amount in addition as fine.

10 He should accept money certified as genuine by the Examiner of Coins. 11 He should cut counterfeit (coins). 12 One who brings (such coins) shall be fined the lowest fine for violence.

13 He should accept corn that is clean, full (in measure) and new. 14 In case the opposite kind is brought in, the fine shall be double the price.

15 By that are explained the commodities, the forest produce and the weapons (to be received in the stores).

16 In all departments, the punishments for officers, subordinates and servants, in cases of defalcation up to one *paṇa* and beyond that (increased by one *paṇa*) upto four *paṇas*, shall be the lowest, the middle, the highest fines and death (respectively). 17 For one in charge of the treasury, execution (shall be the punishment) for robbing the treasury. 18 For those who help them, (the punishment shall) be half the fines. 19 Reproof (only), if they were not aware.

ratna, *sāra* and *phalgu* are described in 2.11 and *kupya* in 2.17. 9 *tacca tāvacca* : Breloer (KSt, III, 283) renders this by ' the quality and the quantity.' A reference to quality is hard to find here.

10 *rūpadarśaka* : see 2.12.25-26 below. 11 *chedayat* : Breloer (KSt, III, 285) understands ' cut off (from currency), i.e., confiscate.' — *āhartuḥ* : Breloer understands ' the user.' Bringing to the treasury is primarily meant.

14 Reading *mūlya-* as in D is preferable to understanding *mūla* in the sense of ' price.'

15 *tena* etc. : i.e., these are to be accepted only if good in quality ; if not, a fine equal to double the price is to be imposed. Breloer (KSt, III, 287 n.2) proposes to read *paṇya-kupyam* ' goods of small value so far as they are commodities.' *kupya*, he says, is already mentioned in s.8. The change is not necessary. Whereas s.8 is general in character and concerns fraud (s.9), this s. is concerned with quality and punishment for low quality.

16 *paṇādi-* etc., i.e., when the misappropriation is of goods up to 1, 2, 3, and 4 *paṇas* in value respectively. *parama* ' maximum ' shows the limit in each of the four cases. *paṇa-dvipaṇa-tripaṇa-catuṣpaṇa-paramāpa-* would have made this explicit. D has something like this with *tripaṇa* missing. Meyer, who has this explanation, would understand *param apahāreṣu*. Cj has ' for one *paṇa* the lowest fine, for two the middle, for four the highest, for five corporal punishment (*vadha*).' Breloer (KSt, III, 290) proposes to read *dvipaṇa-catuṣpaṇāṣṭapaṇa-daśapaṇaparam apahāreṣu* to make this passage conform to 4.9.4 below. The slight discrepancy may, however, be due to this being merely a rough resume, while 4.9.4 gives full details ; perhaps also due to a difference in sources. Cb Cs read *paṇādi-dvipaṇa-catuṣpaṇāḥ param apahāreṣu* and explain ' the fines for the three kinds of servants (*yukta*, *upayukta* and *puruṣa* are 1, 2 and 4 *paṇas* respectively ; for defalcation a second time, the three *sāhasa-daṇḍas* respectively ; if the offence is still repeated, death for all three types of servants.' This is extremely unlikely in view of 4.9.4. 18 *vaiyāvṛtyakara* : cf. 2.8.22 ; 4.8.9 etc. The original word seems to be *vaiyāpṛtya-* from *vyāpṛta*. Prakrit *veyāvacca* is the same word. — *ardhadaṇḍāḥ* is meaningless in the case of *vadha* or *ghāta*. Meyer, following Sorabji, understands ' half (the value of the treasure robbed) as fine.' This is unlikely. *ardhadaṇḍa* is applicable only when a fine is prescribed ; apparently there is no mitigation when death is laid down. Or, *vadha* may be ' corporal punishment ' which can be thought of as reducible.

20 For thieves, in case of breaking open (the treasury), death by torture (shall be the punishment).

21 Therefore, with trustworthy men under him, the Director of Stores should bring the stores into being.

22 He should be conversant with receipts from outside and inside even after a hundred years, so that when asked he would not falter in respect of expenditure, balance and collections.

CHAPTER SIX

SECTION 24 THE SETTING UP OF REVENUE BY THE ADMINISTRATOR

1 The Administrator should attend to the fort, the country, mines, irrigation works, forests, herds and trade-routes (as the main sources of revenue).

2 Custom-duties, fines, standardization of weights and measures, the city-superintendent, the mint master, the superintendent of passports, spirituous liquors, animal slaughter, yarn, oil, ghee, sugars, the goldsmith, the market-establishment, prostitutes, gambling, buildings, the group of artisans and artists, the temple-superintendent, and what is to be received at the gates and from outsiders, —these constitute (the source of income called) 'fort'.

20 *corāṇām abhipradharṣaṇe* : Meyer explains 'for forcible robbing through bandits (with whom the officers are in league).' But the genitive in *corāṇām* as usual points to the offenders themselves, on whom the punishment is to be inflicted. — *citro ghātaḥ* : see 4.11 below. — The s. is repeated in 4.9.7.

22 *bāhya* and *ābhyantara* refer to the countryside and the city respectively. — *na sajjeta* 'would not stick' i.e., would not falter. — *vyaye śeṣe ca saṁcaye* is from D. *vyaya-śeṣaṁ ca darśayet* is colourless. And *saṁcaya* refers to what comes in, a mention of which is necessary.

2.6

The preparation of the budget and fixing of state dues from the various sources are the *samāhartṛ*'s duties mentioned here. For other duties that he has to carry out, see 2.35 below. They show that he is in charge of general administration and is not a mere collector of revenue nor concerned merely with assessment of revenue.

1 *durgam* etc. : these are the principal sources of revenue. — *avekṣeta*, i.e., fix after due consideration.

2 *pautavam* : this evidently refers to prices of weights and measures, inspection fees etc. Cf 2.19. — *nāgarika* : this can only refer to fines imposed by this officer ; no revenue seems to come through him. Cf. 2.36. —*lakṣaṇādhyakṣa* is the mint-master ; see 2.12.24. Perhaps the minting charges and fees for examination of coins are to be understood under this item. — *mudrādhyakṣaḥ* : fees for passports are laid down in 2.34.1. — *surā sūnā sūtram*, i.e., income derived through officers as described in 2.25, 2.26 and 2.23 respectively. These are mostly products of state activity. — *tailaṁ ghṛtaṁ kṣāraḥ* : these apparently are produced in state stores, and income from their sale seems meant. — *sauvarṇikaḥ* : profit from the working of the state goldsmithy is meant ; cf. 2.14. — *paṇyasaṁsthā* i.e., income

3 Agricultural produce, share, tribute, tax, the trader, the river-guard, the ferry, ships, the port, pastures, road-cess, land-survey and thief-catching, —these constitute ' country '.

4 Gold, silver, diamonds, gems, pearls, corals, conch-shells, metals, salt and ores derived from the earth, rocks and liquids, — these constitute 'mines'.

5 Flower-gardens, fruit-orchards, vegetable gardens, wet crop fields, and sowings of roots, —these constitute ' irrigation works '.

6 Enclosures for beasts, deer-parks, forests for produce and elephant forests, —these constitute ' forests. '

7 Cows and buffaloes, goats, and sheep, donkeys and camels and horses and mules, —these constitute ' herds '.

received from the activity of the *paṇyādhyakṣa* of 2.16 and the *saṁsthādhyakṣa* of 4.2. — *veśyā* : obviously income from the department of the *gaṇikādhyakṣa* (2.27) is to be understood. — *dyūtam* : cf. 3.20. — *vāstukam* : imposts mentioned in chapters 3.8-9 appear to be meant. A ' house-tax ' is possible, but there is no specific reference to it elsewhere in the text. According to U. N. Ghoshal, it is ' ground-rent ' (*Revenue Systems* etc. p. 97). — *kāruśilpigaṇaḥ* : a tax on crafts and professions may be understood, though this too is not specifically laid down anywhere. The penalties of 4.1 could be understood. — *devatādhyakṣaḥ* : this officer's duties are not laid down anywhere. Apparently he supervised the management of temples and levied fees. Cj seems to understand collections at temple-fairs (*yātrā*), for which cf. 5.2.39. Temples owned by the state would be a direct source of income. — *dvārabāhirikādeyam*: two ideas are meant, *dvārādeya* and *bāhirikādeya*. The former is mentioned in 2.22.8; the latter is probably a reference to taxes mentioned in 2.4.32 above. Cj understands *bāhirikā* as in 2.4.32 above. D reads *dvāraṁ bāhirikādeyam*; the meaning would apparently be the same, but 2.22.8 might seem to favour the former reading.

3 *sītā* is income from crown lands worked by the *sītādhyakṣa* (2.24). As Cj explains '*sītā svakṛṣiḥ*'. — *bhāgaḥ* 'share' of produce from private lands, usually one-sixth (2.15.3). — *baliḥ* is apparently an occasional levy such as those mentioned in 5.2. — *karaḥ* appears to be a tax paid in cash. It is rather surprising that *bali* and *kara* do not figure under *durga* as well. — *nadīpālaḥ* : such a guard is not mentioned elsewhere. Apparently fines for unauthorised crossing of rivers forming boundaries between states are to be understood ; cf. 2.28.15 ff. — *taraḥ* : see 2.28.21 ff. — *nāvaḥ* : hire for state boats seems meant; cf. 2.28.3 ff. — *pattanam* : evidently port dues are meant. — *vivītam* : 2.34.12 mentions some of these sources of income. — *vartanī* as in 2.21.24. — *rajjuś corarajjuś ca* : according to Cj 'income from the village for fixing measurements (*grāmaparijñāpramāṇam*) and income for finding out thieves by the *pradeṣṭṛ*'s activity.' Cb explains 'what is received from district officers (*viṣayapāla*) and what is given by the village to the thief-catcher.' *rajju* seems to refer to revenue from survey operations, as Ghoshal (*Revenue Systems* etc. p. 53) says. *corarajju* may be 'fine imposed on the territory where the thief is traced' as Breloer (KSt, III, 181) says. Cf. 4.13.10. Stein (AOr, VI, 31 and n.) would omit *rajjuś*, as being due to dittography.

4 *loha* refers to metals other than gold and silver.—*bhūmiprastara*- etc.: see 2.12.1 below.

5 *mūlavāpa* : sowing by root is distinguished from sowing by seed or stem. Ginger, turmeric etc. are meant (Cs). Cj adds -*kanda*- after *mūla* ; that refers to bulbs. Johnston (JRAS, 1929, 99-101) thinks that we should read *mūlāvāpa* ' having hollows (*āvāpa* in the sense of *ālavāla*) for holding water at the base.' This is not very likly. Breloer (KSt, III, 169) construes *mūlavāpa* in the sense of 'plantings' with *puṣpa* and *phala*, these two plantings being then connected with three kinds of fields *vāṭa* ' garden, ' *ṣaṇḍa* ' culture ' and *kedāra* ' water-culture '. Thus he arrives at six kinds of *setu*. This is far from likely. How can flowers and fruits be understood as growing in *kedāra* ?

6 *paśumṛga* i.e.,' *gavaya* etc. and deer etc.' (Cb). Cj's 'domesticated animals and forest animals' is less likely. Meyer understands *paśumṛga* as one, 'antelope'. *paśu* and *mṛga* are, however, distinct. — *parigraha* is an enclosure or preserve, set apart for the various objects.

8 The land-route and the water-route constitute 'trade-routes.' 9 This is the corpus of income.

10 Price, share, surcharge, monopoly tax, fixed tax, manufacturing charge and penalty constitute the heads of income.

11 What is intended for the worship of gods and manes and for charity, gifts for benedictions received, the royal palace, the kitchen, the employment of envoys, the magazine, the armoury, the ware-house, the store for forest produce, factories, labourers, maintenance of foot-soldiers, horses, chariots and elephants, herds of cattle, enclosures for beasts, deer, birds and wild animals, and stores of fuel and grass, — these constitute the corpus of expenditure.

12 The king's (regnal) year, the month, the fortnight and the day, thus the date-entry, the third and seventh fortnights of the rainy season, winter and summer short by one day, the rest full (and) a separate intercalary month, — this is time.

9 *āyaśarīram*, i.e., the total sources of income. Breloer (KSt, III, 174) remarks that *durga* and *rāṣṭra* represent income from administration, *khani*, *setu* and *vana* income from state property and *vraja* and *vaṇikpatha* indirect taxes. *vraja*, however, belongs rather to the second category.

10 *mūlyam* is necessary as in 2.12.35. — *vyājī* is a sort of excess in measure or weight charged when goods are received in the treasury or stores. It amounts to a surcharge of 5% on every transaction. Cf. s. 22 below. It seems to have originated in the idea of a possible shortfall during measuring or weighing, which required to be made good by this surcharge. Breloer (KSt, III, 185) thinks that the object of *vyājī* is to recover the cost of the apparatus used for measuring etc. — *parigha* : 'either money for ferrying (*ātaradravya*) or begging and receiving food' (Cb). Meyer has 'gate-toll', Russ. 'tax for entrance.' Breloer (KSt, III, 433) suggests 'monopoly tax' guaranteeing that the technical production is supervised by the state. This seems a more likely explanation. See 2.12.35. — *klptam* is a fixed tax 'to be paid by a village collectively either in cash or kind' (Cb). Cf. 2.28.2. — *rūpikam* a manufacturing charge of 8%; cf. 2.12.26. — *atyayaḥ* : this would ordinarily include *daṇḍa*. But in 2.12.35 both are separately mentioned. Perhaps there *atyaya* is restricted to penalty for violation of state regulations, while *daṇḍa* is fine imposed by judges and magistrates only. — *āyamukham* refers to heads under which revenue is classified.

11 *devapitṛ-* etc. and *svasti-* etc. are on the king's account. For the latter, Breloer (III, 189) compares the *varṣāsanas* granted to Brahmins by the Peshwas. — *koṣṭhāgāra* etc.: establishment charges are to be understood in these cases. *parigraha* is here clearly upkeep or maintenance. — *vyayaśarīram* : payments to ministers, officers, spies etc. do not seem capable of inclusion here. *vyaya* is not classified into heads or *mukha*. Breloer (KSt, III, 189-193) finds six heads: expenses on cultural things, expenses for court, for treasury administration, for the army, for herds and for parks.

12 The mention of divisions of time is for purposes of account-keeping and budgeting. *rājavarṣam* : the commencement and end of the king's regnal year are apparently made to coincide with those of the works-year of 2.7.6-7 which ended on the Āṣāḍha full moon day. — *vyuṣṭam* : though there is no *iti* before it, it seems to mean the date-entry, by year, month, fortnight and day. In 2.7.31-33, it refers to the period for which the accounts are made up. — *varṣāhemanta* etc. : it seems that *varṣā* includes *śarad*, *hemanta* includes *śiśira* and *grīṣma* includes *vasanta*. In each of these three groups, the 3rd and 7th fortnights have fourteen days, the rest full 15 days. The short fortnights thus are the 1st fortnight in Bhādrapada, Kārttika and so on in every alternate month. This fortnight is the *kṛṣṇa pakṣa*, according to Cj; that is in consonance with Āṣāḍha full moon marking the end of the year and by implication of every month. These statements about short fortnights are not in agreement with the present day practice of calculating the *kṣaya* or *vṛddhi* of a *tithi*. Cs brings *varṣā* into relation with the sun's passing through the zodiacal signs of Leo, Virgo, Libra and Scorpio, and so on. For such an expanation, there is no justification in the

13 The (revenue) estimate, accrued revenue, outstanding revenue, income and expenditure and balance (are items in accounting).

14 The place, the sphere of activity, laying down the corpus (of income), receipts, the total of all (items of) revenue (and) the grand total, — this is (revenue estimate).

15 Deliveries into the treasury, what is taken by the king, and the expenses of the city, (these as) paid in, what is carried forward from last year, what is released by a decree and what is ordered by word of mouth, (these as) not to be remitted, — this is accrued revenue.

16 Acquiring (the fruits) on completion (of an undertaking), the remainder of fines, (these as) what has to be recovered, what is withheld by

text which is unaware of the *rāśis* ; besides, we would thus get solar months in which there can be no question of short or full *pakṣas*. — *pṛthag adhimāsakaḥ* : cf. 2.7.8 below. Cs's ' different from the solar month is the lunar month ' is quite unlikely.

14 *karaṇīya* seems to be a sort of (budget) estimate of revenue, made at the beginning of the year. — *saṁsthānam* ' situation, position ' seems to refer to locality, such as village, district etc. for which the estimate is made. Cb Cs understand ' assessment of revenue for an individual village ' ; Cj has ' regulations (*sthitiḥ*) such as this is to be done by this person only and at this time only, i.e., a royal order stating this.' Some such meaning suits 2.7.2, 3, and is not unlikely even here. Meyer has ' (expenses for the) continuation (of the administration).' — *pracāraḥ* : this seems to refer to the sphere of activity of the particular *adhyakṣa*. The commentators understand ' region (*deśa*).' — *śarīrāvasthāpanam* as in ss. 1-9 above. — *sarvasamudayapiṇḍaḥ saṁjātam* : the former seems to refer to the total of items under each of *durga, rāṣtra* etc., while the latter is the grand total of *durga, rāṣṭra* and others. Cb explains ' the taxable capacity of villages ' and ' the total of different kinds revenue ' respectively. Cj seems to understand ' estimated revenue ' and ' actual recoveries (which may be more or less) ' respectively. — Breloer (KSt, III, 196-197) finds here similarities with the system of budgeting under Peshwas. The final total, according to him, is the *ain jamā* or balance left after deductions are made for revenue officers, Inamdars etc. who received at source. Deductions, however, do not seem intended here. And state officers do not receive at source in this text. There are full salary lists in 5.3.

15 *praviṣṭam* is from Cb (supported by Cj's *praviṣṭaka-*) and seems necessary. It is one kind of *siddha* or accrued income, which is entered, i.e., actually paid in. *arpita* in *kośārpita* favours this reading as against *apraviṣṭam*. — *rājahāraḥ* : apparently some income went directly to the king and not through the treasury. —*puravyayaḥ* : the reference to *vyaya* is strange in this connection. Apparently income ear-marked for city-expenditure also did not go through the treasury. It is not easy to see the reasons for this. Cj has *parutsaṁvatsarā-* ; *parut* in the sense of ' last ' appears better than *parama-*, though it seems possible that the original reading was *carama-*. — *apātanīyam* is the other kind of *siddha* ; it has accured, but is not actually paid in. It may be last year's due not yet received or such as may have been allowed by the king to be paid in later, either by a written or an oral order. The income, however, is not to be dropped or surrendered (*apātaṇīya*) in any case. Cb reads *āpādanīya* ' which has to be brought in and delivered, ' which comes to the same thing. Cs understands this s. to refer to expenditure, not revenue and explains *āpātanīya* by ' to be deducted from revenue.' For *siddha* and *praviṣṭa*, cf. 2.8.18, 21.

16 *śeṣa* seems to refer to outstanding dues. It is also of two kinds *āharaṇīya* and *praśodhya*. — *siddhikarmayogaḥ* is from D and seems to convey the idea of acquiring the fruits of a work on its completion; income from the partly completed work is not immediately available, but would be received only when the whole work is completed. With *prakarma*, Cb has ' loan on interest, ' Breloer (KSt, III, 200-203) ' arrangements (*yoga*) for promotion (*prakarma* smoothening, polishing) of the establishment.' Cj seems to understand ' what is lent for house-building or what is used by an officer from what was given to him.' Cs has 'recovering unpaid taxes when crops etc. are ready,' which in effect is the same as the explanation adopted. — *daṇḍaśeṣam* is, according to Cb Cs, ' surplus left over from the

force and what is used (by officers), (these as) what must be cleared, — this is outstanding revenue, not containing goods of high value, and containing few goods of high value.

17 Current, outstanding and derived from other sources is (the three-fold) income. 18 What comes in from day to day is current (income). 19 What belongs to the preceding year or what is transferred from another sphere of activity, is outstanding (income). 20 What is lost and forgotten, fines imposed on employees, extra income, compensation for loss, gifts, property of a person involved in a riot, property of an issueless person and treasure-trove is income derived from other sources. 21 Balance due to (army-) disbandment and from undertakings (given up) in the middle because of sickness, is return from expenditure. 22 Accretion, viz., increase in the price of commodities at the time of sale, excess in weights and measures called surcharge or the increase in price because of competition for purchase, — this is (also) income.

army.' This hardly fits in here. A *ca* after this would have been better to mark off the two kinds of *āharaṇīya*. — *balātkṛtapratiṣṭabdham* : perhaps *-ṣṭambham* was the original reading ; else *kṛta* is superfluous. Cj understands *balātkṛta* in the sense of *balātkāra*. — *avamṛṣṭam* ' touched ' i.e., used ; ' *yan mukhyādibhir balād upayuktam* ' (Cj). The reading *avasṛṣṭam* ' remitted ' seems hardly appropriate. — The difference between *āharaṇīya* and *praśodhya* is that the former is easily recoverable, the latter only with some effort (Cb).— *asāram alpasāraṁ ca*, i.e., the dues must not contain goods of high value (*sāra*), only *phalgu* and *kupya*, or they must contain only few goods of high value. *vā* would be better instead of *ca*. Cb has ' yielding no fruits though expenses are incurred and yielding small fruit for high expenditure,' as two additional varieties of *śeṣa*. In that case, it is not clear why they are put after *śeṣam*. Cj reads *anādeyam* at the end and explains ' that (from a family, though normally tax-paying) without anything of value or having only few such things — not to be recovered.' This yields a good sense.

19 *parapracārasaṁkrāntaḥ* : this seems to refer to transfer from the sphere of activity of one *adhyakṣa* to that of another. Cb has ' what was due in one officer's time recovered by his successor, or what has come from the enemy's territory.' 20 *pārśvam* : the exact nature of this is not clear. Cb understands a surcharge on the fixed dues, Cp (on 2.15.3) a levy as recommended in 5.2, Breloer an impost for making good a deficit (III, p. 321). Cj Meyer understand a bribe. — *pārihīṇikam* is compensation for loss suffered, rather than ' penalty for failure to carry out the task, or, something received from a mortgagee ' (Cb). — *ḍamara* seems to be ' a revolt ' which would justify the confiscation of property. Cb understands ' booty obtained in a fight ' ; for that the usual word is *vilopa* (cf. 9.2.9. etc.).— *aputrakam* is not to be understood to refer to the son alone ; cf. 3.5.28. Meyer, however, would understand the expression in the literal sense. 21 The s., repeated in 2.15.10, describes lapsed grants. Two reasons for ' return from expenditure ' seem mentioned, *vikṣepa* ' disbandment of the troops ' and *vyādhitāntarārambha* ' undertaking given up midway because of illness or epidemics.' Some such word as *visṛṣṭa* or *parityakta* after *antarā* would have been better. For *vikṣepa*, see 7.9.22 ; 8.5.15 etc. Cb Cs have three items ' balance from army-expenditure, from expenses for medical hall and from other undertakings like *durga*, *antaḥpura* etc.' Provision for medical halls is not mentioned elsewhere. Meyer has ' windfall (*pratyāya*) for purposes of expenditure (*vyaya*) is sickness through bankruptcy or failure (of a private undertaking of the king) (*vikṣepavyādhita*) and remainder from an undertaking given up in the middle (*antarārambhaśeṣa*).' This is highly problematical. — *upajā* primarily refers to increase in the commodities (particularly live-stock) through natural causes ; cf. 2.29.8,11. A natural increase in price is meant here. Cb Cs Meyer undertsand ' what is obtained from prohibited sale.' — *mānonmānaviśeṣo* : this seems to be a description of *vyājī*, in which case it would refer to the 5% surcharge ; see s. 10 above. It is also possible that the expression is unconnected with *vyājī*, and refers to the difference between ordinary weights and measures and those used for receipts in the treasury, as in 2.19.21-23,29. See 2.15.11 below where *vyājī* seems distinguished from *tulāmānāntaram*.

23 Current (expenditure), that arising out of current, gain (and) that arising out of gain, — this is (four-fold) expenditure. 24 What is spent from day to day is current (expenditure). 25 Receipts (by officers, servants etc.) after a fortnight, a month or a year is gain. 26 That arising out of these two is (expenditure) arising out of current (expenditure) and out of gain respectively. This is expenditure.

27 What is left over after calculation of income and expenditure from the total of revenue-items is the balance, received and carried forward.

28 Thus the wise (Administrator) should fix the revenue and show an increase in income and decrease in expenditure and should remedy the opposite (of these).

CHAPTER SEVEN

SECTION 25 THE TOPIC OF ACCOUNTS IN THE RECORDS AND AUDIT OFFICE

1 The Superintendent should cause the Records Office to be built facing the east or the north, with separate halls, (as) a place for record-books.

2 There he should cause to be entered in the record-books: the extent of the number, activity and total (income) of the departments; the amount of increase or decrease in the use of the (various) materials, expenses, excess, surcharge, mixing, place, wages and labourers in connection with factories;

23 The difference between *nitya* and *lābha* is that the former expenditure is incurred from day to day, the latter at fixed intervals of time, a fortnight, a month, a year etc. Breloer remarks (KSt, III, 209-16) that the term *lābha* represents the point of view of the recipient, labourer, officer etc. as in *bhaktavetanalābha*, and that it is a sort of deferred payment. It may also stand for a lump payment. 26 *tayor utpannaḥ*, i.e., items of expenditure of the two types not foreseen at the time of the budget.

27 *saṁjātād āyavyayaviśuddhā*: what is meant is that from the total income the total expenditure is deducted. *saṁjātād āyād vyayaviśuddhā* or *saṁjātāyavyayaviśuddhā* would have been better. Perhaps the latter was the original reading. — *prāptā*, i.e., actually received in the treasury. — *anuvṛttā*, i.e., accrued but not actually delivered into the treasury; it is thus carried forward to the next account period.

28 *sādhayet*, i.e., overcome, remedy, take steps against. It is clear that the *samāhartṛ* fixes the assessment of revenue, prepares the budget and keeps the accounts.

2.7

According to Cj *akṣa* is what is used for counting, such as a pair of scales etc. and *paṭala* is a house (*akṣāṇi gaṇakopakaraṇāni paricchedasādhanatayā indriyāṇīva tulādīni, teṣāṁ paṭalaṁ gṛham*). *akṣa* primarily seems to refer to 'beads' used as counter or tally. As is clear from the Chapter, the *akṣapaṭala* is a records-cum-audit office.

1 *pratyaṅmukham* of G M is unlikely in view of 2.4.7 and other places.

2 *saṁkhyā-* is the total number of departments. — *pracāra* is the activity in which each department is engaged. — *saṁjāta* is the total income from the department; cf. 2.6.14, 27. — *dravyaprayogavṛddhikṣaya* is the increase or loss in weight or volume which

the price, the quality, the weight, the measure, the height, the depth and the container in connection with jewels, articles of high value, of low value and forest produce; laws, transactions, customs and fixed rules of regions, villages, castes, families and corporations; the receipt of favours, lands, use, exemptions, and food and wages by those who serve the king; the receipt of jewels and land (and) the receipt of special allowances and (payments for) remedial measures against sudden calamities, by the king and his queens and sons; and payments and receipts in connection with peace and war with allies and enemies.

3 From that he should hand over in writing the (revenue) estimate, accrued revenue, outstanding revenue, income and expenditure, balance, (the time for) attendance (for audit), (sphere of) activity, customs and fixed rules, to all the departments.

4 And over works of the highest, the middling and the lowest kinds, he should appoint a superintendent of that class, (but) over (works) bringing in revenue, a suitable (officer), by injuring whom (if necessary), the king

raw materials undergo in the process of manufacture as described in 4.1.8 ff. — *prayāma* refers to 'excess' in weight as in 2.19.24 (Cj). It may also refer to additions or extensions to the factory; addition to expenses (Breloer, KSt, III, 227-9) is also possible. — *yoga* is the mixing of materials in the process of manufacture. Cj gives the illustration of the mixing of colouring matter with gold as in 2.14.9. Meyer understands *yogasthāna* as 'the place of employment or work.' — *prativarṇaka* is the standard of quality, also quality. — *saṁghānām* as in D is necessary; cf. 3.7.40. — *dharma* seems to refer to peculiar laws about marriage, inheritance etc. prevalent in a region etc., which are authoritative for that region etc. — *vyavahāra* 'transactions,' i.e., agreements or contracts between parties; cf. 3.1.2-14. This implies that all agreements or contracts are to be registered with the state. Cb explains *vyavahāra* by 'cash and landed property that is inherited.' — *caritra* 'customs, usages,' which, unlike *dharma*, do not have the appearance of having a religious sanction. — *saṁsthāna*: this word cannot mean 'locality' here as it probably does in 2.6.14. Cj explains 'royal order, this should be done, this should not be done and so on (*saṁsthānaṁ saṁsthitī rājājñā atredaṁ kartavyam idaṁ na kartavyam iti*).' Breloer (KSt, III, 251 n.1), comparing this passage with 3.1.39, identifies *saṁsthāna* with *rājaśāsana* there, which is the explanation of Cj. The idea is clearly that of rules fixed by the state. Cb Cs construe *saṁsthāna* 'sticking to convention about' with each of *dharma*, *vyavahāra* and *caritra*. — *pragraha* 'favour, honour'; cf. s. 41 below. — *rājñaś ca patnīputrāṇām*: the *ca* should have come after *-putrāṇām*; if the king is not to be included, *ca* is unnecessary. *nirdeśa* is an extra allowance, according to Cb Cs; what is ordered by the king, according to Cj.— *autpātikapratīkāra* 'taking steps against portents, such as earthquakes etc.' (Cb, which mentions this as a v. l.). Cb's reading is *autpādika* 'money obtained during festivals etc.' It seems better to adopt a reading with which *pratīkāra* can be easily construed.

3 *tataḥ* may be 'from the accounts office' or 'from the record-book.' — *upasthānam*, i.e., time fixed for officers to come and render accounts (Cb). Similarly Breloer (KSt, III, 235-236). Meyer's 'outstanding and accrued income' as in 2.15.11 does not appear likely here. Russ. has 'side-income from office-presence.' — *prayacchet*: the subject is evidently *akṣapaṭalādhyakṣaḥ*. — Apparently the *āya*, *vyaya*, *nīvī* etc. would be those of the preceding year, though the *karaṇīya* would be that of the current year.

4 *tajjātikam*, i.e., an officer of the *uttama* kind for work of the *uttama* type and so on. — *sāmudayikeṣu*: we have to supply *karmasu* and explain with Cj 'of which the purpose is to bring in revenue (*samudayaprayojaneṣu āyasthāneṣu*).' The word is derived from *samudaya* 'revenue.' Cb Cs reading *sāmudāyikeṣu* supply *karmakareṣu* 'from among a large number of workmen capable of doing a work.' This is not satisfactory. — *upahatya*, i.e., inflicting a fine or corporal punishment (Cj), the punishment being for loss of state

would not regret. 5 His co-receivers, sureties, those living on his work, his sons, brothers, wives, daughters and servants shall bear the loss (incurred) in the work.

6 Three hundred and fifty-four days and nights constitute the year of work. 7 He should fix that as ending on the full moon day in Āṣāḍha, (whether) short or full. 8 He should provide the intercalary month with a (separate) bureau.

9 And (he should have) the acitivity (of departments) watched by spies. 10 For, the person in question (viz., the officer) if not conversant with the activity, customs and fixed rules, causes loss of revenue through ignorance, if unable to endure the trouble of (energetic) activity, through laziness, if addicted to the pleasures of the senses, sound and others, through remissness, if afraid of an uproar (among subjects) or of an unrighteous or harmful act, through fear, if inclined to show favour to those who have work with him, through love, if inclined to do them harm, through anger, because of reliance on learning or wealth or the support of a (royal) favourite, through arrogance, (and) because of (deceit in) introducing a difference in weight, measure, assessment or counting, (he causes loss) through greed.

11 'Among those (causes of loss of revenue), the fine is as much as the loss of money, increased by one-fold in each succeeding case according to the order (as stated above),' say the followers of Manu. 12 'In all cases (the fine shall be) eight times (the loss),' say the followers of Parāśara. 13 'Ten times;' say the followers of Bṛhaspati. 14 'Twenty times,' say the followers of Uśanas. 15 '(The fine shall be) in conformity with the offence,' says Kauṭilya.

16 The accounts should come in on the Āṣāḍha full moon day. 17 When the (officers) have come with sealed account books and balances

revenue, through ignorance etc. to be mentioned presently. 5 *sahagrāhiṇaḥ*, i.e., those who have received a share of the state revenue along with the officer. For the expression, cf. 3.11.14. — *karmopajīvinaḥ*, i.e., the staff and workmen. — As Cb Cj say the later one in the list becomes liable in the absence of each preceding one.

6 *karmasaṁvatsaraḥ* : this is the official year for completing the accounts of the various undertakings. 7 *Āṣāḍhīparyavasānam* : *pūrṇīmānta* months are clearly implied. — *ūnaṁ pūrṇaṁ vā*, i.e., whether the work is spread over the full year or only a part of it. Cb has 'in accordance with the period the officer was there.' 8 *karaṇādhiṣṭhitam* etc. : apparently the yearly accounts had only twelve sections, one for each month ; so accounts for the intercalary month were kept separately.

9 *apasarpādhiṣṭhitam* : supply *kuryāt* from the preceeding. 10 *saṁkrośa* 'outcry, uproar' ; cf. 1.17.39 above. — *tutāmāna*- etc. : For the four ways of assessing extent or size, see 2.21.15. — *upadhāna* 'placing near, introducing' implies substitution. Cf. 4.2.22. The word is related to *upadhi* 'fraud.'

11 *teṣām* refers to *ajñāna* etc. — *ekottaraḥ*, i.e., one-fold for *ajñāna*, two-fold for *ālasya*, three-fold for *pramāda* and so on. — *Mānavāḥ* : the rule is not found in the *Manusmṛti*.

17 *samudrapustakabhāṇḍanīvīkānām* : this seems to mean that accounts officers bring accounts in sealed books and works officers bring actual balances in sealed containers. —

in sealed containers, he should impose restriction in one place, not allowing conversation (among them). 18 After hearing the totals of income, expenditure and balance, he should cause the balance to be taken away (to the treasury). 19 And he should make the superintendent pay eightfold whatever may increase in the balance over the total of income (as shown) on the page inside (the account-books) or whatever the (officer) may cause to decrease (from the balance) because of (the inflation of) expenditure. 20 In the reverse cases, it shall fall to the lot of (the officer) himself.

21 For (officers) not coming at the proper time or coming without the account-books and balances, the fine shall be one-tenth of the amount due.

22 And if, when the works officer presents himself, the accounts officer is not ready for audit, the lowest fine for violence (shall be imposed). 23 In the reverse case, the fine for the works officer (shall be) double.

24 The high officers should render accounts in full in accordance with their activity, without contradicting themselves. 25 And among these he who makes a divergent statement or speaks falsely shall pay the highest fine (for violence).

ekatra asaṁbhāṣāvarodham, i.e., the two sets of officers are not to be allowed to converse among themselves. Breloer remarks that this is like treating them as witnesses (KSt, III, 246). 19 *antaraparṇe* is from D supported by Cb. *parṇa* seems to refer to the palm-leaf on which the accounts are written. *antaḥparṇe* would perhaps have been better 'on a leaf inside (the account-book).' Cs explains the reading *antaravarṇe* as 'in the book in which the actual balance is described,' which practically comes to the same thing. Meyer has 'in case of deviation (*antaravarṇe*) of the balance.' Breloer (KSt, III, 246-247) tentatively suggests 'between-counting' (?). —*vyayasya* : supply *agrāt* after this. —*parihāpayet* : *nīvyām* is to be understood with this. The balance is reduced because the expenditure is inflated. 20 *viparyaye*, i.e., when the actual balance is greater than what is shown in the account book or when expenses are shown to be less than those actually incurred. — *tam eva prati syāt*, i.e., the officer shall keep it. Breloer, however, has 'the state keeps the difference of what the officer has counted to his own disadvantage' (KSt, III, 247). The former idea seems better. Cf. the illustration '*yad atra māṁ prati syāt*,' in the *Siddhāntakaumudī*. Cj seems to understand that the officer is not to be punished, since he has spoken the truth. It also refers to the opinion that even this officer is to be fined eight times.

22 *kārmika* is obviously the officer concerned with the carrying out of the work, while the *kāraṇika* is the account-keeper. Cj understands the *akṣapaṭalika* by the latter. — *apratibadhnataḥ*, i.e., not being ready with his accounts. Cb has 'failing to write down.' Cj reads *anupanibadhnataḥ* here as well as in s. 34 below. Because of the high fine, Breloer (KSt, III, 250-1) understands 'not putting in proof, not being able to substantiate a discrepancy (*upasthita*).' This does not seem likely. 23 *dviguṇaḥ* : the fine is double because he has the actual *nīvī* with him and has failed to turn up with it.

24 *samagrāḥ* may be construed with *mahāmātrāḥ*, which is not very happy, or *nīvīḥ* may be understood as the substantive. But *samagrāṇi* (*gāṇanikyāni*) would have been better. — *aviṣamamantrāḥ* : 'not saying what is different,' i.e., not making contradictory statements. Meyer has 'not having dissimilar or unsuitable plans.' Cb Cs read *-mātrāḥ* and the latter explains 'should broadcast (*śrāvayeyuḥ*) all over the countryside (*pracārasamam*) all the related activities or a harmonized statement of income, expenditure and balance.' This is very doubtful. 25 *pṛthagbhūtaḥ* seems to be one whose statements do not tally with those of others, or rather, one who contradicts himself. Cb seems to understand one who has disappeared, made himself scarce.

26 He should wait for one month, if the (officer) has not brought in the day-to-day accounts. 27 After the month, the (officer) shall pay a fine of two hundred *paṇas* increased (by that amount) for each succeeding month. 28 If an (officer) has a little of written balance due (from him), he should wait for five days. 29 If he brings in the day-to-day accounts after that period, preceded by (delivery of the balance into) the treasury, he should look into (the case) with reference to laws, transactions, customs and fixed rules and by totalling up, (and by looking at) the work actually carried out, by inference and the use of spies.

30 And he should check (the accounts) for each day, group of five days, fortnight, month, four months and year. 31 He should check the income with reference to the period, place, time, head of income, source, bringing forward, quantity, the payer, the person causing payment to be made, the recorder and the receiver. 32 He should check the expenditure with reference to the period, place, time, head (of expenditure), gain, occasion, the thing given, its use and amount, the person who orders, the person who takes out, the person who delivers and the receiver. 33 He should check the balance with reference to the period, place, time, head, bringing forward, the article, its characteristics, amount, the vessel in which it is deposited and the person guarding it.

34 If, in an affair of the king, the accounts officer is not ready for audit or disregards an order or changes the income and expenditure in

26 *akṛtāhorūpaharam* : *ahorūpa* seems to refer to the day-to-day accounts, and the expression refers to the officer who fails to bring such accounts. A month is allowed to bring them in. This implies that the day-to-day accounts for a month are allowed to be completed by the end of the next month. 28 *alpaśeṣalekhyanīvīkam*, i.e., when a small part of the balance as arrived at in the account-book is not brought in. This apparently refers to the works officer, while the preceding ss. referred to the accounts officer. — *pañcarātram* apparently in the case of the monthly account. 29 *kośapūrvam ahorūpaharam*: i.e, the balance due is delivered in the treasury and the relevant accounts are brought in after a lapse of five days. Though the accounts officer is also thought of (*ahorūpahara*), the works officer would seem to be principally concerned. — *saṁkalana* evidently refers to the totalling of items in the accounts. — *avekṣeta* : the purpose of this investigation is to find out if the delay in delivery was justified or not. — Ms. D breaks off towards the beginning of this s., there being only one more folio containing 2.11.21-39.

30 *pratisamānayet* : the object is 'accounts.' 31 *vyuṣṭa* refers to the period for which the accounts are made up, '*yathā pravardhamāne pañcadaśarājavarṣe*' (Cj). See 2.6.12 above. — *utpatti* refers to the source included in *āyaśarīra*. — *anuvṛtti* is being brought forward from the preceding period of account. — *pramāṇa* : Breloer suggests *parimāṇa* in conformity with the reading of mss. in the next two ss. However, *pramāṇa* might appear better in all three ss. — *dāpaka* is the person on whose behalf the payment is made. Cb does not seem to have read this word. 32 *lābha*, i.e., payments to employees; cf. s. 2 above — *yoga* 'application,' i.e., use to which the article would be put. — *vidhātṛka* is an emendation suggested by Meyer 'who arranges the delivery.' Of the other readings only *nidhātṛka* 'store-keeper' of Cb Cs conveys any sense. Cj seems to derive its *viyātaka* from *yat* 'to strive'. 33 *anuvartana* is obviously the same as *anuvṛtti*. — *rūpa*, i.e., the article or object constituting the *nīvī*.

34 *rājārthe*: this seems to refer to state undertakings, as distinguished from the work of collecting taxes, fines etc. from subjects. — *kāraṇika*, it is clear, is not an officer in the audit office, as Cj seems to have understood in s. 22 above. — *pratiṣedhayato* : as the fine would appear small if we refer this only to disregarding the king's order, Breloer (KSt,

a way different from the written order, the lowest fine for violence (shall be imposed).

35 For one writing down an item (in the accounts) without any order or in a wrong order or in an illegible manner, or twice over, the fine is twelve *paṇas*. 36 For one writing down the balance (in any of these ways) the fine is double (that). 37 For one who swallows it, the fine is eight-fold. 38 For one who destroys it, the fine is one-fifth of the amount and restitution (of what is lost). 39 In case of a false statement, the punishment is that for theft. 40 If admitted afterwards, (the fine is) double, so also if an item is forgotten and then brought in.

41 The (king) should put up with a minor offence and should be content even when the revenue is small; and he should honour with favours the officer who confers great benefit (on the state).

CHAPTER EIGHT

SECTION 26 RECOVERY OF REVENUE MISAPPROPRIATED BY STATE EMPLOYEES

1 All undertakings are dependent first on the treasury. 2 Therefore, he should look to the treasury first.

3 Prosperousness of activities, cherishing of customs, suppression of thieves, control over employees, luxuriance of crops, abundance of commodities, deliverance from trouble, reduction in exemptions, (and) presents in cash, — these are (the means of) increase in the treasury.

III, 262) understands 'who suppresses an order.' — *ājñānibandha* is the written statement handed out at the beginning concerning heads of income etc., as laid down in s. 3 above.

35 *kramāvahīna* is 'lacking in order,' while *utkrama* is 'in a wrong order.' — *avalikhataḥ* is not necessarily 'who enters wrongly,' for it cannot be understood of *avijñātam*; 'who writes down' is enough. — *vastukam*, i.e., an item in the ledger. 36 *avalikhataḥ* in this case may be understood as 'who writes down less (than the actual balance)' as in Cs, though that is not necessary. The reading *avalihato* is found in this s. in Cj which explains 'who tastes, i.e, swallows a little (*īṣad āsvādayataḥ*).' 38 *pañcabandhaḥ* cannot be five times (Cs Meyer), in view of 2.8.11; 3.1.20; 3.11.33 etc. 40 *pratijñāte*, i.e., when an admission is made that a false statement was made by him earlier. — *dviguṇaḥ* : double the fine for theft might appear too severe in the case of *prasmṛtotpanna*. Meyer therefore thinks of double the 12 *paṇas* prescibed in s. 35. That does not appear very likely.

41 Cj reads *samopakāram* and explains 'who brings in appropriate revenue to the treasury.'

2.8

1 *kośapūrvāḥ* etc. : contrast 8.1.23 and the discussion in 8.1.33-52 below.

2 *pracāra* may, as usual, be understood as departmental activity rather than as 'country' (Cj Cs). — *anugraha* is maintenance, preservation as before. — *pratiṣedha*, i.e., keeping a strict control or check rather than 'dismissal.' — *upasarga* 'troubles' such as fire, floods etc.

4 Hindrance, lending, trading, concealment, causing loss, use, interchange and misappropriation, — these are (the causes of) depletion of the treasury.

5 Failure to carry out a work, failure to realize its fruit, or failure to deliver it (in the treasury), constitutes hindrance. 6 For that the fine is one-tenth (the amount involved).

7 Lending at interest of goods from the treasury is lending. 8 Trading in (state) commodities is trading. 9 In those cases, the fine is double the fruit.

10 If the (officer) makes the due date as not due or the date not due as due, that is concealment. 11 For that the fine is one-fifth.

12 If the (officer) causes a diminution of the revenue fixed or causes an increase in the expenditure sanctioned, that is causing loss. 13 For that the fine is four times the amount lost.

14 The use of the king's goods by oneself or allowing it by others is use. 15 For that, the punishment is execution for use of jewels, the middle fine for violence for use of articles of high value, (restitution of) that and an equal amount as fine for use of articles of small value and forest produce.

16 The appropriation of the king's goods by (the substitution of) other goods is interchange. 17 That is explained by (rules concerning) use.

18 If the (officer) does not deliver the income that has accrued (or) does not pay the expenses put down in writing (or) denies the balance received, — that is misappropriation. 19 For that the fine is twelve times (the amount).

20 Of those (officers) the ways of embezzlement are forty. 21 What has accrued first is realized afterwards, what is to accrue later is realized first, what is to be carried out is not carried out, what is not to be carried out is

4 *avastāra* 'exceeding one's authority' (Russ.).

5 *siddhi* refers to securing the fruits of an undertaking, recovery of revenue, taxes etc. Its *asādhana* is not carrying out the work at all, *anavatāraṇa* is not securing the fruit produced and *apraveśana* is not delivering it into the treasury. Cj explains *anavatāraṇa* by 'not writing down in the accounts (*lekhyākaraṇam*).' — Cp begins with this s. and continues to the end of the Book.

8 *phala*, i.e., the interest received or profit made.

18 *prāptāṁ nīvīm* seems to refer to the balance received by and in the possession of the officer.

20 *catvāriṁśat*: the passage is referred to in the *Daśakumāracarita*, VIII. 21 *pūrvaṁ siddham* etc. : the recovery of the income accrued is delayed, evidently in consideration of gratification received. — *kṛtam*, i.e. made out, represented. — *anyataḥ* refers to the source of the income. — Cs understands *deyaṁ na dattam adeyaṁ dattam* as a single case of misappropriation, similarly *kāle na dattam akāle dattam*. There is little justification for this. — *anyato dattam* : Cs understands *tas* in the sense of the dative; that is better, though the sense of the ablative is also not unlikely. — From *praviṣṭam* onwards offences by treasury and stores officers are mentioned. — *kupyam adattamūlyaṁ praviṣṭam* : Cp Cs explain 'a thing is borrowed at the king's command; after a time a part of the price is paid, making the entry that full price is paid.' There is no reference to part-payment

carried out, what is carried out is made out as not carried out, what is not carried out is made out as carried out, what is carried out a little is made out as much, what is carried out much is made out as little, one thing is carried out while another is made out (as carried out), what is carried out from one source is made out as from another, what is to be paid is not paid, what is not to be paid is paid, payment is not made in time, payment is made untimely, a little paid is made out as much, what is overpaid is made out as little, one thing is given while another is made out as given, what is paid to one is made out as paid to another, what is delivered (into the treasury) is made out as not delivered, what is not delivered is made out as delivered, forest produce for which the price has not been paid is delivered, that for which the price has been paid is not delivered, concentration (of goods) is made out as dispersal, or dispersal made out as concentration, an object of high value is changed for one of low value, or one of low value for one of high value, the price is raised, or (the price is) reduced, the year is made discrepant as to months, or the month discrepant as to days, discrepancy as to source, discrepancy as to head (of income etc.), discrepancy as to workmen, discrepancy in performance, discrepancy in the sum-total, discrepancy in quality, discrepancy in price,

here. It seems that the price is not paid from the treasury, yet the stores officer receives the goods, to be afterwards appropriated by him, the sufferer being the person from whom the goods are received. —*dattamūlyaṁ na praviṣṭam*: Cp Cs have 'a thing purchased at a high price is entered as purchased at a lower price.' There is no reference to high or low price here. The case is clearly one where the price is paid from the treasury, but the goods are not received in the stores. Meyer understands *praviṣṭa* as 'entered in the register' when sales are made from stores to merchants. In the first case, the merchant pays less though the entry shows the regular price. But can *adatta* mean 'paid less'? —*saṁkṣepo vikṣepaḥ kṛtaḥ*: from here onwards, market officers are to be understood. For these terms see 2.16.1. The commentators understand 'aggregate tax to be paid by a village etc.' and 'splitting a tax among individuals (Cp Cs) or collecting it from one individual only (Cb).' In the opposite case, '*vikṣepa*, i.e., a tax to be received from an individual in small instalments and *saṁkṣepa*, i.e., recovering it at one time in a lump sum.' All this seems unlikely. —*mahārgham alpārgheṇa parivartitam*: the purchaser suffers in this case, while in the opposite case the treasury suffers. — *samāropito 'rghaḥ*: the *paṇyādhyakṣa*, who fixes prices (2.16.2-3), might do so to his own advantage. —After *pratyavaropito vā*, Cb Cp and the editions add *rātrayaḥ samāropitāḥ pratyavaropitā vā*. G M do not show these cases; they are also unnecessary in view of *māso divasaviṣamaḥ kṛtaḥ*. And with the deletion of these expressions the number forty is very smoothly arrived at. —*saṁvatsaro* etc.: from here onwards, works-foremen are thought of. The idea in this case is, when there is an intercalary month, that fact is not taken into account when making payments on a yearly basis. —*māso* etc.: the number of days in the month are manipulated to the detriment of the workers. —*samāgamaviṣamaḥ*: here and in the following cases, *viṣama* seems to stand for *viṣamatva*, though it can be understood as an adjective to *upāyaḥ*. *samāgama* seems to be the same as *āgama* and to refer to 'source' (Meyer), though Cp Cs explain it as 'the presence of labourers at the time of payment of wages.' —It is proposed to read *kārmika-* for *dhārmika-*. The latter is explained as defalcation by the *purohita* and his men from amounts sanctioned for charitable purposes like gifts to Brahmins (Cb Cp Cs.). This is unsatisfactory. We expect *dharma-* not *dhārmika-*. And since the preceding and the following cases have reference to some work carried out by an *adhyakṣa*, *kārmika* would appear far more likely. The idea is of discrepancy in the matter of workmen (their number, wages etc.). —*nirvartana-*: Meyer prefers to read *nivartana* 'because of the ceasing of a particular source of income.' In all these cases, however, the reason for the fraud is not stated, only the item in connection with which the fraud is committed. —*piṇḍa* is the total amount of the commodity or income. — Cp shows no explanation of *piṇḍaviṣamaḥ*. —*varṇa* 'class,' i.e., quality of the commodity. Cf. 4.2.22. A reference to the four discrepancy in weighing, discrepancy in measuring, (and) discrepancy as to (container) vessels, — these are the (forty) ways of embezzlement.

22 In these cases, he should interrogate, each individually, the subordinate officer, the store-keeper, the recorder, the receiver, the person who pays, the person who causes the payment to be made, the adviser and the help-mate. 23 And in case of a false statement by these, the fine shall be the same as for the officer (concerned). 24 And he should issue a proclamation in the sphere of his activity, 'Those wronged by such and such an officer should communicate (it to me).' 25 To such as communicate, he should cause payment to be made in accordance with the injury suffered.

26 And in case of many accusations, if the (officer) denies (all charges) and is proved guilty in a single case, he shall be liable for all. 27 In case of partial admission, he shall stand trial in all cases. 28 And in case of misappropriation of a large amount of money, if proved guilty with respect to even a small part of it, he shall be liable for all.

29 An informer, to whom a guarantee is given against reprisal (by the officer), should receive one-sixth part (of the amount involved) if the matter is proved, one-twelfth part if (he happens to be) a state servant. 30 If in an accusation concerning a large amount, only a small portion is proved, he shall receive a share of what is proved. 31 In case it is not proved, he shall receive corporal or monetary punishment, and no favour shall be shown to him.

32 But (if) when the charge is being proved, the informer, at the instigation of the accused (officer), were to throw up the case or to make himself scarce, he shall be condemned to death.

varṇas (Cs) can hardly be understood and 'fineness or touch of gold' (also Cs) unnecessarily restricts the sense to a particular case only.

22 *upayukta* is a subordinate officer (Meyer) rather than a supervising or higher officer (Cp Cs). Cf. 2.5.16. — *nidhāyaka* seems to be the store-keeper as in Cs. — G M read *mantrimantrivaiyā-* etc.; one *-mantri-* is clearly superfluous. It is possible, however, that one *-mantri-* is a corruption of *-mitra-*. Cf. 2.9.25, also 4.8.9 (where we have *sahāya*).

26 *parokṭaḥ* : see 3.1.19 ff. 27 *vaiṣamye*, i.e., when some charges are admitted and others denied (Cp Cs). Cj has alternately 'when different persons bring different charges against him.' — *anuyoga* 'questioning, interrogation' apparently by the *pradeṣṭṛs*. 28 *-apahāre* is to be preferred to *-apacāre* in the context of this Chapter.

29 *sūcaka* who secretly informs against an officer involved in fraud. — *pratighāta* is reprisal by the officer ; cf. 7.6.26; 9.6.27. For *avasthā* 'guarantee,' cf. 8.4.33. Cp has '*avasthaḥ pratibhūḥ*.' 31 *na cānugrāhyaḥ* : this does not necessarily mean 'he is not to be saved from the vengeance of the officer' (Cs).

32 Meyer's construction, supplying *yadi* in the first half, is adopted. That appears to be the construction in Cj as well : *niṣpattau pramāṇaiḥ saṁbhāvitāyām* 'when the charge is likely to be proved.' Cb explains the first half 'when it is proved, the informer should say that the information was given to him by some one else and should remain hidden.' Similarly Cp : 'should transfer the blame of being an informer to treasonable persons or plead an alibi (*ātmānam apavāhayet*)' supplying *dūṣye* in the first half. Cs has 'when the matter is proved, he should cease the accusation and (*vā*) free himself from the bondage of the case (*ātmānam apavāhayet*).' The idea rather seems to be that the informer after making the accusation, withdraws it at the instigation of the accused or fails to appear for proving his charge.

CHAPTER NINE

SECTION 27 INSPECTION OF (THE WORK OF) OFFICERS

1 All superintendents, endowed with the excellences of a minister, should be appointed to works according to (their) capacity. 2 And he should constantly hold an inspection of their works, men being inconstant in their minds. 3 For, men being of a nature similar to that of horses change when employed in works. 4 Therefore, he should be cognizant of the worker, the office, the place, the time, the work to be done, the outlay and the profit in these (undertakings).

5 They should carry out the works according to orders, without concerting together or quarrelling amongst themselves. 6 Concerting together, they might swallow up (the fruits of) the undertakings, quarrelling, they might ruin (them). 7 And they must not commence any work without informing the king, excepting measures against calamities.

8 And in cases of remissness on their part, he should fix a fine double the day's wages and (other) expenses,. 9 And he who, amongst them, caries out the work as ordered or better, should receive a (high) position and honour.

10 'If an (officer) with small income has a large expenditure, he consumes (state revenue). 11 In the reverse case and when an (officer) spends in conformity with his income, he does not consume,' thus say the teachers. 12 Only through spies would (this) be ascertained, says Kauṭilya.

13 He who causes loss of revenue consumes the property of the king. 14 If he causes loss through ignorance and other causes, he should make him pay that, suitably multiplied. 15 He who procures double the (normal) revenue, consumes the countryside. 16 If he brings in (the whole) for the king, he should be warned in case of a minor offence, in case of a major offence

2.9

upayukta ordinarily 'a subordinate officer' is here used for 'officer' in general. The Chapter in fact uses the word *yukta* and does not use *upayukta* even once.

4 *karaṇa* 'office, department' (Cp) seems better than 'way of doing or means of doing' (Cj). Cj seems to add *dravyam* after *karaṇam*. — *prakṣepa* 'investment, outlay' is common in this text. 'Wages of workmen' (Cp Cs) is an unnecessary restriction.

6 Cf. 1.15.37 above.

8 *-vetanavyaya-* 'wages and (other) expenses' rather than 'expenses on wages.'

9 *yathādiṣṭam* etc. : cf. 1.8.13 which is a quotation from Piśuna.

14 *ajñānādibhiḥ* refers to the eight causes mentioned in 2.7.10. — *yathāguṇam*, i.e. 1,2,3 etc. times in case of *ajñāna*, *ālasya*, *pramāda* etc. respectively. In 2.7.11-15, this scale of fines is attributed to the Mānavas, while Kauṭilya himself preferred punishment according to offence. Meyer thinks that we should read *yathāparādham* instead of *yathāguṇam* here as well. Cp Cs understand 'double, three times, etc. according to the offence,' i.e., apparently according to repetition of the offence. This also seems likely.

should be punished according to the offence. 17 He who makes out as expenditure the revenue (he has raised) consumes the works of men. 18 He should be punished according to the offence in cases of loss (or waste) of days of work, the price of goods and the wages of men.

19 Therefore, he who is appointed by an order to a particular department shall communicate to him (i.e., the king) the real nature of that work and the income and expenditure (both) in detail and in the aggregate.

20 And he should keep in check the patrimony-squanderer, the immediate-spender and the niggardly. 21 He who consumes in unjust ways the property inherited from the father and the grand-father is the patrimony-squanderer. 22 He who straightway consumes whatever is produced is the immediate-spender. 23 He who amasses wealth by putting his dependents and himself to suffering is the niggardly. 24 If he has a (large) party (dependent on him), he is not to be deprived of property; in the opposite case, he should be deprived of all property.

25 Of that niggardly officer who, placed in charge of a large amount of revenue, stores it, deposits it or sends it out, — stores it in his own house, deposits it with citizens or country people, sends it out to an enemy's territory, — a secret agent should find out the party of advisers, friends, dependents and kinsmen as well as the coming in and going out of goods. 26 And having

17 *samudayaṁ vyayam upanayati*: Cb Cp Cs Meyer understand 'who brings in the expenditure as income,' i.e., the sanctioned expenditure instead of being spent on the work is returned to the treasury as income from that work. For this we expect *vyayaṁ samudayam (iti) upanayati*. As the parallel ss. 13, 15 show, *samudayam* is the object, not part of the predicate. Moreover, on this explanation, there is no *apahāra* to which the next s. refers. The idea rather is that the income actually raised from the work is represented as expenditure. Thus no benefit is derived by the state and the labour of workmen is wasted so far as the state is concerned. The difference between s. 13 and this s. is that in the former case no revenue (or less revenue) is produced, while in this case revenue is produced, but spent away instead of being brought to the treasury. 18 *karmadivasa-* etc.: with Meyer, three things should be understood, *karmadivasa, dravyamūlya* and *puruṣavetana*. Cp Cs understand two things 'loss of the price fixed for the fruit of the work that would have been achieved on those days and loss of wages by the labourers.' —There is *apahāra* in this case because the net income is pocketed by the officer. It may be calculated on the basis of *karmadivasa* etc. that are lost.

24 Cp Cs understand by *sa* all three. However, only the niggardly seems meant, as Cj shows. The confiscation of property thought of has hardly any scope in the first two cases. — *anādeyaḥ*: according to Cs, though his property may not be seized, he himself is to be removed from office. That is not certain. — *paryādātavyaḥ*: Cb has 'should be removed from office.' Cf. however 5.2.54, 58 where this meaning seems unlikely. The confiscation of all property is meant.

25 *saṁnidhatte...paraviṣaye* has to be understood as parenthetical. It is possible that this is a marginal gloss that has got into the text. 26 *saṁcāram* 'movement,' i.e., coming

insinuated himself into the confidence of that (servant) of his who might be making movements (to and fro) in the enemy's territory, he should find out the secret. 27 When it is fully ascertained, he should cause him to be executed on the pretext of a letter from the enemy.

28 Therefore, his superintedents should carry out the works accompanied by accountants, writers, examiners of coins, receivers of balances and supervisors. 29 Supervisors are those who ride elephants, horses and chariots. 30 Their assistants, endowed with skill and integrity, (should work) as spies over the accountants and others.

31 He should establish (each) department with many heads and without permanency (of tenure of office).

32 Just as it is not possible not to taste honey or poison placed on the surface of the tongue, even so it is not possible for one dealing with the money of the king not to taste the money in however small a quantity.

33 Just as fish moving inside water cannot be known when drinking water, even so officers appointed for carrying out works cannot be known when appropriating money.

34 It is possible to know even the path of birds flying in the sky, but not the ways of officers moving with their intentions concealed.

35 And he should make those who have amassed (money wrongfully) yield it up and should change them in (their) works, so that they do not consume (the king's) property or disgorge what is consumed.

36 But those who do not consume (the king's) goods and increase them in just ways, should be made permanent in their offices, being devoted to what is agreeable and beneficial to the king.

in and going out. — *anupraviśya* : cf. 1.17.39; 1.18.9. 27 *śatruśāsanāpadeśena*, i.e., with a forged letter supposedly written by the enemy to the officer, suggesting that the money sent by the latter was received by him.

29 *uttarādhyakṣāḥ* : these are evidently trained in the army and work as supervisors ostensibly for guarding the works and protecting royal property. They could hardly be 'deputy *adhyakṣas*' as Stein (AOr, 6, 42) thinks.

31 *anityam* implies frequency of transfer from department to department.

32 *arthacara* 'an officer handling money.'

34 *caratām* : Meyer following Sorabji understands the idea of 'grazing, feeding on,' i.e., swallowing, adding that *car* is still used in this sense in India. That is however not certain.

CHAPTER TEN

SECTION 28 THE TOPIC OF EDICTS

1 They declare that as *śāsana* (edict) which is used for giving (directions or) orders. 2 For, kings principally depend on edicts, peace and war being rooted in them.

3 Therefore, the scribe should be endowed with the excellences of a minister, conversant with all conventions, quick in composing, with a beautiful hand and capable of reading a document.

4 He should listen with an attentive mind to the command of the king and set it down in writing, which is precise in meaning, with a courteous mention of the country, the sovereignty, the family and the name in the case of a king, and with the customary mention of the country and the name in the case of one who is not a king.

5 Having taken into consideration, in (every) matter, the caste, the family, the position, age and learning, the profession, property and character, also the place and time and connections by marriage, he should compose the document in conformity with the person (addressed).

6 Arrangement of subject-matter, connection, completeness, sweetness, exaltedness and lucidity constitute the excellences of writing. 7 Among them, arranging in a proper order, the statement first of the principal matter, is arrangement of subject-matter. 8 The statement of a subsequent matter without its being incompatible with the matter in hand, right up to the end, is connection. 9 Absence of deficiency or excess of matter, words and letters, description in detail of the matter by means of reasons, citations and illustrations, (and) expressiveness of words, is completeness. 10 The use of words

2.10

1 *śāsane*, i.e., for issuing directions or orders. It may also mean 'for purposes of administration.' 2 *tanmūlatvāt saṁdhivigrayoḥ*: Stein (ZII, 6, 48) thinks that these words are a gloss, as they do not apply to all *śāsanas* or written documents. However, the clause seems quite genuine as it supports the statement *śāsanapradhānā rājānaḥ* where *rājaśāsana* alone can be thought of.

3 *samaya* may be 'conventions' of writing or customs of different classes of men (Cp Cs); Cp adds that according to some, it means 'script' or 'language.' — *āśugranthaḥ* may be 'quick in composing' or 'quick in writing'. Cj reads *āśugrathanaḥ*, which is better.

4 Cp seems to have read *niścityārtham*.

8 Cp Cj read *prakṛtasya* for *prastutasya*. 9 *udāharaṇa* is, according to Cb Cs, 'conformity with statements in the *śāstras*' and *dṛṣṭānta* 'an instance from actual life.' — *aśrāntapadatā*: according to the commentators, this means 'the use of a word (e.g. *saṁdhatsva*) for a sentence (e.g. *saṁdhiṁ kuru*).' This would be economy of words. The expression literally means 'having words that are not tired or exhausted,' i.e., probably words which retain their power of expression, expressive words. Russ. has 'being without superfluous prolixity.'

with a charming meaning easily conveyed is sweetness. 11 The use of words that are not vulgar is exaltedness. 12 The employment of words that are well-known is lucidity.

13 The letters (in the alphabet) beginning with *a* are sixty-three. 14 A combination of letters is a word. 15 That is four-fold: noun, verb, preposition and particle. 16 Among them, a noun signifies being. 17 A verb, not having a specific gender, is indicative of action. 18 Those that qualify an action, *pra* and others, are prepositions. 19 Indeclinables, *ca* and others, are particles. 20 A collection of words constitutes a sentence, when the sense is completed. 21 A group with a minimum of one word and a maximum of three words should be made, not conflicting with the meaning of the other words.

22 For concluding the writing, the word *iti* and (the sub-script) 'These are the words of so and so' (should be used).

13 *varṇās triṣaṣṭiḥ*: these are 22 vowels (5 short, 8 long and 9 *pluta*), 25 mutes (*k, kh . . . m*), 4 semi-vowels, 4 non-combinables (*anusvāra, visarga, jihvāmūlīya* amd *upadhmānīya*), 4 sibilants, and 4 *yama*-conjuncts (doubles of the first four in each group of mutes before the nasal of the same group). This is according to the *Taittirīya Prātiśākhya* and the *Pāṇinīya Śikṣā*. 14 *varṇasaṁghātaḥ padam*: Stein (ZII, 6, 51-2) thinks that this definition is incomplete and should be corrected to *varṇās triṣaṣṭir varṇasaṁghātaḥ*; *varṇasamudāyo 'kṣaram*; *tatsamudāyaḥ padam*, as in the *Vājasaneya Prātiśākhya* (8.50). There seems little justification for doing so. — *taccaturvidham*: cf. *Nirukta* 1.1.8 ff. Stein points to similarities with the *Vājasaneya* and *Ṛk Prātiśākhyas*, but though he states that the conclusion from all this could be that this text represents pre-Paṇinian knowledge, he adds 'a corresponding chronological deduction can hardly be made.' It is not easy to see why not. 16 *sattva* 'being' is distinguished in the *Nirukta* from *bhāva* 'becoming.' 20 Stein compares the *Tarkasaṁgraha*. 21 *vargaḥ*: according to the commentators this means 'a compound,' and the idea is, it should have 1 to 3 words in addition to the first, i.e., a compound should have 2 to 4 words. The compound should also be in conformity with the later words (2nd to 4th, *parapadārthānuparodhena*). Only Cj understands *parapada* as the principal word, which may be the first (as in *pūrvakāya*) or second (as in *rājapuruṣa*) or both (as in *dharmārthau*) or outside the compound (as in *bahuputra*). Cb offers another explanation 'groups of words should be so formed that they are not likely to be wrongly construed with the preceding or the following words. E.g., after *purāṇaṁ mānavo dharmaḥ svako vedaś cikitsitam, ājñāsiddhāni catvāri*, we should have *hantavyāni na hetubhiḥ*, and not *na hantavyāni hetubhiḥ*; for, in the latter case, *na* is likely to be construed with *ājñāsiddhāni*.' This is referred to as the opinion of 'some' in Cp and is reproduced in Cs. Cs has another explanation in which *eka . . . paraḥ* alone is taken to refer to compounds as above and *parapadārthā-* etc. is understood to mean 'pause, i.e, the sign of a pause, such as a comma etc. should be made, without harming the sense of the following words.' There seems no reason, however, why *ekapada-* etc. should be understood independently of the latter. This explanation of the entire s. may well have been intended. Meyer understands *varga* as 'accumulation' i.e., padding, in order to make the sense of one word clear or to strengthen it. 'A whole with a single meaning' (Russ.) evidently refers to a compound. — *anurodhena* and *anuparodhena* ultimately mean the same thing.

22 *vācikam asya*: Cp Cs have 'when a part of the message is not written down but is to be communicated by the person carrying the letter, the words "oral message should be heard from the bearer of this letter" should be added at the end.' This agrees with *Mudrārākṣasa*, Act 5, but is extremely doubtful here. The reference is only to the writing of the name of the person on whose behalf the letter is written. Cj supplies *śraddheyam* 'the words of so and so must be believed' adding that this is possible only in the case of the *vācikalekha* of s. 43 below.

23-24 Censure, praise, query, statement, request, refusal, reproof, prohibition, injunction, appeasement, help, threatening and propitiation, with these thirteen are matters arising out of writing concerned.

25 Among these, mention of defects concerning birth, body or actions is censure. 26 Mention of the merits of these same is praise. 27 'How is this so?' is query. 28 'Thus (it is)' is statement. 29 'Give (it to me)' is request. 30 'I will not give' is refusal. 31 '(This is) unworthy of you' is reproof. 32 'Do not do (so)' is prohibition. 33 'Let this be done' is injunction. 34 'What I am is you; what object belongs to me is yours' this conciliation is appeasement. 35 Aid in calamities is help. 36 Pointing to the future as full of danger is threatening. 37 Propitiation is threefold, in doing a thing, in case of transgression and during the calamity of a person and so on.

38 Documents of communication, command and gift, documents of exemption and authorization, (the document) giving news of happenings, the document in reply and (the document) applicable everywhere, — these are (types of) decrees.

39 'So and so has communicated; he has said so; hence let it be given if there be truth (in it)', 'He has spoken of an excellent deed in the presence of the king,' this is communication stated to be of various kinds.

40 Where there is the command of the king concerning punishment or favour, especially in the matter of servants, that is the characteristic of a decree of command.

41 Where honour, rendered in accordance with merits, is to be seen, whether in distress or when making a gift, those two become (decrees of) favour.

24 *abhyupapattiḥ* : both here and in s. 35 this is how the word must be read (as in Cj Cp) and not as *abhyavapattiḥ* as in the mss. The latter means 'surrender' as in 12.1.11. — *arthāḥ lekhajāḥ*, i.e., subject-matter of a writing.

37 *arthakṛtau*, i.e., for the sake of getting some work of one's own done. — *atikrame*, i.e., in case of transgression by oneself. — *puruṣādi-*, i.e., when some person is in distress etc. — Stein (ZII, 6,56-7) has pointed out that a partly agreeing list is found in the *Bṛhaddevatā*, 1.35 ff., *Nirukta*, 7.3, *Kāvyādarśa*, 2.30 ff. and the lexicons.

39 According to Cb Cp Cs there are two communications here, one in the first two lines and the other in the third line, both from persons at the court to officers away from court. The first communication is 'some one has told the king (that you have discovered a treasure-trove and have appropriated it); on that the king has said thus (if the officer does not hand it over, I shall recover double from him). So better hand over if there is truth (in the report about the treasure-trove).' The second is 'some one has told the king that you have done a good deed.' Cj seems to understand in the first communication 'you are reported to have a horse worthy of the king; if true, give it to him' and in the second 'I have learnt from the king that your act is approved and you will certainly get some benefit.' — The use of both *ced* and *yadi* is rather strange.

41 Cp understands *paridāne* twice, once as loc. sing. like *ādhau* and again as nom. dual in the sense of *paridānalekhau* with *upagrahau* as adjective to it in the sense of 'occa-

42 The favour, which (is conferred) at the command of the king, on the various castes and on the different cities, villages and regions, the expert should designate as (the decree of) exemption.

43 The delegation of authority in the matter of doing a work and in the matter of issuing orders, this may be a document authorizing (the issuing of) orders or even containing an authorization (for doing a work).

44 With respect to a document, they designate happenings as of two kinds, (viz.,) those associated with the divine, of various kinds, and those concerning men, based on facts.

45 After seeing the document as it really is and then after reading it out, the document in reply should be prepared exactly as the words of the king (may be).

46 That, in which the king asks the princes and officers to ensure protection and comforts for travellers, would be (the decree) called applicable everywhere; it should be known on the road, in the country and everywhere (else).

47 The means are conciliation, gifts, dissension and force.

sions for showing favour.' The difficulty is that *paridāne* is neut., while *upagrahau* is mas. It seems obvious that in s. 38 this document is named *paridāna*, while here it is called *upagraha*. Cs supplies *sa paridānalekhaḥ* at the end of the first half and explains the second half 'these two become the means of showing favour during distress felt by the addressee and when showing compassion towards a servant.' *paridāna* as '*dayāviṣkaraṇa*' seems hardly possible. Cb seems to have read *paridhāne* 'on the occasion of mental distress (*ādhau*) and bodily illness (*paridhāne*).' Meyer suggests *ādhi* as 'pledge' or the same as *upādhi* 'title'; either is unlikely. It seems that a condolence letter and a letter of gift are meant.

43 *kāryakaraṇe* is from Cb. *kāryā* of the mss. implies that instructions about writing are being given. But we have descriptions of documents here, not instructions about writing them. Cj seems to have read *nisṛṣṭisthāpanāṁ kuryāt*. — *vācikalekhaḥ...naisṛṣṭikaḥ*: the translation follows the explanation in Cp Cs, the former as authorization to issue orders in the king's name (corresponding to *vacane*) and the latter as authorization to carry out a work (corresponding to *kāryakaraṇe*). Cb Cj seem to understand *vācikalekha* as only another name for *naisṛṣṭika*. Meyer has 'a document in the very words of the king (*vācika*) or the result of another authorization (*naisṛṣṭika*),' making four varieties in all.

44 *daivasaṁyuktām*, i.e., about divine calamities. — *tattvajām* refers to *mānuṣīṁ pravṛttim* and means 'based on actual happenings,' ('real' Cb). 'Concerning spiritual well-being' (Cs) is little likely.

45 *pratyanubhāṣya* 'reading out' to the king (Cs) rather than to himself (Meyer).

46 *pathikārtham*: Cj understands that the *dūta* or envoy is meant. Other travellers too may be understood. — *īśvarān*: '*durgapāla, antapāla*, etc.' (Cb and others). Feudatory princes seem to have been primarily meant.

47 Cf. 9.5.9 ff. and 9.6.20 ff. — Stein (ZII, 6, 64-5) considers it extraordinary that the four *upāyas* which properly belong to *nīti* 'foreign policy' should have been discussed here. But since royal decrees are under consideration (in the preceding ss.) this discussion is not unnatural here; for, royal documents would be concerned with one or the other of the *upāyas*. The lists in ss. 23-37 above (regarding documents in general) and in ss. 47-56 (regarding royal decrees) are not mutually exclusive. The differences between the present passage and 9.5.10-11 and 9.6.24 are due to difference in context, perhaps also to a difference in sources.

48 Among them, conciliation is five-fold, praising of merits, mention of relationship, pointing out mutual benefits, showing (advantages in) the future, and placing oneself at the (other's) disposal. 49 Amongst these, appreciation of the merits of birth, body, occupation, nature, learning, property and so on, praise, adulation, this is praising of merits. 50 The praising of (common) kinship, marriage relationship, relationship through teaching, relationship through sacrificial performances, (common) family, (affection of the) heart, and (common) friend, this is mention of relationship. 51 The praising of mutual benefits accruing to one's party and the party of the other, this is pointing out mutual benefits. 52 'If this were done in this way, this will happen to us (both)' this raising of hope is showing (advantages in) the future. 53 'What I am is you, what object belongs to me should be used by you in your works,' this is placing oneself at the (other's) disposal.

54 Conferring benefits of money is making gifts.

55 Creating apprehension and reprimanding is dissension.

56 Killing, tormenting and seizure of property constitute force.

57 Absence of charm, contradiction, repetition, incorrect (use of a) word, and confusion, — these are the defects of writing. 58 Among them, (the use of a) black leaf, (and) writing unattractive, uneven and faint letters constitute absence of charm. 59 The incompatibility of the later with the earlier is contradiction. 60 Statement a second time of what is said without any distinction is repetition. 61 The wrong use of gender, number, tense and case is incorrect (use of a) word. 62 The making of a group where there should be no group and not making a group where there should be a group, this reversal of qualities is confusion.

> 63 After going through all the sciences in detail and after observing the practice (in such matters), Kauṭilya has made these rules about edicts for the sake of kings.

49 *guṇagrahaṇam* from Cb is obviously necessary. *guṇāguṇa* as 'merits that are there and that are not there' (Meyer) is hardly convincing. — *praśaṁsā stutiḥ*: one of the words is superfluous. Cs has 'praise of existing merits and mention of non-existent merits.' 50 *kula*, i.e., friendship between the two families without there being any kinship. — *hṛdaya* refers to friendship between the parties themselves, while *mitra* refers to a common friend. 53 *ātmopanidhānam* corresponds to *sāntva* in s. 34 above.

57 *lekhadoṣāḥ*: as Stein (ZII, 6, 65) points out this discussion of defects in writing should preferably have come after that of excellences in ss. 6-12 above. 58 *kālapatrakam*: Cp explains 'writing over a partly written leaf or on a naturally dark leaf (*likhitocchiṣṭe svato vā maline patre likhitam*).' Cb Cj read *kālapatitam* 'writing over a dimmed earlier writing' (Cb), 'rubbed off after writing' (Cj). 62 Here Cp understands *varga* as *yati* 'caesura.' — *guṇaviparyāsaḥ* is only a description of *avarage varga-* etc. (Cb and Meyer).

63 *Kauṭilyena*: Cp says that the implication is that other writers before him had not composed a corresponding section. — *narendrārthe*: there is nothing to show that *narendra* here is a special designation of Candragupta Maurya or that *śāsana* means 'established law,' as V.R.R. Dikshitar (IHQ, III, 178-9) thinks.

CHAPTER ELEVEN

SECTION 29 EXAMINATION OF THE PRECIOUS ARTICLES TO BE RECEIVED INTO THE TREASURY

1 The Superintendent of the Treasury should receive jewels, articles of high value, articles of small value or forest produce, to be received into the treasury, (while) presiding over bureaus of experts in the (various) lines.

2 That from the Tāmraparṇī, that from Pāṇḍyaka-vāṭa, that from the Pāśikā, that from the Kulā, that from the Cūrṇī, that from (Mt.) Mahendra, that from the Kardamā, that from the Srotasī, that from the Lake, and that from the Himavat, these are pearls. 3 The shell, the conch and miscellaneous are the sources (of pearls).

4 (A pearl that is) lentil-shaped, triangular, tortoise-shaped, semi-spherical, with a layer, coupled, cut up, rough, spotted, gourd-shaped, dark, blue, and badly perforated, is defective. 5 (That which is) big, round, without a flat surface, lustrous, white, heavy, smooth and perforated at the proper place is excellent.

6 *Śīrṣaka*, *upaśīrṣaka*, *prakāṇḍaka*, *avaghāṭaka* and *taralapratibaddha*, — these are varieties of (pearl-) strings.

2.11

ratna includes *sāra* and *phalgu* as well, but not *kupya* which is described in 2.17 below, though s. 1 includes it along with the others. — Cb has *prāveśya* also here. — *adhiṣṭhitaḥ*: see 2.5.8.

1 *kośādhyakṣaḥ*: this officer is clearly under the *saṁnidhātṛ*; cf. 2.5.8 where the latter is referred to as receiving articles in the treasury.

2 *pāṇḍyakavāṭaka* : Cb Cp identify Pāṇḍyakavāṭa with Mt. Malayakoṭi in the Pāṇḍya country. H. V. Trivedi (IC, I, 249-50) thinks it is either Negapatam or Ramnad 'the port of embarkation for Ceylon.' — *pāśikya*: the river Pāśikā 'in the Pāṇḍya country' (Cj) seems more likely than 'near Pāṭaliputra' (Cb Cp). — *kauleya*: the river Kulā is near Mayūragrāma in Ceylon (Cb Cp). — *caurṇeya* : the river Cūrṇī is near the town Muracī in Kerala (Cb Cp); river Cūrṇā near Kerala (Cj). — *kārdamika* : river Kardamā is in Pārasīka (Cp), in Conideśa (Cb), in the Uttarāpatha (Cj). — *srautasīya*: river Srotasī is on the shore of Barbara (Cp) or Parpara (Cb). — *hrādīya* 'from a pool called Śrīghaṇṭa in the sea off the coast of Barbara' (Cp) or Parpara (Cb). 3 *prakīrṇakam* : Cp quotes a memorial verse mentioning six such sources, the temple of an elephant, the hood of a serpent etc.

4 According to Cp, *tripuṭa* is also a kind of grain. — *siktakam*: Cb text shows *sikthakam*, but the explanation 'spotted' presupposes *siktaka*. Cs adopting *sikthaka* explains 'having spots of the shape of *siktha* (bees' wax ? or boiled rice ?).'

6 *śīrṣaka* 'with one big pearl in the centre, the rest small and uniform in size' (Cb Cp). — *upaśīrṣaka* 'one big pearl with a small pearl on each side of it,—a series of these' (Cb). — *prakāṇḍaka* 'one big pearl with two small pearls on each side—a series of these' (Cb). Cp seems to understand 'with five pearls as principal, i.e., in the centre.' — *avaghāṭaka* 'a big pearl in the centre with pearls gradually decreasing in size on both sides' (Cb Cp). — *taralapratibaddha* 'a string of uniform-sized pearls throughout' (Cb which, however, reads *-pratividdham*). The readings and explanations of Cj are far from clear. — *yaṣṭiprabhedāḥ* is from the commentators for *-pradeśāḥ* of the mss.

7 One thousand and eight strings make the *indracchanda* (necklace). 8 Half that (number) make the *vijayacchanda.* 9 Sixty-four make the *ardha-hāra.* 10 Fifty-four make the *raśmi-kalāpa.* 11 Thirty-two make the *guccha.* 12 Twenty-seven make the *nakṣatra-mālā.* 13 Twenty-four make the *ardha-guccha.* 14 Twenty (strings) make the *māṇavaka.* 15 Half that (number) make the *ardha-māṇavaka.* 16 These same, with a gem in the centre, become their (respective) *māṇavakas.*

17 (A necklace of) only *śīrṣakas* is an unmixed *hāra.* 18 Like that, are the rest. 19 With a gem in the centre, it is an *ardhamāṇavaka.*

20 One with three strips is a *phalaka-hāra* or one with five strips.

21 A single string is the unmixed *ekāvalī.* 22 The same, with a gem in the centre, is the *yaṣṭi.* 23 Variegated with gold and gems it is the *ratnāvalī.* 24 With gold, gems and pearls at intervals, it is the *apavartaka.* 25 With stringing in a gold thread it is the *sopānaka.* 26 Or, with a gem in the centre, it is the *maṇi-sopānaka.*

27 By that are explained varieties of strings and net-works for the head, hands, feet and waist.

8 After s. 8 Cb adds *śataṁ devacchandaḥ,* explained rather curiously as 'containing 881 strings.' — The commentators add that these varieties are primarily for decoration in temples etc. (*devalavitānādiṣu śobhākaraṇārtham*—Cj). — The *Bṛhat Saṁhitā,* 81.31-36 has a closely parallel passage with a few variations. It has a *hāra* of 108 strings, its *ardhaguccha* has 20 strings, *māṇavaka* 16 and *ardhamāṇavaka* 12 and it adds a *mandara* of 8 strings and a *hāraphalaka* of 5. 16 *ete eva* 'i.e., an *indracchanda* with a gem in the centre instead of a pearl is *indracchanda-māṇavaka* and so on' (Cb Cp); 'e.g., *padmarāgendracchanda* and so on' (Cj). Meyer has 'these have a gem in the centre, therefore they are called *māṇavakas.*' *tat* in the sense of 'therefore' seems doubtful here.

17 *ekaśīrṣakaḥ* etc. 'when in an *indracchanda* we have only *śīrṣaka* strings, we get *indracchandaśīrṣakaśuddhahāra,* and so on' (Cp). This is what seems meant. Cb has 'when there are only pearls in *śīrṣaka* etc. it is called a *śuddha hāra.*' According to Cj there are twenty strings in a *śuddhaśīrṣaka hāra,* but only one according to others mentioned in it. Meyer's 'with one big pearl in the centre and made of bright pearls (*śuddha*) is the Ravisher (*hāra*)' is doubtful. 19 Because of a different *ardha-māṇavaka* in s. 15 above, Meyer regards ss. 17-19 as suspicious.

20 *triphalakaḥ* etc. : *phalaka* seems to be a strip of gold on which pearls or gems are set. A *phalakahāra* (as distinguished from *śuddha hāra*) has 3 or 5 such strips. Thus in the main Cb. Cs reads 19 and 20 as one s. 'an *ardha-māṇavaka* (of s. 15) with a gem in the centre, if accompanied by 3 or 5 strips of gold on which the gem in the centre is inlaid, is called a *phalakahāra.*' This is not unlikely. Cj seems to have 'a ten-stringed *ardha-māṇavaka* with a gem in the centre, with three or five gold-strips inlaid with gems strung in between is a *phalakahāra.*'

21 *sūtram* : according to the commentators, *sūtra* is the name and *ekāvalī* is descriptive of it. The closely parallel *Br. Saṁ.,* 81.36, however, gives *ekāvalī* as the name, adding that it is 1 *hasta* in length. — D has a folio covering ss. 21-39. 23 *hemamaṇi* 'beads of gold' (Cb Cp); 'gold and gems' (Cj as also Meyer, who argues that without an actual gem the name *ratnāvalī* would hardly be justified). — *apavartaka* probably contains a reference to the warding off of the evil eye. 25 *suvarṇasūtrāntaram* 'with gold plates only, without gems' (Cb), 'with gold only in various designs and with holes for threads to be woven in or with catches on both sides for holding the thread' (Cp), 'where a pearl is strung in a single gold thread (*suvarṇasūtreṇa ekena antaritaṁ mauktikaṁ yatra tat*)' (Cj). This last explanation has been adopted. 26 *maṇisopānakam* : Cj says that the name would vary with the gem used, *vaiḍūryasopānaka, vajrasopānaka* and so on. That seems reasonable.

28 Gems come from Koṭi, from the Mālā, and from beyond the sea.

29 The ruby, of the colour of the red lotus, of the colour of saffron, of the (colour of) *pārijāta*-flower, (and) of the (colour of the) morning sun. 30 The beryl, of the colour of the blue lotus, of the *śirīṣa*-flower, of the colour of water, of the colour of (green) bamboo, of the colour of the parrot's wing, yellow-coloured, of the colour of cow's urine (and) of cow's fat. 31 The sapphire, with blue lines, like the *kalāya*-flower, deep blue, having the lustre of the *jambū*-fruit, having the lustre of the dark cloud, the 'delighter' (and) the 'streaming interior.' 32 The pure crystal, of the colour of *mūlāṭa*-flower, shedding a cool shower and the sun-stone. These are the gems.

33 Hexagonal, square or round, of a flashing colour, having a suitable form, clear, smooth, heavy, lustrous, with lustre inside and imparting lustre,— these are the excellences of gems. 34 With a dull colour and lustre, with grains, with a hole in the bloom, broken, badly bored, (and) covered with scratches,— these are blemishes.

35 The *vimalaka*, the *sasyaka*, the *añjanamūlaka*, the *pittaka*, the *sulabhaka*, the *lohitākṣa*, the *mṛgāśmaka*, the *jyotīrasaka*, the *māleyaka*, the

28 *kauṭaḥ* : 'from Koṭi between Malaya and the sea' (Cp), 'from Mt. Kūṭa' (Cb Cj). — *māleyakaḥ* : 'from Malaya' (Cb Cj), 'from Mālā, a part of Malaya also called Karṇīvana' (Cp). — *pārasamudrakaḥ*: 'from Mt. Rohaṇa in Ceylon' (com.).

29-32 The explanation attributed to 'others' in Cp is adopted, *saugandhika*, *vaiḍūrya* and *indranīla* being regarded as *adhikāra-śabdas* or generic names of various types of gems and the words following each understood as varieties of these. This arrangement is found in Russ. Cp itself regards *saugandhika* as only a variety of *māṇikya* or ruby. That is in conformity with the *Mānasollāsa*, 2.475-6. But the *Br. Saṁ.*, 82.1, seems to regard *saugandhika* as a basic variety of gems. —*padmarāgo 'navadya-* is necessary for *padmānavadya-*, as two different types are thought of. —*nīlāvalīyaḥ* is read after *indranīlaḥ* as in D; it is more likely to be a variety of sapphire than of *vaiḍūrya*. — It is to be noted that *marakata* itself is not mentioned. —*puṣyarāga* 'yellow like turmeric' (Cp). —*nandaka* 'white inside and blue outside' (Cp). —*sravanmadhya* 'having rays shooting like flowing water' (Cp). The words *śuddhasphaṭiko mūlāṭavarṇaḥ* are from the commentators, but seem to be genuine. In D they are found before *indranīlaḥ*, clearly out of place. Cj, however, with the same reading as D, understands *śuddhasphaṭika* and *mūlādivarṇa* as two further types of *puṣyarāga*. —*mūlāṭa*, according to Cb Cp is 'curds with the upper layer removed.' It may mean the flower of the *mūlāṭī* plant. — Cb has *vaiḍūrya* of five types up to *śukapatravarṇa*, *puṣyarāga* of two types up to *gomedaka*, then *śuddhasphaṭika* of two types *mūlāṭavarṇa* and *nīlāvalīya*, *indranīla* of four types up to *jīmūtaprabha*, and *nandaka* of three types, *sravanmadhya*, *śītavṛṣṭi* and *sūryakānta*. Cj has *padmarāga*, *vaiḍūrya*, *puṣyarāga*, *indranīla*, *mahānīla*, *nandaka* (i.e., *candrakānta*) and *sūryakānta* as the basic types. — It is also conceivable that from *saugandhika* to *sūryakānta*, we have a single list of gems, without basic types and varieties. The absence of *ca* anywhere except at the end might indicate this.

33 *saṁsthānavān* 'capable of being tied or set' (com.); 'possessed of firmness, hard' (Meyer). The former as implying a suitable form or shape seems better. —*Br. Saṁ*, 82.3, is closely parallel. 34 *puṣpacchidraḥ* 'with a drop in the interior' (Cp), 'with a flower-like whitish spot' (Cb). In the closely parallel *Br. Saṁ.*, 82.4, this word seems to have been replaced by *sadhātu* 'with some mineral.'

35 *vimalaka* 'white-red' (Cb), 'green' (Cp). *sasyaka* 'blue.' *añjanamūlaka* 'dark-blue.' *pittaka* 'of the colour of cow's bile.' *sulabhaka* 'white.' *lohitākṣa* 'black in the centre and red at the fringe.' *mṛgāśmaka* 'white and black.' *jyotīrasaka* 'white-red.'

ahicchatraka, the *kūrpa*, the *pratikūrpa*, the *sugandhikūrpa*, the *kṣīravaka*, the *śukticūrṇaka*, the *śilāpravālaka*, the *pulaka*, the *śuklapulaka*, — these are subsidiary types (of gems). 36 The rest are glass-crystals.

37 Diamonds come from Sabhārāṣṭra, from Tajjamārāṣṭra, from Kāstīrarāṣṭra, from (Mt.) Śrīkaṭanaka, from (Mt.) Maṇimanta and from Indravāna. 38 The mine, the stream, and miscellaneous are the sources.

39 Like the cat's eye, the *śirīṣa*-flower, cow's urine, cow's fat, pure crystal, (or) the *mūlāṭa*-flower, and of the colour of any one of the gems, — these are the colours of diamonds.

40 (A diamond that is) big, heavy, capable of bearing blows, with symmetrical points, (capable of) scratching a vessel, revolving like a spindle and brilliantly shining is excellent. 41. That with points lost, without edges and defective on one side is bad.

42 The coral from Alakanda and from Vivarṇa, red and of the colour of the lotus (is excellent), with the exception of that which is eaten by insects and which is bulging in the middle.

māleyaka (v. l. *maileyaka*) 'vermilion-coloured.' *ahicchatraka* 'of a faint red colour.' *kūrpa* 'with sand-grains inside.' *pratikūrpa* 'of the colour of *sikthaka* (bees' wax?).' *sugandhikūrpa* 'of the colour of the *mudga*-bean.' *kṣīravaka* 'milk-coloured.' *śukticūrṇaka* 'many-coloured.' *śilāpravālaka* 'coral-coloured.' *pulaka* 'with a black interior'. *śuklapulaka* 'with a white interior.' Thus mostly Cp Cs. The names of some of these appear in a different from and the explanations of some differ in Cj. Most of these names have no doubt reference to colour, but *māleyaka* and *ahicchatraka* apparently refer to the place of their origin. 36 *kācamaṇayaḥ*: artificial gems are clearly meant (*yathoktamaṇirāgaprabhānukāriṇaḥ*—Cj). Cp explains by *dhātudravyamaya* 'made of mineral substances.'

37 *Sabhārāṣṭra* is Vidarbha (*vidarbhaviṣaye veṇṇākaṇṭhapārśve jātam sabhārāṣṭrakam* — Cj). Cb reads *mahārāṣṭrakam* identifying the country with Āraṭṭa. — *tajjamārāṣṭrakam*: Cj, reading *tajjumā-*, explains 'from Bhogavallī in the Kaliṅgas.' G M read *madhyamarāṣṭrakam* 'from the Kosalas' (Cp Cs). — *kāstīrarāṣṭrakam*: Cp seems to identify it with Kāśī. Patañjali on Pāṇini 6.1.154 takes Kāstīra to be a Vāhīka-grāma (V. S. Agrawala, *India as Known to Pāṇini* (Lucknow, 1953), p. 65). Cj has '*kāśmīrarāṣṭrakaṁ śūrpākārabhūmijam.*' — *śrīkaṭanakam*: '*Kāñcideśa kaṅkādiṣu* (?) *parvate*' (Cj). According to Oldham (JBORS, 13, 196) the locality is to be sought in the neighbourhood of Jabalpur Dist. 'There are villages called Katanga and Katangi still in the vicinity' (197 n. 2). — *maṇimantakam*: Mt. Maṇimanta is in the Uttarāpatha (Cp); '*śarkabhūmijam* (?)' (Cj). Maṇimantha is mentioned in the *Mahābhārata*, 13.18.83. — *indravānakam* 'from the Kaliṅgas' (Cp), 'from the Kālindī (*kālindyam* ?)' (Cj). Cb's reading seems to be *iṣuvānaka* or *iḻuvānaka*.

40 *bhājanalekhi* 'able to scratch when shaken in a *kāṁsya* vessel containing water' (Cb). — *tarkubhrāmi* : 'though not revolving, yet appearing to revolve' (Cb Cp). *tarku* is a spindle and 'revolving like a spindle' seems also likely. Meyer understands the idea of rays shooting from it like a spindle and would even read *tarkubhrāmibhrājiṣṇu* as one word. 41 *pārśvāpavṛtta* 'slanting on one side' (Cb). The idea seems to be that of one side not being symmetrical with the other sides.

42 *ālakandakam* : Cj reads *ālatsāndrakam*, Cb *ālasāndrakam*. Cb has 'Ālasāndra, a country in the sea off the coast of the Pappar land;' this is Cp's explanation of *ālakandaka*. The latter may possibly contain a reference to the Laccadiv islands. Jayaswal's 'root-coral (*kanda*) with a yellow tinge (*āla*)' (*Hindu Polity*, I, App. C, 212 n. 1) seems little likely. — *vaivarṇikam* : 'Vivarṇa is off the Yavana-dvīpa' (Cp), 'off Coniyadeśa' (Cb). Cj reads *vaivalgukam*. — *garbhiṇikā* 'bulging in the middle' (Cb), 'with a *yaṣṭi* (strip?) in the middle' (Cp); 'with defects in the interior' (Meyer).

43 Sandal-wood from Sātana is red and has the smell of the earth. 44 That from Gośīrṣa is blackish red and smells like fish. 45 The sandal-wood from Hari is of the colour of the parrot's feather and has the smell of a mango, also that from the Tṛṇasā. 46 That from Grāmeru is red or red-black and has the smell of goat's urine. 47 That from Devasabhā is red and has the smell of a lotus, also that from Jāpa. 48 That from Joṅga is red or red-black and smooth, also that from Turūpa. 49 That from the Mālā is whitish red. 50 *kucandana* is rough, black like aloe or red or reddish black. 51 That from Kāla mountain is reddish black or of the colour of saffron. 52 That from Kośāgāra mountain is black or black-variegated. 53 That from the Śītodakā has the lustre of the lotus or is black and smooth. 54 That from Nāga mountain is rough or of the colour of moss. 55 That from Śākala is brown.

56 Light, smooth, not dry, unctuous with oil like butter, pleasant in smell, penetrating the skin, unobtrusive, not losing colour, capable of bearing heat, allaying heat and pleasant to the touch, — these are the excellences of sandal-wood.

57 Aloe from Joṅga is black, black-variegated or variegated with round spots. 58 That from Doṅga is dark. 59 That from beyond the sea has a variegated appearance (and) has the smell of *uśīra* or the fragrance of *navamālikā*.

60 Heavy, smooth, of a pleasant smell, wide-spreading (in fragrance), burning well, without a thick smoke, of a uniform fragrance, capable of standing a rubbing, — these are the excellences of aloe.

61 *Tailaparṇika* (incense) from Aśokagrāma has the colour of flesq and the fragrance of a lotus. 62 That from Joṅga is reddish yellow and has the fra-

43 The description of *sāra* articles begins with this s. — *sātanam* 'from the Sātana country' (Cb), 'from the Sātana mountain' (Cj). 44 *gośīrṣakam* 'from the Gośīrṣa country' (Cb); the name is more likely to be that of a mountain, as in Cj. 45 *haricandanam* 'from the Harideśa' (Cb), 'from the mountain shaped like *hari*, i.e., monkey' (Cj). *hari* may possibly refer to the colour 'tawny.' — *tārṇasam* 'from the mountain on the bank of the river Tṛṇasā' (Cj). 46 Grāmeru is 'a region' (Cb), 'a mountain' (Cj). — *basta* 'goat' is the musk-deer, according to 'some' in the commentators. 47 Jāpa, Joṅga and Turūpa are in Kāmarūpa, the rest of the places mentioned in connection with sandalwood are in the Malaya region (com.). 51 Cb's actual comment shows *raktakālam* before *anavadyavarṇaṁ vā*. That appears to have been original. 53 Śītodakā 'a river' (Cj), 'a country' (Cp).

56 *sarpiḥsnehalepi*: smearing with its oil is compared with smearing with butter. — *tvaganusāri* 'pleasantly penetrating up to the roots of the skin's hair' (Cb). — Cb seems to have read *avikāri* for *avirāgi*. Cf., however, s. 71 below.

58 *doṅgakam* : 'Doṅga is in Kāmarūpa' (Cp). Cj seems to have read *vāṅgakam* 'from the Vaṅgas.'

60 *asaṁplutadhūmam* 'without surging smoke' seems to convey the idea of absence of overpowering smoke, while burning; 'with a steady smoke, *avasthitadhūmam*' (Cj).

61 *tailaparṇika* is a kind of incense. Meyer thinks it is a fragrant oil used as a salve. All the places of origin are in Kāmarūpa (com.).

grance of a blue lotus or the smell of cow's urine. 63 That from Grāmeru is smooth and has the smell of cow's urine. 64 That from Suvarṇakuḍya is reddish yellow and has the smell of the citron fruit. 65 That from Pūrṇakadvīpa has the fragrance of a lotus or the smell of butter.

66 *Bhadraśriya* from beyond the Lauhityā is of the colour of the *jātī*-flower. 67 That from Antaravatī is of the colour of *uśīra*. 68 And both have the smell of *kuṣṭha*.

69 *Kāleyaka* from Svarṇabhūmi is smooth and yellow. 70 That from the northern mountain is reddish yellow.

Thus the objects of high value.

71 Capable of (retaining fragrance when) formed into a lump or boiled or producing smoke, not losing colour, and amenable to mixing (with other substances); 72 and qualities similar to those of sandal-wood and aloe,— these are their excellences.

73 The *kāntanāvaka* and the *praiyaka* are skins from the northern mountain. 74 The *kāntanāvaka* has the lustre of the peacock's neck. 75 The *praiyaka* is variegated with blue, yellow and white lines and spots. 76 Both these are eight *aṅgulas* in length.

77 The *bisī* and the *mahābisī* come from Dvādaśagrāma. 78 The *bisī* is of an indistinct colour, hairy or variegated. 79 The *mahābisī* is rough, mostly white. 80 Both are twelve *aṅgulas* in length.

66 *bhadraśriya* is camphor or *takkola* or *śrīvāsaka* or red sandalwood (Cp). 68 *kuṣṭha* is the name of a medicinal plant, also called *pāribhāvya* (com.).

69 *kāleyaka* is also a kind of fragrant substance. It is *dāruharidrā* (*Amara*, 2.4.101). — Svarṇabhūmi 'Burma' (Cs Meyer), 'Sumatra' (Meyer). 70 *uttaraparvata* is evidently the Himālaya.

71 *piṇḍakvātha-* etc. : the idea of their retaining fragrance when formed into lumps etc. (com.) is preferable to the idea of their capability to form lumps etc. (Meyer). Cj seems to read *gandha* for *dhūma*, 'not losing its fragrance when mixed with something else.' — *yogānuvidhāyi*, i.e., capable of mixing with other substances so as to retain the fragrance. — The adjectives here are in the neuter and would apply only to *tailaparṇika* and *bhadraśriya*, hardly to *kāleyakaḥ*. Perhaps s. 71 should be read after s. 68. And perhaps the words *iti sārāḥ* should be read after s. 72; for ss. 71-72 describe qualities of *sāra*.

73 The description of *phalgu* objects begins with this s. — *kāntanāvakam*: this and *praiyaka* as names of skins are derived from the place of their origin, in the Himālayas (Cj). 76 *aṣṭāṅgulāyāmam* : this comes to about six inches, clearly the skin of a very small animal. According to Cj it is the skin of the Himalayan rat.

77 Jayaswal (JBORS, 18, 97) identifies *bisī* and *mahābisī* with the Little Yūe Chi and the Great Yūe Chi of Central Asia. In another place (*Hindu Polity*, I, 214) he identifies *mahābisī* with the Mahāvṛṣas of the Vedas. These and the following names seem, however, to contain a reference to the animal rather than to the place of their origin. 78 *duhilitikā* 'hairy' (Cb Cp), 'of the shape of a house-lizard (*gṛhagaudhakākārā*)' (Cj). Meyer proposes *dulihitikā* (Prakrit for *dvilikhitikā*) 'having double lines.'

81 The *śyāmikā*, the *kālikā*, the *kadalī*, the *candrottarā* and the *śākulā* are produced in Āroha. 82 The *śyāmikā* is brown or variegated with spots. 83 The *kālikā* is brown or dove-coloured. 84 Both these are eight *aṅgulas* in length. 85 The *kadalī* is rough and one *hasta* in length. 86 The same, variegated with 'moons', is the *candrottarā*. 87 The *śākulā* is one-third the *kadalī* (in length), variegated with circular spots or variegated with natural knots in the skin.

88 The *sāmūra*, the *cīnasī* and the *sāmūlī* are from Bāhlava. 89 The *sāmūra* is thirty-six *aṅgulas* and of the colour of collyrium. 90 The *cīnasī* is reddish black or pale black. 91 The *sāmūlī* is of the colour of wheat.

92 The *sātinā*, the *nalatūlā*, and the *vṛttapucchā* are from Odra. 93 The *sātinā* is black. 94 The *nalatūlā* is of the colour of the flower-panicle of the *nala*-reed. 95 And the *vṛttapucchā* is brown.

These are the varieties of skins.

96 Of skins, the soft, the smooth and the hairy are best.

97 Woollen cloth is white, all red and part red, with threads laid in with the needle, variegated in weaving, with pieces joined together and with broken off threads. 98 The blanket, the *kaucapaka*, the *kulamitikā*, the *saumitikā*, the horse's saddle-cloth, the coloured blanket, the *talicchaka*, the armour, the *paristoma* and the *samantabhadraka* are (varieties of) woollen cloth. 99 Slippery and wet as it were, fine and soft is best.

81 *ārohajāḥ*: Cb has 'Āroṭa in the Himālayas'. 87 *kadalītribhāgā* can hardly be 'three-fourths of *kadalī*' (Meyer). — *koṭha* 'red circles' (Cb). The word may be a Prakrit form of *kuṣṭha* 'a spot on the skin.' Cj seems to have read *naga-* (for *koṭha-*); but its explanation of it '*gāṅgasthānaiḥ*' is far from clear. — *kṛtakarṇikājinacitrā*: the translation follows Cb. Meyer has 'variegated like the antelope's skin when knots are formed in it.' — *vā* seems obviously necessary for *ca* of the mss.

88 *bāhlaveyāḥ*: 'Bāhlava is in the Himālayas' (Cb Cs). Bactria is more likely. Jayaswal asserts (JBORS, 18, 97) that a Central Asian fur is still known as *sāmūra* and is still imported into India.

92 *audrāḥ*: Cp derives it from *udra* in the sense of '*jalacaraprāṇiviśeṣaḥ*'. More likely, however, it contains a reference to the place of origin as in the other cases, perhaps Orissa. Cj has *Udradeśajātāḥ*.

97 *śuddha* 'white' (Cb); *śuddharakta* 'all red' (Cb); *pakṣa-rakta* 'half-red, half-white' (Cb). If *rakta* from *rañj* means 'dyed,' the three terms may also mean 'undyed,' 'fully dyed' and 'part dyed.' Cj has *pakṣmaraktam* 'dyed in (crosswise) threads only.' — *khacita*: the translation is as in Cb, which seems to imply some sort of knitting. — *khaṇḍasaṁghātyā*: as Cj has 'parts are separately made and then joined together.' Cb has 'with many threads left unwoven'. — *tantuvicchinna* seems to refer to some sort of net-work or lace-work. Meyer refers *khacita* etc. also to colours, which seems little likely. 98 *kaucapakaḥ*: Cb, reading *ko-* explains by 'a covering.' Cp has 'helmet for protection from cold.' Cb adds *kapilā* after this word and explains it by 'covering for the head.' — *kulamitikā* and *saumitikā* are housings for elephants, the latter being black (Cb Cp). Cj has '*somitikā karṇatrāṇam*, ear-guard.' — *talicchakam* is a kind of bed-spread (Cp) or carpet (Cj). — *vāravāṇa*: Meyer suggests the etymology from *vāra* 'horses' hair' and *vāna* 'weave', i.e., with a rough texture. — *paristoma* 'a kind of blanket' (Cb), 'a carpet for the elephant' (Cj). Meyer thinks that it is a bed-spread 'tucked in on all sides.' — *samantabhadrakam*: 'belt or hem at the bottom of the armour, *sannāhatalapaṭṭaka*' (Cj). 99 *picchilam*, i.e., 'where the hand slips' (Cj). *iva* may be construed with this word also.

100 The black *bhiṅgisī*, made out of a collection of eight woven strands (and) the *apasāraka* which keeps off rain, —that is (woollen cloth) from Nepāla.

101 The *sampuṭikā*, the *caturaśrikā*, the *lambarā*, the *kaṭavānaka*, the *prāvaraka* and the *sattalikā* are (products from) the hair of animals.

102 The *dukūla* from the Vaṅgas is white and smooth. 103 That from the Puṇḍras is dark and smooth like a gem. 104 That from Suvarṇakuḍya is of the colour of the sun, with gem-smooth water-weave, with a uniform weave and with a mixed weave. 105 Of these, there is cloth with a single yarn or with one and a half yarns or with two, three or four yarns.

106 By that is explained the *kṣauma* from Kāśī and the Puṇḍras.

107 The *patrorṇā*-silk comes from the Magadhas, the Puṇḍras and Suvarṇakuḍya. 108 The *nāga*-tree, the *likuca*, the *bakula* and the banyan tree are the sources. 109 That from the *nāga*-tree is yellow. 110 That from the *likuca* is wheat-coloured. 111 That from the *bakula* is white. 112 The remaining one is of the colour of butter. 113 Of these, that from Suvarṇakuḍya is best.

100 *aṣṭaprotisaṁghātyā* seems to mean 'in which there is a collection (*saṁghātya*) of weaves (*proti*) of eight strands,' apparently suggesting very thick threads. —*bhiṅgisī* is apparently the name of this cloth; so Cb, which, however, reads *tiṁkisī*. —*varṣavāraṇam apasārakaḥ* : in spite of the absence of *ca*, this seems to refer to another type of Nepal cloth, *apasāraka* being the name and *varṣavāraṇa* (despite the difference in gender) descriptive of it. Meyer understands only one type in the whole s., the *apasāraka*. Three (*bhiṅgisī, varṣavāraṇa* and *apasāraka*) are possible, but not very likely.

101 *saṁpuṭikā* 'a guard for shanks' (Cb); *lambarā* and *kaṭavānaka* are kinds of bed-spreads, so is *prāvaraka* also a bed-spread with a fringe on both sides (com.). It may be that *saṁpuṭikā* is 'a bag,' *lambarā* 'a curtain, hanging,' *kaṭavānaka* 'matting or rug,' and *prāvaraka* 'a rug'. *sattalikā* is also a kind of bed-spread. Cp says that to local people, *kaṭavānaka* is known as *bhāṣyaka*, *prāvaraka* as *romāvartaka* and *sattalikā* as *tūlikā*.

102 *dukūlam* : cf. J. Charpentier (ZDMG, 73, 144-145) for the suggestion that this is a case of Prakritism for *dvikūla*, a word primarily descriptive of the cloth 'with two borders' and secondarily of the material. —*Suvarṇakuḍya* 'a region in Kashmir' (Cb). 'Suvarṇakuḍya was subsequently changed to Karṇasuvarṇa, which includes Murshidabad and Rajmahal in Bengal. The soil here is red like gold and hence the name' (Haraprasad Shastri, JBORS, V, 1919, 318). 104 *maṇisnigdhodakavānam* : 'soaking the material in water, then rubbing it with a gem and then weaving' (Cp), 'rubbing with a gem, making wet with water, then weaving' (Cj), 'a weave producing the smoothness of a gem and the transparency of water' (Meyer). — *caturaśravānam* 'weave with one uniform colour' (Cb Cp). A reference to colour seems hardly to be there. Cj has 'unmixed with cotton or silk.' *vyāmiśra-*, i.e., a mixture with cotton or silk or a mixture of colours (com.) The three expressions would seem to describe all three types of *dukūla*. 105 *ekāṁśukam*, i.e., with a single yarn in the warp and the woof; *adhyardhāṁśukam* with a single yarn in the warp and double in the woof; and so on. Cb refers to another explanation where *aṁśu* is understood as 'colour.'

107 *partrorṇā*, literally, 'wool in the leaf' refers to a kind of silk. Joges Chandra Ray (JBORS, III, 216) identifies it with the Eri or Mugā silk of Assam. Lassen mentions 12 kinds of worms native to India, the trees favoured by them being *badarī*, *eraṇḍa* and *pippala* (Meyer).

114 By that are explained the silk and silk-cloth from the land of Cīna.

115 Cotton fabrics from Madhurā, the Aparāntas, the Kaliṅgas, Kāśī, the Vaṅgas, the Vatsas and the Mahiṣas, are best.

116-117 Of precious articles other than these, he should be conversant with the amount, price, characteristics, class and appearance, their storing, manufacture of new ones and repair of old ones, secret treatment, tools, their use according to place and time, and remedies against things destructive (to them).

CHAPTER TWELVE

SECTION 30 STARTING OF MINES AND FACTORIES

1 The Director of Mines, being conversant with the science of (metal) veins in the earth and metallurgy, the art of smelting and the art of colouring gems, or having the assistance of experts in these, and fully equipped with workmen skilled in the work and with implements, should inspect an old mine by the marks of dross, crucibles, coal and ashes, or a new mine, where there are ores in the earth, in rocks or in liquid form, with excessive colour and heaviness and with a strong smell and taste.

114 *cīnabhūmijāḥ*: Jayaswal (*Hindu Polity*, I, App. C, 212 n.) argues that Cīna refers not to China but to Shīṇa, the Gilgit tribe, which still carries on silk manufacture. Cīna, he says, are often mentioned with Darada and other Himalayan or North-western people (Manu, 10.44 etc.). 'Cīna alone cannot jump over thousands of miles away into China.'

115 *mādhuram* 'Madhurā is the capital of the Pāṇḍyas' (Cb); Cj refers to northern Madhurā as well as the southern. —*māhiṣakam* may refer to Māhiṣmatī on the Narmadā or to Mahiṣamaṇḍala. Cb reads *māhiṣmakam*.

117 *karma guhyam*, i.e., colouring, falsification of jewels etc. —*deśakālaparībhogam* 'the proper time and place for manufacture, purchase etc. and the manner of their use' (Cb Cp); but 'use at the proper place and time' would appear a better idea. Breloer (KSt, III, 293) thinks that as the verses deal with the guarding of goods while the chapter is concerned with their inspection, they are probably derived from a different source.

2·12

1 *śulbaśāstra* 'the science of metallic veins in the ground, or that of transmutation of copper into silver or gold' (Cb Cp). Cj has '*bhūmiparīkṣāśātra*.' Breloer (KSt, III, 410) understands 'geometry.' —*rasapāka* 'alchemy and smelting' (Cb); it seems, however, that we have a single idea 'smelting of liquid ores.' Cf. *suvarṇapāka* in 1.18.8 (where *maṇirāga* is also mentioned). —*bhūtapūrvam* implies an abandoned mine. —*bhūmi*, *prastara* and *rasa* are the three types of ore that may be found. —Breloer (KSt, III, 309) refers *atyantavarṇagauravam* to *bhūmi*- and *prastara-dhātu* only and *ugragandharasam* to *rasadhātu* only. That does not seem intended.

2 (Those liquids) that flow inside a hole, a cave, a table-land at the foot, a rock-cut cave, or a secret dug-out in mountains whose regions are known (to contain gold-ore), that are of the colour of the *jambū-* the mango- or the palm-fruit or of a cross-section of ripe turmeric or of jaggery or of orpiment or red arsenic or honey or vermilion or white lotus or of the feather of a parrot or a peacock, that have in their environs water and plants of the same colour, and that are viscous, clear and heavy, are gold-bearing liquids. 3 (If, when) thrown in water, they spread on the surface like oil and absorb mud and dirt, they are capable of transmuting copper and silver up to one hundred (times their own weight).

4 Exactly similar to that in appearance, (but) with a strong smell and taste, he should know to be bitumen.

5 Ores in earth or rocks, which are yellow or copper-coloured or reddish-yellow, which, when broken, show blue lines or are of the colour of the *mudga* or *māṣa* bean or *kṛsara*, which are variegated with spots or lumps as of curds, which are of the colour of turmeric or myrobalan or lotus-leaf or moss or liver or spleen or saffron, which, when broken, show lines, spots or *svastikas* of fine sand, which are possessed of pebbles and are lustrous, which, when heated, do not break and yield plenty of foam and smoke, are gold-ores, to be used for insertion, as transmuters of copper and silver.

6 (Ores) of the colour of a conch-shell or camphor or crystal or butter or a dove or a pigeon, or *vimalaka* (gem) or the peacok's neck, (or) of the colour of *sasyaka* (gem) or *gomedaka* (gem) or jaggery or unrefined sugar, (or) of the colour of the flower of *kovidāra*, or lotus or *pāṭalī*-flower or *kalāya*-flower or the flower of flax or of linseed, (and) containing lead, containing antimony, smelling like raw flesh, when broken (either) black with a white shimmer (or) white with a black shimmer, or all variegated with lines and spots, soft, (which) when being smelted do not split and yield plenty of foam and smoke, are silver-ores.

7 In the case of all ores, when there is increase in heaviness there is increase in metal-content.

2 *gūḍhakhāta* may be one made by robbers. —*guḍa* found in Cb and a v. l. in M2 seems genuine. —*savarṇodaka-* etc. : the liquids evidently affect the colour of water and plants nearby. 3 *veddhāraḥ*: the root *vyadh* seems to have the technical sense of 'to transmute.' Cj has '*suvarṇasya kartāraḥ*' as the paraphrase. In *śatād upari* the idea apparently is that for each 100 units of copper or silver, one unit of this liquid would be sufficient. Meyer compares Kṣemendra's *Kalāvilāsa*, 9.7-8.

5 *pratīvāpārthāḥ* : according to the commentators, this ore in powder form is inserted in copper or silver while boiling.

6 For *vimalaka* and *sasyaka*, see 2.11.35, for *gomedaka* 2.11.30. *vimalaka* is white-red according to Cp here.

8 Of these, those that are impure or dim in the interior flow in a pure form when infused in strong urine and caustic, when formed into lumps with (a paste of) the *rājavṛkṣa*, the banyan tree, the *pīlu*, cow's bile, pigment and the urine and dung of the buffalo, the donkey and the young camel, either mixed with this (during boiling) or smeared with this (paste).

9 The insertion (in the ore) of the bulbous roots of the *kadalī* and the *vajra*, along with the caustic (of the ashes) of barley, *māṣa*-bean, sesamum, *palāśa* and *pīlu* or along with the milk of the cow and the goat, is productive of softness.

> 10 Honey and liquorice, goat's milk with sesamum-oil, mixed with ghee, jaggery and fermenting stuff, together with the *kandalī*, -- with only three infusions in this, a (metal ore) that may have been broken even a hundred-thousand-fold becomes soft.

11 The insertion of (the powder of) the teeth and horns of the cow is the remover of softness (in metals).

12 Ore from rocks or a region of the earth, which is heavy, unctuous and soft (and which is) tawny, green, reddish or red (in colour) is copper-ore.

13 That which is crow-black or of the colour of the dove or yellow pigment or studded with white lines (and) smelling like raw flesh, is lead-ore.

14 That which is grey like saline earth or of the colour of a baked lump of earth is tin-ore.

15 That which is made up mostly of smooth stones, is whitish-red or of the colour of *sinduvāra*-flower is iron-ore.

16. That which is of the colour of *kākāṇḍa* (' crow's egg ') or birch-leaf is *vaikṛntaka*-ore.

8 ***mūḍhagarbhāḥ***, i.e., when the metal content is not clear. — ***mūtra*** of human beings or of the elephant, horse, bullock, donkey and goat (com.). —***kṣāra*** is derived from the ashes of ***kadalī***, ***apāmārga*** etc. (Cb Cj). —***karabha*** 'a young camel' may also mean 'a young elephant.' —Meyer understands an option between ***tīkṣṇa***- etc. and ***rājavṛkṣa***- etc. But the option appears to be only in the matter of ***pratīvāpa*** or ***avalepa***.

9 ***yavamāṣa***- etc. : barley-husks, bean-stalks, sesamum-stalks, and the wood of ***palāśa*** and ***pīlu*** tree are burnt to form the caustic. ***yavakṣāra*** is well-known as salt-petre. —***vajrakanda*** is either ***viṣṇukanda*** or ***vanasūraṇa*** (Cp).

10 The stanza in the middle of the chapter is clearly a quotation from an earlier authority. —***kiṇva*** : its ingredients appear to be described in 2.25.33; cf. 2.25.26. Cb reads -***guḍacūrṇa***- in the sense of 'sandy jaggery.' — ***vibhinnam*** conveys the idea of brittleness.

12 ***bhārikaḥ*** etc. : it may be that ***bhārika***, ***snigdha*** and ***mṛdu*** are to be understood of all metal ores mentioned in ss. 12-16; they differ only as to colour.

15 ***khurumbaḥ*** 'consisting mostly of smooth stones' (Cp); Cb reads ***surumbaḥ*** in the same sense.

16 ***kākāṇḍa*** is 'a kind of tree' identified with ***mahānimba*** in the ***Śabdakalpadruma***. —***bhujapatra*** appears to be corrupted from ***bhūrjapatra***. Apparently reading ***kāṇḍa***-

17   That which is clear, smooth, lustrous, possessed of sound, cold, hard and of a light colour is gem-ore.

18   What is produced from ores, he should put to use in factories for the respective metals.   19   He should establish trade in manufactured goods in a single place, and (lay down) a penalty for those who manufacture, purchase or sell elsewhere.

20   He should make a miner who robs pay eight-fold, except in the case of jewels.   21   The thief and the person who lives (by mining) without permission, he should bind and force to work (in the mines), also the person who offers personal labour in place of a fine.

22   He should let for part-share or on lease a mine that is burden-some in point of expenses or working ; a light one, he should work himself.

23   The Director of Metals should establish factories for copper, lead, tin, vaikṛntaka, brass, steel, bronze, bell-metal and iron, also (establish) trade in metal-ware.

24   The Mint Master should cause to be minted silver coins with one-fourth part copper (and) containing a hardening alloy one māṣa (in weight) of one of the following, (viz.) iron, tin, lead and antimony, (of the denominations

bhūrjapatra-, Cp explains 'kāṇḍaṁ samudrāntaraktaṁ vallīphalam, bhūrjapatraṁ bhūrjā-
bhidhāno vṛkṣas tatphalavarṇam.' — vā seems to show the option between kākāṇḍa and bhujapatra.   — vaikṛntaka : the exact identification of this metal is uncertain. Cj's not very
clear words are 'vaikṛtadhātur acchalohasya dhātur ityarthaḥ; vaikṛtato hi vārakuśale cīnadeśe
pāpam (vāyam ?) utpadyate,' which seems to suggest that the name is derived from some
locality, and may be some special kind of iron or steel.
   17   Cb, reading śītatīvraḥ, explains 'becoming cool immediately on being taken out
of fire.'   Cj seems to read tīvratararāgaḥ.
   19   atyayam : this is 25 paṇas as in s. 26 below, according to Cs.   It may however be 600
paṇas as in s. 31 below and 2.25.2, as it involves a violation of state monopoly rights.
   20   anyatra ratnebhyaḥ : in this case the punishment is death as in 4.9.2.   21   daṇḍo-
pakāriṇam : i.e., the person who, unable to pay the fine, offers personal labour instead, same
as daṇḍapratikartṛ (2.24.2) or daṇḍapratikāriṇī (2.23.2) ; cf. 3.13.18.
   22   In bhāga a fixed share of the actual produce is received; in prakraya a fixed rental
is received whatever the amount of produce.
   23   ārakūṭa, kaṁsa and tāla are alloys of copper with tin or zinc in various proportions.
— loha seems to be used for 'iron' as well metal in general.
   24   lakṣaṇādhyakṣaḥ : lakṣaṇa in this name apparently refers to the emblem of the king
or state stamped on the coins as on the punch-marked coins.   There was obviously no
name or effigy of the ruler.   Cf. Jayaswal, Hindu Polity, I, 42-43.   —Though the actual
weight of the coin is not stated, it is reasonable to suppose that it is the same as karṣa or
suvarṇa, i.e., 16 māṣakas (cf. 2.19.3), as Cp says.   Thus a silver paṇa would have 4 māṣakas
of copper, 1 māṣa (i.e., māṣaka) of bīja or hardening alloy and 11 māṣakas of silver.   In the
lower denominations the same proportions hold good.   But, as Meyer says, though this is
the sense, the wording favours the idea that even in the lower denominations the alloy is to
be 1 māṣaka in each.   — pādājīvam, 'i.e., one-fourth silver, 11 parts copper and 1 māṣa alloy'
(com.).   But the copper māṣa or māṣaka is lower in value than a quarter paṇa and seems
to be 1/16th of a paṇa in value (cf. 4.9.4, 9).   The weight of the copper māṣaka appears
also to be 1 suvarṇa and not 1 māṣaka ; for coins 1/8th of this in weight are mentioned.   A
māṣaka (coin) cannot be supposed to contain 4 māṣas of silver as against 1 3/8th māṣa in an

of) one *paṇa*, a half *paṇa*, a quarter *paṇa* and a one-eighth *paṇa* ; (further), copper coins with one-quarter sustenance (of an alloy), (of the denominations of) one *māṣaka*, a half *māṣaka*, a *kākaṇī* and a half *kākaṇī*.

25 The Examiner of Coins should establish the currency of *paṇas*, for trade and for receipts in the treasury. 26 (He should also fix) a coining fee of eight per cent, a commission of five per cent, an inspection fee of one-eighth per cent, and a penalty of twenty-five *paṇas* for those who manufacture, purchase, sell and examine in other places.

27 The Superintendent of Mines should establish factories for (articles of) conch-shells, diamonds, gems, pearls, corals and caustics as well as commerce in them.

28 The Salt Commissioner should collect at the proper time the share of salt as released after crystallization as well as the lease-rent, also the price, the inspection fee and the surcharge from the sale. 29 Imported salt shall pay one-sixth part (as duty). 30 (Its) sale (shall be allowed) only after the share and the dues are paid (viz.,), five per cent surcharge, the inspection fee and the manufacturing fee. 31 The purchaser shall pay the duty and a protective duty corresponding to the loss sustained by the king's goods ; one who purchases at another place (shall pay) a fine of six-hundred *paṇas* in addition. 32 (A person selling) adulterated salt shall pay the highest fine (for violence), also the person living (by salt-manufacture) without permission, except forest-

aṣṭabhāga paṇa and 2 3/4th *māṣa* in a quarter *paṇa*. There is little doubt that there is no silver in the copper coin, only the *ājīva* or the hardening alloy. Perhaps the original reading was *pādabījam*. Cj seems to imply that the copper coins are also called *paṇa*, *ardhapaṇa* etc. and that it is these that are meant in connection with fines.

25 *vyāvahārikīṁ kośapraveśyāṁ ca* : apparently two sets of currency, one for trade purposes and the other for payments to the treasury are thought of. Breloer thinks (KSt, III, 426) that copper coins were used for trade and silver coins alone came into the treasury. This appears to be Cp's idea. 26 *rūpikam* is manufacturing charges or coining fee, according to the commentators. Meyer understands a sort of commodity tax, on each object (*rūpa*) as such. —*vyājīm* : see 2.6.10. —*atyayam* : according to Cp Cs, the offence is the reduction of metal-content to the extent of 1/8th. There is nothing here to show this, and the fine would appear too small for such tampering with coins. *anyatra* seems to mean 'elsewhere', i.e., not in the royal mint, as in s. 19 above, though here *kartṛ*- etc. is used in the dative or ablative, not genitive. The 25 *paṇas* thus work out as a licensing fee for making coins elsewhere than in a royal mint. With *anyatra* in the sense of 'excepting' Cp understands the fine as 1,000 *paṇas* for *kartṛ*, etc., Cs 'according to offence.' Cb seems to explain 'servants are fined 25 *paṇas* for their offences, except in the case of those who do the things in the proper place.' The nature of the offence is not clear in this case.

27 *kṣāra* : commentators understand alkalis or caustics, Meyer 'mica' or 'quartz.' In view of the mention of *kṣāra* with *lavaṇa* in s. 34 and 2.15.14-15, sugar-cane products are not unlikely even here.

28 *rūpam* is the same as *pārīkṣikam* (com.). 30 *dattabhāgavibhāgasya* : *vibhāga* refers to *vyājī*, *rūpa* and *rūpika* (Breloer). It would have been better, in that case, if *pañcakaṁ... rūpikaṁ ca* were included in the preceding s. —*rūpikam* : if this is 'manufacturing charge', it could hardly apply to imported salt. Perhaps it became a regular impost whether the state manufactured the article or not. 31 *kretā*, i.e., the native trader who purchases from

hermits. 33 Brahmins learned in the Vedas, ascetics and labourers may take salt for their food (without payment). 34 All other varieties of salt and sugar shall pay (only) the duty.

35-36 Thus from the mines he should collect the price, the share, the surcharge, the monopoly tax, penalty, duty, compensation, fine, inspection fee, and manufacturing charges as well as the twelve kinds of metals and commodities (made from them). In this way he should fix the collection (of income) under various heads in the case of all commodities.

37 The treasury has its source in the mines; from the treasury the army comes into being. With the treasury and the army, the earth is obtained with the treasury as its ornament.

CHAPTER THIRTEEN

SECTION 31 THE SUPERINTENDENT OF GOLD IN THE WORKSHOP

1 The Superintendent of Gold should cause to be built a workshop with a court-yard having four work-halls without inter-communication (and) with a single door, for the manufacture of gold and silver. 2 In the middle of the market highway he should establish the Goldsmith, skilled in his profession, of noble birth and trustworthy.

the foreign merchant. Cf. 2.21.7 ff. — *anyatra*, i.e., not at the toll gate. Breloer omits *kretā*, 'in the other case, 600 *paṇas* as an additional impost.' 34 *lavaṇakṣāravargaḥ* : see 2.15.14-15. — *śulkam* and not the other imposts as well.

35-36 Cb's *ca bhāgam* is certainly preferable to *vibhāgam*. — *parigham* : see 2.6.10 above. The commentators here understand inspection fee, which is little likely. As monopoly tax, it would be something fixed on every article made by the state which no one else could make. — *vaidharaṇa*, it would appear, operated when the state goods remained unsold because of competition, or when their prices went down. It was not a regular tax. — *rūpam*: Cb has 'silver and copper coins,' which seems hardly likely in view of s. 30 above; 'inspection fee' is better. — *dvādaśavidham* : commentators supply *samudayam* as the substantive, looking on *dhātu* and *paṇya* as the 11th and 12th items of income. It is, however, better to understand it as an adjective to *dhātum* as in Meyer, who has gold, silver and the metals of s. 23 (*lodhra* of the mss. as *loha* plus another metal). The twelfth metal, however, might well be *maṇidhātu* of s. 17. — *mukha-* refers to *āyamukha* as in 2.6.10. — Breloer (KSt, III, 437) contends that the inclusion of these *kārikās*, which really belong to the province of the *samāhartṛ*, in the Chapter on the Mine-Superintendent shows that the office of the *samāhartṛ* (and also of the *saṁnidhātṛ*) was not differentiated, before Kauṭilya's time, from what was mainly the king's household economy. Kauṭilya may therefore represent, according to him, the attempt to stress the importance of political control. He admits, however, that the differentiation is very old and represents a natural and living division.

37 This stanza, says Breloer (KSt, III, 407), belongs to a simpler conception; *kośa* and *daṇḍa* are among the oldest political ideas. It seems that he finds traces of development where probably none exist.

2.13

The significance of the name *akṣaśālā* for the workshop where gold is purified, assayed etc. is not clear.

2 *sauvarṇikaḥ* : his duties are described in the next Chapter, 2.14.

3 That from the Jambū river, that from (Mt.) Śatakumbha, that from Hāṭaka, that from Veṇu, that produced in Śṛṅgaśukti, that found in a natural condition, that transmuted by means of liquids and that produced from mines, — these are (types of) gold. 4 (Gold) of the colour of the lotus-filament, soft, smooth, not producing a sound and lustrous is best, reddish-yellow is of a middling quality, red of the lowest quality.

5 Of the best (varieties), the pale-yellow and the white are impure. 6 He should cause that because of which it is impure to be removed by means of lead four times that quantity. 7 If it becomes brittle by the admixture of lead, he should cause it to be smelted with dried lumps of cow-dung. 8 If it is brittle because of (its own) roughness, he should cause it to be infused in sesamum-oil and cow-dung.

9 (Gold) produced from the mines, becoming brittle by the admixture of lead, he should turn into leaves by heating and cause them to be pounded on wooden anvils, or should cause it to be infused in the pulp of the bulbous roots of the *kadalī* and the *vajra* (plants).

10 That originating in Tuttha, that from Gauḍa, that from Kambu and that from Cakravāla, — these are (types of) silver. 11 (Silver which is) white, smooth and soft is best. 12 The opposite kind and that which tends to burst is bad. 13 He should purify that with one-fourth part of lead. 14 That in which a crest has appeared at the top, which is clear, lustrous and of the colour of curds is pure.

3 *jāmbūnada* : ' from the Jambū river near Mt. Meru. This gold is used by gods alone and is of the colour of *jambū*-fruit.' (com.). — *śātakumbha* ' from Śatakumbha mountain ' (com.). Meyer thinks that Śatakumbhā may be a river. This gold has the colour of a lotus-filament. — *hāṭaka* contains a reference to the region ; ' of the colour of *kuraṇḍaka* flower ' (Cp), ' of the colour of *pāṭhāṅkurī* or *kusumbha* flower ' (Cb). — *vaiṇavam* ' from Mt. Veṇu ' (com.), ' from river Veṇu ' (Meyer) ; ' of the colour of *karṇikāra* flower ' (com.). — Śṛṅgaśukti is Suvarṇabhūmi (com.) ; ' of the colour of *manaḥśilā* ' (com.). — *jātarūpa* apparently refers to its being found in a naturally pure form. — *rasaviddha* by transmuting copper or silver with the *kāñcanika rasa* of 2.12.2-3. Russ. renders *rasaviddha* by ' obtained from streams.' 4 *anādi* ' not producing a sound ' is from Cb for *anunādi* ' resonant ' of the mss. Cp has *anādi* but refers to the other v.l.

5 *śreṣṭhānāṁ* : Cb Cs read this at the end of s. 4 which makes three kinds of *śreṣṭha*, — *śreṣṭhānāṁ śreṣṭha*, *śreṣṭhānāṁ madhyama*, etc., which is not a happy idea. At the beginning of s. 5, it may refer to the *śreṣṭha* of s. 4 except as regards colour. That also is not convincing. The word *śreṣṭhānāṁ* does not appear to be original and perhaps it might be better to drop it. 6 *yena aprāptakam* etc. ' by lead four times the amount of impurity ' (Cb) ; ' by lead four times the gold itself ' (Meyer, who asks, how can the amount of impurity be calculated beforehand ?). In the latter explanation, *tat* may be taken as referring to the impurity and as the object of *śodhayet*. 8 *niṣecayet* : ' the process of infusion is to be repeated a number of times ' (com.). 9 ' *Gaṇḍiḥ vṛkṣasya mūlācchākhāvadhibhāgaḥ* ' (Hemacandra).

10 Tuttha is a mountain of that name according to the commentators. The sense ' crucible ' does not fit. This silver has the colour of jasmine-flower. — *gauḍikam* : ' Gauḍa is the Kāmarūpa region and silver has the colour of the *tagara*-flower ' (com.). — *kāmbukam* ' from Mt. Kambu, has the colour of the *kunda* flower ' (com.) — *cākravālikam* : ' from Mt. Cakravāla, has the colour of the *kunda*-flower ' (com.) 12 *sphoṭanam* ' liable to burst ' apparently in the process of smelting. 14 *udgatacūlikam* ' with a bud-like form at the top' (Cb).

15 One *suvarṇa* of pure, turmeric-coloured (gold) is the standard. 16 Thence by the substitution of one *kākaṇī* copper onwards (in a *suvarṇa* of gold) up to the limit of four (*māṣakas*), sixteen standards (are obtained).

17 After first rubbing the gold (to be tested) on the touchstone, he should afterwards rub the standard gold (on it). 18 That with a streak of the same colour (as the standard) on places (on the stone) that are neither depressed nor elevated, he should know as properly tested ; what is over-rubbed or lightly rubbed or powdered over with red chalk from underneath the finger-nail, he should know as deception. 19 Gold, touched with the forepart of the hand smeared with *jāti*-vermilion or sulphate of iron dissolved in cow's urine, becomes white. 20 The streak (of the gold) on the touchstone, that has filaments, is smooth, soft and lustrous is best.

21 Stone from the Kaliṅgas or from the Tāpī, which is of the colour of the *mudga*-bean, is the best touchstone. 22 That which shows the exact colour is advantageous for either sale or purchase. 23 That which has the colour of an elephant, with a green tinge, is over-sensitive to colour (and) is advantageous for sale. 24 That which is firm, hard and of uneven colour, is not sensitive to colour (and) is advantageous for purchase.

25 The cut (of gold) that is sticky, of even colour, smooth, soft and lustrous is best. 26 The heating that is uniform outside and inside, (and) has the colour of the lotus-filament or the colour of *kuraṇḍaka*-flower, is best. 27 That which is dark or blue shows impurity.

28 Weights and measures we shall explain in (the Section) ' the Superintendent of Standardisation '. 29 In accordance with those rules he should give and receive silver and gold.

15 *suvarṇaḥ* : this refers to the weight, equivalent to 16 *māṣakas* ; cf. 2.19.3. — *varṇakaḥ* : i.e., touch or fineness of gold. 16 *kākaṇī* and *suvarṇa* are nowhere in the text brought into relation with one another. A *kākaṇī* is a copper coin 1/4th of a *māṣaka* in value (2.12.24). It seems that here it is understood to be 1/4th of a *māṣaka* in weight, though the two *māṣakas* are different ; so that a *suvarṇa* would be eqal to 64 *kākaṇīs*. By substituting 1, 2, 3 etc. *kākaṇīs* of copper in place of gold in a *suvarṇa*, we get 16 touches with proportions of gold and copper ranging from 63 : 1 to 48 : 16 (the 16 *kākaṇīs* in the last make 4 *māṣaka*s which in fact is here stated to be the limit, *ā catuḥsīmāntāt*). Both *māṣaka* and *kākaṇī* appear to be names of weights as well as of coins which apparently are different in weight. That is confusing.

17 *varṇikām*, i.e., one of the 17 standards mentioned above. 19 *jātihiṅguluka* ' a variety of vermilion called *sasada* (Cp) or *haṁsapāda* (Cs).' — *puṣpakāsīsa* seems to be sulphate of iron or blue vitriol.

21 ' River Tāpī in Mahārāṣṭra ' (Cj) ' in Āraṭṭadeśa (Cb). 22 *samarāgī*, i.e., showing the colour of gold as it really is. ' Of a uniform colour ' is less likely. 23 *pratirāgī* , i.e., showing a higher touch than what the gold actually has. 24 *apratirāgī*, i.e., showing a lower touch.

25 *chedaḥ*, i.e., the section where it is cut. 26 *tāpaḥ* : Cb Cs read *tāpe* and that is preferred by Jolly-Schmidt. However, the nom. seems better corresponding to *chedaḥ* above. With *tāpe*, we cannot think of a masculine substantive for *śreṣṭhaḥ* etc., as *suvarṇa* is neuter.

28 *pautavādhyakṣe* in 2.19 below.

30 An unauthorized person shall not approach the workshop. 31 One approaching is to be extirpated. 32 Even an officer, if carrying gold and silver (inside), shall be deprived of the same.

33 Artisans doing the work of setting in gold, bead-making, plating and gilding and ornamental gold, (and) blowers, servants and dust-washers, shall enter and leave after their garments, hands and private parts are searched. 34 And all their tools and uncompleted works shall remain just there. 35 He should hand over the gold received and the work being carried out into the office. 36 In the evening and in the morning, he should deposit (the gold and the articles), marked with the seals of the maker and the overseer.

37 Setting, stringing and minor work, these are ways of working (in gold). 38 Setting is the fixing of binding and so on. 39 Stringing is weaving in threads and so on. 40 (Making) a solid article, a hollow article or one with beads and so on is minor work.

41 In the work of setting, he should use one-fifth part as fastening at base and tenth part as side-fastening. 42 Silver with a quarter part copper, or gold with a quarter part silver is artificial; against that he should guard. 43 In the work of fixing of beads, (there should be) three parts enclosing at

31 *ucchedyaḥ*: Cb Cs understand 'confiscation of entire property.' Cf., however, 1.15.6 above. 32 *tenaiva jīyeta*, i.e., what he has brought with him should be confiscated.

33 Cj drops *-hasta-*. — *kāñcanakāru* seems concerned with setting gems in gold and silver as described in ss. 41-43. The root appears to be *kac, kañc* to bind. The *Trikāṇḍaśeṣa* has '*kācanaṁ patranibandhanam.*' *pṛṣatakāru* seems concerned with the making of gold beads or globules, *tvaṣṭṛkāru* is the gilder and plater as in ss. 44-46, and *tapanīyakāru* is the maker of ornamental gold as in ss. 47 ff. — *caraka* seems to be an ordinary servant. If he has any special duty in the workshop like the others, its nature is not clear. Cj shows *saraka*, which means 'a gem'. But it can hardly be construed with *pāṁsudhāvaka*. Dust-washing is possible in the case of gold, not of gems. 35 *dhṛtaṁ ca prayogam*: Meyer proposes *kṛtam* as a contrast to *aniṣṭhitāḥ*. However, work held in hand under production, is a better concept. Cb explains *dhṛtam* by 'weighed' and *karaṇamadhye* by 'in the presence of witnesses.' *karaṇa* as office appears, however, more likely. 36 *sāyaṁ prātaś ca*: strictly this would imply night shifts as well. Perhaps, however, seals were made in the evening and opened in the morning. — *kartṛ* is the artisan and *kārayitṛ* is the supervisor or '*suvarṇādhyakṣa* himself' (com.)

38 *kācārpaṇa* 'in which *kāca*, i.e., a gem, pearl, diamond or coral is fixed' (Cj). *kāca* would seem to refer rather to the gold in which the gem etc. is set. 39 *sūtravāna*: gold threads arranged in various patterns seem meant.

41 *arpayet*: this position of the verb is unusual. — *pañcabhāgaṁ kāñcanaṁ daśabhāgaṁ kaṭumānam*: Cb has 'one-fifth of the gem should be set in the base and one-tenth in leaves of gold.' Cj explains *kaṭumāna* as 'the covering of wax or lac (*madhūcchiṣṭasya lākṣayā vā pracchādanam*).' Cp, reading *kaṭamānam*, has 'one-fifth as base and one-tenth as binding at the side,' the remaining 7/10th of gold remaining unconnected with the gem as in a ring. This is what seems intended. Meyer suggests *kaṭimānam* as the reading 'side-binding.' G M read only *mānam*. 42 The point of the warning seems to be that artisans frequently use this alloy for setting and that fact cannot be very easily detected. 43 *pṛṣatakācakarmaṇaḥ*: the difference from pure *kācakarman* seems to be that we have gold beads set in this case, or gold beads and gems (Cs Meyer). *paribhāṇḍa* is probably the same as *kaṭumāna*, and *vāstuka* the base. Cb, understanding gems only even in this case, explains *paribhāṇḍa* as 'the lotus-shaped or *svastika*-shaped fixing for the gem.' — *hi* in the s. does

the sides and two parts base, or four parts base and three parts enclosing at the sides.

44 In the work of the gold-plater, he should plate an article of copper with an equal amount of gold. 45 An article of silver, whether solid or hollow, he should cover with half the amount of gold. 46 Or, he should gild (the silver article) with one-fourth part gold by means of the liquid or powder of sand-vermilion.

47 Ornamental gold of the best kind, possessed of excellent colour, passed through an equal amount of lead, turned into leaves by heating (and) made bright with Indus-earth, becomes the base of blue, yellow, white, green and parrot-feather colours. 48 And iron of the colour of the peacock's neck, white at the cut, shimmering, (and) powdered after being heated, is for this (gold) a colouring matter one *kākaṇī* in measure for one *suvarṇa* (of gold).

49 Or, silver, purified, four times in a crucible of bones, four times in one with an equal amount of lead, four times in a dry crucible, three times in a pot-sherd (and) twice in cow-dung, thus passed through seventeen crucibles,

not seem to have any significance. — It is possible that the s. refers to the making of gold beads, *vāstuka* being the interior base, usually of lac and *paribhāṇḍa* the exterior covering of gold. For this *pṛṣatakarmaṇaḥ* would be enough. Or, *vāstuka* may refer to the bead itself and *paribhāṇḍa* to the decorative extension at the sides.

44 *saṁyūhayet* : Meyer has suggested that this is a Prakritism for *saṁ-vyūh*. 45 *suṣiram*: the *ghanasuṣiram* of the mss. is obviously due to repetition from the preceding word. Cf. s. 40 above. 46 *vālukāhiṅgulukasya* etc. ' with the powder of vermilion and sand ' (Cb), ' gold, which is powdered and mixed with mercury, is mixed with the powder of sand-vermilion and melted on straw-fire ' (Cp). It is difficult to see how mercury can be brought in unless *rasena* is read after *cūrṇena*. And mercury dos not seem necessary for the gilding described here. What exactly is meant by *vālukāhiṅguluka* is not clear. See 2.14.34 below. — *vāsayet* from *vas* caus. ' to clothe ' refers to gilding.

47 *tapanīyam* seems to mean ' which is to be turned into ornaments ' by heating, colouring etc. It is here an adjective to *suvarṇam*. — *saindhavikayā* ' with earth from the Saurāṣtra country ' (com.) ; ' earth from Indus ' seems more likely. — *ujjvālitam* probably by rubbing with it, hardly ' by heating along with it ' (Meyer). — *-śukapota-* of the mss. is obviously corrupt for *-śukapatra-* ; cf. s. 56 below. — Some of the colours mentioned here are not referred to in ss. 51-56, while others referred to there are not mentioned here. 48 *asya . . . kākaṇikaḥ suvarṇarāgaḥ*, i.e., one *kākaṇī* of iron is the colouring for one *suvarṇa* of gold (i.e., 1 in 64 as in s. 16 above) as described in s. 47. Meyer has ' a strong (*tīkṣṇa*) form of this gold etc.' It is not easy to see how this strong formis arrived at. — *pītacūrṇitam* 'heated and powdered' (com.). *pīta* may also convey theidea of soaking in water, which may be done after heating. ' *pratāpya udakoṣitaṁ tataś cūrṇitam* ' (Cj). — It is not clear what colour is produced in gold by the insertion of this powder.

49 *tāram upaśuddhaṁ vā* : *tāra* is silver, particularly that used for ornaments ; *upaśuddha* refers to the purification as presently described ; *vā* shows the option with *savarṇa* above ; i.e., this silver also can be a base for colours. Meyer has ' fine silver (*tāra*) or almost pure (*upaśuddha*) silver '. This appears little likely. — *asthitutthe* etc. : Cb Cp understand these terms as descriptive of the crucibles — made of earth mixed with bone-powder, of earth mixed with an equal amount of lead, of earth mixed with sand (*śuṣkatuttha*, i.e., *kaṭaśarkarāmūṣā*), of earth alone and of earth mixed with cow-dung. It may be, however, that *asthi* etc describe the substances along with which the silver is smelted, *śuṣkatuttha* referring to smelting without any mixture. Meyer understands *tuttha* as blue vitriol, a mixture of this with *asthi* and *samasīsa*, and *śuṣka* as dry blue vitriol ; only *kapāla*, he says, he cannot understand. But even in his *gomaya* there is no blue vitriol. Altogether

(and) made bright with Indus-earth (is a base for colours). 50 From this one *kākaṇī* onwards up to two *māṣas* should be inserted in one *suvarṇa* ; afterwards the adding of colouring matter (should follow) ; it becomes white silver.

51 Three parts of ornamental gold, strengthened with thirty-two parts of white silver, it becomes white-red. 52 It makes copper yellow. 53 Making the oranmental gold bright, he should give one-third part colouring ; it becomes yellowish red. 54 (With) two parts of white silver, one part of ornamental gold produces the colour of the *mudga*-bean. 55 When smeared with half a part of black iron, it becomes black. 56 Ornamental gold twice-smeared with an enveloping liquid gets the colour of the parrot's feather. 57 In undertaking that work, he should take a test regarding the various colours.

58. And he should be conversant with the treatment of iron and copper. 59 Therefore, (he should know) also loss in the case of articles made of dia-

his explanation is not satisfactory. 50 *kākaṇyuttaram* etc. : from one *kākaṇī* onwards up to two *māṣas* (i.e., 2 *māṣakas*) of this *tāra* is to be inserted in one *suvarṇa*. This word therefore must be understood as the weight of that name and not as gold. Hence the metal in which the insertion is to be made would appear to be ordinary silver ; this would give nine tints of silver. Thus in the main Cp. Cb, reading *kākaṇyuttarāpasāritā*, understands the insertion to be made in gold. That would make gold *śvetatāra*. This is not very likely ; it also would not fit in with the possibility of *tapanīya* and *śvetatāra* being mixed tegether (s. 51). Meyer understands the removal of 1 *kākaṇī* etc. of silver and insertion of gold in its place. *suvarṇe deyam* makes this hardly possible. — *rāgayogaḥ* : this would appear to be the *tīkṣṇa* as described above.

51 *trayo 'ṁśāḥ* etc. : the grammatical difficulty is best removed by reading *tat* from Cb and retaining *mūrcchitāḥ* of the mss. Cp refers to the following explanation of ' some ' : ' 3 parts of *tapanīya* are added to 32 less 3, i.e. 29 parts of ordinary gold and this mixture is smelted with 32 parts of *śvetatāra*.' It is difficult to see how the words can yield all this meaning. Cb has ' out of 32 parts 3 are *tapanīya*, the rest 29 silver.' Since, however, *mūrch* has the sense of ' to increase, augment,' the proporion of 3 to 32 would appear more likely. It is not altogether unlikely that *dvātriṁśadbhāga* means 1/32nd part, so that the proportion might be 3 to 1/32 or 3 to 3/32. 52 *tāmraṁ pītakaṁ karoti* : Cp has ' 32 parts gold (with 3 parts *tapanīya* as above) with 32 parts copper become yellow.' Cb has ' 3 parts *tapanīya* and 32 parts copper.' That seems to be meant. Meyer has ' 3 parts copper and 32 parts *śvetatāra* '. 53 *rāgatribhāgam* ' 1 *kākaṇī* in 3/4ths of a *suvarṇa*, i.e., in 12 *māṣakas* of gold ' (Cp), ' one-third purified gold in unpurified gold ' (Cb), ' 1/3rd *tapanīya* is inserted in *śvetatāra* ' (Meyer). What seems meant is that in 3 parts of *tapanīya* 1 part of *rāga* of s. 48 is inserted. Cj seems to have read *tāmratribhāgam*. — *pītarāgam* ' yellowish red ' as distinguished from *pītaka* above. 54 *śvetatātra*- etc. : according to Cp, *rāgayoga* is to be understood in addition ; but *śvetatāra* already seems to have it. 55 *kālāyasasya* etc. : ' gold of the colour of *mudga* when mixed with half part (half of 1/3, i.e., 1/6) of colouring, becomes black ' (Cb) ; evidently *kālāyasa* is identified with *tīkṣṇa* and *ardha* is related to *tribhāga* of s. 53. Meyer thinks that *śvetatāra* becomes black in this way, not *tapanīya*. Cb however seems right in understanding the mixture of s. 54. And as it has 3 parts and *rāga* is half a part, the latter does amount to 1/6th of that mixture, though not in the way Cb understands it. 56 *pratilepinā rasena* : Cp has ' liquified iron mixed with mercury.' *pratilepin*, however, is an adjective ' smearing all round, enveloping ' qualifying *rasa*, and the latter can hardly mean ' mixed with mercury.' *rasa* seems to be that of *kālāyasa* or *tīkṣṇa* ; Meyer thinks of *kāñcanika rasa* of 2.12.2. 57 *prativarṇikā* seems to refer to the test on the touchstone to ascertain whether the desired colour is obtained or not.

58 *tīkṣṇatāmra*- etc. : the *suvarṇādhyakṣa* is to be conversant with this, though iron and copper articles are manufactured in separate factories, because these metals are used in the manufacture of gold and silver articles. 59 *tasmāt* : there is nothing in the text to explain this use of ' therefore '. Perhaps it owes its origin to 2.14.43. — *apaneyimānam*

monds, gems, pearls and corals and the amounts required for the making of gold and silver wares.

60-61 Of an even colour, symmetrical, with beads not sticking to each other, firm, well-burnished, not soaked (for a false glitter), divided (into suitable parts), pleasant to wear, not gaudy, full of lustre, with a charming shape, even, and pleasing to the mind and eye, — these are declared to be the excellent qualities of an ornament.

CHAPTER FOURTEEN

SECTION 32 THE ACTIVITY OF THE GOLDSMITH IN THE MARKET-HIGHWAY.

1 The Goldsmith should cause the gold and silver work of the citizens and the country people to be carried out by workshop artisans.

2 They should do the work with the time and the (nature of the) work stipulated, without stipulation as to time when there is the excuse of the (nature of the) work. 3 In case the work is done otherwise (than as ordered) (there shall be) loss of wage and a fine double that (amount). 4 In case the time limit is exceeded, (he shall receive) a wage reduced by one-quarter and a fine double that (amount).

'taking away, removal ' is understood as ' substitution of an inferior for a superior gem ' (Cb). It may also mean ' reduction or loss' in the process of cutting, polishing etc. (Meyer). — *budhyeta* is to be supplied from the preceding s. — *bandhapramāṇāni* refers to ' 3 parts *paribhāṇḍa* etc.' (Cb), ' amount required for plating ' (Cp), ' amount required for making the article ' (Meyer).

60 *samadvandvam* ' having a similar pair,' i.e., symmetrical. — *asaṁpītam* ' not gilded to increase its lustre artificially ' (Cs) ; ' not fabricated ' (Meyer). Cj (with *asaṁvītam*) has ' the colour of which is not obscured by other articles of momentary charm.' — *vibhaktam* seems to refer to proper proportions in the various parts. 61 *abhinītam* ' not gaudy' (Cj), ' tasteful ' (Meyer). It may also convey the idea of ' highly finished.' — *saṁsthāna* seems to mean ' shape or form '. *svasthāna* of M ' in its appropriate place (on the body) ' is also not bad. — *tapanīya* here is clearly ' ornament ', not merely gold. — The *kārikās* more properly belong to the sphere of the *sauvarṇika* of the next Chapter than to that of the *suvarṇādhyakṣa*.

2.14

The *sauvarṇika* or goldsmith is clearly in state service. Apparently private goldsmiths are to work under his supervision.

1. *rūpyasuvarṇam* stands for *rūpyasuvarṇabhāṇḍam* ' gold and silver articles.' There is no reference to gold coins here, as is sometimes supposed. — *āveśanibhiḥ* : these also appear to be in state service.

2 *kāryāpadeśam*, i.e., the nature of the work itself provides a valid excuse for delay. These ss. are repeated in 4.1.4-5, 7. In conformity with that, Cb Cp Cs interchange ss. 3 and 4 here. 4 *pādahīnaṁ vetanaṁ taddviguṇaś ca daṇḍaḥ* : the fine would be ' double the 3/4th wage ' (Cs) rather than ' double the full wage ' or ' double the 1/4th wage that is deducted.'

5 The (artisans) shall deliver in the same condition as to quality and quantity as they receive the entrusted metal. 6 And even after a lapse of time, (customers) shall receive it in the same condition, except what is lost (in manufacture) and worn away (by time.)

7 The (Goldsmith) should be conversant with every detail in connection with the characteristics and the manufacture of gold and its articles by workshop artisans.

8 In the case of gold and silver (used in the manufacture of articles), a loss of one *kākaṇī* in a *suvarṇa* may be allowed. 9 One *kākaṇī* of iron — twice that in the case of silver — is the insertion for colour ; one-sixth part of that is the loss (allowed).

10 In case of diminution of quality to the extent of one *māṣa* at least, the lowest fine for violence (shall be imposed) ; in case of diminution of quantity (to that extent), the middle (fine); in case of deceit in scales and weights, the highest (fine), also in case of fraud in an article manufactured.

11 For a (person) causing the manufacture (of an article) unseen by the Goldsmith or in some other place, the fine shall be twelve *paṇas.* 12 For the artisan, (the fine shall be) double, if there is a valid excuse. 13 If there is no excuse, the (person) shall be taken to the magisterial court. 14 And for

5 *varṇa* is clearly ' quality.' 6 *kālāntarād api*, i.e., ' when delay is caused by illness, disturbances, etc.' (Cb). Cs has ' even if the artisan has gone on a long journey or is dead, his sons must return it in the same condition.' — *anyatra kṣīṇapariśīrṇābhyām* : Cb Cp have 'when there is diminution or wearing away there is a fine.' Cp mentions a fine of 1,000. It seems that *kṣīṇa* refers to loss allowed in manufacture and *pariśīrṇa* to wearing away by time ; in either case there is no fine.

7 *lakṣaṇa* and *prayoga* are to be construed with *suvarṇa* and *pudgala*. In view of 2.18. 35 and s. 11 below ' trade or practice of fraud ' (Cs) is unlikely for *prayoga*.

8 *tapta* seems to be the same as *tapanīya* ornamental gold, and *kaladhautaka* ornamental silver. Cj understands ' during the acts of heating (*tapta*) and washing for rubbing (*kaladhauta*).' — *kākaṇikaḥ suvarṇe* etc. : i.e., loss allowed in the process of manufacture is 1/64th or 1.56 per cent. 9 It seems best to regard *rūpyadviguṇah* as a parenthetical clause as in Meyer. The insertion in the case of silver would be 2 *kākaṇīs* in 1 *suvarṇa*. Cb Cs, reading *rūpyadviguṇā*, explain ' 1 *kākaṇī* of iron with 2 *kākaṇīs* of silver forms the colouring for gold.' Silver, however, is not mentioned as a colouring material in the last Chapter. It is true that the last Chapter does not also refer to 2 *kākaṇīs* as colouring material for silver. Nevertheless the former explanation appears preferable. — *ṣaḍbhāgaḥ kṣayaḥ* : i.e., of 1 *suvarṇa* gold and 1 *kākaṇī rāga* (added to it) loss allowed is 1/64th of gold and 1/6th of *rāga* leaving 63 5/6th instead of 65 *kākaṇīs* ; in silver, 64 2/3rds would remain out of 66 *kākaṇīs*.

10 *māṣāvare*, i.e., one *māṣa* of metal of higher quality (*varṇa*) is reduced to a lower quality (Cp). Meyer has ' when the loss suffered by the customer is of the value of 1 *māṣa*.' This ignores *varṇa*. — *pramāṇahīne* : we have to understand *māṣāvare* with this. — *kṛtabhāṇḍopadhau* seems to refer to fraud after the article is made (*krita*), i.e., during inspection as in s. 44 onwards, though the idea of ' during the making ' is also not unlikely. *māṣāvare* need not be understood with this or the preceding case.

11 *kārayataḥ* seems to refer to the customer, who gets work done on the sly to escape the regular state charges for manufacture. 12 *sāpasāraś cet* is to be understood in s. 11 as well. 13 *anapasāraḥ* : This raises the possibility that the gold may be stolen property and hence the need for investigation by the *pradeṣṭṛ* as in Book 4. 14 *paṇacchedanam* ' cut-

the artisan, (the punishment shall be) a fine of two hundred *paṇas* or the cutting off of the fingers of his hand.

15 They shall purchase the scales and weights from the Superintendent of Standardisation. 16 Otherwise, (there shall be) a fine of twelve *paṇas.*

17 Making solid objects, making hollow objects, plating, coating, fixing and gilding constitute an artisan's work.

18 Fraud in the balance, removal, tapping, boxing and embedding are the means of pilfering (by artisans).

19 (Easily) bending, carved out, with split top, with a subsidiary (false) neck, with bad strings, with defective scales, given to swinging, and magnetic, — these are false balances.

20 Two parts of silver and one part of copper constitute *tripuṭaka.* 21 By means of that, mineral gold is removed; that is 'removal by *tripuṭaka.*' 22 By (substitution of) copper, that is 'removal by copper', by (substitution of) *vellaka,* that is 'removal by *vellaka,*' by (substitution of) gold containing half copper, that is 'removal by gold'.

23 A dummy crucible, foul dross, the 'crane's beak', the blow-pipe, the pair of tongs, the water-vessel, borax, and the same gold, these are the ways of removal. 24 Or, sand made into lumps and placed (there) beforehand, is taken out of the fire-place on the breaking of the crucible.

ting off the fingers of a hand.' *agrahastasya chedanam* (Cj), *pañcāṅgulicchedanam* (Cp). Cf. 4.10.1.

15 *pautava* stands for *pautavādhyakṣa,* 2.19.

17 *ghanaṁ suṣiram* is read as in 2.13.40; see 2.13.45. — *saṁyūhya* is thick plating, while *avalepya* is coating with thin plates; *saṁghātya* is fixing base metal in a precious metal, while *vāsitaka* is gilding.

19 *saṁnāminī* 'bending easily' because it is made of soft metal (Cb); Meyer thinks of a contrivance for bringing the scales down. — *utkīrṇikā* 'hollowed and filled with iron powder (Cj) or mercury (Cb) inside.' — *bhinnamastakā* apparently allows one side to go down easily. — *upakaṇṭhī* apparently has a centre where the scales balance unevenly; 'full of knots or accretions' (Cp). — *śikya* refers to the strings with which the pans (*kakṣya*) are suspended from the beam. *sakaṭu* is uncertain; Cb comment and Cj show only *kaṭu-*. — *āyaskāntā*: the beam has a magnet on one side, so that the metal pan tends to rise towards it.

21 *ākarodgatam*: cf. 2.13.3. 22 *vellaka* 'an alloy of equal parts of silver and iron' (com.).

23 *mūkamūṣā* has a false bottom into which a part of the melting gold drips down. — *pūtikiṭṭaḥ* 'the foul-smelling dross' in which gold may be concealed. Meyer proposes *pratikiṭṭa* 'apparent dross' which does not seem necessary. — *karaṭukamukham* 'a crane's beak' appears to be a kind of pincers with hollow ends for concealing gold. Cj mentions a view according to which it is the passage for wind at the end of the bellows. Cb, reading *karaṭamukham* 'a crow's beak', explains 'a vessel for receiving something.' — *joṅganī* vessel for holding water' (Cb), '*lohakaṭikā* (? iron vessel?)' (Cp); Cj's '*kañcikā vṛttam maryāriṣaṇāgrālohi*' is unintelligible. The root *juṅg* means 'to set aside, exclude.' Can the word mean a sieve, a strainer? — *suvarcikālavaṇam* probably the same as *sauvarcala* 'borax' of 2.15.15. — *tadeva suvarṇam*: the idea seems to be, the presence of the gold itself and its handling create the opportunity for pilfering. 24 *piṇḍavālukāḥ*: these appear like gold particles and are picked up instead of gold, which is recovered later.

25 At the time of fixing together afterwards or at the time of testing the laid-on plating leaf, interchange (of a gold article) by a silver article is tapping, or (the interchange) of sand lumps (containing gold) by sand lumps containing iron.

26 A firm and a removable enclosing is made in cases of plating, coating and fixing. 27 A piece of lead covered with a leaf of gold, (with) the interior fixed with lac, is the firm enclosing. 28 The same, when there are casings of layers, is the removable (enclosing). 29 A leaf that is compact or a twin-leaf is made in cases of coating. 30 Copper or silver is made the interior of leaves in cases of fixing. 31 An article of copper, fixed with a leaf of gold (and) polished is *supārśva* (' with a well-made side '); the same, fixed with a twin-leaf (and) polished, and an article of copper and silver (similarly treated) are *uttaravarṇaka* (' with quality outside ').

32 He should find these two out by heating and testing on the touchstone or by failure of (right) sound and by scratching. 33 The removable (encasing) they set down in the acid of the *badara*-fruit or in salt-water. Thus the 'enclosing '.

34 In a solid or a hollow article, gold-mixed earth or the pulp of *mālukā* and vermilion, when heated, remains (embedded). 35 Or, in an article with

25 *paścād bandhane* : the loc. as in Cb is necessary, not nom. as in the mss. The reference is to joining parts that are first separately made. — *ācitakapatra* is the gold leaf used for plating. — *visrāvaṇam* seems to refer to substitution of one article or piece by another of a lower metal, while in *apasāraṇa* the gold-content is tampered with, not the entire article or piece. — *piṇḍavālukā* here must be supposed to contain gold.

27 *abhyantaram aṣṭakenea baddham* seems to be almost a parenthetical clause. 28 *paṭalasampuṭeṣu* appears to be used as a locative absolute, ' when there are casings of layers '; the idea seems to be that the lead inside is not fixed or soldered and can be removed. There is no fixing with *aṣṭaka* (Cp). *sampuṭa* ' a fold,' a sort of box or casket, hollow inside. 29 *patram āśliṣṭaṁ yamakapatraṁ vā* : ' i.e., on one side of the article or on both sides ' (Cb). The insertion of lead between the gold-leaf and the article in one case and between the two leaves in the other is probably to be understood, though there is no direct reference to that. 31 Following Cb, *supārśva* and *uttaravarṇaka* are understood as two types of *saṁghātya*. In the *uttaravarṇaka* two items are included, a copper article covered with a double gold-leaf and a copper-silver article (either as alloy or in separate parts of the article) covered with gold-leaf. Cs begins the s. with *saṁghātyeṣu kriyate* and understands two types up to the second *pramṛṣṭam*, explaining *tāmratāra*- etc. as ' copper or silver is used as a plating for ironware etc.' or 'a piece of copper is plated with silver.' Meyer seems to find three types of *saṁghātya*,—*supārśva*, *pramṛṣṭa* and *tāmratārarūpa*, ' samples for further work (of fraud) ' being his explanation of *uttaravarṇakaḥ*. Many of the details in these ss. are far from clear.

32 *tad ubhayam*, i.e., the *gāḍha* and the *abhyuddhārya peṭaka*. — *niḥśabda* ' absence of right tone ' (Meyer) seems preferable to ' cutting without a sound ' (Cp). 33 *sādayanti* ' put it down ' ; Cb adds that the article then becomes red in colour.

34 The difference between *peṭaka* and *piṅka* appears to be that in the former a different metal is inserted in the plating of gold, while in the latter a chemical or mineral substance is embedded in the article. — *vā* supports the reading *ghane suṣire* from Cj. Cf. 2.13.40, 45 etc. — *mālukāhiṅguluka*- : perhaps *vālukāhiṅguluka*- should be read as in 2.13.46. Cb comment seems to support it. Cp seems to understand ' pulp of *hiṅguluka* along with *suvarṇamṛd* and *suvarṇamālukā* (these two being kinds of minerals).' This ignores the *vā* that follows. Cp, however, does not show the *vā*. 35 *dṛdhavāstuke* : i.e., the embedding is

a firm base, lac mixed with sand or the paste of red lead, when heated, remains (embedded). 36 Of these two, heating or breaking is the (test of) purity.

37 Or, in an article containing an encircling metal, salt heated by a fire-brand along with soft pebbles, remains (embedded). 38 Boiling is (the test of) its purity.

39 Or, a layer of mica is fixed in an article with a double base by means of lac. 40 Of that, in which the fixing has been covered, one part sinks down when it is placed in water, or it is pierced with a needle in the spaces between the layers.

41 Gems, silver or gold form the embedding in solid or hollow articles. 42 Of that, heating or breaking is (the test of) purity. Thus the embedding.

43 Therefore, the (Goldsmith) should ascertain the class, appearance, quality, quantity, the ornament made and the characteristics of articles made of diamonds, gems, pearls and corals.

44 In the course of testing articles that are made or in the course of repairs to old articles, four ways of stealing (are practised): knocking off, cutting out, scratching out or rubbing off. 45 When under the pretext of (discovering) an ' enclosing ', they cut out a bead or a string or a casing, that is knocking off. 46 Or, when in an article with a double base, they insert

done in the solid base. — *gāndhāra* ' red lead ' evidently named after the country of its origin.

37 *kaṭuśarkarayā* : ' soft stone or pebbles ' (com.). Meyer wonders if it can mean ' hard sugar.' Some kind of sand seems to be intended. 38 *kvāthanam* is done in the *badarāmla* of s. 33 (com.).

39 *dviguṇavāstuke* : i.e., the base has two layers of gold plates, between which mica is fixed with lac. — *vā* shows a new type of *piṅka* ; and it is not necessary, as Meyer thinks, to read *ekavāstuke* at the beginning to justify it. 40 *apihitakācakasya* : *kāca* seems to mean ' embedding ' here, same as *piṅka* ; it is covered with the outer layer of gold. — *udake*, i.e., 'in *badarāmla* ' (com.). — *paṭalāntareṣu vā* : *vā* shows that this is another method of discovering the presence of mica inside. *paṭalāntara* is therefore ' space between layers ' rather than ' other layers, such as copper etc.' (Cp).

41 *maṇayo rūpyam* etc. : ' inferior gems are *piṅka*, i.e., *haraṇopāya* (means of pilfering) for genuine gems, silver for gold, and impure gold for pure gold ' (com.). It seems more likely, however, that an inferior or impure object of the same class constitutes the *piṅka* or embedding in a superior or pure article of that class ; in the case of *maṇi*, it amounts to nothing more than substitution. Meyer seems to understand *maṇayaḥ* etc. as stating the material out of which articles are made, adding ' in their case pasting is practised.' But these words are in the nom. and go with *piṅkaḥ*.

43 Cf. 2.13.59. — *pudgala* ' the ornament made.'

45 *piṭakā* seems related to *peṭaka* and to be some sort of casing. 46 *dviguṇavāstukānām* is strange ; we expect *dviguṇavāstuke* as in s. 39 above. — *sīsarūpam* : this is coated with gold (com. as also Meyer). That may not appear quite necessary. — It seems that in *parikuṭṭana*, some external part is cut out, while in *avacchedana* a part from the inte-

an object of lead and cut the interior out, that is cutting out. 47 When from solid objects they scratch out with a sharp tool, that is scratching out. 48 When after coating a piece of cloth with the powder of one of the following, (viz.,) yellow orpiment, red arsenic or vermilion, or with powder of *kuruvinda* (-stone), they rub the article with it, that is rubbing off. 49 By that articles of gold and silver lose in weight and yet no part of these (articles) gets bruised.

50 Of plated articles that are broken or cut or rubbed off, he should form an inference (as to loss) with the help of a similar article. 51 Of coated articles he should form an estimate by cutting out as much as has been cut out (by the artisan). 52 Or, of those that have changed their appearance, he should do heating and rubbing in (acid) water a number of times.

53 Sudden movement of the hand, the weights, the fire, the wooden anvil, the tool-box, the receptacle, the peacock's feather, the thread, garment, talk, the head, the lap, the fly, attention to one's person, the bellows-skin, the water-platter, and the fire-pan, — these he should know as the means of pilfering.

54 Of silver articles he should know that as fraudulent which smells like raw flesh, easily catches dirt, is rough, very hard or changed in colour.

55 In this manner he should test the new and the old as well as the article that has changed its appearance, and should impose penalties on the (artisans) as prescribed.

rior is cut out. Cj shows *parikartanam* for *parikuṭṭanam*. 48 *kuruvinda* 'a kind of stone' (com.). Is the meaning 'black salt' given in the lexicons possible?

52 *virūpāṇāṁ vā*: Cp renders *vā* by *ca*, perhaps rightly. Cp Cs, reading a stop after *vā*, construe this with the preceding, but instead of supplying *utpāṭyānumānam* as expected, they supply *sadṛśenānumānam*, which is little likely. *virūpa*, 'i.e., made inferior in touch by mixing with an alloy' (Cb).

53 *avakṣepaḥ* 'sleight of hand' (Cb Cs). Cj has '*lāghavena saṁcāraṇam*, moving lightly or quickly.' 'Throwing out (in the rubbish),' to be recovered later, is also not unlikely. — *pratimānam* 'substitution while weighing or adjusting weights' (Cb). — *bhaṇḍikā* 'tool-box' (Meyer), 'vessel for collecting molten gold' (Cb). — *adhikaraṇī* 'an iron vessel' (Cb). — *sūtram* 'the thread for measuring or that in the balance, with wax applied over it' (Cb), 'coil of thread used in making the ornament' (Meyer). — *cellaṁ bollanam*: Cj has *cellacollanam* 'tying the knot with a piece of cloth, *vastrakhaṇḍena nīvībandhanam*.' Cb seems to have *celaṁ pollanam* 'garment and talking.' Cp has *celkaṁ colanam*. Meyer prefers *cellacollanam* 'folding the garment.' Deśī words are evidently used here. — *śiraḥ utsaṅgaḥ* are used for concealing gold. — *kācam* 'means of pilfering' seems a meaning developed from that of s. 40 above.

54 *prastīnam* 'hard.' Cb reads *prastītam* in the same sense.

55 *atyayaṁ yathoddiṣṭam*: actually no penalties are prescribed in this or the preceding Chapter. Perhaps the fines of 4.1.26 ff. are to be thought of. Breloer (KSt, III, 439-440) thinks that the *kārikā* belongs to the duties of the *suvarṇādhyakṣa*, not the *sauvarṇika*. That seems to have been Meyer's view too. As it stands, however, the *sauvarṇika* alone can be thought of in the stanza.

CHAPTER FIFTEEN

SECTION 33 THE SUPERINTENDENT OF THE MAGAZINE

1 The Superintendent of the Magazine should know about agricultural produce, revenue from the countryside, purchase, barter, begging, borrowing, labour in place of taxes, income from other sources, return from expenditure and additional income.

2 The various kinds of grains brought in by the Director of Agriculture constitute agricultural produce.

3 The aggregate tax, the one-sixth share, provisions for the army, tribute, tax, the 'lap', the 'side', compensation for loss, presents, and income from stores constitute revenue from the countryside.

4 The price of grains, disposal of treasury and recovery of what is given at interest constitute purchase.

5 Exchange of different kinds of grains at a different price is barter.

6 Asking for grains from another source is begging. 7 The same, intended to be returned, is borrowing.

8 The work of pounding, splitting (pulses), frying, fermenting, and grinding from those who live by these, the pressing of oil from oilmen using the

2.15

2 *sītā* is produce from state or crown lands. Cf. 2.24 below.

3 *piṇḍakaraḥ*, i.e., received from the village as a whole, not from individual cultivators. Breloer (KST, III, 319) thinks of fixed payments which are less than the regular share-tax, e.g., in amelioration contracts or from land given to officers etc. — *senābhaktam* 'for payment to mercenaries' (Cb); apparently this varied according to the strength of the army. — For *bali* and *kara*, see 2.6.3. — *utsaṅgaḥ* 'presents on festive occasions like a prince's birth' (Cp), 'money given on interest' (Cb), 'maintenance of officers (*āyuktavṛttiḥ*)' (Cj), 'super-tax' (Meyer). — *pārśvam* : see 2.6.20. 'A levy as in 5.2 below' (Cp), 'a surcharge on what has been fixed' (Cb), 'bribe' (Cj), 'impost in case of deficit' (Breloer, III, 321). — *pārihīṇikam* : see 2.6.20. Cj has here 'recovery of ouststandings,' mentioning 'confiscation of the goods of those exiled or gone from the country' as the view of others. — *kauṣṭheyakam* 'income from the stores,' is 'revenue from tanks, parks etc. made by the king' (Cs). Breloer (III, 321) seems to agree with 'receipts from tenants of crown lands' (Cb). — *rāṣṭra* here differs materially from *rāṣṭra* in 2.6.3. Breloer thinks of rulership as land-tax corresponding to *sarkar amal* of modern times (III, 319).

4 *kośanirhāraḥ* 'paying out of the treasury for the purchase of grains' (Com.). Meyer understands selling grains to fill the treasury with cash. The former idea seems better. — The inclusion of recovery of loans under purchase is a bit strange.

5 *arghāntareṇa* 'at different prices'; the quantities would vary according to price in a fair exchange.

8 *rocaka* 'who separates the two halves of pulses' (com.). — *audracākrikeṣu* is from Cj ıor *aurabhra-*. Cj explains 'those who press oil with a machine (*audrā hi puṭikā yantreṇa pīḍayanti*) and those who use the oil-press going round (*cākrikās*) *tu caturṣu pārśveṣu cālyamānena cakreṇa*).' The latter is apparently the *ghānī*; the former was apparently worked by hand. Cb has no explanation of *aurabhra-*; Cs explains 'who do the work of slaughtering the sacrificial ram'; Meyer has 'shepherds'; Breloer has '*auṣṭrika* oil-millers (and *cākrika*

hand press and the round press, and the work of extracting and treating juice of sugar-canes, — these constitute labour in place of taxes.

9 What is lost, forgotten and so on is income from other sources.

10 Balance due to (army-) disbandment and from undertakings (given up) in the middle because of sickness, is return from expenditure.

11 Difference in weights and measures, hand-filling, residue of the heap, surcharge, outstanding (revenue), and earned income, constitute additional income.

12 As regards grains, fats, sugars and salts, we shall state rules concerning grains in the (Section on the) Director of Agriculture.

13 Butter, oil, suet and marrow are fats.

14 Treacle, jaggery, unrefined sugar and granulated sugar constitute the group of sugars.

15 Salt from the Indus-land, sea-salt, *biḍa*-salt, salt-petre, borax and salt from saline soil constitute the group of salts.

16 That made by bees and the juice of grapes, are honey.

17 One of (the following, viz.,) sugar-cane juice, jaggery, honey, treacle, the juice of *jambū*-fruit and the juice of *panasa*-fruit, infused with a decoction of *meṣaśṛṅgī* and long pepper, kept for one month, six months or a year, (and then) mixed with *cidbhiṭa*, *urvāruka*, sugar-cane stalk, mango fruit and myrobalan, or unmixed (with these), constitute the group of fermented juices.

labourers)' (III, 327). — *saṁhanikā* : some sort of derivation is possible for this form and for *saṁhatikā*, hardly for *siṁhatikā* or *siṁhanikā*. The sense, of course, is technical. Russ. renders *siṁhanikā* by 'receipts from treatment of agricultural products.'

10 *vyayapratyāyaḥ* : see 2.6.21. Cj here gives the same explanation as Cb on that s.

11 *tulāmānāntaram* : there are varying sets of weights and measures for trade and for receipts in the treasury; see 2.19.22,29. — *hastapūraṇam* 'holding the hands above the measure so as to take in more grains when measuring out into the treasury' (Cb). It may possibly refer also to the throwing in of a handful or so over and above the grains measured out. — *utkaraḥ* ' what is left over of the heap of grains after the measuring is finished ' (Cb). — *vyājī* : cf. 2.6.10. — *paryuṣitam* : cf. 2.6.19 above. — *prārjitam* ' gains made by trading ' (Cb), ' flowers, betel-leaves etc. raised by the store-keeper himself ' (Cs). The actual comment in Cb shows *upārjitam* as the reading. Breloer understands *paryuṣitaṁ prārjitam* as one ' reclaimed balances of income '(III,329).

12 *sītādhyakṣe* in 2.24 below.

14 Meyer understands *khaṇḍa* and *śarkarā* as two ' candy ' and ' grain-sugar,' which also is possible.

15 *biḍa* ' muriate of soda with small quantities of muriate of lime, sulphur and oxide of iron ' (Monier-Williams : Dictionary). — *udbhedaja* ' derived from saline soil ' (com.), 'from salt-springs or salt-wells ' (Meyer), ' pit-salt ' (Breloer, III, 306).

16 *madhu* need not be assumed to be fermented as Breloer (KSt, III, 306 n.1) thinks.

17 *cidbhiṭa* is a kind of melon. — *urvāruka* is a variety of cucumber. — *avasuta* evidently does not imply infusion over a length of time. — *śukta* seems to be something like vinegar, of which six varieties are mentioned.

18 Tamarind, *karamarda*, mango, pomegranate, myrobalan, citron, *kola*, *badara*, *sauvīraka*, *parūṣaka* and others form the group of sour fruit-juices.

19 Curds, sour gruel and others are the group of sour liquids.

20 Long pepper, black pepper, ginger, cumin-seed, the bitter *kirāta*, white mustard, coriander, *coraka*, *damanaka*, *maruvaka*, the stalk of *śigru* and others constitute the group of spices.

21 And dried fish and dried meat, bulbous roots, roots, fruits, vegetables and others constitute the group of vegetables.

22 From these he should set apart one half for times of distress for the country people, (and) use the (other) half. 23 And he should replace old (stock) with new.

24 He should personally observe the amount of increase or decrease in the grains when pounded, rubbed, ground or fried, and when they are moistened, dry or cooked.

25 Of *kodrava* and *vrīhi*-rice, one-half is the substance, of *śāli*-rice, one-half less (than that), of *varaka*, one-third less. 26 Of *priyaṅgu*, one half is the substance with an increase of one-ninth. 27 *udāraka* has the same mass, also barley and wheat when pounded, and sesame, barley, *mudga* and *māṣa* when rubbed. 28 Wheat increases by one-fifth, also fried barley. 29 *Kalāya*-meal is less by one quarter. 30 (Meal) of *mudga* and *māṣa* is half a quarter less. 31 Of legumes, one-half is the substance, that of lentils, one-third less.

18 *kola*, *badara*, *sauvīraka* and *parūṣaka* are different kinds of edible berries or jujubes.

19 *dhānyāmla* sour gruel 'made from the fermentation of rice-water' (Dict.).

20 *coraka* appears to be anise-seed. — Many of the names in these ss. including the unusual *cidbhiṭa*, *karamarda*, *kustumburu*, *damanaka*, *maruvaka*, etc. have derivatives in Modern Indian Languages.

21 Dried fish and meat are included in *śāka* which ordinarily refers to vegetables only. Anything with which broths are made is evidently included here.

23 See 2.4.28 above.

24 *ghṛṣṭa* 'rubbed' or 'crushed' refers to the splitting of pulses etc.

25 *kodravavrīhīṇām* : we have to understand *kṣuṇṇānām* with this. Cj seems to have read this word. — *ardhabhāgonaḥ* may mean one-half less than the *ardha*, i.e., 1/4th or the same as *ardha* 1/2. In s. 42 the best type of *śāli* for the king has 1/4th. Cb Cj read *aṣṭabhāgonaḥ*, one-eighth less than *ardha*, i.e., 3/8th. — *tribhāgonaḥ* may be 2/3rds (Cb) or 1/2 less 1/3, i.e., 1/6. The latter would be too little. — *kodrava* and *varaka* are inferior kinds of grains. *priyaṅgu* and *udāraka* seem to be varieties of millets. 26 *navabhāgavṛddhiḥ* : 1/2 plus 1/9, i.e., 11/18. 27 *tulyaḥ* 'having the same *sāra* as *priyaṅgu*' (Cb). The idea rather seems to be that the mass remains the same as before pounding. As Breloer (KSt, III, 310) says, we have to think in terms of mass, not weight. — Cb shows no explanation of *yavā godhūmāś ca kṣuṇṇāḥ*, and it is possible that these words are not original. 28 *godhūmaḥ* : we may understand *ghṛṣṭaḥ* with this. 29 *kalāya* refers to peas. — *camasī* 'meal' (com.).

32 Ground flour, uncooked, and *kulmāṣa* become one and a half times (in volume). 33 Barley-meal becomes double, also *pulāka* and cooked flour.

34 Of *kodrava, varaka, udāraka* and *priyaṅgu*, the cooked preparation is threefold, of *vrīhi*-rice fourfold, of *śāli*-rice fivefold.

35 Later grains, when moistened, become double, one half more, when sprouted.

36 (There is) an increase of one-fifth in the case of fried grains. 37 *kalāya* becomes double, also fried rice and barley.

38 One-sixth is the amount of oil from linseed. 29 From *nimba, kuśa*, mango, wood-apple and others, one fifth part (is the amount of oil). 40 Oils from sesame, *kusumbha, madhūka* and *iṅgudī* amount to one-fourth.

41 Of cotton and flax, five *palas* yield one *pala* yarn.

42 Twelve *āḍhakas* of rice-grains from five *droṇas* of *śāli*-rice are for the feeding of a young elephant, eleven for that of vicious elephants, ten for riding elephants, nine for war-elephants, eight for infantry-men, seven for chiefs, six for the queens and the princes, five for kings or one *prastha* of rice-grains, unbroken and cleansed.

43 One *prastha* of rice-grains, one-fourth (of that) broth, a quantity of salt one-sixteenth of broth, (and) one-fourth part (of broth) butter or oil constitute one meal of an Ārya male. 44 One-sixth (of a *prastha*) broth, (and)

32 *piṣṭam* apparently refers to flour of wheat and *saktu*; *yava*-meal is mentioned separately in the next s. — *kulmāṣāḥ*: '*mudga, māṣa* etc.' (Com.), 'grains, particularly rice, moistened and half-cooked' (Meyer), 'cooked rice' (Breloer). It may be a kind of grain. 33 *yāvakaḥ* 'barley-flour' (Cs), 'barley without husk pounded' (Cb), '*yavaudana*, a barley and rice preparation(?)' (Cp). — *pulākaḥ* 'put in water and cooked' (Cb); grains moistened and half cooked are meant for animals; cf. s. 51 below and 2.29.43; 2.30.18.

35 *timitam* 'made wet.' — *aparānnam* '*mudga* and so on, because it is grown later' (Cj). Cp understands *phalāḍhakī, caṇaka* and so on. The reading *avarānnam* in the sense of 'lower kinds of grains' would probably refer to the same, *mudga, māṣa* etc. These are often kept in water for some time. When taken out of water, they sprout after a time (*virūḍha*) and then are used for making broths. Cb has 'the preparation of rice which has become moist in the fields (*timitam*) at the time of ripening and of unripened rice (*aparānnam*) becomes double.' This is doubtful.

39 It is not clear if *kuśa* and *āmra* are to be understood separately or *kuśāmra* as one; cf. 2.17.4.

41 Breloer remarks (KSt, III, 311-2) that this s. may appear to be in the wrong place, but that cotton and flax are required for sacks useful for storing.

42 *pañcadroṇe* etc.: i.e., from 20 *āḍhakas* of paddy we get 12 *āḍhakas* of rice, of the roughest quality. In the best or highly polished, the rice yield is only 1/4th of the paddy. — Breloer remarks that the four, *kalabha, vyāla* etc. refer to classes of animals, not to elephants only, and that the next four refer to classes of men, commoners (*patti*), officers (*mukhya*), court (*devīkumāra*) and king (KSt, III, 313). — *akhaṇḍa . . . prasthaḥ*: this *prastha* is not brought into relation with any amount of paddy as Breloer (III, 313) thinks.

43 It is proposed to add *taṇḍulānāṁ prasthaḥ* at the beginning. The words are necessary to show the amount of rice in the daily ration. They seem to have dropped out because they had occurred just before at the end of the last s. 44 *ardhasneham*: i.e., half that allowed to an Ārya (1/16 *prastha*), i.e., 1/32 *prastha*. If we understand 1/2 of 1/6, i.e., 1/12 *prastha* (as in Cb Cs and Meyer), that would mean the lower classes are to get more fat than the Ārya, which is unlikely. 45 *pādonam* applies to all items of ss. 43 and 44.

half the quantity of fat is for the lower classes. 45 One-quarter less for women. 46 One half for children.

47 For twenty *palas* of meat, half a *kuḍuba* of fat, one *pala* of salt, one *pala* of sugar, two *dharaṇas* of spices and half a *prastha* of curds (should be used). 48 By that higher quantities are explained. 49 For vegetables, one and a half times as much, for dried (meat etc.) twice as much and the same ingredients.

50 We shall state the amount of food ration for elephants and horses in the (Sections on the) Superintendents of these.

51 For bullocks, one *droṇa* of *māṣa* or a *pulāka* of barley (shall be added), the rest as laid down for horses. 52 The special (ration for bullocks is) one *tulā* of oil-cake from the press or ten *āḍhakas* of broken grains and bran. 53 Twice that for buffaloes and camels. 54 Half a *droṇa* for donkeys, spotted deer and red deer. 55 One *āḍhaka* for *eṇa*- and *kuraṅga*-deer. 56 Half an *āḍhaka* for goats, rams and boars or double that broken grains and bran. 57 One *prastha* of boiled rice for dogs. 58 Half a *prastha* for swans, herons and peacocks. 59 For deer, beasts, birds and wild animals other than these, he should cause an estimate to be made from one meal (consumed by them).

60 He should cause charcoal and husks to be taken to metal workshops and for plastering walls. 61 He should give the broken grains to slaves, labourers and broth-makers, (and) things other than these to dealers in cooked rice and in cakes.

62 Implements for weighing and measuring, grinding-stones, pestle and mortar, pounding and crushing machines, scatterer, winnowing basket, sieve, cane-basket, box and broom are the implements.

47 *viṁśatyā* : the instrumental is unusual ; perhaps the *visarga* after it got dropped out. 49 *adhyardha*- etc. : Meyer thinks that this applies to curds only or at most to fat and salt also, but not to *kṣāra* and *kaṭuka*, with which the word generally used is *yoga* ; for we have *yogaḥ* separately mentioned here.

50 *tadadhyakṣe*, i.e., in 2.31 and 2.30 respectively.

51 *pulākaḥ* : see s. 33 above. The amount of *yavas* for making it would also be 1 *droṇa* ; cf. 2.29.43. 53 Repeated in 2.29.44. 54 *ardhadroṇam* : this refers to *māṣa* or *pulāka*, not to oil-cake and bran. 59 *ataḥ* to be construed with *śeṣāṇām*. — *ekabhaktād* 'by inspecting food eaten by them in one day' (com.). It is possible that in s. 43 also *eka bhakta* refers to the day's ration, not a single meal.

61 *kaṇikāḥ* would appear to be larger than *kaṇa* on which the animals are fed. — *ato 'nyad* seems to refer to surplus food from the royal kitchen. It is not clear from *prayacchet* if it was sold.

62 *rocanīdṛṣad* 'the grinding stones,' for which *rocanī* alone is used in 3.8.11. — *kuṭṭakayantra* '*pādakramaṇīyam uṣṭragrīvākāram*' (Cj). — *rocakayantra* 'a machine for crushing pulses etc.' (Cb), '*hastabhramaṇīyam*' (Cj), '*peṣaṇayantram*' (Cp).— *patraka* 'a kind of tray (*caṅgerikā*)' (Cp), 'a wooden pounder' (Cb), 'fan' (Meyer).

63 Sweeper, watchman, weigher, measurer, supervisor of measuring, giver, supervisor of delivery, receiver of tallies, and the group of slaves and labourers, — these are the workmen.

64 On high should be the storing place for grains ; close-knit grass bags for sugar ; earthen jars and wooden casks for fats ; and the earth (should be the storing place) for salt.

CHAPTER SIXTEEN

SECTION 34 THE DIRECTOR OF TRADE

1 The Director of Trade should be conversant with the differences in the prices of commodities of high value and of low value and the popularity or unpopularity of goods of various kinds, whether produced on land or in water (and) whether they have arrived along land-routes or water-routes, also (should know about) suitable times for resorting to dispersal or concentration, purchase or sale.

2 And that commodity which may be plentiful, he should collect in one place and raise the price. 3 Or, when the price is reached, he should fix another price.

4 He should establish in one place trade in royal commodities that are produced in his own country ; in many places, in those produced in foreign lands. 5 And he should cause both to be sold so as to favour the subjects. 6 And he should avoid even a big profit that would be injurious to the subjects. 7 He should not create a restriction as to time or the evil of a glut in the market in the case of commodities constantly in demand.

63 *dharaka* 'holder' of scales, i.e., weigher. Meyer has 'keeper, preserver.' — *māpaka* who supervises measuring. Cb has 'measurer of length.' — *śalākāpratigrāhaka* the receiver of sticks or tallies for counting, an accountant (cf. *salākāgāhaka* of Pali texts). Cj renders by *kalayitā* 'counter.' Cb has 'who supervises grinding and pounding.' — *viṣṭiḥ* : Breloer remarks (III, 304) that 'state worker' is a better rendering of *viṣṭi*.

64 *mūtāḥ* : from *mav* 'to bind' is a woven basket or grass bag. The word is Vedic. Breloer (III, 304-5) says that the Chapter mentions other groups besides these four and hence the *kārikā* seems taken from elsewhere. The four, however, are the principal groups among edibles (cf. s. 12). The other groups (ss. 16-21) are secondary, and needed no special mention for this purpose.

2.16

1 *sāraphalgvarghāntaram* 'differences in the prices of *sāra* and *phalgu* goods' (com.) is better than 'what is *sāra*, what is *phalgu* and fluctuations in their prices' (Meyer). — *vikṣepa* is dispersal of goods in many places for sale, and *saṁkṣepa* is concentration in one place only for sale, as described in this Chapter. — *prayoga* 'use, employment.' Meyer's 'lending at interest' is little likely. Breloer (KSt, III, 332 n.1) proposes *-prayogakalpān* 'the kind and manner (*kalpa*) of actions (*prayoga*) viz., distribution and collection, for purchase and sale.' That is not very happy.

3 *prāpte 'rghe* either because the commodity has ceased to be plentiful or the demand for it is greater. — *arghāntaram*, i.e., a lower price.

4 *ekamukham*, i.e., concentrated in one place. — Foreign goods are to be sold in many centres probably to make them easily available for the country people as well. 5 Cf.

8 Or, traders should sell royal goods in many places with the price fixed. 9 And they should pay compensation in accordance with the loss (sustained).

10 One-sixteenth part is the surcharge in measure by capacity, one-twentieth part in measure by weighing, one-eleventh part of commodities sold by counting.

11 He should encourage the import of goods produced in foreign lands by (allowing) concessions. 12 And to those (who bring such goods) in ships or caravans, he should grant exemptions (from taxes) that would enable a profit (to be made by them). 13 And no law-suit in money matters (should be allowed) against foreign traders, except such as are members (of native concerns) and (their) associates.

14 Officers in charge of (royal) goods shall deposit the price of goods (sold), in one place, in a wooden box having a lid with one opening. 15 And in the eighth part of the day, they should hand it over to the Director of Trade, declaring, 'This much is sold; this is left over.' 16 They should also hand over the implements of weighing and measuring.

17 Thus (the sale of goods) in one's own territory has been explained.

18 In foreign territory, however, he should ascertain the price and the value of the commodity (taken out) and the commodity (to be brought) in exchange and should calculate the profit after clearing expenses for duty, road-cess, escort-charges, picket- and ferry-dues, food and fodder and share.

4.2.27, 35. 6 In view of *api*, *sūkṣmam* would have been better than *sthūlam*. 7 *ajasra-paṇya* 'that are constantly in demand or always sold' (com.); 'which must be fresh' (Breloer, III, 340). Milk, vegetables, etc. are meant. — *saṁkula-* 'crowding,' i.e., glutting the market.

9 *cheda* is the loss suffered by the state because it has not itself engaged in the trade and made the usual profit.

10 According to Cp and 'others' in Cb, *vyājī* goes to the customer. In the text, however, it is evidently a source of state income. Cj has '*ṣoḍaśaprasthān vikrīṇānaḥ ekaṁ nivartayet, krīṇānaḥ saptadaśakam adhikaṁ gṛhṇīyāt*,' i.e., according to it the *vyājī* operates two ways between the trader and the customer. That is unlikely.

12 *āyatikṣamam* : *āyati* is 'income' (2.9.10, 11 etc.) as well as 'future' (2.10.36, 48, etc.). So we may have 'capable of yielding an income, i.e., profit' or 'yielding profit in the future' (Cp). 13 *anabhiyogaḥ*, i.e., the dispute is to be settled by the *paṇyādhyakṣa* himself. — — *sabhyopakāribhyaḥ* : i.e., when they are partners in a native corporation or its associates (or assistants), suits can be filed against them. Cb comment shows *sahopakāribhyaḥ* 'if there is a quarrel between a foreign merchant and a native merchant, the king shall not show partiality (*abhiyoga*); if, however, benefit has been conferred by him, partiality may be shown to him.' *abhiyoga* as 'partiality' is doubtful.

14 *paṇyādhiṣṭhātāraḥ* are clearly salesmen in state service. 15 *ahnaś ca aṣṭame bhāge*, i.e., the last part of the day. Cf. 1.19.6 ff.

18 *paṇyapratipaṇyayoḥ* : *paṇya* is the commodity taken out, and *pratipaṇya* the commodity brought in exchange for it. Breloer seems to understand the opposite 'the ware (asked for) and the counter-ware (offered in return)' (III, 345). — *argha* seems to be the selling price, while *mūlya* is its cost price or value. Breloer understands *argha* of *paṇya* and

19 Should there be no profit, he should see if there is any advantage in taking out goods or in bringing in goods in exchange for goods. 20 Then with a quarter of the goods of high value, he should set going trade by land along a safe route. 21 And he should establish contacts with forest chieftains, frontier officers, and chiefs in the city and the countryside, to secure their favour. 22 In case of a calamity, he should rescue the goods of high value or himself. 23 Or, if he has reached his destination, he should carry on the trade after paying all dues. 24 And on the water-route he should ascertain hire for boats, provisions on the journey, price and amount of (his) goods and of the goods in exchange, seasons suited for voyage, precautions against dangers aud regulations at the ports.

25 And along river-routes, he should ascertain (conditions of) trade from the (port) regulations and should proceed to where there is profit and avoid absence of profit.

CHAPTER SEVENTEEN

SECTION 35 THE DIRECTOR OF FOREST PRODUCE

1 The Director of Forest Produce should cause forest produce to be brought in by guards in the produce forests. 2 And he should start factories for forest produce. 3 And he should fix dues from those cutting produce forests, also penalty, except in cases of distress.

mūlya of *pratipaṇya*. — *ātivāhika* 'escort charges;' cf. 2.28.25 etc. Cb curiously has 'paid to those who go in the morning (?)'. — *gulma* seems to be a sort of police or military picket, stationed in places of danger. Cb has 'paid (*deya*) to those who stay in the forest.' — *bhāga* 'share' claimed by the foreign state as, e.g., in the case of salt, 2.12.29 etc. Cj seems to read *-bhṛtibhakta-* for *-bhaktabhāga-*. — For the s., cf. 2.35.12 below. 19 *bhāṇḍa-nirvahaṇena* : Cp reads *bhāṇḍānirvahaṇena* 'by not taking out'; that is less likely. — *lābham* is some political or strategic advantage. 20. *tataḥ*, i.e., in either case, whether there is profit to be made or some advantage to be secured. — *sārapādena* i.e., 1/4th of the total goods taken out are to be *sāra*, the rest *phalgu*. Cb has 'giving one-fourth of what is agreed upon as profit, i.e., at a cost of 1/4th of the calculated profit,' Meyer 'with strong beasts of burden,' Breloer 'one-fourth of the four types of goods (*ratna, sāra, phālgu, kupya*), viz., *sāra*.' These explanations appear doubtful. 21 Cf. 1.16.7. 22 *āpadi*, e.g., when the caravan is attacked by robbers. 23 *ātmano vā bhumiṁ prāptaḥ* : The reading is from Cp, *ātmanaḥ bhūmi* being understood in the sense of 'his destination'. Cj shows this reading, but explains it by '*svadeśasthaḥ*'. Reading *aprāptaḥ,* Cs also understands by *ātmano bhūmi* the native land of the *paṇyādhyakṣa*, i.e., when he has not come back and is still in the foreign land. *vā* has little significance here. 24 *yānabhāgaka* : Cb's *-bhāṭaka* would appear more appropriate in the sense of 'hire'. Though the state owned boats and hired them out (2.28.3-5) private boats also are thought of, and, in case of need, could be hired by the state. *paṇyapattanacāritra* : cf. 2.28.7 below.

27. *nadīpathe* : apparently, the preceding s. primarily dealt with sea-voyage.

2.17

3. *deyam* : Cb Cs understand 'wages to be paid to those who cut the trees.' However, *deya* usually refers to what is due to the state (cf. 2.16.13, 23), and seems to refer here to fees charged for taking fuel or timber from state forests. — *atyayam* is penalty for taking these things without paying the dues. — *anyatra āpadbhyaḥ* when no charges are recovered.

4 The group of forest produce (is as follows) :

śāka, tiniśa, dhanvana, arjuna, madhūka, tilaka, sāla, śiṁśapā, arimeda, rājādana, śirīṣa, khadira, sarala, tāla, sarja, aśvakarṇa, somavalka, kuśa, āmra, priyaka, dhava and others (constituting) the group of (trees with) hard wood.

5 *uṭaja, cimiya, cāpa, veṇu, vaṁśa, sātina, kaṇṭaka, bhāllūka* and others (constituting) the group of reeds.

6 *vetra, śīkavallī, vāśī, śyāmalatā, nāgalatā* and others (constituting) the group of creepers.

7 *mālatī, mūrvā, arka, śaṇa, gavedhukā, atasī* and others (constituting) the group of fibre-plants.

8 *muñja, balbaja* and others (constituting raw) materials for ropes.

9 The leaves of *tālī, tāla* and *bhūrja.*

10 The flowers of *kiṁśuka, kusumbha* and *kuṅkuma.*

11 Bulbous roots, roots, fruits and others (constituting) the group of medicinal plant products.

12 *kālakūṭa, vatsanābha, hālāhala, meṣaśṛṅga, mustā, kuṣṭha, mahāviṣa, vellitaka, gaurārdra, bālaka, mārkaṭa, haimavata, kāliṅgaka, dāradaka, aṅkolasāra, auṣṭraka,* and other poisons, serpents and insects, these same kept in jars, (all constituting) the group of poisons.

13 Skin, bones, bile, tendons, eyes, teeth, horns, hooves and tails of the lizard, *seraka*, leopard, bear, dolphin, lion, tiger, elephant, buffalo, *camara, sṛmara*, rhinoceros, bison and *gavaya*, and also of other deer, beasts, birds and wild animals.

4. *kuśāmra* is read as in 2.15.39 and understood as two ; otherwise the mango tree would find no mention at all.

5. The commentators thus differentiate : '*uṭaja* with big holes, slender thorns and a rough surface, *cimiya* without holes and with a soft surface, *cāpa* with small holes and very rough, *veṇu* without thorns and fit for the bow, *vaṁśa* with holes and long joints, fit for lutes, *sātina* with many projecting thorns, *kaṇṭaka* with wheat-like fruit, and *bhāllūka* with long joints or with a large circumference.'

6. According to Cb, *śīkavallī* is also called *haṁsavallī* and *nāgalatā* is also called *nāgajihvā*.

11. *auṣadha* is the product of a plant (*oṣadhi*) with a medicinal property.

12. Some of the poisons are well-known ; the identification of others is uncertain. *mārkaṭa* 'so called because the shape of its root is like the monkey's penis' (Cb Cs). — *haimavata, kāliṅgaka* and *dāradaka* are names derived from the regions of their origin, Darada being in North-west India. — *auṣṭraka* 'shaped like a camel's penis' (Cb, which seems to have read *auṣṭrika*). — *kumbhagatāḥ*, i.e., preserved for use against enemies.

13 *seraka* may be the same as *sīraka* 'porpoise'. It is 'the white-skinned *godhā*' (Cs). — *ṛkṣa* after *dvīpi* is from Cb ; it seems genuine. — *sṛmara* 'a kind of deer' (Dict.), 'same as *śarabha*' (Cs). — *asthi* twice as in the mss. is clearly wrong; we have to read *akṣi* in one place. Eyes of animals are of use as is shown by 14.3.1,6.

14 Iron, copper, steel, bronze, lead, tin, *vaikṛntaka* and brass (constituting the group of) metals.

15 Vessels made of split bamboo-cane and of clay.

16 Charcoal, husks and ashes; enclosures for deer, beasts, birds and wild animals and enclosures for fuel and grass.

17 Separate factories making all kinds of goods should be erected, outside as well as inside, by the Director of Forest Produce, for ensuring livelihood and protection of the city.

CHAPTER EIGHTEEN

SECTION 36 THE SUPERINTENDENT OF THE ARMOURY

1 The Superintendent of the Armoury should cause to be made machines for use in battles, for the defence of forts and for assault on the enemies' cities, also weapons, armours and accoutrements by artisans and artists expert in those lines, producing goods with an agreement as to the amount of work, time allowed and wages, and should store them in places suitable for each. 2 He should frequently change their places and expose them to sun and wind. 3 He should store in a different way what is being damaged by heat, moisture or insects. 4 And he should know them by their class, appearance, characteristics, quantity, source, price and place of storing.

5 *sarvatobhadra*, *jāmadagnya*, *bahumukha*, *viśvāsaghātin*, *saṁghāṭī*, *yānaka*, *parjanyaka*, *bāhū*, *ūrdhvabāhu*, and *ardhabāhu* are fixed machines.

14 The metals would come from mines, which are under the *ākarādhyakṣa* (2.12 above). The *kupyādhyakṣa*, in fact, appears to be stationed in the city in charge of the *kupyagṛha*, though the cutting of trees etc. is evidently his concern.

16 *mṛgapaśu* etc. are items of expenditure in 2.6.11.

17 *bahir antaś ca* : i.e., in the country and in the city respectively. Meyer has 'outside and inside the forests.' — *vibhaktāḥ*, i.e., a separate factory for each class of manufacture. Breloer (III, 297 n. 1) has 'not close together' from the strategical point of view so that they do not fall in the enemy's hands all at the same time. — *ājīvapurarakṣārthāḥ*, i.e., 'by providing ploughs, pestles etc. for *ājīva* and machines, weapons etc. for *purarakṣā*' (Cs). — *kupyopajīvin* is the same as *kupyādhyakṣa*, as Cj Cp show.

2.18

1 *ca yantram* is proposed for *cakrayantram* of the mss. and *yantram* of Cb Cj Cp. *ca* is necessary and seems to be read in Cj; *-kra* seems to have been added after it under the impression that all *yantras* are based on the wheel. — *tajjāta* : cf. 2.5.8 etc. — *karmapramāṇa* refers to the amount of work, while *phalaniṣpatti* refers to the type of work to be done, according to Meyer. Cb explains 'who produce articles after an agreement is made that so much work is to be done in so much time for so much wage.' This appears better. 4 Cj reads *-deśa-* after *jāti-*. *nikṣepa* 'scabbards' (Cb) i.e., containers. It may also mean 'a place for storing' corresponding to *nidhāna* of 2.11.116.

5 *sarvatobhadra* 'of the size of a cart-wheel with a sharp rim, placed in the hand of a *gandharva* in a wall and sending stones or arrows all round when turned' (com.). — *jāmadagnya* 'a *dhanuryantra*, discharging big arrows through a hole in the centre' (Cb), 'discharging

6 *pāñcālika, devadaṇḍa, sūkarikā, musalayaṣṭi, hastivāraka, tālavṛnta,* hammer, mace, *spṛktalā,* spade, *āsphāṭima, utpāṭima, udghāṭima, śataghni,* trident and discus are mobile machines.

7 *śakti, prāsa, kunta, hāṭaka, bhiṇḍipāla, śūla, tomara, varāhakarṇa, karpaṇa, kaṇaya, trāsikā* and others are (weapons) with piercing points.

8 Made from *tāla, cāpa,* wood and horn (and known as) *kārmuka, kodaṇḍa* and *drūṇa* are the bows. 9 *mūrvā, arka, śaṇa, gavedhu, veṇu* and sinews (of animals) are bow-strings. 10 *veṇu, śara, śalākā, daṇḍāsana* and *nārāca* are arrows. 11 Their tips for cutting, piercing and striking are made of iron, bone or wood.

weapons of all kinds in various ways' (Cj). —*bahumukha* ' a place for archers on the tower etc., with many holes for shooting from (Cj), ' a tower with 3 or 4 decks with a leather-shield placed on wheels, from which arrows are shot' (Cb).— *viśvāsaghātin* 'a beam outside the city wall placed crosswise and slaying when released by a mechanism ' (Cb). *saṁghāṭī* ' a fire machine made of long beams, for setting fire to turrets' (com). —*yānaka* 'one *daṇḍa* long, on wheels, with planks inside' (Cb). —*parjanyaka* 'a water-machine for putting out fire'(com.). —*bāhū* ' two pillars facing each other, slaying when the mechanism is released.' Cp adds that the pillars are 25 *hastas* long. — *ūrdhvabāhu* ' a single pillar, 50 *hastas* long, slaying by release of mechanism ' (Cp) ; *ardhabāhu* is half in length, i.e., 25 *hastas.* —*sthita* as contrasted with *cala* ; cf. 7.10.7 ; 7.13.8 etc.

6 *pāñcālika* ' a wooden plank thickly studded with iron nails and placed in the moat to obstruct the enemy ' (com.). —*devadaṇḍa* ' a big beam without nails placed on the wall ' (Cp) apparently for hurling down like a bolt from the blue. Cj has ' a stick one *aratni* long discharged by a machine (*yantrakṣepyo 'ratnimātro lakuṭaḥ*).' — *sūkarikā* ' a leather bag stuffed with cotton, wool etc. for protecting turrets etc. from stones ' (Cj), or, ' a pig-shaped cane-bag covered with leather to prevent storming of the wall ' (Cp). —*musalayaṣṭi* ' a pike made of the *khadira* wood '. — *hastivāraka* ' a bar for striking down elephants ' (Cb) ' or, a pike with two or three points ' (Cp). —*tālavṛnta* ' a *vātacakra* ' (com.) apparently producing a strong wind and raising dust. —*mudgara* ' hammer ' and *gadā* ' mace ' are ' *yantrakṣepye* discharged from machines ' (Cj). —*spṛktalā* a mace with sharp nails (Cp); Cj, which reads *spṛktulā* has ' *aśmatulāntaragatāśāvataraṇāt bahir aśmano muñcati* ' which is far from clear. —*āsphāṭima* ' a sort of catapult with four leather-covered pillars ' (com). Cj's *āsphoṭima* might appear to be better. —*utpāṭima* ' a sort of wrench for pulling down pillars.' —*udghāṭima* ' a *mudgara*- shaped machine.' Meyer remarks that *-ima* forms have a passive sense and hence we have to understand weapons that themselves burst or are uprooted or opened. —*śataghni* (for the short *-ghni*, cf. 2.3.34) ' a big pillar studded with big and long nails with a cart-wheel at one end and placed on the wall ' (com.), probably intended to be hurled down.

7 *śakti* ' 4 *hastas* long, all-metal with the tip shaped like the *karavīra*-leaf and the head like a cow's nipple '. *prāsa* '24 *aṅgulas* long, all-metal, with wood inside, having two backs.' *kunta* '7, 6 or 5 *hastas* long,' 'a weapon for horse-riders' (Cj). *hāṭaka* 'similar to *kunta,* but with a three-pointed tip ' (Cj). *bhiṇḍipāla* 'same as *kunta,* but with a broad tip.' *śūla* ' with one point, length not fixed. ' *tomara* ' 4, 4 1/2 or 5 *hastas* long, with an arrow-shaped tip.' *varāhakarṇa* ' same as *prāsa* (*tomara,* Cj) with tip shaped like a boar's ear.' *kaṇaya* ' 20, 22 or 24 *aṅgulas* long, all-metal, with tridents at each end and a grip in the middle.' *karpaṇa* (*kampana* Cj) 'an arrow of the size of *tomara,* 7, 8 or 9 *karṣas* in weight to be thrown by the hand.' *trāsikā* 'all-metal, of the size of *prāsa,* with a tuft at one end. Cj has *prāsikā* ' *prāsārdhaśaktim* '. —*hula-* ' spike ' is more likely than *hala-* 'plough-share' of Cb Cs.

8 *kārmuka-* etc : Meyer thinks that the names correspond to the four types of materials and hence would read *-drūṇaśārṅgāṇi* or understand *dhanus* itself as the name of horn-made bow. However, *kārmuka* seems to contain a reference to *karma* ' action ' and *kodaṇḍa* to its length ' almost a *daṇḍa* ' and not to the material of which they are made. 10 *śalākā* is ' made of wood ,' *daṇḍāsana* is ' *ardhanārāca,*' and *nārāca* is 'all-metal' (com.).

12 *nistriṁśa, maṇḍalāgra* and *asiyaṣṭi* are swords. 13 The horn of the rhinoceros and buffalo, the tusk of the elephant, wood and bamboo-root form the hilts.

14 *paraśu, kuṭhāra, paṭṭasa, khanitra*, spade, saw, and *kāṇḍacchedana* are razor-type weapons.

15 Stones for use in machines, in slings and by hand, and mill-stones are stone-weapons.

16 A coat of mail of metal rings or metal plates, an armour of fabrics, and combinations of skin, hooves and horns of dolphin, rhinoceros, *dhenuka*, elephant and bull, are armours. 17 Helmet, neck-guard, cuirass, robe, coat of mail, breast-plate and thigh-guard, box, leather shield, *hastikarṇa, tālamūla, dhamanikā, kapāṭa, kiṭikā, apratihata* and *balāhakānta* are shields.

18 Objects used in giving training to elephants, chariots and horses, objects used for their decoration and arrangements for their equipment are the accoutrements.

19 Illusion magic and secret practices are (secret) work.

20 And concerning the factories,

the Master of the Armoury should know the desire (of the king), the carrying out of the undertaking, the use, fraud (if practised), gain, loss and expenditure of (the various types of) forest produce.

12 *nistriṁśa* 'has a curved tip' (Cp). The name may contain a reference to length 'beyond thirty (*aṅgulas* ?).' — *maṇḍalāgra* 'straight with a round tip.' — *asiyaṣṭi* 'thin and long.' 13. *viṣāṇa* 'horn' as well as 'tusk.'

14 *paraśu* 'all-metal, 24 *aṅgulas* long'. — *paṭṭasa* 'an axe with a trident at one end or both ends.' — *kāṇḍacchedana* 'a big axe' (Cp), '*kāṇḍāsikā*' (Cb).

15 *goṣpaṇa* : Cb reads *gāvaṇa* and explains *gāvaṇapāṣāṇa* by 'catapult.' — *cāśmāyudhāni* from Cb is clearly preferable to *cārāyudhāni* 'awl-like weapons' of the mss.

16 Commentators read *lohajālajālikā-* etc. Cb explains 'helmet for the head (*lohajāla*), headless armour (*jālikā*), armour (*paṭṭa*) and armour with many flaps or folds (*kavaca*).' Similarly Cp, which construes *loha* with each term up to *kavaca*. It may be, however, that *kavaca* made either of *lohajālikā* or of *lohapaṭṭa* is alone to be understood. — *sūtrakaṅkaṭa* evidently made of cotton cloth with stuffing inside ; they are made by the *sūtrādhyakṣa* as 2.23.10 shows. — *carmakhura-* etc., i.e., the entire skin with hooves, horns etc. is used as an armour. 17 *kūrpāsa* 'with half-sleeves' ; *kañcuka* 'up to the knees' ; *vāravāṇa* up to the ankle' (see 2.11.99 above) ; *paṭṭa* 'without arms and not made of metal' ; *nāgodarikā* 'a thigh-guard' (Cj), '*karāṅgulitrāṇam*' (Cp). — *peṭī* a 'cover made of wood and creepers' ; *hastikarṇa* 'a board used as a cover.' — *tālamūla* ; cf. 2.3.7 above. — *dhamanikā* 'a cloth-bag into which wind is blown' (Cp) ; a leather-bellows may appear more likely. — *kapāṭa* 'a door-fly.' — *kiṭikā* 'made of cane-work and leather.' Meyer has 'a light shield.' — *apratihata*, i.e., *hastivāraka*, warder off of elephants' (Cp), '*hastavāraka* handguard (?)' (Cs). — *balāhakānta* 'same as *apratihata* with iron strips at the end.' Cb shows the form *varāhakānta* 'beloved of the boars.' — *āvaraṇāni* : from *śirastrāṇa* up to *nāgodarikā* we have coverings for the soldiers' persons, from *peṭī* onwards shields or covers as protection.

19 This *karma* or secret work is described in Books 13 and 14 below.

20 *karmāntānāṁ ca* to be construed with the following stanza. — Since the stanza refers to forest produce factories, Cp says that it applies to the preceding Chapter as well. Most of the weapons came from those factories and hence the Armoury Superintendent must be conversant with them. — *vyājam* 'fraud' from Cb Cp is preferable to *vyājīm* ; the latter is out of place. — *uddayam* 'gain, profit' (Cb Cp Cs). Sorabji had proposed *udgamam* 'source, origin.' Meyer proposes *vyājamudriyam* or *vyājamudritam* 'fraud and stamping' or *vyājamad dvayam* 'deceitful duplicity' or *vyājam adbhutam* 'fraud and the wonderful.' None is an improvement. Cj seems to have read *yogaṁ vyājīṁ samuddayam*. Cb's explanation appears least unsatisfactory.

CHAPTER NINETEEN

SECTION 37 STANDARDISATION OF WEIGHTS AND MEASURES

1 The Superintendent of Standardisation should cause factories to be established for the manufacture of standard weights and measures.

2 Ten *māṣa*-beans make one *māṣaka* of gold, or five *guñjā*-berries. 3 Sixteen of these make one *suvarṇa* or *karṣa.* 4 A *pala* is equivalent to four *karṣas.*

5 Eighty-eight white mustard-seeds make one *māṣaka* of silver. 6 Sixteen of these make one *dharaṇa,* or twenty *śimbā*-beans.

7 A *dharaṇa* of diamond weighs twenty rice-grains.

8 A half-*māṣaka,* a *māṣaka,* two, four, eight *māṣakas,* a *suvarṇa,* two, four, eight *suvarṇas,* also ten, twenty, thirty, forty (and) one hundred (*suvarṇas*), (are denominations of weights). 9 By that are explained (denominations of) *dharaṇas.*

10. Weights should be made of iron (or) of stone from the Magadhas or the Mekala hills or such as would not increase in weight by water and smearing or decrease in weight by heat.

11 Beginning with six *aṅgulas* (in length) and rising successively by eight *aṅgulas,* he should cause ten balance-beams to be made, one *pala* of

2.19

pautava is derived from *potu* going back to the root *pū* to purify, refine, rectify. It stands for standardisation of weights and measures.

2 *māṣaka* is the name of a weight (equal to 1/16 *suvarṇa* and also referred to as *māṣa*) as well as of a copper coin (equivalent to 1/16th of a *paṇa* ; 2.12.24). This has led to some confusion. — A *guñjā*-seed is 2 or 1.80 grains (Fleet, JRAS, 1915, p. 228) or 1.8295 grains (A. S. Hemmy, JRAS, 1937, pp. 1-26). A *karṣa,* which is 80 times that comes to a little less than a modern *tolā.* A *karṣa* or *suvarṇa* is the weight of the *paṇa* as well as of the coin *māṣaka* (between which and the weight *māṣaka* there is no relation of identity). '*Karṣa* is the name of a weight in ancient Iran as well. The weight in India was therefore an importation from Western Asia like the Vedic *Manā* or *Minā.*' (F.W. Thomas, JRAS, 1916, p. 366).

5-6 If, as seems very likely, the *pala* of 10 *dharaṇas* (s. 20) is the same as the *pala* of 4 *karṣas* (s. 4) 88 mustard-seeds would be equivalent to 2 *guñjās,* so that the silver *māṣaka* would be 2/5ths of a gold *māṣaka.* Manu, 8.134-135, has the same ratio between the gold *māṣa* and the silver *māṣaka.*

8 Weights of these denominations are meant to be manufactured. 9 For silver, *dharaṇa* would appear in place of *suvarṇa.*

10 Maikala hills are in Madhya Pradesh. — In view of *-maya, -śilā-* for *-śaila-* would have been better.

11 The lengths would be 6,14,22 . . .78 *aṅgulas* and weights 1, 2, 3 . . . 10 *palas* respectively. The beams would be very thin. — *yantram ubhayataḥśikyaṃ vā* : the translation follows the commentators. Cb has 'with pans on both sides of the fulcrum (*yantra*) or a pan on one side only,' understanding by the latter the steelyard type of balance described in the following ss. It is also possible that *yantra* as 'mechanism' refers to the steelyard

metal onwards (in weight) increased successively by one *pala*, with scale-pans on the two sides of the fulcrum or a pan (on one side only).

12 He should cause the *samavṛttā* (balance) to be made of metal thirty-five *palas* (in weight) and seventy-two *aṅgulas* in length. 13 Fixing a ball (of metal) five *palas* in weight (at one end), he should cause the level to be secured (for marking zero). 14 From that (point) onwards, he should cause markings to be made for one *karṣa*, increased by a *karṣa* up to one *pala*, then increased by a *pala* up to ten *palas*, then for twelve, fifteen and twenty *palas*. 15 Thereafter, he should cause markings to be made increased by ten up to one hundred *palas*. 16 In the 'fives' he should cause it to be covered with *nāndī* (the *svastika* mark).

17 He should cause a balance (called) *parimāṇī* to be made with double this amount of metal and ninety-six *aṅgulas* in length. 18 On that he should cause markings to be made beyond one hundred for twenty, fifty and (two) hundred (*palas*).

19 A *bhāra* contains twenty *tulā* weights.

20 A *pala* contains ten *dharaṇas*. 21 One hundred of these *palas* is the revenue measure. 22 Less by five *palas* (successively) are measures for

type of balance and *ubhayataḥśikya* to the pair of scales. Meyer has 'on each of the two sides, there shall be a contrivance (*yantra*) or a scale-pan.' What contrivance is meant is not clear. Russ. has 'on both sides appliances for regulation of scales (*yantram*) or chains for cups (*śikyam*).'

12 This beam would be thicker. *samavṛttā* 'even-rounded' is the name of the balance. 13 *maṇḍalam* etc. : it seems that the steelyard type is described here. According to Cb, a metal ball (*maṇḍala*) weighing five *palas* is to be tied at one end, while the thing to be weighed is to be suspended as the other end ; then the beam is to be lifted with a string, the point at which equilibrium is secured showing the weight of the object in accordance with the markings. It seems that this type of balance is still used in Malabar, being called *tulākkol*. It does not seem possible to understand the fully developed steelyard, in which the beam is suspended from above at a fulcrum dividing it into two unequal arms, the object being at the shorter end and a poise being shifted along the markings on the longer arm to indicate the weight when equilibrium is found. *maṇḍala* can hardly refer to such a poise. — *samakaraṇaṁ kārayet* : this seems to refer to the marking of zero at the point where equilibrium is secured with the *maṇḍala* at one end and nothing at the other (perhaps only a light pan). 14 *tataḥ*, i.e., from the zero thus found and marked. The length between zero and the beam's end is to be divided for markings up to one hundred *palas*. — *akṣeṣu nāndīpinaddham* : *akṣa* is a multiple of five, 5, 10, 15 etc. (com.). *nāndī* is '*svastika*' (Cp), 'a mark of the crow's foot' (Cj), 'mark of the wedge' (Cb). *pinaddha* then would mean 'covered,' i.e., marked, perhaps even carved, engraved. The reading *naddhrī* would mean 'a strap,' *pinaddha* would then be possible in the sense of 'tied' and *akṣa* in the sense of 'the pivot.'. But it is not easy to see pivots, straps etc. in the balance described here. For *tulā*, cf. : 'The balances with which the Hindus weigh things are charistiones, of which the weights are immovable, while the scales move on certain marks and lines. Therefore, the balance is called tulā. The first lines mean the units of the weight from 1 to 5 and further on to 10; the following lines mean the tens, 10, 20, 30 etc.' (Alberuni's India, tr. C. Sachau, I, 164-5).

20 Cp states that this *pala* is bigger than the other *pala* by 1 *karṣa*, i.e., has 5 *karṣas* in it instead of 4. How this relation is arrived at is not clear. However, *tat* in the next s. might suggest that a different *pala* is thought of here. Nevertheless, *āyamānī* is clearly the same as the *samavṛttā*. 22 Thus the *vyāvahārikī* weighs upto 95 *palas*, each *pala* being 9½ *dharaṇas*, beam-metal 33 *palas* and length 66 *aṅgulas*. The values for the other two are 90, 9, 31, 60

trade, for payments and for measuring out to the palace. 23 Of these, the *pala* is (successively) less by half a *dharaṇa*, the metal of the upper (beam, successively) less by two *palas* and the length (successively) less by six *aṅgulas*.

24 In the case of the former two, an excess (in weight) of five *palas* (is to be received) except in cases of meat, metals, salt and gems.

25 The balance made of wood (should be) eight *hastas* (long), provided with markings (or) with weights (and) supported by ' peacock's feet.'

26 Twenty-five *palas* of fire-wood are a means of cooking one *prastha* of rice. 27 This is an indication for more and for less.

28 Thus weights and balances have been explained.

29 Now, two hundred *palas* of *māṣa*-beans make one *droṇa* for revenue measures, one hundred and eighty-seven and a half *palas*, (the *droṇa*) for trade, one hundred and seventy-five *palas*, for making payments, (and) one hundred sixty-two and a half *palas*, for measuring out to the palace.

30 Of these, *āḍhaka*, *prastha* and *kuḍuba* are smaller measures, being each one-fourth of the preceding. 31 Sixteen *droṇas* make one *khārī*. 32 Twenty *droṇas* make one *kumbha*. 33 Ten *kumbhas* make one *vaha*.

and 85, 8½, 29, 54 respectively. The three *tulās* would actually weigh up to 902½, 810 and 722½ *dharaṇas* only instead of 1000 as in the *āyamānī*. Meyer says ' the *dharaṇa* of the trade is greater than that of the revenue measure by 1/20th, that for servants by 2/20th and that for harem by 3/20th ; in 100 *palas* this gives 5, 10 and 15 *palas* more respectively. So that the difference is squared and what is differently weighed is in reality the same (just as in the different systems of Indian philosophy). Thus is reached the highest triumph of the Indian spirit : a refined system.' Where he gets different values for the *dharaṇa* is not clear. And such classifications, with no practical effect whatsoever, cannot, in fairness, be attributed to the author of the present work. Meyer also gives 51, 49, and 47 as the weights of the beams. It is difficult to see how he arrives at these figures. 53 is nowhere mentioned as the weight of the *āyamānī* beam ; 35 is mentioned for the *samavṛttā*. — *antaḥpura-bhājanī* : the smallest measure is for delivery to the palace, apparently because the king could then plead that if he paid to others by a measure smaller than the revenue measure, he himself received by a still smaller measure. The expression may also mean ' for making payments from the palace.' In that case, the king would be the greatest beneficiary.

24 *pūrvayoḥ*, ' i.e., of *samavṛttā* and *parimāṇī* ' (Cp). — *prayāmaḥ* ' extension ', i.e., an addition in weight. This seems to mean in effect that 5% and 2 1/2% respectively are received in addition in revenue receipts. Perhaps this is the same as *vyājī* mentioned elsewhere.

25 *kāṣṭhatulā* ' balance made of hard wood ' (com.) rather than ' balance for weighing fuel ' (Meyer). —*padavatī*, i.e., of the steelyard type, while *pratimānavatī* implies two scale-pans ; the two cannot go together. A *vā* seems necessary after the latter word. —*mayūra-pada*- refers to the frame-work supporting the balance-beam. Nārada, 2.273, describes the *toraṇa*, consisting of two posts 1 or 1½ *hasta* away from each other with a transverse beam on top from which the balance beam is suspended. This *toraṇa* does resemble a peacock's feet.

26 As Cs says this really belongs to the province of the Stores Officer.

29 On the basis of 2 grains to a *guñjā*, a *droṇa* would have 128,000 grains by weight, approximating a capacity of a little over 500 cubic inches or a little less than a quarter bushel or 2 gallons.

33 Meyer, calculating 37 1/2 bushels in a *vaha*, remarks that this amount of a cart-load implies that roads were in a very good condition.

34 He should cause measures to be made of dry, hard wood, even, with one-fourth as top-heap, or with the heap included inside. 35 However, in the case of liquids, wine, flowers and fruits, husk and charcoal, and lime, the measure of the top-heap is an increase that is double.

36 One *paṇa* and a quarter (should be) the price of a *droṇa* ; three-quarters, of an *āḍhaka* ; six *māṣakas*, of a *prastha* ; one *māṣaka*, of a *kuḍuba*. 37 The price of the measures for liquids and others (should be) double. 38 (The price) of the weights (should be) twenty *paṇas*. 39 One-third that the price of the balance.

40 He should cause a stamping (of the weights and measures) to be made every four months. 41 The penalty for unstamped (weights etc.) is twenty-seven *paṇas* and a quarter. 42 (Traders) shall pay a stamping fee amounting to one *kākaṇī* every day to the Superintendent of Standardisation.

43 One-thirty-second part is the surcharge for heating in the case of clarified butter, one-sixty-fourth part in the case of oil. 44 One-fiftieth part is the flow from the measure in the case of liquids.

45 He should cause measures of a half-*kuḍuba*, a quarter-*kuḍuba* and one-eighth *kuḍuba* to be made.

46 Eighty-four *kuḍubas* of clarified butter are known as a *vāraka* ;
but sixty-four (*kuḍubas* make a *vāraka*) of oil; and one-quarter of these is
known as a *ghaṭikā*.

34 *samam* is 'cylindrical in form '. — *caturbhāgaśikham*, i.e., 3/4ths of the actual amount is inside the measure, 1/4th being the heap on the top ; *antaḥśikham* where all four parts are inside the measure and there is no heaping on top. 35 *rasasya tu* : com. understand *antaḥśikham* with this and read a stop here. Perhaps, however, *tu* indicates an exception in the case of *surā* etc. among *rasas* (in whose case *antaḥśikha* is understood *ipso facto*). Of course, *raseṣu* would be better for this. — *dviguṇottarā*, ' i.e., double the 1/4th *śikhā* ; thus in a *prastha* 3 *kuḍubas* inside and 2 in addition ' (Cb). Cp understands all five in the *prastha*. For such an explanation, *śikhāmānasya dviguṇā vṛddhiḥ* would have been better. Cj, reading *śikhāmānadviguṇottarā*, seems to arrive at 75 for *rasa*, 100 for *surā*, 125 for *puṣpa*, 150 for *tuṣāṅgāra* and 175 for *sudhā* as the measure of the *śikhā*. Though this appears to do greater justice to the wording (*uttarā*), it seems highly unlikely that such additions are really intended in these cases.

37 *rasādīnām* : the higher price is due to the measure being larger to account for the greater *śikhāmāna*. 39 *tribhāgaḥ*, i.e., 1/3rd of 20 *paṇas* (' others ' in Cp) ; ' one-third of a *paṇa* for the smallest of the ten *tulās* of s. 11, increased by 1/3 in each successive case,' (Cb. and ' some ' in Cp). On that basis of 1/3 *paṇa* for 1 *pala* metal, the *samavṛittā* would cost 11 2/3 *paṇas*. It seems, however, that the price of the *samavṛttā* alone is stated here as one-third of 20 *paṇas*.

40 *prātivedhanikam*, i.e., stamping as well as inspection regarding stamping. — *caturmāṣikam* of the mss. is clearly wrong, because the fee is laid down, not here, but in s. 42. It comes to 30 *māṣakas* for the four-month period. 42 *prātivedhanika* is here the stamping fee.

43 *taptavyājī* seems to refer to the additional measure of ghee or oil to compensate for the loss suffered by these in the process of liquefaction. Ordinarily the customer would receive this ; but Cb says the king received this as well as the *mānasrāva*. That is likely when these articles are delivered in the state stores. 44 *mānasrāva* is a similar compensation for what sticks to the measure when liquids are measured out.

45 This s. should have come earlier, after s.33. The prices of these should also have been stated.

46 *caturāśītiḥ* of the mss. is metrically easy, but grammatically uncertain ; *caturaśītiḥ* (Cb) is hard on metre but grammatically impeccable.

CHAPTER TWENTY

SECTION 38 MEASURES OF SPACE AND TIME

1 The Superintendent of Measurements should be conversant with the measurements of space and time.

2 Eight atoms make one *rathacakravipruṣ* (chariot-wheel particle). 3 Eight of them make one *likṣā* (nit). 4 Eight of them make one *yūkā* (louse). 5 Eight of them make one *yavamadhya* (barley-middle). 6 Eight *yavamadhyas* make one *aṅgula* (finger). 7 Or, the maximum width of the middle (part) of the middle finger of a middling man is an *aṅgula*.

8 Four *aṅgulas* make a *dhanurgraha*. 9 Eight *aṅgulas* make a *dhanurmuṣṭi*. 10 Twelve *aṅgulas* make a *vitasti* (span) and the height of the shadow-gnomon. 11 Fourteen *aṅgulas* make a *śama*, a *śala*, a *pariraya* and a *pada* (foot).

12 Two spans make an *aratni* (cubit), the *hasta* of Prajāpati. 13 (A *hasta*) with a *dhanurgraha* is the measure (of a *hasta*) for weights and measures and for pastures. 14 (A *hasta*) with a *dhanurmuṣṭi* makes a *kiṣku* or a *kaṁsa*. 15 Forty-two *aṅgulas* make a carpenter's sawing-*kiṣku*, a measure for the camp, the fort and royal property. 16 Fifty-four *aṅgulas* make a *hasta* for (measuring) forest produce.

17 Eighty-four *aṅgulas* make a *vyāma*, a measure for ropes and a *pauruṣa* (man's height) for (measuring) moats (or diggings).

2.20.

1 *mānādhyakṣaḥ* ' same as *pautavādhyakṣa* ' (Cp); Cp adds that he may be an independent officer appointed by the *samāhartṛ*. Measurements of space and time are his concern.

2 *rathacakravipruṣ* : ' this is perceptible to the eye ' (com.). It may be the same as the *trasareṇu* of the Naiyāyikas. 4 *yūkā* is from Cb. *yūkāmadhyaḥ* of the mss. seems influenced by *yavamadhyaḥ*. 5 *yavamadhyaḥ*, i.e., width in the middle, at its widest. (Cf. ' *yavodarair aṅgulam aṣṭasaṁkhyaiḥ* ' — Bhāskarācārya). 7 *madhyamapuruṣa* as described by Cb is ' with a height of 100 of his own finger-widths and a girth of 92 finger-widths.'

8 *dhanurgraha* ' a bow-grip ' in the middle of the bow where the four fingers are clasped round it. 9 *dhanurmuṣṭi* apparently has reference to the fist with the thumb upraised when holding the bow for shooting. 10 *chāyāpauruṣa*, i.e., the height of the *śaṅku* on the sun-dial. A *dvādaśāṅgulaśaṅku* is mentioned in the Atharvaveda (S. B. Dikshit, *Bhāratīya Jyotiṣaśāstra*, p. 367). 11 *śama* appears related to *śamyā* ' yoke-pin ', *śala* to *śalya* ' dart ' and *pada* to ' foot '. The significance of *pariraya* is not clear.

13 *pautavavivītamānam* : Meyer understands a single idea 'measuring pasture-land by the weight-superintendent.' That is unlikely. What is meant is that in the work of the *pautavādhyakṣa* and the *vivītādhyakṣa*, a *hasta* of 14 *aṅgulas* is to be used. 14 *kiṣku* seems to have a reference to the fore-arm. The significance of *kaṁsa* ' cup ' is not clear. Meyer thinks of as much land as can be sown with a *kaṁsa*-ful of seeds. That is doubtful, as this is clearly a linear and not an area measure.

17 *vyāma* is the distance from tip to tip of outstretched hands. — *rajjumānam*, i.e., a unit for measuring ropes. It may refer to the length of rope used for tying cattle, as Meyer thinks. — *khāta* primarily a moat, also a well.

18 Four *aratnis* make a *daṇḍa*, a *dhanus*, a *nālikā*, and a *pauruṣa* for the householder. 19 One hundred and eight *aṅgulas* make a *dhanus*, measure for roads and city-walls and a *pauruṣa* for (measuring) the piling of fire-altars. 20 Six *kaṁsas* make a *daṇḍa*, a measure for gifts to Brahmins and to guests.

21 Ten *daṇḍas* make a *rajju*. 22 Two *rajjus* make a *paridesa*. 23 Three *rajjus* make a *nivartana* on one side. 24 A *bāhu* has two *daṇḍas* more.

25 Two thousand *dhanuses* make a *goruta*. 26 Four *gorutas* make a *yojana*. 27 Thus measurements of space (have been explained).

28 Hereafter (are explained) measurements of time.

29 *tuṭa*, *lava*, *nimeṣa*, *kāṣṭhā*, *kalā*, *nālikā*, *muhūrta*, forenoon and afternoon, day, night, fortnight, month, season, *ayana*, year and cycle (of years) are divisions of time. 30 Two *tuṭas* make a *lava*. 31 Two *lavas* make a *nimeṣa*. 32 Five *nimeṣas* make a *kāṣṭhā*. 33 Thirty *kāṣṭhās* make a *kalā*. 34 Forty *kalās* make a *nālikā*. 35 Or, a hole in a jar (with a dimension) of four *māṣakas* of gold made four *aṅgulas* in length, (with) an *āḍhaka* of water (running through it) measures one *nālikā*. 36 Two *nālikās* make a *muhūrta*.

18 *nālikā pauruṣaṁ ca gārhapatyam* : it is better to read *gārhapatyam* at the end of this s. as in Cb. It can hardly be construed with the following s. The significance of *nālikā*, about 6 feet long, is not clear. Is it possible that the primitive *nālikā* used for measuring time was really a hollow reed 6 feet long from which water flowed out through an aperture at one end during a period of 24 minutes? — *gārhapatya pauruṣa* seems to refer to the average man's (householder's) height. Cb, which adds *matam* after *gārhapatyam*, explains 'the 4-*aratni daṇḍa, dhanus, nālikā* and *pauruṣa* are according to the opinion of Gṛhapati or Viśvakarman.' That is doubtful. Cp reads *gārhapatyam* at the begining of s. 19 and explains it by 'taught by Viśvakarman'. 20 *ṣaṭkaṁso daṇḍaḥ* : Meyer thinks of an area measure.

21-24 Meyer thinks that *rajju* etc. are area measures and finds the mixing of area measures and linear measures confusing. But *daṇḍa*, *rajju* and *bāhu* are clearly only linear measures, so it appears *pradeśa* 'pointing out'. *nivartana*, no doubt, is an area measure later (cf. JBORS, XII, 118 n. 3). But here only the length of one side of the area is mentioned, as shown by *ekataḥ*, i.e., again a linear measure of 30 *daṇḍas* is mentioned. *nivartana* may primarily have reference to the turning back of the bullocks at the plough, a linear conception. *bāhu* may also refer to the length of one side of an area measure; but that is far from certain. Cp reads *ekato* in s. 24.

25 *dvidhanussahasram* : G1's reading *dhanus-* is faulty and Fleet's calculation, on its basis of a *yojana* of 4.54 miles (JRAS, 1912, 234-6) is unacceptable. Fleet also identified his *yojana* with the Persian parasang of 4.76 miles (JRAS, 1912, 462-3). The *yojana*, however, is double that. The name *yojana* seems to have reference to the 'yoking' of bullocks, i.e., distance covered before the yoke is taken off.

29 *tuṭa* is clearly a Prakritism. 31 *nimeṣaḥ* 'time taken to pronounce a short syllable' (Cj). 35 *suvarṇamāṣakāḥ* etc. : the idea is, gold 4 *māṣakas* in weight is made into a wire 4 *aṅgulas* long, the wire's thickness representing the measure of the hole in the jar through which the water is to flow out. The wire itself is of no further use in the *nālikā*. Thus Cb. Cs thinks that the gold is to be turned into a hollow tube, apparently for fixing in the jar, through which the water is to flow out. But unless the thickness of the gold leaf out of which the tube is made is also stated, the diameter would vary from tube to tube. The Punjab reading is derived from Śaṁkarārya on Kāmandaka 5.42 and is clearly only a gloss. Fleet (JRAS, 1915, pp. 213-230) points out that the *Vedāṅga Jyotiṣa* requires 61/64 of a *droṇa* of water to flow in 1 *nāḍikā*, that the *Divyāvadāna* has 1 *droṇa* for 1 *nāḍikā*, the hole however being 1 *suvarṇa* of gold 4 *aṅgulas* long, and that the *Vāyu*, *Viṣṇu* and *Bhāgavata Purāṇas* agree in all details with the present passage. *kumbha* here is simply 'jar', and is not the measure of that name (2.19.32) as H. Jacobi (ZDMG, 74, pp. 250-1) seems to have thought.

37 A day of fifteen *muhūrtas* and a night (of the same length) occur in the months of Caitra and Āśvayuja. 38 After that, one of them (first) increases and (then) decreases by three *muhūrtas* during a period of six months (and vice versa the other).

39 When the shadow (of the gnomon) is eight *pauruṣas*, one-eighteenth part (of the day) is past, when six *pauruṣas*, one-fourteenth part (is past), when three *pauruṣas*, one-eighth part, when two *pauruṣas*, one-sixth part, when one *pauruṣa*, one-fourth part, when eight *aṅgulas*, three-tenth part (is past), when four *aṅgulas*, three-eighth part, (and) when there is no shadow, it is midday. 40 When the day has turned, one should understand the remaining parts in like manner.

41 In the month of Āṣāḍha, the midday loses shadow. 42 After that, in the six months beginning with Śrāvaṇa, the shadow (at midday) increases by two *aṅgulas* in each month and in the six months beginning with Māgha, it decreases by two *aṅgulas* in each month.

43 Fifteen days and nights make a fortnight. 44 That in which the moon waxes is the bright (fortnight). 45 That in which the moon wanes is the dark.

46 Two fortnights make a month. 47 Thirty days and nights make a works month. 48 A half day more makes a solar month. 49 A half day less makes a lunar month. 50 Twenty-seven (days and nights) make a

37 This means that the equinoctial days fall in the months of Caitra (vernal) and Āśvina (autumnal). Cj has '*Caitre meṣādau, Āśvayuje tulādau*; similarly Cp '*meṣatulayoḥ*'. The text, however, does not show acquaintance with the *rāśis*. 38 *tribhir* etc.: as the increase or decrease is from solstice to solstice, we have to understand that the day increases for three months from the vernal equinoctial day in Caitra and decreases for three months thereafter. The longest day at the summer solstice thus amounts to 14 hours 24 minutes. Jacobi (ZDMG, 74, p. 252) states that the longest day of 18 *muhūrtas* is true of North Punjab and is mentioned in the *Vedāṅga Jyotiṣa* and the *Sūryaprajñapti*.

39. *aṣṭapauruṣyām*: the *pauruṣa* of s.10 is to be understood. —*tripauruṣyām* is proposed for *catuṣpauruṣyām* of the mss. in conformity with 1.19.7 and following a suggestion of Jacobi (ZDMG, 74, 253-254). Even *tripauruṣī* is slightly longer than the actual shadow after 1/8th of the day is past. — *acchāyo madhyāhnaḥ*: this is true only of the summer solstice day in Āṣāḍha. Cf. s. 41. Jacobi (ZDMG, 74, pp. 253-4) states that in the first four cases, the actual parts of time at Pataliputra deviate more from those mentioned here than do those at Ujjayini.

41 *Āṣāḍhe māsi* etc.: this can happen only on the Tropic of Cancer, i.e., in Magadha or Bengal or Malwa. 42 *dvyaṅgulottarā*, i.e., 2 *aṅgulas* in Srāvaṇa, 4 in Prauṣṭhapada and so on up to 12 in Pauṣa, decreasing thereafter to the same extent. In Pauṣa in the winter solstice the shadow thus equals the length of the gnomon, again showing a place on the Tropic of Cancer. Jacobi (ZDMG, 74, 255) states that on the Tropic of Cancer the actual length would be 13.08 *aṅgulas* and adds that Kauṭilya's incorrect figures are given as those of the Vāsiṣṭha Siddhānta in the *Pañcasiddhāntikā*, 2.9. This text indeed appears derived from early sources.

47 *karmamāsaḥ* is proposed for *prakarma-* of the mss. as suggested by *karma* for *prakarma* in 2.6.16 and by *karmasaṁvatsaraḥ* of 2.7.6. Cb explains *prakarma-* as 'for calculating wages for labourers.' Cj seems to have read *prakarma* 'for superintendents to commence their work.' 48 *sārdhaḥ*: curiously Cj understands two and a half *pakṣas*, i.e. 37 1/2 days, which is quite unlikely; 30 plus half a day is meant. 49 *ardhanyūnaḥ*: Cj again has 1 1/2 *pakṣas*, i.e , 22 1/2 days. —*balamāsaḥ* is from Cb Cj: 'for giving wages to the army that is dispersed

month of constellations. 51 Thirty-two make a month for the army. 52 Thirty-five, (a month) for maintenance of horses. 53 Forty, (a month) for maintenance of elephants.

54 Two months make a season. 55 Śrāvaṇa and Prauṣṭhapada are the rainy season. 56 Āśvayuja and Kārttika are autumn. 57 Mārgaśīrṣa and Pauṣa are winter. 58 Māgha and Phālguna are the season of frost. 59 Caitra and Vaiśākha are spring. 60 Jyeṣṭhāmūlīya and Āṣāḍha are summer.

61 The *uttarāyaṇa* begins with the season of frost. 62 The *dakṣiṇāyana* begins with the rainy season. 63 Two *ayanas* make a year. 64 Five years make one cycle.

65 The sun takes one-sixtieth part of a day ; thus in one season he brings about the loss of one day, and so does the moon (cause loss of) one (day).

66 Thus in every period of two years and a half the two beget an additional month, the first in summer and the second at the end of (the cycle of) five years.

CHAPTER TWENTY-ONE

SECTION 39 THE COLLECTOR OF CUSTOMS AND TOLLS

1 The Collector of Customs and Tolls should establish the customs house and the flag facing the east or the north in the vicinity of the big gates (of the city).

(*senāvikṣepabhaktadānārthaḥ*)' (Cj), ' for the maintenance of the army ' (Cb). *vala-* is corrupted from *bala-* ; *mala-* seems to be an attempt to correct it. 52-53 *aśvavāhāyāḥ* ... *hastivāhāyāḥ* ' months for calculating the wages of attendants of horses and elephants ' (com.). The reason for such separate calculation is not clear. Fleet had ' for hiring horse-carriages and elephant-carriages.' Elephant-carriages are strange. Meyer in a footnote suggests *vāhā* as ' period of gestation, ' i.e., 10 months of 35 days for mares and 10 months of 40 days for female elephants. He adds that actually 10 months of 60 days are required for elephants and ends by asserting that Indians knew little about the breeding of elephants whom they caught ready. All this seems wide of the mark. The fem. gender and the genitive case of the words are strange. *aśvavāha* ' a horse-attendant ' is referred to in 2.30.3.

61 The *ayanas* apparently begin with the beginning of the season and hence of the month ; they are not brought into relation with the sun's entry into a constellation.

65 *haratyarkaḥ ṣaṣṭibhāgam* because the solar day is longer than the normal day by 1/60th. That is one kind of *haraṇa*. The lunar day is shorter by the same amount ; that is another kind of *haraṇa*.

66 *grīṣme...pūrvam* : this implies that in Grīṣma of the third year, half the year is over ; in other words, the year began with Śiśira and Māgha. — All these details about the five-year cycle and intercalary months agree with those in the *Vedāṅga Jyotiṣa*, 32 (Cf. Fleet, JRAS, 1914, p. 998).

2.21

1 *dhvaja* would apparently bear the emblem of the king. — *mahādvāra-* refers to the four main gates, as implied in 2.4.19.

2 The receivers of duty, four or five in number, should record in writing (details about) traders who have arrived in a caravan, who they are, from what place, with how much merchandise and where the identity-pass (was issued) or the stamping was made.

3 For (goods) without the stamp the penalty is double the dues. 4 For those with a forged stamp, the fine is eight times the duty. 5 For those with broken stamps, the penalty is distraint in the ware-house. 6 In case of change of the royal stamp or of (change in) the name, he should make (the trader) pay a fine of one *paṇa* and a quarter per load.

7 Traders shall declare the quantity and price of the goods that have arrived at the foot of the flag, 'Who is willing to purchase these goods, so much in quantity, at this price?' 8 When it has been thrice proclaimed, he should give it to those who have sought it. 9 In case of competition among purchasers, the increase in price together with the duty shall go to the treasury.

10 If for fear of duty a (trader) declares the quantity of the goods or the price to be less (than it actually is), the king shall confiscate that excess. 11 Or, the (trader) shall pay eight times the duty. 12 He should impose the same (penalty) in case of depreciation of price of a package containing goods by (showing) a sample of lower value and in case of concealment of goods of high value by goods of low value.

13 Or, if through fear of a rival purchaser a (trader) increases the price beyond the (due) price of a commodity, the king shall receive the increase in

2 *abhijñānaṁ mudrā vā* is as proposed by Meyer. The two are different as shown by s. 26 below. The former seems to be a sort of pass for identification of the trader, the latter the stamp or seal made on the package of goods. Both are issued by the *antapāla* (s. 26). In 2.34.1-5, however, *mudrā* means the passport which a person must carry about with him.

3 *amudrāṇām*: supply *paṇyānām* rather than *vaṇijām*. — *deya*, 'i.e., *śulka*' (Cp), '*vartanī*, road cess' (Cb). The former is right. 5 *bhinna-* may refer to accidental breaking. Meyer understands deliberate tampering. — *ghaṭikāsthāne sthānam*: this seems to refer to distraint of goods in the ware-house; the distraint may be for one day (as in one of the explanations in Cp) or till corroboration comes from the frontier (Cj). Cb Cs read *ghaṭikāḥ sthānam*; the former has no explanation, the latter has 'distraint in the toll-house for three *ghaṭikās*, i.e., *nālikās*.' This is extremely doubtful. Meyer (understanding deliberate tampering) thinks of confiscation. 6 *nāmakṛte*: the name would appear to be that of the trader on the passport. — *vahanam* etc.: Meyer thinks that the carriage load is also confiscated. The words can hardly yield this sense. Breloer (III, 461) seems to understand 'make a load pay 1/4th *paṇa* fine for every *paṇa*.' It is difficult to see how this meaning is possible.

7 Imported goods were clearly sold at the gate. Meyer thinks that only confiscated goods were sold there. There is nothing to indicate this. 8 *etat* etc.: the sense requires *etāvatpramāṇam anena argheṇa* etc. Cp does not show ss. 8-9.

12 *niviṣṭapaṇyasya bhāṇḍasya*: *bhāṇḍa* seems to refer to the container in which the goods (*paṇya*) are packed (*niviṣṭa*). It contains goods more precious than the supposed sample (*prativarṇaka*) carried outside the package. In the two cases of this s. the trader would stand to lose by sale at the gate unless he were in collusion with the purchaser. We may understand that not all imported goods are sold at the gates.

13 It is difficult to see any difference between 'competition among purchasers' (s.9) and 'fear of a rival purchaser' (this s.). — *dviguṇaṁ vā śulkam*: apparently this option

price, or make the amount of duty double. 14 The same (penalty) eightfold (shall be imposed) on the Superintendent concealing (the trader's offences).

15 Therefore, the sale of goods should be made by weighing, measuring or counting; an appraisal (of value should be made) of goods of small value and goods enjoying concessions.

16 And for goods that have passed beyond the foot of the flag without the duty being paid, the fine is eight times the duty. 17 Secret agents operating on roads and in places without roads should find out such (evasion).

18 Goods intended for marriage, marriage-gifts accompanying the bride, goods intended as gifts, goods required on the occasion of a sacrifice or a ceremony or a birth and goods used in various rituals like worship of the gods, tonsure rite, initiation for Veda study, hair-cutting rite, consecration for a vow and so on, should go duty-free. 19 For a (person) making a false declaration (in this respect) the punishment for theft (shall be imposed).

20 For the trader taking out a commodity for which duty has not been paid along with one for which duty has been paid, or carrying off a second (commodity) under one stamp after breaking open the package, forfeiture of the same and an equal amount as fine (shall be the punishment). 21 For the (trader) carrying off (goods of high value) from the customs house after securing acceptance of cowdung (cakes) or straw as the basis (for calculating duty), the highest fine for violence (shall be the punishment).

22 For the (trader) taking out any one of the unexportable articles, viz., weapons, armours, coats of mail, metals, chariots, jewels, grains and cattle, there shall be a fine as proclaimed as well as loss of the goods. 23 In case any

operated when the *mūlyavṛddhi* amounted to less than the *śulka*. 14 *aṣṭaguṇam* : eight times the *mūlyavṛddhi* or the *śulka*, according to the two options.

15 *ānugrāhikāṇām* : this conveys the sense of what the state has decided to confer *anugraha* on, i.e., to grant concessions to; cf. 2.22.8. The idea of 'what is beneficial' does not seem intended.

17 *pathika*, i.e., 'disguised as traders' (Cb), and *utpathika*, i.e., 'disguised as shepherds, wood-cutters etc.' (Cb). Cf. 2.36.13.

18 *aupāyanikam* : Meyer understands presents to the king only and compares 2.15.3. — *kṛtya* is independent of *yajña*; cf. 3.8.8; 5.1.43.

20 *nirvāhayato* : this and the following two ss. seem to refer to export; cf. 2.16.19. — *dvitīyam* etc. : 'bringing in another similar-looking package on the strength of a *mudrā* on one (*dvitīyam ekamudrayā*) and breaking open a package on which duty is paid and inserting in it goods on which duty is not paid (*bhittvā puṭam apaharataḥ*).' Thus the commentators, who understand imports as meant. But *nirvāhayataḥ* seems to refer to exports; cf. 2.16.19, also s. 22 below. And it appears that in this s. only a single idea is intended, 'breaking open a package and inserting other goods under the same *mudrā*.' It seems that *apa-har* in this s. and the next, has reference to 'taking out' of the country or the city. *mudrā* may be understood as made even on exported goods. 21 *pramāṇaṁ kṛtvā*, i.e., making a declaration about the goods.

22 *anyatamam anirvāhyam* is proposed for *-tamānirvāhyam* of the mss. as being necessary. The prohibition of the export of these goods is obviously for military and economic reasons. — *nāśa* is to the owner, i.e., confiscation. 23 *ānayana* is import. — *ucchulka* 'duty-

one of these is brought in, its sale (shall be effected) duty-free outside (the city-gate) itself.

24 The frontier officer should charge a road cess of one *paṇa* and a quarter for a cart-load of goods, of one *paṇa* for a one-hoofed animal, of half a *paṇa* for cattle, of a quarter *paṇa* for small animals, of one *māṣaka* for a shoulder-load. 25 And he shall make good what is lost or stolen (on the way). 26 He should send on to the Superintendent a caravan from a foreign land after making an investigaton as to goods of high and low value and giving them an identity-pass and stamp (on the goods).

27 Or, a secret agent appearing as a trader should communicate to the king the size of the caravan. 28 In accordance with that information, the king should tell the Collector of Customs about the size of the caravan, in order to make his omniscience known. 29 Then the Collector, on meeting the caravan, should say, 'These are goods of high and low value belonging to such and such a merchant. It should not be concealed. This is the king's power.' 30 For one concealing goods of low value the fine shall be eight times the duty, (for concealing) goods of high value, confiscation of everything (shall be the punishment).

31 He should cut out goods that are harmful to the country and that are worthless. He should make goods that are highly beneficial duty-free, also seeds that are rare.

CHAPTER TWENTY-TWO

SECTION 39 (Continued) THE TARIFF OF DUTIES AND TOLLS

1 (Goods are) from the countryside, from the city and from foreign lands. 2 That on (goods) going out and that on (goods) coming in is duty.

free,' 'because these confer benefit on the country' (Cb), or because the king is the purchaser of these goods.

24 *vartanī* is a cess on traders for the use of roads. This itself involves the liability to protect and indemnify the trader for loss suffered on the way; separate escort-charges are also thought of, called *ātivāhika*; cf. 2.16.18; 2.28.25 etc. 26 *abhjñānaṁ mudrāṁ ca*: see s. 2 above.

27 *preṣayet* should send word, inform; cf. 12.3.20, etc. 28 *tena pradeśena*: cf. 5.2.38.

31 *ucchindyāt*: this may imply prohibition of import or destruction when imported. — *mahopakāram*: this is regarded as an adjective to *bījam* by com. Meyer regards it first as a separate item 'an object that is highly beneficial' and then also as adj. to *bījam* 'seeds, even if highly beneficial, only if (*tu*) they are rare.' But *ca* of the mss. is preferable to *tu* of the editions, and two items appear intended.

2.22

1 The mss. show the word *śulkavyavahāraḥ* 'the tariff of duty' at the beginning. It really belongs to the colophon of the Chapter and has no place in any s. It has clearly got in by error. — *bāhyam* etc. 'produced in the countryside (*bāhyam*), produced in the city (*ābhyantara*) and foreign (*ātithya*)' (com.). For this explanation, *ca* should have come after *ātithyam*. But though, as the text stands, we can understand *ātithya* as duty on internal

3 On goods coming in (the duty shall be) one-fifth of the price.

4 Of flowers, fruits, vegetables, roots, bulbous roots, fruits of creepers, seeds, dried fish and meat, he should take one-sixth part (as duty).

5 Of conch-shells, diamonds, gems and necklaces of pearls and corals, he should make (a valuation) through men expert in the line, making an agreement with them as to the amount of work, time allowed and wages.

6 On *kṣauma*, *dukūla*, silk yarn, armours, yellow orpiment, red arsenic, antimony, vermilion, metals of various kinds and ores, on sandal-wood, aloe, spices, fermentation, and minor substances, on skins, ivory, bed-spreads, coverings and silk cloth, and on products of goats and rams, (the duty to be charged is) one-tenth part or one-fifteenth part.

7 On clothes, four-footed and two-footed creatures, yarn, cotton, perfumes, medicines, woods, bamboos, barks, leather goods and earthen-ware, and on grains, fats, sugars, salts, wine, cooked food and so on (the duty is) one-twentieth part or one twenty-fifth part.

trade (between city and country) and *śulka* as duty on foreign trade, it seems better to follow the commentators. 2 *niṣkrāmyaṁ* : *pravesyam* : Cb (reading *nai-...prā-*) has 'goods going out of the city into the country and out of the country into foreign lands (*naiṣkrāmya*) and coming from foreing lands into the country and from the country into the city (*prāveśya*).' So Cj. It is possible that foreign exports and imports are primarily meant.

3 *mūlyapañcabhāgaḥ* : 'this implies that the duty on imports was received in cash' (Breloer, III, 451).

4 *ṣaḍbhāgaṁ gṛhṇīyāt* : according to com. ss. 4-7 state exceptions to the 20% ad valorem duty of s. 3. But the exceptions would seem to cover the entire range of dutiable commodities. Breloer refers these to exports and says that this duty was received in kind (III, 450). That seems rignt, though internal movement of goods between city and country is also conceivable in the case of certain commodities.

5 *śaṅkha-* etc. : it seems that *hāra* is to be construed with *muktā* and *pravāla* only, *śaṅkha*, *vajra* and *maṇi* being independent items. — *kārayet* : supply *mūlyam* as the object (Cb). The valuation is necessary for charging duty, for 1/6th part of these things can hardly be fixed off-hand. It is in fact doubtful if duty on jewels etc. was received in kind. And if cash duty fixed after valuation is to be understood, it is possible to suppose that the s. belongs to imports and should be read immediately after s. 3. — *kṛtakarma-* etc. : this is a standard formula for work given on a contract basis ; see 2.18.1. — Breloer (III, 451-3) says that *śaṅkha* etc. come from the king's ground and hence are duty-free ; only the cost of labour increases its value. He seems to understand 'special officers, to whom proceeds (*niṣpatti*) come from the result (*phala*) of the work done, amount, time and wage, see these goods through duty-free.' This appears very doubtful.

6 *krimitāna* seems to be silk yarn, while *krimijāta* appears to be silk cloth. Cf. 2.23.8. — *lohavarṇadhātu* 'minerals of the class of metals, such as red chalk' (Cs), 'metals and colouring material' (Meyer), 'base metals and minerals' (Breloer). For *varṇa* as kind or type, cf. 2.15.5. — *añjana* in the compound is from Cb and appears genuine. — *kiṇvāvarāṇām* is from Cb. *āvaraṇa* 'covering' of the other reading would be in strange company, and the next clause has *prāvaraṇa* which means the same thing. Cb's *-avara* may mean 'a minor substance,' though that too is not quite satisfactory. — *carmadantāstaraṇa-* is again from Cb, so is *ājaiḍakasya*. *nikara* in the other reading is understood as 'cloth' by Cj or 'cloth-sheets' by Breloer. The repetition of *kṣauma* and *dukūla* in it makes it suspicious.

7 *carma* : to obviate the idea of repetition this should be construed with *bhāṇḍa* 'leather goods.'

8 To be received at the gate is one-fifth of the normal duty, or he should fix it with a concession in accordance with the benefit derived by the country.

9 And no sale of commodities (shall be allowed) in the places of their origin. 10 For taking metal goods from mines the penalty is six hundred (*paṇas*). 11 For taking flowers and fruits from flower-gardens and fruit-orchards, the fine is fifty-four *paṇas*. 12 For taking vegetables, roots and bulbous roots from vegetable-gardens, the fine is fifty-one and three quarter *paṇas*. 13 For taking all kinds of crops from fields, (the fine is) fifty-three *paṇas*. 14 One *paṇa* and one *paṇa* and a half is the penalty in case of agricultural produce.

15 From this, he should fix the duties for new and old commodities in accordance with the customs of the country and the community, and penalty according to the offence.

CHAPTER TWENTY-THREE

SECTION 40 THE SUPERINTENDENT OF YARNS (AND TEXTILES).

1 The Superintendent of Yarns should cause trade to be carried out in yarns, armours, cloth and ropes through men expert in the work.

8 *dvārādeyaṁ śulkapañcabhāgaḥ* : this seems to refer to tolls on goods coming into the city ; it is to be one-fifth of the *śulka* as fixed above (Cp). Cj, reading *dvārādeyam*, says that this additional one-fifth of the *śulka* is to be paid at the time of entry into or exit from the city and is over and above the regular *śulka*. Russ. renders *dvārādeya* by 'collections meant for the door-keeper.' — *ānugrāhikam* : this involves an *anugraha* or concession by the state ; cf. 2.21.15. It may be that this option applies not only to the town duty but to all import and export duties as well, as Cp understands it.

9 The purpose of this prohibition is, according to Breloer, to force all goods to the markets and allow the turn-over to be controlled (III, 453-4). In addition, tolls required to be recovered and prices to be regulated by the state. 10 *ṣaṭchatam* : cf. 2.12.31 concerning salt, where also the king enjoys a monopoly. 14 *paṇo 'dhyardhapaṇaś ca sītātyayaḥ* : 'the purchaser pays 1 *paṇa* and the vendor 1½ *paṇa* ' (Cp Cs). Cp adds that this impost is to be paid on every sale whether an offence is committed or not, while according to Cs this is in addition to 53 *paṇas* when the offence is committed. Cb Cj seem to have read *paṇo 'rdhapaṇaś ca*. The former has ' 53 *paṇas* in the case of other grains, a *paṇa* or half a *paṇa* in the case of paddy.' Cj refers to another explanation ' half a *paṇa* fine for grains valued at 1 *paṇa* and so on.' It may be that *sītā* refers as usual to the produce of crown lands (2.15.2). If purchases are made from the field, the penalty is nominal in this case because state goods would be duty-free and sale in the fields would mean no loss of state dues. The two fines may be related to the purchaser and vendor as in Cp, the vendor in this case being a state officer. However, see 5.2.13 below. Russ. renders *sītātyaya* by 'transgression of rules about sowing.

15 *deśajāticaritrataḥ* 'according to the customs of the region and the caste' (com.) appears preferable to 'place, class of goods and custom' (Meyer) or 'land, caste and occupation ' (Breloer). — Concerning stanzas at the end of 2.21 and 2.22 Breloer remarks that they do not show the prolixity of Kauṭilya and are taken from predecessors who were much simpler in their treatment (III, 447). That they are derived from early sources is, of course, very likely ; but they do not reveal simpler or more primitive ideas. They merely lay down guiding principles.

2.23

1 The form *rajju* may be adopted throughout as in 2.17.8 and 2.24.3. — *vyavahāra* usually is ' trade ' ; but the Chapter refers only to manufacture. Actual trade would seem to be in the hands of the *paṇyādhyakṣa*.

2 He should get yarn spun out of wool, bark-fibres, cotton, silk-cotton, hemp and flax, through widows, crippled women, maidens, women who have left their homes and women paying off their fine by personal labour, through mothers of courtesans, through old female slaves of the king and through female slaves of temples whose service of the gods has ceased.

3 He should fix the wage after ascertaining the fineness, coarseness or medium quality of the yarn, and the largeness or smallness of quantity. 4 After finding out the amount of yarn, he shoud favour them with oil and myrobalan unguents. 5 And on festive days, they should be made to work by honouring (them) and making gifts. 6 In case of dim nution in yarn, (there shall be) a diminution in wage, according to the value of the stuff.

7 And he should cause work to be carried out by artisans producing goods with an agreement as to the amount of work, time and wage, and should maintain close contact with them. 8 And when starting mills for the weaving of (cloth from) *kṣauma*, *dukūla*, silk yarn, hair of the *raṅku* deer, and cotton yarn, he should gratify the (workmen) by gifts of perfumes and flowers and by other means of showing good-will. 9 He should bring about the production of varieties of cloth, bed-sheets and coverings. 10 And he should start factories for armours by artisans and craftsmen expert in the line.

11 And those women who do not stir out — those living separately, widows, crippled women or maidens, — who wish to earn their living, should be given work by sending his own female slaves to them with (a view to) support (them). 12 Or, if they come themselves to the yarn-house, he should cause an interchange of goods and wages to be made early at dawn. 13 The lamp (should be there) only for the inspection of the yarn. 14 For looking at the face of the woman or conversing with her on another matter, the lowest fine for violence (shall be imposed), for delay in the payment of wages, the middle fine, also for payment of wages for work not done.

2 *pravrajitā* is one who has left home for good and is living independently. 'Emancipated' is how Breloer (III, 474 and n. 4) renders the word. — *daṇḍapratikāriṇī*: cf. 3.13.18. — *mātṛkā*: see 2.27.5.

5 *tithiṣu* 'on festive days' (Cp). — *pratimānadānaiḥ*, though not very satisfactory, is adopted from Cb for *pratipādanamānaiḥ* of the mss. Cj has *pratimānanadānaiḥ*.

7 *karmapramāṇa-* etc. is a standing formula for piece-rate work; cf. 2.18.1; 2.22.5. — *pratisaṁsargam* amounts to control (Breloer) or a strict watch over them (Meyer).

8 Wool is not mentioned in this connection. — Weavers appear to be treated with special favour. 10 *kaṅkaṭa*: this 'armour' made from fabrics may have been made of wool or other cloth filled with cotton or other stuffing.

11 Ss. 11-15 should preferably have come immediately after s. 6 above. — *proṣitā vidhavā* is emended from *proṣitavidhavā*, and *proṣitā* is understood in the same sense as *pravrajitā* in s. 2 above. Cb understands *proṣita* (in *proṣitavidhavā*) in the sense of *proṣitabhartṛkā*. In any case, *vidhavā* must be understood independently; cf. s. 2 above. — *anusārya*, i.e., sending these to their homes. — *sopagraham*, i.e., by showing favour or by giving support.

15 If a (woman) after receiving the wage does not carry out the work, he should make her forfeit the tongs formed by the thumb (and the middle finger), also those who have misappropriated or stolen and then run away.

16 And in the matter of wages, (there shall be) a fine for workmen in accordance with their offence.

17 And he should himself keep in touch with rope-makers and makers of armours. 18 And he should cause articles, such as straps and others to be manufactured.

19 He should cause ropes to be made of yarn and fibres, (and) thongs of canes and bamboos, as trappings for war and bindings for vehicles and draught-animals.

CHAPTER TWENTY-FOUR

SECTION 41 THE DIRECTOR OF AGRICULTURE

1 The Director of Agriculture, himself conversant with the practice of agriculture, water-divining and the science of rearing plants, or assisted by experts in these, should collect, in the proper seasons, seeds of all kinds of grains, flowers, fruits, vegetables, bulbous roots, roots, creeper fruits, flax and cotton.

15 *aṅguṣṭhasaṁdaṁśam* 'the thumb and middle finger of the right hand' (Cb Cp). Cj seems to understand the two thumbs (*aṅguṣṭhābhyāṁ saṁdaṁśam*). Cb Cp state that the entire thumb and the tip of the middle finger are to be cut. Russ. understands the thumb and the index finger. — *bhakṣitāpa-* etc.: the translation follows the commentators. Meyer objects that the participles cannot be understood in an active sense, as adjectives to *strīṇām*. His rendering 'when anything is used up (*bhakṣita*) or stolen (*apahṛta*) or deliberately ruined (*avaskandita*)' seems, however, hardly plausible.

16 *vetaneṣu . . . daṇḍaḥ*, i.e., the fine is to be recovered from the wages.

17 *rajjuvartakaiḥ*: these may have formed a caste of their own. — *varmakāraiḥ* is from Cp. *carmakāraiḥ* of M Cb does not fit, because even the *varatrās* or thongs seem to be made not of leather, but of cane and bamboo (s. 19). *pūrvākāraiḥ* of G makes little sense. Meyer suggests for it *mūrvākāraiḥ* 'makers of bowstrings.' *varma* 'armour' may refer to accoutrements, including straps etc.

19. Breloer (III, 471-3) thinks that ss. 17-18 and this *kārikā* deal with the manufacture of war-material; the *sūtrādhyakṣa* therefore may, originally, have been an assistant of the Superintendent of Arms and that his independent status here may be due to Kauṭilya himself. This sounds plausible.

2.24

Breloer (I, 74-89, also III, 485-502) is of the opinion that the *sītādhyakṣa* supervised the total cultivation of crops in the realm and that one of his duties was to see that no land remained uncultivated. The Chapter, however, produces the impression that he is concerned with the management of crown lands only. 5.2.8-11 show that it is the *samāhartṛ* and his men who are concerned with sowings by independent farmers. Moreover, the revenue brought in by the *sītādhyakṣa* is called *sītā* and is distinguished from *bhāga* or *ṣaḍbhāga* received from farmers (2.15.2-3 ; 2.6.3).

1. *śulba* 'for finding out if there is water underground' (Cb Cj). This appears to be something like water-divining. — Parāśara or Vṛddha-Parāśara is credited with the authorship of the *Kṛṣitantra* and Agniveśa with that of *Vṛkṣāyurveda*. — Cb seems to have read *saṁgṛhṇīyāt*, which might appear better.

2 He should cause them to be sown in land, suitable for each, which has been ploughed many times, through serfs, labourers and persons paying off their fines by personal labour. 3 And he should cause no delay in (the work of) these on account of ploughing machines, implements and bullocks, and on account of (the work of) artisans, such as smiths, carpenters, basket-makers, rope-makers, snake-catchers and others. 4 In case of loss of fruit of a work (through their negligence), the fine (shall be equal to) the loss of that fruit.

5 Sixteen *droṇas* is the amount of rain in dry lands, one and a half times (that) in wet lands, where sowings are in conformity with (the nature of) the region, thirteen *droṇas* and a half in the Aśmakas, twenty-three in the Avantīs, unlimited in the Aparāntas and the snowy regions, and (unlimited) as to time, in lands where sowings are made with the help of canals.

6 One-third of the (annual) rainfall in the first and the last months (together), two-thirds in the intervening two months, — this is the form of excellence (of the season).

7 Its ascertainment (is made) from the position, motion and impregnation of Jupiter, from the rise, setting and movements of Venus and from modification in the natural appearance of the sun. 8 From the sun (is known)

2. *svabhūmau*, i.e., on land suitable for the crop to be sown. According to Johnston (JRAS, 1929, 90-1), this means 'on crown lands.' That is also possible. — *daṇḍapratikartṛ* cf. 3.13.18. 3 *karṣaṇayantra* contains a single idea, not two 'ploughing and machines' (as Meyer ultimately prefers in the Nachtrag). — *medaka* 'a maker of baskets' (Cb), 'digger' (Cs). Meyer relates it to Meda a mixed caste mentioned in Manu, 10.48, and suggests 'catchers of wild and dangerous animals' as the meaning. 4 *teṣām* refers to *dāsa*, *karmakara* etc., as well as to the craftsmen. — *tatphalahānam* : for the expression, cf. 2.29.33.

5 On the basis of about 511 cubic inches in a *droṇa* and a cylindrical raingauge with a surface area of about 254.3 sq. inches (1 *aratni* about 18″ diameter, 2.5.7), 16 *droṇas* amount to about 32″ of rain ; if the gauge-mouth is understood to be square (18″ by 18″), they would amount to about 25″. — *jāṅgala* are dry tracts as opposed to *ānūpa* or wet lands. Manu, 7.69, recommends *jāṅgala* land for settlement. — *varṣapramāṇam* 'rain-fall necessary for good crops' in such regions (com.). — *deśavāpānām* : Cj Cp Cs understand this as introducing what follows '(amount) required for sowing according to different countries (will now be explained).' *deśavāpa*, however, seems contrasted with *kulyāvāpa*, the former referring to sowing dependent on rain and the nature of the region (whether *jāṅgala* or *ānūpa*), the latter to sowing in irrigated areas (which are not dependent on rain). — *ardhatrayodaśa* is understood by all as 13½, not 12½. — Aśmaka, i.e., 'Mahārāṣṭra' (Cp), 'Āraṭṭa' (Cs). The capital of Aśmaka was Pratiṣṭhāna on the Godāvarī (V.S. Agrawala, *India as known to Pāṇini*, p. 38). — Aparānta 'Koṅkaṇaviṣaya' (Cp). — *haimanya* 'in which there is plenty of snow which makes agriculture possible ; this is near the Himālayas' (Cb). — *kālataḥ* : supply *amitam* with this, the idea being that agriculture is here independent of seasonal rain. Cf. Breloer (III, 493 n. 4). Pran Nath (IA, 60, 111-2) seems to understand *varṣa* as share due to the king, making *kulyāvāpa* an adjective to *haimanya* 'winter crops.' This seems hardly likely.

6 The four monsoon months are Śrāvaṇa to Kārttika according to the commentators. — *suṣamā* '*paramā śobhā*' (Amara, 1.3.17).

7 *garbhādhāna*, i.e., 'dew in Mārgaśīrṣa, snow in Pauṣa, wind in Māgha, clouds in Phālguna, wind and rain in Caitra and rain with wind and lightning in Vaiśākha, together with rain on the days of conception (viz., the first four days of the dark half of Vaiśākha)' (com. which quote mnemonic verses in support). The *Bṛhatsaṁhitā*, 21.7, refers to the impregnation of a cloud 195 days prior to its sending down that rain. — *cāra* 'movement

the successful sprouting of seeds, from Jupiter the formation of stalks in the crops, from Venus rain.

9 Three clouds raining (continuously) for seven days (each), eighty (clouds) showering drops of rain (and) sixty clouds accompanied by sunshine, this rainfall is even and beneficial.

10 Where it rains distributing wind and sunshine properly and creating three (periods for the drying of) cowdung cakes, there the growth of crops is certain.

11 In conformity with that, he should cause crops to be sown, requiring plenty of water or little water. 12 *śāli*-rice, *vrīhi*-rice, *kodrava*, sesamum, *priyaṅgu*, *udāraka* and *varaka* are the first sowings. 13 *mudga*, *māṣa* and *śaimbya* are the middle sowings. 14 Safflower, lentils, *kulattha*, barley, wheat, *kalāya*, linseed and mustard are the last sowings. 15 Or, the sowing of seeds (should be) in conformity with the season.

16 What is left over from sowing, farmers cultivating for half the produce should till, or those who live by personal labour (should work it) for a one-fourth or one-fifth share. 17 The (farmers) shall pay a share for uncultivated land as desired (by the king), except in times of distress.

(of Venus) on the nine days from the 5th to the 13th of Āṣāḍha ' (com.). — *prakṛtivaikṛtāt* ' change in the natural condition ' (com.), ' natural and unnatural appearance ' (Meyer).

9 *saptāhikā*, i.e., sending down rain more or less continuously for seven days. — *aśītiḥ*, i.e., eighty days of light and intermittent showers. — *ātapameghānām*, i.e., rain alternating with sunshine. The total comes to 161 days. Contrast s. 6 above. 10 *karīṣān* ' breaks in the rain long enough to allow the drying of cowdung cakes' (Cb). Cs reads *karṣakān*, but it can hardly mean ' ploughing,' i.e., sowing. And three sowings do not seem intended here.

12 *pūrvavāpāḥ* etc. : in the alternative, this may imply sowings one after another in the same field ; but that does not appear very likely. 15 *yathartuvaśena vā* : seasons for the different crops are suggested by *pūrvavāpa* etc. of the preceding ss. *vā* seems to have little significance.

16 *vāpātiriktam* : this refers to land which the *sītādhyakṣa* has not managed to get cultivated. That is to be leased to tenants on crop-share basis. Breloer understands *vāpātirikta* as ' fallow land.' Johnston (JRAS, 1929, 92) would insert a *vā* after *vāpātiriktam* and explain 'or, land should be let out to cultivators who pay half the produce as rent on the *vāpātirikta* system, under which an amount equal to the seed sown is deducted from the gross produce and handed over to the tenant, the rest being equally divided between the king and the tenant.' This appears too involved. — *svavīryopajīvinaḥ* : Johnston (JRAS, 1929, 95) understands soldiers, policemen, etc. But *vīrya* here is only personal labour, not valour. — In this case, seeds, implements etc. are provided by the state. — *caturtha*- etc. : Johnston understands ' paying 1/4th or 1/5th to the state.' That is hardly likely. Cf. Ghoshal, *Rev. Sys.*, p. 30 n. 2. 17 *anavasitabhāgam* : this is share of the produce from land that has been reclaimed and brought under cultivation for the first time, as described in Chapter 2.1. For *anavasita* referring to *śūnyaniveśa*, see 7.11.1 ff. Cb has ' when half-sharers and others, after agreeing to till, do not do so, they hand over what the king desires, i.e., the entire produce to the state.' This is unlikely ; so is Johnston's 'share other than those set out above (*avasita* as *uparinirdiṣṭa*).' — *yatheṣṭam*, i.e., as desired by the king or *sītādhyakṣa*. This implies the idea of concession to such new settlers. — *anyatra kṛcchrebhyaḥ* : this may mean ' when the state is in distress, concessions may be withdrawn ' or ' when the farmers are in distress, they may be exempted from giving any share.' The former seems meant ; cf. *arthakṛcchra* in 5.2.1.

18 The (farmers) shall pay a water-rate of one-fifth in the case of water set in motion by the hand from their own water-works, one-fourth when set in motion by shoulders and one-third when set flowing in channels by a mechanism, one-fourth when lifted from rivers, lakes, tanks and wells.

19 According to the amount of water (available) for the work, he should decide on wet crops, winter crops or summer crops. 20 *śāli* and others are the best (crops), vegetables middling, sugar-cane worst. 21 For, sugar-canes are fraught with many dangers and require (much) expenditure.

22 (A region) where the foam strikes (the banks) is (suited) for creeper fruits, (regions on) the outskirts of overflows, for long pepper, grapes and sugar-canes, (those on) the borders of wells, for vegetables and roots, (those on) the borders of moist beds of lakes, for green grasses, ridges for plants reaped by cutting, (such as) perfume-plants, medicinal herbs, *uśīra*-grass, *hrībera*, *piṇḍālaka* and others. 23 And on lands suitable for each, he should raise plants that grow on dry lands and that grow in wet lands.

24 Soaking in dew (by night) and drying in the heat (by day) for seven days and nights (is the treatment) in the case of seeds of grains, for three days and nights or five in the case of seeds of pulses, smearing at the cut with honey, ghee and pig's fat, mixed with cowdung in the case of stalks that serve as seeds, (smearing) with honey and ghee in the case of bulbous roots, smearing with cowdung in the case of stone-like seeds, (and) in the case of trees, burning in the pit and fulfilment of the longing with cow-bones and cowdung at the proper time.

18 *svasetubhyaḥ* : Johnston understands state irrigation works. But with *dadyuḥ* as the predicate *sva* can hardly refer to the king. According to the commentators, the king is entitled to a water-rate even when the works are made by the farmers themselves, because he is the owner of all water as well as land, a stanza being quoted to this effect. — *udakabhāgam* : this would naturally mean a share of the produce over and above the regular land-revenue. It is also possible to understand that the regular *bhāga* is 1/6th when no irrigation facilities are available, and that 1/5th, 1/4th etc. are charged instead when the farmers enjoy irrigation facilities (made by themselves), the rates varying according to the nature of the irrigation work. Meyer's idea of a share of the water itself supplied to crown lands from private irrigation works does not appear likely. — *hastaprāvartima*, i.e., drawing water with the hands and carrying it to the fields in pitchers, etc. — *skandha-* are the shoulders or backs of bullocks. — *srotoyantra-* a mechanism for letting water in channels flowing into the fields. — *-udghātam* : com. understand the water-wheel for raising water from river, etc.

19 *karmodaka-* : Meyer's 'amount of labour and water available' would require *karmakara* for *karma*. — *kaidāram* refers to wet crops. Johnston's proposed *kedāre* 'on wet land' (JRAS, 1929, 96) is hardly acceptable.

22 *phenāghātaḥ* : supply *pradeśaḥ* ; 'where the foam strikes' are banks of rivers etc. — *parīvāha* 'overflow, flooding' is, according to Cb, 'another, i.e., a secondary canal.' — *haraṇī* 'moist empty beds of lakes' (Cb Cp), 'canals, channels' (Cs). — *lava* (from *lū* to cut) a plant which when cut continues to grow ; *gandha*, *bhaiṣajya* etc. are illustrations.

24 *kośīdhānya* 'grains in the pods,' i.e., pulses. — *kāṇḍabīja* 'whose seed is the stalk,' that grow from stalk, such as sugar-cane etc. — *gartadāhaḥ*, i.e., burning grass, leaves etc. in the pit in which the seed is to be sown. Meyer construes *go'sthiśakṛdbhiḥ* with *dāhaḥ* and refers *dauhṛda* to the longing of trees imagined by classical poets (*pādāghāta* for *Aśoka* etc.). That is very doubtful. 25 *aśuṣka-* ; Cb reads *śuṣka* 'dried' fish. The *ca*

25 And when they have sprouted, he should feed them with fresh acrid fish along with the milk of the *snuhi*-plant.

26 He should collect (and burn) the seeds of cotton and the slough of a serpent. Serpents do not remain where there is this smoke.

27 However, at the first sowing of all kinds of seeds, he should sow the first handful (after it is) immersed in water containing gold and should recite the following *mantra*:

'Salutation to Kāśyapa, the Lord of Creation and to the god (of rain) always. May the divine Sītā prosper in my seeds and my grains.'

28 To watchmen in vegetable-gardens and in fruit and flower enclosures, to cowherds and serfs and labourers, he should supply food in accordance with persons dependent on them, and pay a wage of one *paṇa* and a quarter per month. 29 To artisans, (he should give) food and wages in conformity with their work.

30 And those learned in the Vedas and ascetics may take flowers and fruits that have fallen on the ground for worship of the gods, rice and barley for the *āgrayaṇa* sacrifice, (and) those who live by gleaning (may take) what is left at the base of a heap (of grains).

31 And at the proper time he should bring in the crops and other things as they are harvested. The wise man should not leave anything in the field, not even husk.

32 (He should make) high walls, or roofs of the same kind. He should not make the tops compact nor very light.

after *-matsyān* is strange. Meyer thinks that some word has dropped out. — *-kṣīreṇa*: with *pāyayet* as the predicate, *-kṣīram* (with *-matsyaiḥ*) would have been better.

26 *-sāra* 'essence,' i.e., seeds. Sorabji mentions a modern practice, burning old rags to keep off serpents.

27 The first line is hypermetric. Meyer proposes *prajāpatye* (for *-pataye*) which is not necessary. Cb's reading appears to be *prajāpateḥ kāśyapāya devalāya namaḥ sadā*. It also reads *madhyamā* for *ṛdhyatām*. — *dhaneṣu* evidently refers to grains, and seems to have been used instead of *dhānyeṣu* for metrical reasons.

28 *-pālaka* is to be construed with each of *ṣaṇḍa-*, *vāṭa-* and *go-*. — *puruṣa-parivāpa* refers usually to retinue or followers; cf. 1.16.5; 3.3.3. Here dependents are evidently to be understood. The state feeds not only the labourer but also his dependents, but he alone gets the cash wage of 1 1/4 *paṇa* a month. — *sapādapaṇikam*: Breloer (III, 505 and n.3) has 'a monthly wage, receiving 5/4ths for every *paṇa*,' i.e, he gets 5/4 times the wage sanctioned for him, the actual amount of the wage not being stated. It is difficult to see how this meaning is possible. For the monthly wage of 5/4 *paṇa*, see 2.27.9. The *ca* after this word is necessary.

30 *āgrayaṇa* is the offering of fresh grains at the end of the rains. — *vrīhiyavam*: *praśīrṇam* is to be understood also with this.

32 *prākārāṇām* is from Cb, also found in G2. It refers to the walls of the shed in which grains are stored. *prakārāṇām* of the mss. hardly suits, also *prakarāṇām* of Cp Cs. — *samucchrāyān*: supply *kurvīta* from the second half. *prākārān ucchritān kuryāt* would have been better. — *valabhīr* 'the thatched roofs' of the shed (Cb). Cb adds that the roof should be made of iron or stones as that gives protection from *piśācas*. — *tathāvidhāḥ*: we have

33 He should make the heaps situated at the border of the circle of the threshing-floor. At the threshing ground, workmen should carry no fire and should be provided with water.

CHAPTER TWENTY-FIVE

SECTION 42 THE CONTROLLER OF SPIRITUOUS LIQUORS

1 The Controlier of Spirituous Liquors should cause trade in wines and ferments to be carried on in the fort, the country or the camp, through persons dealing in wines and ferments, being born to that work, either in one place or in many places or according to (convenience for) purchase and sale. 2 He should fix six hundred *paṇas* as the penalty for those who manufacture, purchase or sell in other places.

3 (He should enforce) prohibition of taking wine out of the village and its accumulation, because of the danger of remissness in duties by those appointed, because of the danger of transgression of the bounds of propriety by Āryas and because of the danger of rash acts by bravoes. 4 Or, those of known integrity may carry out a small quantity, well marked, either one-fourth (of a *kuḍuba*), half a *kuḍuba*, a *kuḍuba*, half a *prastha* or a *prastha*. 5 Or, they should drink in the drinking-houses without moving about.

6 In order to find out things (that are) misappropriated after being received in trust or as a deposit or a pledge and (that are) acquired in undesirable ways, he should, on finding an article or money not belonging to a person, get the person offering it arrested in another place under some (other) pretext, also the person who spends lavishly and the person who spends without having a source of income.

to understand by this *samucchritāḥ*. *vā* seems to have the sense of *ca*. 33 *prakarān* : Cb reads *prākārān* here as well, but it is hard on the metre. And walls of sheds would not be right on the borders of the threshing-floor circle. — Breloer (III, 484) remarks that the *kārikās* are not compressed in style as usual and seem to have had a different source.

2.25

1 *vyavahāra* : here both manufacture and trade seem intended. — *ekamukham* etc. see 2.16.4 above. 2 *anyatra kartṛ-* etc. : cf. 2.12.19, 31.

3 *anirṇayanam* : supply *sthāpayet* from the preceding. — For *sampāta* 'accumulation' of goods, cf. 8.4.36 ; 13.4.38 etc. Cb Cs understand *surā* as 'a drunken man,' *anirṇayana* as 'not going out' and *asampāta* as 'not allowing them to go in a crowd or from house to house.' This appears little likely. 4 *lakṣitam* 'marked' with a seal (Cs). — *vā* : Meyer understands the option to be between *lakṣitam* and *alpam* ; the option however seems to be betweent his s. and the preceding. 5 This s. in effect nullifies the concession of the preceding s. — *asaṁcāriṇaḥ* 'not moving about' when in a state of intoxication.

6 *nikṣepopanidhiproyoga-* : *nikṣepa* is an article entrusted to an artisan for manufacture (3.12.33 ff.). *prayoga* is 'pledging an article' when taking a loan (Cb). Meyer's rendering 'if things are stolen in order to use them (*prayoga* 'use') as an open deposit (*nikṣepa*) or sealed deposit (*upanidhi*)' is quite unlikely. — *kupyam* should be understood to mean some small article, rather than 'forest produce' as usual. — *nikṣeptāram* refers to the customer who passes on the misappropriated article in payment of wine. — *anyatra vyapadeśena*: this is in order that other criminals are not frightened away from the ale-house (Cs).

7 And the (vintner) shall not sell liquor at a different price or on credit, except spoiled liquor. 8 He should get the latter sold in another place. 9 Or, he should pay it as wages for slaves and labourers. 10 Or, he should give it as a strong drink for draught animals or as nourishment for pigs.

11 He should cause ale-houses to be built with many rooms, (and) provided with separate beds and seats, (and) drinking bars provided with perfumes, flowers and water, (and) pleasant in all seasons.

12 Secret agents, placed there, should ascertain the normal and occasional expenditure (of customers) and get information about strangers. 13 They should make a note of the ornaments, clothes and cash of customers who are intoxicated or sleeping. 14 In case of loss of these, the traders shall pay the same and a fine of equal amount. 15 Traders, on their part, should find out through their own female slaves of beautiful appearance, the intentions of strangers and natives, who have the (outward) appearance of Āryas, when they are intoxicated or asleep in secluded parts of the rooms.

16 Concerning the *medaka*, the *prasannā*, the *āsava*, the *ariṣṭas*, the *maireya* and *madhu* : 17 One *droṇa* of water, one-half *āḍhaka* of rice-grains and three *prasthas* of ferment form the mixture for the *medaka*. 18 Twelve *āḍhakas* of flour, five *prasthas* of ferment or the mixture of its class along with the bark and fruit of the *kramuka*, form the mixture for the *prasannā*. 19 One *tulā* of the wood-apple fruit, five *tulās* of treacle, and a *prastha* of honey form the mixture for the *āsava*. 20 One quarter more (of this mixture) is the best (*āsava*), one quarter less the lowest kind. 21 The *ariṣṭas* are as prescribed by physicians for each separate malady. 22 The *maireya* is distilled from a decoction of the bark of the *meṣaśṛṅgī* with the addition of jaggery, having a mixture of long pepper and black pepper or

7 *anargheṇa*, i.e., different from the price fixed by the state ; if higher, the difference is likely to be pocketed by the vintner ; if lower, there is scope for adulteration. — *kālikā* 'on credit' ; cf. 12.4.8. Meyer's 'clearance sale within a limited time' seems less likely. 10 *vāhanapratipānam* : cf. 2.29.43 etc. 'Wages for guarding cattle' (Cs) is little likely. Similarly *sūkaraposaṇam* is hardly 'wages for swine-herds' (Cs).

11 *-śayanāsana-* suggests that these were also lodging houses.

14 *vaṇijaḥ* : these are vintners licensed by the state. 15 *vāstavyānām* may be understood as an adjective to *āgantūnām* or independently as 'residents,' i.e., natives. The latter is better in view of the *ca*.

17 *medaka* may suggest the fattening property of this liquor. — *kiṇva* : see s. 26. 18 *piṣṭa* seems rice-flour, though barley-flour is also possible. Water eight times the amount of flour is to be understood as in the case of *medaka* (com.). — *-kramuka-* is from Cb for *putraka*. Cf. s. 29. — *jātisaṁbhārāḥ* 'mixture belonging to its class, as described in s. 27' (com.). This is an option to the 5 *prasthas* of *kiṇva*. Meyer has 'addition of (*jāti*).' He does not understand this as an option, but renders *vā* by 'according to one's choice.' — The name *prasannā*, may refer to the clearness of the liquor. 19 *āsava* is primarily 'infusion'. The amount of water would evidently be 8 *tulās*. 21 *vikārāṇām* 'maladies' (com.) rather than 'modification (in the ingredients)' (Meyer). The name *ariṣṭa* refers to absence of injury or harm. 22 The significance of the name *maireya* is not clear.

mixed with the three fruits. 23 Or, there should be a mixture of the three fruits in all (liquors) mixed with jaggery. 24 The juice of grapes is *madhu*. 25 Its name derived from the place of origin is *kāpiśāyana* and *hārahūraka*.

26 One *droṇa* pulp of *māṣa*-beans, raw or cooked, with one-third part more rice-grains, mixed with a part weighing one *karṣa* (each) of *moraṭā* and others is the formation of ferment.

27 A mixture weighing five *karṣas* (each) of *pāṭhā, lodhra, tejovatī*, cardamum, *vāluka*, liquorice, *madhurasā, priyaṅgu, dāruharidrā*, black and long pepper is the addition for the *medaka* and the *prasannā*. 28 And *kaṭaśarkarā*, mixed with a decoction of liquorice makes the colour clear.

29 The mixture for the *āsava* is one *karṣa* (each) of cinnamon bark, *citraka, vilaṅga* and *gajapippalī* and two *karṣas* (each) of *kramuka*, liquorice, *mustā* and lodhra. 30 And one-tenth part of these is the formation of the essence.

31 The mixture for *prasannā* is that for white liquor. 32 Mango-liquor, with a higher proportion of juice or a higher proportion of essence, is *mahāsurā*,

23 *triphalā* may be three myrobalans, *harītakī, bibhītaka* and *āmalaka*, or 'nutmeg, areca-nut and clove' (Sorabji and Meyer). According to this s., wherever jaggery is used, *triphalā* should be added. 25 *tasya svadeśo vyākhyānam* is an odd expression. *vyākhyāna* seems used in the sense of designation, name. In that case, we expect *svadeśāt*. — Kapiśa was an ancient capital in the region of the Kabul valley (cf. V. S. Agrawala, *op. cit.*, p. 118 n. 1). Hārahūra is the name of a region or people beyond the North-West of India 'of Scythian or Turkish stock according to Kern' (Weber). Meyer thinks of Hara-Hūṇas. Jayaswal thinks of 'Arachosian wine' (JBORS, II, 79 n.).

26 *kalanī* apparently the same as *kalka*. — *moraṭādīnām* : *ādi* refers to the ingredients mentioned in the first compound in s. 33 below. — *kārṣika-* : 1 *karṣa* of each. — *-yuktam* as going with *droṇam* is preferable to *-yuktaḥ* of the mss.

27 *pañcakārṣikaḥ*, i.e., 5 *karṣas* each. — *saṁbhārayoga* is apparently to be used in place of the *kiṇva*. Cf. s. 18 above. 28 *kaṭaśarkarā* is evidently some plant. Its powder is mentioned in s. 33. Cb reads *kaṇḍaśarkarā* 'pieces of jaggery.' — *varṇaprasādanī*, i.e., the colour of *medaka* and *prasannā* becomes clear (Cb).

30 *daśabhāgaś caiṣām bījabandhaḥ* : the idea apparently is, 1/10th of this mixture is to be added as essence in preparing *āsava* as in s. 19. It amounts to 12/10ths of a *karṣa*, rather a small quantity. Cp reads *ṣaṭkārṣikaḥ* for *kārṣikaḥ* (in s. 29); that gives 32/10 *karṣa*. Meyer construes this s. with the following 'one-tenth of these as the basic deposit and the mixture as in the case of *prasannā* yields white liquor.' For this, a *ca* is necessary after *prasannāyogaḥ*. Understanding *prasannāyogaḥ* as an adjective to *bījabandhaḥ* (Meyer, fn.) is no improvement.

31 According to Cp *śvetasurā* differs from *prasannā* in that it has no *saṁbhāra* and has an equal amount of ferment. According to Cb there is neither *saṁbhāra* nor *bījabandha*. 32 Cp has four kinds, *sahakārasurā* (liquor mixed with mango oil,), *rasottarā* (with jaggery added), *mahāsurā* (with a large amount of *bīja*) and *saṁbhārikī* (with a large amount of *bīja* and *saṁbhāra*). Cb has five, *bījottarā* being distinguished from *mahāsurā*, *bīja* being more in the former, *mātrā* (?) being more in the latter. Neither does justice to the two *vā* in the sentence. Meyer has *mahāsurā* as the name of *rasottarā sahakārasurā* and *saṁbhārikī* as the name of *bījottarā sahakārasurā*. It might appear better to think of *mahāsurā* alone as the name, with three alternatives, *rasottarā, bījottarā* and *saṁbhārikī*, all understood as attributes of *sahakārasurā*, which may be liquor from mango juice, not made by mere addition

or when it contains the mixture. 33 The powder of burnt *kaṭaśarkarā*, infused in a decoction of *moraṭā, palāśa, pattūra, meṣaśṛṅgī, karañja* and *kṣīravṛkṣa*, mixed with half (its quantity) of the pulp of *lodhra, citraka, vilaṅga, paṭhā, musta, kaliṅga-yava, dāruharidrā, indīvara, śatapuṣpā, apāmārga, saptaparṇa, nimba* and *āsphota*, —a handful (of this) with nails invisible, makes one *kumbhī* of those (liquors) clear, fit to be drunk by the king. 34 And jaggery, five *palas* in weight, should be added to it to increase the (sweet) juice.

35 Householders should be free to manufacture white liquor on festive occasions or an *ariṣṭa* for medicinal use, or other (spirituous preparations).

36 On the occasions of festivals, gatherings and fairs, permission to manufacture and sell liquor should be granted for four days. 37 On those days, he should charge a penalty per day from those not permitted, till the end of the festivity.

38 Women and children should make a search for (ingredients used in) liquors and ferments.

39 Dealers in goods not manufactured by the state shall pay a duty of five per cent on *surā, medaka, ariṣṭa, madhu,* sour fruit juices, and sour liquors.

40 And after ascertaining the day's sale and the surcharge on measures and on cash, he should fix the compensation accordingly and should keep going what is customary.

of mango oil. 33 Cb again reads *kaṇḍaśarkarā* 'pieces of jaggery' with which, however, *dagdha* hardly fits in. — *kaliṅgayava* : Cp reads *kālāguru*. Meyer had proposed *kaliṅgayava* for the faulty *kalāgayava* of the editions. — *kalkārdhayuktam*, i.e., the pulp is to be half the *cūrṇa* in quantity. — *antarnakho muṣṭiḥ*, i.e., the fingers are so closed that the nails cannot be seen outside. The amount would be fairly small. — *kumbhīm* 'a pitcher' (Cb). Cs equates it with *khārī*, i.e., 16 *droṇas* (2.19.31). Cp makes out *catuṣṣaṣṭisahasrapalas* (i.e., 1064 ?). 34 *rasavṛddhiḥ*, i.e., the strengthening of *rasa* as against *bīja* or *saṁbhāra*. *rasa* may also suggest 'taste, flavour.'

36 *sauvikaḥ* : the commentators understand not only manufacture and drink, but also selling. 37 *ananujñātānām* : apparently permission could be refused to some persons. What they pay daily for manufacture and sale without premmission amounts to a sort of license fee. Cb reads *anyeṣu ananujñātānām* 'for drinking in places other than the place where the *utsava* etc. is being celebrated, the fine being in conformity with the loss suffered in work on account of the drink.'

38 *vicayam* 'search' for the various ingredients from plants, trees etc. It may also mean 'picking good from bad, selecting.' Com. understand it to mean 'roasting, drying etc.' of the materials.

39 *surakā-* etc. may be construed with the preceding (Cs) or with the stanza that follows (Meyer). The former seems slightly better in view of the *ca* after the first word in the stanza. The *ca* at the end here seems used in spite of the compound.

40 *vyājīm mānahiraṇyayoḥ* : the extra commission for *māna* is 6 1/4% or 5%, and for *hiraṇya* 5% (cf. 2.16.10 and 2.12.26 respectively). — *vaidharaṇam* : the compensation is to be recovered because a state monopoly (manufacture and sale of liquor) has been allowed to be broken ; cf. 2.12.31. The *vyājī* would be taken into consideration when fixing the *vaidharaṇa*. The latter would be apparently reduced to that extent. — *ucitam* 'customary,' rather than 'appropriate.'

CHAPTER TWENTY-SIX

SECTION 43 THE SUPERVISOR OF (ANIMAL-) SLAUGHTER

1 The Supervisor of Slaughter should impose the highest fine (for voilence) for binding, killing or injuring deer, beasts, birds or fish for whom safety has been proclaimed and who are kept in reserved parks, the middle fine on householders (for these offences) in reserved park enclosures.

2 For binding, killing or injuring fish and birds whose slaughter is not current, he should impose a fine of twenty-six *paṇas* and three quarters, (for binding) deer and beasts, double (that). 3 Of those whose slaughter is current (and) who are not protected in enclosures, he should receive one-sixth part, of fish and birds one-tenth part more, of deer and beasts, duty in addition.

4. He should release in sanctuary parks the live one-sixth part of birds and deer.

5 Sea-fish having the form of an elephant or a horse or a man or a bull or a donkey, or those from lakes, rivers, tanks or canals, curlew, osprey, gallinule, swan, ruddy goose, pheasant, *bhṛṅgarāja*, *cakora*, *mattakokila*, peacock, parrot and *madanaśārikā*, which are birds for sport and auspicious (*birds*), also other creatures (whether) birds or deer, should be protected from all dangers of injury. 6 For transgression of (this) protection, the first fine for violence (shall be imposed).

2.26

The *sūnādhyakṣa* is primarily concerned with the safety of game; he is to prevent the slaughter and ill-treatment of animals. He also strictly controls the sale of meat. There is no direct reference to slaughter-houses in the Chapter. '*sūnā* served to carry flesh, RV. 1.16.10, AV 5.17.14, and was probably a braided (*sīv*) basket.' (H. Zimmer, *Altindisches Leben*, p. 271).

1 *pradiṣṭābhayānām*: see 2.2.2 above. — *abhayavana* may also refer to the parks of 2.2.4. — *vadha* is 'killing' and *hiṁsā* 'injury' (Meyer). — *parigraha* 'enclosure'; cf. 2.6.6. — A lesser fine is imposed on householders apparently because the meat would be for personal use, not for sale.

2 *apravṛttavadha*: the slaughter of certain animals may be disallowed by custom (on religious or other grounds) or by the state. Meyer's 'who do not do any harm' seems hardly right. 3 *aparigṛhīta* 'not in the enclosures', i.e., not protected. Meyer's 'who are not caught' is unlikely. If they are not caught, how is the state to receive the sixth part? — *daśabhāgaṁ vādhikam*: Meyer has 'one tenth as fine for killing (*vādhikam* from *vadha*).' So Breloer has 'tax on slaughter' (KSt, III, 534). But this sense is hardly possible with *vādhikam* as adjective to *śulkam*. We have to understand 1/10 in addition to 1/6 in the case of fish and birds, and *śulka* in addition to 1/6 in the case of deer and beasts. The *śulka* would come to 1/20 or 1/25 as shown by 2.22.7. *vā* may be understood as *ca*. It is quite possible that the original reading was *cādhikam*.

4 *pakṣimṛgāṇām*: fish and beasts are omitted probably because they were intended to be consumed even when received alive.

5 It would be better to read *sāmudrāḥ* outside the compound. — *hastyaśva-* etc.: some of the shapes are clearly imaginary. — *vihāra-pakṣiṇaḥ* 'such as cocks, etc.' (Cs). — *maṅgalyāḥ* '*śyāmabhāradvāja* and others' (Cb). — *ābādha* as 'danger' is common in this text. 6 *rakṣātikrame*: the fine is for the *sūnādhyakṣa* (Cs). His subordinates, keepers in the parks, would appear more likely.

7 (Traders) shall sell meat without bones, of deer and beasts freshly killed. 8 For (meat) containing bones, they should give a compensation for loss. 9 For what is short in weight (the fine shall be) eight times the short measure.

10 The calf, the bull and the milch-cow among these (animals) are not to be killed. 11 For one killing (them, there shall be) a fine of fifty *paṇas*, also for (one) torturing (them) to death.

12 They shall not sell (meat that is) swollen, without head, feet and bones, foul-smelling and (of a) naturally dead (animal). 13 Otherwise, there shall be a fine of twelve *paṇas*.

14 Beasts, deer, wild animals and fish, belonging to sanctuaries, should, when harmful, be killed or bound in places other than the place of their protection.

CHAPTER TWENTY-SEVEN

SECTION 44 THE SUPERINTENDENT OF COURTESANS

1 The Superintendent of Courtesans should appoint as a courtesan, with one thousand *paṇas*, a (girl), from a courtesan's family or a family not of courtesans, who is richly endowed with beauty, youth and arts, (and) a deputy courtesan for half the family-establishment.

2 If a (courtesan has) run away or died, her daughter or sister shall run the family-establishment, or the mother shall provide a deputy courtesan. 3 In the absence of these, the king should take away (the establishment).

7 *vikrīṇīran* : the subject is butchers who have observed the rules laid down in s. 3 above. 8 *pratipātam* is from Cb. Cf. 5.2.12. It means compensation for loss, which apparently would be equal to the weight of the bones.

10 *eṣām*, i.e., *mṛgapaśūnām*. 11 *ghnataḥ* is from Cb and is necessary as corresponding to *ghātayataḥ*.

12 *pariśūnam* is an emendation from Meyer for *parisūnam*. The former suggests the diseased condition of the meat. The latter as ' slaughtered or sold outside the slaughter-house ' (com.) is doubtful, as there is no reference to slaughter-houses, or the obligation to slaughter or sell only there. And *pari* as ' outside ' is also uncertain. Russ. has ' not gone through the slaughter-house ' or (in the Notes) ' rejected by the slaughter-house.'

14 *guptisthānebhyaḥ* : these are clearly the *abhayavanas*. The actual slaughter is to be done outside the sanctuaries.

2.27

1 *agaṇikānvayām* : apparently respectable girls could be recruited to the profession when they went astray. — *sahasreṇa*, i.e., by giving 1000 *paṇas* to set up the establishment. The purchase of ornaments, dresses, furniture etc. seems meant. Meyer regards this as the annual salary. The annual salary, however, would seem to be referred to in s. 4 below. — *kuṭumbārdhena* i.e., with 500 *paṇas*.

2 *kuṭumbaṁ bhareta* : this clearly implies the continuation of the establishment. 3 Cp concludes from this that the son of a *gaṇikā* does not inherit from her.

4 In conformity with superiority in point of beauty and ornaments, he should, with one thousand *paṇas*, assign the lowest, middlemost or highest turn (for attendance), in order to add distinction to (attendance with) the parasol, the water-jug, the fan, the palanquin, the seat and the chariot. 5 In case of loss of beauty, he should appoint her as the 'mother'.

6 The ransom price is twenty-four thousand *paṇas* for a courtesan, twelve thousand for a courtesan's son. 7 From the age of eight, the latter should do the work of the king's minstrel.

8 The female slave of a courtesan, whose professional career is over, should do work in the magazine or the kitchen. 9 One, not going (for such work), should, being kept under restraint, (be made to) pay the monthly wage of one *paṇa* and a quarter.

10 He should keep an account of the payment by visitors, gifts, income, expenditure and gains of a courtesan, and should prohibit an act of excessive expenditure.

4 Cb explains 'consistently with the increase in beauty and ornaments duties may be assigned, *uttama*, viz., at *pratihāra*, playing with dice, giving *tāmbūla* etc. for 1000 *paṇas*, *madhyama*, viz., holding fans, chowries etc., at 500 *paṇas* and *kaniṣṭha*, viz., carrying *pīṭha*, washing feet, etc. at 100 *paṇas*. In addition, he should give *chatra* and *bhṛṅgāra* for *kaniṣṭha* duty, fan and chowries in addition for *madhyama* duty and these as well as *pīṭha* and *ratha* for *uttama vāra*.' Cs understands *chatra* and *bhṛṅgāra* as the *kaniṣṭha vāra*, *vyajana* and *śibikā* as *madhyama* and *pīṭhikā* and *ratha* as *uttama*, also 1000, 2000 and 3000 *paṇas* as the nazarana to be paid by the courtesans for the three types of duties respectively. It seems, however, that the amounts are payments made to the *gaṇikā*, not by her to the state. The amounts in Cs appear more likely than those in Cb. As a matter of fact, the text refers to one amount only, 1000 *paṇas*. The idea of the present of the various things to the three types of *gaṇikās* (Cb) is also not suggested by the wording. — *viśeṣārtham* : this may refer to the distinction made in the three types of work, or to the distinction, i.e., lustre added to the task. 5 *mātṛkā* a sort of mother superior of the establishment.

7 *kuśīlava* : cf. 1.12.9.

8 *gaṇikādāsī* : this should be read as a single word as in the commentators 'the female attendant of a courtesan.' Apparently such a *dāsī* carried on the profession of a prostitute. When she can no more do that work (*bhagnabhogā*), she is to be given work in the kitchen etc. Meyer (with *gaṇikā* and *dāsī* as separate words) thinks of the *gaṇikā* herself being *bhagnabhogā* and made to work as a *dāsī* in the kitchen etc. But the *gaṇikā*'s own case seems to have been already considered in s. 5 above. 9 *aviśantī*, i.e., not going to the kitchen etc. for work. Meyer has 'who does not come to the king', because she is *avaruddhā* 'the kept mistress' of some one else. As the reference is to *bhagnabhogā*, this is an unlikely explanation. *avaruddhā* is understood as 'a kept mistress' even in Cp, but in the context, it can only mean 'kept under restraint' as in 1.10.11. — *sapādapaṇaṁ māsavetanam* : this is the monthly cash wage (beside boarding); cf. 2.24.28. She pays the wage to the person who does the work which she has refused to do. The commentators say 'the servant is to pay this amount to the *gaṇikā*, her former mistress.' *vetana* would hardly be used for such payment. Meyer's 'a month's wage and one and a quarter *paṇa*' is doubtful in the absence of *ca*.

10 *dāya* 'gifts by the king or other men' (Cb), rather than 'inheritance from the mother' (Cp Cs), as day to day or month to month accounts are thought of here. — *āyati* seems to refer to some extra income ; that is how Cp understands it. Cb does not seem to have read the word though its text shows it. Cs renders the word by '*prabhāva*, power, capability.'

11 For handing over her ornaments to the keeping of any one else but the mother, the fine shall be four *paṇas* and a quarter. 12 If she sells or pledges her belongings, the fine shall be fifty *paṇas* and a quarter, twenty-four *paṇas* in case of verbal injury, double that in case of physical injury, fifty *paṇas* and a quarter and one *paṇa* and half a *paṇa* for cutting off the ear.

13 In case of violence against a maiden who is unwilling, the highest fine (shall be imposed), the lowest fine for violence, if she is willing. 14 If a (man) keeps under restraint a courtesan who is unwilling, or helps her to run away or spoils her beauty by cutting up a wound, the fine (shall be) one thousand *paṇas*. 15 Or, there shall be an increase in fine in accordance with the importance of her position, up to double the ransom amount. 16 If a (man) causes the death of a courtesan who has been appointed to the office, the fine (shall be) three times the ransom amount. 17 For killing a mother, a daughter or a female slave living by her beauty, the highest fine for violence (shall be imposed).

18 In all cases, the prescribed fine (shall be imposed) for the first offence, double that for the second (offence), threefold for the third (offence), in case of the fourth (repetition of the offence) he may do what he pleases.

19 A courtesan, not approaching a man at the command of the king, shall receive one thousand strokes with the whip, or a fine of five thousand *paṇas*.

20 If a (courtesan), after receiving payment, shows dislike, she shall be fined double the amount of payment. 21 In case she cheats in connection with attendance on visitors staying (overnight), she shall pay eight times the

12 *svāpateyam*, i.e., her personal belongings. Cb reads *svāpadeyam* 'ornaments etc. given at the time of going to bed.' This is not very likely. — *vākpāruṣye* : the offence is by the courtesan against a visitor (com.). Meyer thinks that these are offences against the courtesan. However, the wording clearly favours the former view. — *paṇo 'rdhapaṇas ca* : this goes to the *gaṇikādhyakṣa*, while 50 1/4 *paṇas* go to the state, according to Cp Cs. The total in Cb comes to 50 3/4 *paṇas*. It may be that 1 *paṇa* is the physician's fee and half a *paṇa* charges for medicaments. — *karṇacchedane* : though this is more likely by an irate visitor, this offence against a visitor by a *gaṇikā* is not inconceivable.

13 *kumāryāḥ* : not necessarily a *gaṇikākumārī* ; cf. 4.12.26. 15 *sthāna*, i.e., her position or status, *uttamādivārapradhānyena* (Cp) It can hardly refer to 'the limb of the body where the wound is made' (Cs). — *ā niṣkrayadviguṇāt* : Cb, reading *ā niṣkrayād dviguṇaḥ* has 'for *kaniṣṭha* 24000 *paṇas*, for *madhyana* 48000 *paṇas* and for *uttama* 96000 *paṇas*.' This is little likely. Cb also understands 1000 for *rundhataḥ*, 2000 for *niṣpātayataḥ* and 3000 for *rūpaṁ ghnataḥ*. — *paṇasahasraṁ vā daṇḍaḥ* read after this s. is omitted ; Cp rightly ignores it. S. 14, to which s. 15 states an option, already mentions this same fine. 16. *prāptādhikārām* : i.e., appointed as a courtesan, not necessarily, however, for attendance on the king. 17 *duhitṛkā* is not yet appointed as a *gaṇikā*. — *rūpadāsī* may be the same as or similar in status to the *gaṇikādāsī* of s. 8 above. Cp understands 'one who does work in connection with perfumes, flowers, etc.' — *ghāte* : because of the lighter punishment, Cs thinks of 'beating' rather than 'killing.' But *ghātayato* of the last s. precludes that.

18 This rule seems applicable to all offences, not only to those concerning courtesans. — *syāt* : the subject is *rājā* (Cb).

20 *dviṣatyāḥ* : in effect, 'refusing service.' 21 *vasatibhoga* 'payment for staying with the *gaṇikā*' (Cb), evidently for the night. It seems that in the ordinary *bhoga*, the man does not stay overnight with the *gaṇikā*. It is possible also that *bhoga* is only attendance with

amount of payment, except in case of (her) illness or defects in the man. 22 If she kills a man, (the punishment shall be) burning on the funeral pyre or drowning in water.

23 If a (man) robs a courtesan of her ornaments, her goods or the payment due to her, he shall be fined eight times (the amount).

24 The courtesan shall communicate (to the Superintendent) the payment, the gain and the (name of the) man.

25 By this are explained (rules for) the women of actors, dancers, singers, musicians, story-tellers, bards, rope-dancers, showmen and wandering minstrels, who deal in women, and (women) who follow a secret profession. 26 Their musical instruments, when coming from foreign lands, shall be charged a fee per show of five *paṇas*.

27 (Prostitutes) who live by their beauty, shall pay per month (a tax) double the (normal) fee (charged by them).

28 He should provide maintenance from the king's exchequer to the (teacher) who imparts to courtesans and female slaves who live by the stage, the knowledge of the arts of singing, playing on musical instruments, reciting, dancing, acting, writing, painting, playing on the lute, the flute and the drum, reading the thoughts of others, preparing perfumes and garlands, entertaining in conversation, shampooing and the courtesan's art.

29 And the (teachers) should train the sons of courtesans to be the chiefs of those who live by the stage and also of all types of dancers.

singing, dancing etc. while *vasatibhoga* includes sexual enjoyment. In any case, Meyer's 'when the robbing of the payment is continuous (*vasati* in a locative absolute clause)' is quite unlikely.

24 Cf. s. 10 above.

25 *saubhika* 'a juggler or a shadow-player' (com.). He may be the *saubhika* of Patañjali who puts up a kind of dramatic show. Cf. Winternitz, ZDMG, 74 (1920), 118 ff. Cb Cs include *strīvyavahāriṇām* in the long compound that precedes and understand by it a separate class '*khanariposaka* (?)' (Cb), 'members of a prostitute's family' (Cs). It is better, however, to keep it outside the compound as descriptive of *naṭa*, *nartaka*, etc. — *gūḍhājīvāḥ* : cf. 4.4 below for the secret professions. 26 *prekṣāvetanam* is clearly a sort of license fee.

27 *rūpājīvāḥ* are not in state service. The *gaṇikādhyakṣa* is only concerned with collecting a tax from them. — *bhogadvayaguṇam*, i.e., twice her charge for a single visit. Meyer considers this too little and suggests 'double the monthly income per year', amounting to the usual 1/6th. The words, however, can hardly yield this sense. For *māsam* 'per month', cf. 2.24.28. Cp reads *bhogadvayam* only, which might appear better.

28 *saṁyūhana* in the sense of 'preparing' should be construed with *gandha* and *mālya*, *saṁvādana* being 'art of entertaining in conversation' (Cp). Cs, reading *saṁpādana*, has *gandhasaṁyūhana* and *mālyasaṁpādana*, which is a doubtful construction. — *rājamaṇḍalāt* : this has to be understood as 'from the king's purse.' The circle of kings can hardly be thought of as collaborating and contributing a share towards these expenses.

29 It is proposed to read *-jīvināṁ ca* (implied in Cb's explanation) for *-jīvinā́ś ca* or *-jīvinaś ca* of the mss. The *ca* is really misplaced ; it should come after *gaṇikāputrān*. — Cp reads *-tālāpacarāṁś ca* and construes it with the following stanza ; but the accusative can hardly be right, in view of *teṣām* and *striyaḥ* in that stanza.

30 And their women, who are conversant with various kinds of signs and languages, should be employed, under the lead of their kinsmen, against the wicked, for spying, killing or making them blunder.

CHAPTER TWENTY-EIGHT

SECTION 45 THE CONTROLLER OF SHIPPING

1 The Controller of Shipping should look after activities concerning sea voyages and ferries at the mouths of rivers, as well as ferries over natural lakes, artificial lakes and rivers, in the *sthānīya* and other (towns).

2 Villages on their shores and banks shall pay a fixed (tax).

3 Fishermen shall pay one-sixth (of their catch) as rent for the boats.

4 Traders shall pay a part (of the goods) as duty according as it may be current at the ports, those travelling by the king's ships (shall pay) hire for the voyage.

5 Those fishing for conch-shells and pearls shall pay a rent for the boats, or sail in their own boats. 6 And (the duty of) the Supervisor of these is explained by (that of) the Superintendent of Mines.

7 The Controller of Shipping shall observe the regulations in a port town as fixed by the Commissioner of Ports.

8 He should rescue boats that have gone out of their course or are tossed about by a gale, like a father. 9 He should make goods that have fallen in water either duty-free or pay half the duty. 10 And he should send these (boats) on, as commissioned, at times suitable for voyage from the port.

30 *cāraghātapramādārtham* : three separate ideas seem better than two, the *ghāta* and *pramāda* of enemy's spies (Cs). *anātmasu* already mentions the persons against whom they are to be used. — *bandhuvāhanāḥ*, i.e., under the lead or supervision of kinsmen. Cb has 'their kinsmen are to be given money and honour and then these are to be employed among *dūṣyas*.'

2.28.

The *nāvadhyakṣa* is not a military officer. He is concerned with the control of shipping, management of ports and provision of ferries. Cb on this Chapter is missing.

1 *visaras* is, according to Cs, a lake liable to dry up in summer.

2 *kḷptam* : a fixed tax. Cf. 2.6.10.

3 *ṣaḍbhāgam* : 1/6th part of their catch, as rent for use of state boats. When taken to the city for sale, 1/6th of the remainder as *śulka* would also be due.

4 *śulkabhāgam*, i.e., in accordance with 2.22.4-8. — *yātrāvetanam* would seem to refer to the hire of the boat, including wages for the crew.

5 This implies that pearl-fisheries are not a state monopoly. 6 *adhyakṣaś caiṣām* etc. : this is a reference to 2.12.27. The manufacture and sale of articles made of *śaṅkha* and *muktā* is the concern of the *khanyadhyakṣa*. The *nāvadhyakṣa* has nothing to do with that (as Cs thinks).

8 It is proposed to read *-hatā nāvaḥ* for *-hatāṁ tāṁ* or *-hatānām* of the mss. The pronoun in the former of these is unlikely and the genitive in the latter cannot be properly construed. Cp shows *-hatāṁ nāvam*. Meyer had proposed *-hatatāntam* (or *-tāntāḥ*) 'in distress (*tānta* from *tam*) being buffeted by strong (*mūḍha*) winds.' *mūḍha*, as adjective to *vāta*, is not a happy idea. 10 *yathānirdiṣṭāḥ*, i.e., to their destinations as originally directed.

11 He should demand duty from ships sailing on sea when they come within the domain. 12 He should destroy (boats) that cause harm, also those coming over from the enemy's territory and those violating the regulations of the port.

13 And he should keep in use big boats in charge of a captain, a pilot, a manipulator of the cutter and ropes and a bailer of water, on big rivers that have to be ferried on (even) in winter and summer, small ones on small rivers flowing (only) in the rainy season. 14 And these should have their crossing-places fixed because of the danger of crossing by traitorous persons.

15 For one crossing out of time or elsewhere than at the crossing, (the punishment shall be) the lowest fine for violence. 16 For one who crosses without authority even at the proper time and at the crossing, the penalty for crossing is twenty-six *paṇas* and three quarters. 17 There shall be no penalty for fishermen, (carriers of) loads of wood and grass, attendants at flower-gardens, fruit-orchards and vegetable gardens and cowherds, also for those whose going after an envoy is conceivable, and for those carrying out activity in connection with goods for the army, when these cross in their own barges, as well as for those who ferry across seeds, food-stuffs and articles for household use in villages along the water-courses.

18 Brahmins, wandering monks, children, old persons, sick persons, carriers of royal edicts and pregnant women should cross with a sealed pass from the Controller of Shipping.

11 *kṣetra* seems to refer to the domain of the state. — *śulkaṁ yāceta* : the point of this statement, according to Cs, is that higher rates of duty are not to be charged. The idea, however, seems to be that duty is to be demanded whether the ships discharge the goods in that port or not. These appear more as port dues than duty on goods. 12 *hiṁsrikāḥ*, i.e., piratical ships ; they may or may not belong to an enemy. — *amitraviṣayātigāḥ* 'bound for enemy territory' (com.), 'coming over from the enemy's territory' (Meyer). The latter appears better.

13 *niryāmaka* is a steersman, a pilot. — *dātraraśmigrāhaka* : this would appear to be a single person. Meyer's idea, however, 'the holder of the hook and the rope, i.e., the anchor-thrower' is not very convincing. N. N. Law has 'sailors with sickles and ropes' (IHQ, V, 1929, p. 615).

16 *anisṛṣṭatāriṇaḥ* : the sense of the causal does not seem intended in *-tārin*. — *tar-ātyayaḥ* : the penalty is for violation of the state monopoly of ferrying. 17 *saṁbhāv-yadūtānupātinām* : 'those in pursuit of suspicious characters such as thieves (*saṁbhāvya*) and those who follow royal messengers to supplement their work' (Cp Cs). The meaning given to *saṁbhāvya* is doubtful. 'Those who pursue likely messengers' is possible, but makes little sense. 'Those who are the followers of a likely envoy' or 'those who can be thought of (*saṁbhāvya*) as an envoy's followers' may seem intended, more likely the latter. Apparently, an envoy's followers enjoyed certain privileges. The expression is, however, a bit awkward. — *senābhāṇḍa-* etc. is also an involved expression. Cb Cs read *-cāra* for *-pracāra-*. But the activity of secret agents is hardly likely to be known to the *nāvadhyakṣa*. — *svataraṇais taratām* : this is to be construed with the preceding two clauses. Meyer construes it also with what follows. — *bhaktadravya* as a single idea seems better ; otherwise, *dravya* remains unspecificed. — *tārayatām* shows that the villagers get these things without the help of the state ferry.

18 This implies free use of the ferry.

19 Persons from foreign lands may enter when permission to enter is granted or on the testimony of the caravan. 20 He should cause to be arrested a person carrying off the wife, the daughter or the property of another, a person who is frightened or agitated, a person hiding behind a heavy load, a person concealing (his face) by a load on the head containing heavy goods, a wandering monk who has just put on the marks or who is without the marks, a person whose illness cannot be seen, a person showing a changed appearance because of fear, a person secretly carrying goods of high value, letters, weapons or means of fire, a person with poison in hand, a person who has travelled a long distance and a person without a sealed pass.

21 A small animal and a man with a load (in hand) shall pay one *māṣaka*, a load on the head, a load on the back, a cow and a horse (shall pay) two (*māṣakas*), a camel and a buffalo four, a small vehicle five, one driven by bullocks six, a cart seven, a load of commodities one quarter (of a *paṇa*). 22 By that is explained (fare for) a load of goods. 23 The fare for ferries on big rivers is double.

24 Villages on water-ways shall pay a fixed amount of food and wages (for the ferrymen).

25 At the frontiers, ferrymen should recover the duty, the escort-charges and the road cess, and should confiscate the goods of one going out without a seal, also (those) of a person crossing with a heavy load at an improper time and elsewhere than at the regular crossing.

26 When a boat, that is lacking in men or equipment or is unseaworthy, comes to grief, the Controller of Shipping shall make good what is lost or ruined.

19 *kṛtapraveśāḥ* : cf. 4.10.7. The expression is used predicatively. — *sārthapramāṇā vā* : if *vā* were omitted as in most mss. the guarantee of the caravan would be the reason for granting permission to enter. But that would be applicable only to traders. It seems better to read *vā*. 20 *udbhāṇḍīkṛta* 'tottering under a heavy load' (Cp). Cb (on 2.36.13) explains 'hiding himself with a load on his head.' It seems that this latter explanation from some commentary (*mahābhāṇḍena mūrdhni bhāreṇāvacchādayantam*) has got into the text after *udbhāṇḍīkṛtam*. Else there is tautology. Meyer explains *udbhāṇḍīkṛta* as 'who is excessively stirred up' or 'who is deprived of his tools, vessels etc., helpless.' Neither is satisfactory. — *liṅga* are marks of a monk, *kaṣāyavastra, daṇḍa* etc. — *alakṣyavyādhita* may mean 'whose illness (pretended in order to escape the fare) cannot be seen' (com.), or 'who conceals his illness (either because of wounds or a secret or contagious disease).' The former seems meant. *amudram* : the *mudrā* may be that given by the *mudrādhyakṣa* (2.34.1-4), or by the *nāvadhyakṣa* (s. 18 above). — *upagrāhayet* : perhaps only *grāhayet* should be read.

21 *goliṅgam* : supply *yānam*. — *bhāra* is the weight of 20 *tulās* (2.19.19). 22 *bhāṇḍa*, as distinguished from *paṇya*, refers to other than commercial goods. 'A vehicle drawn by buffaloes, camels etc.' (Cp) is an unusual sense for *bhāṇḍa*.

24 *kḷptam* : this being intended for the ferrymen is apparently different from the *kḷpta* of s. 2 above.

25 *pratyanteṣu*, i.e., where the rivers form the boundaries ; there is no *antapāla* there, only the ferry service. — *nirgacchataḥ* : the goods were being taken out to the foreign country. — *amudradravyasya* : for sealing of goods, cf. 2.21.2-5.

26 *asaṁskṛtāyām*, i.e., not properly built and not kept in good repair ; hence 'unseaworthy' (Meyer). — *abhyāvahet* is from Cb and seems necessary for the sense 'to be responsible for, to be liable for' as distinguished from *abhyābhū* 'to have the right to' (3.9.1).

27 Between the eighth day after the full moon day of Āṣāḍha and that of Kārttika, ferrying (shall be provided). The workman should give a surety and should bring in the regular daily earnings.

CHAPTER TWENTY-NINE

SECTION 46 THE SUPERINTENDENT OF CATTLE

1 The Superintendent of Cattle should know about (cattle) looked after in return for a wage, tended with a tax and a fixed return, become useless and cast off, entered (in the state herds) by payment of a share, the total number of (cattle in) herds, (cattle) that are lost or have perished, and the total produce of milk and ghee.

2 The cowherd, the buffalo-herdsman, the milker, the churner and the hunter should look after one hundred milch-cows, receiving a wage in cash. 3 For, if given a wage in milk and ghee, they might do harm to the calves. These are (cattle) looked after for a wage.

4 One person should look after one hundred animals containing an equal number of aged cows, milch-cows, cows with young, cows with calf for the first

27 *saptāhavṛttām*, i.e., when seven days have passed after the full moon days of the two months. — *taraḥ*: supply *sthāpanīyaḥ*. The commentators interpret *tara* as 'fare for the ferry' and supply *grāhyaḥ*. — Read *kārmikaḥ pratyayam* in the text. This is proposed for *kārmikapratyayam* of the mss. With the latter *taram* or *ātaram* can be understood as the substantive (Meyer Nachtrag), but the idea of the tesimony (*pratyaya*) of workmen for the necessity of a ferry is not very happy. With the proposed emendation, *kārmika* would refer to the officer in charge of the service, who gives a surety (*pratyaya*) to testify to his integrity. For *pratyaya*, cf. 3.12.14; 3.14.34. The commentators have 'the (ferryman) should give information (*pratyaya*) about working days (*kārmika*) to the *nāvadhyakṣa*,' which is hardly satisfactory. — *nityam* i.e., probably as fixed by the rules in ss. 21-23. — *āvahet* 'should bring in' and hand over to the *nāvadhyakṣa*.

2.29

The cattle in charge of this Superintendent clearly belong to the state.

1 *upalabheta*, i.e., should have a record of.

2 *piṇḍāraka* is the original of the modern Pindari and is a Deshi word from *peḍḍā* in the sense of *mahiṣī* (J. Charpentier, IA, 59, 149-51). — *lubdhaka* serves to guard cattle from wild animals. 3 *vetanopagrāhikam*: the *upagraha* may refer to the care bestowed on cattle or the favour of wage received.

4 *paṣṭhauhī*: the form goes back to the *Taittirīya Brāhmaṇa*, 1.7.3.2 and the *Śatapṭaha*, 4.6.1.11. In the latter place it is paraphrased by *prathamagarbhā* 'with calf for the first time.' Cf. A. Hillebrandt, *Vedische Mythologie*, III, p. 93 n.8. The commentators here explain 'who has reached an age when she longs to be covered by a bull.' The word has a Prakrit appearance (from the feminine of *prasthavāḥ*). — *samavibhāgam*: according to Cb, this means 100 of each kind, *jaradgu* etc. That appears doubtful. — *ekaḥ*: this is a sort of a contractor, who makes his own arrangements for tending the cattle. 5 *aṣṭau vārakān*: on the basis of a *vāraka* as 84/64th of a *droṇa* (2.19.46 above), eight *vārakas* amount to about 19.2 gallons; this much ghee would require 16 times milk (s. 35 below) or about 307.2 gallons of milk. As there are only 20 milch-cows (*dhenu*) in the herd, each cow's contribution would be about 15.4 gallons. This may be supposed to be 2 or 3 weeks' yield of milk in the case of good cows. The rest of the milk would obviously be used by the contractor as payment for his services. Meyer, thinking that 8 *vārakas* (72 litres) is too little for the entire herd, understands 800 *vārakas*. He also assumes that there are 50 milk-yielding cows in the herd and arrives at 10 litres of milk per day per cow. It is not easy to follow his reasoning and his figures. And his explanation seems to leave little for the herds-

time and heifers. 5 He should give eight *vārakas* of ghee, one *paṇa* per animal and the hide with the mark, every year. This is tending with a tax and a fixed return.

6 Herdsmen looking after one hundred animals divided into an equal number of cows that are diseased, that are crippled, that do not allow another person to milk them, that are difficult to milk and that kill their calves, should give a share appropriate to that class. These are (cattle) become useless and cast off.

7 Of cattle that have entered (the king's herds) through fear of an enemy invasion or forest-tribes, the (owners) should give one-tenth part according to the law of protection. These are (cattle) entered by payment of a share.

8 Calves, weaned calves, young bulls being broken in, draught-bullocks, and stud-bulls are male cattle ; (buffaloes) drawing a yoked vehicle or a cart, stud-buffaloes, slaughter-buffaloes and those carrying (loads) on their backs and shoulders are male buffaloes ; the heifer, the weaned heifer, the cow with calf for the first time, the cow with young, the milch-cow, the cow that has not borne a calf and the sterile cow, are cows and she-buffaloes ; those a month or two old, are their off-springs (as) calves and heifers. 9 He should mark those that are a month or two old. 10 He should mark an animal that has stayed (in the herd) for a month or two. 11 The (branded) mark, the (natural) mark, the colour, the peculiarity of the horns,—with these characteristics, he should record additions (to the herd). This is the total of (cattle in the) herds.

man. — *paṇikaṁ puccham*, i.e., 100 *paṇas* are paid by him per year as tax in addition. Breloer (III, 519 n.1) understanding *paṇa* as 'stipulation' has '8 *vārakas* of ghee as stipulated per tail.' This also would leave little for the herdsman. And for 'stipulated' *paṇitam* would seem necessary. — *aṅkacarma* : this would apply only when the animal dies. — *karapratikaraḥ* : it seems that *kara* refers to the 8 *vārakas* of ghee and 100 *paṇas* that the herdsman pays to the state and *pratikara* to what he gets for himself out of the herd. It is also possible that *kara* refers to the *paṇika puccha* and *pratikara* to the 8 *vārakas*. The marked hide could hardly have been meant by *pratikara*, as Breloer thinks.

6 *putraghnī* : one that gives birth to a dead calf. — *samavibhāgam* : Cb again has 100 of each kind. — *tajjātikaṁ bhāgam* '1/2 or 1/3 or 1/4 of the 8 *vārakas*, according to the trouble in tending them' (Cb). *vyādhitā nyaṅgā* might yield little or nothing. Breloer thinks of 1/10 as in 5.2.27. But that refers to a part of the cattle themselves and is hardly applicable here.

7 *daśabhāgam*, i.e., one-tenth of their produce (Meyer), hardly 1/10th of the cattle themselves. Cf. 3.13.28. The share is received by the state.

8 *vṛṣā ukṣāṇaḥ* : the commentators understand 'stud-bulls and aged bullocks.' Meyer understands a single idea 'stud-bulls' corresponding to *vṛṣabhāsa ukṣāṇaḥ* of the *Ṛgveda*. The latter seems intended ; cf. 3.10.24 and 4.13.20. — *śakaṭa* appears to be bigger than *yugavāhana* ; cf. 2.28.21. — *dhenuś cāprajātā* : the *ca* is strange ; so is the plural in *vandhyāḥ*. *aprajātā*, i.e., 'who has not borne a calf, but whose sterility is not yet certain' (Cb). — *upajāḥ* 'born near,' i.e., additions. 9 *aṅkayet* : the mark may be some number or *svastika* or sickle, spoon etc. (Meyer, who also refers to cutting or splitting the ears in various ways in Pāṇini 6.3.115). 10 *paryuṣita*, i.e., staying in the king's herds, unclaimed by the owner. 11 *cihna*, as distinguished from *aṅka*, seems to be some natural mark. — *śṛṅgāntaram* 'peculiarity of the horns' (Cb Cp). 'Distance between the horns' is also possible though in either sense *śṛṅgāntara* can be thought of only in connection with fully grown up cattle. — *evam upajāḥ* : Meyer, understanding a single expression, has 'born of such and such a cow and such and such a bull.' It is doubtful if records of pedigrees are meant here.

12 An (animal) that is stolen by thieves, has gone into another herd or has disappeared is lost. 13 An (animal) that has sunk in mud or has got in an inaccessible place, or is struck down by illness or old age or has suffered because of water or food, or is struck by a tree, a bank, wood or rock, or is struck by lightning or killed by a wild animal, a serpent, a crocodile or in a forest conflagration, is destroyed. 14 They should make good (what is lost or destroyed) through negligence.

15 Thus he should be cognisant of the number of animals.

16 He who himself kills (an animal) or incites another to kill or steals or incites another to steal shall be executed.

17 He who changes the cattle of another with the royal mark shall pay the lowest fine for violence per animal.

18 After recovering what is stolen by thieves from cattle belonging to his own country, a person shall receive the animal agreed upon. 19 He who recovers cattle belonging to a foreign country shall receive half (the animals).

20 Cowherds shall (care for and) treat the young, the old and the diseased. 21 They shall graze (the cattle) in a forest from which the fear of danger from thieves, wild animals and enemies has been removed by fowlers and hunters and which is suitable in different seasons. 22 And in order to frighten serpents and wild animals and to know the movements in the pastures, they should tie a bell round the necks of timid animals. 23 They should take (cattle) down to water, to which the descent is even and broad, and which is free from mud and crocodiles, and should guard them (at the time). 24 They should report catt e seized by robbers, w d a imals, serpents or crocodiles and cattle that have died because of disease or old age; otherwise, they shall be liable to pay the price of the animal.

13 *toyāhāra* 'because of defects in water or food' (Cb). — Cb Cs read *vṛkṣātaṭa* and Cs explains *ataṭa* as 'fall from a precipice.' In view of *abhihata* at the end, 'fall' need not be understood. Breloer (III, 526) understands *vṛkṣa* with *kāṣṭha* and *taṭa* with *śilā*. 14. This applies to *naṣṭa* as well as *vinaṣṭa*, not to the latter alone as in Cs. For *abhyāvah*, see 2.28.26 above.

17 *parivartayitā* : apparently the substitution of an inferior animal is thus thought of. — *rūpasya*, i.e., for each animal. It can hardly be construed with *parivartayitā* in the sense of 'appearance'. *rūpa* refers to 'animal' in this Chapter.

18 *paṇitaṁ rūpam*, i.e., the animal that was promised as reward to any one who recovered the stolen cattle. This implies cattle-lifting on a large scale. Cb Cs read *paṇikaṁ rūpam* and explain 'the rescuer should get one *paṇa* per animal'; Meyer agrees and adds that the *go'dhyakṣa* is to be thought of as the rescuer. Such extra remuneration to an officer would be unusual. 19 *mokṣayitā* is evidently the person who successfully lifts cattle from a neighbouring state, or traces such cattle lifted by robbers from that state. He must, of course, inform the state; then he keeps half the cattle, the other half going to the state. Cf. E. H. Johnston, JRAS, 1936, pp. 82-83. Breloer remarks (III, 528 n. 1) that this is according to the law concerning the finding of treasure-trove. *mokṣayitā* cannot be the 'owner of the cattle' (Cs) since these are *paradeśīya*, nor the *go'dhyakṣa* (Meyer).

22 *gocarānupāta-* : *anupāta* clearly means only 'movements.' Meyer, however, has 'pursuit (by wild animals).' That does not seem very likely. — *trasnūnām* : this is 'in order to accustom the timid ones to sound' (Cs). More likely, it is because they would be the first to take fright and attract the herdsman's attention by the sound of the bells, if there is anything amiss.

25 Of (an animal) dying through a valid cause, they shall deliver the marked hide in the case of the cow and the buffalo, the mark on the ear in the case of the goat and the sheep, the tail and the marked skin in the case of the horse, the donkey and the camel, and the hair, skin, bladder, bile, tendons, teeth, hooves, horns and bones (in the case of all). 26 They may sell the flesh, either fresh or dried.

27 They should give the butter-milk to the dogs and pigs. 28 They should bring in the solidified curds as food for the army. 29 The whey is for moistening the oil-cake from the oil-press.

30 The seller of cattle shall pay one quarter (of a *paṇa*) per animal.

31 In the rainy season, autumn and winter, they should milk (the cattle) both times, in the season of frost, spring and summer, once (only). 32 For one milking a second time (then), the cutting off of the thumb (shall be) the punishment. 33 For one allowing the milking time to pass, the fine (shall be equal to) the loss of that fruit. 34 By this are explained (punishments for neglect of proper) times for putting the nose-string, for breaking in, for accustoming to the yoke and for (training in) going round.

35. From a *droṇa* of cows' milk, a *prastha* of ghee (is the normal yield), one-fifth more in the case of she-buffaloes, one-half more in the case of goats and sheep. 36 Or, (actual) churning shall decide the amount in the case of all. 37 For, in accordance with the excellence of the ground, the grass and water, there is an increase in (the yield of) milk and ghee.

38 For one causing a bull of the herd to be hurled down by another bull, the lowest fine for violence (shall be the punishment), for causing his death, the highest (fine).

25 *kāraṇamṛtasya*, i.e., about the cause of whose death there is no suspicion. Meyer proposes to read *kāraṇaṁ mṛtasya* 'as proof (*kāraṇa*), they should bring, of the dead, ear-marks etc.' This seems hardly plausible.

28 *kūrcikām* is from Cb, explained as 'dried coagulated curds' or cheese. Cp seems to have read *rucikām* in the same sense. Cf. '*dadhnā saha ca yat pakvaṁ kṣīraṁ sā dadhi-kūrcīkā* etc.' (*Śabdakalpadruma*).

30 *paśuvikretā* : this might refer to the sale of private cattle and one quarter of a *paṇa* per animal might appear to be a sort of sales tax. We can hardly think of the sale of royal cattle by the herdsman or the *go'dhyakṣa* (Meyer), for there seems to be no reason why these should pay such a tax. If we think of it as a fine for unauthorized sale of state cattle, it would appear to be extremely small for the offence. Breloer (III, 531) thinks of one-quarter of the animal itself (*pādikaṁ rūpam*) as being given to the state. That can apply only to a dead animal. In that case *māṁsavikretā* might appear a better reading and this s. may better be read immediately after s. 26, so that the rule would apply to the sale of meat.

32 *ekakālam*, i.e., in the evening (com., also Meyer). 33 *tatphalahānam*, i.e., equal to the value of the milk lost. Cf. 2.24.4. 34 *etena*, i.e., the *daṇḍa* is to correspond to the *phalahāna*, loss of work-days by bullocks due to delay in their training. — *yugapiṅgana* the root appears to be *piñj* 'to join.' — *vartana* 'going round' is necessary on the threshing floor and in the oil-press.

35 This means that 16 parts of milk yield 1 part ghee. — *pañcabhāgādhikam*, i.e., 1 1/5 part ghee from 16 parts milk; so in the next clause. 37 *kṣīraghṛtavṛddhiḥ* 'increase in milk and ghee' includes the idea of increase in the proportion of the yield of ghee.

39 By grouping according to class, groups of ten (cattle) should be guarded. 40 The arrangements at the place of stay (should be) according to the movements of the cattle or according to the strength of the cattle, and in conformity with capability for guarding.

41 He should cause the wool of goats and sheep to be gathered every six months.

42 By that are explained (rules concerning) herds of horses, donkeys, camels and pigs.

43 For bullocks, with nose-string and capable of driving at the speed of a gentle horse, (the ration shall consist of) half a *bhāra* of green fodder, grass double that, a *tulā* of oil-cake from the press, (or) ten *āḍhakas* of broken grains and bran, five *palas* of rock-salt, one *kuḍuba* of oil for the nose (and) one *prastha* as drink, a *tulā* of meat and an *āḍhaka* of curds, a *droṇa* of barley or of half-cooked *māṣa*-beans ; a *droṇa* of milk or half an *āḍhaka* of liquor, *a prastha* of fat, ten *palas* of sugar and a *pala* of ginger (as) a strength-giving drink. 44 One quarter less (is the ration) for mules, cows and donkeys, double for buffaloes and camels. 45 For bullocks used for work and for milch-cows suckling their calves, the giving of rations (shall be) according to the time of work and the yield (of milk respectively). 46 For all, there shall be abundance of grass and water.

47 Thus is explained the care of herds of cattle.

39 *varṇāvarodhena* : the commentators understand *varṇa* as 'colour,' i.e., cattle should be grouped according to colour for ease in watching. It seems, however, better to understand *varṇa* as 'class, type' such as *jaraagu, dhenu, garbhiṇī* etc. 40 *upaniveśa* 'settlement' for the night (Cb). Stay for a long or short period may also be understood. — *gopracārāt*, i.e., in accordance with ease of movement for the cattle. Cb, however, has 'according to colour, white in the east, black in the south, etc.' This is hardly likely. — *balānvayato*, i.e., according to the strength of the herd. Cb has 'the division should be according to weakness and strength,' i.e., apparently weak on one side and strong on the other.

41 *ajādīnām* : it seems quite clear that *ajāvīnām* should rather be read. Sheep. the principal source of wool, would not just be left to be inferred from *ādi*. Cf. s.48 below.

42 *aśva* in herds are, it seems, the concern of the *go'dhyakṣa*, while those in stables are looked after by the *aśvādhyakṣa* (2.30).

43 *nasya* to be construed with *-vāhin*. — *bhadra* qualifies *aśva* rather than *gati*. — *bhāra*, i.e., 20 *tulās*. As this appears too much, Meyer proposes for *bhāra* the sense of what can be carried in the arms. The rations, however, throughout appear on a very liberal scale. — It appears that a *vā* has dropped out after *daśāḍhakam*, for 10 *āḍhakas* of bran etc. appear as an option to 1 *tulā* of oil-cake in 2.15.52, which is more reasonable. — *mukhalavaṇa* 'salt from the Indus land' (Cs), 'rock-salt' (Meyer). — *māṁsa* as 'meat' being strange, Meyer understands 'pulp of fruit' ; the *Suśruta* (1.324.15) does use *māṁsa* in this sense (*cūtaphale paripakve keśaramāṁsāsthimajjānaḥ*). — *pratipānam* is to whet the appetite (Cs). Cf. 2.25.10. 45 *karmakālataḥ* is to be understood of *karmakarabalīvardas* and *phalataḥ* of *pāyanārtha dhenus*. Cb reads *pāyanārtham* with a stop after it 'for the drinking of workmen's bullocks,' which makes little sense. Cs (reading *karmakarabalīvardānām* at the end of s.44) has *pāyanārthaṁ ca dhenūnāṁ* as a separate sentence 'the drink-ration and the food-ration (understood because of *ca*) are to be double for milch-cows.' This is very doubtful.

47 *gomaṇḍalam* clearly refers to herds of cattle. It is an item of expenditure in 2.6.11.

48 He should provide a herd of one hundred donkeys and horses with five stallions, of (one hundred) goats and sheep with ten rams, and of cows, buffaloes and camels with four bulls.

CHAPTER THIRTY

SECTION 47 THE SUPERINTENDENT OF HORSES

1 The Superintendent of Horses should cause to be registered the total number of horses, received as gift, acquired by purchase, obtained in war, bred (in the stables), received in return for help, stipulated in a treaty or temporarily borrowed, according to their pedigree, age, colour, marks, class and source. 2 And he should report such as are not good or are crippled or diseased.

3 The horse-attendant shall receive from the treasury and the magazine a month's allowance (for the horse) and carefully look after it.

4 He should cause stables to be constructed, in length according to the number of horses, in width double a horse's length, with four doors and a rolling ground in the centre, with an entrance-hall, provided with boards for sitting at the main gate, (and) crowded with monkeys, peacocks, spotted deer, ichneumons, *cakoras*, parrots and *śārikās*. 5 He should cause a stall for each horse to be built, square with the length of a horse, with a flooring of smooth planks, with a receptacle for fodder, with outlets for urine and dung, (and) facing the east or the north. 6 Or, he should arrange the direction according to the (nature of the) stables. 7 For mares, stallions and foals (the stalls shall be) at separate ends.

8 For a mare that has borne a foal, a drink of a *prastha* of ghee (shall be provided) for three nights. 9 After that, a *prastha* of barley-meal and an

48 Breloer (III, 509) remarks 'the sections on cattle-rearing and agriculture are more interspersed with verses than the chapters on trade. The difference lies in the nature of things. The lists in the trade parts were probably not clothed in verse in the original books.' It must be pointed out that there is not a single verse in the body of this Chapter on cattle-rearing.

2.30

The horses under the care of the *aśvādhyakṣa* are those useful in war.

1 *paṇyāgārika* should be understood as 'received as a gift' in conformity with the sense of *paṇyāgāra* in 7.15.20; 9.6.28,29. The Glossary (in Part I) should be corrected accordingly. 'For sale in the market' does not quite suit. — *sāhāyyāgatakam* 'received in return for help rendered' (Cb). 'Received for rendering help' is possible; but these may be supposed to be included in *yāvatkālika*. — *paṇasthitam*, i.e., received as a condition in a treaty. Cb has 'kept as a hostage,' Cs 'kept as a pledge.' — *varga* 'breed, such as Pārasīka etc.' (Cs). It might refer to *uttama*, *madhyama* and *avara* classes.

3 *māsalābham* : this month is one of thirty-five days as in 2.20.52, according to Cp.

4 *aśvāyāmadviguṇavistārām* : as each stall is in length equal to a horse's length (s. 5) and the *śālā* has a width double that, half of the latter would be a sort of corridor behind the row of stalls situated along the four walls.—*upāvartana* may be 'rolling' on the ground, (cf. *luṭhito 'śva upāvṛttaḥ* — *Vaijayantī*), or 'going round' in a ring while in training. — *pragrīva* : cf. 2.5.3. — *pradvārāsanaphalaka-* 'a wooden seat with a back-rest, on both sides

invigorating drink of fat and medicines (shall be given) for ten nights. 10 Thereafter, half-cooked barley or beans, green fodder and a diet according to the season (shall be given).

11 After ten nights (from birth) a foal should have a diet of one *kuḍuba* barley-meal, ghee one-quarter and a *prastha* of milk, till it is six months old. 12 After that, (it should be given) a *prastha* of barley, increased by half (a *prastha*) every month, till it is three years old, (then) a *droṇa* (of barley) till it is four years old. 13 After that, when four-year old or five year old, it is fit for work, being fully developed.

14 The face of the best (type of) horse is thirty-two *aṅgulas*, its length five times the face, its shank twenty *aṅgulas* (and) height four times the shank. 15 Three *aṅgulas* less (successively, are the measurements) for the middling and lowest types. 16 One hundred *aṅgulas* is the girth (of the best type). 17 One-fifth part less (that) of the middling and lowest types (successively).

18 For the best (type of) horse (the ration is) two *droṇas* of *śāli*-rice, *vrīhi*-rice, barley or *priyaṅgu*, either half-dry or half-cooked, or a half-cooked meal of *mudga* or *māṣa* and a *prastha* of fat, five *palas* of salt, fifty *palas* of meat, an *āḍhaka* of juice or double that curds for moistening the lumps (of dry food), a *prastha* of liquor with five *palas* of sugar or double that quantity of milk as an invigo ating drink. 19 And for whetting the appetite of those fatigued by a long journey or a heavy load, a *prastha* of fat (should be given) as a clyster, one *kuḍuba* (of fat) for the nose, half a *bhāra* of green fodder, grass double that or a collection of bundles of grass six *aratnis* in circumference. 20 This, less by one quarter (successively), is for the middling and lowest types.

21 Equal to the best type (in point of ration) is the chariot-horse and the stallion of the middling type. 22 Equal to the middling (are those of) the lowest types. 23 One quarter less (is the ration) for mares and mules. 24 And half of this (is) for foals. 25 These are rules for rations (of horses).

of the door for watchmen' (Cb). For *pradvāra* 'main gate,' cf. 2.36.21. — *vānara*- etc. : some of the creatures are for detection of poison, others for averting the evil eye. 5 *prāṅmukham udaṅmukhaṁ vā* : with the present day method of tying horses, this would imply that there are to be stalls only on the western and southern sides.

11 The *iti* at the end of this s. and the next which is found in the mss. is not necessary. It is proposed to drop it. 12 At the end of the third year, the increase does amount to 16 *prasthas* or a *droṇa*.

14 The length of the horse comes to about 10 feet and the height 5 feet. 15 *tryaṅgulāvaram* : Cb Cp Cs read *dvyaṅgulāvaram*. 17 *pañcabhāgāvaraḥ* : as *pariṇāhaḥ* is to be understood, this is proposed for *-varam* of the mss. One-fifth less comes to 80 and 60 *aṅgulas* respectively. Cb has 80 and 64 (1/5th of 80). Cp Cs have 95 and 90 *aṅgulas*, which seems hardly possible. — The smallest size appears to be more or less that of a pony.

18 *māṁsam* : see 2.29.43 above. — *rasa* seems to be sugar-cane juice. — *kleaanārtham* from Cb is necessary as going with *āḍhakam* and *dviguṇam* ; cf. 2.31.13 below. 19 *khādanārtham* 'to make them eat,' i.e., to whet their appetite. — *anuvāsanam* 'washing the lower intestines by an enema' (com.).

21 *rathyo vṛṣaś ca madhyamaḥ* : Meyer construes *madhyama* with *vṛṣa* alone. It could also be understood of *rathya*. 23 *pādahīnam*, i.e., 1/4th less than that for the male in each class. 24 *ato 'rdham*, i.e., half that of the female in each class.

26 Those who cook the food (for horses), who hold the reins and who treat them should taste the food beforehand.

27 (Horses) incapacitated for work by war, disease, or old age should receive food for maintenance. 28 (Horses) unfit for use in war should be used, as stallions, (to breed) on mares in the interests of the citizens and the country people.

29 Of those fit for use, the best come from Kāmboja, Sindhu, Āraṭṭa and Vanāyu, the middling from Bāhlīka, Pāpeya, Sauvīra and Titala, the rest are inferior. 30 In accordance with their fiery, gentle or dull mettle, he should assign to them work connected with war or riding.

31 The all-sided work of a horse is (work) connected with war.

32 Moving at a gallop, moving at a canter, leaping, moving at a trot, and responding to signals are (movements of) riding-horses.

33 Among them, *aupaveṇuka*, *vardhamānaka*, *yamaka*, *ālīḍhapluta*, *pṛthuga* and *trikacālī* are (varieties of) gallop.

34 The same, with head and ears unaffected, is canter, or it has sixteen (types of) paces. 35 *prakīrṇaka*, *prakīrṇottara*, *niṣaṇṇa*, *pārśvānuvṛtta*,

26 *sūtragrāhaka* 'the rein-holder,' i.e., 'the groom' (com.). — *pratisvāda* : cf. 1.21.10 and 5.1.31. Cp Cs, however, have '(shares in) the ration,' i.e., their food should be prepared along with that of the horses.

27 *piṇḍagocarikāḥ*, i.e., receiving food only for their maintenance.

29 Kāmboja was an ancient kingdom to the north of Gandhāra. The *saṁgha* type of rule prevailing there is mentioned in 11.1.4 below. — Āraṭṭa is a part of the Punjab (Meyer, who compares *Mahābhārata*, 8.44.31-3). — Vanāyu 'Arabia' (the *Vācaspatya*, N. N. Law and K. Nag), 'Persia' (Mallinātha on *Raghu* 5.73, *Halāyudha* and Meyer). Cf. Johnston, JRAS, 1939, 232. — Bāhlīka 'from Bactria.' The origin of *pāpeyaka* is uncertain. — *taitala* 'from Titala' in Orissa (Agrawala, *op. cit.*, p. 61). *Mahābhārata*, 6.90.5, mentions *titiraja* horses (Meyer, who asks if *taitala* refers to these). The Sauvīras are along the Indus to the north of the Sindhus.

30 *aupavāhyaka* refers to riding. Carrying of loads on back seems hardly intended. — *prayojayet*, i.e., train to that type of work.

31 *caturaśram* 'four-sided,' i.e., of all types. A horse's work in warfare is referred to in 10.4.13 and 10.5.53. — *sāṁnāhyam* is predicative, not *caturaśram* (as in Meyer).

32 *aupavāhyāḥ* : the substantive is *aśvāḥ*. Consequently, *valgana* etc. are adjectives descriptive of a horse. *mārgāḥ* 'gaits' is possible as the substantive, but seems less likely. — Meyer suggests *nārāṣṭra* for *nāroṣṭra* 'with a goad (*aṣṭrā*) in the form of a man (*nāra*).' That is possible, but not certain.

33 The exact nature of the various types of a horse's gaits, sometimes even their names, are uncertain. Cb is lacking from s. 21 onwards. Cp is far from clear and does not always appear right. — *aupaveṇuka* 'with a circle (*maṇḍala*) of only one *hasta*' (Cp); this is hardly helpful. — *vardhamānaka* 'jumping in a series of circles of one *hasta* each' (Cp). — *yamaka* 'galloping in two circles simultaneously' (Cp). — *ālīḍhapluta* 'jumping with one leg contracted and the other stretched forward' (Cs). *ālīḍha* is a posture in archery. — *pṛthugaḥ* is in accordance with a suggetion by Meyer for the unlikely form *pṛthagaḥ* of the mss. Cp reads *vṛthādyaḥ* 'jumping with the fore-part of the body.' Cs (with Cb) reads *pūrvagaḥ* in this sense. — *trikacālī* 'jumping with the hind-part of the body' (Cp, the exact reading in it being uncertain).

34 *sa eva*, i.e., the same as *valgana*. — *śiraḥkarṇaviśuddhaḥ* : this apparently means that the head and ears are steady, not moving. — *ṣoḍaśamārgo vā* : '*vā* in the sense of *ca*' (com.). It is possible, however, that this is an alternative view about *nīcairgata*, viz., that it is unrelated to *valgana* and has 16 types. 35 *prakīrṇaka* 'containing a mixture of all gaits'

ūrmimārga, śarabhakrīḍita, śarabhapluta, tritāla, bāhyānuvṛtta, pañcapāṇi, siṁhāyata, svādhūta, kliṣṭa, śliṅgita, bṛṁhita and *puṣpābhikīrṇa* are the paces in canter.

36 Monkey leap, frog leap, antelope leap, one-foot leap, cuckoo move, breast-movement and crane move are (types of) leap.

37 Heron gait, heron-on-water gait, peacock gait, half-peacock gait, ichneumon gait, half-ichneumon gait, boar gait, half-boar gait are (varieties of) trot.

38 Acting in accordance with signals is signal-responding.

39 Six, nine and twelve *yojanas* is the road (covered in a day) for chariot-horses, five *yojanas*, seven and a half, and ten, the road for riding (and pack-) horses.

40 The stride, the (gait) with gentle breath and the load-carrying are the gaits.

41 Striding, galloping, leaping, near-fast and fast are the speeds.

42 Teachers of training should give directions concerning straps and implements for them, and charioteers concerning accoutrements of chariot-horses necessary in war. 43 Physicians of horses (should prescribe) remedies against decrease or increase in (the weight of) the body, and diet varying according to season.

(Cp). — *prakīrṇottara* 'mixed, with one gait prominent' (Cp). — *niṣaṇṇa* 'in which the back is motionless' (Cp). (*viṣaṇṇaḥ* in our text is a misprint.) — *pārśvānuvṛtta* 'a sideways gait' (Cp). — *ūrmimārga* 'heaving the body up and down' (Cp). Referring to Mallinātha on *Śiśupālavadha*, 5.4, Meyer (in the Nachtrag) suggests that some of these gaits are not those of a single horse, but rather movements of cavalry-formation. Thus *prakīrṇaka* 'spread out,' *ūrmimārga* 'wave-like formation' are formations by a number of horses, not the gait of one. This appears plausible. — *tritāla* 'moving with three legs' (Cp). — *bāhyānuvṛtta* 'prancing to the left and the right' (Cp). Meyer proposes *bāhvanuvṛtta* 'harmonious in the fore-legs.' *bāhu* is not very likely for the fore-legs of a horse. — *pañcapāṇi* 'placing three legs on the ground and striking the ground twice with the fourth' (Cp). — Meyer has 'spreading out in five columns.' — *siṁhāyata* 'long like a lion's gait.' — *svādhūta* : 'with very long strides' (Cp). — *kliṣṭa* 'laboured' is '*vivahanavisrabdhagatiḥ* with a steady gait in carrying(?)' (Cp). — *śliṅgita* 'moving with a bent fore-part' (Cp which shows *ślāghita*). — *bṛṁhita* 'with the fore-part raised' (Cp). — *puṣpābhikīrṇa* 'with a zigzag motion' (Cp, which shows *-vakīrṇa*). The expression seems to suggest taking steps very lightly.

36 The expressions are adjectives to *aśvāḥ*. — *ekapādaplutaḥ* 'contracting three legs and jumping with the fourth' (Cp). — *urasya* 'contracting all four legs and jumping with the breast alone' (Cp).

37 *vārikāṅka* : Cb Cs read *vārikāṅkṣa* 'with the gait of a swan,' Meyer proposes *vāri-dhvāṅkṣa* 'water-crow.' The gait of a heron on water may well have been intended.

39 According to Cs, 6, 9 and 12 are for the best, middling and lowest respectively. The reverse might appear more likely.

40 *vikramaḥ* 'taking a stride.' — *bhadrāśvāsaḥ* 'breathing gently,' i.e., not over-exerted. — *bhāravāhya* 'load-bearing,' i. e., with a laboured gait.

41 *vikrama* is the slowest among speeds (Cs). — *upakaṇṭham*, literally, 'near the throat' seems to refer to a leaping run, when the fore-legs come near the throat. — *dhārā* is pace in running or speed.

42 For *bandhana* and *upakaraṇa*, cf. 2.32.12-13 below. — Meyer distinguishes *sāṁgrā-mika alaṁkāra* from *rathāśvālaṁkāra*. That seems hardly intended.

44 The holder of reins, the binder of horses, the fodder-giver, the food-cook, the stall-guard, the hair-trimmer and the specialist in poison-cure, should wait upon horses with their respective duties. 45 And in case of transgression of duties by them, he should cut down their day's wage. 46 For one riding a horse kept apart for the rite of lustration or kept apart (for treatment) by a physician, the fine shall be twelve *paṇas*. 47 In case of a worsening of the disease because of withholding treatment or medicine, the fine shall be double the (cost of) cure. 48 In case of an untoward happening through their fault, the fine shall be the price of the animal.

49 By that are explained (rules for attendance on) herds of cattle, donkeys, camels and buffaloes and goats and sheep.

50 He should cause a bath to be given to horses twice a day, also perfumes and garlands. On the junctures of the dark halves of months, offerings to spirits (should be made) and on those of the bright halves, reciting of blessings (by Brahmins).

51 He should cause the lustration rite to be performed on the ninth day in Āśvayuja, at the beginning or the end of an expedition or in case of illness, being intent on a pacificatory rite.

CHAPTER THIRTY-ONE

SECTION 48 THE SUPERINTENDENT OF ELEPHANTS

1 The Superintendent of Elephants should carry out the guarding of elephant-forests, (and look after) the stables, stalls, places for lying down and the amount of work, food and fodder for male and female elephants and cubs, that are being trained or are competent for work, the assignment of tasks to them, the straps and implements and the accoutrements of war, and physicians, trainers and group of attendants.

44 *sūtragrāhaka* : see s. 26 above. — *aśvabandhaka* who yokes the horse to the chariot or ties it to the post.

46 *nīrājanā* is a purification-rite, performed over arms, horses, elephants etc., with recitation of *mantras*, offering of oblations and waving of lights before them. Cf. s. 51 below. *Bṛ. Saṁ.*, ch. 44, describes the *nīrājana vidhi*.

47 *saṅga* 'attachment,' i.e., not rendering them in time, withholding them.

48 *vailomya* is, in effect, death. — *patra* 'vehicle,' i.e., the horse.

49 *tena*, i.e., the rules in ss. 45 ff. apply, with suitable modifications.

50 *dvir ahnaḥ* : this 'only in summer and autumn' (Cs). — *kṛṣṇasaṁdhi*, i.e., the new moon day and *śuklasaṁdhi*, i.e., the full moon day. 51 The ninth day in Āśvayayuja does not exactly correspond to the Dasara day, which falls on the tenth of the bright half of that month, on which, however, horses are still worshipped in many parts of India.

2.31

1 *hastivanarakṣām* : apparently the *nāgavanādhyakṣa* and his subordinates (of 2.2.7ff.) worked under the *hastyadhyakṣa*. — *karmakṣānta* is one who has completed his training for some particular type of work. Cb has 'who needs rest after training.' — *śayyā* : this is described in s. 4 below. — The form *aupasthāyika* is favoured by Cb Cp. M has *upasathāyuka* here, but *upasthāyika* in 5.8.17.

2 He should cause a stable to be constructed double an elephant's length in height, breadth and length, with additional stalls for female elephants, with an entrance-hall, with a collection of beams, (and) facing the east or the north. 3 He should cause a stall (for each elephant) to be built, square in conformity with an elephant's length, with a smooth tying-post and plank-flooring, (and) with outlets for urine and dung. 4 (There should be) a place for lying down equal (in size) to the stall (and) half in height, in the fort, for elephants used in war and used for riding, outside (the fort) for those under training and rogue-elephants.

5 The first and seventh of the one-eighth parts of the day are times for bath, after that for feeding. 6 In the forenoon is the time for exercise, the afternoon is the time for invigorating drink. 7 Two parts of the night are the time for sleep, one-third part for lying down and getting up.

8 The time for catching (elephants) is in summer. 9 A twenty year old should be caught. 10 A cub, an elephant with small tusks, one without tusks, one diseased, a female elephant with young and a suckling female elephant are not to be caught.

11 A forty year old (elephant) with measurements of seven *aratnis* as height, nine as length and ten as girth is best, a thirty year old one is middling, a twenty-five year old one lowest. 12 For those two, the ration is less by a quarter (than that for the preceding type).

2 *-viṣkambhāyāmām* : that the length of the *śālā* is to be only double an elephant's length (i.e., about 18 *aratnis*) is surprising. We expect it to be in conformity with the number of elephants, as in 2.30.4 above. Perhaps double the length of the number of elephants is to be understood. — *hastinīsthānādhikām*, i.e., with additional, i.e., separate stalls for females. Cb Cs, however, have 'more by six *aratnis*, the stall for a female, i.e., 24 *hastas* long.' How this meaning is arrived at it is difficult to see. — *kumārīsaṁgrahām* 'with a beam placed on the tying post for ease in tying' (com.). As Meyer remarks this should have come in the description of the stall, not of the *śālā*. He has 'a scaffold or framework of beams.' 3 In conformity with 2.30.5 *-starakam* is proposed for *-ntarakam*, and *-tsargaṁ sthānam* for *-tsargasthānam*, as suggested by Meyer. 4 *śayyām* : this seems to refer to temporary sheds, to be used when the number of elephants exceeds the accommodation in the *śālā*. — *ardhāpāśrayām* : this may be understood as 'having half the height (of a *sthāna*) and probably without a roof. Cb has 'with a ceiling 5 *hastas* above the height of the elephant'; Cp 'half, i.e., 4 1/2 *hastas* in height on one side;' Meyer 'with a railing or banister half as high as the elephant.'

6 *pratipānakālaḥ* : Thinking that the whole afternoon is unlikely for drink, Meyer proposes *pratipādanakālaḥ* 'time for exhibition of what is learnt or for recoupment or restoration to normal.' This reading is actually found in the mss., but it does not seem to be original. For *pratipāna* for elephants, see s. 13 below.

10 *vikka* 'a cub that still sucks' (com.). *moḍha* 'with tusks like those of a female elephant' (com.). *makkaṇa* 'a tuskless elephant.' All these are apparently Deshi words.

11 *pramāṇataḥ* etc. : this seems to mean that the *uttama* attains these dimensions at 40; at 30 he is in size like the *madhyama* and at 25 like the *avara*, whose heights at 40 are 6 and 5 *aratnis* respectively. This last in implied in s. 15 below, and this is how Cp understands it; *Mānasollāsa*, 2.222-4, supports the idea. 12 *pādāvaraḥ*, i.e., 3/4ths and 1/2 of the *uttama* respectively. Cb has 3/4ths of the *madhyama* for the *avara*.

13 For each *aratni* (of height), (the ration is) a *droṇa* of rice-grains, half an *āḍhaka* of oil, three *prasthas* of melted butter, ten *palas* of salt, fifty *palas* of meat, an *āḍhaka* of juice or double that quantity of curds for moistening dry lumps, an *āḍhaka* of liquor with ten *palas* of sugar or double that quantity of milk as an invigorating drink, a *prastha* of oil for smearing the limbs, an eighth part (of a *prastha* of oil) for the head and for the lamp, two *bhāras* and a quarter of green fodder and two *bhāras* and a half of dry grass ; of leaves of plants etc., there is to be no limit. 14 Equal in the matter of food to the seven-*aratni* elephant is the eight-*aratni* one when beyond rutting. 15 According to the (size in) *hastas*, the rest, (viz.,) the six-*aratni* and the five-*aratni* ones.

16. A cub, fed on milk and green fodder may be caught for play.

17 With redness formed, covered, with smoothened sides, with an even girth, with flesh spread evenly, level with the back-bone, and with a trough formed, these are appearances (of an elephant).

18 In conformity with the appearance, he should give exercise to the gentle and the dull (elephant) and to the animal with mixed characteristics, in various types of work, or in accordance with the season.

13 *aratnau* : this means that for a seven-*aratni* elephant, each item is to be sevenfold. Meyer thinks this too much and proposes to read *saptāratnau*. But in that case, the genitive case would be expected. Cf. also *yathāhastam*, s. 15 below. It is possible that these are a month's rations; cf. 2.30.3 above. — *kaḍaṅkara* 'branches, leaves etc. of the *sallakī* and other plants' (com.). 14 Cb reads *hastyarālaḥ* for *atyarālaḥ*, and that seems supported by the *Mānasollāa*, 2.222-4, where an *arāla* is 8 *aratnis* tall and *atyarāla* 9 *aratnis*. However, an *arāla* is an elephant in rut and would normally require larger quantities of food; only an *atyarāla* 'beyond the stage of rutting' would have smaller rations.

16 This s. should preferably have come after s. 10.

17 According to Cs *śobhās* are stages in the appearance of an elephant as he grows up, *saṁjātalohitā* being the appearance on the first few days after birth. which is reddish, and so on. Meyer thinks that these are appearances of different types of elephants, true of them throughout life. The explanations in Cb, which reads all the expressions in the plural, seem to show these as stages in the recovery of an elephant after a serious illness. — *saṁjātalohitā* 'who, being emaciated, with bones and skin alone left, has started gaining strength on beginning to take food' (Cb). — *praticchannā* 'covered' apparently with some flesh; 'who has gained strength' (Cb). — *saṁliptapakṣā* 'with sides well-smeared' is 'with a smooth skin and flesh filling up' (Cb). — *samakakṣyā* : *kakṣyā* seems to refer to 'girth.' Cb has 'with full flesh'. — *vyatikīrṇamāṁsā* : Cb has 'with uneven flesh.' Perhaps we should understand *avyatikīrṇa*- 'not scattered,' i.e., evenly spread. — *samatalpatalā* 'with flesh on a level with the back-bone' (Cb). Perhaps the original reading was -*talpalā*, for *talpala* means the back-bone of an elephant; cf. *Śiśupālavadha*, 18.6. — *jātadroṇikā* 'with a *droṇa*-like trough formed,' evidently because of old age. Cb has 'so stout that the *vaṁśa* or spine is covered.' The first and the last expressions seem to support Cs. However, Cb, with which Cp mostly agress, may be right.

18 *vyāyāmam* : training or exercise. — *mṛgaṁ saṁkīrṇaliṅgam* is proposed as suggested by Meyer; that appears to be Cp's reading. This seems necessary whether we understand *mṛga* as the third and *saṁkīrṇaliṅga* as the fourth type, as in the commentators, or *saṁkīrṇaliṅgam* as only a description of *mṛga*, the third type. This latter idea is better. — *vyāla* is not mentioned here, as he is not amenable to *vyāyāma*.

CHAPTER THIRTY-TWO

SECTION 48 (Continued)

The Activity of Elephants

1 Classes (of elephants) corresponding to work are four : one in training, one used in war, one for riding and the rogue-elephant.

2 Among them one under training is of five kinds: getting used to (a man on) the shoulder, getting used to the (tying) post, getting used to the place for catching elephants, getting used to the trap, and getting used to a herd. 3 The accompanying treatment for him is the work of (bringing up) a cub.

4 The war elephant has seven ways of doing work : standing in attendance, going round, marching together, killing and trampling, fighting with elephants, assaulting towns, and fighting in battles. 5 The accompanying treatment for him is the work of (putting) on the girth, the work of (putting on) the neck-chain, and the work of (moving in) a herd.

6 The riding elephant is of eight kinds : one who is led, one ridden with (the help of another) elephant, one trotting, one trained in (various) gaits, one ridden with a stick, one ridden with a goad, one ridden without

2.32

1 *karmaskandhāḥ*, i.e., groups or classes based on the kind of work they do. Cp has 'groups of works;' but the words that follow are attributes of elephants, not of *karma*.

2 *skandhagata*, i.e., allowing a man to sit on his shoulders. — *vārigata* : according to com. *vāri* is the place where elephants are captured; hence *vārigata* is 'trained to catch other elephants.' Meyer has 'trained to go through and in water' or 'accustomed to the tying rope' (fn.). Neither is satisfactory. — *avapāta* 'pit used as a trap for catching elephants' (com.). Meyer has 'getting used to a precipice.' — *yūthagata* 'getting used to the company of trained female elephants' (com.). It may also mean 'getting used to a strange herd and the company of unknown elephants.' 3 *upavicāraḥ*, i.e., the treatment to be given during the period of this training. Russ. has 'preliminary work (necessary for training).' — *vikkakarma* 'i.e., he should be given food (milk, green fodder etc.) fit for a cub' (Cb).

4 *upasthānam* 'standing in attendance' is 'raising and lowering fore- and hind-parts and jumping over fire-brands, bamboos, ropes, etc.' (com.). Meyer has 'standing still (even when there is a loud noise).' — *saṁvartanam* 'going round' is 'lying down, sitting, leaping over pits etc. on the ground' (com.). Cb reads *vartanam*. — *saṁyānam* 'marching together' is 'various gaits, straight, transverse, zigzag, circular, etc.' (com.). — *vadhāvadhaḥ* 'destruction or capture of horses, men or chariots by means of trunk, tusks etc.' (com.). Meyer understands *āvadha* as the second word, which could be rendered by 'trampling.' — *hastiyuddham* is fight between two elephants in an arena. — *nāgarāyaṇam* is breaking down the defences of fortified towns. — *sāṁgrāmikam*, i.e., as in 10.4.14 and 10.5.54. 5 *kakṣyākarma* seems to refer to everything connected with saddling while *graiveyakarma* refers to ornamental chains etc. — *yūthakarma*, i.e., working jointly with other elephants. Com. have 'giving him work according to the type of herd (river, mountain, etc.) from which he came.'

6 *ācaraṇa* 'lowering the fore-part or the hind-part and so on' (Cb), apparently to allow a rider to get on the back. Meyer has 'going rightly or straight.' In the context, 'being led' seems also quite likely. — *kuñjaraupavāhya* 'doing *sāṁnāhya* or *aupavāhya* work with another elephant' (Cb), 'with a man on back, but led with another elephant at the time' (Cs), which seems more likely. Meyer has 'allowing himself to be ridden in the manner of an elephant.'— *dhoraṇa* 'doing all work with one side only' (com.). It might mean 'trotting' as in 2.30.32,37. — *ādhānagatika* 'endowed with two or three types of gaits or capable of imitating the gaits of other elephants' (Cb). Meyer has 'who goes forward in all circum-

any help, and one used for hunting. 7 The accompanying treatment for him is the work of keeping fit, the work of recouping what is lacking and the work of responding to signals.

8 The rogue-elephant has one way of activity : (he is) frightened, restrained, abnormal, in rut, with rut fixed and with a fixed cause of intoxication. 9 The accompanying treatment for him is the work of guarding in solitary confinement. 10 One who is lost for all activity is a rogue-elephant, pure, firmly resolved, vehement and spoiled by all defects.

11 The tying equipment and implements for them should be in accordance with the instructions of trainers. 12 The tying post, the neck-chain, the girth, the stirrup-rope, the foot-chain, the upper chain and so on constitute the tying equipment. 13 The goad, the bamboo, the machine and so on are implements. 14 The *vaijayantī*-garland, the *kṣurapra*-necklace, the covering, the carpet and so on are ornaments. 15 The armour, lance, quiver, machines and so on are accoutrements for war.

16 The physician, the trainer, the rider, the driver, the guard, the decorator, the cook, the fodder-giver, the foot-chainer, the stall-guard, the night-attendant and so on form the group of attendants. 17 The physician, the stall-guard and the cook should receive a *prastha* of boiled rice, a *prasṛti*

stances.' 7 *śāradakarma* : '*śārada* is fourfold, fat, lean, suffering from indigestion and normal; its *karma* is making the fat lean, the lean fat, stimulating digestion and maintaining normalcy' (Cb). Cf. N. N. Law, *Studies* etc., p. 64 n. The general sense seems to be maintaining fitness. — *hīnakarma* 'giving exercise to one who is without it' (com.). Cj seems to read *kṣīṇakarma* 'nourishment etc. of the weak.' — *nāroṣṭra* : see 2.30.38.

8 A re-arrangement of the words is proposed, *śaṅkitaḥ* . . -*viniścayaś ca* being read immediately after -*kriyāpathaḥ*, and *tasyopa*- . . . -*rakṣākarma* treated as an independent s. Thus we get an *upavicāra* with *karma* at the end as usual. *śaṅkita* etc. describe the various reasons why an elephant becomes *vyāla*; his behaviour is always the same, he is *ekakriyāpatha*. Com. and Meyer understand *karmaśaṅkita* etc. as characteristics of one and the same animal, which is not convincing. Cb has '*karmaśaṅkita*, i.e., not obeying orders at the time of training, *avaruddha*, i.e., disregarded as unfit for work, *viṣama*, i.e., whimsical in behaviour, *prabhinna*, i.e., who has become a *vyāla* because of *madadoṣa*, *prabhinnaviniścaya*, i.e., in distress bacause of defects in drink etc. and rut, and *madahetuviniścaya*, i.e., the cause of whose intoxication is known.' Cp agrees. Cb quotes a verse wherein five causes of *mada* are enumerated '*saṁtāpo 'bhijano vyādhiḥ pariṇāmas tathauṣadhiḥ*.' Cj has *aparāddho* for *avaruddho*. 9 *āyamyaikarakṣā* 'guarding alone after being put under restraint.' Cb has 'making him work and thus bringing him under control.' 10 *kriyāvipanna* is another kind of *vyāla*, for whom there is no *upavicāra*. It may mean 'on whom training is lost' or 'unfit for any activity;' 'harmful in his actions' (Cb). — *śuddha* has 18 defects, according to the commentators. — *suvrata* : Cb reads *suvṛtta* and explains 'causes the rider's fall and has 15 defects.' — *viṣama* 'causes the fall of the rider and kills him in addition;' it has 33 defects. — *sarvadoṣapraduṣṭa* has 52 defects in all (com.).

12 *pārāyaṇa* 'a rope for support when mounting an elephant' (Cb). — *uttara* 'a second girth-band, a second neck-chain' (Cb). Meyer has 'smaller, inferior or secondary fetters.' A chain for the upper part of the body may also have been meant. 13 *yantra* 'for cutting tusks' (Cp). 14 *kṣurapramālā* : com. call it *nakṣatramālā*; it may have 27 pieces in it. These, according to Meyer, may be semi-circular metal discs.

16 '*ārohaka* is the *mahāmātra* of elephants who knows the *śāstra*; *ādhoraṇa* has not studied the *śāstra*, but knows by practice; *hastipaka* is an attendant, mahout' (Cb). — *aupacārika* 'who decorates the elephant' (com.). 17 *prasṛti* 'a handful' is about two *palas*.

of fat and two *palas* of sugar and salt, also ten *palas* of meat, excepting the physicians. 18 Physicians shall treat (elephants) afflicted by long journey, illness, work, rut or old age.

19 Uncleanliness of the stall, non-receipt of fodder, making (elephants) sleep on bare ground, striking them at an improper place, mounting by another person, riding at an improper time, (or) on unsuitable land, leading down (to water) where there is no crossing, and a thicket of trees are occasions for penalty. 20 He should take that from their food and wages.

21 Three lustration rites should be performed in the four-monthly junctures of seasons, offerings on the junctures of dark halves (should be made) to spirits and on the junctures of the bright halves to Senānī.

22 Leaving (a length) double the circumference at the root of the tusks, he should cut (these), every two years and a half in the case of those from river-banks, every five years in the case of those from mountainous regions.

CHAPTER THIRTY-THREE

SECTION 49 THE SUPERINTENDENT OF CHARIOTS
SECTION 50 THE SUPERINTENDENT OF FOOT SOLDIERS
SECTION 51 THE ACTIVITY OF THE COMMANDANT OF THE ARMY

1 The (duty of the) Superintendent of Chariots is explained by (that of) the Superintendent of Horses. 2 He should establish factories for (the manufacture of) chariots.

3 One with ten *puruṣas* (of height) and twelve (*puruṣas*) interior is (the biggest) chariot. 4 Less than that by one (*puruṣa*) interior space

This measure is not mentioned is 2.19. — *anyatra cikitsakebhyaḥ* : apparently the physicians came from vegetarian classes.

19 *yavasasya agrahaṇam* refers to the attendant's failure to receive the quota from the stores. — *abhūmau* : Cp supplies *yānam* after it; Cs construes it with the preceding *yānam*; a *vā* should be understood after the word. — *taruṣaṇḍa* is nominative (Meyer) rather than locative (Cs).

21 *cāturmāsyartusaṁdhiṣu* : Cs reads *-syṛtu-* and explains 'on the full moon nights coming every four months (*cāturmāsī*), which stand at the juncture of seasons.' This seems forced; 'junctures of seasons coming every four months' is sufficient. These are the full moons of Kārttika, Phālguna and Āsādha (Cb Cs) at the end of rains, the season of frost and summer. — *senānyaḥ*, i.e., of Skanda or Kārttikeya.

22 The *Bṛhat Saṁhitā*, 79.20, has a close parallel '*dantasya mūlaparidhiṁ dvirāyatāṁ projjhya kalpayeccheṣem, adhikamanūpacarāṇāṁ nyūnaṁ giricāriṇāṁ kiṁcit.*' Its source may partly be the present passage.

2.33

The three sections cover ss. 1-6, 7-8 and 9-11 respectively.

1 The only similarity between the duties of the two *adhyakṣas* seems to be in the matter of equipping their charges for war.

3 *daśapuruṣo dvādaśāntaro* '10 *vitastis* in height and 12 *vitastis* in length (*antaraśabdena āyāmābhidhānāt*)' (Cj). The width would not vary to any great extent in the case of the different *rathas*. *puruṣa* seems used in the sense of *pauruṣa* of 2.20.10, which is the

successively up to six (*puruṣas*) interior space (are smaller ones) ; thus there are seven (sizes of) chariots.

5 He should cause to be made chariots, (such as) temple chariot, festive chariot, war chariot, travelling carriage, chariot for marching against an enemy's city and chariot for training.

6 He should be conversant with arrangements concerning bows, striking weapons, armours and accoutrements, and the employment of charioteers, chariot-attendants and chariot-horses in (various) works, also (look after) food and wages till the conclusion of the works of servants hired and not hired, giving practice to and protecting them, as well as making gifts and showing honour to them.

7 By this is explained the (duty of the) Superintendent of Foot Soldiers. 8 He should be conversant with the strength or weakness of hereditary, hired, banded, allied, alien and forest troops, with military operations in water or on high ground, with open or tactical fighting, in trenches or in the open, by day or by night, and with the employment or absence of employment (of the foot soldiers) in (different types of) work.

9 The Commandant of the Army, trained in the science of all (kinds of) fights and weapons, (and) renowned for riding on elephants, horses or in chariots, should be conversant with the same, (and) with the direction of the work carried out by the four-fold troops. 10 He should look out for suitable ground for one's side, (suitable) season for fighting, arraying a force against (enemy arrays), breaking unbroken ranks, re-forming broken ranks, breaking

same as *vitasti*. Cp Cs paraphrase *antara* by *vistāra*, which may mean 'length' or 'width'. Meyer, regarding a 9-foot width as strange, proposes 'for ten men, with accommodation for twelve (in case of necessity).' This is extremely unlikely. 4 *ekāntarāvarāḥ*, i.e., 11 *puruṣas*, 10, 9 and so on up to 6. This states the length. Cs understands a corresponding diminution in height as well. Meyer's '(with normal accommodation for 9, 8, ...4 but) with accommodation for 11, 10, ...6 in case of necessity)' shows the forced character of his explanation.

5 *puṣyaratha* 'for coronation, marriage etc.' (Cb). Meyer compares Pali *phussaratha*.

6 *iṣvastra* 'quiver of arrows (*iṣu*) and missiles including the bow (*astra*)' (com.). The word often conveys the single idea of 'a bow.' — *abhṛtānām* : this may refer to *dāsa*, bondmen, *daṇḍapratikārin* etc. It may also imply temporary and work-charged servants. — *yogyārakṣā* : Cs has 'protection against enemy's wiles of efficient (*yogya*) officers'. This is hardly likely. *yogyā* is practice, drill, training etc. ; cf. 2.30.42.

7 *etena*, i.e., as in s. 6. The *pattyadhyakṣa* seems concerned with training and care of troops. 8 *maulabhṛta-* etc. : see 9.2.1 ff. — *nimnasthala-* etc. : cf. 7.10.34-7 ; 10.4.2 ; for *nimna* 'water,' cf. 2.3.1. — *vidyāt* after *-vyāyāmaṁ ca* is unnecessary and is dropped.— *ayogam* 'absence of employment.' — *karmasu* : for *padātikarma*, see 10.4.16 and for *pattiyuddha*, 10.5.56.

9 *tadeva* : Cb reads *tathaiva*, which might appear slightly better. — *saṁghuṣṭaḥ* is from Cb and is understood in the sense of 'renowned, well-known.' *saṁpuṣṭaḥ* is the reading of the mss., which is not a happy expression. — *anuṣṭhānādhiṣṭhānam* : Cb has 'his work during fights and disposition of troops in battle ;' Meyer 'the function of the troops and the function of directing.' 'Supervision over the work being done,' may be the meaning intended. 10 *pratyanīkam* apparently refers to arranging one's troops according

compact ranks, destroying broken ranks, destroying the fort and the season for an expedition.

11 Being devoted to the training of the troops, he should arrange signals for the arrays by means of musical instruments, banners and flags, when halting, marching or attacking.

CHAPTER THIRTY-FOUR

SECTION 52 THE SUPERINTENDENT OF PASSPORTS
SECTION 53 THE SUPERINTENDENT OF PASTURE LANDS

1 The Superintendent of Passports should issue a sealed pass for one *māṣaka*.

2 (Only) a person with a sealed pass shall be entitled to enter or leave the countryside. 3 A native of the land, without a sealed pass, shall pay twelve *paṇas*. 4 In case of a forged pass, the lowest fine for violence (shall be imposed), the highest for one not belonging to the country.

5 The Superintendent of Pasture Lands should ask for the sealed pass.

6 And he should establish pasture land in regions between villages. 7 He should clear low lands and forests of the danger of robbers and wild animals.

8 In waterless regions, he should establish wells, water-works and springs, also flower- and fruit-enclosures.

9 Fowlers and hunters should go round in the forests. 10 At the approach of robbers or enemies, they should produce a sound with conch-shells or drums, not allowing themselves to be caught, (either) climbing mountains or trees, or riding swift vehicles.

to the array of the enemy troops. Cs has 'enemy's army,' which can hardly be the object of *senāpatiḥ paśyet*.

11 *sthāne* etc. to be construed with *vyūhasaṁjñāḥ prakalpayet*, not with *vinaye rataḥ*.

2.34

The two *prakaraṇas* are found in ss. 1-4 and 5-12 respectively.

2 *janapadam* : even in cities, passes were issued ; cf. 2.36.38. 4 *tirojanapadasya* 'for a foreigner.' The fine is for forging ; there is no mention of a fine for a foreigner without a pass. Perhaps double the 12 *paṇas* is to be understood.

6 *grāmāntareṣu* is proposed as in 4.13.9 for *bhayāntareṣu* of the mss. With the latter, Cb has 'in places of danger he should employ servants or soldiers to remove it.' Cp Cs have 'in regions within the range of robbers, enemy-spies etc.' Neither explanation is satisfactory. Breloer remarks 'the power of the *vivītādhyakṣa* ends in village territories and before the gates of cities and forts' (III, 512).

9 *lubdhakaśvagaṇinaḥ* : cf. 2.29.21 above. 10 *-vṛkṣādhirūḍhāḥ* from Cb is necessary for the sense.

11 And he should convey to the king movements of enemies and forest-tribes by means of domesticated pigeons carrying sealed letters or by a series of smokes and fires.

12 He should ensure the livelihood of those in produce forests and elephant forests and (secure) the road cess, protection against robbers, escort of caravans, protection of cattle and trade.

CHAPTER THIRTY-FIVE

SECTION 54 THE ACTIVITY OF THE ADMINISTRATOR
SECTION 55 SECRET AGENTS IN THE DISGUISE OF HOUSEHOLDERS, TRADERS AND ASCETICS

1 Dividing the countryside into four divisions, the Administrator should cause to be entered in a register the number of villages, classifying them as best, middling and lowest, (recording) this is exempt from taxes, this provides soldiers, this much is (the revenue in) grains, cattle, cash, forest produce, labour and produce in place of tax. 2 Under his direction, the revenue officer should look after a group of five villages or ten villages.

3 He should record the number of villages by fixing their boundaries, the number of fields by an enumeration of ploughed and unploughed

11 *mudrā-* : here it is a sealed communication, tied round their necks. — *dhūmāgni* 'smoke by day and fire by night' (Cs).

12 *dravyahastivanājīvam* : Cp has 'should receive (*kārayet*, i.e., *upādadīta*) income from produce forests and elephant forests,' Meyer regards this not as an item of revenue received by the *vivītādhyakṣa*, but only as a duty to be carried out by him 'maintenance of labourers in the two forests.' That appears better. — *vartanīm* : this is usually received by the *antapāla* (2.21.24). — *corarakṣaṇam* is more likely a duty laid down than 'a fee for protection from robbers '(Cp). In 4.13.9 the *vivītādhyakṣa* is made responsible for theft committed between villages. — *sārthātivāhyam* : Cp has 'charges for escorting '. — *gorakṣyam* 'a fee for protection of cattle ' (Cp). — *vyavahāram* refers to trade in the region. Breloer, however, understands judicial functions (III, 514). That is far from certain. Some of these items appear as duties laid down for the *vivītādhyakṣa* and can hardly be looked upon as sources of revenue. That may be true of all, as Meyer understands it.

2.35

The two *prakaraṇas* are found in ss. 1-7 and 8-15 respectively.

1 *caturdhā* etc. : Breloer (III, 105-6) remarks, '*janapada* was the territory of a people or tribe, then the kingdoms of Pañcāla, Matsya etc. Pāṇini refers to divisions, two-fold or four-fold of these, Pūrvapañcāla, Aparapañcāla etc. (7.3.12-3 ; 4.2.125 ; 4.3.7 ; 6.2.103) with rules for the formation of a name for a resident of such divisions. This shows that the division in four provinces is very old.' — *āyudhīya* 'supplying soldiers.' Exemption from land-revenue may seem implied. Cf. Ghoshal, *Rev. Sys.*, etc., p. 43. Breloer (III, 117-118) seems to understand 'village, the revenue of which is set apart for provisions of the army,' corresponding to provision for *śibandi* among the Marathas. — *pratikara* : 'a fixed tax' (com.). It may also mean 'produce (or work) in place of a tax.' — *gopaḥ* : the name suggests a pastoral economy. In the agricultural economy, he has become a revenue official, concerned with the keeping of records.

3 *sīmāvarodhena* : cf. 4.13.11. — *sīmnāṁ kṣetrāṇāṁ ca* : these words are difficult to construe with *maryādāraṇya-*. Meyer regards them as a marginal gloss that has got into the text. That seems possible. — *gṛhāṇāṁ ca* : supply *nibandhān kārayet*. 4 *karṣaka-* etc. is classification according to occupation over and above that according to *varṇa*. —

(fields), dry and wet fields, parks, vegetable gardens, (flower and fruit) enclosures, forests, structures, sanctuaries, temples, water-works, cremation grounds, rest-houses, sheds for drinking water, holy places, pasture lands and roads, (and) in conformity with that he should keep records of the size of boundaries, forests and roads, and of grants, sales, favours and exemptions, concerning village-boundaries and fields, and (keep records) of houses by an enumeration of tax-payers and non-tax-payers. 4 And in them, (he should record) so many are persons belonging to the four *varṇas*, so many are farmers, cowherds, traders, artisans, labourers and slaves, so many are two-footed and four-footed creatures, and so much money, labour, duty and fines arise from them. 5 And of males and females in the families, he should know the number of childern and old persons, their work, customs and the amount of their income and expenditure.

6 And in the same manner, the divisional officer chould look after a fourth part of the countryside.

7 In the head-quarters of the revenue and divisional officers, magistrates should carry out their duties and secure the recovery of dues.

8 And agents in the guise of householders, directed by the Administrator, should find out the number of fields, houses and families in those villages in which they are stationed,—fields with respect to their size and total produce, houses with respect to taxes and exemptions and families with respect to their *varṇa* and occupation. 9 And they should find out the number of individuals in them and their income and expenditure. 10 And

iaaṁ caiṣu is from Cp and is quite necessary. Cb Cs drop *eṣu*. — *daṇḍa* ' fine ' rather than ' army ' (Cs) ; the other items are revenue items. 5 *karma* is ' occupation ', while *ājīva* here seems to refer to income. Breloer (III, 138-140) understands *karma* as *arthamānakarma* ' honour and gifts ' by the state to the subjects (as in 5.3.30), *caritra* as ' private incomes ' and *ājīvavyaya* (as a single idea) ' payments by the state to those whom it is its duty to maintain (in accordance with 2.1.26).' The meaning given to *caritra* is doubtful, also that given to *karma*, in view of the latter's use in s. 8 below.

6 Breloer (III, 123) insists that the *gopa* receives his instructions and authority from the *samāhartṛ*, and not from the *sthānika*. But the latter cannot do his work without the registers prepared by the *gopas*, who must be supposed to pass them on to the *sthānika* and not to the *samāhartṛ* directly.

7 *pradeṣṭāraḥ* : see Book 4. — *balipragraham* ' recovery of dues' (one explanation in Cp, Meyer), *āyānāṁ grahaṇam* (Cj) ; ' suppression of the powerful ' (another explanation in Cp). Cb has ' 1/20th of what is due to him and moreover what is taken from robbers etc.' It seems that dues were ordinarily brought to the treasury by the assessees themselves, but the recalcitrant were dealt with by the *pradeṣṭṛ*, who saw to the recovery of the dues. Apparently the *gopa* and the *sthānika* had no executive authority.

8 This is a check on the *gopa*'s registers. — *gṛhapatikavyañjanāḥ* : cf. 1.11.9-10. Breloer (III, 145 n. 1) maintains that these are not spies, tnat *vyañjana* is not disguise, and that the activity of these persons was known and honoured. *vyañjana*, he says, shows an individual of a class, like *-viśeṣa*, *-bheda*, etc. However, 1.11 above leaves little room for doubt that these are secret agents. Breloer's view that '*gṛhapati* appears more and more like a zamindar ' (III, 152 n. 1) is hardly acceptable. — *praṇihitāḥ*, i.e., appointed for duty. — *saṁjāta* : Cb reads *saṁjñāta*, but explains it as ' yield.' — *bhoga* ' tax ' (Cb Cs). The usual sense of ' use,' i.e., possession, is possible ; but the commentators seem right. *bhoga* and *parihāra* correspond to *karada* and *akarada* in s. 3 ; cf. Ghoshal, *Rev. Sys.*, etc., p. 51. 9 *jaṅghāgra* : cf. 2.36.3. 10 *prasthitāgatānām* : Cp understands four cases,

they should find out the reason for departure and stay of those who have gone on a journey and those who have arrived (respectively), as also of men and women who are harmful, and (find out) the activity of spies.

11 In the same manner, spies in the guise of traders should find out the quantity and price of the king's goods produced in his own country, obtained from mines, water-works, forests, factories and fields. 12 And in activities concerning goods of high and low value produced in foreign lands (and) imported along a water-route or a land-route, they should find out the amount of duty, road cess, escort charges, dues at the police station and the ferry, share, food and gifts.

13 In the same manner, agents in the guise of ascetics, directed by the Administrator, should ascertain the honesty or dishonesty of farmers, cowherds and traders and of the departmental heads.

14 And assistants disguised as old thieves should find out the reasons for entry, stay and departure of thieves and brave men of the enemy, in sanctuaries, cross-roads, deserted places, wells, rivers, pools, river crossings, temple compounds, hermitages, jungles, mountains, forests and thickets.

> 15 Thus the Administrator, being ever diligent, should look after the countryside ; and those establishments (of spies) should also look after (it), also other establishments having their own (different) origin (should look after it).

prasthita, *āgata*, *prasthitāgata* and *āgataprasthita*. This is unnecessarily elaborate. — *anarthyānām* : cf. 1.7.2 above. Cb has *anarthya* of three types ' those addicted to *strī*, *dyūta*, *madya* etc., those who spend more than their income, and actors, dancers etc. ' After *strīpuruṣāṇām* we have to supply *pravāsāvāsakāraṇam*, since a construction with *cārapracāram* is hardly likely because of the other *ca* after the latter. — *cāra* may be state spies or enemy spies.

12 *karmasu ca* : these words are not quite necessary. *karma* is ' sale, purchase and other activity ' (com.). Cb Cs read a stop after *ca* supplying *parimāṇam arghaṁ ca vidyuḥ*. But *parabhūmijātānām* etc. is to be construed with *śulkavartanī-* etc. as shown by 2.16.18 where these terms recur. It would be better to drop *kamasu ca*. — *paṇyāgāra* should be understood as ' gifts ' to the king etc., as in 7.15.20 etc.

13 The *adhyakṣas* thus would appear to be under the surveillance of the *samāhartṛ*.

14 *śūnyapada* : Cb reads *śūnyabhadra* ' a deserted house (*śūnyagṛha*) and a deserted town (*śūnyabhadra*, with *bhadra* as ' a small town ').' — *śailavanagahana* : Cb Cs understand *śailagahana* and *vanagahana*. Three separate terms could well have been meant.

15 *saṁsthās tāḥ*, i.e., the agents referred to above. For *saṁsthā*, see 1.11.22. — *saṁsthāś cānyāḥ svayonayaḥ* : Cb has ' they should find out about enemy spies of the same class.' The enemy spies could hardly be understood by *saṁsthā*. Cp Cs have ' establishments of the same class should watch over these establishments (*saṁsthāḥ* as acc. plu.).' Spying over spies seems hardly intended here. The ' other *saṁsthās* ' seem to be *udāsthita* and *kāpaṭika* of 1.11 who have not been mentioned here. *svayonayaḥ* seems to imply the idea of these having their own different origin. If *sva* could refer to the *samāhartṛ*, it would yield a better idea. Breloer remarks (III, 153) ' the smallest station in each village is *saṁsthā*, then *sthāna* for *gopa*, *sthānika* and *pradeṣṭṛ*, finally *sthānīya* for *samāhartṛ*. All these words may be rendered by depot, magazine.' *saṁsthā* is hardly an open depot, in view of 1.11.22.

CHAPTER THIRTY-SIX

SECTION 56 RULES FOR THE CITY-SUPERINTENDENT

1 The City-superintendent should look after the city in the manner of the Administrator. 2 The section officer (should look after) a group of ten families or twenty or forty families. 3 He should find out the number of individuals, men and women, in that (group), according to caste, family-name and occupation, also their income and expenditure.

4 In the same manner, the divisional warden should look after a fourth part of the fortified city.

5 Officers in charge of charitable lodging-houses should allow lodging to heretical travellers after informing (the section officer), and to ascetics and Brahmins learned in the Vedas, after satisfying themselves (about their bona fides). 6 Artisans and artists should lodge persons of their own (profession) in their own places of work, and traders (should lodge) each other in their own places of work. 7 They shall report one who sells goods at an unauthorized place or time, as well as one without a title (to the goods).

8 Vintners, vendors of cooked meat, vendors of cooked rice, and prostitutes shall give lodging (only) to one thoroughly known (to them). 9 They shall report one who spends lavishly and one who does a rash deed.

10 The physician, after reporting to the section officer and the ward officer, a person who has made him treat a wound secretly and a person who does an unwholesome act, would become free, and so would the house-owner; otherwise, he shall be (held) equal in guilt. 11 And (the house-owner) shall report those who have departed and those who have arrived; otherwise he shall be held liable for any offence committed during the night. 12 On safe nights, he shall pay three *paṇas*.

2.36

1 *samāhartṛvat*, i.e., as in 2.35, not as in 2.6. — *nāgarikaḥ*: Pāṇini (*rakṣati* 4.4.33) gives *nāgarika* in the sense of *nagaraṁ rakṣati*, while *nāgaraka* is given in the sense of 'a bad person' or 'a skilled person' (*nagarāt kutsanaprāvīṇyayoḥ*, 4.2.128). The former is the only correct form here.

2 *gopaḥ*: this is an extension of the name from the country administration to that in the city; cf. 2.35.2. — Cb reads *triṁśatkulīm* in addition after *viṁśatikulīm*. — *āya-vyayau*: this is for revenue purposes.

4 *sthānikaḥ* also is an importation from the country administration; cf. 2.35.6.

5 *dharmāvasatninah* are managers appointed by owners of the charitable lodging houses; they are not state servants. — *svapratyayāś ca*, i.e., after satisfying themselves that they are really *tapasvins* etc. They are to be held responsible if they are proved wrong and if harmful persons or spies are found to have been given lodging. For *svapratyaya* cf. 3.14.34; 8.4.33. 7 *svakaraṇa* 'proof of ownership, title;' cf. 3.1.15; 3.16.17-18 etc.

8 Separate vegetarian and non-vegetarian eating houses are indicated.

10 The position of *gṛhasvāmī ca* is awkward; the words should come after *mucyeta* or *tulyadoṣaḥ syāt* as Cp seems to have read. It is possible that the words have got into the text from the margin. 12 *kṣemarātriṣu*, i.e., when no crime is reported during the night.

13 And agents operating along roads and away from roads should arrest, outside the city and inside, in temples, holy places, forests and cremation grounds, a person with a wound, one with harmful tools, one hiding behind a heavy load, one agitated, one in a long sleep, one tired after a journey or a stranger. 14 Similarly, inside the city, they should make a search in deserted places, work-shops, ale-houses, cooked-rice houses, cooked-meat houses, gambling dens and quarters of heretics.

15 And (citizens shall take) steps against (an outbreak of) fire in summer. 16 In the two middle quarters of the day, one-eighth (of a *paṇa*) is the fine for (kindling) fire. 17 Or they should do their cooking outside (the house). 18 One quarter (of a *paṇa* is the fine) for not providing five jars, also a big jar, a trough, a ladder, an axe, a winnowing-basket, a hook, a 'hair-seizer' and a skin-bag. 19 The (City-superintendent) should remove things covered with grass or matting. 20 He shall make those who live by (the use of) fire reside in one locality.

21 House-owners should live near the front doors of their own houses, not collecting together at night.

22 Collections of water-jars should be placed in thousands on roads and at cross-roads, gates and in royal precincts.

23 For the owner, not running to save the house on fire, the fine (shall be) twelve *paṇas*, six *paṇas* for a tenant.

24 In case of (houses) catching fire through negligence, the fine (shall be) fifty-four *paṇas*. 25 The incendiary should be put to death by fire.

26 For throwing dirt on the road the fine (shall be) one-eighth (of a *paṇa*), for blocking it with muddy water, one quarter. 27 On the royal highway, (the fines shall be) double.

13 *pathikotpathika* : see 2.21.17 above. — *udbhāṇḍīkṛta* : see 2.28.20 above. Cj seems to have read *udbhāṇḍam* '*tṛṇādibhārapracchāditabhāṇḍam*.'

15-16 The punctuation adopted is supported by the actual comment in Cb, though not its text. We have to supply *kuryuḥ* from the last s., with householders or citizens as the subject. Cs reads the stop after *caturbhāgayoḥ*, Meyer proposes it after *ca*. 17 *bahiḥ* 'outside' the houses. Cb understands 'outside the city.' 18 *pādaḥ pañcaghaṭīnām* to be contrued with *akaraṇe* as in Cb Cj. Cp Cs understand 'one-fourth *paṇa* fine during five *ghaṭikās* round mid-day.' Meyer agrees with this. *ghaṭī* as a measure of time is not mentioned elsewhere in the text. And for this explanation, we should have the locative, not the genitive of *ghaṭī*. — *kacagrahaṇī* 'a long pole with curved-finger-like iron hooks at the end for pulling the enemy by the hair' (Cp). Cf. 9.2.27. 19 *channa* 'things covered' seems to refer to the coverings or thatchings themselves. 20 Cj shows *agnijīvino na hyairakasthān āvāsayet*. G. Harihara Sastri understands *erakā* 'grass'. The idea of anyone likely to be settled on grass would be strange. The reading is an obvious corruption.

21 *asampātinaḥ* 'not collecting together.' The prohibiton is apparently intended to prevent conspiracies, also to ensure the presence of owners if their houses catch fire at night.

22 *rājaparigraha*, according to Cb, refers to the *kośagṛha*, *kupyagṛha*, *koṣṭhāgāra*, *paṇyagṛha* and *āyudhāgāra* ; that seems right.

23 '*vakrayiṇaḥ* is from Cb ; its correctness is shown by 3.8.24.

28 Fines for voiding faeces in a holy place, in a place for water, in a temple and in royal property are one *paṇa* rising successively by one *paṇa*, half these for passing urine. 29 If (these are) due to medicine, illness or fear, (the persons are) not to be fined.

30 For throwing the dead body of a cat, a dog, an ichneumon or a serpent inside the city, the fine shall be three *paṇas*, for (throwing) the dead body of a donkey, a camel, a mule, a horse or cattle, six *paṇas*, for a human corpse, fifty *paṇas*.

31 In case of a change of route or in case of taking the corpse out by a gate other than the gate for corpses, the lowest fine for violence (shall be imposed). 32 (The fine) for gate-keepers (allowing this, shall be) two hundred (*paṇas*). 33 For depositing and burning (a corpse) elsewhere than in a cremation ground, the fine (shall be) twelve *paṇas*.

34 The watch-drum (shall be sounded) at both ends of the night excluding a period of six *nālikās*. 35 At the sound of the drum, punishment for (moving at) the prohibited time, near the king's palace, is (a fine of) one *paṇa* and a quarter, in the first and the last watches, double (that) in the middle watch, four times (that) inside (the palace-grounds.)

36 He should question a (person) arrested in a suspicious place or with a suspicious mark or because of a previous offence. 37 For approaching royal property and for scaling the city's fortifications, the middle fine for violence (shall be imposed). 38 (Those moving at night) on account of a woman in delivery, for a doctor, on account of a death, with a lamp, in a carriage, at the City-superintendent's drum, for a show or on account of a fire, and those moving with sealed passports are not to be arrested.

28 Cb Cs include *rājamārge* here from the last s. and have '1 *paṇa* on *rājamārga*, 2 in a *puṇyasthāna* and so on.' This seems hardly right. Only four places are intended.

33 *nyāse* seems to refer to burial rather than merely leaving the corpse there.

34 *viṣaṇṇālikam ubhayatorātram*, i.e., six *nālikās* after sunset and six *nālikās* before sunrise. The latter expression is adverbial; the former may also be treated as adverbial or as an adjective to *yāmatūryam*. Cj reads *ṣaṇṇālikam*. Meyer proposes *dviṣaṇṇālikam* and tr. 'the closing signal instrument (*yāmatūrya*) fixes twice six *nālikās* reckoned from midnight on both sides.' For this *dvi* is not necessary when *ubhayato* is there, and *rātra* can hardly refer to *madhyarātra*. 35 *akṣaṇa*: '*kṣaṇaḥ anujñātaḥ kālaḥ, akṣaṇo niṣiddhaḥ*' (Cp); prohibited period,' i.e., movement during the prohibited period; cf. 3.12.46; 4.9.26. Cj has *rakṣaṇa* for *akṣaṇa-*. *tāḍanam* '*daṇḍaḥ*' (Cp). — *prathama-* etc.: it is clear that three *yāmas* (*prathama*, *madhyama* and *paścima*) are thought of between the two beats of the drum; in other words the *yāma* here is a period of 6 *nālikās* or 2 hours 24 minutes. Cp Cs, understanding the usual *yāma* of 3 hours, have 'in what remains of the 1st and last watches' and *madhyama*, i.e., 'the 2nd and 3rd watches.' There is hardly any justification for supplying *śeṣa* or understanding two watches as constituting the *madhyamayāma*. Meyer, who has a period of 12 *nālikās* for restricted movement, has *prathama yāma* as the 1st *nālikā*, *paścima* as the 12th *nālikā* and *madhyama yāma* as the intervening 10 *nālikās*. This is clearly unlikely. — *antaḥ* is from Cb for *bahiḥ*. The latter as 'outside the city' could hardly be the *nāgarika*'s concern, and is by itself unlikely.

36 *pūrvāpadāne*: *apadāna* is used in the sense of 'offence'; cf. 3.12.35; 4.5.11 etc.

38 *-pradīpayāna-* as two separate items is better as in Cb. Cp does not show *-yāna-*. — *nāgarika-tūrya* apparently sounded to call attention to some danger or threat. — *mudrā* apparently issued by the *nāgarika* or his subordinates.

39 During nights of (unrestricted) movements, those disguised in dress or in a dress contrary (to their sex), wandering monks, and men with sticks and weapons in hand, shall be punished in accordance with their offence.

40 For guards preventing what ought not to be prevented and not preventing what ought to be prevented, the fine (shall be) double that for (movement during) the forbidden watches. 41 For (guards) misbehaving with a woman who is a slave, the lowest fine for violence (shall be imposed), with one not a slave, the middle fine, with one in the exclusive keeping (of some one), the highest, with a woman from a respectable family (the punishment shall be) death.

42 For (a guard) not reporting to the City-superintendent an offence committed during the night whether by the animate or the inanimate, the punishment shall be in conformity with the offence, also in case of negligence.

43 Constant inspection of places supplying water, roads, water-courses, covered paths, ramparts, parapets (and other) fortifications, and the guarding of what is lost, forgotten or has run away (are the duties of the Superintendent).

44 And in the prison house, (there should be) a release of children, old persons, the sick and the helpless on the day of the (king's) birth-constellation and on full moon days. 45 Persons of a pious disposition or persons bound by an agreement may give a ransom for the offence.

39 *pravrajitāḥ*: apparently these are suspected enemy spies in disguise. Cp seems to understand exiles, *ājñayā niṣkrāntāḥ*. — *doṣataḥ*: the *doṣa* may be *pracchannaveṣatva* etc. itself, or theft etc. that might be committed during the night.

40 *akṣaṇadviguṇaḥ*, i.e., 2 *paṇas* and a half. Cj has *rakṣaṇa-* as before. 41 *adāsīm*, i.e., 'a courtesan' (Cs).

42 *aśaṁsataḥ*: we should supply *rakṣiṇaḥ* and understand *nāgarikasya* in the sense of the dative. Cp supplies *nagaravāsijanasya*, while Cs understands *nāgarika* as 'citizen.' Meyer has 'if the *nāgarika* does not report,' apparently, to the king. The guard is more likely in view of *pramādasthāne*.

43 *bhrama* etc.: cf. 2.4.2.

44 *jātanakṣatra-* etc.: the day on which the moon is in the *nakṣatra* in which it was at the time of the king's birth. There would be one such day in each month. With the *paurṇamāsī*, there would be two days for jail clearance every month. The expression can hardly mean 'on the full moon day when the moon (or sun) is in the constellation of birth.' There would be only one such day in a year. 45 *puṇyaśīlāḥ* those who are charitably disposed. — *samayānubaddhāḥ* 'bound (with the prisoner) by an agreement' to be recompensed for the ransom they pay now. It is possible to understand also 'who were bound to the prisoner to pay ransom for him.' — *doṣaniṣkrayam* 'a ransom in accordance with the crime' for which they are in prison. The commentators explain the s.: 'Holy persons inadvertently committing an offence should pay a ransom after binding themselves for future conduct (*samayānubaddhāḥ*); if they do not do this (*vā*), they must remain in prison.' This is extremly unlikely. — For *niṣkraya* in place of corporal punishment, see Chapter 4.10. That is available to anyone, not to *puṇyaśīla* or *samayānubaddha* persons only. Ransom in place of imprisonment is mentioned only here. In fact, imprisonment is scarcely prescribed anywhere in the text.

46 Every day or every five days, he should clear out those in prison by (getting them to do) work, by (inflicting) corporal punishment or by (receiving) the favour of cash (in ransom).

47 On the occasion of the acquisition of a new territory, on the occasion of the installation of the crown prince or on the occasion of the birth of a son (to the king), a release of (all in) the prison is ordained.

Herewith ends the Second Book of the Arthaśāstra of Kauṭilya,
'THE ACTIVITY OF THE HEADS OF DEPARTMENTS'

46 *viśodhayet* 'should clear out,' i.e., set free. Meyer compares *cāragasohaṇa* in Jain literature.

BOOK THREE

CONCERNING JUDGES

CHAPTER ONE

SECTION 57 DETERMINATION OF (VALID AND INVALID) TRANSACTIONS

SECTION 58 FILING OF LAW-SUITS

1 Three judges, (all) three (of the rank of) ministers, should try cases arising out of transactions at frontier posts, in the *saṁgrahaṇas*, *droṇamukhas* and *sthānīyas*.

2 They should declare as invalid transactions concluded in absence, inside a house, at night-time, in a forest, by fraud or in secret. 3 For one who concludes (such a transaction) or induces its conclusion, the lowest fine for violence (shall be the punishment). 4 The fines shall be half for witnesses, each one of them. 5 For trustworthy persons, however, (there shall be only) annulment of the object.

The Third Book, which lays down the duties of judges, gives us, in effect, the entire law according to Kauṭilya. — *dharmastha* 'a judge' has reference to the enforcement of law (*dharma*). This name is generally unknown to the Smṛtis; only the *Manusmṛti* in 8.87 makes a casual reference to it.

3.1

The two *prakaraṇas* in this Chapter extend from ss. 1-16 and 17-47 respectively. — *vyavahāra* is primarily a transaction between two or more parties, which may form the basis of a suit in a court of law. Some transactions are invalid by their very nature. *sthāpanā* refers to a consideration of their admissibility in the court. — *vivādapada* is a suit concerning a matter in dispute. It has no reference to the 'title of law.' The section deals with the filing of a suit and the procedure to be followed thereafter.

1 *trayo 'mātyāḥ* : it is best to regard these as parenthetical as in Meyer, the idea being that the three judges (who are to sit in each court) should possess the qualifications of an *amātya* as mentioned in 1.9.1-2. Cj has '*trayaḥ* is repeated to show that there are to be three is every place.' Cb understands three ministers in addition to three judges. Cs renders *amātya* by 'sitting together,' i.e., constituting a bench. N. N. Law (*Studies*, p. 118 and n.) supplies a *vā* 'three persons grounded in the *śāstra* or three ministers.' This is hardly likely. — *janapadasaṁdhi*, i.e., frontier towns and forts. For *saṁgrahaṇa* etc., see 2.1.4. — *vyāvahārikān arthān* : this shows that the judges are to deal with cases involving transactions between two parties. These are, therefore, all cases concerning civil law. There is no reference to different grades among judges in small and large towns. Nor is there a reference to possible differences of opinion among the three judges or to appeals from one court to another.

2 *tirohita*, i.e., in which a party to the transaction is absent or the object involved in it is not there at the time. — *kṛtān* is to be construed with *antarāgāra* onwards. — *pratiṣedhayeyuḥ*, i.e., no suit can be admitted on the basis of such a transaction. 5 *śraddheya* apparently refers to those who are parties to such a transaction in good faith, being unaware that they are invalid. — *dravyavyapanayaḥ*, i.e., the transaction is declared null and void ; no fine is, however, imposed in this case.

6 Contracting a debt with a pledge in its absence or transactions in absence that are accepted as free from blame shall succeed.

7 Those concluded inside a house, concerning inheritance, things handed over, deposits and marriage, (or) by women who do not stir out (of their homes), or by sick persons who are not unsound in mind, shall succeed.

8 Those concluded at night, concerning forcible seizure, trespass with criminal intent, strife, marriage and a royal order, (or) by persons carrying on their business in the fore-part of the night, shall succeed.

9 Those concluded in the forest, by persons moving in forests, from amongst caravans, herds, hermitages, hunters and wandering minstrels, shall succeed.

10 And among persons earning a secret livelihood, those fraudulently made shall succeed.

11 And in case of secret association, those concluded in secret shall succeed.

12 (Transactions) other than these shall not succeed, also those concluded by dependents, (such as) by a son dependent on the father, by a father dependent on the son, by a brother excluded from the family, by a younger son whose share has not been allotted to him, by a woman dependent on her husband or son, by a slave or a person kept as a pledge, by a minor or a person

6 *parokṣeṇa* etc. 'contracting a debt by mortgaging one's property such as a house or a field when the property is not seen at the time' (Cb Cj). For this *sādhikarṇagrahaṇam* would have been better. Meyer has 'contracting a debt in addition to one already contracted (*adhika ṛṇa*),' which is less likely. — *avaktavyakarāḥ* 'accepted by the people as valid, e.g., where people say that such and such a property may be dealt with by such and such a person even in the absence of the owner' (Cb Cs). Meyer has 'where the contracting parties need not be named'; Breloer (KSt, II, 133) has 'where through witnesses certainty is reached (that the agreement was intended by the absent party). Russ. has 'which do not deserve consideration, i.e., petty.'

7 For *nikṣepa*, see 3.12.33 ff., for *upanidhi*, 3.12.1 ff. — *aniṣkāsinīnām*: see 2.23.12 above. — *amūḍhasaṁjña* would seem to mean 'not of unsound mind' rather than 'who have not lost consciousness.'

8 *anupraveśa*: Cb has 'entering the house and stealing'; trespass with criminal intent seems meant; cf. 3.19.71. Meyer compares Vasiṣṭha, 19.38 and Āpastamba, 2.10.26.18. —Cj, reading *-vicāra-* for *-vivāha-*, explains '*viruddhaś cāro vicāraḥ saṁgrahaṇam*,' which is doubtful. — *rājaniyoga*: Cb Cs restrict this to measures for guarding the city, at the king's order. There seems to be no reason for such a restriction. —*pūrvarātra-* etc., i.e., prostitutes vintners, innkeepers etc.

9 *-madhyeṣu araṇyacarāṇām*, i.e., when any of these are at the time moving through the forest or staying in it.

10 *gūḍhājīviṣu*: cf. 4.4 for such persons. Curiously, that Chapter includes corrupt judges too in this category.

11 *mithaḥsamavāya*: Cb Cs restrict this to the Gāndharva marriage. Any secret association would seem meant, its secrecy being regarded as necessary and legal.

12 *pitrā putravatā*, i.e., when the father has retired and the son is looking after the affairs. — *niṣkula*, i.e., separated from the family. Cj reads *niṣkalena*, explaining it by 'impotent'; *kalam iti bījaparyāyaḥ*. — A minor is one under 16 (cf. 3.3.1) and *atītavyavahāra* is 'over seventy' (Cb Cs). — *abhiśasta*: one 'accused' of some offence by another

grown too old for doing any business, and by a person accused of a crime, by a wandering monk, by a cripple or by one overcome by a calamity,—excepting by those to whom authority for the transaction has been given. 13 Even among such, transactions concluded by a person in rage, a person in distress, an intoxicated person, an insane person or a person in another's power, shall not succeed. 14 For those who conclude, who induce the conclusion of and who bear witness to (such transactions), the fines (shall be) as prescribed for each one separately.

15 All transactions, however, in each respective group, concluded with full title at the proper place and time, with all formalities duly observed, with admissible evidence, with the appearance, marks, quantity and qualities duly noted, shall succeed. 16 And in their case, the last document shall be authoritative, except in the case of direction and pledge.

Thus ends the determination of (valid and invalid) transactions.

17 After writing down the year, the season, the month, the fortnight, the day, the office, the place, the debt, and the country, village, caste, family, name and occupation of the plaintiff and the defendant, who have given adequate sureties, the (clerk) shall put down the questions (with answers) to the plaintiff and the defendant, in due order of the subject-matter. 18 And he shall look into them when put down.

person. Cf. 4.8.1,7. — *vyasanin* is hardly 'addicted to vice' (Cb Cs); cf. s. 34 below. 13 *tatrāpi* seems to refer to all valid transactions, not to *nisṛṣṭavyavahāras* only as in Cs. — *avagṛhīta* 'suppressed, held in power'; cf. 5.6.47. Cs explains it as 'a convicted person,' Meyer as 'possessed by a spirit' or 'become abnormal in some way,' corresponding to *aprakṛtiṁ gataḥ* of Nārada, 1.40.

15 *varge*, i.e., community, caste (Cb Cj Cs); an economic group, *karṣaka*, *vaidehaka* etc. may also be thought of. — *svakaraṇa* : cf. 2.36.7; 3.16.17,18. — *sampūrṇācārāḥ* : *ācāra* seems to refer to the customary formalities to be observed when entering into a transaction. — *deśa* 'witnesses' (Cb Cj Cs). In s. 19 below, *deśa* seems distinguished from *sākṣin*. It may be understood as evidence in general. Meyer renders it by 'a point' in a statement. — *rūpalakṣaṇa-* etc. refers to the object concerning which the transaction takes place. — Yāj., 2.31-32, appear to be a metrical summary of this passage; so Nārada, 1.40-41 and Intro. 1.43. 16 *karaṇa* seems to refer to evidence or proof in general (cf. 4.8.13), but here a document may well be thought of. — *ādeśa* : see 3.12.18. It means 'a direction' or instruction to a person to take a thing entrusted to him to another person. In view of that, 'receiving a gift or purchase' (Cb Cs) seems little likely. They seem to be influenced by Yāj., 2.23, and Nārada, 1.97. But 'purchase' at least can hardly be on the same footing as a pledge in this connection.

17 *karaṇa* here can hardly refer to 'evidence,' so early in the list. Cs refers it to 'half a *tithi* called *bava* etc.' That is uncertain. Cb does not explain, only mentions *dharmakaraṇa* and *arthakaraṇa*. Probably something like 'department, office' is to be understood. Jayaswal's 'cause of action' (*Manu and Yāj.*, p. 121) is doubtful in view of the specific mention of *ṛṇam*. — *adhikaraṇam* : the place where the court is situated, then the court itself. Jayaswal has 'statement of the case' (*loc. cit.*). — *ṛṇam* : this shows that the law of procedure is based on the law of debts, the prime cause of action. — It is not certain if *avedaka* or *āvedaka* is to be understood in the sense of 'the defendant.' — For *avastha* 'surety.' cf. 2.8.29; 3.18.11. The surety is for ensuring payment of the fine. 18 *avekṣeta* : though the writing down is done by the *lekhaka* (cf. 4.9.17), and this examination may be supposed to be by the judge, that is not made quite clear. Of course, the subject for *avekṣeta* may also be *lekhakaḥ* understood.

19 A (party to a suit) who gives up the dispute as put down and changes to another dispute, does not corroborate the first statement by a subsequent matter, remains (silent) after challenging an unchallengeable statement of the other (party), after making an affirmation does not indicate the evidence when asked to do so, indicates weak evidence or false evidence, produces evidence other than that indicated, when evidence is produced denies a statement in the matter saying 'it is not so', does not accept what is confirmed by witnesses, talks secretly with witnesses in a place where no conversation is allowed,—these are reasons for loss of suit.

20 The fine for loss of suit is one-fifth the amount (in dispute). 21 The fine for one who voluntarily admits is one-tenth.

22 Wages for the servant shall be one-eighth part (of a *paṇa*). 23 Food on the way (will be) according to the prices (at the time). 24 The defeated party shall pay both these.

25 The accused shall not file a counter-complaint, except in cases of strife, forcible seizure and association in caravans. 26 And there shall be no suit against the accused (by another party).

27 If the plaintiff, to whom a reply has been given (by the defendant), does not counter-reply on the same day, he shall lose the suit. 28 For, it is the plaintiff, who has decided (beforehand) what is to be done, not the defen-

19 *vādam* is preferred to *pādam*, as in the actual comment in Cb. It is also supported by Nārada Intro, 2.24 (*pūrvavādam parityajya* and *vādasaṁkramaṇād*). And as Meyer points out, *pāda* does not mean 'a title of law.' Nor can *padam* be read as in Cj, for *pada* in *vivādapada* does not refer to the 18 titles of law. — *deśam* : see s. 16 above. Breloer (II,155) understands 'place' in the usual sense. — *hīnadeśam* 'a smaller number of witnesses than those cited' (Cs). — *adeśam* 'those unfit to be witnesses, such as kinsmen etc.' (Cb Cs). — *nirdiṣṭād deśād* is from Cb and is necessary. Breloer, however, prefers *nirdiṣṭoddeśād*, understanding *uddeśa* as 'a leading statement at the commencement of a discussion, what is to be proved' as in 15.1.15-16 (II, 155). This is extremely doubtful. *anyaṁ deśam* that follows makes this reading quite unlikely. — *arthavacanam* : Cb Cs read *arthavacane* as adjective to *deśe* 'when he has deposed truthfully.' Breloer (II, 155) understands it in the sense of 'an official account'. — *parokta* 'a person against whom a decision is given (*parā-ukta*).' Manu, 8.53-57, are clearly based on this passage.

20 *pañcabandhaḥ* cannot be 'five times' as Meyer translates. For 'so many times' we have *-guṇa* ; cf. *bandhacaturguṇaḥ*, 3.11.7. 21 *svayaṁvādin* : this refers to one who voluntarily admits what is urged against him. This is principally to be understood of the defendant. Cf. s. 46 below. Cb implies that the admission is made before the witnesses have deposed, which seems reasonable. Cs has 'who has filed a suit without witnesses,' Meyer 'who has offered to make a false deposition as a witness,' Breloer 'the same as *tavāhaṁvādin*, i.e., the unfree man' (III, 247 n. 6). None of these explanations seems intended.

22 *puruṣa* as 'judge' (Cb) is quite unlikely. The court servant who summons witnesses etc. is clearly to be understood. 23 *pathibhaktam* is in the nature of a travelling allowance. — *argha-* is definitely preferable to *artha-*. With the latter, Meyer has 'according to the peculiarity of the case.'

25 *sārthasamavāyebhyaḥ* : Meyer proposes *mithaḥsamavāyebhyaḥ*. That is quite unnecessary. Association between members of a caravan can conceivably lead to complaints and counter-complaints. 26 *abhiyogaḥ*, apparently, by a third party. Breloer (II, 140), however, understands the same party, the idea being that a suit about a matter can only be filed once.

dant. 29 If the latter does not reply, a period of three days or seven (may be allowed). 30 After that, the (judge) shall impose a fine of three *paṇas* minimum and twelve *paṇas* maximum. 31 After three fortnights, if he does not reply, the (judge) shall impose the fine for loss of suit and indemnity the plaintiff from goods belonging to him, excepting the tools of his profession. 32 He shall impose the same (pen lty) on the defendant who absconds. 33 In the case of the plaintiff, there shall be loss of suit the moment he absconds.

34 The statement of a witness who dies or suffers from a misfortune is without value.

35 The (successful) plaintiff may, after paying the fine, make (a poor defendant) work (for him). 36 Or, the (defendant) may keep a pledge, if he so desires. 37 Or, he may indemnify him by work, guarded by charms destructive of evil spirits, with the exception of a Brahmin.

> 38 When all laws are perishing, the king here is the promulgator of laws, by virtue of his guarding the right conduct of the world consisting of the four *varṇas* and four *āśramas*.

29 Three days or seven would depend on the circumstances of the case. Nārada Intro., 2.3, has a similar rule. 31 *pratipādayet* 'make him receive,' i.e., pay him. — For the rule, cf. Manu, 8.58, Yāj., 2.12, Nārad Intro., 1.44-45. 32 Cf. Manu, 8.55, Yāj., 2.16.

34 The translation follows Meyer, with his proposed *-vacanam asāram* though *sākṣiṇaḥ* outside the compound would have been still better. The idea is, if a witness, after giving evidence, dies or suffers some great misfortune, he is presumed to have given false evidence. Cf. Manu, 8.108. In the Nachtrag, Meyer proposes *sākṣivacanāt* with a stop after it, construing *asāram* with the next s. 'a party becomes *parokta* on the (false) testimony of a witness who dies or is in calamity. If the accused is poor (*asāra*) the complainant shall pay the fine etc.' Even for this *sākṣiṇaḥ* outside the compound is necessary. That, however, is Cj's construction. Its explanation of s. 34 is 'if after an accusation is made, the complainant dies or disappears, (truth should be ascertained and punishment meted out) according to the testimony of witnesses.' A number of things have to be supplied in this explanation. Cb Cs, reading *sākṣivacanāḥ sāram*, explain 'the sons etc. of a deceased or a suffering party shall be entitled to receive or liable to pay the amount in dispute (*sāram*) on producing witnesses (*sākṣivacanāḥ*).' It is extremely doubtful if heirs could be so brought in without any prior mention. And why should a *vyasanin* not receive the amount himself? The s. may also be understood as 'if a party to a suit dies or suffers a misfortune, the testimony of his witnesses has no value.' But this is colourless.

35 *daṇḍaṁ dattvā*: the state must receive the *daṇḍa*, if need be from the successful party. 36 *sa* refers to *abhiyukta*, hardly to *abhiyoktā*. 37 *rakṣoghnarakṣitam*: perhaps *abhiyoktāram* is to be supplied, hardly *ādhim*. — *pratipādayet*: the subject may be *dharmasthaḥ* as in s. 31, though *abhiyuktaḥ* is also possible. — *anyatra brāhmaṇāt* is odd, for the defendant, of whom alone the *brāhmaṇatva* can be thought of, is not specifically referred to in the s. It is quite possible that the whole s. is a marginal gloss that has intruded into the text. It is unnecessary in view of s. 35. — *iti* read in the mss. in such places is often derived from some commentary. At any rate, a pious Kṣatriya cannot be understood on its strength as is done in Cs.

38 *ayam*: *asya* as going with *lokasya* would be better. There is little point in *ayaṁ rājā*. — *naśyatāṁ sarvadharmāṇām* is a case of genitive absolute. Meyer objects that this construction is unknown to this text and suggests *nāśena* or *nāśanāt* and *sarvādharmāṇām*, 'by destroying all impieties.' This is unnecessary. Cb Cs construe the genitives with *pravartakaḥ*. — *rājā dharmapravartakaḥ*: M Cb Cs read *rājadharmaḥ pravartakaḥ*. But a *dharma* as a *pravartaka* of *dharma* is not a happy idea. And *ācārarakṣaṇa* is more likely of *rājā* than of *rājadharma*. The idea seems to be, because the king gives protection, he can lay down law when the traditional laws have become inoperative. The commentators' idea seems to be that a king can revive laws that are languishing, by protecting the right conduct of subjects. That also is possible.

39 A matter in dispute has four feet, law, transaction, custom and the royal edict; (among them) the later one supersedes the earlier one.

40 Of them, law is based on truth, a transaction, however, on witnesses, customs on the commonly held view of men, while the command of kings is the royal edict.

41 (Carrying out) his own duty by the king, who protects the subjects accroding to law, leads to heaven; of one who does not protect or who inflicts an unjust punishment, (the condition) is the reverse of this.

42 For, it is punishment alone that guards this world and the other, when it is evenly meted out by the king to his son and his enemy, according to the offence.

43 For, a king, giving decisions in accordance with law, transaction, settled custom and edict as the fourth, would conquer the earth up to its four ends.

44 He shall decide, with the help of law, a matter in which a settled custom or a matter based on a transaction contradicts the science of law.

39 Compare the paraphrase in Bṛhaspati: *dharmeṇa vyavahāreṇa caritreṇa nṛpājñayā catuṣprakāro 'bhihitaḥ saṁdigdhe 'rthe vinirṇayaḥ.* *vyavahāra* seems to mean only 'a transaction' throughout. We may also think of 'judicial process.' — *paścimaḥ pūrvabādhakaḥ*: this seems to mean that the later one in the list supersedes the earlier one. Thus Cj. According to Cb Cs, only the last supersedes the first three. Cf., however, Nārada Intro., 1.10, *uttaraḥ pūrvabādhakaḥ.* 40 *satya* seems to refer to truth in the sense of eternal truth, that is supposed to be the basis of *dharma*. Breloer (II, 49-53) thinks that we should read *smṛtyāṁ sthito* or *smṛtisthito* 'based on tradition.' Though for the sake of uniformity in the meaning of *dharma* in these verses and in 43-44, this is what should be understood by *dharma*, *satye sthitaḥ* is quite likely and is supported by Nārada Intro., 1.11. — *saṁgrahe*, i.e., in the view commonly accepted by men. Cb has 'unanimity among witnesses.'

41-42 These stanzas are out of place and are clearly derived from a different source. They belong to 1.4 above.

43 *anuśāsad*: cf. *anuśiṣṭa*, 4.9.15. — *dharmeṇa*: by this *dharmaśāsrtra* law is clearly to be understood, as shown by s. 44. — *saṁsthayā*: this is probably the same as *caritra* above, as in Cj. Cb has '*lokācāra*.' — *nyāyena*: this refers to *rājaśāsana*. Meyer relates the word to *nīti* or *naya* in the sense of 'a royal measure.' It is possible that the difference in terminology stems from a difference in sources.

44 Though with the reading *saṁsthā yā*, as proposed by Meyer, we get two relative pronouns in the same clause, that appears preferable to *saṁsthayā*. It may be that *saṁsthā vā* should be read. The idea is, when *saṁsthā* or *vyavahāra* is in conflict with *dharma*, the latter prevails. With *saṁsthayā* as the reading there would be a reference to a conflict between *saṁsthā* and *vyavahāra* without a solution being offered for it. This stanza clearly contradicts s. 39, if the terms in the two places are regarded as identical, unless *paścimaḥ pūrvabādhakaḥ* is understood as in Cb. — The use of the word *śāstra* in connection with *vyavahāra* is strange. Cb seems to understand *vyāvahārika śāstra* as *rājavacana*. That is not very likely. Cs has 'royal edict (*śāstra*) or the evidence of witnesses (*vyāvahārika*).' This is doubtful.

45 Where (a text of) the science may be in conflict with any edict in a matter of law, there the edict shall prevail; for, there the written text loses its validity.

46 A (distinctly) seen offence, a voluntary admission, straightforwardness in questions (and answers) to one's own and the opposite party, reasoning, and oath lead to a decision in a case.

47 In case of contradiction between an earlier and a later statement, in case of the blameworthiness of witnesses and in case of escape from the custody of the prison-guard, loss of suit shall be decreed.

CHAPTER TWO

SECTION 59 CONCERNING MARRIAGE

(*i*) The Law of Marriage; (*ii*) Rules Concerning Woman's Property; (*iii*) Concerning Supersession (of a Wife) by a Second Marriage

1 (All) transacrions begin with marriage.

2 Making a gift of the daughter, after adorning her (with ornaments) is the Brāhma form of marriage. 3. The joint peformance of sacred duties

45 *dharme nyāyena* of M seems preferable to *dharmanyāyena*, though *dharma* has then to be understood as 'a matter of law.' *dharmanyāya* is confusing. Cb understands *dharma* and *nyāya* as two separate things. Cs has 'custom which is just in every way.' Breloer (II, 131) explains 'a reflection or judgment (*nyāya*) which follows from the same holy law.' In that case, the conflict between the *śāstra* and this *nyāya* would hardly arise. — *tatra pāṭho hi naśyati*: Breloer (II, 131) translates 'for the text underlies the change.' He adds that the judge is thus given the opportunity to build up new legal sentences outside of and even contrary to the holy law.

46 *dṛṣṭadoṣaḥ*: in view of the predicate *arthasādhakaḥ*, this should be understood as a Karmadhāraya rather than as a Bahuvrīhi. — *svapakṣa-* etc. is to be construed with *anuyogārjavam* in the second half, as in Cb Cs. Meyer construes it with *svayaṁvādaḥ*, making *dṛṣṭadoṣaḥ* the predicate in the first half 'the defect of a voluntary statement by one or the other party is seen above (in s. 21 ?).' This is hardly possible. Breloer proposes (II, 132 n. 4) *svayaṁvādasvapakṣa-* etc. as one 'when the guilt is brought to light through his own admission or through the evidence of the other party.' This also seems doubtful.

47 *sākṣivaktavyakāraṇe*: *vaktavya* seems used for *vaktavyatva*. 3.11.28-9 enumerate persons ineligible as witnesses. Breloer's 'when there are witnesses whom the judge has brought himself' (II, 132) is hardly possible. — *cāra* is obviously the jailor or prison-guard ; cf. *cāraka* 4.9.22. It may also refer to the secret agent of the court, who has traced the party and is bringing him to the court. For *niṣpāta* 'running away' cf. s. 33 above. Breloer's 'by going over (*niṣpāte*) by means of secret police' is not quite clear. — The *kārikās* have clearly a miscellaneous origin.

3.2

The 59th *prakaraṇa* is spread over three Chapters, 3.2-4, and contains a number of sub-sections. The three sub-sections in this chapter are to be found in ss. 1-13, 14-37 and 38-48 respectively. — Cb Cs quote a mnemonic verse according to which Manu begins with the law of debts, Uśanas with property, Bṛhaspati with deposits and Kauṭilya with marriage. Meyer has shown very clearly how Kauṭilya's is the most rational arrangement of the topics of law.

1 *vyavahāra* 'dealing', i.e., in effect, civil life.

is the Prājāpatya. 4 On receiving a pair to cattle (from the bride-groom) it is the Ārṣa. 5 By making a gift (of the daughter) to the officiating priest inside a sacrificial altar, it is the Daiva. 6 By a secret association (between lovers) it is the Gāndharva. 7 On receiving a dowry, it is the Āsura. 8 By forcible seizure (of a maiden), it is the Rākṣasa. 9 By the seizure of a sleeping or intoxicated (maiden), it is the Paiśāca.

10 The first four are lawful with the sanction of the father, the remaining with the sanction of the father and the mother. 11 For, those two receive the dowry of the daughter, or one of them in the absence of the other. 12 The woman shall receive the second dowry.

13 In the case of all (forms of marriage), giving pleasure (to the bride by means of gifts) is not forbidden.

Thus ends the law of marriage.

14 Maintenance and ornaments constitute woman's property. 15 Maintenance is an endowment of a maximum of two thousand (*paṇas*); as to ornaments, there is no limit.

16 It is not an offence for the wife to use that for the maintenance of her sons and daughters-in-law or if no provision is made when (the husband is) away on a journey, (or) for the husband (to use it) for taking steps against

3 ' The *mantra* containing the admonition to practise *dharma* together is recited in the Prājāpatya ' (Cb). — The Smṛtis have closely parallel definitions of these forms of marriage.

10 *pitṛpramāṇāḥ* : apparently the will or consent of the mother is unnecessary. — *dharmyāḥ* conveys the idea of not only ' lawful ', but also ' holy, pious '. *dharmiṣṭha* or *dharmavivāha* conveys the same idea. — *mātāpitṛpramāṇāḥ* : the consent is obtained evidently after the event in three of these four cases. 11 *śulkaharau* : evidently *śulka* was received when consent was given in these cases. 12 *dvitīyaṁ śulkam* : Cb paraphrases by ' *prītidāna* ' ; so Cs understands gifts given to the bride at the time of marriage. It is possible that the second dowry may be that received when the woman happens to marry again, after the first husband's death.

13 *sarveṣām*, i.e., ' by all relations of the bridegroom and others ' (Cb Cs) ; Cb in fact appears to regard this *prītyāropaṇa* as the second dowry. *sarveṣām*, however, may refer to forms of marriage, in all of which gifts are allowed, though not *śulka*. And it is possible that this *prītyāropaṇa*, e.g., in a Brāhma marriage, is the *dvitīya* or secondary *śukla*. — It is proposed to read *iti vivāhadharmaḥ* here and not after s. 18 as in the mss. They are clearly misplaced there.

14 *ābandhyam* : this form from Cb is more likely (from *bandh* ' to bind '). The lexicons show the forms *ābaddha* and *ābandha*. 15 *paradvisāhasrā* : we expect *dvisahasraparā* for the sense ' a maximum of two thousand *paṇas* '. — *sthāpyā* is another name for *vṛtti* (cf. s. 19 and 3.3.12), ' what is set apart, an endowment.'.

16 *ātma-* to be construed with *putra* and *snuṣā*. Her own case is covered by the next expression. — *bhaya* ' danger ' as a separate item is better. — It is proposed to read a stop after *prajātayoḥ* (supplying *bhoktum adoṣaḥ*). Cb Cs regard *saṁbhūya. . . . nānuyuñjīta* as constituting a single sentence and restrict the rule to pious marriages and a three-year use only. The presence of both *vā* and *ca* in the same clause would be strange. And the genitive of *dampatyoḥ* implies construction with *bhoktum adoṣaḥ* like that of *patyuḥ* in the preceding clause. Meyer has ' when the couple has put it together as common property, when they have begotten a son and a daughter and when it is used as common property for three years. '. This is reading too much in the words. Kane (HD, III, 786) seems to have

robbers, diseases, famine (and other) dangers and for religious acts, or for the couple (to use it) jointly when they have begotten a son and a daughter. 17 And if it has been used for three years, the (wife) shall not question, in the case of the pious marriages. 18 If used in the Gāndharva and Āsura marriages, the (husband) shall be made to return both with interest, if used in the Rākṣasa and Paiśāca marriages, he shall pay (the penalty for) theft.

19 When the husband is dead, the (widow), if desirous of leading a life of piety, shall forthwith receive the endowment and oranments and the remainder of the dowry. 20 If, after receiving (these), she marries again, she shall be made to return both with interest. 21 If, however, she is desirous of having a family, she shall receive, at the time of remarriage, what was given to her by her father-in-law and her (late) husband. 22 We shall explain the time for remarriage in 'Long absence from home.' 23 If she remarries against the wishes of her father-in-law, she shall forfeit what was given her by her father-in-law and her (late) husband.

24 If the (widow) is snatched away from the protection of her kinsmen, the kinsmen (by the new marriage) shall return (her woman's property of the first marriage) as it may have been received (by her). 25 If she has approached (for remarriage) in a legitimate manner, the acceptor shall protect her woman's property (of the first marriage).

26 A (widow) remarrying shall forfeit what was given by her (late) husband. 27 She shall use it if desirous of a pious life. 28 If a (widow) who has sons marries again, she shall forfeit her woman's property. 29 The

read *aprajātayoḥ* 'so also if there be no children of the marriage and the husband expends *strīdhana* without objection by the wife, then also no complaint would be entertained.' 17 *trivarṣopabhuktam*, i.e., if the husband has used it for three years without complaint by the wife. The idea that no complaint shall be entertained after a lapse of three years after it was spent is less likely. 18 *ubhayam*, i.e., *vṛtti* and *ābandhya*, hardly *śulka* and *strīdhana*. *savṛddhikaṁ dāpyeta*, i.e., it is treated as a loan. — *steyaṁ dadyāt*, i.e., he has no right at all to its use.

19 *sthāpyābharaṇam* is necessary as shown by 3.3.12; 3.4.16 and s. 15 above. — *śulkaśeṣam* : Cs has 'what is left after joint use by the couple.' But the *śulka* goes to the bride's parents (s. 11). It may be that the parents who receive the *śulka* hold it in trust for the daughter. Meyer understands payment of *śulka* in instalments, the unpaid instalments going to the wife and not her parents. This seems supported by 3.4.15,33. 21 *kuṭumba-kāmā* : she desires a son who would belong to her late husband's family. The husband's full brother is to be her first preference for remarriage (3.4.38). 22 *dīrghapravāse*, i.e., in the subsection in 3.4.37-42.

24 The first *jñāti-* refers to the kinsmen of the late husband, while the second *jñātayaḥ* refers to those of the new husband. Meyer understands by both the woman's father, brother etc. and proposes *abhisṛṣṭāyāḥ*, 'handed over, made over' in place of *abhimṛṣṭāyāḥ*. That seems little likely. — *yathāgṛhītam*, i.e., as she had received at the time of the first marriage. 25 *strīdhanam* is evidently that of the first marriage.

26 *patidāyam* would normally be 'what she has inherited from her husband.' But the wife does not appear among heirs in 3.5.9-12. Some kind of inheritance can be understood here to distinguish this from *patidatta* of s. 21. But 'gift' appears better. Cb has 'food and clothing given by the husband.'

sons, however, shall receive that woman's property. 30 Or, if she remarries for the maintenance of her sons, she shall augment (the woman's property) for the sake of the sons.

31 The (woman) shall settle on sons born (to her) from many husbands her woman's property as given by the respective fathers.

32 A (widow) marrying again shall settle on her sons her woman's property even when she is entitled to do what she pleases with it.

33 A (widow) without sons, remaining faithful to her husband's bed, shall use her woman's property in the proximity of elders, till the end of her life. 34 For, a woman's property is meant for calamities. 35 After (her death), it shall go to the heirs.

36 If a woman dies while her husband is living, her sons and daughters shall divide her woman's property among themselves, daughters (only) if she had no sons, in the absence of these the husband (shall receive it). 37 The dowry, the post-marriage gifts and other things given by her relations, the relations shall receive.

Thus end rules concerning woman's property.

38 The (husband) shall wait for eight years if the wife does not bear offsprings or does not bear a son or is barren, for ten if she bears dead offspring, for twelve if she bears only daughters. 39 After that, he may marry a second wife with the object of getting a son. 40 In case of transgression of that (rule), he shall hand over the dowry, the woman's property and half (that) as compensation for supersession, and (pay) a fine of twenty-four *paṇas* maximum.

32 *kāmakaraṇīyam* : it is not stated what *strīdhana* can be so described. Perhaps the *saudāyika* of later Smṛtis 'gifts by brothers and father before or after marriage' may be understood.

33 *gurusamīpe strīdhanam* etc. : Kane (III, 708 n. 1357) seems to read *strī dhanam* and comments that this passage is probably the first to propound clearly the characteristics of the Hindu Widow's estate. It is doubtful if in this section *strīdhanam* can be read as to two words, the latter understood as referring to other property as well. The next s. mentions the technical *strīdhana* only, and it gives the reason for the rule in this s. — *dāyādam*, i.e., the husband's heirs. Kātyāyana reproduces this rule word for word.

36 *vibhajeran*, evidently in equal shares. In the matter of succession to *strīdhana*, this text does not make a distinction between the forms of marriage as the Smṛtis do (Manu, 9.196-7 ; Yāj., 2.145 ; Nārada, 13.9). It refers to them in a different connection (ss. 17-18 above). 37 *śulkam* : this is received by the parents (s. 11). — *anvādheyam* 'what is given by blood relations after marriage.' Kātyāyana includes gifts from the husband's family as well. — Yāj., 2.144, is an echo of this rule.

38 *aprajāyamānā* 'who bears a child once and does not conceive again' (Cb Cs). It may also mean 'who does not bear (because of miscarriages).' — *aputrām* may mean whose son died and who has not borne a child thereafter. 40 *ardham* 'half the *strīdhana*' (Cb) ; 'half the *śulka* and *strīdhana*' is also possible. Meyer prefers to read *artham* 'money as compensation for the second marriage.' Yāj., 2.148, repeats the rule and has *ardham*.

41 By paying the dowry, the woman's property, (and) in the case of a wife without a dowry or woman's property of her own a compensation for supersession equal in amount to that, and a suitable maintenance he may marry even a number of wives. 42 For, wives are (necessary) for having sons.

43 And in case of simultaneity of the menstrual periods of these, he shall approach according to (the time of) marriage, first that (wife) whom he had married first, or the wife who has living sons.

44 In case of concealment of the period or failure to approach at the time, ninety-six (*paṇas* shall be) the fine.

45 The (husband) may not approach a (wife) who has sons, who is desirous of a pious life, who is barren, who bears dead offspring or whose menstruation has stopped, if she is unwilling. 46 And if unwilling, the man may not approach a (wife) who is leprous or insane. 47 A woman, however, shall approach a (husband) even of this type, for bearing a son.

> 48 A husband, who has become degraded or gone to a foreign land or has committed an offence against the king or is dangerous to her life or has become an outcast or even an impotent one may be abandoned.

41 *tatpramāṇam* 'equal to the *śulka* and *strīdhana* of any of the other wives' (Meyer). Cs has 'equal to the expenses of the new marriage,' which appears less likely. 42 Cf. Manu, 9.26; Nārada, 12.19.

43 *yathāvivāham*, i.e., according to the form of marriage, first a wife married according to the Brāhma form and so on (com.). A man only rarely would marry different wives according to different forms. Manu, 9.85-87, lays down seniority according to the *varṇa* of the wives. *yathāvivāham* can be construed with *pūrvoḍhām* 'married first according to the time of marriage'; this appears more likely.

44 *tīrthagūhanāgamane*: the commentators understand the two offences by the wife, Meyer by the husband. It is possible also to understand the first as the wife's offence and the second as the husband's.

45 *dharmakāmām* is to be understood independently, not to be construed with *vandhyām* as in Cs. — Cb Cs remove the stop after *upeyāt* and read it after *na cākāmaḥ puruṣaḥ*, adding a *na* before *gacchet* in the next s. The punctuation has little to commend it. A man could hardly avoid his duties during the *ṛtu* merely because he was unwilling. Cf. 3.4.36. 47 *vā* has the force of *api*. — The reason for the discrimination seems to be that the husband could easily marry again, not so the wife.

48 *nīcatvam*: construe with *prasthitaḥ*. It is not stated what makes a man degraded. Following some degraded profession or becoming a drunkard or a rake may be understood. — *rājakilbiṣī*: this seems to refer to one committing an offence against the king, i.e., a seditious person. Cb has 'this is of three kinds, the king's *purohita*, the person receiving a gift from the king, and a consumptive person.' The consumptive is possible, but the other two are strange, particularly as there is no reference to their crime. — *tyājyaḥ*: Jayaswal (*Manu and Yāj.*, p. 230) says that *tyāga* denotes separation from conjugal intercourse, as opposed to *mokṣa*, the technical divorce.

CHAPTER THREE

SECTION 59 (Continued)

(*iv*) Marital Duty; (*v*) Maintenance; (*vi*) Cruelty; (*vii*) Disaffection; (*viii*) Misconduct; and (*ix*) Prohibition of Favours and Dealings

1 A woman twelve years of age attains majority, a man when sixteen years of age. 2 If after this there is a failure to carry out marital duties, there shall be a fine of twelve *paṇas* for the woman, twice that for the man. Thus ends (the topic of) marital duty.

3 When maintenance is not (payable) at stipulated (intervals of) time, the (husband) shall give (the necessary) food and clothing according to the dependents or more in a generous measure. 4 If (payable) at stipulated (intervals of) time, he shall calculate the same and pay in instalments. 5 And also in case she has not received a dowry, a woman's property and compensation for supersession, (the same procedure shall be followed).

6 If the (wife) is staying in her father-in-law's family or has become separated, the husband is not to be sued. Thus ends (the topic of) maintenance.

3.3

2 The colophon *iti śuśrūṣā* is added in conformity with those of the other subsections in this Chapter.

3 *bharmaṇyā* seems clearly to mean the allowance given for the maintenance of a wife separated from the husband. — *anirdiṣṭakālā* 'the time for which is not stated' seems to refer to payment of the alimony in one lump sum, while *nirdiṣṭakālā* seems to be that paid in instalments at stated times. — *grāsācchādanam* is the usual expression for 'maintenance' given to a person; cf. 3.5.32; 3.7.19. — *vā dhikam*: *vā* is misplaced; it should come after *adhikam*. — *puruṣaparivāpa*: see 1.16.5; 2.24.28 etc. — *saviśeṣam* may refer to quality while *adhikam* refers to quantity. Cb explains the s. thus 'when a woman is appointed to look after the household (*bharmaṇyā*) and there is no restriction on her as to time that so much amount is to be spent in so much time, she should be given provisions for running the household according to the number of persons in it.' Cs mostly follows. The idea is very strange. Russ. has 'if one keeps a lady-in-waiting (*bharmaṇyā*) for an indefinite period, then one should give her food and clothing as much as one gives to one's servant-men (*yathāpuruṣaparivāpam*) or even more than that'. 4 Meyer understands *nirdiṣṭakālā* as 'to be given for a definite period,' which appears less likely. — *tadeva*, i.e., *grāsācchādanam*, probably excluding the idea of *adhikam*. — *bandham* seems to refer to 'part, portion' of an amount, as in *pañcabandha*, *daśabandha* etc.; cf. also 3.9.20; 3.12.16. *ca* is unnecessary. Meyer understands *bandha* as 'surety.' That also is not unlikely. The commentatotrs have 'if the wife takes the matter (of provisions) to the court and fails, she is to give 1/5th or 1/10th part of the provisions (to the state ?).' This appear still more strange. 5 *-ādhivedanikānām* is from Cb and quite necessary for the sense. *adhyāvahanika* 'gifts received at the time of going from the father's to the husband's place' would hardly be intended in this context. Since we have to supply *bandhaṁ dadyāt* in this s., Cs adds 'she has to pay even when she has not received *śulka* etc., how much more would she be liable to pay if she has received that ?' The commentators appear to be clearly on a wrong track.

6 *śvaśurakulapraviṣṭāyām*: the wife, though having no relations with the husband, stays in the family. Meyer thinks that she may have married the husband's brother. In the alternative, he proposes *śvaśurakulāpraviṣṭāyām*, signifying an appointed daughter (*putrikā*) who is not a member of her father-in-law's family. Neither suggestion seems necessary. — *vibhaktāyām*: apparently in this case, she has received some share of the property. — *nābhiyojyaḥ*: the claim would be about maintenance, hardly about *śulka* (as in Cb).

7 The inculcation of modest behaviour (shall be done) without the use of expressions such as 'thou lost one,' 'thou ruined one,' 'thou cripple', 'thou fatherless one' or 'thou motherless one.' 8 Or, striking on the back three times with one of (the three, viz.,) a split bamboo cane, rope or hand (may be done). 9 In case of transgression of this fines half those for verbal and physical injury (shall be imposed).

10 The same (shall be the punishment) for the wife whose offence against her husband is well-known. 11 On occasions of (her) enjoying herself outside (the home) out of jealousy, the penalty shall be as laid down. Thus ends (the topic of) cruelty.

12 A wife disliking her husband (and) not adorning herself (for fulfilment of marital duty) during seven menstrual periods, shall forthwith set down her endowment and ornaments and consent to her husband lying with another woman.

13 A husband disliking the wife shall consent to her staying alone in the family of one of (the following, viz.,) a female mendicant, a guardian or a kinsman.

14 One who speaks a falsehood, when indications are clear, when there is a refusal of intercourse or when an approach is made to a person

7 *naṣṭe vinaṣṭe* is from the actual comment in Cb. *vinagne* at least is suspicious. — *anirdeśena* 'without using these expressions, but using other words of admonition' (Cb). Cs has 'addressing her with these abusive expressions.' That is less likely. 8 Cf. Manu, 8.299-300. 9 *vāgdaṇḍa-* etc.: as in 3.18 and 3.19 below.

10-11 It is proposed to read *prasiddhadoṣāyāḥ* with a stop after it and *īrṣyayā* at the beginning of the next s. — *tadeva*, i.e., the *ardhadaṇḍāḥ*. — *doṣa* would be abuse or beating of the husband. — *bāhyavihāreṣu dvāreṣu*: i.e., when the wife goes away from home to enjoy herself; *dvāra* is 'an occasion'. — *yathānirdiṣṭaḥ*, i.e., as laid down in ss. 20-22 below or 3.4.1-23. Cb Cs explain 'the same amount of cruelty (*naṣṭa* or *nagna* etc. and *trir āghāta*) is allowed to a chaste (*adoṣā*) wife when her jealousy is aroused by such occasions (*dvāreṣu*) for harsh treatment towards the husband as his wandering outside (for prostitution etc.). In case of transgression she pays full fines (not half like her husband).' With *īrṣyāyām*, Meyer tr. 'the same holds good in case of jealousy by the wife towards the husband when there is no open offence (*prasiddhāyām adoṣāyām*). Punishment for wandering outside the house or at the doors, as prescribed in each case.'

12 *sthāpyābharaṇam*: see 3.2.15. — *anuśayīta* 'should sleep nearby on a lower level' (Cb), 'should wait upon the husband full of remorse' (Cs). Mere consent would seem meant, without the idea of claiming *ādhivedanika*.

13 *anvādhi*: Cb understands 'a trustee of the *strīdhana*'. It may simply mean 'a guardian'. — *-kulānām*: in the case of the *bhikṣukī*, this implies only staying with her. — *dviṣan*, as qualifying *bhartā*, is necessary. Because of *vā*, Meyer would find here something new about the disaffected wife; hence, he proposes a stop after *vā* 'or, (she shall give freedom) when she stays with *bhikṣukī*, etc. The husband, hating, shall give freedom if he has only one wife in her.' *ekām* need not be so understood. It merely refers to her staying separately from her husband.

14 *dṛṣṭaliṅge maithunāpahāre* 'who denies or conceals intercourse (with another woman) when signs of such are distinctly visible' (Cb Cs). It seems better, however, to understand the two terms separately as in Meyer and to construe *mithyāvādī* with each of them. *liṅga* refers to signs of disaffection or hatred, not of intercourse. — *apahāra* seems to have the sense of refusal (to have intercourse). *mithyāvādī* 'one who speaks a falsehood,' i.e., denies these things, hardly, 'who falsely accuses' (as in Meyer). — *savarṇāpasarpopagame*

of the same *varṇa* through a secret emissary, shall pay a (fine of) twelve *paṇas*.

15 A disaffected wife is not to be granted divorce from the husband who is unwilling, nor the husband from the wife. 16 By mutual disaffection (alone) a divorce (shall be granted). 17 Or, if the husband seeks divorce because of the wife's offence, he shall give to her whatever he may have taken. 18 Or, if the wife seeks divorce because of the husband's offence, he shall not give her whatever may have been received. 19 There is no divorce in pious marriages. Thus ends (the topic of) disaffection.

20 The wife who, (though) prohibited, indulges haughtily in the sport of drink, shall pay a fine of three *paṇas*. 21 In case she goes by day to a show by women or on a pleasure-trip with women, the fine (shall be) six *paṇas*, for going to a show by men or on a pleasure-trip with men, twelve *paṇas*. 22 At night, (the fines shall be) double.

23 For leaving home when the (husband) is asleep or intoxicated and for not opening the door to the husband, twelve *paṇas* (is the fine). 24 For going out at night, (the fine is) double.

25 If a man and a woman, with sexual intercourse in view, indulge in gestures with limbs or indecent conversation in secret, twenty-four *paṇas* is the fine for the woman, double that for the man.

'when the husband's misdeeds are found out through a friend sent to him as a spy' (Cb), 'who has approached for intercourse a female emissary who is a friend (of the wife)' (Cs). This latter is clearly influenced by classical poetry. Meyer has 'when she has acknowledged (*upagama*, i.e., *abhyupagama*) before a wife of the same caste that she dislikes her husband.' Perhaps the only idea is 'approaching a person of the same *varṇa* through an intermediary' for shelter or aid, rather than for intercourse, in which case the punishment would have been more severe. The offence is conceivable more of the wife than of the husband ; *mithyāvādī*, however, is masculine. Russ. reads 'if he makes false statements (*mithyāvādī*) that he has clear proof (*dṛṣṭaliṅge*) that she refuses intercourse (*maithunāpahāre*) or that she tells him through a woman similar to herself used as an informer (that she refuses intercourse).' 17-18 It is strange that when the wife is in the wrong, she gets her *śulka*, *strīdhana* etc., while she gets nothing if forced to seek divorce through the man's wrong. Apparently, the only test is who seeks divorce. It is not unlikely, however, that *asyai* and *nāsyai* have changed places in the two ss. ; or perhaps we should read *asau* (for *asyai*) and *nāsau* (for *nāsyai*). 19 *dharmavivāhānām*, i.e., the first four forms. — *dveṣaḥ* is added from Cb in the colophon, for uniformity.

20 *darpamadyakrīḍāyām* 'haughty play (*darpakrīḍā*) and the sport of drinking' (Cb Cs Meyer). A single idea might appear preferable. 21 *strīprekṣāvihāra* : we have to understand *strīprekṣā* 'a show put up by women only' and *strīvihāra*. *vihāra* is '*udyānagamana*' (Cb). — Cf. Manu, 9.84.

23 *suptamattapravrajane* : it is necessary to read *matta* as in Cb, as it describes the husband. *pravrajana* is 'leaving home, going out.' — *adāne*, i.e., not opening, when, for example, the husband returns home at night. 24 *niṣkasane* is the same as *pravrajane*.

25 *maithunārthenāṅga-* : Cb text shows *maithunārthe 'naṅga-*, which Cs adopts ; the actual comment in Cb, however, implies the former reading. *anaṅga* is superfluous, when *maithunārtha* is there. For the instrumental case of the latter word, cf. 3.4.21 below.

26 For touching the hair, the knot of the lower garment, teeth or nails, the lowest fine for violence (shall be imposed), double (that) for the man.

27 And in case of conversation in a suspicious place, punishment by whipping may be substituted for the fine in *paṇas*. 28 To women, the Caṇḍāla shall give five strokes with the lash in the region between the sides (i.e., on the back) in the centre of the village. 29 Or, she may free herself by paying a *paṇa* for each stroke.

Thus ends (the topic of) misconduct.

30 When a man and a woman, who are forbidden, make a gift to one another of small articles, a fine of twelve *paṇas* (shall be imposed), if of big articles, twenty-four *paṇas*, if of money or gold, a fine of fifty-four *paṇas* for the woman, double (these) for the man. 31 Half these same fines (shall be imposed) in case the two are unapproachable (for each other), also in cases of forbidden dealings with men.

Thus ends (the topic of) prohibition.

32 On account of disaffection towards the king, and misconduct, and by wilfully runing away, a woman loses her ownership over the woman's property, what she has brought (from her kinsmen) and dowry.

26 Cb Cs interpret *ālambana* as '*kṣatakaraṇa*' when construing it with *danta* and *nakha*. But *danta* and *nakha* would rather appear to be those of the other party, like *keśa* and *nīvī*. Meyer proposes *hasta* for *danta*, or *stanasakthyava-* for *dantanakhā-*. It must be admitted that *danta* and *nakha* are strange and can only be thought of in the commentators' sense. *hasta* for *danta* and *sakthyā-* for *nakhā-* might appear better.

28 *strīṇām* : this would imply that males were exempt from this whipping. — *pakṣāntare* is from Cb *pakṣāntaram* cannot be properly construed. The expression seems to refer to the back. Cb. Cs however explain by 'on each side', which would be an unusual sense. Meyer's suggestion 'at intervals of half a month' (Nachtrag) is hardly acceptable. 29 *paṇikam*: as this comes to a small fine, Meyer thinks that *pañca* has dropped out before *paṇikam*. For one lash as the equivalent of five *paṇas*, he compares 2.27.19. That appears plausible. — *atīcāraḥ* : other *aticāras* are dealt with in 4.13.

30 *kṣudrakadravya* : see 3.17.6. — *sthūlakadravya* : see 3.17.7-8. 31 *agamyayoḥ* : between whom a sexual relationship is prohibited. — *pratiṣiddhapuruṣavyavahāreṣu* : Cs has 'dealings between two men between whom dealings are forbidden.' It seems that the wife's dealings (such as purchasing, borrowing etc.) with a forbidden man are meant. Jolly-Schmidt have the curious note ' "in the case of forbidden intercourse with them." An apparent allusion to homosexuality.' That is an *aticāra* mentioned in 4.13.40, not here.

32 *rājadviṣṭa* is 'treason.' — *aticāra*, as treated above in this Chapter, does not lead to loss of *strīdhana*. — *ātmāpakramaṇena* seems to be running away from home. In 3.4.15, one case of *niṣpatana* is said to lead to loss of *strīdhana*. Cb has 'stealing the husband (?).' — The *kārikā* is evidently derived from a different source.

CHAPTER FOUR

SECTION 59 (Continued)

(*x*) Leaving Home; (*xi*) Going Away (with a Man); (*xii*) Short Absence from Home; and (*xiii*) Long Absence from Home.

1 For a woman who leaves the house of her husband, the fine is six *paṇas*, except in case of ill-treatment. 2 If she was forbidden (to do so), (the fine is) twelve *paṇas*.

3. If she has gone to a neighbour's house, (the fine is) six *paṇas*. 4 In case a neighbour, a mendicant or a trader gives her shelter, food or goods (respectively), the fine shall be twelve *paṇas*. 5 If (these have been) forbidden, the lowest fine for violence (shall be imposed).

6 If she has gone to the house of a stranger, (the fine is) twenty-four *paṇas*. 7 In case a (stranger) gives shelter to another man's wife, a fine of a hundred *paṇas* (shall be imposed), except in cases of distress. 8 In case he has prohibited (her) or is ignorant (about her coming), he is guiltless.

9 'There is no offence in going to the house of one of (the following, viz.,) a kinsman of the husband, a trustee, the village headman, a guardian, a female mendicant or her own kinsman, if there are on males in it, on account of the husband's ill-treatment,' say the teachers.

10 'To the house of a kinsman, even if there are males in it. 11 For, how can there be deceit by a chaste woman? 12 This is easy to understand,' says Kauṭilya.

3.4

1 *viprakāra* is clearly by the husband.

3 *atigata* is simply 'gone to', not 'gone beyond (the neighbour's house).' 4 It is proposed to read *-paṇyadāne* for *-paṇyādāne* of the mss. The offence of the neighbour is that he gives shelter to the wife, of the *bhikṣuka* that he gives food to her and of the *vaidehaka* that he gives goods to her. This in the main is how Cb understands, except that it understands a *pāṣaṇḍa bhikṣu* and an evil trader. There is no reason for the restriction. With the reading of the mss. Cs understands *dāna* with *avakāśa* and *bhikṣā*, but *ādāna* with *paṇya*. This appears hardly legitimate. 5 *pratiṣiddhānām* refers to the neighbour, etc.

7 *śatyo daṇḍaḥ*: the heavy fine is in view of the man being a total stranger, not a known neighbour. Meyer has 'a wife giving an opportunity (*avakāśa*) to another man's wife,' which is hardly likely. 8 *vāraṇa* 'preventing,' i.e., prohibiting her from coming in.

9 *sukhāvastha* 'a surety for happiness' is a sort of trustee for the wife's happiness. He has the responsibility of maintaining her for some time during the husband's absence (s.26). According to Cb 'he has brought about the match.' Meyer treats it as an adjective to *grāmika* 'in affluent circumstances.' — *anvādhi*: see 3.3.13 above. — *apuruṣam*: apparently males other than the heads of the families are meant.

10 *jñātikulam*: this excludes *sukhāvastha* and others. 11 *chalam* 'deceit' rather than 'contention about trifles, word-jugglery' (Meyer). The latter meaning, however, suits in 3.5.24. 12 *etad*, i.e., the fact that chaste women would not cheat, or, the deceit if practised by a woman.

13 Going to the house of a kinsman on the occasion of death, illness, calamity or childbed is not at all forbidden. 14 For the (husband) preventing her on such an occasion, the fine is twelve *paṇas*. 15 If even on such occasions she conceals hereself, she shall forfeit her woman's property, or the kinsmen, concealing (her, shall forfeit) the balance of the dowry.

Thus ends (the topic of) leaving home.

16 In case a (wife) leaving the house of her husband, goes to another village, the fine is twelve *paṇas* as well as the loss of her endowment and ornaments. 17 Or, in case she goes in the company of a man with whom sex-intercourse is permissible, the fine shall be twenty-four *paṇas* and the loss of all rights, excepting the giving of maintenance and approaching during the period. 18 For the man (the punishment is) the lowest fine for violence, if equal or superior (in *varṇa*), the middle (fine) if inferior. 19 A blood-relation is not to be punished. 20 In case there is prohibition, half the (above) fines (shall be imposed on him).

21 In case she goes to a secret place midway on her way or if she accompanies on the way, with carnal intentions, a man who is suspected or forbidden, one should know that as adultery.

22 Accompanying a man on the way is no offence in the case of (the women of) dancers, wandering minstrels, fishermen, fowlers, cowherds, vintners and others who give freedom to their women. 23 Or, in case of prohibition, for the man taking the woman with him or the woman going with him, the fines (shall be) half the same as above.

Thus ends (the topic of) going with a man.

13 *garbha* may be her own confinement or rather that of some other female relation. 15 *gūhamānā*, in effect, amounts to a refusal to return to the husband's house. — *śulka-śeṣam* implies payment of the dowry in instalments.

16 *sthāpyā-* : see 3.2.15. 17 *gamyena*, i.e., not within prohibited degrees of relationship. — *sarvadharma-*, i.e., all social and religious rights and privileges. — *anyatra bharmadānatīrthagamanābhyām* : this means that she is entitled to these two privileges, both of which involve the husband's duties towards her. Cs has 'except when she goes for the maintenance of the household or for the sake of the period.' The latter would imply freedom to ignore the husband during the *ṛtu*. Meyer's 'except when she creates (i.e., seeks) livelihood or makes a pilgrimage' is also little likely. In the footnote, Meyer suggests *bharmādāna* as 'receiving maintenance', and 'adultery by the wife during the *ṛtu*' as the meaning of *tīrthagamana*. Neither is necessary. 18 *tulyaśreyasoḥ* : Cb reads *tulyaśreyasaḥ* evidently to make it conform with *puṁsaḥ*, and explains 'one equal in *varṇa*' only. But two persons are clearly to be thought of. 20 *pratiṣedhe*, i.e., when the *bandhu* is asked not to go with that woman.

21 *vyantare* seems to mean 'in the middle' while she is on the way (*pathi*). Cb has 'away from the road.' Meyer thinks that *aṭavyantare* 'inside a forest' is to be read. — *maithunārthena* : Cb supplies *vidyāt* after this and understands it with the preceding case. Cs follows. It seems better, however, to construe this word with what follows, particularly with *pathyanusaraṇe*. — *pathyanusaraṇe* is proposed for *pathyanusārena* of the mss., in conformity with the next s. and the title of the sub-section. — Besides proposing *aṭavyantare*, Meyer also proposes *gūḍhadeśe vābhigamane* for *-deśābhigamane*. His tr. is 'if she approaches with carnal intentions a man on the road, either in the middle of the forest or in a secret place, or if she accompanies etc.' which is not very happy. — *saṁgrahaṇam* : for the punishments Cb refers to 4.12.33.

22 *prasṛṣṭastrīkāṇām*, i.e., among whom women enjoy a greater freedom of movement than among the other communities. 23 *ta eva*, i.e., those of ss. 17-19 above.

24 The wives of a Śūdra, a Vaiśya, a Kṣatriya and a Brahmin, who are away on a short journey, shall wait for a period (of one year) increased successively by one year, if they have not borne children, for one year more, if they have borne children. 25 Those who are provided for (shall wait) for double the period. 26 The trustees shall maintain those unprovided for, kinsmen for four or eight years after that. 27 Thereafter, they shall release (them) after taking back according as they had given.

28 The (wife) shall wait for a Brahmin who is away studying, for ten years if she has no child, for twelve if she has a child, for a royal servant (she shall wait) till the end of her life. 29 And if she bears a child from a man of the same *varṇa*, she shall not incur blame.

30 Or, when the affluence of the family has disappeared, she, being released by the trustees, may marry again as she desires, or when she is in distress, for the sake of livelihood.

31 After a pious marriage, the maiden shall wait for her husband who has gone away without informing her, for seven periods if no news is heard about him, for one year if news is heard. 32 If he has gone away after informing her, she shall wait for five periods when no news is heard, for ten if news is heard. 33 If he had paid only a part of the dowry, she shall wait for three periods if there is no news, seven periods if there is news about him. 34 If he had paid the dowry (in full), (she shall wait) for five preriods if there is no news, ten if there is news. 35 After that, she may remarry as she desires, with the permission of the judges. 36 'For, frustration of the period is destruction of sacred duty,' says Kauṭilya.

Thus ends (the topic of) short absence from home.

24 *saṁvatsarottaram*, i.e., 1, 2, 3 and 4 respectively. — *saṁvatsarādhikam*, i.e., 2, 3, 4 and 5 years. 25 *dviguṇaṁ kālam*, i.e., double the two sets in the last s. 26 *sukhāvasthāḥ* : see s. 9 above. These maintain for the periods stipulated in ss. 24–25. — *param*, i.e., after this stipulated period, the *jñātis* take upon themselves the responsibility. *sukhāvasthāḥ* is understood as an adjective to *jñātayaḥ* by Meyer 'kinsmen in affluent circumstances' which is hardly right. 27 *pramuñceyuḥ* : i.e., she may then marry again ; cf, s. 30 below. Cb Cs understand 'release' to go to her parents' house if she so desires, which appears hardly adequate.

28 *rājapuruṣam* : A Brahmin would seem meant primarily. 29 *savarṇataś ca prajātā* : apparently this applies to the *rājapuruṣa*'s wife only, though Cb Cs make it applicable to all cases. Because of *ca* 'from a higher *varṇa*' is also to be understood according to them.

30 *kuṭumbarddhilope* : in this case, even before the stipulated period is over, she may be allowed to remarry. — *sukhāvasthair vimuktā* : it is obvious that the *sukhāvasthas* have been able to maintain her out of the family funds only. When these dwindle, they give her freedom to marry again.

31 *kumārī* and *parigrahītāram* both imply that the marriage has not been consummated. — *sapta tīrthāni* : the counting may start from the day of departure or from the day on which he was expected back. 33 *ekadeśadattaśulkam* : payment of *śulka* in instalments is clearly implied. It is to be noted that the reference to *śulka* here is in connection with *dharmavivāhas*. 34 This is naturally a repetition of s. 32. 35 *dharmasthair visṛṣṭā* : we may conclude that the permission of the judges is necessary if a virgin wife in the first four forms of marriage wishes to marry again. 36 Apparently the maxim in this form is Kauṭilya's own.

37 The wife of a (man) who has gone away on a long journey or has become a wandering monk or is dead shall wait for seven periods, for one year if she has borne children. 38 After that she may approach (for marriage) a full brother of the husband. 39 If there are many (such brothers, she should approach) one who is proximate (to the husband), one who is pious, one capable of maintaining her, or the youngest if without a wife. 40 In the absence of these, even one who is not a full brother, a *sapiṇḍa* or a member of the family who is near. 41 Among these, this alone shall be the order (of preference).

42 In case she marries setting aside these heirs of her husband, (or) in case she has a lover, the lover, the woman, the bestower (of the woman) and the man who marries her receive the penalty for adultery.

CHAPTER FIVE

SECTION 60 PARTITION OF INHERITANCE

(*i*) Order of Inheritance

1 Sons, having fathers, — with the father and mother alive, — are not masters (of the property). 2 After the father's death, there may be a partition of the father's property among them.

3 What is acquired by oneself is not to be divided, except what is brought into being out of the father's property.

37 *dīrghapravāsinaḥ* : apparently in the case of a 'long' journey no time limit for return is fixed. — *sapta tīrthāni* : if the period of waiting is to start from the day of departure in the case of the *dīrghapravāsin*, as is only to be expected, there would be little material difference between the short and long journey. It probably lay in the distance from home of the intended destination. 39 *pratyāsanna*, i.e., proximate to the husband in point of age. — *kaniṣṭham abhāryam* : Cs understands two distinct brothers. But 'the youngest if unmarried' (Cb) is better, since a descending order of preference is intended. Meyer has the latter explanation, but offers another, '*dhārmika bharmasamartha kaniṣṭha* is the second and *abhārya* is the third alternative.' 40 *kulyam* a member of the husband's family beyond the *sapiṇḍa*-relationship. *āsannam* is to be construed with this word as shown by 3.6.22. 41 The Smṛtis recommend this order for *niyoga*, not for re-marriage. Cf. Manu, 9.59.

42 *jārakarmaṇi* : Meyer manages to get from *jātakarmaṇi* of G the same meaning as *jārakarmaṇi*. A *vā* or *ca* is to be understood ; else *vedana* itself would be *jārakarma*. But the second half mentions *jāra* as well as *vettṛ* 'one who marries.' — *atyayam* : the punishment of 4.12.33 is apparently to be thought of.

3.5

The 60th *prakaraṇa* is also spread over three Chapters, 3.5-7.

1 *pitṛmantaḥ sthitapitṛmātṛkāḥ* : it seems clear that the latter expression is a marginal gloss explaining *pitṛmantaḥ* that has got into the text. The gloss probably owes its origin to Manu, 9.104. To get over the tautology Cs has '*pitṛmantaḥ*, i.e., having excellent parents,' Meyer '*pitṛmantaḥ*, who are still under the father's protection.' 2 *ūrdhvaṁ pitṛtaḥ* : partition during the father's lifetime is, however, also thought of in s. 16 below. Russ. has 'parents directly (i.e., without anyone suggesting it) divide inheritance among them (the sons').

3 The Smṛtis refer to *vidyādhana*, *śauryadhana*, etc. in this connection.

4 Sons or grandsons up to the fourth generation shall be receivers of shares of (goods) come down without a partition from the father's property. 5 Till then the (funeral) cake remains unbroken. 6 When the cake is discontinued, all shall divide in equal shares.

7 Those who had received no property from the father or those who had divided the father's property, when they live together, may divide again. 8 And he, through whom the (property) may arise, shall receive two shares.

9 Full brothers or those living with him shall receive the property of a sonless man, and daughters (shall receive it).

10 The sons (shall inherit) the estate of a man with sons, or the daughters, born in the pious marriages. 11 In the absence of these, the father if alive. 12 In the absence of the father, the brothers and sons of brothers.

13 And a brother's sons, if without their father, shall receive only a single share of the father, even if they are many in number, along with the brothers.

14 Of uterine brothers born of more than one father, the partition of inheritance is to be from the (respective) father.

4 *avibhaktopagatānām* : supply *dravyāṇām*, 'goods come down without there having been a partition before.' Cs has 'of those who died (*upagata*) without dividing the property.' This is hardly possible. *upagata* is not *uparata*. — *ā caturthād*, i.e., sons, grandsons and great-grandsons. — *aṁśa* seems to refer to the unequal shares as described in the next Chapter. The idea apparently is that a son, or a grandson would be entitled to the preferential share to which his deceased father or grandfather was entitled. 5 *tāvad avicchinnaḥ* etc. : cf. Manu, 9.186.

7 *apitṛdravyāḥ* 'who had received no property from the father' when they had decided to live separately, the reason probably being that there was then no property that could be partitioned. — *saha jīvantaḥ* : these are the *saṁsṛṣṭins* of the Smṛtis. They are referred to in this text much too early. 8 *dvyaṁśam* : Meyer would prefer to read *ṛddhyaṁśam* 'a portion corresponding to the addition.' *ṛddhi* is not 'addition', and we should have *anurūpa* for 'corresponding'. — The rule is made applicable in the Smṛtis to the case where a son through his efforts recovers ancestral property that was mortgaged etc. Cf. Vasiṣṭha, 17.51. Bṛhaspati, however, agrees with this text in applying it to *saṁsṛṣṭins*. (Cf. Jolly, ZDMG, vol. 71, p. 233).

9 *sodaryāḥ* : these may or may not be living with him. — *sahajīvino vā* : these may not be *sodarya*. — *kanyāś ca* : the *ca* shows that the daughters are to get a share whichever type of brother inherits. Her share would apparently be equal to that of an uncle. Cs understands only an amount for marriage. But the *prādānika* is mentioned in s. 21 below.

10 *riktham* : it is difficult to find any distinction between *riktha* and *dravya* of s. 9. Perhaps s. 9 refers to *saṁsṛṣṭins*, this s. to the first partition. — *duhitaro vā*, i.e., the daughters inherit if there are no sons. *vā* can hardly be understood as *ca*. This s. places the daughter before the brother, not together with him as in s. 9. — *dharmiṣṭheṣu* etc. : the implication is that in the case of the last four forms of marriage, the daughters are excluded from inheritance even in the absence of sons. 12 *bhrātaro bhrātṛputrāś ca* : these share jointly. — Contrast Manu, 9.185-7 (daughter not admitted), Yāj., 2.135 (wife between sons and daughters), Nārada, 13.50-51 (father, brothers and their sons not mentioned).

13 *apitṛkā bahavo 'pi* goes primarily with *bhrātṛputrāḥ* and *pitur ekam aṁśam* has reference to them only. A deceased brother's sons, even if many, receive, amongst them, only the share which their father, if alive, would have received along with his brothers. This is partition *per stirpes*.

15 As between the father, the brother and the son, so long as the earlier one is alive, they do not depend on the later one, and so long as the eldest is alive, on the youngest even if he had received wealth.

16 In the case of partition during his life-time, the father shall not show special favour to any one. 17 And he shall not, without ground, exclude any one from inheritance.

18 When there is no property of the father, the eldest shall support the younger brothers except those who are wrongly behaved.

19 There is partition only among those who have attained majority. 20 They shall deposit with the mother's kinsmen or with village elders, the share of those who have not attained majority, clearing it of debts, till they come of age, also the share of one who is away on a journey.

21 To (brothers) who are not established (in life) they shall give an amount for their marriage, equal to that of those already settled, and to daughters an amount for bestowal in marriage.

22 There is to be an equal division of debts and property.

23 'Those without any property shall divide even water-vessels,' say the teachers. 24 'This is play with words,' says Kauṭilya. 25 There is division of an object that exists, not of one that does not exist.

26 He should cause partition to be made in the presence of witnesses, declaring with specific mention, 'so much property is joint, of that so much is each one's share.'

27 They shall divide again what is wrongly divided, what is robbed by one from the other, what is hidden, or what, being unknown, comes to light (later).

15 Apprently this s. refers to the manager in a joint family. Seniority determines it. Cb, reading *arthagrāhiṇaḥ*, explains 'those who had given the loan (*arthagrāhiṇaḥ*) should demand it of the father, the brother and the son of the debtor in this order.' Cs makes this clear by understanding *ṛṇadātāraḥ* as the subject and explaining *arthagrāhiṇaḥ* as gen. sing. 'of the man who had taken the debt.' The idea seems out of place here and does not agree with the rule in 3.11.14. — *arthagrāhiṇam* 'who had received wealth' apparently by his own endeavour. The force of *api* is to be understood with this.

17 *akāraṇāt*: a valid *kāraṇa* would be *patitatva* etc. of s. 30 below.

20 The *ā* is necessary before *vyavahāraprāpaṇāt*. — Baudhāyana, 2.2.42, is an exact parallel (cf. Kane, HD, III, 573 n. 1077).

21 *naiveśanikam*: the expenses for marriage would be over and above their regular share.

22 *riktha* is understood by Cb Cs as debt owed to the family by strangers. This can hardly be right in the context. Cf. Yāj., 2.117; Manu, 9.218.

23 The *ācāryas* seem to be rather keen on formalities to avoid future trouble. 24 *chalam* 'play with words' as in the Nyāya system (Meyer). Cs has 'contradiction in terms: if they are *niṣkiṁcana*, they cannot have water-jugs.'

26 *anubhāṣya*, i.e., specifying the share. — *kārayet*: the subject seems to be *dharmasthaḥ*. A village elder or an elderly kinsman is also possible.

28 The king shall take that to which there are no heirs, excluding maintenance for the wife and what is needed for funeral rites, with the exception of the property of a Brahmin learned in the Vedas. 29 He shall bestow that on those well-versed in the three Vedas.

30 An outcast, a son born to an outcast and an impotent person are not entitled to a share, also an idiot, a lunatic, a blind and a leprous person. 31 If these have a wife, their progeny, not of the same kind (as the father), shall receive a share. 32 The others (shall receive only) food and clothing, excepting the outcasts.

> 33 And if, after they have been married, their potency is lost, the kinsmen shall beget sons (for them, and) he shall assign shares to them.

CHAPTER SIX

SECTION 60 (Continued)

(*ii*) Division into Shares

1 Among sons of the same wife, the (special) share of the eldest (is to be) goats in the case of Brahmins, horses in the case of Kṣatriyas, cattle in the case of Vaiśyas and sheep in the case of Śudras. 2 One-eyed or lame among them (are to be) the share of the middlemost (and) those of mixed colours the share of the youngest. 3 In the absence of animals, the eldest shall receive one part of every ten articles, with the exception of jewels. 4 For, he has the fetters of (the duty of offering) oblations to the manes tied round him. 5 This is the partition recommended by Uśanas.

6 From the personal belongings of the father, the carriage and ornaments (are to be) the share of the eldest; the bed and seat, and bell-metal dishes

28 *strīvṛtti*: only the wife seems meant. — *pretakārya* from Cb is distinctly preferable to *pretakadarya* of the mss. which hardly yields a sense. Meyer proposes to emend it to *pretakarmadeya*. Kane (III, 763 n.1469 and 810-1 n.1586 and 1587) would understand *kadarya* in the sense of *bhṛtya* 'a dependant' as in Kātyāyana (*yoṣidbhṛtyaurdhvadehikam*). That would be a very unusual meaning for the word.

31 *sati bhāryārthe teṣām* refers to *jaḍonmattāndhakuṣṭhinaḥ* only. 32 *patitavarjāḥ*: the *patita* is not entitled to maintenance; his son, however, would be entitled.

33 *bāndhavāḥ*: for this *niyoga*, the order of 3.4.38-40 would apparently operate; cf. above 3.7.6.

3.6

1 *brāhmaṇānām ajāḥ* 'because the goats are useful in sacrifices' (Cs). Baudhāyana, 2.2.3.9, assigns cattle to Brahmins and goats to Vaiśyas. 2 *kāṇalaṅgāḥ*: Cb comment implies this reading though its text shows *-liṅgāḥ*, which is adopted by Cs and explained 'characterised by one-eyedness,' which is quite unsatisfactory. — The question whether, when there are none of such animals, the junior sons are to go without them, is not answered. 5 *auśanaso vibhāgaḥ*: Cb Cs state that as this view is not contradicted, it is acceptable to Kauṭilya. But the following ss. mention an alternative arrangement, and, as is often the case, the last mentioned view may well be that of the author.

6 *kṛṣṇaṁ dhānyāyasam*: Cb reads *kṛṣṇadhānyā-*. Āpastamba, 2.6.14.7-8, mentions *kṛṣṇa bhauma* in the share of the eldest. 7 *ekadravyasya*: such as the work of a single

used for meals, the share of the middlemost; black grains, iron (objects), household furnishing and the bullock-cart, the share of the youngest. 7 Of the remaining articles or of a single article (there is to be) an equal division.

8 The sisters do not inherit, receiving (only) a share of the bell-metal dishes used for meals and ornaments from the mother's personal belongings.

9 The eldest, if devoid of manly qualities, shall receive (only) a third of an eldest son's share, one-fourth (only) if he behaves in an unjust manner or has given up religious duties. 10 If he behaves wantonly, he shall forfeit the whole.

11 By that are explained the middlemost and youngest sons. 12 Among these, he who is endowed with manly qualities shall receive a half of an eldest son's (special) share.

13 In the case of sons of different wives, however, seniority (is to be) in accordance with priority of birth, in the absence of one wife married according to the sacrament and another not married according to the sacrament, and in the absence of one wife married while a virgin and another married when she had lost her virginity, (also) among two sons born of the same wife or among twins.

14 In the case of the Sūta, the Māgadha, the Vrātya and the Rathakāra, partition (is to be) in accordance with mastery (in the profession). 15 The rest shall live under him. 16 If (all are) without mastery, they shall receive equal shares.

slave, the water of a single well etc. (Jolly-Schmidt). Cs interprets *vā* as *api*. Meyer prefers *etaddravyasya* 'of this whole property.' The idea of *sarva* can hardly be brought in in this way. — The rule about the rest of the property would also apply to Uśanas's scheme. — For special shares, cf. Manu, 9.112 ff., Āpastamba, 2.6.14.10-11. They are among *kalivarjyas* later.

8 *adāyādā bhaginyaḥ* : this can be reconciled with 3.5.10 if we suppose here that daughters do not inherit when there are sons. Meyer thinks of special shares being denied to them. That is not unlikely. Manu, 9.118, Yāj., 2.114, allow 1/4th of a son's share to a daughter.

9 *mānuṣa*, i.e., capacity to earn, to manage the household etc. — *jyeṣṭhāṁśād* : he loses a part of the special share ; his regular share is not affected. — *anyāyavṛttiḥ* is from Cb. *anāyavṛttiḥ* of the mss. could mean 'living without earning an income,' but does not appear a likely reading. 10 *sarvaṁ* refers to *jyeṣṭhāṁśa* only.

12 *jyeṣṭhāṁśād ardham* : this would come from the estate, or from the eldest son's special share, if the latter is *mānuṣahīna*.

13 *saṁskṛtāsaṁskṛtayoḥ (abhāve)* : i.e., the son of a *saṁskṛtā* wife would be senior to that of an *asaṁskṛtā*, irrespective of age. *asaṁskṛtā* 'one married by the Gāndharva and other forms' (Cb). — *-kṛtakṣatayor* is from the comment in Cb for *-kṛtakriyayor*. Cs understands by the latter the same as *kṛtakṣatā*. But in 3.7.4, *kṛtakriyā* is 'one married in the proper way.' Meyer proposes *kanyākṛtākṛtakriyayor*, i.e., *kanyākṛtakriyā* and *kṛtākṛtakriyā* (*kṛtā* meaning 'violated'). This is hardly satisfactory. The idea, of course, is that the son of a wife who was a virgin at the time of marriage is senior to that of a wife not virgin at the time, irrespective of age. — *yamayor* : cf. Manu, 9.125-6.

14 *aiśvaryato*, i.e., according to proficiency in the profession.

17 Among (a Brahmin's) sons from wives beloning to the four *varṇas*, the son of the Brahmin wife shall receive four shares, the son of the Kṣatriya wife three shares, the son of the Vaiśya wife two shares, the son of the Śūdra wife one. 18 By that is explained partition among sons from wives belonging to three and two *varṇas* of a Kṣatriya and a Vaiśya (respectively).

19 A Brahmin's son born of a wife belonging to the immediately next *varṇa* is to have an equal share. 20 That of a Kṣatriya or a Vaiśya is to have half a share, or an equal share if endowed with manly qualities.

21 The only son among two wives, one of the same *varṇa* (as the husband) and the other of a different *varṇa*, shall receive everything, and shall maintain the kinsmen.

22 In the case of Brahmins, however, the son born of a Śūdra wife shall receive (only) one-third (of the property) as his share, a *sapiṇḍa* or a proximate member of the family (shall receive) two-thirds for the sake of offering the funeral oblations. 23 In the absence of these, the father's teacher or pupil (shall receive the two-thirds).

24 Or, a person appointed, either a mother's kinsman or a person of the same *gotra*, may beget on his wife a *kṣetraja* son; to him he shall allot that property.

CHAPTER SEVEN

SECTION 60 (Continued)

(*iii*) Classification of Sons

1 'Seed, dropped in the property of another, belongs to the owner of the field,' say (some) teachers. 2 'The mother is (only) a leather-bag (for holding the seed); who owns the seed, to him belongs the child,' say others. 3 'Both are to be found,' says Kauṭilya.

18 *kṣatriyavaiśyayoḥ* : the ratios would be 3 : 2 : 1 and 2 : 1 respectively. Cf. Manu, 9.152-3, Yāj., 2.125.

19-20 This seems to be an alternative to ss. 17-18. In this arrangement a Kṣatriya's son from a Vaiśya wife gets less than in the preceding arrangement. According to Cs, this arrangement operates when there are no sons from the other wives. There is nothing to indicate this. Cb seems to refer *aṁśa* to *jyeṣṭhāṁśa*.

22 *pāraśavaḥ* : see 3.7.21. Cb states that according to others this rule applies by *upalakṣaṇa* also to a Kṣatriya's son from a Śūdra wife. 23 *ācāryo 'ntevāsī vā* : the Smṛtis mention these in the regular list of heirs before the king ; cf. Manu, 9.187, Yāj., 2.135. Their mention in the present context is more appropriate.

24 *asya*, i.e., the Brahmin who has only a *śūdrāputra*. — *mātṛbandhuḥ* : this is because a *sapiṇḍa* or a *kulya* is not there. — *tad dhanam*, i.e., the 2/3rds share.

3.7

3 *vidyamānam ubhayam* : Cb has 'since both *kṣetra* and *bīja* are necessary, the offspring belongs to both.' The idea rather is, in certain circumstances, it belongs to the owner of the *kṣetra*, in others to the *bījin*. By agreement, he belongs to both, when he is called *dvyāmuṣyāyaṇa* ; cf. s. 7 below. Cf. Manu, 9.32 ff., for a full discussion.

4 A (son) begotten by oneself on a duly married wife is the legitimate son. 5 Equal to him is the son of the appointed daughter.

6 A (son) begotten on the wife (of a man) by a person appointed, whether of the same *gotra* or of a different *gotra*, is the *kṣetraja* son. 7 If the begetter has no other son, he belongs to both fathers or both *gotras* and offers funeral offerings to and inherits property from both. 8 With the same duties and rights as he, is the (son) secretly born, who is, however, secretly begotten in the house of the kinsmen.

9 One abandoned by the kinsman is the cast-off, a son to him who performs the sacraments for him. 10 The offspring of a maiden is the 'maiden's son.' 11 The (son) of a bride married when *enceinte* is 'brought with the marriage.'

12 The (son) of a woman remarried is 'the remarried woman's son.' 13 If begotten by oneself, he becomes an heir to his father and kinsmen. 14 If begotten by another, (he is an heir) only to him who performs the sacraments for him, not to the kinsmen. 15 With the same rights is the adopted son, given with water by the parents.

16 One who himself or through his kinsmen has offered to be a son is the son who has approached. 17 One appointed to the position of a son is the son made. 18 One purchased is the son bought.

19 When, however, a legitimate son is born, (the others), if of the same *varṇa*, receive a one-third share, if not of the same *varṇa*, receive only food and clothing.

4 *kṛtakriyā* is one who is duly married. Cf. 3.6.13 above. 5 *putrikāputraḥ* : cf. Manu, 9.127 ff.

6 *anyagotreṇa* : this would refer to *mātṛbandhus* ; cf. 3.6.24, also 1.17.50. 7 *dvigotro vā* : *vā* has the sense of *ca* (Cs). This is the *dvyāmuṣyāyaṇa* of the later texts. — Cf. Manu, 9.132, Yāj., 2.127. Baudhāyana, 2.2.21, is an exact parallel and Kātyāyana has a metrical rendering of this rule. 8 *bandhūnām* : Meyer proposes *bandhunā* 'by a kinsman,' which is not necessary. — *tu* has no significance.

9 *saṁskartuḥ* : the *upanayana saṁskāra* is primarily meant. 10 *kānīnaḥ* : cf. Manu, 9.172 (he belongs to the man who marries the mother), Yāj., 2.129 (he belongs to the mother's father).

13 *svayaṁjāta*, i.e., begotten by the second husband, and *parajāta*, i.e., a son by the first husband, who is accepted by the second husband. Cb Cs refer them to the *aurasa*, and *kṣetraja* and others respectively. There is no reason why these should be understood here. Two kinds of *paunarbhava* are clearly to be understood. — *pitur bandhūnāṁ ca* is as proposed by Meyer. It is obviously the original reading. 15 *tatsadharmā* : Cb Cs refer *tat* to *svayaṁjāta*. Normally it should refer to *parajāta*. On this view, the rights of the adopted son would appear restricted.

16 *bandhubhir vā* : because he has no parents he is given by the kinsmen. — For the sons, cf. Manu, 9.158-179, Yāj., 2.128-132 (closely agreeing with this text), Nārada, 13.45-47.

19 Baudhāyana, 2.3.11, agrees, using the same words (cf. D. R. Bhandarkar, *Some Aspects* etc., p. 59).

20 The sons of a Brahmin and a Kṣatriya born of a wife belonging to the immediately next *varṇa* are of the same *varṇa* (as the father), of a wife belonging to the next but one *varṇa*, are not of the same *varṇa*. 21 A Brahmin's son from a Vaiśya wife is Ambaṣṭha, from a Śūdra wife a Niṣāda or a Pāraśava. 22 A Kṣatriya's son from a Śūdra wife is Ugra. 23 A Vaiśya's son (from a Śūdra wife) is nothing but a Śūdra. 24 And of these (three *varṇas*) sons begotten on wives of the same *varṇa* by those who have not practised the vows, are Vrātyas. 25 These are the 'right order' sons.

26 From a Śūdra (are born of a Vaiśya, a Kṣatriya and a Brahmin wife respectively) the Āyogava, the Kṣatta and the Caṇḍāla. 27 From a Vaiśya (are born) the Māgadha and the Vaidehaka (of a Kṣatriya and a Brahmin wife respectively). 28 From a Kṣatriya (is born) the Sūta (of a Brahmin wife). 29 The Sūta and the Māgadha mentioned in the Purāṇa, however, are different, a special type from the Brahmin and the Kṣatriya.

30 These are the 'reverse order' sons, who come into existence because of the transgression of his own duties by the king.

31 From an Ugra on a Niṣāda wife is begotten the Kukkuṭa; in the opposite case, the Pulkasa. 32 From an Ambaṣṭha on a Vaidehaka wife is born the Vaiṇa; in the opposite case, the Kuśīlava. 33 From an Ugra on a Kṣatta wife is born the Śvapāka. 34 These and others are the intermediate castes.

35 A Rathakāra is a Vaiśya, (so called) because of his profession.

36 Among them, marriage (is to be) in their own (caste of) origin, there is to be the observance of precedence and the pursuit of the hereditary

20 Manu, 10.6, considers all three *anantarāputras* as *sadṛśa*. Yāj., 1.91 ff., differs and gives names for the mixed castes so formed, which are unknown to Manu, Nārada and Kauṭilya. 21 *niṣāduḥ pāraśavo vā* : Meyer says the former is an offspring of a regular marriage, the latter is a bastard, and refers to Baudhāyana, 2.2.29-30, for support. 24 *acaritavratebhyaḥ* : the *vrata* is principally *upanayana*. Manu, 10.20, also seems to derive *vrātya* from *vrata* 'vow, sacred rite'. Meyer would derive it from *vrāta* 'a group,' either as 'those wandering in groups' or 'those fallen from their group.'

26 This text does not specifically prohibit *pratiloma* marriages, though s. 30 implies that. The women are likely to be wives, not mistresses. 29 *paurāṇikas tvanyaḥ* etc. : Cs understands by Sūta Sauti Romaharṣaṇa, the narrator of the *Mahābhārata*, who is said to have sprung from a sacrificial altar ; so was Māgadha, according to the *Viṣṇu Purāṇa*, 1.3. They are superior to Brahmins and Kṣatriyas respectively (Cs). This is very doubtful. In fact the s. is suspicious. *viśeṣaḥ* or *viśeṣataḥ* cannot be properly construed in the sentence. The s. appears to be a late marginal comment that has got into the text. Cb seems to understand the Sūta as springing from a Brāhmaṇa and Māgadha from a Kṣatriya.

35 *vaiśyo* is from Cb from *vainyo* of the mss. The latter cannot be right because the Vaiṇya and the Rathakāra follow different professions. As Cb remarks 'according to some Rathakāra is an *antarāla* community, but he is only a Vaiśya called by this name because of the profession.' — This theory of the origin of mixed castes is, of course, open to many serious objections.

36 *pūrvāparagāmitvam* seems to refer to precedence in social matters, in accordance with the origin of the mixed castes. Cb Cs, reading *pūrvāvara-*, understand the rule of hypergamy, a man of a higher community marrying a woman of a lower one. If this is meant, we should have a *vā* after it, showing an option to *svayonau vivāhaḥ*. — It is proposed

occupation. 37 Or, they are to have the same special duties as the Śūdra, expecting the Caṇḍāla.

38 Only the king, behaving in this manner, obtains heaven, otherwise hell.

39 In the case of all intermediate castes, partition is to be in equal shares.

40 Whatever be the customary law of a region, a caste, a corporation or a village, in accordance with that alone shall he administer the law of inheritance.

CHAPTER EIGHT

SECTION 61 CONCERNING IMMOVABLE PROPERTY

(*i*) Concerning Dwelling-places

1 Disputes concerning immovable property (are to be decided) on the testimony of neighbours.

2 A house, a field, a park, an embankment, a tank or a reservoir is immovable property.

3 Along the house (is to be) a boundary, fixed with iron wires in pillars at the corners. 4 He should cause the house to be made in conformity with the extent of the boundary. 5 Or, he should cause a new fixing of the boundary to be made two *aratnis* or three *padas* away from the wall of a neighbour's house.

to omit *svadharmaṁ sthāpayet* read after *ca* in the mss. Those words require *rājā* as the subject, whichc an be understood neither in the preceding nor the following clause. These clauses show that *pūrvāpara-* etc. are in the nominative, not accusative. 37 *anyatra caṇḍālebhyaḥ*, i.e., a Caṇḍāla is not to follow the professions of a Śūdra. Cf. Manu. 10.51-56.

38 This also is a spurious s., obviously a marginal comment by the same hand that added *svadharmaṁ sthāpayet* above. No reference is made to the king's conduct in this Chapter to justify the words *evaṁ vartamānaḥ*.

39 Cb seems to imply that males and females all get equal shares. Meyer points out the contrast with 3.6.14-15 above. But the *antarālas* are probably only those in ss. 31-33, which do not include those of 3.6.14.

40 Manu, 8.41, makes the rule applicable to all matters, not to inheritance alone.

3.8

The 61st *prakaraṇa* is also spread over three Chapters, 3.8-10.

3 *karṇakīlāyasasaṁbandho*: Cb has 'having a fixing of durable substances with copper wires in the pillars (*kīla*) at the corners (*karṇa*).' Cs has iron instead of copper (*āyasa*). Meyer has 'an iron joining with pegs (*kīla*) that have ears (*karṇa*, i. e., barbs ?).' 'Pointed iron pegs' is possible, but the commentators may be right. Perhaps *-saṁbaddho* is to be read for *-saṁbandho*. — *setuḥ* here is 'a boundary' or 'boundary-mark' as in 3.9.10 ff. 4 *bhoga* is here 'expanse, extent' (Cs). 5 For *pada* and *aratni*, sec 2.20.11 and 12. — *deśabandha* is evidently 'fixing of the limit or boundary'. Cb reads *pāde bandham*, paraphrased by '*nemibandha*, fixing of the circumference'. Cs understands *pāde bandham* as 'foundation.' That reading, however, is uncertain.

6 (He should make) the dung-hill, the water-course or the well, not in a place other than that suited to the house, except the water-ditch for a woman in confinement till the end of ten days (from delivery). 7 In case of transgression of that, the lowest fine for violence (shall be imposed).

8 By that are explained the work of cutting fire-wood and channels for water used for rinsing on festive occasions.

9 He should cause to be made a deep-flowing water-course or one falling in a cascade, three *padas* away (from a neighbour's wall) or one *aratni* and a half (away). 10 In case of transgression of that, the fine is fifty-four *paṇas.*

11 He should cause to be made a place for carts and quadrupeds, a fire-place, a place for the large water-jar, the grinding mill or the pounding machine, one *pada* away or one *aratni* (from a neighbour's wall). 12 In case of transgression of that, the fine is twenty-four *paṇas.*

13 Between all two structures or two projecting rooms, (there is to be) an open lane one *kiṣku* (wide) or three *padas.* 14 Between them, the distance between the eaves of roofs (is to be) four *aṅgulas,* or one may over-lay the other.

15 He should cause to be made a side-door in the intervening lane, measuring one *kiṣku,* for making repairs to what is damaged, not (allowing) crowding. 16 For light, he should cause a small window to be made high up. 17 When the dwelling is occupied, he should cause it to be covered.

6 *vā na* is from Cb, so is the additional *anyatra* ; but *gṛhocitād* is proposed for its *gṛhocitam.* The ablative is clearly necessary for the sense. The *gṛha* is more likely that of a neighbour. The idea is that the dung-hill etc., are not to cause nuisance to the latter. — *anyatra sūtikākūpād* : i.e., the neighbours have to put up with the nuisance of waste water from a lying-in chamber for a period of ten days from delivery.

8 *tena,* i.e., ' by the rule of the *sūtikākūpa* ' (Cb Cs). It seems, however, that *tena* would refer to the principal rule rather than to the exception to it. Perhaps, *indhanāvaghātana* corresponds to the principal rule, while *kalyāṇakṛtyeṣu* to the exception. *-kṛtam* after *-ghātana* is not necessary. Meyer would look upon it as a separate word and construe it with *kalyāṇakṛtyeṣu* ' arrangements for joyous festivities.' That is not very happy. — *ācāmodaka* : Meyer has ' water strained after rice is cooked.' That is one of the meanings of *ācāma* ; but ' water used for rinsing the mouth after meals ' seems better.

9 It is proposed to omit *praveśya* after *aratniṁ vā.* That is supported by its absence in the parallel s. 11. The word seems to have got in from some comment in the margin. *prasravaṇaprapātam* from Cb is an alternative to *gūḍhaprasṛtam,* hardly to *udakamārgam* itself as in Cs. It would mean ' which flows in a cascade.' Cb, however, has ' where everything falls and flows,' Cs ' a place where all water-streams can fall.' *udakamārga* is for drinking water as distinguished from *bhrama* which is for waste water ; see 2.4.2.

11 *cakricatuṣpada* ' carts and quadrupeds.' Cf 10.2.16. The quadrupeds can hardly be ' elephants, etc .' (Cb). ' Goats and bullocks (*cakrin*) and elephants, etc. ' (Cs) is improbable. Meyer's ' with a foundation of four circular (*cakrin*) *padas* ' as adjective to *agniṣṭham* is altogether unlikely.

13 *prākṣiptaka* seems to mean ' projecting ' beyond the area of the house ; by such *śālās* are meant *cakricatuṣpadasthāna* etc.

15 *khaṇḍaphullārtham asampātam* ' for making repairs to what is damaged and for not allowing people to move in and out easily ' (Cb). Meyer has ' causing no knocking together when opened wide,' which appears less likely. *asampāta* may mean ' where there can be no crowding.' 17 *avasita,* lit., ' finished, completed,' conveys the sense of ' occupied ' ; cf. its opposite *anavasita,* 3.16.31. — *chādayet* ' should cover ' apparently with curtains, as Jolly suggests.

18 Or, house-owners, by mutual agreement, may get things done as desired, (and) should avoid what is undesirable.

19 And he should cause that part above the verandah which requires protection, to be covered by matting, or a wall touching (the roof), for fear of damage by rain. 20 In case of transgression of that, the lowest fine for violence (shall be imposed), also in case of obstruction by doors or windows contrary to natural arrangement, except on royal high-ways and roads. 21 (The same fine is to be imposed) in case of obstruction outside (the house) by parts of a ditch, stair-case, water-channel, ladder or dung-hill and in case of prevention of the use (of their rights by others).

22 For one causing damage to the wall of another's house the fine is twelve *paṇas*, double that in case of spoiling it with urine or dung.

23 A free flow of water (must be allowed) in the channels when it is raining, else the fine is twelve *paṇas*.

24 And (the same fine shall be imposed) on one staying on when forbidden and on one ejecting a tenant, except in cases of (verbal and physical) injury, theft, forcible seizure, adultery and wrongful use. 25 The (tenant) leaving of his own accord shall pay the balance of the annual rent.

26 For one not rendering help in a common dwelling, for one obstructing a thing used in common and in case of prevention of (rightful) use (by others), twelve *paṇas* is the fine. 27 Double that (is the fine) for destroying (what is used in common).

28 Of sheds, court-yards and latrines, of fire-places and pounding-sheds, and of all open (spaces), use in common is desired.

19 *vānalaṭī* is the '*gṛhavaraṇḍaka*' (Cb, which shows the form *vānalāṭī*). Meyer would understand 'a stick or pole (*laṭi* from *yaṣṭi*) which supports the net-work (*vāna*) of straw-matting' or 'a pole of dried fruit.' Neither seems intended. — *āvāryabhāgam* is from Cb; *āhāryabhoga-* yields little sense. Meyer's suggestion of *ahāryabhoga* 'whose use cannot be taken away,' that is, durable, hardly improves matters. — *avamarśabhittiṁ vā*: Cb Cs understand 'a small wall,' supplying *kaṭapracchannām* with it and treating *vā* as *ca*. The expression may mean 'a wall touching (the roof)' which would imply an enclosed verandah. Meyer interprets the reading *avamadbhaktim* as 'not leaking at the joints.' 20 *pratiloma* etc.: i.e., which impinge on the rights of neighbours. — *anyatra* etc.: this would imply that encroachments (*bādhā*) on *rājamārga* etc. are allowed, which is strange. Perhaps in their case a higher fine is to be thought of, though that is not specified.

23 *praṇālīmokṣaḥ*, i.e., not blocking the free flow in the channels.

24 *avakrayiṇam*: cf. 2.36.23. 25 *varṣāvakrayaśeṣam*: clearly a yearly contract of tenancy is implied.

26 *sāmānyam*, i.e., things shared in common as in s. 28 below. — *ca* is necessary after *bhoganigrahe* and has been added. The text in Cb has *bhogaṁ ca gṛhe*, but the actual comment presupposes *bhoganigrahe* or *bhogaṁ ca nigṛhṇataḥ*.

28 *koṣṭhaka* 'door of the house' (Cb Cs). It may be the same as *vāhanakoṣṭha* 'a shed for vehicles' of 3.9.25. — *varcānām*: cf. 2.5.6. The word means 'a latrine.' Cb, adopting *varjānām*, renders it by 'rubbish-heap.' Meyer's proposed *vrajānām* 'cattle-herds' is quite unlikely.

CHAPTER NINE

SECTION 61 (Continued)

(*ii*) Sale of Immovable Property; (*iii-v*) Fixing of Boundaries; (*vi*) Concerning Encroachment and Damage.

1 Kinsmen, neighbours and creditors, in this order, shall have the right to purchase landed property (on sale). 2 After that, others who are outsiders (may bid for purchase).

3 (Owners) shall proclaim a dwelling (as for sale) in front of the house, in the presence of members of forty neighbouring families, and a field, a park, an embankment, a tank or a reservoir (as for sale) at the boundaries, in the presence of village elders who are neighbours, according to the extent of the boundary, saying 'at this price who is willing to purchase?' 4 What has been thrice proclaimed and not objected to, the purchaser shall be entitled to purchase.

5 Or, in case of increase in price because of competition, the increase in price together with the tax shall go to the treasury. 6 The (successful) bidder at the sale shall pay the tax. 7 In case of a bid by one who is not an owner, the fine shall be twenty-four *paṇas*. 8 If the (bidder) does not come (to take possession), the owner whose property was auctioned may sell (again) after seven days. 9 In case of transgression by one whose property was auctioned, the fine is two hundred *paṇas* in the case of immovable property, a fine of twenty-four *paṇas* in other cases.

Thus ends (the topic of) sale of immovable property.

10 A group of neighbouring five villages or ten villages shall decide a dispute regarding boundaries between two villages, by means of boundary-marks, immovable or artificial.

3.9

1 *abhyābhaveyuḥ*: cf. 2.28.26 for the distinction in meaning from *abhyāvah*.

3 *-kulyeṣu* is proposed for *-kulyāḥ* of the mss. in conformity with the locative in the parallel *-grāmavṛddheṣu*. Cb understands the sense of the locative. The subject for *śrāvayeyuḥ* is *svāminaḥ* understood. — *sāmanta* is an adjective to *grāmavṛddha*, and not to *grāma*. — *setubhoga*: cf. 3.8.4 above. — For an exactly parallel procedure, cf. 2.21.7-8. 4 *avyāhatam* 'not objected to' by any one claiming the right of pre-emption, etc. Meyer has 'without hindrance' construing it with *kretuṁ labheta*. — Since the sale is by auction, Meyer thinks of it as carried out under a court decree. In 2.21.7-9, however, there is no question of a court decree. In fact, all sales are controlled by the state and taxed.

7 *asvāmi-*: Meyer thinks of a broker or an agent. Cs has 'one who has no right to land.' The former seems intended. 9 *pratikruṣṭātikrama* is not handing over possession to the purchaser. — *anyatra*, i.e., property other than immovable. Contrast 3.15.1 (which apparently applies only to traders).

10 The sub-section *sīmavivāda* is to be found in ss. 10-14, *kṣetravivāda* in ss. 15-20, *maryādāsthāpana* in ss. 21-23, and *bādhābādhika* is ss. 24-38. The colophon for *maryādāsthāpana* alone is found. — *sāmantā* as an adjective to *pañcagrāmī* and *daśagrāmī* is from Cb and quite necessary. — *sthāvaraiḥ*, i.e., trees, rivers etc. — *kṛtrimaiḥ* i.e., mounds, things buried underground etc.

11 Elders among farmers and cowherds, or outsiders who formerly had possessions (there), conversant with the boundary-marks, either many or even one, should, after declaring the boundary-marks, point out the boundary, putting on a contrary dress. In case the boundary-marks as declared are not found, the fine shall be a thousand (*paṇas*). 13 He shall impose the same (fine) on those who, after the boundary is pointed out, remove the boundaries or destroy the boundary-marks.

14 Or, the king shall fix, according as it may be beneficial, the boundary, the extent of the marks of which is lost.

15 Village elders who are neighbours shall decide disputes concerning fields. 16 In case of difference of opinion among them, they shall arbitrate in favour of that in favour of which are the majority, the honest or the approved, or they shall follow the middle course. 17 The king shall take that property to which the claim of both is rejected, also that the owner of which has disappeared. 18 Or, he may allot it as it may be beneficial.

19 In case of forcible seizure, the fine for theft (shall be imposed) in the case of immovable property. 20 In case of seizure on good grounds, he shall pay an amount (to the owner) after calculating his labour and profit.

21 For removing the boundary (marks) the lowest fine for violence (shall be imposed). 22 For breaking the boundary, twenty-four *paṇas* (shall be the fine).

23 By that are explained disputes concerning penance-groves, pasture lands, highways, cremation grounds, temples, sacrificial grounds and holy places.

Thus ends (the topic of) fixing of boundaries.

11 Cb seems to have read *-gopālakalubdhakāḥ*. — *pūrvabhuktikā vā bāhyāḥ* : in view of *vā*, this should be understood as an option to *karṣaka-* etc. Cb, however, reads *abāhyāḥ* and contrues *pūrvabhuktikāḥ* with *karṣaka-* etc. — *abhijñāḥ* from Cb is quite necessary for *anabhijñāḥ* of the mss. — *viparītaveṣāḥ*, i.e., putting on a female dress; cf. 2.36.39. 12 *sahasram* : the fine appears to be rather exorbitant. 13 *setucchidām* : trees are primarily thought of.

15 Here, too, *sāmanta* is an adjective to *grāmavṛddha* rather than an independent substantive. Cf s. 3 above. 16 *bahavaḥ śucayo 'numatā vā* : Cs understands *vā* as *ca* 'majority who are honest and approved by the people.' It seems, however, that there is an option between *śucayaḥ* and *anumatāḥ*, the latter being 'acceptable to both parties to the dispute'. Cf. 3.11.26-7 in connection with witnesses, also 3.11.39. — *madhyam gṛhṇīyuḥ*, i.e., in effect divide the disputed portion equally. 17 *ubhayaparoktam* is proposed for *ubhayaṁ paroktam* of the mss. As adjective to *vāstu*, the emendation is obviously necessary, the meaning being 'to which the claim by both parties is disallowed or lost (*parā-ukta*).' Cb explains the other reading 'if the two parties are unable to come to terms'; Cs has 'if both decisions, viz., the majority and the middle course are rejected by suitors.' Neither is happy. For *parokta* (used of a party to a dispute), see 3.1.19 ff.

20 *kāraṇādāne*, e.g., when received as a pledge for debt etc. — *bandham* is clearly 'an amount', which is arrived at by deducting from the produce of the field charges for his own labour and a legitimate profit on the working of the field. The sense of surety does not suit here. See 3.3.4 above.

21 Whereas *sīman* refers to boundaries between villages, *maryādā* refers to those between fields, etc.

24 All disputes whatever (shall be decided) on the testimony of neighbours.

25 As between a pasture land, dry land, wet-crop field, a vegetable garden, a threshing floor, a shed and a stall for vehicles the earlier one may suffer encroachment from the later one. 26 Dry regions (are those) with the exception of groves for Vedic study and *soma*-sacrifices, temples and holy places.

27 In case of damage to the ploughing or seeds in another's field by the use of a reservoir, channels or a field under water, they shall pay compensation in accordance with the damage. 28 In case of mutual damage to fields under water, parks and embankments, the fine (shall be) double the damage.

29 A tank on a lower level, constructed afterwards, shall not flood with water a field watered by a tank on a higher level. 30 A (tank) constructed on a higher level shall not prevent the flooding with water of a lower tank, except when its use has ceased for three years. 31 For transgression of that, (the punishment shall be) the lowest fine for violence and the emptying of the tank.

32 The ownership of a water-work, not in use for five years, shall be lost except in cases of distress.

33 When tanks and embankments are newly constructed, an exemption (from taxes) for five years (should be granted), when those that are ruined and abandoned are renovated, an exemption for four years, when those that are over-grown with weeds are cleared, for three years, when dry land is newly brought under cultivation, for two years. 34 He is free to mortgage or sell.

35 (Owners) may give (water) in return for a share of produce of various kinds from sowings in fields, parks and gardens watered by (their) dug-out

24 *sarva eva vivādāḥ* : this has reference to disputes about damage to property which are now about to be discussed.

25 *veśma* seems to be a shed for storing grains etc., though a residential building is also likely. Meyer understands *khalaveśma* as one . Cf., however, 3.10.29 below. 26 The idea apparently is that these *sthala* regions are not to suffer encroachments by *kedāra* etc. It seems likely that the s. is a marginal gloss by some pious hand which has got into the text.

27 *ādhāraparivāhakedāropabhogaiḥ* : in view of the plural, three ideas appear better than a single idea, viz., 'the use of wet-fields receiving water by channels from a reservoir.'

30 *uparinivistam* : *paścāt* may be understood with this, but is not necessary.

33 *parihāraḥ* : the exemption would be from land revenue as fixed in 2.24.18. — *samupārūḍhānām* 'overgrown with weeds etc.' (Cb). It could hardly mean 'overflowing their banks (and thus damaged)' (Meyer). — *sthalasya* : as we have to understand *navapravartane* with this also, new land brought under cultivation for the first time is obviously meant. 34 *svātmā* : '*svāmī* would have been better' (Cs). The idea is that the concessions do not affect rights flowing from ownership.

35 The s. seems to refer to lending water from one's water-works in return for a stipulated share of the produce. It would be better to read *-taṭākodakam* or at least *-taṭākam*. — *khātaprāvṛttima* 'set in motion by digging' evidently refers to canals. *nadīnibandhāyatana* may mean 'a structure, i.e., an arrangement dependent on a river (such as a dam).' *taṭāka* is a tank. From these, water is given to *kedāra, ārāma* and *ṣaṇḍa*. *sasyavarṇa* 'var-

channels, structures based on rivers or tanks, or to others as it may be advantageous.

36 And those who use these on lease, on hire, as a pledge, for a share or with authorization for use, shall keep (them) in repair. 37 In case of failure to repair, the fine in double the loss.

38 For one letting out water from the dams out of turn, the fine shall be six *paṇas*, also for one obstructing, through negligence, the water of others when it is their turn.

CHAPTER TEN

SECTION 61 (Continued)

(*vii*) Damage to Pastures, Fields and Roads

SECTION 62 NON-OBSERVANCE OF CONVENTIONS

1 If one obstructs a customary water-course in use or makes (a new one) that is not customary, the lowest fine for violence (shall be imposed), also if one constructs in another's land a dam, a well, a holy place, a sanctuary or a temple. 2 If a (person) himself or through others puts to mortgage or sale a charitable water-work, continued since old times, the middle fine for violence (is to be imposed), the highest on witnesses, except when it is in ruins and abandoned.

3 In the absence of the owner, villages or persons of a pious disposition should repair (these).

ious kinds of produce' from *kedāra*, *ārāma* and *ṣaṇḍa*. With the last two, *sasya* as 'grains' is not quite suitable. *-uttarika* has reference to 'the return' received. Meyer, in the main, has this explanation. Cb, however, has 'water from a well (*khāta*), from a river (*nadyāyatana*), from canals from a river-dam (*nibandhāyatana*), from a tank (*taṭāka*), from a field (*kedāra*), from a garden (*ārāma*), or from plantations (*ṣaṇḍa*), may be given in such a way that the quality (*varṇa*) and quantity (*bhāga*) of the crops are improved (*uttarika*).' *ārāma* and *ṣaṇḍa* as sources of water are doubtful. And *kedāra*, *ārāma* and *ṣaṇḍa* are hardly on the same footing as *taṭāka* etc. — *anyebhyo*, i.e., to owners of fields other than *kedāra*, *ārāma* and *ṣaṇḍa*, and others to whom the water would be useful.

36 *prakraya* 'lease'; cf. 2.12.22. In view of that, 'purchase' (Cs) is not right. — *bhoganisṛṣṭa* 'what is allowed for use' for the time being. — *pratikuryuḥ*, i.e., repair any damage caused by them.

38 *avāre* and *vāre* from Cb are preferable to *apāre* and *pāre* of the mss. It is doubtful if *pāra* can mean 'a sluice-gate' (Meyer). *vāra* is 'a turn' for receiving water from a tank etc. used in common.

3.10

The last sub-section of the 61st *prakaraṇa* is contained in ss. 1-34, while the short 62nd *prakaraṇa* is found in ss. 35-46. — *samaya* is more of a convention than a consciously made agreement between parties, though that also seems included.

1 The stop after *niveśayataḥ*, instead of after *sāhasadaṇḍaḥ*, is as in Cb. 2 *dharmasetu* is a tank or other water-work made by some charitable person.

3 *svāmyabhāve*: Cb restricts the rule to *dharmasetu* only.

4 The size of roads has been explained in the 'Lay-out of the Fort'. 5 For encroaching on a path for small animals or men the fine is twelve *paṇas*, on a path for large animals twenty-four *paṇas*, on a road for elephants or fields fifty-four *paṇas*, on a road to a dike or a forest one hundred and six, on a road to a cremation ground or a village two hundred, on a road in a *droṇamukha* five hundred, on a road in a *sthānīya*, the countryside or pasture land one thousand.

6 In case of reducing the size of these (roads), the fines are one-quarter of the fines (mentioned). 7 In case of ploughing (on them, the fines are) as prescribed.

8 If the owner of the field takes away the field or the tenant leaves it at the time of sowing, the fine shall be twelve *paṇas*, except in cases of defect, calamity or unbearable conditions.

9 Tax-payers shall mortgage or sell (only) to tax-payers, Brahmin owners of gift-lands (only) to Brahmin owners of gift-lands. 10 Otherwise, the lowest fine for violence (shall be imposed). 11 Or, (the same fine is to be imposed) on a tax-payer settling in a village exempt from taxes. 12 But one settling in a tax-paying village shall have freedom to get all things, excepting a house. 13 That also he may give him.

14 If one does not till land that is inalienable, another may use it for five years and return it after receiving compensation for his exertions.

15 Non-tax-payers, living in a different place, may live on the produce (of their fields).

16 Tenants shall accompany, by turns, the village headman journeying on village business. 17 Those who do not accompany shall pay a (penalty per) *yojana* of one *paṇa* and half a *paṇa*.

4 *durganiveśe*: in 2.4.3-5 above. 5 *rundhataḥ*: encroachment on the road is to be understood. — *ṣatchataḥ* cannot be 'six hundred,' in view of its place in the rising scale; 'one hundred and six' is possible, though unusual. Cb seems to have read *śatyaḥ* 'one hundred,' which might appear better.

6 *atikarṣaṇe* 'reducing in size (from what is recorded in the documents)' (Cb). Perhaps *atikarśane* was the original reading. Meyer proposes *abhikarṣaṇe* 'ploughing up close to the road' (Nachtrag).

8 *upavāsa*, as distinguished from *kṣetrika*, is clearly 'a tenant.' — *doṣopanipātāviṣahyebhyaḥ*: see 3.15.2-4. Here *doṣa* is defect in the field, tools etc., *upanipāta* some calamity and *aviṣahya* some unbearable condition of work, such as incapacity, illness etc.

9 *brahmadeyikāḥ*: cf. 2.1.7. 12 *prākāmyam* is not a right to first choice, as Meyer thinks. It is only a right to obtain things. 13 *dadyāt*: the subject is apparently *grāmikaḥ*, the headman of the village.

14 Apparently the owner cannot claim it back within five years if he has not been tilling it, nor can the other use it for more than five years.

15 The implication may be that tax-paying farmers cannot be absentee landlords.

16 *grāmika* is clearly the village headman; cf. s. 18 below. His duties are not described anywhere. — *upavāsāḥ* 'tenants' are 'farm labourers' according to Russ. 17 *paṇārdhapaṇikam* is understood as 1/1/2 *paṇas*. It is also possible to understand an option between 1 *paṇa* and half a *paṇa* at the discretion of the headman.

18 For the village headman ejecting from the village one who is not a thief or an adulterer, the fine is twenty-four *paṇas*, for the village the highest (fine for violence). 19 The entry of one who has been ejected is explained by trespass.

20 He should cause a fence to be made with pillars all round the village at a distance of one hundred *dhanuses* from it.

21 They shall live on pasture land, intended for the grazing of cattle, by cutting (the grass).

22 They shall receive one quarter (of a *paṇa*) per animal in the case of camels and buffaloes that have grazed on the pasture and moved away, half a quarter in the case of cattle, horses and donkeys, one-sixteenth part in the case of small animals. 23 If after grazing, the (animals) sit down, these same fines shall be double, fourfold if they stay overnight.

24 Bulls belonging to village temples or a cow within ten days of her calving, and stud bulls are exempt from fines.

25 In case the (cattle) eat the crops, he shall make (their owner) pay double the damage to the crops after calculating it in accordance with the harvest. 26 And if the owner allows the (cattle) to graze without informing (the owner of the field), the fine shall be twelve *paṇas*, twenty-four *paṇas* if he lets them loose. 27 For herdsmen the fines shall be half (of these). 28 The same (fines) he shall impose in case the cattle eat (the produce in) plantations. 29 (The fines shall be) double if the fence is broken, also if the (cattle) eat grains in the sheds or the threshing circle.

18 Apparently, only a thief or an adulterer could be exiled, and that by the headman or the entire village. 19 *abhigamena* is proposed for *adhigamena* in conformity with 4.13.3-4 to which alone the reference in *vyākhyātaḥ* can be understood.

20 *upasāla* is a small rampart (*sāla*), a sort of fence ; it provided an open space round the village and also served as a defence.

21 *vivītamālavanena* : this is understood as *vivītam ālavanena* (by cutting the grass). Cb on this s. is missing. Cs has *vivīta*, *māla* (table-land or wood near the village) and *vana*. So Meyer, who has 'they shall provide these for grazing.' The compound in the singular would be strange in that case. — *upajīveyuḥ* : the subject is 'grass-cutters'. It is because these have an interest in the *vivīta* that fines are laid down in the following ss. which go to the grass-cutters and not to the state. They may be supposed to pay a rent for the right to cut the grass in the pasture land. These seem to correspond to the wood-cutters of 2.17.3.

22 *rūpam* : cf. 2.29.4,6. — *gṛhṇīyuḥ* : the subject is 'grass-cutters.' We cannot think of any state officers who can be the subject of this plural verb.

24 *ukṣāṇo govṛṣāś ca* 'old bulls and stud-bulls' (Cb Cs). Meyer's 'stud-bull' for the whole might appear better here. Cf. 2.29.8. Manu, 8.242, a close parallel, does not refer to old bullocks.

26 *svāminaḥ* : the owner of the cattle is more likely than that of the field. — *cārayataḥ* 'making them graze' (Cb), 'leading them through the field' (Meyer). In the context the former is better despite 4.9.28. 27 *pālinām* : perhaps we should read *pālānām*.

30 He shall take steps against injury (to cattle). 31 Animals from reserved parks or those that are protected, if found eating, should, after intimating the owner, be so driven off as not to cause injury to them.

32 Cattle should be driven off with a piece of rope or a whip. 33 For causing injury to them in other ways, the fines for physical injury (shall be imposed). 34 Those that attack or whose offence is clear may be restrained by all (possible) means.

Thus ends (the topic of) damage to fields and roads.

35 The village itself shall receive the penalty of a farmer who, after accepting (residence in) a village, does not do (his share of) work. 36 He shall pay double the wage for the work if he does not do work, double each individual's share if he does not contribute money, and a double share if he does not contribute food and drink on festive occasions.

37 One who does not contribute his share in a stage-show shall not witness it with his people. 38 If he listens to or witnesses it secretly, he shall perforce give a double share, also in an undertaking beneficial to all.

39 They shall obey the orders of one who proposes what is beneficial to all. 40 For not carrying them out the fine is twelve *paṇas*. 41 If, on the other hand, they conspire together and beat him, the punishment for each severally shall be double the (prescribed punishment for the) offence. 42 (The punishment shall be) severe for those who injure him.

43 And seniority among them shall be fixed from the Brahmin downwards. 44 And in their festivities, Brahmins, if unwilling, may not do any work and yet receive (their) share.

30 *hiṁsāpratīkāram* is prevention of injury to cattle, which is a new topic that now begins. 31 *abhayavana-* : cf. 2.2.2, also 2.26.1. — *parigṛhītāḥ* : cf. 2.26.3. — *svāminaḥ* : this, in effect, would be the king in the case of animals in the reserved parks.

34 *prārthayamānāḥ* : for the root, cf. 1.17.39.

35 *grāmam abhyupetya* : i.e., accepting obligations consequent on his settling in the village and becoming a member of the community. — *akurvataḥ* : the object is *svakarma*. — *grāma eva* and not the state. 36 The readings and explanations adopted are from Cb. *adāne* is necessary with *hiraṇya-* and *bhakṣyapeya-* to constitute an offence.

38 *nigraheṇa* : Cb explains 'for obstructing the work.' In that case, the locative should have been used rather than the instrumental. The word seems used adverbially in the sense of 'by force, forcibly.' Cf. Manu, 8.220, where we have *nigṛhya*.

41 *hanyuḥ* : the root seems used only in the sense of 'to beat, to strike.' 42 *upahantṛṣu* 'those who cause death' (Cb Cs). It may be that 'those who cause serious injury' are meant.

44 *brāhmaṇā nākāmāḥ*, an emendation in the Punjab edition, is necessary instead of *brāhmaṇe nākāmāḥ* ; with the latter reading Cs explains 'in the case of a Brahmin, they shall not apportion any share to him without first ascertaining his wishes.' This is hardly satisfactory. — *aṁśaṁ ca labheran* : Cs explains 'may contribute, if they are willing.' This is hardly possible. Cb has no comment on this s. Possibly it is a marginal gloss.

45 By that is explained the non-observance of conventions in the case of a region, a caste, a family and a corporation.

46 The king should do what is agreeable and beneficial to these, when they build dikes that are of benefit to the country or bridges on roads or carry out works beautifying the villages or defences (of the villages).

CHAPTER ELEVEN

SECTION 63 NON-PAYMENT OF DEBTS

1 One *paṇa* and a quarter is the lawful rate of interest per month on one hundred *paṇas*, five *paṇas* for purposes of trade, ten *paṇas* for those going through forests, twenty *paṇas* for those going by sea. 2 For one charging or making another charge a rate beyond that, the punishment shall be the lowest fine for violence, for witnesses, each one of them, half the fine. 3 If, however, the king is unable to ensure protection, the (judge) should take into consideration the usual practice among creditors and debtors.

4 Interest on grains (shall be) up to a half, on the harvesting of crops; thereafter it may increase being turned into capital. 5 Interest on capital (shall amount to) half the profit, to be paid for one year, being set apart in a

45 *saṁgha* is an independent term, not to be construed with each of *deśa*, *jāti* and *kula*, as K. P. Jayaswal (*Hindu Polity*, II, 65) thinks. Cf. 3.7.40 above. — *anapākarma* is failure to carry out or observe.

46 *saṁkrama* 'a bridge, a causeway'; cf. 2.3.30 above.

3.11

As in the *Manusmṛti*, the question of the evidence of witnesses is discussed in the section on debts. The law of evidence was indeed formulated primarily in connection with debts.

1 *dharmyā. . . vyāvahārikī* can hardly mean 'according to sacerdotal law' and 'according to secular law' as Jayaswal (*Manu and Yāj.*, p. 15) thinks. — *kāntāragāṇām* from Cb seems supported by Yāj., 2.38. 3 *caritram*, i.e., practices usual among the two parties. These are to be taken into consideration because the traders venture into regions where the king's protection cannot be assured. Cb has 'in such a manner as to suit the debtor and the creditor.' Meyer proposes to read *apakṣīyeta* 'the whole relationship between creditors and debtors breaks down' i.e., creditors charge exorbitant rates and debtors hardly repay. This is unlikely. Russ. follows Meyer. Breloer (II, 49-53) renders *rājani ayogakṣemavahe* by 'so far as it is useful to the king's fiscus or treasury,' i.e., local usage in the matter is to be taken into consideration only if the king's treasury does not suffer thereby. This seems hardly possible. Cf. 1.13.7-8 above.

4 *upārdhā*: i.e., half the amount of grains lent as interest. Cb Cs have 'one and a half times.' That would include the grains lent. —*param*, i.e., if at harvesting time the loan in grains is not returned. — *mūlyakṛtā*, i.e., the loan in grains with the interest is turned into a money loan. Meyer, reading *upārdhāvaram* and a stop after *sasyaniṣpattau*, has 'interest in grains will be due when crops ripen. It may, after the fixing of the price, increase at least to half.' Breloer has 'up to a half of the ripening field. After the crops have ripened, the interest is half the produce' (II, 85-7). Neither seems meant. 5 *prakṣepa* is capital or investment; cf. 4.2.36 etc. In this case money is lent to the farmer, the interest being half the produce. — *saṁnidhānasannā* 'accumulated in a store' (Breloer, who compares *saṁnidhatte svaveśmani* in 2.9.25). Meyer's 'if capital is sunk in the vicinity' is less likely, as the expression describes *vṛddhi*, not *prakṣepa*. Cb, reading *saṁnidhānasan-*

store. 6 One away on a long journey or become obstinate (in making payments) shally pay double the capital.

7 For one recovering interest without fixing it or increasing its rate or claiming through witnesses the capital with interest added to it, the fine shall be four times the (one-fifth or one-tenth) part. 8 For claiming through witnesses a small amount (that was never lent), the fine shall be four times the non-existent (amount). 9 Of that, the receiver shall pay one-third, the rest he who helped him to receive it.

10 Debt shall not increase in the case of a person confined in a long sacrificial session or by illness or in the preceptor's house, or in the case of a minor or an insolvent.

11 For one not receiving back the debt being paid off, the fine shall be twelve *paṇas*. 12 If (it is done) by pleading a valid reason, it shall remain in another's custody with (further) interest stopped.

13 A debt not taken notice of for ten years shall be irrecoverable, except in the case of a minor, an aged person, a sick person, a person in a calamity, a person away on a journey or in case of migration from the country or disorder in the kingdom.

14 Sons shall pay the debt with interest of a deceased person, or heirs inheriting the property or co-debtors or sureties. 15 (There shall be) no other suretyship. 16 The suretyship of a minor is void in law.

nā vārṣikī deyā as an independent s., has 'if interest is not taken for a number of years it should be calculated for one year only.' *vārṣikī* 'for one year' may, however, imply yearly interest, so long as the capital is not paid. 6 *stambhapraviṣṭaḥ* : *stambha* refers primarily to haughtiness which may lead to obstinacy in the matter of paying the debt. Cf 8.4.30. Cb, reading *saṁstambha*, seems to understand 'paralysis' by it. Meyer has '(money) absorbed (*praviṣṭa*) in frozen capital,' which is little likely, since with *dadyāt* as the predicate, *arthaḥ* can hardly be understood as the subject. — *mūlyadviguṇam* : according to Cb, this is the maximum even if many years have elapsed.

7 *śrāvayataḥ* : in view of *śrotṛ* 'a witness,' this obviously means 'claiming with the help of witnesses.' — *bandha* is the usual one-fifth or one-tenth, the fine for loss of suit (3.1.20-1). Four times that is meant. Cf. 3.12.6. Breloer (II, 87) who follows G1 in not reading *vardhayato*, has 'if one deposes that the capital (*vā mūlya*) or the interest (*vā vṛddhi*) is higher than is actually the case (*āropya*, i.e., having enhanced) he is fined four times the enhanced amount (*bandha*).' That appears doubtful. 8 *-catura-* is omitted as in Cb. It may convey the idea of fraud, but does not appear genuine. *tuccha* 'insignificant' conveys the idea of a non-existent loan, in view of *abhūta* that follows. *śrāvaṇā* is a claim with the help of witnesses. 9 *ādātā* is obviously the false claimant, while *pradātā* is the witness who would have helped him to get it. Thus Breloer (II, 88). Cb has the debtor and creditor respectively, and curiously has 1/4th and 3/4th (for *tribhāgam* and *śeṣam*).

10 *asāram* 'indigent,' i.e., an insolvent. Breloer (II, 85) seems to render it by 'an old man.' — *narṇam anuvardheta*, i.e., interest shall cease during that period.

12 *anyatra*, i.e., with some reliable person as a deposit.

13 *daśavarṣo-* etc. : cf. 3.16.30.

14 Breloer (II, 85) treats *sahagrāhiṇaḥ* as an adjective to *pratibhuvaḥ*.

15 *anyat*, i.e., suretyship for producing the debtor etc. Cf. Yāj., 2.53. 16 *asāram* : cf. 3.1.34. Cb has 'if the surety is insolvent he need not pay when the debtor dies.' It is not easy to see how this meaning is possible.

17 But sons, grandsons or heirs inheriting the property shall (be liable to) pay a (debt about the repayment) of which the place and the time are not fixed.

18 Sons or grandsons shall bear liability for suretyship concerning life, marriage or land, to which no restriction as to place or time applies.

19 In case many debts become due at the same time, two (creditors) shall not simultaneously sue one (debtor), except when he is about to leave (the place). 20 Even in that case, he shall secure payment in the order of contracting the debts or first the dues of the king and of a Brahmin learned in the Vedas.

21 The debt mutually contracted between a husband and a wife or a father and a son or between undivided brothers, is irrecoverable (through a court of law).

22 Agriculturists and the king's servants are not to be held at the time of their work. 23 And the wife (shall not be held liable) for the debt incurred by her husband, if she has not assented to it, except in the case of cowherds and farmers tilling for half the produce. 24 The husband, however, shall be held liable for the debt incurred by the wife, if he has gone abroad without providing for her.

25 In case of admission (of the claim), it is best. 26 In case of non-admission, however, witnesses shall decide, those who are trustworthy, honest or approved, three at least in number. 27 Or, two (will suffice) if both parties agree, but never a single witness in the case of debt.

28 Not allowed (as witnesses) are a wife's brother, an associate, a dependent, a creditor, a debtor, an enemy, a cripple, and a convicted person, also those mentioned before as unfit for transactions. 29 The king, a Brahmin learned in the Vedas, a village servant, a leper and a wounded man, an outcast, a Caṇḍāla, a person following a despised profession, a blind, deaf, dumb or self-invited person, a woman and a king's officer (shall not be cited as witnesses)

17 *asaṁkhyāta-* etc. : the substantive is *ṛṇam* (Cb) rather than *prātibhāvyam* (Meyer). With the former, *dadyuḥ* is used, with the latter *vaheyuḥ* as in s. 18. — This is different from s. 14 in that here grandsons are also made liable, and *sahagrāhiṇaḥ* and *pratibhuvaḥ* are excluded.

18 *jīvitapratibhū* seems to be a guarantor of a man's life, while *vivāhapratibhū* seems to be the same as *sukhāvastha* of 3.4.9, 26. *bhūmipratibhū* may be a guarantor for the return of land by tenants. — The s. implies that *ṛṇaprātibhāvya* does not pass on to sons and grandsons.

22 *agrāhyāḥ* : *grah* is primarily 'to seize, to arrest'; but liability to pay the debt is intended in the following ss. 23 *anyatra* etc. : i.e., the wives of these become liable even if their assent was not secured.

25 *uttamaḥ* : supply *pakṣaḥ* (Cb), *upāyaḥ* (Cs.) Meyer proposes *uttamam*, which is not necessary. 26 *śucayo 'numatā vā* : the option is between *śucayaḥ* and *anumatāḥ*, *prātyayikatva* being compulsory. Cf. 3.9.16 above.

28 *anvarthin* seems to mean 'a dependent.' Cb has 'one who says that such and such a person has taken a loan.' — *pūrve* etc. : a reference to 3.1.12. 29 *ahaṁvādin* : who offers to give evidence without being cited. — *svavargebhyaḥ*, i.e., a *śrotriya* for a *śrotriya* and so on.

except in the case of their own groups. 30 In cases of (verbal and physical) injury, theft and adultery, however, (all may be cited as witnesses) except an enemy, a wife's brother and an associate. 31 In the case of secret transactions, one woman or man, who has heard or witnessed it, may be cited as a witness, excepting the king or an ascetic.

32 Masters may bear testimony for servants, priests and preceptors for disciples, and parents for sons, without being forced, or the latter (may do so) for them. 33 And in case of their suing each other, the betters, if defeated, shall pay one-tenth (as fine), the inferiors, one-fifth.

Thus ends the topic of witnesses.

34 The (judge) should exhort witnesses in the presence of Brahmins, a water-jar and fire. 35 In that connection, he should say to a Brahmin (witness), 'Speak the truth.' 36 To a Kṣatriya or a Vaiśya (he should say), 'Let there be no fruit of sacrificial and charitable deeds for you (if you speak untruth); you would go, potsherd in hand, begging for alms to the house of your enemy.' 37 To the Śūdra (he should say), 'Whatever the reward of your merit between birth and death, that would go to the king and the king's sin come to you in case of a false deposition, and punishment will also follow; even afterwards facts as seen and heard would be found out; being of one mind, bring out the truth.' 38 For those who do not bring out (the truth), the fine shall be twelve *paṇas* after seven days; after three fortnights, they shall pay the (amount of the) suit.

39 In case of differences among witnesses, the (judges) should decide in favour of that party in whose favour are the majority, honest or approved, or should follow the middle course. 40 Or, the king should take that object.

41 If witnesses testify to an amount less than (that claimed in) the suit, the plaintiff shall pay a part of the excess (claimed, as fine). 42 If, on the other hand, they testify to a larger amount, the king should take that excess.

32 *anigraheṇa*, i.e., without being forced. 33 For the terms, see 3.1.20-21. — Breloer (II, 90) seems to understand by *uttama* and *avara* higher and lower classes in general, not only those in s. 32. That is unlikely in view of *eṣām*.

37 *vaḥ . . . yuṣmān* : the plural may show that the Śūdras are exhorted jointly, while the others are abjured individually. — *anubaddhaḥ* as an adjective is clearly necessary, not *anubandhaḥ*. — *upaharata* is from Meyer which is better for sense than *avaharata*. The prepositions *ava* and *upa* are often interchanged due to scribal errors. 38 *anupaharatām* refers to refusal to bear testimony. False testimony is mentioned later. — *saptarātrād ūrdhvam* : Cb Cs add that the 12-*paṇa* fine is for each day after the seventh. — *abhiyogam* 'the amount of the suit plus 1/10th as fine' (Cb), apparently because the state must receive its charges.

39-40 *sākṣibhede* etc.: cf. 3.9.16-17.

41 *bandham* seems to be one-fifth; one-tenth is inapplicable in this case.

43 What was badly heard or badly written through the folly of the plaintiff, or the affidavit of a person (since) deceased, shall, after investigation, be decided only on the testimony of witnesses.

44 'In case of divergent (replies to) questions through the folly of witnesses themselves, they shall be fined the lowest, middlemost and highest fines, with regard to (testimony about) place, time and the matter (respectively),' say the followers of Uśanas. 45 'False witnesses who bring into being a non-existent thing or ruin an existing thing, shall pay ten times that (thing) as fine,' say the followers of Manu. 46 'Or, if through folly they lead to a wrong judgment, death by torture (is to be the punishment),' say the followers of Bṛhaspati. 47 'No,' says Kauṭilya. 48 For, witnesses have to testify to what is the truth. 49 For those who do not testify (to the truth) the fine is twenty-four *paṇas*, half that for those who do not speak out.

50 The (plaintiff or defendant) shall produce witnesses who are not at a great distance in place or time. He may secure those who are at a distance or are unwilling to come, with a summons from the king.

CHAPTER TWELVE

SECTION 64 CONCERNING DEPOSITS

1. The law of deposits is explained by that of debts.

2 If the fortified city or the countryside is pillaged by enemy forces or forest tribes, or the village, the caravan or the herd is plundered by robbers,

43 *duḥśrutaṁ durlikhitam* by the writer when the document (the promissory note) was prepared. — *pretābhiniveśaṁ* : this is clearly a statement by a person since dead. Cb's 'distraction of the writer's mind by grief caused by death in the family' is hardly likely.

44 *anuyoge* : questions as well as replies to them. Cf. 3.1.46. 45 The omission of *kuryur bhūtam* in the mss. is due to a scribal error. Cf. 4.9.20. 46 *visaṁvādayatām* : because of the causal, 'causing a false judgment' is better than 'tendering contradictory evidence.' 48 Cb Cs read *dhruvā hi sākṣiṇaḥ śrotavyāḥ* and explain *dhruva* as 'a member of the neighbouring forty families' who are liable to be witnesses, apparently as in 3.9.3. This is doubtful. *śru* would mean in the context 'to bear testimony'. 49 *abruvāṇānām* i.e., those who refuse to give evidence. The fine agrees with that in s. 38 . Cb Cs read *adhruvāṇām* 'those outside the forty families.' Russ. has 'half that if (they emphasize) the testimony of unreliable witnesses (*adhruvāṇām*).'

50 *pratipādayet*: the subject would be *abhiyoktā* or *abhiyuktaḥ*. — Distant in time are such, e.g., as are engaged in a long sacrificial session. — *aprasārān* 'who do not come,' being unwilling. — *svāmi-* 'king' (Meyer) rather than the 'judge' (Cs). The summons would presumably be issued by the judge in the name of the king.

3.12

Along with *upanidhi* 'deposits' after which it is named, this *prakaraṇa* deals with allied topics, such as pledge, borrowing etc. All these, like debt, have this common element, that they involve the placing of one person's goods in the temporary possession or charge of another.

1 The rules particularly applicable would seem to be those in 3.11.11-24 concerning receiving it back, liability of heirs etc.

2 *cakrayuktanāśe* is proposed for *cakrayukte nāśe*. *cakrayukta* means 'a carriage' as shown by 4.10.8 ; 4.13.22. Hence the proposed reading or *cakrayukte naṣṭe* is necessary. *cakra* can hardly be 'fraud' (Cs) or 'army' (Meyer) here. — It is proposed to omit

or there is loss of the wheeled carriage, or the (deposit) is enveloped by flames or by the current in a calamity of fire or floods in the midst of the villege, or the boat has sunk or is plundered, the (depositary), if himself involved, shall not be liable for the deposit.

3 The user of the deposit shall pay charges for use in accordance with the place and the time, and a fine of twelve *paṇas*. 4 He shall be liable for what is lost or has perished in consequence of the use and (shall pay) a fine of twenty-four *paṇas*, or, if the (deposit) runs away for some other reason. 5 He shall not be liable for a deposit that dies or is in distress.

6 And in case of a mortgage, sale or denial of the deposit, the fine shall be four times one-fifth (its value). 7 In case of substitution or helping it to run away, (the fine shall be) equal to its value.

8 By that are explained the loss, use, sale, mortgage and misappropriation of a pledge.

9 A pledge, yielding benefit, shall not be forfeit nor shall its capital bear interest, except when allowed. 10 A pledge, not yielding a benefit, may be forfeit and its capital shall bear interest.

11 For one not returning the pledge to (the owner) who has come (to redeem it) the fine shall be twelve *paṇas*. 12 Or, in the absence of the creditor, the (debtor) may recover his pledge after depositing the redemption amount with village elders. 13 Or, the pledge, with further interest stopped and its value at that time fixed, may remain just there or in the charge of the office for prevention of loss and destruction. 14 Or, in the absence of the

kiṁcid... dravye vā read in the mss. between *-bādhe* and *jvālā-*. It is obvious that *grāmamadhyāgnyudakābādhe* and *jvālāvegoparuddhe* go together and cannot be understood separately. The omitted words cannot be easily construed with these. *kupya* in them is odd, and we have to suppose that irremovable objects could be spared by fire or floods. With *ekadeśamuktadravye* 'when fire or floods have spared part of the goods,' there should have been a statement about the depositary's liability in the form of an exception. This expression can hardly mean 'when all goods are placed in one place' (Meyer). Cf 3.4.33 for *ekadeśa*. The omitted words are clearly derived from some marginal gloss. — *abhyāvahet*: cf. 2.28.26 for the distinction between this root and *abhyābhū*.

4 *niṣpatane* implies a live deposit, an animal or a slave. *pretam* (s. 5) has the same implication. — *anyathā* seems to refer to ill-treatment, which makes the deposit run away.

6 *caturguṇapañcabandho*, i.e., four-fifths of the value of the deposit. Compensation to the owner would be distinct from this fine. Cb Cs have 'four times as reparation to the owner and 4/5ths as fine.' There is no reason for a four-fold restitution. 7 *parivartane* 'change', i.e., substitution.

9 *sopakāraḥ*, e.g., a cow whose milk can be used by the creditor. — *sīdet*: *sad* seems to have the sense of 'to be forfeit, to be lost to the owner,' if the owner is unable to redeem it within the stipulated period. — *anyatra nisargāt* implies a case where the benefit from the pledge is not sufficient to cover the expected interest. Cb Cs read these words in s. 10 where they are inappropriate. G2 and M omit s.10.

12 *niṣkrayam* 'redemption amount' is, in effect, the capital lent plus interest as it may be due. 13 *tatraiva*, i.e., in the creditor's house. — *anāśavināśakaraṇa* seems to be something like a lost property office. 14 *dhāraṇikāsaṁnidhāne* is an emendation that is necessary for the sense. Cf. Yāj., 2.63. — *udgatārgham* 'with a raised price,' i.e.,

debtor, the (creditor), if afraid of destruction (of the pledge), may sell it, with the judges' permission, at the highest price, or to the satisfaction of the Guardian of Deposits.

15 But an immovable (pledge) that can be enjoyed after labour or enjoyed in its fruits (without labour), may bring in a profit over and above the value of the interest on the capital, without causing a reduction in the capital. 16 He who enjoys it without authorization shall surrender the profit after deducting the value (of the interest due) and a part (as fine).

17 The rest is explained by the law of deposits.

18 By that are explained the direction and the commission.

19 Or, if a person in whose charge is the object to be handed over, does not reach the place indicated while going with a caravan, or is plundered and abandoned by robbers, he shall not be liable for the object in his charge. 20 Or, if he dies on the way, even his heir shall not be liable.

21 The rest is explained by the law of deposits.

22 They shall return, in the same condition in which they received it, a thing borrowed or a thing hired. 23 They shall not be liable for a thing given with restriction as to place or time, if it is lost or ruined through deterioration or some sudden calamity.

24 The rest is explained by the law of deposits.

the highest price obtainable. *ādhipālapratyayo vā* : *vikrīṇīta* is evidently to be understood, so that *pratyaya* refers to his satisfaction that the sale is above board and that a fair price is obtained for the pledge. — It is possible that the *ādhipāla* is also in charge of the *anāśavināśakaraṇa*.

15 *prayāsabhogyaḥ*, e.g., a field. — *phalabhogyaḥ*, e.g., a rented house, the rent of which is received by the creditor as interest. — *prakṣepa-* etc. : the idea seems to be that if the benefit from such an *ādhi* is more than the interest due, the whole of it may be enjoyed by the creditor and the excess may not be calculated towards repayment of the capital. In *prakṣepavṛddhimūlya*, *mūlya* is ' value ', while in *amūlyakṣayeṇa*, *mūlya* is the ' capital ' lent, the same as *prakṣepa*. Meyer, in the main, has this explanation, though he understands the first *mūlya* also as ' capital.' 16 *anisṛṣṭopabhoktā*, i.e., when the debtor does not want him to enjoy the whole fruit but only as much as would amount to the interest. — *mūlyaśuddham* is evidently the same as *prakṣepavṛddhimūlyaśuddham* above. — *bandham*, i.e., 1/5th or 1/10th as fine. — Breloer remarks (II, 113-4) that in ancient India only a mortgage was usual, that a hypothec in which the debtor remained in possession of the *ādhi*-goods was unknown and that hence Megasthenes' statement that in India no civil hypothec-suits took place is quite correct.

18 *ādeśa* seems to be a ' direction,' e.g., to a servant to take a thing to some person not far away, while *anvādhi* is ' a commission ' to take a thing to some distant place. Breloer thinks that in the latter case, the person commissioned placed an *ādhi* with the person who handed the goods to him. These two, he says, are guarantee-contracts (II, 114-115).

19 Cs has a single case, plundered etc. by robbers while with the caravan and hence unable to reach the destination. This ignores the *vā*.

23 *bhreṣa* ' deterioration ' ; cf. the use of the root in 3.20.18. — *deśakāloparodhi* : Cb reads *deśakālāvarodhi*. The idea is the same. The thing is given for use in a specified place and for a specified period of time.

25 Concerning sale through agents, however, salesmen selling the commodity at the proper place and time shall pay (to the owner) the price as received and the profit. 26 Or, if (the price is) lower because of their missing the proper place and time, they shall pay the price according to the rate at the time of giving (the goods to them for sale) and the profit. 27 Or, if selling (the goods) as agreed upon they do not make a profit, they should pay only the price. 28 Or, if the price is lower because of a fall in prices, they should give the lower price as reduced. 29 Or, in the case of dealers, who are trustworthy and free from blame so far as the king is concerned, they may not pay even the price of what is lost or ruined through deterioration or a sudden calamity. 30 But of commodities removed in space or time they shall pay the price and profit after deducting losses and expenses, and a separate share in the case of each of the different kinds of goods.

31 The rest is explained by the law of deposits. 32 With this is explained (the topic of) sale through agents.

33 And the trust (is explained) by the law of deposits.

34 If he hands it over to one when it was entrusted to him by another, it shall be (treated as) lost.

35 In case of misappropriation of a thing entrusted, a former offence (of the trustee) and the persons entrusting it shall lead to decision. 36 For, artisans are dishonest. 37 There is no rule regarding trusts prevailing among them which requires evidence beforehand.

38 If he denies a thing entrusted without evidence, the person who had entrusted it may make witnesses, secretly stationed behind walls, learn about it

25 For *vaiyāvṛtya-* see 2.5.18 ; 2.8.22. We have here sale through agents, who may be receiving a commission on sales. — *śeṣam upanidhinā vyākhyātam* after s. 25 is out of place and must be omitted. 26 *parihīṇam*, i.e., sold at a lower price. 27 *yathāsaṁbhāṣitam*, i.e., carrying out their part of the agreement as to place and time. 28 *arghapatane* which is due to other causes, over which the salesmen have no control. 29 *sāṁvyāvahārika* seems to mean nothing more than 'a dealer, a trader.' — *arājavācyeṣu* suggests that the whole section has primarily in view the sale of royal goods. 30 *deśakālāntaritānām*, i.e., those to be sold in foreign lands or those to be sold after a lapse of time. — *paṇyasamavāyānāṁ ca pratyaṁśam* : this apparently means that when the agent handles many kinds of goods at the same time, he is to render a separate account of each. Meyer thinks of a number of agents of the same merchant selling the same kind of goods, each being responsible for his share. Such a rule does not seem necessary.

33 *nikṣepa* is a thing given in trust and primarily refers to raw material given to artisans for manufacture into articles. Cf. '*nikṣepaḥ śilpihaste tu bhāṇḍaṁ saṁskartum arpitam*' (Kṣīrasvāmin on Amara ; cf. Kane, III, 454 n. 766).

34 *hīyeta*, i.e., it is to be treated as lost and the usual compensation and fine are to be given. Breloer thinks that *hīyeta* means 'shall redeem itself,' i.e., the keeper is not liable. This would be so only if the other person is the heir of the entruster, since deceased, as in Manu, 8.185-6.

35 *pūrvāpadānam* : cf. 2.36.36 and see 1.8.16. 37 *karaṇa-* 'evidence', particularly in the form of witnesses.

38 It is proposed to read *rahasi praṇi-* for *rahasyapraṇi-* ; the latter can hardly mean by making witnesses listen to the secret with a request' (Cs) or 'by making them enter (*praṇipāta*) into the secret' (Meyer). The customer entreats the artisan when the latter

by soliciting him in private or in a park by creating confidence on the occasion of a drinking party.

39 Some aged or sick trader should entrust to him in secret an object that is marked and go away. 40 At his direction, his son or brother should approach and demand the thing entrusted. 41 If he returns it he is honest, else he shall give the thing (originally) entrusted and a fine for theft.

42 Or, some credible person, about to leave home, should entrust to him a marked object and then leave. 43 Then returning after some time he should ask for it. 44 If he returns it he is honest, else he shall give the thing enttrusted and a fine for theft.

45 Or, he should (himself) bring him round with a marked object.

46 Or, a person appearing foolish by nature should, through fear of (arrest for) king's dues or movement at forbidden time, entrust to him at night an object of high value and go away. 47 Being in prison, he should ask him for it. 48 If he returns it he is honest, else he shall give the thing entrusted and a fine for theft.

49 And by means of a recognition-mark, he shall demand both of people in his house. 50 If either (of the two) is not given, (punishment etc.) as stated before.

thinks that there is no one about (*rahasi*), when he may say something implying that he had received the article. That the concealed witnesses are spies (Meyer) is quite possible. *vanānte* : *vana* is *upavana*, where picnics are arranged. *madyaprahavaṇa* is obviously a drinking party arranged in the park. Wine might loosen the artisan's tongue.

39 *apagacchet*: Cs has 'should die'; the artisan is to get this impression, as the man was *vṛddha* or *vyādhita*; the man himself, however, only goes away, i.e., disappears for the time being.

42 *pravrajyā* may refer only to leaving home, not necessarily becoming a monk. Cf. *pravrajitā* 2.23.2 above. — *śraddheya* suggests that the artisan must believe in the bona fides of the man about his intention to leave home or become a monk.

45 *pratyānayet*: the subject seems to be the customer. According to Cs he points to a mark already there in the original article. Perhaps the reading should be *pratyāyayet* 'should convince' the artisan that it really belongs to him. This presupposes, of course, that the article is found when a search is made.

46 *rājadāyikākṣaṇabhītaḥ* is uncertain in meaning. Two things may be understood—afraid of dues (*dāyika*) to the king, and afraid of *akṣaṇa* (as in 2.36.35). Meyer has 'fear of harm (*akṣaṇa*) from the king or inheritors (*dāyaka*) laying claim to the valuables' or 'fear of king, inheritance or harm.' With *-kāṅkṣaṇa*, Cs has 'fear of a demand on him (*kāṅkṣaṇa*) by a minister, etc. who wants to present it to the king (*rājadāyin*).' Cb has no explanation; its text has *-kāṅkṣaṇa*. Meyer also suggests *rājadvārikākṣaṇa* 'fear of the forbidden hour (*akṣaṇa*) of the royal door-keepers (at the royal gate).' That is not unlikely. 47 *bandhanāgāra-* etc.: i.e., on the plea that he wants to pay for his release.

49 *asya gṛhe janam*: this applies when the artisan is dead (Cs). — Meyer thinks that the s. is mutilated, a portion stating that an agent should deposit two things, one with marks and another without, has got dropped; that would explain *ubhayam*. It is also possible that *ubhaya* refers to the *nikṣepa* and the *kṛtalakṣaṇa dravya* of ss. 39, 42, or the *sāra* of s. 46.

51 And the (judge) should question the source of the objects used (by the defendant), and inquire into indications of that object being involved in the transaction, as well as the capacity of the complainant to (own) the object.

52 By this is explained association in secret.

53 Therefore, one should make (a deal), with one's own people or with strangers, in the presence of witnesses, in an open manner, properly declaring it with respect to place, time, quantity and quality.

CHAPTER THIRTEEN

SECTION 65 LAW CONCERNING SLAVES AND LABOURERS

1 For one selling or keeping as a pledge a minor Ārya individual except a slave for livelihood, the fine is twelve *paṇas* for a kinsman in the case of a Śūdra, double that in the case of a Vaiśya, three times in the case of a Kṣatriya, four times in the case of a Brahmin. 2 For a stranger, the lowest, the middle and the highest fines and death are the punishments (respectively), also for purchasers and witnesses.

3 It is not an offence for Mlecchas to sell an offspring or keep it as a pledge. 4 But there shall be no slavery for an Ārya in any circumstances whatsoever.

5 Or, after keeping as a pledge an Ārya when the family has bound itself in times of distress of Āryas, they shall, on finding the redemption-amount, redeem first a minor or one who renders help.

51 *upaliṅganam* : cf. 3.13.37 etc. Meyer's 'circumstantial evidence about the thing being connected with the artisan's business (*vyavahāra*)' is rather involved.

52 That is, similar tricks are to be used if one party denies a secret agreement.

53 *vibhāṣitam* 'declared in words.' — *agra* 'number,' i.e., quantity, and *varṇa* 'class,' i.e., quality.

3.13

A part of this section is found in the next Chapter also.

1 *udaradāsa* : he is one who, in distress, lives with another person in better circumstances and works as a slave in return for food. A minor may be so handed over for his maintenance. There is no actual sale in this case, only stay for the time being. — *ārya-prāṇam* : a Śūdra is clearly included among Āryas. — *aprāptavyavahāram* : see 3.3.1. — *parajana*, i.e., one not related to the minor.

3 *mlecchānām* would seem to refer to foreigners as well as tribals not absorbed in Āryan society. Mixed castes would be on a par with a Śūdra (3.7.37). Breloer (II, 37-41) remarks that this corroborates the fact that the bondmen were of foreign origin. 4 This means that a minor's *dāsabhāva* is null and void. The *dāsatva* of a major Ārya is, however, implicit in the Chapter.

5 What seems meant is this : there is distress among Āryas (*āryāṇām āpadi*), so a whole family pledges itself to some one more happily placed (*kulabandhane*) ; then a minor may be included as a pledge (*āryam ādhāya*). That *āryam* refers to a minor seems clear from *athavā*, which implies an option to the preceding rule. — *sāhāyyadātāram* is probably one who has been helpful in procuring the ransom amount. Cs has 'who has agreed to be a pledge.'

6 A person pledging himself shall be forfeit if he runs away once, one pledged by another if (he runs away) twice, both at the first attempt, if about to leave for a foreign land.

7 Or, for one depriving a slave of his Āryahood, when he has stolen money, the fine shall be half (the above fines).

8 The pledger shall be liable for the capital, if the pledge has run away or is dead or is in calamity.

9 Making a pledge pick up a corpse, dung, urine or leavings of food, and making women (pledges) give bath to a naked person, giving corporal punishment to them and dishonouring them shall result in the loss of the capital, and shall result in freedom for a nurse, a female attendant, a woman tenant tilling for half the produce and a maid. 10 The going away of an attendant who has begotten an offspring is valid (in law).

11 For one approaching a nurse who is pledged, when she is unwilling, (the punishment shall be) the lowest fine for violence if she is under his control, the middle if she is under the control of another. 12 If one, himself or through another, defiles a maiden who is pledged, he shall lose the capital, pay (her) dowry and a fine double that.

13 The progeny of one who sells himself shall be known as Ārya. 14 He shall get what is earned by himself without detriment to his work for

6 *sīdet*: cf. 3.12.9. What seems meant is that he ceases to be a pledge and becomes a *dāsa*. The former had a number of rights denied to the latter; an absconding pledge lost these. Cs has 'i.e., he must return the debt at once.' But if he could have paid the debt, why need he have run away? Breloer (II, 41-43) understands by 'running away' not only returning to the master but also demanding in law his liberation on account of illegal treatment. If the suit failed he had to go back. A law-suit by the pledge in this form seems hardly implied.

7 This s. is in the middle of ss. that deal with the *āhitaka*, not the *dāsa*. Perhaps *āhitakasya* should, therefore, be read for *dāsasya*, the idea being, a pledge who steals money might be reduced to the status of a slave by the pledgee; that makes the latter liable to half the fines of s. 1. Cb Cs have 'a slave stealing his master's money is to pay a fine half that for a thief stealing the money (*bhāva*) of an Ārya.' This is doubtful. Meyer has 'for a slave stealing money, the fine is to be half that for depriving a man of his Āryahood.' The fine would appear too small for the offence. He also suggests 'for stealing a slave's money, half the fine for deprivation of Āryahood' or 'for a slave stealing, half that for an Ārya stealing.' Neither seems likely. The exact meaning of the s. is uncertain.

8 *mūlyaṁ bhajeta*, i.e., pay off the debt or furnish a fresh pledge.

9 *upacārikā* appears to be a more personal attendant than a *paricārikā*. 10 *upacārakasya abhiprajātasya*: despite the gender, a female attendant bearing a child to the creditor is to be understood. If she leaves, no fresh pledge need be given. A male pledge begetting a child on some female in the creditor's house is possible, but appears less likely. Cb Cs understand the husband of the *dāsī*, who maintains her and serves her master for the same wage; if he begets a child on her, he may run away. This is rather involved. Meyer thinks of sexual misbehaviour with a male pledge and suggests *abhimehitasya* as the reading. That is quite unlikely. For *abhiprajāta*, cf. 3.15.13.

11 *vā* is often used only to introduce a new rule. — *svavaśām* 'under his control' as in Meyer rather than 'not under her husband's control' (Cb Cs). So *paravaśā* is 'not under his control'; i.e., a man other than the creditor himself has relations with her.

13 From this s. onwards the *dāsa* proper is dealt with. 15 *āryatvaṁ gacchet*: contrast Nārada, 5.37 'an *ātmavikrayin* can never be free.'

the master, also his paternal inheritance. 15 And he shall become an Ārya by paying the price.

16 By that are explained the slave for livelihood and the person pledged. 17 And his ransom-amount is to be in conformity with the capital.

18 One on whom a fine is imposed may pay off the fine by work.

19 An Ārya individual captured under the banner should be freed by suitable work for a specified period or for half the price.

20 If one employs in vile work or in a foreign land, a slave less than eight years of age, without kinsmen and unwilling (to do that work), from among any of the four types, —(a slave) born in the house, received in inheritance, obtained (as a present) and purchased,—or if one sells or pledges a female slave who is *enceinte* without providing for the nourishment of the foetus, the lowest fine for violence (shall be imposed), also on purchasers and witnesses.

21 If a person does not make a slave an Ārya for a suitable ransom, the fine is twelve *paṇas*, and confinement (for him) till he does it.

22 Kinsmen shall inherit the property of a slave, in their absence the master.

23 The offspring begotten by the master on his own female slave shall be known as free along with the mother. 24 If the mother is attached to the house and looks after the affairs of the family, her brother and sister also shall be free.

16 That is, their progeny is Ārya, they can earn and inherit and be free by paying ransom. 17 *asya* evidently refers to the *āhitaka* only, for in the case of an *udaradāsa*, no debt is incurred. — Breloer (I, 70-71 ; II, 43-5) says that half the wage earned by the *dāsa* by working for his master is counted towards liberation price. The present text shows no such rule. But it is clear that the *dāsa* could earn a wage and from the savings made out of his earnings, he could procure his freedom.

18 This is obviously the *daṇḍopakārin* (2.12.21) or *daṇḍapratikartṛ* (2.23.2 ; 2.24.2). He is a state slave and the whole of his wage goes towards his ransom amount.

19 *karmakālānurūpeṇa* : we have to supply *niṣkrayeṇa*. The idea is, after doing work assigned for a specific period he becomes free. For the expression cf. s. 27 below. — *mūlyārdhena*, i.e., for half the usual price of a *dāsa*. Cb Cs have ' for half the price fixed in conformity with the work and time.' This ignores the *vā*. Breloer has (II, 45) ' through a fixed work or a fixed time or half the cost of the work (provided he can produce this amount immediately).'

20 *gṛhejāta-* etc. refer to the *caturvarga* of Nārada, 5.29. — *videśe* : after this a *vā* seems necessary. With this clause *nayataḥ* is to be understood from the following clause.

21 *saṁrodhaś cākaraṇāt* is in conformity with 3.14.1 as proposed by Meyer. With *ākāraṇāt*, Cb Cs have ' he should be called (*ākāraṇa*) and surrounded by kinsmen (*saṁrodha*) taunted and thus forced to give freedom.' This is very doubtful. Russ. (with *cākāraṇāt*) has ' and the same fine for one who puts obstacles (to liberation) without sufficient cause.'

22 Contrast Manu, 8.416 ' a slave cannot own property.'

23-24 Kātyāyana has a closely parallel rule.

25 If, after ransoming a male or a female slave, a person again sells or pledges him, the fine is twelve *paṇas*, except in the case of those who themselves agree.

Thus ends the law concerning slaves.

26 Those who are near shall note a labourer's engagement in work.

27 He should receive a wage as agreed upon, in conformity with the work and time (if the wage is not agreed upon). 28 A cultivator, a cowherd (and) a trader should receive one-tenth part of the crops, of butter (and) of the goods dealt in by them (respectively) if the wage is not agreed upon. 29 But if the wage is agreed upon, then as agreed upon.

30 But the group of those who work in hope (of remuneration) such as artisans, artists, minstrels, physicians, professional story-tellers, attendants and others should get a remuneration as others of that type do or as experts fix.

31 (Disputes) shall be settled only on the testimony of witnesses. 32 In the absence of witnesses, the (judge) should inquire at the place where the work (was carried out).

33 In case of non-payment of the wage, the fine is one-tenth or six *paṇas*. 34 In case of denial, the fine is twelve *paṇas* or one-fifth.

35 If a person in distress, overcome by the current of a river or flames or robbers or wild animals, calls a rescuer with the promise of all possessions or sons and wife or himself and is rescued, he should give a reward as directed by experts. 36 By that are explained retractions of promises made in distress in all cases.

25 *punar vikrayādhānaṁ nayataḥ* : Cs thinks that the person who pays the ransom price is meant, Meyer that the person who receives the ransom price is meant. The former seems better. Breloer thinks (II, 57 n. 5) that *aniṣkrīya* is to be read ' so long as he or she is not freed.' This does not fit in with the exception in *svayaṁvādin* ' who himself agrees to be sold or pledged.' — *dāsakalpaḥ* : *dāsa* includes the *āhitaka*. They both differ from the *karmakara*. The former are under the sway of some one ; the latter only does work for a wage. For slavery in ancient India, cf. Breloer II, 7-60.

26 *āsannāḥ* appear to be some sort of foremen, who are on the spot.

28 The wage mentioned in 2.24.28 for *gopālaka* etc. appears to be for those in state service ; here those working for private citizens seem meant. *gopālakaḥ sarpiṣām* : cf. 2.29.7 above.

30 *āśākārika* is an unusual word ; it seems to mean one who works in the expectation of a lump remuneration or reward, not a wage. These persons are not labourers, but belong to a higher category. — *yathānyas tadvidhaḥ*, i.e., at the usual rates, these varying according to circumstances.

33 *daśabandho daṇḍaḥ ṣaṭpaṇo vā*, i.e., if 1/10th amounts to less than six *paṇas* the latter fine is imposed. With his explanation of *bandha* as ' so many times ' Meyer is forced to suggest that *daśabandha* and *pañcabandha* are to be interchanged in the two ss. 34 *apavyayamāne*, i.e., denying that any wage is due from him.

37 A harlot should get a fee in accordance with the indications of union ; but she who makes an exorbitant demand shall lose it, also if she shows evil-mindedness or lack of modesty.

CHAPTER FOURTEEN

SECTION 65 (Continued)

Duties of Servants

SECTION 66 UNDERTAKINGS IN PARTNERSHIP

1 For a labourer not doing the work after receiving the wage, the fine is twelve *paṇas*, and detention till it is done.

2 If he is incapable or if the work is vile or if he is ill or in calamity, he shall get annulment (of the agreement) or (the right) to get it done by another. 3 Or, at his cost, the employer shall have the right to get it done.

4 If, when there is a restriction ' You shall not give this work to another, nor shall I do any one else's work,' the employer does not get work done by him or the labourer does not do the work, the fine shall be twelve *paṇas*. 5 If the (labourer) has received wages from another person than the employer, he may not, on completion of the work, do (additional) work for him if unwilling.

6 ' If the (employer) does not give work when the labourer has presented himself, the work shall be considered as done,' say the teachers. 7 ' No,' says Kauṭilya. 8 A wage is for work done, not for what is not done. 9 If after allowing even a little to be done, he does not allow it to be done (further), his work shall be considered as done.

37 *puṁścalī* is not mentioned in 2.27. — *upaliṅganāt* : cf. 3.12.51 above. — The stanza is not in keeping with the rest of the Chapter and seems derived from a different context.

3.14

The rest of section 65 is found in ss. 1-17 and section 66 is found in ss. 18-38. The two are closely connected.

1 *saṁrodhaś cākaraṇāt* : see 3.13.21 above. With *cākāraṇāt* Russ. has ' if he obstructs work without cause.'

3 *vyayakarman* ' cost, expense ' ; cf. 2.1.23.

4 *avarodhe* from Cb is necessary for the sense. Meyer proposes *virodhe* ' when there is prohibition,' because of 3.15.7. But even in the latter place we have to read *avarodhena* for *avirodhena* of the mss. 5 *karmaniṣṭhāpane* etc. : the idea seems to be that the employer may want the labourer to do additional work after the contracted work in hand is completed by him ; if in the meanwhile the labourer has accepted another man's work (receiving payment beforehand), he may refuse to do the additional work for the first employer. Suggesting *karmāniṣṭhāpane* as the reading, Cs has ' when the work is uncompleted, the labourer who has received wages from another shall not work for the latter if the first employer is unwilling to allow.' *asakāmaḥ* is queerly understood in this. Meyer has ' If the master has assigned his work to some other person and if he has also received the wage, then if unwilling he may not do it.' This sense for *niṣṭhāpana* is uncertain. Cb is missing on *bhartur akārayato. . . nāsakāmaḥ kuryāt.*

6 *kṛtaṁ vidyāt* : i.e., a claim for wage can be successfully made.

10 In case the labourer misses the proper place and time or does the work in a wrong manner, he may not, if unwilling, allow the work as done. 11 In case more work is done than agreed upon, he shall not make the effort vain.

12 By that are explained labourers from unions. 13 The (workman) kept (on the work) from among them shall remain for seven nights. 14 After that, the (union) shall provide another and secure the completion of the work.

15 And without informing the employer, the union shall not remove any one or bring in any one. 16 In case of transgression of that, the fine is twenty-four *paṇas*. 17 For the person removed by the union, the fine shall be half (that).

Thus ends the topic of labourers.

18 Labourers from unions or partners in an undertaking shall divide the wages as agreed upon or in equal proportions.

19 Or, cultivators and traders shall give to a (partner) who has become ill in the interval between the commencement and completion of (work connected with) crops and goods (respectively) an individual share corresponding to work as done by him. 20 In case a substitute is provided, they shall give the full share. 21 But if he has fallen ill when the goods put together have brought success, they shall give his individual share there and then. 22 For, success or failure on the way is common.

23 But if when the work has begun a (partner) goes away even if in good health, he shall be fined twelve *paṇas*. 24 Nor shall he have the freedom to keep away.

10 *-pātanena* : *-pātane* locative as usual would have been better. 11 *prayāsaṁ na mogham* from Cb is quite necessary. *na* seems to have dropped out through a scribal error. *prayāsam amogham* is also possible.

12 *saṁghabhṛtāḥ* : obviously these are members of a labour union. They get work and also their wages through the union, not directly from the employer. 13 *ādhiḥ* : in effect, this means a workman sent by the *saṁgha* to do the work. The similarity with the 'pledge (*ādhi*)' is that like the latter he does work for another at the behest of a third party (viz., the union). — *saptarātram* : change of workmen every seven days may be to prevent direct and close relations being established between individual workmen and the employer. 14 *karmaniṣpākam* : apparently the idea is that the *saṁgha* is responsible for finishing the work and not any individual member. Russ. renders ss. 13-14 : 'the time given to such a union is weekly ; thereafter agreements are allowed with others and work given for carrying it out.'

17 *saṁghena parihṛtasya* : the workman is to be fined apparently because he leftn without informing the employer when withdrawn (from the work) by the union. The unio may be supposed to indemnify him.

18 The labour union is a sort of partnership and hence the easy transition to the new section.

19 *sannasya* 'who has become ill' (Cb). 20 *upasthāne* : we expect *upasthāpane*.

21 *saṁsiddha* 'has succeeded', i.e., has brought in a profit. Cb, however, has 'is ready to start.' In that case *pratyaṁśa* would refer to the man's goods returned to him before starting. However, in the next s. which, with its *hi*, gives the reason for this rule, *saṁsiddha* seems referred to in *pathi siddhi*.

24 *na ca prākāmyam*, i.e., he shall be forced to work. Cf. 2.1.22.

25 But he should cause a misappropriator to be caught by (a promise of) a share for the work, preceded by a promise of safety, (and) he should give him the share and safety. 26 In case he steals again, he shall be exiled, also if he goes elsewhere. 27 In case of a very serious offence, however, he should deal with him as with a traitor.

28 Sacrificial priests shall divide the fees as agreed upon or in equal shares, excepting objects received for each one's special duties.

29 And in the *Agniṣṭoma* and other sacrifices, a priest falling ill after the consecration ceremony shall receive one-fifth (of his share), after the sale of *soma* one-fourth, after the heating of the *pravargya*-vessel on the middle *upasad* day one-third, after the middle *upasad* day half the share, after the morning pressing on the day of *soma*-pressing three quarters of the share. 30 After the mid-day pressing, he shall receive the full share. 31 For (at that time) the fees are carried. 32 Except in the case of the *Bṛhaspatisava,* fees are indeed given at each pressing.

33 By that are explained fees for sacrifices lasting for many days.

34 The remaining hired (priests) should do the work of those who have fallen ill, up to ten days and nights, or others trusted by themselves (should do it).

35 Should, however, the sacrificer fall ill before the sacrifice is completed, the priests should complete the work and receive the fees.

36 But if when the work is incomplete one leaves the sacrificer or the priest, the lowest fine for violence (shall be imposed).

37-38 One owning a hundred cows but not keeping the sacred fires,
one owning a thousand cows but not performing a sacrifice, a drunkard,

25 *coram* : this evidently refers to a partner in a joint undertaking who is suspected of stealing the earnings. *abhayapūrvaṁ karmaṇaḥ pratyaṁśena* implies a promise when his first offence is discovered that no harm would come to him and he would get his share, if he agrees to improve. *grāhayet* is not quite appropriate, as there does not seem to be any arrest at this time. Cs thinks of a guild of robbers, one of them betraying the others. But *dūṣyavad ācaret* in s. 27 is hardly possible in the case of a robber. Some important citizen or dignitary can alone be thought of. 26 *punaḥsteye* implies a reprieve on the earlier occasion. — *anyatra gamane*, i.e., abandoning the work and going away altogether. 27 *dūṣyavat*, i.e., as in 5.1 below.

29 *tṛtīyam* rom Cb is obviously necessary for *dvitīyam* of the mss. — *madhyamopasada ūrdhvam* is read in comformity with the actual comment in Cb, though its text shows *madhyād ūrdhvam.* 32 This s. serves little purpose and seems to be a marginal gloss by some one who did not agree with s. 31. *hi* in the s. cannot establish a relationship with the preceding. — For the rules, cf. Manu, 8.210.

33 This s. is unnecessary, and may not be original. Cb has no comment on it.

34 *ādaśāhorātrāt* : Meyer thinks of the days of impurity ; that is possible if *sanna* implies actual death. — *svapratyayāḥ* : *sva* may refer to the other priests, who have trust in these. Cb refers *sva* to the *yajamāna* 'according to his own wish.' Cf. 2.36.5 ; 8.4.33.

35 *samāpayya* : the casual shows that the heir or relation isi nduced to complete the sacrifice.

37 The first half occurs in Manu, 11.14, in another connection. — *vṛṣalī* is a heretic woman, not necessarily a Śūdra. Cf. 1.12.5. — The nominatives in this and the follow-

one who has married a heretical woman, a slayer of a Brahmin, a violator of an elder's bed, one addicted to receiving gifts from evil persons, a thief, a priest working for a degraded person, — (in the case of these) there is no harm in abandoning each other, because of the certainty of impurity attaching to (such sacrificial) work.

CHAPTER FIFTEEN

SECTION 67 RESCISSION OF SALE AND PURCHASE.

1 If, after selling an article, one does not deliver it, the fine shall be twelve *paṇas*, except in cases of defect, a sudden calamity or unsuitability. 2 A defect in the article is defect. 3 Trouble from the king, thief, fire or water is a sudden calamity. 4 What is lacking in many qualities or what is done by one in distress is unsuitable.

5 For traders a period of retraction of one day (may be allowed), for agriculturists three days, for cowherds five days. 6 In the case of the sale of the means of livelihood by (persons of) mixed and the highest *varṇas*, (a period of retraction of) seven days (may be allowed).

7 For perishable goods, a retraction may be allowed with the restriction 'It shall not be sold elsewhere.' 8 In case of transgression of that, the fine is twenty-four *paṇas* or one-tenth part of the goods.

9 If, after purchasing an article, one does not receive it, the fine is twelve *paṇas*, except in cases of defect, a sudden calamity or unsuitability. 10 And rescission of purchase is similar to retraction by a seller.

11 In the case of marriages, however, revocation is valid up to the ceremony of clasping the hand in the case of the first three *varṇas*, and up to

ing stanza cannot be easily construed with the predicate at the end ; we should supply *eteṣām* with it. 38 *saṁkara* is defect, i.e., impurity.

3.15

4 *bahuguṇahīnam* 'lacking in many qualities' is according to Cs 'with its value diminished many times,' according to Meyer 'disadvantageous from many points of view.' — *ārtakṛtam* may convey the idea of what is done under duress. — The same three conditions operate for rescission of purchase as well (s. 9 below).

6 *vṛttivikraye* is from Cb. For concern about *vṛtti*, cf. 3.1.31. *vivṛtti-* of the mss. conveys little sense. Meyer suggesting *nivṛtti-* for it and thinking *varṇānām* to be an error for *paṇyānām* has 'for cancellation (*nivṛtti*) or sale (finally confirmed) of goods mixed or of the highest quality.' This is little likely.

7 *ātipātika* which must be disposed of quickly, perishable goods, such as milk, curds, flowers etc. (Cb). — *avarodhena* is proposed for *avirodhena* of the mss. Cf. 3.14.4. *avirodhena* can hardly mean 'so as to enable the goods to be preserved' (Cs) or 'when there is no prohibition to sell elsewhere' (Meyer). Meyer's other explanation (with *avirodhe na*) 'there shall be no retraction (*na anuśayaḥ*) except when there is no prohibition (*avirodhe*)' is not possible. There is nothing in the text for 'except when.'

10 *samānaḥ*, i.e., as in s. 5.

consummation in the case of Śūdras. 12 Even in the case of those whose hand-clasping ceremony is completed, revocation is valid on discovering a defect connected with sex. 13 But under no circumstances (will revocation be valid) when they have begotten children.

14 For giving a maiden in marriage without mentioning the maiden's defect in connection with sex, the fine is ninety-six *paṇas* and the return of the dowry and woman's property. 15 Or, for the suitor marrying without mentioning the bridegroom's defect, the fine is double, and the loss of the dowry and woman's property.

16 In the case of bipeds and quadrupeds, however, for declaring dull, diseased and unclean ones as energetic, healthy and clean (respectively) the fine is twelve *paṇas.* 17 In the case of quadrupeds revocation (is allowed) up to three fortnights, up to a year in the case of human beings. 18 For, it is by that time that purity or otherwise can be known.

19 The members of the court should so allow revocation in the matter of a gift or a purchase that neither the giver nor the receiver is harmed.

CHAPTER SIXTEEN

SECTION 68 NON-CONVEYANCE OF GIFTS

SECTION 69 SALE WITHOUT OWNERSHIP

SECTION 70 THE RELATION OF OWNERSHIP

1 The non-delivery of gifts is explained by the non-payment of debts.

2 A gift, not negotiable, shall remain in revocation in one place.

11 *pāṇigrahṇāt*: the sense of *ā* is to be understood with the ablative. Cf 3.5.20. — *prakarmaṇaḥ*: again *ā* is to be understood. *prakarman* is sexual intercourse, i.e., consummation. 12 *doṣam aupaśāyikam*, e.g., impotency, loss of virginity etc. (Cb).

14 *strīdhana* could be returned by the parents if it is in their possession. For *strīdhana*, see 3.2.14-15. 15 *varayituḥ* refers to the bridegroom himself, since it goes with *vindataḥ* 'who marries.' — Manu also includes marriage-sale under this head.

16 It is proposed to read *kuṇṭha-* for *kuṣṭha-* of the mss., as it provides the necessary contrast to *utsāha*. *kuṇṭha* is found in Cb. — We expect *sotsāha* and *svastha*, adjectives like *śuci*. 18 *śaucāśauce* is attested by Cb. Physical as well as mental cleanliness is implied. — Sale of human beings is clearly mentioned here.

19 *sabhāsadaḥ* are apparently the same as *kuśalāḥ* of 3.16.5, where this rule is repeated; experts consulted by the court in technical matters are meant.

3.16

The three short *prakaraṇas* are found in ss. 1-9, 10-28 and 29-42 respectively.

2 *avyavahāryam* which cannot be the object of a transaction of gift. — *ekatra anuśaye varteta* : Meyer has 'belongs solely to revocation, (i.e., to the chapter on revocation of sale and purchase).' This seems hardly meant. The idea seems to be, it stands revoked automatically, with the donor.

3 If, after promising to give his whole property, his sons and wife or himself, one revokes, the (judge) shall allow it. 4 And (the judge shall annual) a gift of piety to wicked persons or for destructive actions, a gift of wealth to those who are not useful or are harmful, and a gift of love to unworthy persons.

5 And experts shall fix revocation in such a way that neither the donor nor the receiver is harmed.

6 For one who accepts a gift made in fear—through fear of punishment or fear of abuse or fear of a calamity—the punishment shall be that for theft, also for him who makes it. 7 (That applies also to) a gift in anger for injuring another and a gift made in haughtiness above that of kings. 8 In that case the fine shall be the highest.

9 The son or heir inheriting the property may not pay, if unwilling, obligations of suretyship, balance of a fine or dowry, a gambling debt, a debt for drinks and a gift of love.

Thus ends the topic of non-conveyance of gifts.

10 As to sale without ownership, however, on finding a lost or stolen article, the owner shall cause it to be seized by the judge. 11 Or, if the place and time are likely to be missed, he should himself seize it and bring it (to the judge). 12 And the judge should question the possessor, 'Where did you get this?' 13 If he were to show a legitimate method (of purchase), but not the vendor, he shall be acquitted on handing over that article. 14 If the vendor were found, he shall pay the price (to the pruchaser) and a fine for theft. 15 If he were to find a means of exoneration, he may clear himself (and so on) till the means of exoneration are exhausted. 16 When these are exhausted, the (last person unable to exonerate himself) shall pay the price and fine for theft.

3 *sarvasvam* etc.: cf. 3.13.35. These are the *avyavahārya* gifts. — *prayacchet*: the subject seems to be the judge, rather than the receiver. In the next s., the judge is clearly to be thought of as ordering annulment of gifts. 4 *karmasu ca*: the *ca* should preferably have come after *dharmadānam*.

5 Cf. 3.15.19.

6 *ākrośa* 'reviling, abusing'; cf. 3.18.12; also 4.11.14. 7 *rājñām*: the plural may suggest inclusion of members of the royal family.

9 *prātibhāvyam*: cf. 3.11.15 ff. — *śulkaśeṣam*: cf. 3.4.33; 3.2.19. The readings from Cb are obviously necessary. — Manu, 8.159, is identical.

10 *āsādya*, i.e., when the owner finds or comes across his lost article in some one else's possession. — *grāhayet*: the object is 'the article' lost. 11 *deśakālātipattau*, i.e., if delay means that the article may be lost sight of. Cf. 7.18.11. 12 *svāminam* can only refer to the person in whose possession the article is found. The use of the same word for the claimant as well as the suspect in consecutive ss. is confusing. 13 *ācārakramam*: perhaps the reading should be *ācārakrayam*, as is shown by *vikretāram*,. 14 *mūlyam* would naturally go to the suspect, whose bona fides are thus proved. 15 *apasāra* 'a means of escape,' i.e., a person who makes it possible for another to exonerate himself.

CHAPTER SEVENTEEN

SECTION 71 FORCIBLE SEIZURE

1 Forcible seizure is a deed of force in the presence (of the owner). 2 In the absence (of the owner) it is theft, also in case of denial.

3 'In case of the forceible seizure of jewels, articles of high value, of low value and forest produce, the fine shall be equal to their value,' say the followers of Manu. 4 'Double the value,' say the followers of Uśanas. 5 'In accordance with the offence,' says Kauṭilya.

6 '(In the case) of flowers, fruits, vegetables, roots, bulbous roots, cooked food, leather goods, wicker-baskets, earthenware and other trifling articles, the fine is a minimum of twelve *paṇas* and a maximum of twenty-four *paṇas*. 7 In the case of articles of iron, wood and ropes, small animals, cloth and other big articles, the fine is a minimum of twenty-four *paṇas* and a maximum of forty-eight *paṇas*. 8 In the case of articles of copper, steel, bronze, glass and ivory and other big articles, the lowest fine for violence, (i.e.) a minimum of forty-eight *paṇas* and a maximum of ninety-six *paṇas* (shall be the punishment). 9 In the case of large animals, human beings, fields, houses, money, gold, fine cloth and other big articles, the middle fine for violence, (i.e.) a minimum of two hundred and a maximum of five hundred (shall be the punishment). 10 For one who binds or causes another to bind or releases from bondage a woman or a man by using force, (the punishment shall be) the highest fine for violence, (i.e.) a minimum of five hundred and a maximum of one thousand,' say the teachers.

11 'He who causes another to commit an act of force, saying "I accept (responsibility)," shall pay double (the fine). 12 (He who causes it) saying "I shall give as much money as will be required," shall pay a fourfold fine. 13 He who causes it by stating the amount in the words "I shall give so much money," shall pay the money as stated as well as the fine,' say the followers of Bṛhaspati. 14 'If he were to plead anger, intoxication or delusion, he shall impose on him the (single) fine as prescribed,' says Kauṭilya.

3.17

sāhasa, derived from *sahas* 'force,' is primarily a forcible seizure of another's articles.

1 *anvayavat*: *anvaya* is the presence of the owner when the article is seized. Cf. Kullūka on Manu, 8.332, which is an exact echo of this s. The idea of connection (*anvaya*) between the article and the person seizing it is possible, but seems less likely. The idea of common ownership (Cs, following Yāj. 2.230) also does not seem likely.

3 *mānavāḥ* : there is no such rule in the *Manusmṛti*.

10 The worst case of *sāhasa* involves human beings, and force is used to tamper with their condition of liberty or bondage. — *ityācāryāḥ*: Kauṭilya apparently agrees with them.

15 In all cases of fine one should know that there is an impost of eight *paṇas* per hundred, but in those above one hundred, a surcharge in addition of five *paṇas* per hundred.

16 Because of the large number of crimes by subjects or because of a defect in the condition of kings, the impost and the surcharge, which are illegal, (are current) ; but the basic fine is (alone) known to be legal.

CHAPTER EIGHTEEN

SECTION 72 VERBAL INJURY

1 Defamation, vilification and threat constitute verbal injury.

2 Of (defamation pertaining to) body, character, learning, profession and country, in case of defamation pertaining to body, such as one-eyed, lame and so on, the fine is three *paṇas* if (the defect is) a fact, the fine is six *paṇas* in case of a false imputation (of the defect).

3 In case of censure masquerading as praise of one-eyed, lame and other (persons), such as ' with beautiful eyes ', the fine shall be twelve *paṇas*.

4 And in case of vilification referring to leprosy, madness, impotence and so on, when it is true, false and contains ironical praise, the fines are twelve *paṇas* increased by twelve *paṇas* successively (in the three cases, if it is) towards equals. 5 If towards superiors the fines shall be double, if towards inferiors half the fines, if towards wives of others double, (but) half the fines if it is due to a mistake, intoxication, delusion and so on.

6 Of leprosy and madness, physicians and men staying near are the authority, of impotency, women, foam on the urine and sinking of ordure in water (shall constitute proof).

15 *rūpam* : this impost of 8% on the fine is different from the *rūpa* understood as the inspection fee of 1/8% in 2.12.28, 30, 35. It corresponds to the *rūpika* of 2.12.25. — *śatāt pareṣu* is proposed for *śatāt pare* of the mss. which show a metrically short *pāda*. The pural is necessary in conformity with *karmasu*. It is clear that *ṣu* of *pareṣu* got dropped out through a scribal error. Cb reads *śatāvareṣu* and explains ' more than a hundred.' It can hardly mean ' less than a hundred ' (Cs). — *vyājīm* : see 2.6.10 etc. 16 *bhāva*- ' nature, condition.'

3.18

1 *upavādaḥ* etc. : it is clear that *upavāda* is reviling a person with reference to some defect in body, character etc., while *kutsana* has reference to some serious malady, like leprosy, impotency etc. Thus Cb.

2 *śarīropavāde* : the locative is proposed in keeping with the usual practice for the instrumental of the mss.

3 *śobhanākṣimantaḥ* : the plural shows irony. *-dantaḥ* is clearly out of place. Meyer suggests *-krāntaḥ* ' gait ' for it.

4 *tulyeṣu*, i.e., of the same *varṇa*, though ' equal in status ' is not unlikely.

5 *dviguṇāḥ* etc. : the plurals are necessary as in 3.19.4.

6 *mūtrapheno* : it is the absence of the foam on the urine that shows the *klība*.

7 In case of libel concerning character, among Brahmins, Kṣatriyas, Vaiśyas, Śūdras and the lowest born, the fines are three *paṇas* increased by three *paṇas* successively (if it is) of the earlier by the later, decreasing by two *paṇas* successively up to two *paṇas* if of the later by the earlier, also in case of vilification like 'low Brahmin' and so on.

8 By that are explained defamation concerning the learning of professional story-tellers, slander of the profession of artisans and actors, and libel of the country of those from Prājjūṇa, Gandhāra and so on.

9 The person who threatens another with doing (something), saying, 'I shall do this to you,' shall pay, in case he does not (actually) do it, a fine half that prescribed for the doing of it. 10 If he is incapable (of carrying out the threat) or pleads anger, intoxication or delusion, he shall pay a fine of twelve *paṇas*. 11 If he has feelings of enmity and is capable of doing harm, he shall furnish a surety till the end of his life.

12 A person deserves the lowest fine (for violence) for reviling his own country and village, the middle fine for reviling his own caste or corporation, the highest for reviling gods and sanctuaries.

CHAPTER NINETEEN

SECTION 73 PHYSICAL INJURY

1 Touching, menacing and striking constitute physical injury.

2 For one touching (another's) body below the navel with the hand, mud, ashes or dust, the fine shall be three *paṇas* ; with those same when they are impure and with the foot or with spittle, six *paṇas* ; with vomit, urine, ordure and so on, twelve *paṇas*. 3 (For touching) above the navel (the fines shall be) double, on the head four-fold, in the case of equals. 4 (The fines shall be) double in the case of superiors, half in the case of inferiors, double in the case of wives of others, half if due to a mistake, intoxication, delusion and so on.

7 *tripaṇottarāḥ*, i.e., 12, 9, 6 and 3 if an Antāvasāyin vilifies a Brahmin, a Kṣatriya, a Vaiśya and a Śūdra, 9, 6 and 3 if a Śūdra vilifies the upper *varṇas*, and so on. — *dvipaṇādharāḥ*, i.e., 8, 6, 4 and 2 if a Brahmin offends a Kṣatriya, Vaiśya, Śūdra and Antāvasāyin, 6, 4 and 2 if a Kṣatriya offends and so on. — *kubrāhmaṇādibhiś ca kutsāyām* : the fines are milder (basis of 2, not 3) because there is no specific reflection on character.

8 *Prājjūṇaka* : Cb reads *Prāgghūṇaka* explained as 'the kingdom of the Caṇḍālas.' Cs renders this reading by 'the Eastern Huns.' That seems doubtful. At any rate, finding a reference in this to the Huns under Toramana and drawing a conclusion from that as to the date of this work (Pran Nath, IA, 60, 121) seem hardly justified. *Prājjūṇa* may be Prakrit for Prārjuna, perhaps related to the Ārjunāyanas of the inscriptions.

9 *karaṇe daṇḍaḥ*, i.e., as laid down in the next Chapter. 11 *avastha* 'surety;' cf. 3.1.17.

12 *devacaityānām* : *sva* may or may not be understood with this. — Cf. Yāj., 2.211.

3.19

3 *sameṣu*, i.e., *tulyeṣu* of 3.18.4 above. 4 Cf. 3.18.5.

5 For holding (another) by the feet, the garment, the hand and the hair, the fines shall be six *paṇas* increased successively by six *paṇas*.

6 In cases of pressing, squeezing (in one's arms), bending, dragging and sitting on (another), the lowest fine for violence (shall be imposed). 7 For going away after throwing down, the fine shall be half.

8 The (judge) shall cause the limb of a Śūdra with which he strikes a Brahmin to be cut off. 9 For menacing a ransom (may be allowed), for touching the fine is half. 10 By that are explained Caṇḍālas and (other) impure persons.

11 For menacing with the hand the fine shall be three *paṇas* minimum and twelve *paṇas* maximum, double (for menacing) with the foot, the lowest fine for violence with an object causing hurt, the middle with one endangering life.

12 For one causing hurt without blood with any one of objects made of wood, earth, stone, or metal, or a stick or rope, the fine shall be twenty-four *paṇas*, for causing a bleeding wound double, except in the case of impure blood. 13 For one beating (another) to the point of death without causing bleeding, or causing dislocation of the hand or foot, (the punishment shall be) the lowest fine for violence, also for breaking hands, feet or teeth, cutting off the ear or nose and opening up wounds, excepting festering wounds. 14 For breaking the thigh or neck or piercing the eye and in cases of (hurt leading to) obstruction in speech, movement or eating, (the punishment shall be) the middle fine for violence and the expenses for treatment and cure. 15 In case of death, he shall be taken for trial as a criminal by a magistrate.

16 If a number of persons beat one person, the fine shall be double for each one (of them).

6 *-añcana-* 'bending' is proposed for *-añjana-*, as suggested by Meyer. The latter word hardly conveys a suitable meaning. 7 *-daṇḍaḥ* singular is proposed, as it refers only to *pūrva sāhasadaṇḍa*.

8-10 As Meyer argues, these ss. appear to be interpolated. They break the order. After *sparśana*, we expect a discussion of *avagūrṇa* and then of *prahata*. Besides, the four *varṇas* with the Antāvasāyin would have been mentioned as in 3.18.7, not only Brahmins and Śūdras. The animus against the Śūdra found here is unknown to this text, which looks upon him as an Ārya. The interpolation seems derived from Yāj., 2.215 with Manu, 8.279-84. — *Caṇḍālāśucayaḥ* : an *ādi* was expected after *Caṇḍāla* in the compound.

11 *tripaṇāvaro dvādaśapaṇaparo* evidently refers to the four *varṇas* and Antāvasāyins as in 3.18.7.

12 *anyatra duṣṭaśoṇitāt*, i.e., in this case the fine is not double. 13 *pārañcikam* seems derived from *parā-añc* 'to bend away,' though the form appears irregular. — *vraṇavidāraṇe* : this may refer to making a fresh wound or opening an old wound. — *anyatra duṣṭavraṇebhyaḥ* : this seems to imply that if the wound is very serious, a higher punishment is to be inflicted. Perhaps a similar idea is to be understood in *duṣṭaśoṇitāt* in s. 12. 14 *samutthāna* 'curing' by a physician. 15 *kaṇṭakaśodhanāya* etc. : apparently 4.11.1 ff. would apply.

17 'An old scuffle or trespass with criminal intent shall not be a cause for a suit,' say the teachers. 18 'There is no going scot-free for an offender,' says Kauṭilya.

19 'In case of a scuffle, he who comes first (to the court) wins, for (only) one unable to put up (with the injury) runs (to the court),' say the teachers. 20 'No,' says Kauṭilya. 21 Whether one has approached first or later, witnesses (alone) are to help in deciding the case; if there are no witnesses, the injury or the indications of the scuffle (are to decide).

22 If one does not reply to an accusation of injury, he shall be convicted on the same day.

23 For taking away in a scuffle an object (of another), the fine shall be ten *paṇas*, for destroying a small object, the same and an equal amount as fine, for destroying a big object, the same and double that as fine, for destroying clothes, ornaments, money and gold articles, the same and the lowest fine for violence.

24 For one causing the wall of another's house to shake by striking at it, the fine shall be three *paṇas*, for breaking or cutting it six *paṇas* and (payment of the cost of) repairs. 25 For one throwing into another's house an object causing hurt the fine shall be twelve *paṇas*, an object dangerous to life the lowest fine for violence.

26 For causing hurt to small animals with wood and other things, the fine shall be one *paṇa* or two *paṇas*, double that for causing bleeding. 27 For these same offences concerning big animals, the fine shall be double and (payment of) expenses for treatment and cure.

28 For cutting the shoots of trees in city parks that bear flowers or fruit or yield shade (the fine shall be) six *paṇas*, for cutting small branches twelve *paṇas*, for cutting stout branches twenty-four *paṇas*, for destroying trunks the lowest fine for violence, for uprooting (the tree) the middle (fine).

17 *anupraveśaḥ*: see 3.1.8.

21 *ghātaḥ* 'injury.' — *upaliṅganam*: cf. 3.12.51; 3.13.37.

22 *tad ahar eva*: for the period usually allowed, see 3.1.29. *paścātkāra* 'setting aside' refers to conviction.

23 *daśapaṇo*: Cb comment implies the reading *dviśatapaṇaḥ*. — *tat* would apparently be restitution to the owner.

24 Cb Cs add *pātanabhañjane dvādaśapaṇaḥ*. It is not easy to see the difference between *bhañjana* of this and *chedana* or *bhedana* already mentioned. 25 *anyaveśmani* from Cb appears better, though *asya* of the mss. could refer to *para* in the last s.

26 At the end of this s. Cb has a long additional passage, not all of which appears genuine. In particular, the distinction in it between *śākhāṅga* and *varāṅga* is suspicious. It seems that Yāj., 2.225-6, is responsible for the addition. However, the plural in *sthāneṣu* in the next s. suggests that some part of the addition, particularly *vraṇavidāraṇe caturguṇaḥ*, may be original.

29 In the case of bushes and creepers bearing flowers or fruit or yielding shade the fines shall be half, also in the case of trees in holy places, penance-groves and cremation grounds.

30 In the case of trees at the boundaries, in sanctuaries, and of trees that are prominent, these same fines doubled shall be imposed, also (in the case of trees) in royal parks.

CHAPTER TWENTY

SECTION 74 GAMBLING AND BETTING

SECTION 75 MISCELLANEOUS

1 The Director of Gambling should cause gambling to be carried on in one place. 2 For one gambling with dice in another place, the fine shall be twelve *paṇas*, in order to find out those who follow a secret profession.

3 'In a suit concerning gambling, the lowest fine for violence (shall be imposed) on the winner, the middle on the loser. 4 For, this (latter), being of a foolish nature and anxious to win, cannot bear a loss,' say the teachers. 5 'No,' says Kauṭilya. 6 If the loser is punished with a double fine, no one will approach the king (for justice). 7 Gamblers indeed are generally fraudulent players.

8 Masters (of gambling halls) shall provide for them clean cowrie-shells and dice. 9 For substituting other cowrie-shells or dice the fine shall be twelve *paṇas*, for fraudulent play the lowest fine for violence and confiscation of winnings, for cheating fine for theft in addition.

29 *ca* clearly implies that *puṇyasthāna-* etc. is to be construed with the preceding. Meyer, influenced by Yāj., 2.227-9, would construe it with the following stanza.

30 *ālakṣita* is clearly the same as *viśruta* of Yāj., 2.228. — Yāj. often gives only a metrical rendering of ss. found in this section.

3.20

The two *prakaraṇas* are found in ss. 1-13 and 14-24 respectively. Manu, 9.223, explains the difference between *dyūta* 'gambling' and *samāhvaya* 'challenge' with a bet. The former is done with inanimate objects (dice etc.), the latter with living creatures (cocks etc.).

1 The *dyūtādhyakṣa* is not included among the *adhyakṣas* discussed in Book 2. — *ekamukham* : cf. 2.16.4 ; 2.25.1. 2 *gūḍhājīvijñāpanārtham* : it is obvious that these words should have come at the end of s.1, as stating the reason for gambling being allowed only in one place. Cf. Yāj., 2.203 *dyūtam ekamukhaṁ kāryaṁ taskarajñānakāraṇāt*, which is an exact echo of the present passage. For *gūḍhājīvin*, see 4.4 below.

3 *jetuḥ* : who has won in gambling ; if he loses the suit, he is clearly held to have cheated at play. That he should get off with a lighter fine is obviously unreasonable.

9 *upadhau steyadaṇḍaś ca* from Cb is clearly necessary. Cb understands *upadhi* to refer to fraud in making payments, to distinguish it from *kūṭakarman*. — 4.10.9 prescribes a heavier punishment for these offences.

10 The master (of the hall) shall take five per hundred of the winnings, as well as hire for cowrie-shells, dice, leather-straps and ivory-cubes and charges for water, ground and the act (of gambling). 11 He shall carry out the pledging and sale of articles. 12 For not prohibiting offences concerning dice, ground or (the use of) hand, the fine shall be double.

13 By that is explained 'a challenge' except challenges concerning learning or art.

14 As to miscellaneous, however—

For not returning at the proper place and time a thing borrowed, hired, pledged or entrusted, for missing the place or time of meeting or staying together at a watch (of the night) or shadow (of the gnomon by day), for one making a Brahmin pay duty at the police post or fare at the ferry, and for inviting over the heads of the immediate and the next-but-one neighbours, the fine shall be twelve *paṇas*.

15 For one not handing over an object which he is enjoined (to deliver), for one touching the brother's wife with the hand, for one going to a prostitute in the exclusive keeping of another, for one purchasing goods claimed by another, for one breaking open a sealed house, and for one doing harm to members from forty neighbouring families, the fine shall be forty-eight *paṇas*.

10 *arālā* is rendered by *paṭṭa* in Cb ; Cs understands something like a leather-strap. — *śalākā* 'a rod that demarcates the places of the two players' (Cb), 'an ivory cube' (Cs). Pāṇini 2.1.10 refers to *akṣa* and *śalākā* as implements of gambling. 11 *ādhānam* : the *adhyakṣa* himself may be the pledgee. 12 *dviguṇaḥ* : apparently double those of s. 9 are meant. Cs has 'double the five per cent,' which appears less likely.

13 *anyatra vidyāśilpasamāhvayāt* : i.e., challenges with bets concerning learning, or skill in art, are not subject to state control and may be freely indulged in. — Manu forbids gambling as such.

14 In the miscellaneous section offences are arranged according to the amount of fines they carry. Some of the offences mentioned here could well have been included under one or the other of the heads discussed earlier. — *yāma*, i.e., time by night and *chāyā*, i.e., time by day. — *samupaveśa* and *saṁsthiti* seem to refer to meeting or staying in a place at the direction of the state. A failure to keep a private engagement could hardly be an offence. Cb seems to understand 'failure to do work as promised at the time and place. *saṁsthiti* may also possibly mean 'regulations, conventions etc.' regarding meeting (*samupaveśa*). — *taradeyam* etc. : 2.28.18 shows that Brahmins are not to be charged at ferries. — *anuveśa* from Cb is clearly necessary for *anupraveśa*. It seems that according to Cb *anuveśa* is the immediate neighbour and *prativeśa* the next neighbour. — *nimantraṇa* 'invitation' for meals etc. on ceremonial occasions. It seems that a list of offences carrying a fine of twenty-four *paṇas* has dropped out. That has usually a place in the scale of fines. Cf. 3.17.6 etc.

15 *saṁdiṣṭam* has reference to *ādeśa* of 3.12.18 ; it hardly means 'promised' (Cs). — *paravaktavyam* : this seems to mean 'promised to others' or 'claimed by others' ; in either case, the vendor would be at fault, not the purchaser. Perhaps we have to read *vikrīṇānasya* (for *krīṇānasya*). The expression could mean 'blamed or condemned by others.' Even then the vendor would be at fault.

16 For the receiver of the family treasure denying it, for one forcibly violating a widow living by herself, for a Caṇḍāla touching an Ārya lady, for one not rushing to rescue (another) close by in distress, for one rushing without cause (and) for one feeding Śākya, Ājīvaka and other heritical monks at rites in honour of gods and manes, the fine shall be one hundred *paṇas*.

17 For one putting questions (to suspects) on oath without authorization, and for one, not an officer, doing the work of an officer, for one castrating males used for stud purposes among small animals, and for one causing the abortion of a female slave by medicines, (the punishment shall be) the lowest fine for violence.

18 As between father and son, husband and wife, brother and sister, maternal uncle and nephew or teacher and pupil, for one abandoning the other when not an outcast, (and) for one abandoning another going together in a caravan in the middle of a village, the lowest fine for violence (shall be the punishment), if in a forest the middle fine, for causing harm to him thereby the highest fine ; for others going with the caravan, half the fines (shall be the punishment).

19 For one binding or making another bind a man not deserving to be bound or releasing a (man from) bondage, (and) for one binding or causing another to bind a child that has not attained majority, the fine shall be one thousand *paṇas*.

20 Special fines should be imposed according to the special nature of men and offences.

21 The head of a religious order, an ascetic, a sick person, one exhausted by hunger, thirst or a journey, a foreigner, one groaning under a fine, and an indigent person should be shown leniency.

16 *āryām* : Yāj., 2.234, has *uttamān spṛśan* making it an offence of untouchability only. — *niṣkāraṇam*, i.e., when there is no *āpad*. — Ājīvakas are the followers of Gosāla Makkhaliputta. Obviously this sect was prominent in the author's day. They are mentioned in Aśoka's inscriptions. — *vṛṣala* : it is clear that this word refers to heretics and has nothing to do with Śūdras.

17 *vākyānuyoga* : see 4.8.1-5. Yāj., 2.235, has *ayuktaṁ śapathaṁ kurvan ayogyo yogyakarmakṛt*, which shows a clear misunderstanding of the present text.

18 *sārthābhiprayātam* from Cb is necessary. *svārtha-* has little significance. The fine is for the leader of the caravan abandoning a member on the way. — *bhreṣayataḥ*, i.e., for causing harm to him, either physically or materially. — *sahaprasthāyiṣu* : these are other members of the caravan who have acquiesced in the leader's action.

19 Compare 3.17.10 above.

20 *puruṣaviśeṣa* and *aparādhaviśeṣa* are to be understood. The former are mentioned in what follows.

21 *tīrthakaraḥ* seems to be 'the head of a religious order,' rather than 'a pilgrim.' Cb renders it by *dānaśīla* 'a charitable person.' — *tirojanapadaḥ* : cf. 2.34.4. Cb seems to have read *vṛddhaḥ* before *vyādhitaḥ*. — *daṇḍakhedin* : *daṇḍa* seems to refer to fines, rather than physical punishment, though that is not unlikely.

22 The judges themselves shall look into the affiairs of gods, Brahmins, ascetics, women, minors, old persons, sick persons, who are helpless, when these do not approach (the court), and they shall not dismiss (their suits) under the pretext of place, time or (adverse) possession.

23 And men are to be honoured on account of excellence in learning, intellect, valour, noble birth and deeds.

24 In this way the judges should look into affairs, without resorting to deceit, being impartial to all beings, worthy of trust and beloved of the people.

Herewith ends the Third Book of the Arthaśāstra of Kauṭilya
'CONCERNING THE JUDGES'

22 *anāthānām* : this qualifies the preceding compound as in 2.1.26. — *atihareyuḥ*: cf. 4.9.15.

23 This is a direction to the judges concerning persons appearing before them.

24 *bhāveṣu*, i.e., towards beings or persons.

Book Four

THE SUPPRESSION OF CRIMINALS

CHAPTER ONE

SECTION 76 KEEPING A WATCH OVER ARTISANS

1 Three magistrates, (all) three (of the rank of) ministers, shall carry out the suppression of criminals.

2 Employers of artisans capable of making good an article, those good at entrusting materials, (and) artisans working with their own capital should accept entrusted material with the guarantee of the guild. 3 In case of death, the guild shall be responsible for the entrusted material.

The Fourth Book deals with criminal offences of various kinds. *kaṇṭaka* a thorn' refers to criminals who are thorns in the side of the body politic. These include thieves, dacoits, murderers etc. as well as artisans, craftsmen, traders and others who cheat the public. Only Manu, 9.253-293, among the Smṛtis, has a rambling discussion on some of these topics. Yājñavalkya gives many of these rules under *steya*, *sāhasa* or *saṁgrahaṇa*, i.e., under the regular *vyavahārapadas*.

4.1

For *rakṣaṇa* 'guarding against, keeping a watch over,' cf. 1.17 above.

1 *pradeṣṭāraḥ* : as is clear from the contents of this Book these officers are principally magistrates who punish criminals. They are also concerned with the investigation of crimes. As 2.35.7 shows they are also authorized to enforce payment of state dues. That they are subordinate to the *samāhartṛ* is clear from 4.4.1, 4.5.13 as well as from 2.35.7. — *trayo 'mātyāḥ* : see 3.1.1 above.

2 *arthyapratīkārāḥ* is obscure. Meyer renders it by 'who can make good anything connected with the object entrusted.' That appears possible, though not very satisfactory. Cb Cs read *arthyaprakārāḥ* and explain 'whose nature (*prakāra* in the sense of *svabhāva*) is honest.' Breloer renders that reading by 'people from the class of the rich' (KSt, III, 372). This sense, or the meaning of *arthyapratīkārāḥ* as understood by Meyer, would appear suitable, if the expression is understood as descriptive of *kāruśāsitāraḥ*. These are apparently 'employers of artisans,' i.e., some sort of master-artisans with assistants working under them. — *saṁnikṣeptāraḥ* : understood literally, this means 'who are good entrusters of materials'; that would be a description of the customers, not of the artisans. Since, however, the predicate is *nikṣepaṁ gṛhṇīyuḥ*, the expression must be interpreted so as to describe artisans. We may understand some sort of middlemen, who receive material from customers and then entrust the work to artisans. In that case, the expression may be understood as a further description of *kāruśāsitāraḥ*. — *svavittakāravaḥ* appears to refer to artisans who work on their own and deal directly with customers; they have started their workshop with their own capital. Cb seems to explain the word as follows 'those who treat other people's gold (with the same care) as their own gold.' — *śreṇīpramāṇāḥ*, i.e., with the guild standing guarantee for the artisan's reliability and honesty. This would seem applicable to all the earlier cases or at least to the last case of *svavittakāravaḥ*. Cb Cs understand all five expressions as describing different traits which are necessary in an artisan. But it is doubtful if one and the same artisan can be described as *kāruśāsitṛ* and *svavittakāru*

4 And they shall carry out the work with the place, time and (nature of the) work stipulated, without stipulation as to place or time if the nature of the work can be pointed out (as the reason). 5 For exceeding the time-limit, (there shall be) a reduction in the wage by one quarter and double that as fine. 6 They shall be liable for what is lost or destroyed except in case of deterioration or a sudden calamity. 7 For carrying out a work otherwise than as ordered, (there shall be) loss of wage and double that as fine.

8 Weavers shall increase yarn to the extent of eleven (*palas*) from ten. 9 For diminution in increase, the fine shall be double the diminution.

10 The wage for weaving (shall be equal to) the value of the yarn, one and a half times in the case of *kṣauma* and *kauśeya*, double in the case of *patrorṇā*, blankets and *dukūla*.

11 For shortness in measure, (there shall be) a reduction in wage equal to (the value of) the short measure and double that as fine, for short weight the fine (shall be) four times the deficiency, for change of yarn (the fine shall be) double its value. 12 By that is explained the weaving of double cloth.

13 In one *tulā* of wool, a reduction in carding to the extent of five *palas* (is allowed), and (the same amount of) reduction in the hair (when carded).

14 Washermen shall wash garments on wooden boards or smooth slabs of stone. 15 Those washing on anything else shall pay for damage to garments and a fine of six *paṇas*.

15 (Washermen) wearing a garment other than one marked with the sign of the club shall pay a fine of three *paṇas*. 17 For selling, hiring out or pledging the garments of others the fine shall be twelve *paṇas*, for change of garment (the fine shall be) double the price and the return of the garment.

at the same time. Breloer finds in the expressions five different categories of artisans. That appears doubtful at least in the case of *śreṇīpramāṇāḥ*, which has to be understood of *svavittakāravaḥ*. It seems that only two classes are meant, *kāruśāsitāraḥ* and *svavittakāravaḥ*. Russ. has four categories 'honest leaders of artisans (*arthyaprakārāḥ kāruśāsitāraḥ*), trusted depositaries (*saṁnikṣeptāraḥ*), independent workmen (*svavittakāravaḥ*) and those having authority in their unions (*śreṇīpramāṇāḥ*).' 3 *vipattau*, i.e., in case the artisan dies. Cf. s. 56 below and 3.19.15 for this sense.

4 See 2.14.2, which shows that -*kālaṁ kāryāpadeśam* is necessary. 5 Cf. 2.14.4. 6 Cf. 3.12.23. 7 Cf. 2.14.3.

8 *daśaikādaśikam*, i.e., the ten *palas* of yarn are expected to yield eleven *palas* of cloth ; the addition would come from the sizing material used. 9 *chedadviguṇaḥ*, i.e., double the value of the short weight in cloth. Meyer, who does not read the stop after *daṇḍaḥ*, includes *sūtramūlyam* and *vānavetanam* also in the fine. That is quite unlikely.

12 *dvipaṭavānam*, i.e., weaving with a double yarn. For other kinds of weaves, see 2.11.105.

13 *ūrṇātulāyāḥ* : a *tulā* is a weight of one hundred *palas* ; see 2.19.21. — *romacchedaś ca* : as 2.11.101 shows, the hair of animals wereused for making rugs etc. The loss would occur during carding and spinning rather than during weaving (as in Cs). It would have been better if we had *romatulāyāś ca* instead.

16 *mudgarāṅkād anyad* etc. : it is the washermen's own clothes that are to carry the mark. The emblem may stand for the club used for beating the clothes during the washing operations.

18 They shall return a garment, which is white like a bud, which is cleansed on a slab of stone, which has the colour of washed yarn, and which is bleached white, after one day increased successively by one day. 19 One with a light red colour (may be returned) after five days, one dyed blue after six days, a precious garment dyed in (saffron) flower, lac-juice or *mañjiṣṭhā* the treatment of which is arduous and which has to be worked upon with great care, after seven days. 20 After that they shall lose their wage. 21 In cases of dispute concerning dyeing, trustworthy experts shall fix the wage.

22 For the most precious (garments) the wage (shall be) one *paṇa*, for middling one half, for lowest one-quarter, for rough (garments) one *māṣaka* or two *māṣakas*, double for dyed (garments).

23 At the first washing there is a loss of one-fourth (of the value of the garment), at the second of one-fifth. 24 By that are explained later (losses in value).

25 By washermen are explained tailors.

26 For goldsmiths purchasing silver (or) gold in the same form from the hands of a disreputable person without informing (state officers) the fine is twelve *paṇas*, if in a changed form twenty-four *paṇas*, if from the hands of a thief forty-eight *paṇas*. 27 In cases of purchase at a low price in secret or what is changed in appearance there shall be the punishment for theft, also in case of deceit in the article manufactured.

28 For (the goldsmith) stealing one *māṣaka* from one *suvarṇa* (of gold) the fine shall be two hundred *paṇas*, for stealing one *māṣaka* from one *dharaṇa* of silver twelve *paṇas*. 29 By that are explained higher (values).

18 *mukulāvadātam* : this and the following expressions seem to convey four kinds of whiteness each succeeding one brighter than the preceding one, washermen being allowed 1, 2, 3 and 4 days respectively for producing the different grades of whiteness. 19 *pañcarātrikaṁ tanurāgam* : the dyeing operation makes a longer period necessary. — *guruparikarma* 'the treatment of which (dyeing) is heavy, i.e., long and arduous (e.g., printing in various colours etc.).'

23 *pañcabhāgaḥ*, i.e., '1/5th of 3/4ths' (Cb Cs). It may also mean 1/5th in addition to the 1/4th of the original price. 24 *uttaram*, i.e., 1/6th at the third washing and so on.

25 Only a few of the above rules would apply to tailors, perhaps ss. 17-20 with modifications.

26 *aśuci* is a disreputable person with a suspicious character rather than a slave, labourer etc. (as in Cb Cs). — *rūpyaṁ suvarṇam* : it seems that we should read *rūpyasuvarṇam* as in 2.14.1. Ornaments of silver and gold are thought of. — *anākhyāya* : the information is apparently to be given to the *sauvarṇika* of 2.14. The *pradeṣṭṛ* also may have been meant. 27 *pracchanna-* etc. : Meyer has 'in secret, in a changed form or at a low price,' i.e., three ideas. Cs has 'at a low price what is secretly changed.' It seems, however, that *pracchanna* and *virūpa* are unrelated to each other, but *mūlyahīnakraya* is to be understood of both.

28 For the weights mentioned see 2.19.2-6.

30 For one securing an (artificial) enhancement of colour or practising removal or mixture (with base metals), the fine shall be five hundred *paṇas*. 31 In case of fraud in connection with these two (metals), he shall treat it as (a case of) removal of colour.

32 One *māṣaka* is the wage for one *dharaṇa* of silver, one-eighth part (of a *paṇa*) for one *suvarṇa* (of gold). 33 In accordance with special skill, the wage may be increased to double. 34 By that are explained further rates.

35 In the case of copper, steel, bell-metal, *vaikṛntaka* and brass, the wage is five (*paṇas*) per hundred (*palas*).

36 A lump of copper has a loss of one-tenth part (in working). 37 In case of reduction to the extent of one *pala* (beyond this), the fine shall be double the (value of the) loss. 38 By that are explained further cases. 39 A lump of lead or tin has a reduction of one-twentieth part. 40 And one *kākaṇī* is the wage for one *pala* of it. 41 A lump of iron has a reduction of one-fifth. 42 And two *kākaṇīs* is the wage for one *pala* of it. 43 By that are explained further cases.

44 For the Examiner of Coins rejecting an established currency of *paṇas* which does not deserve to be rejected or not rejecting one deserving to be rejected the fine is twelve *paṇas*. 45 The currency of *paṇas* is effective when cleared of the payment of surcharge. 46 For one accepting one *māṣaka* on a *paṇa* (sent into circulation) the fine is twelve *paṇas*. 47 By that are explained further cases.

48 For one causing a counterfeit coin to be made or receiving it or sending it into circulation the fine is one thousand *paṇas*, for inserting it in the treasury (the penalty is) death.

30 *varṇotkarṣam* refers to an artificial glitter given to gold and silver ornaments. — *apasāraṇam* is proposed in accordance with a suggestion by Meyer for *apasārāṇām* of the mss. and *asārāṇām* of Cb Cs. *apasāraṇa* is described at length in 2.14.20-24. Cb understands *asāra* in the sense of an inferior alloy ; this is given a polish (*varṇotkarṣa*) to make it appear as gold or silver ; or it is mixed with gold or silver (*yoga*). This explanation also appears possible. 31 *tayoḥ*, i.e., of gold and silver. — *rāgasya apahāram* : as 4.4.22 shows, this is a very serious offence. It would seem then that *apacaraṇa* implies a complete substitution of gold or silver by a base metal.

32 *aṣṭabhāgaḥ* is one-eighth of a *paṇa*, not of a *māṣaka* (as in Cs Meyer). Cb understands one-eighth of a gold *māṣaka*. No such coin is known to the text.

41 *kālāyasa* is not mentioned in the Chapter on metals, 2.12, but is known to the text; cf. 3.17.7.

44 *rūpadarśaka* : see 2.12.25. — *akopyām* : the root *kup* in the causal has the sense of 'to cause to be shaken, to disturb,' i.e., to find fault with, to reject. 45 *vyājī* : this is 5% as laid down in 2.12.26. It seems that the *rūpika* of 8% and the *pārīkṣika* of 1/8% mentioned there are also to be understood. 46 *paṇān māṣakam upajīvataḥ* : this appears to be a bribe of one *māṣaka* for every *paṇa* certified. The trader pays 1/6th, i.e., 6¼% and escapes 5 plus 8 plus 1/8, i.e., 13⅛%. Cb Cs think that it is the *lakṣaṇādhyakṣa* who misappropriates a *māṣa* of silver from 1 *paṇa* at the time of minting. That officer, however, is not mentioned here. Moreover, that would be a counterfeit coin for making which the fine is very heavy (s. 48).

49 Attendants and dust-washers should receive one-third of articles of high value (found by them), the king two-thirds and gems (when found). 50 For stealing a gem, (the punishment is) the highest fine (for violence).

51 In cases of information about mines, gems and buried treasure, the informant shall receive one-sixth part, one-twelfth part (if he be) a servant (of the state). 52 A treasure-trove over one hundred thousand (*paṇas*) shall go to the king. 53 If less, he shall give one-sixth part (to the finder). 54 A native of the land, who is upright, shall receive the entire treasure-trove buried by his forefathers after producing proof of ownership. 55 In the absence of proof of ownership, the fine is five hundred (*paṇas*), one thousand for appropriating it secretly.

56 For the physician undertaking treatment involving danger to life without informing (the authorities), the fine is the lowest fine for violence in case of death, the middle fine in case of death through a mistake in treatment. 57 In case of injury to a vital part or causing a deformity, the (magistrate) shall treat it as (a case of) physical injury.

58 Actors shall live in one place during the rainy season. 59 They shall avoid excessive gifts of love by one person and excessive praise of one. 60 For transgression of that, the fine is twelve *paṇas*. 61 They may, at will, entertain by making fun of the (customs of) countries, castes, families, schools and love-affairs.

62 By actors are explained wandering minstrels and mendicants. 63 For them the punishment shall be as many lashes with the whip as the number of *paṇas* the (judges) may pronounce as the fine, to be inflicted with an iron rod (i.e., mercilessly).

49 *caraka-* is proposed in conformity with 2.13.33. Cf. Breloer, III, 370 n.3. Cb Cs read *saraka* which means 'a jewel.' That meaning does not fit in the context. The actual comment in Cb contains no reference to any jewel.

53 *ṣaṣṭham aṁśaṁ dadyāt* : according to Cs it is the finder who gives one-sixth to the king. That is due to Yāj. 2.35. But Yāj. presupposes that the treasure-trove belongs to the finder, which is not the case here. 54 *svakaraṇena* : cf. 2.36.7 ; 3.1.15 etc. — Manu (8.35-37) allows only the Brahmin to take the whole ; the rest are to give one-sixth to the state.

57 *marmavadhavaiguṇyakaraṇa* may be understood as a single idea 'causing a physical deformity through injury to a vital part' or as two separate ideas, *marmavadha* and *vaiguṇyakaraṇa*. *-vedha* (Cb Cs) for *vadha-* is perhaps better. — *daṇḍapāruṣyaṁ vidyāt*, i.e., the punishments of 3.19.12-14 would operate.

58 This is in order to prevent their disturbing agricultural operations (Cs). Cf. 2.1.34. 59 *kāmadānam* : this would be received by the *kuśīlavas* from some patron, hardly given by them to some one. 60 *dvādaśaguṇo* of the mss. would apply to *kāmadāna*, but not to *ativāda*. We should read *dvādaśapaṇo* with Cb. 61 The mss. read *-avabhāsena* ; Meyer's suggestion to read *-avahāsena* is adopted as being preferable to it. Cb Cs read *-apahāne* 'by avoiding (the ridicule of).' In 3.18.8 we have *upavāda* 'reviling' which is different from *avahāsa* 'joking about, making fun of' here. And the form *apahāna* is not convincing.

63 *ayaḥśūlena* 'with an iron rod' ; but since *śiphā* is there, this has to be understood figuratively. Cf. *āyaḥśūlika* in *Kāvyaprakāśa*, 10. Cb explains 'if any one pierces the vitals of *kuśīlavas* and *cāraṇas* and takes money from them he is to be punished with lashes.' This is doubtful. Cs has 'in case they wound the feelings of others which is like piercing the vitals with an iron dart,' which seems little likely.

64 In the case of the remaining kinds of work, he shall lay down wages for artists in accordance with what they produce.

65 In this manner the (king) should prevent thieves who are not known as thieves such as traders, artisans, actors, mendicants, jugglers and others from oppressing the country.

CHAPTER TWO

SECTION 77 KEEPING A WATCH OVER TRADERS

1 The Superintendent of Markets should set up the pledging or sale of old wares which are furnished with proof of ownership in the market-place. 2 And he should inspect the weights and measures because of (likely) fraud in the standard of weights and measures.

3 In the case of the *parimāṇī* and the *droṇa*, half a *pala* less or more is no offence. 4 For one *pala* less or more the fine is twelve *paṇas*. 5 By that is explained the increase in fine for each successive *pala*. 6 In the case of a *tulā*, one *karṣa* less or more is no offence. 7 For two *karṣa*s less or more the fine is six *paṇas*. 8 By that is explained the increase in fine for each successive *karṣa*. 9 In the case of an *āḍhaka*, half a *karṣa* less or more is no offence. 10 For one *karṣa* less or more the fine is three *paṇas*. 11 By that is explained the increase in fine for each successive *karṣa*. 12 From this, he should form an estimate of (the fines for deviations in) other types of weights and measures.

64 The idea seems to be that in the case of the work of artisans not mentioned in the Chapter, their remuneration should be fixed in accordance with the type of work they do. Cs has *śeṣa* as ' additional work ' for which remuneration is to be according to work done. This meaning for *śeṣa* seems hardly likely. According to Breloer (III, 370 n.2) we should read a *ca* after *karmaṇām* and understand ' for the classes of artisans not mentioned in this Chapter, the wages should be as given to artists.' He adds that artists (*śilpin*) do not belong to this Chapter and artisans not mentioned here should be treated like artists, i.e., their wages are not fixed by rules, but according to the object. It is not certain that such a distinction between two sets of artisans is really intended. What seems meant is only that artists' wages depend on the type of work they do.

65 Breloer (III, 371) considers it noteworthy that wood- and leather-workers, clay-workers and house-builders are missing in this Chapter. According to his reasoning on the last s. these would be treated on a par with artists. It is likely that these are not mentioned because fraud or cheating is not measurable in their case, also because their misdemeanour does not quite constitute a social crime. The fact that they belong to a more primitive economy seems to have little to do with their non-mention in this Chapter. — *kuhaka* is a ' magician ' according to Cb.

4.2

1 *saṁsthādhyakṣaḥ* : this officer's duties are not described in the Second Book. It is not clear if he is to work under the *paṇyādhyakṣa* (2.16) who appears towards the end of this Chapter. *saṁsthā* refers to the *paṇyasaṁsthā* ' the market-place.' — *purāṇabhāṇḍānām* : this does not mean that the officer is concerned with old or second-hand goods only. He supervises the whole market, where old goods (that are likely to be stolen goods) may also be on sale. 2 *pautava-* : see 2.19.1.

3 *parimāṇī* and *droṇa* each measures two hundred *palas* (2.19.17-18 and 29). So the deviation allowed is to the extent of 1/400th. 6 *tulā* is one hundred *palas* and a *karsa* is 1/4th of a *pala* (2.19.12-15 and 4) ; so the same deviation is allowed. 9 *āḍhaka* is 1/4th of a *droṇa* (2.19.31).

13 For the trader, purchasing with larger weights and measures and selling with smaller ones, these same fines are to be doubled. 14 For one robbing to the extent of one-eighth part of the price of the goods in the case of goods sold by counting, the fine is ninety-six *paṇas*.

15 For the trader effecting the sale or pledging of an article made of wood, metal or gems, or made of ropes, leather or clay, or made of yarn, bark or hair, which is not genuine by declaring it to be genuine, the fine is eight times the price. 16 For the trader effecting the sale or pledging of an article not of high value as an article of high value or of an article not of a particular class as an article of that class or of an article which is given a false shine or in which there is fraud or the container of which is changed, the fine is fifty-four *paṇas* if the price is trifling, double if the price is one *paṇa*, two hundred (*paṇas*) if the price is two *paṇas*. 17 By that is explained the increase in fine in case of increase in price.

18 For artisans and artists who by conspiring together bring about a deterioration in the quality of a work or (increase in) profit or a hindrance to purchase or sale, the fine is one thousand *paṇas*.

19 For traders, too, who by conspiring together hold back wares or sell them at a high price, the fine is one thousand *paṇas*.

20 As to difference in weight or measure or difference in price or quality, for the weigher or measurer who by a trick of the hand brings about (a difference to the extent of) one-eighth part in (an article) priced at one *paṇa*, the fine is two hundred (*paṇas*). 21 By that is explained the increase in fines by two

13 *atiriktābhyāṁ krītvā* etc.: the purchase is made with a weight larger by more than 1/400th, while the sale is made with a weight smaller by more than 1/400th, i.e., the difference in weight is more than double the deviation allowed and therefore the fines are doubled. 14 *paṇyamūlyeṣu aṣṭabhāgam*: perhaps in conformity with s. 20 below, *paṇamūlyeṣu* may have been the original reading; however, we have no reference in this case to a rising scale of fines as we have there.

15 Yāj., 2.246 is an exact paraphrase. 16 *tajjāta* is 'of a particular class' rather than 'made at a particular place' (Cs Breloer). Cf 4.6.3. — *samudgaparivartimam*, i.e., given from a different container. The reading *samutpari-* meaning 'changed in appearance' is less likely. Cf Yāj., 2.247-8. — *hīnamūlyam*, i.e., valued at less than one *paṇa*.

18 *kāruśilpinām* etc.: evidently the *saṁsthādhyakṣa* was also responsible for preventing craftsmen and artists whose shops were in the market from joining together for exploiting customers. Meyer thinks that traders inducing craftsmen etc. to join together may also be understood. But that does not seem right. Cf. Yāj., 2.249. From 4.1.64 and this s. Breloer (III, 382) concludes that the separation of artisans from traders was not usual before Kauṭilya. For *ājīva* 'profit' cf. s. 28 below.

19 Yāj., 2.250 is an exact reproduction.

20 The expression *tulāmānāntaram arghavarṇāntaraṁ vā* at the beginning are understood as something like *adhikāraśabdas* introducing the topic. This is how Cb apparently understands it. It explains *antara* by 'special gain (made through *tulā* etc.).' The two words could have been understood with *aṣṭabhāgam* in the s., but though the former is possible with *hastadoṣeṇa*, it is difficult to conceive of *arghāntara* or *varṇāntara* being brought about by *hastadoṣa*. And the case of *varṇāntara* is separately mentioned in s. 22. Cs supplies 'should be written down in a book' after the expression, but it is not easy to see the purpose of such records. — *dharakasya* etc.: as Breloer (III, 396-400) says these are servants in the royal store-houses, where these offences are to be understood as being committed. Cf. 2.15.63. That explains the heavier fine. 21 *dviśatottarā daṇḍavṛddhiḥ*: this may mean

hundred (*paṇas*) successively. 22 For mixing things of a similar kind with objects such as grains, fats, sugars, salts, perfumes and medicines, the fine is twelve *paṇas*.

23 The Merchant should fix, after calculating their total earnings for the day, what the (sales-agents) should live on with permission.

24 What falls in between the purchaser and the seller becomes different from what is received. 25 With that they may make stores of grains and commodities, when permitted to do so. 26 The Director of Trade should confiscate what is accumulated otherwise by them. 27. With that he should trade when selling grains and commodities to the advantage of the subjects.

28 And he should fix a profit for them of five per hundred over and above the permitted purchase-price in the case of indigenous commodities, ten (per hundred) in the case of foreign goods. 29 For those who increase the price beyond that or secure (a profit beyond that) during purchase or sale, the fine shall be two hundred *paṇas* for (an additional profit of) five *paṇas* in one hundred *paṇas*. 30. By that is explained the increase in fine in case of increase in price.

31 And in case of the joint purchase by them remaining unsold, he shall not allow another joint purchase. 32 In case of damage to commodities, he should show them favour.

that in the case of an article valued at two *paṇas*, the fine is four hundred *paṇas* and so on or that if the difference is to the extent of 1/4th of the price the fine is 400 and so on (Cs). The former is obviously intended. 22 *samavarṇopadhāne*: this literally implies mixing with goods of the same or similar quality. Meyer thinks we should read *asamavarṇo-* 'not of the same quality,' which seems supported by *hīnaṁ prakṣipan* in Yāj.'s paraphrase of this s. (2.245). But the smallness of the fine seems to indicate only a mixing with similar quality goods. The fine is prescribed because goods in royal stores are tampered with.

23 *yan nisṛṣṭam* etc.: it seems that from this s. onwards we have to think of the *paṇyādhyakṣa* as the officer concerned and not the *saṁsthādhyakṣa*. The former is mentioned in ss. 26 and 33. Moreover, *upajīveyuḥ* could have for its subject sales-agents, referred to as *paṇyādhiṣṭhātāraḥ* in 2.16.14-16, who work under the *paṇyādhyakṣa*. It is he who fixes their day's remuneration. *vaṇik*, therefore, seems to be the *paṇyādhyakṣa*; he is the state Trader-in-Chief as 2.16 shows.

24 *kretṛvikretor antarapatitam* is an odd expression. What seems meant is 'the difference between purchases and sales,' i.e., goods remaining unsold. *krayavikrayayor* would have been better. — *ādāyādanyad* 'other than, i.e., different from what is received (as commission or profit).' The idea seems to be that unsold goods cannot be treated as remuneration or profit and the agent deprived of the latter with that excuse. It must be admitted that this sense for *ādāya* would be unusual. It is not unlikely that ss. 24 and 25 formed a single sentence and we originally had *antarapatitam ādāya yad bhavati tena dhānyapaṇya-* etc. Cs reads *adāyādanyaṁ* 'not liable to be divided among heirs (but to be taken by the king alone),' which is extremely doubtful. Meyer proposes *ādāya adainyaṁ bhavati* 'no difficulty would arise by taking it,' i.e., it would be useful in times of distress. There seems little point in such a statement here. 26 *anyathānicitam*, e.g., by setting aside a part of the goods given to them for selling and making up the price by charging more for the rest. 27 *anugraheṇa prajānām* : cf. 2.16.5 above.

28 *-kraya* is clearly 'purchase-price'. 29 *bhāvayatām* : the object is 'gain or profit.' — *paṇaśate pañcapaṇād*, i.e., for an additional 5%.

31 *nānyaṁ saṁbhūyakrayam* : Cb Cs understand 'to other merchants.' However, 'to the same merchants' is also likely. A sort of monopoly in sale is thought of here, care being taken to see that there is no cornering of the commodity.

33 If there is a glut of commodities, the Director of Trade should sell all goods in one place. 34 So long as these are unsold, others shall not sell (those goods). 35 The (agents) shall sell those for a daily wage for the benefit of the subjects.

36 In the case of commodities distant in place and time, however, the (Director of Trade), expert in fixing prices, shall fix the price after calculating the investment, the production of goods, duty, interest, rent and other expenses.

CHAPTER THREE

SECTION 78 REMEDIAL MEASURES DURING CALAMITIES

1 There are eight great calamities of a divine origin: fire, floods, disease, famine, rats, wild animals, serpents and evil spirits. 2 From them he should protect the country.

3 In summer, the villages shall do the cooking outside (the houses) or being protected by a collection of ten fire-fighting implements.

4 Prevention of fire is explained in 'Rules for the City Superintendent' and in connection with royal possessions in 'Rules for the Royal Residence.'

5 And on *parvan*-days, he should cause worship of the fire to be made with offerings, oblations in fire and recitals of benedictions.

33 *paṇyabāhulyāt*: Cs reads this with the preceding s.; but the construction is far from happy. The comment in Cb supports the other construction. — *ekamukhāni*: cf. 2.16.4. 34 *anye*, i.e., other independent traders. 35 *anugraheṇa prajānām*: cf. s. 27 above.

36 The prose is to be construed with the following stanza, showing a common authorship. — *paṇyaniṣpattim* refers to the amount of goods produced. Cs has 'time taken for production.' — *arghavit* is clearly the *paṇyādhyakṣa*, as 2.16.1-3 show. He can hardly be the *saṁsthādhyakṣa* as Cs and Breloer think.

4.3

The inclusion of this Chapter in this Book is rather strange. Perhaps *kaṇṭaka* stands for everything causing trouble to subjects. The *pradeṣṭṛs* may be concerned with some of the measures recommended, but often the king appears to direct the operations himself.

3 *grīṣme* etc.: cf. 2.36.15-17 above. — *daśamūlīsaṁgraheṇa adhiṣṭhitāḥ*: this is far from clear in meaning. The translation follows a suggestion by N. N. Law (*Studies*, p. 101) that *daśamūlī* refers to the fire-fighting tools of 2.36.18, though it must be pointed out that we have only nine objects mentioned there, not ten, since *kacagrahaṇī* is a single item, not two as Law thinks. Cb Cs read *daśakulī-*; the idea seems to be that groups of ten families hold themselves responsible for fires in their area and that probably they kept a watch by turns while cooking was in progress. This might also appear to be a likely idea. Cb seems to imply that the *gopa* (in charge of ten families) is to look after the prevention of fire.

4 *nāgarika-* etc., i.e., in 2.36.15-27 above. — *niśāntapraṇidhau*, i.e., in 1.20.4.

5 *parvasu*, i.e., on the new moon and full moon days.

6 In the rainy season, villages situated near water should live away from the level of the floods. 7 And they should keep a collection of wooden planks, bamboos and boats. 8 They should rescue a (person) being carried away (by the flood) by means of gourds, skin-bags, canoes, tree-stems and rope-braids. 9 For those who do not go to the rescue, the fine is twelve *paṇas*, except in the case of those without canoes.

10 And on *parvan*-days he should cause worship of the rivers to be carried out. 11 Experts in the practice of magic or those versed in the Vedas should use spells against rain.

12 In case of drought, he should cause worship of the Lord of Śacī, the Ganges, the Mountains and Mahākaccha to be made.

13 The calamity of disease, (magicians and others) should counteract with secret means, physicians with medicines or holy ascetics with pacificatory and expiatory rites.

14 By that is explained the epidemic. 15 He should cause to be instituted bathing in sacred places, worship of Mahākaccha, milking of cows in cremation grounds, burning of effigies and a night (festival in honour) of gods.

16 In case of disease or epidemic among cattle, he should order lustration rites in connection with the sheds and objects (connected with them) and worship of their respective deities.

17 During a famine, the king should make a store of seeds and foodstuffs and show favour (to the subjects), or (institute) the building of forts or water-works with the grant of food, or share (his) provisions (with them), or entrust the country (to another king). 18 Or, he should seek shelter with allies, or cause a reduction or shifting (of the population). 19 Or, he should migrate with the people to another region where crops have grown, or settle

7 *upagṛhṇīyuḥ* is proposed for *apa-* as being necessary for sense. 8 *gaṇḍikā* is a tree-stem, sometimes used as an anvil; cf. 2.13.9. — *veṇikā* is a rope (which has the appearance of a braid). Cf. 10.2.14. Law (*Studies*, p. 84) thinks that *gaṇḍikā* is a floating device made of the skin of a rhinoceros and that *veṇikā* is a float of reeds etc. woven together. The former at least is doubtful in this text.

12 *mahākaccha* : see 3.16.38. According to Cb it means 'the sea.'

13 *siddhatāpasāḥ* seems to convey a single idea 'ascetics who have attained *siddhis*.'

15 *mahākacchavardhanam* : see 3.16.38.

16 *sthānārtha-* is proposed for *sthānānyartha-* of the mss. *sthānāni* outside the compound would be strange. *sthāna* by itself can hardly mean 'keeping in another place' (Cb). Meyer suggests *sthānānyārtha-* 'sheds and other (*anya*) objects,' which is doubtful. He also suggests *senānyartha-* or *senānyarchā-*, which are hardly likely. — *svadaivata* 'i.e., Subrahmaṇya of elephants, Aśvinau of horses, Paśupati of cattle, Varuṇa of buffaloes, Vāyu of donkeys and mules, and Agni of goats' (Cb Cs).

17 *deśanikṣepam* : this amounts to entrusting the region to the care of another king who may be better placed. *nikṣepa* implies receiving back after a time. 18 *karśana* is reduction in population by inducing migration to foreign lands, while *vamana* is shifting

along the sea, lakes or tanks. 20 He should make sowings of grains, vegetables, roots and fruits along the water-works or hunt deer, beasts, birds, wild animals and fish.

21 In case of danger from rats, cats and ichneumons should be let loose. 22 For catching or killing these, the fine shall be twelve *paṇas*, also for not restraining dogs, except in the case of foresters. 23 He should strew grains smeared with the milk of *snuhi*-plants or such as are mixed with secret mixtures. 24 Or, he should institute a tax in rats. 25 Or, holy ascetics should perform pacificatory rites. 26 And on *parvan*-days, he should order worship of rats.

27 By that are explained remedies against danger from locusts, birds, and insects.

28 In case of danger from wild animals, he should leave carcasses of cattle mixed with a stupefying liquid or intestines (of cattle) filled with *madanakodrava*. 29 Fowlers or hunters should busy themselves with concealed cages and pits. 30 Armoured men, weapons in hand, should kill wild animals. 31 For one not going forth to help, the fine shall be twelve *paṇas*. 32 The same shall be the reward for one slaying a wild animal. 33 And he should order the worship of mountains on *parvan*-days.

34 By that are explained remedies against herds of deer or beasts, swarms of birds and crocodiles.

35 In case of danger from serpents, experts in poison-cure should act with charms and medicines. 36 Or (persons) coming together should kill snakes. 37 Or, experts in the Atharvaveda lore should use magic spells. 38 And on *parvan*-days, he should order worship of cobras.

39 By that are explained remedies against danger from aquatic creatures.

40 In case of danger from evil spirits, experts in the Atharvaveda lore or experts in the practice of magic should perform rites for destroying evil spirits. 41 And on *parvan*-days, he should order worship of *caitya*-trees with offerings of raised platforms, umbrellas, food, small flags and goats.

population from one region to another in the kingdom itself. Cf. 2.1.1. 20 *ārambhān* in the context refers to hunting, catching etc.

22 *teṣām*, i.e., of cats and ichneumons. — *śunām* : these might drive away the cats.
24 *mūṣikakaram*, i.e., so many dead rats as tax per head.

28 *madanarasa* : see 14.1.16-17. — *madanakodrava* appears to be a poisonous variety of the *kodrava* grains ; or *kodrava* grains treated with poison may be understood. 29 *kūṭa* as an adjective 'concealed' is preferable to a substantive 'a snare' (Meyer); cf. 2.3.15 ; 4.10.3 etc.

35 *jāṅgulīvidaḥ* : cf. 1.21.9 etc. 36 *vāpi sarpān* is proposed for *vopasarpān*, which is evidently corrupt.

41 *ullopikā* appears to be a kind of food, as in Cb. The *Mahābhārata* (5.191.21) has the form *ullāpika* (from *lap* 'address' to the spirits when offering food to them). Utpala on *Bṛ. Saṁ.* 48.28 has *ullāpika*, but on 46.16 *ullopikā*. — *hastapatākā* is a flag carried in the hand. a small flag.

42 In cases of all (kinds of) danger, they should make offerings day and night, saying 'We offer you the oblation.' 43 And in all cases, he should favour the stricken (subjects) like a father.

44 Therefore, experts in the practice of magic, (and) holy ascetics, capable of counteracting divine calamities, should live in the kingdom, honoured by the king.

CHAPTER FOUR

SECTION 79 GUARDING AGAINST PERSONS WITH SECRET (MEANS OF) INCOME

1 In 'Rules for the Administrator' the protection of the country has been described. 2 We shall (now) explain the weeding of thorns in that (country).

3 The Administrator should station in the country (secret agents) appearing as holy ascetics, wandering monks, cart-drivers, wandering minstrels, jugglers, tramps, fortune-tellers, soothsayers, astrologers, physicians, lunatics, dumb persons, deaf persons, idiots, blind persons, traders, artisans, artists, actors, brothel-keepers, vintners, dealers in bread, dealers in cooked meat, and dealers in cooked rice. 4 They should find out the integrity or otherwise of village-officers and heads of departments. 5 And whomsoever among these he suspects of deriving a secret income he should cause to be spied upon by a secret agent.

6 A secret agent should say to a judge in whom confidence is inspired by him, 'Such and such a relation of mine is accused (before you); save him in this misfortune and accept this amount.' 7 If he were to do so, he should be exiled as one given to receiving bribes. 8 By that are explained magistrates.

42 *carāmaḥ* from Cb Cs seems preferable to *carāmi* of the mss.

4.4

gūḍhājīvinām : the genitive conveys the sense of the ablative. — *rakṣā* is the same as *rakṣaṇa* in 4.1 and 4.2 above.

1 *samāhartṛpraṇidhau* : the actual title of the section in 2.35 is *samāhartṛpracāraḥ*.

3 *samāhartā* : it is clear that this officer is ultimately responsible for the *kaṇṭakaśodhana* and that the *pradeṣṭṛs* work under him. — Russ. renders *pracchandaka* by 'mediators or middle-men' or (in the Notes) 'those who carry secret messages.' 4 *grāmāṇām* obviously refers to officers stationed in the villages. 5 *gūḍhājīvinam* is proposd for *gūḍhajīvinam* in conformity with the use of the former form found throughout elsewhere ; cf. 3.1.10 ; 3.20.2 etc., as well as the title of this section. The actual comment in Cb shows the correct form. — *sattriṇā* is proposed for *sattrisavarṇena* of the mss. *savarṇa* 'of the same *varṇa*' has little significance in the context ; and its place in the compound is also suspicious.

6 It is proposed to omit *pradeṣṭāraṁ vā* read after *dharmastham* is the mss., in view of s. 8 which follows. 7 *pravāsyeta* : the idea is of 'exile,' not of 'execution,' in the present Chapter.

9 A secret agent should say to a village chief or a departmental head, 'Such and such a rogue has plenty of wealth; this misfortune has befallen him; by using that, extort money from him.' 10 If he were to do so, he should be exiled as an extortioner.

11 Or, (an agent) pretending to be an accused should induce those, who are known to bear false testimony, with plenty of money. 12 If they were to do so, they should be exiled as false witnesses. 13 By that are explained those who cause false evidence to be given.

14 Or, if he considers any one as a user of occult means for winning love with incantations or rites with herbs and rites in cremation grounds, a secret agent should say to him, 'I am in love with so and so's wife, daughter-in-law or daughter; make her reciprocate my love and take this money.' 15 If he were to do so, he should be exiled as a user of occult means for winning love. 16 By that are explained practisers of black magic and sorcery.

17 Or, if he considers any one who prepares, purchases or sells poison or who deals in medicines or food, as an administerer of poison, a secret agent should say to him, 'So and so is my enemy; bring about his death and take this money.' 18 If he were to do so, he should be exiled as a poison-giver. 19 By that is explained the dealer in stupefying mixtures.

20 Or, if he considers any one as an utterer of false coins, (being) a frequent purchaser of various metals and acids, of coals, bellows, pincers, vices, anvils, dies, chisels and crucibles, with indications of hands and clothes smeared with soot, ashes and smoke, (and being) possessed of blacksmith's tools, a secret agent should expose him by insinuating himself into his confidence as a pupil and by carrying on dealings with him. 21 If exposed, he should be exiled as an utterer of false coins. 22 By that is explained the remover of colour (from precious metals) and the dealer in artificial gold.

9 *grāmakūṭam*: the word does not occur elsewhere. It means probably the same as *grāmika* (3.4.9) and seems to be the village headman. — *āhārayasva*: cf. 1.6.7 etc. 10 *utkocaka* is one who extorts money rather than one who takes a bribe.

13 *-śrāvaṇakārakāḥ*: for *śrotṛ* 'witness' cf. 3.1.4,14 etc.

14 *saṁvadana* is how all mss. read the word here and in the next s., also apparently in 4.5.6, but in 4.5.1 and 4.13.28 they show *saṁvanana*. The *Atharvaveda* knows *saṁvanana* (6.9.3) and *saṁvananī* (a plant for winning love, 6.139.3). The *Mahābhārata* (3.222.56-57) shows *saṁvanana* in the Critical Edition, though a number of mss. have *saṁvadana*; the lexicons have *saṁvadana*. The latter form has been adopted throughout. 16 *kṛtyā* appears to be connected with spirits, while *abhicāra* is sorcery.

19 *madanayoga*: cf. 14.1.16-17.

20 *muṣṭikā* appears to be a kind of hand-vice. — *bimba* the 'die' from which coins are made. — *-saṁsargam* is read for *-saṁvargam* in conformity with (*upakaraṇa-*) *saṁsargam* in 4.6.2 and 18. — *saṁvyavahāra*: cf. 1.9.3. — *anupraviśya*: cf. 1.17.39 etc. 22 *rāgasyāpahartā kūṭasuvarṇavyavahārī ca*: it seems that a single offender is intended, one who deals in artificial gold and robs precious metals of their genuineness. *vyākhyātaḥ* also implies a single individual. The *ca*, therefore, does not seem to be right.

23 But the thirteen (persons), having secret ways of income, when engaged in doing injury (to others), should be exiled or they shall pay a redemption-amount in accordance with the gravity of the offence.

CHAPTER FIVE

SECTION 80 DETECTION OF CRIMINALS THROUGH SECRET AGENTS IN THE DISGUISE OF HOLY MEN

1 After the employment of spies, (secret agents) appearing as holy men should entice criminals by means of lores favourite with criminals, (viz.,) robbers by means of charms inducing sleep, making invisible or opening doors, adulterers by love-winning charms.

2 When these have been enthused (to see the power of the charms), they should take a large band of them at night and proposing to go to one village should go to another village in which men and women are prepared beforehand, and say, 'Right here you can see the power of our lore ; it is difficult to go to the other village.' 3 Then opening the gates by means of a gate-opening charm, they should say, 'Enter.' 4 By means of an invisibility charm they should make the criminals go safely through the midst of wakeful guards. 5 Sending guards to sleep with a sleep-inducing charm they should cause them with their beds to be moved by the criminals. 6 With a love-winning charm they should make the criminals enjoy (harlots) appearing as other men's wives. 7 When these are convinced of the power of their lores, the should prescribe the performance of preliminary rites and so on, so that they may be recognized.

8 Or, they should get them to do their work in houses in which goods have been marked. 9 Or, they should get them caught in one place after winning their confidence. 10 They should get them arrested while engaged in purchasing, selling or pledging articles that are marked or when they are intoxicated with drugged liquor.

23 *trayodaśa* : we get the number thirteen only if we understand a single offender in s. 22. See above. — *pravāsyāḥ* : this again is exile, not execution, since redemption is allowed.

4.5

māṇava 'an evil man' is a criminal, particularly a dacoit or robber. Patañjali on Pāṇini, 4.1.161, explains the formation of the word in this sense. Cf. Sten Konow, *Indian Culture*, III, 3.

1 *māṇavān* is proposed for *māṇavā* of the mss. as suggested by Meyer. The accusative as the object for *pralobhayeyuḥ* is quite necessary. The *siddha* agents themselves are not criminals. If they were former criminals, we should have had *purāṇamāṇavā*. Cb comment presupposes *māṇavān*. — *saṁvadana* : see 4.4.14 above.

2 *kṛtakastrīpuruṣam* : Meyer proposes *kṛtasaṁketastrīpuruṣam* ; that does not seem quite necessary. 7 *abhijñānārtham* : the idea apparently is that while engaged in the rites, the dacoits would be off their guard and hence easy to apprehend. It seems quite possible that this expression is to be construed with *kṛtalakṣaṇa-* etc. in the next s.

11 When they are arrested, he should question them concerning former offences and their associates.

12 Or, (secret agents) appearing as old thieves should, after winning their confidence, get thieves to do their work in the same manner and get them arrested. 13 When they are arrested, the Administrator should point them out to citizens and country people, saying, ' The king has studied the lore of catching thieves ; it is under his instructions that these thieves have been caught ; I shall catch others too ; you should (therefore) restrain your kinsmen who may have criminal tendencies.'

14 And if he were to come to know through the information of the spies that some one among them has stolen a (trifle like a) yoke-pin, goad and so on, he should declare (that about) him among them, saying, ' This is the king's power.'

15 Old thieves, cow-herds, fowlers and hunters, winning the confidence of forest thieves and foresters, should induce them to attack caravans, herds or villages with plenty of articles made of artificial gold and forest produce. 16 When the attack is made, they should get them killed by concealed soldiers or through provisions for the journey mixed with stupefying liquids. 17 (Or), they should get them arrested while sleeping after being tired by a long journey carrying a heavy load of stolen goods or when they are intoxicated by drugged liquor at festive parties.

18 And having caught them, the Administrator should show them as before (to the people), causing a proclamation of the king's omniscience to be made among the inhabitants of the kingdom.

CHAPTER SIX

SECTION 81 ARREST ON SUSPICION, WITH THE (STOLEN) ARTICLE AND BY (INDICATIONS OF) THE ACT

1 After the practices of holy men comes (the topic of) arrest on suspicion, with the articles and because of the act.

9 *anupraviṣṭā* in the nominative is proposed as suggested by Meyer in place of the accusative in the mss., in view of the usual sense of this word. Cf. ss. 12 and 15 below. — The s. is misplaced ; it may be read after s. 7. For ss. 8 and 10 go together.

11 *pūrvāpadāna* : see 2.36.36 ; 3.12.35 etc.

14 *pratyādiśet* : cf. 1.11.4.

16 *pathyadanena* is read in conformity with the reading in 2.16.24 above. All mss. read here *pathyādanena*, as all read *pathyadānena* in 7.17.59.

18 *sarvajña-* stands for *sarvajñatva-*. Cf. 1.8.6 for a similar use.

4.6

rūpa refers to the stolen article found with a person. *karma* is the act of theft.

1 *siddhaprayogād ūrdhvam* : the succession is of topics only. The *siddhas* have nothing to do with the contents of this Chapter.

2 He should suspect as being either a murderer, or a thief, or one living on a secret income by appropriating buried treasure or entrusted article or through employment by enemies (the following persons, viz.,) one whose inheritance and family (income) are exhausted, one with a small wage, one falsely declaring his country, caste, family, name or occupation, one whose profession or work is hidden, one addicted to meat, wine, eating of food, perfumes, garlands, clothes and ornaments, one who spends lavishly, one addicted to prostitutes, gambling or drinking in bars, one travelling frequently, one whose stay and departure are unknown, one moving at an odd time in a solitary place or a forest or a house-garden, one holding long consultations and meeting frequently in a secret place or in a place with a (likely) victim, one secretly getting treatment for recently inflicted wounds, one always staying inside the house, one proceeding (stealthily ?), one devoted to a beloved, one making frequent inquiries about other people's possessions (such as) women, goods, or houses, one in possession of tools of a condemned occupation or lore, one moving stealthily in the shadow of walls at an odd hour of the night, one selling at an improper place and time goods that are changed in appearance, one who entertains a feeling of hostility, one with a low occupation or caste concealing his appearance, one, not a monk, having the marks of a monk, or a monk with a different mode of life, one who had formerly committed an offence, one shown up by his own deeds, one who, at the sight of the City-Superintendent or a big officer, conceals himself, runs away, sits without breathing, becomes agitated or has his voice and complexion of the face dry and changed, (and) one shying at a crowd of men carrying weapons in hand. Thus ends (the topic of) arrest on suspicion.

3 As to arrest with the article, however, what is lost or stolen and is not found, he should communicate to those who deal in wares of that class. 4 If they, on coming by the article communicated, were to conceal, it, they shall be liable for the offence of being accessories. 5 If they are ignorant about it, they shall be acquitted on giving up the article. 6 And they shall not pledge or sell old wares without informing the Market Superintendent.

2 *-sthānagamanam* : *paṇya* found in the mss. at the end of this compound is dropped as in Cb Cs. It does not go well with *sthāna* and *gamana*. — *-pratīkārakārayitāram* is proposed for *pratīkārayitāram*, in conformity with 2.36.10 above. — *abhyadhigantāram* is uncertain in meaning. Cb explains 'one suddenly turning aside when some person is coming towards him.' Cs follows. It may also mean 'one who stealthily approaches other people or their houses.' — *kutsitakarmaśāstropa-* : Cs has *-śastra-* for *-śāstra-*. Cb comment presupposes *śastra*. However, *kutsita* seems more likely of a lore such as magic than of a weapon. — *hīnakarmajātiṁ vigūhamānarūpam* : the expressions may be understood together or separately. — *liṅgin* is one who has the marks of a monk. — *pūrvakṛtāpadānam* ; cf. 4.8.26 etc. — *svakarmabhir apadiṣṭam* : this person is not caught in the act ; only his actions in general are suspicious. — *nāgarikamahāmātradarśane* is to be understood right up to *-mukhavarṇam*. — *-paraprayoga* seems to mean 'employment by the enemy (as an agent).' Cb Cs read *varaprayoga*. Cb has '*śastrayukta*, armed' ; it is not unlikely that this is corrupt for *śatruprayukta*. Cs explains 'use of a weapon in consequence of anger (*vara*, i.e., *krodha*).' This latter is doubtful. — *apahāra* and *prayoga* are the means of *gūḍha ājīva* or 'secret income.'

4 *sācivyakara* 'one who renders help,' an associate. 5 Cf. 3.16.13. 6 Cf. 4.2.1.

7 If the article about which information has been given is found, he should question the person arrested with the article concerning its acquisition 'Whence did you get this?' 8 If he were to plead 'I got it in inheritance, obtained it as a gift, purchased it, got it made, (or) received it as a secret pledge from so and so; this is the place and time of its acquisition; this is its price, quantity, marks and value,' he shall be acquitted on his (statements about the) acquisition being corroborated. 9 If the person who lost the article were also to prove the same, he shall hold the article as belonging to him whose possession of it was earlier and long or whose title is clear. 10 For, even among quadrupeds and bipeds there is a similarity in appearance and marks; how much more then would it be in the case of forest produce, ornaments and (other) articles produced from materials from the same source and by the same manufacturer?

11 If he were to plead 'This is a borrowed or hired article, a pledge, a trust, a deposit or goods given for sale on agency basis, belonging to so and so,' he shall be acquitted on corroboration by the person proving his innocence. 12 If that person were to say 'It is not so,' the person arrested with the article shall justify the reason for the other person giving it, the reasons for his accepting it or get the indications corroborated by the giver, the one who causes to give, the recorder, the receiver and those who have witnessed or heard (the transaction).

13 In the case of an (article) that is left, has disappeared (or) run away and is (afterwards) found, (there shall be) clearance (from guilt) by proof concerning place, time and acquisition. 14 If not cleared, he shall pay that and as much again as fine. 15 Otherwise, he shall be liable to punishment for theft. Thus ends (the topic of) arrest with the article.

7 For this passage, cf. 3.16.12 ff. 8 *ādhipracchannam* seems to mean 'concealed as a pledge,' i.e., a secret pledge. This is distinguished from *āhitaka* 'a thing pledged' of s. 11 below. — *upasaṁprāpteḥ* is an emendation of Meyer for *upasaṁprāptaḥ*; the genitive is quite necessary. — *argha* is the price fixed for sale, while *mūlya* is its cost price. 9 For *deśa* 'title, proof of ownership', cf. 3.16.29. 10 It seems better to understand *ekayoni* with *dravya* and *eka* alone with *kartṛ*.

11 *vaiyāvṛtyakarma*: for sales-agents, see 3.12.25 ff. — *apasāra*: see 3.16.15. 12 *upaliṅganam*: cf. 3.12.51; 3.12.37. It primarily means 'a sign or indication that proves something.' In the next s., it refers to proof or production of proof.— *dāyakadāpaka-* etc.: in 2.7.31 some of these terms are used in connection with receipts in the treasury. — *upadraṣṭṛbhir* is an emendation suggested by Meyer for *upadeṣṭṛbhir*. That it is necessary is shown by 3.11.31. *upadeṣṭṛ* can hardly mean 'one who dictates to the writer' (Cs). Cb seems to understand 'one who tells the person that the object is in his possession.'

13 *upaliṅganena*: see s. 12 above. 15 *anyathā*: the difference between this case and that in the last s. seems to be that in this case, the person cannot plead any excuse, howsoever invalid, for the possession of the object.

16 As to arrest because of the act, however, in the case of a house that has been robbed, entry or exit otherwise than by a door, the piercing of the door with a hole or by uprooting, the breaking of a latticed window or eaves of an upper chamber, the crumbling of a wall while climbing up or descending, or the digging up (of the ground) as a means of burying or robbing objects secretly, he should hold (these) as committed by one inside the house, if (things stolen) could be known through information supplied, and if the cutting, the rubbish, the breaking and the tools are on the inside. 17 In the reverse case (he should hold these) as committed by an outsider, if (these are) on both sides as committed by both (inmates and outsiders).

18 If the offence is committed by an insider, he should examine a man closely related, who may be addicted to vice, may have ruthless associates or may be in possession of a thief's tools, or a woman from an indigent family or attached to another (man), or an attendant of a similar conduct, who is sleeping excessively, overpowered by sleep, agitated, with voice and face dry and changed, restless, prattling too much, with limbs stiffened by climbing high up, with body or clothes cut, crushed, broken or torn, with hands and feet having scars or stiffened, with hair and nails full of dust or with hair and nails cut and bent, or who is thoroughly bathed and anointed, with limbs rubbed with oil, or with hands and feet just washed, whose foot-prints are similar to those (found) in dust or wet surfaces, or who has flowers, wine, perfumes, bits of cloth, unguents or perspiration similar to those (found) at the entrance and exit. 19 He should hold (him) to be a thief or an adulterer.

20 The magistrate, along with the village and divisional officers, should make a search for thieves outside, and the City-Superintendent (should do it) inside the fort, according to indications (just) mentioned.

16 *saṁdhinā bījena vā vedham* : since *vedha* 'piercing' implies the idea of making an opening, *saṁdhi* and *bīja* are obviously means to that end. *saṁdhi* seems to be 'making a hole,' but *bīja* is uncertain ; it may signify 'uprooting.' Cb seems to understand the removal of some sort of a wooden latch for opening the door. Cs renders *saṁdhi* by '*suruṅgā*, underground tunnel,' which is doubtful; its explanation of *bīja* by '*vedhasādhana*' is not helpful. Meyer's 'at the joints (*saṁdhi*) or at the hinges (*bīja*)' is possible ; but the locative would have been preferable to the instrumental in that case. Besides, for *saṁdhi* as 'making a hole, or, a hole,' cf. the *Mṛcchakaṭika*, Act 3. — *upadeśopalabhyam* : this and the next clause are the only indications of the effort being made from the inside. — *abhyantara-* goes with each of *cheda*, *utkara*, *parimarda* and *upakaraṇa*.

18 *tadvidhācārum*, i.e., *vyasaninam* etc. — *saṁrabdha* means 'swollen,' also 'stiffened'; the latter seems preferable, for *śūna* is used for 'swollen' in the next Chapter. Cb has 'sprained.' — *vilūnabhugnakeśanakham* : *bhugna* 'bent, curved' does not seem quite appropriate with hair or nails ; perhaps *bhagna* is to be read, *vilūna* going with *keśa* and *bhagna* with *nakha*. Cb's explanation is 'worn out, cut,' which seems to presuppose *bhagna*. 19 *pāradārikam* : the adulterer may also break into a house like a thief.

20 *sagopasthānikaḥ* : cf. 2.35.1-6 above. — *nirdiṣṭahetubhiḥ* refers to the indications mentioned in this Chapter for arrest on suspicion etc.

CHAPTER SEVEN

SECTION 82 INQUEST ON SUDDEN DEATHS

1 He shall examine a (person) dying suddenly, after smearing (the body) with oil.

2 (One) with urine and ordure thrown out, with the skin of the abdomen filled with wind, with swollen hands and feet, with eyes open, with marks on the throat, he should hold as killed through the stopping of breathing by strangulation. 3 The same, with arms and thighs contracted, he should hold as slain by hanging.

4 (One) with hands, feet and abdomen swollen, with eyes sunk in, with the navel turned out, he should hold as impaled.

5 (One) with the anus and eyes closed, with the tongue bitten, with the belly swollen, he should hold as dead by (drowning in) water.

6 (One) bespattered with blood, with limbs broken or dislocated, he should hold as slain with sticks or stones.

7 (One) with limbs shattered and burst, he should hold as hurled down (from a height).

8 (One) with dark hands, feet, teeth and nails, with loose flesh, hair of the body and skin, with the mouth covered with foam, he should hold as killed by poison. 9 The same, with bloody marks of bite, he should hold as killed by a snake or an insect.

10 (One) with clothes and limbs thrown about, with excessive vomiting and motions, he should hold as killed by a stupefying mixture.

11 He should find out if the (person) is killed in one of these ways, or, if after being killed, he is hanged or has his throat cut, through fear of punishment.

4.7

1 *tailābhyaktam* : this is in order that injuries, swellings, etc. may become clear. — *parīkṣeta* : it may be presumed that the inquests were held by the *pradeṣṭṛs* in the country and by the *nāgarika* in the city, as suggested by 4.6.20.

4 *avaropitam* : this is uncertain in meaning. Cb Cs have 'impaled'; though for that *āropita* would be expected, that meaning seems preferable to Meyer's 'choked with a gag', or 'asphyxiated by some object being stuck into the mouth' of Russ.

5 *nistabdha* : Cs has 'come out, protruding'; Meyer 'pressed, closed.' The latter seems more likely. The word also means 'paralysed.'

6 *kāṣṭhair aśmabhir vā* from G1 Cb seems preferable to *kāṣṭhai raśmibhir vā* of the other mss. For, breaking or dislocation of limbs is more likely with stones than with ropes.

10 *madanayoga* : see 14.1.16-17.

11 *udbandhanikṛttakaṇṭham* : it seems necessary to read *udbaddha* here as a participle rather than *udbandha* as a noun which cannot be properly construed with the other words in the compound. The idea is that the murderer makes it appear as a case of suicide either by hanging or by cutting the throat.

12 He should examine through birds the remainder of the meal of one (suspected of being) killed by poison. 13 Or, if what is taken from the heart and thrown in fire produces a crackling sound and becomes rainbow-coloured, he should hold that as poisoned, or if he sees the heart not burning when the body is cremated.

14 He should seek his servant who may have received a severe verbal or physical injury (at the hands of the deceased), or a woman stricken with grief or attached to another, or a kinsman coveting inheritance, livelihood or a woman.

15 He should investigate the same in the case of one (suspected of being) hanged after being murdered. 16 Or, in the case of one who has hanged himself, he should find out (if) any improper wrong (has been done to him).

17 In the case of all, an offence concerning a woman or property, rivalry in profession, hostility towards a rival, or association in a market place, or one of the heads of dispute in a law-court is an occasion for anger. 18 Murder is caused by anger.

19 He should investigate, through those proximate, the murder of a (person, whether he is) killed by (some persons) themselves or through agents appointed, or by thieves for the sake of money, or by enemies of some one else because of similarity. 20 He should question him by whom he had been called, with whom he had stayed or gone, or by whom he was brought to the place of murder. 21 And he should question those moving near him at the place of murder, each one separately, 'Who brought him here? Who killed him? Did you see any one with a weapon in hand or hiding himself or agitated?' 22 As they might reply, so should he question (further).

23-24 Observing the objects used on the person of the helpless (deceased), his belongings, clothes, dress or ornaments, he should question those who deal in those articles, concerning their meeting (with him), their residence, the reason for their stay, their occupation and dealings, and then carry on the investigation.

12 *vayobhiḥ*: see 1.20.7-8. 13 *hṛdayād*: Meyer understands this to refer to the 'stomach.' But that does not seem necessary. The heart also would be affected.

14 There can be no doubt about *vāgdaṇḍapāruṣyātilabdham* being the original reading. Cs renders *atilabdha* by 'oppressed'; its literal meaning 'who has received in excess or severely' is also conceivable. — *dāyavṛtti-* is proposed for *dāyanivṛtti* of the mss., as indicated by *strīdravyavṛttikāmo vā* in Yāj. 2.281. *dāyanivṛtti* can hardly mean 'reversion of inheritance (on somebody's death)' (Cs). Cb has no explanation of *nivṛtti*. — For *abhi-man* 'to covet, entertain a longing for,' cf. 1.6.5 etc.

15 *hatodbaddhasya* for *hatodbandhasya* of the mss. is found in Cb. The dot indicating a double conjunct in a ms. is often mistaken for an *anusvāra*. 16 *viprakāram*: this wrong might have been the cause of the suicide.

17 *paṇyasaṁsthāsamavāyaḥ*: Cb has 'disputes in trade and disputes about importance in partnerships' as two things. Cs follows with 'trade (by fraud etc.) and forming groups by violating seniority (*samavāya*).' This is doubtful. Either association or partnership in trade or rivalry in the market as a single idea seems meant.

19 *ādiṣṭa* 'ordered,' i.e., commissioned or hired to do the murder.

23 *veṣam*, as distinguished from *vastram*, seems to imply some special dress. 24 *saṁyogaṁ nivāsam* etc.: these are those of the dealers, rather than those of the deceased.

25-26 If a person, under the influence of passion or anger, or a woman infatuated by sin, were to kill himself (or herself) by means of a rope, a weapon or poison, he should cause them to be dragged with a rope on the royal highway by a Caṇḍāla ; there is to be no cremation-rite for them nor obsequies by kinsmen.

27 If, however, some kinsman were to perform for them the rites in connection with the dead, he should meet with the same fate afterwards, or should be abandoned by his relations.

28 A person having dealings with an outcast loses caste himself after one year, by sacrificing for them, by teaching them or by entering into marriage relations with them ; so does another having dealings with these.

CHAPTER EIGHT

SECTION 83 INVESTIGATION THROUGH INTERROGATION AND THROUGH TORTURE

1 In the presence of the robbed person and of witnesses, external and internal, he should question the accused about his country, caste, family, name, occupation, wealth, associates and residence. 2 And he should compare these with statements (of others). 3 Then he should question him concerning his movements on the previous day, and place of stay during the night up to the time of arrest. 4 In case of corroboration by persons proving his innocence, he shall be cleared of guilt ; otherwise, he shall be put to torture.

26 *rajjunā* : Cs remarks that the masculine is archaic and adds that the reading was probably *rajjvā vā*. — *tāṁś Caṇḍālena* is proposed for *tāṁ Caṇḍālena* of the mss. As *teṣām* in the following line shows, the woman alone is not meant.

27 *-kriyāvidhim* : *kriyā* and *vidhi* both are not necessary. — *tadgatim*, i.e., having their bodies dragged through the streets and absence of rites. — *svajanād vā pramucyate* : *vā* seems to have the sense of *ca* . We expect *pramucyeta* in the potential mood.

28 The stanza occurs in Manu, 11.80, with slight changes, also in Vasiṣṭha, 1.22, as a quotation. The readings here seem original, though the stanza may have been derived from some earlier source.

4.8

karma is this Chapter has the technical sense of ' torture. ' It has been suggested that it means only ' corporal punishment ' inflicted on the guilty, and not torture inflicted for getting a confession from a suspect (K. P. Jayaswal, *Manu and Yājñavalkya*, pp. 86-87). But *anuyoga* ' questioning, investigation ' cannot be understood with *karma* in that sense. The use of secret agents recommended as an alternative to *karma* (ss.15-16,19) and the mention of *vākyānuyoga* as an alternative to it (s. 18) also imply the sense of torture for the sake of securing a confession.

1 *sākṣiṇām* : after this we have to supply *saṁnidhau* from the preceding compound. Meyer favours *sākṣiṇam* or *sākṣiṇaḥ* ; but it is the suspect who is to be interrogated, not the witnesses. 2 *apadeśa* seems used in the sense of ' statement, declaration,' as explained in 15.1.21. 4 *apasārapratisaṁdhāne* : see 4.6.11.

5 After three nights, the suspect shall not be liable to arrest, because of the inadmissibility of interrogation (after that interval), except when tools (of the crime) are found (with him).

6 For one calling another, who is not a thief, a thief, the punishment shall be that for a thief, also for one hiding a thief.

7 One accused of (being) a thief shall be cleared of guilt, if implicated out of enmity or hatred. 8 For one keeping under restraint one cleared of guilt, the lowest fine for violence (shall be the punishment).

9 In the case of one about whom suspicion has arisen, he should produce tools, counsellers, accomplices, (stolen) articles and agents. 10 And he should compare his action by reference to his entry, receiving of goods and division into shares (of the stolen goods).

11 In the absence of corroboration of these grounds (showing guilt), he should hold a person, though prattling, as not a thief. 12 For, it is observed that even one not a thief, meeting by chance thieves on their way, is arrested because of similarity with the thieves in dress, weapons or goods or on account of his being found near the thieves' goods, as for instance Aṇi-Māṇḍavya declaring himself to be a thief though not a thief, because of the fear of the pain of torture. 13 Hence he should punish only such in whose case proof is fully obtained.

14 He shall not put to torture a person whose offence is trifling, or who is a minor or aged or sick or intoxicated or insane or overcome by hunger, thirst or travel, or who has overeaten or whose meal is undigested or who is weak. 15 He should cause them to be secretly watched by persons of the same character, prostitutes, attendants at water-booths, givers of advice, accommodation and food to them. 16 In this way should he outwit them, or as explained in connection with misappropriation of entrusted articles.

5 *anyatra upakaraṇadarśanāt* can hardly mean 'because of the possibility of finding tools of theft elsewhere than with a thief' (Cs).

7 *coreṇa* obviously is used for *cauryeṇa*. — *apadiṣṭakaḥ* 'about whom a declaration is made (that he is a theif).' 8 *parivāsayataḥ* : this clearly refers to the investigating officer continuing to keep the person in custody.

9 *niṣpādayet*, i.e., should try to find such circumstantial evidence as possession of tools, etc. 10 *karmaṇaś ca* : this refers to the acts of the suspect and his associates, viz., *praveśa*, *dravyādāna* and *aṁśavibhāga*. It would have been better if we had *karmabhiś ca*. — *praveśa* 'entry' into the house for theft.

11 *vipralapantam*, i.e., though he may himself declare himself to be a thief. 12 In view of *dṛśyate* at the beginning of the s., it is proposed to drop *dṛṣṭaḥ* found in the mss. after *gṛhyamāṇaḥ*. — *upavāsena* seems used in the literal sense 'staying near.' — *Aṇi-Māṇḍavya* : Cf. the *Mahābhārata*, 1.101, where, however, there is no mention of the fear of torture, only observance of the vow of silence by the sage. 13 *karaṇa* : cf. 3.12.37,38.

14 *āmakāśitam* from Cb Cs 'whose meal is undigested' is preferable to *ātmakāśitam* of the mss. which can only mean 'shining by himself, appearing by himself.' 15 *prāpāvika* is understood as in Meyer, who would, however, read *prāpāpika*. Cb Cs read *prāvādika* 'one who wrangles' or 'clever in languages,' which is not convincing. M reads *prāvāpika* ; its meaning is uncertain. — *kathā-* : with this, too, *dātṛ* is to be understood : that is rather unusual. *kathā* here may be advice or directions or information. The text does not seem quite all right. 16 *nikṣepāpahāre*, i.e., in 3.12.38-50 above.

17 He should put to torture one whose guilt is found to be probable, but under no circumstances a pregnant woman or a woman within one month of delivery. 18 For a woman, however, there is to be only half the torture, or only examination by interrogation.

19 For a Brahmin there is to be the use of secret agents if he is learned in the Veda, also for an ascetic. 20 In case of transgression of this (rule), the highest fine (shall be imposed) on one who gives and who causes him to give the torture, also for causing death by torture.

21 The ordinary fourfold torture is: six strokes with a stick, seven lashes with a whip, two suspensions from above and the water-tube.

22 In the case of very grave offenders, (there may be): nine strokes with a cane, twelve whip-lashes, two thigh-encirclings, twenty strokes with a *nakta-māla*-stick, thirty-two slaps, two scorpion-bindings, and two hangings up, needle in the hand, burning one joint of a finger of one who has drunk gruel, heating in the sun for one day for one who has drunk fat, and a bed of *balbaja*-points on a winter-night. 23 This is the eighteen-fold torture.

24 He should ascertain the tools, the amount, the (manner of) infliction, the determining and the limiting of it from the *Kharapaṭṭa*.

17 *āptadoṣam*, i.e., when the presumption of guilt is strong, but there is no definite proof. 19 Though the text of Cb has *sattriparigrahaḥ*, the actual comment shows *satya-parigrahaḥ*, i.e., making the Brahmin take an oath. But that would come during *vākyānu-yoga*, which precedes *karmānuyoga* and would not be a substitute for the latter as meant here. — It seems that *śrutavataḥ* is to be construed with *brāhmaṇasya*, and not to be understood independently. 20 *kārayituḥ*: this would be the higher officer, directing the operation.

21 *vyāvahārika* seems to convey the idea of 'normal, ordinary, usual.' — *dvau uparinibandhau*: Cb has 'tying two hands above; and tying the head along with the hands.' It seems, however, that suspension from a height by a rope twice is all that is meant. — *udakanālikā* 'pouring salt-water through the nose' (Cb Cs).

22 *dvādaśa kaśāḥ* is proposed for *dvādaśakam*. The space after *-kam* in M suggested this. — *dvāvūruveṣṭau* from Cb Cs is obviously the only reading possible. Cb Cs explain 'tying the feet with a rope, and tying the head along with that.' Giving the *ūruveṣṭa* twice is also possible. — *dvau vṛścikabandhau*; Cb Cs explain 'tying the left hand and foot together at the back, and doing the same with the right hand and foot.' Tying both hands and feet at the back and doing this twice is also possible. — *ullambane ca dve*: the *ca* here is strange. Cb Cs have 'hanging straight with hands tied, and the same with feet tied and upside down.' — *sūcī hastasya* 'pricking with a needle under the finger-nails' (Cb Cs). — *yavāgūpītasya*: understanding this independently, Cb Cs explain 'making a person drink gruel and then preventing him from passing urine.' It is not easy to see how the latter part of the explanation is arrived at. It seems better to construe the expression with what follows. — *snehapītasya* is to be construed with the following (Cb Cs) rather than with the preceding (Meyer). 23 *aṣṭādaśakam*: Meyer finds the eighteen in s. 22, Cs in 21 and 22 together. The latter is decidedly better. But the fourteen is s. 22 are not easy to fix. Cb Cs have *navavetralatādvādaśakam* 'twelve strokes with a cane nine *hastas* long' as the first item in the s. But a cane 13½ feet long seems unlikely and the reading itself is doubtful. Perhaps, we have to count *dvau* or *dve* as two in the three cases (contrary to *dvau* in s. 21). One cannot be quite certain.

24 *pradhāraṇam* seems to refer to the determination of the suitability of the person for the torture. — *avadhāraṇam* may refer to limiting or restricting the torture. — *khara-paṭṭād*: *Kharapaṭṭa* appears to be the name of a work on torture. According to Cs, it is the name of an author on the science of theft. Meyer suggests that we should read *kharapāṭavād dyamayet* 'should regulate according to the hardness or softness of the culprit.' That does not sound convincing.

25 He should cause torture to be given on alternate days and one only on one day.

26 He should cause torture to be used collectively, separately or repeatedly in the case of one who is a former offender, who, after confessing, retracts, with whom a part of the (stolen) goods are found, who is arrested because of the act or with the article, who conceals the king's treasury or who is to be killed by torture at the king's order.

27 In all offences, a Brahmin is not to be tormented. 28 On his forehead shall be a branded mark of the guilty to exclude him from all dealings, —(the mark of) a dog in case of theft, a headless trunk in case of murder of a human being, the female organ in case of violation of an elder's bed, the vintner's flag in case of liquor-drinking.

29 Proclaiming a Brahmin of sinful deeds and making the scar of the mark on him, the king should exile him from the country or settle him in mines.

CHAPTER NINE

SECTION 84 KEEPING A WATCH OVER (OFFICERS OF) ALL DEPARTMENTS

1 The Administrator and the magistrates should first keep in check the heads of departments and their subordinates.

2 For an (officer) stealing an article of high value or a gem from mines or factories for articles of high value, simple death (without torture, shall be the punishment). 3 (For stealing) an article of low value or an implement from factories for articles of low value, the lowest fine for violence (shall be the punishment).

26 *pūrvakṛtāpadāna* : cf. 4.6.2, also 2.36.36 etc. — *avastṛṇantam* : this root seems to have the sense of ' to cover, conceal, i.e., to misappropriate.' Cf 4.10.13 below.

27-28 Meyer thinks that these ss. are likely to be interpolations, suggested by Manu, 9.237 (where, however, branding is laid down for all *varṇas*, not for Brahmins alone). It is true that these ss., which speak of punishment for offences, are not in keeping with the contents of the Chapter which are concerned with the interrogation of a suspect and other means of extracting a confession from him. The passage, therefore, may not be original, though the idea contained in these ss. and in the stanza that follows appears to be quite ancient.

4.9

For *rakṣaṇa*, cf. 4.1 above.

1 It is clear again that the *samāhartṛ* with the *pradeṣṭṛs* working under him, is ultimately responsible for the maintenance of a clean administration. Even the judges are under his surveillance. Cf. 4.4 above.

4 For one stealing from places (of production) of articles a king's commodity, above one *māṣa* in value up to one-fourth (of a *paṇa*) in value, the fine is twelve *paṇas* ; up to two-quarters in value, twenty four *paṇas* ; up to three-quarters in value, thirty-six *paṇas*; up to one *paṇa* in value, forty-eight *paṇas* ; up to two *paṇas* in value, the lowest fine for violence ; up to four *paṇas* in value, the middle fine ; up to eight *paṇas* in value, the highest ; up to ten *paṇas* (and above) in value, death (shall be the punishment). 5. For misappropriation of forest produce, goods or tools from magazines, ware-houses, stores of forest produce and armouries, these same fines (shall be imposed) for articles half in value (of those above). 6 (For misappropriation) from the treasury, store-rooms and the Goldsmith's workshop, these same fines shall be doubled for articles one-quarter in value. 7 For thieves, in case of breaking open (the treasury etc.) death by torture (shall be the punishment). 8 Thus have been explained offences concerning the king's possessions.

9 But in the case of other properties, for an (officer) stealing secretly by day from a field, a threshing floor, a house or a shop, forest produce, ware or tool above one *māṣa* in value and up to one-quarter (of a *paṇa*) in value, the fine is three *paṇas* or smearing him with cow-dung and proclaiming his guilt ; up to two-quarters in value, six *paṇas* (fine) or smearing with cow-dung and ashes and proclaiming his guilt ; up to three-quarters in value, nine *paṇas* (fine) or smearing with cow-dung and ashes and proclamation of his guilt or with a girdle of potsherds (round his body) ; up to one *paṇa* in value, twelve *paṇas* (fine) or shaving of the head and exile ; up to two *paṇas* in value, twenty-four *paṇas* (fine) or driving him out (of the city) with a piece of brick after shaving him ; up to four *paṇas* in value, thirty-six *paṇas* (fine) ; up to five *paṇas* in value, forty-eight *paṇas* ; up to ten *paṇas* in value, the lowest fine for violence ; up to twenty *paṇas* in value, two hundred *paṇas* (fine) ; up to thirty *paṇas* in value, five hundred *paṇas* (fine) ; up to forty *paṇas* in value, one thousand (fine) ; up to fifty *paṇas* in value (and above) death (shall be the punishment). 10 For one stealing forcibly by day or at night during the (forbidden) watches, these same (shall be imposed) for articles half in value. 11 For one robbing forcibly, by day or night, with weapons, these same fines shall be doubled for articles one quarter in value.

4 Cf. 2.5.16, which shows some variations. These may be due to the fact that 2.5.16 is a very brief abstract of these detailed rules, perhaps also due to a difference in sources. 7 The s. is repeated in 2.5.20. It is not necessary to understand, with Meyer, that officers instigating robbers to break open stores, etc. are meant. Robbers themselves seem meant. 8. *rājaparigraheṣu*, i.e., from *koṣṭhāgāra*, *paṇyāgāra* etc. just mentioned.

9 *bāhyeṣu* : we have to supply *parigraheṣu*, i.e., in the case of property not belonging to the state, but to the subjects. — *ā catuṣpaṇamūlyād* : according to Cs, in this and the higher cases, *muṇḍana* and *pravrājana* with brickbats have to be understood, though not mentioned. That appears likely. 10 *antaryāmikam*, i.e., during the watches when movement is forbidden as in 2.36.34-35. The mss. read *dviguṇā* in s. 10 ; it is proposed to transfer it to s. 11 in conformity with ss. 5-6 above.

12 For making counterfeit documents and seals of householders, superintendents, principal officers and the king, the punishment is the lowest, the middle, the highest (fines) and death (respectively), or in accordance with the offence.

13 If the judge threatens, upbraids, drives away or browbeats a litigant, he shall impose the lowest fine for violence on him, double that in case of verbal injury. 14 If he does not question one who ought to be questioned, questions one who ought not to be questioned, or after questioning dismisses (the statement), or instructs, reminds or prompts him, he shall impose the middle fine for violence on him. 15 If he does not ask for evidence which ought to be submitted, asks for evidence that ought not to be submitted, proceeds with the case without evidence, dismisses it under a pretext, carries away one tired with delays, throws out of context a statement which is in proper order, gives to witnesses help in their statements (or) takes up once again a case which is completed and in which judgement is pronounced, he shall impose the highest fine for violence on him. 16 In case the offence is repeated, double (the fine) and removal from office (shall be the punishment).

17 If the clerk does not write what is said, writes what is not said, writes correctly what is badly spoken, writes inaccurately what is well spoken, or modifies the sense conveyed, he shall impose the lowest fine for violence on him or (punishment) in accordance with the offence.

18 If the judge or the magistrate imposes a money fine on one not deserving to be fined, he shall impose on him double the fine imposed, or eight times the shortfall or excess (over the prescribed fine). 19 If he imposes corporal punishment (wrongly), he shall himself suffer corporal punishment or pay double the (normal) redemption-amount. 20 Or, he shall pay a fine eight times the just claim which he disallows or unjust claim which he allows.

12 *mukhya* 'a principal officer.' Cf 5.1.3 etc. Restriction to 'village headman' (Cb Cs) is not right. — *svāmin* is the king, hardly the *samāhartṛ* (Cb Cs).

13 *abhigrasate* 'swallows' is understood in Cs as 'receives money from.' That would appear to be a very serious offence, for which a light punishment is not likely. Cf. 4.4.6-7. The root may convey the idea of 'to over-awe, brow-beat' or 'to silence.' — *pṛcchyam* may refer to the person who is to be questioned or the question that ought to be put. — *visṛjati* 'dismisses' the statement made, rather than the person himself. — *pūrvaṁ dadāti* gives the earlier part,' i.e., prompts. 15 *deśam*: see 3.1.15,19. — *chalena atiharati*: cf. 3.20.22. — *apavāhayati* 'carries him away,' i.e., prevents his coming to the court. — *tārita* 'which is taken to the end,' i.e., completed. Manu 9.233 has the form *tīrita*. — *anuśiṣṭa* 'in which judgment is given'; cf. 3.1.43. 16 *vyavaropaṇam*: *vi-ava* appears better with *ruh* than *vi-apa*, in the sense of 'to pull down, remove, dismiss.'

17 The prepositions *upa* and *ut* convey opposite senses with the root *likh*.

18 *hairaṇyadaṇḍam adaṇḍye* is proposed for the readings of the mss., as being quite necessary for sense. — *hīnātiriktāṣṭaguṇam*: if the fine imposed is less (*hīna*) or more (*atirikta*) than that prescribed by law, eight times the difference between the prescribed and the imposed fines is to be the fine for the erring judge or magistrate. 19 *niṣkraya* amounts are laid down in the next Chapter. 20 *bhūtam artham* etc.: cf. 3.11.45. *artha* refers to the amount involved in the suit.

21 For the hindrance of sleep, sitting down, meals, answering calls of nature or movement and for binding, in a judge's lock-up or in a prison-house, the fine shall be three *paṇas* increased successively by three *paṇas* for him who does it and for him who causes it to be done.

22 For the (jailor) setting free or allowing the escape of an accused from the lock-up (the punishment shall be) the middle fine for violence and the payment of the (amount in the) suit, from the prison-house (confiscation of) the entire property and death.

23 For the superintendent of the prison-house allowing movement to a prisoner without informing (the judge or magistrate) the fine is twenty-four *paṇas*, for using torture double (that), for making him submit to another position or withholding food and drink ninety-six *paṇas*, for tormenting or maiming him the middle fine for violence, for killing him one thousand (*paṇas* as fine).

24 For the (jailor) violating a married woman prisoner who is a slave or a pledge (the punishment shall be) the lowest fine for violence, the wife of a thief or a rioter the middle, an Ārya woman prisoner the highest. 25 Or, for a prisoner (doing this, there shall be) execution there and then. 26 He shall understand the same (punishment for the offence) in connection with an Ārya woman caught in the prohibited period (of the night), in connection with a female slave the lowest fine for violence.

27 For one helping a (prisoner) to escape from the lock-up without breaking it (the punishment shall be) the middle (fine), by breaking it death, from the prison-house (confiscation of) the entire property and death.

21 It is proposed to read *dharmasthīye cārake bandhanāgāre vā* for the reading of the mss. ; *niḥsārayataḥ* occurring in that reading is quite unlikely in this s. which refers to the offences of *śayyārodha, āsanarodha* etc. And the offence of *niḥsāraṇa* is far more serious, for which the fines mentioned in this s. would hardly appear adequate. — *saṁcārarodha-* is read as proposed by Meyer. *rodha* is to be construed with each of the preceding words, while *bandhana* is to be understood independently. The fine for *bandhana* comes to 18 *paṇas*. — *kartuḥ kārayituḥ* : the former would be the warder, the latter the prison superintendent. — It seems that *cāraka* is a sort of lock-up where those convicted by the *dharmastha* are kept, while the *bandhanāgāra* is for criminals convicted by the *pradeṣṭṛs*. In either case, the convicts are kept there mostly because of their inability to pay the money fine or the redemption amount.

22 *abhiyogadānam* seems to mean the payment of the amount in dispute including the fine imposed. — *bandhanāgārāt* etc. is repeated in s. 27 below.

23 Cb Cs (also Meyer) construe *anākhyāya* with *bandhanāgārādhyakṣasya* and understand the offences as committed by the warders. — *cārayataḥ* seems to refer to allowing freedom of movement short of setting the prisoner free. Cb understands 'making him render service.' — *karma* as in 4.8.21-23 above. — *sthānānyatvam* : this seems to imply not merely a change of place (for which *sthānāntaram* would have been sufficient) but also a difference in status or class to which the transfer is made. —*utkoṭayataḥ* has the sense of 'one who breaks or maims' ; that is preferable to the reading *utkocayataḥ* in Cb Cs.

24 *dāmarika* : cf. *ḍamaragataka* in 2.6.20. 25 *tatraiva ghātaḥ* : it seems that this would apply only in case of violation of an Ārya woman prisoner, not of a *dāsī* etc. 26 *akṣaṇagṛhītāyām* : for *akṣaṇa* see 2.36.34-35. Cb reads *adhyakṣeṇa gṛhītāyām*, but its comment is not clear. — Similar punishments are laid down for guards misbehaving with women in 2.36.41.

27 Cb comment presupposes *uttamaḥ* for *vadhaḥ*. This s. seems to apply to outsiders, while s. 22 refers to prison officers.

28 In this manner the king should first correct those (officers) who deal in money matters by means of punishment; and they, being corrected, should correct the citizens and the country people by means of punishments.

CHAPTER TEN

SECTION 85 REDEMPTION FROM THE CUTTING OF INDIVIDUAL LIMBS

1 In case of the first offence of thieves at holy places, pick-pockets and those with raised hands, (the punishment shall be) the cutting off of the middle finger and thumb or a fine of fifty-four *paṇas*; in case of the second, the cutting off of five fingers or a fine of one hundred; in case of the third, cutting off of the right hand or a fine of four hundred; in case of the fourth, death as desired (by the magistrate).

2 In cases of theft of cocks, ichneumons, cats, dogs or pigs less than twenty-five *paṇas* (in value) or in case of killing (any of these, there shall be) a fine of fifty-four *paṇas* or the cutting off of the tip of the nose; half the fines for Caṇḍālas and forest-dwellers.

3 For carrying away deer, beasts, birds, wild animals or fish, caught in snares, nets or concealed pits, (the punishment shall be) that and an equal amount as fine. 4 In case of theft of deer or objects from deer-parks or produce-forests, (there shall be) a fine of one hundred.

5 In case of theft of deer or birds (intended) for show or pleasure or in case of killing these, the fine shall be double.

6 In case of theft of small articles belonging to artisans, artists, actors or ascetics, (there shall be) a fine of one hundred; for theft of large articles, two hundred, also for theft of agricultural goods.

28 *arthcarān*: cf.2.9.32.

4.10

niṣkrayaḥ: it appears that the various types of corporal punishments prescribed for theft and similar offences came to be replaced by money fines, which are called 'redemptions' from the corporal punishments.

1 *tīrthaghāta* 'who lifts articles at sacred places on festive occasions' (Cb Cs) is more likely than 'cash-chest-breaker' (Meyer). *tīrtha* as 'cash' is doubtful. —*granthibheda*: money was often tied in a corner of the upper garment; one who cuts open that and steals seems meant. — *ūrdhvakara*: Cs has 'who breaks the upper part or roof of a house.' This is uncertain. Meyer suggests *ūrdhvahara* in the sense of a 'pick-pocket'. The basic idea may well be that of lifting up things 'with a raised hand.' — *saṁdaṁśa* 'the thumb and the middle finger' as in Cp on 2.23.15. 'The thumb and the index finger' (Cb Meyer) is supported by the *Mitākṣarā* on Yāj., 2.274. — *paṇa* refers to the five fingers of the hand. Cf. 2.14.14. — Manu, 9.277 and Yāj., 2.274 are exact paraphrases of this s. — *yathākāmī vadhaḥ*, i.e., simple death or death by torture as the magistrate may wish.

2 *hiṁsā* is 'killing' rather than mere injury. — *ardhadaṇḍāḥ*: the singular would have been better; *ardha* does not apply to *nāsāgracchedana*.

3 *ādāne*, i.e., theft by one, other than the person who set the trap etc. 5 *bimbavihāra-*: Cs renders *bimba* by 'the variegated *kṛkalāsa* or chameleon,' which is very doubtful. Meyer suggests the idea of 'a show' in some sort of a zoo. That appears better. *vihāra* should be understood independently of that. — There is no comment on this s. in Cb.

7 For one, who is not given permission to enter, entering a fort, or one going out through a hole in the city-wall taking an entrusted article with him, (the punishment shall be) the cutting of the sinews (of the feet) or a fine of two hundred.

8 For one stealing a cart, a boat or a small animal, (the punishment shall be) the cutting off of one foot or a fine of three hundred.

9 For one cheating with false cowrie-shells, dice, leather-straps, ivory-cubes or by sleight of hand, (the punishment shall be) cutting off of one hand or a fine of four hundred.

10 In case of aiding a thief or an adulterer, and for a woman caught in adultery, (the punishment shall be) the cutting off of ears and nose or a fine of five hundred; for a man double (that).

11 For one stealing a big animal or one male or female slave, or for one selling articles from a corpse, (the punishment shall be) the cutting off of both feet or a fine of six hundred.

12 In case of striking with hands or feet persons of the highest *varṇa* and elders, and in case of mounting the royal carriage, riding animal and so on, (the punishment shall be) the cutting off of one hand and one foot or a fine of seven hundred.

13 For a Śūdra calling himself a Brahmin, for one concealing temple property, for one ordering what is treasonable and for one blinding both eyes (of another, the punishment shall be) blindness by means of poisonous collyrium or a fine of eight hundred.

14 For one setting a thief or an adulterer free, for one writing a royal edict with omissions or additions, for one kidnapping a maiden or a female slave together with money, for a fraudulent dealer, and for one selling unclean meat, (the punishment shall be) the cutting off of the left hand and both feet or a fine of nine hundred.

7 *akṛtapraveśasya* : cf. 2.28.19 for *kṛtapraveśa* used of foreigners allowed to enter. — *nikṣepam* : Meyer thinks of what is stolen and buried near the city-wall, to be taken away at night-time. That is possible, but the usual idea of what is entrusted to a person may also have been meant. — *kāṇḍarā* : the lexicons give *kaṇḍarā* as the form in the sense of 'sinew, tendon.' Cb does show 'two tendons at the back of the foot.'

8 *cakrayuktam* : the reading *cakrayuktām* (Cb Cs) would be an adjective to *nāvam* which is impossible. For *cakrayukta* 'cart,' cf. 3.12.2.

9 *arālīśalākā-* : see 3.20.10.

10 *saṁgṛhītāyāḥ* : 'who is caught in adultery,' though in 4.12.30,31 the word seems to have the sense of 'kept under guard.'

12 *varṇottamānām* : Meyer thinks that this word is interpolated. Yāj. 2.303 has only *guru*. That seems possible. — *laṅghana* is obviously 'striking with.' Yāj., has *tāḍayituḥ*.

13 *avastṛṇataḥ* : cf. 4.8.26. — *yogāñjanena* : see 14.1.15 for collyrium causing blindness.

14 *sahiraṇyam* : this is adverbial. It is not necessary to read *sahiraṇyām* as proposed by Meyer. *hiraṇya* is 'money', not 'gold' in this text. Cf. 4.12.24. *kūṭavyavahāriṇaḥ* : on the authority of Yāj. 2.297 Meyer thinks that we should read *kūṭasuvarṇavyavahāriṇaḥ*. But all dealers who indulge in fraud may well have been meant. Yāj. is derived from this text; sometimes it adds, at other times it misunderstands. — *vimāṁsam* as described in 2.26.12.

15 In case of sale of human flesh, death (is the punishment).

16 For one stealing cattle, images, persons, fields, houses, money, gold, gems or crops belonging to a temple, (the punishment shall be) the highest fine or simple death.

17-18 After taking into full consideration the person and the offence, the motive, seriousness or lightness (of the offence), the consequences, the present (effects), and the place and time, the magistrate shall fix the highest, the lowest and the middle in the matter of punishment, remaining neutral between the king and the subjects.

CHAPTER ELEVEN

SECTION 86 THE LAW OF (CAPITAL) PUNISHMENT, SIMPLE AND WITH TORTURE

1 For one killing a person (on the spot) during a scuffle, (the punishment shall be) death with torture. 2 In case of death within seven days simple death (shall be the punishment), within a fortnight the highest (fine), within a month five hundred, and the cost of treatment.

3 For one striking (another) with a weapon, the fine shall be the highest (for violence). 4 If (that is done) in intoxication, the hand shall be cut off; if through delusion, a fine of two hundred (shall be imposed). 5 In case of death (resulting), death (shall be the punishment).

6 For one causing abortion with a blow the fine shall be the highest, with medicine the middle, by causing suffering (to the woman) the lowest fine for violence.

7 They shall impale on the stake those who beat a man or a woman with force, who rush upon them, who hold them down, who threaten (to kill), who attack them and who pierce them, also robbers on highways and house-thieves, and those who kill or steal an elephant, a horse or a chariot belonging to the king. 8 And if any one were to cremate or remove them (from the stake), he shall receive the same punishment or the highest fine for violence.

16 *manuṣya*, i.e., slaves attached to temples.

17 *anubandha* can hardly mean 'motive' as in Manu, 8.126 (as Jayaswal *Manu and Yāj.*, 83-84, thinks). Cf. 9.7.14 ff.

4.11

The *citra vadha* involves some sort of torture accompanying or leading to death.

2 *samutthānavyayaḥ*: the expenses for treatment would have to be borne whether the man dies within seven days or a fortnight or a month after the fight. For the expression cf. 3.19.14,27.

7 *ghātaka*: considering the other terms in the compound which show different forms of assault, *ghātaka* seems to mean simply 'who beats up,' not actually 'who slays.' — *abhisāraka* from Cs is certainly preferable to *adhīsāraka* which hardly yields any sense. The former seems to mean 'who rushes at'. — *nigrāhaka*: Cs has 'who cuts ears and nose.' That appears to be Cb's explanation of *avaghoṣaka*;; it does not show an explanation of *abhisāraka*. Perhaps it simply means 'who holds down or restrains' by force. — *avagho-*

9 For supplying murderers or thieves with food, accommodation, tools, fire, or giving counsel or rendering service (to them), the fine shall be the highest ; reprimand (only) in case of ignorance. 10 He should let go the sons and wives of murderers or thieves if not in concert, should seize them, if in concert.

11 He shall cause to be slain by setting fire to hands and head one who covets the kingdom, who attacks the king's palace, who rouses foresters or enemies, or who causes rebellion in the fortified city, the country or the army. 12 He shall make a Brahmin (in such a case) enter darkness.

13 He shall cause to be slain by setting fire to the skinless head one who has killed his mother, father, son, brother, preceptor or an ascetic. 14 For reviling these, (the punishment shall be) the cutting of the tongue ; for wounding a limb, he shall be deprived of the (corresponding) limb.

15 For killing a person by accident, and in case of theft of a herd of cattle, (the punishment shall be) simple death. 16 And he should know a herd to contain ten (heads of cattle) at least.

17 For one breaking a dam holding water, drowning in water at the same spot (shall be the punishment), the highest fine for violence if it was without water, the middle if it was in ruins and abandoned.

18 He shall drown in water a man giving poison (to another) and a woman slaying a man, if not pregnant ; if pregnant, at least a month after delivery. 19 He shall cause to be torn by bullocks a woman who kills her husband, an elder or her offsprings or who sets (a house etc.) on fire or gives poison or breaks into a house.

20 He shall cause to be burnt in fire one who sets on fire a pasture, a field, a threshing ground, a house, a produce-forest or an elephant forest.

ṣaka : the word does not seem right. Cs has 'who threatens that he would kill.' Meyer suggests *avagoraka* 'who threatens' or *avaghoṭaka* 'who hurls down.' The former is possible (cf. 3.19) but not quite certain. The different forms of attack cannot be clearly distinguished from one another. — *pathiveśma* : Cb understands 'a shed by the road-side for giving water.'

11 *antaḥpurapradharṣakam* : as *antaḥpura* refers to the royal apartments, the offence is political, not sexual. 12 *tamaḥ praveśayet* seems to mean 'should make blind' (Meyer) rather than 'confine in a dark cellar for good' (Cs). Cf. Āpastamba, 2.10.27.16-17. It is possible that this s. is a marginal gloss due to Āpastamba.

13 *atvakchiraḥprādīpikam* is understood as in Cb Cs. The head is skinned first and then set on fire. Meyer has 'burning the skinned hands tied over the head.' There is nothing to show the hands. 14 *abhiradana* is 'wounding' or 'breaking.'

17 *bhagnotsṛṣṭakam* : cf. 3.9.33 ; 3.10.2.

19 *pāṭayet* : Cb Cs read *pādayet* explained as 'should cause to be trampled underfoot.' — Yāj., 2.278-279 reproduce these rules, but include dam-breaking with offences of s.19, so that only females breaking dams can be understood, which is absurd and shows up the character of Yāj.

20 Cf. 2.36.25.

21 He shall cause the tongue to be rooted out of one who reviles the king or divulges secret counsel or spreads evil news (about the king) and one who licks anything in a Brahmin's kitchen.

22 He shall cause to be slain with arrows the stealer of weapons or armours, if he is not a soldier. 23 For the soldier, the highest fine (shall be the punishment).

24 Of one injuring the generating organ or testicles (of another) he shall cause these same (limbs) to be cut off.

25 For injuring the tongue or the nose, the cutting of the middle finger and the thumb (shall be the punishment).

26 These painful punishments have been laid down in the texts of high-souled (authors); but in the case of crimes that are not painful, simple death is prescribed as lawful.

CHAPTER TWELVE

SECTION 87 VIOLATION OF MAIDENS

1 For one violating a maiden of the same *varṇa* who has not attained puberty, (the punishment shall be) the cutting off of the hand or a fine of four hundred. 2 In case she dies, death (shall be the punishment).

3 Of one violating a maiden who has attained puberty, the middle and index fingers shall be cut off or a fine of two hundred (imposed). 4 And he shall make good the loss to her father. 5 And he shall not have the right (to marry her) if she is unwilling. 6 If she is willing, (there shall be) a fine of fifty-four *paṇas*; half that, however, for the woman. 7 If she has been reserved by the dowry of another, (there shall be) the cutting off of the hand or a fine of four hundred, as well as the payment of the dowry.

8 A bride-groom not receiving the bride after the betrothal, when she has had seven menstrual periods, shall have the right (to her) by having relations with her, and he shall not make good the father's loss. 9 The (latter) forfeits his ownership by (his acts) making her periods vain.

21 *brāhmaṇamahānasāvalehinaḥ*: Meyer thinks that this is an interpolation, since even Yāj., 2.302 does not reproduce this offence. That seems likely.

25 *saṁdaṁśa*: see 4.10.1 above.

26 *mahātmanām*: these are the author's predecessors, from whom he has derived his material.

4.12

prakṛ has obviously the sense of 'to violate, to deflower, to have sexual relations with.'

4 *pituś cāvahīnam*: this refers to the dowry. 5 *prākāmyam* refers to the freedom or right to marry her.

8 *alabhamānaḥ*: Cs reads *alabhamānām* and explains 'if the girl does not find the man who wooed her, another man may have relations with her and do what he pleases.' This appears less likely. It is the groom-elect who would be given the liberty, because the girl's

10 It is no offence for a maiden having menstruation for three years to approach a man of the same *varṇa*, after that even a man not of the same *varṇa* provided she goes without her ornaments. 11 For taking her father's property, she shall be liable for theft.

12 If a man intending (a maiden) for another, secures her (for himself), the fine shall be two hundred. 13 And he shall not have the right (to her) if she is unwilling.

14 For showing one maiden and giving another, the fine shall be one hundred if she is of the same *varṇa*, double (that) if she is of a lower *varṇa*.

15 For a (bride) not a virigin at the time of consummation, the fine shall be fifty-four *paṇas*, and (she) shall return the dowry and (marriage) expenses. 16 If after maintaining that kind (of condition) she fails, she shall pay double. 17 For substituting other blood, the fine shall be two hundred, also for the man falsely accusing (the bride of loss of virginity). 18 And he shall lose the dowry and the expenses. 19 And he shall not have the right (to her) if she is unwilling.

father is postponing the marriage. *prākāmī* refers to the right to marry, even if the father is unwilling. *prakāmī* (Cb) appears to be a more likely form. 9 *ṛtupratirodhibhiḥ* : supply *karmabhiḥ*. 'In consequence of robbers (*pratirodhin*) in the form of menstrual periods' (Cs) is fanciful. Cf. Manu, 9.93, which reproduces this s. in full.

10 *tulyo gantum adoṣaḥ* : we except *tulyam*. — *tataḥ param* : how long she is to wait for *tulya* is not stated. — Cf. Manu, 9.90-92, which reproduce these rules, omitting, however, the reference to *atulya*.

13 *na ca prākāmyam akāmāyām*, i.e., the marriage would be void and the girl free to marry a different person altogether.

15 *prakarmaṇi* etc. : this is understood as in Meyer, the idea being that if the girl is found not to be a virgin at the time of the consummation of marriage (*prakarmaṇi*), she is to be fined 54 *paṇas*, and the husband is to get back the *śulka* and the marriage expenses. Cb Cs include *avasthāya* in this s. and explain 'for violating a virgin maiden who is betrothed (*akumārī*, i.e., *dattā*), the fine is fifty-four *paṇas*, and he shall give the dowry to the first groom and the marriage expenses to the marriage-negotiator or surety (*avastha*).' The difficulty is that the fine is obviously meant for the girl, as is shown by the genitive of *akumāryāḥ* ; if the violator were intended, we would have had as usual *akumārīṁ prakurvataḥ*. Moreover, *pratidadyāt* implies that one who received the dowry is to return it ; the girl's father is more likely in that case to be the person who would be asked to do that. Again in the next s. the double fine seems intended for the girl herself as is shown by the subject *kṛtā*. All of which shows that the offence thought of is one committed by the girl. Such an offence could be her being not a virgin. The fines, of course, may ultimately be supposed to be paid by the father. 16 This s. is understood to mean that if the girl maintains that she is a virgin, but if, on investigation, she is found not to be a virgin, she is to be fined 108 *paṇas*. *paścātkṛtā* is one who has failed to prove her case ; cf. *paścātkāra* in 3.9.22. *tajjātam* 'of that kind' may be understood to refer to the condition of virginity. *avasthāya* may be understood in the sense of 'having maintained,' though perhaps *avasthāpya* in the causal would have been better. Meyer has 'if she makes herself a virgin again (*paścāt kṛtā*) with blood from that (*tajjātam*, *tat* being the female organ).' This is extremely doubtful. Cb Cs explain 'if she is afterwards (*paścāt*) accepted (*kṛtā*) by another person, then a double fine is be to paid.' It is not clear who is to pay the fine. There appears to be no reason why tnis third person who accepts the girl should be penalised. And the girl cannot be supposed to be fined in this s., when in the last s. the fine, according to Cb Cs, is meant for the violator. 17 *anyaśoṇitopadhāne* : this apparently refers to the girl's attempt to prove her virginity by soiling her garment with blood from another source (to indicate the rupture of the hymen). According to Cs, she does this to prove that she is violated and is not a virgin. — *mithyābhiśaṁsinaḥ puṁsaḥ* : this is obviously the husband who falsely accuses the wife of not being a virgin. 19 *na ca prākāmyam*, i.e., she shall be free to leave him and marry some one else ; cf. s. 13 above.

20 A (maiden) deflowered by a woman shall pay a fine of twelve *paṇas*, if a willing party and of the same *varṇa*; the violating woman (shall pay) double. 21 If (the maiden was) unwilling, she shall pay a fine of one hundred and her dowry, for (the satisfaction of) her passion.

22 A maiden deflowering herself shall become the king's slave.

23 In case a maiden is violated outside the village and in case of a false accusation, the fine shall be double.

24 For one abducting a maiden by force, (the fine is) two hundred; if with gold (ornaments), the highest. 25 For many (persons) abducting a maiden, the fines shall be as prescribed for each one separately.

26 For one deflowering a courtesan's daughter, (the punishment shall be) a fine of fifty-four *paṇas* (and) a dowry to the mother sixteen times the rate for a visit. 27 For one deflowering the daughter of a male or a female slave, who is not a slave (herself), the fine is twenty-four *paṇas* and the payment of dowry and ornaments (for her). 28 For one violating a female slave due for redemption, the fine is twelve *paṇas* and the payment of clothes and ornaments.

29 For giving help or accommodation, the punishment shall be the same as for the offender.

30 The husband's kinsman or his servant should keep under guard the wife who misbehaves when the husband is away on a journey. 31 Kept under guard, she should wait for the husband. 32 If the husband were to tolerate, both should be set free. 33 In case he does not tolerate, (the punishment shall be) the cutting off of the ears and nose for the woman, and the lover shall meet with death.

34 For one making out a paramour as a thief, the fine shall be five hundred; for one releasing him with money, eight times that (as fine).

35 Adultery (shall be understood as committed) when there is mutual caressing of the hair, or from indications of bodily enjoyment, or from (the opinion of) experts, or from the woman's statement.

21 The fine is for the *prakartrī*, to whom the *ātmarāga* refers. — Cf. Manu, 8.369-370, which prescribe severe corporal punishment.

24-25 Cf. Yāj., 2.287, which varies the punishment according to *varṇa*.

26 *bhogaḥ*: cf. 2.27.10 ff. Sixteen times the rate for a visit is to be the amount of the *śulka*. 27 *ābandhya*: see 3.2.14,15. 28 *niṣkrayānurūpām* 'who is worthy of, i.e., due for redemption,' a rather unusual expression. For *niṣkraya*, see 3.13.17, 21.

30 *saṁgṛhṇīyāt*: this obviously implies holding in confinement. Even the paramour is so held as shown by *ubhayam* in s. 32. — Yāj., 2.301 is an exact reproduction.

34 *abhiharataḥ* 'carrying off,' i.e., trying to save him; as a thief he would get a lighter punishment. Perhaps we have to read *abhivyāharataḥ*, 'calling, declaring.' — *tadaṣṭaguṇaḥ*: *tad* refers to the *hiraṇya* offered, not the fine of five hundred.

35 *upaliṅganād*: cf. 3.13.37. — *tajjātebhyaḥ* 'experts,' who know how to interpret gestures etc. (Cb), rather than 'marks produced by the act' (Meyer). The latter would not be different from *upaliṅgana*. — *strīvacanād*: *strī* is the woman concerned herself.

36 After rescuing a stranger woman, who was being carried off by enemy troops or foresters, or carried away by a current, or was abandoned in a forest or during a famine, or was left under the impression of her being dead, a man may enjoy her as agreed upon. 37 If she is superior in caste (to him) or is unwilling, or has children, he shall give (her back) for a ransom.

> 38-40 After having rescued a woman belonging to others from the hands of robbers, from the current of a river, from a famine, from a disturbance in the country, from a forest, or when she is lost or left as dead, a man may enjoy her as agreed, but not one who is saved through the power of the king or by her kinsmen, nor one higher (in caste) nor one unwilling, nor again one who already has children ; such a one, however, he should restore (to her kinsmen) in return for a suitable ransom.

CHAPTER THIRTEEN

SECTION 88 PUNISHMENTS FOR TRANSGRESSIONS

1 For one making a Brahmin consume drink or food which is unfit for human consumption the fine shall be the highest, the middle for (making) a Kṣatriya (do so), the lowest for making a Vaiśya (do so), a fine of fifty-four *paṇa*s for making a Śūdra (do so). 2 Those consuming (such things) of their own accord shall be exiled from the country.

3 In case of trespass in another's house by day (the punishment shall be) the lowest fine for violence, by night the middle. 4 For one entering with a weapon by day or by night, the fine shall be the highest. 5 A mendicant and a trader, an intoxicated and an insane person, very close neighbours when threatened by force or in a calamity, and those whose entry is customary, are not to be punished except when prohibited. 6 For one climbing the enclosing fence of his own house after midnight (the punishment shall be) the lowest fine for violence, that of another's house middle, also for one breaking the hedge of a village park.

36 *yathāsaṁbhāṣitam* : according to Cb Cs, the agreement is to make her the wife or slave. That need not necessarily be understood.

38-40 The stanzas repeat the ideas of ss. 36-37, adding the line *na tu rājapratāpena* etc. The line implies that if the rescuer happens to be a state servant or the woman's kinsman, he cannot claim this privilege. The stanzas seem derived from an earlier source and ss. 36-37 seem to be a prose rendering of the same. — *apavāhayet* 'have her carried away (by her kinsmen),' i.e., restore her to them.

4.13

1-2 *apeyam abhakṣyam* does not seem to refer to food etc. forbidden in the Smṛtis on sacramental grounds. That has mostly to do with Brahmins only. Yāj., 2.296 is an exact reproduction.

3 *abhigamana* obviously conveys the idea of trespass. 5 *balād āpadi ca* are to be construed with *atisaṁnikṛṣṭāḥ*, which refers to very close neighbours rather than close relations. 6 *virātra* here is obviously 'midnight'. Cf. 4.6.2.

7 Traders in caravans may stay inside the villages when their valuables are made known (to village officers). 8 What is stolen or killed from among these, the master of the village shall make good, if it has not gone out at night. 9 What is stolen or killed between villages, the Superintendent of Pastures shall make good. 10 In regions without pastures, the officers for catching thieves (shall make good). 11 If they are unprotected even then, the (villages) shall allow a search according to the boundaries as fixed. 12 In the absence of a fixing of boundaries, a group of five or ten villages (shall allow the search).

13 In case of injury (caused) by making a rickety house, a cart with the pole at the head unsupported, a weapon without covering, an uncovered hollow or well or a concealed pit, he shall hold it to be a case of physical injury.

14 One shouting 'get out of the way' when cutting a tree, leading by the rope an animal under training, using or riding the untamed among quadrupeds, throwing about pieces of wood, clods of earth, stones, sticks, arrows or arms, and in a collision in a carriage or with an elephant, is not to be punished.

15 One (desiring to be) killed by an enraged elephant shall give one *droṇa* food, a jar of wine, flowers and unguents and a piece of cloth for wiping the tusks. 16 Death by an elephant is equal to a bath at the end of the horse sacrifice; hence this washing of the feet. 17 In case of death of one not desirous (of such a death), the highest fine (shall be imposed) on the driver.

18 For the owner not rescuing a person being injured by a horned or tusked animal of his, the lowest fine for violence (shall be the punishment); the middle if he was called to come to the rescue. 19 For one allowing horned or tusked animals to kill one another, the fine shall be that and as much again.

20 For one riding a temple animal, a stud bull or a cow not yet calved the fine shall be five hundred, for killing (these) the highest. 21 In case of theft of small animals useful for their hair or milk or for riding or stud-purposes, the fine shall be that and as much again, also for killing these, except for rites in honour of gods and the manes.

7 There can be little doubt about *grāmeṣvantaḥ* being the correct reading, those in M and G1 being corruptions of the same. 8 *pravāsitam* 'killed' rather than 'driven out,' as is shown in Yāj., 2.271. That seems also the meaning in ss. 20, 21 below. — *grāmasvāmī*: evidently some one like a jāgirdar or sardar is to be thought of. 'The village headman' is possible, but for that the usual word is *grāmika*. 9 *grāmāntareṣu*: this is the province of the *vivītādhyakṣa*; see 2.34.6. 10 *corarajjuka* is evidently some officer operating in regions outside villages and pasture-lands, i.e., in forest lands etc., his duty being the rounding up of robbers etc. 11 *sīmāvarodhena*: cf. 2.35.3. — *pañcagrāmī daśagrāmī vā*: this is the jurisdiction of the *gopa*; cf. 2.35.2. It seems that we have to supply *vicayaṁ dadyuḥ* rather than *muṣitaṁ dadyuḥ*.

14 *yāne hastinā ca saṁghaṭṭane*: this does not seem quite right. We expect *yānena* like *hastinā*. — Cf. Yāj., 2.298.

15 *droṇānnaṁ madyakumbham* is emended from the readings of M and G1. 16 *pādaprakṣālanam* is an offering to a guest, of which water for washing the feet forms the starting point.

20 *ṛṣabham ukṣāṇam*: cf. 2.29.8, also 3.10.24. 21 *anyatra deva-* etc.: this means that the taking or killing of small animals not belonging to oneself is to be condoned, if that is done for religious purposes.

22 In case of injury when the cart has the nose-strings (of the bullocks) cut or the yoke broken or when it moves crosswise towards (some one) or recedes backwards, or when there is a crowd of animals and men, the driver is not to be punished. 23 Otherwise he shall be liable to punishment as prescribed in case of injury to men and animals. 24 And in case of death of non-human animals, the payment of the animal (as well shall be enforced).

25 When the driver is a minor, the owner if in the carriage is to be fined; if the owner is not there the person in the carriage or the driver if he has attained majority. 26 The king shall confiscate a carriage in charge of a minor or one without a man in it.

27 What a (magician) brings about to another by witchcraft and black magic, that shall be meted out to him. 28 The use of love-winning magic may be allowed towards a wife who does not like (her husband) or towards a maiden by a suitor or towards the husband by the wife. 29 Else, in case of injury, the middle fine for violence (shall be imposed).

30 For one carnally approaching the sister of his mother or father, his maternal aunt, his preceptor's wife, his daughter-in-law, daughter or sister, (the punishment shall be) the cutting off of the generating organ and testicles and death (thereafter). 31 The woman, if willing, shall receive the same, also a woman who has had relations with a slave, a servant or a pledged man.

32 For a Kṣatriya (having relations) with a Brahmin woman, not guarded, the fine shall be the highest, for a Vaiśya (confiscation of) the entire proerty; a Śūdra shall be burnt in a fire of straw.

33 For having relations with the king's wife, the (punishment) in all cases (shall be) cooking in a big jar.

34 For having relations with a Śvapāka woman, the man shall go to another land, with the mark of the headless trunk branded (on his forehead), or shall become a Śvapāka himself if he is a Śūdra. 35 For a Śvapāka having relations with an Ārya woman there shall be death, for the woman the cutting off of the ears and nose.

22 It is proposed to read *yātā paśu-* for *yātapaśu-* or *yānapaśu-*. *cakrayuktam* cannot properly be construed with *adaṇḍyaḥ* which requires a subject like *yātā*. The yoke etc. breaks and injury is caused while the cart is being driven and the driver has no control over the happening. 23 *abhyāvahet*: see 2.28.26. This verb also requires *yātā* as the subject.

25 *prāptavyavahāro vā yātā* is superfluous when *bāle yātari* is there. Perhaps it is a marginal gloss.

28 *dārārthino* in the genitive singular is proposed to correspond to *bhāryāyāḥ*. In the alternative, we should have *dārārthinā* and *bhāryayā* in the instrumental in both cases.

30 *triliṅga-*: Yāj., 3.232-3 has only *liṅga*. 31 *tadeva* apparently refers only to the punishment of death. Cs, however, includes *triliṅgacchedana* as well, understanding by it 'cutting of the organ and the two breasts.' That appears highly questionable. — *-bhuktā* seems to imply the woman's consent.

32 *aguptāyām*: Meyer thinks that *guptāyām* alone would be correct. However, Manu, 8.374-378, shows that the former is quite likely.

34 *śvapākatvaṁ vā śūdraḥ*: this implies that there is no branding for the Śūdra, but there is a fall in the social scale for him.

36 For having relations with a woman who has left her home, the fine is twenty-four *paṇas*. 37 If willing she shall receive the same.

38 For enjoyment of a prostitute by force, the fine shall be twelve *paṇas*. 39 For many (men) enjoying (forcibly) one (prostitute), the fine shall be twenty-four *paṇas* for each one separately.

40 For one approaching a woman elsewhere than in the female organ the lowest fine for violence (shall be imposed), also for one misbehaving with a man.

> 41 A fine of twelve *paṇas* is prescribed for the senseless wretch who carnally approaches lower animals, and double (that) for misbehaving with images of gods.
>
> 42 In case punishment is inflicted on those not deserving to be punished, thirty times that as a fine for the king shall be placed in water for Varuṇa and given to Brahmins after that.
>
> 43 Thereby the sin of the king arising from the mistake in inflicting punishment is purified. For Varuṇa is the chastiser of kings who behave wrongly towards men.

Herewith ends the Fourth Book of the Arthaśāstra of Kauṭilya
'THE SUPPRESSION OF CRIMINALS'

36 *pravrajitā* : as the punishment is too light, the word can hardly refer to 'a nun' ; it seems to mean 'who has left her home' as in 2.23.2.

39 *adhicaratām* : we have probably to understand *prasahya* from the preceding s. with this.

42 *tataḥ param* shows that the Brahmins are to be the real recipients, the offering to Varuṇa being ceremonial.

43 *rājñām* is from Cb Cs for *rājā* of the mss. It is true that *Varuṇo rājā* is a conception that goes back to the Vedas ; but it seems better to have *rājñām* as the substantive for *vyācaratām*, to be construed with *śāstā*.

BOOK FIVE

SECRET CONDUCT

CHAPTER ONE

SECTION 89 CONCERNING THE INFLICTION OF (SECRET) PUNISHMENT

1 The 'weeding of thorns' from the fortified city and the country has been explained. 2 We shall now explain that from the king and his rulership.

3 The remedy against those principal officers, who live on the king by holding him in their power or who are in league with the enemy, is the employment of secret agents or winning over of seducible parties, as explained before, or secret instigation or spying, as we shall explain in (the section on) the capture of an enemy's town.

4 But against those treasonable principal officers, who cause harm to the kingdom, (and) who, being favourites or being united, cannot be suppressed openly, he should employ 'silent punishment,' finding pleasure in (doing his) duty.

5 A secret agent, after inciting a brother of the treasonable high officer, not honoured by him, should show him to the king. 6 The king should induce him to fight against the treasonable officer by granting the use of the treasonable man's property. 7 When he has acted with a weapon or poison, he should cause him to be executed on that very ground, declaring 'He is a murderer of his brother.' 8 By that are explained the *pāraśava* and the son of a female attendant.

The secret conduct (*yogavṛtta*) described in this Book is that of the king in the first two Chapters and that of the servants in Chapters 4 to 6. Chapter 3 does not fit in. Cb remarks that the title really is true of the First Chapter (5.1), but is applied to the whole *adhikaraṇa*, because that is the most important Chapter in it. Breloer (I, 77-78 n.) relates *yoga* to *yogakṣema* and understands the whole state mechanism as intended, Ch. 2 referring to state income and Ch. 3 to expenditure. The other chapters, however, hardly fit in.

5.1

2 *rājarājyayoḥ* : the offenders, viz., traitorous persons are like thorns to the king and his rulership. For *rājya* see 8.2.1.

3 *avagṛhya* : cf. 1.8.21 etc. — *gūḍhapuruṣapraṇidhiḥ* is described in 1.12, and *kṛtyapakṣopagrahaḥ* in 1.13. — *yathā ca pāragrāmike vakṣyāmaḥ* : the *ca* is unnecessary and it is proposed to drop it. *upajāpa* and *apasarpa* are in fact some of the ways recommended in the *pāragrāmika* section ; see 13.1 and 13.3.

4 This s. refers to *rājyakaṇṭakas*, as the preceding one referred to *rājakaṇṭakas*. — *dūṣyāḥ* literally 'who can be spoiled,' is used of treasonable persons or suspected traitors. Cs understands the idea to be 'who are to be somehow destroyed.' Russ. refers to Mallinātha's paraphrase by *tyājya* "who ought to be eliminated' on Māgha's *Śiśupālavadha*, 2.56.

5 *asatkṛtam* by his brother, the traitorous officer. Cb reads *satkṛtam*, but the actual comment implies the reading *asatkṛtam*. 6 *atisargeṇa*, i.e., by promising the grant of his

9 Or, a brother, instigated by a secret agent, should demand inheritance from the treasonable officer. 10 As he lies down at the door of the treasonable man's house at night, or when he is staying elsewhere, an assassin, slaying him, should declare, 'This claimant of the inheritance is killed.' 11 Then, giving support to the slain man's party, the (king) should suppress the other.

12 Or, secret agents, staying near the treasonable officer, should threaten the brother claiming inheritance with death. 13 As he at night and so on, as before.

14 When of two treasonable officers, a son has relations with the father's wife or a father with the son's wife or a brother with that of a brother, a fight between the two started by a sharp pupil is explained by the preceding.

15 Or, a secret agent should instigate a son of the treasonable officer thinking highly of himself, (suggesting) 'You are really the king's son, kept here through fear of the enemy.' 16 When he believes that, the king should honour him in private, 'Though the time for installing you as the crown prince has come, I am not crowning you through fear of the officer.' 17 The secret agent should induce him to murder the officer. 18 When he has acted, the (king) should cause him to be executed on that very ground, declaring 'He is a parricide.'

19 Or, a female mendicant (agent), having won the confidence of the wife of the treasonable officer by means of love-winning potions, should cheat (them) by the use of poison.

20 Thus end the stratagems through kinsmen.

21 He should despatch the treasonable high officer with a weak army containing assassins, for destroying foresters or an enemy's town or for establishing a district officer or a frontier officer in a region separated by a wilderness or for suppressing the domain of a city-officer that has risen in revolt or for seizing a caravan-route on the frontier along with land easily recoverable (by the enemy). 22 In the fight, taking place by day or night, assassins or agents

property after the officer's death. 7 *tatraiva*, i.e., on the charge of fratricide. 8 *pāraśavaḥ* : see 3.7.21.

10 *upaśayānam* seems to include the idea of fasting also besides staying at the door till the demand is granted. 11 *upagṛhya* is quite necessary for the sense ; *ri* after *upa-* in the mss. has evidently got in through a scribal error. For *upagrah*, cf. 7.2.19 etc. Cb shows *parigṛhya* which also yields the sense required.

13 *iti samānam*, i.e., as in ss. 10-11.

14 *adhicarati* : cf. 4.13.30 etc. — *kāpaṭika* : see 1.11.2-4. — *pūrveṇa vyākhyātaḥ*, a *tīkṣṇa* kills one in the name of the other, who is then charged with murder.

15 *upajapet* is preferable to *upacaret*. The former is commonly used with *sattrī*.

19 *sāṁvadanikībhiḥ* is necessary in view of the form *saṁvadana* adopted elsewhere; see 4.4.14. — *saṁvāsya*, literally 'having made her live with herself,' refers to winning of confidence. — *rasena* : the poison is administered to the husband in the belief that it is a love potion.

20 *āpyaprayogaḥ* a trick in which use is made of a kinsman of the suspected traitor.

21 *sārthātivāhya* is usually the escorting of caravans and the fee charged for it ; cf. 2.34.12. Here the caravan-route seems to be meant. — *pratyādeya* is territory which, even if seized by one, can be easily recovered by one's enemy ; cf. 9.4.5-6.

appearing as highway robbers should kill him, announcing, 'He was killed during the attack.'

23 Or, when he has gone to a fair or on a pleasure-trip, the (king) should invite treasonable officers to see him. 24 These, entering together with assassins with concealed weapons shall allow a search of their persons in the middle hall for being allowed to enter inside. 25 The assassins, seized by the door-keepers, should say, 'We are engaged by the treasonable officers.' 26 After proclaiming that, they should kill the treasonable men. 27 In place of the assassins, others (i.e., criminals) should be executed.

28 Or, going on a pleasure-trip outside (the city), he should honour the treasonable men by giving them quarters near him. 29 A woman of bad character, appearing as the queen, should be caught in their quarters at night and so on, as before.

30 Or, he should request the treasonable officer for food by praising 'Your cook or food-preparer is good,' or for a drink, when out on a journey some time. 31 Mixing both those with poison, he should urge the two themselves to taste them first. 32 Having announced that, he should cause them to be slain as poison-givers.

33 Or, an agent appearing as a holy man should make the (officer), if he is given to black magic, believe 'You will attain your desires by eating one of the following: a lizard, a tortoise, a crab or an ox with broken horns, which is endowed with auspicious marks.' 34 When he agrees, he should get him killed in the course of the rite by poison or iron clubs, announcing, 'He was killed by a mishap in the rite.'

35 Or, an agent appearing as a physician, after establishing a malignant or incurable disease for the treasonable person, should cheat him with poison in the preparations of medicine or food.

36 Or, agents employed as cooks or food-servers, should cheat the treasonable person by means of poison.

37 Thus ends (the topic of) suppression by secret means.

38 As to suppression of two treasonable persons, however: 39 He should despatch one treasonable person himself accompanied by a weak army and assassins to where the (other) treasonable person is to be suppressed, (saying) 'Go, raise an army or money in that fortified city or region; or extract

23 *yātrā* may be a religious fair or a military expedition. The former seems intended here.

29 *devīvyañjanā vā duḥstrī*: *vā* is unnecessary. Meyer suggests *prāduṣkṛtā strī* 'a bad woman' or 'a decorated woman', or *kācit strī* 'some woman' in place of *vā strī* — *samānaṁ pūrveṇa*, i.e., he should be slain as *devīkāmuka*.

33 *-prāśanena* is from Cb Cs; though it is not altogether satisfactory, it is preferable to *-prakāśanena* of the mss. The latter may mean 'exhibiting', i.e., placing at the cross-roads or some such thing. Cb explains *prāśana* by 'eating the remnants of the meat offered in a sacrificial fire in the cremation ground.'

35 *daurātmika* 'malignant' as adj. to *vyādhi* is unusual.

money from the favourite; or, kidnap the favourite's daughter; or, carry out any one of the undertakings, viz., building a fort or an embankment, making a trade-route, settling on new land, starting mines, raising material-forests or elephant-forests; or, carry out the work of a provincial officer or frontier officer; and whoever prevents you or does not give you help should be imprisoned.' 40 In the same way he should send word to the others, 'The transgression of so and so should be prevented (by you).' 41 When he may be disputing on these occasions for strife or on account of hindrances in his work, assassins should secretly kill him by bringing down their weapon (on him). 42 For that offence, the others should be punished.

43 Or, when strife ensues or is raised by assassins on occasions of injury to property, implements, crops or vehicles in connection with boundaries of villages, fields, threshing-floors or houses in treasonable cities, villages or families, or on occasions of shows, ceremonies or festivals, the assassins should bring down their weapons and say 'Thus are dealt with those who dispute with this person.' 44 For that offence the others should be punished.

45 Or, assassins should set fire to the fields, threshing-floors or houses, or bring down their weapons on the kinsmen, relations or draught-animals of those treasonable persons whose mutual quarrels are deep-rooted, and say, 'We were engaged by so and so.' 46 For that offence the others should be punished.

47 Or, secret agents should induce treasonable officers in the fortified city and in the country to be one another's guests. 48 There poison-givers should give poison. 49 For that offence the others should be punished.

50 Or, a female mendicant (agent) should suggest to a treasonable chief in the country, 'The wife, the daughter-in-law or the daughter of (that) treasonable chief in the country is in love with you.' 51 When he consents, she should take his ornaments and show them to the master, saying 'That chief, puffed up with youth, has designs on your wife, daughter-in-law or daughter.' 52 (In) the quarrel between the two at night and so on, as above.

53 As to treasonable (vassals) surrendering with troops, however, —the crown prince or the commander-in-chief should do some wrong and, after going away, show fight. 54 Then the king should despatch (against him)

43 *dūṣyāṇām* qualifies *purāṇām* etc. Cs makes out the dispute to be between *dūṣya* on the one hand and *pura* etc. on the other. That appears less likely. — *sīmā* is a boundary between villages, while *maryādā* is a boundary between fields, houses etc. Cf. 3.9.10-23.

45 *saṁbandhin*, as distinguished from *bandhu*, is a relation by marriage.

47 *āveśanika* 'who lives in the residence,' is obviously 'a guest.' *durgadūṣya* as guests of *rāṣṭradūṣya* and vice versa are to be understood.

51 *svāmine*, i.e., to the husband, father-in-law or father as the case may be. — *abhiman*; cf. 1.6.5 etc.

53 *daṇḍopanata* ordinarily would mean 'who has submitted to force'; but 7.3.23-26 show that *daṇḍopanata* involves the surrender of one's troops. — *apakṛtya* from Cb Cs is

the treasonable vassals themselves with a weak army containing assassins and so on,—all the stratagems as above. 55 And among their sons surviving them, he who is not disloyal should get the patrimony.

56 In this way, the kingdom continues in the succession of his sons and grand-sons, free from dangers caused by men.

57 He should employ 'silent punishment' towards his own party or that of the enemy, without hesitation, being possessed of forbearance in respect of the future and the present.

CHAPTER TWO

SECTION 90 REPLENISHMENT OF THE TREASURY

1 The (king) without a treasury should collect a treasury, when difficulties concerning money have arisen.

2 He should demand a third or a fourth part of the grains from a region, whether big or small in size, that is not dependent on rains and yields abundant crops; from a middling or inferior one, according to yield. 3 He should not make a demand on (a region) useful for building a fort or embankment or trade-routes or new settlements or mining or material forests or elephant forests, or on (a region) small in size which is on the frontier.

clearly necessary for *upakṛtya* of the mss. 55 *anukṣi* here is 'to survive,' but in 13.5.17 it seems to have the sense of 'to brood over (the death of), to think constantly of.'

56 *asya* refers to the king, hardly to the vassal of the preceding ss.

57 *āyatyāṁ ca tadātve ca kṣamāvān*, i.e., showing forbearance, bearing in mind future consequences and immediate results.

1 *pratyutpannārthakṛcchraḥ* 'who is in difficulties in respect of money or some object to be achieved (*artha*).' Cf. 7.8.5. Breloer (I, 78-81), arguing that this Chapter describes only normal sources of revenue, not special levies, considers this s. as without any significance for the rest of the Chapter; in the alternative, he proposes to translate 'in times of peace, he should provide for a treasury against times of distress (with *-kṛcchram* as adjective to *kośam*).' The translation appears quite unlikely, as is the reading *-kṛcchram*. To his question, how can the king collect treasury when there is general distress, the answer is that there is no reference to any general distress here. The king's treasury is depleted because of some undertaking like war etc., and it has to be replenished for some other undertaking. It is not only money that constitutes the *kośa*; it consists of *ratna*, *sāra*, *phalgu* and *kupya*, as 2.11.1 shows, where there is no mention of cash. Stores, in fact, from an integral part of the treasury. It is true that ss. 4-7 mention monetary help given by the king; that is possible because the king, though lacking in *kośa* in the full sense of the term, may have some cash with him. And *artha* in *arthakṛcchra* need not refer to cash only. In any case, it is not possible to agree that the Chapter refers to normal sources of revenue. The various dubious ways of making collections described in ss. 31-68 can hardly be regarded as normal ways of collecting revenue.

2 It is better to read *adevamātṛkam* (with the *avagraha*) as in 6.1.8 — *tṛtīyaṁ caturthaṁ vā*: as E. H. Johnston (*JRAS*, 1929, 97) has pointed out, we have to think of levies from the stocks with the cultivators, not a share of the crops as land revenue. The latter is *bhāga*; here we have *aṁśa*, besides *yāceta*. — *sāra*, i.e., quality of the soil and the amount of its yield. 3 *pratyantam . . . na yāceta*: the reason is, the frontier people, if disgruntled because of the levy, may go over to the neighbouring king.

4 He should provide one making a new settlement with grains, cattle, money and other things.

5 He should purchase for money a fourth part of the grains after allowing for seeds and livelihood. 6 He should exempt forest produce and the property of a Brahmin learned in the Vedas. 7 Even that he may purchase so as to favour them.

8 Or, in case that does not serve the purpose, officers of the Administrator should cause preparation of the fields for sowing to be made by farmers in summer. 9 At the time of (sowing) seeds, they should make a deed of (the grant of) seeds, laying down a penalty double that which may be lost through negligence. 10 When the crops have ripened, they should prevent the taking of green or ripe (grains), except handfuls of vegetables or grains plucked by hand for the purpose of worship of gods and manes and for charity or for the sake of cows. 11 And they should leave remnants of the heap for mendicants and village servants.

12 For one appropriating his own crops, compensation for loss shall be eight-fold. 13 For one stealing another's crops, the penalty for grains shall be fifty-fold, if he is of the same class ; death, however, if he is an outsider.

14 They should take a fourth part of grains, a sixth part of wild produce and of goods made of silk-cotton, lac, linen, barks, cotton, wool and silk, medicines, perfumes, flowers, fruits and vegetables, also of wood, bamboos, meat and dried meat, one half of ivory and skins. 15 For one selling these without permission, (the punishment shall be) the lowest fine for violence.

16 Thus ends (the topic of) making demands on farmers.

4 Cf. 2.1.13 above. The purpose of the new settlements is to increase agricultural revenue. The state is not absolutely bankrupt and is in a position to provide even cash for the purpose.

8 *tasya akaraṇe*, i.e., when these measures do not bring in the necessary grains in the stores. The idiom is unusual. — *samāhartṛpuruṣāḥ*, i.e., the *gopas* and the *sthānikas*. See 2.35.1-6. Cb has *sītādhyakaṣa* and others. Breloer (I, 78-89), holding that all land belongs to the state, thinks that the *sītādhyakṣa* works under the *samāhartṛ*. — *udvāpam* : as Johnston (JRAS, 1929, 99) says this refers to preparation of the land for sowing. He thinks that clearing fresh land is also intended ; that, however, seems doubtful. 9 *bījakāle bījalekhyaṁ kuryuḥ* : Breloer explains 'when seedlings appear, the officers of the *samāhartṛ* are to make a survey.' This appears doubtful. *bījalekhya* only shows that the state has a record of the amount of seeds given and has thus an idea of the crops expected. — *kaṭabhaṅga* 'corn plucked by the hand.' 11 Cf. 2.24.30.

12 *pratipātaḥ* : cf. 2.26.8. The compensation is for loss suffered by the state which is entitled to a larger share of the crops than the usual one-sixth. 13 *sītātyayaḥ* : cf. 2.22.14, which has reference to normal times. — *svavargasya*, i.e., if he is himself a farmer.

14 *gṛhṇīyuḥ* : the subject may be *samāhartṛpuruṣāḥ*, though some of the items mentioned are unconnected with farming. 15 *tad* may refer to *dantājinam* only ; the inclusion of the other items is, however, also possible.

16 For *praṇaya* as a special levy, cf. Rudradāman's Junagadh Inscription, where it is used beside *kara* and *viṣṭi*.

17 Dealers in gold, silver, diamonds, gems, pearls, corals, horses and elephants shall pay a tax of fifty. 18 Dealers in yarn, cloth, copper, steel, bronze, perfumes, medicines and wines shall pay a tax of forty. 19 Dealers in grains, liquids and metals and those carrying on trade with carts shall pay a tax of thirty. 20 Traders in glass and major artisans shall pay a tax of twenty. 21 Minor artisans and keepers of harlots shall pay a tax of ten. 22 Dealers in articles of wood and bamboo, stoneware, earthenware, cooked food and green (vegetables), shall pay a tax of five. 23 Actors and prostitutes shall pay half their wage.

24 They shall recover a tax in cash from those skilled in work, and shall not overlook any offence of theirs. 25 For, these might sell (something) by representing it as not belonging to them.

26 Thus ends (the topic of) making a demand on dealers.

27 (Owners of) cocks and pigs shall give half; small animals one-sixth; cows, buffaloes, mules, donkeys and camels one-tenth.

28 Keepers of harlots should replenish the treasury through female servants of the king, possessed of great beauty and youth.

29 Thus ends the making of demands on breeders of animals.

30 The (demand) is to be made once only, not twice.

31 Or, in case that does not serve the purpose, the Administrator, pointing to some work to be done, should ask citizens and country people for contributions. 32 And secret agents should then first give large amounts. 33 Referring to that, the king should ask the citizens and country people (for corresponding contributions). 34 And sharp pupils should reproach those who give little.

17 *pañcāśatkarāḥ* seems to mean 'paying a tax of fifty (*paṇas*).' Meyer understands 50% of the profit as tax. There is, however, no reference to profit or percentage. Cb Cs have '1/50th (of profit? or of commodities?)' under the influence of Manu, 7.130, which, however, refers to normal times. 21 *bandhakīpoṣakāḥ* from Cb Cs seems necessary. Cf. s. 28. *vardhakipoṣakāḥ* of the mss. is unlikely. Meyer suggests *vardhakitakṣakāḥ*; but either would be included in *mahākāru* or *kṣudrakāru*. 23 *vetanārdham*, i.e., half their monthly wage; half the annual income is hardly conceivable.

24 *hiraṇyakaraṁ karmaṇyān*, the reading proposed, alone yields a reasonable sense. The idea is, those skilled in work or efficient (*karmaṇya*, cf. 5.3.6) are likely to cheat the state; so they must be made to pay the cash tax; *ā-hṛ* to make one pay, to extort. With *akarmaṇyān* Cs (following Cb) explains 'should make those not engaged in work (i.e., living by selling grass, water etc., — Cb) pay a levy in cash, viz., one *varāṭa* (one *kāṇa*—Cb) per head.' This coin is unknown to the text. And s. 25 with its *hi* cannot be understood with this explanation. 25 *aparigṛhītam* 'not possessed or owned by themselves (but belonging to some one else).' Cf. *parigraha* 'possessions'. Cb Cs read *aparagṛhītam* 'taken by others.' — an *iti* before *abhinīya* would be better. Pleading that the goods do not belong to them, they evade the tax.

27 *ardham*, i.e., half the stock of fowl etc.

28 *bandhakīpoṣakāḥ*: in s. 21 these contribute from their own income, while here they help indirectly in raising money.

29 *yonipoṣaka*: Meyer compares *asatīpoṣaṇa* in Hemacandra's *Yogaśāstra*, 3.111, which includes the keeping of animals as well as of prostitutes. Cf. *asaījaṇaposaṇayā* in the Jaina Canon.

31 *tasyākaraṇe*: see s. 8 above.

35 Or, he should ask money of the rich according to their wealth, or according to benefits (conferred on them), or whatever they may offer of their own will. 36 He should bestow on them position, umbrella, turban or decorations in consideration of money.

37 Administrators should bring (to the treasury) the property of heretical corporations or the property of temples not intended for use by a Brahmin learned in the Vedas, declaring that it was deposited with a person who is dead or whose house is burnt.

38 The Superintendent of Temples should collect the treasures belonging to temples in the fort and in the country in one place, each separately, and bring them (to the treasury) in the same manner.

39 Or, after raising at night a god's temple or a sanctuary of a holy person as a miraculous happening, he should live on fairs and festive gatherings (at the place). 40 Or, he should proclaim the presence of a divinity by means of a tree in a sanctuary-park endowed with flowers and fruits out of season. 41 Or, agents appearing as holy men after showing danger from an evil spirit in a tree demanding the tax of a human being, should ward it off for the citizens and the country people for money. 42 Or, in a well connected by a subterranean passage, he should show a cobra with a number of hoods in return for a gift of money. 43 In a sanctuary hole or an ant-hill hole, (he should point to) the manifestation of a snake in an image of a cobra concealed inside, and after 'arresting its consciousness' by means of food, should show it to the credulous. 44 To those who do not believe, he should administer poison when they are sipping water or washing themselves and declare it to be a curse of the divinity, or should cause a person condemned to death to be bitten.

36 *sthāna* 'position' is evidently in state service. A mere title does not seem meant.

37 *kṛtyakarāḥ* : the context suggests the obvious meaning of 'administrators.' These appear to be state officers, or at least amenable to state influence. — *dagdhagṛhasya* : the idea is, the property was supposed to have been kept in the house and burnt along with it, being of course secretly removed to the treasury. The reading *dagdhahṛdayasya* is impossible. There is no question of a man's heart burning in torture, as Meyer thinks.

38 *yathāsvam ekastham*, i.e., the property of *durgadevatās* in one place and that of *rāṣṭradevatās* in another. — *tathaiva*, i.e., as in s. 37, which makes *upaharet* necessary in place of *apaharet* of the mss. Cb reads *āharet*.

39 *aupapādikam* 'that has suddenly arisen.' The *vā* should have come before instead of after this word, for the option is between *daivatacaitya* and *siddhapuṇyasthāna*, either of which could be *aupapādika*. Cs, with *bhaumavādikam*, explains 'associated with the rumour that it has appeared out of the ground at the holy place.' This is hardly satisfactory. Cb has the same reading, but its explanation contains no reference to *bhūmi*. 41 *manuṣyakaram*, i.e., demanding the tax of one human being per day. 42 *suruṅgā* is for a person who remains concealed there for manipulating the many-headed cobra to show that it is alive. 43 It is proposed to read *antaśchannāyām* for *antaśchidrāyām*. The *nāgapratimā* is concealed in a hole in the *caitya* or in an ant-hill hole. There is little sense in making the image of the cobra have holes inside (*antaśchidrā*). Cs, however, has 'in a cobra image sufficiently hollow inside (*antaśchidrā*) to allow a real snake to remain inside,' reading the words at the end of the last s., instead of at the beginning of this s. Cb reads the words in this s. and understands that a live serpent is shown in the hollow of the *nāga*-image. There seems little point in keeping a snake image as well as a live snake in it. — *sarpadarśanam* : Meyer proposes to read *sarpam* only ; that does not seem necessary. Even with the former we may understand *rūpayitvā* or the like. — *āhāreṇa* : Cs understands some magical rite. 'Food' might also do. — *pratibaddha* 'arrested, stopped.'

45 Or, he should replenish the treasury by (offering) remedies against occult manifestations.

46 Or, an agent appearing as a trader should trade with plenty of goods and assistants. 47 When he has amassed wealth by entrusted deposits and loans against the value of goods, he should get him robbed at night. 48 By this are explained the Examiner of Coins and the Goldsmith.

49 Or, an agent appearing as a trader, with well-known dealings, should secure on loan or hire a large number of gold and silver articles on the occasion of a festive party. 50 Or, in a festive gathering he should obtain plenty of money and gold as a loan by a display of his entire goods, and also (collect) the price of each article. 51 Both these, he should cause to be stolen at night.

52 Or, after infatuating men suspected of treason with women appearing as pious ladies, and catching them in the houses of those same women, they should confiscate their entire property.

53 Or, when a dispute has arisen between members of treasonable families, poison-givers, who are employed there, should give poison. 54 For that offence, the others should be deprived of their property.

55 Or, a person condemned to death should demand of a treasonable person, on a credible pretext, a commodity or entrusted money or a loan given or an inheritance. 56 Or, he should address the treasonable person as a slave, or his wife, daughter-in-law or daughter as a slave or as wife. 57 As he lies down at the door of the treasonable person's house or when he stays elsewhere, an assassin, slaying him, should declare 'This fellow, longing for property, has been killed.' 58 For that offence, the others should be deprived of their property.

59 Or, an agent appearing as a holy man, after luring a treasonable person with magical lores, should say to him, 'I know the rite for inexhaustible wealth, for opening the doors of the king's palace, for winning a woman's heart, for causing disease to the enemy, for securing a long life or for getting a son.' 60 When he consents, he should cause him to make an offering of plenty of

45 *yogadarśana* 'an occult or miraculous manifestation.' The s. is repeated in 13.2.38.

47 *paṇyamūlye* : this seems to provide the security for the deposits and loans secured ; it does not appear to be another means of becoming *upacita*, as Meyer thinks. In that case it would have been in the instrumental, like *nikṣepaprayogaiḥ*. 48 The *rūpadarśaka* collects coins for inspection, and gets himself robbed ; so does the Goldsmith with the citizens' gold and silver.

50 *sarvapaṇyasaṁdohena* : this again provides security for the loan. —*pratibhāṇḍamūlyam* can hardly mean 'capital for counter-wares (to be brought from foreign lands),' as Meyer thinks. 51 *ubhayam*. i.e., the *ṛṇa* and the *mūlya*.

52 *sādhvī* may convey the idea of a nun.

54 *paryādātavyāḥ* : cf. 2.9.24.

57 *arthakāmukaḥ* is an emendation from Meyer for *itthaṁ kāmukaḥ* of the mss. The latter would not include the cases mentioned in s. 55 ; and even s. 56 does not show *kāmukatva* in all cases. *artha* as 'object, property' would do in all cases. Cf. 5.1.10 above.

59 *akṣayahiraṇyam* is also an emendation by Meyer ; it is necessary as an adjective to *karma*. 61 *ekarūpam* : Meyer thinks that this is a false coin. That is possible, because the person is to be arrested while making purchases with that coin. Meyer, in fact, suggests

wine, meat and perfumes in a sanctuary at night time. 61 And from a place, where money consisting of a single coin is buried beforehand (and) where a limb of a corpse or the corpse of an infant may have been placed, he should show him the money and say, 'This is too little.' 62 (He should add) 'For plenty of money, offering must again be made; hence, with this very money you yourself purchase to-morrow plenty of articles of offering.' 63 He should be arrested while purchasing articles of offering with that money.

64 Or, (a treasonable person) should be charged by a female agent appearing as a mother, saying, 'You have killed my son.' 65 During his night sacrifice or a sacrifice in a forest or when sport in a forest has started, assassins, killing a condemned man due for execution, should smuggle him in.

66 Or, an agent working as a servant of the treasonable person should throw in a false coin in the money received as wages and point that out.

67 Or, an agent appearing as a workman should, while working in the house, place the implements of a thief or a maker of false coins there, or an agent appearing as a physician (should place) poison there in the guise of medicine.

68 Or, a secret agent close to the treasonable person should communicate through a sharp pupil (the presence of) articles for coronation and a letter from an enemy (secretly) planted there and should mention their purpose.

69 Thus he should behave towards treasonable and unrighteous persons, not towards others.

70 He should take from the kingdom fruits as they ripen, as from a garden; he should avoid unripe (fruit) that causes an uprising, for fear of his own destruction.

the reading *kūṭarūpam*. Russ. has 'money of one particular type.' — *pretāṅgam* etc. is there only to mark the place where the coin is buried before. 63 *gṛhyeta*: the arrest may be because of the false coin or perhaps also because the purchases are supposed to show that the person is engaged in the practice of black magic (which is an offence; cf. 4.4.14-16).

64-65 The readings of Cb Cs with *mātṛvyañjanayā* in the instrumental and *avarūpitaḥ* in the sense of 'shown up, i.e., accused' are adopted. *saṁsiddham* is to be understood as an adjective to *abhityaktam* in the sense of of 'ready' for execution. — It seems that *vanayāge* is due to dittography and is not original. — *atinayeyuḥ*, i.e., secretly plant the corpse in the sacrifice, to make it appear as the 'son' killed by the *dūṣya*. The 'son' is supposed to be intended as a victim in the occult rite.

67 *garam agadāpadeśena*, which is shown by Meyer's translation, is clearly necessary. *gadam agadā-* or *garam agarā-* are both unlikely. The poison implicates the *dūṣya* as a poison-giver.

68 *abhiṣekabhāṇḍam*: this is supposed to be for the coronation of the enemy, with whom the *dūṣya* is to be charged with being in league. In all these cases, the confiscation of the property of the *dūṣya* is to be understood. That would help in replenishing the treasury.

69 This is an important safeguard against arbitrary extortions.

70 *ātmaccheda-* from Cb Cs is clearly preferable to *āmaccheda-* of the mss. The danger is of the king himself being destroyed in a possible revolt (*kopa*).

CHAPTER THREE

SECTION 91 CONCERNING THE SALARIES OF (STATE) SERVANTS.

1 In accordance with the capacity of the fortified city and the countryside, he should fix (wages for) the work of servants at one quarter of the revenue, or by payment to servants that enables the carrying out of works. 2 He should pay regard to the body (of income), not cause harm to spiritual good and material advantage.

3 The sacrificial priest, the preceptor, the minister, the chaplain, the commander-in chief, the crown prince, the king's mother and the crowned queen should receive forty-eight thousand (*paṇas*). 4 With this much remuneration, they become insusceptible to instigations and disinclined to revolt.

5 The Chief Palace Usher, the Chief of Palace Guards, the Director (of labour corps), the Administrator and the Director of Stores should receive twenty-four thousand. 6 With this much, they become efficient in their work.

7 The princes, the mothers of princes, the commandant, the city-judge, the Director of Factories, the council of ministers, the provincial officer and the frontier officer should receive twelve thousand. 8 For, with this much, they help in strengthening the entourage of the master.

9 Heads of banded troops, commandants of elephants, horses and chariot corps, and magistrates should receive eight thousand. 10 For, with this much, they are able to carry their groups with them.

11 Superintendents of infantry, cavalry, chariots and elephants and Guardians of material and elephant forests should receive four thousand.

1 *samudayapādena* is from Cb Cs for *-vādena*, which makes little sense. — *-lābha* is what is received by the servant; cf. 2.6.23 and Breloer referred to there. 2 *śarīram*, i.e., *āyaśarīram*, (2.6.1-9). The idea of 'body politic' (Meyer) does not seem intended.

3 *aṣṭacatvāriṁśatsāhasrāḥ*: this is obviously a year's salary in *paṇas*. N. N. Law (IHQ, V, 780 ff.) thinks of monthly salaries. That is possible only if a copper *paṇa* is understood; but a copper *paṇa* is not known to this text.— It seems better to understand *bharaṇena* instead of *bharaṇe*. With the latter, *nānāsvādyatvam* is left, explained as 'having many kinds of tasteful dishes' (Cs). That does not appear a happy idea. The expressions seem to have in view the advantage to the state rather than to the recipients. *anāspadyatvam* (*anāspadat vam* might perhaps have been better; cf. *pareṣām āspadabhayāt*, 1.13.21) refers to these persons being not susceptible to enemy instigations, just as *akopakam* refers to their being not likely to rise in revolt. *anāsvādya* (with its passive sense) cannot be understood in the sense of 'not given to misappropriation' as suggested by 2.9.32. And persons mentioned here in s. 3 could not have been meant in 2.9.32.

5 *praśāstṛ*: for this and other officers mentioned in these ss., see 1.12.6. The *rāṣṭrapāla*, mentioned only here, seems to be an officer in charge of a province or a district; cf. 5.1.21,39. 8 *paribandha* seems to mean 'entourage, retinue.'

10 *svavargānukarṣiṇaḥ*, i.e., able to secure the loyalty and obedience of their subordinates.

12 The chariot-fighter, the elephant trainer, the physician, the horse-tamer and the carpenter and breeders of animals should receive two thousand.

13 The fortune-teller, the soothsayer, the astrologer, the narrator of Purāṇas, the charioteer and the bard, the chaplain's men and all superintendents should receive one thousand.

14 Foot-soldiers trained in the (fighting) arts and the groups of accountants, clerks and others should receive five hundred.

15 But actors should receive two hundred and fifty, and makers of musical instruments should receive double the wage of these.

16 Artisans and artists should receive one hundred and twenty.

17 Servants, valets, attendants and guards of quadrupeds and bipeds and foremen of labourers should receive a wage of sixty, also riders, bandits and mountain-diggers supervised by Āryas, as well as all attendants.

16 Teachers and learned men should receive an honorarium as deserved, a minimum of five hundred and a maximum of one thousand.

19 The average envoy should receive ten *paṇas* per *yojana*, a double wage beyond ten (*yojanas*) up to one hundred *yojanas*.

20 The ' king ' should receive three times the fee of those equal in learning at the Rājasūya and other sacrifices.

21 The king's charioteer should get one thousand.

12 *rathika* : cf. 2.33.6. Cb here has ' chariot-fighter.' — *vardhaki* seems to be the officer mentioned in 10.1.1,17. — *yonipoṣakāḥ* : cf. 5.2.29. These here appear in state employ ; 5.2.29 does not visualise that.

14 *śilpavantaḥ* should be understood with *pādātāḥ*, since *śilpins* are separately mentioned in s. 16 below.

15 *tūryakara* seems to be the maker of musical instruments, though a player on musical instruments is not unlikely. Cb comment shows ' chief (*pradhāna*) ' in explanation of this word.

17 It is proposed to add a *ca* after *sarvopasthāyinaḥ* and read a stop here. The *upasthāyinaḥ*, who can only be attendants, cannot be brought into relation with *pūjāvetanam* ; only the *ācāryāḥ* and *vidyāvantaḥ* can be thought of as receiving it. Nor can *sarvopasthāyinaḥ* be brought into relation with *ācāryāḥ*. — *āryayukta* seems to mean working under the supervision of Āryas, *ārohaka* etc. being themselves non-Aryans. Russ. has *āryayukta* ' those in the service of Aryas.' *ārohaka* may mean ' a rider ' or ' a climber.' — *māṇavaka* : see 4.5 above ; here these are to be supposed as being in state service.

19 *daśapaṇika* etc. : if *dūta* is an ordinary messenger, the rates, as Meyer says, would appear exorbitant. He proposes to read *daśayojane* for *yojane*, i.e., 10 *paṇas* for the first 10 *yojanas* and 20 up to 100 *yojanas*. This also is unlikely. Perhaps the *dūta* is the envoy of 1.16, *madhyama* being the *parimitārtha* of 1.16.3. The rates given here would cover the travelling expenses for the envoy and his retinue. The envoy is usually of the rank of a minister ; it is possible that he would be entitled to his regular salary, over and above these expenses. — *ā yojanaśatād* : evidently a distance of 100 *yojanas* or about 900 miles was the maximum that was considered likely.

20 *rājā* is the *adhvaryu* priest who deputises for the ruler during a long sacrificial session, as shown by *Āpastamba Śrauta Sūtra*, 20.2.12.3 and *Baudhāyana Śrauta Sūtra*, 15.4. Cf. Kane, HD, III, 28.

21 *sārathiḥ* : this does not seem to have anything to do with the *kratus* of the last s., as Cb Cs think.

22 Sharp pupils, monks fallen from vow, and agents appearing as householders, traders and ascetics should get one thousand.

23 Village servants, secret agents, assassins, poison-givers and female mendicants should get five hundred.

24 Those moving about for spying should get two hundred and fifty or should have their wage increased according to their efforts.

25 Supervisors of groups of one hundred and one thousand (troops) should carry out the payment of food and wages to them, give directions and order their dispersal. 26 There is to be no dispersal in the case of royal property and guarding the fortifications in the city and the country. 27 They shall have permanent heads and many (such) heads.

28 Of those dying while on duty, the sons and wives shall receive the food and wages. 29 And their minor children, old and sick persons should be helped. 30 And he should grant them money and do honour on occasions of death, illness and birth ceremonials.

31 If he has a small treasury, he should give forest produce, cattle and fields and a little money,. 32 Or, if he has undertaken the settlement of new lands, he should give only money, not a village, in order that transactions that have taken place in the village may be stabilised.

33 In this manner he should fix different (amounts of) food and wages for regular and casual servants according to their skill and work.

34 Fixing one *āḍhaka* for a (servant with a) wage of sixty, he should fix food in accordance with the cash wage.

35 Infantry, cavalry, chariots and elephants should carry out practice in their arts outside (the city) at sun-rise, except on juncture-days. 36 The king should constantly attend to that, and should frequently inspect their arts.

23 *grāmabhṛtaka*, i.e., washerman, barber, etc. (Cb).

24 *cārasaṁcāriṇaḥ*, i.e., the lower staff of the spy establishment. Cf. 1.12.7-14.

25 *vikṣepam* ' dispersal ' seems to refer to discharge, not to transfer to another place. Cf. especially 7.9.22 ff. Troops are to be thought of even here. Cb has ' *vikṣepa*, i.e., assigning suitable work.' 26 Cb has *avikṣepe* ' when there is no work.' 27 Cf. 2.4.29, 30.

30 *pretavyādhita-* etc. : this also seems to refer to those of the *karmasu mṛta*, hardly to those of all state servants.

32 *grāmasaṁjāta-* etc. : The idea is to prevent old established dealings from being disturbed by the new owners. Money is given, so that new villages may be founded instead. Cb seems to mention as the reason the possibility that if the village were required to give something (to the new owner) business in it might come to a stop.

33 *abhṛta* are those not in regular service.

34 *ṣaṣṭivetanasya āḍhakaṁ kṛtvā* : this seems to mean that to a servant entitled to a wage of 60 *paṇas* a year, a ration of one *āḍhaka* of grains is to be given as part payment per day, the cash wage being correspondingly reduced ; cf. 2.24.28. And apparently this is restricted to menials entitled to this wage only, hardly to those with 48,000 a year, for example. One could understand 1 *āḍhaka* of grains per day as payment in lieu of the entire 60 *paṇas* per year. But *bhakta* alone without some cash payment is unlikely. It is not possible to regard 1 *āḍhaka* of grains as the equivalent of a wage of 60 (copper) *paṇas* a month (Kane, HD, III, 124 ff). There is no copper *paṇa* in this text. Moreover, 1 *āḍhaka* of grains would just about suffice for only four meals of a single individual. Cf. 2.15.43.

35 Ss. 35-44 and 47 are not relevant to the topic of this Chapter.

37 He should allow weapons and armours that are stamped with the king's insignia to be brought into the armoury.

38 (People) shall move about unarmed, except those permitted with a sealed licence. 39 He shall pay double what is lost or destroyed. 40 And he shall keep an account of what has perished.

41 Frontier officers should seize the weapons and armours of caravan traders or allow them to pass after sealing them.

42 Or, when deciding on an expedition, he should make the army ready. 43 Then agents appearing as traders should give all goods to the soldiers at the time of the expedition to be recovered double (later). 44 Thus is made the secret sale of the king's goods as well as the recovery of wages.

45 Looking after income and expenditure in this manner, he does not suffer a calamity of the treasury and the army.

46 Thus (are explained) different rates of food and wages.

47 And secret agents, prostitutes, artisans and actors as well as elders of the army should ascertain, with diligence, the loyalty or disloyalty of soldiers.

CHAPTER FOUR

SECTION 92 CONDUCT (PROPER) FOR A DEPENDENT

1 One, conversant with the ways of the world, should seek service with a king, endowed with personal excellences and the excellences of material constituents, through such as are dear and beneficial (to the king). 2 Or, he should have recourse to even one lacking in material constituents, if he thinks, 'Just as I am desirous of service, so is he desirous of training and is endowed with qualities of one easily approachable,' but never one lacking in personal excellences. 3 For, one lacking in qualities of the self, comes to an end even after receiving mighty sovereignty, as a result of contempt for the political science or as a result of association with harmful persons.

37 This s. should have been included in 2.18. — *praveśayet* : the subject is *āyudhāgārādhyakṣaḥ*.

38 *aśastrāḥ* : this apparently refers to ordinary citizens, not to soldiers. 39, 40 The subject is again *āyudhāgārādhyakṣaḥ*.

43 *yātrākāle* is to be construed with *dadyuḥ*. — *dviguṇapratyādeyāni* : the agreement is to receive double the normal price of the article at the end of the expedition. The soldiers would apparently agree because they want to provide for their families during their absence, and payment is not to be made immediately. Evidently, if the soldiers were to die in the expedition, their relatives would be held liable for the double charge. 44 *vetanapratyādānam* : this is in the form of the extra price charged, which could come only from the soldiers' salaries.

46 *-vikalpaḥ* : perhaps we should read *-kalpaḥ* 'the law of, rules about.'

5.4

anujīvin is principally an aspirant to ministership.

1 For *ātmasaṁpad* see 6.1.3-6, and for *dravyaprakṛtisaṁpad* 6.1.8-11. 2 *ābhigāmikaguṇa* : see 6.1.3. 3 *anarthya* : see 1.7.2, also 8.3.15.

4 After securing an audience with a (king) endowed with qualities of the self, he should give a test in the (political) science. 5 For, he attains stability of position by not contradicting (the science). 6 Questioned about matters requiring intelligence, he should state what is associated with spiritual and material benefit in the present and in future (and) what is possible (of achievement), like an expert, without being afraid of the assembly.

7 If approved, he should stipulate, 'You should not question those, who are not distinguished, concerning spiritual and material well-being, nor inflict punishment on those who are associated with powerful (persons) nor inflict punishment on the instant on those associated with me ; you should not harm my party, my livelihood and my secrets ; and by signs I shall prevent you from inflicting punishment under the influence of passion or anger.'

8 If appointed, he should, with permission, enter the place indicated, and should sit at the (king's) side neither very near nor far, on another seat. 9 He shall not indulge in bellicose talk, nor make statements that are uncultured or not based on personal knowledge or untrustworthy or untrue, nor indulge in loud laughter when there is no joke nor break wind or spit with a sound. 10 He should avoid a secret talk with another, a quarrelsome remark during a discussion among men, a dress fit for a king or that of gaudy men or clowns, an open request for some jewel or a special favour, contracting one eye or lip, knitting of eye-brows and cutting short a remark when (another person is) speaking, opposition to those associated with the powerful, association, working for a common objective and union with women, persons (frequently) meeting women, envoys of neighbouring princes, persons belonging to the party of the inimical, persons dismissed and harmful persons.

> 11 He should declare without loss of time what is in the king's interest, in the company of those dear and beneficial (to the king) what is in his own interest, at the proper place and time what is in the interest of another, (always) what is connected with spiritual and material well-being.

5 *avisaṁvādāt*: the *avisaṁvāda* is with the *śāstra* (Cs) rather than with the king (Meyer). 6 *samartham*, i.e, capable of being carried out. Cb comment shows '*sambandhārtham*, what is relevant.'

7 *aviśiṣṭa* 'not distinguished' for learning or experience and hence not competent to advise on *dharma* and *artha*. — *balavatsaṁyukteṣu daṇḍadhāraṇam*: we have to supply *na kuryāḥ*. Meyer supplies *kuryāḥ* and proposes *abalavat-* 'you must punish criminals before they attain prominence (*aviśiṣṭeṣu*), before they are associated with the mighty.' This is quite unlikely. — *matsaṁyoge tadātve ca* etc.: this is to be understood together 'no punishment for my people at once'; 'no punishment for my associates and no instantaneous punishment' is possible, but seems less likely.

8 Cb reads *āyuktapradiṣṭāyām*. It seems that *āyuktaḥ* should be read instead of *ādiṣṭaḥ*. — *saṁnikṛṣṭaviprakṛṣṭaḥ* is from Cs for *saṁnikṛṣṭaḥ viprakṛṣṭaḥ* of the mss. In fact the sense requires *asaṁnikṛṣṭaḥ aviprakṛṣṭaḥ* 'not too near nor too far,' as in Cb. — *parāsanam*: Cs reads *varāsanam* and places it at the beginning of the next s. But then it has to be construed with *na kuryāt*, which is far from happy. Cb has the same punctuation with *parāsanam* 'a seat intended for some one else.' 10 *dvandvakathanam*

12 When asked, he should declare what is agreeable and beneficial, should not declare what is harmful but agreeable; or, he may, with permission, declare in private what is disagreeable but beneficial, when the (king) is prepared to listen.

13-14 Or, when making a reply he should remain silent and should not mention enemies and others. Those cast out from his affection may, though competent, become even disagreable (to him), and harmful persons are known to have become favourites as they act according to their knowledge of his inclinations. He may laugh at laughable things, and avoid frightful laughter.

15 He should turn away from another frightful (words by the king), and should not himself use frightful words to another, and should tolerate (such words) addressed to himself, being full of forbearance like the earth.

16 For, self-protection must always be first secured by the wise (person) for, the conduct of those serving a king has been stated to be like (remaining) in fire.

17 Fire, when it reaches another, may burn a part or (at most) the whole body; but a king might kill one along with sons and wife or might cause one to prosper.

CHAPTER FIVE

SECTION 93 CONCERNING PROPER BEHAVIOUR (FOR A COURTIER)

1 When assigned work, he should show income cleared of expenses. 2 And he should specify a business that is inner or outer, open or secret, urgent or brooking delay, by saying 'This is of this nature.'

'quarrelsome talk,' rather than 'talk between two'; cf. *dvandvin* 1.13.2. — *atiśaya* seems to refer to some special favour as Meyer says. — *avakṣipta*: cf. 1.10.2,5. — *saṁghāta* 'union' is more intimate than *ekārthacaryā* 'working for a common object.' All three, *pratisaṁsarga* etc., are to be construed with each of *strībhiḥ*, *strīdarśibhiḥ* etc. The *strīs* would appear to be those in the harem.

13-14 The second half of st. 13 and the first half of st. 14 from a single *śloka* and are quoted as such in the *Daśakumāracarita*, VIII. It is possible that there has been some disarrangement of the lines in the text here. — *prativākye* 'when giving a reply' rather than 'when a reply is being given by the king.' — *abhihāsyeṣu* is from Cb Cs for *alihāsyeṣu*, which yields little sense.

15 *ghoram*, i.e., *ghoravacanam* by the king.

17 *paraṁ gataḥ* 'when it reaches another' may also mean 'when it reaches its maximum' (Meyer).

5.5

2 *ābhyantaram*, i.e., pertaining to the city or the palace and *bāhyam*, i.e., pertaining to the outlying regions. See 9.5 below.

3 He should not humour him by (false) praises when he is addicted to hunting, gambling, wine or women. 4 And remaining near, he should endeavour to wean him from the vice, and should guard him from enemy's instigations, cheating and fraud.

5 And he should observe his gestures and expressions. 6 For, a wise man shows, with his gestures and expressions, a reversal of the pairs of feelings viz., liking and hatred, joy and distress, resoluteness and fear, for concealing his secret counsel.

7 The (king) is pleased at his sight, accepts his statement, gives him a seat, gives an audience in private, does not over-suspect on an occasion of suspicion, takes pleasure in his talk, pays regard to him in matters that are to be communicated, tolerates wholesome words spoken, appoints him to a task with a smile, touches him with the hand, does not ridicule him in a praiseworthy matter, speaks of his virtues in his absence, remembers him during meals, goes with him on a pleasure trip, helps him in a calamity, honours those devoted to him, tells him his secret, increases his honour, does what is advantageous to him, wards off what is harmful, — thus is known when the king is satisfied (with him).

8 These same reversed (are signs) of a dissatisfied (king) ; and we shall state more (such signs) : 9 Anger at sight of him, not listening to and prohibition of his statements, not giving him a seat and not looking at him, change in complexion and voice, contraction of one eye, eye-brow or lip, appearance without cause of sweat, sighs or smile, consultation with another, going away suddenly, making another prosper, scratching the ground or limbs, goading another (against him), showing contempt for his learning, *varṇa* or country, censure of those with a like offence, censure of every single offence, praise of those against him, not paying regard to his good deeds, mentioning his evil deeds, paying attention at the back, extreme indifference, telling him a falsehood, and a difference in the behaviour towards him of those who frequently see the king.

3 *nainam anuvarteta* is proposed for *caivam anuvarteta* or *caivānuvarteta*. Considering the next s. and the general spirit of this section, it is little likely that advice would be given to humour the king in his vices ; the reverse is far more likely. And *evam* or *eva* in the other readings has no significance.

5 *iṅgitākārau* : see 1.15.7-9. 6 *vyavasāya* has almost the sense of 'courage,' being the opposite of *bhaya*. — *prājñaḥ* is as suggested by Meyer. The reading of the mss. is obviously corrupt.

7 *ślāghye nopahasati* : Cs reads *ślāghyena upahasati* 'when a praiseworthy thing is done by the minister, he jokes in his presence' ; this appears to be Cb's explanation too. But it appears less likely. Meyer proposes *aślāghye nopahasati* or *ślāghye ślāghate marmaṇi nopahasati* ; neither seems necessary. — *abhyupapadyate* is read in place of *abhyava-* ; cf. 2.10.24 above. — *tadbhaktīn*, i.e., those loyal to the minister.

9 *paramantraṇam* is from Meyer for *parimantraṇam*, though Cs gets the same meaning 'talking with another' from the latter. Meyer also suggests *aparimantraṇam* 'not talking with him,' as supported by the *Kāmasūtra*. — *pratidoṣanindā* seems to be due to dittography. There is no comment on it in Cb. — *pṛṣṭhāvadhānam* 'paying attention at the back (and not in front where the minister is).' — *atityāgaḥ*, i.e., having nothing to do with him.

10 And he should observe the change in behaviour even of non-human beings. 11 'He is sprinkling (water) from on high,' with this (thought) Kātyāyana left (his king's service); 'The heron (is flying) towards the left,' with this Kaṇiṅka Bhāradvāja (left); 'Ah, grass,' with this Dīrgha Cārāyaṇa left); 'The garment is cold,' with this Ghoṭamukha (left); 'The elephant has sprinkled water,' with this Kiñjalka (left); 'He has praised the chariot and horse,' with this Piśuna (left); at the barking of the dog, the son of Piśuna (left).

12 And in case of deprival of emoluments and honour, leaving (the service of the king is recommended). 13 Or, knowing the master's character and his own offence, he should remedy it. 14 Or he should approach his ally who may be close to him.

15 And staying there, he should, through friends, carry out the removal of his offence towards the master; then he should return again while the king is alive or when he is dead.

CHAPTER SIX

SECTION 94 CONTINUANCE OF THE KINGDOM
SECTION 95 CONTINUOUS SOVEREIGNTY

1 The minister should take steps in case of a calamity of the king in the following manner:

11 *ayam uccaiḥ siñcati*: according to Cb, followed by Cs, the minister found the gardener watering from on high instead of from the usual low level and thus making him wet; that served as a warning that the king wanted to kill him, because he thoughtthat the minister had divulged a secret. This sounds plausible though the warning may only be about the king's displeasure. — *'krauñco' pasavyam*: this is even ordinarily an evil omen; the detailsin Cb Cs need not be necessarily accepted. — *kaṇiṅko bhāradvājaḥ*: it is possible that this Bhāradvāja is the same as the author of a work on the Arthaśāstra frequently quoted in this text. Kaṇiṅka Bhāradvāja's discourse on politics is found in the *Mahābhārata*, 12.138. — *tṛṇam iti Dīrghaś Cārāyaṇaḥ*: it seems that grass appeared in a place where it was not expected and that set the minister thinking. According to Cb Cs, the king sent a plateful of food covered with grass; that would be too obvious an indication of displeasure. The story narrated in the *Nandī Sūtra* does not appear intended here. — *sītā śāṭī*: a cold garment when a warm one was expected apparently set the minister thinking. — *hastī pratyaukṣīt*: the unusual occurrence of an elephant sprinkling him with water set the minister thinking. — *rathāśvaṁ prāśaṁsīt*: the praise of the chariot and horse by the king is understood as a hint that the minister should depart. — *piśunaḥ*: cf. 1.8.11. Piśuna is the name of Duṣyanta's minister in the *Śākuntala*. — *pratiravaṇe śunaḥ*: the barking of the dog is taken as a hint of the king's displeasure. — *piśunaputraḥ*: he may be the son of the Piśuna mentioned earlier.

12 This s. is not to be construed with the preceding s., and hence the emendations in the Punjab text are unacceptable. — *avakṣepa* 'deprival' rather than mere 'diminution.' 14 *upakṛṣṭam* 'near (to the king)' both figuratively and literally.

15 *jīva* as adjective 'living' is known to the *Ṛgveda* (*jīvā jyotiraśīmahi*, 7.32.26). Cb Cs read *jīved* for *jīve*. The latter, however, appears better.

5.6

The two sections are closely related; the dividing line between them, which is not quite distinct, may be found at s. 22.

1 *rājavyasanam*, i.e., a seriousillness or death of the king. Mostly, death is thought of.

2 Even before there is fear of the danger of (the king's) death, he should, by winning the support of those dear and beneficial (to the king), establish audience (with the king) at intervals of one month or two, under the pretext that 'The king is engaged in a rite for removing the troubles of the country or for destroying enemies or for securing long life or for getting a son.' 3 He should show, at a time when the appearance cannot be distinguished, a person appearing like the king to the subjects and to the envoys of allies and enemies. 4 And he should hold suitable conversation with them through the minister. 5 And through the Chief Usher and the Chief of Palace Guards, he should cause the king's daily duties to be carried out as described (before). 6 And towards those who do harm, he should cause disfavour or favour to be shown as it may be pleasing to the subjects, favour only towards those who have conferred benefits.

7 He should cause the treasury and the army to be collected in one place, in the fortified city or on the frontier, in charge of trustworthy men, also (bring together) members of the (royal) family, princes and principal officers under some pretext.

8 And if any principal officer, with a (strong) party, stationed in the fort or a forest, were to show hostility, he should get him won over. 9 Or, he should send him on an expedition full of dangers or to an ally's family.

10 And he should cause that vassal, from whom he apprehends danger, to be brought under control under the pretext of a festival, a wedding, an elephant hunt, a horse-sale, or grant of land, or through his own ally. 11 Then he should enter into a treaty that would be inviolable. 12 Or, he should bring about enmity (of the vassal) with forest chiefs or enemies. 13 Or, he should win over a pretender from his family or a prince in disfavour by (the promise of) a part of (his) territory.

14 Or, winning the support of members of the (royal) family, princes and principal officers, he should show a prince as already crowned.

15 Or, he should cause the administration to be carried on by weeding out the thorns of the kingdom in the manner described in (the section) 'Infliction of (secret) Punishment.'

2 *upagraha* 'winning over,' i.e., securing the support of. 3 *rājavyañjanam*, i.e., some one who is the king's double. — *arūpavelāyām* is proposed in conformity with 7.17.11; the actual comment in Cb supports the emendation. The meaning is 'at a time when the form cannot be clearly seen,' i.e., when it is dark. 4 He, i.e., the person appearing like the king. 5 For *dauvārika* and *āntarvaṁśika*, see 1.12.6. — *yathoktam*, i.e., as described in 1.19.

7 *kulya* is independent of *kumāra*, not an adjective to it.

8 *upagrāhayet*: this seems to mean 'should have him won over' as in s. 13 below, hardly 'should have him seized or imprisoned' as in 2.28.20.

11 *adūṣyam* seems to mean 'which cannot be violated'; it may also mean 'which would not make him treasonable.' 13 *takulīnam aparuddhaṁ vā*: cf. 1.10.3. These cannot be members of the dying king's family as Meyer thinks.

14 *abhiṣiktam eva*, i.e., already crowned before the news of the king's death is announced.

15 *dāṇḍakarmikavat*, i.e., as in 5.1 above.

16 If, however, any principal officer or any one of the vassals were to rise in revolt, he should invite him, saying, 'Come here, I shall make you the king,' and get him killed. 17 Or, he should get rid of him by (using) ' Remedies against Troubles.'

18 Or, after gradually transferring the burden of the kingdom to the crown prince, he should announce the calamity of the king.

19 In case the calamity has befallen the king in enemy territory (during war), he should secure a treaty with the enemy through an ally posing as a foe and retire. 20 Or, he should place one of the vassals in his fort and retire. 21 Or, after crowning the prince, he should fight back. 22 Or, if attacked by the enemy, he should use ' Remedies against Troubles ' as described.

23 ' In this way the minister should secure continuous sovereignty,' says Kauṭilya.

24 'Not so', says Bhāradvāja. 25 'When the king is dying, the minister should make members of the family, princes, and principal officers fight against one another or against (other) principal officers. 26 When any one fights, he should get him slain by a rising of the subjects. 27 Or, getting rid of members of the family, princes and principal officers by silent punishment, he should seize the kingdom himself. 28 For, for the sake of the kingdom, the father fights with sons and the sons with the father, what to say then of the constituent, namely, the minister, the one support of the kingdom ? 29 He should not disdain that when it has come to him of its own accord. 30 "A woman approaching of her own accord curses if discarded," such is a saying among the people.

> 31 'Time comes but once to a man waiting for an opportunity ; that time is difficult for that man to get again when he wants to do his work.'

16 A *vā* would seem necessary after *anyatamaḥ*. 17 *āpatpratīkāreṇa*, i.e., as in 9.5 below.

18 *rājyabhāram āropya* : this is without crowning him as king.

19 *mitreṇa amitravyañjanena* : such an ally is able to secure better terms from the enemy. 20 *asya*, i.e., *śatroḥ*. This implies that a fort of the enemy was captured before the king's death. 21 *kumāram abhiṣicya* : this is done in the enemy's fort.

23 *evam ekaiśvaryam* etc. shows that the preceding ss. are also concerned with ' continuity of sovereignty ', and the two *prakaraṇas* can hardly be separated.

24 *bhāradvājaḥ* : he is a ruthless and cynical teacher ; cf. 1.17.4-6. 25 *pramriyamāṇe vā* : Meyer suggests that *vā* may be understood as *eva*, or that *mṛte* may be suposed to have dropped out before it or that *vā* shows an alternative in Bhāradvāja's work, from which we have here an extensive quotation. The last suggestion seems reasonable. — *kulyakumāramukhyān* : it seems that the original reading was *kulyakumārān* only, as is shown by *mukhyeṣu* that follows. 28 *abhidruhyanti*, i.e., become enemies and fight. — *ekapragrahaḥ* : cf. 1.10.3. The *amātya* thought of in this Chapter is the chief minister. 29 *tat*, i.e., *rājyam*. 30 *strī* : *rājyaśrī* is figuratively a woman. 31 This stanza marks the end of the quotation from Bhāradvāja's work ; an *iti* after it would have been better Cb mentions the stanza as a śloka of Bṛhaspati. It is found with slight variations in the *Mahābhārata*, 12.104.20 and in the *Tantrākhyāyika*, 3.74.

32 'This incites subjects to revolt, is unrighteous and uncertain as to result,' says Kauṭilya. 33 He should place on the throne a prince possessed of qualities of the self. 34 In the absence of one so endowed, he should call together high officers and, introducing a prince not addicted to vice or a princess or the queen *enceinte*, should say, 'This is a trust with you; pay regard to his father as well as to your goodness and noble birth ; he is only an emblem, you alone are masters ; or, what (else) should be done ?' 35 When he says this, secret agents (among them) should say, 'Who else but this king, with you to guide him, would be able to protect the four *varṇas* ?' 36 Saying 'So be it,' the minister should invest with authority the prince or the princess or the *enceinte* queen and should introduce (him or her) to kinsmen and relations and to the envoys of allies and enemies.

37 He should cause an increase in the provisions and salaries of ministers and soliders, and say, 'When grown up, this (prince) will again give a rise.' 38 Thus he should speak to the principal officers in the fort and the country, and to parties of allies and enemies (he should speak) as deserved.

39 And he should strive to give training to the prince.

40 Or, after getting an offspring begotten on the princess by a man of the same caste, he should crown him. 41 Through fear of change of the mother's mind, he should keep near her a member of the family with small spirit and a young boy with auspicious marks. 42 And during the (monthly) periods he should guard her.

43 And he should not cause any excellent object of pleasure to be made for his own use. 44 For the king, however, he should cause belongings like carriages, riding animals, ornaments, dresses, women and houses, to be provided.

32 The difficulty posed by Bhāradvāja saying 'not so' to Kauṭilya's opinion (s. 24) and Kauṭilya then refuting the former's opinion may be eased by supposing that *naivam* in s. 24 is not from Bhāradvāja's work, but is put in his mouth only for emphasis, or that *naivam* has reference to all that is stated in ss. 1-22 which was there in the works of Bhāradvāja's predecessors and is not directed against the statement in s. 23. Keith's supposition (JRAS, 1916, 135-137) that this text was produced in Kauṭilya's school which was conversant with the master's views does not get over the difficulty of Bhāradvāja, a predecessor, refuting views attributed to Kauṭilya.

34 *vyasaninam,* which Cb Cs read for *avyasaninam,* seems hardly likely in the context.

40 *kanyāyām* etc. : this would operate when there is no prince. 41 *mātuḥ* : this is the *kanyā* of the last s. The danger is that she may waver and find some lover, ignoring the interests of the state and her own young prince. — *kulyam alpasattvam,* apparently as a check on the princess without involving any risk of himself enticing her. — *chātraṁ ca* : in view of the *ca,* this is different from the *kulya,* being apparently 'a young boy' intended as a companion to the young prince. Cb seems to understand a Brahmin boy, the excuse for keeping him being worship of the gods. — *upanidadhyāt* is used in the literal sense. 42 *ṛtau* etc. : this is to prevent another offspring, now that the continuity of the line is assured.

44 *parivāpa* 'personal belongings'; cf. 3.6.6.

45 And when he has attained youth, he should ask for rest, to find out his inclination ; he should leave him if he is not satisfied and continue to guard him if he is satisfied.

46 Or, if he has fallen from favour, he should repair to a forest or engage in a long sacrificial session after instructing select secret retinue to guard the prince.

47 Or, if the king is under the influence of principal officers, he, well conversant with the science of politics, should enlighten him through historical and mythological tales, with the support of those dear (to the king).

48 Or, putting on the appearance of a holy man and resorting to secret practices, he should get hold of the king and after getting hold of him should employ 'the Infliction of Punishment' against the treasonable.

Herewith ends the Fifth Book of the Arthaśāstra of Kauṭilya
'SECRET CONDUCT'

45 *yauvanastham* from Cb Cs is obviously necessary.

46 *sāra* 'of the best kind, select'; Cb renders it by '*pitṛpaitāmaha*, hereditary.' *parigraha* clearly is 'an attendant, servant.' — *arucyatāṁ gataḥ* 'come to be disliked' by the prince.

48 *siddhavyañjanarūpaḥ* : *rūpa* does not seem quite necessary. — *yogam*, i.e., secret practices.

Book Six

THE CIRCLE (OF KINGS) AS THE BASIS

CHAPTER ONE

SECTION 96 EXCELLENCES OF THE CONSTITUENT ELEMENTS

1 The king, the minister, the country, the fortified city, the treasury, the army and the ally are the constituent elements (of the state).

2 Among them, the excellences of the king are :

3 Born in a high family, endowed with good fortune, intelligence and and spirit, given to seeing elders, pious, truthful in speech, not breaking his promise, grateful, liberal, of great energy, not dilatory, with weak neighbouring princes, resolute, not having a mean council (of ministers), desirous of training,—these are the qualities of one easily approachable.

4. Desire to learn, listening, learning, retention, thorough understanding, reflecting, rejecting (false views) and intentness on truth,—these are the qualities of intellect.

5 Bravery, resentment, quickness and dexterity,—these are the qualities of energy.

6 Eloquent, bold, endowed with memory, intellect and strength, exalted, easy to manage, trained in arts, free from vices, able to lead the army, able to requite obligations and injury in the prescribed manner, possessed

The Sixth Book deals with the circle of kings (*maṇḍala*) and their constituents. Cb Cs explain *maṇḍalayoniḥ* as 'the *maṇḍala*, which is the *yoni*, i.e., basis of the six measures (*ṣāḍguṇya*).' That is supported by 7.1.1. The description of the *maṇḍala* in this Book serves as an introduction to the next Book which deals with *ṣāḍguṇya*. The expression, as a Tatpuruṣa compound, might also mean 'the source, i.e., the basic elements of the circle.'

6.1

1 Gl and Ml both have the faulty *-daṇḍadurgāṇi*, which shows that the two are derived from the same exemplar.

3 *avisaṁvādakaḥ* 'one who does not contradict,i.e., is consistent or actsas he speaks.' — *śakyasāmantaḥ* : as 7.10.9-10 show, *śakya* has the sense of *durbala*, the point being that the neighbouring princes are not a source of trouble. By *śakya*, Cb understands *pīḍanīya*, *karśanīya* and *ucchedanīya* of 6.2.16. — Cb reads *dṛḍhabhaktiḥ* for *dṛḍhabuddhiḥ*.—*akṣudra*- seems to refer to the quality of the ministers, hardly their number.

4 Cf. 1.5.5.

6 *svavagrahaḥ* 'easy to control' is usually used of an enemy or a servant ; cf. 1.9.1. In the case of the master, it may convey the sense of 'easy to lead or guide (along the right path),' as suggested in 1.7.8. — *avyasanaḥ* : Cb Cs read *vyasane* and construe it with *daṇḍanāyī*. But leadership of the army at all times is definitely a better idea. And freedom from *vyasanas* would be an independent qualification. Perhaps *avyasanī* should be read. — *daṇḍanāyī* is 'able to lead the army', hardly 'inflictor of punishment' ; in the latter sense, the root used is *pra-nī*. — *dṛṣṭapratīkārī* : as Cb Cs explain, *dṛṣṭa* is *śāstradṛṣṭa*, as laid down in the science of politics. Meyer has 'who knows how to requite etc.' ; but

of a sense of shame, able to take suitable action in calamities and in normal conditions, seeing long and far, attaching prominence to undertakings at the proper place and time and with appropriate human endeavour, able to discriminate between peace and fighting, giving and withholding, and (observance of) conditions and (striking at) the enemy's weak points, well-guarded, not laughing in an undignified manner, with a glance which is straight and without a frown, devoid of passion, anger, greed, stiffness, fickleness, troublesomeness and slanderousness, sweet in speech, speaking with a smile and with dignity, with conduct conforming to the advice of elders,—these are personal excellences.

7 The excellences of a minister have been stated before.

8 Possessed of strong positions in the centre and at the frontiers, capable of sustaining itself and others in times of distress, easy to protect, providing excellent (means of) livelihood, malevolent towards enemies, with weak neighbouring princes, devoid of mud, stones, salty ground, uneven land, thorns, bands, wild animals, deer and forest tribes, charming, endowed with agricultural land, mines, material forests and elephant forests, beneficial to cattle, beneficial to men, with protected pastures, rich in animals, not depending on rain for water, provided with water-routes and land-routes, with valuable, manifold and plenty of commodities, capable of bearing fines and taxes, with farmers devoted to work, with a wise master, inhabited mostly by the lower *varṇas*, with men loyal and honest,—these are the excellences of a country.

for this *dṛṣṭapratīkāraḥ* would be necessary. With the suffix *-in*, *dṛṣṭa* can only be an adjective to *pratīkāra* in a Karmadhāraya compound. — *āpatprakṛtyor viniyoktā* 'who makes appropriate use of, i.e., takes suitable action in calamities and normal times.' — *deśakāla-* etc.: Cb Cs understand importance attached to each of *deśa*, *kāla*, *puruṣakāra* and *kārya* separately. It seems better, however, to understand importance given to *kārya*, which is done at the proper place and time, with requisite human effort. — *saṁdhivikrama-* etc.: Cb Cs regard *saṁyamapaṇa* as a single idea, 'collection of treasury as in Chapter 5.2 (*paṇa* as coins?) without creating disaffection among the subjects (*saṁyama* as absence of troublesomeness?).' This is doubtful. As Meyer says, there are three contrasted pairs, the second being *tyāga* and *saṁyama*, and the third *paṇa* and *paracchidra*; between each pair, the king must be able to distinguish or discriminate (*vibhāgin*). *tyāga* refers to giving something to the enemy etc., *saṁyama* to withholding it. *paṇa* refers to the terms of a treaty, i.e., the observance of the terms, and *paracchidra* implies the idea of striking at the enemy's weak point, even by violating the terms of a treaty. — *saṁvṛtaḥ* refers primarily to the guarding of the *mantra*. — *ajihma-* etc.: we have to understand *ajihma* and *abhrukuṭi* as describing the *īkṣaṇa*. Cb understands *ajihma* as describing *bhrukuṭi*. That also is possible. — *upatāpa* is harassment of the subjects, as in Cb Cs. — *śaktaḥ* outside the compound, as in Cb Cs, is better, though the compound *smitodagrābhibhāṣī* is a bit odd. Meyer suggests *śaktaḥ smitavādī agrābhibhāṣī*. But neither *śaktaḥ* nor *agrābhibhāṣī* appears likely.

7 *purastāt*: in 1.9.1 above.

8 *sthānavān*: *sthāna* obviously refers to positions of strength, such as a fort etc.— *āpadi* is to be construed with the preceding (Meyer) rather than with the following *svārakṣaḥ* (Cb Cs). — *kaṇṭaka* may be understood in the figurative sense of the Fourth Book or in the literal sense. — *adevamātṛkaḥ* 'not depending on the god (of rain)', having perennial sources of water supply, such as rivers etc. — *daṇḍakara-* etc.: *daṇḍa* can hardly be 'army' (Meyer). Cf. 1.13.3,8. — *abāliśasvāmī*: on the strength of Kāmandaka, 4.54, Meyer would read *bāliśasvāmī* 'having foolish lords.' But *svāmin* clearly refers to the king himself and not to other landlords (Kāmandaka has *nāyaka*); and even foolish landholders would hardly be an excellence in a *janapada*. Cf 7.10.23-25. — *avaravarṇa* primarily refers to the Śūdras. Cf. 2.1.2.

9 The excellences of a fort have been stated before.

10 Acquired lawfully by the ancestors or by oneself, consisting mostly of gold and silver, containing various kinds of big jewels and cash, (one) that would withstand a calamity even of a long duration in which there is no income,—these are the excellences of a treasury.

11 Inherited from the father and the grandfather, constant, obedient, with the soliders' sons and wives contented, not disappointed during marches, unhindered everywhere, able to put up with troubles, that has fought many battles, skilled in the science of all types of war and weapons, not having a separate interest because of prosperity and adversity shared (with the king), consisting mostly of Kṣatriyas,—these are the excellences of an army.

12 Allied from the days of the father and the grandfather, constant, under control, not having a separate interest, great, able to mobilise quickly,—these are the excellences of an ally.

13 Not of royal descent, greedy, with a mean council (of ministers), with disaffected subjects, unjust in behaviour, not applying himself (to duties), vicious, devoid of energy, trusting in fate, doing whatever pleases him, without shelter, without a following, impotent, ever doing harm (to others),—these are excellences in an enemy. 14 For, an enemy of this type becomes easy to exterminate.

15 Excluding the enemy, these seven constituent elements have been described with each one's excellences manifest ; those, when they operate, become subordinate to the excellences of the king.

9 *purastāt* : in 2.3 above.

10 *anāyatim* : this is an adjective to *āpadam*. For *āyati* ' income, revenue ', cf. 2.9.10, 11 etc.

11 *bhṛta* are the hired soldiers ; cf. *bhṛtabala* 9.2.3 etc. — *pravāseṣu avisaṁvāditaḥ* not contradicted in long marches,' i.e., not frustrated or disappointed during such marches. Cf. 10.3.38. This appears to be the explanation in Cb, though its text shows the reading *pravāseṣvapi saṁpāditaḥ*. Cs explains this as ' receiving its customary comforts even during marches.' — *advaidhya* may mean ' having no separate interests of its own ' or ' not resorting to duplicity or double-dealing ' ; the former seems meant. Cf. s. 12 below and 7.9.43.

12 Cf. 7.9.38 and 7.9.9 ff.

13 *ayuktaḥ* seems ' one not applying himself ' diligently to his duties (*utthānahīna*,—Cb), rather than ' one without servants ' or ' improperly behaved.' — *agatiḥ* ' without support when being exterminated ' (Cb). — *ananubandhaḥ* : this may mean ' having no following ' or ' having no connections.' *anubandha* in this text usually refers to what follows from something, a consequence. Cf. 9.7.14.

15 It seems best to look upon *uktāḥ* as the predicate for the first half, as in Cb Cs ; in the second half *pratyaṅgabhūtāḥ* may be regarded as the predicate, with *prakṛtāḥ* in the sense of ' which function or operate ' understood as descriptive of the constituent elements. The idea seems to be that the other constituents are dependent on the king and his qualities. Russ. renders the second half : ' they appear as composite parts on which is dependent the well-being of the state ;' and in the Notes it is suggested that we should read *rājyasaṁpadaḥ* for *rāja-*.

16 A king endowed with personal qualities endows with excellences the constituent elements not so endowed. One not endowed with personal qualities destroys the constituent elements that are prosperous and devoted (to him).

17 Then that (king) not endowed with personal qualities, with defective constituent elements, is either killed by the subjects or subjugated by the enemies, even if he be ruler up to the four ends of the earth.

18 But one possessed of personal qualities, though ruling over a small territory, being united with the excellences of the constituent elements, (and) conversant with (the science of) politics, does conquer the entire earth, never loses.

CHAPTER TWO

SECTION 97 CONCERNING PEACE AND ACTIVITY

1 Peace and activity constitute the source of acquisition and security. 2 Activity is that which brings about the accomplishment of works undertaken. 3 Peace is that which brings about security of enjoyment of the fruits of works.

4 The source of peace and activity is the six-fold policy. 5 Decline, stability and advancement are the consequences of that (policy).

6 (Acts) of human agency are good policy and bad policy ; of divine agency good fortune and misfortune. 7 For, it is acts of human and divine agency that make the world go. 8 That caused by an unseen agency is the divine (act). 9 In that, the attainment of the desired fruit is good fortune; of undesired (fruit), misfortune. 10 That caused by a seen agency is the human (act). 11 In that, the coming into being of well-being is good policy ; (its) ruin, bad policy. 12 That can be thought about ; the divine is incalculable.

16 Breloer (III, 269 n.2) thinks that the word *ātmavān* indicates that the verses are derived from Bṛhaspati.

17 *duṣṭaprakṛtiḥ*: in the context, *prakṛti* is a constituent element (Cs), rather than 'nature' (as in Meyer) or 'subjects', though in *prakṛtibhiḥ* in the second half, subjects are clearly to be thought of. — *cāturantaḥ* : cf. 1.6.4.

6.2

The Section, though named *śamavyāyāmikam*, actually describes the nature of the circle of kings. That is because peace and activity in a state, which are necessary for its well-being, depend on its relations with the circle of neighbouring states.

2 *yogārādhanaḥ* : this can hardly mean 'exertion and making it fruitful' (Meyer) ; it seems to mean 'what secures the acquisition or accomplishment (of the works).' So *kṣemārādhanaḥ* is hardly 'peacefully making it fruitful' (Meyer).

5 *udayāḥ* 'fruits,' i.e., consequences.

6 *mānuṣam* : supply *karma*. 7 *yāpayati*, i.e., keeps it going. 9 *aya* as 'good fortune' seems restricted to this science. Cf. *Raghuvaṁśa*, 4.26.

13 The king, endowed with personal excellences and those of his material constituents, the seat of good policy, is the would-be conqueror. 14 Encircling him on all sides, with territory immediately next to his is the constituent called the enemy. 15 In the same manner, one with territory separated by one (other territory) is the constituent called the ally.

16 A neighbouring prince possessed of the excellences of an enemy is the foe ; one in calamity is vulnerable ; one without support or with a weak support is fit to be exterminated ; in the reverse case, fit to be harassed or weakened. 17 These are the different types of enemies.

18 Beyond him, the ally, the enemy's ally, the ally's ally, and the enemy's ally's ally are situated in front in accordance with the proximity of the territories ; behind, the enemy in the rear, the ally in the rear, the rear enemy's ally and the rear ally's ally (one behind the other).

19 One with immediately proximate territory is the natural enemy ; one of equal birth is the enemy by birth ; one opposed or in opposition is the enemy made (for the time being).

20 One with territory separated by one other is the natural ally ; one related through the mother or father is the ally by birth ; one who has sought shelter for wealth or life is the ally made (for the time being).

21 One with territory immediately proximate to those of the enemy and the conqueror, capable of helping them when they are united or disunited and of suppressing them when they are disunited, is the middle king.

22 One outside (the sphere of) the enemy, the conqueror and the middle king, stronger than (their) constituents, capable of helping the enemy, the

14 *samantato maṇḍalībhūtā* : this would imply not one king, but all those whose territories are contiguous to that of the *vijigīṣu* ; they are his *aris*. — It is to be noted that in 15.1.51-52, where this passage is quoted, we have *prathamā prakṛtiḥ, dvitīyā* and *tṛtīyā* in place of *vijigīṣuḥ, ariprakṛtiḥ* and *mitraprakṛtiḥ* here. What is more, those terms are there called *svasaṁjñāḥ* 'one's own technical terms.' Apparently, the numerical terms were first thought of by Kauṭilya. But he has used them only on a few occasions, as in 7.6.1 and 7.7.1. Cf. also 7.18.1-2.

16 *anapāśrayaḥ* : the shelter is either a fort or an ally. — *viparyaye*, i.e., when he has a strong support.

18 *pārṣṇigrāhaḥ* 'the heel-catcher', who attacks in the rear when one is fighting in front. — *ākranda* may contain a reference to 'crying out for help' on the part of the *vijigīṣu* So *āsāra* 'ally' has reference to 'moving forward' for helping or rescuing.

19 Cb Cs regard *prakṛtyamitra* and *tulyābhijana* as two types of *sahaja* enemy ; that is doubtful in the absence of a *ca* or a *vā*. And the literal sense of *sahaja* would restrict the term to the *tulyābhijana* only. This term seems to refer to some member of the same royal family as the *vijigīṣu*.

20 As before, Cb Cs regard *prakṛtimitra* also as a type of *sahaja* ally.

21 For the *madhyama* and *udāsīna*, cf. N. N. Law (IHQ, IX, 770-783). As he points out, these two are powerful rulers who could easily upset the balance of power in the circle of kings.

22 *-madhyānāṁ bahiḥ prakṛtibhyo balavattaraḥ* : the comment in Cb omits the reference to *madhyama* and understands *daṇḍa* and *kośa* by the *prakṛtis*. Cs understands 'outside the constituents of' ; for this, *bahiḥ* should have come after *prakṛtibhyaḥ* ; and 'outside the

conqueror and the middle king when they are united or disunited and of suppressing them when they are disunited, is the neutral king.

23. These are the constituents (of the circle of kings).

24. Or, the conqueror, the ally and the ally's ally are the three constituents of this (circle of kings). 25 They, each individually united with its five constituent elements, the minister, the country, the fort, the treasury and the army, constitute the eighteen-fold circle. 26 By that is explained a separate circle (for each of) the enemy, the middle and the neutral kings. 27 Thus there is a collection of four circles.

28 There are twelve constituents who are kings, sixty material constituents, a total of seventy-two in all. 29 Each of these has its own peculiar excellences.

30 Power and success (are to be explained). 31 Power is (possession of) strength. 32 Success is (obtaining) happiness.

33 Power is three-fold : the power of knowledge is the power of counsel, the power of the treasury and the army is the power of might, the power of valour is the power of energy.

34 In the same way, success is also three-fold : that attainable by the power of counsel is success by counsel, that attainable by the power of might is success by might, that attainable by the power of energy is success by energy.

35 Thriving with these, the (king) becomes superior ; reduced (in these), inferior ; with equal powers, equal. 36 Therefore, he should endeavour to endow himself with power and success, or, if similar, (to endow with power and success) the material constituents in accordance with their immediate proximity or integrity. 37 Or, he should endeavour to detract (these) from treasonable persons and enemies.

constituents ' does not make much sense. Meyer has ' stronger than the outer *prakṛtis* ' ; but such a description of the *prakṛtis* is uncertain. Outside the sphere of the three kings is what seems meant. Russ. has ' standing independently away from *ari*, *vijigīṣu* and *madhyama* and stronger than these on the basis of his own state (*prakṛtibhyaḥ*) '. This rendering of *prakṛtibhyaḥ* is extremely doubtful. *ud-āsīna* seems to contain a reference to his being outside the group of kings. He is the most powerful monarch thought of.

24 In these ss. we have a different arrangement of the twelve kings forming the circle. The text follows the earlier arrangement ; *pārṣṇigrāha*, *ākranda*, etc. are frequently mentioned, the allies etc. of the *madhyama* or *udāsīna* hardly ever.

30 *śaktiḥ siddhiś ca* : these are *adhikāraśabdas* in as Cs; they cannot be construed with *sampadaḥ* (regarded as genitive singular) as in Meyer or with *tāsām* of the preceding s.

35 *jyāyān* etc. : the comparison is with the enemy, the *vijigīṣu*'s rival. 36 *sādhāraṇo vā* : this refers to the *vijigīṣu* and his enemy being both endowed with personal excellences. The sense of ' common, mediocre ' is possible but seems less likely. 37 *apakraṣṭum* : the object is *śaktiṁ siddhiṁ ca*.

38 Or, if he were to see, 'My enemy, possessed of power, will injure his subjects with verbal or physical injury or appropriation of their property, or, when endowed with success, will become negligent because of (addiction to) hunting, gambling, wine or women, thus with subjects disaffected or (himself) become weakened or remiss, he will be easy to overpower for me; or, being attacked in war, he will remain in one place or not in his fort, with all his troops collected togther, thus with his army brought together, (and himself) separated from his ally and fort, he will be easy to over-power for me; or, he will render help to me when I am attacked by a strong king, (thinking) "the strong king is desirous of exterminating my enemy elsewhere; after exterminating him, he might exterminate me," or (help me) when my undertakings have failed;' and when seeking to seize the middle king (the enemy's help is needed); —for these and other reasons, he may wish power and success even to the enemy.

39 Making the kings separated by one (intervening territory) the felly and those immediately proximate the spokes, the leader should stretch himself out as the hub in the circle of constitutents.

40. For, the enemy situated between the two, the leader and the ally, becomes easy to exterminate or to harass, even if strong.

Herewith ends the Sixth Book of the Arthaśāstra of Kauṭilya
'THE CIRCLE (OF KINGS) AS THE BASIS'

38 There are three situations visualised in the thoughts of the *vijigīṣu*, the fourth *madhyamalipsāyām* being added after that. — *vāgdaṇḍa-* etc.: these are *kopaja vyasanas*; cf. 8.3.23. — *mṛgayā-* etc.: these are *kāmaja vyasanas*; cf. 8.3.38. — *sarvasaṁdoha* refers to collecting the whole army together in one place. — *ekastho 'durgastho vā*: the *avagraha* is clearly necessary as in Meyer's translation; that is shown by *-durgaviyuktaḥ* that follows. — *balavān vā* etc. contain the enemy's thoughts in his own words, which the *vijigīṣu* can surmise. *balavān rājā* is a third king, the *śatru* in the enemy's thoughts being the *vijigīṣu*. — *māṁ ucchindyāt* is as proposed by Meyer. With *na* before these words as in the mss. we may have 'he may not exterminate me.' But without *na* the sense becomes more emphatic. —*madhyamalipsāyāṁ ca*: it is the *vijigīṣu* who wishes to overcome the *madhyama* king; for that he would require the enemy's help; hence he wishes *śakti* and *siddhi* to the enemy. The expression cannot be construed with *vipannakarmārambhasya vā* etc. in the preceding clause, as in Cs. *lipsā* is not 'expectation of help from'; it is desire to seize or overcome'; cf. 7.1.32, also 7.18.5ff. For *madhyamalipsā* see 7.13.26.

39 *netā* is the same as the *vijigīṣu*. — *nābhim*: Cf. *Raghu*. 9.15.

40 *madhye hyupahitaḥ* from Cb Cs is obviously the only correct reading.

BOOK SEVEN

THE SIX MEASURES OF FOREIGN POLICY

CHAPTER ONE

SECTION 98 ENUMERATION OF THE SIX MEASURES OF FOREIGN POLICY

SECTION 99 DETERMINATION OF (MEASURES IN) DECLINE, STABLE CONDITION AND ADVANCEMENT

1. The circle of constituent elements is the basis of the six measures of foreign policy.

2. 'Peace, war, staying quiet, marching, seeking shelter and dual policy constitute the six measures,' say the teachers.

3. 'There are (only) two measures', says Vātavyādhi. 4 'For, out of peace and war the six measures come into being.'

5. 'These are really six measures, because of differences in the situations,' say Kauṭilya.

6 Among them, entering into a treaty is peace. 7 Doing injury is war. 8 Remaining indifferent is staying quiet. 9 Augmentation of (powers) is marching. 10 Submitting to another is seeking shelter. 11 Resorting to peace (with one) and war (with another) is dual policy. 12 These are the six measures of foreign policy.

13 When in decline as compared to the enemy, he should make peace. 14 When prospering, he should make war. 15 (When he thinks) 'The enemy is not able to do harm to me, nor I to him,' he should stay quiet.

The Seventh Book deals with the use of the six measures that can be adopted by a state in its relations with foreign states. *guṇa* has the technical sense of a measure to be adopted as a policy.

7.1

The two Sections are to be found in ss. 1-19 and 20-38 respectively.

1 *prakṛtimaṇḍalam*, i.e., the twelve kings and their constituents as mentioned in 6.2.13-29.

3 *Vātavyādhiḥ*: see 1.7.20. 4 The idea is that peace and war are the basic policies, the others being only variations of these. There is some truth in this point of view.

5 *avasthābhedāt*, i.e., the different situations warrant a six-fold division. Cf. Kāmandaka, 11.40.

6 *paṇabandhaḥ* 'the framing of terms or conditions,' i.e., entering into a formal treaty with specific clauses. 9 *abhyuccayaḥ*: the cause is used in place of its consequence (marching). 11 *saṁdhivigrahopādānam*: as is clear from the text, this is peace with one king and war with another; cf. s. 37 below. See K. Nag (*Les Theories Diplomatique* etc., p. 78). Cs has in this s. 'peace outwardly, but war secretly', but has the former explanation in s. 37. Meyer accepts the view that *dvaidhībhāva* is duplicity, making peace for the time being with a view to making better preparations for war against the same enemy. The text does not seem to support that explanation.

16 When possessed of a preponderance of excellent qualities, he should march. 17 Depleted in power, he should seek shelter. 18 In a work that can be achieved with the help of an associate, he should resort to a dual policy. 19 Thus are the measures established.

20 Of them, he should follow that policy by resorting to which he may be able to see, 'By resorting to this, I shall be able to promote my own undertakings concerning forts, water-works, trade-routes, settling on waste land, mines, material forests and elephant forests, and to injure these undertakings of the enemy.' 21 That is advancement. 22 Perceiving 'My advancement will be quicker or greater or leading to a greater advancement in the future, the reverse (will be) that of the enemy', he should remain indifferent to the enemy's advancement. 23 In case the advancement takes the same time or bears an equal fruit (for both), he should make peace.

24 He should not follow that policy by resorting to which he were to see the ruin of his own undertakings, not of (those of) the other (party). 25 This is decline. 26 Perceiving 'I shall decline after a longer time or to a lesser extent or in such a way that I shall make a greater advancement, the enemy (will decline) in the reverse manner,' he should remain indifferent to his decline. 27. In case the decline lasts for the same period or leads to equal results (for both), he should make peace.

28 The policy, following which he were to see neither the advancement nor the decline of his own undertakings, constitutes stable condition. 29 Perceiving 'I shall remain stable for a shorter period or in such a way that I shall make a greater advancement, the enemy (will do so) in the opposite way,' he should remain indifferent to his stable condition. 30 'In case the stable condition lasts for the same period or leads to equal consequences (for both), he should make peace,' say the teachers. 31 This is not disputed, says Kauṭilya.

18 *sahāyasādhye kārye* : the help sought is from one who is ordinarily the *vijigīṣu's* enemy ; but his help is necessary for getting the better of another enemy ; hence the treaty with the former and war with the latter. Cf. 7.7.1-2 below.

20 *durgasetu-* etc. : Meyer thinks that agriculture is missing here from the usual list of the eight-fold *karma*. He would therefore read *karṣa* for *karma* or add *kṛṣi* after *setukarma*. Despite Manu, 7.154, however, that is unacceptable, because *karma*, as fully described in 7.12, does not include *kṛṣi*. 22 *vṛddhyudayatarā* (adjective to *vṛddhiḥ*) 'which brings about a greater advancement (for the *vijigīṣu*) in the future.' For *vṛddhyudaya*, see 9.4.20. 23 *tulyakālaphalodayāyāṁ vā* : it seems that *vā* shows the option between *tulyakālā* and *tulyaphalodayā* in the compound. A single idea 'which requires the same time for the appearance of the result' (as in Meyer) does not seem meant in view of *āśutarā* and *bhūyastarā* used separately above.

26 *vṛddhyudayataram* is adverbial.

31 *vibhāṣitam* : Cb Cs have '*viśeṣeṇa bhāṣitam*', i.e., stated with a special distinction. K. Nag (*op.cit.*, p. 78) has 'unreasonable.' Meyer has 'option, alternative' as in grammar, the idea being, *sthānam upekṣeta* and *saṁdhim upeyāt* come practically to the same thing. *vibhāṣita* may also mean 'contradicted, disputed.'

32 Or, if he were to see, 'Remaining at peace, I shall ruin the enemy's undertakings by my own undertakings bearing abundant fruits; or, I shall enjoy my own undertakings bearing abundant fruits or the undertakings of the enemy; or, by creating confidence by means of the peace, I shall ruin the enemy's undertakings by the employment of secret remedies and occult practices; or, I shall easily entice away the persons capable of carrying out the enemy's undertakings by (offering) a greater remuneration from my own undertakings, with facilities of favours and exemptions; or, the enemy, in alliance with an extremely strong king, will suffer the ruin of his own undertakings; or, I shall keep prolonged his war with the king, being at war with whom he is making peace with me; or, he will harass the country of the king, who is in alliance with me (but is) hostile to me; or, his country, laid waste by his enemy, will come to me, so that I shall achieve advancement in my undertakings; or, the enemy, with his undertakings ruined (and himself) placed in a difficult situation, would not attack my undertakings; or, with my undertakings started elsewhere, I shall achieve advancement in my undertakings, being in alliance with both; or, by making peace with the enemy I shall divide from him the circle (of kings) which is attached to the enemy, (and) when divided, I shall secure it (for myself); or, by giving support to the enemy by favouring him with troops when he seeks to seize the circle, I shall create hostility towards him, (and) when he faces hostility I shall get him destroyed by that same (circle),' he should secure advancement through peace.

33 Or, if he were to see, 'My country, consisting mostly of martial people or fighting bands, or secure in the protection of a single entrance through a mountain-fort, a forest-fort or a river-fort, will be able to repulse the enemy's attack; or, taking shelter in an impregnable fort on the border of my territory, I shall be able to ruin the enemy's undertakings; or, the enemy,

32 *yogopaniṣatpraṇidhibhiḥ*: Meyer understands *praṇidhi* in the sense of 'a spy' (so Nag, p. 79). But the word by itself does not convey that sense. It is to be construed with *yoga* and *upaniṣad* in the sense of 'employment, use.' — *-saukaryam* is adverbial. Cs treats it as an adjective to *-janam*. Meyer proposes to join this expression to the following compound *phalalābha-* etc. — *balinā, timātreṇa*: Cs has 'with a very rich king, by offering him excessive tribute (*atimātreṇa*).' But *atimātreṇa* seems to be adverbial, going with *balinā* (or *balavatā*, the other v. l.). — *parataḥ pravṛttakarmārambho vā*: this describes the *vijigīṣu*, who wants to start some undertaking away from the enemy's territory, but near the territory of some other king. *tābhyāṁ saṁhitaḥ* has reference to peace with the enemy and this other king (near whose territory the *vijigīṣu* is active). Meyer construes *parataḥ pravṛtta-* etc. with the preceding (*karmasu na me vikrameta*) and translates *tābhyām* by 'in either eventuality.' This is far from happy. Nag (*op. cit.*, p. 80) has 'with the two adversaries of my enemy'; but it is difficult to see who these two adversaries of the enemy could be. — *daṇḍānugraheṇa* cannot mean 'by favours or punishment' (Nag., *op. cit.*, p. 80). This is lending of troops to the enemy so as to encourage him to fight the *maṇḍala* to his own ultimate ruin. — *lipsā* 'desire to seize, dominate or control.'

33 The difference between *āyudhīya* and *śreṇī* seems to be that the former do not form a close-knit group or band like the latter. — *śailavana-* etc.: the fort itself constitutes the one entrance into the country (*eka-dvāra*). — *apavāhayitum*: cf. 2.1.1; 8.2.8 etc. It can hardly mean 'to attack' (Cs).

with his energy sapped by the troubles caused by a calamaity, has reached a time when his undertakings face ruin ; or, when he is fighting elsewhere, I shall be able to carry off his country,' he should secure advancement by resorting to war.

34 Or, if he were to think, 'The enemy is not able to ruin my undertakings nor am I able to ruin his undertakings ; or, (when) he is in a calamity, or (engaged) as in a conflict between a hound and a boar, I shall advance (myself), being intent on carrying out my own undertakings,' he should secure advancement by staying quiet.

35 Or, if he were to think, 'The ruin of the enemy's undertakings can be brought about by marching, and I have taken steps to secure the protection of my own undertakings,' he should secure advancement by marching.

36 Or, if he were to think, 'I am not able to ruin the enemy's undertakings nor to avert the ruin of my own undertakings,' he should seek shelter with a strong king and by carrying out his own undertakings, should seek to progress from decline to stable condition and from stable condition to advancement.

37 Or, if he were to think, 'I shall promote my own undertakings by peace on one side and ruin the enemy's undertakings by war on the other side,' he should secure advancement through a dual policy.

38 Situated in the circle of constituent elements, he should, in this manner, with these six measures of policy, seek to progress from decline to stable condition and from stable condition to advancement in his own undertakings.

34 *vyasanam asya* and *kalahe* are the two occasions when the *vijigīṣu* can carry out his own works and augment his own power. The *kalaha* is between his enemy and some other king ; it is a life and death struggle, but whatever its outcome, the *vijigīṣu* stands to benefit. Cf. 9.2.6. The *kalaha* is not between the *vijigīṣu* and the enemy (as in Cs). How can the *vijigīṣu* carry out his works if he is engaged in a life and death struggle ? Meyer proposes to read *kalaho* 'a calamity which I cause to him (*vyasanam asya*) is like a hound and boar fight.' But if the *vijigīṣu* were to be active in causing such a calamity, that would not be in consonance with the advice to stay quiet. — *vā* (after *-nuṣṭhānaparo*) shows the option to the situation in *na me śaktaḥ paraḥ* etc.

36 *balavantam* : some mss. show the faulty *balavattam* ; Meyer therefore thinks that *balavattaram* is more likely. *balavantam*, however, seems all right.

37 *ekataḥ . . . ekataḥ*, i.e., with one enemy and with another. This is not duplicity or double-dealing with the same king.

CHAPTER TWO

SECTION 100 CONDUCT WHEN SEEKING SHELTER

1 If there is equal advancement in peace or war, he should resort to peace. 2 For, in war there are losses, expenses, marches away from home and hindrances. 3 By that is explained (preference for) staying quiet, as between staying quiet and marching.

4 As between dual policy and seeking shelter, he should resort to dual policy. 5 For, he who resorts to the dual policy, giving prominence to his own undertakings, serves only his own interests, while he who takes shelter (with another) serves the interests of the other, not his own.

6 He should seek shelter with one whose strength is superior to the strength of the neighbouring (enemy). 7 In the absence of one superior in strength to him, he should seek shelter with the (enemy) himself and, remaining out of sight, should try to serve him with any one of the (three): treasury, army and territory. 8 For, union with one superior in strength is a great danger to kings, except when he is at war with an enemy.

9 If this be impossible, he should behave like one submitting with troops. 10 And when he sees that the enmy is afflicted by a fatal disease or is facing an internal revolt or a growth in power of his enemy or a calamity of his ally and (sees) thereby his own advancement, he should go away under a plausible pretext of illness or the performance of a religious duty. 11 Or, if he is in his own territory, he should not go to him. 12 Or, if near him, he should strike in his weak points.

13 Or, if situated between two stronger kings, he should seek shelter with one capable of protecting him, or with one whose intervening weak neighbour he may be, or with both. 14 He should resort to the potsherd-treaty,

7.2

The 100th Section really begins at s. 6. The earlier ss. dealing with relative superiority among the six measures form a sort of an introduction.

2 *-pratyavāyāḥ*: Meyer regards *kṣaya, vyaya* and *pravāsa* as three 'hindrances.' *pratyavāya* may, however, be understood independently of the three. — Cf. 7.8.2.

6 *sāmantaḥ* is the neighbouring enemy, whose growing power makes the *vijigīṣu* seek shelter. 7 *adṛṣṭaḥ*, i.e., himself remaining away from the enemy, not surrendering his person. 8 *anyatra arivigṛhītāt*: the idea seems to be that when the strong king is at war with some one else, he would remain grateful for the support given by the weak king and not treat him with contempt or in a high-handed manner.

9 *aśakye* is from Cb Cs for *aśakyo*. For the latter, *aśakto* is conceivable, but *aśakye* is better. The idea is 'when the strong neighbour cannot be made to accept *daṇḍa* etc. without the surrender of his person.' Meyer translates 'towards an enemy who cannot be so managed'; but a locative absolute might appear better. — *daṇḍopanatavat*, i.e., as in 7.15.21 ff. 12 *chidreṣu* can hardly mean 'by means of secret coups' (Nag, *op. cit.*, p. 82).

13 *antardhiḥ*: 7.13.25 defines this king; he serves as a buffer to a powerful king, who would consequently refrain from totally exterminating him. Cb Cs read *anantardhiḥ* and explain 'who may be next to him, not separated from him.' That does not seem very likely. 14 *kapālasaṁśrayaḥ*: this appears to be a reference to the *kapālasaṁdhi* of 7.3.30,

declaring one (to the other) as plotting to seize his patrimony. 15 Or, he should employ dissension between the two by falsely implicating one against the other, and (use) silent punishment when they are in discord.

16 Or, if situated at the side of two strong kings, he should take steps against immediate danger. 17 Or, taking shelter in a fort, he should resort to the dual policy. 18 Or, he should act on motives for resorting to peace or war. 19 He should give support to the treasonable officers, the enemies and forest chiefs of both. 20 Going over to one of these two, he should strike in the other's calamity with these same (treasonable officers, etc.).

21 Or, if pressed by both, he should resort to the circle (of kings) for shelter, or find shelter with the middle or the neutral king. 22 Together with him, he should support one and exterminate the other, or (exterminate) both.

23 Or, if exterminated by both, he should find shelter with the justly behaved from among the middle king, the neutral king or kings belonging to their parties. 24 From among those equally just, (he should resort to that king) whose constituents would give him happiness or by staying with whom he would be able to raise himself or where his ancestors may have been accustomed to go or he may have close connections (or) where there may be many or very powerful friends.

> 25 He to whom he may be dear or he who may be dear to him, which one among these two (should he approach for shelter)? He should go to him to whom he may be dear. This is the best course for seeking shelter.

in which the weak king is advised to avoid meeting the exorbitant demands made on him under the pretext that his undertakings are ruined. The expression can also mean ' resorting to the begging bowl, ' in which case *ubhau vā* may be included in this s. from the last, as Cb seems to do. — *mūla-* refers to the base, i.e., the kingdom, also the capital. — *apadiśan* involves the idea of a false declaration. 15 *-apadeśa* again implies a false implication.

16 *pārśvasthaḥ*, as contrasted with *madhyagataḥ* of s. 13. 17 *dvaidhībhūtaḥ*, i.e., making peace with one and fighting with the other. 18 *saṁdhivigrahakramahetubhiḥ*: the reference is to 7.1.32,33. *krama* serves little purpose; it seems to stand for *ātiṣṭhet* of that passage. Cb comment presupposes *saṁdhivikramahetubhiḥ* and that was obviously the original reading. 20 *gacchan* ' going to ', i.e., joining hands with. It can hardly mean ' engaging in fight ' (Cs); *anyataram* and *anyatarasya* do not refer to the same king, but to the two powerful kings, like *itaram* and *itarasya* in s. 14. Meyer's proposed *yacchan* (for *gacchan*) in the sense of ' restraining ' is not very likely.

21 *upahataḥ* is as proposed by Meyer for *upahitaḥ*. The latter can hardly mean ' pressed, harassed ', which is the sense required.

23 *tatpakṣīyāṇām*: *tat* refers to the *madhyama* and *udāsīna*. 24 *bhūyāṁsyatiśaktimanti* is as proposed by Meyer for *bhūyāṁsīti śaktimanti*; the *iti* in the latter is little likely. Perhaps we should read only *bhūyāṁsi śaktimanti*.

25 We have to supply *āśrayaṇīyaḥ* at the end of the first half. The question is, when a choice for purposes of *saṁśraya* is available between *yasya asau priyaḥ* and *yaḥ asya priyaḥ*, whom should he prefer? The answer given is, he should go to the former.

CHAPTER THREE

SECTION 101 ADHERENCE TO POLICIES BY THE EQUAL, THE WEAKER AND THE STRONGER (KINGS)

SECTION 102 PEACE-TREATIES BY THE WEAKER KING

1 The conqueror should employ the six measures of policy with due regard to his power. 2 He should make peace with the equal and the stronger; he should make war with the weaker. 3 For, going to war with the stronger, he engages as it were in a fight on foot with an elephant. 4 And (at war) with the equal, he brings about loss on both sides, like an unbaked jar struck by an unbaked jar. 5 (At war) with the weaker, he attains absolute success, like a stone with an earthen vessel.

6 If the stronger were not to desire peace, he should resort to the conduct of one submitting with troops or measures recommended for the weaker king.

7 If the equal were not to desire peace, he should do harm to him in return to the extent that he may have done to him. 8 For, heat is the means of joining together. 9 Metal that is not heated does not become joined with metal.

10 If the weaker were to remain submissive in all respects, he should make peace with him. 11 For, heroism born of grief and resentment makes one fight bravely like a forest fire. 12 And he becomes the object of favour of the circle (of kings).

13 If, when at peace, he were to see, 'The enemy's subjects, who are greedy or impoverished or rebellious, do not come over (to me) through fear of being seized again (by the enemy),' even the weaker should make war.

14 If, when at war, he were to see, 'The enemy's subjects, greedy, impoverished or rebellious, do not come over, being frightened of war,' even the stronger should make peace, or should allay the fear of war.

7.3

The two Sections are found in ss. 1-20 and 21-36 respectively; the latter is entirely in verse.

2 *saṁdhīyeta* : the passive is without significance. 5 *ekāntasiddhim* : Meyer justifies the reading *ekāntaḥ siddhim* ('the exclusive king, i.e., alone, single-handed, attains success') on the ground that the text recommends war only as a last resort. But apart from the very unlikely rendering of *ekāntaḥ*, the war with *hīna* is actually recommended in s. 2 and this s. merely explains why it should be undertaken.

6 *daṇḍopanatavṛttam* as in 7.15.21 ff. — *ābalīyasaṁ yogam* as in Book 12.

13 *apacaritāḥ* is the only correct reading as shown by 7.5.12-15 and s. 14 below. It means 'disaffected, rebellious.' *prakṛti* refers to the subjects, particularly to principal officers and men. — *pratyādānabhayāt* : the idea is that these would-be seceders from the strong king's side do not go over to the weak king when there is peace between them, for they are afraid that the strong king would easily capture and punish them ; in war, however, their going over would strengthen the weak king in his fight with their former master. The *vā* after this word has little significance ; a *mām* or *mā* should be understood after it, as in the next s.

14 *vigrahodvignā vā* : here, too, *vā* serves little purpose.

15 Even in case of simultaneity of calamities, if he were to see, 'I am in a greater calamity; the enemy, in a lighter calamity, will easily overcome his own calamity and attack (me),' even the stronger should make peace.

16 If by resorting to peace or war, he were not to see the weakening of the enemy or increase in his own strength, then even the stronger should stay quite.

17 If he were to see the enemy's calamity to be irremediable, then even the weaker should march against him.

18 Even the stronger, whose immediate calamity is irremediable, should seek shelter.

19 If he were to see success in his work by peace in one place and war in another, then even the stronger should resort to the dual policy.

20 Similar is the use of six measures by the equal.

21 With regard to that, however, the special points are:

22 A weak king, over-run by a strong king who has set his armies in motion, should quickly submit, seeking peace with (the offer of) his treasury, army, himself or territory.

23 That he himself has to wait upon (the enemy) with a stipulated number of troops or according to the strength of the army, this treaty is known as 'one with himself as prey.'

24 That the commander-in-chief or the (crown) prince has to wait upon (the enemy), this would be 'the treaty through another person,' not through himself, hence one in which he himself is saved.

15 *pratikṛtya vyasanam* from Cb Cs is quite obviously necessary for *prakṛtyavyasanam* of the mss.

18 *apratikāryāsannavyasano vā*: Because of *vā* we may understand two kinds of calamities, *apratikārya* and *āsanna*, in the compound; or, we may understand the *āsanna-vyasana* to be *apratikārya*. The latter appears better, *vā* being then understood as being without much significance. It cannot indicate an option to the last s., as the two ss. refer to two different kings.

20 *samasya*: this can hardly mean '*sarvasya*' (Cs) in view of *sama-* in the title of the Section. Meyer's 'taking together' (gerund from *sam-as*) or 'briefly' (Russ.) is also unlikely. With *evam* understood as 'in this same manner' there need be no difficulty.

21 *tatra* has reference to *ṣāḍguṇyopayoga* and has nothing to do with *sama*. — *prati-viśeṣaḥ*: the special case is that of the weak king forced to surrender to the strong king.

22 *-daṇḍātma-*: *ātmopanatasaṁdhi* is not separately treated in the sequel; it is included in the *daṇḍopanatasaṁdhi*.

23 *daṇḍasya vibhavena* 'in accordance with the strength of the army' implies that a large part of the army is to be surrendered. The expression can hardly mean 'with the entirety of his army' (Meyer). — *upasthātavyam* implies that the king is to surrender in person. Hence the name *ātmāmiṣa* 'with himself as the prey or victim.'

24 *puruṣāntarasaṁdhiḥ*: this treaty seems also called *puruṣasaṁdhi*: cf. 12.1.26. Cb seems to regard *ātmarakṣaṇa* as the name of the treaty.

25 Either himself or the army has to go elsewhere alone; this treaty is 'with persons unseen', in which the army chiefs and he himself are saved.

26 In the first two (treaties), he should bring about a marriage alliance of the chiefs; in the last, however, he should secretly get rid of the enemy. These are treaties with troops submitted.

27-28 The release of the rest of the constituents by handling over the treasury would become the treaty 'purchase.' And the same, when it is to be delivered in parts many times, at one's convenience, should be known as the treaty 'support'; the tribute restricted as to time and place, would be support.

29 Tolerable because of payment of a bearable amount in future, even because of a marriage alliance, it would be the 'golden treaty', bringing about union through (mutual) confidence.

30 The reverse would be the 'potsherd' (treaty), so called because of excessive payments received. In the first two (treaties), he should deliver forest produce, or elephants and horses that are poisoned.

25 *ekena*, i.e., either the king alone or the army alone. — *anyatra*, i.e., not where the enemy is stationed or operating, but elsewhere, though that is to serve the enemy's interest. — *svayaṁ daṇḍena vā*: in the former case, the king in person goes with a small army; in the latter case, the army is sent under the *senāpati* or the *kumāra*. — *adṛṣṭapuruṣaḥ*, so called because the king in one case and the *senāpati* etc. in the other are not within sight of the enemy, as they operate elsewhere independently. For *adṛṣṭa*, cf. 7.2.7. Cb seems to look upon *daṇḍamukhyātmarakṣaṇa* as the name of the treaty.

26 ***mukhyastrībandhanam***: the *mukhya* would appear to be the *senāpati* and *kumāra* of s. 24, hardly the king himself; *strībandhana* is obviously a marriage alliance with the strong king. — *sādhayed gūḍham* implies assassination. — *daṇḍopanata*: in view of *kośopanata* and *deśopanata* that follow, this means 'in which the army is surrendered,' though the idea of 'subdued by force' is sometimes to be understood by this expression.

27 ***sa eva ca yathāsukham***: this is to be construed with ***skandhopaneyaḥ*** in s. 28. Meyer understands these words of the *parikraya saṁdhi*, 'it can be entered into when it appears good to him.' This is hardly likely. 28 ***skandhopaneyo***: this may mean 'to be carried on the shoulder.' It seems, however, that *skandha* as 'branch' has reference to parts or instalments in which the tribute is to be paid; thus Cb. — ***atyayaḥ syād upagrahaḥ***: Cs regards *atyaya* as the name of another *saṁdhi*. However, there are only four *kośopanata saṁdhis* (s. 31). Meyer understands two types of *upagraha*, viz., *skandhopaneya* and *atyaya*. It seems, however, that the second half only explains the term *skandhopaneya*, the instalments being fixed as to place and time. *atyaya* 'penalty' has here the sense of 'tribute.' — *upagraha* conveys the idea of instalments serving as 'a support' or 'help' to the weak king. Cb looks upon *upagraha* and *atyaya* as two varieties of *parikraya*, referred to by *pūrvayoḥ* in s. 30. Russ. renders the second half: 'concluding such a treaty where the place and time are not suitable is a mistake (*atyayaḥ*).' This seems hardly possible.

29 ***āyatyām*** 'in future' to be construed with *viṣahyadānāt* (Meyer) rather than with *kṣamaḥ* (Cs).

30 ***viparītaḥ*** implies not only *atyādāna*, but also immediate payment (as opposed to *āyatyām*). — ***kapālaḥ*** evidently has reference to the king being beggared by the payment. — ***atyādānābhibhāṣitaḥ***: Cb Cs read *-dabhāṣitaḥ* 'not recommended in the *śāstra* because of excessive levies.' This is unlikely, as the treaty is actually mentioned, and s. 36, which is a summing up, makes no exceptions. Russ. renders the former reading by 'dictated with extreme demands for payment.' — ***vā garānvitam*** from Cb Cs is supported by 12.1.25.

31 In the third, he should pay the amount; in the fourth, he should tarry telling him of the decline of undertakings. These are treaties with treasury submitted.

32 The saving of the rest of the constituents by the surrender of a part of his territory is the 'directed' treaty, desirable in the case where one wishes to injure through secret agents and robbers.

33 The surrender of lands from which all riches have been removed, with the exception of his base, is the 'exterminated' treaty, desirable in the case where one hopes for a calamity for the enemy.

34 The saving of lands by the surrender of the produce is the 'hire' treaty; that with the produce completely surrendered from lands is the 'ruinous' treaty.

35 He should resort to waiting in the first two, in the last two, however, to 'practices of the weaker king', taking the produce (himself). These are treaties with territory surrendered.

36 These three types of treaties by the weaker king recommended for use at the proper place and time in accordance with one's own undertakings, should be entered into as 'practices of the weaker king.'

31 *artham*: Cb Cs have *ardham* in the sense of 'some part'. But since the payments in this treaty are reasonable, and the relations are cordial, *artha* as the whole amount appears preferable. — *kathayan* etc. is to be construed with *tiṣṭhet caturthe* as in Meyer, and not with the preceding.

32 *gūḍhastenopaghātinaḥ*: Meyer's 'who would secretly destroy robbers' is little likely. As the idea is to harm the enemy to whom the land is ceded, *gūḍha*, i.e., *gūḍha puruṣa* and *stena* would appear to be the means of doing so.

33 *mūla-* the 'base' is the weak king's capital. — *ucchinna* may have reference to the lands being deprived of riches.

34 *phalātimukto bhūmibhyaḥ*: this seems to mean 'in which the produce is completely given away from the lands.' Cb Cs read *phalātibhukto* and explain 'in which more than the actual produce of the lands is promised'; this is not convincing. Meyer translates, with that reading, 'bound up with an over-feeding on the produce'; but the enjoyment of more than what the lands produce would appear to be a doubtful idea. The former reading seems better. Meyer does not find a new *saṁdhi* in the second half, only a further description of *avakraya*. But s. 35 implies four *deśopanata saṁdhis*. — *paridūṣaṇah* is as proposed by Meyer for *paradūṣaṇah*. The reading is found in Cb. The names of the treaties have the weak king's standpoint in view or mention their effect on him and do not refer to the enemy directly.

35 *pūrvau paścimau*: the accusatives are strange, when locatives are expected. Perhaps *pūrve paścime* is to be read, as referring to the *avakraya* and the *paridūṣaṇa* only; in the case of *ādiṣṭa* and *ucchinna*, the steps to be taken are already stated in *gūḍhasteno-* and *paravyasana-* etc. respectively. — *ādāya* can hardly be 'presenting it to the enemy' (Cs). *ādāya phalam* is to be construed with the preceding and not with *deśopantasaṁdhayaḥ*, as Meyer does, 'these are *deśopanata* treaties in which the produce is carried away.'

36 *ābalīyasikāḥ* 'associated with *ābalīyasa*, the practices of the weak king' as in Book 12.

CHAPTER FOUR

SECTION 103 STAYING QUIET AFTER MAKING WAR
SECTION 104 STAYING QUIET AFTER MAKING PEACE
SECTION 105 MARCHING AFTER MAKING WAR
SECTION 106 MARCHING AFTER MAKING PEACE
SECTION 107 MARCHING TOGETHER (WITH OTHER KINGS)

1 Staying quiet and marching in peace and war are (now) explained.

2 Remaining still, staying quiet and remaining indifferent are synonyms of staying quiet. 3 The distinction, however, is: when there is (only) a part of the excellences present, it is remaining still; staying quiet is for attaining one's own advancement; non-employment of the means is remaining indifferent.

4 When the enemy and the conqueror, desirous of over-reaching each other, are unable to injure each other, staying quiet after making war or after making peace (is recommended).

5 Or, when he were to see, 'With my own troops or the ally's troops or forest troops, I can weaken the equal or stronger king,' then he should make war and stay quiet after taking precautions in the outer regions and in the interior.

6 Or, when he were to see, 'My constituents, full of energy, united and thriving, will carry out their works unhindered or will destroy the works of the enemy,' then he should make war and stay quiet.

7 Or, when he were to see, 'The enemy's subjects, rebellious, impoverished, greedy, or harassed by (the enemy's) own troops, robbers or foresters, will come to me of their own accord or through instigations; sources

7.4

The five short Sections are to be found in ss. 1-12, 13, 1-17, 18 and 19-22 respectively.

1 *vyākhyātam*: the sense required is that of *vyākhyātavyam*; for the policies stated are being explained in this Chapter.

3 *guṇaikadeśe*: *guṇa* clearly means the 'excellence' of the constituents, as in 6.1.15 and 7.1.16. It can hardly mean 'the policy of *āsana*' (Cb Cs); nor can the expression mean 'remaining in one particular kind of political behaviour' (Meyer). The idea is when one is weaker, *sthāna* is recommended. In *āsana*, one is equal.

4 *atisaṁdhānakāmayoḥ* is as proposed by Meyer for *iti* (end of s. 3) *saṁdhānakāmayoḥ*. The actual comment in Cb presupposes the emended reading. The conqueror and the enemy cannot be described as *saṁdhānakāma*, when *vigṛhya āsana* is also recommended, nor does it fit in with *upahantum aśaktayoḥ*. The corruption is easily explained.

5 *kṛtabāhyābhyantarakṛtyaḥ*: Cb Cs understand *kṛtya* as likely seceders as in 1.13 and 14. But *kṛta* would be unusual with it; *upagṛhīta* would have been used in that case.

6 *svakarmāṇi*: M has *svakarmaṇi*; but if the locative were intended, we should expect *svakarmasu*

7 *netaram*: the *itara* is the enemy, though we should expect *para*. Perhaps we should read *netarathā*. — *mitraṁ mitrabhāvi* is defined in 7.9.43. — *bahvalpakālam*: Meyer has 'in a longer or shorter time'; it seems, however, that *bahu* goes with *artham*, though we

of livelihood in my state are flourishing, those of the enemy ruined, (hence) his subjects stricken by famine will come to me ; sources of livelihood in my state are ruined, those of the enemy flourishing, my subjects will not go over to him (only if there is war), and after making war I shall plunder his grains, cattle and cash ; or, I shall keep out the enemy's goods that are harmful to my own goods, or highly valuable goods will come to me from the enemy's trade-route, when he is at war, (and) will not go to the other ; or, when at war, he will not suppress his traitors, enemies or forest-tribes, or will be involved in war with these same ; marching against my ally having the nature of a true ally, he will obtain abundant wealth in a short time, with small losses and expenses or excellent land which can be easily seized ; or, wishing to march with all troops mobilised in disregard of me, he must not somehow be allowed to march,' then in order to hinder the advancement of the enemy and to affirm his valour, he should make war and stay quiet. 8 'Turning back, he might swallow him up,' say the teachers. 9 'No,' says Kauṭilya. 10 He would only cause a weakening of the (conqueror, if he is) not in a calamity, but when augmented by the (acquisition of the) enemy's prosperity, (he would cause) extermination. 11 (If he acts) thus, the vulnerable foe of the enemy would render help to him, being not destroyed. 12 Therefore, he should make war on one acting with all troops mobilised, and stay quiet.

13 In cases the reverse of the motives for staying quiet after making war, he should make peace and stay quiet.

14 When grown in power on the occasions for staying quiet after making war, he should make war and march, except when the enemy has mobilised all his troops.

15 Or, when he were to see, 'The enemy is in a calamity ; or, a calamity of his constituent cannot be remedied by the remaining constituents ; or, his subjects, harassed by his own army, or disaffected with him, are easy to entice, being weakened, without energy or divided among themselves ; the

expect *bahum* in that case. — *guṇavatīm ādeyāṁ vā* : *vā* shows the option to *artham*, not an option between *guṇavatīm* and *ādeyām*. For *ādeya*, see 9.4.5. — *kathaṁ na yāyāt* is rather awkward as put in the *vijigīṣu's* thoughts. Either *kathaṁ yāyāt* or *na yāyāt* would have been better. — *pratāpārtham* is more applicable to the last case than to the others. 8 *tameva* etc. : the discussion has reference to the last case (*sarvasaṁdohena* etc.) only. — *grasate* : we expect *graseta*. Possibly that was the original reading. 10 *paravṛddhyā* : the *para* is the enemy of the *vijigīṣu's* enemy against whom the latter proposes to march with all troops. Meyer translates the s. thus, 'the conqueror should cause only the weakening of the enemy, if he is not in a calamity ; if strengthened by complete prosperity (with the reading *parivṛddhyā*) he should exterminate him.' This is quite unlikely. It constitutes no reply to the teachers. 11 *evam*, i.e., when the *vijigīṣu* has declared war. — *parasya yātavyaḥ* is the enemy of the *vijigīṣu*'s enemy.

13 According to Cb, in *vigṛhyāsana* the enemy's undertakings are to be destroyed and one's own furthered ; in *saṁdhāyāsana* only one's own undertakings are to be furthered.

14 *sarvasaṁdohavarjam* : this is the last case of s. 7 ; in that case, there is to be no marching, only staying quiet.

enemy has his draught-animals, men, stores and fortifications reduced in consequence of fire, floods, disease, epidemic or famine,' then he should make war and march.

16 Or, when he were to see, 'My ally in front and my rear ally have brave, prosperous and devoted subjects, the enemy, the rear enemy and the rear enemy's ally have subjects the reverse of this, I shall (therefore) be able to march after engaging the enemy's ally in a fight with my ally or my rear enemy in a fight with my rear ally,' then he should make war and march.

17 Or, when he were to see that the fruit can be attained by a single person within a short time, then he should make war on the rear enemy and his ally and march.

18 In the reverse cases, he should make peace and march.

19 Or, when he were to see, 'It is not possible to march alone, but it is necessary to march,' then joining forces with confederates, equal, weaker or stronger (than himself), he should march, for a stipulated share if in one place, for an unstipulated share if in more than one place. 20 In case there is no confederacy with them, he should request for troops from one of them in return for a fixed share. 21 Or, (the troops) should be hired by (a promise of) marching together (with them), with a fixed share when the gain is certain, with a portion of the gain when it is uncertain.

22 A share in conformity with troops is of the first type, in conformity with efforts is best; or plunder, as obtained (by each), (should be the share), or a share in conformity with the amount lent.

16 *pārṣṇigrāhaḥ* etc.: for these kings, see 6.2.18 above. — *mitreṇa āsāram*: the *āsāra* is the enemy's *āsāra* or helpmate; from the *vijigīṣu*'s stand-point he is the *arimitra*, with territory beyong that of the *mitra*. Even from the enemy's stand-point, he is really his *ākranda*, not *āsāra*. But the latter is a general term for an ally.

17 *ekahāryam*, i.e., obtainable without the help of the *mitra* or *ākranda*. — *pārṣṇigrāhāsārābhyāṁ vigṛhya*: the reason for not taking the help of allies appears to be to avoid any sharing of the spoils of the expedition.

18 *saṁdhāya yāyāt*: this is downright duplicity, making peace and then attacking the enemy when he is least expecting such an attack.

19 *ekatra* seems to refer to an expedition for a single specific objective, while *anekatra* refers to more than one objective requiring fighting in many places. 20 *niviṣṭa* 'laid down, fixed.' 21 *saṁbhūyābhigamanena vā nirviśyeta*: the subject is *daṇḍaḥ*. The idea in *saṁbhūyābhigamana* seems to be that when hiring the troops the *vijigīṣu* agrees to march with them along with his own troops and not to send them alone on the expedition. Cs understands a promise to march in future with the other king when the latter wants his troops. With the reading *nirdiśyeta* Meyer translates 'a share should be fixed as the price for the joint expedition.' The reading itself is doubtful. The difference between ss. 19 and 21 is that in the former there is no hiring, but a confederacy of kings who join forces and receive agreed shares.

22 *pūrvaḥ* seems to convey the idea of lowest. — *prakṣepa* 'investment' is the *kośa* or money lent for the expedition. Though the text does not make it clear, it is possible that the second half mentions the *madhyama* kind of *aṁśa*.

CHAPTER FIVE

SECTION 108 CONSIDERATIONS REGARDING AN ATTACK ON A VULNERABLE KING AND THE (NATURAL) ENEMY

SECTION 109 CAUSES LEADING TO DECLINE, GREED AND DISAFFECTION AMONG THE SUBJECTS

SECTION 110 REFLECTION ON CONFEDERATED ALLIES

1 In case the calamities of two neighbouring princes are alike, (should one march) against the vulnerable king or the enemy? — in such a case, he should march against the enemy; after subduing him, against the vulnerable king. 2 For, the vulnerable king might give him help in subduing the enemy, not the enemy in subduing the vulnerable king.

3 (Should one march) against a vulnerable king in a serious calamity or the enemy in a light calamity? 'He should march against the one in a serious calamity, because of ease (in subjugating),' say the teachers. 4 'No,' says Kauṭilya. 5 He should march against the enemy with a light calamity. 6 Even a light calamity becomes dangerous to him when attacked. 7 True, even a serious (calamity) becomes more serious (in that case). 8 But the enemy with a light calamity, if not attacked, might easily overcome his calamity and go to the rescue of the vulnerable king, or might attack in the rear.

9 In case there are many vulnerable kings at the same time, (when the choice is) between one in a serious calamity but justly behaved and one in a light calamity but unjustly behaved or with disaffected subjects, he should march against the one with disaffected subjects. 10 The subjects help the king who is justly behaved but suffering from a serious calamity, when he is attacked; remain indifferent to one unjustly behaved, suffering from a light calamity; but if disaffected, exterminate even a strong king. 11 Therefore, he should march only against one with disaffected subjects.

12 (When the choice is) between one with impoverished and greedy subjects and one with rebellious subjects, 'He should march against the one with impoverished and greedy subjects; for, impoverished and greedy subjects easily yield themselves to instigations or harassment, not the rebellious who can be overcome by the suppression of their leaders,' say the teachers. 13 'No,' says Kauṭilya. 14 For, impoverished and greedy subjects, when

7.5 The three Sections are to be found in ss. 1-18, 19-37 and 38-39 respectively.

1 *yātavya* is a neighbouring prince who is in a calamity; cf. 6.2.16. 2 *amitrasiddhau* is not to be understood as a locative absolute, but as meaning 'in the conquering of the enemy.'

8 *vā* after *pārṣṇim* is quite necessary as in Cs.

9 There are three alternatives, the third *viraktaprakṛti* apparently not suffering from any calamity. 11 As between the *guruvyasana nyāyavṛtti* and *laghuvyasana anyāyavṛtti*, s. 10 suggests that the latter should be preferred for an attack.

12 *apacarita* is stronger than *virakta*; the subjects are not only disaffected but also rebellious. — *pīḍām upagacchanti*, i.e., they can be easily harassed. 14 *anurāge sārvaguṇyam* is apparently a maxim quoted in support of the statements made. Cf. 8.2.24 below.

devoted to their master, remain steadfast in what is beneficial to the master or make the instigations futile, on the principle, 'Where there is love, all qualities (are present).' 15 Hence he should march only against one with rebellious subjects.

16 (When the choice is) between a strong king unjustly behaved and a weak king justly behaved, he should march against the strong king unjustly behaved. 17 The subjects do not help the strong unjust king when he is attacked, they drive him out or resort to his enemy. 18 But the subjects support in every way the weak but just king when he is attacked or follow him if he has to flee.

19-26 For, by discarding the good and favouring the wicked, and by starting unrighteous injuries not current before, by discontinuing customary practices that are righteous, by indulgence in impiety and suppression of piety, and by doing acts that ought not to be done and by ruining rightful acts, and by not giving what ought to be given and securing what ought not to be given (to him), and by not punishing those deserving to be punished and punishing those not deserving to be punished, by seizing those who ought not to be seized and not arresting those who ought to be seized, and by doing harmful things and destroying beneficial things, and by failing to protect from thieves and by robbing (them) himself, by ruining human exertions, by spoiling the excellence of works done, by doing harm to principal men and by dishonouring those worthy of honour, and by opposing the elders, by partiality and falsehood, by not requiting what is done and by not carrying out what is settled, through the negligence and indolence of the king and because of the destruction of well-being, — (through these causes) decline, greed and disaffection are produced among the subjects.

27 Subjects, when impoverished, become greedy; when greedy they become disaffected; when disaffected they either go over to the enemy or themselves kill the master.

28 Therefore, he should not allow these causes of decline, greed and disaffection among the subjects to arise, or, if arisen, should immediately counter-act them.

17 *niṣ-pat* 'to flee' is common in this text.

19-26 The causes of impoverishment etc. of subjects seem to have been incorporated in a metrical form since early days; hence the stanzas in the middle of the Chapter. — *hiṁsānām*: this refers to injuries in general, not merely actual killing. 22 *upagrāha*, as the opposite of *anabhigraha*, clearly means 'seizing, arresting', as pointed out by Meyer. Cb has '*agrāhya*, i.e., thieves etc. and *upagrāha*, i.e., favouring them.' 24 *guṇadūṣaṇaiḥ*: *dūṣaṇa* seems to be 'spoiling, ruining', not merely 'censuring.' 25 Cb has *bhṛtyānām vṛddhānām*. — *apratikāra* conveys the idea of failure to requite (what is done by some one for you). — *sthitasya* 'of a settled custom, such as the Śakra-festival' (Cb Cs). *sthita*, however, may mean 'what is agreed upon'; cf. *yathāsthitakārī*, s. 39 below. 26 *ca* should preferably be read for *vā* as in Cb.

29 (Which are worst), subjects that are impoverished or greedy or disaffected? 30 The impoverished, through fear of harassment or extermination, prefer an immediate peace or fight or flight. 31 The greedy, dissatisfied because of greed, willingly respond to the enemy's instigations. 32 The disaffected rise in revolt when there is an enemy attack.

33 Among them, the exhaustion of money and grains is destructive of everything and difficult to remedy, the diminution of draught animals and men can be remedied with money and grains. 34 Greed, restricted to a part, being confined to the principal men, can be directed to spend itself on the enemy's possessions or can be removed. 35 Disaffection can be overcome by suppression of the leaders. 36 For, subjects, without leaders, become easy to rule, not susceptible to instigations by others, become, however, incapable of putting up with troubles. 37 But those divided into many groups by the favouring of the leaders of the subjects, become protected and able to put up with troubles.

38 Even among confederated allies, he should consider the grounds for making peace or war and march after joining forces with those possessed of power and uprightness. 39 For, the powerful king is capable of attacking in the rear or rendering help in the expedition, the upright one carries out what is settled, in success as well as in failure.

40 Among them, as between marching after joining forces with one stronger king or two equals, it is better (to march) with two who are equals. 41 For, with a stronger, he moves over-powered by him; with two equals,

30 *yuddham*: this is preferred apparently to escape harassment by their own king. — *rocayante*: the sense of the causal does not seem intended.

34 *aikadeśiko mukhyāyattaḥ*: the idea is, only a part of the populace is affected by greed; the greed of the *mukhyas* alone has any bearing on state policy. Meyer would read *amukhyāyattaḥ* 'not dependent on the leaders, (but a natural tendency of the average citizen)'; that seems hardly likely. — *ādātum*: this seems to refer to giving satisfaction to the greedy by giving them something. Meyer thinks of taking the greedy in service. 35 *anāpatsahās tu*: Meyer construes these words with the next s. and translates 'those that are unable to bear calamities would become divided because of the seizure (*pragraha*) of leaders of common people, well-protected and able to bear troubles.' This is quite unlikely in view of another *tu* after *pragrahaiḥ* and the meaning assigned to *pragraha*. Cf. also 7.11.19. 37 *bahudhā bhinnā*: each leader with his followers is separately shown favour, so that there is no unity among the disaffected parties. — Meyer thinks that of the three troubles, *kṣaya*, particularly of grains and money, is regarded as the worst, the other two being remediable. According to Cs each later trouble is more serious than the preceding one. That is right so far as danger to the state is concerned.

38 *śaktiśaucayuktaiḥ* is proposed for *-yuktau* of the mss. Cb Cs read *-yuktena*; but the plural seems necessary in view of the many confederates. 39 *pārṣṇigrahaṇe*: the *pārṣṇi* is that of the *vijigīṣu*; by taking him along, a potential threat is averted. *pārṣṇi* of the intended victim of the expedition is possible, but that would be included in *yātrāsāhāyyadāna* and would not have been separately mentioned. Cs has 'in keeping off the enemy in the *vijigīṣu*'s rear,' which is hardly likely. — *-sthita-* is 'what is settled, agreed upon' at the start of the expedition, hardly 'what is just' (Cs) or 'what is right' (Meyer).

41 *atisaṁdhānādhikye vā*: we have to supply *carati*. The *vā* serves little purpose. Meyer, however, proposes *atisaṁdhāna* (=*ne*) *ādhikye vā* 'by over-reaching or by becoming superior.' This does not seem meant, as in the next s. there is no reference to the *vijigīṣu* becoming more powerful. Russ. renders 'over the (two) equals one might gain

with a greater (possibility of) over-reaching. 42 For, they are easy to divide from each other, and if one (of them) becomes treacherous, he is easy to restrain for the two or to seize through dissensions.

43 As between one equal and two weaker kings, it is better (to march) with two weaker kings. 44 For, they carry out two tasks and remain under control.

45 However when the undertaking has succeeded,

he should secretly go away under some pretext from the stronger who has achieved his object, if he is not upright; in the case of the upright, however, he should wait till he is sent away.

46 Or, from a dangerous situation he should move away with effort, after removing his women-folk. For, even from the equal who has achieved his object there might be danger to the trusting one.

47 And even the equal who has achieved his object tends to be stronger, and when augmented in power, untrustworthy; prosperity tends to change the mind.

48 Even if he receives a small share or even no share from a superior, he should go away with a contented face; then striking at him when in his power, he should recover double.

49 But the leader, when he has himself achieved his object, should send away the confederated allies; he should, if need be, forgo (his dues), not score (over them). Thereby he would be liked by the circle (of kings).

superiority and benefit.' Cb Cs construe the expression with what follows 'or, when he gets superiority through resort to subterfuge, the two can be easily divided.' This ignores the *hi* in the next s. 42 *bhedopagraham copagantum* seems to refer to the capture of the king through dissensions in his ranks.

45 *kṛtārthājjyāyaso* from Cb Cs is obviously quite necessary for *kṛtārthā jyāyaso* of the mss. Cf. 7.8.31. — *aśuceḥ* is to be construed with the first half as in Cb Cs. Meyer construes it with what follows 'from the dishonest, who shows himself honest in his conduct,' which is hardly possible.

46 *sattrād*: for *sattra* 'ambush' as a dangerous situation, cf. 10.3.24.

47 *jyāyastve cāpi*: etc.: Meyer understands 'being raised to a superior position (*jyāyastve*), he becomes changed in mind (with *viparikalpate* as the reading).' But *samo 'pi parikalpate* is obviously a better reading, despite the presence of another *api* in the same half.

48 *aṅke prahṛtya*: *pragṛhya* is an unlikely reading. *aṅka* conveys the idea of 'one's control, one's power'; cf. *aṅkam upasthita* 7.18.40, and *aṅke kuryāt* 1.17.10. The idea is, when the strong king comes under his power some time, he should strike. Cb Cs render *aṅka* by *randhra*.

49 *netā* is the *vijigīṣu*; cf. 6.2.39.

CHAPTER SIX

SECTION 111 CONCERNING THE MARCH OF TWO (KINGS) WHO HAVE ENTERNED INTO A TREATY OF ALLIANCE

SECTION 112 TREATIES WITH STIPULATIONS, WITHOUT STIPULATIONS AND WITH DESERTERS

1 The conqueror should over-reach the second member (of the circle of kings) in this manner. 2 He should induce the neighbouring king to march after entering into a treaty, 'You march in this direction, I shall march in that; the gains shall be equal.' 3 In case the gains are equal, there should be peace, if unequal, fight.

4 A treaty is with stipulations or without stipulations. 5 'You march to this region, I shall march to this,' this is treaty with stipulations as to place. 6 'You operate for this length of time, I shall operate for this length of time,' this is treaty with stipulations as to time. 7 'You carry out this much work, I shall carry out this much work,' this is treaty with stipulations as to objects to be achieved.

8 If he were to think, 'The enemy will march against a region, with a mountain-fort, a forest-fort or a river-fort, separated by a forest, with supplies of grains and men and allied troops cut off, deficient in fodder, fuel and water, unknown, far distant, or with natives hostile, or one in which land is not available for the operations of the army, (and) I (shall march) against a region the reverse of this,' in such a situation he should enter into a treaty with stipulations as to place.

9 If he were to think, 'The enemy will operate at a time when there is excessive rain, heat or cold, when there is plenty of illness, when food and other articles of use are exhausted, which is a hindrance to the operations of the army, which is too short or too long for accommplishing the work, (and) I at a time the reverse of this,' in such a situation, he should enter into a treaty with stipulations as to time.

7.6

The two Sections may be said to extend over ss. 1-3 and 4-41 respectively; but they are really very closely connected.

1 *dvitīyāṁ prakṛtim*, i.e., *arim*; cf. 6.2.14. 2 *sāmanta* is again the *ari*. — *saṁhita-prayāṇe* : the *vijigīṣu* and the *ari* make a treaty for a common expedition against some other king or kings. 3 *vaiṣamye* : according to Cb Cs, the *vijigīṣu* has got more out of the expedition; he attacks because he is now superior. It may also be that it is the *ari* who has got more; hence the recommendation to fight him. If the *vijigīṣu* has got more, he has thereby already over-reached the enemy, and there would be no need to fight. See, however, s. 12 below.

8 *vīvadha* stands for supplies (grains, men etc.) from his own land; cf. 10.2.6. According to the *Siddhāntakaumudī* on Pāṇini 4.4.71, *vivadha* or *vīvadha* is a contrivance for carrying loads, a pole with slings at both ends carried on the shoulder. — For *āsāra*, see 10.2.7. — *deśya* 'natives of the country' that is to be attacked; these are *anyabhāva* 'with different, i.e., hostile feelings' towards the attacker.

10 If he were to think, 'The enemy will achieve an object, easily recoverable (from him), causing revolt among the subjects, taking a long time, involving heavy losses and expenses, insignificant, bound up with troubles in future, unwholesome, unlawful, opposed by the middle or neutral king, or ruinous to his own ally, (and) I (shall achieve) the reverse of this,' in such a situation, he should enter into a treaty with stipulations as to objects to be achieved.

11 By the fixing, in this manner, of place and time, of time and object, of place and object, and of place, time and object, the treaty with stipulations becomes seven-fold.

12 In the case of that (treaty), he should start and establish his own undertakings right in advance and attack the enemy's undertakings.

13 Wishing to over-reach an enemy, who is vicious, hasty, contemptuous, slothful or ignorant, he should create confidence with a treaty, saying 'we are in alliance,' without the fixing of place, time or object, and after finding the enemy's weak point, strike at him ; this is (treaty) without stipulations.

14 In that connection, the following occurs :

> 15 The wise (conqueror), making one neighbouring king fight with another neighbouring king, should seize the territory of another, cutting off his party on all sides.

16 Of a treaty, (there are) the desire to make a (treaty) not yet made, clinging fast to a treaty made, spoiling a treaty made and repair of what is broken. 17 Of war, there is open war, concealed war and silent war. 18 Thus (we have) treaty and war.

19 The examination of a new treaty in relation to conciliation and other means with their consequences, and the fixing of equal, weaker and stronger kings according to their strength, is the desire to make a (treaty) not made.

20 The observance, on both sides, of a (treaty) made, by means of what is agreeable and beneficial, and the carrying out of conditions as agreed upon and their safe-guarding (by seeing) that he may not be divided from the other party, is clinging fast to a treaty made.

10 *pratyādeyam* : cf. 9.4.5-6 ; for the other terms, too, see 9.4.16-22.

13 *vyasana* seems here ' vice ' (Cb) rather than ' calamity.'

14-15 These ss. appear to be out of context. They make no reference to *saṁdhi*, which is the topic under discussion. They might fit in with 7.4.16. It may be that they have got into the text at the wrong place. It is also possible that it is a marginal comment which has got into the text. 15 *anyasya* : this would seem to be the *ari*, who is attacked by another king at the *vijigīṣu*'s instance.

19 *paryeṣaṇam* ' thorough investigation ' of the possible consequences of a treaty and of the possibility of using *sāman*, *dāna* etc. if the treaty is made. — *akṛtacikīrṣā* is a preliminary investigation before a treaty is actually made.

20 *nibandhana* ' binding ', i.e., terms, conditions. — *kathaṁ parasmān na bhidyeta* has the appearance of an indirect construction.

21 Violation (of the treaty) after establishing that the enemy deserves to have the treaty with him broken, by cheating (him) through treasonable persons, is spoiling a treaty made.

22 Becoming reconciled with a servant or an ally who had deserted through some fault is repair of what is broken. 23 In that case, the deserter returning is of four kinds : one deserting and returning on good grounds, the reverse of this, one leaving on good grounds and returning without such grounds, and the reverse of this.

24 One deserting because of the master's fault and returning because of his virtue, (or) deserting because of the enemy's virtue and returning because of his fault, is one deserting and returning on good grounds, fit to be made peace with.

25 One deserting and returning because of his own fault ignoring the virtues of both, is one deserting and returning without ground, unfit to be made peace with, being fickle in mind.

26 One deserting because of the master's fault and returning from the enemy because of his own fault is one deserting on good grounds and returning without ground, about whom he should reflect, 'Has he come with the intention of doing harm at the enemy's instigation or through his own evilmindedness, or knowing my enemy to be an exterminator of his enemy (returned) through fear of reprisal, or leaving the enemy, who is planning to exterminate me, returned out of a feeling of compassion ?' 27 On finding out, he should honour one with benevolent intentions, should keep away at a distance one with different intentions.

28 One deserting because of his own fault and returning because of the enemy's fault is one deserting without ground and returning on good grounds, about whom he should reflect, 'Will he make good my weak point ? Is he accustomed to live here ? Do his people not find pleasure at the enemy's place ? Is he in alliance with my allies ? Is he at war with my enemies ? Is he frightened of the greedy or cruel (enemy) or of (the enemy) in alliance with

21 *dūṣyātisaṁdhānena* : it seems that the *vijigīṣu* is to encourage his own *dūṣyas* to get in touch with the enemy ; if the latter were to entertain any proposals by these, his *apasaṁdheyatā* would thereby be established.

22 *avaśirṇakriyā* 'repairing what is broken' is the same as *apasṛtasaṁdhi* in the title.

26 *parasya ucchettāram amitraṁ me jñātvā* : the deserter knows that the enemy to whom he had gone is severe on his enemies and fears severe punishment from him as he himself is at fault (*svadoṣeṇa āgataḥ*) ; hence he returns to his old master. Meyer proposes *mām* for *me*, his idea being that the deserter realises that the *vijigīṣu* would uproot the enemy to whom he has gone over; hence fearing reprisals he returns. This is little likely. The *vijigīṣu* in his thoughts would not refer to himself as *amitra*.

28 *chidraṁ me pūrayiṣyati* : these are in the form of questions. The explanation in Cs 'he will widen my weak points, so that the enemy may easily strike at them' is quite unlikely. This deserter has returned because of the enemy's fault ; he could not be supposed to serve the enemy's interests. — *śatrusaṁhitād* : the *śatru* is the deserter's enemy (Cb).

his enemy ?' 29 On finding out, he should keep him in accordance with his intentions.

30 'Destruction of what one has done, diminution of power, treating learning as a commodity, despair in hopes, eagerness for (seeing) different lands, lack of trust, or conflict with a powerful person are the occasions for leaving (the master),' say the teachers. 31 'Fear, lack of livelihood (and) resentment (are the main occasions),' says Kauṭilya.

32 Among these, one who has done harm to him should be abandoned, one who has done harm to the enemy should be made peace with, regarding one who has done harm to both, he should reflect as before.

33 In case, however, it is absolutely necessary to make peace with one unfit to make peace with, he should take precautions with regard to that wherein the (other) has might.

34 In repairing what is broken, he should station one who belongs to the enemy's party, if (on coming to him) he has conferred benefits, away (from himself), guarded till the end of his life.

35 Or, he should make him fight against his master, or, if completely secured, make him a leader of the army against the enemy or forest tribes or station him on one side on the frontier.

36 Or, if not secured, he should sell him as a commodity, or (sell) even a secured one concealed by that one, blaming him with the fault of that (other one) himself, for the sake of making peace with the enemy.

30 *śaktihāniḥ*: the *śakti* seems to be that of the deserter rather than that of the king. Cb looks upon all these as defects of the king, not of the deserter. — *vidyāpaṇyatvam*, e.g., a clever minister going over to the enemy for higher emoluments. — *deśalaulyam*: this can hardly mean 'trouble in the country from flies, mosquitoes, etc.' (Cb Cs). — *balavadvigrahaḥ*: the *vigraha* is that of the would-be deserter, hardly that of the king.

33 The reading *asaṁdheyatvena* of the mss. is quite obviously faulty. — *yataḥ prabhāvaḥ tataḥ*, i.e., in that (*kośa, daṇḍa* etc.) in which the returning deserter may be powerful.

34 *āyuḥkṣayād iti*: *iti* seems used because of *ā*; Meyer suggests *ati* or *adhi* for it; that is hardly an improvement. — *aripakṣīyam*: though *avaśīrṇakriyāvidhau* indicates a prime deserter from the *vijigīṣu*, it seems that in most of these stanzas a deserter from the enemy is to be understood. Cs understands an enemy's servant coming to the *vijigīṣu*, going back to the enemy and returning to the *vijigīṣu* a second time. This seems hardly intended.

35 *bhartari*: this is clearly the *ari*. — *siddham* who has been secured, i.e., about whose loyalty there is no more any doubt. — *amitrāṭavīṣu*: with this we have to construe *daṇḍacāriṇam*: the deserter may be sent to fight enemies or forest tribes. Meyer has 'being given a command over alien troops or forest tribes.' Cs construes *amitrāṭavīṣu* with *kṣipet* 'should send him against enemies or forest tribes.' It seems better, however, to look upon the last quarter as containing a separate clause.

36 *paṇyaṁ kuryāt* 'should sell him,' i.e., hand him over to the enemy, the deserter's old master, for a price. Cb Cs, however, explain 'should send him with goods for selling them.' That appears hardly possible in view of the usual meaning of this expression. Cf. 9.3.27 etc. — *siddhaṁ vā tena saṁvṛtaṁ tasyaiva doṣeṇa ādūṣya*: this seems to mean that even the deserter proved loyal (*siddham*) may be sold to the enemy, his old master, in place of or along with the one proved disloyal (*tena*, i.e., *asiddhena* and *saṁvṛtam* covered, concealed); the loyal one is charged with the offence really committed by the *asiddha* one. This is to be done in order that peace may be made with the enemy, who insists on the

37 Or, he should do away with him silently for the sake of the future; and finding that the deserter who has returned is desirous of killing him in future, he should slay him.

38 One who has come from the enemy is a danger, caused by his staying with the enemy; being of the nature of staying with a serpent, it suffers from the defect of constant fear.

39 He becomes a cause of constant fear and dangerous even afterwards like (danger) to a *śālmali* tree from a pigeon feeding on *plakṣa* seeds.

40-41 Open war is fighting at the place and time indicated; creating fright, sudden assault, striking when there is error or a calamity, giving way and striking in one place, are types of concealed warfare; that which concerns secret practices and instigations through secret agents is the mark of silent war.

CHAPTER SEVEN

SECTION 113 PEACE AND WAR CONNECTED WITH THE DUAL POLICY

1 The conqueror should accept as ally the second member (of the circle of kings) in this manner. 2 He should march against a neighbouring king after joining forces with the neighbouring enemy if he were to think, '(Thus)

surrender of the loyal one (*parasaṁdheyakāraṇāt*). The explanation in Cb seems to be, 'if the deserter, after making a secret agreement with the enemy, were to kill the *dūṣya* etc. of the enemy and thus show to the *vijigīṣu* that he had suppressed (or weakened) the enemy (and is therefore an honest deserter), the *vijigīṣu* should proclaim this offence (of trying to cheat him) and kill him, in order that this may serve as a lesson to other *dūṣyas* of the enemy who may think of deserting to him.' This hardly appears meant. Russ. reads 'Otherwise if he is unreliable (*asiddham*) he may be made into a commodity for sale or handed over under the supervision of a reliable person so that he may not have contact with the enemy, by the way he to whom he is entrusted can be spoiled by him.'

37 *hanyāt* may refer to open execution as against *upāṁśunā śamayet*.

38 *doṣaḥ*, i.e., a source of danger.

39 *plakṣabījāśāt kapotād*: nominatives would have been better, in view of the comparison of the *abhyāgata* with the *kapota*. *plakṣa* is the *ari* of the *śālmali*, which is uprooted by the former's seeds taking root at its base, being dropped there by the *kapota*.

40 *nirdiṣṭe deśe kāle ca*: Cf. 10.3.26. — *vibhīṣaṇam* appears to be the same as *vibhīṣikā* of 10.4.14. 41 *ekatra tyāgaghātau*: this seems to refer to the tactics of making a show of yielding in one place and, when the enemy forces are lulled by a sense of victory or are scattered, striking back in force at the same place; cf. 10.3.4,6. Meyer would read *ekasya* 'leaving in the lurch or killing one who is alone (*eka*).' This is not mentioned in 10.3, the Section on *kūṭayuddha*. Russ. has *ekatra tyāgaghātau* 'abandoning (a bogus ally) and destruction of him when alone.' — *mātṛkā* 'source, womb,' i.e., types. — *yogagūḍhopajāpārtham*: *artham* is rather strange; we expect the nominative; we cannot render it by 'for the sake of.' *yoga* and *gūḍhopajāpa* are described at length from 12.2 to 13.4 below. The reading *gūḍhāpa-* is obviously faulty.

7.7

Cb is missing on Chapters 7.7 to 7.13.

1 *dvitīyāṁ prakṛtim*: see 7.6.1 above. — *upagṛhṇīyāt* 'should secure support' from him, by making a pact of alliance with him. 2 *sāmantam*: this is a third king against

he will not attack me in the rear, will ward off my rear enemy, will not go to the help of the king against whom I am marching, there will be double troops at my disposal, he will provide me with supplies and reinforcements, will prevent these from (reaching) the enemy, will crush for me the thorns on the way full of many dangers, will operate with his army against (the enemy's) retreats in forts or forests, will place the king I am marching against in an unbearable danger or bring him to terms of peace, or as he receives his share of the gain, will create confidence in my other enemies.'

3 Or, resorting to the dual policy, he should seek to obtain from one of the neighbouring kings troops in return for treasury or treasury in return for troops. 4 Among them, from the stronger for a larger share, from the equal for an equal share, from the weaker for a smaller share, — this is an equal pact. 5 In the reverse case, it is an unequal pact. 6 By receiving a special gain in these two, there is over-reaching.

7 A weaker king may bargain with a stronger king with the offer of a gain equal to his troops, when he is in a calamity or is addicted to what is harmful or is in trouble. 8 He with whom the bargain is made should fight if capable of doing harm to him; else he should make the pact.

9 A weaker king, when in the same situation, may bargain with a stronger king with the offer of a gain greater than what is equal to the troops, for the sake of recouping his diminished powers and might or for the sake of guarding his base or rear when going after an object which it is possible to secure. 10 He with whom the bargain is made should help one with honourable intentions, else fight.

11 A weaker king, entrenched in a fort or supported by an ally, may bargain with a stronger king on whom a calamity has fallen or who has a weak point among his subjects or to whom troubles have come, with the offer of a gain less than what is equal to his troops, when intending to march against an

whom the *vijigīṣu* would march in alliance with his enemy (*sāmantena saṁbhūya*). — *bala-dvaiguṇyam* from Cn Cs is absolutely necessary. — *durgāṭavyapasāreṣu* : a *durga* or *aṭavī* would provide a place of refuge (*apasāra*) for the *yātavya*.

3 *dvaidhībhūtaḥ*, i.e., making a pact with his usual enemy in order to make war on another king. 5 *viparyaye* : there are two *viparyayas* in each case; e.g., from a *jyāyān*, a *sama aṁśa* or a *hīna aṁśa*, instead of *adhika*. There are thus six *viṣama saṁdhis*. — *viśeṣalābhād* : according to Cn, the *viśeṣa* lies in quality rather than quantity, e.g., gain of money rather than of ally or of land rather than of money, as in 7.9.1. — *atisaṁdhiḥ* 'excessive treaty,' is over-reaching or cheating, which is what the word usually means.

7 *anarthinam* : for *anartha* see. 9.7.7. — *balasamena*, i.e., in proportion to the number of troops, desired from him. This is a *viṣama saṁdhi* as the stronger king is offered not *adhika*, but *sama aṁśa*. 8 *paṇitaḥ* is the *jyāyān* in difficulties. Advice is given to both sides in this text.

9 *evaṁbhūtaḥ*, i.e., when he is *vyasanin* etc. as in s. 7. — *saṁbhāvyārtha-* is an object that can conceivably be achieved. — *jyāyāṁsaṁ viśiṣṭena* ; this thus is a *sama saṁdhi*.

11 *jātavyasanaprakṛtirandhram* : this should be understood as containing two ideas, *jātavyasanam* and *jātaprakṛtirandhram*. Thus Cn, which, however, refers *randhra* to *kruddha*, *lubdha* etc. who are likely seceders. It is more likely that the reference is to *kṣīṇa*, *lubdha* and *virakta* (and *apacarita*) as constituting the *randhra* of the subjects. Meyer has a single idea 'in whom a weak point in the form of a calamity of a constituent has appeared.' —

enemy over a short route or when intending to secure a gain without a fight or (a gain) of which the attainment is certain. 12 He with whom the bargain is made should fight if capable of doing harm to him, else make the pact.

13 A stronger king, (even when) without a weakness or a calamity, may accept a lesser gain when intending to make (a weaker king) who made a bad start in his undertaking suffer greater losses and expenses, or when intending to get his own treasonable troops killed, or when intending to bring to his side (the weaker king's) treasonable troops, or when intending to cause trouble to (his own enemy) fit to be harassed or exterminated through the weaker king, or if he, attaching importance to peace, has honourable intentions. 14 Joining forces with one who has honourable intentions, he should seek to achieve his object, else fight.

15 In the same way, an equal should over-reach or help an equal.

16 An equal may bargain with a gain equal to the troops, for (troops) capable of fighting against the particular kind of the enemy's troops or against those of the ally or forest troops, or for (troops) that would serve as a guide in terrains unfavourable to the enemy or for guarding his base or rear. 17 He with whom the bargain is made should help one with honourable intentions, otherwise he should fight.

18 An equal may bargain with the offer of a gain less than equal to the troops with one on whom a calamity has fallen or who has a weak point among his subjects or who is opposed by many (kings) or when he himself can get help from another source. 19 He with whom the bargain is made should fight if capable of doing harm to him, else make the pact.

20 An equal, in this situation himself, should bargain with the offer of a gain greater than what is equal to the troops, if his affairs are dependent on

durgamitrapratiṣṭabdho vā : it seems that *vā* shows the option between *durga* and *mitra* in the compound. This expression can hardly be understood as an option to what follows as in Cn. It describes the situation of the *hīna* and not his intentions. — *śatrum* as another object to *yātukāmaḥ* is rather odd. It is unnecessary. — *jyāyāṁsaṁ hīnena* is a *viṣama saṁdhi*.

13 *arandhravyasano vā* : again *vā* may show the option between *randhra* and *vyasana*. This expression is the negative of *jātavyasana*- etc. in s. 11. — *yoktukāmaḥ* : the sense of the causal seems implicit. — *pravāsay* is here ' to kill,' hardly ' to send into exile.'

15 *evam*, i.e., as in ss. 13-14.

16 *parānīkasya pratyanīkam*, i.e., the kind of troops that would be suitable for use against the troops that the enemy would be using. Considerations mentioned in 9.2.26-28 would seem to apply. — *mitrāṭavīnām* : we have to supply *pratyanīkam*. The ally and forest troops are those of the enemy. — *vibhūmi* ' terrain which is unsuitable.' — *deśika* seems to mean ' who can point out,' i.e., able to guide. — *balasamena* is proposed for *samabalena* in conformity with the reading in ss. 20, 24, 27 and 29. *samabala* is inappropriate with *lābha*. Similarly, *balasamād* is proposed in s. 18.

18 *anyato labhamāno vā* : if the king wanting troops can get them from another source, the *sama*, with whom negotiations are going on, may find the *vijigīṣu* getting more powerful without himself getting any gain; he might therefore prefer a smaller gain. Meyer (in the Berechtigung) finally prefers *alabhamānaḥ* ' if the *vijigīṣu* cannot get help from any other source.' In that case, offering a smaller gain is quite inconceivable.

20 *kartavyabalaḥ* : the building up of an army is meant. — This and the last case are *viparyayas* of the second kind of *sama saṁdhi* (*samāt samena*).

the neighbouring king or when his strength is to be built up. 21 He with whom the bargain is made should help one with honourable intentions, otherwise fight.

22 One may ask for more (gain) from a stronger, a weaker or an equal, if intending to strike at him when a calamity has befallen him or his subjects show a weakness, or if intending to ruin his undertaking that may have been well started or that may be sure of success, or if intending to strike at his base or expedition, or if he is getting more from the king against whom (the other) is marching. 23 The one, asked for more, may give more for the sake of protecting his own troops when intending to crush another's unassailable fort or allied or forest troops by means of enemy troops, or when intending to make the enemy troops suffer losses and expenses on a distant or prolonged expedition, or when intending to exterminate the enemy himself after growing in power through his troops, or when intending to take the enemy troops himself.

24 A stronger king may bargain with a weaker king with the offer of a gain greater than what is equal to the troops, when intending to get him in his power under the pretext of the enemy to be attacked, or when intending to exterminate him after exterminating the enemy, or when, after making the bestowal, intending to recover it (later). 25 He with whom the bargain is made should fight if capable of doing harm to him, otherwise make the pact. 26 Or, he should enter into an alliance with the king to be attacked (by the other), or should give treasonable or alien or forest troops.

27 A stronger king, suffering from a calamity or a weak point among his subjects, may bargain with a weaker one with the offer of a gain equal to the troops. 28 He with whom the bargain is made should fight if capable of doing harm to him, otherwise make the pact.

29 A stronger king may bargain with a weaker one who is in this situation with the offer of a gain less than what is equal to the troops. 30 He with whom the bargain is made should fight if capable of doing him harm, otherwise make the pact.

31 The one to whom a pact is proposed and the one proposing the pact should first find out the motives ; then after reflecting on both sides, he should follow the course wherein lies his well-being.

22 *bhūyo yāceta* : this seems to imply a demand for additional gain some time after the pact is made. — *yātavyād bhūyo labhamāno* : the threat held out is, if you do not give me more, I can get it from your enemy and help him with troops to fight against you. 23 *paradaṇḍam ādātukāmaḥ*: Cn Cs think that *para* is the *yātavya*. But *para* as the enemy whose troops are borrowed is definitely better; it is these troops that are to be appropriated.

24 *jyāyān vā* for *jyāyāṁsaṁ vā* is from Cs. The latter is unlikely as the case of *jyāyāṁsaṁ viśiṣṭena lābhena* is discussed already in s. 9 — *yātavyāpadeśena* : the idea is, the request for troops for fighting a *yātavya* is only a pretext ; the real intention is to weaken the *hīna* by taking his troops and thus get him in his power. — *tyāga* is that of the higher gain. — This and the case in s. 27 are *viparyayas* of the third *sama saṁdhi* (*hīnād hīnena*).

31 *ādau* : Cn has *ato*, Cs *āto*. But *ādau* seems better. — *kāraṇam*, i.e., motives of the other party. — *ubhayataḥ* 'on both sides' may refer to the two sides of the *paṇita* and the *paṇamāna*, or to the two alternatives of peace and war (Cn Cs). Cn remarks that *paṇita* and *paṇamāna* refer to the different situations in which the *vijigīṣu* may find himself.

CHAPTER EIGHT

SECTION 114 CONDUCT (PROPER) FOR THE KING ABOUT TO BE ATTACKED
SECTION 115 DIFFERENT KINDS OF ALLIES FIT TO BE HELPED

1 The vulnerable king, about to be attacked, should bargain with one of the confederates with the offer of double the gain, with the intention of removing the motive of the alliance or of destroying it. 2 Proposing the bargain, he should describe to him (likely) losses, expenses, marches, hindrances, benefits to enemies and danger to his person. 3 If he agrees, he should bestow wealth on him. 4 Or, making him entertain enmity towards the others, he should divide him (from them).

5 When intending to make one who has made a bad start in his undertaking suffer further losses and expenses, or when intending to obstruct the success of his expedition that has begun well, or when intending to strike at his base or expedition, or when intending to ask for more again after becoming allied with the king to be attacked, one may accept a small gain in the present and a large gain in the future, even when difficulties of money have arisen or he has no confidence in that (other king).

6 When he sees a benefit to his ally or harm to his enemy, with a continuity of advantage to himself, or when he intends to make the king who has helped him before help him further, he should forgo a great gain in the present and seek a small gain in the future.

7 When he wants to save a king engaged in a fight with traitors or enemies or with a stronger king seeking to seize his kingdom, or when he wants to make

7.8

The two Sections are contained in ss. 1-4 and 11-34 respectively. Ss. 5-10 do not belong to either, but continue the topic of the last Chapter (Section 113). — *yātavyavṛttiḥ* : Cn Cs and Meyer have ' conduct of as well as conduct towards the *yātavya*.' Of the latter there is little trace.

1 *saṁdhikāraṇam* ' the reason why the alliance was made,' viz., the gain. — *ādātukāmaḥ* ' to take away,' i.e., to remove it. How to do this is explained in ss. 2-3 (Cn). — *vihantukāmaḥ* : this is explained in s. 4 (Cn). 2 *paṇamānaḥ* is from Cn for *prapaṇitaḥ* of the mss. Cf. 7.7.31 above. Cs reads *prapaṇitā*. — *kṣayavyaya-* etc. : cf. 7.2.2. 4 *visaṁvādayet* : make him disagree with the others and thus divide him from them.

5 *svārabdhāṁ vā yātrāsiddhim* : strictly *svārabdhā* goes with *yātrā*, not with *siddhi* ; this is an *ekadeśin* compound. Meyer prefers the reading *svārabdham . . . -siddham* and understands *svārabdham* as an accusative of relation 'when a thing has well begun.' That is doubtful. — *prahartukāmaḥ* is read as in 7.7.22 for *pratihartukāmaḥ*. It seems supported by Cn. — *pratyutpannārthakṛcchraḥ*: the sense of *api* is to be understood with this expression, as also with *aviśvastaḥ*. The two expressions do not refer to any ulterior motives like the earlier clauses. For the former expression, cf. 5.2.1. — This s. can hardly be regarded as describing the behaviour of a confederate towards the *yātavya*, as in Cs. *yātavyasaṁhitaḥ* in one of the clauses precludes that.

6 *arthānubandham* : as 9.7.14 shows, this should be regarded as an adjective to *mitropakāram* and *amitropaghātam*. — *kārayitukāmaḥ* : the object *upakāram* has to be understood. *bhūyaḥ* should have come before this word, not after.

7 *mūlahareṇa* : see 7.2.14 above. — *tathāvidham upakāram*, i.e., the saving of himself when there may be need for it in the future. — *saṁbandhāvekṣī* : Cs reads *-pekṣī* and explains

(that king) render the same kind of help (to himself) or when he takes relationship into consideration, he should not accept a gain in the present and in the future.

8 When after making a pact he intends to violate it, or when he intends to bring about the impoverishment of the enemy's subjects or the breaking up of his alliance with his allies or foes, or when apprehensive of any attack by the enemy, he should demand a gain not received or more. 9 With respect to that, the other should consider the order (of preference) in the present and in the future. 10 By that are explained the earlier (cases).

11 But when the enemy and the conqueror help each his respective ally, a special advantage (results) from an ally whose undertaking is possible or sound or productive or who is resolute in his undertakings or who has loyal subjects. 12 One with a possible undertaking starts a work capable of accomplishment, one with a sound undertaking (starts a work) free from defects, one with a productive undertaking what leads to goods results. 13 One resolute in his undertakings does not stop without completing his work. 14 One with loyal subjects accomplishes his work even with a little help, since he has (already) good helpmates. 15 These (allies), when they have achieved their objects, easily and abundantly oblige (in return). 16 The reverse of these should not be helped.

17 In case the two give help to the same individual, he who helps his ally or a better ally (of his) over-reaches (the other). 18 For, from the ally he attains his own advancement, the other (gets only) losses, expenses, marches and beneficence to enemies. 19 And the enemy, on achieving his object, becomes hostile.

20 But when the two help the middle king, he who helps the middle king when he is his ally or a better ally, over-reaches (the other). 21 For, from the ally he attains his own advancement, the other (gets only) losses, expenses, marches and beneficence to enemies. 22 If the middle king, after being helped, turns hostile, the enemy over-reaches (the conqueror). 23 For,

'expecting a marriage alliance with the *yātavya*.' It is doubtful if the *yātavya* comes into the picture at all.

8 *parābhiyogāt*: the *para* appears to be the enemy who is asking for troops. To prevent an attack on himself with the help of his own troops, a large amount is demanded. — *śaṅkamānaḥ*: a *vā* after this seems necessary. — *aprāptam* implies demand for immediate payment of what was agreed. 9 *tam* is merely an accusative of reference, 'with reference to him.' — *kramam*, i.e., what would be best to do in the present and in future. 10 *pūrve* refers to the cases of ss. 5-7.

12 *ārabhate* in the indicative is from Cn for *ārabheta*; that is in keeping with the verbs in the following ss. 16 *pratilomā* is again from Cn. For *pratilome* of the mss. we should expect *prātilomye*.

17 *mitrataram*: though an ally of both, he is more friendly towards one of them. 19 *śatruḥ*: this is the *mitra* or *mitratara* of the other party. — *vaiguṇyam* has the sense of 'hostility.' Cf. *viguṇa* in s. 22 below.

he obtains (as an ally) the enemy of the middle king, who had made exertions, (but) who has now deserted (him) and come to him with a common goal.

24 By that is explained help to the neutral king.

25 In the matter of giving a portion of one's troops to the middle or neutral king, he who gives troops that are brave, skilled in the use of weapons, able to put up with troubles or loyal, is over-reached. 26 The opposite kind over-reaches.

27 Where, however, the troops, when sent, can accomplish that object as well as others, he should give any of the hereditary, hired, banded, allied or forest troops, when the place and time are known, or alien and forest troops, when the place is distant and time long.

28 But if he were to think of a king, 'On achiving his object, he will appropriate my troops, or will camp them among alien or forest troops or in an unsuitable region or season, or might render them unserviceable,' then he should not help him on the pretext that his troops are engaged (elsewhere). 29 If, however, he has necessarily to be given help in this manner, he should give him troops able to put up with that occasion (only). 30 And till the end (of the campaign) he should get them to encamp and fight (in another place ?) and guard them from the calamities of an army. 31 And when the other has achieved his object, he should, under some pretext, get them removed from him. 32 Or, he should give him treasonable, alien or forest troops. 33 Or, making a treaty with the king to be attacked, he should over-reach him.

34 For, when the gain is equal there should be peace, when unequal war is considered (desirable) for the equal, weaker and stronger kings. Thus have peace and war been described.

23 *kṛtaprayāsam* etc. : it is the *vijigīṣu* who had made the effort to help the *madhyama* ; but since the latter has turned hostile (*viguṇa*), he has become his enemy (*madhyamāmitram*); so he deserts the *madhyama* (*apasṛta*) and makes common cause with his usual enemy, who thus scores over him. *ekārtha* is hostility towards the *madhyama*.

25 Cn specifically adds that this does not apply to troops lent to one's allies.

27 *daṇḍaḥ prahitaḥ* etc. : the mss. read *pratihataḥ*. One may understand that the troops given are repulsed, being cowardly etc., and so better troops are demanded of him. He may give such, if more objects can be achieved. But in the text there is no mention of a fresh demand or a demand for better troops. The idea is simply that when a number of objects can be attained by sending troops, good troops may be given. This is an exception to s. 25 as shown by *tu*. — *taṁ vā cārtham* : the *vā* is unnecessary. — *upalabdha* ' acquainted with ' (Cn) ; rather ' known '.

28 *aphalaṁ kuryāt* : cf. 9.2.11, which shows that ' might deprive it of the reward due after the enemy's defeat' (Cn Cs) is not likely. What is meant is rendering them unserviceable or useless for fighting by neglecting to take proper care of them, — *-deśena nainam* from Cs is quite necessary for the sense. 29 *tatkālasaham* may mean ' capable of fighting in that season only ' or ' enabling him to tide over that occasion.' Meyer has 'raised at that time only ', i.e., not seasoned. 30 *vāsayed* etc. : it seems some such word as *anyatra* (i.e., at a place away from where the other king's troops are operating) or *āsannam* (near himself) has dropped out. — *balavyasanas* are enumerated in 8.5 below.

34 The stanza forms the conclusion of the discussion in the last Chapter, the two Sections in this Chapter being only special cases of the Section in that Chapter. — *uktāḥ saṁdhivikramāḥ* : the plurals are from Cn Cs, supported by the title of Section 113.

CHAPTER NINE

SECTION 116 PACTS FOR (SECURING) AN ALLY, MONEY, LAND AND AN UNDERTAKING

(i) Pact for an Ally (ii) Pact for Money

1 When marching after making a pact, of the gains of an ally, money and land, the gain of each later one is preferable to that of each earlier one. 2 For, an ally and money come from the gain of land, (and) an ally from the gain of money. 3 Or, that gain, which when secured helps in securing one of the remaining two (is preferable).

4 'Let us two secure an ally each,' this and the like is an equal pact. 5 'You secure an ally (I, one of the other two),' this and the like is an unequal pact. 6 By securing a special gain in these two (cases), there is over-reaching.

7 In an equal pact, however, he who secures an excellent ally or an ally in the ally's difficulty, over-reaches. 8 For, troubles produce firmness in friendship.

9 Even in the case of an ally's difficulty, (when there is a choice) between one who is constant but not under control and one inconstant but under control, 'The constant, though not under control, is preferable; for he, though not helping, does not do harm,' say the teachers. 10 'No,' says Kauṭilya 11 One under control, though inconstant, is preferable. 12 As long as he helps, he becomes an ally; for, the characteristic of an ally is conferring benefit.

13 Even between two allies under control, (when there is a choice) between one rendering abundant help but inconstant and one rendering small help but constant, 'The one rendering abundant help, though inconstant, is preferable; one rendering abundant help, though inconstant, gives great help in a short time and provides against large items of expenditure,' say the teachers. 14 'No,' says Kauṭilya. 15 The constant one, though giving small help, is preferable. 16 The inconstant, though capable of great help,

7.9

Section 116 is spread over the four Chapters 9 to 12.

4 *tvaṁ cāhaṁ ca mitram*: the same king is not sought as an ally by both; each seeks a different king as his ally. — *tvaṁ mitram*: we have to supply *ahaṁ hiraṇyaṁ bhūmiṁ vā*.

7 *sampannam*, i.e., possessed of *mitrasaṁpad* as in 6.1.12. — *mitrakṛcchre*, i.e., when the king whose alliance is sought is in difficulties (Cn Cs). Meyer has 'when the *vijigīṣu* is in need of an ally.' This is unlikely; the *āpad* in the next s. is not that of the conqueror, for the question of his own firmness in friendship is irrelevant when it is a matter of scoring over the rival.

12 Russ. compares *Śiśupālavadha*, 2-37: *upakartrā 'riṇā saṁdhir na mitreṇāpakāriṇā, upakārāpakārau hi lakṣyaṁ lakṣaṇam etayoḥ.*'

13 *mahābhogam*: *bhoga* 'enjoyment (of his resources)' conveys the sense of help received from him. 16 *upakārabhayād*: the fear is that he may really have to give the help expected of him.

deserts through fear of (having to render) help or after giving help strives to take it back. 17 The constant one, giving a small help, rendering the small help continuously, renders great help over a long period of time.

18 As between a big ally mobilising slowly and a small ally mobilising quickly, 'The big ally, mobilising slowly, gives great prestige, and when he does mobilise, he secures the object,' say the teachers. 19 'No,' says Kauṭilya. 20 A small ally mobilising quickly is preferable. 21 The small ally mobilising quickly does not allow the time for action to pass, and because of his weakness becomes fit to be used at one's will, not so the other, with an extensive territory.

22 As between dispersed troops and troops not under control, 'Dispersed troops can be collected together again, being under control,' say the teachers. 23 'No,' says Kauṭilya. 24 Troops not under control are better. 25 For, uncontrolled troops can be brought under control by conciliation and other means; the other (kind), being engaged in their work, cannot be collected together.

26 As between an ally giving the help of men and one giving the help of money, 'The ally giving the help of men is preferable; the ally giving the help of men gives prestige and when he mobilises, he achieves the object,' say the teachers. 27 'No,' says Kauṭilya. 28 The ally giving the help of money is preferable. 29 For, the use of money is made at all times, only sometimes that of troops. 30 And with money, troops and other objects of desire are obtained.

31 As between an ally giving the help of money and one giving the help of land, 'The one giving the help of money, being possessed of mobility, enables one to meet all expenses,' say the teachers. 32 'No,' says Kauṭilya. 33 That an ally and money come from the acquisition of land has been stated before. 34 Therefore, the ally giving the help of land is preferable.

18 *gurusamutthaṃ* 'heavy to rise,' i.e., taking a long time to get his troops ready. — *pratāpa*, as Meyer points out, refers to prestige among the kings. — Ss. 20-23 are missing in M1 showing that it was not the exemplar for G1. — *prakṛṣṭabhaumam*: Cs renders *prakṛṣṭa* by 'distant', Meyer by 'extensive, wide-flung.' The latter appears better in the present context. Cf., however, 7.6.8. The *taddhita* form of *bhauma* has little significance.

22 *vikṣiptasainyam*: though the discussion is about allies, and we can easily supply *mitram* after this, the ss. that follow consider the question of troops as such. The fact that the ally's armies are primarily meant can be easily understood. *vikṣipta* 'scattered,' i.e., dispersed in more than one place, not necessarily on different missions (as Cs has it). Cf. 9.2.11. 25 *kāryavyāsaktam*: the *kārya* seems to refer to the normal peaceful avocations of the soldiers. *vikṣepa* thus almost amounts to disbandment.

29 *yogaḥ* 'union with' refers to the use to which it can be put.

31 There can be no doubt that *gatimattvāt* from Cn is the correct reading. The question of the ally's prudence (*matimattvāt*, which Meyer prefers) is hardly relevant. Of course, it is *hiraṇya* that is mobile, the ally only secondarily so. 33 *purastāt*: in s. 2 above.

35 When help in men (from two allies) is equal, valour, ability to put up with troubles, loyalty or the gain of all troops from the side of the ally becomes a special advantage.

36 When the help in money is equal, getting the things asked for, plentifulness, smallness of exertion and continuity become a special advantage.

37 With respect to that, the following occurs :

38 A perfect ally is said to have six qualities, namely, constant, under control, quickly mobilising, hereditary, great and not given to double-dealing.

39 One, that is protected and that protects out of love, without (consideration of) money, with relationship grown since old times, is called the constant ally.

40 One under control is said to be three-fold, helping with all, with various or with great resources ; giving help on one side, on both sides and on all sides is another (three-fold ally under control).

41 One who, whether receiving or giving (help), lives by doing harm to (one's) enemies, and is possessed of a fort or forest as a place of retreat, is a constant ally, (but) not under control.

42 He who, when engaged in war with another or even when only in a light calamity, makes a pact for help, is an ally under control, but not constant.

43 Now one related by a common objective, helpful and never changing, is the ally endowed with the nature of an ally, not given to double-dealing in times of trouble.

35 *sarvabalalābhaḥ* may be 'getting all types of troops' or 'getting all the troops the ally has.' — *mitrakulād* : *kula* does not seem to have much significance.

36 *sātatyaṁ ca* from Cn Cs is obviously preferable to *sātatyāc ca*.

37 It is possible that this passage in ss. 37-49 is not genuine, like the other passage (7.6.14-15) introduced with the words *tatraitad bhavati*. It is not the usual practice of this text to introduce quotations in this manner. The stanzas have the appearance of being explanatory comments on expressions used in the text, which, however, do not stand in need of much explanation.

38 This is a repetition of 6.1.12.

40 For the terms see 7.16.10-15 below. — *aparam* : we have to understand *trividhaṁ vaśyam*.

41 *durgāṭavyapasāri* : cf. 7.7.2.

42 *upakārāya* : a pact for mtual aid seems meant.

43 It is proposed to read *ekārthenātha saṁbaddham* for *ekārthenārthasaṁbandham* of the mss. One *artha* in the latter is superfluous. For the expression, cf. 7.8.23, also 9.2.17, which make *ekārthānartha-*, (i.e., with *artha* and *anartha* common) of Cn Cs less likely, though possible in itself.

44 The ally is permanent because of (exclusive) feelings of friendship, fickle because of (his feelings) being common to the enemy, indifferent when not interested in either, with feelings for both when interested in the two.

45 That ally, (really) an enemy of the conqueror, who has become a buffer (between two strong kings), does not help, being not placed under obligations or being unable to help.

46 The ally who, (though) dear to the enemy or deserving to be protected or honoured by him or related to him, gives help, is common to the enemy.

47 The (ally) with an extensive territory, contented, strong and indolent becomes indifferent, (also) one disrespected because of a calamity.

48 One who, because of his weakness, is subservient to the prosperity of the enemy and the leader and is not treated as an enemy by either, should be known as (the ally) with feelings for both.

49 He, who would remain negligent about an ally who had deserted with or without reason and who has returned with or without reason, embraces death.

44 The explanation of Cn is followed in the first half, understanding *asādhāraṇāt* (with *mitrabhāvāt*) in the description of a *dhruva* ally and understanding *mitrabhāvāt* (after *śatrusādhāraṇāt*) in that of a *cala* ally. In the second half, Cn understands *udāsīnam* as only a description of the *ubhayabhāvin*. However, not only in this stanza but also in 47 and 48 *udāsīna* seems distinguished from *ubhayabhāvin*. Meyer translates this s. 'an ally, firm because of his friendly feelings, but vacillating because he has common interests with the enemy, indifferent to neither of the two, is *ubhayabhāvin*.' That the ally can be *dhruva* and *cala* at the same time is doubtful.

45 *amitram* seems used in the neuter because it is in apposition to *mitram*. — *antardhitāṁ gatam* : cf. 7.13.25. The idea is, an enemy of the conqueror, finding himself between two strong kings and in the position of a buffer to the *vijigīṣu*, becomes his ally. Such an ally, of course, is unhelpful. — It is proposed to read an *avagraha* with *niviṣṭam* corresponding to *'śaktam* in Cs. With *niviṣṭam*, Cs has 'resolved on helping, but incapable of doing so,' which seems little likely. *upakāre aniviṣṭa* may be understood in the sense of 'not placed under obligations'; cf. 7.18.37 for the idiom. Being an *amitra*, he had not been helped by the *vijigīṣu* before.

46 It is proposed to read *pūjyaṁ saṁbaddham*. With *pūjyasaṁbandham*, Cn Cs explain 'related to one worthy of honour (by the *vijigīṣu* himself).' It seems, however, that in view of *vā*, *parasya* is to be construed with these words, in which case the reading proposed would be definitely better.

47 *prakṛṣṭabhaumam* : see s. 21 above. — Cn Cs understand each single term in the first half as making a type of *udāsīna*. — *vyasanād* : the calamity seems to be that of the *vijigīṣu*. Cn has 'in the ally's calamity'; for that *vyasane* would be expected. Cs also has 'because of the ally's vice.'

48 Cn Cs regard *ubhayabhāvin* as the name for all types mentioned in ss. 44-48. It seems, however, that *ubhayabhāvin* is restricted only to this s., except for a different description in s. 44. Cf. 7.18.34 ff., where *ubhayabhāvin* is not mentioned at all. In fact, 7.18.29 makes the present discussion superfluous and hence suspect. It also seems clear that the stanzas are derived from different sources.

49 *kāraṇākāraṇa-* : a *vā* is implied between *kāraṇa* and *akāraṇa*. Most mss. show *kāraṇākaraṇa-* 'when a cause has not arisen,' which is not happy. Cf. 7.6.23 ff.

50 As between a small but quick gain and a large gain after a long time, 'The small but quick gain is preferable, if in consonance with the undertaking, the place and the time,' say the teachers. 51 'No,' says Kauṭilya. 52 A large gain after a long time is preferable, if not liable to disappear (and if) of the nature of a seed; in the reverse case, the former.

53 On thus perceiving the presence of excellence in a gain or a portion of a gain, which is definite, he should march after making pacts with confederates, being intent on achieving his own object.

CHAPTER TEN

SECTION 116 (Continued)

(iii) Pact for Land

1 'Let us two obtain land,' this is a pact for land.

2 Of the two, he who obtains land possessed of excellences, when need for it has arisen, over-reaches.

3 In case there is an equal acquisition of excellent land, he who obtains land after attacking a strong king over-reachers. 4 For, he secures acquisition of land, weakening of the enemy and prestige. 5 It is true that in obtaining land from a weak king, there is ease. 6 But the gain of land is poor and his neighbour, (who was) an ally, becomes an enemy.

7 In case the strength (of kings overthrown) is equal, he who obtains land after uprooting a firmly entrenched enemy, over-reaches. 8 For, the acquisition of a fort brings about the protection of his own land and the repulsion of enemies and forest tribes.

9 In case of acquisition of land from a moving enemy, (there is) special advantage from a weak neighbour. 10 For, (land) with a weak neighbour has its well-being and security quickly augmented. 11 Land with a strong neighbour is the opposite of this and becomes ruinous to the treasury and the army.

50 This s. and the following two ss. refer to *hiraṇyasaṁdhi*. 52 *bījasadharmā*, i.e., yielding abundant gains in the future. — *viparyaye*, i.e., if it is *vinipātī* and not *bījasadharmā*.

53 *dhruve* is to be construed with *lābhe* as well as *lābhāṁśe*.

7.10

2 *saṁpannām*, i.e., possessed of the excellences of a *janapada* as in 6.1.8.

4 *śatrukarśanam* : *śatru* is the strong king of the last s., whose land he has conquered. 6 *tatsāmantaḥ*, i.e., the neighbour of the weak king whose overthrow has brought the *vijigīṣu* into contiguity with him; so by theory, he becomes the *vijigīṣu*'s enemy, when formerly he was his ally, being one state away.

7 *sthitaśatru* is clearly one who has a fort; so *calāmitra* is an enemy without a fort. 8 *amitrāṭavī-* from Cn Cs is quite necessary. Cf. 1.13.15.

9 *śakya* is obviously paraphrased by *durbala*. 10 *bhavati* in the singular is necessary; *bhūmiḥ* is used in the singular throughout.

12 As between excellent land with permanent enemies and one with few excellences without permanent enemies, 'The excellent land with permanent enemies is preferable; for, excellent land enables one to secure treasury and army, and these two destroy enemies,' say the teachers. 13 'No,' says Kauṭilya. 14 In acquiring land with permanent enemies, there is a greater acquisition of enemies. 15 And a permanent enemy remains an enemy whether he is obliged or injured; the impermanent enemy, however, ceases to be so through obligations (conferred on him) or by desisting from injury (to him).

16 The land, whose frontiers have many forts (beyond them) and are never devoid of robber-bands or Mleccha forest tribes, is one with permanent enemies; in the reverse case, it is one without permanent enemies.

17 As between a small proximate land and a big land that is distant, the small proximate land is preferable. 18 For, it is easy to obtain, to protect and to get it to rescue (oneself). 19 The distant one is the opposite of this.

20 Even of two distant lands, as between land held by troops and one held by itself, the one held by itself is preferable. 21 For, it is held by the treasury and the army produced within itself. 22 That held by troops is the opposite of this, (being merely) a station for troops.

23 As between acquisition of land from a foolish king and from a wise king, the acquisition of land from a foolish king is preferable. 24 For, it is easy to obtain and protect and cannot be taken back. 25 That from a wise king is the opposite of this, being loyal (to him).

26 As between an enemy fit to be harassed and an enemy fit to be exterminated, acquisition of land from an enemy fit to be exterminated is preferable. 27 For, the king fit to be exterminated, being without support or with a weak support, is deserted by his subjects when, on being attacked, he wishes to flee taking with him the treasury and the army, not the one fit to be harassed, entrenched in a fort or supported by an ally.

28 Even of two kings entrenched in a fort, one in a land-fort and the other in a river-fort, the acquisition of land from one in a land-fort is preferable. 29 For, a land-fort is easy to besiege, to storm and to assault suddenly and does not allow the enemy to slip out. 30 A river-fort, however, causes

16 *mlecchāṭavībhiḥ*: *mleccha* is an adjective to *aṭavī*, not an independent substantive.

18 *abhisārayitum* from the causal of *abhi-sṛ* 'to make (the land) go to the rescue of'; as Cs makes clear, 'to make it a refuge in times of distress.'

22 *daṇḍasthānam*, i.e., a sort of a place for the camping of the army.

26 *pīḍanīya*: see 6.2.16.

29 *avamarda* is described in 13.4. — *aniḥsrāvi-* with the *visarga* as in Cs is to be preferred. 30 *udakaṁ ca pātavyam* 'there is water fit for drinking' (Cn Cs Meyer); this does not have the look of being a hardship for the *vijigīṣu*, which is what is expected to be mentioned; the whole river could not be enclosed in the fort to prevent the *vijigīṣu* from using its water. *pātavyam* can also mean 'to be guarded', but that seems less likely.

double exertion, and water has to be drunk and it yields livelihood to the enemy.

31 As between an enemy in a river-fort and an enemy in a mountain-fort, acquisition of land from one in a river-fort is preferable. 32 For, a river-fort can be conquered by means of elephants, bridges of wooden posts, embankments and boats, it is of varying depth and its water can be made to flow away. 33 A mountain-fort, however, is easy to protect, difficult to lay siege to, difficult to climb; and even if one (part) is breached, the destruction of all does not follow; and (there can be) throwing down of rocks and trees on those doing great damage.

34 As between those who fight in water and those who fight on land, the acquisition of land from those who fight in water is preferable. 35 For, those fighting in water are restricted as to the place and time (of fighting); fighters on land, however, can fight in all places and in all seasons.

36 As between fighters in trenches and fighters in the open, acquisition of land from trench-fighters is preferable. 37 For, trench-fighters fight with both trenches and weapons, those fighting in the open, with weapons alone.

38 The (king) conversant with the science of politics, acquiring land from kings like these, secures a special advantage over confederates and enemies.

CHAPTER ELEVEN

SECTION 116 (Continued)

(iii a) Pact for Unsettled Land

1 'Let us two settle waste land,' this is a pact for unsettled land.

2 Of the two, he who causes settlement on land possessed of excellences as mentioned, when the need for it has arisen, over-reaches (the other).

Perhaps *pārayitavyam* 'to be crossed' is to be read? — *vṛttikaram* perhaps because of fish in it or because supplies can come along the river.

32 *stambhasaṃkrama* 'a bridge of pillars.' Cf. 10.2.14. Cn Cs understand planks fixed on pillars (in the river-bed). Tree-steams thrown across rivers may also appear possible. — *avasrāvyudakam*: cf. 13.4.9. 33 *bhagne caikasmin* 'when a part of the fortifications is breached' (Meyer) appears preferable to 'when some warriors are killed by arrows etc.' (Cn Cs). — *duruparodhi*: it seems that *avarodha* and *uparodha* both mean 'a siege,' though the former is favoured in 12.5.9 and 13.3.37.

34 *nimna* obviously means 'water'; cf. 2.3.1.

37 *khātena śastreṇa ca*, i.e., they require not only weapons but also trenches, and there may be no time to dig trenches before the fight begins. That would be a handicap to the fighters.

7.11

1 *anavasita* is 'unoccupied, untenanted.' Cf. *avasita* in 3.8.17. The discussion in this Chapter is part of *bhūmisaṃdhi*, and is about qualities necessary in land to be acquired for fresh settlement.

2 *pratyupasthitārthaḥ*: Cn Cs explain 'who has all the necessary materials ready at hand for the settlement.' It seems better, however, to stick to the meaning 'when a need for it has arisen' as in 7.10.2 above. The need might arise when there is excess population, part of which is to be shifted. Cf. 2.1.

3 Even in that case, as between a dry tract and land abounding in water, a small land abounding in water is preferable to a large dry tract, because of the continuousness and fixity of produce.

4 Even between two dry tracts, one with plentiful earlier and later crops, with crops ripening with a little rain, with undertakings not held up, is preferable.

5 Even between two tracts abounding in water, one with sowings of grains is preferable to one not conducive to the sowing of grains.

6 In the case of the smallness or largeness of these two, a large tract, (though) unfavourable to crops, is preferable to a small one favourable to crops. 7 For, in a large tract, there are plants growing on land and those growing in water. 8 And undertakings like the fort and so on are carried out in plenty. 9 For, the qualities of land are such as are contrived by man.

10 As between the benefit of mines and that of grains, the benefit of mines brings the treasury into being, that of grains brings the treasury and the magazine into being. 11 For, the undertaking of works like the fort and so on is dependent on grains. 12 Or, the benefit of mines, with an extensive sale (of their produce), is preferable.

13 'As between the usefulness of a material forest and an elephant forest, the use of a material forest is the source of all undertakings and able to secure plenty of stores, the reverse is the use of an elephant forest,' say the teachers. 14 'No,' says Kauṭilya. 15 It is possible to plant many material forests in many tracts of land, not so an elephant forest. 16 For, the destruction of an enemy's forces is principally dependent on elephants.

17 As between the use of a water-route and that of a land-route, the use of a water-route is not constant, the use of a land-route is constant.

18 As between land with people disunited and one with people in bands, that with people disunited is preferable. 19 One with people disunited becomes easy to enjoy, not susceptible to the instigations of others, is, however, unable to bear difficulties. 20 One with people in bands is the reverse of this, full of danger when there is a revolt.

3 *sthalam* 'which gets water only from the rains' (Cn). — *audakam* 'having a river with flowing water' (Cn).

4 *alpavarṣapākam* : it is not necessary to read *karṣa* or *karma* for *varṣa* in the compound, as Meyer proposes to do. Russ. adopts *alpakarṣapākam* from Meyer. — *asakta* 'not sticking,' i.e., not obstructed, not held up.

10 *khani-* etc. : the reference to *khani*, *vana* and *vaṇikpatha* (in ss. 10-17) here is from the point of view of the land, whether it is better to have a mine or fields on the land and so on. Their intrinsic merits are considered in 7.12.6-28. 12 *mahāviṣayavikrayaḥ*, i.e., for whose sale there are many customers (Cn). Cf. 7.12.25.

16 *hastipradhāno* etc. : cf. 2.2.13.

18 *śreṇīmanuṣyā* : the *śreṇī* is a compact group following the same profession ; some of the groups followed the profession of arms when occasion required it. It is these that are meant here. 19 *anāpatsahā* : Cf. 7.5.36.

21 In the matter of settling the four *varṇas* on that (land), one consisting mostly of lower *varṇas* is preferable because of its capacity to yield all (kinds of) benefits, one with farmers (being preferable) because of plentifulness and definiteness of agriculture, one with cowherds because of its starting agriculture and other undertakings, one with rich traders because of the benefit of stores of goods and loans.

22 Of the excellences of land, affording shelter is best.

23 As between land with the support of a fort and one with the support of men, the one with the support of men is preferable. 24 For, a kingdom is that which has men. 25 Without men, like a barren cow, what could it yield?

26 But when intending to acquire land, the settlement of which would entail heavy losses and expenses, he should first make a bargain with a purchaser, who is weak, or not of royal blood, or without energy, or without a party, or unjustly behaved, or vicious, or trusting in fate, or who does whatever pleases him.

27 For, a weak king, (though) of royal blood, settling on land, the settlement of which entails heavy losses and expenses, perishes with his subjects bound to him by ties, because of the losses and expenses. 28 One not of royal blood, (though) strong, is deserted by his subjects not bound by ties to him, through fear of losses and expenses.

29 One without energy, however, not using force even when possessed of troops, is broken along with his troops because of the losses and expenses.

30 One without a party, though possessed of a treasury, does not achieve anything, being deficient in conferring the benefit (on the land) of losses and expenses.

21 *cāturvarṇyaniveśe* is from Cn; *-abhiniveśe* in the reading of the mss. is not likely. — It is proposed to read *karṣakavatī*, corresponding to *gorakṣaka-* and *vaṇik-* in the following clauses; these are the practitioners of the three-fold *vārttā*. Cn seems to have read *karṣaṇa-*, *gorakṣya-* and *vāṇijya-*, which refer to *vārttā* directly. But a reference to the inhabitants seems better in connection with *cāturvarṇyaniveśa*, though the four *varṇas* as such are not mentioned. — *ṛṇa*: loans by the traders to the state appear also a possible idea.

23 *puruṣāpāśrayā* 'having the support of men,' i.e., with plenty of men to sustain the kingdom, and ensure its security. 25 *gauḥ*: there may be a pun on the word, 'cow' and 'earth'; cf. s. 45 below.

26 *pūrvam eva*: the idea is, the land would be seized from the purchaser by the *vijigīṣu* after the former is broken in the attempt. If the land remains undeveloped, the only gain of the *vijigīṣu* would be the sale-price.

27 *sagandhābhiḥ*: this means in effect that the subjects are attached to the dynasty for generations. Cf. 1.8.16 ff.

29 *daṇḍa* is 'army' as well as 'force.'

30 *kṣayavyayānugraha-*: the 'benefit' of *kṣaya* and *vyaya* is conferred on the land, which only then yields fruits; and *vyaya* etc. cannot be made in the absence of people (party) to support him in the undertaking. — *na kutaścit prāpnoti*, i.e., does not get anything out of the land.

31 The unjustly behaved would cause even settled land to be laid waste. 32 How could he cause settlement on unsettled land ? 33 By that is explained the vicious king.

34 One trusting in fate, being devoid of human endeavour, perishes, because he does not start undertakings or his undertakings have miscarried.

35 One doing whatever pleases him does not achieve anything. 36 And he is the worst of them all. 37 'One undertaking any work whatever, may perchance find a weak point of the conqueror,' say the teachers. 38 'As (he may find) a weak point, so he may meet with destruction as well,' says Kauṭilya.

39 In case he does not find (any of) these, he should settle the land as we shall explain in 'securing the enemy in the rear.'

40 This is a pact for fixing.

41 When asked by a strong king to sell land which is possessed of excellences or which can be seized (by him), he should give it after making a pact. 42 This is an open pact. 43 When asked by an equal, he should give after considering grounds for doing so : 'The land is easily recoverable by me or under my control ; being tied to it, the enemy will come under my control ; or, through the sale of the land, I shall get an ally and money, which will strengthen my undertakings.' 44 By that is explained a weaker king purchasing (land from him).

45 A king knowing the science (of politics), acquiring in this manner an ally, money and land with men and without men, over-reaches the confederates.

37 The *hi* shows that the *ācāryas* are justifying a view which does not agree that *yatkiṁcanakārī* is the worst of these. We have obviously a quotation here from an early source discussing this point. 38 There is a little sarcasm here.

39 *pārṣṇigrāhopagrahe*, i.e., as described in 7.16.16 below.

40 *abhihita* 'spoken' seems rather to have reference to 'fixing' or fastening the land on some one through the treaty. Russ. renders by 'with pre-conditions.'

41 For *ādeyā*, cf. 9.4.5. 42 *anibhṛta*, i.e., open or public ; there is no intention to over-reach the strong king. 43 *mitrahiraṇyalābhaḥ* : an ally is secured in the *sama* king, and the price realised from the sale is the *hiraṇya* that is secured.

CHAPTER TWELVE

SECTION 116 (Continued)

(iv) Pact for an Undertaking

1 'Let us two build a fort,' is a pact for an undertaking.

2 Of the two, he who causes a fort to be built that is nature-made, unassailable, (and) requires small expenses in making, over-reaches. 3 Even among them, of a land-fort, a river-fort and a mountain-fort, each later one is preferable to each earlier one.

4 Of two water-works, one with naturally flowing water is preferable to one into which water has to be brought. 5 Even among two water-works with naturally flowing water, one with an extensive region for sowing is preferable.

6 Of two material forests, he who fells (for his use) a material forest, which is large, has forest land rich in materials of high value, is on the border of his territory and is watered by a river, over-reachers. 7 For, that which is watered by a river has easy means of livelihood and becomes a refuge in times of trouble.

8 Of two elephant forests, he who raises an elephant forest, with many brave animals, with weak neighbours, causing endless trouble (to enemies), on the border of his territory, over-reaches. 9 Even in that case, 'As between one with many but dull (elephants) and one with few but brave, the one with few but brave elephants is preferable; for, on the brave depends the fight; the few brave rout the many dull, (and) those routed become the destroyers of their own troops,' say the teachers. 10 'No,' says Kauṭilya. 11 The many dull are preferable; because of their use in the army, they carry out many tasks, become the refuge of their own troops in battle and unassailable

7.12

1 *tvaṁ cāhaṁ ca* etc.: each separately proposes to build his own fort. — Other types of *karma* such as *setubandha* would be covered by similar pacts.

3 For forts of different kinds, see 2.3.1-2.

4 *āhāryodaka* refers principally to reservoirs for storing rain-water (Cs). Cf. 2.1.20 for these terms.

6 *chedayati* apparently refers to the cutting of trees which is the prime use of these forests. We expect, however, a reference to the laying out of these forests rather than to their cutting.

8 *durbalaprativeśam*: this is because if the neighbouring king is strong, he might seize the elephant forest. Cs has 'where there is less comfortable residence than in the fixed stables,' which seems doubtful. — *anantāvakleśi*: the troubles would evidently be caused to neighbouring kingdoms. Cs has 'with numerous exits and entrances' which again is doubtful. Meyer proposes *-avakledi* 'having a perennial source of moisture, i.e., water,' which also is unconvincing. Russ. adopts Meyer's *-kledi* 'possessing considerable humidity.' 9 *kuṇṭha* primarily means 'dull, indolent' and does not quite mean 'craven, cowardly,' though it is replaced by *aśūra* in the sequel. 11 *skandhaviniyogāt*: the word *skandha* seems to mean 'troops, armed forces' as in 12.3.16; 12.4.20; cf. *skandhāvāra* 'an enclosure for troops, a camp.'

and frightful to the enemies. 12 For, to the many dull, bravery can be imparted by means of training, but numerousness cannot be created at all in the few brave.

13 Of two mines, he who causes a mine to be opened, yielding plenty of valuable ores, with roads not inaccessible, and operated with small expenditure, over-reaches. 14 Even in that case, as between few things of high value and plenty of things of small value, 'The few things of high value are to be preferred, for, diamonds, rubies, pearls, corals and gold and silver ores swallow up the many objects of small value by their excessively high value,' say the teachers. 15 'No,' says Kautilya. 16 A purchaser for an object of high value is rare and found after a long time, while there are plenty for objects of small value because of a constant demand.

17 But that is explained the trade route.

18 Even as to that, 'As between a water-route and a land-route, the water-route is preferable, involving little expenditure and exertion and yielding plenty of goods,' say the teachers. 19 'No,' says Kauṭilya. 20 The water-route is restricted in movements, not usable at all times, a source of great dangers and without remedies; the land-route is the opposite of this.

21 In the case of a water-way, however, as between a route along the shore and one on high sea, the route along the coast is preferable because of the large number of ports, or a river-route, because of perennial use and because the dangers in it can be withstood.

22 Even in the case of a land-route, 'The route to the Himavat is preferable to the southern route, for the commodities of elephants, horses, perfumes, ivory, skins, silver and gold are of very high value,' say the teachers. 23 'No,' says Kauṭilya. 24 (These) with the exception of the commodities of blankets, skins and horses, besides the commodities of conch-shells, diamonds, rubies, pearls and gold are more plentiful on the southern route.

25 Even in the case of the route to the south, the trade-route with many mines, with commodities of high value, with well-secured movements, or requiring little expenditure and exertion, is preferable, or one with commodities of small value, with an extensive scope (for sale).

14 *grasate* 'swallows up', i.e., surpasses in usefulness. 16 *sātatyād*, i.e., because there are always customers for them.

18 *prabhūtapaṇyodayaḥ* 'in which there is the securing of many commodities,' appears better than 'in which great profit (*udaya*) is secured on commodities.' 20 *prakṛṣṭabhaya-yoniḥ*: sea-voyage is primarily thought of.

21 *saṁyānapatha* is clearly voyage on the high seas. Cf. 2.28.1. — *paṇyapattana* is read in conformity with earlier passages, 2.6.3; 2.28.4,12 etc.

22 *dakṣiṇāpatha* 'route to the south' is not the name of a region here. The standpoint is that of a person in the midlands, neither a southerner nor a northerner. 24 Apparently trade to the south was more developed in Kauṭilya's days than in those of the earlier teachers.

25 *prasiddha-* seems to have the sense of 'well-secured,' not infested by robbers, etc. It may also mean 'well-known,' i.e., well-established. — *prabhūtaviṣayaḥ*: see 7.11.12.

26 By that are explained the trade-routes to the east and the west.

27 Even in that case, as between a wheel-track and a foot-path, the wheel-track is preferable, as it enables undertakings on a large scale, or the path for donkeys and camels in conformity with the place and time. 28 By these is explained the 'shoulder' path.

29 The flourishing of an enemy's undertaking is decline for the leader, advancement in the reverse case; when the course of undertakings is equal, that should be known by the conqueror as his own stable condition.

30 Smallness of profit and excess of expenditure is decline, advancement in the reverse case; equality of income and expenditure in undertakings should be known as the stable condition for himself.

31 Therefore, from among a fort and so on, he should secure an undertaking requiring little expenditure and yielding large profit and get a special advantage. Thus have been described pacts for undertakings.

CHAPTER THIRTEEN

SECTION 117 CONSIDERATIONS REGARDING THE KING ATTACKING IN THE REAR

1 Of the conqueror and the enemy, who, joining together, intend attacking in the rear two enemies who have attacked their enemies, he, who attacks in the rear a king rich in powers, over-reaches (the other). 2 For, one, rich in powers, might, after exterminating the enemy, exterminate the attacker in the rear, not the one, weak in power, who has not obtained any gain.

27 *cakrapatha* is obviously 'a track for carriages'; it can hardly mean 'for a wheel-barrow carried about by a man' (Cs). — *pādapatha* appears to mean 'a road for draught-animals' as in Meyer. 28 *aṁsapatha* seems to be a path for men carrying goods on their shoulders; *aṁsabhāra* in 2.12.24. The word can hardly mean 'path for bullocks etc. yoked to carts' (Cs).

29 *karmapathe*: perhaps the original reading was *karmaphale.*

30 This description is independent of any comparison with a rival enemy.

31 *viśiṣṭaḥ syād*: this has reference to *viśiṣṭa lābha* that is to be secured.

7.13

The question discussed is, when is it profitable to attack an enemy in the rear while he is engaged in fighting in front?

1 The discussion assumes a rivalry between the *vijigīṣu* and his enemy in the matter of *pārṣṇigrahaṇa*; each has an enemy engaged in a fight elsewhere and each can attack his own enemy in the rear. The situation is likely to occur only rarely in actual life. But for purposes of discussion, visualisation of such situations is more convenient and is hence availed of in these Chapters beginning with 7.6. — *saṁhatya* 'joining together' refers only to a common understanding between the two. There is no joining of forces nor a pact between the two. — *atisaṁdhatte*: Meyer thinks that here and in some places in this Chapter we have to read *atisaṁdhīyate.* That is not right. The next s. points out the necessity of attacking a powerful king in the rear; the king who does that definitely gains an advantage. The *pārṣṇigrahaṇa* in this case is preventive in character, to avert a future disaster.

3 In case of equality of power, he, who attacks in the rear one with an extensive undertaking, over-reaches. 4 For, one with an extensive undertaking, might, after exterminating the enemy, exterminate the attacker in the rear, not the one with a small undertaking, with his army stuck.

5 In case of equality of undertakings, he, who attacks in the rear one marching with all troops mobilised, over-reaches. 6 For, with his base denuded (of troops), he becomes easy to overpower for him, not the one marching with a part of the troops only, who has made provision for guarding his rear.

7 In case of equality of troops raised, he, who attacks in the rear one marching against a moving enemy, over-reaches. 8 For, one marching against a moving enemy might, after easily attaining success, exterminate the attacker in the rear, not the one marching against an entrenched enemy. 9 For, that (king), if he is repulsed by the fort and turns round against the attacker in the rear, is checked by the entrenched enemy.

10 By that are explained the earlier (kings).

11 In case of equality of the enemies, he, who attacks in the rear one attacking a righteous king, over-reaches. 12 For, one attacking a righteous king is hated by his own people and by others, one attacking an unrighteous king is liked (by them).

13 By that is explained the attack in the rear of one who squanders his patrimony, one living in the present and the niggardly one.

3 *vipulārambha* refers to a military operation on an extensive scale. That being likely to yield results, a preventive *pārṣṇigrahaṇa* is recommended. Here too Meyer has *atisaṁdhīyate*. Russ. follows Meyer in this case. 4 *saktacakraḥ* 'whose army is stuck (i.e., being small, is unable to achieve its object).' There is thus no future danger for the king in the rear. Cs has 'whose army is dispersed (*vikṣipta*),' which is doubtful.

6 *śūnyamūlo* etc.: this is an aggressive *pārṣṇigrahaṇa*.

7 *calāmitram*, i.e., an enemy without a fort. — Meyer has *atisaṁdhīyate* here. 9 *pratinivṛttaḥ sthitena* is as proposed by Meyer for *pratinivṛttasthitena*. Cs explains the latter 'if the rear is attacked (*pārṣṇigrāhe*, i.e., *pārṣṇigrahaṇe kriyamāṇe sati*), the heel-catcher is suppressed by the enemy who has turned back, being foiled by the fort.' This is unlikely. The subject for *avagṛhyate* cannot be different from *asau durgapratihataḥ*. The idea here seems to be, there is no future danger that needs to be averted by the preventive action of *pārṣṇigrahaṇa*; it is, therefore, unnecessary. For the enemy would be foiled by the fort; and even if he were to turn back against the rear enemy (who might have attacked him) he would be held in check by the enemy in the fort, who may be supposed to be the ally of the *pārṣṇigrāha* and who, in any case, would harass the repulsed enemy who had attacked him.

10 *pūrve* seems to refer to the *hīnaśakti*, the *alpārambha* and the *ekadeśabalaprayāta* of ss. 2, 4, and 6 in whose case also the *pārṣṇigrahaṇa* is unnecessary.

11 After *sveṣām*, it is proposed to add *pareṣām* as in 9.4.10; that is shown by the *ca*. — The motive here is ease in orverthrowing the enemy.

13 *mūlahara-* etc.: cf. 2.9.21-23; though the definitions there refer primarily to state servants, they can also apply to kings. The idea evidently is, one who attacks such kings becomes *saṁpriya* and hence his *pārṣṇigrahaṇa* is inadvisable. According to Cs, as between the attacker of a *mūlahara* and that of a *tādātvika*, the former should be preferred for attack in the rear, while as between the attacker of a *tādātvika* and that of a *kadarya*, the latter should be preferred for an attack in the rear. This is hardly likely. The preference for the former in one case and for the latter in the other would be very strange. And no comparison between these seems intended.

14 The same motives (hold good) for attacking in the rear those attacking their allies.

15 As between one attacking his ally and the other attacking his enemy, he, who attacks in the rear the one attacking his ally, over-reaches. 16 For, one attacking an ally, might, after easily obtaining success, exterminate the attacker in the rear. 17 For, it is easy to make peace with an ally, not with an enemy.

18 As between one uprooting an ally and one uprooting an enemy, he, who attacks in the rear one uprooting an enemy, over-reaches. 19 For, one uprooting his enemy, with allies grown in strength, might exterminate the attacker in the rear, not the other, destroying his own party.

20 In case the two (enemies) have come away without obtaining a gain, that attacker in the rear, whose enemy is frustrated in securing a great gain or whose enemy has suffered heavy losses and expenses, over-reaches. 21 In case they have come after obtaining a gain, that attacker in the rear, whose enemy is weaker in point of gain or power, over-reachers, or in whose case the enemy against whom (his enemy) had marched might do harm to the enemy in battle.

22 Even of two kings attacking (their enemies) in the rear, he who is superior in raising troops for an undertaking capable of achievement, or who is an entrenched enemy, or who is situated on the flank (of the enemy), over-reaches. 23 For, one situated on the flank can go to the rescue of the king to be attacked and is dangerous to the (enemy's) base, one situated in the rear is only dangerous to the base.

14 *te eva hetavaḥ*, i.e., all considerations mentioned in ss. 1-13 in connection with *parābhiyoginau* would also apply to *mitrābhiyoginau*, enemies who attack their own allies.

15 *mitrābhiyoginaḥ* : Meyer would read *amitrābhiyoginaḥ* or in the alternative *atisaṁdhīyate*. The correctness of *mitrā-* is, however, shown by the next s.

18 *amitroddhāriṇaḥ* is from Cs : its correctness is shown by the next s. — The difference between *abhi-yuj* and *ud-hṛ* seems to be that in the latter the enemy is completely exterminated, and his territory seized. — *vṛddhamitraḥ* : apparently the success in uprooting the enemy brings in new allies.

20 *yasya amitraḥ* : the *amitra* is not the *vijigīṣu's* rival as Meyer thinks, but the king who is to be attacked in the rear. 21 *lābhena śaktyā hīnaḥ* : a *vā* seems necessary after *śaktyā*. Meyer, however, has 'who has lost in power because of the gain,' which seems hardly likely. — *yasya vā* etc. : *yasya* refers to the attacker in the rear; *śatroḥ* refers to the enemy whose rear he would attack ; and *yātavya* is the king attacked by this *śatru*. Cs has 'that *pārṣṇigrāha* gets an advantage to whose enemy (viz., the *vijigīṣu*) the enemy attacked (viz., the *ari*) is able to do harm in battle.' This is quite unlikely ; the *vijigīṣu* and *ari* are themselves thought of as *pārṣṇigrāhas* in this Chapter. See s. 1.

22 *śakyārambha-* etc. : a single idea 'raising troops for an undertaking which can succeed' (Cs) is better than two ideas 'possible undertakings and the raising of troops' (Meyer). — *pārśva* is not the side of the *yātavya* (Cs), but of the attacking king. Cf. s. 24 below.

24 Three kinds of attackers in the rear should be known as impeding the activity of the enemy : the group of neighbouring kings in the rear and the two neighbours on the two flanks.

25 The weak king situated between the leader and the enemy is called a buffer ; he is a hindrance to the strong, if possessed of a fort or a forest as a place of retreat.

26 But when the conqueror and the enemy, intending to secure the middle king, attack the middle king in the rear, he who, when that king returns after securing the gain, divides the middle king from his ally and secures a former enemy as an ally, over-reaches. 27 The enemy who helps is fit to be allied with, not the ally who has renounced his friendly feelings.

28 By that is explained the intention to secure the neutral king.

29 'But in the case of attack in the rear and march against an enemy, prosperity results from diplomatic fight. 30 For, in a fight with military operations, there is loss of prosperity for both sides because of losses and expenses. 31 For, even after winning, a king with his army and treasury depleted becomes a loser,' say the teachers. 32 'No,' says Kauṭilya. 33 Even with very great losses and expenses, the destruction of the enemy must be brought about.

24 *sāmantaḥ* is an emendation from Meyer ; the singular is preferable in view of *vargaḥ* with which it should be construed. — Cs understands the three to be (i) *sāmantāḥ*, (ii) *pṛṣṭhatovargaḥ* and (iii) *prativeśau* at the sides. This is unlikely. A *sāmanta* who can be described as a *pārṣṇigrāha*, cannot be in front and if he is in the rear or at the side, he would be included in (ii) or (iii) of Cs.

25 *pratighātaḥ* : Cs reads *pratighāte* and explains 'when the strong king attacks him, he has a refuge in a fort or a forest,' adding that *antardhi* is so called because he disappears in this way (cf. *antardhāna*). *pratighāta* is, however, an obstacle, a hindrance, hardly an attack. And *antardhi* seems to be from *antar-dhā* 'to place between two.' Cf. 7.18.29, where curiously Cs quotes the present passage with the reading *pratighātaḥ*. — *durgāṭavyapasāravān* : cf. 7.7.2.

26 *madhyamaṁ lipsamānayoḥ* : both the *vijigīṣu* and the *ari* are anxious to get the *madhyama* in his own control ; one of them is an ally of the *madhyama*, the other is not. In this situation, the *madhyama* launches an attack on a third king; the *vijigīṣu* and the *ari* each wants to attack him in the rear. The one who is not in alliance with the *madhyama* scores over the other who is his ally. For, the *madhyama* would naturally be angry with the latter who despite the alliance had attacked him in the rear ; he would leave that ally and make an alliance with the rival of that old ally. He might regard the latter's *pārṣṇigrahaṇa* as understandable because he was known to be originally hostile. — *amitram*, i.e, *madhyamam*. 27 *śatruḥ* is the *pārṣṇigrāha* who formerly was not in alliance with the *madhyama*. — *upakurvāṇaḥ* suggests that the attack in the rear by this former enemy was nominal, and even aid may have been surreptitiously given by this *pārṣṇigrāha* to the *madhyama*. Meyer thinks that it is the *vijigīṣu* and the *ari* who return with the gain (*labdhalābhāpagamane*). That is unlikely. It is the attacking king who would be returning with the gain, not the *pārṣṇigrāha*. Cf. ss. 20, 21 above. — In s. 26 Cs has *gṛhṇataḥ* for *gṛhṇatoḥ* ; but *yaḥ* presupposes the dual. The idea (in Cs) that the *madhyama* is engaged in helping one (*vijigīṣu* or *ari*) while the other attacks him in the rear does not seem likely when both of them are *lipsamāna* in respect of the *madhyama*.

29 For *mantrayuddha*, cf. 12.2. The ancient teachers seem to be averse to actual fighting. 33 *abhyupagantavyaḥ* used in the literal sense, 'should be brought about.'

34 When losses and expenses are equal, he who, after first bringing about the destruction of his own treasonable troops (and) becoming free from thorns, would afterwards fight with troops under control, over-reachers. 35 Even of two, securing first the destruction of their treasonable troops, he, who would secure the destructon of a large number, of more powerful and extremely treacherous troops, over-reaches.

36 By that is explained the destruction of alien and forest troops.

37 When the conqueror may become the attacker in the rear, the attacker in front or one marched against, then in those cases, he should carry out the following course for a leader.

38 The leader should attack in the rear the enemy attacking his ally, after first making (the enemy's) ally in (his) rear become engaged in a fight with the rescuer of the attacker in the rear (i.e., of himself).

39 When attacking (in front) he should keep off the enemy in his rear by his ally in the rear, similarly (keep off) the ally of the enemy in the rear by the ally of his ally in the rear.

40 And in front he should make his ally engage in fight with the enemy's ally, and should keep off the ally of the enemy's ally by the ally of his own ally.

41 When attacked, he should cause the rear of the attacker to be attacked by his ally and keep off the rear ally (of the attacker) from the attacker in the rear by the ally of his ally.

34 *purastāt . . . ghātayitvā*, i.e., by placing them in front to bear the enemy's first onslaught. — The *atisaṁdhi* is on the hypothetical basis of rivalry between the *vijigīṣu* and *ari*, hardly between combatants in the same fight.

37 The *vijigīṣu* may find himself in three situations, as a *pārṣṇigrāha* or as an *abhiyoktā* (aggressor) or as a *yātavya* (victim of aggression). The three situations are discussed in ss. 38, 39-40 and 41 respectively. Meyer thinks of two cases, an *abhiyoktā* becoming a *pārṣṇigrāha* of the conqueror and a *yātavya* becoming the conqueror's *pārṣṇigrāha*. This is quite unlikely. How can kings supposedly in front attack in the rear?

38 The *śatru* attacks the *vijigīṣu*'s ally; hence the *vijigīṣu* attacks the *śatru* in the rear; he becomes his *pārṣṇigrāha*. — *ākranda* is the *śatru*'s ally in the rear; he is really the *vijigīṣu*'s rear enemy, his *pārṣṇigrāha*. He is engaged in fight by the *vijigīṣu*'s own rear ally, who is called *pārṣṇigrāhābhisārin*, because the *vijigīṣu* has become the *pārṣṇigrāha*. These terms are not rigid as Meyer supposes, but differ according to each particular situation. In this stanza, the enemy as the attacker becomes the centre and the *vijigīṣu* becomes his *pārṣṇigrāha*. Meyer's translation 'after he has made his own ally in the rear engage in fight the ally of his rear enemy' does not show what the *vijigīṣu*'s *pārṣṇigrāha* himself is to do.

39 *ākrandena* is to be construed with *nivārayet*, not with *abhiyuñjānaḥ* (as in Meyer).

40 *avaghaṭṭayet*, i.e., make him engage in fight. — Stanzas 39 and 40 go together.

41 Whereas *mitra* and *mitramitra* are from the *vijigīṣu*'s point of view, *ākranda* and *pārṣṇigrāha* are from the attacking enemy's point of view; the latter are the *vijigīṣu*'s *arimitra* and *mitra* respectively. Meyer who understands fixed princes by these terms (from the *vijigīṣu*'s point) finds himself in deep waters. He asks, how can the *mitramitra*, three states away in front, help the *ākranda* one state away in the rear? His rendering of *nivārayet* 'should rescue' or 'should warn,' unlikely in itself, is of no help.

42 In this way, the conqueror should establish in the rear and in front, a circle (of kings) in his own interest, with the excellences of the constituent, called the ally.

43 And in the entire circle, he should ever station envoys and secret agents, becoming a friend of the rivals, maintaining secrecy when striking again and again.

44 The affairs of one, who cannot maintain secrecy, even if achieved with particular success, undoubtedly perish, like a broken boat in the ocean.

CHAPTER FOURTEEN

SECTION 118 RECOUPMENT OF POWERS THAT HAVE BECOME WEAK

1 When attacked by confederates in this manner, the conqueror should say to the one who is the principal among them, 'With you, I would make peace; here is money and I shall be an ally, you will (thus) have a double advancement; it does not behove you to let your enemies, masquerading as friends, thrive at your cost; for, these, when grown powerful, will overthrow you yourself.'

2 Or, he should sow dissensions, saying 'Just as I, who had done no harm, am attacked by these kings joining together, so will they, with their forces combined, attack you also, when at ease or in a calamity; for, strength changes the mind; prevent that (strength) of theirs.'

3 When they are divided, he should support the principal and make him fight with the weaker (confederates) or giving help to the weaker make them fight with the principal, or so (act) as he may consider better (for himself). 4 Or, making one entertain enmity towards the others, he should divide him from them.

5 Or, secretly offering a greater gain to the principal, he should get peace made (through him). 6 Then agents in the pay of both, pointing to the

42 *mitraprakṛti-*, i.e., the ally himself as a *prakṛti* rather than the constituents of the ally.

7.14

1 *pradhānaḥ*: this is the foremost among the confederates, their leader. — *dviguṇā* because he would be getting the money and also securing a new ally. There is nothing to show that double the amount is promised, as Cb Cs imply.

2 *svasthā vyasane vā*: perhaps we should read *svatham*; both the expressions would then refer to the king addressed. *svasthāḥ* is odd as it is descriptive of the other confederates.

3 *anugrāhya* refers to the lending of troops in particular; cf. 7.8.28-29. 4 *vairaṁ vā* etc. is repeated from 7.8.4 above.

5 *phalabhūyastvena*, i.e., by the promise of more than what he would be getting from the confederacy. 6 *ubhayavetanāḥ*: see 1.12.17-18. — *uddūṣayeyuḥ*: the idea is of poisoning

greater gain, should poison the minds of the confederates, saying 'You have been cheated.' 7 When they have become vitiated, he should violate the treaty. 8 Then agents in the pay of both should bring about a further discord among them, saying 'This is what we had pointed out.' 9 When they are divided, he should act by supporting one of them.

10 In the absence of a principal (among them), he should secure from among the confederates one who had roused them, or one persevering in his undertakings, or one with loyal subjects, or one who had joined the confederacy out of greed or fear, or one afraid of the conqueror, or one bound to his kingdom, or his ally or a moving enemy, the earlier ones in the absence of the later ones (in this list), — one who had roused them by a surrender of himself, one persevering in his undertakings by bowing down with conciliation, one with loyal subjects by offering and accepting girls in marriage, the greedy one by double the share, one afraid of them by helping him with treasury and army, one afraid of himself by creating confidence by the giving of a surety, one bound to his kingdom by becoming one with him, his ally by doing what is agreeable and beneficial to both or by giving up benefits (received), the moving enemy by reassuring him by desisting from doing harm and rendering help (to him). 11 Or, by whichever means any of them may be separated, by that he should secure him, or by means of conciliation, gifts, dissension and force, as we shall explain in (the section on) troubles.

their minds against the *pradhāna*. 7 *saṁdhim* : the treaty mentioned in s. 5. — *dūṣayet*, i.e., should not pay what he had agreed to pay under the treaty. 8 *evaṁ tad* : they argue, 'we told you that you were cheated; this is the proof. He is not giving you anything because he is giving more to the *pradhāna*.' This brings about the *bheda* of the other confederates from the *pradhāna*. Cs (mostly following Cb) explains 'he should violate the treaty and not give anything to the *pradhāna* on the plea that the confederates had violated it. Then the agents should say to the confederates that the *pradhāna* has brought about this violation of the treaty since he did not get the promised higher gain and since he wants to act again after joining our confederacy.' All this seems a little strange. How can the *pradhāna* be said to have brought about the violation of the treaty ? And so long as he has not received anything, he would probably be able to prove his innocence. The reasoning thought of would not necessarily lead to *bheda*. — *anyatamopagraheṇa* : the *vā* after this is unnecessary and has been dropped.

10 *pūrvān uttarābhāve* : this reading from Cb Cs is now read in the text for *pūrvānyatarābhāve*, which is an odd compound. The idea is that the later kings in the list should be tackled first for the purpose of bringing about *bheda* in the confederacy. The reason for that is that it is easier to tackle them. Thus the *calāmitra* and the *mitra* can be more easily divided from the confederacy than the earlier kings. Cb Cs, however, think that each later king is to be tackled first because he is more dangerous to the *vijigīṣu* than the earlier one, and tackling him would be more advantageous. That is not correct. The *mitra* and the *calāmitra*, mentioned last in the list, are certainly not more dangerous than those mentioned earlier. — *kanyādānayāpanābhyām* : Cb Cs have *ādāna* 'receiving' and *yāpana* 'giving.' It is likely, however, that *kanyādāna* has the usual meaning of 'giving a girl' in marriage ; cf. 7.16.6. *yāpana* can mean 'receiving, accepting.' — *viśvāsya* is from a suggestion of Meyer for *viśvāsayet* of the mss. The actual comment in Cb presupposes a form in the absolutive. A finite verb in the midst of clauses all connected with *sādhayet* is quite unlikely. — *upakāratyāgena* : the benefit received or expected from the ally might have caused estrangement ; hence it is to be given up. Cs has 'giving up tribute which he used to receive from the ally.' The idea of a regular tribute would be unusual in the case of *upakāra*. Meyer suggests *apakāratyāgena*, which does not appear necessary. — *avadhṛtam* 'held,' i.e., given assurances. 11 *ayogam* 'separation.' — *āpatsu*, i.e., in 9.5-7.

12 Or, when in a hurry because of harm caused by a calamity, he should enter into a treaty with the (surrender of his) treasury and army, stipulating the place, the time or the work. 13 After making the treaty, he should (try to) remedy his weakness.

14 If weak in a party, he should create a party of kinsmen and allies, or an unassailable fort. 15 For, one entrenched in a fort or supported by allies, becomes worthy of honour by his own (people) and by those of others.

16 If weak in the power of counsel, he should get a large number of wise men in service or asssociate with elders in the sciences. 17 For, in that way, he attains immediate good.

18 If weak in might, he should endeavour to secure the welfare of his subjects. 19 The countryside is the source of all undertakings; from them comes might. 20 The abode for it and for himself, when in trouble, is the fort. 21 Water-works are the source of crops. 22 For, ever continuous is the benefit (as) from an excellent rainfall to sowings watered by irrigaton. 23 A trade-route is the means of over-reaching the enemy. 24 For, along the trade-route is made the carrying over of troops and secret agents (into enemy territory) and the purchase of weapons, armours, carriages and vehicles, as well as bringing in and taking out. 25 Mines are the source of implements of war; material forests, of fortification work and of carriages and chariots; elephant forests, of elephants; and herds, of cattle, horses, donkeys and camels. 26 In case of their non-availability, obtaining them from groups of kinsmen and allies (should be resorted to).

27 If weak in energy, he should secure the services, as they may be available, of heroic men from bands, robber-bands, foresters and Mleccha tribes, and of secret agents capable of doing harm to enemies.

28 Or, he should employ against the enemies 'steps against an enemy-mixed trouble' or 'the conduct of the weaker king.'

29 Being thus enriched with a party, with counsel, with material resources and army, he should march out to overthrow the suppression of himself by enemies.

12 *avadhṛtam* 'fixed' as to place, time etc.

18 For *prabhāva* in this and the next s. the mss. curiously show *prabhava*. 20 *tasya*, i.e., *janapadasya*, implying the inhabitants in it; Cf. 8.1.25. *tasya* can hardly be *prabhāvasya* (Cs). 22 The idea is, what good rain secures in the monsoon, irrigation secures all the year round. 24 *atinayana*: Cf. 13.3.48. — Cb comment shows *-krayavikrayaś ca*. — *praveśo nirṇayanaṁ ca* 'bringing in and taking out' of the goods just mentioned and other goods. A general 'entrance and exit' is possible, but seems less likely. 25 *-rathoṣṭrāṇām* of the mss. is obviously corrupt for *-kharoṣṭrāṇām*. — Ss. 19-25 refer to undertakings as the sources of *prabhāva*.

27 *parāpakāriṇām* is an adjective to *gūḍhapuruṣāṇām* (Cs) rather than an independent substantive (Meyer).

28 *paramiśrāpratīkāram* as in 9.6.11 ff. Cb Cs read *paramiśraḥ pra-* 'having made peace with the enemy etc.' Cb comment shows *paramitraḥ* 'turning his enemy into an ally'; neither of these is likely. 9.6.11 was obviously lost sight of. — *ābalīyasam* as in Book 12.

29 *parāvagraham ātmanaḥ* can hardly mean 'for the putting down of his enemies' (Meyer). For such a sense *ātmanaḥ* would be quite unnecessary.

CHAPTER FIFTEEN

SECTION 119 REASONS FOR ENTRENCHING ONESELF (IN A FORT) AFTER MAKING WAR WITH A STRONG KING

SECTION 120 CONDUCT (PROPER) FOR THE KING SURRENDERING WITH HIS TROOPS

1 A weak king attacked by a strong king, should resort for shelter to one with strength greater than his, whom the other would not over-reach by the power of counsel. 2 Among those with an equal power of counsel, superiority (comes) from the excellence of men under them or from association with elders.

3 In the absence of one of greater strength, he should stay joining forces with kings equal in strength or with oligarchies equal in strength to the strong king, whom he would not over-reach with powers of counsel and might. 4 Among those with equal powers of counsel and might, superiority (comes) from extensiveness of undertakings.

5 In the absence of those equal in strength, he should stay joining forces with kings inferior in strength who are upright, energetic and opposed to the strong king, whom he would not over-reach with powers of counsel, might and energy. 6 Among those with an equal power of energy, superiority (comes) from the attainment of terrain suitable for one's own (mode of) fighting. 7 Among those with an equally suitable terrain, superiority (comes) from the attainment of a season suited to one's own (mode of) fighting. 8 Among those with equally suitable terrains and seasons, superiority (comes) from draught-animals, weapons and armours.

9 In the absence of help-mates, he should find shelter in a fort where the enemy, even with a large army, would not cut off his food, fodder, fuel and water, and would himself meet with losses and expenses. 10 Among forts

7.15

The two closely related Sections are to be found in ss. 1-20 and 21-30 respectively.

2 *tulyamantraśaktīnām* : Cb Cs read *-bala-* after *tulya-*. But *bala* is out of place here. — *āyattasaṁpadaḥ* : it is possible that the original reading was *amātya-*, who are principally to be understood by *āyatta*. Cf., however, 9.6.7. These expressions describe characteristics of the weak king's possible ally.

3 Most mss. read *tulyabalasaṁkhyaiḥ*, which Cs explains 'having the same number of troops.' This does not differ from *samabala*. Meyer has 'who are his equals (*tulya*) in point of number of troops.' Equality with the king attacked is beside the point. *-saṁghaiḥ* is definitely better, the reference being to states mentioned in Book 11. — *yān na* is proposed for *yāvan na* of the mss. *yāvat* is unlikely. The actual comment in Cb seems to support *yān na* ; it has no explanation of *yāvat*. Cs has 'should fight (*tiṣṭhet*) so long as the enemy does not succeed in over-reaching him', i.e., the king is to go on fighting till the enemy divides his helpmates from him which is a strange idea. Meyer's 'till he is able to over-reach his enemy by *mantra* and *prabhāva* etc.' is also little likely. The parallel s. 1 shows that it is the strong king who might try to over-reach, not the king attacked. The latter intends to strengthen his position by alliances, which the former might try to break up.

5 *yān na* is again proposed for *yāvan na* as in s. 3. 6 *sva-* in this and the next s. refers to the helpmate, not to the king attacked.

equally impregnable, superiority (comes) from stores and refuge. 11 'For, one should seek a fortress with men, rich in stores and provided with refuge,' says Kauṭilya.

12 He should resort to that (fort) for these reasons : 'I shall win over the enemy in the rear or his ally or the middle king or the neutral king ; or, I shall cause his kingdom to be seized or destroyed by one of these, viz., his neighbouring king, a forest chief, a pretender from his family and a prince in disfavour ; or, by supporting the party of likely seceders, I shall raise a revolt in his fort, country or camp ; or, I shall kill him as I please, when he comes near, by the use of weapons, fire or poison or by occult means ; or, I shall put him to losses and expenses on account of secret practices employed by myself; or, I shall succeed in gradually instigating (against him) the group of his allies or his army, when they are severely afflicted by losses, expenses and long marches ; or, by destroying his supplies, reserves and foraging parties, I shall bring about the subjugation of his encamped army ; or by taking out troops, I shall create a weak point in him and strike with all troops mobilised ; or, I shall secure a treaty with him as desired when his energy is damped ; or, while he is engaged in a struggle with me, insurrections will rise all round him ; or, I shall cause his base, denuded of reserves, to be devastated by my ally's troops or forest troops ; or, staying in this fort, I shall protect the welfare of a vast territory ; or, if I stay here, my own dispersed troops and those of my ally will collect in one place and be irresistible ; or, my army skilled in fighting in water, in trenches or at night, being freed of the dangers of (marches on the) roads, will carry out operations when the (enemy) is near ; or, coming here on a terrain and in a season adverse to him, he will himself cease to be because of losses and expenses, (as) this region can be approached only with heavy losses and expenses because of the abundance of forts and forests as places of refuge, is full of sickness for foreigners and without a suitable terrain for the operation

10 According to Cb, this s. represents the opinion of the ancient teachers. 11 *manuṣyadurgam*, i.e., a fort with men to defend it. — *apasāra* is a place of refuge for the king as well as the subjects. A means of escape from the fort does not seem intended here. — *iti Kauṭilyaḥ* : this does not show a material difference of opinion, except that the presence of men, i.e., troops in the fort is insisted upon.

12 *pratipādayiṣyāmi* 'will secure them,' i.e., win them over and get their help. — *aupaniṣadikaiḥ* : supply *yogaiḥ*. This expression should preferably be understood independently rather than as an adjective to the preceding *śastrāgnirasapraṇidhānaiḥ*. — *svayam* refers to the *vijigīṣu* (Cs) ; a reference to the enemy (Meyer) appears less likely. — *daṇḍopanayena*, i.e., by secretly sending out some troops into the enemy's encamped forces ; that would create a weak point (*randhra*) in the enemy's army, making a sudden assault on it advantageous. The enemy must be supposed to remain unaware of the arrival in his camp of these troops. It is also possible that the troops are not sent into the camp itself, but to a place where they would create a diversion. — *āsanne* : this can hardly mean 'when the time comes.' *āsanna* refers to the enemy who has approached near. — *mahākṣayavyayābhigamyo* etc. is understood in Cn as only an explanation of *viruddhadeśa-* etc., and not as a separate *kāraṇa*. That is supported by the absence of *vā*. In fact, it seems that this whole passage beginning with *mahākṣayavyayā-* etc. up to *nirgamiṣyati* seems to be a marginal gloss in explanation of the preceding clause. — *āpadgato pravekṣyati* 'will enter when in dire

of their troops, (and hence) he will enter it (only) when in trouble, and will not get out of it if he enters.'

13 'In the absence of (such) reasons, or when the enemy has very great strength, he should leave the fort and go away. 14 Or, like a moth in fire, he should fall (desperately) on the enemy. 15 For, achievement of one thing or the other is certain for one giving up all hope of himself,' say the teachers. 16 'No,' says Kauṭilya. 17 Finding out suitable conditions for peace between himself and the enemy, he should make peace. 18 In the reverse case, he should seek peace after a fight or seek escape. 19 To one with whom peace is possible, he should send an envoy. 20 Or, if one is sent by him, he should welcome him with money and honour, and say, 'These are gifts for the king, these for the queen and princes from my queen and princes ; this kingdom and myself are at your disposal.'

21 After obtaining shelter, he should behave towards the suzerain as in (the section on) 'proper behaviour.' 22 And he should carry out undertakings like the fort and others as well as the accepting and giving of princesses in marriage, coronation of the prince, purchase of horses, catching of elephants, holding sacrificial sessions or fairs and going on pleasure-trips, (only) when permitted. 23 Agreements with constituents remaining in his own territory or punishment of deserters, — he should carry out all, when permitted.

24 Or, if his citizens and country people have turned hostile, he should request for another land, being justly behaved. 25 Or, he should deal with them by silent punishment, as with treasonable persons. 26 He should not accept even suitable land being given to him from his ally.

27 When the suzerain cannot be seen, he should see one of these, viz., (his) minister, chaplain, commander-in-chief and crown prince, and should confer obligations on them as far as he is able.

straits and there is no other go ' (Cn) is to be preferred to 'as soon as he enters he will be in trouble '(Cs.)

15 *anyatarasiddhiḥ*, i.e., victory or death (and consequent heaven). 18 *vikrameṇa saṁdhim* : the idea apparently is, the strong king may be impressed by his valour and agree to come to terms. — *apasāram* is here escape to a fort or forest. 20 *paṇyāgāram* refers to goods sent as gifts.

21 *labdhasaṁśrayaḥ*: the shelter obtained is with the strong king himself as suggested in ss. 19-20. — *samayācārikavat*, i.e., as in 5.5. 22 *āvāhavivāha* 'receiving and giving girls in marriage ' (Cs). The other way about is also possible. — *yātrā* can hardly mean 'a military expedition ' in this context. 23 *prakṛti* would be ministers in particular ; *saṁdhi* with them would be agreements or instructions about carrying out work in his own former state.

24 *nyāyavṛttir* is from Cb Cn Cs ; *nyāyavṛttim*, which would be an adjective to *bhūmim*, is much less likely. 26 *ucitāṁ vā* : *vā* has the sense of *api* (Meyer). A former ally must not be antagonised.

27 *adṛśyamāne bhartari* : Cn Cs have 'should see his own minister etc. only when the suzerain is not there.' His own ministers etc. are unlikely in view of *upakuryāt* that follows. Meyer proposes *dṛśyamāne bhartari* 'only when the suzerain is there,' the ministers being those of the vassal. That also is unlikely. The idea clearly is, when the suzerain cannot be seen, his minister etc. may be seen. This appears to be the explanation in Cb.

28 On occasions of worship of deities and recitations of blessings, he should cause blessings to be pronounced on him. 29 In every case, he should speak of his surrender as an excellent thing.

30 One surrendering to force should thus behave towards the suzerain in a steadfast manner, waiting on the strong, united (with him) and opposed to those suspected and so on (by him).

CHAPTER SIXTEEN

SECTION 121 CONDUCT (PROPER) FOR THE KING SUBJUGATING (OTHER KINGS) BY FORCE

1 The strong king, desirous of conquering one causing harassment, though the terms of the treaty were accepted (by him), should march in that direction in which there is suitable terrain, suitable season and livelihood for his own troops, in which the enemy is without the refuge of a fort and without (protection in) the rear and the help of an ally. 2 In the reverse case, he should march after taking protective measures.

28 After *daivata-*, *pūjā* is to be understood. 29 The idea is, he should not show dissatisfaction with his condition. The explanation in Cs 'to all people he should speak of his surrender and should praise the virtues of his sovereign' is little likely. Cb has a similar explanation.

30 *saṁyuktabalavat* : these are the ministers etc. of the sovereign (Cn Cs). — *avasthitaḥ* may mean 'firm, steadfast.' If *evam* could be construed with it (instead of with *varteta*) we could understand 'placed in this situation.'

7.16

Cn Cs point out that *daṇḍopanāmin* would be a more appropriate name for this king as shown by s. 3. Meyer's idea that *daṇḍopanāyin* is the weak king taking his troops to the strong king is unlikely in the light of the contents of the Chapter.

1 It is proposed to read *anujñātasaṁdhipaṇodvegakaram* for *anujñātastaddhiraṇyo-* of the mss. The idea understood is that the weak king, though he had consented to the terms of the treaty, has started ignoring them, and causing harassment or trouble to the strong king, (*anujñātasaṁdhipaṇaḥ api udvegakaraḥ*). We may also understand *udvega* as 'shaking,' i.e., violation (*anujñātasaṁdhipaṇānām udvegakaram*, causing violation of the terms of the treaty accepted by him.) Cn reads *ananujñātasaṁdhipaṇyodvegakaram* 'who has not accepted (*ananujñāta*) the terms of peace (*saṁdhipaṇya*) and is therefore causing harassment (*udevga*).' *paṇya* is unusual in this sense, for which *paṇa* is the usual word. Otherwise, the meaning arrived at in Cn is also good. It adds that the reading of the mss. is an *apapāṭha* and that those trying to explain it are to be pitied. Thus Cs (mostly following Cb) has 'who causes trouble because of money promised but not paid (*adattahiraṇya*) by him, (i.e., by the strong king) though he had agreed to do so (*anujñātaḥ* as ablative singular of *anujñā*, agreement or promise).' Meyer understands the expression as an adjective to *karma* (supplied), and, with the vassal king in view, translates 'when permitted (*anujñātaḥ*) to carry out an undertaking bringing money and formidable might (*udvega*) to him, (*tad*, i.e., his suzerain), he who has surrendered, after growing strong (*balavān*) and wishing to conquer etc.' This is hardly possible. — *svartuvṛttiḥ* : *vṛtti* is 'livelihood, food etc.' (Cn Cs). — *apārṣṇir anāsāraś ca* : These expressions also describe the *śatru*, i.e., the weak *yātavya*. He should have no *pārṣṇi*, i.e., a rear which is well guarded and no *āsāra*, i.e., help expected from some ally. Thus the commentators. That seems better than understanding the expressions as describing the *balavān* king, with *pārṣṇi* understood as the *pārṣṇigrāha* and *āsāra* as the *pārṣṇigrāhāsāra* of the strong king.

3 He should subjugate the weak by means of conciliation and gifts, the strong by means of dissension and force. 4 And he should secure the members (of the kings' circle) who are immediately next to him and who are separated by one intervening state, by the exclusive use, the alternative use or the combined use of the (four) means.

5 The protection of those dwelling in villages and forests, of cattle-herds and trade-routes, and the handing over of those who are discarded, who have deserted and who have done harm, — thus should he practise conciliation. 6 The giving of land, money and girls, and the promise of safety, — thus should he practise gifts. 7 Making a demand for treasury, troops, land or inheritance by supporting one of these, viz., a neighbouring prince, a forest chief, a pretender from the family and a prince in disfavour, — thus should he sow discord. 8 Subjugation of the enemy in open, concealed or silent war or through 'means for taking a fort,' — thus should he make use of force.

9 Thus he should place those full of energy in such a way that they are helpful to the army, those possessed of might so that they are helpful to the treasury, those endowed with intellect so that they are helpful to the land.

10 Among them, he who helps in many ways with gems, articles of high value, of low value and forest produce produced in his ports, villages and mines, or with carriages and vehicles arising from material forests, elephant forests and herds, is (the ally) of varied usefulness. 11 He who gives substantial help with troops or treasury is one of great usefulness. 12 He who helps with troops, treasury and land is one of all-sided usefulness.

13 He who withstands one's enemy on one side is the (ally) useful on one side. 14 He who withstands the enemy and the enemy's ally on the two sides is one useful on both sides. 15 He who withstands the enemy, his ally, the neighbour and the forest chief on all sides is one useful on all sides.

16 And if an enemy in the rear, — a forest chieftain, a principal officer of the enemy or the enemy (himself) — be found capable of being secured by

3 *upanamayet* : it is this root that is found in *daṇḍopanata* : hence Cn's preference for *daṇḍopanāmi*- in the title. 4 *niyoga* etc. : cf. 9.7.73-76. — *anantaraikāntarāḥ* : see 6.2.14 ff.

7 Land and inheritance would be demanded on behalf of the *tatkulīna* and *aparuddha*. 8 *kūṭayuddha* : see 10.3. — *tūṣṇīṁyuddha* : see 12.4 and 12.5. — *durgalambhopāya* is Book 13.

9 *daṇḍopakāriṇaḥ* 'helpful to the army (of the *balavān*).' — The connection between *prajñā* and *bhūmi* is not quite obvious. *mantraśakti* may be helpful for administration of the territory.

10 *phalgu* had clearly got dropped out from the exemplar of the mss. through a scribal error. — *yad* . . . *tad* has the neuter *mitram* in view. 12 *-bhūmībhiḥ* is as proposed by Meyer, and is obviously quite necessary in view of the instrumentals in the parallel ss. 10-11.

14 *cobhayataḥ pratikaroti* is as proposed by Meyer ; that is obviously supported by the parallels in the other ss.

16 *pārṣṇigrāhaś ca* etc.: the translation follows Meyer in regarding *āṭavika*, *śatrumukhya* and *śatru* as three types of *pārṣṇigrāha* of the *balavān* ; and for this the reading *śatrumukhyaḥ śatrur vā* from Cb Cs is preferred to *śatrur mukhyaśatrur vā* (or *mukhyaḥ śatrur*) of the mss.

a gift of land, he should win his support with (the grant of) land without excellences ; one stationed in a fort, with land not continguous ; a forest chief, with land not yielding livelihood ; a pretender from the family of the enemy, with recoverable land ; a prince in disfavour of the enemy, with land snatched ; one with banded troops, with land having permanent enemies ; one with compact troops, with land having strong neighbouring kings ; one opposing in war, with land having both these characteristics ; one with energy, with land where military operations are not possible ; one belonging to the enemy's party, with waste land ; one enticed away, with impoverished land ; a deserter who has returned, with land the settlement of which would involve great losses and expenses ; the deserter (from the enemy) who has come over, with land without shelter ; with land that cannot be occupied by any one else, he should secure the support of its master himself.

17 He should allow to continue (as before) that one among them who is of great help and unchanging in loyalty. 18 He should silently do away with the contrary one. 19 He should gratify, according to his power to help, one who has helped him. 20 And in conformity with his efforts, he should bestow wealth and honour on him, and give help in calamities. 21 To those coming of their own accord, he should grant interviews as desired and make arrangements (for receiving them). 22 He should not use towards them insults, injuries, contemptuous words or reproaches. 23 And after promising them safety, he should favour them like a father.

24 And if any of them were to do him harm, he should proclaim his guilt and slay him openly. 25 Or, because of fright (likely) among others, he should act as in 'infliction of secret punishment'. 26 And he shall not covet the land, property, sons or wives of the slain one. 27 He should place in their appropriate positions even the members of his family. 28 He should place on the throne the son of one killed in action.

Cb Cs understand *pārṣṇigrāhaḥ* independently as the first of four kings mentioned. But the s. has in view *pārṣṇigrāhas* of different types. For, it is this s. which seems to be referred to as *pārṣṇigrāhopagraha* in 7.11.39. — *apratisaṁbaddha*, i.e., far away from the fort. — *apacchinnayā* is as suggested by Meyer. The land snatched may be from the enemy himself. — *śreṇībalam* and *saṁhatabalam* (*saṁghabalam* in Cb) are descriptive of a king. Cb Cn Cs understand these as substantives, i.e., such armies themselves are to be understood, the former being without a leader, the latter with a leader (Cb Cn Cs). — *apavāhitam* 'carried off,' i.e., enticed to come over. Cb Cs have 'distressed by the fight'; Cn 'with whom a treaty was first made, but who was then made to violate the treaty.' Cf., however, 12.3.14. — *pratyapasṛtam* : a deserter from the enemy who has come over to him. Cf. 13.4.51. — *bhartāram*, i.e., the owner of the land. This can hardly mean 'the sovereign' in the context, as Meyer thinks. He is clearly on a wrong track in this Chapter.

17 *anuvartayet*, i.e., allow him to continue in his own realm as before. 'Secure his obedience' is possible, but seems less likely. 21 *pratividhāna* seems to refer to 'arrangements' for receiving them, rather than to 'steps for protecting (himself from them)' (Cb Cs). 22 *ativāda* may mean 'excessive praise' (Cb Cn Cs) as in 4.1.59. However, 'reproach, reproof' appears more likey in the context. Cf. *ativādāṁs titikṣeta*, Manu, 6.47.

25 *dāṇḍakarmikavat*, i.e., as in 5.1. 27 *pātreṣu* 'in suitable positions' is an unusual sense.

29 In this way, the princes surrendering to force remain loyal to his sons and grandsons.

30 But the circle (of kings), being frightened, rises to destroy one who were to kill or imprison those who have submitted and covet their land, property, sons or wives. 31 And those ministers, who are under his control in their own lands, become frightened of him and resort to the circle. 32 Or, they themselves seek to take his kingdom or life.

> 33 And therefore, kings, protected in their own territories by means of conciliation, become favourably disposed towards the king, remaining obedient to his sons and grandsons.

CHAPTER SEVENTEEN

SECTION 122 THE MAKING OF PEACE
SECTION 123 LIBERATION OF THE HOSTAGE

1 Peace, treaty, hostage, these are one and the same thing. 2 The creation of confidence among kings is (the purpose of) peace, treaty or hostage.

3 'Plighting one's troth or taking an oath is an unstable pact, a surety or a hostage is stable,' say the teachers. 4 'No,' says Kauṭilya. 5 Plighting one's troth or taking an oath is a pact stable in the next world as well as here, a surety or a hostage is of use only in this world, depending on strength.

6 'We have made a pact,' thus kings of old, faithful to their word, made pacts by plighting their troth. 7 In case of (fear of) its transgression, they touched fire, water, a furrow in the field, a clod of earth from the rampart, the shoulder of an elephant, the back of a horse, the box of a chariot, a weapon, a gem, seeds, a fragrant substance, a liquid, gold or money, affirming with an oath, 'May these kill or abandon him who would break the oath'.

31 *ye cāsyāmātyāḥ svabhūmiṣvāyattāḥ* : these ministers are those of the vassals, *svabhūmiṣu* being the respective territories of the latter, and *asya*, referring to the sovereign, to be construed with *āyattāḥ*. Cb Cn Cs understand the ministers to be those of the sovereign, engaged in work (*āyatta*, i.e., *vyāpṛta*) in the vassals' territories. But if *asya* refers to the sovereign, *sva-* can hardly refer to the vassals. Meyer suggests *anāyattāḥ* 'his viceroys, unconnected with lands under their control (*svabhūmiṣu*).' *svabhūmiṣu* can hardly be understood in this way. Cf. s. 33 below.

7.17

The two Sections are to be found in ss. 1-31 and 32-61 respectively.

1 *samādhi* 'hostage' is related to *ādhi* 'pledge.' A *saṁdhi* may or may not contain a stipulation as to *samādhi*. And there can be *śama* without a *saṁdhi*.

3 *pratigraha* 'acceptance (of a hostage),' i.e., a hostage. 5 *balāpekṣaḥ* : the strength is the relative strength of the parties to the transaction. Russ. understands 'dependent on the measure of strength of him who gives them.' The explanation in Cb Cs 'the surety can be trusted only when he is strong, and the hostage only when he is the object of love (*snehapātra*) of the king who hands him over,' is hardly acceptable.

7 *agni* etc. might kill, *ratna* etc. might leave.

8 In case of (fear of) transgression of oath, the binding to suretyship of great men, ascetics or principal men constitutes surety. 9 With respect to that, he who receives sureties capable of suppressing the enemy, over-reaches. 10 The opposite of this is over-reached.

11 The holding of a kinsman or a principal officer, is receiving a hostage. 12 With respect to that, he who gives a treasonable minister or a treasonable child, over-reaches. 13 The opposite of this is over-reached. 14 For, the enemy strikes without compunction at the weak points of one who is trustful because of receiving a hostage.

15 When keeping a child as a hostage, however, as between giving a son and a daughter, he who gives a daughter over-reaches. 16 For, a daughter is not an heir, and is of use to others only and cannot be harassed. 17 A son is the reverse of this.

18 Even of two sons, he who gives a son legitimately born, wise, brave, trained in the use of weapons, or an only son, is over-reached. 19 The opposite of this over-reaches. 20 For, it is better to hand over as a hostage an illegitimate son than a legitimate one, because of the loss of continuity of heirs (in his case), an unwise son than a wise one, because of the absence of the power of counsel, a son not brave than a brave one, because of the absence of the power of energy, one not trained in the use of weapons to one trained in their use, because of the absence of the ability to strike, one not an only son than an only son, because of the absence of expectations (being centred in him alone).

21 As between a legitimate son and a wise son, the attribute of sovereignty goes with one who is legitimate though unwise, the function of counsel (goes) with one who is wise though illegitimate. 22 Even in the matter of counsel, the legitimate over-reaches the wise through association with elders.

8 *mahatām* should be understood independently of *tapasvinām*. 9 *atisaṁdhatte*: comparison between two similarly placed kings is to be understood here as before. 10 *viparītaḥ*, i.e., who does not receive sureties that are *parāvagrahasamartha*.

11 *bandhumukhya* can hardly be 'a distinguished relation' (Meyer) in view of *amātya* and *apatya* in the next s. 14 *paraḥ* is the one who gives the hostage. — *nirapekṣaḥ*, i.e., not caring for what happens to the hostage.

16 *adāyādā* from Cb Cn Cs is the only correct reading. Meyer's remark (in the Nachtrag) that even the daughter inherits in the absence of a son is beside the point; the question here is as between a son and a daughter when both are there whom to give as a hostage? His further discussion regarding the conqueror's responsibility to get the conquered king's daughters married has little relevance here. — *pareṣām*, i.e., of the husband and his family. — *akleśyā* not liable to be troubled as a male is. With *kleśāya* Cb has 'a trouble to her father because of money he has to spend on her.'

18 *yo* is added as being necessary as usual. 20 *luptadāyādasaṁtānatvāt*: Cs has 'because he cannot have an offspring who can inherit.' But the illegitimate son himself would also be unable to inherit. — *prahartavyasaṁpad*: Cn Cs have 'excellence in using weapons (*prahartavya* as *praharaṇa*)'; Meyer has 'capacity when it is necessary to strike'; 'excellence in hitting or striking' may appear sufficient.

21 *aiśvaryaprakṛtiḥ*, i.e., a natural ability to rule or a naturally majestic bearing. Cf. 8.2.23. — *mantrādhikāraḥ*, i.e., ability to give counsel and make use of it. 22 This means that as between a *jātya* and a *prājña*, the latter should preferably be given.

23 As between a wise son and a brave son, the possession of acts of intelligence belongs to the wise though cowardly, the function of valour to the brave though unwise. 24 Even in the matter of valour, the wise one overreaches the brave, as the hunter does the elephant.

25 As between a brave son and one trained in the use of weapons, valorous behaviour belongs to the brave though untrained in the use of weapons, the power to hit the target (comes) to one trained in weapons though not brave. 26 Even in the matter of hitting the target, the brave one overreaches the trained one, because of his firmness, quick understanding and watchfulness.

27 As between a king with many sons and a king with an only son, the one with many sons, handing over one and supported by the rest, can violate the pact, not the other.

28 If the pact is on condition of giving the son who is his all, advantage (comes) from the offspring of the son. 29 Between two, equally having offspring from a son, advantage (comes) from the power to procreate. 30 Even between two, possessing the power to procreate, advantage (comes) from the birth being close at hand.

31 But when there is a capable only son, he should hand over himself, if he has lost the power of procreation, but should not give the only son.

32 When grown in strength, he should bring about the liberation of the hostage.

33 Secret agents disguised as artisans or artists, carrying out works in the proximity of the prince, should dig up a subterranean passage at night and carry away the prince.

23 *matikarmaṇāṁ yogaḥ*, i.e., association with acts requiring intelligence. 24 That is, a *śūra* should be given, rather than a *prājña*.

26 *asaṁmoṣa* 'watchfulness in protecting oneself' (Cn) is better than 'absence of bewilderment or delusion (*asaṁmoha*)' (Cs). 26 That is, a *kṛtāstra* should be given rather than a *śūra*.

27 *śeṣapratiṣṭabdhaḥ*: both *pravṛtti* and *vṛtti* in place of *prati* are unlikely. For *pratiṣṭabdha*, cf. 7.7.11; 7.10.27.

28 *putrasarvasva* is the only son, who is the all in all of the father. Meyer's 'all the sons he has' is little likely. *putraphalataḥ*, i.e., if the son to be given as a hostage has a son. The grandchild would be there to continue the line. Meyer's 'when there is power to procreate sons (in the king himself)' is little likely. 29 *samaphalayoḥ*: comparison is again thought of; when two kings give each an only son, and this son has an offspring. — *śaktaprajananataḥ*: the capacity to procreate is that of the king himself (Cn) rather than that of the only son (Cb Cs). Cf. *luptaputrotpattir ātmānam*, s. 31 below. The question of the son's capacity to procreate would appear to be premature. Meyer has 'whose progeny is capable.' There is little point in that. 30 *upasthita-* etc.: Meyer's 'with progeny which is already capable of doing work (*upasthita*, i.e., ready for work)' is altogether beside the point and is unlikely in itself.

33 *upakhānayitvā* is an archaic form.

34 Or, actors, dancers, singers, musicians, reciters, minstrels, rope-walkers and showmen, stationed (there) beforehand, should wait upon the enemy. 35 They should (then) wait upon the prince one after the other. 36 He should fix for them entry, stay and departure without restriction as to time. 37 Then, disguised as one of them, he should leave at night. 38 By that are explained courtesans and women appearing as wives.

39 Or, he should go out carrying the box of their musical instruments or (other) articles.

40 Or, he should be carried out by cooks, waiters, bath-attendants, shampooers, bed-preparers, barbers, toilet-attendants or water-servers along with boxes of materials, dresses and articles, beds and seats after they have been used.

41 Or, he should go out at a time when the appearance cannot be distinguished, disguised as a servant, carrying something with him, or (go out) through a subterranean passage with (materials for) a night oblation. 42 Or, he should practise the trick of Varuṇa in a reservoir of water.

43 Or, secret agents disguised as traders should administer poison to guards by selling cooked food and fruits.

44 Or, on the occasion of offerings to deities or worship of manes or picnic parties he should administer food and drink mixed with a stupefying mixture or poison, and depart, or (he should leave) by seducing the guards.

45 Or, secret agents disguised as gallants, minstrels, physicians or vendors of cooked food should set fire at night to houses of the rich or of the

34 *naṭanartaka-* etc. : cf. 1.12.9, also 2.27.25. — *saubhika*, one who puts up a show on the stage. Cf. 11.1.34. — *pūrvapraṇihitāḥ*, i.e., stationed in the enemy territory before the hostage was given. 36 *sthāpayet* : the subject is *kumāraḥ*. 37 *tadvyañjano vā* : *vā* serves no purpose. Meyer thinks that some words like *tair nirhriyeta* have dropped out. It is not necessary to suppose that. 38 *bhāryāvyañjanāḥ*, i.e., female agents posing as the wives of the prince ; as wife, the agent would be allowed unrestricted entry ; then the prince is to leave in her garb.

39 *teṣām* refers to *naṭanartaka-* etc. as well as *rūpājīvāḥ* etc. ; hence *tāsām* is not necessary as Meyer thinks. For *phelā*, cf. 13.2.48.

40 *sūdārālika-* etc.: cf. 1.12.9. — One is reminded of the trick used by Shivaji to escape from Aurangzeb's custody in Agra ; he was carried out in a fruit basket. — *saṁbhogaiḥ*, i.e., when they are sent out after use.

41 *arūpavelāyām* ' at a time when the form is indistinguishable ', i.e., when it is dark. — *suruṅgāmukhena vā niśopahāreṇa* : Cn Cs have ' sending all attendants away on the pretext that he wants to offer night oblations.' Cb has a similar explanation. We may also understand the offering of night oblations as a pretext for his leaving the residence alone and then arriving at the opening of an underground passage through which to escape. This *suruṅgā*, unlike that in s. 33, is not made by his agents and starts at a place away from his residence. Meyer proposes *niśāpahāreṇa* ' by a nocturnal removal through a tunnel' *apahāra* does not go well with *nirgacchet*. 42 *vāruṇaṁ yogam* : Cn Cs refer to 13.1.3-4. The idea rather is that of remaining submerged in water for a long time and coming up at a very distant place from where he plunged in (apparently for a bath).

43 *rasam* from Cn Cs is quite necessary.

44 *madanayoga* : see 14.1.16,17. — *protsāhana* is inducing them to let him go ' by a promise of gifts ' (Cn Cs) rather than ' by stirring up a fight amongst them ' (Meyer).

45 *nāgaraka* ' a gallant ' is different from *nāgarika*. — *ārakṣiṇām* : Cb Cn have no comment on this word. Cs puts it in brackets without comment. If it is to be read, a *vā*

guards. 46 Or, those disguised as traders should set fire to the market-place. 47 Or, after throwing another body inside, he should set his own residence on fire, for fear of pursuit. 48 Then he should leave through a hole in the wall, a channel or a subterranean passage.

49 Or, disguised as a carrier of loads of goods in jars suspended in slings from a pole, he should leave at night.

50 Or, entering the roving camps of ascetics with shaved heads or matted hair, he should leave at night disguised as one of them, or with the help of one of these, viz., change of appearance, inducing a malady and the disguise of a forester.

51 Or, made to appear as a corpse, he should be carried out by secret agents. 52 Or, dressed as a woman, he should follow (the funeral procession of some) one dead.

53 And agents appearing as foresters should direct (pursuers) to another direction when he is going in one. 54 Then he should go in another direction. 55 Or, he should escape through groups of carts of cartmen.

56 And when pursuit is close on his heels, he should remain hidden. 57 In the absence of a hiding place, he should scatter on both sides of the road money or poisoned food-stuffs. 58 Then he should go away in another direction.

59 If caught, he should over-reach the pursuers with conciliation and other means, or with poisoned food on the way.

60 Or, in the trick of Varuṇa and in acts of setting fire, he should place another body and accuse the enemy, 'You have killed my son.'

> 61 Or, taking up weapons secretly (brought), and falling on the guards at night, he should escape on quick-marching (horses) along with secret agents.

after it is necessary, *gṛhāṇi* being supplied from the preceding. The prince would escape when the guards are busy putting out the fire. 47 *anyad vā śarīram* etc. : one is reminded of the escape of the Pāṇḍavas from the lac-house. 48 *khāta* : cf. 3.8.21.

49 *kāca* is a contrivance for carrying loads on the shoulder, consisting of a pole with slings at the two ends, a contrivance still in common use in India. Cb, however, has '*kācabhāra*, i.e., carriers of grass, fuel etc., *kumbhabhāra*, i.e., carriers of water and *bhāṇḍabhāra*, i.e., dealers in horses etc.' Cs follows.

50 *virūpakaraṇa* : see 14.2.4 ff. — *vyādhikaraṇa* is described in 14.1. The disease would, however, be only apparent ; the pretence of illness may induce the guards to allow him to go ostensibly for treatment.

55 *śakaṭavāṭaiḥ* : *vāṭa* usually 'an enclosure,' seems used in the sense of 'group' (Cn Cs), *samūha* (Cb).

56 *sattram* is a place where one can hide oneself, particularly for lying in ambush ; cf. 10.3.24.

59 *pathyadānena* read in the mss. is obviously not right ; cf. 2.16.24.

60 The subject for *abhiyuñjīta* is the father of the prince, while that for *ādhāya* would be the secret agents ; the sense of the causal may therefore be understood in *ādhāya*. — *abhiyuñjīta* 'should accuse' may also suggest the idea of attacking.

61 *śīghrapātaiḥ* : Cn supplies *aśvaiḥ*, Cb *yānaiḥ*.

CHAPTER EIGHTEEN

SECTION 124 CONDUCT TOWARDS THE MIDDLE KING

SECTION 125 CONDUCT TOWARDS THE NEUTRAL KING

SECTION 126 CONDUCT TOWARDS THE CIRCLE OF KINGS

1 With respect to the middle king, he himself, the third and the fifth constituents are friendly elements. 2 The second, the fourth and the sixth are unfriendly elements.

3 If the middle king were to help both these, the conqueror should be favourably inclined towards the middle king. 4 If he does not help (either), he should remain favourable to the friendly elements.

5 If the middle king were to desire to seize an ally of the conqueror having the feelings of a friend, he should save the ally by rousing the allies of the ally and his own allies, and dividing his allies from the middle king. 6 Or, he should incite the circle : 'This middle king, grown very powerful, has risen for the destruction of all of us ; let us join together and frustrate his expedition.' 7 If the circle were to favour that, he should, by the suppression of the middle king, augment himself. 8 If it were not to favour, helping the ally with treasury and army, he should win over by conciliation and gifts one — the principal or the proximate — from among the kings inimical to the middle king, who, many in number, may be helping each other, or of whom, by winning over one, many would be won over, or who, being afraid of each other, would not rise. 9 Being thus double, (he should win over) a second king ; being three-fold, a third king. 10 Augmented in power in this way, he should suppress the middle king. 11 Or, if place and time were to lapse, he should make peace with the middle king and be helpful to the ally, or make a pact for an undertaking with the treasonable (officers of the middle king).

7.18

The three Sections are found in ss. 1-25, 26-27 and 28-44 respectively.

1 *madhyamasya* : this word seems out of place here. This and the next s. describe the *prakṛtis* and the *vikṛtis* of the *vijigīṣu*, not of the *madhyama*, as Cb Cs understand. For, *ubhayam* in s. 3, who are likely to be favoured by the *madhyama*, cannot include his own enemies ; and the *prakṛtis* in s. 4, to whom the *vijigīṣu* is advised to be favourably disposed if the *madhyama* does not help either party, can be the *prakṛtis* of the *vijigīṣu* himself, not those of the *madhyama*. If at all the word *madhyamasya* is read at the beginning of this s., it should be understood in some such sense as 'in relation to, with respect to, the *madhyama* king.' — *ātmā* as a separate word is quite necessary as in the commentators. It refers to the *vijigīṣu* himself, the third and fifth *prakṛtis* being his *mitra* and *mitramitra*. 2 The second, fourth and sixth *prakṛtis* are the *ari*, *arimitra* and *arimitramitra* of the *vijigīṣu*.

8 *ye madhyamadveṣiṇo rājānaḥ* is to be understood with each of the following three clauses (Cn Cs) rather than as a separate fourth clause (Meyer). — *nottiṣṭheran* 'not rise (against the *madhyama*),' though they are hostile (*dveṣin*) to him. — *āsannam* 'proximate' to himself or to the ally who is to be saved. 11 *deśakālātipattau*, i.e., when the matter is urgent. Cf. 3.16.11. — *sācivyaṁ kuryāt* : by secretly helping the ally with troops and money, as in Cn ; cf. s. 16 below. — *dūṣyeṣu* ; these are clearly those of the middle king. — *karmasaṁdhim* : see 7.12.

12 If the middle king were to desire to seize an ally of his deserving to be weakened, he should sustain him, saying 'I will save you,' till he is weakened. 13 He should save him when weakened.

14 If the middle king were to desire to seize an ally of his deserving to be exterminated, he should save him when weakened through fear of the increase of the middle king's power. 15 Or, if he is exterminated, he should get him in his power by the grant of land, through fear of his going elsewhere.

16 If the allies of his ally, deserving to be weakened or exterminated, were to be helpful to the middle king, he should have peace made through another person. 17 Or, if the allies of those two were capable of suppressing the conqueror, he should make peace (with the middle king).

18 If the middle king were to desire to seize his (i.e., the conqueror's) enemy, he should make peace. 19 Thus his own ends are secured and the middle king is also pleased.

20 If the middle king were to desire to seize his own ally having friendly feelings, he should have peace made through another person. 21 Or, if he were to care (for the conqueror), he should dissuade him, saying ' It does not behove you to exterminate an ally.' 22 Or, he should remain indifferent, thinking ' Let the circle be enraged with him on account of the destruction of his own party.'

23 If the middle king were to desire to seize his own enemy, he should help him with treasury and army, unseen.

24 If the middle king were to desire to seize the neutral king, he should give him aid, thinking ' Let him be divided from the neutral king.' 25 Of the middle and the neutral kings, he should resort to the one who is liked by the circle of kings.

12 *asya*, i.e., *vijigīṣoḥ*. Similarly in ss. 14 and 18.

14 *madhyamavṛddhibhayāt* : the fear is that if his ally were totally crushed, the *madhyama* would be very strong. 15 *anyatra*, i.e., in the enemy's camp (Cn Cs).

16 *sācivyakarāṇi* : they render aid against their own ally, clandestinely. — *puruṣāntareṇa saṁdhīyeta* : this refers to 7.3.24, a treaty in which the *senāpati* or the *kumāra* is surrendered to the enemy. Here the *senāpati* or *kumāra* would appear to be that of the ally. The causal would have been preferable to the passive of *saṁdhīyeta*.

20 *saṁdadhyāt* : apparently the *vijigīṣu* induces the *madhyama* king's ally to make a treaty of this kind. *saṁdhiṁ kārayet* would have been better. 21 *sāpekṣam* seems to mean 'if the *madhyama* has regard for him (the *vijigīṣu*).' Cn has ' *anucchedarucim* if he is disinclined to exterminate.' Meyer treats it as an adverb ' respectfully, discreetly.'

23 *enam*, i.e., to the enemy of the *madhyama*.

24 After *lipseta*, the words *asmai sāhāyyaṁ dadyāt* are added as in Cn ; the comment in Cb also presupposes those worlds. In their absence, the words that follow, *udāsīnād* etc. (including those in s. 25 in that case), cannot be construed with the preceding clause. And s. 25 very clearly contains a new idea, unconnected with words in s. 24. For *bheda* implied by *bhidyatām* cannot be brought about by what is recommended in s. 25. The help given might encourage the *madhyama* to take a strong line against the *udāsīna*. — *asmai* is *madhyamāya* ; he is weaker than the *udāsīna* , and his strengthening would be necessary for *bheda*. — *udāsīnād bhidyatām* cannot mean 'turn away from the *udāsīna* ' as words addressed by the *madhyama* to the *vijigīṣu*, as Meyer thinks.

26 By conduct towards the middle king is explained conduct towards the neutral king.

27 If the neutral king were to desire to seize the middle king, he should turn to that side where he would over-reach his enemy or render help to his ally or secure the neutral king for rendering aid with troops to himself.

28 Augmenting himself in this way, he should weaken the constituent, enemy, and support the constituent, ally.

29 Though there are feelings of enmity (among all), the enemy (in front) not self-possessed (and) constantly doing injury, or the enemy in the rear in league with the enemy (in front), one vulnerable, being in a calamity, or one attacking the leader in his calamity, these are (neighbouring kings) with a hostile disposition; one marching for a common objective, one marching for a separate object, one marching after joining forces, one marching after making a pact, one marching for his own object, one rising together (with the leader), one purchasing or selling either treasury or troops as he resorts to a dual policy, these are with a friendly disposition; the neighbour placed in between or at the side as a hindrance to the strong king, or one in the rear of the strong king, one who has submitted to force, either submitting of his own accord or submitting because of the might, these are neighbours with a dependent's feelings. 30 By these are explained those separated by one intervening state.

> 31 Of these, that ally who would make common cause with him in case of hostility with the enemy, he should help with power, with which he would withstand the enemy.
>
> 32 He should get that ally, who after conquering the enemy, might grow in strength and go out of control, into conflict with the two constituents, the neighbour and the one separated by one state.

27 *udāsīnaṁ vā*: Cb Cs add *madhyamam* before this. But though possible, the *lābha* of the *madhyama* does not seem intended here.

29 All neighbouring kings (*sāmantāḥ*) normally tend to be inimical, possessed of *amitrabhāva*: yet three classes are distinguished here, *aribhāvin*, *mitrabhāvin* and *bhṛtyabhāvin*. — *anātmavān* and *nityāpakārī* are descriptions of *śatru* as well as of *pārṣṇigrāha* and not independent categories (as in Cs and Meyer). So *śatrusaṁhitaḥ* is an adjective to *pārṣṇigrāhaḥ* and not an independent category. — *vyasanī yātavyaḥ* is one king; cf. 6.2.16. — *aribhāvinaḥ*: the substantive is *sāmantāḥ* at the end. — *sva* in *svārthā-* etc. seems to refer to the *vijigīṣu*, not to the *sāmanta*. The latter's *artha* is mentioned in *pṛthagartha*. — *dvaidhībhāvikaḥ* is the *sāmanta* who makes peace with the *vijigīṣu*, when engaged in war elsewhere; while making the peace, he purchases or sells *daṇḍa* or *kośa* to the *vijigīṣu*. Hence *kośadaṇḍayor* etc. does not constitute a category independent of *dvaidhībhāvika*. — *balavataḥ pratighātaḥ* is a description of the *antardhi* and the *prativeśa*, and not a separate type of king as Cb Cs think. Cf. 7.13.24-25. There is no definition of *pratighāta* in 7.13.25 as Cs states here (though not while commenting on the passage itself). *svayamupanata* and *pratāpopanata* are two types of *daṇḍopanata*, and not separate categories.

31 *ekārthatāṁ vrajet* cannot mean 'would make common cause, i.e., peace (with the enemy)' (Cb Cs). Cn rightly has '*vijigīṣuṇā saha*.'

32 *sāmantaikāntarābhyāṁ prakṛtibhyām*: these would be those of the ally himself, hardly those of the *vijigīṣu*.

33 Or, he should cause his territory to be seized by a pretender from his family or a prince in disfavour or so act that he would remain under control in consideration of help (received).

34 That ally, who being much weakened might not help or might go over to the enemy, he, well-versed in polities, should keep neither weak nor strong.

35 That unstable ally, who for the sake of his own ends makes peace (with him), — he should remove the reason for his leaving, so that he would not waver.

36 That ally who remains common to the enemy (and himself), he should divide that rogue from the enemy, (and) when divided, exterminate him, thereafter (exterminate) the enemy.

37 And he should get that ally, who would remain indifferent, into conflict with neighbouring kings ; then when he is severely distressed by the fight, he should place him under (his) obligations.

38 That weak ally, who goes to the enemy and the conqueror (for support), he should help with troops, so that he would not turn away from him.

39 Or, removing him from that (territory) he should settle him in another land, after first settling another (ally) there because of help with troops (received from him).

40 That ally who might do harm or who, though capable, would not help in times of trouble, he should certainly exterminate him, when trustingly, he comes within his reach.

41 When the enemy has risen, unrestrained, because of a calamity of the ally, he should be got over-powered by that ally himself, with his calamity removed (by him).

33 *anugrahāpekṣam* may be 'in expectation of help' or 'in consideration of help received.' The latter seems meant.

34 *arthavid* seems to be *arthaśāstravid*, hardly 'who knows his interests.'

35 *arthayuktyā* 'with the purpose of securing his own interests.' Cf. 8.1.59.

37 *upakāre niveśayet*: the same idiom as in 'place under obligation.' It can hardly mean 'take him into favour and allow him to render service (to himself)' (Meyer) or 'should make him serve oneself anew' (Russ.).

39 *tatra*, i.e., in the territory of the weak king, who is shifted from there. — *daṇḍānugraha* is help of troops already received from him, hardly that expected from him.

40 *aṅkam upasthitam*, i.e., come within his reach or in his power. Cf. 1.17.10.

41 Meyer understands the *vā* in this stanza in the sense of *iva* or *yathā*, and construes this stanza (as containing a comparison) with the next stanza, 'just as an enemy, rising because of an ally's calamity can be put down through the ally, so an ally rising because of an enemy's calamity should be put down through the enemy etc.' This is not likely. There is no *tathā* or *evam* in s. 42. And *vā* as *iva* is doubtful. And even though s. 41 speaks of the *ari*, the mention of the *mitravyasana* and of the *vijigīṣu*'s duty towards the ally show that the context of 'ally' is not violated.

42 That ally who, after rising because of a calamity of the enemy, becomes disaffected, is over-powered through the enemy himself, by overcoming the calamity of the enemy.

43 He, who is well-versed in the science of politics, should employ all the means, viz., advancement, decline and stable condition as well as weakening and extermination.

44 He who sees the six measures of policy as being interdependent in this manner, plays, as he pleases, with kings tied by the chains of his intellect.

Herewith ends the Seventh Book of the Arthaśāstra of Kauṭilya

'THE SIX MEASURES OF FOREIGN POLICY'

42 *prasidhyati* is used with the sense of the passive voice.

44 *anyonyasaṁcāram* 'moving to each other,' i.e., connected with each other, bound up with one another.

BOOK EIGHT

CONCERNING THE TOPIC OF CALAMITIES

CHAPTER ONE

SECTION 127 THE GROUP OF CALAMITIES OF THE CONSTITUENT ELEMENTS

1 In case of simultaneity of calamities (the question arises) should one march or guard (oneself) because of ease, hence a consideration of calamities (is necessary).

2 A calamity of a constituent, of a divine or human origin, springs from ill luck or wrong policy.

3 Inversion of excellences, absence, a great defect, addiction, or affliction constitutes a calamity. 4 It throws out a person from his good, hence it is called *vyasana*.

The Eighth Book deals with the calamities that affect the various constituents (*prakṛtis*) of the state. It is necessary to take precautions against these before one can start on an expedition of conquest, which is to be described in the following Books.

8.1

1 *vyasanayaugapadye* : for the purpose of the discussion of the calamities befalling the different *prakṛtis*, it is assumed that the *vijigīṣu* and the *ari* are both suffering from a calamity affecting one of their *prakṛtis*. The relative seriousness of the calamities befalling the various *prakṛtis* being pointed out, it becomes easy for the *vijigīṣu* to decide whether he should march against the *ari* or should stay quiet. If his calamity is lighter, he is to march; if it is more serious, he is to remain quiet. — *saukaryataḥ* 'because of the ease,' i.e., with ease in the carrying out of the policy either of *yāna* or of *sthāna*. — *yātavyaṁ rakṣitavyaṁ vā* : the *vā* is from Cn Cs ; it is to be preferred to the *ca* of the mss. The two policies of *yāna* and *sthāna* (i.e., *āsana*) cannot be pursued simultaneously. There can be no doubt that *rakṣitavyam* refers to the policy of *sthāna*, as is clearly shown by 8.2.26. With *ca*, Meyer has 'going forth (*yātavyam*) and finding means of protection (*rakṣitavyaṁ ca*).' He supposes that the two or more calamities have befallen the *vijigīṣu* himself. That is hardly right. Meyer further suggests that *yātavyam* may mean 'he should run away' or that *pātavyam* should be read instead. *yā* cannot mean 'to run away' in this case and there would be no difference between *pātavyam* and *rakṣitavyam*.

2 For *anaya* and *apanaya* see 6.2.6-12.

3 *guṇaprātilomyam*, i.e., the possession of qualities the opposite of those regarded as constituting the excellences of the various *prakṛtis* as in 6.1. Cn Cs give an alternative explanation 'the wrong use of the six *guṇas* or policies.' But that is not right. This and the following expressions are attributes of the *prakṛtis* which represent a *vyasana* in their case. And *guṇa* in connection with *prakṛtis* can only refer to their qualities, not to the six-fold *guṇa* ; cf. s. 62 below. Besides, the wrong use of *guṇas* (or policies) is *apanaya*, as stated in 9.5.1 ; and *apanaya* is the cause of *vyasana* (s. 2 above), is not itself a *vyasana*. — *abhāvaḥ* is the absence of any of the *prakṛtis*, such as absence of *durga* or *kośa*. — *pradoṣaḥ* 'a great defect' refers to spoiling or deterioration of a *prakṛti*. Material elements may get ruined; human beings may become *dūṣya*. — *prasaṅgaḥ* is applicable to human beings only. — *pīḍā* is the same as the *pīḍana* of 8.4.1 ff.

5 'Of calamities befalling the king, the minister, the country, the fort, the treasury, the army and the ally, that of each earlier one is more serious.' say the teachers.

6 'No,' says Bhāradvāja. 7 'Of calamities befalling the king and the minister, the calamity of the minister is more serious. 8 Deliberation in counsel, securing the fruits of deliberation, carrying out undertakings, managing income and expenditure, infliction of punishment, warding off of enemies and forest tribes, protection of the kingdom, taking steps against calamities, guarding of princes and the installation of princes, are (all) dependent on ministers. 9 In the absence of these, those (activities) are lacking, and there is loss of all activity on the part of the king, as of a (bird) with clipped wings. 10 And in the calamities (of these), secret instigations by the enemy are close at hand. 11 And if these are hostile, there is danger to (the king's) life, since they move near the person of the king.'

12 'No,' says Kauṭilya. 13 It is the king alone who appoints the group of servants like the councillor, the chaplain and others, directs the activity of departmental heads, takes counter-measures against the calamities of constituents, whether human or material, and secures their advancement. 14 If the ministers are suffering from calamities, he appoints others who are not in calamities. 15 He remains ever diligent in honouring those worthy of honour and suppressing the treasonable. 16 And when the king is possessed of excellences, he makes the constituents perfect with their respective excellences. 17 What character he has, that character the constituents come to have, being dependent on him in the matter of energetic activity and remissness. 18 For, the king is in the place of their head.

19 'Of calamities befalling the minister and the country, the calamity of the country is more serious,' says Viśālākṣa. 20 'The treasury, the army, forest produce, labourers, means of transport and stores spring from the country. 21 In the absence of the country, there would be lack of these,

5 Manu, 7.294-295, puts *pura* (i.e., *durga*) before *rāṣṭra* (i.e., *janapada*); that agrees with the view of the Pārāśaras (s. 24 below).

8 *daṇḍapraṇayanam* refers to infliction of punishment, rather than to the raising or disposing of an army (as Cn Cs understand it). Cf. 1.4.11-12 for *daṇḍa* with *pra-nī*. — *daṇḍāpraṇayanam* of the mss. is obviously faulty. — *kumārarakṣaṇam*: according to Cn Cs this is 'guarding against princes' as in 1.17. However, 'protection of the princes, appears more likely here. 9 *tadabhāvaḥ*: Cn seems to have read *tadabhāvāt* 'because there would be no *mantra* etc. in the absence of ministers, there would be *ceṣṭānāśa*.' This would dispense with the necessity of *ca* after *ceṣṭānāśaḥ*. But in 15.1.39, where this passage is quoted, the *ca* is read; on the strength of that, *ca* is added here and in consequence *tadabhāvaḥ* is retained. 11 For *vaiguṇya* 'hostility,' cf. 5.6.8; 7.8.19. — *prāṇāntika-*: *prāṇa* here is the person of the king. *antika* has nothing to do with *anta* and the expression cannot mean 'life-threatening,' i.e., fatal (Meyer).

13 *edhanam* is that of the two kinds of *prakṛtis*. 14 Cn seems to have read *vyasaniṣu cāmātyeṣu*, which might appear better. 16 *sampannaḥ* and *svasampadbhiḥ* refer to excellences as described in 6.1 and elsewhere. 17 *utthāne pramāde ca*: cf. 1.19.1-2. 18 *kūṭa* is 'peak, head' rather than 'root cause' (Cn Cs).

20 *vāhanam* refers to bullocks and carts in particular. 21 *svāmyamātyayoś cānantaraḥ*: we have to supply *abhāvaḥ* from the preceding, the idea being, if there is no country

and (the disappearance) of the king and the minister (would follow) immediately thereafter.'

22 'No,' says Kauṭilya. 23 All undertakings have their origin in the ministers, (viz.), successful execution of works in the country, bringing about its well-being and security from one's own and from the enemy's people, taking counter-measures against calamities, settlement of new lands and their development, and (bringing in) the benefit of fines and taxes.

24 'Of calamities befalling the country and the fort, the calamity of the fort (is more serious),' say the followers of Parāśara. 25 'For, it is in the fort that the treasury and the army spring up and a place (secured) for the country people in times of trouble. 26 And city-dwellers are stronger than the country people and being steadfast (in loyalty) are helpful to the king in times of trouble. 27 Country people, on the other hand, are common to the enemy.'

28 'No,' says Kauṭilya. 29 The undertakings of the fort, the treasury, the army, water-works and the occupations for livelihood have their source in the country. 30 And bravery, firmness, cleverness and large numbers are (found) among the country people. 31 And mountain forts and island forts are not inhabited because of the absence of the country. 32 However, in a country inhabited mostly by agriculturists, the calamity of the fort (is more serious), while in a country inhabited mostly by martial people, the calamity of the country (is more serious).

33 'Of calamities befalling the fort and the treasury, the calamity of the treasury (is more serious),' says Piśuna. 34 'For, dependent on the treasury

and therefore no treasury etc., there will soon be no king and no minister. Cn Cs, however, treat this as a new s., 'the country should really occupy the position between the king and the minister in the list of *prakṛtis*.' For this, *antarā* would be necessary, and *janapadaḥ* would have to be supplied from *janapadābhāve*. It is extremely doubtful if *anantaraḥ* can mean 'placed in between.' The clause, as naturally understood, does not imply that the *janapada* is superior to the king, as Cn objects.

23 *daṇḍakara-*: cf. 1.13.8, though here *daṇḍa* may also mean 'army' (Meyer).

25 *durge*: Cn reads *durgāt*. 26 *paurā jānapadebhyaḥ* from Cs is clearly necessary in place of *paurajānapadebhyaḥ* of the mss. — *nityāḥ*: Cn seems to understand this independently 'steadfastly loyal'; in view of the position of *ca*, it seems better to understand it as the reason for their being *āpadi sahāyāḥ*. 27 *amitrasādhāraṇāḥ*: this is because when they are over-run by the enemy they easily transfer their allegiance to him.

31 *parvatāntardvīpāḥ durgāḥ*: see 2.3.1-2. 32 *karṣakaprāye tu* etc.: this is a partial agreement with the view of the Pārāśaras. We have to supply *janapade* after *karṣakaprāye* and understand *garīyaḥ* after *durgavyasanam*. Thus Cn. Cs explains 'in a land with a few warriors and many agriculturists there is trouble in the absence of a fort; that trouble can be avoided in a land of warriors, but even they cannot ward off the calamity of the land; hence calamity of the land is more serious.' All this could hardly have been meant. Meyer supplies *durge* after *karṣakaprāye*, 'on the one hand, the preponderance of agriculturists in a fort is a calamity; on the other, the preponderance of soldiers on the land is a calamity for the countryside.' This also appears extremely doubtful. Russ. reads 'if the people consist for the most part of farmers then is felt the calamity in relation to the fortified place; if the countryside consists mostly of fighters then the country suffers similarly (because soldiers take away the resources).'

34 *durgasaṁskāraḥ*: cf. 2.4.31. — It is proposed to read, with Meyer, *janapada-*. . . *vyavahāraḥ* in this s., instead of after *pareṣām* at the end of the next s. The words transposed

are building of the fort, protection of the fort, control over the country, the allies and the enemies, incitement of those away from the land, and the use of armed forces. 35 A fort is susceptible to secret instigations by enemies with money. 36 And in a calamity, it is possible to go away with the treasury, not with the fort.'

37 'No,' says Kauṭilya. 38 Dependent on the fort are the treasury, the army, silent war, restraint of one's own party, use of armed forces, receiving allied troops, and warding off enemy troops and forest tribes. 39 And in the absence of a fort, the treasury will fall into the hands of enemies. 40 For, it is seen that those with forts are not exterminated.

41 'Of calamities befalling the treasury and the army, the calamity of the army (is more serious),' says Kauṇapadanta. 42 'For, dependent on the army are restraint of allies and enemies, rousing alien troops to action, and reinforcement of one's own troops. 43 And in the absence of an army, the loss of the treasury is certain. 44 And in the absence of a treasury, it is possible to collect an army with forest produce or land or by allowing seizure of enemy's land by each for himself, and to collect a treasury, when one has an army. 45 And being in close proximity to the king, the army has the same characteristics as the minister.'

46 'No,' says Kauṭilya. 47 The army, indeed, is rooted in the treasury. 48 In the absence of a treasury, the army goes over to the enemy or kills the king. 49 And the treasury, ensuring (the success of) all endeavours, is the means of deeds of piety and sensual pleasures. 50 In conformity with the place, the time and the work, however, one of the two, treasury and army, becomes important. 51 For, the army is the means of acquiring and protecting the treasury, the treasury that of the treasury and the army.

can be construed with *kośamūlaḥ*, but not with *durgaḥ*. — *deśāntarita* may be natives who have gone away or foreigners in their own lands. — *daṇḍabalavyavahāraḥ* : Cn has 'forcing some one to send troops (*bala*) by threats of punishment (*daṇḍabhayāt*)'; Cs 'dealing in, i.e., giving and receiving of troops'; this sense does not suit s. 38 or 9.2.4; see also 13.3.15. Meyer has 'activity and maintenance (*vyavahāra*) of professional troops (*daṇḍabala*).' 'The use of armed forces' would appear to be sufficient in all places where the expression occurs.

38 *daṇḍabalavyavahāraḥ* : Cn here has 'disposition of troops sent through fear of use of force.' — *āsāra* is the ally's troops; cf. 10.2.7.

42 *paradaṇḍotsāhanam* : the alien troops are part of one's army. Meyer proposes *utsādanam* for *utsāhanam*; that does not seem necessary. The idea of urging them to fight is better. — *svadaṇḍapratigrahaḥ* : *pratigraha* means 'reserves' which are used to reinforce the troops engaged in fighting; cf. 10.2.20. Cn's explanation seems to imply the idea of raising troops. Cs has 'acceptance of one's army as attacking the enemy's troops,' i.e., apparently its use for attack. Meyer has 'possession of one's army' or mastery over it. Russ. has 'taking punitive measures in his own land.' 44 *kośābhāve ca* : we expect a *tu* in place of *ca*. — *svayaṁgrāha* : cf. 8.4.23; 9.3.17. 45 *rājñaḥ āsannavṛttitvād* : this is because the army is directly under the king. For the idea, cf. s. 11 above.

49 *sarvābhiyogakaraḥ* : it seems that *abhiyoga* is used in the sense of 'effort, endeavour.' Cs has 'capable of carrying out attacks against all neighbours' which is hardly appropriate in the case of *kośa*. Cn seems to have read *-taraḥ* 'capable of saving from attacks by all.' These explanations might suit *daṇḍa* but the expression cannot be included in the preceding

52 Because it brings into being all objects, the calamity of the treasury is more serious.

53 'Of calamities befalling the army and the ally, the calamity of the ally (is more serious),' says Vātavyādhi. 54 'The ally does the work without being paid and at a distance, repels the enemy in the rear, his ally, the enemy and the forest chief, and helps with treasury, army and territory, remaining united in conditions of calamity.'

55 'No,' says Kauṭilya. 56 When one has an army, one's ally remains friendly, or (even) the enemy becomes friendly. 57 However, in a work that can well be performed either by the army or the ally, advantage comes from their strength (and) the attainment of suitable place and time for their own type of warfare. 58 But an ally is of no avail in a speedy expedition against enemies or forest chiefs and in a rising in the interior. 59 An ally looks to the securing of his own interests in the event of simultaneity of calamities and in the event of the growth of the enemy's power.

60 Thus has been stated the determination of (the seriousness of) calamities befalling the constituents.

61 But in accordance with the peculiar nature of the calamity, the numerousness or loyalty or strength of parts of the constituent leads to the accomplishment of a work.

s. 50 This is a partial concession to Kauṇapadanta's view. 52 *sarvadravya-* : Cn Cs understand the *dravyaprakṛtis*.

54 *vyasanāvasthāyogam* as an adjective to *mitram* rather than to *vijigīṣum* 'who has fallen in a state of misfortune' (Meyer). With *upakaroti*, we generally have the genitive, not the accusative.

56 Cn reads a *hi* after *daṇḍavato*. 57 *sādhāraṇe*, i.e., which can be carried out either by the army or the ally. Cs understands *kārya* in the sense of *kāryasādhakatva* and construes *sārataḥ* 'in point of strength' with it. That is unnecessary. — For *sāra* 'strength,' cf. 10.5.14 ff. — After *-lābhāt* a *ca* or *vā* would seem necessary. 58 *amitrāṭavikān* is proposed as the object of *śīghrābhiyāne*, since *kope* cannot be construed with *amitra* or *āṭavika*. *kopa* refers to a revolt in the kingdom. For *abhyantarakopa*, see 9.3.12. 59 *vyasanayaugapadye*, i.e., when the *vijigīṣu* and the enemy are both in calamity, as in s. 1. — *arthayuktau* : cf. 7.18.35.

61 *prakṛtyavayavānām* is construed with *bahubhāvaḥ* etc. in the second half and *vyasanasya viśeṣataḥ* understood as an independent clause. The idea is, it would depend on the nature of the particular calamity whether *bahubhāva* or *anurāga* or *sāra* of parts of the *prakṛti* would be helpful in overcoming the calamity. Meyer has 'in the case of a calamity (*vyasanasya*) befalling single parts of a constituent, it is in accordance with the peculiar nature (*viśeṣataḥ* of the calamity) that numerousness etc. leads to success.' It is not necessary to understand the *vyasana* to be that of parts of a *prakṛti*. Cn has two explanations, the second of which is adopted in Cs. According to it, 'the numerousness etc. of parts of constituents is more effective than the greater or less importance (*viśeṣa*) of the calamity affecting those parts.' Cn adds 'if, for example, the *vijigīṣu* has *janapadavyasana* and the enemy has *durgavyasana*, the former (even though in a greater calamity) would succeed, if his *janapada* has numerousness etc. and if the *avayavas* of the enemy's *durga* (such as *dhānvana*, *vana*, etc.) do not have *bahubhāva* etc.' This is reading too much in the words. It is also doubtful if a comparison between the calamities of two kings is intended in this stanza. Cn's first explanation is 'on account of the greater or less importance (*viśeṣataḥ* i.e., *balīyastvāt*) of the calamities of the members (*avayava*), viz., the constituents (i.e., with *prakṛtayaḥ eva avayavāḥ*) being thus declared, the numerousness etc. (of a later *prakṛti*, whose calamity is lighter) brings success.' The first half does not seem properly understood. — 9.7.48-49 show that *bahubhāva* and *anurāga* belong to *avayavas* of *puruṣaprakṛtis*, while *sāra* to those of *dravyaprakṛtis*.

62 But when the calamity of two (constituents) is equal, the difference (arises) from a decline in qualities, if the possession of excellences by the rest of the constituents is not rendered unserviceable.

63 But where the destruction of the rest of the constituents is likely to follow from the calamity of one, that calamity would be more serious, whether of the principal or of (some) other (constituent).

CHAPTER TWO

SECTION 128 CONSIDERATIONS REGARDING THE CALAMITIES OF THE KING AND KINGSHIP

1 The king and (his) rule, this is the sum-total of the constituents.

2 For the king, there is (danger of) revolt in the interior or in the outer regions. 3 Because of danger as from a snake, a rising in the interior is a greater evil than a rising in the outer regions, and a rising of ministers of the interior (a greater evil) than a rising in the interior. 4 Therefore, he should keep the power of the treasury and the army in his own hands.

62 It is proposed to read *nāvidheyakam* for *nābhidheyikam* of the mss., and *avidheyaka* is understood as 'not under control, not effective, etc.'; *nāvidhāyakam* may also be read in this sense. *dvayoḥ* refers to two constituents of the same state. *guṇataḥ* is construed with *kṣayāt*, the idea understood being that the difference arises from a greater or less deterioration in the excellences of the *prakṛtis*. Cn has two explanations, the first of which is 'when the same *prakṛti* of the conqueror and the enemy is in a calamity, the difference is due to absence of *bahubhāva* and other qualities; but if the remaining *prakṛtis* possess their excellences, that renders the absence of *bahubhāva* and other qualities ineffective (*guṇokṣayasya avidhāyakaṁ bhavati*).' In the second, Cn has 'the distinction is according to presence of qualities (*guṇataḥ*) or their absence (*kṣayāt*), provided the excellences of the remaining *prakṛtis* mentioned above (*abhidheyakam*, i.e., *abhidhāya viṣayīkṛtam*) are not present in those of the enemy.' There seems little justification for supplying *parasya* in the second half. Cs differs from the second explanation in Cn only in referring *guṇataḥ* to the conqueror and *kṣayāt* to the enemy or *vice versa* instead of referring both to the *vijigīṣu*. In this s. *dvayoḥ* can be understood to refer to two rival kings; however, it appears better to understand two *prakṛtis* of the same state by it. Meyer construes *kṣayāt* with the second half, 'if after deterioration of a constituent, the remaining constituents are in an excellent condition, the calamity is not worth mentioning (*nābhidheyikam*).' This last is extremely doubtful. Russ. follows Meyer.

63 *ekavyasanād* shows that *dvayoḥ* in the last stanza refers to *prakṛtis* rather than to rival kings. — *pradhānasya*, i.e., of the king.

8.2

The Chapter deals with *rājavyasana* and *rājyavyasana* in ss. 2-4 and 5-25 respectively. The former is concerned with danger to the king's person, the latter with abnormal forms of rule.

1 *rājā rājyam*: this is not the same thing as 'l'état c'est moi' of Louis XIV. *rājya* refers to rulership or rule and does not mean 'kingdom'. The idea here is, the king and his rule constitute the sum-total of *prakṛtis*. The other *prakṛtis* are subservient to that. The supreme importance of the king and his rule is thus emphasised. Because of this importance, the question of the *vyasanas* befalling them is taken up first. Cn Cs (agreeing in this with Kāmandaka, 15.1) understand by *rājya* all the other *prakṛtis* from *amātya* to *mitra*. But *rājya* in this Chapter has nothing to do with those *prakṛtis*. Cf. also 5.1.2 and the contents of that Chapter.

2 *abhyantara kopa* and *bāhya kopa* are described in 9.3.12 and 22 respectively. 3 *ahibhayāt*: a simile is implied; the ablative shows *hetu*. — *antaramātyakopa* is defined in 9.3.20 and refers to a rising of palace officials like *dauvārika*, *antarvaṁśika* etc. — *antaḥkopa* is the same as *abhyantarakopa*.

5 'As between rule by two and rule without the (legitimate) king, rule by two is destroyed by hatred and loyalty towards each other's parties or by mutual rivalry; rule without the (legitimate) king, on the other hand, looking to the winning of the hearts of the subjects, is enjoyed by the others as it exists,' say the teachers.

6 'No,' says Kauṭilya. 7 Rule by two, (e.g.), by father and son or by two brothers, continues to exist, with well-being and security equally shared and with ministers held in check. 8 Rule without the (legitimate) king, on the other hand, snatching what belongs to another still living, and thinking, 'This does not belong to me,' impoverishes it, carries it off or sells it or, if (still) disaffected, leaves it and goes away.

9 As between a king blind and a king deviating from the science, 'The king, blind because he is without the eye of science, doing whatsoever pleases him, obstinately resolved, or led by others, ruins the kingdom with (his acts of) injustice; but one deviating from the science is easy of persuasion in those cases where his mind has strayed from the science,' say the teachers.

10 'No,' says Kauṭilya. 11 The blind king can be made to follow any course of action through the excellence of his associates. 12 One devia-

5 *dvairājya* : as the sequel shows, this is joint rule by two kings, not a partition of a kingdom into two, as is the case in *Mālavikāgnimitra*, Act 5. — *vairājya* 'being without the king' is in effect rule by one other than the legitimate ruler of the state. Some enemy, after conquering a state, has driven out its ruler and started ruling over it from his own state. The text does not justify the thesis of Jayaswal (*Hindu Polity*, I, 92) that this means a kingless state and that it implies a real democratic constitution, nor is *vairājya* an aristocracy (*vi-rāj*) ruling under authority from *janapada* or the entire body of the people (H. K. Deb, IHQ, XIV, 372 ff.). — *anyaiḥ* cannot mean 'by the subjects' (Cs) or 'by everybody' (Deb, *loc. cit.*, p. 370). It refers to those who have forcibly seized the kingdom.

7 *tulyayogakṣemam* is a reply to *parasparasaṁgharṣeṇa* ; if welfare is equally shared, there need be no rivalry. Cn rightly adds '*mitho virodhāsaṁbhavāt*' by way of explanation. — *amātyāvagraham* is from Cn Cs. It means 'where the ministers are held in check' and is a reply to *anyonyapakṣadveṣa-* etc. Cn, however, has 'if a conflict does arise, the ministers can set it right'; Cs has 'the ministers can prevent double rule from coming into existence,' which is hardly likely; the question of preventing *dvairājya* is not being discussed here. V. Raghavan (Proceedings of the All-India Oriental Conference, Nagpur, 1946, pp. 103-4) proposes *mitho' vagraham*, regarding *tulyayogakṣemam* as a reply to *anyonyapakṣa-* etc. and *mitho 'vagraham* as a reply to *parasparasaṁgharṣeṇa*. He thinks that the *amātyas* have no place here. But *anyonypakṣa-* does contain a reference to such officers in both parties. And *tulya-* etc. appears more likely as a reply to *paraspara-* etc. The case of *Mālavikāgnimitra* 5.14 (*parasparāvagrahanirvikārau*) is not exactly parallel. The two kings there rule over two halves of Vidarbha independently and are both vassals to another sovereign. 8 *vairājya* does not necessarily refer to rule by foreigners from outside India, as Meyer thinks. The foreign ruler is only from a neighbouring state in India. Though the subject for *karśayati* etc. is *vairājyam*, we have to understand the foreign ruler as meant. Cn Cs read *vairājye* for *vairājyam*. The construction becomes easy in that case, though the subject for *karśayati* etc. has then to be supplied. — Jayaswal's translation of the s. (*Hindu Polity*, I, 94) 'nobody feels in a Vairājya government the feeling of "mine" (with regard to the state), the aim of political organism is rejected, any one can sell away (the country), no one feels responsible, or becoming indifferent leaves the state' does too much violence to the text.

9 For *aśāstracakṣur andhaḥ*, cf. 1.14.7 — *calitaśāstra* is one who deliberately flouts the teaching of the *śāstra*.

ting from the science, however, with his mind firmly fixed on what is contrary to the science, ruins the kingdom and himself with his injustice.

13 As between a sick and a new king, 'The sick king meets with (the danger of) the overthrow of his rule caused by ministers or danger to his own life caused by (carrying on the) rule ; the new king, on the other hand, busies himself with acts like observance of his duties, showing favours, granting exemptions, bestowing gifts and conferring honour, which please and benefit the subjects,' say the teachers.

14 'No,' says Kauṭilya. 15 The sick king carries on the kingly duties as they were going on before. 16 The new king, however, thinking the kingdom, won by force, to be his, behaves as he likes without restraint. 17 Or, being in the power of his associates in revolt, he tolerates the ruin of the kingdom. 18 Not being rooted among the subjects, he becomes easy to uproot.

19 With respect to the sick king, there is this distinction, one afflicted by a foul disease and one not so afflicted. 20 With respect to the new, also, (the distinction is) one of noble birth and one not of noble birth.

21 As between a weak king of noble birth and a strong king not of noble birth, 'The subjects yield with difficulty to the overtures of the weak though nobly-born king, having regard to his weakness, but easily (yield) to those of the strong though low-born king, having regard to his strength,' say the teachers.

22 'No,' says Kauṭilya. 23 The subjects submit of their own accord to a weak king of noble birth, as a natural capacity to rule devolves on one of noble birth. 24 And they frustrate the overtures of the strong but low-born king since in love are all virtues present. 25 The loss of the crops is

13 *prāṇābādhaṁ vā rājyamūlam* : this clearly means that carrying on the rule would be too much for the health of the king and he might die, as Meyer says. Cn has 'the people consider him unfit to rule and overthrow him.' — *prakṛtirañjanopakāraiḥ* is an adjective to the preceding expression.

15 *rājapraṇidhim* as in 1.19. 16 *balāvarjitam* and *sāmutthāyikaiḥ* (s. 17) show that 'new king' means a usurper. The difference from *vairājya* is that in this case the new ruler is not a foreigner, but a usurper from the same land, perhaps even a scion of the same family to which the ousted king belonged.

19 *pāparogī*, i.e., suffering from foul disease such as leprosy and so on. — The idea in these two ss. appears to be that in connection with the choice between a sick king and a new king, the preference indicated above need not be mechanically followed, but the nature of the illness and the nobility or otherwise of birth of the new king should also be taken into account.

21 *upajāpa* is usually 'secret instigation' in order to win a person over to one's side. Here it refers to overtures, not necessarily secret, made for that purpose.

23 *jātyam* etc. is repeated from 7.17.21. 24 *anurāge sārvaguṇyam* from Cn Cs is found in 7.5.14 in the same connection. The reading of the mss. *anuyoge sāḍguṇyam* yields little relevant sense. 25 *prayāsavadhāt* etc. : Cn Cs regard the two statements in this s. as dealing with troubles caused by foreign invasion and divine calamities respectively. But this seems hardly right. Such a discussion would be out of place here ; it would have been included in 8.4, under *pīḍanavarga*. The two things are unconnected with *rājavyasana* or *rājyavyasana*, which form the topic of this Chapter. The s. seems to contain two maxims

a greater evil than the loss of sowings, as it involves loss of efforts, drought (a greater evil) than excessive rain, as it involves loss of livelihood.

26 The relative seriousness or otherwise of calamities of the constituents, (taken) two at a time, has been set forth in the traditional order, as the ground for marching or staying quiet.

CHAPTER THREE

SECTION 129 THE GROUP OF THE VICES OF MAN

1 Absence of training in the lores is the cause of a man's vices. 2 For, an untrained person does not see the faults in vices. 3 We shall set them forth.

4 A group of three (vices) springs from anger, a group of four springs from lust.

5 Of the two, anger is more serious. 6 For, anger acts everywhere. 7 And mostly kings under the influence of anger are known to have been killed by risings among the subjects, those under the influence of lust (are known to be killed) by enemies and diseases as a result of losses.

8 'No,' says Bhāradvāja. 9 'Anger is behaviour proper for a good man, (a means of) requiting enmity, extirpation of insults and keeping men in dread. 10 And resort to anger is ever needed for putting down evil. 11 Lust is (a means of) attainment of success, conciliation, generosity of nature and being lovable. 12 And resort to lust is ever needed for the enjoyment of fruits of works done.'

pertaining to rule by a weak king and a strong king. Rule by the latter is like *sasyavadha* or *avṛṣṭi*, that by a weak king like *muṣṭivadha* 'destruction of sowings' or *ativṛṣṭi*. This is intended to support the view that rule by the *durbala* noble king is preferable. It is not unlikely that the s. is a marginal comment that has got into the text. — Meyer finds here the words of experience of Candragupta's minister, who, having fallen from the 'rains (of favour)' to the gutter, is bitter against the low upstart whom he helped to power. It is as difficult to agree with this inference as with Jolly's opposite inference that the author could not have been the minister who had helped an upstart to power. Personal experience need not be understood as reflected in this passage.

26 The stanza is unrelated to the contents of this Chapter, but forms a summing up of the discussion in the last Chapter; it should have preferably come at the end of 8.1. — *yāne sthāne* refers to *yātavyaṁ rakṣitavyam* of 8.1.1. Hence Meyer's proposal to read *sthāne sthāne* 'in each case' is unacceptable.

8.3

3 *tān* has in view *doṣān*; hence the masculine.

7 *kṣayanimittam* is read as in Cn, and *arivyādhibhiḥ* is preferred to *ativyādhibhiḥ*. As Cn explains *kṣaya* refers to losses of *kośa* and *daṇḍa* (in the case of *ari*) and to decay of the body (in the case of *vyādhi*). *vyaya* does not have such a double significance and does not appear authentic. *ativyādhi*, though possible (cf. 7.6.9), seems less likely. — *iti*: Meyer thinks that the name of the teacher or school holding this view is lost. Perhaps *ācāryāḥ* was originally there after *iti*.

9 *vairayātanam* and *avajñāvadho* from Cn Cs are quite obviously the only correct readings. 11 *siddhilābhaḥ*: a strong desire or urge often leads to success. — Bhāradvāja does not regard *kopa* and *kāma* as vices and is therefore unconcerned with their relative seriousness.

13 'No,' says Kauṭilya. 14 Becoming hated, making enemies, and association with pain, that is anger. 15 Humiliation, loss of wealth, and association with harmful persons like thieves, gamblers, hunters, singers and players on instruments, that is lust. 16 Of these, being hated is a greater evil than humiliation. 17 One humiliated is held in their power by his own people and by others; the hated one is exterminated. 18 Making enemies is a greater evil than loss of wealth. 19 Loss of wealth endangers the treasury, making enemies endangers life. 20 Association with pain is a greater evil than association with harmful persons. 21 Association with harmful persons can be remedied in a moment, association with pain causes prolonged distress. 22 Therefore, anger is more serious.'

23 Verbal injury, violation of property and physical injury (are vices springing from anger).

24 'As between verbal injury and violation of property, verbal injury is worse,' says Viśālākṣa. 25 'For, a spirited man, spoken to harshly, retaliates with energy. 26 The barb of offensive speech, embedded in the heart, inflames the spirit and afflicts the senses.'

27 'No,' says Kauṭilya. 28 Honouring with money removes the dart of speech, but violation of property means loss of livelihood. 29 Not giving (what belongs to the other), taking away, destroying or abandoning property is violation of property.

30 'As between violation of property and physical injury, violation of property is worse,' say the followers of Parāśara. 31 'Spiritual good and pleasures are rooted in money. 32 And the world is tied up with money. 33 Its destruction is a greater evil.'

34 'No,' says Kauṭilya. 35 Even for a very large sum of money, no one would desire the loss of his life. 36 And through physical injury a person incurs that same danger at the hands of others.

37 This is the group of three (vices) springing from anger.

38 The group of four (vices) springing from lust, however, is, hunting, gambling, women and drink.

39 Among them, 'Of hunting and gambling, hunting is worse,' says Piśuna. 40 'For, in it, the danger of robbers, enemies, wild animals, forest

14 *śatruvedanam* 'finding enemies,' i.e., making enemies. Meyer's 'feeling enmity towards others' does not quite fit s. 19 — *duḥkhāsaṅgaḥ*: *āsaṅga* is close contact, association. 15 *pāṭaccara* 'a thief' is explained in Cn as 'a drunkard.' 21 *muhūrta-pratīkāro*: Cn Cs read *muhūrtaprītikaro*; but the former presents a better contrast to *dīrghakleśakaro*.

25 *pratyārohati* 'climbs back,' i.e., retaliates.

29 *parityāgaḥ*, i.e., 'non-protection of goods entrusted to one's care' (Cn Cs).

fires and stumbling and loss of way as well as hunger and thirst constitute a danger to life. 41 In gambling, however, there is only winning for one expert in dice, as it was for Jayatsena and Duryodhana.'

42 'No,' says Kauṭilya. 43 Of the two (parties in gambling) there is also loss for one, as is illustrated by Nala and Yudhiṣṭhira. 44 And the same money, won at gambling, becomes a bait and leads to formation of enmities. 45 Uncertainty as to existing wealth and obtaining non-existing wealth, loss before a thing is enjoyed and getting illness due to retention of urine, motions of the bowel, hunger and so on, are the evils of gambling. 46 But in hunting, there is exercise, getting rid of phlegm, bile, fat and (a tendency to) perspiration, practice in hitting the targets of moving and stationary bodies, knowledge of the minds of animals in anger, fear and condition of ease, and (only) occasional marching.

47 'Of the vices of gambling and women, the vice of gambling (is worse),' says Kauṇapadanta. 48 'For, continuously, at night in lamplight, and (even) when the mother has died, the gambler goes on playing. 49 And if questioned in difficulties, he becomes enraged. 50 But in case of indulgence in women, questioning concerning spiritual and material well-being is indeed possible on occasions of bath, toilet and meals. 51 And it is possible to employ a woman in what is beneficial to the king or to turn her away by means of silent punishment or disease or to make her go away.'

52 'No,' says Kauṭilya. 53 Deliverance is possible in gambling, without deliverance is addiction to women. 54 Failure to show himself, aversion for work, absence of material good and loss of spiritual good by allowing the right time to pass, weakness in administration and addiction to drink (result from addiction to women).

40 *prāṇābādhaḥ* is the predicate for *stenāmitra-* etc. and *kṣutpipāse*. 41 Jayatsena is apparently the name of Nala's brother. According to the *Mahābhārata*, 3.56.4 ff., however, Nala had lost to Puṣkara.

44 *āmiṣam* 'a bait' which lures other gamblers to covet it (Meyer) rather than 'a prey, i.e., an object of enjoyment for all (not for himself)' (Cn Cs). — *vairānubandhaḥ* from Cn is a better expression than *vairabandhaḥ* of the mss. 45 *vipratipattiḥ* 'conflict' seems to refer to uncertainty, rather than 'misuse' (Cn). Meyer has 'slipping out of one's hand'. 46 *kopabhayasthāneṣu* is from Cn. Cn explains *sthāna* as 'condition of ease.' With *-sthānehiteṣu* of the mss., Cs understands *īhita* in the sense of 'activity'. Meyer prefers to read *hiteṣu* as a separate word 'in conditions of well-being,' which is not very happy. — *anityayāna*, i.e., you do not have to go out always ; only occasionally you go hunting. Meyer thinks that *nityayānam* 'being always on the move' is better. But that would hardly be a point in favour of hunting.

51 *upāṁśudaṇḍena* : Meyer's attempts to get over the difficulty of 'silent' punishment for women, occasioned by his belief that Indians looked upon a woman's murder as a ghastly sin, are all unsuccessful. We have to face the fact that one teacher, Kauṇapadanta, at least had no scruples on that score. — Cn construes *vyāvartayitum* with *upāṁśudaṇḍena*, and *avasrāvayitum* with *vyādhinā*. That is also likely.

53 *sapratyādeyam*, i.e., from which a person can be reclaimed. 'The losses of which can be recovered' is much less likely. 54 In view of the *ca* after *dharmalopaḥ*, *anartho* is read as a separate word. The compound *anarthadharmalopaḥ* is awkward.

55 'Of the vices of women and drink, indulgence in women (is worse),' says Vātavyādhi. 56 'For, harmfulness among women is of various kinds as explained in (the Section on) rules for the royal residence. 57 In drink, on the other hand, there is the enjoyment of pleasures of the senses, such as sound and others, making gifts of love, honouring attendants, and the removal of fatigue caused by work.'

58 'No,' says Kauṭilya. 59 In the case of indulgence in women there is begetting of an offspring and protection of oneself with wives at home, the opposite of this with outside women, ruin of everything with women unapproachable (for one). 60 Both these (evils) are there in the vice of drink. 61 The excellences of drink are: loss of consciousness, insane behaviour of one not insane, appearing like a corpse when not deceased, exposing private parts to view, loss of learning, intellect, strength, wealth and friends, separation from the good, association with the harmful, and attachment to skill in lute and song, destructive of wealth.

62 Of gambling and wine, gambling (is worse). 63 The success or failure of one side, due to the stakes, leads to strife among the subjects by creating two factions concerning animate and inanimate objects. 64 And in particular, in the case of oligarchies and of royal families having the character of an oligarchy, there are dissensions caused by gambling and destruction caused by that; hence it is the most evil among vices, as it favours evil men, (and) since it leads to weakness in administration.

65 Lust means the favouring of evil persons, anger, the suppression of good persons. Because of the multitude of evils (resulting from them), both are held to be a calamity without end.

66 Hence, the self-possessed (king) should give up anger and lust, the starting point of all calamities, the destroyers of the patrimony, by waiting upon elders and gaining control over his senses.

56 *bāliśyam* is not mere foolishness, but harmfulness, as shown by the contents of 1.20.14-17. — As the quotation from Vātavyādhi refers to the section on *niśāntapraṇidhi*, it is reasonable to suppose that his work contained a section similar to 1.20 above.

60 *tad ubhayam*, i.e, the *viparyaya* (viz., absence of offspring and absence of self-protection) and *sarvocchittiḥ* 'ruin of everything.' 61 *pānasampad*: *sampad* appears to be used ironically.

62 Cn, followed by Cs, reads *ekeṣām* at the end of this s., explaining it by 'in the opinion of some.' It then adds *anyeṣām* after *vināśa iti* in s. 64, interpreting *asatpragraha* there as 'indulgence in drink'. That is quite unlikely, as is shown by the fact that s. 64 is quoted in 15.1.43-44 as an illustration of *vyākhyāna*, where *anyeṣām* is not to be found, showing that right up to the end of s. 64 we have only *dyūta* in view and nowhere *pāna*. It is therefore better to read *ekeṣām* at the beginning of s. 63 in the sense of 'of one party (to the game)'. 63 *prāṇiṣu* refers to betting on animal fights, races etc., while *niścetaneṣu* refers to dice etc. 64 *saṁghānām*: see 11.1 below. — *saṁghadharmiṇāṁ rājakulānām*: this refers to the *kulasaṁgha* of 1.17.53 in which all male adults of the dynasty form a condominium over the state.

66 *mūlaharam*: *mūla* refers to the inherited kingdom, as Cn points out. Cf. 2.9.20 ff. — *vṛddhasevī jitendriyaḥ*: cf. 1.5-7 above. — For *vyasanas*, cf. Manu 7.45-52, which show some expansion and much difference as compared to the present text.

CHAPTER FOUR

SECTION 130 THE GROUP OF AFFLICTIONS
SECTION 131 THE GROUP OF HINDRANCES
SECTION 132 THE GROUP OF STOPPAGES OF PAYMENT TO THE TREASURY

1 Visitations from the gods are: fire, floods, disease, famine and epidemic.

2 'Of fire and floods, the affliction of fire is irremediable and all-consuming, while the affliction of floods is such that escape from it is possible and its dangers can be tided over,' say the teachers. 3 'No,' says Kauṭilya. 4 Fire burns (at most) a village or half a village; floods, on the other hand, carry away hundreds of villages.

5 'Of disease and famine, disease ruins undertakings by hindering the activity of workers who die or are sick or afflicted, whereas famine does not ruin undertakings and yields taxes in money and cattle,' say the teachers. 6 'No,' says Kauṭilya. 7 Disease afflicts only one region and remedies can be found for it, while famine afflicts the whole country and leads to absence of livelihood for living beings.

8 By that is explained epidemic.

9 'Of the loss of common men and that of chiefs, the loss of common men brings about insecurity of undertakings, the loss of chiefs is characterised by a hindrance to the carrying out of works,' say the teachers. 10 'No,' says Kauṭilya. 11 The loss of common men can be made good because of the very large number of common men, not the loss of chiefs. 12 For, among thousands there is one chief or not (even one), because of the high degree of spirit and intelligence (necessary, and) because of the dependence of common men on him.

8.4

The first of the three Sections in this Chapter, which is mainly concerned with *janapada-vyasana*, extends up to s. 47, the other two being disposed of in a single s. each.

1 Cf. 4.3.1 for eight calamities of a divine origin. Rats, serpents etc. mentioned there are calamities of much less importance. — *maraka* is a pestilential epidemic.

2 *śakyāpagamanam* from Cn is certainly preferable to *śakyopagamanam*; the idea is of possibility of escaping from the floods. — *uktam*, which appears in the reading of the mss., is due to a scribal error.

5 *-vyādhitopasṛṣṭa* is read as in Cs for *-vyādhitāpasṛṣṭa*. It seems that *upasṛṣṭa* should be understood in the sense of 'afflicted,' i.e., incapacitated for work because of the illness. Cf. *rogopasṛṣṭa* (*Raghuvaṁśa*, 8.94). Cs, understanding it in the sense of 'sick,' explains *upasṛṣṭaparicāraka* by 'who nurse the sick'. *paricāraka*, however, is to be construed with *preta* and *vyādhita* as well and evidently refers to workmen employed on works. *apasṛṣṭa* may mean 'who is relieved of his work' (Meyer), 'discharged, dismissed' (Russ.), or 'who has left'; but *upasṛṣṭa* is a better reading.

8 *tena* seems to refer to famine as in Cs rather than to disease as in Cn.

9 *kṣudraka*: cf. 1.13.13. — *mukhya* refers to principal officers and cheftains, including feudatories. 12 *sattvaprajñādhikyāt*: Cs makes this the reason for *kṣudrakāṇām tadāśrayatvam*. Cn does not read *tadāśrayatvāt kṣudrakāṇām*, and it seems very likely that these words are only a marginal comment that has crept into the text. They do not provide the reason for the statement in *bhavati eko na vā*, as the use of the ablative is expected to do.

13 'Of one's own army and an enemy's army, one's own army harasses by excessive violence and levies, and cannot be warded off, whereas an enemy's army can be given a fight or can be escaped from by means of flight or by a treaty,' say the teachers. 14 'No,' says Kauṭilya. 15 Harassment by one's own army can be avoided by winning over or destroying the leaders among the principal officers or it afflicts (only) a part of the country, whereas the enemy's army, which afflicts the whole country, ruins it by plunder, slaughter, burning, destroying and carrying (people) off.

16 'Of strife among subjects and strife in the royal family, strife among subjects, creating a split among subjects, invites attacks by enemies, while strife in the royal family brings about double food, wages and exemptions for the subjects,' say the teachers. 17 'No,' says Kauṭilya. 18 Strife among subjects can be averted by winning over the leaders among the subjects or by removal of the cause of strife. 19 And subjects, contending among themselves, benefit (the king) by their mutual rivalry. 20 Strife in the royal family, on the other hand, leads to harassment and destruction of the subjects and can be overcome (only) with a double exertion.

21 'Of indulgence in pleasures by the country people and that by the king, indulgence in pleasures by the country people brings about the destruction of the fruits of works for all three times, whereas indulgence in pleasures by the king confers benefit on artisans, artists, actors, reciters, prostitutes and traders,' say the teachers. 22 'No,' says Kauṭilya. 23 Indulgence in pleasures by the country people consumes little for the sake of the removal of fatigue caused by work and, after consuming, leads to application to work once again, whereas indulgence in pleasures by the king afflicts (the subjects) through seizure of what he pleases, demands, gifts and seizure of works by (the king) himself and by his favourites.

24 'Of the king's beloved and the prince, the prince harasses through seizure of what he pleases, demands, gifts and seizure of works by himself and by his favourites, the king's beloved through enjoyment of pleasures,'

13 *daṇḍakarābhyām*: in spite of its use along with *kara*, *daṇḍa* here is obviously 'force' rather than 'fines'. — *apasāreṇa*: the flight is by the people rather than by the king. 15 *prakṛtipuruṣamukhya*: it seems that *prakṛtipuruṣa* means a principal officer, and *mukhya* refers to leaders or the foremost among them. Cf. 12.3.14. Cn seems to have read only *prakṛtimukhya* and explained it by 'chief among ministers'. — *apavāhanaiḥ* from Cn Cs is clearly necessary. Cf. 2.1.1, also 8.2.8.

16 *'rājavivādaḥ* is strife among members of the royal family for power. 18 *upagraha* is conciliation, winning over. 20 *dviguṇavyāyāma*, i.e., effort double that required for putting down strife among subjects.

21 *traikālyena* 'e.g., crops sown in the past are not cared for, sowings in the present are not made and preparation of land for future sowing is not made' (Cn). — *-rūpājīvā-*, found in Cn Cs, is missing in the mss. It seems quite authentic. 23 *gacchati*: as the subject is *-vihāraḥ*, *gamayati* would appear better. — *svayaṁgrāha*: cf. 8.1.44. — *praṇaya*: cf. 5.2.16 etc. — *paṇyāgāra* is a present consisting of goods. Cf. 7.15.20 etc. — *kāryopagraha*: Cn has 'receiving bribes for allowing any work to be done'. Meyer has 'seizure of works', i.e., appropriation of their fruits. That would appear to be better.

24 *subhagā* 'beloved' of the king. In 12.2.15, the word is used as an adjective to *mahiṣī*. Here a queen or a mistress may be understood.

say the teachers. 25 'No,' says Kauṭilya. 26 The prince can be held in check through the minister and the chaplain, not the king's beloved, because of her foolishness and association with harmful persons.

27 'Of a band (of fighting units) and a chief, the band, impossible to suppress because of large numbers, harasses through robbery and forcible seizure, the chief through favouring and destroying undertakings,' say the teachers. 28 'No,' says Kauṭilya. 29 A band is easy to restrain because of common character and vices or through the winning over of the chief or a part of the band. 30 The chief, full of hauteur, harasses by destroying the lives and property of others.

31 'Of the Director of Stores and the Administrator, the Director of Stores harasses by finding fault with what is done and by (imposing) penalties, while the Administrator, supervised by a bureau, enjoys (only) the fruit assigned,' say the teachers. 32 'No,' says Kauṭilya. 33 The Director of Stores receives as admissible in the treasury what is guaranteed by others, whereas the Administrator first secures wealth for himself, then collects revenue for the king or allows it to perish, and in the matter of receiving others' property he acts on his own authority.

34 'Of the frontier officer and the trader, the frontier officer harasses a trade-route by allowing the activity of robbers and charging excessive duties, whereas traders promote (a trade-route) through benefits conferred by goods carried out and goods brought in exchange,' say the teachers. 35 'No,' says Kauṭilya. 36 The frontier officer maintains (a trade-route) by favouring the bringing together of goods, whereas traders, joining together and raising or lowering the (prices of) goods, make a profit of one hundred *paṇas* on one *paṇa* or of one hundred *kumbhas* on one *kumbha*.

37 As between land seized by a person of noble birth and land occupied by herds of cattle, 'Land seized by a person of noble birth, though yielding

27 *śreṇī* is clearly a band or community of fighting men, normally carrying on some peaceful occupation. Cf. 7.11.18. For *mukhya*, cf. ss. 9-12 above. 29 *samānaśīlavyasanatvāt*: the idea seems to be, if one of them can be won over, the others would follow suit. The idea in Cs is, they can be restrained by other men of the same character and vices. 30 *stambha* 'haughtiness'; cf. 1.9.1,3 etc.

31 *karaṇādhiṣṭhitaḥ*: this can mean 'under the control of a bureau' as in Breloer (III, 223), and that sense better suits the context here, though in 2.5.8 and 2.11.1, the expression seems to mean 'presiding over an office'. 33 *kṛtāvastham*: for *avasthā* 'guarantee,' cf. 2.8.29. — *svapratyayaḥ* 'trusting in himself,' i.e., acting on his own authority. Cf. 2.36.5; 3.14.34. — Breloer (III, 101-102) makes this comment: 'The *ācāryas* look only at the goods; what the *samāhartṛ* pilfers is for the private individuals to see, the state is not harmed thereby. Kauṭilya, on the contrary, looks upon harm to the people and to the economy as harm to the state, a sort of state socialism.' It is doubtful it this view can be sustained on the strength of this passage.

34 *coraprasarga* 'letting loose thieves,' i.e., encouraging them. Cn Cs read *-prasaṅga*, understanding it as 'instigation'. — *paṇyapratipaṇya*: cf. 2.16.18 etc. 36 *saṁpāta* 'coming together' or 'bringing together'. — *vartayati*: the object is *vaṇikpatham*. — *paṇe paṇaśatam* is a profit of 10,000%; this is an exaggeration, as pointed out in Cn. — *ājīvanti* 'live on' as well as 'make a profit of.'

37 *abhijāta* is a man from a noble family, particularly from the royal family itself. Cf. 13.5.19. — *uparuddha* 'blocked', i.e., occupied, seized. — *mahāphalā 'pi āyudhī-*

abundant produce, is not fit to be retrieved (if) useful in providing soldiers, because of the fear of the danger of a calamity, while land occupied by herds of cattle, being suited for agriculture, is fit to be reclaimed. 38 For, pasture-land is made to yield before fields,' say the teachers. 39 'No,' says Kauṭilya. 40 Land seized by a person of noble birth, even if yielding extremely great benefit, is fit to be retrieved because of the fear of the danger of a calamity, whereas that occupied by herds of cattle, of benefit to the treasury and useful for transport, is not fit to be reclaimed, except in case of obstruction to the sowing of crops.

41 'Of highway robbers and forest tribes, highway robbers, operating at night and lying in wait, attack men's bodies, are a constant danger, rob hundreds of thousands (in cash) and stir up principal men, (while) forest tribes, operating in forests on the frontier far away, are openly known and move before the eyes of all, and harm only a part of the country,' say the teachers. 42 'No,' says Kauṭilya. 43 Robbers rob only the negligent, are few in number, powerless and easy to know and capture, whereas forest tribes, living in their own territory, are many in number and brave, fight openly, seize and ruin countries, having the same characteristics as a king.

44 Of deer parks and elephant forests, deer, being plenty in number, yield the benefit of abundant meat and skins, cause little trouble about fodder and are easy to control. 45 Elephants are the reverse of this when being caught, and if rogues, they lead to the ruin of the country.

yopakāriṇī: the contribution of fighting men which the land is likely to make is not to be understood as the great *phala* derived from it. — *vyasanābādhabhayāt*: Cn Cs understand the danger to be that soldiers would not be available in times of calamities (i.e., *vyasane ābādhabhayāt*). But if the land is recovered, the fighting men in it would certainly be available. The danger would rather appear to be that of a fight in case an attempt is made to rescue it; such a conflict would be a calamity. *vyasanābādha* may be understood as 'the danger of a calamity'. — Meyer has an altogether different explanation. He reads *amahāphalā*, interprets *abhijāta* as 'cultivable plants' and translates, 'land fully covered by cultivable plants, even though not yielding great produce, should not be freed, being useful for service in war.' This is highly doubtful. Russ. follows Meyer. 40 *atyantamahopakārā*, because it supplies a very large number of fighting men. There is no reference to *phala* here. — *vyasanābādha-*: the danger is of the *abhijāta* becoming very powerful and attempting to seize the kingdom for himself.

41 *rātrisattracarāḥ*: it is true that *rātri* is one of the *sattras* mentioned in 10.3.24 and that therefore a single idea 'operating under cover of night' is possible; nevertheless, two ideas 'operating at night and after lying in wait' seem better. *rātrisattra* can hardly mean 'nocturnal assemblies (of thieves, robbers etc.)' as J. Charpentier (JRAS, 1934, 113-4) thinks it means in *Saundarananda*, 2.28. With these words, *-carāḥ* from Cn Cs is to be preferred to *-parāḥ*. — *nityāḥ*: Cn does not seem to have read this word. Meyer suggests *anityāḥ* 'never in one place'; Charpentier suggests *nityam*.

43 *kuṇṭhāḥ*: cf. 7.12.9,13. — *rājasadharmāṇaḥ*, i.e., as dangerous as an enemy king.

44 *mandagrāsāvakleśinaḥ*: Cs has 'eating little fodder and hence causing little trouble in catching them.' It may simply mean 'causing little trouble about food.' 45 *gṛhyamāṇāḥ*: Cs construes this with *duṣṭāś ca*: it seems, however, that the latter begins a new clause. Meyer proposes *agṛhyamāṇāḥ* 'if they are not caught and if they are wicked etc.' However, *gṛhyamāṇāḥ* appears better. — Meyer thinks that ss. 44-45 contain the opinion of the *ācāryas* and that its refutation by Kauṭilya has been lost. The latter, he argues, would not be so hard on his favourite elephants. However, when it is a question of *pīḍana* or affliction, even Kauṭilya could not possibly have argued that elephants are less troublesome than deer.

46 Of benefit conferred on one's own *sthānīya* and that conferred on an enemy's *sthānīya*, the benefit conferred on one's own *sthānīya*, (viz.,) the benefit of grains, cattle, money and forest produce, is capable of sustaining the lives of the country people in times of trouble. 47 The reverse is the benefit conferred on an enemy's *sthānīya*.

Thus ends the topic of afflictions.

48 Internal (hindrance) is hindrance by the chiefs, external the hindrance caused by enemies or forest tribes.

Thus ends the topic of hindrances.

49 Affected by those two (hindrances) and by the afflictions as described, appropriated by chiefs, impaired by exemptions, scattered, wrongfully collected, (and) carried off by neighbouring kings and forest tribes, — these are stoppages of (payment to the) treasury.

50 The (king) should strive to prevent the afflictions from arising and to overcome those that have arisen, as well as to destroy the hindrances and stoppages (of payment) for the sake of the country's prosperity.

CHAPTER FIVE

SECTION 133 THE GROUP OF CALAMITIES OF THE ARMY
SECTION 134 THE GROUP OF CALAMITIES OF THE ALLY

1 The calamities of the army are: (the state of being) unhonoured, dishonoured, unpaid, sick, newly arrived, come after a long march, exhausted, depleted, repulsed, broken in the first onslaught, caught in an unsuitable season, caught on an unsuitable terrain, despondent of hope, deserted, with women-folk inside, with 'darts' inside, with a rebellious base, split inside, run away, widely scattered, encamped near, completely absorbed, blocked,

46 *sthānīya*: see 2.3.3, also 2.1.4. The *upakāra* is help rendered in times of difficulty. Cn explains '*durbhikṣādiṣu krayavikrayavyavahāraḥ*'. Such help may be given even to an enemy's *sthānīya*. The *upakāra* on a *sthānīya* is regarded as a *pīḍana*, perhaps because it is done at the cost of the rest of the country. However, such an *upakāra* on one's *sthānīya* is said to sustain *jānapadas* in times of difficulty. It seems, therefore, that *jānapada* means only 'natives' as contrasted with foreigners in the *parasthānīya*.

48 *stambha* refers to hindrances or obstructions caused to state undertakings by officers themselves or by enemies etc. — As suggested by Meyer an *avagraha* should be read after *bāhyo*, so that *amitra* is understood, not *mitra*. Forest tribes are invariably mentioned together with enemies, not with allies. — It may be that this *vyasana* is principally that of a *durga*; for the *vyasanas* of this *prakṛti* are not mentioned elsewhere in this Book.

49 *saktaḥ* 'clinging to', i.e., misappropriated, not paid into the treasury.

8.5

The two Sections are to be found in ss. 1-21 and 22-30 respectively.

1 Here and in s. 9 below Meyer's proposal to read *kalatragarbhi* (for *-garhi*) has been adopted, being necessary for the sense required. It is supported by Kāmandaka, 14.69,80. — *parikṣiptam* is from Cs for *upakṣiptam*; it is supported by s. 13; cf. also Kāmandaka, 14.67,73.

encircled, with supplies of grains and men cut off, dispersed in one's own land, dispersed in an ally's land, infested by treasonable men, with a hostile enemy in the rear, with its base denuded (of troops), not united with the master, with head broken, and blind.

2 Among these, as between an unhonoured and a dishonoured (army), the unhonoured would fight when honoured with money, not the dishonoured, with resentment in its heart.

3 As between an unpaid and a sick (army), the unpaid would fight if given pay at once, not the sick, unfit for work.

4 As between a newly arrived (army) and one that has come after a long march, the newly arrived would fight after learning about the region from others and being mixed with old troops, not the one that has come after a long march, being troubled by the long march.

5 As between an exhausted and a depleted (army), the exhausted would fight after getting refreshed with bath, food and sleep, not the depleted, with its draught-animals and men reduced in a fight elsewhere.

6 As between a repulsed (army) and one broken in the first onslaught, the repulsed, thrown back in the first encounter, would fight, being rallied by heroic men, not the one broken in the first onslaught, with its heroic men slain in the first encounter.

7 As between an (army) caught in an unsuitable season and one caught on an unsuitable terrain, the one caught in an unsuitable season would fight when equipped with vehicles, weapons and armours suited to the season, not the one caught on an unsuitable terrain, with its foraging raids and operations impeded.

8 As between an (army) despondent of hope and a deserted one, the despondent would fight when its desires are fulfilled, not the deserted one, from which its chiefs have run away.

9 As between an (army) with women-folk inside and one with darts inside, the one with women inside would fight after getting rid of the women, not the one with darts inside, having enemies inside it.

2 *kṛtārthamānam* : 'which is honoured by giving money' seems better than 'given money and shown honour' (Meyer).

4 Here, as in s. 1, the mss. show *dūrayāta* : but *dūrāyāta* from Cs seems preferable. It is supported by Kāmandaka, 14.67,76. Cn seems to have read *dūrāgata*.

7 *yathartuyugya-* is as proposed by Meyer for *yathartuyogyayugya-*. When *yathā* is there, *yogya* is unnecessary. — *prasāra* 'a foraging raid'; cf. 10.2.5.

8 *apasṛtamukhyam* is from Cs. Cn seems to have read *parisṛtamukhyam*. — Meyer remarks that *parisṛptam* is a mistake for *parasṛṣṭam* 'abandoned'. Kāmandaka, 14.69,83, has *avamukta* for *parisṛpta*.

9 The explanation of the reading *kalatragarhi* in Cs is 'finding fault with the women-folk, i.e., the retinue, for being a burden and a hindrance in the work of fighting'; that is highly problematical.

10 As between an (army) with a rebellious base and one split inside, the one with a rebellious base would fight when its resentment is overcome by conciliation and other means, not the one split inside, divided from one another.

11 As between an (army) run away and one widely scattered, the army that has run away, having crossed over to a single realm, would fight with diplomacy and military activity, finding shelter in a fastness or an ally, not the widely scattered one, gone to more than one realm, because of there being many dangers.

12 As between an (army) encamped near (the enemy) and one completely absorbed (in his forces), the one encamped near, having separate marches and halts, would fight by over-reaching the enemy, not the one completely absorbed, with its halts and marches one with the enemy.

13 As between a blocked and an encircled (army), the blocked one would fight the obstructor by getting out in another direction, not the encircled one, obstructed on all sides.

14 As between an (army) with supplies of grains cut off and one with reserves of men cut off, that with supplies of grains cut off would fight after bringing grains from elsewhere or by subsisting on animal and vegetable food, not the one with reserves of men cut off, being without help.

15 As between an (army) dispersed in one's own land and one dispersed in an ally's land, that dispersed in one's own land, being disbanded in one's own territory, can be collected together in case of trouble, not the one dispersed in an ally's land, because of the distant place and time.

16 As between an (army) infested by treasonable men and one with a hostile enemy in the rear, that infested by treasonable men would fight when

10 *kupitamūlam*: Cn Cs understand *mūla* in the sense of 'principal officers'; that is better than understanding it in the sense of "the hereditary army (*maulabala*) as in Meyer, though in Kāmandaka, 14.70,83, *kruddhamaula* appears for *kupitamūla*.

11 It seems that the army has run away or been scattered, because it is defeated and the kingdom is conquered. In *apasṛta*, the whole of it goes into one other land; in *atikṣipta* it is split up and scattered in many lands. — *sattra* is, in particular, a fortress.

12 *upaniviṣṭam*: this happens when there is a joint expedition. Meyer's 'on whose neck the enemy has sat, i.e., hard-pressed by the enemy' is not possible. — *atisaṁdhāyārim* is proposed for *atisaṁdhākāram* (or *-tāram*). The mention of *ari* in the next clause suggests its use also in this. And the question is not of fighting the enemy trying to cheat (*atisaṁdhātṛ*), but a third king along with the enemy. — *samāptam* 'completely joined', because under a single command of the enemy. It cannot mean 'captured' (Meyer). — Kāmandaka, 14.84, regards *upaniviṣṭa* also as incapable of fighting.

14 *anabhisāram*: *abhisāra* refers to help or rescue. Cn reads *anāsāram* which comes to the same thing.

15 *vikṣipta* is explained in Cn Cs as 'sent on some mission or task'. However, no mission or task can be thought of in 9.2.11 and other places. — *ārāhayitum* from Cn provides the action necessary in the case of *vikṣipta*, not *avasrāvayitum*. The latter can hardly mean 'to bring together' as Cs interprets it; cf. 8.3.51. For *āvāhay* in this sense, cf. 7.7.13.

16 *asaṁhatam*, i.e., kept as a separate unit. Meyer suggests *adūṣyasaṁhatam* and thinks that Kāmandaka, 14.85, presupposes *saṁpūtam* 'purged'. Cn seems to have read *mitho 'saṁhatam*.

officered by trustworthy men and kept apart, not the one with a hostile enemy in the rear, being frightened of an attack in the rear.

17 As between an (army) with a denuded base and one not united with the master, that with a denuded base would fight with full mobilisation, after protection is secured through the citizens and the country people, not the one not united with the master, being without the king or the commander-in-chief.

18 As between an (army) with head broken and a blind (army), the one with head broken would fight under the command of another (commandant), not the blind one, being without a guide.

19 Removal of defects, insertion of (fresh) troops, over-reaching by remaining in a strong place, and peace with a superior party, are the means of overcoming the calamities of an army.

20 Being ever active, he should protect his own army, in its calamity, from the enemies; and being ever active, he should strike at the weak points of the army of the enemies.

21 The (king), ever diligent, should take steps right beforehand against that cause because of which he might suffer a calamity of the constituents.

22-27 An ally against whom one has marched oneself after joining forces (with others) or under the influence of others, or who is deserted through weakness or greed or regard (for another), or who is sold to the attacker by turning away from the battle or by planning to march against another enemy in another direction when pursuing the dual policy, or

17 *śūnyamūlam* : *mūla* is the country and its capital from which the troops have come; these are now without troops. — It is clear that *svāmin* refers to the commander-in-chief besides the king.

18 *kūṭa* 'head' is the commandant; his death is implied in *bhinna*.

19 *sattrasthānātisaṁhitam* from Cn Cs is metrically preferable, though the *bhāve kta* is a little awkward. A single idea seems intended 'over-reaching the enemy after taking up a position in a strong place like a fort,' though the commentators understand two ideas 'remaining in a strong place and over-reaching.' Russ. has 'placing oneself in a concealed place and thus getting an opportunity to outwit the enemy.' — *uttarapakṣasya*: we expect the instrumental, 'with the stronger party,' i.e., with the enemy, if he is stronger. Russ. renders the word by 'one who can take counter-action (against a rebellious army).'

21 Cn Cs read this stanza at the end of the chapter, after the discussion of the *mitravyasanas*. That may appear reasonable since *mitra* also is one of the *prakṛtis*. Nevertheless, the present place would seem all right for the stanza as it refers to the *prakṛtis* that are part of the same state, regarding which steps can be taken right before calamities overtake them. A *mitra* is not on the same footing. A provision for preventing a *mitravyasana* is separately mentioned in stanza 30. — *yatonimittam* is a bit awkward as an adjective to *vyasanam*. Perhaps *yato nimittād* would simplify the construction.

22 *svayam* etc.: Cn Cs understand three cases 'oneself in one's own interest (*svayam*), in combination with others (*saṁbhūya*) and at the instigation of another (*anyavaśena*).' It seems, however, that *svayam* is to be understood in any case and the alternative is only between *saṁbhūya* and *anyavaśena*.

23 *abhiyuñjāne*, i.e., to the enemy who has attacked one's ally. — *saṁgrāme apavartinā* refers to one method of 'selling'; instead of going to the ally's help, the *vijigīṣu* turns away from the fight, leaving the attacker free to overcome the ally. This would be for some

who after being inspired with confidence is over-reached either in a separate or a joint march, or who is not rescued from a calamity through fear or disrespect or laziness, or who, being kept out of his own lands, has gone away from one's side through fear, or who is humiliated by snatching (something) away (from him) or by not giving (something) to him or even by giving (something to him), or whose wealth is extorted from him by oneself or through another's agency, or who, being assigned a very heavy task, is broken (in the attempt) and has gone over to the enemy, or who, neglected because of weakness, is antagonised after making a request, (such an ally) can be secured with difficulty, and (even) when secured becomes quickly disaffected.

28-29 An ally, who has exerted himself or is worthy of honour, but is not honoured through one's folly, or is not honoured in a suitable manner, or who is prevented from gaining strength, or who is frightened because of harm done to (another) ally, or who is suspicious of oneself making a treaty with the enemy, or who is divided (from onseself) by treasonable persons, is easy to secure and remains (loyal, when) secured.

30 Therefore he should not allow these defects harmful to allies to arise, or, when they have arisen, he should remove them by qualities capable of removing the defects.

Herewith ends the Eighth Book of the Arthaśāstra of Kauṭilya
'CONCERNING THE TOPIC OF CALAMITIES'

consideration; that is the price received for the sale. — *dvaidhībhāvena*: Cn reads *dvaidhībhūtena*, which is slightly better. The idea is, the *vijigīṣu*, in following the dual policy, makes peace with the attacker of his ally because he wants to march against some enemy (*anyam amitram*) of his own elsewhere (*anyataḥ*); the ally is thus 'sold' to his attacker. Because of the second *vā* (after *yāsyatā*), Cn Cs find two situations in the second half; but the two situations as explained in them do not differ at all. The *vā* seems used a second time merely for the sake of metre.

25 *avaruddham* etc: the idea seems to be that the ally is obstructed when returning to his own land; he thus gets frightened and manages to escape from the *vijigīṣu*'s side. The two were apparently on a joint expedition on the *vigigīṣu*'s account. — *ācchedanāt* of the ally's land. — *adānāt* of what was due to him for his part in the expedition.

26 *atyāhāritam*: cf. 1.6.7. — *bhanktvā* seems used intransitively 'being broken' in attempting the very heavy task, and then gone over to the enemy, who had proved to be very strong. Cn Cs have 'who is set a very heavy task when he has just broken the enemy.' It is doubtful, however, if the *vijigiṣu* would think of dictating terms to a victorious ally. — *upasthitam* from Cn is preferable to *avasthitam*.

27 *upekṣitam* etc.: Cs has 'who, though treated with indifference because of his weakness, approaches again with a proposal for alliance but is antagonised.' It is doubtful if *mitram* can be the subject for *prārthayitvā*. The *vijigīṣu* alone can be thought of as making the proposal. Cn's reading *prārthayitrā* makes this clear. It is, in any case, a bit strange that a proposal for alliance should antagonise the ally. Perhaps that is because of the *upekṣā* that has led to resentment. Understanding *prārthay* in the sense of 'to attack' (Meyer in a foot-note) appears to improve matters; but that case seems covered by *abhiyātaṁ svayam* in s. 22.

28 *śaktito vā nivāritam*: Cn Cs read *bhaktito* for *śaktito* and explain 'weaned away from his devotion to the *vijigīṣu* by others.' That is possible, but 'prevented from growing strong' might appear slightly better.

29 *arisaṁhitāt*: when the *vijigīṣu* has made a treaty or pact with his enemy.

BOOK NINE

THE ACTIVITY OF THE KING ABOUT TO MARCH

CHAPTER ONE

SECTION 135 ASCERTAINMENT OF THE (RELATIVE) STRENGTH OR WEAKNESS OF POWERS, PLACE AND TIME

SECTION 136 SEASONS FOR MARCHING ON AN EXPEDITION

1 After ascertaining the (relative) strength or weakness of powers, place, time, seasons for marching, time for raising armies, revolts in the rear, losses, expenses, gains and troubles, of himself and of the enemy, the conqueror should march if superior in strength, otherwise stay quiet.

2 'Of (the powers of) energy and might, energy is superior. 3 For, the king himself, if brave, strong, healthy, trained in the use of missiles, is able to conquer a king possessed of might with the aid of the army alone. 4 And even his small army becomes capable of achieving its object because of its spirit. 5 But a king without energy, though possessed of might, perishes when overpowered by valour,' say the teachers.

6 'No,' says Kauṭilya. 7 The king, possessed of might, over-reaches the king possessed of energy, by his might, by inviting another king superior to him (in energy), by hiring or purchasing heroic men. 8 And his army, richly endowed with abundant might, horses, elephants, chariots and equipment, moves unhindered everywhere. 9 And winning over and purchasing men of energy, those possessed of might, even women, children, lame and blind persons, have conquered the world.

10 'Of (the powers of) might and counsel, might is superior. 11 For, one, though richly endowed with the power of counsel, has only barren wisdom,

The Ninth Book deals with preparations to be made before starting on an expedition and the precautions that have to be taken at the time.

9.1

The two Sections are to be found in ss. 1-33 and 34-52 respectively.

1 *śaktideśa-* etc. contains a list of all the topics discussed in this Book.

3 *daṇḍadvitīyo 'pi*: the point of *api* is, he may have no other resources except an army; particularly he may have no treasury. Meyer proposes *adaṇḍa-* 'even without an army'. That is not likely. The next s. refers to this king's army though it may be small. And Kāmandaka, 18.44, does speak of the use of an army (*daṇḍam adhike nayet*), though he gives the illustration of Paraśurāma.

7 *tadviśiṣṭam*: *tad* would refer to *utsāha*, not to *bala* or forces (Cn Cs). The king is already *prabhāvavān*; he will not be in need of superior forces. *bhṛtvā* is proposed for *hṛtvā*, in accordance with the explanation in Cs 'having hired for wages'. *hṛ* in its usual sense is little likely in the case of brave warriors. 9 *utsāhavataḥ* in the accusative as in Cn Cs is quite necessary. — *jitvā* 'winning over' rather than 'conquering in battle.'

if without might. 12 And lack of might ruins his works decided upon after deliberation, as lack of rain ruins the grains in the womb (of the earth),' say the teachers.

13 'No,' says Kauṭilya. 14 The power of counsel is superior. 15 For, the king with the eyes of intelligence and science, is able to take counsel even with a small effort and to over-reach enemies possessed of energy and might, by conciliation and other means and by secret and occult practices.

16 Thus the king, superior in each later one among the powers of energy, might and counsel, over-reaches (the enemy).

17 Place means the earth. 18 In that, the region of the sovereign ruler extends northwards between the Himavat and the sea, one thousand *yojanas* in extent across. 19 There the various types (of land are): forest land, village land, mountainous land, marshy land, dry land, level land and uneven land. 20 In them, he should start work that would augment his own strength.

21 That in which there is terrain suitable for the operations of one's own army and unsuitable for those of the enemy, is the best region, the opposite kind is the worst, alike to both is middling.

22 Time is of the nature of cold, heat and rain. 23 Its various parts are: night, day, fortnight, month, season, half year, year and *yuga*. 24 In them, he should start work that would augment his own strength.

25 That in which the season is suitable for the operations of one's own army, unsuitable for those of the enemy, is the best time, the opposite kind is the worst, alike to both is middling.

26 'Of power, place and time, however, power is superior,' say the teachers. 27 For, one possessed of power is able to counter-act (the difficulties of) marshy or dry region and (those of) time with cold, heat or rain. 28 'Place is superior,' say some. 29 'For, a dog on land drags a crocodile,

15 *prajñāśāstracakṣuḥ*: *prajñā* is one eye and *śāstra* the other. — *-prabhāvataś ca* of the mss. is an obvious corruption. — *yoga* is described in Books 12 and 13 and *upaniṣad* in Book 14.

18 *udīcīnam* 'to the north,' i.e., from the sea in the south to the Himālayas in the north. *tiryak* is explained as 'between the eastern and the western ocean,' i.e., the extent breadthwise (Cn). The extent of 1,000 *yojanas* would be that of the breadth rather than that between the north and the south; it could possibly apply to both, but hardly to north-south alone. Usually, however, 1,000 *yojanas* is given as the extent from north to south; cf. *kumārīpurāt prabhṛti bindusarovadhi yojanānāṁ daśaśatī cakravartikṣetram* — *Kāvyamīmāṁsā* p. 92 (Kane, HD, III, p. 66, fn. 96). In either case one thousand *yojanas* which is a little more than nine thousand miles is far outside the actual measurements. Russ. prefers the reading *atiryak* in the sense of 'breadthwise' on the ground that *tiryak* means 'cross-wise, i.e.,' north to south' and that in ancient references South India is hardly included. It is quite impossible to accept *navayojanasahasrapramāṇam* as the reading on the strength of the quotation in Śaṁkarāya on Kāmandaka, 1.39 (D. R. Bhandarkar, *Some Aspects* etc., p. 96). — The *cakravartikṣetra* does not seem intended to include regions beyond the borders of India.

27 *nimna* refers to water, watery regions.

a crocodile in water drags a dog.' 30 'Time is superior,' say some (others). 'By day a crow kills an owl, at night an owl kills a crow.' 32 'No,' says Kauṭilya. 33 Power, place and time are mutually helpful.

34 Grown superior in these, keeping a third or a fourth part of the army as protection in the base, in the rear, and in forests on the borders and taking with him treasury and troops capable of carrying out the undertaking, he should march against the enemy, whose old stocks of food are exhausted, who has not yet collected the new food-grains and whose fort is unrepaired, on an expedition in Mārgaśīrṣa, with a view to destroy his monsoon crops and winter sowings. 35 He should march on an expedition in Caitra, with a view to destroy his winter crops and spring sowings. 36 He should march on an expedition in Jyeṣṭha, against the enemy, whose stores of grass, timber and water are exhausted and whose fort is unrepaired, with a view to destroy his spring crops and monsoon sowings.

37 He should march in winter against a country which is very hot or which has little fodder, fuel and water. 38 He should march in summer against a country with showers of snow, or consisting mostly of deep water or with dense grass and trees. 39 He should march when it is raining against a country suited to the operations of his own army and unsuited to those of the enemy.

40 He should march on an expedition of long duration between the Mārgaśīrṣa and the Pauṣa full moon days, on one of medium duration between the Caitra and the Vaiśākha full moon days, on one of short duration between the Jyeṣṭha and the Āṣāḍha full moon days, on the fourth (expedition), if desirous of burning up (the enemy) in his calamity. 41 Marching in (the enemy's) calamity has been explained in (the Section on) 'marching after making war'.

42 And in general the teachers advise, 'One should march in the enemy's calamity.' 43 'On accession of strength one should march, there being uncertainty as to calamities,' says Kauṭilya. 44 Or, he should march when by marching he would be able to weaken or exterminate the enemy.

34 *mūle*, i.e., in the kingdom from which the expedition starts. 35 In this case there is no reference to the enemy's difficulties. Perhaps in Caitra, conditions described in *kṣīṇapurāṇa-* etc. are not expected to arise. 36 Meyer thinks that Jyeṣṭha is absurd and that Śrāvaṇa was expected. But monsoon sowings so late as in Śrāvaṇa are not very likely. And s. 40 supports Jyeṣṭha, as it supports Mārgaśīrṣa and Caitra.

38 *tuṣāradurdinam* 'always having showers of snow' (Cn Cs) is preferable to 'rich in mist and clouds' (Meyer).

40 *Mārgaśīrṣīm* etc.: the feminines refer to the full moon days. Cs reads *Mārgaśīrṣam* etc., as names of months. But with *antareṇa* 'between', particular days appear preferable to months. — *upoṣiṣyan* (from *upa-uṣ* 'to burn') should be construed with *vyasane* rather than with the preceding *hrasvakālām* (as in Cn Cs). — *caturthīm* is from Cn Cs. We have to supply *yātrāṁ yāyāt*. The point seems to be that it is different from the three just mentioned in not being restricted as to duration and season. The only occasion is the enemy's calamity. Meyer supplies *pūrṇimām* 'on the fourth full moon day'. But in view of *antareṇa*, the full moon days themselves are not to be thought of as days for starting. 41 *vigṛhya yāne*, i.e., in 7.4 above.

45   At a time when excessive heat is over, he should march with elephant divisions for the most part.   46   For, elephants, sweating inside, become leprous.   47   And not getting a plunge in water or a drink of water, they become blind through internal secretion.   48   Hence in a region with plenty of water and when it is raining he should march with elephant divisions for the most part.   49   In the reverse case, (he should march) with troops consisting mostly of donkeys, camels and horses, in a region with little rain and mud.   50   In a region mostly desert, he should march with the fourfold army when it is raining.

51   He should regulate the expedition in accordance with the evenness or unevenness of the road, the presence of water or land on it, or the shortness or length of the march.

52   Or, all expeditions should be of short duration in conformity with the lightness of the undertaking, or of long duration in conformity with the heaviness of the undertaking, and (then there may be) camping during rains in the foreign land.

CHAPTER TWO

SECTION 137   OCCASIONS FOR THE EMPLOYMENT OF (THE DIFFERENT KINDS OF) TROOPS
SECTION 138   MERITS OF EQUIPPING FOR WAR (THE DIFFERENT KINDS OF TROOPS)
SECTION 139   THE WORK OF (EMPLOYING SUITABLE) TROOPS AGAINST ENEMY TROOPS

1   Occasions for the employment of the hereditary, the hired, the banded, the ally's, the alien and the forest troops are :

2   When hereditary troops are in excess of what is required for the defence of the base ; or, when hereditary troops, being over-strewn with treasonable men, might create trouble at the base ; or, the enemy has plenty of loyal hereditary troops or a strong army, (hence) it is necessary to fight with

43   *anaikāntikatva* ' uncertainty ' as to there being a *vyasana* at all and as to any benefit that can be derived from it.

45   *atyuṣṇopakṣīṇe kāle*, i.e., when summer is past.   Cs explains ' which ends in excessive heat, i.e., in summer,' and consequently reads *ahastibalaprāyaḥ* ' without elephants '. Such a negative description of troops to be used does not appear very likely.   49   Cs removes the stop after -*paṅkaṁ*, so that *olpavarṣapaṅkaṁ* goes with *maruprāyaṁ*.   But the order of words favours the other punctuation.

51   *sama*- etc. stand for *samatva*- etc.

52   *yātavyāḥ* is used as a substantive in the sense of *yātrāḥ*.

9.2
The three Sections are to be found in ss. 1-12, 13-24 and 25-29 respectively.

1   *samuddāna* is synonymous with *upādāna*.

2   *maula* is derived from *mūla*, the kingdom or the capital, of which the troops are natives.   The word, however, conveys the sense of hereditary troops loyal to the dynasty from generation to generation. — *atyāvāpa* : see 10.5.28. — *bahulānuraktasaṁpāte* : the mss. show -*saṁpādite*, which would imply that the many loyal troops of the *vijigīṣu* create (*saṁpādita*) distrust in his mind (*aviśvāsa*) regarding *bhṛta* and other troops.   This would

military operations; or, because on a long march or on one of long duration, hereditary troops can bear losses and expenses; or, when plenty of loyal troops being got together, no trust can be placed in other troops, hired and other, through fear of secret instigations by the enemy against whom one is marching; or, when the strength of all (other) troops is depleted;—these are occasions for the use of hereditary troops.

3 (When he thinks), 'I have a large hired army and only a small hereditary army; or, the enemy has a small or disaffected hereditary army or a hired army consisting mostly of weak troops or without strong troops; or, it is to be a fight with diplomacy with slight military operations; or, the distance is short or duration brief, involving few losses and expenses; or, my army is with few treasonable men in it, with secret (enemy) instigations frustrated, and trustworthy; a small raid of the enemy is to be repelled;'—these are occasions for the use of hired troops.

4 (When he thinks), 'I have a large army of warrior bands, capable of being used at the base and in the expedition; the distance is short, the enemy, having mostly an army of warrior bands, intends to fight with diplomacy and military operations; use of armed forces is to be made;'—these are occasions for the use of an army consisting of bands.

5 (When he thinks), 'I have a large allied army that can be used at the base and in the expedition; the distance is small and war with military operations is to be more extensive than diplomatic war; or, having first engaged in fight the forest troops or the site of the capital or the allied troops of the enemy with my allied troops, I shall then engage them in fight with my own troops; or, my undertaking is shared in common with the ally; or, the success of my undertaking is dependent on the ally; or, my ally is close to me, deserving to be favoured; or, I shall destroy the excess of traitors (in his troops) for him;'—these are occasions for the use of an ally's troops.

appear to be a very strange idea. Meyer therefore proposes *bahulānanuraktasaṁpādite* 'created by many faithless troops'. With *-saṁpāte*, Cn Cs understand 'the coming (*saṁpāta*) of many loyal agents of the enemy and their engaging in *upajāpa*.' The idea would rather appear to be 'when a large number of loyal troops (of the *maula* type) can be collected (*saṁpāta*) and other troops cannot be trusted because of instigations etc.' The expression is a little odd. Russ. reads 'not trusting hired and other troops at their presence in large numbers and their devotion as there is danger that they may succumb to the instigations of the enemy.'

3 *alpāvāpam* is proposed in the sense of 'with few treasonable men in it' as contrasted with *atyāvāpam* 'having many treasonable men in it' (10.5.28). Cs reads *alpasaṁpātam* 'to which few secret agents from the enemy come'; Russ. renders this reading by 'which does not fail in spirit, indifferent to temptations.' Cn seems to have read *alpasaṁghātam* or *-saṁvādam* in the sense understood in Cs. *alpasvāpam* 'with little sleep' hardly suits even in a figurative sense. — *prasāraḥ*, primarily a foraging raid (10.2.5), refers to a raid or advance.

4 Whereas in *bhṛtabala* the soldiers are recruited individually, the *śreṇībala* is a band of fighting men under its own leader. — *daṇḍabalavyavahāraḥ*: cf. 8.1.34,38. This seems to be an independent substantive. Cn Cs treat it as an adjective to *pratiyoddhā* 'who has to fight with troops (*bala*) sent to him by his enemy through fear of chastisement (*daṇḍa*).' 'when the enemy uses the army under fear of punishment' (Russ.). Meyer renders *daṇḍabala* by 'professional troops'.

5 *atyāvāpam*: see 10.5.28.

6 (When he thinks), 'I have a large alien army, with alien troops I shall fight at the site of the (enemy's) capital or against (his) forest troops, in that case I shall gain in either eventuality, as does the Caṇḍāla in a fight between a dog and a boar; or, I shall make these the means of crushing the thorns among allied or forest troops;'—or, when they have grown excessively large, he should always station alien troops in close proximity (to himself) for fear of a revolt, except in case of fear of a rising in the interior;—and when the time for (one's own) fighting is later than that for the enemy's fighting;—these are occasions for the use of alien troops.

7 By that are explained occasions for the use of forest troops. 8 When useful for showing the way; when suited for the terrain of the enemy; when capable of counter-acting the enemy's mode of fighting; or when the enemy has mostly forest troops, (on the principle) 'let the Bilva-fruit be destroyed by the Bilva-fruit'; when a small raid is to be repelled;—these are (further) occasions for the use of forest troops.

9 An army not in one unit, coming from many regions, which, whether asked or unasked, gets ready with the object of getting plunder is the volunteer army, not given food and wages, carrying out plunder, doing labour and heroic deeds, liable to be divided by the enemies, (but) not liable to be divided if consisting mostly of persons from the same region, caste or profession, united and large in number. These are occasions for the use of (various kinds of) troops.

10 Of these, he should remunerate alien and forest troops with forest produce or with booty. 11 Or, when an occasion has arisen for the enemy to raise troops, he should keep alien troops in his control, or send them elsewhere, or render them ineffective, or keep them dispersed, or should release them when the time for them is past.

12 And he should obstruct such raising of troops by the enemy and secure that for himself.

6 *śvavarāhayoḥ* etc.: cf. 7.1.34. — *atyupacitaṁ vā* etc. up to *-kopaśaṅkāyāḥ* is misplaced. The passage does not state any occasion for the use of alien troops. That they are not, however, a late gloss is shown by the fact that they are quoted in 15.1.50. The words should preferably be read after s. 11 below. — *anyatra* etc. i.e., if stationing the alien troops near him were to lead to a rising by *mantrin*, *senāpati* etc. For *abhyantarakopa*, see 9.3.12. — *śatruyuddhāvara-* etc., i.e, when the *vijigīṣu* wants to fight after the enemy (from whom the troops are received) has finished his own fighting.

8 *ariyuddhapratilomam*: it is not necessary to read *-apratiloman* 'not averse to fighting' as Meyer proposes. *pratiloma* can mean 'able to fight against'.

9 *anekam* 'not in one unit,' i.e., 'not under one leadership' (Cn Cs). — *anekastham* is read as in Cn. *anekajātīyam* would also be possible, but not *anekajātīyastham* as found in the mss. — *vilomavṛṣṭi-* is an obvious corruption of *vilopaviṣṭi*. — Cn Cs interpret *-pratāpakara* as 'carrying out the king's orders'. That would be an unusual sense.

11 *śatrubalam* is proposed for *śatrum*; that is necessary. — *aphalam* etc.: cf. 7.8.28. Cn Cs understand 'should not give the stipulated money for the troops.' But 'should render them unserviceable' appears better. — *vikṣiptam*: cf. 7.9.22 etc.

13 And it is better to equip for war each earlier one among these than each later one.

14 Because of their having the same feelings as the king and because of constant enjoyment of his regard (for them), hereditary troops are better than hired troops.

15 Being always proximate to him, quick in rising for action, and under control, hired troops are better than banded troops.

16 Being native to the country, actuated by a common purpose, and having the same rivalry, resentment, success and gain (as the king), banded troops are better than allied troops.

17 Being not restricted as to place and time and because of having a common purpose, allied troops are better than alien troops.

18 Being under the command of Āryas, alien troops are better than forest troops. 19 These two have plunder as their objective. 20 When there is no plunder or when there is a calamity, there might be danger from them as from a snake.

21 'Among Brāhmaṇa, Kṣatriya, Vaiśya and Śūdra troops, each earlier one is better for equipping for war than each later one, on account of superiority of spirit,' say the teachers. 22 'No,' says Kauṭilya. 23 By prostration, an enemy may win over Brāhmaṇa troops. 24 A Kṣatriya army, trained in the art of weapons, is better, or a Vaiśya or a Śūdra army, when possessed of great strength.

25 Therefore, he should raise troops keeping in mind 'The enemy has these troops; for them these would be counter-troops.'

26 That with elephants, machines and carts at the centre, equipped with lances, javelins, spears, reeds and arrows, is a counter-force against elephant

13 *saṁnāhayitum* 'to equip with armour,' i.e., to make it ready for fight, to use it for fighting.

14 *tadbhāvabhāvitvāt*: Cn Cs understand *bhāva* as 'existence', and explain 'whose existence depends on that of the king.' *bhāva* as 'feeling' would also do; cf. *mitrabhāvin*, *aribhāvin* etc., 7.18.29. — *-satkāra-* from the commentators is preferable to *-saṁskāra-* of the mss. Cn reads *-anurāgāt* in place of *-anugamāt*. Kāmandaka, 19.4, *satkārād anurāgāc ca* seems to support that.

16 *ekārthopagatam*: Cn understands the common purpose to be that of members of the *śreṇī* among themselves, not as that of the *vijigīṣu* and the *śreṇībala*. — Cs includes *aparimita-...-gamāc ca* from the next s. at the end of this s., making *ekārthopagamāt* an adjective to *mitrabalāt*. That is hardly right. With that punctuation there would be no statement of reasons for preferring a *mitrabala* to an *amitrabala*.

18 Clearly forest troops had their own non-Āryan or Mleccha commanders. 20 *ahibhayam*: cf. 1.17.9.

24 *bahulasāram* 'possessed of great strength,' is understood as 'having many brave men in it' (Cn Cs Meyer).

26 It would be better to read *śakaṭagarbham* separately as in the quotation in Śaṁkarārya on Kāmandaka, 19.26. Cn interprets *śakaṭagarbha* (in the compound) as 'a centre consisting of carts,' understanding *hasti* and *yantra* as two things or *hastiyantra* as one (machine against elephants? or machine to be used from elephants?). — *hāṭaka* is from

divisions. 27 The same, equipped mostly with stones, clubs, armours, hooks and 'hair-seizers', is a counter-force against chariot divisions. 28 The same is a counter-force against cavalry, or mailed elephants or mailed horses. 29 Mailed chariots and armoured infantrymen are a counter-force against the fourfold troops.

30 Thus he should carry out the raising of troops so as to withstand enemy troops, in conformity with the strength of his own troops, (and) in accordance with the various types of divisions (that may be necessary).

CHAPTER THREE

SECTION 140 CONSIDERATION OF REVOLTS IN THE REAR

SECTION 141 COUNTER-MEASURES AGAINST RISINGS OF CONSTITUENTS IN THE OUTER REGIONS AND IN THE INTERIOR

1 As between a small disturbance in the rear and a large gain in front, the small disturbance in the rear is of greater importance. 2 For, when he is gone, treasonable men, enemies and foresters augment the small disturbance in the rear on all sides, or a rising of the constituents (augments it). 3 And if this happens servants, allies, losses and expenses eat up the large gain in front even if obtained. 4 Therefore, the advantage from a gain in front being one in a thousand or (at most) one in a hundred when there is a disturbance in the rear, he should not march. 5 'Misfortunes, indeed, have the mouth of a needle' is a saying among the people.

the commentators for *bharvataka*. It is 'of the size of the *kunta* and has three points' (Cn Cs). — *veṇu* 'a long whip' (Cn Cs). — *śalya* 'an iron club with spikes all round' (Cn Cs). It may also mean 'a dart, an arrow'. 27 *kacagrahaṇī*: cf. 2.36.18. It is 'a long, broad bamboo with a hook' (Cn Cs). 28 *tadeva* 'i.e. *rathapratibala*, according to some, *hastipratibala*, according to others' (Cn). — *varmiṇo vā hastino 'śvā vā varmiṇaḥ*: Cn Cs include these words in the next s. and explain 'mailed elephants against elephants, mailed horses against cavalry, mailed chariots against chariots and armoured infantrymen against infantry, this in general should be the counter-force against the fourfold army.' For this, the two *vās* should be dropped or a *vā* read after *kavacinaḥ* and *āvaraṇinaḥ*. Even so the explanation does not appear convicing. The punctuation adopted is found in the quotation in Śaṁkarārya on Kāmandaka, 19.26. — The *ca* after *pattayaḥ* is from Cn; it seems to have dropped out because of the following *ca* (in *caturaṅga*).

30 *parasainyanivāraṇam* is an adjective to *samuddānam*. — *aṅgavikalpaśaḥ*, i.e., according as one or the other of the four *aṅgas* may be needed.

9.3

The two Sections are very closely related and it is difficult to find a demarcation line betwen the two.

2 *prakṛti* refers to such officers etc. as are mentioned in ss. 12, 15, 20 and 22 below. It may also refer to subjects. 3 *bhṛtyamitrakṣayavyayāḥ* is 'servants, allies, losses and expenses' rather than loss of servants and allies and expenses.' — *bhṛte* in G1 is due to dittography. 4 *sahasraikīyaḥ* etc.: Cn explains 'the gain in front is one-thousandth, while trouble in the rear is one-hundredth (with *paścātkopoḥ* nominative).' Thus Cs. *vā* does not seem properly explained in this. Cn has another explanation 'when the gain is one thousand and loss (*-ayogaḥ*) one; similarly when gain is one hundred and loss one.' Meyer (with *paścātkope* locative) has 'advantage from a gain is one in a thousand, or (at most) one in a hundred when there is trouble in the rear.' That explanation is adopted. For *śataikīya* in this sense, cf. *Rājataraṅgiṇī*, 8.1272 (*śataikīyo yo 'vaśiṣṭo viplavakṣayite jane*).

6 In case of revolt in the rear, he should make use of conciliation, gifts, dissension and force. 7 For the gain in front he should make the commander-in-chief or the crown prince the commandant of the troops. 8 Or, if strong (and) capable of suppressing the revolt in the rear, the king (himself) should march to secure the gain in front.

9 In case of suspicion of a revolt in the interior, he should march taking with him the suspected persons, or in case of suspicion of a revolt in the outer regions, (taking with him) the sons and wives of these.

10 He should march after suppressing the (revolt in the) interior and appointing a regent with many types of troops under more than one chief, or he may not march. 11 That a revolt in the interior is a greater evil than a rising in the outer regions has been stated before.

12 A revolt by one of (the following), the minister, the chaplain, the commander-in-chief and the crown prince, is a revolt in the interior. 13 He should overcome that by giving up his own faults or in accordance with the power and offence of the other. 14 In the case of the chaplain, even when his offence is great, the punishment should be confinement or exile, in the case of the crown prince, confinement or death, if there is another virtuous son.

15 He should overcome, with energy, a son, a brother or another member of the family, planning to seize the kingdom ; if lacking in energy, by acquiescing in what is seized and by entering into a pact (with him), for fear that he might join the enemy. 16 Or, he should create confidence in him by grants of land to others like him. 17 Or, he should send (against him) troops superior to him, that are permitted to seize what they can, or a neighbouring vassal or a forest chieftain, (and) should over-reach him when he is fighting with these. 18 Or, he should make use of ways for securing a prince in disfavour, or secret ways of capturing an enemy's town. 19 By this are explained the minister and the commander-in-chief.

9 Cn Cs include *abhyantarāvagrahaṁ kṛtvā* at the end of this s., not at the beginning of the next. That is far from happy. *avagraha* can mean only 'suppression'; and the idea of keeping the wives and sons of *bāhyas* in charge of (*avagraha*) *abhyantaras* is quite unlikely Moreover, s. 11 would have significance only if the words are read in s. 10.

11 *purastāt* : in 8.2.3 above.

14 *nigrahaḥ* : 'death' (Cn Cs) seems clearly intended. — *tābhyāṁ mantrisenāpatī vyākhyātau* found in the mss. after s. 14 are clearly an interpolation. The *mantrin* is not on the same footing as the *purohita* nor the *senāpati* on the same footing as the *yuvarāja*. Moreover, their case is specifically mentioned in s. 19.

15 *putram* : son other than the *yuvarāja*. — *utsāhena*, i.e., by energetic action. 17 *tadviśiṣṭam*, i.e., superior to the rebel's troops. It can hardly mean 'commanded by the rebel' (Cs) ; that would be very risky. Meyer has '(after creating confidence) he should send him against one who is superior to him (*tadviśiṣṭam*) for plunder (*svayaṁgrāham*) or for execution of punishment (*daṇḍam*).' This is unlikely. *daṇḍa* cannot be understood in this sense ; in fact, *svayaṁgrāhaṁ daṇḍam* conveys a single idea. And Meyer's construction shows three accusatives (*tadviśiṣṭam, enam* and *svayaṁgrāham*) with *preṣayet*, which is very unlikely. 18 *aparuddhādānam* as in 1.18.13-16. — *pāragrāmikaṁ yogam* as in 13.1.

20 A revolt by any one of the officers of the interior except the minister and others is a rising of ministers of the interior. 21 In their case, too, he should use means as deserved.

22 A revolt by one of (the following), the chief of the countryside, the frontier officer, the forest chieftain and the vassal surrendering to force, is a revolt in the outer regions. 23 He should cause that to be suppressed through one another. 24 Or, if he is strongly entrenched in a fort, he should cause him to be suppressed by any one of (the following), a neighbouring prince, a forest chieftain, a pretender from his family or a prince in disfavour. 25 Or, he should make his ally win him over, so that he does not go over to the enemy.

26 Or, a secret agent should divide him from the enemy, (saying), 'This (enemy), looking upon you as a secret agent, will make you fight against the king himself, (and) with his object achieved, will employ you, in charge of troops, against his enemy or forest chieftain or in a difficult undertaking, or will post you at the frontier, separated from wife and sons. 27 If you fail in the fight (against your king), he will sell you to the king, or making peace through you, will conciliate the king himself. 28 You should go to his best ally.' 29 If he agrees, he should honour him by the fulfilment of his wishes 30 If he does not agree, the (agent) should divide the support from him, (saying), 'He is kept as a secret agent against you.' 31 And the secret agent should get him killed on the strength of letters carried by men condemned to death or through secret agents. 32 Or, he should win back warriors, who had left along with him, by granting their wishes. 33 The secret agent should (then) declare them as having been employed by him. 34 Thus is success to be achieved.

35 And he should cause these revolts to arise for the enemy, and suppress those against himself.

20 *antaramātya* : '*dauvārika, antarvaṁśika* and others' (Cn), i.e., palace officials.

22 *rāṣṭramukhya* would principally include the *samāhartṛ*. 24 *tatkulīna* and *aparuddha* show that the rebel has the status of a king ; a vassal seems primarily thought of.

26 *ayam* refers to the enemy, whose aid the rebel has sought or is likely to seek. 27 *tvayā vā saṁdhiṁ kṛtvā* : in this, no material gain is derived as in *paṇyaṁ kariṣyati* ; in either case, the rebel is handed over to his former master. 28 *upakṛṣṭaṁ vā* : the *vā* is due to 5.5.14, where it is necessary. Cs reads *gacchet* as in 5.5.14 ; but the potential form is quite unlikely here. 30 *saṁśrayam* is the enemy with whom the rebel has found shelter. *abhityakta* : this is the usual form of the word for 'a person condemned to death' ; that is adopted throughout on the authority of Cn Cs. The mss show *abhivyakta*, which, if genuine must be understood in the same sense. *abhivyaktaśāsana* cannot mean 'a letter brought to light' (Meyer) ; cf. 9.6.29 and 13.4.28. A man condemned to death is preferred for carrying the implicating letter, as the enemy is likely to kill the person carrying it. 32 *āvāhayet* is the usual word ; cf. 7.7.13. 33 *tena*, i.e., by their old master. As they have gone back, they are proved to have been his agents ; the rebel also, therefore, must be one such.

36 Secret instigations (to revolt) should be made to one who is capable of starting or putting down a revolt.

37 A response to instigations (to revolt) should be made to one who is true of promise, capable of helping in carrying out the undertaking and securing its reward and of saving in case of failure, and about him one should form a conjecture as to whether he has honest intentions or is a rogue.

38 A roguish officer from the outer regions instigates an officer in the interior (to revolt) with these motives : ' If after killing the king, he will make me accepted (as king), I shall make a double gain, death of the enemy and acquisition of land ; or, the enemy will kill him, so that the party of kinsmen of the officer put to death and those frightened of punishment because of a like offence, will become for me a very large non-seducible party ; or, the (king) will be suspicious even of others like him, and (then) I shall get his other chiefs killed one by one through letters carried by men condemned to death.'

39 Or, a roguish officer from the interior instigates an officer in the outer regions (to revolt) with these motives : ' I shall appropriate his treasury or I shall destory his troops, or I shall get the wicked king killed by him ; when he responds I shall make the officer from the outer regions fight against the enemy or forest chieftains (with the idea), "Let his army get stuck, let his enmity be firmly fixed, then he will be in my power, then I shall conciliate the king himself or shall seize the kingdom myself" ; or, after imprisoning him, I shall secure both--the territory of the officer from the outer region and the territory of the king ; or, inviting the officer from the outer region, when he has become hostile (to the king) and is full of trust (in me), I shall get him killed; or, I shall seize his base when it is without him.'

40 One with honest intentions, however, instigates (others to revolt) in the interests of those who live with him.

41 One should make a pact with one of honest intentions ; agreeing ' So let us do,' one should over-reach a roguish one.

36 This and the following ss. contain advice to rebels ; the king comes in only as a victim of their intrigues.

38 *pratipādayiṣyati* : cf. 1.10.3. — *tulyadoṣa*- etc. need not be understood as an adjective to *hatabandhupakṣaḥ* ; in view of *ca*, a separate idea is better. — *bhūyānakṛtya*- is as proposed by Meyer for *bhūyāt na kṛtya*- of the mss. and *bhūyān kṛtya*- of Cn Cs. *akṛtya* implying that they cannot be seduced from his side by the king is preferable to *kṛtya* implying that he will have to make efforts to win them over to his side. — *asya*, i.e., of the king. — *abhityaktaśāsanena* : see s. 31 above.

39 *vairam* is apparently with the king. — *svayaṁ vā rājyam* : Cn Cs think that this is the kingdom of the *bāhya* ; that, however, is referred to in *śūnyaṁ vā asya mūlam* later on. This is the master's kingdom. — *āvāhayitvā* ; the invitation to come is as a fellow-conspirator.

40 *sahajīvyartham* : *sahajīvin* seems to refer to fellow officers who live in the same state and are fed up with the king. Cs makes *sahajīvī* ' living in close association with fellow-conspirators ' an adjective to *kalyāṇabuddhiḥ* and understands *artham* ' what is beneficial ' as the object of *upajapati*. That is not happy.

42 Understanding all this,

the wise (king) should guard others from others, his own people from his own people, his own people from others, and others from his own people, and always guard himself from his own people and from others.

CHAPTER FOUR

SECTION 142 CONSIDERATION OF LOSSES, EXPENSES AND GAINS

1 The diminution of draught-animals and men is loss. 2 The diminution of money and grains is expense.

3 He should march when the gain is superior, because of many good points, to these two.

4 That which can be seized, which can be recovered, which is pleasing, which is rousing to anger, which requires a short time, which involves small losses, which requires small expenses, which is great, which leads to further increase, which is safe, which is lawful and which is foremost,—these are the excellences of gain.

5 That which is easy to obtain and protect, and cannot be recovered by the enemies is the (gain) which can be seized. 6 In the reverse case, it is one that can be recovered. 7 One, seizing it or staying there, meets with destruction.

8 If, however, he were to see, 'After seizing the recoverable gain, I shall cause (the enemy's) treasury, army, stores and fortifications to disappear; I shall make the mines, the produce forests, the elephant forests, water-works and trade-routes denuded of all valuables; I shall impoverish his subjects, carry them away or conciliate them by suitable means, (while) the (enemy) will afterwards rouse them by contrary means; or, I shall sell this (gain)

42 *evam upalabhya* is to be construed with the stanza; it is thus that the *vijigīṣu* is brought into relation with the discussion on rebel conspirators. — *pare sve*: Cn remarks that *pare* in effect refers to *bāhyas* and *sve* to *abhyantaras*. That is possible in the context; 'those hostile' and 'those loyal' would, however, appear more likely. — *rakṣyāḥ* can hardly mean 'should keep the roguishness etc. of one a secret from the others' (Cs). That is impossible with *ātmā* with which also *rakṣyaḥ* is to be understood.

9.4

3 *bahuguṇaviśiṣṭe* 'superior (to *kṣaya* and *vyaya*) because of many excellences'; we can also understand 'greater by many times (than the two).' But s. 24 shows that *guṇa* refers to qualities like *ādeyatva* etc.

7 *tatrastho*: the *lābha* thought of is that of land.

8 *apavāhayiṣyāmi*: cf. 8.2.8. That makes *āvāhayiṣyāmi* of Cs little likely. The idea is, when the enemy recovers it, he would find it impoverished and deserted. — *āyogena*: this seems contrasted with *pratiyogena* that follows and may be understood as 'suitable means', while *pratiyoga* may be 'contrary means'. Meyer has 'application (to duty)'; Cn has 'not taking away their gains'. *āyoga* may also mean 'employing (them)' as in 9.5.11. — *param*, i.e., when the enemy tries to recover it; his ways would alienate the subjects, who would then support the *vijigīṣu* and prevent the recovery. Cn seems to have read *paraḥ*, though its explanation has '*paścāt*.' — *mitram aparuddhaṁ vā*: the *mitra* is that of the

to his rival or make his ally or a prince in disfavour accept it; or, remaining here, I shall take steps against the harassment of my ally's or my own territory by robbers and enemies; or, I shall make his ally or support realise his deficiency, so that being disaffected with the enemy, he will accept a member of his family; or, I shall honour him and return the land to him, so that I shall have an ally bound to me and acting with me for a long time;' in such cases, he should seize even a recoverable gain.

9 Thus the gains that can be seized and that can be recovered have been explained.

10 The gain, being obtained by a righteous (king) from an unrighteous one becomes pleasing to his own people and to others. 11 The reverse rouses to anger.

12 A gain, not being obtained on the advice of ministers, leads to a rising, (as they think), 'He has been made to undergo losses and expenses by us.' 13 A gain, being obtained in disregard of treasonable ministers, leads to a rising, (as they think), 'Having achieved his object, he will destory us.' 14 The reverse is the gain that pleases.

15 Thus the gains that please and that rouse have been explained.

16 Because it can be secured by merely going (there), the gain is one requiring a short time. 17 Because it can be secured by diplomacy, it is

enemy (Meyer) not of the *vijigīṣu* (Cs); the idea is to alienate the enemy's ally from him. — *vaiguṇyaṁ grāhayiṣyāmi*: *vaiguṇya* is usually 'hostility'; cf. 5.6.8; 8.1.11. But here it seems to mean 'deficiency'. The idea is, the fact that his land is occupied by the *vijigīṣu* would show the enemy's weakness to his ally, who would thereupon be *amitravirakta* and extend his support to another member of the enemy's family (*tatkulīnam*) who may have a claim to the throne. Thus Cs; this explanation appears the least unsatisfactory. Hence *amitraviraktaṁ* is read in the text as in Cs, in place of *amitraṁ viraktam*. of the mss. With the latter reading, *amitra* could refer to the enemy's enemy and *virakta* could qualify *tatkulīna*; even then a *vā* would be necessary to show the option between *amitra* and *tatkulīna*. Cn mentions *pratipatsye* or *pratipatsyate* as the reading, explaining 'I shall get that ally (*tad*) for myself, as he is disaffected with the enemy (*amitraviraktam*)'; or 'that ally with take that (*tad*, i.e., the enemy's kingdom), being disaffected with the enemy'. In neither explanation does *tatkulīnam* find a place. Meyer has 'I shall bring his ally to harm (*vaigunya*)' and then separately 'that (*tad*, i.e., gain) will fall to the lot of one hostile to him (*amitram*) or to one disaffected with him (*viraktam*) or to a pretender from his family (when the gain is ultimately recovered from me).' It is doubtful if *tad* can refer to the *lābha*, and if *pratipatsyate* could have *lābhaḥ* for its subject.

12 *lābho 'labhyamānaḥ kopako bhavati*: the situation is: the king fails in an adventure recommended by the ministers and has incurred losses and expenses in the expedition. This is *kopaka*. This word is understood in Cs as 'producing hatred (*pradveṣa*) in the king and fear in the ministers'; Cn has '*bhayahetuḥ* (cause of fear among the ministers)'. Though the sense suits, that is not the usual meaning of *kopaka*. It would mean either 'rousing to anger', which does not suit, or 'leading to a rising' by the ministers, who apparently think of revolting in order to forestall the king's anger; there may be hopes of the rising succeeding, as the king is weakened by losses and expenses. This latter meaning for *kopaka* is necessary in the next s. There the *dūṣyas* would rise in order to prevent the king from obtaining the gain and then wreaking his vengeance on them. 14 *viparītaḥ*, i.e., *labhyamānaḥ* in the first case and *alabhyamānaḥ* in the second (Cs).

one involving small losses. 18 Because there is only the expense of food, it is one requiring small expenses. 19 Because of vastness in the present, it is great. 20 Because it leads to continuity of advantage, it is one that leads to further increase. 21 Because it is free from dangers, it is one that is safe. 22 Because it is obtained in a praiseworthy manner, it is one that is lawful. 23 Because it comes without restrictions in the case of confederates, it is one that is foremost.

24 When the gain is equal (from two expeditions), he should consider the place and the time, powers and means, agreeableness and disagreeableness, speed and absence of speed, nearness and distance, the present and consequences in the future, valuableness and continuousness, and abundance and richness in qualities, and seize that gain which is possessed of many good points.

25 Hindrances to gain are: passion, anger, nervousness, pity, shyness, ignobleness, haughtiness, a sympathetic nature, regard for the other world, piousness, illiberality, abjectness, jealousy, contempt for what is in the hand, wickedness, lack of trust, fear, failure to counter-act, inability to endure cold, heat and rain, and fondness for auspicious days and constellations.

26 The object slips away from the foolish person, who continuously consults the stars; for an object is the (auspicious) constellation for (achieving) an object; what will the stars do?

27 Men, without wealth, do not attain their objects even with hundreds of efforts; objects are secured through objects, as elephants are through elephants set to catch them.

22 *praśastopādānāt* refers to such ways of acquisition as conquest, purchase etc.
23 *sāmavāyikānām anirbandhagāmitvāt*: this seems to mean that one of the confederates receives a higher share in the joint expedition, without restrictions or objections by others. Russ. shows this explanation. Cn seems to understand 'a higher share (*bhāgāntarotkṛṣṭaḥ*) because there is no restriction as to each one's gain (*svasvalābhotkarṣanibandhābhāvāt*).' In 9.7.59, *apuroga* is used of a confederate who is not the leader. We need not, however, understand that the *puroga* or leader alone gets a *puroga* share. Any one of the confederates may appropriate a higher share if the others do not object. Meyer has 'one in which one need not march (*gam*) together with the allies any further,' which hardly suits.

24 *priyāpriyau*, i.e., *priyatva* and *apriyatva* of the *lābha*. — *sāratvasātatye*: for the contrast implied in the two terms, Cn compares 7.12.16.

25 *kāruṇya*, according to Cn Cs, leads to aversion to fighting, while *sānukrośatā* leads to forgiveness for an offender. — *hrīḥ*: it prevents the use of force when the offenders cry for mercy (Cn Cs); it is the noble feeling that recoils from soiling itself with evil (Meyer). — For *atyāgitvam*, Cs reads *atyāśitvam* 'consuming more than one's share'. — *apratīkāraḥ* is from Cn; Cs reads *anikāraḥ* 'absence of contempt for the enemy'.

27 *nādhanāḥ* is from Cs for *sādhanāḥ* of the mss. The latter has to be understood as *sādhanavantaḥ* and even then *yatnaśatair api* cannot be construed naturally with it. The *Mahābhārata*, 12.8.20 (*adhanenārthakāmena nārthaḥ śakyo vivitsatā, arthair arthā nibodhyante gajair iva mahāgajāḥ*) supports *nādhanāḥ*.

CHAPTER FIVE

SECTION 148 DANGERS FROM (OFFICERS IN) THE OUTER REGIONS AND THE INTERIOR

1 The use of peace and other policies not in the prescribed manner is wrong policy. 2 From that spring dangers (of conspiracy or revolt).

3 Originating in the outer region and responded to from the interior, originating in the interior and responded to from the outer region, originating in the outer region and responded to from the outer region, (and) originating in the interior and responded to from the interior : these are the (four types of) conspiracies.

4 Where those in the outer regions instigate those in the interior, or those in the interior instigate those in the outer regions, in these cases where there is association between the two types, success over the one who responds is of greater advantage. 5 For, those who respond are full of guile, not those who instigate. 6 When they are subdued, the instigators would not be able to instigate others. 7 For, those in the interior are difficult to instigate for those in the outer regions, or these for the former. 8 There is a waste of great effort for the others and a continuous advantage for oneself.

9 When those in the interior respond, he should make use of conciliation and gifts. 10 Giving a position and showing honour is conciliation. 11 Favours and exemptions or employment in works is gifts.

12 When those in the outer regions respond, he should make use of dissension and force. 13 Secret agents, posing as friends of those in the outer regions should communicate to them (the following, as) secret information spied out, 'This king intends to over-reach you through these posing as treasonable men ; beware.' 14 Or, secret agents, posing as treasonable men,

9.5

As Meyer observes *āpad* in this Chapter refers to conspiracies against the king or the state.

1 *ayathoddeśa-*, i.e., not as recommended in Book 7 above.

3 For *abhyantara* and *bāhya*, see 9.3.12,22.

4 *ubhayayoge* : *ubhaya* refers to *abhyantara* and *bāhya*, at the two ends of the realm. 5 *suvyājāḥ* : Cn explains *vyāja* by '*abhyupagamanimitta*, an indication that he agrees', such as a bribe received, etc. That is not very happy. Meyer's 'easy to cheat (for the authorities)' seems also less likely. It seems we have to understand 'full of deceit or guile'. Success over them may be not easy, but for that very reason would be specially advantageous. 8 This s. seems to mention further advantages of overcoming the *pratijapitṛs*. The instigators are referred to in *pareṣām*, while *ātmanaḥ* refers to the king. Cn, however, regards the s. as stating the reason why *upajāpa*, though difficult, should still be attempted : thereby the efforts of others are frustrated and one attains one's own objective. This hardly seems intended. Cs adds *anyaḥ* after *ātmanaḥ* and explains '(if the *pratijapitṛs* were to reveal the plot to the king) there is great loss of effort (of the *upajapitṛ*), a great gain, viz., favour of the king to the others (*pareṣām*, i.e., *pratijapitṝṇām*) and the opposite of that (*anyaḥ*), i.e., disaster for himself (i.e., the *upajapitṛ*).' This appears even less likely. There is no reference to the revealing of the plot ; and *anya* can hardly be 'opposite, reverse'.

13 *vā* here as well as in s. 21 has no significance. — *cāram* : cf. 1.12.7 etc. Hence 'use of a secret trick (by the king)' (Cn Cs) is less likely. 14 *dūṣyān bāhyair bhedayeyuḥ* :

employed with the treasonable men (in the interior), should divide the treasonable men from those in the outer regions or those in the outer regions from the treasonable men (in the interior). 15 Or, assassins, insinuating themselves, should slay the treasonable men with weapon or poison. 16 Or, after inviting (to the capital) those from the outer regions, they should get them killed.

17 Where those in the outer regions instigate others in the outer regions or those in the interior instigate others in the interior, in these cases, where there is association at one end only, success over the instigator is of greater advantage. 18 For, when the evil (of treason) is removed, there remain no treasonable men. 19 But when treasonable men are over-come, the evil again makes others treasonable.

20 Therefore, when those in the outer regions are instigators, he should make use of dissension and force. 21 Secret agents, posing as friends, should say, 'This king himself intends to seize you; you are at war with this king; beware.' 22 Or, assassins, insinuating themselves in the troops of the envoy of the one responding, should strike at their weak points with weapon, poison and so on. 23 Then secret agents should accuse the one responding (of that crime).

24 When those in the interior instigate others in the interior, he should make use of the means as deserved. 25 He should use conciliation in the case of one discontented though showing signs of contentment, or the reverse of this. 26 Honouring under the pretext of (appreciating) integrity or capability or by showing consideration in a calamity or on a happy occasion, is the use of gifts. 27 Or, an agent posing as a friend, should say to them, 'In order to find out your feelings, the king will put you to test; you should disclose them to him.' 28 Or, he should divide them from each other, saying, 'So and so is thus whispering to the king about you'; thus is dissension (to be brought about). 29 And force should be used as in the infliction of (secret) punishment'.

it seems that the instrumental is used in the sense of the ablative. In any case, 'through the *bāhyas* who have instigated' (Cn Cs) is quite unlikely in the context where the *bāhyas* are the *pratijapitṛs*. The instigators are the *abhyantaras*, referred to here as *dūṣyas*. 15 *anupraviṣṭāḥ*: insinuating themselves in their service is primarily meant, though the idea of first winning their confidence is also possible. Cf. 1.17.39 etc. 16 *ghātayeyuḥ*: the singular would have been better, with the king as subject. As it is, *sattriṇaḥ* may be the subject, hardly *tīkṣṇāḥ* in view of the causal.

17 *ekāntayoge* from Cn Cs is read in conformity with *ubhayayoge* above. *ekānta* is one end of the realm, either the interior or the outer regions. 18 *doṣa* is the evil of treason that is there in the *upajapitṛs*. 19 *dūṣya*, i.e., *pratijapitṛ*.

21 *ādātukāmaḥ*: i.e., the king will seize you through the *pratijapitṛs* who are really his agents. 22 This s. describes the use of *daṇḍa* and hence is unrelated to s. 21; *tataḥ* found in the mss. has therefore no place in this s. and it is proposed to drop it. It seems to have been repeated here from the next s. by some copyist. The attempts in Cn Cs to explain *tataḥ* are far from satisfactory. — *eṣām*, i.e., *upajapitṝṇām*. 23 *abhiśaṁseyuḥ*: the accusation is of murder of the *upajapitṛs*.

27 *upadhāsyati* refers to the *upadhās* of 1.10. — *tad*, i.e., 'your mind' (Cn Cs). — *upajapati* seems used in the literal sense 'whispers'. Meyer proposes *upajalpati*, since the former has a technical sense. That, however, is not necessary. 29 *daṇḍakarmikavat*, i.e., as in 5.1 above.

30 Of these four conspiracies, he should first deal with that in the interior. 31 That a rising in the interior is a greater evil than a rising in the outer regions because of danger as from a snake has been stated before.

32 Of the conspiracies, he should know each earlier one as a less serious conspiracy than each later one, or that starting from strong men as more serious, the reverse as less serious.

CHAPTER SIX

SECTION 144 (DANGERS) CONNECTED WITH TRAITORS AND ENEMIES

1 (That) from the treasonable only and (that) from the enemies only: this is the two-fold unmixed (danger).

2 In the case of unmixed (danger) from the treasonable, he should use against the citizens and the country people the (various) means excepting force. 3 For, force cannot be used against a multitude of people. 4 Even if used, it might not achieve its object and at the same time might bring on another disaster. 5 But against the leaders among them, he should act as in 'the infliction of (secret) punishment'.

6 In the case of unmixed (danger) from enemies, he should seek success by conciliation and other means in that place where the enemy, whether the principal or the subordinate, is. 7 Success over the principal is dependent on the king, success over dependents in dependent on ministers, (and) success over the principal and the dependents is dependent on both.

30 *abhyantarām* 'where the *abhyantaras* are the *upajapitṛs*' (Cn); 'where both instigators and responders are *abhyantaras*' (Meyer). 31 *purastāt* in 8.2.8.

32 *pūrvāṁ pūrvām* as enumerated in s. 3 above. — Meyer, preferring the faulty *śuddhim* for *gurvīm* translates 'should know the removal (*śuddhi*) of the conspiracies to be, however (*vā*), easy (*laghvīm*) against opponents (*viparyaye*) when it (i.e., *śuddhi*) springs from the powerful (king, *balavadbhyaḥ*).' This is quite unlikely.

9.6

We have to supply *āpadaḥ* as the substantive in the title, as is clear from the colophon after 9.7.66. Meyer understands 'events, situations', with the result that he is often misled in this Chapter. Cn Cs supply *bāhyābhyantarāh* as well; but that is not intended.

1 *śuddhā* in the singular is necessary. This *āpad* is contrasted with *āmiśrā* and *paramiśrā*. In this Chapter *āpad* is more 'danger' than 'conspiracy'.

2 *paureṣu jānapadeṣu vā*: this shows that sedition is not restricted to officers. In this, *dūṣyaśuddhā* differs from *bāhyābhyantarā āpad*; also there is no *upajāpa* apparent in it. 5 *mukhyeṣu*: these would be ring-leaders, not necessarily officers.

6 *śatruśuddhā* is nothing more than an actual or impending attack by an enemy, including intrigues by him to oust the king. — *yataḥ śatruḥ* etc.: Cn Cs have 'on whom is dependent (*yataḥ*) the enemy or his minister (*pradhānaḥ*) or an officer other than the minister (*kārya*), these being the ally etc., the enemy himself and the minister respectively.' This seems doubtful; *yataḥ* can hardly mean '*yasmin adhīnaḥ*'. And the next s. does not speak of *śatrusiddhiḥ*, as would have been expected if three persons were intended in this s. It seems therefore that *pradhānaḥ kāryo vā* is merely in elucidation of *śatruḥ* — the principal enemy, i.e., the enemy king in person, or his *kārya*, i.e., dependent, such as a minister or general. *yataḥ . . . tataḥ* may refer to the place or the situation, 'there . . . where' or 'in respect of that . . . which'. 7 *āyatta* is used as a substantive as well as an adjective in this s. — Meyer remarks that this is strange wisdom. Over-zealousness in classification is responsible for what are often quite obvious statements.

8 Because the treasonable and the non-treasonable have joined hands, it is mixed (danger). 9 In the case of mixed (danger) success (should be sought) through the non-treasonable. 10 For, in the absence of the support, the supported do not exist.

11 Because allies and enemies have become one, it is (danger) mixed with the enemy. 12 In the case of enemy-mixed (danger), success (should be sought) through allies. 13 For, peace is easy to make with an ally, not with an enemy.

14 If the ally were not to desire peace, he should constantly instigate him secretly. 15 Then dividing him from the enemy through secret agents, he should win the ally. 16 Or, he should win over the (king) situated on the border of the confederacy of allies. 17 When one situated on the border is won over, those situated in the centre become divided. 18 Or, he should win over one situated in the centre. 19 When one situated in the centre is won over, those situated on the border do not remain united.

20 And he should use such means as would secure the defection of the support of these (confederates).

21 He should conciliate a pious king by extolling his birth, family, learning and conduct, by (mention of) relationship of ancestors (of both) or by rendering service and refraining from injury in all three times. 22 He should win over by conciliation one whose energy has left him, one weary of war, one whose efforts are frustrated, one distressed by losses and expenses and by the expedition abroad, one seeking another (ally) with (his) integrity, one afraid of another or one of honourable intentions, attaching prominence to friendship.

23 He should win over a greedy or a weakened king with gifts after first making an ascetic or a chief stand surety. 24 Gift is five-fold : relinquishing what is due, acquiescence in what is taken, return of what is received, bestowal of one's own goods not given before, and permission to seize what he can from others' goods. 25 This is making gifts.

26 He should divide one frightened because of mutual hatred or enmity or afraid of seizure of his land, through one of these (causes of fear). 27

8 *dūṣyādūṣyāṇām* : both the *dūṣya* and the *adūṣya* are state subjects. For the time being they have joined in a conspiracy.

11 *paramiśrā* : Meyer thinks that *parimiśrā* with a preposition would be better as the name, like *āmiśrā*. That is possible, but not certain. 13 Cf. 7.13.17.

16 Cs reads *mitrāmitrasaṁghasya* for *mitrasaṁghasya*. But that is not necessary. It is a confederacy of allies from their own point of view, not that of the *vijigīṣu*.

20 Cn has *vaiṣām* for *caiṣām* ; that might appear better. — *āśraya* is the chief among the confederates.

22 It seems that *kalyāṇabuddhim* is to be construed with *maitripradhānam* only, not with *nivṛttotsāham* and others. Thus Meyer.

23 *-avasthāpanā* has reference to giving a surety. *tapasvin* and *mukhya* are to be distinguished ; cf. 7.17.8.

(He should divide) a timid king by (threat of) reprisals, 'After making peace, this king will take action against you; his ally has been sent (to negotiate); you are not in the peace (negotiations) even.'

28 Or, when for any king goods from his own land or from another's land should come as presents, secret agents should spread reports, 'These have been received from the king against whom we are to march.' 29 When (the report) is spread wide, he should send a letter with a man condemned to death, 'These goods have been sent by me to you as a present; attack your confederates or desert them; then you will receive the rest of the stipulated amount.' 30 Then secret agents should make the others realise, 'This was given by the enemy.'

31 Or, an article, well-known as belonging to the enemy, should go, unknown, to the conqueror. 32 Secret agents appearing as traders from him should sell it among enemy chiefs. 33 Then secret agents should make the others realise, 'This commodity was given to the enemy.'

34 Or, after favouring with money and honour persons who have committed great crimes, he should employ them against the enemy with weapon, poison and fire. 35 Then he should make one minister (seemingly) desert. 36 Taking his sons and wife under protection, he should have it proclaimed, 'They were killed at night.' 37 Then the minister should disclose those (criminals) one by one to the enemy. 38 If they were to act as directed, he should not get them seized. 39 Or, if unable (to do as told), he should get them seized. 40 Securing the position of a trusted counsellor, the (minister) should speak of the necessity of (the enemy) being on his guard against the

27 *pratighātena* 'by counter-attack,' i.e., by a threat of reprisals. — ***nisṛṣṭam***: cf. *nisṛṣṭārtha dūta* in 1.16.2. — *saṁdhau vā nābhyantaraḥ*: we have to understand ***tvam*** as the subject. The idea is, you have no place in the negotiations, and, further, the terms of the treaty will not cover you, so that you will be at the mercy of the ***vijigīṣu***.

28 *paṇyāgāra* is 'a present, primarily consisting of goods'; cf. 7.15.20. — *cārayeyuḥ*, i.e., spread the report as news secretly spied out. 30 *grāhayeyuḥ* 'should make them understand.' The object can hardly be ***śāsanam*** here, in view of *aripradattam*, which can be understood of the goods only.

31 *śatruprakhyātaṁ paṇyam* is curious: *śatroḥ prakhyātam* would be better. — ***avijñātam***, i.e., in effect, by theft. 33 *grāhayeyuḥ*: it can hardly mean 'have the goods seized by the guards' (Cn Cs). There is no need for seizing the goods. — ***aripradattam***: this may mean 'given to the enemy' by the particular confederate, or 'given by the enemy' to the traders. As *ari* is the ***vijigīṣu***, with whom the particular confederate is thus proved to have been in league, the former meaning appears slightly better.

34 *mahāparādhān*: these seem to be ordinary criminals, who are pardoned and in return for that are asked to act as agents for killing the enemy. These are not likely to be *amātyas*, as Cn Cs think. *amātyas* would hardly be asked to serve as assassins. 35 *ekam amātyam*: this in reality is a very trustworthy minister who is assigned the task of bringing about *bheda*. He could not be *mahāparādha* in reality. One is reminded of Bhāgurāyaṇa in the *Mudrārākṣasa*. — ***niṣpātayet***: the desertion of the minister and the consequent disappearance of his wife and sons are only a pretence, used to outwit the enemy; he might think the desertion etc. to be real. For this trick, cf. 13.3.11-14 below. 37 *tān*, i.e., the ***mahāparādhas***. — *prarūpayet* 'point out, disclose'; cf. 4.5.18; 11.1.49. This is done one by one as they may be found to have failed in their mission of secretly killing the enemy. Thus the *amātya* wins the enemy's confidence; he is not concerned with the fate of the ***mahāparādhas*** at the hands of the enemy. 38 The two ss. 38 and 39 are pointless; it seems likely that they are a marginal gloss that has got into the text. 41 ***amitraśāsanaṁ mukhyopaghātāya***

chief (confederate). 41 Then an agent in the pay of both should get an order of the enemy for the chief's destruction seized.

42 Or, he should send a letter to one possessed of the power of energy, 'Seize the kingdom of so and so; our treaty stands as before.' 43 Then secret agents should have it seized among the enemies.

44 Or, (agents) should destroy the camp or supplies or allied troops of one (of the confederates). 45 Speaking of friendship with the others, they should suggest to him, 'You are sought to be destroyed by these.'

46 Or if a great warrior or an elephant or a horse of some one were to die or to be killed or carried away by secret agents, (other) secret agents should declare him as destroyed by others. 47 Then he should send a letter to the one who is accused, 'Do more of this; then you will receive the rest of the stipulated amount.' 48 Agents in the pay of both should get that seized.

49 When they are thus divided, he should secure one of them.

50 By that are explained (dissensions among) commanders-in-chief, princes and commandants of armies.

51 And he should make use of dissensions as for oligarchies. 52 This is the work of creating dissensions.

53 Secret agents should dispose of a fiery or energetic enemy or one in a calamity or one entrenched in a fort, by weapon, fire, poison and so on, or one of them (should do so) because of ease in doing it. 54 For, an assassin, single-handed, may be able to achieve his end with weapon, poison and fire. 55 He does the work of a whole army or more.

56 This is the group of four means. 57 In that, each earlier one is lighter than each later one. 58 Conciliation is one-fold. 59 Gifts are two-fold, being preceded by conciliation. 60 Dissension is three-fold, being preceded by conciliation and gifts. 61 Force is four-fold, being preceded by conciliation, gifts and dissension.

is from Cn. *amitra* is the enemy with whom the *vijigīṣu*'s minister is staying. The letter may be addressed to his officer or agent; 'to another confederate' (Cn) appears less likely. — *grāhayet* is here 'cause it to be seized,' i.e., let it fall into their hands. The *ubhayavetana* does this, as he is really the *vijigīṣu*'s agent, working also as the enemy's agent. Cf. 1.12.18-19. — The idea is to divide the enemy from the chief confederate and others.

45 *itareṣu maitrīṁ bruvāṇāḥ*: it is better to consture these words with the following than with the preceding *ghātayeyuḥ* (as in Cs). For the *ghāta*, mention of friendship with others is unnecessary, but it is necessary for the *upajāpa*.

50 *tena* etc.: this means that the *senāpati* of one should be similarly divided from the *senāpati* of the other confederates and so on. This is when the armies of the confederates are led not by the respective kings, but by *senāpati*, *kumāra* and so on.

51 *sāṁghikaṁ bhedam*, i.e., ways of dissension recommended in the case of *saṁghas* in 11.1 below.

53 *tīkṣṇam*: cf. 1.14.5. — *sthitaśatrum*: see 7.10.7. — *saukaryataḥ* 'because of the ease in doing'. 55 *sarvasaṁdoha*, i.e., the full army mobilised; cf. 6.2.38 etc.

57 *laghiṣṭhaḥ*: the comparative would have been better. *laghu* 'light', i.e., easy to employ.

62 Thus has been declared (what is to be done) against those who attack.

63 But the same means (are to be used) against those in their own territories. 64 Special steps, however, are: 65 He should frequently send well-known envoy-chiefs with presents to one of the (confederates) who are in their own territories. 66 They should urge him to a treaty or to kill another (confederate). 67 If he does not agree, they should announce, 'We have made a treaty.' 68 Agents in the pay of both should communicate that to the others (adding) 'This king of yours is treacherous.'

69. Or, if any of them has fear of or enmity towards or hatred of another, (agents) should divide him from the other, (suggesting), 'This king is making peace with your enemy; presently he will over-reach you; make peace yourself very quickly and try to restrain him.'

70 Or, establishing relationship by accepting or giving (girls) in marriage, he should divide those not so related.

71 He should cause their kingdoms to be destroyed by a neighbouring prince or a forest chieftain or a pretender from his family or a prince in disfavour, or (destroy) their caravans, herds and forests or troops approaching to render help. 72 And guilds of castes, supported by one another, should strike at their weak points, and secret agents (should strike) with fire, poison and weapon.

73 And in case of enemy-mixed danger, he, being deceitful, should kill the enemies by secret practices like a (fowler using a) cloak and a bait (to lure birds) by creating confidence and offering a bait.

62 *abhiyuñjāneṣu*: when the kings forming the confederacy have already attacked his territory.

65 *abhijñātān dūtamukhyān*: these envoys would be well-known to the other kings as those coming from the *vijigīṣu*. 67 *kṛto naḥ saṁdhiḥ*: apparently the denial of the king would not convince the other confederates, because the envoy was known to have frequently gone to him with *paṇyāgāra*.

69 Meyer construes *purā tvām atisaṁdhatte* 'before he deceives you' with the following clause; cf. 1.14.8.

70 *āvāhavivāhābhyām*: see 7.15.22.

71 *rājyāni ghātayet* is from Cn's comment '*janapadādīni*'; Cs has *rājyam* in the singular. — *sārthavrajāṭavīr vā* is from Cn Cs for *-ṭavībhir vā* of the mss. The instrumental in the latter is unlikely. These are objects to be destroyed, not means of destruction. — *abhisṛtam* 'come for rescuing' the *rājya*, *sārtha* etc. 72 *jātisaṁghāḥ* 'corporations or guilds of castes'. This could hardly be a reference to the ruling *saṁghas*, Licchivika and others mentioned in 11.1.4-5 below, as Cn Cs understand it. Clearly, castes were spread over many states and often caste loyalties transcended those to the state. These are intended to be exploited.

73 *vītaṁsagila-* is proposed as the most likely reading. *vītaṁsa* is given in the lexicons the sense of 'a trap or snare for binding or catching birds and deer' or 'a cloak worn by fowlers to create confidence among birds and deer (when catching them).' The latter meaning is adopted as in Cn Cs. *gila* is 'a bait'. The idea is that the *vijigīṣu* should act like a fowler who uses a *vītaṁsa* or a *gila* for catching birds. The two correspond to *viśvāsena* and *āmiṣeṇa* respectively. Meyer, with *-gala*, explains 'like a fowler who produces from his throat (*gala*) imitative luring cries.' That does not sound very likely. — *paramiśrāyām*: the *paramiśrā āpad* is nothing but an attack by confederates. The situation is similar to that in 7.8.1-4 (*yātavyavṛttiḥ*) and in 7.14.1-11, the present passage on *paramiśrā* being in fact only an expansion of the latter Section (*hīnaśaktipūraṇam*).

CHAPTER SEVEN

SECTION 145 (DANGERS) ASSOCIATED WITH ADVANTAGE, DISADVANTAGE AND UNCERTAINTY (AS TO EITHER)

SECTION 146 OVERCOMING THESE (DANGERS) BY THE USE OF THE DIFFERENT MEANS

1 Immoderation, such as passion and so on, rouses one's own constituents, wrong policy (rouses) foreign (constituents). 2 Both those amount to demoniacal conduct. 3 A change in one's own people is revolt.

4 In cases that cause advancement of the enemy, there may be advantage that is dangerous, disadvantge or uncertainty.

5 That gain, which when not obtained leads to the prosperity of the enemy, or when obtained is recoverable by enemies, or when being obtained gives rise to losses and expenses, is a dangerous advantage. 6 For example, a gain which is a tempting morsel for neighbours being caused by a calamity of the neighbour, or a gain sought by the enemy obtainable (by him) by its very nature, or a gain in front contested by a rising in the rear or an enemy in the rear, or a gain repugnant to the circle (of kings) because of the extermination of an ally or the violation of a treaty, is an advantage that is dangerous.

7 The rise of danger from one's own people or from enemies is a disadvantage.

8 Concerning these two, 'Is it an advantage or no?' 'Is it a disadvantage or no?' 'Is the advantage a disadvantage?' 'Is the disadvantage an

9.7

The two Sections are found in ss. 1-66 and 67-84 respectively. In the first of the two Sections we have to supply *āpadaḥ* as the substantive.

1 *kāmādir utsekaḥ*: see 1.15.11. — *bāhyāḥ* are foreign states, hardly state officers in the outer regions (Cs). The contrary of *bāhyāḥ* here is *svāḥ*, not *abhyantarāḥ*. 3 Cn Cs read ss. 3 and 4 together, explaining 'revolt, which is change in the feelings of the subjects, when it leads to the prosperity of enemies, is an *āpad*, which may be an *artha* or an *anartha* or a *saṁśaya*.' It seems, however, that s. 3 only defines *kopa* and is quite unconnected with the discussion on *āpad*s that follows, in which *svajanavikāra* has no place at all. A *kopa* can hardly be described as an *āpad* which may be an *artha*. Moreover, ss. 5-6 show that *āpadartha* is to be understood as a single idea '*āpadrūpaḥ arthaḥ*, an advantage that may turn out to be disastrous'; a *kopa* cannot be so described. It is also possible that s. 3 is a marginal gloss.

5 *aprāptaḥ*: because you do not seize the *artha*, the enemy grows stronger; its non-seizure is an *āpad*. 6 *sāmantānām āmiṣabhūtaḥ sāmantavyasanajaḥ*: one *sāmanta* is in a calamity; other *sāmanta*s are waiting to benefit from it. If you do not seize the *artha*, some other *sāmanta* will; that will be an *āpad* (as this other *sāmanta* will be growing strong). It seems that this illustrates *śatruvṛddhim aprāptaḥ karoti* of s. 5. Cn Cs, however, understand two types here, *āmiṣabhūtaḥ* and *-vyasanajaḥ*, though there is no *vā*. — *śatruprārthito* etc.: this illustrates *prāptaḥ pratyādeyaḥ* etc. of s. 5. Hence the *vā* after *svabhāvādhigamyo* should be dropped as in Cn Cs.

7 *svataḥ parato vā bhayotpattiḥ*: Cn Cs have 'danger when a gain (*artha*) is taken away from oneself and danger arising while one is seizing a gain from one's enemy (*parataḥ*).' It is not easy to see why *artha* should be brought in at all. The latter at least would be an *āpadartha*, not an *anartha* pure and simple.

8 *artho na veti* (in this s.) and ss. 11-12 are from the commentators. There can be no question about their authenticity. — *artho 'nartha iti* i.e., is what appears to be an *artha*

advantage ?" is uncertainty. 9 (Thus) stirring up an ally of the enemy is uncertainty as to whether it is an advantage or no. 10 Inviting alien troops with money and honour is uncertainty as to whether it is a disadvantage or no. 11 Seizing land with a strong neighbour is uncertainty as to whether the advantage is a disadvantage. 12 Marching after joining forces with a superior king is uncertainty as to whether the disadvantage is an advantage. 13 Among these, he should act in the case of the uncertainty associated with advantage.

14 Advantage followed by advantage, advantage without a consequence, advantage followed by disadvantage, disadvantage followed by advantage, disadvantage without a consequence, disadvantage followed by disadvantage : this is the group of six consequences. 15 Seizing the enemy in the rear after uprooting the enemy (in front) is advantage followed by advantage. 16 Helping the neutral king with troops in return for reward is advantage without a consequence. 17 Uprooting a buffer king of the enemy is advantage followed by disadvantage. 18 Helping the enemy's neighbour at the side with treasury and troops is disadvantage followed by advantage. 19 Desisting after stirring up a weak king is disadvatnage without a consequence. 20 Desisting after rousing a superior king is disadvantage followed by disadvantage. 21 Of these, each earlier one is better for attaining than each later one.

22 Thus has been laid down the nature of enterprises.

23 The presentation of advantages simultaneously from all sides is the danger of advantages from all sides. 24 The same, when contested by the enemy in the rear, is the danger of uncertainty concerning advantages from all sides. 25 In the case of these, success (should be sought) by securing the support of the ally and the rear ally.

in reality an *anartha* ? 9 *śatrumitram utsāhayitum* : the enemy's ally is roused against him ; this would ordinarily be an *artha*, as it would weaken the enemy and place him in danger. The uncertainty arises because the enemy's ally may not be quite reliable. 10 Inviting enemy troops is ordinarily an *anartha* ; but if treated with honour etc., they may prove loyal. 11 Seizing land is an *artha*, but if it has strong neighbours, it may turn out to be an *anartha*. 13 *arthasaṁśayam* : Cn Cs understand only the first type. The third type could also be understood.

14 *anubandhaṣaḍvargaḥ* from Cn Cs is quite obviously necessary. *anubandha* is 'a consequence.' 16 *phalena*, i.e., for money received when giving troops. 17 *antar* is the *antardhi*, as in Cn Cs. Exterminating another king is ordinarily an *artha*, but if thereby you remove the buffer between you and a powerful king, that would be an *anartha*. 18 Giving *kośa* or *daṇḍa* without receiving anything in return is an *anartha*, but if it helps in putting down your enemy, that is a result to be welcomed. 21 *pūrvaḥ pūrvaḥ śreyān* : Cn Cs understand in the last three cases (*anarthatrivarga*) the earlier one as preferable for avoiding. That cannot be right. An *anartha* leading to *artha* cannot be 'more fit to avoid' than one without a further consequence and most certainly not than one leading to a further *anartha*. All six cases are arranged in a descending order for purposes of preference.

22 *kārya* 'the enterprise,' i.e., whether it is to be undertaken or not.

23 *samantato'rthāpad* : this is an *āpad* apparently because one cannot decide which *artha* to secure first. But it is an *āpad* only technically. 25 *tayoḥ* : it would be better to read *tasyām*, for, the case of *samantato'rthā* is referred to in ss. 30-31 below and steps recommended here do not apply to it.

26 The appearance of danger from enemies from all sides is danger of disasters from all sides. 27 The same, when checked by the ally, is the danger of uncertainty concerning disasters from all sides. 28 In the case of these, success (should be sought) by securing the support of a mobile enemy and the rear ally or taking the steps (recommended) against enemy-mixed danger.

29 When there is gain from one side and gain from another side, that is danger of advantage from two sides. 30 In that and in the one with advantages from all sides, he should march to obtain the object possessed of the excellences of a gain. 31 If excellences of the gains are equal, he should march to secure that which is prominent or proximate or not brooking delay or in which he may be deficient.

32 When there is disaster on one side and disaster on another side, that is danger with disasters on two sides. 33 In that and in the one with disasters on all sides, he should seek success through allies. 34 In the absence of allies, he should overcome the disaster on one side with a less important constituent, the disaster from two sides with a more important (constituent), the disaster from all sides with his base. 35 If that is impossible, he should leave everything and go away. 36 For, the coming back to the throne of one continuing to live is observed as in the case of Suyātra and Udayana.

37 When there is gain on one side and an attack on the kingdom on the other, that is danger with advantage and disaster on the two sides. 38 In that, he should march to secure that object which would overcome the disaster. 39 Otherwise, he should ward off the attack on the kingdom. 40 By that is explained the danger with advantage and disadvantage on all sides.

41 When there is disaster on one side and uncertainty as to advantage on the other, that is danger with disaster and uncertainty as to advantage on the two sides. 42 In that, he should first overcome the disaster; when that is overcome, (he should seek) the uncertain gain. 43 By that is explained the danger with disaster and uncertainty as to gain on all sides.

28 *tayoḥ* : here, too, *tasyām* would be better. For, measures in the case of *samantato-'narthā* are stated in ss. 33-36 below. — *calāmitra* is an enemy who has no fort. Cf. 7.10.9. Such a foe, being easy to manage, should be tackled first; cf. 7.14.10. — *paramiśrāpratīkāraḥ* as recommended in 9.6.11 ff.

31 *anatipātinam*, i.e., urgent. — *ūno vā yena bhavet*: Cs has 'which, if not secured, would render him weak'. A more direct 'in which he may be deficient' appears, however, preferable.

34 *laghīyasyā*, i.e., by surrendering *daṇḍa* before *kośa*, the latter before *durga* and so on. — *mūlena*, i.e., by a surrender of the kingdom. 35 The mss. show *samutsṛjya* for *sarvam utsṛjya*. The latter is definitely better and is supported by the quotation in the *Nāṭyadarpaṇa*, p. 36. 36 *jīvataḥ* : Cs reads *jīvatā* to correspond to the instrumental in *Suyātrodayanābhyām*. It would perhaps be better to read *-dayanayoḥ* in the genitive in the latter word, as the quotation in the *Nāṭyadarpaṇa* (p. 36) has it. Suyātra is Nala (Cn Cs).

39 *vārayet* : Meyer proposes *kārayet*, 'otherwise, he would be bringing about an attack on his kingship.' In spite of *hi*, however, this does not seem likely. The idea is simply, if the *artha* is not *anarthasādhaka*, steps to ward off the *anartha* itself should be taken first.

44 When there is gain on one side and uncertainty as to disaster on the other, that is danger with gain and uncertainty as to disaster on the two sides. 45 By that is explained one with gain and uncertainty as to disaster on all sides. 46 In that, he should strive to rescue each earlier one among the constituents from the possibility of disaster in preference to each later one. 47 For, it is better that the ally remain in peril of disaster, not the army, or the army, not the treasury. 48 If the entire (constituent) cannot be saved, he should strive to rescue parts of the constituents. 49 Then of constituents consisting of men, (he should rescue) the more numerous or the loyal, excepting the sharp and the greedy, of material constituents, that of high value or of great benefit. 50 By peace or staying quiet or the dual policy, (he should rescue) the insignificant ones, by the opposite (of these) the important ones. 51 And of decline, stationary condition and advancement, he should seek to attain each later one in preference to each earlier one. 52 Or, he may see a special advantage in the future by seeking decline and others in the reverse order.

53 Thus has been laid down place (in the matter of dangers)

54 By this is explained meeting with gain, disaster and uncertainty at the start, in the middle or at the end of an expedition.

55 And because gain, disaster and uncertainty are immediately effective, it is better to obtain gain at the start of an expedition, (as) it becomes (useful) for overcoming the enemy in the rear and his ally, for reimbursing losses, expenses and marches and for guarding the base. 56 Similarly, a disaster or an uncertainty becomes bearable to one staying in his own territory.

57 By this is explained meeting with gain, disaster and uncertainty in the middle of an expedition.

58 At the end of an expedition, however, after weakening an enemy fit to be weakened or exterminating one fit to be exterminated, it is better to meet with a gain, not a disaster or uncertainty, because of the fear of danger from an enemy.

44 Meyer thinks that a s. to the effect 'in that case, he should try to overcome the real *anartha* and then the things that threaten *anartha*', is missing after s. 44. If at all a missing s. is to be understood, it should rather be to this effect, 'in that he should first overcome the *anarthasaṁśaya* and then proceed to secure the *artha*.' 49 *tīkṣṇa-*: it is not necessary to read *kṣīṇa-* for this, as Meyer proposes. Cf. 1.14.5; 9.6.53. 50 *laghūni...gurūni*: this seems common gender to cover *prakṛti* feminine and *avayava* masculine. 52 *prātilomyena*, i.e., by seeking *kṣaya* rather than *sthāna* or *vṛddhi* and so on. For a full discussion of this, see 7.1.20 ff.

54 *yātrādi-*: *ādi* is necessary in view of the discussion that follows. — *upasaṁprāptum* 'to meet with'.

55 *nirantarayogitvāt*, i.e., because *artha* etc. produce their effect or results immediately. Cs's 'in case all three simultaneously present themselves' seems unlikely. Meyer's 'because the three are intimately connected with each other' seems also little likely. — *pārṣṇigrāhā-* etc.: having three separate expressions in the locative appears better in view of *ca* than having a single long compound. 56 *svabhūmiṣṭhasya*: this is the case *yātrādau*.

58 The point seems to be that *karśana* etc. should be resorted to only if it leads to *artha*, not if it leads to *anartha* or *saṁśaya*. — *parābādha*: the *para* is some other enemy, hardly the *karśanīya* etc. himself.

59 But for one not the leader among confederates, it is better to meet with disaster or uncertainty in the middle or at the end of an expedition, because of its affecting (all) without restrictions.

60 Material gain, spiritual good and pleasures : this is the triad of gain. 61 Of that, it is better to attain each earlier one in preference to each later one.

62 Material loss, spiritual evil and misery : this is the triad of disaster. 63 Of that, it is better to remedy each earlier one in preference to each later one.

64 'Is it material gain or loss ?' 'Is it spiritual good or evil ?' 'Is it pleasure or pain ?' : this is the triad of uncertainty. 65 Of that, it is better to secure the first alternative after overcoming the second (in each case).

66 Thus has been laid down time (in the matter of dangers).

Thus ends the topic of dangers.

67 The means of overcoming these are :

68 In the case of a son, a brother or a kinsman, overcoming (dangers from them) through conciliation and gifts is appropriate, in the case of leaders among citizens, country people and in the army, through gifts and dissension, in the case of neighbouring princes and forest chieftains, through dissension and force. 69 This is the natural method; in the reverse case, it is unnatural.

70 In the case of allies and enemies, success (should be sought) by a combination (of the means). 71 For, the means help each other.

72 Conciliation used in the case of ministers under suspicion of the enemy renders unnecessary the use of the remaining (means), gifts used in the case of treasonable ministers, dissension used in the case of confederates, (and) force used in the case of the powerful (render other means unnecessary).

59 *apurogasya*, i.e., an ordinary or subordinate member of the confederacy.— *anirbandhagāmitvāt* is proposed as in 9.4.23 and as suggested by Meyer. The idea seems to be that the *anartha* etc. would not be restricted to him, and would be shared by the confederates with him, or, if he alone is in trouble the confederates would come to his rescue. Meyer, however, explains 'because then there is no urgent need further to march', which seems hardly meant. Cn Cs, with *anibandha-*, explain 'because he can go elsewhere being unrestricted in his movements.' This is doubtful. The confederates could hardly be so free.

60 It is significant that *artha* is placed before *dharma* ; cf. 1.7.6-7 ; also s. 81 below.

66 *ityāpadaḥ* is a sort of colophon for all three Sections 143-145 which deal with the various kinds of *āpads*.

69 *anulomā*, i.e, natural. It can hardly mean 'to be used in normal cases, i.e., when the sons etc. are obedient' (Cn Cs). In that case, there is no need to use any remedy at all. — *viparyaye*, i.e., when *sāmadāna* is not used of sons etc., but *bhedadaṇḍa* instead.

72 *dūṣyāmātyeṣu* : with this also *śatroḥ* is to be understood. — *saṁghāteṣu* i.e., confederacies.

73 And in accordance with the seriousness or lightness of the dangers, there is restriction or option or combination (in the use of means). 74 With this (means) only, not with another: this is restriction. 75 With this (means) or with another: this is option. 75 With this and with another: this is combination.

77 Of these, the use of one means at a time is four-fold, so is the use of three at a time; the use of two at a time is six-fold; the use of four at a time is single. 78 Thus there are fifteen (ways of using the) means. 79 The same number (of using them are there) in an unnatural way.

80 Of these, success with one means is single success, with two, two-way success, with three, three-way success, with four, four-way success. 81 And since material wealth is the root of spiritual good and has pleasure for its fruit, that attainment of material gain which continuously results in spiritual good, material gain and pleasures, is attainment of all gains.

These are ways of overcoming (dangers).

82 Caused by providence are the troubles: fire, floods, disease, epidemic, panic, famine and demoniacal creation. 82 Overcoming them is through prostration before gods and Brahmins.

84 When there is excessive rain or drought or demoniac creation, then the means of overcoming it are rites prescribed in the Atharvaveda and undertakings by holy men.

Herewith ends the Ninth Book of the Arthaśāstra of Kauṭilya
'THE ACTIVITY OF THE KING ABOUT TO MARCH'

79 *pratilomāḥ*, i.e., when the means are used in an unnatural or wrongful manner.

81 *dharmamūla-* is a Tatpuruṣa compound rather than a Bahuvrīhi. Cf. ss. 60-61 above.

82 Cf. 4.3.1 and 8.4.1. Strictly speaking, fire, floods etc. are *pīḍanas* (8.4), hardly *āpads*. The reference to them here is unnecessary. — *pramāraḥ* is clearly the same as *maraka*. — *vidrava* 'running away in panic'. — *āsurī sṛṣṭiḥ*: rats, serpents, spirits etc.

84 *ativṛṣṭir avṛṣṭir vā* is from Cn; the reading of the mss., *asṛṣṭir atisṛṣṭir vā*, is impossible.

BOOK TEN

CONCERNING WAR

CHAPTER ONE

SECTION 147 SETTING UP OF THE CAMP

1 On a site, approved by experts in the science of building, the commandant, carpenters and astrologers should cause the camp to be set up, circular, rectangular or square or in conformity with the nature of the ground, with four gates, six roads and nine divisions, endowed with a moat, a rampart, a parapet, gates and towers, when there is danger and when the army has to halt.

2 In the ninth part to the north of the central (should be erected) quarters for the king, one hundred *dhanus*es in length and half that in width, (with) the royal residence in the western half of that. 3 The palace guards should be stationed on the borders. 4 In front (should be erected) the audience-hall, to the right the treasury and offices for issuing orders and carrying out works, to the left the place for elephants, horses and chariots intended for the king's use.

10.1

The description of the *skandhāvāra* shows that it is a strongly fortified cantonment area where troops raised are stationed over a long period before starting on an expedition. The standing army, at other times, must also have been stationed there.

1 *vāstuka* : cf. 1.20.1 ; 2.3.3. — *nāyaka* is the general who marches at the head of the army ; cf. 10.2.4, also 10.6.45. — *navasaṁsthānam* : apparently, *saṁsthāna* is the same as *bhāga* in the next s. According to an alternative explanation in Cn, *saṁsthāna* is a square formed by intersection of roads. That fits in with six roads. — *khāta* etc. : cf. 2.3.4 ff. *sāla* here is the same as *prākāra* there. — *bhaye sthāne ca* : these are the two occasions when the setting up of a camp is recommended.

2 *madhyamasya uttare navabhāge* : perhaps we have to understand this in the same sense as *vāstuhṛdayād uttare navabhāge* in 2.4.7, i.e., in the ninth part to the north of the central one-eighty-first part on the *paramaśāyika* plan of 81 squares. And by the ninth part we have probably to understand the one-eighty-first part lying to the north of the central square. Cf. Śaṁkarārya on Kāmandaka, 17.5. — *rājavāstukam* : the quotation in Śaṁkarārya shows *rājavāstuniveśaṁ kārayet* in place of *rājavāstukaṁ* ; that reading is adopted in the Punjab edition. — Whereas *rājavāstuka* refers to palace grounds as a whole including the *upasthāna* etc. of s. 4, *antaḥpura* refers to the actual royal residence. Cf. 1.20.1. 3 *antarvaṁśikasainyam* : cf. 1.20.13 and 1.21.3. 4 *śāsanakaraṇa* can hardly be the *akṣapaṭala* (Cn Cs) ; the record-cum-audit office (2.7) is hardly likely to be shifted to the camp. Moreover, *śāsana* would seem to refer to the decrees or orders, the issuing of which would be so necessary in the camp. Similarly, *kāryakaraṇa* can hardly be 'dispensation of justice' (Cn Cs), in view of the separate mention of the *upasthāna*. It may be the staff headquarters for control of the camp.

5 Beyond this at a distance of one hundred *dhanus*es from each other (there should be) four enclosures, with carts, stretches of thorny branches, pillars and the parapet.

6 In the first (enclosure) in front, the councillor and the chaplain (should be encamped), to the right the magazine and the kitchen, to the left the store for forest produce and the armoury. 7 In the second, (there should be) quarters for hereditary and hired troops, for horses and chariots and for the commander-in-chief. 8 In the third, elephants, banded troops and the camp-superintendent (should be encamped). 9 In the fourth, the labour-corps, the commandant and allied, alien and forest troops under the command of their own officers (should be encamped). 10 Traders and courtesans (should be encamped) along the highways.

11 Outside (the camp), fowlers and hunters (should be stationed) with drums and fire, as well as secret guards.

12 In the path of the march of enemies he should cause to be placed (hidden) wells, concealed hollows and barbed wires.

13 He should cause a change of guards to be made in the eighteen groups. 14 And he should cause watches to be kept (even) by day in order to discover spying.

15 He should prohibit disputes, drinking, festive gatherings and gambling and secure the guarding of the seal.

16 The regent shall arrest a soldier returning from the army without a written order.

5 *methīpratati* 'stretches of thorny branches' (Cn Cs). *methī* means 'a post, particularly at the threshing floor'; but in view of *stambha*, which is also used here, that sense is
not very likely. Meyer understands *pratatistambha* as one, 'posts with creeper-entangle-
ments'.

6 *mahānasam* : this is meant for the palace, hardly for the entire camp; cf. 2.4.8.
7 It is possible but not certain that in this and the following two ss., we have to understand
purastāt, dakṣiṇataḥ and *vāmataḥ* respectively of the three groups mentioned in each s. 8
śreṇyaḥ : this clearly refers to the *śreṇībala* ; a reference to Kāmboja, Surāṣṭra and other
saṁghas of 11.1.4-5 (Cn) can hardly be understood. — *praśāstā* : see s. 17 below. He is
obviously not the same as the *praśāstṛ* mentioned in 5.3.5 and 1.12.6.

12 *āpāte* 'in the path of advance'. — *kūpa-* etc.: cf. 2.3.15. *kaṇṭakinī* here is probably the same as *kaṇṭakapratisara* there. Cs explains by 'planks with thorns'. *kaṇṭakinī* is also the name of some thorny plants.

13 *aṣṭādaśavargāṇām* : Cn Cs have 'the six kinds of troops, each threefold because
of the leaders, *padika*, *senāpati* and *nāyaka* (of 10.6.45).' This is not very convincing.
Perhaps the positions mentioned in ss. 6-9 above can be understood, with *aśvaratha* as one,
and *mitra-*, *amitra-* and *aṭavī-bala* each separately. Or, places mentioned in ss. 2-4 may
also be included for arriving at the number eighteen.

15 *mudrārakṣaṇam* may refer to allowing entry or departure only with a sealed pass, also perhaps to preventing fraud in connection with the seal.

16 *senānivṛttam* from Cn Cs alone makes sense. — *śūnyapālaḥ* also from the commentators is preferred to *antapālaḥ* of the mss. As the camp is obviously still inside the
state territory, a deserter from it is hardly likely to come across the *antapāla*. As the king
is in the camp, a *śūnyapāla* or regent would be appointed to deputise for him.

17 The camp-superintendent should march ahead on the road, and should make carpenters and labourers prepare arrangements for protection and for water in the proper manner.

CHAPTER TWO

SECTION 148 MARCH FROM THE CAMP
SECTION 149 GUARDING (TROOPS) DURING THE CALAMITIES OF THE ARMY AND AT THE TIME OF ATTACK

1 After calculating the halts on the way in villages and in forests, in accordance with the supply of fodder, fuel and water, and (calculating) the time for camping, halting and marching, he should start on the expedition. 2 He should cause food and equipment to be transported in double the quantity required to meet the case. 3 Or, if unable to do so, he should assign it to the troops, or should store them at intervals on the route.

4 In front (shall march) the commandant, in the centre womenfolk and the king, on the flanks horses as repellers as with arms, at the end elephants or extensive raids, in the rear the commander-in-chief shall march (and) encamp.

5 Getting supplies from forests on all sides is a raid. 6 The flow (of equipment and men) from one's own country is supplies. 7 An ally's army is help. 8 The place where the women-folk are kept is a place of retreat.

17 *rakṣaṇāni* is from Cn Cs for *grahaṇāni*: the latter may mean 'taking up positions' for the halts on the way. But *rakṣaṇa* 'securing protection' on the way appears preferable. The commentators understand levelling of roads, removal of wild animals etc. — *yāyāt* should have come before *samyak*; for the latter and *rakṣaṇāni* are to be construed with *kārayet*.

10.2

The two Sections are to be found in ss. 1-16 and 17-20 respectively. *skandhāvāra-prayāṇam* is 'march from a camp' rather than 'march to a camp' (Cn Cs).

1 *sthāna* 'a halt of two or three months' (Cn), 'a long halt of a month or a fortnight' (Cs); *āsana* 'a halt of five or six days' (Cn Cs); *gamana* 'halt for the night' (Cn Cs). 3 *āyojayet* from Cs is preferable to *prayojayet*; Cn seems to have read *sainyeṣu vāyojayet*.

4 The arrangement of ss. 4-12 is as in Cs, except that *paścāt senāpatir yāyāt niviśeta* is read at the end of s.4. not after s. 8 as in Cs; also with *sarvato* in s. 5 instead of after *prasāravṛddhir vā* (s. 4) as in Cs. Thus we get a description of the order of the march in one place. — *bāhūtsāraḥ*: this seems to convey the idea of spreading out on the flanks and repelling an attack in those quarters, as a man does with his arms. Cf. 10.4.13-14. Russ. understands by it 'reconnoitring by the infantry.' — *cakrānteṣu* refers to the rear ends of the army (Cn Cs). — *prasāravṛddhir vā*: this is an option to *hastinaḥ*. It is horses that carry out *prasāravṛddhi* (10.4.13). If there are no elephants, raids by horses in large numbers are recommended. If *cakrānteṣu* in the sense of the rear ends is to be understood with this, *sarvataḥ* is less likely to be used with it. — *senāpatir yāyāt niviśeta*: a *ca* seems obviously necessary. Cs, however, reads *paryāyāt* (for *yāyāt*) and explains 'in the rear (*paścāt*) of their respective army-divisions (*svasvasenāpaścādbhāgakramāt*)'. It is doubtful, however, if more than one *senāpati* is meant in this passage. Cf. 10.1.7 above. *paryāyāt* cannot be understood in the sense of 'by turns' as Meyer in the Nachtrag suggests. *yāyāt* is found in Kāmandaka, 19.47.

5 *vanājīvaḥ* 'living on the forests'; *vana*, it seems, stands for all places where supplies of food can be found, and *prasāra* seems to imply a foraging raid; often, however, an ordinary raid seems intended. 8 This definition of *apasāra* is not found in the mss. It may well be that all the definitions in ss. 5-8 are derived from some marginal gloss. Those of *vīvadha*, *āsāra* and *apasāra* are uncalled for here.

9 In case of an attack in front he should march in the crocodile array, in the rear, in the cart array, on the two flanks, in the thunderbolt array, on all sides, in the 'excellent-on-all-sides' array, in a region where march in a single file alone is possible, in the needle array.

10 In case of two alternate routes, he should march in a region suitable to himself. 11 For, those on terrain suitable to themselves effectively resist those on unsuitable terrain.

12 One *yojana* is the slowest (rate of marching), one and a half middling, two *yojanas* fastest, or, the rate of march may be as possible (for him).

13 When steps have to be taken against an enemy in the rear, his ally, the middle or the neutral king, who may give shelter (to the enemy) and destroy (one's) rich lands; when a difficult path has to be cleared; when the treasury, the army, allied, alien or forest troops, labourers or a suitable season has to be awaited; when (he thinks) 'There will come about a deterioration in the fortifications made (by the enemy), in his stores and in his precautions for protection, a feeling of despondency in his purchased troops and a feeling of despondency in his ally's troops; or, the instigators are not very quick; or, the enemy will fulfil my desires;' (then) he should march slowly, in the reverse case, quickly.

14 He should make the army cross waters with (the help of) elephants, pillar-bridges, embankments, boats, rafts of wood and bamboos and by means of gourds, leather baskets, skins, canoes, tree-stems and ropes. 15 In case the ford is seized (by the enemy), he should get (the army) across at another place at night with the help of elephants and horses and lie in ambush.

9 *abhyāghāte* seems to refer to an expected attack from the enemy, rather than one planned by the *vijigīṣu* himself. — *makareṇa* : for the arrays, see 10.6.8 ff.

11 *pratilomāḥ* 'contrary', i.e., able to fight effectively against the others.

12 With *sambhāvyā cāgatiḥ*, Meyer translates 'and in accordance with that, one should calculate the arrival (*āgatiḥ*, at a particular place)'. This is unlikely.

13 *āśrayakārī sampannaghātī* : these are not independent occasions when a slow march is recommended (as in Cn Cs), but are only adjectives qualifying *pārṣṇiḥ āsāraḥ* etc. The idea is, when any of these is likely to give shelter to the enemy or to lay waste one's rich lands during one's absence, precautions are necessary beforehand (*pratikartavyaḥ*); hence a slow march is recommended. *āśrayakārī* can hardly mean 'when one is seeking a shelter for oneself' or *sampannaghātī* 'when one plans to destroy the rich territory of the enemy.' In the latter case, it is not clear why one should march slowly. Meyer, understanding the passage up to *pratīkṣyāḥ* independently of *śanair yāyāt*, translates, 'precautions have to be taken against the *āśrayakārī* and the *sampannaghātī*, no less than against the *pārṣṇi* etc.' This is unlikely in the absence of *api* and *yathā . . . tathā*. And there is little doubt that the entire passage is to be understood with *śanair yāyāt*. — *vṛṣṭir* of the mss. (for *viṣṭir*) would seem to be included in *ṛtu*. — *upajapitāro nātitvarayanti* : these are his own agents trying to wean the enemy's officers etc. from their loyalty to him. These can hardly be 'the treacherous elements of the enemy' with whom the *vijigīṣu* is conspiring (Cn Cs). *upa-jap* is 'to instigate to treason in order to win over to one's side'. — *abhiprāyam* etc. : this will be without having to fight.

14 *stambhasaṁkrama* : see 7.10.32. — *carmakaraṇḍa* 'a wicker basket covered with hide' (Cn). — *dṛti* 'animal skin filled with water'. 15 For *sattra*, see 10.3.24 below.

16 And in a waterless region, he should make carts and animals carry water according to their capacity, in conformity with the length of the route.

17 He should guard his own army when on a long march in a wilderness, when without water, when lacking in fodder, fuel and water, when marching on a difficult road, when broken by an attack, when exhausted by hunger, thirst or a long march, when engaged in crossing rivers deep in mud and water or climbing up and down valleys and mountains, when crowded on a road where march in a single file alone is possible or in a region uneven with mountains or in a narrow place, when without equipment whether in the camp or on the march, when engaged in meals, when tired after a long march, when sleeping, when troubled by diseases, epidemics or famine, when infantrymen, horses and elephants are ill, when not on terrain suitable to it, or when any of the calamities of an army has befallen it; and he should strike at the enemy's troops (when they are in these predicaments).

18 Ascertainment of the strength of the enemy's army (is made) by counting the number of troops marching out along a route allowing a march in a single file only, their fodder, foodstuffs, beds spread out, cooking fires laid out, banners and weapons. 19 He should conceal (all) that in his own case.

20 After securing a mountain fort or a forest fort in the rear, with means of retreat and reserves, he should fight and encamp on land suitable to himself.

16 *adhvapramāṇena* from Cn Cs is preferable to the locative *-pramāṇe*.

17 *anudakam* seems superfluous when the next expression has *-udakahīnam*. Cn remarks that this shows that waterlessness is the greatest calamity. Meyer proposes to read *anugatam* 'pursued', or *dīrghakāntārāmanuṣyakam* 'when in the widlerness superhuman beings (*amanuṣya*) threaten it'. This last is quite fanciful. — The participle in *-praskannam* (Cn Cs) is preferable to the noun *-praskandanam*. — *-gambhīrāṇām* goes with *nadī-* only in the compound. Cn seems to have read *-gambhīranadī-*, the whole in a single compound. That might appear better. — *-avayāne*, as Meyer says, might appear better than *-apayāne*. — *abhūmiṣṭham* is from Cn Cs for *abhūyiṣṭham*; the latter is unlikely though *-dvipabhūyiṣṭham* is conceivable. — *balavyasana*: see 8.5.1-18.

18 *senāniścāra* 'marching out of the army' and *grāsāhāra* 'fodder and food' are both from the commentators. The other readings are obviously faulty.

20 *vanadurgaṁ vā* is from Cn Cs for *vānadurgaṁ vā* of G M. *vā nadīdurgam* is unlikely. 2.3.2 mentions *vanadurga* as a place of retreat in difficulties, *apasāra* being mentioned there. — *pratigraha* seems to refer to the place in the rear where the king remains with reserves. Cf. 10.5.58. In view of that passage, 'where the king meets the attacking enemy forces' (Cn Cs) seems less likely.

CHAPTER THREE

SECTION 150 VARIOUS TYPES OF COVERT FIGHTING
SECTION 151 ENCOURAGING ONE'S OWN TROOPS
SECTION 152 DISPOSITION OF ONE'S TROOPS TO COUNTER-ACT ENEMY TROOPS

1 When he is superior in troops, when secret instigations are made (in the enemy's camp), when precautions are taken about the season, (and) when he is on land suitable to himself, he should engage in open fight. 2 In the reverse case, (he should resort to) concealed fighting.

3 He should strike at the enemy on the occasions of the calamities of his troops and on occasions for assault, or when he is on unsuitable terrain, being himself on suitable terrain, or (even) one on suitable terrain, if (he himself is) possessed of the support of constituents.

4 Or, feigning a rout with treasonable, alien and forest troops, he should strike at the (pursuing enemy when he has) reached unsuitable ground.

5 He should break compact ranks through elephants.

6 He should strike by turning round at the (enemy) who is pursuing when a rout is first feigned and who is broken (in the attempt), himself remaining unbroken.

7 Or, striking in front, he should strike in the rear with elephants and horses, when the (enemy) is reeling or has turned back. 8 Striking in the rear, he should strike in front with strong forces, when the (enemy) is reeling or has turned back. 9 By these are explained attacks on the flanks. 10 Or, he should strike at the point where the treasonable or weak troops (of the enemy) may be stationed.

11 If the ground in front is uneven, he should strike in the rear. 12 If uneven in the (enemy's) rear he should strike in front. 13 If uneven on one flank, he should strike at the other flank.

14 Or, after first engaging (the enemy) in fight with treasonable, alien and forest troops, he should strike at him when he is exhausted, himself remaining fresh.

10.3

The three Sections are to be found in ss. 1-25, 26-47 and 48-57 respectively.

1 *prativihitakartuḥ* of the mss. is faulty. Meyer's proposal to read *prativihitadurgaḥ* is unlikely, as a reference to *durga* is out of place here. 2 *śakaṭa-* for *kūṭa-* is also faulty.

3 *avaskandakālas* are occasions mentioned in 10.2.17. — *prakṛtipragrahaḥ*: the *prakṛti* would appear to be his own constituents (Meyer), rather than those of the enemy (Cs).

4 *bhaṅgaṁ dā* has the sense of 'to make a show of being broken in ranks, to feign a rout'. — Most of the *kūṭayuddhas* are nothing but normal tactics common on the battlefield, and there is nothing wrong about them.

6 *abhinnaḥ* is proposed for *abhinnam* as suggested by Meyer. That is in conformity with s. 22 and other parallel expressions.

15 Or, making a show of a rout himself through treasonable troops, he should strike at the enemy, who is confident that he has won, by resorting to ambuscade, being himself on his guard.

16 Remaining ever vigilant he should strike at the (enemy) negligent when engaged in plundering a caravan, a herd of cattle, an encampment or transport.

17 Or, with strong troops concealed by weak troops, he should enter the ranks of enemy warriors and slay them.

18 Or, luring enemy warriors with (prospects of) cattle seizure or hunting wild animals, he should, concealed in an ambush, strike at them.

19 After keeping (enemy troops) awake at night by a sudden assault, he should slay them by day when they are overpowered by sleep or are asleep.

20 Or, he should make an attack on those asleep (at night) with elephants having leather-cases on their feet.

21 He should strike in the latter part of the day at troops exhausted by keeping fighting equipment on for the day.

22 Or, he should strike at the enemy, whose elephants and horses are made ineffective through herds of cattle, buffaloes and camels carrying sacks of dry skins containing round pebbles and taking fright, who is broken and has turned back (in flight), remaining unbroken himself.

23 Or, he should strike at all (kinds of troops) when they are facing the sun or the wind.

24 A desert, a forest, a strait path, a muddy place, a mountain, a marshy place, uneven ground, a boat, cattle, a cart array, mist and night : these are places for ambush.

25 And the occasions for assault mentioned before are also occasions for concealed fighting.

15 *sattra*, i.e., one of the places mentioned in s. 24 below.

16 *saṁvāha* is understood in Cn Cs as 'guarding'; but troops engaged in guarding can hardly be described as *pramatta*. *saṁvāha* as 'transport' seems better, as another object of plunder.

17 *-cchannasārabalo* is proposed for *-cchannaḥ sārabalo*. Cf. Kāmandaka, 19.63 (*phalgusainyapraticchannaṁ kṛtvā vā sāravad balaṁ*).

18 *gograhaṇena*, i.e., 'for seizing cattle on the *vijigīṣu*'s side' (Meyer) rather than 'for preventing *vijigīṣu*'s men from seizing the enemy's cattle' (Cn Cs). So *śvāpadavadhena* is 'for engaging in hunting' rather than 'for preventing the *vijigīṣu*'s men from hunting in enemy territory' (Cn Cs). One is reminded of Udayana lured with hunting.

20 The leather-coverings on the feet of elephants are for protection against thorns etc. or 'against *śvadaṁṣṭra*' (Meyer).

22 The idea seems to be that the herds are frightened (*trasnu*) by the noise of the pebbles (*śarkarā*) in the sacks they carry and run helter-skelter, thus creating confusion in the ranks of the enemy's elephants and horses.

23 *sarvam* : Meyer thinks that we should read *kharvam* 'crippled', i.e., unable to see clearly. That is extremely doubtful.

25 *praharaṇakālāḥ* are those of 10.2.17.

26 Open warfare, however, in which the place and time (for the fighting) are indicated, is most righteous.

27 Collecting the troops together, he should address them, 'I receive a wage like you; this kingdom is to be enjoyed together with you; the enemy should be attacked by you at my request.'

28 Even in the Vedas, on the occasions of the concluding baths of sacrifices in which fees have been fully received, it is declared, 'That will be your condition after death, which is obtained by the brave (fallen on the field).' 29 Moreover, there are two stanzas in this connection:

> 30 Brave men, giving up their lives in good battles, reach in one moment even beyond those (worlds), which Brahmins, desirous of heaven, reach by a large number of sacrifices, by penance and by many gifts to worthy persons.
>
> 31 A new vessel, filled with water, properly consecrated, with a mantle of *darbha* grass—may this not be the share of him and may he go to hell, who would not fight for the sake of the lump of food received from the master.

32 He should make the minister and the chaplain encourage the warriors by (pointing out) the excellences of the array.

33 And the group of his astrologers and others should fill his own side with enthusiasm by proclaiming his omniscience and association with divine agencies, and should fill the enemy's side with terror.

34 When 'to-morrow is the fight', he should observe a fast and sleep beside his weapons and vehicles. 35 He should offer oblations in the fire with Atharva-*mantras*. 36 He should make (Brahmins) recite blessings invoking victory and securing heaven. 37 And he should consign himself to (the care of) Brahmins.

26 The punctuation is as in Cs, with a stop after *dharmiṣṭhaḥ*, Open warfare is recommended as righteous. *dharmiṣṭha* as descriptive of the king in the next s. is not so happy.

27 *mayā 'bhihitaiḥ* is from Cn; that is preferable to *mayā 'bhihitaḥ* 'specified by me' or *mayā 'bhihataḥ* 'attacked by me'.

28 It seems that the passage in ss. 28-31 is a later addition. It is not part of the king's exhortation as is clear from the *iti* at the end of s. 27, nor can it be understood as part of the encouragement to be attempted by the *mantrin* and *purohita* mentioned in s. 32. In any case, it is quite unlikely that anyone would say on the battlefield '*apīha ślokau bhavataḥ*', in the manner of an expository treatise. The whole passage is obviously a marginal gloss that has crept into the text. The question of the indebtedness of this text to Bhāsa's *Pratijñāyavgandharāyaṇa*, where in Act 4, s. 31 occurs, is therefore hardly relevant. 31 *navaṁ śarāvam* clearly refers to the vessel from which libations of water are offered to the deceased.

32 *vyūhasaṁpadā* is included at the end of this s. as in Cn; it states the ground on which the minister and chaplain encourage the troops. It could hardly be appropriately used with *kārtāntikādiḥ vargaḥ* in the next s.

33 *sarvajña-*, i.e., *sarvajñatva-*. Cf. 1.8.6 etc. — *daivatasaṁyoga* is read as in 13.1.1,3.

38 He should make troops that are possessed of bravery, skill, nobility of birth and loyalty and that are not cheated in the matter of money and honour, the centre of the ranks.

39 A bare army, without standards, consisting of warriors related as fathers, sons and brothers, should be the place for the king. 40 An elephant or a chariot should be the vehicle for the king, guarded by cavalry. 41 He should mount that (vehicle), of which the army mostly consists or in which he may be trained. 42 One appearing as the king should be stationed at the head of the array.

43 Bards and panegyrists should describe the attainment of heaven by the brave and the absence of heaven for cowards, and sing praises of the caste, corporation, family, deeds and conduct of the warriors. 44 Assistants of the chaplain should speak of the use of sorcery and black magic, mechanics, carpenters and astrologers (should speak) of success in their own works and failure in those of the enemy.

45 The commander-in-chief should address the ranks after they are carefully made well-disposed with money and honour, 'One hundred thousand (shall be the prize) for killing the (enemy) king, fifty thousand for killing the commander-in-chief or a prince, ten thousand for killing a foremost warrior, five thousand for killing an elephant or chariot warrior, one thousand for killing a horseman, one hundred for killing a chief of infantrymen, twenty per head (of infantrymen killed), beside double the wage and whatever one seizes.' 46 Heads of groups of ten should ascertain that about them.

47 Physicians, with surgical instruments, apparatus, medicines, oils and bandages, and women in charge of food and drink and capable of filling men with enthusiasm, should be stationed in the rear.

48 He should arrange his ranks in a battle-array on ground suitable to himself in such a way that it does not face the south, has the sun at the back and the wind favourable. 49 And in a battle-array on land suitable to the enemy, they should set the horses moving.

39 *muṇḍānīkam* 'like a shaven head, because of the absence of crest-like flags' (Cn). It cannot mean 'like the head, i.e., the principal army' (Cs). 42 *vyūhādhiṣṭhānam* is from Cn Cs; the reference is to the most prominent place in the array, 'the head' (Cs).

44 *kṛtyābhicāram*: this is for the destruction of the enemy. — *yantrika* is from Cn, 'mechanics who had manufactured the machines of war like *jāmadagnya* etc.' *sattrika*, as secret agents, would hardly go about speaking of the success of their work. — *mauhūrtika* is in strange company with *yantrika* and *vardhaki*.

45 *śatasāhasraḥ*: we cannot understand gold coins in the higher cases as Cn Cs do; *paṇa* must be understood throughout. — *bhogadvaiguṇyaṁ svayaṁgrāhaś ca* need not be restricted to the *viṁśatika*, as Meyer does. 46 *daśavargādhipatayaḥ*, i.e., *patika*, *senāpati*, and *nāyaka* as in 10.6.45.

47 *śastrayantra* is a reference to surgical instruments and other apparatus, hardly to weapons and machines. — *uddharṣaṇīya* has the sense of the active voice; '*uccair harṣaṇahetavaḥ*' (Cn).

49 *aśvāṁś cārayeyuḥ*: this is in order to prevent the enemy arranging his battle-array there.

50 Where a firm stand and speed in movements of the array have no favourable terrain, there he would be conquered in either case, whether standing firm or moving quickly. 51 In the reverse case, he wins in either case by standing firm or moving quickly.

52 Ground being level, uneven or mixed, its nature in front, on the flanks and in the rear should be ascertained. 53 On level ground (there should be) the staff and circle arrays, on uneven the snake and diffuse arrays, on mixed mixed arrays.

54 After breaking an (enemy) superior in strength he should ask for peace. 55 If sued for peace by one equal in strength, he should make peace. 56 He should continue to strike at one inferior in strength, but not at all at one who has reached his own land or is ready to sacrifice himself.

> 57 The vehemence of one returning again to the fight and despairing of his life becomes irresistible; therefore, he should not harass a broken enemy.

CHAPTER FOUR

SECTION 153 GROUND SUITABLE FOR FIGHTING
SECTION 154 FUNCTIONS OF THE INFANTRY, THE CAVALRY, THE CHARIOTS AND THE ELEPHANTS

1 Suitable ground is desirable for infantrymen, horses, chariots an elephants, for fighting and for camping. 2 Battle-fields and seasons for men fighting in deserts, forests, water or dry lands and for those fighting in trenches, on open ground, by day or by night, and for elephants from rivers, mountains, marshes and lakes, and for horses are desirable for each as suited to him.

3 Level, firm, clear, not causing jolting, not causing wheels or hooves to get stuck, not obstructing axles, not broken with trees, thickets, creepers, tree-stems, fields under water, pits, ant-hills, sand and mud, and free from clefts, this is ground for chariots, beneficial (also) to elephants and horses as well as men, for fighting and for camping, in normal and in difficult (situations)

50 *abhūmir vyūhasya* is one of the readings in Cn; that is better than *abhūmi* (Cs); *abhūmau* might be better still; but perhaps *sthāne prajave ca abhūmir* would be best.

57 Cf. *Mahābhārata*, 12.100.13 '*punarāvartamānānāṁ nirāśānāṁ ca jīvite, vegaḥ suduḥsaho rājaṁs tasmānnātyanusārayet.*'

10.4

The two Sections are found in ss. 1-12 and 13-18 respectively.

3 *abhikāśā*, i.e., clearly visible. — *acakrakhurā 'nakṣagrāhiṇī*: Meyer thinks that the original reading was *asaktacakra-* etc. It is also possible that it was *acakrakhurākṣagrāhiṇī* as a single compound 'not catching wheels, hooves or axles'. — Both here and in s. 6 Cn has *-bhaṅguradaraṇahīnā* in a continuous compound, *bhaṅgura* being understood as 'a wavy surface'. The word, however, is more likely to be an adjective 'broken'. — *same viṣame* seem to refer to normal and abnormal situations. In the locative masculine or neuter the words can hardly refer to *bhūmiḥ* for elephants etc. (as Meyer has it). We also cannot supply *deśe* after the words (as in Cs), since the *bhūmi* is described as *samā* only.

4 That with small stones and trees, with small pits that can be jumped over, and with the blemish of small clefts is the ground for horses.

5 That with big tree-stems, stones, trees, creepers, ant-hills and thickets is the ground for infantrymen.

6 That with traversable mountains, water and uneven places, with trees that can be uprooted and creepers that can be cut, broken with mud and free from clefts is the ground for elephants.

7 Without thorns, not very uneven, with room for retreat, this is excellence (of ground) for infantrymen.

8 With double the room for retreat, free from mud, water and bogs and devoid of pebbles is excellence for horses.

9 With dust, mud, water, reeds and growth of rushes, free from 'dog s teeth', and free from obstruction by big branches of trees, is excellence for elephants.

10 Possessed of water-reservoirs and shelters, not causing jolting, without fields under water, and enabling a turn round, is excellence for chariots.

11 Ground (suitable) for all has been declared. 12 By this camping and fighting of all kinds of troops becomes explained.

13 Investigation of the ground, the halting place and forests, securing land without unevenness, water, ford, wind and sun's rays, destruction of supplies and reserves or their protection, cleansing and steadying the army, extension of raids, repelling as with arms, making the first attack, penetration, breaking through, comforting, capturing, setting free, causing a change in the

6 *gamyaśailanimnaviṣamā* is from Cn Cs. The idea is of land dotted with hills and streams which can be easily traversed by elephants and with uneven regions (*viṣama*) which elephants can easily cross. Kāmandaka, 20.14, supports the interpretation of *viṣama* as a noun in the sense of 'an uneven place' (Cn Cs). — Cn reads *bhañjanīya-* for *chedanīya-*. *paṇkabhaṅgurā*, i.e., 'having mud in places' seems supported by the reference to the presence of *kardama* in the best kind of land for elephants in s.9.

7 Cn seems to have read *bahuviṣamā* for *abahuviṣamā*. The latter appears better. — *pratyāsāra* is a place for retreat in the rear; '*vyūhasya paścādbhāgaḥ*' (Cn).

9 *śarādhāna* appears to mean 'growth of grass, rushes etc.' Cn seems to understand 'pointed roots of grass'. — *śvadaṁṣṭra* is the plant *gokṣura*, according to Cn Cs. Cf. 2.3.15.

10 *-apāśraya* which is found in Cn for *-āśraya* is the usual word. — *vyāvartana* is turning round.

13 *-vicayaḥ* in the sense of 'search' is preferable to *-nicayaḥ* which means 'collecting'. — *aviṣama* is from a reading in Cn, understood in the sense of 'land without unevenness.' *viṣama* as 'land inaccessible to the enemy' appears less likely. — *ghātaḥ* is that of those of the enemy, while *rakṣā* is that of those of oneself. — *viśuddhiḥ* is clearing the wounded etc. from the army, hardly clearing it of treasonable elements. — *sthāpanā* is steadying of the army. — *prasāravṛddhir bāhūtsāraḥ* as two separate items are necessary. Cf. 10.2.5. — *vyāvedhanam* 'piercing' refers to 'breaking through'. — *grahaṇam*, i.e., making prisoners; *mokṣaṇam* setting one's own prisoners free. — *mārgānusāravinimayaḥ*, i.e., making the enemy give up his pursuit of one's troops by going to his rear and pursuing him in turn. — *kośakumāra-* may be those of the enemy or of oneself; the latter are carried off to safety. —

path of pursuit, carrying off the treasury or the prince, assault on the rear and tips, pursuit of the weak, accompanying, and the work of rallying, these are the functions of cavalry.

14 Marching in the van, making new roads, halting places and fords, repelling as with arms, crossing and descending in water, remaining steadfast, marching forward and descending, entering difficult and crowded places, setting fire and extinguishing it, securing victory single-handed, reuniting broken ranks, breaking up unbroken ranks, protecting in a calamity, assault, frightening, causing terror, showing magnificence, capturing, setting free, breaking ramparts, gates and towers, bringing in and carrying away treasury, these are the functions of elephants.

15 Guarding one's own troops, repelling the four-fold army in battle, capturing, setting free, reuniting broken ranks, breaking up unbroken ranks, causing terror, showing magnificence, and making a frightful din, these are the functions of chariots.

16 Bearing arms in all places and seasons, and military activity are the functions of infantrymen.

17 The work of clearing camps, roads, water-works, wells and fords, carrying machines, weapons, armours, implements and food, and removing from the battle-field weapons, armours and wounded men are the functions of labourers.

18 A king, with few horses, should yoke bullocks and horses to chariots; similarly, one with few elephants, should make the centre consist of carts driven by donkeys and camels.

hīnānusāraṇam : the causal does not seem to have any significance. Meyer thinks that we should read *dīnānusaraṇam* as in Kāmandaka, 20.6. That does not appear necessary. — *anuyānam* is simply accompanying one's troops in order to guard them. Cn Cs have ' pursuing the fleeing enemy '. *anu-sṛ* is the usual root for ' to pursue.' — *samāja* is ' getting together,' i.e., rallying.

14 The first *avataraṇa* (with *toya*) refers to getting in water, while the second refers to descending from a height. — *viṣamasaṁbādhapraveśaḥ* as a single word (as in Cn Cs) is distinctly better than the three words separately. — *ekāṅgavijaya* is ' victory with one arm of the army, viz., with the elephants ' (Cn Cs) ; it can hardly mean ' victory over a single element of the enemy ' (Meyer). — *abhighātaḥ* may be construed with *vyasane* or understood independently. — *vibhīṣikā* is ' frightening at mere sight ', while *trāsanam* is by frightful deeds (Cs). — *audāryam* is lending grandeur or magnificence to the army. — *kośavāhanāpavāhanam* is from Cn Cs. According to Cn some read *upavāhana* as the last word in the compound in the sense of ' carrying (king and others) on the back '. *apavāhana* would refer to carrying away the enemy's treasury.

15 *saṁgrāme* is to be construed with the preceding *-pratiṣedhaḥ* (Cn Cs), rather than with the following *grahaṇam* etc. (Meyer).

16 *vyāyāmaḥ* refers to actual fighting.

18 *gavāśvavyāyogam*, i.e., yoking horses to some chariots and bullocks to others.

CHAPTER FIVE

SECTION 155 ARRANGEMENT OF BATTLE-ARRAYS IN WINGS, FLANKS AND FRONT IN ACCORDANCE WITH THE STRENGTH OF TROOPS

SECTION 156 DISTRIBUTION OF STRONG AND WEAK TROOPS

SECTION 157 MODES OF FIGHTING OF THE INFANTRY, THE CAVALRY, THE CHARIOTS AND THE ELEPHANTS

1 He should engage in fight after establishing a fortified place at a distance of five hundred *dhanus*es, or in accordance with the nature of the ground.

2 The commander-in-chief and the commandant should arrange the army in a battle-array, with chiefs assigned different positions, after detaching it out of sight (of the enemy).

3 He should place a foot-soldier at a distance of one *śama* (from the next), a horseman at a distance of three *śama*s, a chariot or an elephant at a distance of five *śama*s. 4 Or, he should arrange with double or treble the distance. 5 Thus one should fight in comfort, without being crowded.

6 A *dhanus* is five *aratni*s. 7 At that distance (from the next) he should place an archer, at a distance of three *dhanus*es a horseman, at a distance of five *dhanus*es, a chariot or an elephant.

8 Five *dhanus*es (should be) the juncture of the divisions of wings, flanks and centre.

10.5

The three Sections are to be found in ss. 1-40, 41-52 and 53-56 respectively.

1 It is proposed to read *-pakṛṣṭaṁ durgam* as separate words, so that *durgam* alone can be understood with *bhūmivaśena vā*. If a single compound is read as in the mss. the option in *bhūmivaśena vā* would have no meaning. The *durga* is a fortified place (not a regular fort) which is inaccessible to the enemy. It seems to be the same as *pratigraha* of s. 58, though that is 200 *dhanus*es behind the army, while the *durga* is 500 *dhanus*es away. The difference in distance as well as nomenclature may be due to a difference in sources.

2 *mokṣayitvā*, i.e., detaching the main army from the reserves in the rear.

3 *śama* is a distance of 14 *aṅgula*s; cf. 2.20.11. The distance is between two soldiers in a row. 4 *dviguṇāntaram*: According to Cn, the greater distances are recommended when foot-soldiers are few in number and elephants etc. are of the middling or best types (as against lowest types in s. 3).

6 *pañcāratni*: the ordinary *dhanus* is 4 *aratni*s; cf. 2.20.18. Meyer thinks that ss. 6-7 are interpolations. Kāmandaka, 20.22, however, presupposes them. It is possible that these distances are for fighters with bow and arrow, while those in ss. 3-4 are for those fighting with swords, spears etc.

8 *anīkasaṁdhiḥ*: *anīka* seems used of the divisions of an array, such as *pakṣa*, *kakṣa* etc., and *saṁdhi* is the open space betweeen any two of these. '*pakṣa*s are outside in front, *kakṣa*s inside at the back and *urasya* is in the middle' (Cn Cs). The terms are suggested by the figure of a flying bird.

9 For a horse, (there are) three soldiers as fighters in front. 10 (There are) fifteen for a chariot or an elephant, as well as five horses. 11 The same number of foot guards should be arranged for horses, chariots and elephants.

12 He should place as the centre a division of three rows of three chariot-units, a flank and a wing of the same size on either side. 13 There are thus forty-five chariots in a chariot division, two hundred and twenty-five horses, six hundred and seventy-five soldiers as fighters in front and the same number as foot-guards.

14 This is the uniform array. 15 It may increase in size by two chariot-units at a time up to twenty-one chariot-units. 16 Thus the odd numbers become the ten bases of the uniform array.

17 In case of an unequal number in the wings, the flanks and the centre as compared to one another, there is uneven array. 18 It may also increase in size by two chariot-units at a time up to twenty-one chariot-units. 19 Thus the odd numbers become the ten bases of the uneven array.

20 Troops left over after this array should be made an insertion. 21 He should insert two thirds of the chariots in the (outer) parts, the

10 *rathasya hastino vā*: chariots and elephants are generally not used together. Here a unit is based either on chariots or on elephants. 11 *tāvantaḥ* i.e., 3 for a horse and 15 for a chariot or an elephant. Cs understands *tāvantaḥ* to mean 5, which seems hardly correct. Cn thinks that there are 5 horses and 15 foot-guards for a chariot, making 10 horses and 30 foot-soldiers in the unit. That also is hardly right. As each horse has 3 *pratiyoddhṛs* and 3 *pādagopas*, that would give 60 foot-soldiers, not 30. Meyer arrives at 1 chariot, 5 horses and 90 infantrymen. That is unlikely, as shown by s. 13 below.

12 *trīṇi trikāṇi*, i.e., three rows of three chariot-units each. 13 In view of the explicit statement here, 450 horses (in Cn) or 4050 foot-soldiers (in Meyer) cannot be right. — *rathavyūhe*, which is read in the Punjab edition is quite necessary. Here we have a description of a *rathavyūha* only. — It is proposed to drop *vājirathadvipānām* found after *pādagopāḥ* at the end. The expression is unlikely here in a description of a *rathavyūha*; it is clearly repeated by a copyist from s. 11 above.

14 *sama-*, i.e., one in which each of the five divisions of the *vyūha* has the same number of units. 15 *dvirathottarā* is from Cn Cs. It seems that each row of chariots (*trika* of s. 12) is to increase successively by two, 5, 7, 9, etc., up to 21 chariots. The actual number of chariots in each of the five divisions of the array comes to 9, 15, 21 and so on up to 63, and in the array as a whole to 45, 75, 105, and so on up to 315. In the largest array we get 315 chariots, 1575 horses and 9450 foot-soldiers. 16 *ojāḥ*: 3, 5, 7 etc. are odd numbers.

17 *mitho* is from Cn for *ato*, which has little significance. The unevenness of numbers is with reference to one another (*mithaḥ*), e.g., 9 in *urasya*, 15 in *pakṣa*, 17 in *kakṣa* and so on; the permutations can be very large in number. 18 *tasyāpi* etc. means little more than that the series 3, 5 to 21 is available for each of the five divisions in different numbers. 19 These *prakṛtis* do not differ in any way from those of s. 16.

20 *āvāpaḥ* 'an insertion'. The idea seems to be that of reinforcing or strengthening of the array. 21 *dvau tribhāgau aṅgeṣu* etc.: this would disturb the character of a *sama vyūha*; for, while in the latter the *urasya* has only one-fifth of the whole, the addition to *urasya* is to the extent of one-third of it. — It may be assumed that the chariots added are accompanied by the usual number of horses and foot-soldiers. 22 *tribhāgonaḥ* etc.: the idea seems to be that the insertion is to be less by one-third, i.e., up to two-thirds; thus in an array with 45 chariots, the addition is to be of 30 chariots only (20 of these being in the wings and flanks and 10 in the centre). Thus Cn. Cs seems to understand that the total addition is to be less than one-third, e.g., less than 15 in a unit of 45. Meyer thinks that this s. only sums up the preceding statement; two-thirds in the *aṅgas* is the only

rest he should place as the centre. 22 Thus an insertion of chariots less by one-third should be made.

23 By that is explained the insertion of elephants and horses. 24 The insertion should be so made that it does not cause crowding in the fighting of horses, chariots and elephants.

25 Excess of troops is insertion. 26 Excess of infantry is counter-insertion. 27 Excess of one arm is side-insertion. 28 Excess of treasonable troops is over-insertion.

29 Insertion should be made according to the strength of the troops up to four times or up to eight times the insertion or counter-insertion of the enemy.

30 By the chariot-array is explained the elephant-array.

31 Or, (the array may be) mixed, of elephants, chariots and horses—elephants at the ends of the army, horses on the flanks, chariots in the centre. 32 A centre of elephants, flanks of chariots and wings of horses—this is (an array) breaking with the centre. 33 The reverse is one breaking with the ends.

34 But the unmixed (array) of elephants is—war-elephants at the centre, riding elephants in the rear, vicious elephants at the tips.

35 (An unmixed) horse-array is—a centre of armoured horses, flanks and wings of unarmoured.

36 (An unmixed) infantry-array is—armoured soldiers in front, archers behind. 37 Thus the unmixed (arrays).

āvāpa ; one-third placed at the centre is not to be considered an *āvāpa*, because it is not inserted in between any two parts. It is to be noted that in the quotation in Śaṁkarārya on Kāmandaka, 20.40, this s. is not to be found ; it is therefore quite possible that it is a marginal gloss that has got into the text.

25 *bāhulyam* 'excess, i.e., surplus left over after the array is formed' (Cn). This is the means of *āvāpa*. Cs has '*bāhulya*, i.e., strengthening by the insertion of the excess.' This sense of *bāhulya* does not fit in the case of *dūṣyabāhulya*.

29 The mss. read the *ca* after *ā*; it is proposed to read it before, to make the construction smoother. The idea seems to be that the *āvāpa* is to be four times or eight times that of the enemy's *āvāpa* and *pratyāvāpa*. It seems that *āvāpa* refers to chariot (or elephant) units, while *pratyāvāpa* to foot-soldiers. — *vibhavataḥ sainyānām* is not a third option as Cn seems to understand it.

30 This clearly shows that a *rathavyūha* as described so far contains no elephants.

31 *hastirathāśvānām* : as Cn remarks, horses here are those used independently of chariot or elephant units. — *cakrānteṣu* : Cn Cs read *cakrāntayoḥ* 'in the wings'. The dual is not quite necessary. — The mss. add *mukhyā* after *aśvā* ; Cs has *aśvamukhyā* in a compound. It is proposed to drop *mukhyā*, as it is unlikely either with *aśvā* or *rathā*. — Cn adds that after *urasye*, the words *ayaṁ pakṣabhedī* have to be read, having dropped out through a scribal error. It then reads *antarbhedī* in s. 33, understanding *antar* in the sense of *kakṣa*. However, it seems better to stick to the readings of the mss. Kāmandaka, 20,37-38, has only *madhyabhedī* and *antabhid*. And *madhya* and *anta* are the usual terms of contrast ; cf. 9.6.16-19. 33 *viparītaḥ*, i.e., with horses in the centre and elephants in the wings, as shown by Kāmandaka, 20.38. Cn Cs have 'horses in centre, elephants on the flanks and chariots in the wings.' The objection in Cn that the other arrangement would not differ from that in s. 31 is not quite valid ; and it is not necessary to provide for the case where elephants are in the flanks (as Cn also objects).

34 *jaghana*, i.e., *kakṣa* and *koṭi*, i.e., *pakṣa* (Cn).

38 Foot-soldiers (should be) in the wings, horses on the flanks, elephants in the rear, chariots in front, or a reversal of this (may be made) in accordance with enemy's army. 39 This is disposition of troops with two arms. 40 By that is explained disposition of troops with three arms.

41 In the case of men, the excellences of an army constitute the best troops. 42 In the case of elephants and horses, special excellences are: pedigree, breed, mettle, youthfulness, vigour, height, speed, spiritedness, training, firmness, loftiness, obedience and possession of auspicious marks and good conduct.

43 He should place one-third of the best among foot-soldiers, horses, chariots and elephants as the centre, two-thirds as flanks and wings on the two sides, behind them the second best, against the order the third best, weak troops against the order. 44 Thus he should make use of all.

45 By placing weak troops at the ends, he becomes able to over-power (the enemy) with his vehemence.

46 Placing the best troops in front he should place the next best at the ends, the third best in the rear, (and) weak troops in the centre. 47 Thus it becomes capable of resisting.

48 After arranging the battle-array, however, he should strike with one or two out of the wings, flanks and centre; with the remaining he should support (the attack).

49 He should attack with plenty of best troops that army of the enemy which is weak, lacking in elephants and horses, with treasonable officers in it or seduced by secret instigations. 50 Or, when the enemy's army is most

38 *pattayaḥ* etc.: Cn Cs understand two arrays here, infantry and horses alone in one and elephants and chariots alone in the other. It seems rather that the s. states the general position of each of the four arms in an array whenever two arms are used, irrespective of the usual division into *kakṣa*, *pakṣa* and *urasya*. In any case, a combination of elephants and chariots alone would hardly be recommended. Meyer proposes *caturaṅga-* for *dvyaṅga-* in the next s. As, however, the preceding ss. 34-37 have referred to *ekāṅgabalavibhāga*, a reference to *dvyaṅgabalavibhāga* would seem expected. Nevertheless, the arrangement might appear applicable to *caturaṅgabala* also.

41 *daṇḍasaṁpat* etc.: when men are possessed of qualities mentioned in 6.1.11, they make the best army (*sārabala*). 42 *udagratā*: Cn Cs have 'having a high or uplifted face.' A lofty bearing is what seems intended.

43 *anulomam* 'in the natural order', i.e., behind the best troops. — *pratilómam*, i.e., in front of the *sārabala*, the *phalgubala* being stationed right in front of all.

45 *vegābhihūlikaḥ* is an emendation suggested by Meyer for *-hūlitaḥ*; it is also found in G2. The former may mean 'who wears down the enemy's vehemence, who withstands his vehemence' or 'who overpowers the enemy by his vehemence'. The latter reading would mean 'who is overpowered by vehemence', which is inapt in the context. Cn seems to read *vegābhihutaḥ*, Cs *vego 'bhihutaḥ*, the explanation being 'the enemy's vehemence is burnt up as an oblation in the fire of weak troops.' Cs overcomes the grammatical difficulty in his reading by understanding *yudhyamānena* after *avadhāya*. Cn Cs mention another reading *vego 'bhihataḥ* 'the vehemence of the enemy becomes shattered.'

46 *koṭiṣu*: the plural shows that the two wings alone are not intended. See s. 34 above.

48 *pratigṛhṇīyāt*: Cn Cs understand 'should hold (the enemy's attack)'. In view of *pratigraha* as used in s. 58 below, also in 12.4.19 and 13.3.46, the root *prati-grah* seems to have the sense of 'to support an attack (made by oneself)'. The idea here may be that of supporting the attack (already made) at a later stage.

strong, he should attack it with double that number of best troops. 51 He should reinforce that arm of his which has few best troops with a large number of them. 52 He should arrange the troops near the place where the enemy has suffered a loss, or whence there may be danger.

53 Rushing forth, rushing about, rushing beyond, rushing back, holding together after pounding, enclasping, moving zigzag, encircling, scattering, turning back after fleeing, guarding broken ranks along the lines, in front, on the flanks (and) in the rear, pursuing broken ranks—these are modes of fighting for horses.

54 These same with the exception of scattering, (and) destruction of the four arms whether combined or separate, smashing of wings, flanks and centre, making a sudden assault, and attacking those asleep—these are modes of fighting for elephants.

55 These same with the exception of holding together after pounding, (and) marching forth, marching away, fighting in a stationary position on land suitable to them — these are modes of fighting for chariots.

56 Striking in all places and at all times, and silent punishment are the modes of fighting for foot-soldiers.

57 In this manner he should arrange battle-arrays, odd and even, in such a way that the strength of the four arms becomes suitably used.

58 Retiring to a distance of two hundred *dhanus*es, the king should remain in the rear; from that (comes) the rallying of broken ranks; he should not fight without reserves in the rear.

50 *dviguṇasāreṇa*: as the enemy's troops are *sāriṣṭha*, 'double' can only refer to quantity. 51 *bahunā*: we should supply *sāreṇa*, rather than *aṅgena* (Cn Cs).

53 *unmathyāvadhānam*: Cn Cs have 'holding together, keeping together (*avadhānam*) after pounding the enemy.' Russ. has 'a destructive raid.' Meyer understands *avadhāna* as 'throwing down' or *apadhāna* as 'driving away'. — *valayaḥ* is a sort of pincer movement with two *daṇḍa* arrays (cf. 10.6.21). — *maṇḍalam* 'encirclement' of a part of enemy troops after cutting them off (Cn Cs). — *prakīrṇikā* 'scattering' is 'the use of all the above movements together' (Cn Cs). — *vyāvṛttapṛṣṭham* seems to refer to making a show of flight (*pṛṣṭha*) and then turning round to attack. — *anuvaṁśam* seems used adverbially to be construed with *bhagnarakṣā*. Cn Cs, however, understand it independently 'following one's troops that face the enemy' or 'retiring and coming back to fight'; Russ. has 'turning back of a part of one's troops before the enemy.'

54 *vyastasamastānāṁ vā*: the *vā* obviously shows the option between *vyasta* and *samasta*.

55 *sthitayuddha*: this can hardly mean 'fighting after remaining for a long time round the enemy's fortified wall (*prākāra*)' (Cs). It only refers to fighting without manoeuvring or movements.

56 *karmāṇi* in 10.4.13-16 differ from *yuddhāni* here in that they include functions not involving actual fighting.

57 *yugmān*, i.e., even. The Chapter itself has mentioned only odd *vyūhas*. — *sadṛśaḥ* 'suitable', i.e., suitably distributed or used.

58 *pratigrahe* is from Cn Cs; *pratigrahaḥ* in the nominative would have to be construed with *rājā*, which would be odd. *pratigraha* is 'rear of the army' according to Cn Cs. It is the place where reserves are kept; these are to be used to reinforce the fighting troops when need for it arises — *bhinnasaṁghātanaṁ tasmāt* should be understood as a separate sentence. In the quotation in Saṁkarārya on Kāmandaka, 20.15, we have *bhinnasaṁdhāraṇaḥ* (with *pratigrahaḥ* for *-grahe*); in that case *tasmāt* in the sense of 'therefore' can be construed with the last clause *na yudhyetāpratigrahaḥ*.

CHAPTER SIX

SECTION 158 ARRANGING THE STAFF, THE SNAKE, THE CIRCLE AND THE DIFFUSE ARRAYS

SECTION 159 ARRANGING COUNTER-ARRAYS AGAINST THEM

1 Two wings, a centre and reserves—this is the arrangement of a battle-array according to Uśanas. 2 Two wings, two flanks, a centre and reserves—this is according to Bṛhaspati.

3 According to both, arrays with wings, flanks and centre are the basic arrays, the staff, the snake, the circle and the diffuse. 4 Among them, that with crosswise operations is the staff array. 5 Operation of all (divisions) one after the other is the snake array. 6 Operation on all sides of advancing (divisions) is the circle array. 7 The separate operation of divisions as stationed is the diffuse array.

8 That operating evenly with wings, flanks and centre is the staff (array). 9 That, marching beyond with the flanks is the 'splitter'. 10 The same falling back with wings and flanks is the 'strengthener'. 11 The same, marching out with the wings is the 'unbearable'. 12 Marching out with the centre keeping the wings stationary is the 'falcon'. 13 In the reverse case, (these four become) the 'bow', the 'bow-flank', the 'established' and the 'well-established' (respectively). 14 That with wings of

10.6

The two Sections are found in ss. 1-41 and 42-44, the rest of the ss. being miscellaneous in character.

1 In 15.1.41-42, this s. is quoted as an illustration of *anumata* 'another's opinion which is not contradicted'. However, *kakṣa* which is not mentioned by Uśanas is frequently referred to in the text. — *pratigrahaḥ*: see 10.5.58 above.

3 *prapakṣa-* etc.: Cn Cs explain 'with wings etc. arranged (*pra* as *pravibhakta*) as described below.' That is not very satisfactory. Perhaps the original reading was *sapakṣa-*. — *ubhayoḥ*, i.e., according to both Uśanas and Bṛhaspati. This is strange, as Uśanas does not mention *kakṣa* at all in his scheme. Perhaps the word has wrongly got into the text. 4 *tiryagvṛttiḥ*: *vṛtti* seems to refer to the mode of operations during the fight, though Cn Cs render it by '*avasthāna*, taking up a position'. *tiryak* may refer to the crosswise movements of the divisions, though the use of *tiryak* in describing something called *daṇḍa* does not seem quite appropriate. Perhaps *atiryak* is to be read; *samam* in s. 8 might seem to support this. Russ. has *tiryagvṛttiḥ* 'exactly according to the length of the front.' — *samastānām*: supply *anīkānām*. — *anvāvṛttiḥ* 'coming one behind the other' as in a serpent's body. The idea seems to be that the divisions operate one behind the other. 6 *saratām* from Cn Cs is preferable to *sutarām*, which has little significance. *saratām* presents a contrast to *sthitānām* in the next s.

8 Cn Cs state that these definitions are in accordance with Bṛhaspati's ideas whereas the earlier ones were acceptable to both. This is hardly convincing. The two sets of definitions do not quite agree with each other. — *samaṁ vartamānaḥ* may refer to simultaneity of operations by the various divisions, though 'operating in a straight line' may well have been meant. 9 *kakṣātikrāntaḥ* 'breaking through with the flanks,' the *urasya* and *pakṣas* remaining in their positions. 10 *pakṣakakṣābhyām*: Cn Cs have *pakṣābhyām* only. But the former is supported by Kāmandaka, 20.45. — *pratikrāntaḥ* 'falling back'; this is obviously the opposite of *atikrāntaḥ*. 11 *sa evātikrāntaḥ* is from Cn Cs, supported by Kāmandaka, though *niṣkrāntaḥ* of the mss. would mean the same thing. 12 *pakṣāvavasthāpya*: perhaps *pakṣakakṣāvavasthāpya* is to be read. 13 *viparyaye*, i.e., with *pratikrānta* for *atikrānta* and vice versa in the earlier four cases. 14 *cāpapakṣaḥ*: this

bows is the 'conqueror'. 15 The same, marching out with the centre, is the 'victory'. 16 That with wings like big ears is the 'pillar-eared'. 17 That with double pillars in the wings is the 'extensive-victory'. 18 That with wings augmented threefold is the 'army-face'. 19 In the reverse case, it is the 'fish-mouth'. 20 The staff, in a straight line, is the 'needle'. 21 Two staffs is the 'bracelet'. 22 Four staffs is the 'invincible'. 23 These are staff arrays.

24 That operating unevenly with wings, flanks and centre is the snake array. 25 It is 'moving-like-a-serpent' or 'cow's-urination'. 26 That with two (divisions) at the centre and staffs in the wings is the 'cart'. 27 In the reverse case, it is the 'crocodile'. 28 The cart, inter-mixed with elephants, horses and chariots is the 'flying-about'. 29 These are snake arrays.

30 When the wings, flanks and centre become one, it is the circle array. 31 That with faces on all sides is the 'good-on-all-sides.' 32 That with eight divisions (or faces) is the 'invincible.' 33 These are circle arrays.

may mean 'with wings shaped like bows' or 'with a *cāpavyūha* in each of the wings'; in the latter case, there would be five divisions in each of the wings, besides the other three (2 *kakṣas* and an *urasya*), i.e., 13 in all, as Śaṁkarārya points out on Kāmandaka 20.46. It is not certain that this is really meant. 16 It is proposed to read *sthūlakarṇapakṣaḥ* as a single compound. According to Kāmandaka, 20.47, each of the wings has two *anīkas* instead of one. 17 *dviguṇapakṣasthūṇaḥ*: tihs seems to mean that the size of the *pakṣa* is twice that in the *sthūṇākarṇa*, i.e., 4 *anīkas* in each. Kāmandaka's definition is *dvisthūṇaḥ*, which Śaṁkarārya understands as two *sthūṇākarṇas* one beyond the other, with 14 *anīkas* in all. 18 *tryabhikrāntapakṣah*: Cn has 'when the wings go beyond three'; does this mean 'with more than three *anīkas* in each wing'? Śaṁkarārya in fact understands four *anīkas* in each wing, and eleven *anikas* in all. It is possible that we have to understand 'with three *anīkas* in each wing'. 19 *viparyaye*, i.e., with the *urasya* and *kakṣa* threefold. 20 *ūrdhvarājiḥ daṇḍaḥ*, i.e., a *daṇḍa* going in a straight line. This seems to mean that the five divisions move one behind the other. 21 *dvau daṇḍau*: *daṇḍa* here is evidently as arranged for *sūcī*. Two parallel columns seem to be meant, each with five divisions. 22 *catvāraḥ*, i.e., four *sūcī*-formations.

24 *viṣamaṁ vartamānaḥ* 'moving unevenly', i.e., apparently not in a straight line. 25 According to Cn Cs (also Kāmandaka, 20.48) *sarpasārī* and *gomūtrikā* are names of two varieties of the *bhoga vyūha*; their definitions are not given, because the names are self-explanatory. The difference between the two is that in the former the divisions are close to each other, while in the latter they are broken and of various sizes (*bahudhā vibhinnākārāḥ*). Meyer thinks that these are not varieties of *bhoga*, only other names by which also it is known. 26 *yugmorasyo daṇḍapakṣaḥ*: Śaṁkarārya on Kāmandaka, 20.49, understands a double-sized *urasya* and the *pakṣa* and *kakṣa* arranged one behind the other as in *daṇḍa*, on either side, with six *anīkas* in all. Cn Cs have 'with the centre shaped as a *daṇḍa* split into two and each wing like a full *daṇḍa*.' This would seem to give 15 divisions, if *daṇḍa* of the *sūcī* type is to be understood. — *viparyaye*, i.e., *daṇḍorasyaḥ* and *yugmapakṣaḥ*. Śaṁkarārya does not explain beyond saying that it too has six *anīkas*. Perhaps he would understand two *anīkas* in the centre one behind the other and a *kakṣa* and a *pakṣa* on each side in a line. Cn Cs have '*urasya* like one *daṇḍa* and the wings of the shape of a split *daṇḍa*.' 'A *daṇḍa* (five divisions one behind the other) in the centre and two divisions in each wing' seems more likely. The exact nature of many of these arrays is far from clear. 28 *vyatikīrṇaḥ*: this seems to imply that an *āvāpa* of these is made in the regular *śakaṭa* array.

30 *ekībhāve*, i.e., when the distance between them (10.5.8) is not there. 32 *aṣṭānīkaḥ*, i.e., 2 *urasyas*, 2 *kakṣas* and 4 *pakṣas* (Cn Cs). Śaṁkarārya has 2 *urasyas*, 4 *kakṣas* and 2 *pakṣas*. — Meyer thinks that we have four types of *maṇḍala vyūha*, without the description of any one of them. That is probably because of the plural *-vyūhāḥ*, in s. 33. Cs states that the plural may serve to include varieties not mentioned here. Kāmandaka, 20.50, also has only two types. — *durjaya* figures also among *daṇḍavyūhas* (s. 22).

34 Because of the disjoined nature of the wings, flanks and centre it is the diffuse array. 35 By the formation of the figure with five divisions, it is the 'thunder-bolt' or the 'lizard'. 36 With four (divisions), it is the 'hearth' or the 'crow's-feet'. 37 With three, it is the 'half-moon' or the 'crab-horned'. 38 These are diffuse arrays.

39 One with chariots at the centre, elephants on the flanks and horses in the rear is the 'unharmed' array. 40 Foot-soldiers, horses, chariots and elephants, one behind the other is the 'immovable' array. 41 Elephants, horses, chariots, and foot-soldiers, one behind the other is the 'unrepulsed'.

42 Among these, he should counter-act the 'splitter' with the 'strengthener', the 'strengthener' with the 'unbearable', the 'falcon' with the 'bow', the 'established' with the 'well-established', the 'conqueror' with the 'victory', the 'pillar-eared' with the 'extensive-victory', the 'flying-about' with the 'good-on-all-sides'. 43 With the 'invincible', he should counter-arrange against all other arrays.

44 Of foot-soldiers, horses, chariots, and elephants, he should strike at each earlier one with each later one and an inferior arm with a superior arm.

45 The one commander of ten single units is the lieutenant, the one (commander) of ten lieutenants is the general, the one (commander) of these is the commandant. 46 With drum-beats, flags and banners, he should establish signals for the divisions of the array, for dividing (themselves) into sections, for joining together, for halting, for marching, for turning back and for attacking.

47 In case the (opposite) arrays are equally matched, success (comes) from the possession of suitable place, time and strength.

34 *asaṁhatāt*, i.e., *asaṁhatatvāt*. 35 *ākṛtisthāpanāt*, i.e., the five divisions are so arranged that they present the appearance of a *vajra* and so on. The figure of the *vajra* is not at all clear. The description in Śaṁkarārya on Kāmandaka, 20.52, does not throw much light. 36 *uddhānakaḥ* is from Kāmandaka as suggested by Meyer for *udyānakaḥ*. The former is a fire-place or hearth; the latter suggesting a park is not likely when some *ākṛti* is expected. Whereas the *uddhānaka* would appear to be a square, the *kākapadī* would appear to be diamond-shaped with the tip in front. 37 *ardhacandrakaḥ*, i.e., with the centre moved forward of the two side-divisions. This seems meant, since in the *karkaṭakaśṛṅgī* the sides would obviously be moved forward, not the centre.

39 Cn Cs state that in this array, the foot-soldiers are in the wings. That is possible, but not certain. 40 Cn Cs have 'infantry in the wings, cavalry in the centre, chariots in the flanks, and elephants in the rear.' The idea of *urasya*, *kakṣa* etc. does not seem intended in this s. and in the next. 41 Cn Cs have 'elephants in the wings, cavalry in the centre, chariots in the flanks and infantry in the rear.' — These arrays seem to be unconnected with the four basic *vyūhas* and are, therefore, separately mentioned.

43 *durjaya* may be the one of s. 22 or of s. 38.

45 *aṅgadaśakasya* : the *aṅga* is the unit as described in 10.5.9-11, viz., 1 chariot (or elephant), 5 horses and 30 infantrymen. — *patikaḥ* : this form is from Cn for *padikaḥ*; it is more appropriate, since it is applicable to all arms. *padika* would refer to an infantry officer only. As Meyer says, this officer corresponds to the lieutenant. — *senāpatiḥ* : this officer here is clearly subordinate to the *nāyaka* and hence cannot be identified with the usual *senāpati* who is one of the highest dignitaries of the state. — The *nāyaka* thus commands 1,000 units as described above. 46 *dhvaja* is a big flag, while *patākā* is smaller.

47 The word *-sāra-* is from the commentators. It seems to be authentic.

48-50 He should strike terror in the enemy with machines, by the employment of occult practices, through assassins slaying those engaged in something else, by magical arts, by (a show of) association with divinities, through carts, by frightening with elephants, by rousing the treasonable, through herds of cattle, by setting fire to camps, by attacks on the tips and in the rear, by creating dissensions through agents appearing as messengers (saying), 'Your fort has been burnt down or captured; a revolt by a member of your family has broken out; or, your enemy or a forest chieftain has risen (against you).'

51 An arrow, discharged by an archer, may kill one person or may not kill (even one); but intellect operated by a wise man would kill even children in the womb.

Herewith ends the Tenth Book of the Arthaśāstra of Kauṭilya
'CONCERNING WAR'

48 *yantraiḥ* is from Cn Cs for *daṇḍaiḥ*; the latter is hardly ever used in the plural. — *śakaṭair hastibhīṣaṇaiḥ* : *-bhīṣaṇaiḥ* is proposed for *-bhūṣaṇaiḥ*. With the latter Cn Cs have 'with carts whose appearance is concealed by accountrements etc. proper for an elephant', i.e., carts decked as elephants. That appears a very strange idea. Meyer proposes *kapaṭair hastidūṣaṇaiḥ* 'with tricks destroying the enemy's elephants.' *bhīṣaṇa*, however, would appear better in view of *vibhīṣikā* and *trāsana* being mentioned among *hastikarmāṇi* in 10.4.14. 49 *goyūthaiḥ* seems to be a reference to 10.3.22. 50 *durgaṁ dagdham* : ordinarily the word *durga* is masculine. — *kopaḥ kulyaḥ* seems to contain a single idea rather than two, 'an insurrection has broken out; a pretender from your family has arisen' (Meyer).

BOOK ELEVEN

POLICY TOWARDS OLIGARCHIES

CHAPTER ONE

SECTION 160 (WAYS OF) RESORTING TO THE POLICY OF (SOWING) DISSENSIONS

SECTION 161 FORMS OF SILENT PUNISHMENT

1 The gain of an oligarchy is best among gains of an army and an ally. 2 For, oligarchies being closely knit are unassailable for enemies. 3 He should win over those of them who are friendly with conciliation and gifts, those hostile through dissensions and force.

4 The Kāmbojas, the Surāṣṭras, the Kṣatriyas, the Śreṇīs and others live by an economic vocation and the profession of arms. 5 The Licchivikas, the Vṛjikas, the Mallakas, the Madrakas, the Kukuras, the Kurus, the Pāñcālas and others make use of the title of kings.

saṁgha is a form of rule evolved from clan rule. Fairly big states were formed with councils of elders to rule over them. The Chapter clearly shows that a *saṁgha* had more than one chief or *mukhya*. In some *saṁghas*, the chiefs styled themselves *rājan* or king. *saṁgha* is best rendered by 'oligarchy'. It seems to be assumed in the Chapter that the *vijigīṣu* has or proposes to have suzerainty over the *saṁghas*, The Chapter is concerned with showing how he should maintain strict control over them.

11.1

The two Sections may be found in ss. 1-30 and 31-54 respectively.

1 *-lābhānām uttamaḥ*: the use of the comparative would have been better. Having a *saṁgha* under you and loyal to you is preferable to having an army of one's own or an ally. Meyer identifies *saṁgha* with *śreṇībala*. But that would be part of *daṇḍa*; moreover, the *saṁghas* enumerated in ss. 4-5 cannot be looked upon as constituting the *śreṇībala* of any king. 2 *saṁhatatvāt*: this is so because the ultimate basis of a *saṁgha* is the clan. 3 *anuguṇa* 'favourable', i.e., friendly to the *vijigīṣu*. — For *viguṇa* in the sense of 'hostile', cf. 7.8.22.

4 *Kāmboja-Surāṣṭra-Kṣatriya-Śreṇyādayaḥ*: As K.P. Jayaswal (*Hindu Polity*, I, 62) argues, the position of *ādi* in the compound is against our understanding 'Kāmboja, Surāṣṭra and other Kṣatriya bands', and that Kṣatriya and Śreṇi must also be understood as proper nouns. He identifies Kṣatriyas with the Xathroi of the Greek historians and Śreṇīs with 'sinae' in Agesinae (i.e., agra-Śreṇī) of those historians. One cannot be sure about the latter. Cn has 'Kṣatriya bands such as Kāmboja and Surāṣṭra and (bands of) other (*varṇas*).' Even for this, *ādi* should have come before *Śreṇī*. — *vārttāśastropajīvinaḥ* i.e., following agriculture and other vocations in peace time, but taking to arms in case of need. 5 *Licchivika-* etc.: for these, see Jayaswal (*op. cit.*, 58-60). The Licchivis, the Vṛjis and the Mallas are well-known from Buddhist and other sources. Kukuras are a member of the Andhaka-Vṛṣṇi league according to the *Mahābhārata*. The Kurus and the Pāñcālas are monarchies in the *Mahābhārata*. Jayaswal has further pointed out that the suffix *-ka* indicates a political group, not a tribe, since it implies loyalty (*bhakti*) to other than one's country of origin, according to Pāṇini 4.3.95-100 and Kātyāyana thereon (*op. cit.*, 120-121). — *rājaśabdopajīvinaḥ*: this simply means that the chiefs who formed the ruling council of the *saṁgha* styled themselves '*rājan*'. Russ. has 'who derive benefit from their royal rank itself.' — Most of the *saṁghas* mentioned belong to the north and the north-west of India. It is also clear that the second group is politically more developed; it is this group that seems to have had a ruling council, which wielded political authority. Kāmboja and others do not seem to have gone much beyond the state of a clan.

6 In the case of all, secret agents close to them should find out one another's defects, and occasions for mutual hatred, enmity or strife among members of the oligarchy, and should sow discord in one who is gradually brought round to believe (them, saying), 'So and so is slandering you.' 7 When resentment is thus built up on both sides, agents serving as teachers should start quarrels among pupils concerning learning, skill, gambling and pleasure sports.

8 Or, assassins should start quarrels among the followers of the chiefs in the oligarchy by praising the opponents in brothels and taverns, or by supporting seducible parties.

9 They should stir up princelings enjoying low comforts with (a longing for) superior comforts.

10 And they should prevent inter-dining or inter-marriage of the superior with the inferior. 11 Or, they should urge inferiors to inter-dining or inter-marrying with superiors. 12 Or, (they should urge) the very low ones to obtain a position of equality in the matter of family, valour or change of status.

13 Or, they should nullify a transaction that is settled by establishing its opposite.

14 Or, in cases of legal dispute, assassins should start quarrels by injuring objects, cattle or men at night.

15 And in all cases of strife, the king should support the weak party with treasury and troops and urge them to kill the rival party. 16 Or, he should carry away those that have been divided. 17 And he should settle groups of five families or ten families of them on land suitable for agriculture.

6 *saṁghānām*, i.e., *saṁghamukhyānām*. It is not a question of one *saṁgha* being set up against another, but of one *mukhya* being set up against another in the same *saṁgha*. — *nyaṅga* seems to stand for *nyaṅgatva*, some defect or deformity. Cn Cs render the word by 'slander', which is doubtful. — *kramābhinītam* 'who has been gradually made to believe what is being suggested to him'. 7 *vaihārika* seems derived from *vihāra* 'pleasure sport'. Cn Cs, however, have 'answering riddles, recondite questions etc.' — *bāla* 'pupils' are the chiefs, who are learning from the so-called *ācāryas*.

8 *saṁghamukhyamanuṣyāṇām* : this may refer to the sevants or followers (*manuṣya*) of the different chiefs in the *saṁgha* or to the chiefs themselves ; in the latter case, *manuṣya* would be superfluous. In the former case, we can understand that the quarrels between the followers would be taken up by the chiefs. — *kṛtyapakṣa* : cf. 1.14.

9 *chandikā* 'pleasure, comfort'. Cn explains by '*paricchada*, retinue, paraphernalia'.

10 *ekapātraṁ vivāhaṁ* as separate words (cf. the next s.) with a *vā* after them are necessary. — It is clear that inter-dining and inter-marriage were not easy even among members of the same *saṁgha*. 12 *avahīnān* : these are apparently even lower than the *hīna*. We have to supply *yojayeyuḥ*.

13 *vyavahāram* 'transaction', rather than 'a legal case' (Cs). — *niśāmayeyuḥ* 'should extinguish,' i.e., make it inoperative. Cs has 'should let the litigant concerned know, by justifying the contrary view'. But *sthāpana* can hardly be mere *samarthana*. It is the upsetting of the *vyavahāra* that is likely to lead to quarrels. 16 *apavāhayet*, i.e., carry them to his own kingdom. That would weaken the *saṁgha*. 17 It is proposed to omit the words *ekadeśe samartān vā niveśya* found in the mss. before *bhūmau*. They contradict s. 18; and *niveśya* and *niveśayet* in the same sentence do not appear likely. — *bhūmau ca* etc. explains what is to be done after *apavāhana*.

18 For, if stationed in one place, they might be capable of bearing arms. 19 And he should fix a penalty if they come together.

20 He should appoint as crown prince a nobly born member of the (ruling) families, who is in disfavour or has been discarded by those using the title of king. 21 And the group of his astrologers and others should declare among members of the oligarchy the possession of marks of royalty by him. 22 And he should instigate the pious chiefs of the oligarchy, (saying) 'Observe your duties towards the son or brother of such and such a king.' 23 When they have agreed, he should send money and troops for supporting the seducible party. 24 At the time of fighting, agents appearing as vintners should offer, in hundreds, jars of wine mixed with a stupefying liquid, as libation to the deceased, under the pretext of the death of a son or wife.

25 And secret agents should point out the depositing (of an object) after an agreement, (such as) sealed (bags) with money and vessels containing money, at the gates of sanctuaries or temples and near fortified places. 26 When members of the oligarchy are seen (approaching), they should declare, 'These belong to the king.' 27 Then he should make an attack.

28 Or, borrowing for temporary use vehicles or money from members of the oligarchy, he should give a well-known article to a chief of the oligarchy. 29 When it is demanded back by them, he should say, 'It has been given to such and such a chief.'

30 By this is explained (the method of creating) dissensions in the (enemy's) camp and among forest chieftains.

20 *rājaputratve sthāpayet*, i.e., should give him recognition as the crown prince. 24 *madanarasa* : cf. 1.18.9 etc.

25 *samayakarmanikṣepam* : this seems to refer to the placing of certain things at the places mentioned for one of the chiefs with whom the king is supposed to arrive at an agreement (*samaya*). The objects placed would seem to be referred to in *sahiraṇya-* etc. In view of *ca*, two things are evidently to be understood, sealed packets with money inside or vessels full of coins. The places mentioned must be supposed to be in charge of the chief who is to be implicated. When the other chiefs find the articles to have come from the king, they come to believe that the particular chief has been bribed. Thus is dissension created. For this *rājakīyāḥ* from Cn is to be preferred to *vikrītāḥ*, which conveys little sense. — *sahiraṇyābhijñānamudrāṇi* : some noun conveying the sense of a bag or packet has to be understood with this. It may also be that we have to read only *bhājanāni* (for *hiraṇyabhājanāni*), and omit the *ca* after it; in this case the compound *sahiraṇya-* etc. would qualify *bhājanāni*. 26 *rājakīyāḥ* : we expect the neuter as describing *bhājanāni*. In the masculine it may refer to the chiefs; in that case, the plural might suggest that a number of chiefs come to take the hoard, these then are declared to be partisans of the king. This, however, appears to be a less likely idea. 27 *avaskandam* : the attack would be in support of the chief implicated, with whom the others may be supposed to have quarrelled. It may also be that the attack is for recovery of the hoard which belongs to the king; but that seems less likely.

28 *prakhyātam* : cf. 9.6.31. Meyer proposes *aprakhyātam*, comparing 9.6.31; but there we have *prakhyātam* and *avijñātam*. — We have to assume that the chief who has received the article does not inform his colleagues. That would lead to strife.

30 This is incidental, unconnected with *saṁghas*.

31 Or, a secret agent should make a son of a chief of the ruling council, who thinks highly of himself, come to believe, 'You are the son of such and such a king, kept here through fear of the enemy.' 32 When he agrees, the king should support him with treasury and troops and make him fight the members of the oligarchy. 33 When his object is achieved, he should get him also slain.

34 Keepers of prostitutes or acrobats, actors, dancers or showmen, employed as agents, should make chiefs of the ruling council infatuated with women possessed of great beauty and youth. 35 When passion is roused in them, they should start quarrels by creating belief (about their love) in one and by going to another, or by forcible abduction (by the other). 36 During the quarrel, assassins should do their work, saying, 'Thus has this passionate fellow been slain.' 37 Or, if the one frustrated puts up with his disappointment, the woman should approach him and say, 'Such and such a chief is harassing me, who am in love with you ; so long as he is alive, I shall not stay here,' and thus urge his murder. 38 Or, the woman, if forcibly abducted, should get the abductor murdered at night by an assassin at the edge of the park or in a pleasure house, or should herself kill him with poison. 39 Then she should proclaim, 'My lover has been killed by so and so.'

40 Or, an agent appearing as a holy man should create confidence in a chief, in whom passion is roused, by means of love-winning herbs and then killing him with poison should disappear. 41 When he has gone away, secret agents should declare that as the act of the other.

42 Or, female secret agents (posing as) rich widows or living by a secret profession, and contending for inheritance or a deposit should infatuate chiefs of the ruling council, or Aditikauśika women or dancers or songstresses

31 *ātmasaṁbhāvitam* etc. : cf. 5.1.15-18 ; some of the tricks mentioned in this Chapter have parallels in Chapter 5.1 33 *pravāsayet* 'should kill' (Cn).

34 *bandhakīpoṣakāḥ* : cf. 5.2.21,28. — *saubhika* would appear to be one who puts up a dramatic or other show on the stage ; cf. 7.17.34. 36 *tīkṣṇāḥ* : these claim to have been employed by the other chief. 39 *amunā* etc. : the other chief is thus implicated in the murder.

40 For the trick and expressions used, cf. 5.1.19. 41 *para*, i.e., the other chief, the rival in love.

41 *ādhyavidhavā* etc. : it seems that *yogastriyaḥ*, i.e., female secret agents, are to pose as rich widows or carry on some secret profession (such as of a sorceress, a counterfeiter of coins etc., as in 4.4). As rich widows they contend for *dāya*, and as *gūḍhājīvāḥ* they contend for a *nikṣepa*. — *aditikauśika-* is from the commentators, read as in 1.17.19. They understand 'women earning their living by showing pictures of deities, and female snake-charmers (*kauśika*)'. But a single idea, 'females dedicated to some deity' might appear better. Russ. renders by 'actresses'. V. Raghavan (*Journal of Oriental Research*, vol. XV, December, 1945, pp. 110-116) objects that mendicant women are very unlikely in the context and suggests that Kauśika (a variant of Kaiśika) is the name of a community devoted to the arts of music, dancing, toilet etc., and frequently engaged in aiding love-affairs ; he compares Kauśikī of the *Mālavikāgnimitra*. But the Kauśikas are Brahmins, and it is extremely doubtful if the women-folk of any Brahmin community were engaged in the sort of work expected of them here. It is impossible to believe that the noble Kauśikī of the *Mālavikāgnimitra* could have played such a role as the one described here. How-

(should do so). 43 When they have agreed and come to secret houses for the night's meeting, assassins should kill them or carry them off imprisoned.

44 Or, a secret agent should describe to a chief of the oligarchy who is fond of women, 'In such and such a village, the family of a poor man has migrated; his wife is fit for a king; seize her.' 45 When she is seized, after a fortnight, an agent appearing as a holy man should cry out in the midst of the chiefs of the treasonable oligarchy, 'That chief has violated my wife or daughter-in-law or sister or daughter.' 46 If the ruling council were to chastise him, the king should support him and make him fight against those hostile to him. 47 If he is not punished, assassins should slay at night the agent appearing as a holy man. 48 Then others appearing in the same disguise should cry out, 'So and so is a Brāhmin-slayer and the paramour of a Brahmin woman.'

49 Or, an agent appearing as an astrologer, should describe a maiden chosen as the bride by one (chief) to another, 'The daughter of so and so is destined to become the wife of a king or the mother of a king; get her by spending all you have or by force.' 50 If she cannot be obtained, he should rouse the other party. 51 If she is obtained, the strife is (at once) brought about.

52 Or, a female mendicant should say to a chief fond of his wife, 'Such and such a chief, conceited by reason of youth, sent me to your wife; through fear of him I have brought a letter and ornaments from him; your wife is innocent; steps against him should be taken secretly; in the meantime I shall accept (on your wife's behalf).'

53 On these and other occasions of strife, whether the strife has arisen of its own accord or has been created by assassins, the king should support the weak party with treasury and troops and make him fight against those hostile to him, or should carry him away.

ever, *kaiśikastriyaḥ* may appear possible. 43 *-praviṣṭān* in the accusative as in Cs is necessary for sense.

44 *apasṛtam*: this has to be understood in the sense of 'that has come away (from some other place).' It is also possible that the idea to be understood is that of *apasṛtamukhyam* 'with the head of the family away from home'. Cn Cs understand 'gone away elsewhere for livelihood'. In the context of what follows that appears less likely. 45 *dūṣyasaṁghamukhyamadhye* is read as suggested by Meyer instead of *dūṣyaḥ saṁgha-* etc. Outside the compound, *dūṣyaḥ* would be a description of the *siddhavyañjana*. But it is doubtful if a real *dūṣya* would be employed to serve as a secret agent in this manner. It is, however, possible that an *abhityakta*, a man condemned to death and apparently reprieved, might be asked to undertake such work. — *asau me* etc.: cf. 5.1.51. — *mukhyo* for *mukhyām* is also from Meyer, and is necessary. *mukhyām* is pointless. 47 *siddhavyañjanaṁ pravāsayeyuḥ*: if the *siddhavyañjana* is not an *abhityakta* as suggested above, this would be a case of a state servant being sacrificed for reasons of state. Perhaps that is why the mss. read *dūṣyaḥ* in s. 45 above. 48 *tadvyañjanāḥ*, i.e., *siddhavyañjanāḥ*.

50 *para*, i.e., the one who had chosen her as his bride.

52 *pratipatsyāmi*, i.e., will make a show of accepting his proposal on your wife's behalf, so that a meeting may be fixed, giving you an opportunity to have your revenge. It can hardly mean 'I shall be by your side till you kill him' (Cs).

54 The single monarch should deal with oligarchies in this manner.

55 The oligarchies also should thus guard themselves against these deceitful tricks by the single monarch.

56 And the head of the oligarchy should remain just in behaviour towards the members of the oligarchy, beneficial (and) agreeable (to them), self-controlled, with devoted men, and following the wishes of all.

Herewith ends the Eleventh Book of the Arthaśāstra of Kauṭilya
'POLICY TOWARDS OLIGARCHIES'

54 *ekarājaḥ* : Kātyāyana on Pāṇini, 4.1.168, distinguishes *ekarāja* the single monarch from a *saṁgha* in which rule is shared by a number of persons. Cf. Jayaswal, *op. cit.*, I, 84.

55 With its usual impartiality, the text offers advice to both sides. — *ekarājād* in the ablative, as read in Cs, is necessary, unless we read *ekarājasya*. — *rakṣeyuḥ* : the object is *ātmānam*.

56 *nyāyavṛttir hitaḥ* as in Cn is decidedly better than *nyāyavṛttihitaḥ* of the mss. — *yukta* may be 'diligent in their work', perhaps also 'attached to him'.

BOOK TWELVE

CONCERNING THE WEAKER KING

CHAPTER ONE

SECTION 162 THE MISSION OF THE ENVOY

1 'A weak king, attacked by a stronger king, should everywhere remain submissive showing the characteristics of a reed. 2 For, he submits to Indra who submits to a stronger king,' says Bhāradvāja.

3 'He should fight with the mobilisation of all troops. 4 For, valour overcomes a calamity. 5 And this is a Kṣatriya's special duty, whether there be victory or defeat in war,' says Viśālākṣa.

6 'No,' says Kauṭilya. 7 One submissive everywhere lives despairing of life like a ram (strayed) from a herd. 8 And one fighting with only a small army perishes like one plunging in the ocean without a boat. 9 He should, however, act finding shelter with a king superior to him or in an unassailable fort.

10 There are three kings who attack: the righteous conqueror, the greedy conqueror and the demoniacal conqueror. 11 Of them, the righteous conqueror is satisfied with submission. 12 He should submit to him, also when there is danger from others. 13 The greedy conqueror is satisfied with the seziure of land and goods. 14 He should yield money to him. 15 The demoniacal conqueror (is satisfied only) with the seizure of land, goods, sons, wives and life. 16 By yielding land and goods to him, he should take counter-steps, remaining out of reach himself.

ābalīyasam is 'what concerns the *abalīyas*, one who is not stronger'. Meyer understands *ā-balīyasam* 'till one gets stronger', which seems grammatically doubtful. The Book, for the most part, expands ideas already found elsewhere, particularly in 7.14-17 above.

12.1

1-2 Cf. *Mahābhārata*, 12.67.11 '*etayopamayā dhīraḥ saṁnameta balīyase, Indrāya sa praṇamate namate yo balīyase.*'

3 *saṁdohena*: cf. 7.4.7,14.

7 *kulaiḍakaḥ*: Meyer proposes *akulaiḍakaḥ* 'a sheep lost from the herd'. Cn Cs get the same meaning from *kulaiḍaka*. Cf. 13.1.16. 9 *tadviśiṣṭam*: *tad* is the *balavān* king. Cf. 7.15.1. — *durgam*: cf. 7.15.9.

10 *dharmalobhāsura-* from Cs is in accordance with the order that follows. 12 *pareṣām api bhayāt*: i.e., even when the *dharmavijayin* is not threatening him, but danger from another source is feared.

17 When one of these is making ready to start, he should make a countermove through peace or diplomatic war or concealed warfare. 18 (He should win over) the party inimical to him with conciliation and gifts, his own party through dissension and force.

19 Secret agents should destroy his fort, country or camp with weapons, poison or fire. 20 He should cause his rear to be attacked from all sides. 21 Or, he should cause the kingdom to be destroyed through forest tribes or to be seized by a pretender from his family or a prince in disfavour. 22 And at the end of (such) injurious acts, he should send an envoy (for peace). 23 Or, peace (may be sued for) without doing any injurious act.

24 If he marches even then, he should sue for peace with a successive increase of one-quarter of the treasury and troops or a successive increase of a day and night.

25 If he were to sue for peace with the offer of troops, he should give him dull elephants and horses, or such energetic ones as are administered poison.

26 If he were to sue for peace with men, he should give him treasonable, alien or forest troops under the command of secret agents. 27 He should so manage that the destruction of both would take place. 28 Or, he should give him troops with a fiery temper which, when insulted, would injure him, or hereditary, loyal troops that would injure him in his calamity.

29 If he were to sue for peace with treasury, he should give him articles of high value, for which he would not find a purchaser, or forest produce that is unfit for use in war.

30 If he were to sue for peace with land, he should give him land which can be easily recovered, or which has constant enemies, or which is without a shelter, or such that settlement on it would involve heavy losses and expenses.

17 *mantrayuddhena* as in 12.2 below. — *kūṭayuddha* does not seem to refer to the tactics on the field described in 10.3 ; for, there is no attack yet on the weak king. Perhaps secret murders are to be understood, as detailed in 12.2-5 below. 18 *asya*, i.e., of the stronger king. — *sva-* also refers to the stronger king. We have to understand the idea of *sādhayet* in the sentence.

24 *pādottaram*, i.e., 'by offering him one quarter more than what was offered before but not accepted ; thus one lac and a quarter if one lac is not accepted or 125 horses if 100 are not accepted' (Cn Cs). — *ahorātrottaram* : Cs has 'increasing the period during which to do a work by more days'. This is not satisfactory. Meyer suggests period for disbanding or surrendering troops to be reduced successively by one day, (i.e., in 9 days instead of 10). This gives a good sense, but it is doubtful if *uttara* can be so understood.

25 *saḥ* : in view of *yāceta*, this is the weak king (Cn Cs), hardly the attacking king (Meyer). The acceptance of the terms by the latter is implied. — *daṇḍa*, as distinguished from *puruṣa* (in s. 26), refers to horses and elephants. — *kuṇṭham* 'ineffective' or 'cowardly'; cf. 7.12.9 ff. — *gara* 'poison, which would kill after a month or a fortnight' (Cs). Cf 14.1.6-7. For the idea, cf. 7.3.30.

27 *ubhaya*, i.e., the enemy as well as the *dūṣyabala* etc.

29 *sāram* etc. : cf. 7.12.16.

30 *nityāmitrām* : cf. 7.10.12. — *anapāśrayām* : the shelter meant is a fortress.

31 Or, he should sue a stronger king for peace with the offer of all his possessions, with the exception of the capital.

32 That which the other might seize by force, he should offer through one of the means. He should preserve his body, not wealth; for, what regret can there be for wealth that is impermanent?

CHAPTER TWO

SECTION 163 FIGHT WITH (THE WEAPON OF) DIPLOMACY

SECTION 164 ASSASSINATION OF (THE ENEMY'S) ARMY CHIEFS

1 If he were not to accept a peace-treaty, he should say to him, 'Such and such kings under the influence of the group of six enemies, have perished; it does not behove you to follow in the foot-steps of those who were without self-control. 2 You should pay regard to spiritual and material well-being. 3 For, those are really enemies, wearing the mask of friends, who make you undertake a rash deed, an impious act and the forgoing of material good. 4 To fight with brave men who have given up all hope of life is a rash deed, to bring about the loss of men on both sides is an impious act, to give up a good in hand and to forsake a blameless ally is forgoing of material good. 5 And that king has allies and with this object he will raise more allies, who will attack you from all sides. 6 Nor is he forsaken by the middle and neutral kings or by the circle of kings; you, however, are forsaken (by them), since, while you are ready to fight, they are looking on (with the idea), "Let him meet with further losses and expenses, let him be divided from his ally; then we shall easily exterminate him when he has left his kingdom". 7 It does not behove you, therefore, to listen to enemies masquerading as friends, to frighten your allies and to confer good on your enemies and to face the risk of (losing your) life and meet with disaster;' thus he should (try to) restrain him.

8 If he starts even then, he should engender a revolt among the constituents as explained in the 'policy towards oligarches' and in 'drawing out

32 *upāyataḥ*: particularly by resorting to *saṁdhi*, as in Cs.

12.2

The first of the two Sections is restricted to ss. 1-7, the rest of the Chapter together with the next is concerned with the other Section. — *mantrayuddha* amounts to cajoling, warning, threatening etc. through an envoy.

1 *sa cet*: this is in continuation of the last Section; *saḥ* is the stronger king. — *śatruṣaḍvarga-*: see 1.6. 3 *mitramukhāḥ* from Cs is quite necessary. *mitramukhyāḥ* of the mss. is unlikely. 5 *sa rājā* is the weak king, for whom the envoy is speaking. — *etena arthena* 'with this object that was offered to you by him, but rejected by you.' *yat tvā* from M is preferable to *ye tvā*. The *ye* in the latter would refer to *madhyama* etc., hardly to *mitramukha amitra* of the next s. as Meyer understands it. — *yacchet*: this seems to be from *yam* 'to restrain, to check'. Cs has 'should give (the object that was offered before)'; but this pressupposes acceptance of the suggestions on the enemy's part.

8 *saṁghavṛtte*: actually in 11.1 there is little about stirring constituents or subjects (*prakṛti*) to revolt. — *yogavāmane*, i.e., in 13.2. 10 *ātmarakṣitake*, i.e., in 1.21.

by means of stratagems'. 9 And he should employ assassins and poison-givers. 10 He should employ assassins and poison-givers at those points which have been declared as fit to be guarded in 'concerning self-protection'.

11 Keepers of prostitutes should make the (enemy's) army chiefs infatuated with women possessed of great beauty and youth. 12 When many or two of the chiefs feel passion for one woman, assassins should create quarrels among them. 13 (Agents) should urge the party worsted in the strife to go away elsewhere or to render help to their master in the expedition.

14 Or, agents appearing as holy men should cause poison to be given to those among the chiefs who are under the influence of passion, along with love-winning medicines, in order to overreach them.

15 Or, an agent appearing as a trader should shower wealth on an intimate maid of the favourite queen (of the enemy) for the sake of love and then leave her. 16 An agent appearing as a holy man, recommended by an agent appearing as an attendant of that same (trader), should give a love-winning medicine, saying, 'This should be placed on the person of the trader.' 17 When this has succeeded, he should advise this remedy also to the favourite queen, saying, 'This should be placed on the king's person.' 18 Then he should overreach with poison.

19 Or, an agent appearing as an astrologer should declare to a high officer, whose confidence has been gradually won, that he is possessed of the marks of a king. 20 A female mendicant (should declare) to his wife, 'You will be the wife of a king or the mother of a king.'

21 Or, a female agent who is the wife of a high officer should say to him, 'The king wants to keep me in his harem; this letter and these ornaments have been brought to your house by a female mendicant.'

11 *bandhakīpoṣakāḥ*: cf. 11.1.34. 13 *bhartuḥ* 'to the master (of the agents)', i.e., to the weaker king.

14 *kāmavaśān vā*: it would have been better if *mukhyeṣu* had come before *kāmavaśān*. Cn seems to have read *kāmavaśād vā*, which cannot be construed properly. In any case Jolly-Schmidt's rendering of it 'under the pretext of giving them an aphrodisiac' is altogether unlikely. Meyer proposes *kāmavaśāḥ (strīḥ)* 'make women under the influence of love administer poison etc.' But it is doubtful if the women, who are merely agents, have to be themselves in love in order that the *siddhavyañjana* may make use of the love-winning potion on the *mukhyas*. The *mukhya* is in love and wants it to be reciprocated by the woman and therefore uses the potion to make himself loved by her. Cf. 11.1.40 for the same trick. If we suppose that the *mukhya* is cold and his passion is to be roused, it is difficult to see how the *siddhavyañjana* could induce him to drink the potion.

16 *vaidehakaśarīre 'vadhātavyā*: in this case, the medicine is apparently used on the person of the individual in whom passion is to be roused. — The *vaidehaka*, of course, pretends to be in love again, so that the power of the medicine is proved. That would induce the queen to try it on the king.

19 *kramābhinītam*: cf. 11.1.6. 20 Cf. 11.1.49.

21 *bhāryāvyañjanā*: we must suppose that a female agent had earlier got herself married to one of the high officials of the enemy; this is a long term plan. The idea that an agent appears in the garb of a wife of the officer is less likely, as the officer would certainly see through the disguise of any one posing as his wife. — *avarodhayiṣyati* clearly refers to making her an inmate of the harem. — *lekhyam ābharaṇam*: cf. 11.1.52.

22 Or, an agent appearing as a cook or a waiter should inform (a chief) about the king's instruction for administering poison (to him) and the money offered to tempt him (to do so). 23 An agent appearing as a trader should corroborate that (information) of his, and should speak of the success of the undertaking.

24 Thus with one or two or three means, he should incite the high officers one by one to fight or to desert him.

25 And in his fortified cities, secret agents serving in close proximity to the Regent, should declare among citizens and country people, (as if) out of friendship, 'The Regent has said to warriors and heads of departments, "The king is in a difficult position; he may or may not come back alive; obtain wealth by force and slay your enemies."' 26 When the rumour has spread far and wide, assassins should rob citizens at night and slay chiefs, (saying at the time), 'Thus are dealt with those who do not obey the Regent.' 27 And they should leave blood-stained weapons, articles and binding ropes in the quarters of the Regent. 28 Then secret agents should proclaim, 'The Regent is slaying and robbing (the subjects).'

29 In the same manner, they should divide the country people from the Administrator. 30 But assassins should kill the subordinates of the Administrator in the midst of villages at night and say, 'Thus are dealt with those who oppress the countryside unrighteously.'

31 When trouble has (thus) started, they should cause the Regent or the Administrator to be killed by a rising of the subjects. 32 They should get a pretender from his family or a prince in disfavour accepted as a ruler.

33 They should set fire to royal palaces and city gates, to stores of articles and grains, or should kill those (officers there) and, crying piteously should declare that as done by him,

22 *rājavacanam* from Cs is necessary in view of the *ca* after *artham*. The enemy king is himself represented as planning the officer's murder through the cook etc. — *abhinayet*: cf. 5.2.25. 23 *kāryasiddhim*, i.e., 'the effectiveness of the poison in killing instantaneously' (Cn Cs). Meyer has 'the successful outcome of the affair (by the officer taking revenge on the king)'; this is little likely. It may simply mean 'success in his work (of selling the poison)'.

24 *ekaikamasya*: *ekaikasya* of the mss. is quite obviously faulty.

25 *maitrīnimittam*: the friendship pretended is for the persons addressed. It can hardly mean 'in order to produce loyalty towards the *śūnyapāla*' (Cs). This loyalty, in fact, is to be undermined. — *bahulībhūte*: the subject is 'report' or 'rumour'. Cf. 12.3.2. — Jayaswal's translation 'when the Pauras held a general meeting (*bahulībhūte*) to give their votes on the subject, the leaders were to be done away with secretly' (*Hindu Polity*, II, 88 ff.) has little relation either to the context or to the words used. — *evaṁ kriyante* etc.: this is in order to throw the blame for the robberies and murders on the *śūnyapāla*.

29 Apparently, the *śūnyapāla* had jurisdiction only in the fort; the *samāhartṛ* continued to wield power in the countryside. 30 *samāhartṛpuruṣān*, i.e., *gopa*, *sthānika* etc.

32 *pratipādayeyuḥ*: cf. 1.10.3.

33 *-dvāram* is a Samāhāradvandva. — *tān* refers to officers stationed there. — *asya* refers to the *śūnyapāla* or the *samāhatṛ* on whom the blame for the fire and murder is to be thrown. It can hardly refer to 'citizens and country people' (Cs).

CHAPTER THREE

SECTION 164 (Continued)

SECTION 165 STIRRING UP THE CIRCLE OF KINGS

1 Secret agents working in close proximity to the (enemy) king and the king's favourites should inform those in the position of friends to chiefs of infantry, cavalry, chariots and elephants that the king is enraged with these, by showing confidence as in a friend. 2 When the rumours have become thick, assassins, after taking precautions against (dangers arising from) moving at night-time, should go to their houses and say, 'At the king's order, come (with us).' 3 They should slay them even as they come out and say to those near, 'This is the king's message.' 4 And to those who have not been slain, secret agents should say, 'This is what we had told you; he who wants to remain alive should go away.'

5 And to those to whom the king does not give (something) when asked for it, secret agents should say, 'The Regent was told by the king, "Such and such persons are asking me for something that ought not to be asked for; refused by me, they have joined the enemy; strive to exterminate them."' 6 Then he should act as before.

7 And to those to whom the king gives (something) when asked for it, secret agents should say, 'The Regent was told by the king, "Such and such persons ask me for something that ought not to be asked for; I gave it to them to ensure trust (in me); they are in league with the enemy; strive to exterminate them."' 8 Then he should act as before.

9 And to those who do not ask him for something that ought to be asked for, secret agents should say, 'The Regent was told by the king, "Such and such persons do not ask me for something which ought to be asked for; what else (could there be) but their being apprehensive because of their own guilt? Strive to exterminate them."' 10 Then he should act as before.

11 By this is explained the whole party of seducible persons.

123.

Section 165 is to be found only in ss. 18-21 as a sort of a tag at the end; it is really a continuation of the preceding topic.

1 *suhṛdviśvāsena*, i.e., divulging it as a secret, which could be done only to a trusted friend. — *mitrasthānīyeṣu*, i.e., to those who are the friends of the *mukhyas* (with whom the king is supposed to be angry). 2 *kṛtarātricārapratīkārāḥ*: e.g., providing themselves with passes for moving in the camp at night time. 3 *āsannān* is from Cs; *āsannāḥ* of the mss. can only go with *tīkṣṇāḥ*, which makes little sense. 4 *ye cāpravāsitāḥ* is as suggested by Meyer. *pravāsita*, either as 'murdered' or 'gone away' does not fit in with *apakrāntavyam* addressed to them.

5 *cāsau* from Cs is missing from the mss. through a scribal error; that it is necessary is shown by ss. 7 and 9. 6 *pūrvavat*, i.e., assassins killing some officers ostensibly under orders from the Regent and frightening away others, as in ss. 2-4.

9 *svadoṣa-*: the *doṣa* is that of treason.

11 *kṛtyapakṣaḥ*: see 1.14 above.

12 Or, a secret agent, serving in close proximity, should give the (enemy) king to understand, 'Such and such a high officer is in communication with men of the enemy.' 13 When this is believed, he should show treasonable men carrying letters from him and say, 'This is it.'

14 Or, after tempting with land or money the principal officers among the chiefs of the army, he should make them fight their own people or should carry them away.

15 He should cause that son of his, who may be staying near or in a fort, to be instigated through a secret agent, 'You are a son possessed of greater personal excellences, yet you have been set aside; why then are you indifferent? Fight and seize (the kingdom); the crown prince will soon destroy you.'

16 After tempting with money a pretender from his family or a prince in disfavour, he should say to him, 'Crush his troops inside (the kingdom) or the troops on the frontier or the frontier fort.'

17 After winning the forest chieftains with money and honour, he should cause his kingdom to be destroyed.

18 Or, he should say to the enemy in the rear of the (enemy), 'This king, after exterminating me, will indeed exterminate you; attack him in the rear; if he turns round on you, I shall attack him in the rear.'

19 Or, he should say to the allies of the (enemy), 'I am your dam; with me broken, this king will overwhelm all of you; let us join together and frustrate his expedition.'

20 And he should send (letters) to those united with him and to those not united, 'This king, after uprooting me, will indeed take action against you; beware; it is better for you to help me.'

12 *saṁbhāṣate*: the passive in the reading of the mss. (*saṁbhāṣyate*) is unnecessary.
13 *dūṣyān* etc.: the bearers of letters are treasonable men, whose rough treatment by the enemy when they are caught would be welcome to the weak king. — *asya*, if referring to the weak king, would be construed with *śāsanaharān*; if referring to the enemy, it would be construed with *darśayet*.

14 *senāmukhyaprakṛtipuruṣān*: this seems to contain a single idea, 'the principal officers (*prakṛtipuruṣa*) among the army chiefs'. Cf. 8.4.15, where we have *prakṛtipuruṣamukhya*. Meyer, in the Nachtrag, has 'army officers and administrative officers in the army'. Russ. has 'army chiefs and officials'. In any case, 'army chiefs, ministers (*prakṛti*) and servants (*puruṣa*)' (Cn Cs) is quite unlikely.

15 *samīpe*, i.e., near the weak king's territory. — *durge*, i.e., in the strong king's capital fort. — *ātmasaṁpannataraḥ*: the comparison is with the *yuvarāja*. — *purā vināśayati*: for the idiom, cf. 9.6.69, also 1.14.8.

16 *antarbalam*, i.e., troops left for the protection of the kingdom. — *antam* seems to refer to the frontier fort, the place for the *antapāla*. Cn explains it by *janapada* etc.; Cs reads *anyam*, supplying *skandham* from the preceding, 'other troops'. That is far from happy.

18-19 Through an obvious copyist's slip, the words *eṣa khalu . . . vā 'sya brūyāt* (in ss. 18-19) are missing in the mss., showing that they are all derived from a single exemplar. Cn presupposes the passage which is quite necessary. *ahaṁ vaḥ setuḥ* could not be addressed to a *pārṣṇigrāha*.

20 *abhyupapattum* is read for *abhyavapattum*; the latter has the sense of 'to submit to, to surrender', from which the former must be distinguished. Cf. 2.10.24,25 and 5.5.7.

21 He should send (appeals) to the middle king or again to the neutral king, according as the one or the other may be near, making a surrender to him of all possessions, in order to be saved.

CHAPTER FOUR

SECTION 166 SECRET USE OF WEAPONS, FIRE AND POISON

SECTION 167 DESTRUCTION OF (THE ENEMY'S) SUPPLIES, REINFORCEMENTS AND FORAGING RAIDS

1 And those agents who are living disguised as traders in the fortified towns of the (enemy), disguised as householders in his villages, disguised as cow-herds and ascetics in the frontier posts of the country, should send, along with presents (word) to a neighbouring prince, a forest chief, a pretender from his family or a prince in disfavour, 'This region can be seized.' 2 And when secret agents of these have come to the fortified town, they should welcome them with money and honour and show them the weak points of the constituents. 3 They should strike at those (weak points) along with them.

4 Or, an agent appearing as a vintner in his camp, showing a person condemned to death as his son and killing him by poison at the time of an attack should offer, in hundreds, jars of wine as libation in honour of the dead. 5 He should give on the first day unadulterated wine or wine with one quarter (poison), on the next, (wine) mixed with poison. 6 Or, giving unadulterated wine to the army chiefs, he should give them (wine) mixed with poison when they are in a state of intoxication.

7 Or, an agent, serving as a chief in the army, (should show) a condemned person as a son and so on, as before.

8 Or, agents disguised as dealers in cooked meat or cooked rice or vintners or dealers in cakes, should advertise their special goods and, in mutual ri-

21 *sarvasvena tadarpaṇam*: what seems meant is *sarvasvasya tadarpaṇena*. Cs seems to have read *tvadarpaṇam*, though its text shows *tadarpaṇam*. One can hardly look upon *tadarpaṇam* as the object of *prahiṇuyūt* as in Cn Cs.

12.4

The whole Chapter really contains a single Section, the second of the two Sections being disposed of in half of s. 20 in the middle of the Chapter.

1 *janapadasaṁdhi*: see 3.1.1. — *paṇyāgāra*: cf. 7.15.20 etc. — *ayaṁ deśaḥ*: this is some region in the enemy's country. 2 *durge*, i.e., in the enemy's fortified capital.

4 For the trick, cf. 11.1.24. — *madanamadya-* found in the mss. is unlikely in view of the details given in the next s. *madya-* alone is therefore proposed. 5 *pādyam* seems to mean 'with one-quarter *madanarasa*, the rest wine'. Cs has 'with a quarter of the dose sufficient to kill a person'. Meyer's suggestion to read *māndyam* 'very mild' seems hardly plausible. The expression is odd; it is quite possible that the words *pādyaṁ vā madyam* are due to a scribal error and are not authentic. Cn does not show them.

7 *daṇḍamukhyavyañjano*: this presupposes a secret agent serving in the enemy's army as an officer for quite some time. A mere disguise would not be convincing and might even arouse suspicion.

8 *kālikam*: cf. 2.25.7. — *apacārayeyuḥ* is read and understood in the sense of 'mix'.

valry, call the enemies, proclaiming 'This is given on credit, this is very cheap,' and mix their goods with poison.

9 Or, women and children, purchasing wine, milk, curds, butter or oil from dealers in these commodities, should pour them in their own vessels containing poison. 10 (Saying) 'Give us at this price, or give us of better quality again,' they should pour that back in the same place. 11 Agents appearing as traders or those who bring goods for sale (to the camp, should sell) these same articles (after mixing them with poison).

12 Those near should mix poison with the fodder and grass for elephants and horses. 13 Or, agents appearing as workmen should sell grass or water mixed with poison.

14 Or, cattle-traders, long associated (with the camp), should let loose herds of cattle or of sheep and goats on the occasion of an attack, in places likely to cause confusion among the enemies, also (should let loose) the vicious among horses, donkeys, camels, buffaloes and other animals. 15 Or, agents appearing as above (should let loose) animals whose eyes have been smeared with the blood of musk-rats. 16 Or, those appearing as hunters should let loose wild animals from their cages, or snake charmers, serpents with deadly poison, or those living by elephants, elephants. 17 Or, those living by fire should set fire to things.

18 Or, secret agents should kill the chiefs of infantry, cavalry, chariots or elephants when they have turned back, or should set fire to the quarters of the chiefs.

19 Those appearing as treasonable or alien or forest troops, being employed (with the enemy), should make an attack on the rear or give support to the (weak king's) attack.

9 *tadvyavahartṛhasteṣu* is from Cs, though *hasta* is not quite necessary. Perhaps *tadvyavahartṛṣu* should be read, as in ms. T. In either case, however, we expect the ablative rather than the locative. 10 *viśiṣṭam*, i.e., better in quality. — *tatraiva*, i.e., in the containers of the shopkeepers. The whole stock of the shopkeepers becomes poisoned, to be sold later to the troops by the unsuspecting shopkeepers. 11 *etānyeva* seems to refer to *surā, ksīra* etc., 'poisoned' being understood and *vikrīṇīran* being supplied. The liquids as poisoned by the women need not be understood; for, the *vaidehakavyañjanas* could themselves procure poisoned goods. — *paṇyavikrayeṇa āhartāraḥ* seems to mean something like hawkers, as Meyer implies. *paṇyāni vikrayārtham āhartāraḥ* is what seems intended. — Cn comes to an end with this s.

14 *mohasthāneṣu* 'in places where the enemy ranks are thereby likely to be thrown into confusion'. Cs has 'when the enemy is at his wit's end as to what to do'. 15 *tadvyañjanāḥ*: *tad* refers to the *govāṇijaka*. — *cucchundariśoṇitāktākṣān*: apparently this makes the animals mad. Cf. 14.1.29.

18 *vimukhān* 'who are turning back from the battle, who are in flight'.

19 *dūṣyāmitrāṭavikavyañjanāḥ*: the idea is, loyal troops go over as deserters from the weak king, some of them his own troops pretending to be treasonable, others alien and still others forest troops. The unsuspecting enemy welcomes them. — *pratigraha* is 'giving support'. Cf. 13.3.46.

20 Or, those concealed in forests should lure out troops on the frontier and slay them, or (should destroy) the supplies, the reinforcements and foraging raids on a path where march in a single file alone is possible.

21 Or, on the occasion of a night-battle, they should strike many drums, fixed beforehand as a signal, and announce, ' We have entered it ; the kingdom is won.'

22 Or, entering the king's quarters, they shoud kill the king in the tumult. 23 Or, if he is trying to escape, leaders of Mleccha and forest troops, on all sides, should kill him, taking cover in places of ambush or taking cover behind hedges of tree-stems. 24 Or, agents appearing as hunters should, in the tumult of an attack, strike at him on occasions fit for secret fight. 25 Or, they should strike at him when he is on a path where march in a single file alone is possible or on a mountain, or behind a hedge of tree-stems or in a marshy place or inside water, in accordance with the favourableness of the terrain to themselves. 26 Or, they should drown him through a rush of water by breaking dams in rivers, lakes and tanks. 27 Or, if he is in a desert fort, a forest fort or a water fort, they should destroy him with poisonous fire and smoke. 28 Assassins should do away with him by fire when he is in a narrow place, by smoke when he is in a desert, by poison if he is in his residence, by frightful crocodiles or persons moving in water if he has taken a plunge in water, or (kill him) as he is coming out of his quarters set on fire.

29 He should overreach the enemy, clinging to the places mentioned, by forcing him out through trickery and by secret practices or by using one of the secret tricks.

21 *saṁketa* is a signal fixed with the weak king before the night attack. — *brūyuḥ* : the subject seems to be the so-called deserters from the weak king. We must suppose them to be somewhere else in the enemy's kingdom, probably in the capital. When they cry *labdhaṁ rājyam*, the enemy may be expected to give up the fight and return to the kingdom to save it.

23 *stambhavāṭa* seems to mean a hedge or fence made of tree-stems. 24 *gūḍhayuddha* is not the same as *kūṭayuddha* (10.3). It is murder pure and simple. 25 Some mss. show *stambhavanā-* here for *stambhavāṭā-* (Cs). The latter may be preferred in view of s. 23. — *khañjana* : cf. 10.4.8. 26 It seems that *setubandhabheda* is to be construed with *nadī*, *saras* and *taṭāka* though *vega* is conceivable of a river even without a dam breaking. 27 *yogāgnidhūma* : see 14.1.4-14. 28 *nidhāna* is little more than ' residence, abode ' ; ' storehouse ' or ' treasure-house ' seems less likely. — *udakacaraṇaiḥ* : see 13.1.3-5 for ways of moving in water.

29 *yogavāmana* is described in 13.2 below. — *yoga* refers to the *yogātisaṁdhāna* of the next Chapter (Cs). — *yogenānyatamena vā* : this *yoga* would seem to refer to the tricks described in this Chapter. — *uktāsu bhūmiṣu* seems to refer to *saṁkaṭa* etc. of s. 28, perhaps also to ss. 23 ff.

CHAPTER FIVE

SECTION 168 OVER-REACHING (THE ENEMY) BY TRICKERY

SECTION 169 OVER-REACHING (THE ENEMY) BY FORCE

SECTION 170 VICTORY OF THE SINGLE KING

1 On the occasion of a festival in honour of a deity, (there may be) many places for the enemy's coming to worship because of his devotion. 2 In those places, he should practise secret tricks on him. 3 When he has entered the temple, he should cause a concealed wall or a huge stone to fall on him by the release of a mechanism. 4 Or, he should cause to be dropped down on him a shower of stones and weapons from an upper chamber, or a door panel thrown down or a door-bar placed in a wall and fixed at one end. 5 Or, he should cause the image, the banner and the weapons of the deity to fall upon him. 6 Or, in the places where he stays, sits or moves about, he should cause poison to be used along with the cow-dung smearing or with the scented water used for sprinkling on the floor, or with the offering of flowers and fragrant powder. 7 Or, he should carry over to him poisonous smoke concealed by perfume. 8 Or, he should make him drop down, by the release of a pin, into a well with spikes or a pit, underneath the bed or seat, where the floor is fixed by a mechanism.

9 Or, when the enemy has come near, he should carry over (into the fort) persons capable of withstanding a siege from the countryside. 10 And from the fort he should remove those incapable of withstanding a siege or send them to the enemy's territory which is easily recoverable. 11 And he should place the country people in one place in a mountain fort, a forest fort or a river fort, or in regions separated by forests, in charge of a son or a brother.

12.5

The three Sections are closely inter-related and there is no clear demarcation line between them; at most we can say that the third begins at s. 43. *eka* in *ekavijayaḥ* refers to the king being alone, with his fort in the enemy's possession.

1 *daivatejyāyāṁ yātrāyām* : Cs Meyer have 'on the occasion of the worship of a deity or of a festival'; however, in the absence of a *ca* or a *vā*, a single idea would appear better. — *pūjāgama-* is proposed for *pūjyāgama-* ; *pūjya* in the latter is little likely. — *bhaktitaḥ* : Meyer construes this word with the next s. That seems less happy. 2 *ubjayet* : Cs paraphrases by *prasārayet* 'should spread'. Cf. s. 15 below. 6 *puṣpacūrṇa-* : these would be offered as *prasāda* to the enemy. 7 For poisonous smoke, cf. 14.1.9-14. 8 *yantrabaddhatalam* : the *tala* is the floor of the room ; it sinks down when the pin is removed, and the bed or seat topples down into the well full of spikes.

9 *avarodhakṣamam* : Cs has 'people from the enemy's country who are fit to be put in confinement'; that appears very strange. 10 *anavarodhakṣamam* etc. : the explanation in Cs 'should set free those not deserving to be confined, yet confined by the enemy' is still more strange. Can the weak king be supposed to bring about the release of such men when the enemy is drawing near ? —*pratyādeyam* etc. : this is his own land, now in enemy occupation, which he hopes to recover later. 11 *putrabhrātṛ-* : these are those of the weak king. Cs, however, understands the enemy's son etc. being placed in charge of his territory after dividing it. Would the weak king be able to do so ? Cs is on a wrong track. The idea here is of preparing for a siege.

12 Reasons for entrenching oneself in a fort have been explained in 'the conduct of one surrendering with troops'.

13 He should cause grass and wood to be burnt up to one *yojana* (all round the fort). 14 And he should cause waters to be spoiled and to flow away. 15 And he should place wells, concealed pits and barbed wires outside.

16 Making an underground passage with many openings up to the enemy's camp, he should cause the chiefs of stores to be carried away, or the enemy (himself). 17 Or, if an underground passage is made by the enemy, he should cause the moat to be dug deeper till its water reaches the passage, or a well-shed along the rampart. 18 In suspected places, he should cause to be placed jars of water or bell-metal vessels, in order to find out any digging done there. 19 When the underground passage is known, he should cause a counter-passage to be dug. 20 Breaking it in the middle, he should let in smoke or water.

21 Or, making arrangements for the defence of the fort, and appointing a kinsman (as regent) in the base, he should go in the direction opposite to that of the (enemy), or where he might be united with allies, kinsmen or forest chiefs or with great enemies and traitors of the enemy, or where, by going there, he might be able to separate him from his allies or to attack him in the rear or cause his kingdom to be seized or to prevent his supplies, reinforcements and foraging raids, or from where he might be able to strike at him with a foul throw like a gambler, or from where his kingdom may be protected or he might be able to strengthen the base. 22 Or, he should go there where he might be able to secure desirable peace.

23 Or, those who have left (the fort) with him should send (word) to the (enemy), 'This enemy of yours has fallen in our hands; on the pretext of (the purchase of) a commodity or of (doing) injury, send money and a strong

12 *avarodha-* is found here as in s. 9. However, since the title of the 119th Section has *uparodhahetavaḥ*, we should retain *uparodha-* here. The *hetus* are enumerated in 7.15.12.

15 *kūpakūṭāvapāta-* etc.: cf. 2.3.15 and 10.1.12. — *ubjayet*: see s. 2.

16 *nicayamukhyān* 'chiefs of stores' is not very satisfactory. Perhaps 'supplies (*nicaya*) and army-chiefs (*mukhya*)' is meant; but then the compound would be unusual. Cs has *vicayamukhyān* 'chief inspecting officers' which is little better. 17 *udakāntikīm* 'ending in water' implies water reaching down to the *suruṅgā* and flooding it. — *kūpa-śālām*: i.e., a well is to be dug for flooding the passage. *śālā* is unusual with *kūpa*. 18 *toyakumbhān* is proposed for *atoyakumbhān*; since *kāṁsyabhāṇḍāni* may be supposed to contain no water, indicating only by their vibrations if digging is going on, *atoyakumbhas* would not materially differ from them. The water in the *toyakumbhas* may be supposed to indicate digging by its movement or by spilling over. 20 *madhye bhittvā*: the enemy's tunnel is breached and then flooded.

21 *mūle*, i.e., in the fort. — *ākṣikavad apakṣepeṇa* 'with a foul throw like a gambler'. This is not very satisfactory; but that appears to be the only meaning possible. Meyer's suggested *āśmikapādapakṣepeṇa* 'by throwing stones and trees' is quite fanciful.

23 *paṇyam*: the idea is that the weak king, who is supposed to be held in custody by his associates, is offered to the besieging king for a price, as a commodity for sale. For the

force, to which we should hand him over, bound or killed.' 24 When he agrees, he should appropriate the money and the strong force.

25 Or, the commander of a frontier fort, by offering the surrender of the fort, should get a part of the (enemy's) troops inside and destroy them when full of trust.

26 Or, (the regent) should invite a division of the enemy's army to destroy the country people stationed in one place. 27 Taking it to the enclosed region, he should destroy it when full of trust.

28 Or, an agent posing as a friend should send (word) to the besieger, 'In this fort, grains, fats, sugar or salt is exhausted; (new stocks of) it will come in at this place and time; seize it.' 29 Then treasonable, alien or forest troops should bring in poisoned grains, fats, sugar or salt, or others condemned to death (should bring it in). 30 By that is explained the seizure of all goods and supplies.

31 Or, making peace, he should give him a part of the (tribute-) money, the rest after a long delay. 32 Then he should cause his fortifications to be weakened. 33 Or, he should strike with fire, poison or weapon. 34 Or, he should favour those of his favourites who (come to) receive the money.

35 Or, if quite exhausted, he should surrender the fort to him and depart. 36 He should go out by an underground passage or an opening in the rampart, breaking through the side.

37 Making a sudden assault at night, he should remain if successful; if not successful he should go out by some stratagem. 38 In the disguise of a heretical monk, he should go out with a small retinue. 39 Or, he should be carried out decked as a corpse by secret agents. 40 Or, wearing a woman's garb, he should follow a funeral procession. 41 Or, (he should go away)

idea, cf. 8.2.8 etc. The *hiraṇya* asked for represents this price. The army is asked for ostensibly for taking charge of the weak king and to fight if the latter's troops offer any resistance.

25 *balaikadeśam atinīya* : these come in to take over the surrendered fort.

26 *āvāhayet* : the subject would be the son or the brother of s. 11, who is in charge of the people and is a sort of a regent in the place. 27 *avaruddhadeśam* : this apparently refers to the region to which the people have been taken, as in s. 11.

28 *bāhya* is the king outside the fort who has laid siege to it. 29 *dūṣyāmitrāṭavikāḥ* : these, if caught by the enemy, would not be a source of worry to the besieged king.

32 *rakṣāvidhānāni* ; these are arrangements for the defence of his kingdom by the enemy. — *avasrāvayet* : cf. 9.4.8. 34 *hiraṇyapratigrāhiṇaḥ* : Cs has 'who are used to receiving bribes' with *anugṛhṇīyāt* as 'should give a bribe (so that they may strike at their master)'. This is little likely. *hiraṇya* is the stipulated tribute which the *vallabhas* come to receive; the bribe is given so that they may go back without the tribute.

36 *kukṣipradareṇa* etc. : apparently, the enemy troops are mainly concentrated at the gates for entering the fort, so that an escape through a hole in the side of the wall would not be noticed.

37 *pārśvena* 'by the side', i.e., by a stratagem or trick to be presently described (Cs). 38 For this and the following tricks, cf. 7.17.50-52 and 44. 41 The stop after *avasṛjya* is as proposed by Meyer; Cs reads ss. 41-42 as one. It is doubtful, however, if the two ideas,

leaving behind poisoned food and drink on occasions of offerings to gods, obsequial rites or festivals.

42 After making secret instigations, he should come out with apparently treasonable troops and strike with the concealed army.

43 Or, if his fort is thus seized, he should, after setting up a sanctuary with plenty of food to eat, remain concealed in a hollow inside the image of the deity or in a hollow wall or in an underground chamber endowed with the image of a deity. 44 When (things are) forgotten, he should enter the king's chamber at night by an underground passage and kill the sleeping enemy. 45 Or, loosening something that can be loosened by a mechanism, he should make it fall down (on him). 46 Or, as the enemy is sleeping in a house smeared with a poisonous fire-mixture or in a lac-house, he should set it on fire. 47 Or, when the (enemy) is careless in a place of recreation in a pleasure park or other recreation grounds, assassins, entering through underground chambers or tunnels or hollow walls, should slay him, or those employed in secret service (should do so) by poison. 48 Or, when he is sleeping in a secluded place, female secret agents should drop on him serpents or poisonous fire and smoke.

49 Or, when an occasion arises, he should, moving about secretly, use everything that may be possible against the enemy staying in the palace. 50 Then he should go away in a secret manner, and give signals to his own men.

51 Calling by signals of drums door-keepers, eunuchs and others secretly employed with the enemy, he should get the rest of the enemies killed.

Herewith ends the Twelfth Book of the Arthaśāstra of Kauṭilya
'CONCERNING THE WEAKER KING'

leaving poisoned food and attacking with a concealed army can be combined. After *avasṛjya*, we should supply *nirgacchet*. For this idea, cf. 7.17.44. The king would allow the poisoned food to fall into the hands of enemy troops who come in, while he makes good his escape.

42 The idea seems to be that secret agents assure the enemy that the army of the weak king is *dūṣya*; the officers, in fact, are in touch with the enemy, pretending to be traitors. When he comes out for the attack with these supposed traitors, the enemy thinks that the troops will desert and come over to him; as he is negligent in view of this expectation, the troops, firm in loyalty, overwhelm him. *gūḍhasainyaḥ* seems to mean that the army is concealed in the appearance of *dūṣyas*. An army concealed somewhere outside the fort is conceivable, but does not appear very likely.

43 *prāśyaprāśam* seems intended as an adjective to *caityam*. The expression is awkward. As two words it could mean 'having eaten food' which is hardly likely. — *daivatapratimāchidram*: cf. 13.1.3. The image must be assumed to be fairly big, with openings for ventilation. — *gūḍhabhittim* 'a hollow wall' in the palace itself. — *daivatapratimā-* etc. the cellar has the image of a deity covering its entrance, so that its existence is not suspected by the enemy occupying the palace. Cf. 1.20.2. 45 *yantraviśleṣaṇam*: a substantive such as *kapāṭam* or *parigham* is to be understood. 46 *avaliptaṁ gṛham* as well as *jatugṛham* would be prepared before leaving the palace.

50 *apagacchet*: the reason for this is not obvious, perhaps to escape being regarded as a murderer. It is possible that *āgacchet* was the original reading. — *svajanasaṁjñām*: the signals are fixed with his own men in the palace, who continue in service with the occupying enemy.

51 *pare* is from Cs; *paraiḥ* of the mss. is unlikely. Similarly, *ghātayet* from Cs is preferable to *kārayet*. In any case, Meyer's 'should make (*kārayet*) only a few enemies left (*dviṣaccheṣāṇi*)' is hardly possible.

Book Thirteen

MEANS OF TAKING A FORT

CHAPTER ONE

SECTION 171 INSTIGATION TO SEDITION

1 The conqueror, desirous of capturing the enemy's (fortified) town, should fill his own side with enthusiasm and fill the enemy's side with terror, by getting his omniscience and association with divinities proclaimed.

2 The proclamation of omniscience, however, (is to be made thus): after ascertaining secret information from their houses, communicating it to the chiefs; after finding out through spies used in suppression of criminals, bringing to light traitors to the king; announcing a request or a present (about to be made) through unnoticed signs and other things according to the science of association; (showing) knowledge of news from foreign lands on the same day through a domestic pigeon carrying a sealed communication.

3 The proclamation of association with divinities, however, (should be arranged thus): conversing with and worshipping agents appearing as deities in fire-sanctuaries, who have entered the hollow images of deities in fire-sanctuaries by an underground passage; or, conversing with and worshipping agents appearing as Nāgas or Varuṇa risen from the water; showing a row of fires at night inside water by placing a container with sea-sand; standing on a boat held down by slings containing stones; application to the nose of

Cj (on 1.1.15) says '*lambha* for *lābha* is a wrong form grammatically.' — The capture of enemy forts is recommended mostly through stratagems.

13.1

1 *grāma* refers to the *durga* or the fortified capital. The reference to *pāragrāmika yoga* in 1.18.10 and 9.3.18 and to the *pāragrāmika* Section in 5.1.3 is clearly to details found in this Book. — *sarvajña-* stands for *sarvajñatva-*, as elsewhere.

2 *pratyādeśaḥ* 'communicating'; for this sense of the root, cf. 1.11.3, also 4.5.14. — *-avagamena* is proposed for *-āgamena* or *-apagamena* of the mss. For the sense 'knowing, finding out,' *avagama* is clearly preferable. — *vijñāpyopāyana-* seems to contain two ideas 'a request to be made (*vijñāpya*) and presents to be given (*upāyana*).' It could hardly mean 'a present about to be offered (*vijñāpya*)' (Cs) or 'information (*upāyana*) yet to be communicated to the king (*vijñāpya*)' (Meyer). — For *saṁsargavidyā*, see 1.12.1. *adṛṣṭa* is to be construed with *saṁjñā*, in the sense of 'not noticed by others'. — *gṛhakapotena*: this would be sent by agents working in foreign lands.

3 *agnicaityadaivatapratimā* is clearly an image of the fire-god in a temple dedicated to him. The image must be assumed to be fairly big to accommodate a human being inside. — *-hariṇa-* in the mss. for *-varuṇa-* is an obvious corruption. — *samudravālukākośam* is not clear. Cs has 'bags of sand with their mouths sewn up'; how these are to produce fire in water is not explained. 14.2.36 states that *samudraphena* smeared with oil floats on water and burns. Perhaps that is meant here, though the words contain no reference to it. *kośa* seems to mean 'container'; *-kośān* in the plural might have been expected to create the illusion of *agnimālā*. — *udaka-* is strange with *basti*. Perhaps some aquatic animal is meant;

oil boiled a hundred times with the entrails of a spotted deer or the fats of crabs, crocodiles, dolphins and otters, to a person whose head without the nose is covered with water-bladder or an embryo-covering. 4 With that, the group of nocturnal creatures moves about. 5 These are ways of moving in water. 6 Through them (there is) use of speech by Varuṇa or by Nāga maidens and conversation (with them, and) the emitting of fire and smoke from the mouth on occasions of anger.

7 Soothsayers, interpreters of omens, astrologers, reciters of Purāṇas, seers, and secret agents, those who have helped and those who have witnessed it, should broadcast that (power) of the (king) in his own territory. 8 In the enemy's territory, they should speak about his meeting with divinities and the acquisiton of a treasury and army from a divine source. 9 And when interpreting questions to deities, omens, crows' flight, the science of the body, dreams and utterances of animals and birds, they should predict victory for him, the reverse of it for the enemy. 10 And they should point to a meteor in the enemy's constellation with a beat of drum.

11 Agents working as envoys, speaking to the chiefs of the enemy out of friendship, should tell them of the king's high regard for them, of the strengthening of his own party and the deterioration of the enemy's party. 12 They should tell ministers and soldiers of the same well-being and security (as before). 13 He should show consideration for them in calamities and on festive occasions, and honour their children.

udakāhi of 14.3.67 is possible, but not certain. — *śirovagūḍhanāsaḥ* is also an odd expression. What seems meant is that the head is covered, leaving the nose out (to make it appear blazing). 'With the nose covered along with the head' (Cs) could hardly have been meant. As *nastaḥ prayogaḥ* is obviously to be construed with this expression, the genitive would have been better; or should we read *-nasaḥ* (in the genitive singular from *nas* 'nose')? — *-vasābhir vā*: the *vā* apparently shows the option between *pṛṣatāntra* and the *vasā* of the various animals. — *tailam*: we expect the instrumental, since it is this oil applied to the nose that will apparently make it glow. The whole clause appears loosely constructed. 5 *udakacaraṇāni*, i.e., moving in water or on the surface of water. 6 *agnidhūmotsargaḥ* as described in 14.2.34.

7 *sācivyakarāḥ*, i.e., those who have helped him in manipulating these tricks. 9 *vāyasa* is 'crows' flight' rather than their cries. — *aṅgavidyā*: see 1.12.1. 10 *sadundubhim* cannot be included in s. 9 (as is done in Cs), as fortune-telling with drum-beats does not appear likely. — *ulkām*: this is managed artificially as in 14.2.30. — *parasya nakṣatre* i.e., when the moon is in the birth constellation of the enemy.

11 *svāmisatkāram*, i.e., regard felt by the *vijigīṣu* for the particular *mukhya* of the enemy; it can hardly mean 'honour done to the *dūta*-agent (described so as to tempt the *mykhya*)' (Cs). — *svapakṣabalādhānam*: this and the following expression are construed in Cs with *tulyayogakṣemam* in the next s., the explanation being 'should declare *svapakṣabalādhāna* and *parapakṣapratighāta* as leading to a gain and security (*yogakṣema*) for ministers and soldiers, equal to that of the king himself (*tulyam*, i.e., *rājñā samānam*)'. This is hardly satisfactory, particularly the equality with the king. Meyer understands by *tulya* the same prosperity for ministers and soldiers, which would hardly tempt the *mukhyas*. *tulya* seems to refer to the same position as now enjoyed by them, though it must be confessed that this by itself would hardly be a sufficient temptation to change sides. 13 *apatyapūjanam*: according to Cs, this is done after the death of the *mukhya*. This is unlikely; the *vijigīṣu* would not be interested in their children for their own sake. Honouring the children is only a means of winning over the father.

14 In that way he should stir up the enemy's party (against him) as explained before. 15 And we shall explain further. 16 (He should stir up) the diligent by (speaking of) the ordinary donkey ; the leaders of the army, by the stick and the striking of the branch ; those frightened, by the ram (strayed) from the herd ; those insulted, by a shower of thunder-bolts ; those with hopes frustrated, by the cane bearing no fruit, balls of rice to crows and the cloud created by magic ; those receiving the reward of honour, by decoration of a disliked wife by one who hates ; those secretly put to test, by the tiger-skin and the death-trap ; those who constantly oblige, by the eating of the *pīlu*-fruit, the hail, the female camel and churning of the she-donkey's milk.

17 Those who agree (to desert), he should endow with money and honour. 18 And in their difficulties regarding goods and food, he should favour them with gifts of goods and food. 19 In the case of those not accepting (these), they should bring ornaments to their women and children.

20 And on occasions of famine, or troubles by robbers or forest tribes, secret agents, stirring up the citizens and the country people, should say, 'Let us ask the king for help ; if we do not get help, let us go elsewhere.'

21 When, saying 'All right', they agree, help should be given to them by the grant of goods and grains. Thus there is this great miracle of secret instigation.

14 *purastāt*, i.e., in 1.14.6 ff. 16 *sādhāraṇagardabhena*, i.e., by comparing them with a donkey that labours without getting adequate compensation. — *lakuṭaśākhāhananābhyām*, i.e., comparing them to a stick which strikes a branch so that others may get the fruits ; so a general fights so that the king may enjoy himself. — *kulaiḍakena* : cf. 12.1.7 ; the suggestion is, like such a ram, he may be caught any time and killed. — *aśanivarṣeṇa* implying that an insult is like a thunder-bolt. — *vidulena avakeśinā*, i.e., by comparing the enemy king with a reed that promises but does not bear fruit. — *vāyasapiṇḍena* i.e., by comparing what is given by the king with an offering to a crow, suggesting its meagreness as well as contempt for the recipient. Cs understands *vā āyasapiṇḍena* 'or, an uneatable lump of iron'; that is very doubtful. — *kaitavajameghena* : by comparing the king with a magic cloud from which there is no rain. — *durbhagālaṁkāreṇa dveṣiṇeti* (this last is from Cs for *dveṣiṇo 'ti*) The king is compared to a husband who dislikes his wife and yet provides her with ornaments etc.; *dveṣiṇā* describes the king or the husband. *dvesiṇaḥ* in the other reading would describe the *mukhyas*, who would also appear as *atipūjāphalān*. But if they are already full of hate for the king, no instigation would be necessary in their case. *atipūjā* also appears doubtful. The explanation in Cs 'those honoured by the king, by speaking of the gift (*alaṁkāra*) being defective (*durbhaga*) or that the king is displeased (*dveṣiṇā*)' is however, quite unlikely. *durbhagā* is contrasted with *subhagā* of 8.4.24 etc. Cf. '*durbhagā patisneharahitā*' (*Trikāṇḍaśeṣa*). — *vyāghracarmaṇā*, i.e., suggesting that the king is ferocious like a tiger. — *upahitān* : this has reference to the *upadhās* of 1.10. — *pīluvikhādanena* : *pīlu* is a kind of fruit which apparently provides no nourishment, but is only a source of trouble ; so is *upakāra* conferred on this king. — *karakā* 'hail' is understood as a kind of bitter vegetable in Cs, as a water-jug by Meyer. A hail-stone may signify harmfulness or uselessness. — *uṣṭryā* : this also is a kind of bitter plant, according to Cs. One may understand the female camel as being useless for purposes of milk. — *gardabhī-* etc. apparently signifies great effort with no return. — *dhruvopakāriṇaḥ* is an emendation from Meyer. *dhruvāpakāriṇaḥ* 'constantly doing harm' seems little likely in the context.

18 *chidra* clearly refers to want or lack of the things mentioned.

21 *parigraha* seems to have the sense of 'favouring', i.e., granting or giving.

CHAPTER TWO

SECTION 172 DRAWING OUT (THE ENEMY) BY MEANS OF STRATAGEMS

1 An ascetic with shaven head or with matted locks, living in a mountain cave, (and) declaring himself to be four hundred years old, should stay in the vicinity of the city with plenty of disciples with matted locks. 2 And his disciples, approaching with roots and fruits, should induce the ministers and the king to pay a visit to the holy master. 3 And, visited by the king, he should speak of identification marks of former kings and their countries, (adding), 'When every one hundred years of my life are completed, I enter fire and become a child again; so here in your presence, I shall enter fire for the fourth time; you have necessarily to be honoured by me; choose three boons.' 4 When he agrees, he should say, 'You should stay here with sons and wife for seven nights, after arranging a festival with shows.' 5 He should attack him while he is staying there.

6 Or, an agent appearing as a seer of underground objects, with shaven head or with matted hair, having plenty of disciples with matted hair, should place in an ant-hill a bamboo-strip smeared with goat's blood, after smearing it with gold powder, in order that ants may follow it, or (place there) a hollow tube of gold. 7 Then a secret agent should tell the king, 'That holy man knows a flowering treasure-trove.' 8 Questioned by the king, he should say, 'Yes,' and point out that proof, or after placing more money in the earth. 9 And he should say to him, 'This treasure-trove, guarded by a cobra, can be obtained through worship.' 10 When he agrees, 'for seven nights' and so on as before.

11 Or, as an agent appearing as a seer of underground objects, with his body enveloped in a burning fire at night, is staying in a solitary place, secret

13.2

vāmana 'emptying' refers to forcing the enemy king out of his fort and then getting him killed. Meyer understands 'emptying' to imply weakening of the king. But *vamana* refers to movement from one place to another; cf. 2.1.1. *vāmana* is the causal of that.

1 *nagara-* is the enemy's capital. 3 *abhijñānāni*: these are, of course, learnt from history. — *bhavān mānayitavyaḥ* is from Cs; *bhavānānayitavyaḥ* of the mss. is an obvious corruption. 5 *avaskandeta*: the subject is the *vijigīṣu*.

6 *sthānika*, as the context shows, seems to mean one who is able to see what is underground in any particular place (*sthāna*); the usual meaning of a divisional officer is out of the question. Russ. has *sthāṇika* 'one who constantly stays in one place.' — *bastaśoṇita-* is from Cs for the unlikely *vastraśoṇita* of the mss. — *upajihvikānusaraṇārtham*: apparently the ants would be attracted by the goat's blood and their presence may be regarded as an indication of a treasure-trove there. It is however, quite likely that the absence of ants would indicate the presence of a cobra and the treasure guarded by him and that the goat's blood is in order to drive away ants. For this *-apasaraṇārtham* would have to be read. 7 *puṣpitaṁ nidhim*: On the strength of parallels from other folk-tales, Meyer thinks that a light is supposed to appear at the place, indicating that the treasure is flowering, i.e., shooting forth and growing, the flower being the *śalākā* or *nālikā*. 8 *bhūyo vā hiraṇyamādhāya*: this may be in place of or in addition to the *śalākā* or *nālikā* of s. 6. 10 *samānam*, i.e., as in ss. 4-5.

11 *tejanāgni* is described in 14.2.18-26. — *kramābhinītam*: 'faith in whom is gradually created'; the meaning is slightly different from that in 11.1.6 and 12.2.19. — *sāmedhikaḥ*: cf. 1.11.16.

agents should say to the king after making him gradually entertain faith (in him), 'That holy man is able to secure prosperity.' 12 Promising to ensure what object the king were to ask for, (the seer should say), 'for seven nights' and so on as before.

13 Or, an agent appearing as a holy man should tempt the king with magical lores. 14 'What object the king' and so on as before.

15 Or, an agent appearing as a holy man, finding shelter in (the temple of) an honoured deity of the country, should, by frequent festivities, win over the chiefs among the constituents and gradually overreach the king.

16 Or, as an agent appearing as an ascetic with matted locks, all white, is staying in water, with means of getting away to an underground tunnel or chamber under the bank, secret agents should tell the king, after gradually making him believe, that he is Varuṇa or the King of Nāgas. 17 'What object the king' and so on as before.

18 Or, an agent appearing as a holy man, living on the border of the country, should induce the king to have a sight of the enemy. 19 When he agrees, he should make an effigy and invoke the enemy, and should kill the king, in a secluded spot.

20 Agents appearing as traders, coming with horses for sale, should invite the king to purchase or receive horses as a gift, and kill him while engrossed in inspecting the goods or when mingled with horses and should strike with the horses.

21 Or, assassins, climbing a sacred tree near the city at night-time and blowing into jars through stalks or reeds, should say indistinctly, 'We shall eat the flesh of the king or the chiefs; let worship be offered to us.' 22 Agents appearing as interpreters of omens and astrologers should make that (utterance) of theirs known.

15 *abhyarhitām*, i.e., worshipped by all the people there. — *abhisaṁvāsya*: making them stay with him and thus creating confidence in him. Cf. *saṁvāsya* 5.1.19; 11.1.40.

16 *taṭasuruṅgā-* from Cs is clearly necesary; *tadasuruṅgā-* of the mss. conveys little sense.

18 *śatrudarśanāya*: the *darśana* is for working on his effigy for black magic. 19 *bimbam* is the enemy's effigy, and *āvāhayitvā* refers to 'invoking' the enemy to come and be present in the effigy. It is this 'presence' that is apparently to be held responsible for the death of the king. Cs has 'giving a sign (*bimba*) and bringing in the enemy (in person)'. It is doubtful if the *vijigīṣu* is intended to be brought face to face with the enemy.

20 *paṇyopāyananimittam*: two separate purposes, sale and gift, are intended. — *aśvaiś ca prahareyuḥ*: after killing him themselves, they get him trampled upon by horses, so that his death would appear as being due to a stampede of horses.

21 *caityam*, i.e., *caityavṛkṣam*. — *nālīn vā vidulāni*: the *vā* is misplaced; it should have come after *vidulāni*. The idea seems to be to muffle the voice by blowing through hollow reeds into jars, so that it would sound as the voice of a spirit. Cs, reading *vidalāni*, has 'by burning as incense (*dhamantaḥ*) grain-stalls (*nālīn*) and splinters of wood (*vidalāni*)'. It is doubtful if incense-smoke can be supposed to be created by spirits. Meyer suggests *vādayantaḥ* in place of *vā* 'playing on the reeds in the pots or blowing into rattan-sticks'. This does not seem meant. 22 After this, some rite is recommended to the enemy, during the course of which he is to be murdered. See ss. 33-34 below.

23 Or, agents appearing as Nāgas, with their bodies smeared with burning oil, should, at night-time, pound together iron clubs and pestles in a holy lake or in the middle of a tank and utter in the same way.

24 Or, agents robed in the skins of bears, giving out fire and smoke (from the mouths), and having the appearance of Rākṣasas, should go three times left-wise round the city and utter in the same way, in the intervals between the cries of dogs and jackals.

25 Or, making the image of a deity in a sanctuary burn at night with burning oil or with fire covered by a layer of mica, (agents) should utter in the same way. 26 Others should make that known.

27 Or, with blood (of animals) they should cause an excessive flow (of blood) from honoured images of deities. 28 Then others should declare defeat in battle in consequence of the flow of the blood of the deity.

29 Or, on the nights of the month's junctures, they should point out a sanctuary in a prominent part of the cemetary as with men eaten standing. 30 Thereafter an agent appearing as a Rākṣasa should demand the offering of a human being. 31 And whoever, calling himself brave or some one else, were to come there to see, others should kill him with iron pestles, so that it would be known that he was killed by the Rākṣasas. 32 Those who have witnessed it and secret agents should report that miracle to the king. 33 Then agents appearing as interpreters of omens and astrologers should prescribe pacificatory and expiatory rites (adding), 'Otherwise a great disaster will befall the king and the country.' 34 When he has agreed, they should say, 'In these (manifestations), for seven nights the king himself should make offerings of oblations with *mantras* on each single day.' 35 Then as before.

36 Or, showing these tricks practised on himself, he should overcome them, in order to convince the enemies. 37 Then he should employ the tricks (against them).

23 *tejanataila* as described in 14.2.25.

24 *agnidhūmotsarga* from the mouth, as described in 14.2.34. — *apasavyam*: see 1.20.4. — *śvasṛgāla-* is from Cs for *śivāsṛgāla-*: the latter may mean 'female and male jackals'; but the expression appears doubtful. The cries of the animals may be supposed to have been also imitated.

25 *abhrapaṭalacchannena agninā*: Meyer thinks that the mere application of mica would make the image burn at night. But the wording presupposes an inflammatory substance covered by mica.

29 *saṁdhirātriṣu*, i.e., full moon and new moon nights, particularly the latter. — *ūrdhvabhakṣitair* 'eaten upright', i.e., eaten while they are alive, as in Meyer. Cs has 'with the upper part of the body eaten ' which appears less likely. 34 *eteṣu* refers to all the manifestations mentioned above in ss. 21 onwards. — *ekaika* seems to refer to *bali* or *homa* on each one of the seven days. Meyer has 'one single chant, offering and oblation, for seven days.'

36 *Pareṣām upadeśārtham*, i.e., to show to the enemy that the manifestations can be successfully overcome and so to induce him to take the same measures when the manifestations are produced in his state, so that he could then be done away with. *pareṣām* can hardly refer to his own men, as Cs understands. It is unlikely that the king would be teaching these tricks to his servants. Meyer proposes *apadeśārtham* 'in order to have a pretext for using them against the enemies'; that is not necessary at all.

38 Or, by overcoming occult manifestations, he should replenish the treasury.

39 Keepers of elephant forests should tempt the (enemy) fond of elephants with an elephant possessed of auspicious marks. 40 When he agrees, they should take him to a dense forest or a path allowing only one person to march at a time, and kill him, or carry him off imprisoned. 41 By that is explained the (enemy) fond of hunting.

42 Or, secret agents should tempt the (enemy) greedy of money or women with rich widows (or) women possessed of great beauty and youth, taken to him for the sake of inheritance or deposit. 43 When he agrees, they should, concealed in ambush, kill him with weapon or poison at the time of the meeting.

44 Or, on the occasions of his frequent visits to holy men, mendicants, images of deities in sanctuaries and *stūpas*, assassins, concealed in underground chambers or passages or inside hollow walls, should strike at the enemy.

45 In those places, in which the king himself is witnessing a dramatic show, or is enjoying himself in a festival or where he is sporting in water;

46 On all occasions of speaking words of reproof and so on, during sacrifices and festive parties, during birth-rites, funeral rites and illnesses, on occasions of love, sorrow or fear;

47 Or, when at a festival of his own people he, being full of trust, becomes careless, or when he moves about without a guard, on a rainy day or in crowds;

48-49 When he has strayed from the route, or when there is a fire or when he has entered a place without any men in it, assassins, entering with packages of clothes, ornaments and flowers, with beds and seats, or with vessels containing wine and food or with musical instruments, should strike at the enemy along with those employed there beforehand.

38 This s. is repeated from 5.2.45 and is really out of place here.

39 Cs rightly compares the capture of Udayana by Pradyota's men.

42 As it appears that women of great beauty and youth are to be distinguished from rich widows, it would be better to read the *vā* after *paramarūpayauvanābhiḥ* instead of after *āḍhyavidhavābhiḥ*. It is also possible, however, that *paramarūpa-* etc. only further describes the rich widows themselves. — *dāyanikṣepārtham* is proposed as in 11.1.42; there is little doubt that *dāyāda* 'heir' is unlikely. A *vivāda* with respect to *dāya* or *nikṣepa* is meant. 43 *sattracchannāḥ* is as proposed by Meyer; *sattricchannāḥ* of the mss. is little likely., *sattracchanna* is, in fact, a paraphrase of *sattrin*.

45 *yāḥ* (in *yāḥ prekṣāḥ*) has little significance. — *yātrāvihāre*: Meyer thinks that we should read *yatra vihāre*, since *yātrā* as 'festival' is not common in this text. But that is not correct. For *yātrāvihāra*, cf. 7.15.22 and for *yātrā* 1.21.28 and 12.5.1.

46 *dhiguktyādiṣu sarveṣu*: Cs reads *cāṭūktyādiṣu kṛtyeṣu* 'on occasions of panegyrics and on ceremonial occasions.' Meyer proposes *ṛguktyādiṣu* 'on occasions when *ṛcs* are recited.' This is little likely.

48 *viprasthāne*, i.e., when he has missed the road and is lost. 49 *abhigatāḥ* is an emendation from Meyer; *abhihataiḥ* of the mss. implies that drums would be beaten when killing the enemy, which would be strange. And *abhigatāḥ* is necessary in itself. — *arim* in the singular is also from Meyer; that is in conformity with the singulars in the earlier clauses.

50 And in the same way as they may have entered on the occasions for an ambush of the enemy, they should depart. Thus has been described the drawing out (of the enemy) by stratagems.

CHAPTER THREE

SECTION 173 EMPLOYMENT OF SECRET AGENTS

1 He should make a trustworthy chief of a band (ostensibly) desert him. 2 Finding shelter with the enemy, he should bring over helpmates and associates from his own country on the pretext of their being his (own) party. 3 Or, bringing about an influx of secret agents, he should, after securing the enemy's consent, destroy a treasonable town of his master, or an army devoid of elephants and horses with treasonable officers, or a (treasonable) ally in the rear (of his master), and should send word to the enemy. 4 Or, he should resort to a part of the country or a band or forest chiefs for obtaining help. 5 Winning (the enemy's) confidence he should send word to his master. 6 Then the master, pretending (an expedition for) catching elephants or destruction of forest tribes, should attack secretly.

7 By this are explained ministers and forest chiefs.

8 After making friends with the enemy, he should dismiss (some) ministers. 9 They should send a request to his enemy, 'Propitiate the master for us.' 10 He should upbraid the messenger whom he might send (with such a request), 'Your master is dividing me from the ministers; you should not come here again.' 11 Then he should make one minister desert him. 12 Finding shelter with the enemy, he should bring to the notice of

50 *dviṣataḥ*: Cs understands this as accusative plural construed with *praviśeyuḥ*; that is not a happy construction. It is obviously genitive singular to be construed with *sattrahetubhiḥ*. These latter refer to the occasions enumerated in the preceding stanzas. — *tathaiva*, i.e., with the *phelās* as in ss. 48-49.

13.3

1 *śreṇī* here obviously refers to the *śreṇībala*. — *niṣpātayet*: cf. 9.6.35. That passage describes a similar stratagem. See also ss. 11 ff. below. 3 *vītahastyaśvaṁ dūṣyāmātyam*: cf. 10.5.49. — With *ākrandam*, we have to understand *dūṣya* from the preceding. — The object is two-fold, to get rid of the *dūṣyas* and at the same time to convince the enemy that he really has become hostile to his old master. 4 *janapadaikadeśam* etc.: this seems to mean that instead of attacking the *dūṣyagrāma* etc. of his old master, he goes to the countryside of the enemy to raise troops for him. These troops would be under him, so that he is in a position to get them destroyed by inviting a secret attack by his old master. Cs, however, understands the idea in this and the next s. as follows, 'he should secretly go to the country etc. to receive them as helpmates for his old master; when after receiving them he feels confidence in them, he should send them to his old master.' This is altogether unlikely. *viśvāsa* in the next s. refers to the trust which the enemy would be placing in the 'deserter', not the latter's confidence in the troops. And *preṣayet* is as usual only 'should send word'; cf.12.5.23, also ss. 9,10,17 below. Besides, it is unlikely that enemy's men are here intended to be won over to the *vijigīṣu*'s side. The idea here is that of preparing for a secret attack on the enemy. 6 *gūḍham eva praharet*: the 'deserting' *śreṇīmukhya* would, of course, be helping in this attack to destroy the enemy's troops.

8 *avakṣipet*: cf 1.10.2. 10 *sa yam* from Cs is clearly necessary for *svayam*. 11 *athaikam* etc.: for this stratagem, cf. 9.6.35-41. 12 *yogāpasarpa* seems to mean 'agents who have turned traitors' to the *vijigīṣu*. These and the *aparakta* and *dūṣya* are brought

the enemy treacherous spies, the disaffected and the treasonable, who are weak, or robbers and forest chiefs who harass both (kingdoms). 13 Winning (thus) a position of trust, he should bring to his notice the offence of brave men (of the enemy, such as) a frontier officer or a forest chief or a leader of the army, saying, 'So and so is surely in league with your enemy.' 14 Then afterwards he should get them killed through letters carried by men condemned to death.

15 Or, he should get him destroyed by rousing the enemy with the use of armed forces.

16 Or, by supporting the seducible party, he should make the king who is the enemy's enemy do injury to himself and then should attack him. 17 Then he should send word to the enemy, 'This enemy of yours is doing injury to me; come, let us join forces and destroy him; you will have a share in (his) land or money.' 18 If he agrees and comes after honouring (these words), he should get him killed by the enemy in a sudden assault or in open battle. 19 Or, under the pretext of giving land or crowning his son or giving protection, in order to create confidence, he should get him seized. 20 Or, if he is unassailable, he should get him killed by silent punishment. 21 If he were to lend a force and not come himself, he should get it destroyed by his enemy. 22 Or, if he were to desire to march with troops, but not with the conqueror, even then he should get him destroyed by a squeezing from both sides. 23 Or, if, full of distrust, he were to wish to march, each separately, or were desirous of seizing a part of the territory of the king against whom they are marching, even then he should get him killed by the enemy or by mobilising all his troops. 24 Or, when he is engaged in a fight with the enemy, he should get his base seized from another direction by sending troops (there).

25 Or, he should bargain with the ally with the (offer of the) enemy's land, or with the enemy with the (offer of the) ally's land. 26 Then making the ally do injury to himself when seeking to seize the enemy's land, he should attack him and so on, all the tricks exactly as before.

to the notice of the enemy by the deserting *amātya* in order to win his confidence. — *aśaktimataḥ*: the point seems to be that even if the enemy takes them in service, they will not be much use to him. — *parasya upaharet* can hardly mean 'should present to the enemy as helpmates'; it could not possibly apply to the *stena* and *āṭavika* who harass both kingdoms. 13 *pravīrapuruṣopaghāta* is 'injury by brave men,' i.e., some offence of theirs. *antapāla* etc. illustrate *pravīrapuruṣa* and *śatruṇā saṁdhatte* illustrates the *upaghāta*.

15 *daṇḍabalavyavahāreṇa*: cf. 8.1.34,38. — *śatrum* seems to be the enemy's enemy, though there is no *asya* to show that. The ss. that follow illustrate this s. The enemy himself as the object of *udyojya* appears little likely in the context.

16 *kṛtyapakṣopagraha* is the reason why the enemy's enemy would be doing injury to the *vijigīṣu*, who would then attack in retaliation. 17 *parigrahaḥ* 'allotment' or assignment of a share. 19 *abhiviśvāsanārtham*: this is when he is not killed, but is successful in defeating his enemy. He is invited to receive the promised share of land or get his son crowned there and so on. 20 *aviṣahyam* refers primarily to the fort in which he is safe. 22 *ubhyataḥsaṁpīḍanena*, i.e., between himself and the enemy's enemy.

25 *mitram*: this is the *vijigīṣu*'s ally as in Cs. 26 *sarva eva yogāḥ*, i.e., those of ss. 17-24, substituting *me mitram* for *te vairī* in 17.

27 Or, he should help with troops the enemy, who has agreed, when he is seeking to seize the ally's land. 28 Then he should overreach him, as he marches against the ally.

29 Or, after taking remedial measures, he should show a calamity for himself, and rousing the enemy through the ally, should get him to attack himself. 30 Then he should destroy him by squeezing or, catching him alive, make an exchange of the kingdom (for his life).

31 If, sheltered by the ally, the enemy were to wish to remain out of reach, he should get his base seized by a neighbouring prince and so on. 32 Or, if he were to seek to protect it with troops, he should cause those to be destroyed.

33 If the two were not to become estranged, he should quite openly bargain with each other's land. 34 Then agents posing as friends or those in the pay of both should send messengers to one or the other, 'This king wants to seize your land, being in league with the enemy.' 35 (If) one of them is filled with apprehension or anger, he should act as before.

36 Or, he should banish chiefs of the fort or the country or the army, after proclaiming the grounds for their being the seducible party. 37 They should overreach the enemy in a battle or a sudden assault or a siege or a calamity. 38 Or, they should bring about his estrangement from his own groups. 39 They should get corroboration through letters carried by men condemned to death.

40 Or, secret agents appearing as hunters, remaining at the gates for the sale of meat, and given shelter by gate-keepers, should win the enemy's confidence by informing him of the approach of dacoits two or three times, (then) getting their master's army stationed in two places, one for destroying a town and the other for a sudden assault, should say to the enemies, 'A band

29 *tataḥ pratividhānena* of the mss. is not right, since this trick is not connected with the preceding as would be implied by *tataḥ*. — *mitreṇa* : this again is the *vijigīṣu*'s ally ; he is to urge the enemy to attack the *vijigīṣu* because of the pretended *vyasana*. 30 *sampīḍanena*, i.e., between his ally and himself ; cf. s. 22.

31 *mitreṇa āśritaḥ* : this is equivalent to *mitram āśritaḥ*, the ally being that of the enemy. The latter has gone to the ally's capital. — *agrāhye* 'in a position where he cannot be captured'. *agrāhyaḥ*, might appear better as in 12.1.16. — *trātum* : the object is *mūlam*.

33 *tau*, i.e., the enemy and his ally. — *-bhūmyā* in the instrumental is preferable to *-bhūmyām* ; cf. s. 25. 34 *parasparam* is not from the enemy to the ally and *vice versa*, but to the enemy or to the ally from third parties. — *mitravyañjanā ubhayavetanā vā* : in view of *vā*, two separate words are proposed in place of a single compound. 35 *jātāśaṅkārosaḥ* etc. : we have to supply *cet* with this, for the subject for *ceṣṭeta* is *vijigīṣuḥ*.

36 *kṛtyapakṣahetus* are mentioned in 1.14. — *pravrājayet* : the banishment is for hoodwinking the enemy, who unsuspectingly gives them shelter. 37 *avarodha* : cf. 12.5.9, 10. 38 *svavargebhyaḥ* : these would be the enemy's own chiefs or officers.

40 *māṁsavikrayeṇa dvāḥsthāḥ* : apparently the hunters remained outside the gates to avoid duty. — *grāmavadhe* : one part of the *vijigīṣu*'s troops is assigned the task of attacking a town (other than the *durga*) as dacoits, the other is intended for an assault on the

of robbers is close by; there is a great din; let a large force come.' 41 Handing that over to the troops (of their master) meant for destroying the town and taking the other troops to the gates of the fort at night, (they) should say, 'The band of robbers is killed; the troops, successful in the expedition, have come back; open the gate.' 42 Or, those secretly employed there beforehand should open the gates. 43 Along with them they should strike.

44 Or, he should station in the enemy's fort soldiers disguised as artisans, artists, heretical monks, actors and traders. 45 Agents appearing as householders should bring to them weapons and armours in carts carrying wood, grass, grains and other goods, or in flags and images of gods. 46 Then those disguised like them (should carry out) the slaughter of the unwary, the supporting of sudden assault, or a strike in the rear, or should announce by the sound of conches and drums, 'The (army of the enemy) has come in.' 47 They should open rampart-gates and towers, divide the enemy's divisions or destroy them.

48 The carrying over of troops (into the enemy's fort) is to be along with those moving in caravans or groups, with escorts, with those accompanying brides, with dealers in horses, with carriers of implements, with sellers or purchasers of grains, with those bearing the marks of monks and with envoys; peace is to be made (during the period) for creating confidence.

49 These are secret agents for (outwitting) the king.

durga. — *dviṣataḥ*: the plural has in view the officers in the enemy's fort. 41 *tad*, i.e., the large force of the enemy. — *arpayitvā* suggests absence of any fight, as the enemy's troops realise that they have been tricked. — *itarad*, i.e., that meant for the *avaskanda*. — The explanation in Cs is much beside the point and bristles with difficulties. The *pratyaya* won is supposed to be that of the master (not of the enemy), *grāmavadhe* and *avaskande* are understood as 'for defending against an attack on the town and against an assault,' the handing over is supposed to be for the purpose of warding off the attack on the town, and the hunters themselves are supposed 'to kill the enemy troops so that those who want to leave the fort may do so easily'; all this implies that a real attack by robbers is visualised, which is hardly conceivable.

44 *āyudhīyān* here and *praharaṇāvaraṇāni* in the next s. are from Cs and are obviously the only correct readings. 45 *dhvaja*: spears could be brought in with flags. 46 *tadvyañjanāḥ*: *tad* may refer to *kāru* etc. and *gṛhapatika*. It is also possible that it has reference to enemy troops, suggesting the putting on of their uniform. — *pṛṣṭhataḥ*: after this *kuryḥ* is to be understood. In fact, the words *pramatta* - . . . *pṛṣṭhataḥ* do not seem to to belong to this s. and should preferably be read at the beginning of the next s. In that case *tadvyañjana* might refer to putting on the appearance of those whose duty it is to announce something to the sound of conches etc. Cs construes *pramattavadham* etc. with *praviṣṭam* 'should announce that *pramattavadha* etc. has appeared in the rear.' That is extremely doubtful. — *vā* seems to show the option between *śaṅkha* and *dundubhi*. 47 *ghāta* is preferable to *pāta* in connection with the *anīkas*.

48 *ātivāhikaiḥ*: these are escorts for merchants etc. A fee is charged for this; cf. 2.16.18. Cs has 'those who want protection on difficult roads', treating it as an adjective to the other six clauses. That is quite unlikely. — *-kretṛvikretṛbhir vā*: in view of the *ca* at the end, *vā* seems to show the option between *kretṛ* and *vikretṛ*. — *dyūtaiḥ* in the mss. is an obvious corruption. — *atinayanam*: cf. 7.14.24. Cs has 'carrying enemy troops very far by pretending to escort them'. It would be a very strange army that would allow itself to be led astray by bridal processions and grain merchants. — *saṁdhikarma*: this is while the soldiers are being smuggled in.

50 These same are agents for forest tribes, also those mentioned in 'the suppression of criminals'. 51 Secret agents should cause a herd of cattle or a caravan in the vicinity of a forest to be destroyed by robbers. 52 And making the food and drink placed there, in accordance with an agreement, mixed with a stupefying liquid, they should go away. 53 Then cowherds and traders should cause the robbers carrying loads of stolen goods to be attacked when the stupefying liquid is having its effect.

54 Or, an agent appearing as an ascetic with shaven head or with matted locks and posing as a devotee of god Saṁkarṣaṇa, should overreach (the forest robbers) by using a stupefying liquid after holding a festival. 55 Then he should make an attack.

56 Or, an agent appearing as a vintner should overreach foresters by using a stupefying liquid on the occasion of the sale or presentation of wine during festivities in honour of gods or funeral rites or festive gatherings. 57 Then he should make an attack.

58 Or, after scattering in many groups the forest tribes that have come for plundering the town, he should destroy them. Thus secret agents for robbers have been described.

CHAPTER FOUR

SECTION 174 THE WORK OF LAYING SIEGE (TO A FORT)
SECTION 175 STORMING (A FORT)

1 The work of laying siege (to a fort) should be preceded by weakening (the enemy).

2 He should grant safety to the countryside as it may have been settled. 3 He should induce those, who have risen, to settle down through favours

51 *apasarpāḥ* etc. : the agents win the confidence of the robber-bands and get them to attack a caravan etc. At the same time they get the merchants etc. to agree to poison their food etc. and let it fall in the hands of the robbers, who would be partaking of that, to their own cost. 52 *apagaccheyuḥ* : the subject would be *gopālakavaidehakāḥ*, rather than *apasarpāḥ*. It would be better to read *gopālakavaidehakāḥ* at the beginning of s. 52 instead of s. 53. 53 *corān* and *-bhārān* in the accusative is an emendation from Meyer ; the accusative is quite necessary, as object for *avaskandayeyuḥ*.

54 *Saṁkarṣaṇadaivatīyo* is from Cs ; *-yogā* at the end is a corruption. Saṁkarṣaṇa or Balarāma is represented as fond of wine, which may be supposed to be freely used in a festival in his honour. — Both here and in s. 56, *-yogena* is read for *-yogām* or *-yogābhyām*, in conformity with 1.18.9. There is no point in the use of the dual.

56 *upāyana* 'present' rather than 'bringing in (for sale)' (Cs) or 'arrival (of the vintner for sale)' (Meyer). Cf. 13.2.20 above.

58 *apasarpāḥ* are principally agents who ingratiate themselves with persons whose ruin is to be brought about.

13.4

The two Sections are found in ss. 1-24 and 25-53 ; the last few ss. discuss the order in which conquest of lands should be made.

1 *karśana-* is described in ss. 6-7.

2 *abhaye* from Cs is clearly the original reading. 3 *utthitam* : the rising is not in revolt against the conqueror, but only to get out of his way to make room for military operations.

and exemptions, excepting those who go away. 4 He should settle them on land away from the battle-field or make them stay in one region. 5 For, there is no country without people and no kingdom without a country, says Kauṭilya.

6 He should destroy the sowings or crops of one entrenched in an inaccessible fort, also his supplies and foraging raids.

> 7 By cutting off foraging raids and supplies, also by destroying sowings and crops, by removing (from their place) and by secret murder, a deterioration of the constituents takes place.

8 (When he thinks), 'My troops are fully supplied with abundant and excellent grains, forest produce, machines, weapons, armours, labourers and ropes ; the season is favourable (to me), unfavourable to the enemy ; (he is suffering from) a deterioration of his stores and fortifications through diseases and famine, there is weariness among his purchased troops and weariness among the ally's troops ; ' then he should lay siege.

9 After securing the protection of the camp, of supplies and reinforcements and of the roads, he should encircle the fort along the moat and the rampart, defile the water, empty the moats or fill them, and cause the parapet and the rampart to be taken by means of an underground passage and storming by troops, and the breach by means of elephant-armour. 10 He should fill hollows with piles of earth. 11 He should destroy with machines

Russ. has *utthita* 'who love their work', obviously connecting it with *utthāna* 'energetic activity.' — *anugraha-* etc. : cf. 2.1.15. — *anyatra apasarataḥ* : the exception is that of those who wish to go away and do not wish to live under the conqueror. 4 *saṁgrāmād anyasyāṁ bhūmau* (*saṁgrāmād* is from Meyer for *saṁgrāmam*) : the idea seems to be that the people who are to be settled should be settled where there is going to be no battle. With *saṁgrāmam*, Russ. has *anyasyām* 'other than where agriculturists live.' It is possible to construe *anyatra apasarataḥ* with this s., i.e., those who move away from their lands should be settled in a place where there is going to be no battle. Meyer, who has this punctuation, explains 'those who have run away from other places'; for this last clause, *anyataḥ* would be expected. Cs reads *samagram* and has 'those over and above (the number engaged in agriculture, *utthita*)'. This is highly problematical. 5 The point of this dictum is that the *vijigīṣu*, while engaged in conquest, should see to it that the country is not ravaged nor the people exterminated ; otherwise the conquest will be fruitless.

6 *viṣama* refers to the inaccessible fort, not to any difficulty or danger.

7 *vamanād* : cf. 2.1.1. — *prakṛti* 'constituents' rather than 'subjects'.

8 *raśmi* may be ropes (for scaling ?) or reins. — *vyādhi* and *durbhikṣa* are the causes that have led to the *kṣaya* of *nicaya* and *rakṣā*. — For some of the expressions, cf. 10.2.13.

9 *suruṅgābalakuṭikābhyām* is obscure. In spite of the dual, Cs has a single idea 'army huts (*sainyapallībhiḥ*) dug crosswise in the ground'. What this means is hard to make out. Meyer renders *balakuṭikā* by 'a sort of vinea (?)' ; he also suggests 'a false wall' or 'a strong hammering'. Russ. has 'dug-outs (mud-huts) for one's own troops.' Can it mean 'a sudden storming by troops'? — *dāram* : this refers to a breach in the wall. With this *hārayet* is to be understood from the preceding. Cs understands *ācchādayet* from what follows and, with *gula* in the sense of 'a lump for covering', has 'should cover the breach with a lump'. Why the besieger should cover the breach is not clear. *guḍa* (which is the form preferred) is given the sense of 'an elephant's armour' in the *Medinī* ; it is possible to understand the storming of the breach with armoured elephants. *gulena* 'with unwieldy objects' (Russ.) Meyer proposes *dvāram* for *dāram*, in which case we can understand the idea of storming the gate with elephants. *bahulena* is a faulty reading. 10 *nimnaṁ vā* : *vā* serves

what is guarded with many troops. 12 Dragging out (soldiers) from the runway exit, they should strike with horses. 13 And in the intervals between fighting, he should seek success by the exclusive, alternate or combined use of the (four) means.

14 Getting hawks, crows, pheasants, kites, parrots, *śārikās*, owls and pigeons, with nests in the fort, caught, he should release them in the enemy's fort with fire-mixtures tied to the tails. 15 Or, from the camp stationed at a distance (from the fort) he should set fire to the enemy's fort with human fire, being guarded by bows with flags raised aloft. 16 And secret agents, serving as guards inside the fort, should place a fire-mixture in the tails of ichneumons, monkeys, cats and dogs, and let them loose in stores of reeds, fortifications and houses. 17 Placing fire in the interior of dried fish or in dried meat, they should have it carried in through birds by offering it to crows.

18 Balls of *sarala, devadāru*, 'stinking-grass', bdellium, pine-resin, *sāla* resin and lac and the dung of donkeys, camels, goats and sheep, are (good) retainers of fire.

19 The powder of *priyāla*, the soot of *avalguja*, wax and the dung of horses, donkeys, camels and bullocks make a fire-mixture which can be thrown (into the fort).

20 Or, the powder of all metals, of the colour of fire, or the powder of *kumbhī*, lead and tin, mixed with the flowers of *pāribhadraka* and *palāśa*,

little purpose. 12 *niṣkirād* is read as in 2.3.14. Cs, reading *niṣkarād*, has 'by means of a trick (*kapaṭāt*)' or 'by making the elephant put forth his trunk (*kara*)'. The second explanation is quite fanciful. — *aśvaiś ca prahareyuḥ*; the *ca* and the plural of the verb seem due to repetition from 13.2.20. — *niyoga-* etc.: see 9.7.73-86. — Cs reads *durgavāsinaḥ* at the end of this s. instead of at the beginning of the next and understands it as genitive singular 'of the enemy in the fort' over whom he is to seek success. It is, however, distinctly better to understand the word as describing the birds in the next s.

14 *naptṛ* is '*viṣkira*' (Cs); the lexicons give the latter as 'a cock' or 'a pheasant'. 15 The camp is to be at some distance (from the fort) so that it is not affected by the fire. — *-dhanvārakṣo* in the singular is read to conform with the verb *ādīpayet* of the mss. — *ucchritadhvajadhanvārakṣo vā*: the purpose of the raised flags is not clear. Apparently they are intended as a sort of protection from the human fire that is being used. Cs breaks the compound at *-dhanvā* (singular), with *ārakṣāḥ* (plural) as the option to it, understanding *ādīpayeyuḥ* with the latter. This is far from happy. Meyer suggests *ucchritasthadhanvākṣepāḥ* 'throwers of fire by means of bows, stationed on high ground', his verb being *ādīpayeyuḥ* in the plural. The suggestion is not satisfactory. — *mānuṣeṇa agninā* as described in 14.2.38. 16 *antardurga-* is as suggested by Meyer; *antadurga-* of the mss. would refer to a frontier fort, which has no propriety here. — *kāṇḍa* 'reed', used as an arrow.

18 *pūtitṛṇa* is apparently some kind of grass. — *śrīveṣṭaka* is 'the resin of *sarala*-pine' (Cs). — It is not clear if the balls and the dung are to be mixed together or not; perhaps not.

19 *avalgujamaṣī-*: Cs understands *maṣī* as a variety of the *śephālikā* plant, instead of as 'soot'. All substances mentioned in this s. together form an incendiary compound, that can be hurled with the hand.

20 *agnivarṇam*: how the powder of all metals is to get the colour of fire is not at all clear. Meyer suggests *agnipūraṇam* 'with fire in it', which is not convincing. — *kumbhī* is 'the *śrīparṇī*' (Cs); the latter means 'the silk cotton tree'. Meyer thinks that *kumbhī*

the soot of *keśa*, oil, wax and pine-resin makes a fire-mixture, one that kills the trusting. 21 An arrow smeared with it (and) covered with hemp and the bark of *trapusa*, is a (means of) setting on fire.

22 However, when fighting is possible, he should not at all make use of fire. 23 For, fire is unreliable and is a divine calamity, the destroyer of innumerable creatures, grains, animals, money, forest produce and goods. 24 And a kingdom, with stores exhausted, even if obtained, leads only to loss.

Thus ends (the topic of) laying siege (to a fort).

25 (When he thinks), ' I am fully provided with equipment and labourers for the undertaking ; the enemy is ill, has the constituents estranged because of secret tests, or has made no fortifications or stores ; being without reinforcements or with reinforcements, he will soon make peace with allies ; ' that is the time for storming (the fort).

26 When a fire is accidentally caused or is produced (by agents), when there is a festival, when troops are engaged in witnessing a show, during quarrels caused by drink, when troops are tired by constant fighting, when his men are wounded or killed in many battles, when people, tired of keeping awake, are asleep, when it is raining or the river is flooded or there is a thick fog, he should storm (the fort).

27 Or, abandoning the camp, (and) hiding in a forest, he should kill the enemy as he sallies out.

28 Or, one posing as the chief ally or helpmate should make friendship with the besieged and send a man condemned to death as a messenger, saying, ' This is your weak point ; these men are treasonable ; ' or ' This is the weak

may be some metal. — *-keśamaṣī-* : ' *keśa* is the *hrībera* and *maṣī* is a variety of *śephālikā* ' (Cs). Meyer understands ' soot ' not only of the *keśa* plant, but also of the flowers of *pāribhadraka* and *palāśa*. — *śrīveṣṭakayuktaḥ* : the masculine seems due to *agniyogaḥ* ; actually the compound qualifies *-cūrṇam* neuter. — *viśvāsaghātī vā* : the *vā* is strange ; for, *viśvāsaghātī* is only a description of the *agniyoga*, not an option to it. In 2.18.5, *viśvāsaghātin* appears as a *sthitayantra* ; it may have been used for throwing fire into the fort. Meyer reads *viśvāsa-* etc., at the beginning of the next s., which is no improvement. 21 *trapusa* is a kind of plant. — *bāṇa* can hardly mean ' *arjunavṛkṣa* ' (Cs) in the context.

23 *apratisaṁghāta-* of the mss. yields little sense. *apratisaṁkhyāta-* is necessary.

25 *upadhāviruddhaprakṛtiḥ* : as *upadhā* has a technical sense (cf. 1.10), *prakṛti* would refer primarily to ministers. Meyer thinks of *upadhā* as ' deceit ' and *prakṛti* as ' subjects '. — *purā mitraiḥ saṁdhatte* : the idea apparently is that he might make fresh alliances with a view to raise the siege with their help ; to prevent that, an immediate assault is to be made. Meyer's translation presupposes *purā amitraiḥ* ' make peace with his other enemies ' ; that does not yield a better sense. For the idiom with *purā* cf. 9.6.69 and 12.3.15.

26 *prekṣānīkadarśanasaṅga* : what seems meant is *prekṣādarśanānīkasaṅga* ' engrossment of the troops in seing a theatrical show '. In a foot-note Meyer suggests *prekṣāyām anīkadarśanasaṅge* ' when in a show, the sight of the troops is obstructed'. The inability of the troops to see a show would hardly be a reason for storming the fort.

27 Cs reads *śatruḥ sattrāt* for *śatrum*, and understands that the enemy is hiding in a forest. That the enemy, who is besieged, would be hiding in a forest is altogether unlikely.

28 *mitrāsāramukhyavyañjano vā* is from Cs. *vā* shows the option between *mitra* and *āsāra* ; cf. s. 30. *mukhya* does not mean merely ' a chief officer ' (Cs). It refers to the principal one among the kings who are supposed to be the enemy's allies. *vyañjana* shows that this king is in reality in league with the *vijigīṣu* — *ime dūṣyāḥ* : these innocent men

point of the besieger ; this is the seducible party for you.' 29 As he comes out with a return messenger, the conqueror should seize him and proclaiming his offence, slay him and go away. 30 Then the one posing as an ally or a helpmate should say to the besieged, 'Come out to save me,' or 'Kill the besieger along with me.' 31 When he agrees, he should destroy him by squeezing from both sides, or, catching him alive, make an exchange of the kingdom (for his life). 32 Or, he should demolish his capital city. 33 Or, forcing out his best troops he should strike.

34 By that are explained the king surrendering with troops and forest chieftains. 35 One of the two, a king surrednering with troops or a forest chieftain, should send word to the besieged, 'This besieger is ill, (or) he is attacked by an enemy in the rear, (or) another weak point has appeared, (or) he wants to go to another land.' 36 When he has agreed, the besieger should set fire to the camp and go away. 37 Then he should act as before.

38 Or, making a collection of merchandise, he should overreach him with goods mixed with poison.

39 Or, one posing as a helpmate should send a messenger to the besieged, 'Come out to attack the enemy outside, already attacked by me.' 40 When he agrees, he should act as before.

41 Entering the fort under the pretext of (seeing) a friend or a kinsman, with sealed passes in hand, secret agents should get it seized (by the besieger).

42 Or, one posing as a helpmate should send word to the besieged, 'At such and such a place and at such and such a time, I shall strike at the camp ; you also must fight (then)'. 43 When he agrees, he should show the tumult of an attack as mentioned and destroy him as he sallies out of the fort at night.

44 Or, he should invite an ally or a forest chieftain (and) incite him, 'Fight against the besieged and seize his land.' 45 When he fights, he should get him slain through the subjects or by supporting his treasonable chiefs, of kill him himself with poison, achieving his object (of implicating the enemy), 'He is the slayer of his ally'.

being removed by the enemy on this suggestion, he thereby becomes weakened. 29 *apagacchet*: go away with the ostensible object of attacking the *mitra* or *āsāra* who had given information about his *kṛtyapakṣa* to the enemy. 31 *ubhayataḥ* - etc. : cf. 13.3.22 and 30. 33 *sārabalaṁ vā vamayitvā*, i.e., when the enemy, instead of coming out in person, sends a strong force in response to the appeal of the *mitra* or *āsāra*.

34 *daṇḍopanata* : see 7.15. He is to pretend to be dissatisfied with his suzerain, the *vijigīṣu* ; so is the *āṭavika* to pretend. 37 *pūrvavat*, i.e., as in ss. 31-33.

38 *paṇyasaṁpātam* 'an accumulation of goods' ; this may be done when leaving the camp, as Meyer thinks, or by simply allowing goods to fall in the enemy's hands.

39 *bāhyam* is from Cs ; for the word, cf. 12.5.28.

41 *śāsanamudrā* : this seems to be merely a sealed pass allowing entry in the fort, it being, of course, forged.

44 *mitram* : this is the ally of the besieged enemy. 45 *prakṛtibhiḥ* seems to be 'subjects'. — *dūṣyamukhya*- are those of the ally or forest chief. — *mitraghātakaḥ* describes the enemy on whom the blame is thrown for the murder, so that the other allies may leave him.

46 Or, one posing as a friend should inform the enemy about (the ally etc.) wanting to attack. 47 Securing a position of trust, he should get his brave warriors slain.

48 Or, making peace with him, he should induce him to settle the country. 49 When settled, he should, unknown, destroy his country.

50 Or, after causing an injury to be done and getting part of the (enemy's) troops led against treasonable or forest troops, he should capture the fort by a sudden assault.

51 Treasonable, alien and forest troops, hostile men and deserters (from the enemy) who have come over, being given money and honour and supplied with signals and signs, should attack the enemy fort.

52 When attacking the enemy's fort or camp, they should grant safety to those fallen down, those turning back, those surrendering, those with loose hair, those without weapons, those disfigured by terror and to those not fighting.

53 After obtaining the enemy's fort, he should enter it after it is cleared of the enemy's party and after precautions against silent punishment are taken inside and outside.

54 After thus conquering the enemy's territory, the conqueror should seek to seize the middle king, after succeeding over him, the neutral king. 55 This is the first method of conquering the world.

56 In the absence of the middle and neutral kings, he should overcome the enemy constituents by superiority of policy, then the other constituents. 57 This is the second method.

46 *vikramitukāmam* refers to *mitram āṭavikaṁ vā* of s. 44. 47 This is done as in 13.3.13-14 and other places, through faked letters.

49 *janapadaṁ hanyāt* : this goes counter to Kauṭilya's own opinion as stated in ss. 2-5 above. The tricks seem to be simply repeated from earlier writers.

50 The idea seems to be that the *vijigīṣu* causes some injury to the enemy through his *dūṣya* and *āṭavika* troops ; the enemy would send a part of of his troops against them, whereupon the fort, with depleted troops, may be seized. For *balaikadeśam atinīya*, cf. 12.5.25. *atinīya* has the sense of the causal. The usual idea of smuggling troops into the fort, which Meyer understands, does not seem meant here.

51 *pratyapasṛta* is apparently a deserter (from the enemy) who has come over to him ; cf. 7.16.16. Meyer construes this word with each of the other words in the compound ; that is not likely. — *saṁjñā* is a signal for acting at a particular time or place ; *cihna* is a sign for recognizing one's own side.

52 *abhipanna* : cf. 1.18.6. — *-śastra-* is to be construed with the preceding *mukta*, rather than with the following *bhaya*.

56 *guṇātiśayena* : *guṇa* would seem to refer to the 'policy' pursued, though 'qualities in himself and his constituents' is not unlikely. — *ariprakṛtīḥ*, i.e., the enemy and his allies. — *uttarāḥ*, i.e., the other kings of the circle.

58 In the absence of the circle he should overcome by squeezing from both sides the ally through the enemy or the enemy through the ally. 59 This is the third method.

60 He should first overcome a weak or a single neighbouring prince; becoming doubly powerful through him a second prince; three times powerful, a third. 61 This is the fourth method of conquering the world.

62 And after conquering the world he should enjoy it divided into *varṇas* and *āśramas* in accordance with his own duty.

63 Secret instigation, secret agents, drawing out (of the fort), laying siege and storming, these are the five means of taking a fort.

CHAPTER FIVE

SECTION 176 PACIFICATION OF THE CONQUERED TERRITORY

1 The (object of the) conqueror's activity is two-fold : forests and so on, and a single city and so on. 2 Its acquisition is of three kinds : new, formerly possessed and inherited.

3 After gaining new territory, he should cover the enemy's faults with his own virtues, his virtues with double virtues. 4 He should carry out what is agreeable and beneficial to the subjects by doing his own duty as laid down, granting favours, giving exemptions, making gifts and showing honour. 5 And he should cause the (enemy's) seducible party to be favoured as promised, and more if they had exerted themselves. 6 For, he who does not keep his promise becomes unworthy of trust for his own and other people, also he whose behaviour is contrary to that of the subjects. 7 Hence he should adopt a similar character, dress, language and behaviour (as the subjects). 8 And he should show the same devotion in festivals in honour of deities of the country, festive gatherings and sportive amusements.

58 *maṇḍalasya abhāve*, i.e., when there are only two states to be tackled, one friendly, the other hostile.

60 *śakyam* : cf. 6.1.8. — *ekam*, i.e., without an ally.

62 *svadharmeṇa* refers to the king's own duties rather than to those of the *varṇas* and *āśramas*, as in Cs.

63 These are the titles of the Sections in the first four Chapters of this Book.

13.5

1 *samutthānam* refers to engaging in military and allied activity for conquest; *aṭavī* etc. are its objects. — *aṭavyādikam* refers to extensive dominion over all kinds of territory, while *ekagrāmādikam* refers to the capture of a single city or fort. 2 *pitryam* 'inherited from the father'. Cs has 'lost by the father and recovered by the son'. That is not meant.

4 *svadharmakarma*, i.e., carrying out tasks prescribed as his special duty; cf. 1.4.16.

5 *upagrāhayet*, i.e., do for them what he has promised in return for their help against their master. The causal has little significance. 8 It seems that *utsava* is to be construed with *deśadaivata* and *samāja*, while *vihāra* is to be understood independently.

9 Secret agents should frequently point out the enemy's misconduct to chiefs in the country, towns, castes and corporations, the master's great good fortune and love for them, and the master's great regard for them. 10 And he should make use of them by looking after their customary rights, exemptions and protection.

11 And he should cause the honouring of all deities and hermitages, and make grants of land, money and exemptions to men distinguished in learning, speech and piety, order the release of all prisoners and render help to the distressed, the helpless and the diseased. 12 (He should order) the stopping of slaughter for half a month in every four months, for four nights (and days) on the occasions of full moon nights, for one night (and day) on the days of the constellations of the king and the country. 13 He should prohibit the killing of females and young ones and the destruction of a male's virility.

14 And discontinuing whatever custom he might regard as harmful to the treasury and the army, or as unrighteous, he should establish a righteous course of conduct.

15 And he should cause a change of residence, not in one place, of those in the habit of robbing and of Mleccha communities, and of chiefs of forts, country and army. 16 And he should cause ministers, chaplains and others favoured by the enemy, to reside on the enemy's frontiers, not in one place. 17 He should put down by silent punishment those capable of injuring or those brooding on the master's destruction. 18 In the places of those removed, he should establish men from his own country or those in disfavour with the enemy.

19 And if any pretender from the (enemy's) family be capable of seizing easily recoverable territory, or a nobleman staying in a frontier forest be capable of troubling him, he should give him worthless land or a fourth part of valuable land, after fixing a tribute in treasury and army, such that while paying it he would rouse the citizens and country people to revolt. 20 He should get him killed through these, when they are roused. 21 He should remove one denounced by the subjects or station him in a dangerous region.

9 *deśajāti-* etc. : cf. 3.10.45. *saṁgha* is not to be construed with *deśa, grāma* and *jāti*, as Jayaswal (*Hindu Polity*, II, 65 ff.) thinks.

11 *vidyāvākyadharmaśūra* : it seems better to understand *śūra* with the preceding as 'brave in i.e., distinguished in', rather than independently as 'brave'. 13 *yonibāla-* refers to females and young ones of all species, particularly animals. Meyer has 'female children' only ; Russ. has 'young females' ; K. Nag has 'girls and the newly born' (*Les Théories* etc., p. 112). — *puṁstva* is also that of all creatures.

15 In view of the position of *ca*, *coraprakṛtīnām* is different from *mlecchajātīnām*. 17 *anukṣiyataḥ*, in the context, has the sense of 'brooding over'. Cf. 5.1.55 for the normal sense of 'to survive'. 18 *aparuddhān* 'in disfavour', not necessarily thrown in prison, as in Cs.

19 *kośadaṇḍadānam avasthāpya* : the amount is not stated, but must be assumed to be exorbitant. It cannot be supposed to be stated in *caturbhāgam* 'one-fourth of the produce' as Meyer thinks. That would hardly lead to a rising of the people. 21 *upakruṣṭam* : this would apply to any officer, not to *tatkulīna* or *abhijāta* alone.

22 In the case of territory formerly possessed (and reconquered), he should cover up that defect of the constituents because of which he had to leave and should strengthen that quality on the strength of which he has returned.

23 In the case of inherited territory, he should cover up the father's defects and display his virtues.

24 He should institute a righteous custom, not initiated before and continue one initiated by others; and he should not institute an unrighteous custom, and should stop any initiated by others.

Herewith ends the Thirteenth Book of the Arthaśāstra of Kauṭilya
'MEANS OF TAKING A FORT'

23 For *labdhapraśamana* in the case of an inherited kingdom, cf. *Raghuvaṁśa* 4.14 and preceding verses. We need not suppose *pitrya* to have been lost by the father and recovered by the son, as that passage clearly shows.

BOOK FOURTEEN

CONCERNING SECRET PRACTICES

SECTION 177 SECRET PRACTICES FOR THE DESTRUCTION OF ENEMY TROOPS

1 For the sake of protecting the four *varṇas*, he should use secret practices against the unrighteous.

2 The group of poisons, *kālakūṭa* and others, should be introduced into articles used on his person by the enemy, by approved men and women of the Mleccha communities, disguised as humpbacks, dwarfs, Kirātas, dumb or deaf persons, idiots, or blind persons, in an appearance credible as to country, dress, profession, language and birth.

3 Secret agents should introduce weapons in the articles for the (enemy) king's sports and in objects from the stores used by him, and agents following a secret activity, moving about at night, and those living by fire, should put fire (in those objects).

4 The powder of the speckled frog, the insects *kauṇḍinyaka* and *kṛkaṇa*, the *pañcakuṣṭha* and the centipede, the powder of *uccidiṅga*, *kambalī*, *śatakanda*, *idhma* and the lizard, the powder of the house-lizard, the 'blind reptile', the *krakaṇṭaka*, the 'stink-insect', and the *gomārikā*, mixed with the sap of *bhallātaka* and *avalguja*, causes instantaneous death, or the smoke of these (causes it).

The Fourteenth Book describes various secret remedies and occult practices intended for the destruction of the enemy. A great deal of magical and other lore is incorporated here.

14.1

We have in this Chapter recipes intended to kill, maim or disfigure a person. The ingredients cannot often be identified; in fact, sometimes it is not even clear if a name stands for a plant or some creature. The efficacy of the recipes cannot, of course, be tested.

1 It may be noted that these preparations are to be used against the unrighteous, the object being the protection of the four *varṇas*.

2 *viṣavargaḥ*: see 2.17.12. — *śraddheya-* etc.: cf. 1.12.6. — *mlecchajātīyaiḥ* suggests that Aryans were not favoured for the work of administering poison. — *abhipretaiḥ* 'liked', i.e., enjoying the confidence of the king on whom poisoning is to be tried. — *śarīropabhogeṣu* 'articles used on the person' appears better than 'on the body and in the articles used by him.'

3 *rājakrīḍā-* etc.: *upabhoga* can be construed with *krīḍābhāṇḍa* 'articles for sport' and *nidhānadravya* 'goods from stores'; but it seems preferable to understand it with *nidhānadravya* only. — *śastranidhānam*: *nidhāna* 'placing' is practically 'using' the weapon. — *sattrājīvinaḥ* is little more than *sattriṇaḥ*. — *rātricāriṇaḥ*: the agents appear as night watchmen etc.

4 *pañcakuṣṭha* is, according to Cs, the five products of the *kuṣṭha* plant (bark, leaf, flower, fruit and root). It may, however, be the name of some insect. The other words in the compound refer to insects. — *idhma* 'fuel of *palāśa*' (Cs). Meyer has *idhmakṛkalāsa* as one 'a lizard living in fuel'. *idhma*, however, seems to be the name of a plant or a creature. Cf. s.10. — *andhāhika* 'blind reptile' is a kind of fish, according to Cs. — *gomārikā* 'some sort of reptile' (Meyer); 'a kind of herb' (Cs). — *avalguja* is as suggested by Meyer for *avalgukā* of the mss. *avalguja* is the name of a plant, known to this text; cf. 13.4.10.

5 Or, any one of the insects, boiled along with the black serpent and *priyaṅgu*—one should dry up (this mixture); this mixture is believed to cause instantaneous death.

6 The root of *dhāmārgava* and *yātudhāna*, mixed with the powder of *bhallātaka* flowers (is a preparation) for bringing on death in a fortnight.

7 The root of *vyāghātaka*, mixed with the powder of *bhallātaka* flowers (and) a mixture of insects, brings on death in a month.

8 Only a minute portion (is the dose) for men, double for donkeys and horses, four times for elephants and camels.

9 The smoke of *śatakardama*, *uccidiṅga*, *karavīra*, the bitter gourd and fish, with the stalks of *madana* and *kodrava* or with the stalks of *hastikarṇa* and *palāśa*, when carried forth in a breeze blowing forward, kills everything to which it blows.

10 The powder of the 'stink-insect', fish, bitter gourd, *śatakardama*, *idhma* and the *indragopa* insect, or the powder of the 'stink-insect', *kṣudrā*, *arālā*, *hema* and *vidārī*, mixed with the powder of the horns and hooves of a goat, makes a smoke that blinds (one).

11 The leaves of *pūtikarañja*, yellow orpiment, red arsenic, *guñjā*-seeds and stalks of red cotton plant, made into a dough with the sap of *āsphoṭa*, *kāca* and cow-dung, make a blinding smoke.

12 The slough of a serpent, the dung of the cow and the horse and the head of a 'blind reptile', make a blinding smoke.

13 The urine and dung of pigeons, frogs and carnivorous animals and of elephants, men and boars, green sulphate of iron, asafoetida, the husk and broken and whole grains of barley, the seeds of cotton, *kuṭaja* and *kośātakī*, the roots of *gomūtrikā* and *bhāṇḍī*, bits of *nimba*, *śigru*, *phaṇirjaka*, *akṣīva* and *pīluka*, the skin of a serpent and a female *śaphara* and the powder of the

5 *taptaḥ* 'heated' seems to mean 'boiled' with *kṛṣṇasarpa*- etc. We expect *kīṭam* ... *taptam* as the object of *śoṣayet*; that is probably why Cs has 'an insect by itself would dry up a person (*śoṣayet*); when mixed with black serpent and *priyaṅgu* it kills immediately'. It is doubtful, however, if *śoṣayet* contains a reference to the effect produced by the recipe; moreover, the construction is far from natural.

6 *ārdhamāsikaḥ*: we have to understand *prāṇaharo yogaḥ* (Cs). — It seems *kīṭayogaḥ* is to be understood in this s. as in s. 7; the word seems to have dropped out accidentally from this s.

7 *kīṭayogaḥ* refers to the mixture of insects mentioned in s. 4.

8 *kalā*: this measure is not mentioned in 2.19, clearly suggesting a difference in sources.

9 Cs understands *śata* and *kardama* as two plants. — *palāla* 'stalks' or 'grass'; it is this that makes the smoke. — *pravātānuvāte*, i.e., when the wind is blowing forward towards the enemy. — *praṇītaḥ* 'led, directed'.

11 *kāca* 'a variety of salt produced from salty ground' (Cs).

13 *kravyāda*: perhaps any carnivorous animal would do. — *pratyekaśaḥ* to be construed with *mārayati* (Meyer). Cs understands the smoke of each one of the objects

nails and tusk of an elephant—the smoke of this produced with the stalks of *madana* and *kodrava* or with the stalks of *hastikarṇa* and *palāśa*, kills each singly, wherever it moves.

14 The roots of *kālī*, *kuṣṭha*, *naḍa* and *śatāvarī*, or the powder of the serpent, *pracalāka*, *kṛkaṇa* and *pañcakuṣṭha*—this smoke produced in the manner mentioned before or with half-wet, half-dry stalks, (and) directed to (the enemy's) coming on the battle-field or crowding in a sudden assault, by men who have taken precautions for their own eyes with 'washing water', destroys the sight of all creatures.

15 The dung of the *śārikā*, the pigeon, the heron and the crane, kneaded with the milk of *arka*, *akṣi*, *pīluka* and *snuhi* plants is a blinding eye-salve and a polluter of water.

16 A mixture of the roots of barley and *śāli*-rice, the fruit of *madana*, nutmeg leaves and man's urine, mixed with the roots of *plakṣa* and *vidārī*, (and) mixed with a decoction of *mūka*, *udumbara*, *madana* and *kodrava*, or mixed with a decoction of *hastikarṇa* and *palāśa*, is a stupefying preparation.

17 A mixture of *śṛṅgi*, the *gautama*-tree, *kaṇṭakāra* and *mayūrapadī*, a mixture of *guñjā*, *lāṅgalī*, *viṣamūlikā* and *iṅgudī*, a mixture of *karavīra*, *akṣi*, *pīluka*, *arka* and *mṛgamāraṇī*, mixed with a decoction of *madana* and *kodrava*, or mixed with a decoction of *hastikarṇa* and *palāśa* is a stupefying preparation.

18 Or, all these are polluters of fodder, fuel and water.

19 The smoke of *kṛtakaṇḍala*, the lizard, the house-lizard and the 'blind reptile' causes loss of eyesight and madness.

20 A mixture of the lizard and the house-lizard causes leprosy. 21 The same, mixed with the entrails of the speckled frog and honey brings on a disease of the bladder; mixed with human blood, (it causes) consumption.

mentioned, used singly; that appears less likely in view of ***ityeṣa dhūmaḥ*** coming after the enumeration of all the ingredients.

14 ***pūrvakalpena*** (from Cs) refers to ***madanakodravapalālena*** etc. — ***ārdraśuṣka-*** may be 'half-wet, half-dry' or 'wet or dry'; the former seems preferable. — ***nejanodaka*** is proposed as in 14.4.2. ***tejanodaka*** in Cs is little likely.

16 ***mūka*** : Cs paraphrases by '***āvilaṁ jalam***, turbid water', which is doubtful. Meyer suggests ***musta*** in place of ***mūka***. — ***madanayogaḥ*** 'a mixture that causes stupefaction or swoon'. Cs has '*cittavibhramakaraḥ*, causing madness'.

17 ***śṛṅgi-*** etc. : Cs has 'the fat (***gautama***) of the ***śṛṅgi***-fish and the ***lodhra*** tree (***vṛkṣa*** as ***lodhra***)'. This is very doubtful.

18 *samastāḥ* 'all these', i.e., each singly, not all mixed together, as Meyer thinks.

19 *kṛtakaṇḍala* seems to be the name of some reptile. Cs, however, has 'whose muscles have been cooked' as adjective to ***kṛkalāsa*** etc., or 'mixed with the ***kapikacchūka*** plant'. Neither is satisfactory. Meyer thinks of ***kṛṣakā*** a magic bird mentioned in the ***Pāraskara Gṛhya Sūtra***, 1.19.10.

21 ***śoṣam*** 'drying up', i.e., consumption.

22 The (poison) *dūṣīviṣa* and the powder of *madana* and *kodrava* is a preparation for bringing on paralysis of the tongue.

23 A mixture of *mātṛvāhaka*, *añjalikāra*, *pracalāka*, the frog, *akṣi* and *pīluka* causes cholera.

24 A mixture of *pañcakuṣṭha*, *kauṇḍinyaka*, the flowers of *rājavṛkṣa* and honey, causes fever.

25 A mixture of (the flesh of) *bhāsa* and *nakula* and (the plants) *jihvā* and *granthikā*, kneaded with the milk of a female donkey, makes one dumb and deaf, in a month or half a month.

26 Only a minute portion for men and so on as before.

27 The administration of a decoction of bits in the case of plants, powder in the case of creatures, or the administration of a decoction in all cases, thus it becomes more potent. 28 These are the excellences of mixtures.

29 The man, whom an arrow, prepared with the seeds of *śālmalī* and *vidārī*, joined with *mūla* and *vatsanābha* and smeared with the blood of musk-rat, hits, bites, when wounded (by it), other ten persons, and those bitten bite other ten persons each.

30 The decoction of *elaka*, *akṣi*, *guggulu*, and *hālāhala*, together with the flowers of *bhallātaka*, *yātudhāna*, *avānu*, *dhāmārgava* and *bāṇa*, mixed with the blood of a goat and man, is a preparation causing biting. 31 A measure of one-half *dharaṇa* of this preparation, introduced in water with barley meal and oil-cake, poisons a reservoir of water, one hundred *dhanus*es in extent. 32 For, a shoal of fish bitten or touched by this, becomes poisonous, also whoever drinks this water or touches it.

33 An iguana, placed along with red and white mustard seeds in a camel-shaped vessel buried in the ground for three fortnights, (and) taken out by a man condemned to death, kills wherever it casts its glance, or a black serpent (does so).

22 *dūṣīviṣam* : 'in medicinal works, a dry vegetable poison which does not cause death, but remains long in the system' (Jolly-Schmidt). Cs has 'poison whose potency has been removed by herbs etc.'; that is unlikely in view of 14.4.1. — *apajihvikā* 'removal of the tongue' seems to refer to loss of its use. Cs, reading *upajihvikāyogaḥ*, includes it along with *dūṣīviṣam* etc. in the next s. in the sense of 'a mixture of ants'. That does not sound plausible.

25 *jihvā* and *granthikā* are understood as names of plants; may it be that the tongue and the muscles of *bhāsa* and *nakula* are to be understood? — *māsārdhamāsikaḥ* : this seems to mean 'effective in a month or in a fortnight', though 'effective in a month and a half' is also possible; cf. 14.2.4 below.

29 *dhānya* 'grains', i.e., seeds. Cs understands *kustumburu* by it.

30 *avānu* is uncertain and seems due to a corruption of the text; Cs drops it but reads *apāmārga* for *dhāmārgava*; for the latter, however, cf. s. 6. — *daṁśayogaḥ* : probably the same idea as in s. 29 is to be understood. 31 For *dharaṇa*, see 2.19.5-6. 32 *daṣṭa* in the case of fish probably means only drunk by them, and thus introduced in their system.

34 A charcoal burnt by lightning or a flame (caused by it), caught and fed with wood burnt by lightning — this fire, with offerings made into it under the Kṛttikās or the Bharaṇīs in a rite in honour of Rudra, burns, when directed (towards an enemy), without there being any remedy for it.

35 Bringing fire from a blacksmith, he should offer honey in it separately, wine in the fire from the vintner, and ghee in the fire from the roads;

36 And, (he should offer) garland-flowers in the fire from a woman devoted to her husband, mustard seeds in the fire from a harlot, curds in the fire from a woman in confinement and rice-grains in the fire from one who has kept the sacrificial fires;

37 Meat in the fire from a Caṇḍāla, human flesh in the fire from a funeral pyre, the fat of a goat and human *dhruva* in all these together.

38 He should offer the wood of *rājavṛkṣa* with *mantra*s in honour of Agni. This is a fire against which there is no remedy, which confounds the eyes of enemies.

39 O Aditi, a salutation to thee; O Anumati, a salutation to thee; O Sarasvati, a salutation to thee; O God Savitṛ, a salutation to thee. 40 To Agni, hail! To Soma, hail! Earth hail! Atmosphere hail!

34 *-pradagdho 'ṅgāro jvālo vā* is proposed for the corrupt *-pradagdhodgārojvālo vā.* Cs has *ajvalo*; but in view of *vā, jvālo* (masculine) as 'flame' appears preferable to *ajvāla* (adjective) 'without flame' describing *aṅgāra.* — *anuvāsitaḥ*, i.e., maintained for some days. — *raudreṇa karmaṇā*: Meyer refers to the Atharvaveda Pariśiṣṭa, 1. 406, 415.

35 *mārgato 'gnim* is a very tentative suggestion for *bhāgaṁ yo 'gnim* of the mss. Meyer proposes *bhāgato 'gnim*, but his explanation 'fire from a brothel (*bhāga* from *bhaga* the female organ)' is quite fanciful. Cs reads *bhārgyāyognim* 'the fire from *ayas*, i.e., *ayaskāra*, with the offering of the *bhārgī*-plant and ghee.' But *ayaskāra* could hardly be different from *karmāra*, already mentioned. One might also suggest *bhārgavāgnim* 'fire of archers', *mārgaṇāgnim* 'the fire of a beggar', *mārgikāgnim* 'the fire of a hunter', or *bhārikāgnim* 'the fire of a porter.' But none is satisfactory.

36 *sūtikāsu*: the locative is strange.

37 *samastān*: i.e., after the separate offerings are made, all fires are put together and the offering of *bastavasā* etc. made. — *mānuṣeṇa dhruveṇa ca*: Cs understands *dhruva* in the sense of the banyan tree, *mānuṣa* being human flesh. Meyer proposes *sraveṇa* 'urine' for *dhruveṇa*, or in the alternative *manuṣyarudhireṇa ca* as the last quarter. *dhruva*, among others things, means 'tip of the nose', but it can hardly be understood here. Can it mean flesh? Russ. understands 'flat cakes.'

39-40 These are evidently formulas to be repeated after the offerings in the fire. They themselves do not constitute the *agnimantra*. The deities are mostly Vedic.

CHAPTER TWO

SECTION 178 DECEIVING (BY MEANS OF OCCULT PRACTICES)

(*i*) Working of Miracles

1 The powder of *śirīṣa, udumbara* and *śamī*, mixed with clarified butter, is a recipé against hunger, effective for half a month. 2 That, prepared out of *kaśeruka*, the bulbous root of the lotus, the root of sugar-cane, lotus-fibres, *dūrvā* grass, milk, ghee and cream, is effective for one month.

3 Drinking, with milk and ghee, the powder of *māṣa*-beans, barley, *kulattha* and the roots of *darbha* grass, or *vallī*, milk and ghee boiled together in equal quantities, (or) the paste of the roots of *sāla* and *pṛśniparṇī* along with milk, or partaking of milk boiled together with that, along with honey and ghee, one is able to fast for a month.

4 Oil, prepared from mustard seeds kept for seven nights in the urine of white goats and kept in a bitter gourd for a month and half a month, is a means of disfiguring quadrupeds and bipeds.

5 The oil of white mustard seeds, boiled with barley-grains (taken) from the dung of a white donkey fed on butter-milk and barley, after seven nights, is a means of disfiguration.

6 Mustard oil, boiled along with the urine and dung of either of these two, with the addition of the powder of *arka, tūla* and *pataṅga*, is a means of making (a person) white.

7 A mixture of the dung of a white cock and a boa constrictor, is a means of making white.

8 White mustard seeds, kept in the urine of a white goat for seven nights, butter-milk, the milk of *arka*, salt and grains — this mixture kept for a fortnight is a means of making white.

14.2

The 178th Section is spread over this and the next Chapter. *pralambhana* is 'deceiving, deluding.'

1 *kṣudyogaḥ* is a remedy for keeping off hunger. Apparently the mixture is to be taken only once at the start of the fortnightly period. 2 Meyer has *kandekṣu* as a kind of grass.

3 A *vā* seems necessary after *payasā*, so that we get four recipes in all. In the absence of *vā*, Meyer, proposing *vallīkṣīraghṛtābhyām*, has 'drinking as a drink (*payasā pītvā*) the pulp of the roots of *sāla* and *pṛśniparṇī* prepared in equal quantities with the juice of *vallī* and ghee.' The rendering of *payasā pītvā* is doubtful.

4 *māsārdhamāsa-*: *sārdhamāsa* would have been better for the sense intended. 'A month or half a smonth' is possible, but seems less likely.

5 *leṇḍayavaiḥ* 'barley-grains picked from the dung' (Meyer) is preferable to 'dung and barley-grains' (Cs).

6 *etayoḥ* i.e., of the white goat or white donkey. — *pataṅga* 'moth' (Meyer), '*śāliḥ*' (Cs). — *pratīvāpa*: cf. 2.25.22.

8 In this recipe, Cs has in addition *arka, tūla, kaṭuka, matsya* and *vilaṅga*, but no *lavaṇa* and *dhānya*. — After this, Cs has two additional recipes for making white: 'A mixture of

9 The flour of white mustard seeds, kept for half a month in a bitter gourd while still on the creeper, is a means of making hair white.

10 The insect that is known as *alojuna* and the white house-lizard — hair smeared with this paste would become as white as a conch-shell.

11 One, with his body rubbed with cow-dung or with the pulp of *tinduka* and *ariṣṭa*, (and) smeared with the sap of *bhallātaka*, gets leprosy within a month.

12 *Guñjā*-seeds kept for seven nights in the mouth of a black serpent or in the mouth of a house-lizard is a means of causing leprosy.

13 Application all over the body of the bile and the liquid of the egg of a parrot is a means of causing leprosy.

14 A decoction of the pulp of *priyāla* is a remedy for leprosy.

15 One, eating (food) containing the roots of *kukkuṭa*, *kośātakī* and *śatāvarī*, becomes fair-complexioned in a month.

16 One, bathing in a decoction of *vaṭa* (and) smeared with the pulp of *sahacara*, becomes black.

17 Yellow orpiment and red arsenic, mixed with the oil of *śakuna* and *kaṅgu*, are a means of making dark.

18 The powder of the fire-fly, mixed with mustard oil, burns at night.

19 The powder of the fire-fly and the insect *gaṇḍūpada*, or the powder of the flowers of *samudra-jantus*, *bhṛṅgakapālas*, *khadira* and *karṇikāra*, mixed with the oil of *śakuna* and *kaṅgu*, is a powder that makes (an object) glow.

20 The soot of the bark of *pāribhadraka*, mixed with the fat of a frog, is a means of making limbs burn with fire. 21 The body, smeared with the pulp of the bark of the *pāribhadraka* and sesamum seeds burns with fire.

the female sea-frog, conch-shell, *sudhā*, i.e., *mūrvā* grass, *kadalī*, salt and butter-milk, is a means of making white. The soured juices of *kadalī*, *avalguja* and *kṣāra*, mixed with wine, butter-milk, *arka*, *tūla*, *snuhi*, and salt and the sour gruel of grains, — this mixture kept for a fortnight is a means of making white.' The ss. seem to be derived from the mss. which cannot be traced now. These recipes may well be genuine, though the possibility of addition by later copyists cannot be ruled out.

9 For *gatam* Cs reads *nagaram* which is explained as 'dried ginger'; this is very doubtful.

10 Cs has *arkatūlo 'rjune kīṭaḥ* in the first quarter, '*arka*, *tūla*, two kinds of *arjuna* (viz., *kakubha* and *yavasa*) and an insect (to be learnt from tradition).' This is not very convincing.

14 *kalkakaṣāyaḥ* 'decoction of the pulp' (Cs); 'pulp and decoction' (Meyer).

15 Cs reads *kukkuṭī-* for *kukkuṭa-*. Either word must be understood as referring to some plant.

17 *śakunakaṅgu* 'vulture and the *priyaṅgu*-plant' (Cs); 'the fins of birds' (Meyer). If *śakuna* means a bird, *taila* would apparently refer to its fat.

19 *samudrajantu* etc. appear to be names of plants, as *puṣpacūrṇam* is to be understood of them, though Cs construes the latter only with *khadirakarṇikārāṇām* (looking upon *samudrajantu* as sea-creatures, *bhṛṅga* as the *kaliṅga* bird and *kapāla* as skull). — *tejanacūrṇam* 'powder that makes an object glow'; cf. 13.2.23. Cs, interpreting it as 'the powder of bamboo', construes it with the next s., which does not appear right.

22 A lump, consisting of the soot of the bark of *pīlu*, burns in the hand. 23 Smeared with the fat of a frog, it burns with fire. 24 The body, smeared with that, or, sprinkled with the oil of the *kuśāmra* fruit (and) mixed with the powder of a female sea-frog, sea-foam and *sarja*-exudation, burns.

25 Oil, boiled with equal quantities of the fat of the frog, crab and so on, causes the blazing of limbs with fire all over.

26 The body, smeared with the roots of bamboo and moss, (and) smeared with the fat of a frog, burns with fire.

27 One, with his feet smeared with oil boiled together with the fat of a frog and the pulp of the roots of *pāribhadraka*, *pratibalā*, *vañjula*, *vajra* and *kadalī*, walks on burning charcoal.

28-29 One should prepare oil from the pulp of these, namely, *upodakā*, *pratibalā*, *vañjula* and *pāribhadraka*, by boiling together with the fat of a frog; after smearing one's clean feet with this (oil), one may walk on a heap of burning charcoal as on a heap of flowers.

30 Lamps of reeds, tied to the tails of swans, herons and peacocks or of other big birds swimming in water, is a manifestation of meteors at night.

31 Ashes caused by lightning are a means of extinguishing fire.

32 *Māṣa*-beans, soaked in a woman's menstrual fluid (and) the root of *vrajakulī*, mixed with the fat of a frog, is a means of preventing cooking even when the oven is burning. 33 Cleansing the oven is the remedy for it.

34 A ball made of *pīlu*, with fire in the interior, with a knot of the root of *suvarcalā* or with a knot of thread, encircled by cotton, is (a means of) emitting fire and smoke from the mouth.

35 Fire, sprinkled with the oil of the *kuśāmra* fruit, burns in rain and in strong winds.

36 Sea-foam soaked in oil, burns floating on water.

37 Fire, kindled by churning a speckled bamboo-reed in the bones of swimming birds, is not put out by water, (but) burns with water.

23 *-digdho*: we have to supply *piṇḍaḥ* from the preceding, hardly *hastaḥ*. 24 *kuśāmra-* etc. and *samudra-* etc. constitute a single *yoga*, an option to *tena* (*piṇḍena*) *pradigdham*.

25 *maṇḍūkakulīrādīnām* is proposed for *maṇḍūkavasākulīrādīnām* of the mss. *vasayā* is there outside the compound; its use also in the compound is unlikely. — *abhyaṅgam* is proposed for *abhyaṅgo*; there is no word in the masculine with which the latter can be construed. — The repetition of s. 23 after this s. is clearly due to a scribal slip.

28 Apparently, *upodakā* is the same as *vajra* of s. 27, of which these two stanzas appear to be only a versification.

30 *ulkā* may mean 'a meteor' or a 'fire-brand, a flame' floating on water.

34 *pīlumayo maṇiḥ*, i.e., a ball made of *pīlu* wood, which is hollow inside. It cannot be the lump of the soot of its bark mentioned in s. 22, as Meyer thinks. — *granthi* refers to the stopper at the mouth of the ball; this *granthi* encircled by cotton (*picu*) burns and produces the fire and smoke coming out of the mouth.

37 *plavamānānām* is proposed for *plavamānām* of G M; *plavaṅgamānām* 'of monkeys' is not very likely in the context.

38 Where a fire kindled by churning a speckled bamboo-reed in the ribs from the left side of a man slain with a weapon or impaled on the stake, (or) a fire kindled by churning the rib of a human being in the bones of a woman or a man, goes round three times left-wise, there no other fire burns.

39 The musk-rat, the wag-tail and the salt-insect are ground to powder ; mixed with the urine of a horse, (they are) a means of breaking chains.

40 Or, the load-stone, made doubly powerful by the smearing of the fats of the crab, the frog and the salt-insect, (is a breaker of chains).

41 The foetus of a calf, ground together with the sides of the heron and the *bhāsa*, lotus and water, is a foot-salve for quadrupeds and bipeds.

42 Smearing sandals made of camel-hide with the fat of the owl and the vulture, covering them with leaves of the banyan tree, one walks fifty *yojana*s without being fatigued.

43 The bone-marrow or the semen of the hawk, the heron, the crow, the vulture, the swan, the plover and the *vīcīralla* (enables one to walk untired) for one hundred *yojana*s, or the bone-marrow or semen of the lion, the tiger, the leopard, the crow and the owl.

44 After pressing in a camel-shaped vessel the aborted foetuses of all the *varṇas* or dead infants in the cemetary—the fat produced from that (enables one to walk untired) for one hundred *yojana*s.

45 He should cause fright to the enemy with (these) evil, miraculous portents ; because it is for the consolidation of the kingdom, a similar blameworthy conduct is recommended when there is a revolt.

38 This is the *mānuṣa agni* ; cf. 1.20.4.

39 Meyer remarks that *khāra-* here and in the next s. is a Prākṛtism for *kṣāra-* ; that appears plausible.

40 *kulīra-* is from Meyer for *kuliṇḍa* ; Cs has *kulīrāṇḍa*, where *aṇḍa* would appear oddly placed in the compound. — We have to supply *nigalānāṁ bhañjanam* as the predicate. Cs, however, has a stop after *pāṣāṇaḥ* (so that this itself is a means of breaking chains), and includes the rest in the next s. Meyer reads a stop after *pradehena* and another after *nārakagarbhaḥ* of the next s. He explains 'it becomes doubly powerful when human fat (*nārakagarbha*) is added to it'. This is very doubtful.

41 *nārakagarbhaḥ* : the *Medinī* gives *nāra* in the sense of a fresh-born calf ; that sense may be understood for *nārakagarbha*. Cs, reading *dāraka-*, explains it by 'pig'. — *utpala* is a kind of fish (Cs).

44 *abhiṣūya* refers to infusing or distilling.

45 *ārājyāya* : this seems to mean 'for securing the kingdom on all sides, consolidating the kingdom'. — *nirvādaḥ* 'censure, blame', i.e., blameworthy conduct implicit in the use of these manifestations. — *kope*, i.e., when there is revolt among the officers etc. Cs construes *ārājyāya* 'for depriving (the enemy) of his kingdom' with the first half and then goes on 'this activity is common (to the *vijigīṣu* and the enemy) when passions are aroused (*kope*) ; hence it is described here (*ucyate*)'. Among a bewildering variety of explanations and suggestions offered by Meyer (here and in his *Über das Wesen* usw., p. 400 n.) one is to read *ā rājyāya* 'till the kingdom is obtained' or *svarājyāya*, further *nirvāhaḥ* (for *nirvādaḥ*) as 'means of doing things'. This latter suggestion appears not unreasonable. Russ. renders the second half : 'but if rumour spreads that (such an action) does not serve the interests of the state, then there will be a general uprising.'

CHAPTER THREE

SECTION 178 (Continued)

(*ii*) The use of Medicines and Spells

1 Taking the right and the left eyes of one, two or more of (the following), the cat, the camel, the wolf, the boar, the porcupine, the flying fox, the *naptṛ*, the crow, the owl or other creatures roaming at night, one should prepare two separate powders. 2 Then anointing the right eye with (the powder of) the left (eye) and the left with (that of) the right, one is able to see at night and in darkness.

> 3 One *amlaka*-fruit, the eye of a boar, the fire-fly, the black *śārivā*—
> one with his eyes anointed with this (preparation), sees objects at night time.

4 After fasting for three (days and) nights, one should sow, on the *puṣya* day, barley-seeds in earth in the skull of a man killed with a weapon or impaled on the stake, and sprinkle them with sheep's milk. 5 Then wearing a garland of the sprouts of barley, one is able to move about with one's shadow and form invisible.

6 After fasting for three (days and) nights, one should, on the *puṣya* day, powder separately the right and the left eyes of a dog, a cat, an owl and a flying fox. 7 Then anointing the eyes with the (powder of the) corresponding (eyes), one moves about with shadow and form invisible.

8 After fasting for three (days and) nights, one should prepare, on the *puṣya* day, a pin and a salve-container out of the thigh-bone of a murderer. 9 Then, with eyes anointed with the powder of the eyes of any one of these, one moves about with shadow and form invisible.

10 After fasting for three (days and) nights, one should prepare, on the *puṣya* day, an iron salve-container and a pin. 11 Then, filling the skull of any one of the night-roaming creatures with an eye-salve, one should insert it in the vagina of a dead woman and cause it to be burnt. 12 Taking out that

14.3

1 *vāgulī* appears to be a Prākṛtism for *valgulī*, the flying fox. — *vāmāni cākṣiṇi* is emended as in Meyer for *vāmāni vākṣiṇi*. The former is necessary as shown by what follows as well as s. 6.

3 *amlaka* '*lakuca*, the bread-fruit' (Cs); 'tamarind' (Meyer). — *kālaśārivā* is 'a black plant known as *bhadrā*' (Cs). Meyer thinks that we should read *kālaśārikā*.

4 *yavān āvāsya*: for the correctness of this reading from Cs, cf. the parallels in ss. 64 and 79 below. 5 *yavavirūḍha*-, i.e., the sprouts of the barley sown as above.

7 *yathāsvam*, i.e., the powder of the right eyes in the right eye and that of the left in the left.

8 *kāṇḍaka* means a thigh-bone or an arm-bone. 9 *anyatamena* seems to refer to any one of the creatures mentioned in s. 6. If the option were between the powder of the right eyes and that of the left eyes, we would have had *anyatareṇa*. Meyer's proposal to read *tatra nyastena* (for *tato 'nyatamena*) is unnecessary.

salve on the *puṣya* day, one should keep it in that salve-container. 13 With eyes anointed with that, one moves about with shadow and form invisible.

14 Where one sees a Brahmin, who has maintained the sacred fires, cremated or burning on the pyre, there, after fasting for three (days and) nights, one should, on the *puṣya* day, make a bag out of the garment of a man who has died naturally and fill it with the ashes of the funeral pyre ; wearing that (bag), one moves about with shadow and form invisible.

15 The skin of a serpent, filled with the powder of the bones and marrow of that bull which is slaughtered in the funeral rites of a Brahmin, is a means of making animals invisible.

16 The skin of a *pracalāka*, filled with the ashes of one bitten by a serpent, is a means of making deer invisible.

17 The skin of a serpent, filled with the powder of the tail, the dung and the knee-bones of an owl and a flying fox, is a means of making birds invisible.

18 These are the eight recipes for making invisible.

19 'I bow to Bali, the son of Virocana and to Śambara of the hundred guiles, to Bhaṇḍīrapāka, to Naraka, to Nikumbha, as well as to Kumbha.

20 I bow to Devala (and) to Nārada ; I bow to Sāvarṇi Gālava. According to the prescription of these this great sleep has been brought on you.

21 As the boa constrictors sleep, as also the *camūkhalas* sleep, so may men sleep, also those who, in the village, are curious.

22 With a thousand vessels and with a hundred fellies of chariots, I shall enter this house; let the vessels remain silent.

23-24 Bowing to Manu and tying the dog-kennels, and (bowing) to those who are gods in the worlds of the gods and are Brahmins among men, to holy men who have completed their study and to ascetics on the Kailāsa-mountain, (bowing) to all these holy men, this great sleep has been brought on you.

14 *svayaṁmṛtasya* : cf. 2.2.9. — *citābhasmanā* : this is that of the Brahmin.

15 *bhastrā* is a bag made of the creature's skin. — *paśūnām* : these are other than *mṛga*, referred to in the next s.

17 *jānvasthi* can hardly be 'knee and bones' (Cs) ; knee-bones would appear meant.

19 The spells are clearly *prasvāpana-mantras*, intended primarily for thieves. Asuras and sages are invoked to send people to sleep. 20 *anuyogena* : this seems to mean 'teaching, instruction, prescription'. 21 *camūkhalāḥ* is obscure. Some creature is apparently meant. Meyer proposes *ca mūrkhalāḥ* 'and fools,' which is not convincing. 22 *bhaṇḍaka* seems to be the same as *bhāṇḍaka* 'vessel' in which apparently the loot is to be carried away. Meyer would read *bhaṇḍakānām* 'something for the dogs (from *bhaṇḍ* to bark), i.e., kennels' and understand *bhāṇḍakāḥ* at the end as 'dogs'. This is very doubtful. — *āsantu* : the Parasmaipada is archaic. 23 *phelakāḥ* 'boxes, caskets' may refer to kennels ; can it

25 As I go beyond, may all together go away.

26 O Alitā, O Valitā, hail to Manu!'

27 The method of using this is: 28 After fasting for three (days and) nights, one should, on the fourteenth of the dark half of a month with (the moon in) conjunction with the *puṣya*-constellation, purchase from a Śvapāka woman the scrapings made by *bilakhas*. 29 Placing them with *māṣa*-beans in a basket, one should bury it in an uncrowded cremation-ground. 30 Taking it out on the fourteenth of the next fortnight and getting it pounded by a maiden, one should make pills out of it. 31 Then wherever one throws one pill after reciting this *mantra* over it, there one sends all to sleep.

32 In this same manner, one should bury the quill of a porcupine with three black and three white lines in an uncrowded cremation-ground. 33 Taking it out on the fourteenth of the next fortnight, wherever one throws it along with ashes from the burning ground, reciting this *mantra* over it, one sends all there to sleep.

34 'I bow to Brahmāṇī with the golden flowers and to Brahman with the flag of *kuśa*-grass and to all the deities; and I bow to all the ascetics.

35 May Brahmins come under my control, and may the Kṣatriyas who protect the earth; may the Vaiśyas and the Śūdras be ever under my control.

36 Hail! O Amilā, O Kimilā, O Vayucārā, O Prayogā, O Phakkā, O Vayuhvā, O Vihālā, O Dantakaṭakā, hail!

37 May the dogs sleep happily, and those who, in the village, are curious; and this quill of the porcupine, white in three places, is created by Brahman.

38 For, all successful men are asleep; this sleep has been brought on you, up to where the end of the boundary of the village is and till the rising of the sun.

39 Hail!'

40 The use of this (*mantra* is as follows): 41 The quills of a porcupine with three white lines (should be taken); after fasting for seven (days and)

possibly mean 'muzzles'? Russ. has *śunakaphelakāḥ* 'a pack of hounds'. 26 *Alite* may be a corruption of *Adite*, and *Valite* only a name formed by analogy.

28 *bilakha* 'a mouse-like burrowing creature' (Cs). The word literally means 'a hole-digger'. 29 Russ. has *asaṁkīrṇe* 'not desecrated'.

34-39 also contain a *prasvāpana-mantra*. 36 The names of these female spirits are unknown elsewhere; the correct form of the names is also uncretain. 38 *siddhāḥ* may be the same as *siddhārthāḥ* (s. 46), i.e., successful or wealthy men.

41 After *triśvetāni*, Cs supplies *ādahane nikhānayet* as in s. 32. But there is no reference in the sequel to 'taking out' as there is in s. 33 there. Meyer supplies *gṛhṇīyāt* or *gṛhītvā*; that appears better. — *aṣṭaśatasaṁpātam*: this means little more than that 108 sticks of

nights, one should, on the fourteenth of the dark fortnight, offer into the fire sticks of *khadira* accumulating them to one hundred and eight, along with honey and ghee, reciting this *mantra.* 42 Then where at the village-gate or the door of a house, one of these is buried, with the recitation of this *mantra,* one sends all there to sleep.

43 ' I bow to Bali, the son of Virocana and to Śambara of the hundred guiles, to Nikumbha, to Naraka, to Kumbha, to Tantukaccha, the great Asura ;

44 (I bow) to Armālava, to Pramīla, to Maṇḍolūka, to Ghaṭodbala, and to the service of Kṛṣṇa and Kaṁsa, and to Paulomī, the successful.

45 Consecrating with *mantras*, I take the dead *śārikā* for the sake of success ; may it succeed, and it does succeed ; salutation to quill-beings. Hail !

46 May the dogs sleep happily, and those who, in the village, are curious. May those who have achieved their object—the object which we seek—sleep happily till the rising (of the sun) after its setting, till the object is mine as the fruit.

47 Hail ! '

48 The use of this (*mantra* is as follows) : 49 One who has fasted for four meals should make an offering in an uncrowded cremation-ground on the fourteenth of the dark fortnight, and taking, with this *mantra*, a dead *śārikā* should tie (it in) a bag made of a hog's snout. 50 Piercing it in the middle with the quill of a porcupine, where it is buried with this *mantra*, one sends all there to sleep.

51 ' I seek refuge with Agni and the deities, the ten quarters ; and may all go away, may they be ever under my control.

52 Hail ! '

khadira are to be offered in the *agni*. Cs interprets *sampāta* as *homa* ' offering as oblation ' and adds that the quills are to be dug out after the *homa* is over. That is possible, though there is no reference to burying and digging out, as there is in ss. 55-56 below.

43-47 is again a *prasvāpana-mantra.* 44 *kṛṣṇa-kaṁsopacāram* ' the service of Kṛṣṇa and Kaṁsa, i.e., those who wait upon these two spirits ' (Meyer). That Kṛṣṇa and Kaṁsa here are unrelated to the heroes of the *Harivaṁśa* is likely, though not certain. So Paulomī may or my not refer to *Śacī*, Indra's wife. 45 *siddhyartham* is proposed for *siddhārtham* ; if the latter is ' mustard seeds ', there is no reference to them in the *prayoga* that follows. 46 *siddhārthāḥ* refers to wealthy men in the town. — *yāvad astamayād udayo*, i.e., from sunset to sunrise. — *artham* neuter is unusual ; Meyer remarks that *artha* neuter is found in the *Mahābhārata*, 12.142.14. The Critical Edition of the *Mahābhārata* (12.140.14), however, has *atha*, not *artham* in that passage. It is possible to look upon *yāvadartham* as an adjective to *phalam* ' in which the total (*yāvat*) wealth is secured.'

49 *caturbhaktopavāsī* would mean ' who fasts for four meals ', i.e., fasts for two days, rather than ' abstaining from four days' food ' (Cs); for the latter, we would have had *catūrātropoṣitaḥ* like *trirātropoṣitaḥ* above. — *pautrīpoṭṭalikam* : *potrī* means ' a hog's snout'; *pautri* seems used in the same sense. Cs reads *potrī-* but undeserstands by it ' a piece of garment ' ; Russ. understands ' a bundle of pigs' bristles '. *poṭṭalika* is an obvious *deśī* word.

53 The use of this (*mantra* is as follows): 54 After fasting for three (days and) nights, one should, on the *puṣya* day, make an aggregate of twenty-one pebble-stones and offer oblations of honey and ghee (in the fire). 55 Then, worshipping them with incense and flowers, one should bury them. 56 Taking them out on the next *puṣya* day, one should consecrate one pebble with this *mantra* and strike a door-panel with it. 57 Within four pebbles, the door is opened.

58 After fasting for four meals, one should, on the fourteenth of the dark fortnight, make a bull out of the bone of a broken man, and should consecrate it with this *mantra*. 59 A bullock-cart with two bullocks yoked is brought to him. 60 Thereafter, he moves about in the sky. 61 Becoming akin to the sun, he penetrates everything beyond the gate-bar.

62 'Thou art possessed of the bitter strength of the pitcher-gourd of a Caṇḍāla woman, and possessed of a woman's organ; hail!' 63 This is a means of opening locks and sending (all) to sleep.

64 After fasting for three (days and) nights, one should, on the *puṣya* day, sow *tuvarī*-seeds in earth in the skull of a man killed with a weapon or impaled on the stake, and sprinkle them with water. 65 When grown, he should take them on the *puṣya* day itself and twist them into a rope. 66 Then, the cutting of it in front of bows and machines fitted with strings causes the snapping of (those) strings.

67 One should fill the skin of a water-snake with the earth into which a woman or a man has breathed; this is a means of blocking the nostrils and choking the mouth.

54 *ekaviṁśatisampātam*: cf. s. 41 above. Though *agni* is not mentioned here, the offering of *madhu* and *ghṛta* could only be in fire. 57 The interpretation in Cs 'a hole four *śarkarās* in diameter is made in the door' seems quite unlikely.

58 *bhagnasya* evidently refers to a murdered man. Meyer suggests *magnasya* 'drowned' for it. 61 *ravisagandhaḥ parigham ati sarvaṁ pṛṇāti* is proposed with hesitation and understood to mean that the person is able to move about in the sky like the sun, flying over the bars of city-gates. With *sadā raviraviḥ sagaṇḍaparighāti sarvaṁ bhaṇāti*, Cs in-includes this in the *mantra* in s. 62. But the next *mantra* seems addressed to the gate-bar or lock and has *asi* in the Second Person, whereas in this s., we have *bhaṇāti* in the Third Person. Russ. reads 'and announces everything that appears under the sun and up to the limit of the horizon.' Meyer in the Nachtrag ultimately agrees with Cs (only proposing *bhṛṇāti* for *bhaṇāti*) and explains 'always as loud roarer (*raviraviḥ* from the frequentative of *ru* to cry) the full-cheeked (*sagaṇḍaḥ*) or the stinking (with *sagandhaḥ*) bar bears above everything else'. This is far from satisfactory. The s. appears better as a further description of *ākāśe vikrāmati* of s. 60.

62 *-kumbhītumba-* and *-sāraughaḥ* are tentatively proposed for the uncertain *-kumbīttamba-* and *-sārīghaḥ*. Meyer understands *Caṇḍālīkumbā* 'the petticoat of a Caṇḍāla woman' as a separate *upamāna*. He also proposes *parigha* (for *sārīghaḥ*) and looks upon it and *-kaṭuka* as vocatives, i.e., 'o bar! you who are bitter like a Caṇḍāla woman's petticoat and like a gourd etc.' Russ. reads 'o bolt, you have a sharp smell like the skirt or milk-bucket of a Caṇḍāla woman.' — *sanārībhagaḥ*: this apparently has reference to the hole in the side-wall in which the bar is fixed when the gate is closed; it may also refer to the hoop-like brackets fixed to the gates through which the bar is passed when the gate is closed.

64 *tuvarīḥ* refers to a kind of pulse. 66 The idea is, when this rope is cut in front of the enemies' bows, etc., the latter have their strings cut automatically.

67 *nāsikābandhanam* (from Cs) is preferable to *-vardhanam* 'growth', or 'cutting'. — *mukhagraha* refers to obstruction of the functions of the mouth.

68 Filling the skin of a boar with breathed-in earth, one should tie it with a monkey's tendons; this is a means of causing suppression of urine and stools.

69 On the fourteenth of the dark fortnight, one should anoint (the eyes of) an effigy of the enemy made out of *rājavṛkṣa* wood with the bile of a tawny-coloured cow killed with a weapon; this is a means of making (him) blind.

70 One who has fasted for four meals should make an offering on the fourteenth of the dark fortnight and make pins out of the bones of a man impaled on the stake. 71 One of these planted in the dung or urine (of an enemy) causes suppression of stools and urine, planted in his foot-step or seat it kills by consumption, planted in his shop, field or house, it destroys the source of his livelihood.

72 With this same procedure are explained wedges made out of a tree burnt by lightning.

> 73-74 He, in whose house the *punarnava* turned downwards, the *nimba* and the *kāmamadhu*, the hair of a monkey and the bone of a human being, tied up in the garment of a corpse, are buried, or to whose foot-step one takes it after seeing it, does not survive beyond three fortnights with his sons and wife and his wealth.
>
> 75-76 He, in whose foot-step are buried the *punarnava* turned downwards, the *nimba*, the *kāmamadhu*, the *svayaṁguptā* and the bone of a human being, at the gate of the house or army (camp) or village or city, does not survive beyond three fortnights with his sons and wife and his wealth.
>
> 77 One should procure the hairs of a goat and a monkey, of a cat and an ichneumon, of Brahmins and Śvapākas, and of a crow and an owl; the ordure (of an enemy) pounded with this causes immediate destruction.

68 *varāhabhastrām* is proposed for *varāhahastim* of M. Cs reads *varāhahastibhastrām*, where *-hasti-* seems unlikely. *ānāha* 'suppression of urine and stools'.

69 *pratimām añjyāt*: the collyrium is put in the eyes of the effigy.

71 *pade* is proposed for *pāde* as suggested by Meyer, supported by ss. 74, 75 and 78. *pada*, however, can hardly mean 'the place where he moves about, i.e., the living room' (Meyer).

72 *etenaiva kalpena* is emended from *etena lepakalapena* of the mss. Cs drops *eva*, which, however, may appear necessary for emphasis; cf. s. 32 above.

73 *punarnavam* may be the same as the plant *punarnavā*; cf. 14.4.2. — *avācīnam* 'turned downwards' is not clear; may it be the name of some plant? 74 *dṛṣṭvā vā yatpadaṁ nayet*: (*yatpadam* is proposed for *yaṁ padam*). The object of *dṛṣṭvā* as of *nayet* is *padam*. It is clear that *padaṁ nayet* means the same as *pade nikhānayet*. Cs reads *piṣṭvā vā yaṁ prapāyayet* 'whom he gives it as a drink after grinding it'. There seems to be nothing in the prescription that can be given as a drink. For *dṛṣṭvā*, Meyer suggests *dviṣṭvā* or *sṛṣṭvā* or *sṛṣṭyā* (by placing), all unnecessary.

76 *dvāre* from Cs is better than *pāre*; in the case of *senā*, it would refer to the entrance to the camp.

77 *viṣṭhā-* is clearly right, not *piṣṭā-*.

78 He, in whose foot-step are buried flowers removed from a corpse, fermenting stuff, the hairs of an ichneumon and the skins of a scorpion, a bee and a snake, becomes immediately impotent so long as that is not removed.

79 After fasting for three (days and) nights, one should, on the *puṣya* day, sow *guñjā*-seeds in earth in the skull of a man killed with a weapon or impaled on the stake, and sprinkle them with water. 80 When they have grown, one should cause the *guñjā*-creepers to be taken on the new moon night or full moon night when there is conjunction (of the moon) with the *puṣya*-constellation, and make rings out of them. 81 Vessels with food and drink, placed on them, are never exhausted.

82 When a night show is going on, one should cut out the udders of a dead cow and burn them in the flames of a lamp. 83 When burnt, he should grind them with the urine of a bull and smear a new jar inside (with it). 84 When one takes it round the village leftwise, whatever butter may have been kept there by those (villagers), all that comes (into it).

85 On the fourteenth of the dark fortnight when there is conjunction (of the moon) with the *puṣya*-constellation, one should insert into the vulva of a bitch in heat an iron signet ring. 86 One should pick it up when fallen of its own accord. 87 Fruits from trees come to one when called with it.

88 Practices accompanied by *mantras* and medicines and those that are caused by illusion—with them he should destroy the enemies and protect his own people.

78 *vṛścikālyahi-* : Cs understands *alī* 'a variety of scorpion', not *ali* 'a bee'.

79 It is proposed to drop the *ca* found in the mss. after *udakena*. Cf. s. 64 above.
80 *maṇḍalikāni* 'rings' on which vessels are placed so that they may remain steady and upright whether on the ground or on the head and the contents do not spill over.

84 *eṣām* clearly refers to the villagers.

85 *śuno lagnakasya* : Cs has 'the masculine is not intended; hence a bitch is to be understood'.

88 *yogā māyākṛtāś ca* from Cs is quite necessary in place of *yogamāyā-* etc. of the mss. It provides the substantive *yogāḥ*.

CHAPTER FOUR

SECTION 179 COUNTER-MEASURES AGAINST INJURIES TO ONE'S OWN TROOPS

1 Counter-measures against *dūṣīviṣa* and other poisons used by the enemy against one's own party (should be taken as follows) :

2 Washing water, mixed with a decoction of *śleṣmātaka, kapittha, danti, dantaśaṭha, goji, śirīṣa, pāṭalī, balā, syonāga, punarnavā,* and *śvetāvaraṇa,* (and) mixed with sandalwood and the blood of a female hyena, is a wash for the private parts of women to be enjoyed by the king and an antidote against the poisoning of the army.

3 The powder of *mahīrājī,* mixed with the bile of the speckled deer, the ichneumon, the peacock and the iguana, (and) the mixture of *sinduvārita, varaṇa, vāruṇī, taṇḍulīyaka,* the tips of *śataparvan* and *piṇḍītaka,* remove the evil effects of a stupefying mixture.

4 A drink of the decoction of one or of all of the roots of (the following), *sṛgālavinnā, madana, sinduvārita, varaṇa, vāraṇa,* and *vallī,* together with milk, removes the evil effects of a stupefying mixture.

5 The oil of *kaiḍarya, pūti* and sesame removes madness, when used in the nostrils.

6 The mixture of *priyaṅgu* and *naktamāla* cures leprosy.

7 The mixture of *kuṣṭha* and *lodhra* cures whiteness of hair and consumption.

8 The powder of *kaṭaphala, dravantī* and *vilaṅga,* used as snuff, removes headaches.

9 The mixture of *priyaṅgu, mañjiṣṭhī, tagara,* lac-juice, liquorice, turmeric and honey, is a means of bringing back to consciousness those who have lost it through rope (strangling), water (drowning), poison, beating or fall.

14.4

1 *dūṣīviṣa* : cf. 14.1.22. *gara* would refer to poisons other than this.

2 *senāyāś ca* : Cs construes this with the preceding *guhyaprakṣālanam* ; it seems better, however, to construe it with *viṣapratīkāraḥ* as in Meyer.

3 It seems better to read *-yuktam* separately. — *mahīrājī* : Cs reads *maṣīrājī* and explains 'the blue *śephālikā* (*maṣī*) and the royal mustard (*rājī*)'. *mahīrājī* appears to be the name of a single plant. — *śataparvan* is 'a bamboo'.

4 *vāraṇa* is '*gajapippalī*' (Cs).

7 *pākaśoṣaghnaḥ* : Cs has 'whiteness of the hair (*pāka*) and consumption (*śoṣa*)'. Meyer thinks of 'suppuration and consumption' or 'scrofulous tuberculosis'.

8 *kaṭaphala* : Cs reads *kaṭphala* ; Meyer proposes *kaṭuphala*. — *nastaḥkarma* is here 'a snuff'.

9 The mss. favour the form *mañjiṣṭhī* ; Cs reads *mañjiṣṭhā*.

10 A measure of one *akṣa* (is the dose) for men, double for cattle and horses, four times for elephants and camels.

11 And a pill made of these, with gold inside, removes (the evil effects of) all poisons.

12 A pill made of *jīvantī, śvetā, muṣkaka* and *puṣpavandākā* (and) of *aśvattha* growing on moist soil, removes (the evil effects of) all poisons.

13 The sound of drums, smeared with these, destroys poison; by looking at a flag or a banner, smeared with these, one becomes free from poison.

14 After using these remedial measures for the safety of his own troops and himself, he should use against enemies poisonous smoke and pollution of water.

Herewith ends the Fourteenth Book of the Arthaśāstra of Kauṭilya
'CONCERNING SECRET PRACTICES'

10 *akṣa* is not mentioned among the weights in 2.19. According to Cs it is equal to 16 *māṣas*. The lexicons show this measure.

11 *eṣām* refers to *priyaṅgu* etc. of s. 9.

12 Cf. 1.20.5. We should read *akṣīve* as in that s. Cs understands *puṣpa* as a separate plant here. — The *maṇi* is apparently to be worn round the neck or the wrist as an amulet.

13 *liptadhvajaṁ patākāṁ vā*: perhaps it might be better to read *liptaṁ dhvajam* and understand *liṅgavipariṇāma* in the case of *patākām*. — The difference between *dhvaja* and *patākā* is hardly that the former refers to the staff and the latter to the cloth, as Cs has it. The difference seems due to their size or purpose. Cf. 10.6.46.

14 *viṣadhūmāmbudūṣaṇān*: we have to supply *yogān*, because *-dūṣaṇān* appears in the masculine.

Book Fifteen

THE METHOD OF THE SCIENCE

CHAPTER ONE

SECTION 180 DEVICES USED IN THE (TREATMENT OF THE) SCIENCE

1 The source of the livelihood of men is wealth, in other words, the earth inhabited by men. 2 The science which is the means of the attainment and protection of that earth is the Science of Politics.

3 That contains thirty-two devices of treatment: topic, statement (of contents), employment (of sentences), meaning of words, reason for (establishing) something, mention, explanation, advice, reference, application, indication, analogy, implication, doubt, (similar) situation, contrary (corollary), completion of a sentence, agreement, emphasising, derivation (of a word), illustration, exception, one's own technical term, the *prima facie* view, the correct view, invariable rule, reference to a future statement, reference to a past statement, restriction, option, combination, and what is understood.

4 The object, with respect to which a statement is made, is the topic. 5 For instance: 'This single (treatise on the) Science of Politics is composed mostly by bringing together (the teachings of) as many treatises on the Science of Politics as have been composed by the ancient teachers for the acquisition and protection of the earth.' (1.1.1)

15.1

The Fifteenth Book, in a single Chapter, explains and illustrates the various stylistic devices used to elucidate a scientific subject. *tantra* means a science. The *Suśrutasaṁhitā* (Uttaratantra, Ch. 65) describes closely allied 32 *tantrayuktis*; we read there '*dvātriṁśad yuktayo hyetās tantrasāragaveṣaṇe, mayā samyag vinihitāḥ śabdanyāyārthasaṁyutāḥ*.' The *Carakasaṁhitā* (Siddhisthāna, Ch. 12) enumerates 34 *tantrayuktis*; the two additional seem to be *pratyuccāra* (repetition) and *saṁbhava* (possibility). S. Vidyabhusan (*History of Indian Logic*, pp. 24-25) remarks that the *tantra-yukti* 'was compiled possibly in the 6th century B.C. to systematize debates in *pariṣads* or learned assemblies. It is distinctly stated in the *Suśrutasaṁhitā*: *asadvādiprayuktānāṁ vākyānāṁ pratiṣedhanam, svavākyasiddhirapi ca kriyate tantrayuktitaḥ*.'

1 *vṛtti* is livelihood, i.e., means of livelihood. It may also mean 'existence', i.e., men's existence on earth (Cf. Jayaswal, *Hindu Polity*, I, 5 n.3). According to P Masson-Oursel (*Ancient India*, p. 106) *vṛtti*, which is the basis of *vārttā*, refers to the whole of human activity; *artha* raises the question of ends, *vārttā* that of means. The idea here is, the earth inhabited by men following various occupations constitutes *artha*; the science dealing with such an earth is Arthaśāstra. Its main concern is, how to obtain such earth and how to protect it; in other words, it is the Science of Politics. Russ. renders the s.: 'Riches, valuables sustain human existence; (in the present case) valuability is land populated by people.' 2 *pṛthivyāḥ* etc.: cf. 1.1.1.

4 The illustration implies that by *adhikaraṇa* the subject-matter of the entire work is to be understood. It may be presumed, however, that the definition would cover the subject-matter of each of the fifteen *adhikaraṇas* in the text.

6 A serial enumeration of the sections of the science is statement (of contents). 7 For instance : 'Enumeration of the sciences, association with elders, control over the senses, appointment of ministers,' and so on. (1.1.3)

8 The arrangement of a sentence is employment (of sentences). 9 For instance : 'The people, of the four *varṇa*s and in the four *āśrama*s.' (1.4.16)

10 That which has its limit in the word is the meaning of the word. 11 For instance : *mūlahara* is the word. 12 'He who consumes in unjust ways the property inherited from the father and the grandfather is *mūlahara*,' (2.9.21) is the meaning.

13 A reason proving a thing is the reason for (establishing) a thing. 14 For instance : 'For, spiritual good and sensual pleasures depend on material well-being.' (1.7.7)

15 A statement in brief is mention. 16 For instance : 'Control over the senses is motivated by training in the sciences.' (1.6.1)

17 A detailed statement is explanation. 18 For instance : 'Absence of improper indulgence in (the pleasures of) sound, touch, colour, taste and smell by the senses of hearing, touch and sight, the tongue and the sense of smell, means control over the senses.' (1.6.2)

19 'One should behave in this manner,' is advice. 20 For instance : 'He should enjoy sensual pleasures without contravening his spiritual good and material well-being ; he should not deprive himself of pleasures.' (1.7.3)

21 'So and so says this' is reference. 22 For instance : '"He should appoint a council consisting of twelve ministers," say the followers of Manu. "Sixteen," say the followers of Bṛhaspati. "Twenty," say the followers of Uśanas. "According to capacity," says Kauṭilya.' (1.15.47-50).

23 Setting forth (a thing) with what is already said is application. 24 For instance : 'Non-conveyance of gifts is explained by the non-payment of debts.' (3.16.1)

25 Setting forth (a thing) with what is going to be said is indication. 26 For instance : 'Or, by means of conciliation, gifts, dissension and force, as we shall explain in (the Section on) troubles.' (7.14.11)

6 *vidhāna* appears to be little more than a table of contents.

8 *vākyayojanā* seems to refer to a syntactical arrangement of words so as to form a sentence, though the illustration does not give a complete sentence. The illustration does not justify the explanation 'arrangement of sentences, so as to establish a mutual relation between them'.

21-22 The inclusion of Kauṭilya among those referred to as *asau* is taken to imply that he himself could not have been the author of this work. But *asau* is 'so and so', not 'some other person'; and if an author has chosen to refer to himself in the third person, there would be nothing strange in referring to himself as *asau*.

27 Setting forth an unknown (thing) with the help of the known is analogy. 28 For instance: 'He should, like a father, show favours to those whose exemptions have ceased.' (2.1.18)

29 That which, though not stated, follows as a matter of course is implication. 30 For instance: 'One conversant with the ways of the world should resort to a king endowed with personal excellences and the excellences of material constituents through such as are dear and beneficial (to the king).' (5.4.1) 31 That he should not resort through one who is not dear and beneficial follows as a matter of course.

32 A thing with reasons on both sides is doubt. 33 For instance: '(Should one march) against a king with impoverished and greedy subjects or a king with rebellious subjects?' (7.5.12)

34 A thing common to another topic is (similar) situation. 35 For instance: 'In a place assigned (to him) for agricultural work and so on, exactly as before.' (1.11.10)

36 Setting forth (a thing) with the help of the opposite is contrary (corollary). 37 For instance: 'The opposite, as those of one displeased.' (1.16.12)

38 That by which a sentence is completed is completion of a sentence. 39 For instance: 'And there is loss of all activity on the part of the king, as of a (bird) with clipped wings.' (8.1.9) 40 There, 'of a bird' is the completion of the sentence.

41 The statement of another, not contradicted, is agreement. 42 For instance: 'Two wings, a centre and reserves,—this is the arrangement of a battle-array according to Uśanas.' (10.6.1)

43 The description of a speciality is emphasising. 44 For instance: 'And in particular, in the case of oligarchies and of royal families having the character of an oligarchy, there are dissensions caused by gambling and destruction caused by that; hence it is the most evil among vices, as it favours evil men and leads to weakness in administration.' (8.3.64)

45 Deriving the meaning of a word through its components is derivation. 46 For instance: 'It throws out a person from his good, hence it is called *vyasana*.' (8.1.4)

47 Exemplifying by means of an example is illustration. 48 For instance: 'For, going to war with the stronger, he engages as it were in a fight on foot with an elephant.' (7.3.3)

41-42 The author, however, recognizes two *kakṣas* in addition to what is supposed to be approved by him. See 10.6.1.

48 As 7.3.3 shows, *hastinā* is to be read as in Cs for *hastinaḥ* of the mss.

49 Taking away from a rule of universal application is exception. 50 For instance: 'He should always station alien troops in close proximity (to himself), except in case of fear of a rising in the interior.' (9.2.6)

51 A word, not agreed to by others, is one's own technical term. 52 For instance: '(The would-be conqueror is) the first constituent; one immediately next to his territory is the second; one separated by an intervening territory is the third.' Cf. 6.2.13-15).

53 A statement to be rejected is the *prima facie* view. 54 For instance: 'Of calamities befalling the king and the minister, the calamity of the minister is more serious.' (8.1.7)

55 A statement giving the final view on that is the correct view. 56 For instance: 'being dependent on him; for, the king is in the place of the head.' (8.1.17-18)

57 What is applicable everywhere is invariable rule. 58 For instance: 'Therefore, he should himself be energetically active.' (1.19.5)

59 'This will be stated afterwards' is reference to a future statement. 60 For instance: 'Weights and measures we shall explain in (the Section on) the Superintendent of Standardisation.' (2.13.28)

61 'This has been stated before' is reference to a past statement. 62 For instance: 'The excellences of a minister have been stated before.' (6.1.7).

63 'Thus and in no other way' is restriction. 64 For instance: 'Therefore, he should instruct him in what conduces to spiritual and material good, not in what is spiritually and materially harmful.' (1.17.33)

65 'Either in this way or in that' is option. 66 For instance: 'Or, daughters, born in the pious marriages.' (3.5.10)

67 'In this way and in that' is combination. 68 For instance: 'Begotten by oneself, the (son) becomes the heir to his father and kinsmen.' (3.7.13)

49 *abhipluta* 'what is spread all over' refers to a rule of general or universal application; *vyapakarṣaṇa* is 'taking away' from it.

51 *asamitaḥ* 'not agreed to, not accepted;' *paraiḥ* would seem to refer to other sciences, rather than to other authors of this science. The passage given in illustration is found with some variations in 6.2.13-15. We have there *vijigīṣuḥ*, *ariprakṛtiḥ* and *mitraprakṛtiḥ*, not *prathamā prakṛtiḥ* etc. But *dvitīyā*, *tṛtīyā* and other terms are known to the text; cf. 7.6.1; 7.7.1 · 7.18.1-2. The discrepancy in quotation is, however, difficult to explain. Understanding *sva* to refer to Kauṭilya alone (and not to the science), Meyer thinks that the use of the word *prakṛti* for princes is an innovation by Kauṭilya. That could hardly be right.

59 *anāgatāvekṣaṇa* differs from *pradeśa* (s. 25) in that a future statement is not made applicable to a present case; there is only a reference to a future discussion. Similar is the difference between *atikrāntāvekṣaṇa* (s. 61) and *atideśa* (s. 23).

63 For *niyoga*, *vikalpa* and *samuccaya*, cf. 9.7.73-76 above.

64 *dharmyam* etc. is read here as in the actual passage, 1.17.33.

68 *svayaṁjātaḥ* is read here as in the actual passage (3.7.13) for *svasaṁjātaḥ*, which, however, means the same thing.

69 The doing of what is not expressly stated is what is understood.
70 For instance : 'And experts shall fix revocation in such a way that neither the donor nor the donee is injured.' (3.16.5)

71 Thus this science, expounded with these devices of a science, has been composed for the acquisition and protection of this world and of the next.

72 This science brings into being and preserves spiritual good, material well-being and pleasures, and destroys spiritual evil, material loss and hatred.

73 This science has been composed by him, who in resentment, quickly regenerated the science and the weapon and the earth that was under the control of the Nanda kings.

Herewith ends the Fifteenth Book of the Arthaśāstra of Kauṭilya
'THE METHOD OF THE SCIENCE'

(Seeing the manifold errors of the writers of commentaries on scientific treatises, Viṣṇugupta himself composed the *sūtra* as well as the *bhāṣya*).

HEREWITH ENDS THE ARTHAŚĀSTRA OF KAUTILYA

70 As the actual passage shows, we have to read *yathā ca* for *yathāvad* of the mss.

71 *parasya ca* : with this *pālane* is not to be understood, only *avāptau*.

73 *śāstraṁ ca śastraṁ ca* : apparently the Science of Politics had fallen into neglect in the author's day. The *uddhāra* of *śastra* or weapon seems to refer to his 'raising' it for striking down enemies. It could hardly mean a resurrection of the science of fighting. Meyer would interpret *śastra* as 'the prime minister's office (from *śas* to rule)'. That does not appear possible. — Kāmandaka, 1.6, refers to the fact that Viṣṇugupta extracted (*uddadhre*) the nectar of Nītiśāstra from the vast ocean of Arthaśāstra.

The stanza that follows the colophon of the final Book is clearly a later addition. It refers to the text as containing a *sūtra* as well as a *bhāṣya* on it by the same author. But the text contains only *sūtra*s and no *bhāṣya*. It is erroneous to look upon the titles of the *prakaraṇa*s as constituting the *sūtra* portion and the entire text as a *bhāṣya* on it, as the commentators do. The fact that the author is referred to in the stanza by his personal name Viṣṇugupta and not by his *gotra* name Kauṭilya used throughout in the text also raises doubts about the genuineness of the stanza.

INDEX OF PRINCIPAL TOPICS

Accounts, checking of, 2.7.16-40.
Adultery, see Sexual offences.
Agents, secret, 1.11-12.
Agreements, see Conventions.
Agricultural operations, 2.24.
Ally, types of, 7.9 ; calamities affecting, 8.5.22-30 ; treatment of, 7.18.31-42.
Ānvīkṣikī, study of, 1.2.10-12.
Armoury, 2.5.5 ; 2.18.
Army, excellences of, 6.1.11 ; march of, 10.2 ; mobilisation of, 9.2.1-9 ; troubles affecting, 8.5.1-18.
Arrays for battles, 10.5.1-47 ; 10.6.1-43.
Arrest on suspicion etc., 4.6.
Artisans and craftsmen, control over, 4.1.
Āśramas, 1.3.9-13.
Audit and Records Office, 2.7.

Balances (for weighing), kinds of, 2.19. 11-28 ; defective, 2.14.19.
Battle-arrays, see Arrays.
Battle, see Fighting.
Belligerency, see Hostility.
Betting, 3.20.13.
Boats, 2.28.
Boundaries, disputes concerning, 3.9.10-23.
Buildings, regulations about construction of, 3.8 ; sale of, 3.9.1-9.

Calamities, natural, steps to overcome, 4.3 ; affecting constituents of the State, 8.
Camp, setting up of, 10.1.
Capital, see City.
Castes, mixed, 3.7.20-40.
Cattle, care of, 2.29 ; trespass and damage caused by, 3.10.22-34.
Census in rural areas, 2.35.1-10 ; in the city, 2.36.1-4.
Chariots for war, 2.33.1-6 ; 10.4.15 ; 10.5.55.
Charms, occult, 14.3.
Circle of Kings, 6.2.13-29.
City, fortified, lay-out of, 2.4 ; administration of, 2.36.
Coins, minting of, 2.12.24.
Conciliation, policy of, 9.5.10 ; 9.6.21-22 ; 9.7.68-81 ; 2.10.48-53.
Confederacies, forming of, 7.4.19-22. ; 7.5.38-49 ; dealing with, 7.14.1-13.
Conquered territory, treatment of, 13.5.
Conquerors, types of, 12.1.10-16.
Conspiracies, 9.5.
Constituents of the State, 6.1.
Conventions, non-observance of, 3.10.35-46.
Corruption, see Officers.
Cotton cloth, 2.11.115 ; manufacture of, 2.23.
Council of Ministers, 1.15.47-59.
Councillors, appointment of, 1.15.1-46.
Country, excellences of, 6.18.
Courtesans, 2.27.
Crimes, miscellaneous, 4.13.1-29.
Criminals, suppression of, 4.
Customs-duties, 2.22.1-8.
Custom-house regulations, 2.21.

Dacoit gangs, rounding up of, 4.5.
Daṇḍanīti, study of, 1.4.3-16.
Death, sudden, investigation of, 4.7.
Debts, law of, 3.11.1-24.
Decrees, writing of, 2.10.
Defamation, see Injury, verbal.
Defence against a confederacy, 7.8.1-10 ; against a strong enemy, 7.15.1-12 ; 12.1-5.
Departments, activity of heads of, 2.
Deposits, law of, 3.12.1-7.
Deserters who return, dealing with, 7.6.22-41.
Diplomatic fight, 12.1 ; 12.2.1-7.
Disaffection, between husband and wife, 3.3.12-19 ; among subjects, 7.5.19-27.
Dissensions, policy of creating, 9.5.12-28 ; 9.6.26-52 ; 9.7.68-81 ; 2.10.55.
Divisions of space and time, 2.20.
Documents, types of, 2.10.38-46.
Drinks, spirituous, manufacture and use of, 2.25.
Dual policy, 7.7.
Duties, custom and excise, 2.22.
Duties of *varṇas* and *āśramas*, 1.3.

Elders, association with, 1.5.
Elephants, care and training of, 2.31-32 in war, 10.4.14 ; 10.5.54.
Embezzlement, ways of and steps against, 2.8.
Emergency affecting treasury, steps in, 5.2.
Enemy, types of, 6.2.16,19 ; outwitting by making agreements, 7.6 ; 7.8.11-34 ; 7.9-12.
Envoys, duties of, 1.16.
Espionage, see Agents, secret.
Evidence, law of, 3.11.25-50.
Excise duties, 2.22.
Exemptions from taxes, 2.1.7-18 ; 3.9.33.
Expeditions, preparing for, 9.1-2 ; gains from, 9.4.
Expenditure, State, 2.6.11,23-26.

Factories, metal, 2.12 ; forest goods, 2.17 ; textile, 2.23.
Ferries, 2.28.
Fighting, kinds of, 7.6.40-41 ; modes of, 10.5.53-56 ; diplomatic, 12.1 ; 12.2.1-7 ; tactical, 10.8.1-25 ; secret, 12.2-5.
Fines, scales of *sāhasa*-, 3.17.8-10.

Fire, precautions against, 2.36.15-25.
Food-rations for men, 2.15.43-49 ; for cattle and other animals, 2.15.51-58 ; 2.29.43-46 ; for elephants, 2.31.13-15 ; for horses, 2.30.18-25.
Force, use of, 9.6.53-55 ; 9.7.68-81 ; 2.10.56.
Forcible seizure, 3.17.
Forest produce, 2.17.
Forts, construction of, 2.3 ; laying siege to and capture of, 13.3-4.
Fraud by artisans and craftsmen, 4.1 ; by traders, 4.2.

Gambling, control of, 3.20.1-12.
Gems, 2.11.28-42.
Gifts, making, as a policy, 9.5.11 ; 9.6.23-25 ; 9.7.68-81 ; 2.10.54 ; non-conveyance of, 3.16.1-9.
Gold, mining and treatment of, 2.12 ; 2.13.1-27 ; working in, 2.13.30-61 ; 2.14.
Goldsmith, Royal, 2.14.
Government service, see Service.
Grammatical terms, 2.10.13-21.

Horses, care of, 2.30 ; in war, 10.4.13 ; 10.5.33.
Hostage, keeping of, 7.17.1-31 ; escape of, 7.17.32-61.
Hostility, policy of, 7.1.14,33 ; 7.4.5-12, 14-17.
Houses, see Buildings.
Husband and wife, relations between, 3.3-4.

Income, secret ways of earning, 4.4 ; State, 2.6.1-10,17-22.
Infantry, training of, 2.33.7-8 ; in war, 10.4.16 ; 10.5.56.
Inheritance, law of, 3.5-7.
Injury, physical, 3.19.
Injury, verbal, 3.18.
Investigation of theft, 4.6 ; 4.8 ; of sudden death and murder, 4.7.
Irrigation-works, 2.1.20-24 ; 3.9.32-38 ; 3.10.1-2.

Judges, concerning, 3.

King, calamities affecting, 8.2 ; daily life of, 1.19 ; excellences of, 6.1.2-6 ; safety of person of, 1.20 ; 1.21 ; training of, 1.
Kings, Circle of, 6.2.13-29.

Labourers, conditions of work by, 3.14.1-11 ; wages of, 3.13 27-37 ; unions of, 3.14.12-17.
Land, acquisition of, 7.10 ; new settlement on, 2.1 ; 7.11.
Law and its administration, 3.
Lay-out of the capital, 2.4.
Legal procedure, 3.1.17-37.
Liquor, see Drinks.
Lost property, recovery of, 3.16.10-23.

Madhyama king, 6.2.21 ; 7.18.1-25.
Magistrates, 4.1.1.
Maidens, violation of, 4.12.
Manifestations, supernatural, 13.1.1-10.
March on expedition, 10.2.
Marching, policy of, 7.1.16,35 ; 7.4.14, 18.
Markets, control of, 4.2.
Marriage, law of, 3.2-4.
Measurements of space and time, 2.20.
Measures, capacity, 2.19.29-45.
Metal-ores, 2.12.
Method of the science, 15.1.
Mines, working of, 2.12.
Ministers, choice of, 1.8 ; excellences of, 1.9.1-2 ; secret tests for probity of, 1.10.
Miracles, 14.2 ; 14.3.
Murder, investigation of, 4.7.

Offences, miscellaneous, 3.20-14-19 ; sexual, 4.12 ; 4.13.30-41.
Officers, corruption among, 2.9 ; offences by, 4.9 ; salaries of, 5.3.
Oligarchies, see Saṁghas.
Ornaments, manufacture of, 2.14.
Ownership, law concerning, 3.16.29-36.

Pacification of conquered territory, 13.5.
Palace, construction of, 1.20.1-13.
Partnership, law of, 3.14.18-38.
Passports, 2.34.1-4.
Pastures, care of, 2.34.5-12.
Peace, policy of, 7.1.13,32 ; 7.3.
Pearls, 2.11.2-27.
Pledges, law concerning, 3.12.8-17.
Police officers, 4.1.1.
Policy, six measures of, 7.1.6-19.
Post-mortem examination, 4.7.1-13.
Power, threefold, 6.2.33 ; 9.1.2-16.
Practices, secret and miraculous, 14.
Precious stones, 2.11.28-42.
Prices, regulation of, 2.16.1-10; 4.2.28-36.
Prince, in disfavour, 1.18 ; treatment of, 1.17.
Prisoners, maltreatment of, 4.9.21-27.
Procedure, law of, 3.1.17-37.
Property, sale of, 3.9.1-9 ; see Lost property.
Prostitutes, see Courtesans.
Punishments, capital, 4.11 ; corporal, 4.10.
Purohita, 1.9.9-11.
Purchase, rescission of, 3.15.9-18.

Quiet, staying, policy of, 7.1.15,34 ; 7.4.2-13.

Rainfall, 2.4.5-10.
Rain-gauge, 2.5.7.
Ransom, see Redemptions.
Rations, see Food-rations.
Rear, attacks in the, 7.13.
Records, 2.7.1-2.
Redemptions from corporal punishments, 4.10.
Remarriage of women, 3.4.24-42.
Remedies, destructive and harmful, 14.1 ; 14.2.

Republics, see Saṁghas.
Revenue, State, 2.6.
Revolts, 9.3.
Rule, preservation of dynastic, 5.6.
Rulership, abnormal, 8.2.

Salaries, 5.3.
Sale, rescission of, 3.15.1-8 ; without ownership, 3.16.10-23.
Sales-agents, 3.12.25-32.
Saṁghas, subjugation of, 11.1
Sandalwood and fragrant substances, 2.11.43-72.
Seasons for expedition, 9.1.34-52.
Seducible persons, 1.14.
Seizure by force, 3.17.
Senses, control of, 1.6.
Service, State, seeking and retaining, 5.4 ; 5.5.
Settlements, new, 2.1.
Sexual offences, 4.12 ; 4.13.30-41.
Shelter, seeking, policy of, 7.1.17,36 ; 7.2.
Shipping, control of, 2.28.
Silk and allied cloth, 2.11.102-114.
Silver, working in, 2-14.
Skins, 2.11.73-96.
Slander, see Injury, verbal.
Slaughter of animals, 2.26.
Slaves, law concerning, 3.13.1-25.
Sons, different kinds of, 3.7.4-19.
Sovereignty, continuity of, 5.6.
Spells, magical, 14.3.
Spies, see Agents, secret.
Stores, State, 2.5 ; 2.15.
Stratagems against an attacking enemy, 12.2,3,4,5.
Strīdhana, 3.2.14-37.
Succession to rulership, 1.17.53-53 ; 5.6.33-48.
Superintendents, activity of, 2.

Taxes during emergencies, 5.2.2-30.
Terrains suitable for fighting, 10.4.1-12.
Territory, see Country, Land.
Tests of integrity, 1.10.
Textiles, manufacture of, 2.23.8-10.
Thefts, investigation of, 4.6 ; 4.8.
Tortures for eliciting confession, 4.8.
Trade in State goods, 2.16.
Traders, control over, 4.2.
Training of the ruler, 1.
Traitors (Treasonable persons), dealing with, 5.1.
Transactions, valid and invalid, 3.1.2-16.
Treasure-trove, finding of, 4.1.51-55.
Treasury, replenishment of, 5.2.
Treaties, kinds of, 7.3.22-36 ; 7.6.4-13.
Tricks for destroying an attacking enemy, 12.5 ; for recovering entrusted articles, 3.12.35-51 ; for replenishing the treasury 5.2.31-68.
Troubles affecting the State, 8.4 ; from hostile elements and enemies, 9.6.

Udāsīna king, 6.2.22 ; 7.18.25-27.
Unions of workmen, 3.14.12-17.

Varṇas, 1.3.5-8.
Vārttā, study of, 1.4.1-2.
Vassals, conduct appropriate to, 7.15.21-30 ; treatment of, 7.16.
Vedas, study of, 1.3.
Vices of man, 8.3.

War, preparations for, 9.1-2 ; see also Fighting.
Water-rate, 2.24.18.
Water-works, see Irrigation-works.
Weapons, 2.18.
Weighing machines, 2.19.11-28.
Weights, 2.19.8-10
Wife, offences by, 3.3.10-32 ; 3.4.1-23 ; maintenance of, 3.3.3-5.
Witnesses, evidence by, 3.11.14-37.
Woman's property, see Stridhana.
Woollen cloth, 2.11.97-100.
Workmen, see Labourers.
Writing, defects of, 2.10.57-62 ; excellences of, 2.10.6-12.

Yarn, manufacture of, 2.23.